Dictionary of Composers
for the Church in Great Britain and Ireland

Dictionary of Composers
for the Church in
Great Britain and Ireland

Maggie Humphreys
and
Robert Evans

MANSELL

First published 1997 by
Mansell Publishing Limited, *A Cassell Imprint*
Wellington House, 125 Strand, London WC2R 0BB, England

PO Box 605, Herndon, VA 20172

British Library Cataloguing-in-Publication Data
Humphreys, Maggie
　　Dictionary of composers for the church in Great Britain and Ireland
　　1. Church musicians – Dictionaries 2. Church music – Dictionaries
　　I. Title II. Evans, Robert
　　781.7'1'0922

ISBN 0 7201 2330 5

Library of Congress Cataloguing-in-Publication Data
Humphreys, Maggie.
　　Dictionary of composers for the Church in Great Britain and
　　Ireland / Maggie Humphreys and Robert Evans.
　　　　p. cm.
　　Includes bibliographical references (p.) and index.
　　ISBN O-7201-2330-5
　　1. Church music—British Isles—Bio-bibliography. 2. Composers—
　　British Isles.　I. Title
　　ML102.C5H86 1997
　　781.71'0092'241—dc20
　　[B]　　　　　　　　　　　　　　　　　　　96-41998
　　　　　　　　　　　　　　　　　　　　　　　　　CIP
　　　　　　　　　　　　　　　　　　　　　　　　　MN

Printed and bound in Great Britain by Bookcraft, Midsomer Norton.

Contents

Foreword

by The Very Revd. Patrick Mitchell, Dean of Windsor

Nobody knows how many composers have written for the worship of the Church in Great Britain and Ireland; but Maggie Humphreys and Robert Evans have done a great service in this Dictionary by allowing us to sample the range of output and talent. How varied it is!

Household names, such as Byrd, Purcell, Wesley, Stanford and Britten, confront us expectedly; but they are interspersed with less familiar figures such as lay vicars or lay clerks from the cathedral and collegiate foundations, or faithful but unremembered parish organists. Their contributions vary from ambitious anthems to humble hymn tunes or responses. Do we still think of Crotch as a serious rival to Mendelssohn?

Here we can browse and find such surprises as a 17th-century Earl of Abingdon, who was an amateur flute-player and once wrote an anthem; but I have failed to find the composer who (according to legend) once set the Churching of Women to music in five parts, including the memorable words 'all men are liars'.

Apart from the fun to be had by browsing through this book, this will be a serious contribution to musical scholarship. Musicians, worshippers and historians alike can look with renewed pride at the riches of our Christian heritage.

Foreword

by Bernard Barrell

The title of this volume exactly describes its function. It features almost 3,000 composers of church music from ancient times to the present day, with brief biographies, notes on the music and reference to composers' secular works as well. (Few now compose exclusively for the Church.)

This book will be a godsend to organists and choirs, who should know something about the composers whose works they perform - likewise the clergy. It ought to be a 'standard fitting' in churches, colleges, libraries and schools. Congregations, too, may well take an added interest in the subject, whilst the casual reader may find unexpected and absorbing information leading to increased respect for those involved in church music - and we, the composers, will surely be encouraged that our work is not in vain, whether it be for cathedral or tiny village church, for the same care is required in both contexts. As Dr. Peter Aston so aptly pointed out in an article about the composer and the Church, the shortest item has no right to be trivial.

The compilers have toiled long and hard to produce this indispensable book: their finest reward will be its ready acceptance and continual use to the benefit of all concerned. It is, indeed, a great privilege to be asked to write this Foreword (from the composer's point of view) and I wish a very warm welcome to a unique publication.

Bon Voyage!

Preface

The tremendous growth of interest in church music of all types, not least as a consequence of what has become popularly known as the 'hymn explosion', has led both the interested bystander and the serious student to an increasing number of reference books. The opportunity to obtain background and biographical information within one volume, regardless of the barriers of denomination and the niceties of churchmanship, is a major aim of the present publication. Entries are limited to composers of Great Britain, Northern Ireland and the Irish Republic who are native-born or who have spent a significant part of their working lives in these islands. Each has written music intended primarily for use in public Christian worship, although few have composed exclusively for the Church.

Remarkable misunderstandings and misattributions have arisen over the years, partly due to limitations of space on the music lists of choral foundations and in the notes for concert programmes and recordings. Among those who have suffered as a result is the composer H.C. Stewart, nearly all of whose anthems and settings are still credited to Charles Hylton Stewart. Welsh surnames are another minefield to trap the unwary enthusiast. Unfortunately, once an error has been made, the reverence accorded to the printed word and the infallibility attributed to its author usually ensure that it is replicated and compounded through subsequent publications. Although the Dictionary is not intended as an exhaustive catalogue, we have attempted to set the record straight on misattributed works of note whenever the opportunity presented itself.

A conscious decision has been made to avoid subjective discussion of the merits of individual composers and of specific works, but where that most fickle of commodities – popular taste – has become involved, then some comments have been reproduced. Where possible, the selection from the composer's output quoted towards the end of each entry has been that which is currently available either in print or by archive reprint. Some music in everyday use is only obtainable in volumes or anthologies. In as many cases as possible, where the works of living composers are cited, the selection given is the choice of the composer.

The heritage of the church music of these islands is one of the glories of Western civilisation. With the onset of a welcome catholicity of experience in worship, the music of other nationalities (often sung in the original language) has sometimes displaced our native inheritance. Names of once fashionable musicians quietly disappear from musical dictionaries once they are perceived as no longer useful. On the other hand, information on the composers of today, or tomorrow, can prove elusive for upwards of a generation, leading to the unfortunate situation where the music is well known but the composer is not. The neglected and the progressive are of as much interest as the famous and often very much harder to research. Our aim has been to do justice to them all.

One aspect of a work of this kind, spanning a long period of time, is the problem of citing place names. A hundred or more years ago, migration from within the County of London into surrounding areas of Kent, Middlesex and Surrey gave rise to the concept of Greater London as a single region. The London County Council was set up in 1888 but the constituent counties remained, and in many cases, so did the association with the towns that they had given up. In our own times, the Local Government Act of 1974 had far-reaching effects within England and Wales. Some ancient counties such as Rutland simply ceased to exist after 1 April 1974. London remained unchanged, but the remainder of England and Wales was divided into 54 enlarged metropolitan and non-metropolitan counties, which were themselves divided into metropolitan and non-metropolitan districts. With this in mind, we have attempted to cite place names in such a way as to avoid anachronism and to aid clarity. It would, for instance, read strangely if we were to suggest that the 19th-century composer J.B. Dykes was born in Humberside, but there are instances where it would be equally unhelpful to use counties that disappeared some time ago and whose names are almost forgotten. We have therefore used whatever method seemed most appropriate in its context.

Certain conventions have been adopted and followed throughout the work. Ordained ministers of the various churches are simply styled 'Reverend'. Wherever possible, the Christian name by which the composer was or is known has been used. When cross-referencing, if the preferred name is a middle name, then the preceding initial is not reproduced, and neither is the title. Thus, when referring to the entry for Sir Walford Davies, we have simply used Walford Davies rather than Sir H. Walford Davies.

Of those who gave their time and expertise during the project, we are indebted in particular, to The Very Revd. Patrick Mitchell, Dean of Windsor, and to Mr. Bernard Barrell, whose endorsements of our efforts in the form of a Foreword we treasure and gratefully acknowledge. Dr. Christopher Kent, senior lecturer in music at the University of Reading, offered lines of enquiry for details of some of the less well-documented composers, and thanks are also due to Dr. Margaret Laurie and Mr. Melvyn Bird of the University of Reading Music Library, where much of the research was carried out. Mr. Simon Lindley, organist of Leeds Parish Church, responded with his usual boundless enthusiasm, made available his knowledge of the cathedral repertoire and of church music in general, and offered suggestions as to the scope of the book. Similarly, Dr. Donald Webster, one of today's leading hymnologists, formerly of Huddersfield University and of Napier University, Edinburgh, reviewed and commented in detail on a draft version.

Mr. Jonathan Rees-Williams, director of music of St. George's Chapel, Windsor Castle, gave advice and drew upon personal knowledge to enable us to fill out some of the entries. Further information was supplied by the composer, Mr. Paul Edwards.

We enjoyed the comfortable facilities and drew freely upon the expertise and kindness of the staff at a number of libraries around the country. These include the public libraries of Bracknell, City of London (Barbican), Cheam, Dundee, Leeds, Maidenhead, Putney, Reading, Sutton (Surrey), West Hill (Wandsworth), and Westminster; we wish to mention and thank specifically Ms. Sue Mills and Ms. Jennifer Thorpe of the Angus Library, Regent's Park Baptist College, Oxford.

Information was gathered at the Royal College of Organists, London, and thanks are due to Dr. Michael Nicholas and his staff. Assistance was also forthcoming from the British Music Information Centre and from Ms. Roisin Maher of the Contemporary Music Centre, Dublin. Facilities were offered, and gratefully accepted, at the Welsh National Folk Museum, St. Fagan's, Cardiff.

Finally, we received a most heartening response from the contemporary composers themselves. When asked for details about themselves or for verification of the draft, the composers responded with warmth and commitment to the project. It is clear that today's composers are engaged in a continuing process of renewal, mindful of the legacy of the past and of the evolving needs of today's congregations, and in sincere pursuit of those special qualities required of music for the worship of God.

Maggie Humphreys
Robert Evans
August 1996

Bibliography

Books

ATKINS, Harold and NEWMAN, Archie. *Beecham stories*. London: Robson Books, 1987.

Australian dictionary of biography. Melbourne: Melbourne University Press, 1972.

BACHARACH, A.L. (editor). *British music of our time*. London: Pelican Books, 1946.

BAILEY, Cyril. *Hugh Percy Allen*. Oxford: Oxford University Press, 1948.

BAYLISS, Colin (editor). *The music of Anthony Hedges*. Hull: Humberside Leisure Services, 1990.

B.B.C. Musical Library choral and opera catalogue (Volume I: composers). London: B.B.C., 1967.

BIRD, Enid. *Twentieth century cathedral organists*. Published privately, 1990.

BOHLE, Bruce (editor). *The international cyclopaedia of music and musicians*. London: J.M. Dent & Sons, 1975.

BONNER, Carey and WHITLEY, W.T. *Handbook to The Baptist Church Hymnal revised*. London: Psalms and Hymns Trust, 1935.

BOWERS, Roger, *et al*. The organs and organists of Wells Cathedral (7th edition). Wells: The Friends of Wells Cathedral, 1979.

BOYLAN, Henry. *A dictionary of Irish biography*. Dublin: Gill and Macmillan, 1978.

BRADLEY, Ian. *The Penguin book of hymns*. London: Penguin Books, 1989.

BROWN, James Duff and STRATTON, Stephen S. *British musical biography: a dictionary of musical artists, authors and composers born in Britain and its colonies*. Published privately, 1897.

BRYANT, Giles. *The Healey Willan catalogue*. Ottawa: National Library of Canada, 1972.

The catalogue of printed music in the British Library. Munich: K.G. Saur, 1980.

CHARLTON, Peter. *John Stainer and the musical life of Victorian Britain*. Newton Abbot: David and Charles, 1984.

COHEN, Aaron I. *International encyclopaedia of women composers*. New York: Books and Music Inc., 1981.

COLLES, H.C. *Walford Davies: a biography*. Oxford: Oxford University Press, 1943.

The concise dictionary of national biography. Oxford: Oxford University Press, 1992.

COOMBS, James Martin. *Dictionary of musicians* (2nd edition). London: Novello, 1827.

COPLEY, Ian. *Robin Milford*. London: Thames Publishing, 1984.

COWARD, Henry. *Reminiscences of Henry Coward*. London: Curwen, 1919.

COWLEY, Russell. *The full names, dates and countries of 3,500 composers of organ and sacred choral music*. New Zealand: Invercargill, published privately, 1984.

CRISP, Alan and CLARKE, Ron (compilers). *Hark the sound: A history of the Free Church Choir Union*. Place unspecified: Free Church Choir Union, 1995.

CUMMINGS, W.H. *Purcell*. London: Sampson, Low, Marston & Co., 1942.

DANZIGER, Danny. *The cathedral*. London: Viking, 1989.

DAUBNEY. Brian Blyth. *Benjamin Burrows 1891–1966: The life and music of the Leicester composer*. Leicester: University of Leicester, 1979.

DAWE, Donovan. *Organists of the City of London 1666–1850*. Published privately, 1983.

DEXTER, Harold. *Student's dictionary of composers*. Woodford Green: International Music Publications, 1984.

DIBBLE, Jeremy, *C. Hubert H. Parry: his life and music*. Oxford: Oxford University Press, 1993.

Dictionary of national biography. London: Smith Elder and Co., 1885.

Dictionary of national biography. Oxford: Oxford University Press, 1968.

Dictionary of organs and organists (2nd edition). London: George Mate and Company, 1921.

The dictionary of Welsh biography down to 1940. London: The Honourable Society of Cymmrodorion, 1959.

EVANS, H. Turner. A *bibliography of Welsh hymnology to 1960*. Cardiff: Welsh Library Association, 1977.

EWEN, David (editor). *The complete book of classical music*. London: Robert Hale, 1966.

FELLOWES, E.H. *The catalogue of manuscripts in the library of St. Michael's College, Tenbury*. Tenbury: Dyer, 1934.

FELLOWES. E.H. *English cathedral music*. London: Methuen, 1969.

FELLOWES, E.H. *Memoirs of an amateur musician*. London: Methuen, 1946.

FELLOWES, E.H. *Organists and masters of the choristers of St. George's Chapel in Windsor Castle*. London: S.P.C.K., 1939.

FOSTER, Myles Birket. *Anthems and anthem composers*. London: Novello, 1901.

FROST, Maurice (editor). *Historical companion to* Hymns Ancient and Modern. London: Proprietors of Hymns Ancient and Modern, 1962.

GATENS, William J. *Victorian cathedral music in theory and practice*. Cambridge: Cambridge University Press, 1986.

GAUNTLETT, Catharine T. *Memoirs of Henry Gauntlett*. London: Seeley and Burnside, 1835.

GLOVER, Raymond F. *A commentary on new hymns* (Hymnal Studies 6). New York: Church Hymnal Corporation, 1987.

GREENE, Harry Plunket. *Charles Villiers Stanford*. London: Edward Arnold, 1935.

GRIFFITHS, Paul. *New sounds, new personalities: British composers of the 1980s*. London: Faber Music Ltd., 1985.

GRIFFITHS, Paul. *Thames and Hudson encyclopaedia of 20th century music*. London: Thames and Hudson, 1986.

GRINDLE, W. H. *Irish cathedral music*. Belfast: Queen's University Belfast, 1989.

The new Grove 20th century English masters. London: Macmillan, 1986.

HAYDEN, Andrew J. and NEWTON, Robert F. *British hymn writers and composers: a check list*. Place unspecified: Hymn Society of Great Britain and Ireland, 1977.

HILL, David G. *Henry Smart (1813–1879): neglected 19th century organ master*. London: de Mixtuur, 1938.

HINRICHSON, Max (compiler). *Organ and choral aspects and prospects*. London: Hinrichson, 1958.

HOLD, Trevor. *The walled-in garden: A study of the songs of Roger Quilter (1877–1953)*. London: Triad Press, 1978.

HUNT, Donald. *Samuel Sebastian Wesley*. Bridgend: Seren Books, 1990.

International who's who in music. Cambridge: International Who's Who in Music, 1985 and 1990.

JACOBS, Arthur. *A short history of western music*. London: Penguin Books, 1981.

JACOBS, Arthur. *Arthur Sullivan: a Victorian musician*. Oxford: Oxford University Press, 1986.

JULIAN, John. *Dictionary of hymnology*. New York: Dover Publications, Inc., 1892.

KENNEDY, Michael. *The Oxford dictionary of music*. Oxford: Oxford University Press, 1985.

KINGTON, Beryl. *Rowley rediscovered: The life and music of Alec Rowley*. London: Thames, 1993.

KNIGHT, Gerald and REED, William L. *The treasury of English church music*, Volumes 4 & 5. London: Blandford Press.

Le FLEMING, Christopher. *Journey into music*. Bristol: Redcliffe Press, 1982.

Le HURAY, Peter. *Music and the Reformation in England 1549–1660*. Cambridge: Cambridge University Press, 1978.

LEACH, Gerald. *British composer profiles*. Newbury: British Music Society, 1980.

LIGHTWOOD, James T. *Hymn tunes and their story*. London: Charles H. Kelly, 1905.

LLOYD, Stephen. *H. Balfour Gardiner*. Cambridge: Cambridge University Press, 1984.

LONG, Kenneth. *The music of the English church*. London: Hodder and Stoughton, 1991.

LONGMIRE, John. *John Ireland: portrait of a friend*. London: John Baker, 1969.

LUFF, Alan. *Welsh hymns and their tunes*. London: Stainer and Bell, 1990.

MAGNUSSON, Magnus. *Chambers biographical dictionary*. Edinburgh: Chambers, 1993.

MOFFAT, Rev. Prof. James. *Handbook to* The Church Hymnary. Oxford: Oxford University Press, 1927.

MOORE, Gerald Northrop. *Edward Elgar: a creative life*. Oxford: Oxford University Press, 1984.

NORRIS, Gerald. *A musical gazetteer of Great Britain and Ireland*. Newton Abbot: David and Charles, 1981.

PALMER, Christopher (editor). *Dyson's delight: An anthology of Sir George Dyson's writings and talks on music*. London: Thames, 1989.

PARRY, K.L. (editor). *Companion to* Congregational Praise. London: Independent Press Ltd., 1953.

PATTON, John. *Eighty-eight years of cathedral music 1898–1986*. Winchester: published privately, 1994.

PATTON, John. *Eighty-eight years of cathedral music 1898–1986 – an addendum*. Winchester: published privately, 1995.

PERRY, David W. *Hymns and tunes indexed*. Croydon: The Hymn Society of Great Britain and Ireland and the Royal School of Church Music, 1980.

PHILLIPS, C. Henry. *The singing church*. London: Mowbrays, 1979.

RAVENSCROFT, W. *Some Ravenscrofts*. London: Telford and Stone, 1929.

xii

RENNERT, Jonathan. *George Thalben-Ball*. Newton Abbot: David and Charles, 1979.

ROCHE, Jerome and ROCHE, Elizabeth. *A dictionary of early music*. London: Faber Music Ltd., 1981.

Roll of the Union of Graduates in Music. London: Union of Graduates in Music, editions of 1910, 1915, 1920 and 1925.

ROUTLEY, Erik. *The musical Wesleys 1703–1876*. London: Herbert Jenkins, 1968.

SADIE, Stanley (editor). *The new Grove dictionary of music and musicians*. London: Macmillan, 1980.

SAMUEL, Irene. *Musical maestros*. London: Rosters Ltd., 1987.

SCHOLES, Percy A. *The Oxford companion to music* (10th edition). Oxford: Oxford University Press, 1984.

SCHOLES, Percy A. *The Puritans and music in England and New England*. Oxford: Oxford University Press, 1969.

SEARLE, Muriel. *John Ireland: The man and his music*. Tunbridge Wells: Midas Books, 1979.

SHAW, H. Watkins. *The succession of organists of the Chapels Royal and the cathedrals of England and Wales from c1538*. Oxford: Oxford University Press, 1991.

SHERWIN BAILEY, Derek. *Wells Cathedral Chapter Act Book 1666–1683*. London: H.M.S.O., 1973.

SIDDONS, James. *Anthony Milner: A bio-bibliography*. Westport, Connecticut: Greenwood Press, 1989.

SLONIMSKY, Nicholas. *The concise Baker's biographical dictionary of composers and musicians*. New York: Simon and Schuster, 1988.

THOMSON, Andrew. *The life and times of Charles-Marie Widor (1844–1937)*. Oxford: Oxford University Press, 1987.

THOMSON, Ronald W. *Who's who of hymn writers*. Manchester: Epworth Press, 1967.

TOMLINSON, Fred. *A Peter Warlock handbook* (Volume I). London: Triad Press, 1974.

TOVEY, Donald F. and PARRATT, Geoffrey. *Walter Parratt, master of the music*. Oxford: Oxford University Press, 1941.

VAUGHAN WLLIAMS, Ursula. *A biography of Ralph Vaughan Williams*. Oxford: Oxford University Press, 1988.

WATSON, Richard and TRICKETT, Kenneth (editors). *Companion to* Hymns and Psalms. Peterborough: Methodist Publishing House, 1988.

WEBSTER, Donald. *'Parish' past and present (275 years of Leeds Parish Church music)*. Leeds: Leeds Parish Church Old Choirboys' Association, 1988.

WEST, John Ebenezer. *A record of the succession of organists of the cathedrals, chapels royal and principal collegiate churches of the United Kingdom*. London: Novello, 1921.

WHITTLE, Tyler. *Solid joys and lasting treasure*. London: Ross Anderson Publications, 1985.

Who's who in music. London: Shaw Publishing Co., 1915 and 1937.

Who's who in music, and musicians' international directory. London: Burke's Peerage Ltd., 1962.

WILLIAMS, Peter and OWEN, Barbara. *The new Grove organ*. London: Macmillan, 1988.

WOOD, Sir Henry J. *My life of music*. London: Victor Gollancz, 1946.

YOUNG, Percy M. *A history of British music*. London: Ernest Benn, 1967.

Hymn books

Church Hymns. London: S.P.C.K., 1874.

Congregational Hymnary. London: Congregational Union of England and Wales, 1916.

Congregational Praise. Congregational Union of England and Wales, 1950.

Hymns Ancient and Modern. London: The Proprietors of Hymns Ancient and Modern, Standard Edition, 1916; New Standard Edition (4th impression), 1985.

The Church Hymnary with Supplement (Revised edition). Oxford: Oxford University Press, 1927.

With one voice: A hymn book for all the churches. London: Collins, 1985. (First published as *The Australian Hymn Book,* 1977.)

Y caniedydd cynulleidfaol newydd. London: The Bookroom of the Welsh Independents, 1921.

Journals

The Berkshire Organist (1984–1991).

Musical Times (1899 onwards).

Miscellaneous

ARCHER, Malcolm. Sleeve notes for record of organ music, including A.H. Brewer. Aylesbury: Priory Records, 1986.

FINGLETON, David. Sleeve notes on Geoffrey Burgon. London: Hyperion Records.

JACKSON, Francis. *Sir Edward Bairstow*. Lecture delivered to the Church Music Society on 5 July 1986.

Programme of the Charles Wood Summer School. Armagh, 1996.

A

ABDEY, Dr. Alfred William (1876-?)
Born in Brentford, Middlesex in 1876.
Received his musical education privately; graduated B.Mus. at
New College, Oxford (1907). Later became an Oxford D.Mus.
Assistant director of the London College of Music. Bandmaster to
the Hampshire Regiment (1917-1919).
Organist and choirmaster of the Sussex institutions of St. Andrew's
Church, Burgess Hill (1898-1903); the Chapel Royal, Brighton
(1903-1910) and St. Augustine's Church, Brighton (from 1910). A
local operatic society conductor.
Composed a Te Deum in G (1908), and works for piano and for
organ.

ABERNETHY, Dr. Frank Nicholson (1864-1927)
Born in Lambeth, London in 1864; died in East Dulwich, London
on 29 January 1927. Graduated B.Mus. (1890) and D.Mus. (1895)
at New College, Oxford. Held appointments in London as organist
of St. Saviour's Collegiate Church, Southwark (1882-1897) - now
elevated to cathedral status - and as organist and choirmaster of St.
John's Presbyterian Church, Forest Hill (1898-1927). Joint editor
of *Church Praise* (1907) with John Borland. Composed church
music including a Magnificat and Nunc Dimittis in C (1895), the
anthem 'I have made God my hope' (?1894), hymn tunes and
works for organ.

ABINGDON, Willoughby, Earl of (1740-1799)
An amateur flute player and composer, whose works include the
anthem 'Grant, we beseech Thee'.

ABRAM, Dr. John (1840-1918)
Born in Margate, Kent on 7 August 1840; died in Hastings, Sussex
on 17 January 1918. Educated privately in music, graduating
B.Mus (1868) and D.Mus. (1874) at New College, Oxford.
Organist of the Churches of St. John, Torquay, Devon
(1864-1866); SS Peter and Paul, Wantage, Berkshire (1866-1869);
St. Paul's, St. Leonards-on-Sea, Sussex (1869-1890) and the
nearby All Saints, Hastings from not later than 1893 until after
1897. Composed the oratorio *The Widow of Nain* (1874); anthems
for Easter-tide, 'Christ is risen' (1897) and Harvest-tide, 'The earth
is the Lord's' (1897); services, including a chant setting of the Te
Deum (1865); piano items and songs.

ABYNGDON (Abyndon), Henry (c1420-c1497)
Believed to have lived from 1420 to 1497, both years being
approximate although some sources claim a precise date of 1
September 1497 for his death.
The first person known to have graduated Mus.B. at the University
of Cambridge, in 1464.
A successful and celebrated singer and organist both within and
outside the pre-Reformation English church, his earliest known
appointment was that of lay clerk at Eton College (1447-1451). He
moved to a similar position at the Chapel Royal in 1451, later
serving as master of the choristers there (1455-1478).
Known to have been succentor of Wells Cathedral and to have held
other positions, including that of master of St. Catherine's
Hospital, Bristol in 1478.
Believed to have written music for the church, but his compositions
have not survived.

ACFIELD, William (c1832-1916)
Born around the year 1832; died in Gunnersbury, near Chiswick,
London on 15 October 1916. Composed the words and tune of 'O
Summer-Land!' (1896), Vesper Hymn Number One (1892) - the
first of a short series - and other hymn tunes.

ACLAND, Arthur Henry Dyke
See **TROYTE,** Arthur Henry Dyke.

ADAMS, Robert (16th century)
Few personal details are known of Robert Adams, except that he
lived during the middle years of the 16th century. He was a
musician of the Chapel Royal, and he is known to have composed a
Venite and Nunc Dimittis.

ADAMS, Thomas (1785-1858)
Born possibly in London and baptised on 5 September 1785; died
on 15 September 1858.
Studied music under **Thomas Busby** from the age of 11.
Held a number of London organistships, beginning with the
Carlisle Chapel, Lambeth (1802-1814), followed by St. Paul's,
Deptford (1814-1824). In 1824, the new Church of St. George,
Camberwell was built: Thomas Adams became its first organist
(1824-1858), composing an anthem 'O how amiable' for the

consecration service. Additionally, organist of St. Dunstan-in-the-West, Fleet Street (1832-1858).

Thomas Adams was often called upon by organ manufacturers to test their new instruments prior to dismantling and despatch.

'O how amiable' is one of several anthems he composed, in addition to organ fugues and voluntaries, items for piano, hymns and sacred songs.

ADAMS, Thomas (?-1918)

Died on 4 November 1918. Organist of the London Church of St. Alban, Holborn, where he designed the new organ, for more than 20 years. Composed settings of the Magnificat and Nunc Dimittis in F (1884) and in C (1894), and anthems including 'Sing we merrily unto God' (1904).

ADCOCK, James (1778-1860)

Born in Eton, Berkshire on 29 June 1778; died in Cambridge on 30 April 1860. A chorister of St. George's Chapel, Windsor Castle (1786-1796), first under William Webb and subsequently under **Theodore Aylward** (c1730-1801), and at Eton College under **William Sexton**. Became a lay clerk at St. George's Chapel (1797) and at Eton College (1799). Moved to Cambridge and sang in the Choirs of St. John's College, Trinity College and King's College. Published *The Rudiments of Singing*. He composed an Evening Service in B-flat and another in D, anthems including 'My soul truly waiteth still upon God' and 'Thou knowest, Lord, the secrets of our hearts' glees, and songs.

ADCOCK, John (1838-1919)

Born in Loughborough, Leicestershire on 31 August 1838; died in Nottingham on 12 January 1919. Worked in Spalding, Lincolnshire from the age of 16 as a school usher; became the choirmaster of the chapel and conductor of the local choral society. Moved in 1858 to Nottingham, where he sold sheet music, later becoming manager of the shop. For 21 years he was choirmaster of the Castle Gate Congregational Church in the city. Compiled *The School Hymnal Tune Book* (1882), in which were some of his own tunes; wrote a book on pronunciation for singers which was published in 1878. Won two guineas (£2.10) for a hymn tune composed for the Nonconformist Choir Union Festival of 1894. His tune 'Woodbrook' was used in the Revised Edition (1927) of *Church Hymnary* with the hymn 'If I come to Jesus' by Frances van Alstyne. The tune is also used in *Hymns of Faith* (1964).

ADDISON, John (c1765-1844)

Born in London around the year 1765; died in Camden Town, London on 30 January 1844.

As a child, John Addison learned to play the flageolet, flute, bassoon and violin. He played the cello in Vauxhall Gardens and the double bass at the Italian Opera, the Concerts of Ancient Music and the Vocal Concerts. His wife, the singer Miss Willems, whom he married in 1793, became an accomplished opera singer; the couple lived and worked for a time in Liverpool, Bath, Dublin and Manchester. John Addison worked briefly in the cotton trade while living in Manchester. However his principal occupation was as an orchestral cellist, double bass player and teacher of singing. He later concentrated on the double bass

Composed the operas *Sleeping Beauty* (1805) and *The Russian Impostor* (1809) and a sacred musical drama. Items by him were included in *A Collection of Psalms and Hymns for... Parish Churches* (1790).

ADDISON, Robert Brydges (c1860-?)

Born in Dorchester, Dorset around the year 1860. Studied at the Royal Academy of Music under **George Macfarren**, where and under whom he was later a sub-professor; also a professor of harmony and composition at Trinity College of Music, London (from 1892). Composed songs, the motet *Save me, O Lord* and the anthem, based on Psalm 126, 'They that sow in tears'.

AGUTTER, Dr. Benjamin (1844-1913)

Born in St. Albans, Hertfordshire on 2 April 1844; died in Fritwell, Oxfordshire on 7 June 1913.

Attended St. Albans Grammar School. Studied singing under Manuel Garcia, organ playing and composition under **E.J. Hopkins** and harmony and composition with **Henry Wylde**. Graduated B.Mus. at Exeter College, Oxford in 1870. The Lambeth D.Mus. was conferred upon him in 1891.

Precentor, organist and choirmaster of St. Peter's Church, Streatham, London (1867-1905).

Composed Masses *of St. Alban* and *of St. Peter*, 10 Holy Communion settings including versions in E (1906) and in B-flat (1874), a Magnificat and Nunc Dimittis in A-flat (1888), anthems including 'Blessed be the man that provideth for the sick and needy' (1870), hymn tunes and carols.

AINGER, Revd. Geoffrey (b.1925)

Born in Mistley, near Manningtree, Essex on 28 October 1925.

Educated at Brackendale School, Norwich, Norfolk; Richmond College and the Union Theological Seminary in New York City.

A minister of the Methodist Church, in Loughton, Essex (1958-1962) and Notting Hill, London during the 1960s. Notting Hill attracted a number of other composers including **Ian Calvert**, **Sydney Carter**, **June Boyce-Tillman** and **Donald Swann**. A group of these and other composers issued private collections of hymns and songs for use in Christian worship, including *Songs from Notting Hill* and *Songs from the Square*, referring to Trafalgar Square, London, where the music was sung.

Was then a school teacher before returning to the Methodist Circuit in south east London. Now retired.

Wrote the hymn or worship song 'Born in the night' and composed the tune 'Mary's Child' to accompany it. The tune has been used in three major hymnals including *Hymns and Psalms* (1983).

AINLEY, William Clark (1834-?)

Born in Kirkheaton, Yorkshire on 13 July 1834.

A chorister of his local parish church from the age of 10.

Studied music privately, graduating Mus.B. at the University of Cambridge (1885).

Appointed organist and choirmaster of the Yorkshire Parish Churches of Kirkburton (1856), Kirkheaton (1863), Mold Green (1865) and Mirfield (1874); also music master of Batley Grammar School.

Composed anthems including 'O give thanks' and 'Behold, O God our Defender', the latter being written for the Diamond Jubilee of Queen Victoria in 1897. His services include a Te Deum, a Holy Communion Service in G and an Evening Service in E. Also composed pieces for organ.

AINSCOUGH, Juliana Mary (b.1957)

Julie Ainscough was born in London on 25 April 1957.

Attended Trinity College of Music (1975-1979) where she studied organ, piano and composition. From 1981 until 1984 she undertook part-time study at Goldsmiths' College, London, graduating M.Mus. in composition.

Visiting piano teacher of the Francis Holland School, London (from 1980).

Organist in Putney, London of the churches of St. Margaret (1981-1983) and SS Peter and Paul (from 1983).

Her church music includes the anthems 'De profundis' (1978) and 'Super flumina Babylonis' (1980). She has composed chamber works, including a Quintet (1976), a Piano Sonata (1978) and songs. Awarded the composition prize of the Royal Philharmonic Society in 1978.

AINSLIE, John (b.1942)
Editor of *The Simple Gradual for Sundays and Holy Days* (1969). His hymn tune 'Worlebury' was used with 'Reap me the earth as a harvest to God' in the New Standard Edition (1983) of *Hymns Ancient and Modern* and has also been used in the collections *New Church Praise* (1975) and *Praise The Lord* (1972).

AKERMAN, Richard Frank Martin (c1876-1938)
Died in 1938 at the age of 62. Assistant organist of St. George's Chapel, Windsor Castle and one of the first students of the Royal College of Music. Martin Akerman was assistant music master of Eton College, one of a number of appointments that he held in and around Windsor, Berkshire. The first editor of *The Year Book Press* series of anthems and church music (1911). His anthems include 'I call and cry to Thee, O Lord' (1900) and 'Lo! my Shepherd is divine' (1902) for Men's Voices. Also known for his arrangement of Bach's 'Jesu, Joyaunce of my heart' for Trebles.

AKEROYD, Arthur Thomas (1862-?)
Born in Bradford, Yorkshire on 10 March 1862. An articled pupil of **Frederic Atkinson**. Organist of the Parish Churches of Oswestry, Shropshire (1879-1881) and Ellesmere, Shropshire, (1881-1889); St. Paul's Church, Bradford, Yorkshire (1889-1899) and St. Margaret's Church, Ilkley, Yorkshire (1899-1904). Organist and director of the choir of St. Mark's Church, Harrogate, Yorkshire. A teacher of music at Bradford Girls' Grammar School (from 1895) for more than 39 years. Singing master of Harrogate Ladies' College (from 1908). A local vocal and orchestral society conductor. Composed works for piano and organ, an opera *The Professor* (1891) and anthems including 'They that put their trust'.

AKEROYD (Akeroyde), Samuel (c1650-?)
Born, probably in Yorkshire, around the year 1650; he probably died early in the 18th century. A musician-in-ordinary of James II and William I (1687-1690). In 1695 he was a wait of the City of London. Composed many songs. Some of his hymn tunes were included in *The Divine Companion* (1701).

Alaw Ddu
See **REES,** William Thomas.

Alawydd
See **ROBERTS,** David Alawydd.

ALBERT, Prince Consort (1819-1861)
Born in Rosenau, Germany on 26 August 1819; died in Windsor, Berkshire on 14 December 1861.
Married the reigning monarch, Queen Victoria, in February 1840.

He played the organ, sang, and composed, although it is sometimes suggested that he had discreet professional help with his writing. An edition of his work, published in 1880, includes a Morning Service.

Two of his anthems were sung at Queen Victoria's jubilees. In *Church Hymns* (1874), edited by **Arthur Sullivan**, Prince Albert's tunes 'Coburg' and 'Gotha' are used with the hymn 'Jesus calls us o'er the tumult' by Mrs. Cecil Frances Alexander and 'Praise the Lord, His glories show' by Henry Lyte.

ALCOCK, Gilbert A. (1870-1954)
Born in London in 1870; died on 10 January 1954. The younger brother of **Walter Alcock**. Trained at Westminster Abbey: articled to **Frederick Bridge**. Studied with Herbert Sharpe. Organist of Holy Trinity Church, Eastbourne, Sussex for six years, and then organist and choirmaster of St. John's, Eastbourne for 48 years. Composed a Magnificat and Nunc Dimittis (1936), a set of alternative chants for the Psalms appointed for the fourth evening of the month (1914), Chants for the Te Deum (1905 and 1915), a carol 'Follow the star' (1933), and songs.

ALCOCK (Allcock), Dr. John (1715-1806)
Born near St. Paul's Cathedral, London on 11 April 1715; died in Lichfield, Staffordshire in February 1806 and was buried on the 23rd.

A boy chorister and colleague of **William Boyce** from the age of seven (1722-1729) at St. Paul's Cathedral under **Charles King**. From 1729, at the age of 14, he was apprenticed to the blind organist **John Stanley** at the Temple Church, London. He graduated B.Mus. (1755) and D.Mus. (1761), at the University of Oxford, submitting for his doctorate the anthem 'Sing unto the Lord'.

Served as deputy to John Stanley in London at St. Andrew's Holborn and at the Temple Church (1734). Early in his career he was a parish church organist at All Hallows, London (1735-1737); St. Andrew's, Plymouth, Devon (1737-1741) and St. Laurence, Reading, Berkshire (1742-1749).

During his time at Reading wrote *The Life of Miss Fanny Brown*, a work that was in part autobiographical, under the pseudonym of John Piper (piper being colloquial at the time for organist). Private organist at some time to the Earl of Donegal.

In January 1750 he took up the position of master of the choristers and organist at Lichfield Cathedral at a salary of only £4 per annum, and of vicar choral.

In 1758, 10 vicars choral of Lichfield complained to the authorities of Alcock's rudeness and lack of Cupertino towards the choir and his lack of reverence during services. They claimed that he played the organ perversely in order to confound them musically during worship. Alcock received a warning about his conduct from the Dean and Chapter to which he later responded in a foreword to a collection of anthems: he claimed that the choir was unfit to sing the services, citing both poor attendance and lack of ability.

The impasse could not continue, and by 1765 Alcock had resigned in disenchantment from the position of organist. Rheumatism had been a further problem and his resignation might have been expected some years earlier. He remained in the choir as a vicar choral and continued to live in the Cathedral Close while he resumed his work within the diocese as a parish church organist, being appointed to Sutton Coldfield (1761-1786) and Tamworth (1766-1790).

In publishing a set of anthems (1771) he expressed exasperation that in 10 years at the cathedral he had never found a book in the organ loft fit for use, other than those he had provided at his own expense. Part of the problem had been the quality of the little material that had been available to him, which was full of copyists' mistakes. In 1752 he decided to publish quarterly collections of services by composers such as **William Byrd**, **Orlando Gibbons** and **Thomas Tallis** as well as works of his own and called for like-minded people to submit good quality scores.

Maurice Greene had already embarked on a similar project and when Alcock learned of this he handed over his own collection to the other (1752). Greene had undertaken to provide all the principal choirs in the country with a copy of his collection. Although Greene died before the work was complete it was incorporated by William Boyce within his *Cathedral Music*, published in three separate volumes between 1760 and 1773. Alcock published a collection of hymn tunes, many of which were adaptations, in *Harmony of Jerusalem*.

Alcock had begun to compose while still in his teens. His musical output for the church consisted of some 59 chants, services including Canticles in F, which are still sung at Lichfield Cathedral, a setting to the Latin version of Psalm 51 and a book of 26 anthems which he published in 1771. Various other anthems were composed between 1754 and 1798. An example of his anthems is 'Wherewithal shall a young man cleanse his way'.

His Chant in B-flat was used in the Revised Edition (1927) of *Church Hymnary*. In addition, he wrote for harpsichord and won Catch Club prizes for composition between 1770 and 1778.

ALCOCK, John (1740-1791)

Born in Plymouth, Devon where he was baptised on 28 January 1740; died in Walsall, Staffordshire on 30 March 1791.

A chorister under his father of the same name at Lichfield, acting as deputy to him from the age of 12. Graduated B.Mus. at the University of Oxford (1773).

Organist and master of the song school at Newark, Nottinghamshire (1758-1768); became organist of St. Matthew's Church, Walsall in 1773.

As well as church music - which included anthems and a Double Chant in E-flat - Alcock published songs, cantatas and instrumental music. Collaborated with his father in the publication of the collection *Six New Anthems...* (?1795). His works include the anthems 'Arise, O Lord, and lift up', and 'The Lord is King'.

ALCOCK, Stanley (1871-1964)

Born in Twickenham, Middlesex in 1871; died in Chieveley, Berkshire on 7 January 1964. Composed a motet *Bone Pastor* (1960), a Missa Brevis (1943), and the words and tune of the hymn 'Faith of our fathers'.

ALCOCK, Sir Walter Galpin (1861-1947)

Born in Edenbridge, Kent on 29 December 1861; died in Salisbury, Wiltshire on 11 September 1947.

Educated privately before becoming Society of Arts scholar (1876-1881) at the National Training School of Music (which was superseded by the Royal College of Music in 1882), studying under **John Stainer**, **Arthur Sullivan**, **John Francis Barnett** and **Eaton Faning**. Graduated B.Mus. (1896) and D.Mus. (1905) at the University of Durham.

Became renowned as an organ recitalist, his improvisations drawing special praise. He was the 'A' of the 'ABC' trio of organists at the 1937 Coronation, the others being **George Thalben-Ball** and G.D. Cunningham.

Earned the distinction of taking a key part in the music of three Coronations at Westminster Abbey: Edward VII (1902), George V (1911) and George VI (1937). After the second of these he was appointed M.V.O., and he was knighted in 1933.

He held the posts of assistant organist (1873-1879) and organist (1881) at St. Mary's Church, Twickenham, Middlesex and in London at the Quebec Chapel (later known as the Church of the Annunciation) in Bryanston Street (from 1882), and Holy Trinity, Sloane Street (1895-1902) where he succeeded Edwin Lemare. From 1896 his assistant at Holy Trinity was the youthful **John Ireland**, who subsequently became an academic and composer.

Organist and composer to the Chapels Royal (1902-1916). From 1896 to 1916 he held an appointment as an assistant to **Frederick Bridge** at Westminster Abbey although he had served unofficially since 1886.

The question as to why Alcock did not succeed to the organistship of Westminster Abbey has often been raised. It is possible that the authorities were concerned about his health prospects and lack of robustness following serious illness A more likely explanation is that which circulated at the time, that the Dean and Chapter had told Alcock that they would in due course be looking for a younger man who was not steeped in the traditions of the Abbey, and who would be an eminent choir trainer rather than an organist.

In any event, Alcock did not wait for the Abbey organistship to fall vacant. He was appointed organist of Salisbury Cathedral in 1917, where he remained until his death. In addition he was a professor of organ at the R.C.M., where he had taught since 1893.

Walter Alcock was known among his friends as a model railway enthusiast with a layout that he built and ran in his garden at Salisbury. Alcock had a flair for engineering, and had intimate knowledge of the technical intricacies of the organ. That same ability was applied to the building of his models, the parts for which he turned on his own lathe.

Hubert Parry dedicated his Third Fantasia to Walter Alcock who returned the compliment by contributing to the collection in Parry's memory of miniature works by leading composers of the day, *For the little Organ Book*.

He wrote church music, including settings of the Morning Canticles in B-flat (1914), and in G (1936), and a version for Men's Voices in D (1889). He composed the anthems 'And I heard a great voice', written for the 700th anniversary of Salisbury Cathedral in 1920, and 'When the Lord turned'.

His hymn tune 'Bryant' was used in the Revised Edition (1927) of *Church Hymnary* with the hymn 'There were ninety and nine that safely lay' by Elizabeth Clephane. His Double Chant in D is found in *Baptist Hymn Book* (1962).

A number of his organ works are still performed today, including his Introduction and Passacaglia and the Fantasia *Impromptu*.

ALDEN, Dr. John Hewlett (1900-1976)

Born in Hornsey, London on 22 February 1900; died in Devizes, Wiltshire on 6 November 1976.

His formal education was entirely in Oxford, at New College School where he was a chorister, Magdalen College School and New College. His degrees included M.A. and D.Mus.

Director of music at the Diocesan College, Cape Town, South Africa (1923-1926). He then taught music at various English establishments and was assistant director of music at Harrow School (1927-1930); director of music at Bradfield College,

Berkshire (1930-1934 and 1946-1953); Eastbourne College, Sussex (1940-1945) and the Royal Naval College, Dartmouth, Devon (1946-1947).

Organist of St. Martin-in-the-Fields, London (1934-1938) and Bradfield College, Berkshire (1947-1953).

Part-time lecturer in education at the University of Reading, Berkshire (1957-1974).

Composed a setting of the Magnificat and Nunc Dimittis (1929). His hymn tune 'Shepherd boy's song' is used with the hymn 'He that is down needs fear no fall' by John Bunyan in the compilation *Hymns and Psalms* (1983).

ALDRICH, Revd. Dr. Henry (1647-1710)
Born in Westminster, London in January 1647; died in Oxford on 14 December 1710.

Attended Westminster School and Christ Church, Oxford (1662), where he was to remain in various capacities for the rest of his life. Graduated B.A. (1666), M.A. (1669) and D.D. (1682).

Although his career was devoted to church music he was also an architect, cathedral administrator, classical scholar, heraldist and theologian.

After ordination he was appointed vicar of Wem, Shropshire but continued to live at Christ Church where his career prospered. In 1681 he was appointed canon and, in 1689, dean (a position he held until his death). He later became vice chancellor (1692-1695).

Aldrich enjoyed good company and was notorious for his passion for smoking a pipe. He accumulated a valuable collection of musical manuscripts which he bequeathed to the college.

His anthems, including those not written entirely by him, number some 50 including 'Not unto us, O God' and 'Out of the deep'. A Single Chant in A was included in *Cathedral Psalter Chants* (1875). His Services in A, in E Minor and in G remained popular well into the 19th century.

ALEXANDER, Alfred (1844-?)
Born in Rochester, Kent on 6 May 1844.

A chorister and pupil of **John Hopkins** at Rochester Cathedral. Graduated B.Mus. at the University of Toronto (1889).

At the age of 17 he succeeded **Frederick Bridge** as organist of Shorne Parish Church, near Rochester. In 1865 he took up a similar appointment in the same county at Strood. He was also organist to the Earl of Mar and Kellie.

Succeeded **Langdon Colborne** as organist of St. Michael's College, Tenbury, Worcestershire (1874-1877), proceeding in the latter year to Wigan Parish Church, Lancashire and later to France where he was organist of the American Church at Nice (1891-1892) before returning to Lancashire as organist of St. Andrew's Church, Southport.

He composed services including three settings dating from 1890 of the Benedicite in B-flat, in E-flat and in C; anthems including 'Put me not to rebuke' (1908); six Kyries (1899); cantatas; chamber works; songs and part songs.

ALFORD, Revd. Dr. Henry (1810-1871)
Born in Bloomsbury, London on 7 October 1810; died in Canterbury, Kent on 12 January 1871. His father was rector of Aston Sandford.

Educated at Ilminster Grammar School, Somerset and Trinity College, Cambridge.

Curate at his father's church in Winkfield, Wiltshire. Also served a curacy at Ampton. Following his ordination as priest he was vicar of Wymeswold, Leicestershire for 18 years, and incumbent (from 1853) of the Quebec Chapel, Portman Square, London (later renamed the Church of the Annunciation). In 1857 he became dean of Canterbury Cathedral.

He is best known for his writings which included sermons, poetry and a major work of scholarship on the New Testament but was also an editor, translator and composer of tunes. Of his hymns, 'Come, ye thankful people, come' has long been associated with the tune 'St. George's Chapel' by a former chorister of Canterbury Cathedral, **George Elvey**. Author of the hymn 'In token that Thou shall not fear' (1832), which appeared in successive editions of *Hymns Ancient and Modern*. Edited *The Year of Praise* (1867), a collection of hymns and tunes for Canterbury Cathedral.

ALISON (Allison), Richard (?-c1610)
Described himself as a 'gentleman practitioner in the art of musicke'. He was active in the period eight years or so each side of the year 1600.

A composer of madrigals and songs. Wrote and harmonised Psalm tunes and metrical Psalms. His original intention was to provide a musical supplement to the Sternhold and Hopkins version of the Psalter. In 1592 he harmonised the edition of Psalms by Thomas East and in 1599, he published *The Psalmes of David in Meter*. In 1606 followed *An Howres Recreation in Musicke*, in which he imposed a formal metre upon melodies from **John Day**'s version of the Psalter (1579) and added harmonies.

Richard Alison is also known for his hymn tune 'Playford', and the anthems 'Behold, now praise the Lord' and 'The sacred choir of angels'. In *Church Hymns* (1874), edited by **Arthur Sullivan**, Alison's tune 'Wearmouth', also known as 'Old 81st', is the setting to the hymn 'O Sight for angels to adore' by William Walsham How. His hymn tunes are found in a number of 19th-century collections, and may have been adapted from their original form.

ALLAN, James (1842-1885)
Born near Falkirk, Stirlingshire, Scotland on 27 July 1842; died in Glasgow on 10 August 1885.

Lived and worked in Glasgow as a lithographer, and precentor of the Sydney Place United Presbyterian Church and the Kelvinside Free Church. Composer of the anthem 'He shall feed His flock' (1928). His hymn tunes include 'Vevay', which is found in *Free Church Hymnal*. Also composed part songs.

ALLCHIN, William Thomas Howell (1843-1883)
Born in Oxford in 1843; died at Oxford on 8 January 1883.
Graduated B.Mus. at New College, Oxford (1869).

Organist of three Oxford Parish Churches, including the University Church of St. Mary and subsequently of St. John's College, Oxford (from 1875). A teacher and examiner in music, and a leading figure in the music of the city.

Composed as his B.Mus. exercise a sacred cantata *The Rebellion of Korah*. Also composed hymn tunes, carols and songs although the total of his output is quite small.

ALLEN, George Benjamin (1822-1898)
Born in London on 21 April 1822; died in Brisbane, Australia on 30 November 1898.

A chorister at the church of St. Martin-in-the-Fields, London (from 1830), and at Westminster Abbey (from 1832). Graduated B.Mus. at the University of Oxford (1852).

A bass singer in the Choir of Armagh Cathedral (from 1843). On returning to London he was organist of All Saints' Church, Kensington. He then emigrated to Australia where he took up an organistship at Toorak, Melbourne but returned to England and formed a comic opera company, in whose repertory the Savoy operas of Gilbert and Sullivan featured prominently.

Composed a two-act opera *Castle Grim* (1865), cantatas, many songs, part songs, pieces for organ and for piano and services including a Te Deum and Jubilate in F (1866). A book of 15 oh his anthems was published in 1853. His anthems include 'I will worship toward Thy holy temple' (1887).

ALLEN, Sir Hugh Percy (1869-1946)
Born in Reading, Berkshire on 23 December 1869; died in Oxford on 20 February 1946 following an accident involving a motor cycle.

Educated at Kendrick School (now Reading School). Organ scholar at Christ's College, Cambridge (from 1892), graduating Mus.B. (1893), B.A. (1895), Mus.D. (1898) and M.A. (1899). Later in life the academic honours bestowed upon him included the Litt.D. (Sheffield, 1926).

The playing of **Frederick Read** who at the time was organist of Christ Church, Reading had inspired Allen at the age of eight to learn the organ from Dr. Read. He took up local parish church organistships from the age of 11, at St. Saviour's, Coley (1880); Tilehurst (1884) and Eversley (1886). Read subsequently became organist of Chichester Cathedral and made Allen his assistant (1886-1892) when appointed organist. During this time, Hugh Allen was assistant music master at Wellington College, Berkshire (1887-1892).

Held the three appointments as cathedral or collegiate organist of St. Asaph's, Wales (1897-1898); Ely (1898-1900) and New College, Oxford (1901-1918), the latter being the post to which he had always aspired and for which he competed successfully against his powerful fellow-candidates **Edward Bairstow**, organist at the time of Wigan Parish Church and subsequently of York Minster, and Hubert Hunt, organist of Bristol Cathedral.

Allen's biographer, **Thomas Wood**, described Allen's playing of the organ at New College as 'eaten up with energy'. Allen apparently saw no harm in transposing the daily service up by a minor third, commenting 'There's nothing like putting a choir on its beam ends'.

Succeeded his friend **Hubert Parry** as director of the Royal College of Music (1919-1937). In his term of office he brought about an increase in the number of students from 200 to 600 within two years and introduced new teaching methods. For these and other services he was knighted in 1920 and appointed G.C.V.O. (1935).

Professor of music at the University of Oxford (1918-1946) in succession to **John Goss**. It was Allen who finally established the faculty of music at the university. During his term of office, he and **Ralph Vaughan Williams**, his fellow examiner, failed **William Walton** in the B.Mus. composition paper.

Director of music (1908 -1918) at University College, Reading (later, the University of Reading).

Since the 1890s Allen had been a champion of Bach. He directed the Bach Choir (1907-1921), taking over the position from **Walford Davies**. He had charge of the Oxford Bach Choir (1901-1926) and conducted festivals of communal hymn singing at the city's Sheldonian Theatre.

While at Chichester, Allen had composed a lively Magnificat and although it was prepared for performance, it was vetoed by the clergy. Allen's hymn tune 'Midian' appeared in *New College Hymn Book* (1911) with 'Christian, dost thou see them?'. 'Qui laborat orat' was composed for 'Come, labour on'.

Another tune, 'Kingley Vale', was used in *Hymns Ancient and Modern* (New Standard Edition) with 'Thanks to God whose Word was spoken' and elsewhere with the hymn 'Lord dismiss us with Thy Blessing' by Henry Buckoll. He harmonised a number of accompaniments for plainsong melodies, and compiled a new college hymnal for Cheltenham Ladies' College, where he was director of music. But by far his best known work is his arrangement of Bach's Cantata 147 to words by the poet laureate, Robert Bridges, beginning 'Jesu, Joy of man's desiring'.

Henry Wood wrote of him that he knew of no-one else with a greater capacity for making and keeping friends, nor anyone else with such a happy and genial temperament, but to others, his strong personality could be somewhat intimidating.

ALLEN, Revd. Peter John Douglas (b.1935)
A minister of the Church of Scotland. Until December 1992 he was senior chaplain to Sedburgh School, at which time he became priest-in-charge of St. Ninian's Church, Edinburgh. The hymn tune 'Feed us now' is used in the hymnal *With One Voice* (1978) with 'Feed us now, O Son of God'. Both hymn and tune are by Peter Allen. He has also composed the anthem 'O Son of God'.

ALLEYN, Alfred Hopkins (1867-1949)
Born in 1867; died in Exeter, Devon on 24 February 1949.
Few details of his life and career are known. Author of the novel *Combechester* (1939). Compiler of the hymnal *A little Primer for Home and School* (1935), in which his translation of the hymn 'Ales diei nuntius' was set to his tune 'Vernham Dean'. Later, the tune was used in the Revised Edition (1950) of *Hymns Ancient and Modern*.

ALLINSON (Allanson), Thomas (?-1705)
Died in Lincoln in 1705. Organist of Lincoln Cathedral (1693-1704). Composed the anthems 'Behold, God is my Helper' and 'Have mercy upon me'.

ALLISON, Dr. Horton Claridge (1846-1926)
Born in London on 25 July 1846; died on 17 October 1926.
Studied at the Royal Academy of Music (from 1856), where he became a piano pupil of **W.H. Holmes** and at the Leipzig Conservatory (1862-1865), where his teachers were Louis Plaidy, Ernst Richter, Carl Reinecke, Moritz Hauptmann and Ignaz Moscheles.

Graduated Mus.B. at St. John's College, Cambridge, and B.Mus. and D.Mus. at the University of Dublin, all in the same year: 1877.

On his return to London in July 1865 he began to give piano concerts. He was also organist of the Church of St. James, Piccadilly (from 1867). He then moved to Manchester where he taught music and was organist of the Lancashire Churches of St. Paul, Bolton (from 1868) and St. Paul, Kersal (from 1869). A professor at the Royal Manchester School of Music, being appointed at its foundation in 1892.

From 1884 he was a government schools inspector, specialising in music.

His compositions include anthems such as 'O praise the Lord O ye nations' (1873) and a work drawing on the text of Psalms 107, 110 and 134 for Solo Voices, Chorus and Strings (1876); items for piano and for organ; songs and part songs.

ALLITSEN, Mary Frances Bumpus (1849-1912)
Born in 1849; died in London on 2 October 1912. Attended Guildhall School of Music and became a concert singer in 1882, but her voice later failed and she took up teaching. Before attending G.S.M., Frances Allitsen had composed music but was unable to set down her works on paper. She sought advice from the principal, Weist Hill, who offered her a free scholarship to study music theory. Her compositions include the anthem 'Praise thou the Lord, O my soul' (1908) and a Psalm of Thanksgiving. Her works include an orchestral overture, *Undine*, with which she took the Lady Mayoress's Prize for Composition, and songs including *Christmas song* (1901). Her Edwardian ballad 'There's a land, a dear land' was popular during World War II.

ALLMAND, Frank (1858-1948)
Born in Wrexham, Wales in 1858; died in Liverpool on 8 September 1948. Composed hymn tunes, including a collection of five for use in the local Congregational Church in 1903.

ALLUM, Dr. Charles Edward (1852-?)
Studied under Yates, the organist of Bisham Abbey, Buckinghamshire. A pupil of, and assistant to William Ringrose. Graduated B.Mus. (1883) and D.Mus. (1887) at the University of Dublin. Organist and choirmaster of the Holy Trinity Episcopal Church, Stirling, Scotland (from 1874). Municipal organist to the boroughs of Stirling and Alloa and a captain in the 4th Stirlingshire volunteer battalion. Composed a setting of the Benedicite (1906), a Te Deum in B (1907), the anthems 'Come ye disconsolate' (1917) and 'O Lord, how manifold' (1917) and an oratorio *The Deliverance of Israel*.

ALWOOD (**Allwood, Alwoode, Allwoode**), Richard (16th century)
A composer and priest of the early 16th century. Composed a six-part Mass. Five items of sacred music by him were included in the *Mulliner Book*, a collection of more than a hundred musical pieces of the 16th century assumed to have been compiled by Thomas Mulliner, a mid 16th-century organist of St. Paul's Cathedral. Alwood also composed keyboard music.

AMBER, Daniel (1782-1871)
Composer of the anthem 'O Lord God, Thou Holy One of Israel', about whom little is known.

AMNER, Revd. John (1579-1641)
Baptised in Ely, Cambridgeshire on 24 August 1579; buried in Ely on 28 July 1641.
Graduated B.Mus. (1613) at the University of Oxford and Mus.B. (1640) at Cambridge. In March 1617 he was ordained deacon.
A contemporary of **Orlando Gibbons** and **Thomas Tomkins**. His uncle and possibly his brother already had connections with Ely Cathedral, where he was appointed in succession to **George Barcroft** as master of the choristers (1610-1641), organist (1615-1641) and, soon after his ordination in 1617, minor canon.
His *Sacred Hymnes*, 20 pieces for voices and viols, were published in 1615 and became popular. He is also known to have written two sets of Preces, three services including the work known as *Caesar's* Service, dedicated to Rev. Henry Caesar, dean of Ely (1614), 41

anthems including the verse anthem 'O ye little flock' and a Chant to Psalm 89. Many of his anthems are lost.

AMOTT, John (1798-1865)
Born in Monmouth, Wales in 1798; died in Gloucester on 3 February 1865. A pupil of **William Mutlow**, organist of Gloucester Cathedral. Organist of St. Chad's, the Abbey Church of Shrewsbury (1822-1832). Succeeded William Mutlow at Gloucester (1832-1865). Conducted the Three Choirs' Festival on the occasions when it was held in Gloucester; edited an account of the festivals in 1864. Composed anthems, services and a Sanctus in G. A collection of Kyries and chants was compiled by him.

AMPLEFORTH, Laurence
See **TERRY**, Richard Runciman.

AMPS, William (1824-1910)
Born in Cambridge on 18 December 1824; died in Cambridge on 20 May 1910. Educated at Peterhouse College, Cambridge, where graduated B.A. (1858) and M.A. (1862). For a time he was organist at Peterhouse and he held similar posts at King's College (1855-1876) and Christ's. He was also organist of St. Peter's Church, Cambridge and conductor of the university music society. Amps composed piano works including Sonatas in B-flat and in G Minor, and part songs. He is also known for the hymn tune 'Venice', which was first published in Thorne's *Selection of Psalms and Hymn Tunes* (1853) and continued to be popular with hymnal compilers into the present century. Also composed an anthem 'Thy God hath commanded thy strength' (1862).

ANDERSON, Dr. James Smith (1853-1945)
Born in Crail, Fife, Scotland on 30 June 1853; died in Edinburgh on 17 January 1945.
Studied with **George Martin** in Edinburgh and with **Albert Peace** in Glasgow. Graduated B.Mus. (1878) and later, D.Mus. at the University of Oxford.
Held organistships in Edinburgh at the Wesleyan Chapel, Nicolson Square (1872-1877); Abbey Parish Church (1877-1879); St. Thomas's Episcopal Church (1879-1881) and St. Andrew's Parish Church (from 1881). He taught music at schools in Edinburgh and gave piano instruction at the Moray House Training College and School (from 1892). A member of the Revision Committee for the 1927 Edition of *Church Hymnary*.
The hymn tunes 'Fingal' was used initially with the hymn 'I am not worthy, Holy Lord' and it has been used in five major hymnals including *Christian Worship* (1976). He also composed operettas, songs and items for the piano, including a Nocturne in A-flat (1884).

ANDERSON, Revd. William (1799-1872)
Born in Kilsyth, Stirlingshire, Scotland on 6 January 1799; died in Uddington, near Glasgow on 15 September 1872. Minister of the United Presbyterian Church in Glasgow, and pastor of a church in John Street. In 1841 he published a collection of hymns and tunes, including his own tunes 'Thanksgiving', 'Trinity' and 'Sacred Choir'.

ANDREWS, Dr. Herbert Kennedy (1904-1965)
Born in Comber, County Down, Northern Ireland on 10 August 1904; died in Oxford on 10 October 1965.

Kennedy Andrews was educated at Bedford School. Studied composition with **Ralph Vaughan Williams** at the Royal College of Music. Graduated B.Mus. (1935) and D.Mus. (1935) at Trinity College, Dublin.

Beverley Minster, where his assistant was **Gordon Reynolds**, was his first major appointment as organist (1934-1938), followed by New College, Oxford (1938-1956). At New College, where he graduated D.Mus. (1942), he studied modern history, taking the degrees of B.A. (1943) and M.A. (1944).

lectured in music at the University of Oxford, taught at the R.C.M., and was the author of much-admired works on Palestrina (1958) and Byrd (1966). He contributed articles to Grove's *Dictionary of Music and Musicians*. His *Oxford Harmony Volume II* (1950) deals exclusively, and in depth, with chromatic chords.

His compositions include motets, an Evening Service in D (1953) and others in D Minor and in G (1958), and the anthems 'He is the lonely Greatness of the world' (1956) for Good Friday, and 'The spacious firmament' (1949). He composed the motet *Ah see the fair chivalry come* on a poem for All Saints' Day by Lionel Johnson. His other works include songs.

ANDREWS, Richard Hofmann (1803-1891)
Born in London on 22 November 1803; died in Longsight, Manchester on 8 June 1891. A child actor, appearing at the Theatre Royal, Birmingham and elsewhere. At the age of nine he was apprenticed to the leader of the band of the Manchester Theatre. A teacher and, later, a music publisher in Manchester; also a concert violinist. Gave a concert, in 1885, in his 82nd year. Author of the book *Music as a Science* (1885) and the editor of a large quantity of piano items. Composed anthems including 'O Lord Thou art my God' and 'Praise ye the Lord', piano works and glees including 'Hail, fair peace'.

ANGEL, Alfred (1816-1876)
Born in 1816; died in Exeter, Devon on 24 May 1876. A chorister of Wells Cathedral, where he was later assistant organist. On the advice of **Stephen Elvey**, he was appointed organist of Exeter Cathedral (1842-1876) in succession to **S.S. Wesley**. Also master of the choristers at Exeter Cathedral, and a lay vicar (from 1864). Angel's 'Blow ye the trumpet in Zion' won him the Gresham Prize for composition in 1842. He also composed hymn tunes, part songs including 'Arise my fair and come away' (1861), and songs.

ANSON, Hugo Vernon (1894-1958)
Born in Wellington, New Zealand on 18 October 1894; died in London on 4 August 1958. Attended school in Wanganui. Came to England at the age of 18 in order to study at the Royal College of Music (1912-1913 and 1920-1921). He attended Trinity College, Cambridge, where he studied economics (1913-1920) but during the war years he was absent on military service. He eventually graduated M.A. and Mus.B. Music director at Alleyn's School (1922-1925). Registrar of the Royal College of Music (from 1939), where he had taught since 1925. His church compositions include a Benedictus (1930), a Magnificat and Nunc Dimittis, a Te Deum and carols. A composer of chamber and piano music.

ANSTEY, Thomas (19th century)
Thomas Anstey is believed to have been alive around the year 1830, when his collection *Sacred music...* was published, in two volumes. Composed the anthems 'Awake my glory' and 'By the waters of Babylon'.

APPELBY (Appleby), Thomas (c1488-c1562)
Thomas Appelby's life is believed to have spanned the years 1488 to 1562, both years being approximate. In 1536 he became acting organist, while already a vicar choral, of Lincoln Cathedral. He was formally appointed to the position in April 1538, serving until the following year. From July 1539 until 1541 one 'Applebie' was master of the choristers of Magdalen College, Oxford. Returned to Lincoln Cathedral in 1541 and resumed his former position, holding the appointment until 1562. Composed two Masses and a Magnificat.

APPLEFORD, Revd. Patrick Robert Norman (b.1925)
Born in Croydon, Surrey on 4 May 1925.
Educated at Hurstpierpoint College, Sussex and Trinity College, Cambridge where he graduated B.A. (1949) and M.A. (1954). Studied for the ministry of the Church of England at Chichester Theological College, Sussex, being ordained deacon in 1952, priest in 1953.
Dean of Lusaka Cathedral, Zambia (1966-1972). Priest-in-charge at the parishes of Sutton St. Nicholas and Sutton St. Michael in Hereford Diocese (1973-1975). Diocesan director of education at Chelmsford (1975-1990), and a residentiary canon of Chelmsford Cathedral (1978-1990). Retired in the latter year.
His tune 'Living Lord' is used in *Hymns Ancient and Modern* (New Standard Edition) and elsewhere with his 'Lord Jesus Christ, You have come to us'. Another popular combination is 'Henfield' with 'Jesus our Lord, our King and our God'. His Communion settings include the Mass of Five Melodies (1961) and the *New English* Mass (1973).

ARBUTHNOT, Dr. John (1667-1735)
Born in Arbuthnot, Scotland in 1667; died in London on 27 February 1735.
Graduated with a doctorate in medicine at the University of St. Andrews (1696), having undertaken at least part of his studies at the University of Aberdeen.
John Arbuthnot was at Epsom, Surrey when Prince George of Denmark, the husband of Queen Anne, fell ill. Arbuthnot's timely and competent intervention led to an appointment as physician extraordinary in 1705 to Queen Anne. When a position of physician in ordinary fell vacant (1709), Arbuthnot was preferred.
He helped found the Scriblerus Club (1714) whose objectives were to satirise abuses of the privileges of education. Among his friends were **Handel**, whom he befriended during Handel's litigation with his publishers, and Jonathan Swift. The latter became Dean of St. Patrick's Cathedral, Dublin and Arbuthnot recommended a number of prospective choristers as positions arose.
A composer of anthems.

ARCHER, Malcolm David (b.1952)
Born in Lytham St. Annes, Lancashire on 29 April 1952.
Attended King Edward VII School, Lytham. Royal College of Organists' scholar at the Royal College of Music (1970-1972) with Ralph Downes and **Herbert Sumsion**. Organ scholar at Jesus College, Cambridge (1972-1975), studying with Gillian Weir and Nicolas Kynaston. Graduated B.A. (1975) and M.A. (1979). Assistant organist of Magdalen College School, Oxford (1976-1978), in London at St. Clement Danes Church and Hampstead Parish Church, and at Norwich Cathedral to **Michael Nicholas** (from 1978).

Organist of Bristol Cathedral (1983-1989) and of Wells Cathedral (from 1996), composing and giving recitals during the intervening period.

Has composed more than 100 published works, mainly organ or choral, including a Requiem, the *Chichester* Service; various Mass settings including the *Christchurch* Mass and *St. Albans* Mass; a set of Responses and the anthems 'The Lord is my Shepherd' and 'My song is love unknown'. Other works include the musical *Walter and the Pigeons*.

ARGENT, William Ignatius (1844-?)

Born in Colchester, Essex on 26 August 1844. Organist of the Little Oratory, Brompton, London (1859-1860). From 1868 he lived in Liverpool and in Birkenhead. Organist of the Church of St. Lawrence, Birkenhead and St. Anne's Roman Catholic Church, Edge Hill, Liverpool. Conductor of local choral societies. Music critic of the *Liverpool Albion* (1873-1880) and *Liverpool Mercury* (1886-1890). Contributed to *Musical Times*, and compiled a modern history of Liverpool. Composed a Mass in A (1875), a Mass in B-flat dedicated to St. Benedict (1886), motets and anthems.

ARKWRIGHT, Dr. Marian Ursula (1863-1922)

Born in Norwich, Norfolk on 25 January 1863; died in Highclere, near Newbury, Berkshire on 23 March 1922. Graduated B.Mus. (1895) and D.Mus. (1913) at the University of Durham. Composed a Requiem Mass (1915). Her symphonic suite *The Winds of the World* won a prize for orchestral works offered by the magazine *The Gentlewoman*.

ARMES, Dr. Philip (1836-1908)

Born in Norwich, Norfolk on 15 August 1836; died in Durham on 10 February 1908.

A boy chorister at Norwich Cathedral (1846-1848) under **Zechariah Buck**. When his father became a lay clerk at Rochester Cathedral, Philip Armes took a place in the same choir (1848-1850). Famous for his beautiful voice. On leaving the choir in 1850 he was given the proceeds of a public testimonial in the form of a piano.

A pupil and articled assistant of **J.L. Hopkins** at Rochester (1850-1856). Graduated B.Mus. (1858) and D.Mus. (1864) at the University of Oxford, the first Oxford B.Mus. candidate to be required to submit to a *viva voce* examination. Received an honorary M.A. (1891) and a D.Mus. (1874) from the University of Durham.

His first parish church organist appointment was at Trinity Church, Milton, Gravesend, Kent (1855-1857). Succeeded **John Foster** (1827-1915) at St. Andrew's Church, Wells Street, London (1857-1861) where the performance of the music was said to be of cathedral standard. On Armes's departure for the organistship of Chichester Cathedral (1861), he was succeeded at Wells Street by **Joseph Barnby**.

Armes's tenure of the post at Chichester was brief, for he moved in the same year to Durham Cathedral (1861-1907). In the 1880s he indexed the manuscript part books at the Cathedral, some of which included works by **Thomas Tallis** and **Henry Purcell**. In 1890 he was appointed examiner in music at the University of Durham, becoming the university's first professor of music in 1907.

Composed a Morning, Evening and Holy Communion Service in G (1882-1889), a Cantate Domino and Deus Misereatur in A (1894)

and Holy Communion services, each published in 1920, in A, in B-flat and in G.

His hymn tunes 'St. Bede' and 'Galilee', originally used in the 1875 Edition of *Hymns Ancient and Modern* are still known today, the latter being associated with 'Jesus shall reign where'er the sun' in several hymnals. Wrote oratorios including *Hezekiah*, anthems including 'We wait for Thy loving kindness' (1912) and 'Give ear O ye heavens' (1876) which were popular in Victorian times. Composed Single Chants in A, in F and in G that were included in *Cathedral Psalter Chants* (1875), and services.

W.H. Monk praised him as one of a select group of composers producing music 'worthy of perpetual preservation' in contrast to other material which Monk characterised as effeminate.

ARMISTEAD, Dr. James (1877-1935)

Born in 1877; died in Burnley, Lancashire on 30 August 1935.

Educated at the Royal Manchester College of Music and then at Owen's College, Manchester. Graduated B.Mus. (1908) and D.Mus. at Queen's College, Oxford.

Organist in Burnley at the Wesleyan Church, Brierfield (1908) and Holy Trinity Church (1909).

Composed the anthem 'Our day of praise is done' (1910). His hymn tune 'Pro Patria' was published in 1912 in Novello's *Parish Choir Series* to the hymn 'To Thee our God we fly' by William Walsham How. The same combination was also used in *Hymns Ancient and Modern*.

ARMSTRONG, Revd. James (1840-1928)

Born in 1840; died in Castle Rock, County Derry, Northern Ireland on 30 April 1928. Graduated B.A. (1864) at Trinity College, Dublin, where he passed the Divinity Test with a category of first class (1865). Ordained deacon (1865) and priest (1866); graduated M.A. in 1870. Incumbent of Castle Rock (1868); a canon of Derry Cathedral from 1900. Known today for the hymn tune 'Newland', which he wrote at the request of Mrs. Cecil Frances Alexander, while she was staying at Newland, to her hymn 'Do no sinful action', for the 1889 Supplement to *Hymns Ancient and Modern*. He also composed a patriotic song 'The voice of the Empire'.

ARMSTRONG, Sir Thomas Henry Wait (1898-1994)

Born in Peterborough, Cambridgeshire on 15 June 1898; died on 26 June 1994.

The son of a local church musician. His own son, Lord Armstrong of Ilminster, was secretary to the Cabinet.

A chorister at the Chapel Royal, St. James's Palace. Attended King's School, Peterborough. In 1916 he became organ scholar of Keble College, Oxford, interrupting his studies to serve in the British Expeditionary Force (1917-1919). After the war he resumed at Keble College and read modern history. Organ scholar at the Royal College of Music (1922-1928) where he studied with **Gustav Holst**, **Walter Parratt** and **Ralph Vaughan Williams**; also under Ernest Read at the Matthay School.

Graduated B.A. (1922), B.Mus. (1923), M.A. (1925) and D.Mus. (1928) at the University of Oxford. In 1963 he received the honorary D.Mus. from the University of Edinburgh.

Thomas Armstrong was knighted in 1958.

Organist of Thorney Abbey (from 1914) and sub organist at Peterborough Cathedral (1914-1916) where he was articled to **Haydn Keeton**.

Sub organist of Manchester Cathedral (1921-1922). Organist of St. Peter's Church, Eaton Square, London (1922-1928), before taking up the two Cathedral organistships of Exeter (1928-1933) and Christ Church, Oxford (1933-1955), where he succeeded **William Harris**.

In 1937, Thomas Armstrong became choragus of the university and a lecturer and tutor in music. Conductor of the Oxford Bach Choir (1933-1955) and of the Oxford Orchestra. Took over the B.B.C. schools' broadcasts following the death of **Walford Davies**. Principal of the Royal Academy of Music (1955-1968).

His musical output includes choral and chamber music, and works for the church including a Magnificat and Nunc Dimittis in D Minor (1936), the anthems 'Christ, whose glory fills the skies' (1933), to words by Charles Wesley, and 'Lord it belongs not to my care' (1959). Continued to compose late in life.

ARNE, Dr. Thomas Augustine (1710-1778)
Born in Covent Garden, London on or around 12 March 1710; died in London on 5 March 1778. Educated at Eton, where he learned flute, harpsichord and violin. Studied violin under John Festing. Graduated D.Mus. at the University of Oxford (1759). Composer to the Drury Lane Theatre in London (from 1738); later, composer to all the principal London theatres. Often considered the foremost English composer of the 18th century, his output included songs including 'Under the greenwood tree' and oratorios, the airs from several of which were later arranged as hymn tunes. Arne wrote sacred music for the liturgy of the Roman Catholic Church. The hymn tune 'Hymn of Eve' is still known today but Arne remains most famous for the rousing 'Rule, Britannia'.

ARNOLD, Dr. George Benjamin (1832-1902)
Born in Petworth, Sussex on 22 December 1832; died in Winchester, Hampshire on 31 January 1902.
Studied under **George Chard** and **S.S. Wesley**, successive organists of Winchester Cathedral, and graduated B.Mus (1855) and D.Mus. (1861).at the University of Oxford.
Organist of St. Columba's College, Dublin (from 1852); Rathfarnham College, County Dublin (1853-1856) and of St. Mary's Church, Torquay, Devon (from 1856). A concert pianist.
Organist of New College, Oxford (1860-1865) and of Winchester Cathedral (1865-1902), where he succeeded S.S. Wesley, his former teacher.
His compositions include piano music, part songs, oratorios, of which an example is *Ahab* (1864), a Magnificat and Nunc Dimittis in F (1910), a Holy Communion Service in G and a Jubilate Deo in C (1899). He composed anthems including 'Praise the Lord' (1874) and 'Let the righteous be glad'.

ARNOLD, John (c1720-1792)
Some confusion surrounds the date and place of John Arnold's birth. It is believed that he was born in Essex some time within the period 1715 to 1720. He died in Great Warley, Essex and was buried on 14 February 1792. Very active as a composer, he was well known for his popular collections of Psalm tunes. He also wrote songs and catches, as well as *The Compleat Psalmodist* (1741), and he harmonised the hymn tune 'Windsor'.

ARNOLD, Dr. John Henry (1887-1956)
Born in St. Pancras, London on 29 May 1887; died in Stanmore, Middlesex on 19 June 1956.
Attended Dulwich College, London, and studied with **Martin Shaw** and Harvey Grace.
Awarded the Lambeth D.Mus. (1914).

Organist of the London Churches of St. Alphege, Southwark (from 1914) and Christ Church, Streatham Hill. Assistant organist to **Geoffrey Shaw** at St. Mary's Church, Primrose Hill, Hampstead (1920-1932). Counsellor in liturgy and music to the Church of John Keble, Mill Hill, London (from 1932).

Prominent in both the Church Music Society (where he was a member of the Executive Committee) and the Plainsong and Medieval Music Society. From time to time notices by him appeared in *Manchester Guardian*. An expert on typography and on the delivery of the written word.

During World War II, he worked in Salisbury, Wiltshire. Following a bout of severe illness he restricted his professional activities to teaching at the Royal School of Church Music, at colleges of theology, and at summer schools.

Arnold devised plainsong accompaniments to *Songs of Praise*, *Plainsong Hymnbook* and the Second Edition of *English Hymnal*. Edited the Advent Antiphons on the Magnificat, one of which is by tradition sung daily in the week before Christmas. Harmonised plainsong melodies for use as hymn tunes, some of which are still used today. Composed a Simple 3-Part Magnificat and Nunc Dimittis (1938) and a Benedicite (1953).

ARNOLD, Dr. Samuel (1740-1802)
Born in London on 10 August 1740; died in London on 22 October 1802. Buried in Westminster Abbey near **Henry Purcell** and **John Blow**.
Learned music as a boy at the Chapel Royal under Bernard Gates and **James Nares**. As a boy he was said to have been noticed and advised by **Handel**. Graduated both B.Mus and D.Mus. at the University of Oxford in 1773.
Organist of the Royal Female Orphan Asylum; composed a number of anthems for use in the chapel. Bought the Marylebone Gardens, London (1769) and promoted concerts there, a venture that proved unsuccessful financially.
Organist and composer to the Chapel Royal (1783-1793) in succession to James Nares; organist of Westminster Abbey (1793-1802), succeeding **Benjamin Cooke**. At Westminster Abbey his responsibilities excluded the position of master of the choristers, a responsibility held by **Richard Guise**. Became conductor of the Academy of Ancient Music. One of the founders of the Glee Club, with **John Wall Callcott**. Harpsichordist (1764) and later composer of the Covent Garden Theatre. Conductor of the Academy of Ancient Music (from 1789).
In 1761 he published a collection of Psalm tunes, *Compleat Psalmodist*, not to be confused with a collection of the same name by **John Arnold**. He was highly critical of composers who had not studied composition but presumed nevertheless to compose Psalm tunes. In 1791 he published his own continuation of Boyce's *Cathedral Music* but it fared badly, selling only some 120 copies. George III encouraged him to edit the entire work of Handel, a project that yielded a set of 40 volumes.
A prolific composer, among his works are a completion of the Magnificat and Nunc Dimittis in A by **William Boyce** (the work being subsequently known as Boyce and Arnold in A), other services, and anthems including 'God is our Hope' and 'Who is this that cometh from Edom?'. A Single Chant in B-flat was included in *Cathedral Psalter Chants* (1875). His hymn tunes include 'Llandaff Tune' (also known as 'Leamington') and his other works comprise operas, pantomimes and oratorios, of which *The Prodigal Son* is one. Later commentators have assessed him as outstanding in an age of compositional mediocrity and credited

him with maintaining the standard of cathedral music at a time of general decline.

ARNOLD, William (1768-1832)
Born in 1768; died in Hampshire in 1832. A shipwright in Portsmouth Dockyard, and choirmaster of the Daniel Street Wesleyan Chapel. He composed, sometimes at work. It is said that he noted down his compositions on a piece of wood with a carpenter's pencil. His hymn tunes 'Josiah', 'Sarah' and 'Job' were included in his collection *Original Psalm and Hymn Tunes* (c1810).

ARNOTT, Dr. Archibald Davidson (1870-?)
Born in Glasgow on 25 February 1870.
Moved with his parents to London at the age of 10.
Fond of music but did not study it seriously until around the age of 20. Spent a year at the Royal College of Music under **C.V. Stanford** and **Hubert Parry**. Afterwards studied under **Frederick Corder**. Graduated B.Mus. (1891) and D.Mus. (1901) at the University of Durham.
Organist of the London Churches of St. George, Perry Vale; Trinity Church, Forest Hill; St. Gabriel, Pimlico and St. Paul, Forest Hill (1904) before moving to Glasgow and becoming organist and choirmaster of Queen's Park Parish Church (1905).
Composed a Morning Service in F (1897), the anthems 'Blessed are the pure in heart' (1900) and 'Come unto Me, all that labour' (1932), operas including *Angelo, a noble of Venice* (1895), song cycles and overtures.

ARTHUR, Edward
See **EVANS,** David.

ASHEWELL (**Ashwell, Asshwell, Aswell, Hashewell**), Thomas (15th/16th century)
Lived before and around the beginning of the 16th century. A chorister at St. George's Chapel, Windsor Castle (1491-1493). A singer at Tattershall College, Lincolnshire (1502-1503), where he may have taught **John Taverner**. Later, master of the choristers of Lincoln Cathedral (from 1508 or before to 1513). Cantor of Durham Cathedral (1513), remaining true to his Roman Catholic faith throughout his life. Composed a number of Masses; some motets are preserved in manuscript at Oxford.

ASHFIELD, Dr. Robert James (b.1911)
Born in Chipstead, Surrey, on 28 July 1911.
Attended Tonbridge School, Kent (1925-1929) and the Royal College of Music (1929-1936). Graduated B.Mus. (1936) and D.Mus. (1941) at the University of London.
Organist of St. John's Church, Smith Square, London (1934-1941). Organist of Southwell Minster (1946-1956) and Rochester Cathedral (1956-1977).
Taught at the R.C.M. (from 1957), where he was appointed a professor of theory in 1958. A special commissioner to the Royal School of Church Music.
Has written chamber music, songs and an opera. His church music includes the anthems 'The fair chivalry' (1949) and 'Heralds of Christ', and the *People's* Communion, a setting of the Rite A version in the 1980 *Alternative Service Book*. Composed a Benedicite in F (1955), and there are Evening Services in D, in E Minor, in D and in G Minor.

ASHLEY, Anthony William (1803-1877)
Master of St. Katherine's Hospital, Regent's Park, London. Composed anthems including 'Haste Thee, O Lord' and 'Let Thy merciful ears, O Lord'.

ASHTON, John (1830-1896)
Born near Trefeglwys, Montgomeryshire, Wales in 1830; died in New Zealand on 31 December 1896. A shoemaker by trade but following an accident he joined the police force. Emigrated to New Zealand (1874). Composed the hymn tune 'Trefeglwys' (1857), songs and part songs.

ASPINWALL (**Aspinall**), Joseph (18th century)
Composed the anthems 'Give ear, O Lord' and 'I will judge you', both to words by Joseph Addison.

ASQUITH, John (19th century)
Graduated Mus.B. at the University of Cambridge (1878). Organist of Barnsley Parish Church, Yorkshire. Composed services including a Chant setting of the Venite (1882); anthems; four sets of Responses to the Commandments (1880); works for organ and songs.

ASTON (Ashton), Hugh (c1485-1558)
Born around the year 1485; believed to have died in November 1558. The details below may be a composite picture of contemporaries who cannot be distinguished and identified with certainty.
Graduated B.A. (1505 or 1506), M.A. (1507) and B.Mus. (1510) at the University of Oxford, having studied music for eight years. Following his M.A. he studied canon law at the University of Cambridge.
In 1509 he became prebend of St. Stephen's Church, Westminster, London. In 1515 he became archdeacon of York. He was probably master of the choristers of the St. Mary Newarke Hospital and College, Leicester from around 1525 until 1548.
Wrote music for the virginal and for use in the church, including two Festal Masses and a Te Deum. In 1929, **P.C. Buck** published a collection of material by various composers including Hugh Aston.

ASTON, Dr. Peter George (b.1938)
Born in Edgbaston, Birmingham, on 5 October 1938.
Studied at the Birmingham School of Music and the University of York and took private lessons in composition with Wilfrid Mellers. Awarded the D.Phil. at the University of York.
Lecturer in music at Anstey College (1961-1964); lecturer (1964-1972) and senior lecturer (1972-1974) at the University of York. Since 1974 he has been professor and head of music at the University of East Anglia, where he was dean of the School of Fine Arts and Music (1981-1984).
Director of the Tudor Consort (1959-1965), and conductor of the English Baroque Ensemble (1967-1970) and of the Aldeburgh Festival Singers (1975-1988). Performs regularly in the USA and has been principal guest conductor at the Sacramento Bach Festival, California, since 1993.
Joint founder and artistic director of the Norwich Festival of Contemporary Church Music (from 1981).
His written works include *The Music of York Minster* (1972) and, as co-author, *Sound and Silence* (1970) and *Music Theory in Practice* (3 volumes, 1992-1993).

Peter Aston gave evidence to the Archbishops' Commission on Church Music, which sat for four years from October 1988. The Commission heard a wide range of opinions: Dr. Aston's evidence pointed to the conclusion that the church should take care not to become a musical museum. The leading composers of the day should be persuaded to write for the church, and active church composers ought to be encouraged to write in a truly modern idiom.

An honorary member of the Royal College of Music (1992), and an honorary fellow of the Curwen Institute (conferred 1987). An honorary fellow (1995) and chairman of the Academic Board (from 1996) of the Guild of Church Musicians.

Has composed a Magnificat and Nunc Dimittis in F (1973); settings of the Series III Rite of Holy Communion (1973) and of the 1662 Version of the Holy Communion Service (1987); anthems including 'For I went with the multitude' (1970), 'O sing unto the Lord a new song' (1976) and 'Where shall wisdom be found?' (1991); and carols among which are 'Make we joye' (1976). His other works include an opera.

ATKINS, Sir Ivor Algernon (1869-1953)
Born in Llandaff, Cardiff on 29 November 1869; died in Worcester on 26 November 1953.

As a boy, Atkins was a chorister at Cardiff Parish Church and was educated at Roath, privately with his father and with **Charles Lee Williams**. Graduated Mus.B. (1892) at Queens' College, Cambridge. Also a Cambridge Mus.D. (1920).

Knighted in 1921.

G.R. Sinclair engaged him as a pupil at Truro Cathedral, and from 1885 to 1886 as his assistant. Following Sinclair's departure for Hereford Cathedral, Atkins made a similar move and was assistant organist at Hereford Cathedral (1890-1893) before taking up full musical responsibility at the Collegiate Church, Ludlow (1893-1897). .

In 1897 he became organist at Worcester Cathedral, a position he held for the next 53 years. He changed the musical flavour of the services as soon as he arrived, dropping much of the Victorian material and re-introducing compositions by the Tudor composers and by J.S. Bach despite the misgivings of some. His influence on cathedral music was considerable in his own time and is still widespread today.

As conductor-in-chief triennially of the Three Choirs' Festival it was at his insistence in 1902 that Elgar's newly-published *Dream of Gerontius* was performed. There had been opposition to the work because of the defection of its author, J.H. Newman, to the Roman Catholic Church. The festival was discontinued during World War I and it was almost entirely due to Atkins that it was successfully revived in 1920. The re-establishment of the festival and his other achievements led to his knighthood.

Among his editorial work was a collaboration with Elgar, his life-long friend, on the *St. John Passion* and the *St. Matthew Passion*. These collaborative editions, together with his own version in English of the Brahms *Ein Deutches Requiem*, are regarded by some as the definitive versions and are widely used today.

His compositions include the hymn tune 'St. Wulstan', which was used in the Standard Edition (1916) of *Hymns Ancient And Modern* with the hymn 'I lift my heart to Thee' by Charles Mudie. He also wrote songs, anthems, part songs and services, the latter including an Evening Service in G (1904).

Atkins wrote festival settings of the Evening Canticles for Chorus and Orchestra for use at the Three Choirs' Festivals of 1903 and

1904. His anthems include 'God be in my head' (1940) and 'Abide with me', a work that has been described as 'expressive and spiritually-confident'. Published the *Worcester Psalter* in 1950. He was himself a prolific composer of chants, and modern collections commonly include some four or five.

ATKINS, Robert Augustus (1811-1889)
Born in Chichester, Sussex on 2 October 1811, the son of Robert Atkins, a lay vicar of Chichester Cathedral; died in St. Asaph, Wales on 3 August 1889. A chorister of Chichester Cathedral, later becoming assistant organist there; subsequently cathedral organist of St. Asaph for more than 50 years (1834-1889). Composed Services in A and in G, chants, anthems and other items of church music.

ATKINSON, Frederic Cook (1841-1896)
Born in Norwich, Norfolk, on 20 August 1841; died in East Dereham, Norfolk on 30 November 1896.

A chorister of Norwich Cathedral, where he later studied under **Zechariah Buck** and became assistant organist. Graduated Mus.B. at the University of Cambridge (1867).

Taught music at Tonbridge School, Kent before moving to Bradford, Yorkshire and taking up organistships at St. Luke's Church, Manningham, Bradford and elsewhere.

Succeeded Buck as organist of Norwich Cathedral (1881-1886).

Organist of St. Mary's Church, Lewisham, London (1886-1896).

Composed anthems such as 'Rend your hearts and not your garments' (1882), services including a Magnificat and Nunc Dimittis in D (1881), instrumental items including pieces for piano and hymn tunes. His 'Hellespont', also known as 'Morecambe', was composed during his time at Manningham. It was published in 1870 on a leaflet and is used in *Hymns and Psalms* (1983) with 'O God, our Father, who dost make us one'.

ATTWATER, John Post (1862-1909)
Born in Faversham, Kent on 26 June 1862; died in Clapham Common, London on 10 April 1909

Studied under **Charles Frost**, Charles Pearce and others. Graduated B.Mus. at the University of Durham (1905).

At the age of 11, he became organist of the Faversham Wesleyan Church. Moved to London in 1884, where he became organist of the Studley Road Congregational Church, Clapham. The following year, he became organist and choirmaster of Grafton Square Congregational Church. Principal of the music department of Battersea Polytechnic. A singer and violinist, and the conductor of a music club of some one hundred male voices.

Composed anthems including 'Abide with me' (1890) and 'Rock of ages' (1896), songs, piano music and a setting of Psalm 34 'I will alway give thanks unto the Lord' for Solo Voices, Chorus and Organ.

ATTWOOD, Thomas (1765-1838)
Born in London, where he was baptised on 23 November 1765; died in Chelsea, London on 24 March 1838 and was buried in St. Paul's Cathedral.

The son of a coal merchant who also played the trumpet in the Royal Band of George III.

A boy chorister for five years from the age of nine at the Chapel Royal under **James Nares** and his successor **Edmund Ayrton**.

Following a performance before the Prince of Wales - who as George IV reigned from 1820 to 1830 - he studied in Naples with

Filippo Cinque and Gaetano Latilla (1783-1785) and in Vienna, with Mozart (1785 -1787). On his return to London in 1787, Attwood was appointed organist of the Church of St. George the Martyr, Queen Square. He also met Haydn in London and struck up a friendship with Mendelssohn, acting as host to him in his home in Norwood, London. Mendelssohn dedicated his Three Preludes and Fugues to Attwood.

Organist of St. Paul's Cathedral (1796-1838) and of George IV's private chapel in Brighton, Sussex (from 1821). Held two positions in the Chapel Royal - in June 1796 he succeeded **Thomas Dupuis** as composer and in 1836 he took over from **John Stafford Smith** as organist.

Taught music to various members of the Royal Family including the Duchess of York and the Princess of Wales. In 1823 he became one of the professors at the opening of the Royal Academy of Music. A founder of the London Philharmonic Society and a conductor of some of the Society's concerts.

His early music was mostly written for the theatre and included 28 operas. It was later in life that he produced most of his work for the church. He is said to have composed the anthem 'Come Holy Ghost' in a gig on Trinity Sunday 1831 between Brixton and St. Paul's Cathedral where it was used immediately in a service of ordination. The melody was subsequently used as a hymn tune and known as 'Attwood'. It is found in the Revised Edition (1927) of *Church Hymnary* and elsewhere with the hymn 'Creator Spirit! By whose aid'. There are some 12 other anthems including the two coronation pieces 'I was glad' for George IV and 'O Lord, grant the King a long life' for William IV.

Church Hymnary also uses his Sanctus and his Double Chant in E-flat. His services include settings in the keys of A, C, D and F.

Attwood's work was perceived as significant by the Victorians. **John Stainer** praised him for attaching worthy music to powerful texts, while Joseph Bennett discerned in his work a softening of style compared with other compositions of the Georgian period. Two of his pupils whom he profoundly influenced were **John Goss** and **T.A. Walmisley**. Among the budding composers in his charge and inevitably under his influence at the Chapel Royal and St. Paul's were **S.S. Wesley** and **E.J. Hopkins**.

AUSTEN (Guthrie), Augusta Amherst (1827-1877)
Born in London on 2 August 1827; died in Glasgow in 1877. Educated at the Royal Academy of Music. Organist of Ealing Church, London (1844-1846) and of the Paddington Chapel, London. Composer of hymn tunes.

AUSTIN, David (b.1932)
Born in Southend-on-Sea, Essex, on 10 October 1932.
Attended Alleyn Court School, Westcliff, Essex and St. Edward's School, Oxford before going up to Brasenose College, Oxford. Taught for 30 years at Wotton-under-Edge, Gloucestershire (1957-1987), before returning to Alleyn Court as director of music.
His hymn tune 'Day by day' is used with 'Day by day, dear Lord' in *Hymns and Psalms* (1983).

AUSTIN, Frederic (1872-1952)
Born in London on 30 March 1872; died in London on 10 April 1952. His brother was Ernest Austin, a composer of chamber music. His son is Richard Austin, the conductor, musician and academic.
Studied music with his mother, his uncle, **William Hunt**, and with Charles Lunn.

An organist, baritone, opera director and composer. A church organist before joining the staff of the Liverpool College of Music where he remained until 1906. At the same time he studied singing under Charles Lunn. He made his London concert debut in 1902, following which he took part in many local music festivals.

In 1924 he became artistic director of the National Opera Company, having already been a singer and producer there. For a time he was a professor of singing at the Royal Academy of Music. He was a leading authority of his day on the interpretation of modern music.

He composed orchestral, choral and incidental music as well as material for the church such as his Te Deum in F (1945). His instrumental works include a Spring Rhapsody and in lighter vein he composed the refrain in augmentation for the fifth verse of the popular Christmas song 'The twelve days of Christmas' - the line 'Five gold rings'.

AVISON, Charles (1710-1770)
Born in Newcastle-on-Tyne, and baptised on 16 February 1709; died in Newcastle on 9 or 10 May 1770.
Little is known of his education other than that he was a pupil of Francesco Geminiani in London.
In July 1736 he was appointed organist of St. John's, Newcastle, moving in October of that year as organist to the parish church of St. Nicholas (which in 1882 was elevated to cathedral status), where he remained until his death.
In his *Essay on Musical Expression* (1752) he ascribed to music uplifting qualities which were not sinful as long as they were properly used. The second and more controversial part of his essay praised French and Italian music at the expense of German music including that of **Handel**.
His case was scholarly and well argued and Charles Burney saw it as the beginning of musical criticism in the form that it is known today. Among those who studied the essay was Charles Wesley. Such views were bound to be controversial and the topic of musical superiority continued to be debated hotly for some time.
He organised a series of subscription concerts in Newcastle, which were among the first such events in this country.
Avison is the subject of a poem by Robert Browning.
He wrote 50 organ and orchestral concertos as well as church music, which included the anthem 'Sound the loud timbrel', a hymn (c1760) and a chant to Psalm 107 (1849).

AYLEWARD, Richard (1626-1669)
Born in Winchester, Hampshire in 1626; died in Norwich, Norfolk, on 15 October 1669.
A chorister at Winchester Cathedral, where his father was a minor canon, under **Christopher Gibbons** (1638-1639).
At the Restoration he was appointed organist and master of the choristers at Norwich Cathedral, where he served from March 1661 until the middle of 1664, and from December 1666 to 1669.
His church music includes a Short Service and other settings of the Canticles, anthems and a set of Responses still in current use in many places. His anthems include 'The King shall rejoice', written expressly for the Service of Thanksgiving for the Restoration on 20 May 1666 in Norwich Cathedral, and 'I was glad'.

AYLOTT (Thomas), Lydia Georgina Edith (b.1936)
Born in Finningham, Suffolk on 28 January 1936.
Studied music at Weymouth College of Education, Dorset. Studied harmony in Sydney with Muriel King (1968-1969 and at Trinity

College of Music, where she received tuition in composition from Richard Arnell.

From 1959 until 1970 she lived in Sydney, Australia. She was a teacher, initially in primary schools and then from 1968, in secondary schools.

Began to compose in 1967. Many of her early works were for school children. Her compositions include an *English* Mass (1973) and the *Fitzherbert School* Mass (1972).

AYLWARD, Dr. Theodore (c1730-1801)

Born in or around the year 1730, probably in Chichester, Hampshire; died in London on 27 February 1801 and was buried at Windsor, Berkshire in St. George's Chapel.

Said to have sung as a boy at the Drury Lane Theatre, London. Graduated B.Mus. at the University of Oxford (1791) followed two days later by D.Mus. Organist of the London Churches of Oxford Chapel (from around 1760); St. Lawrence, Jewry (1762-1788) and St. Michael's, Cornhill (1768-1781). Private organist to Queen Charlotte. Gresham professor of music (from 1771).

In 1784 he helped to organise the Handel Commemoration in Westminster Abbey and in 1788 he succeeded **Edward Webb** as organist of St. George's Chapel, Windsor Castle, where he was simultaneously appointed succentor, at the age of 58. One of his innovations at St. George's was to introduce excerpts from The *Messiah* into the services.

Theodore Aylward composed two chants, and his Chant in D-flat was included in *Cathedral Psalter Chants* (1875). His other works include songs, duets glees and organ pieces. Among his five anthems is 'Ponder my words'. Composed an Evening Service in E-flat and a Morning Service in D. Most of his church compositions were never published, although he had some success as a composer for the theatre.

AYLWARD, Theodore Edward (1844-1933)

Born on 28 February 1844; died in Cardiff on 6 February 1933.

The son of William Price Aylward, organist of the Churches of St. Martin, and later, St Edmund, Salisbury. The great-great-nephew of **Theodore Aylward**. Studied at Salisbury Cathedral under **C.J. Read**, with **S.S. Wesley** to whom he was articled, and **George Macfarren**. Aylward continued to work his articles with Wesley after the latter's appointment to Gloucester Cathedral.

Organist of the Church of St. Matthew, Cheltenham; St. Columba's College, Rathfarnham, County Dublin (from 1866); St. Martin's, Salisbury and St. Mary's, Spring Grove, in the Diocese of London. Organist of Llandaff Cathedral (1870-1876) and Chichester Cathedral (1876-1886).

Organist of St. Andrew's Church, Cardiff (1886-1925).

Known for the hymn tunes 'Nutbourne' and for his tune 'Duci cruento martyrum', composed for the hymn of the same name in *Sarum Hymnal* (1869) of which he was musical editor, compiling it during his time at Salisbury. This tune was later used in *Hymns Ancient and Modern* and in *Irish Church Hymnal* (1960). The compilation by **Arthur Sullivan** *Church Hymns* (1874) sets 'Lord of the living harvest' by J.S. Monsell to Aylward's 'Sarum'.

Composed sets of Preces and Responses, festal and ferial, and a Litany, published as a collection in 1877.

AYRTON, Dr. Edmund (1734-1808)

Born in Ripon, Yorkshire, baptised on 19 November 1734; died in Westminster, London on 22 May 1808 and was buried in Westminster Abbey.

Younger brother of William Ayrton, who later became organist of Ripon Cathedral.

In April 1756, having already begun work, he was granted leave for three months to further his musical education with **James Nares** at York Minster. Graduated Mus.D. at the University of Cambridge (1784). Awarded his Oxford doctorate in music in 1788.

It was originally intended that he would become a minister of the church but it was as a musician within the church that his career developed.

Auditor, organist and rector chori in succession to **William Lee** at Southwell Collegiate Church (later to become the Minster) from October 1755. Also a singing man at Southwell. A gentleman (from 1764) and master of the children (1780-1805) of the Chapel Royal, and vicar choral of St. Paul's Cathedral (from 1767) and of Westminster Abbey (from 1780), the latter in succession to James Nares.

Composed a quantity of secular vocal music, including catches and glees, all of which is lost. His church music includes morning and evening services and anthems including 'Unto Thee, O Lord'.

'Begin unto my Lord with timbrels' for Singers and Orchestra, which was his Mus.D. exercise, was used shortly afterwards on 27 July 1784 at the Service of Thanksgiving for the cessation of the American War of Independence.

A Single Chant in E was included in *Cathedral Psalter Chants* (1875).

B

BACON, Revd. Robert (?-1759)
Graduated B.A. at the University of Oxford (1738). A priest vicar of Salisbury Cathedral (from 1753). A Single Chant in A is found in *Cathedral Psalter Chants* (1875) and he is known to have composed others. Anthems include 'My soul truly waiteth' and 'The Lord is King'.

BADEN-POWELL, Revd. James (1842-1931)
Born in Speldhurst, Kent on 3 December 1842; died in Crowborough, East Sussex on 6 April 1931. A cousin of the scout founder, Lord Baden Powell. Educated at Exeter College, Oxford; ordained in 1867. For nine years he was incumbent of St. Paul's Church, Lorrimore Square. He was then precentor of St. Paul's Church, Knigtsbridge, for 25 years. Chaplain of the Hostel of God, Clapham, (from 1907) until his retirement in 1925. Composer of hymns and anthems.

BAILDON, Joseph (1727-1774)
Born in 1727; died in London on 7 May 1774.
A chorister of St. Paul's Cathedral and a pupil of **Charles King**.
A gentleman of the Chapel Royal, and a lay vicar of Westminster Abbey. Organist of the London Churches of St. Luke, Old Street and All Saints, Fulham (from 1762).
Contributed Psalm tunes to the collection *Parochial Music Corrected* (1762) by **William Riley**; composed the anthem 'Behold, how good and joyful', glees and catches.

BAILEY, E. Rawdon
See **BONNER,** Carey.

BAILEY, John (1749-1823)
Born in Chester in 1749; died on 26 November 1823.
A chorister of Chester Cathedral under Edward Orme, to whom he was related.
Bailey was Orme's assistant organist before assuming the organistship in 1776. He remained in the position until 1803 when he was succeeded by his brother, Edward. Bailey had also been a conduct (singing man) of the cathedral.
He composed anthems and chants, which were used in the worship at the cathedral. His songs include 'Delia'.

BAILEY, Judith Margaret (b.1941)
Born in Camborne, Cornwall on 18 July 1941.
Studied composition, piano and clarinet at the Royal Academy of Music, following which she has worked as a performer, conductor, lecturer and composer.
She has been conductor of the Petersfield Orchestra and the Southampton Concert Orchestra, Hampshire and of the Haslemere Orchestra, Surrey.
Has lectured at the Open University and has taught woodwind instruments.
Her compositions include the anthems 'Praise my soul' (1967) and 'From East to West' (1982), two Symphonies (1980 and 1982) and chamber works such as a String Quartet.

BAINTON, Dr. Edgar Leslie (1880-1956)
Born in London on 14 February 1880; died in Sydney, New South Wales on 8 December 1956.
Attended Henry VIII Grammar School, Coventry, Warwickshire. A pupil of **C.V. Stanford, Walford Davies, Charles Wood** and Franklin Taylor at the Royal College of Music, where he won an open scholarship for piano playing (1896) and the Wilson scholarship for composition (1899). Awarded the honorary degree of D.Mus. at the University of Durham in 1933.
First appeared in public as a piano recitalist at the age of eight.
From 1901 he was a pianist and teacher at the Newcastl-on-Tyne School of Music and in 1912 he was appointed principal.
Interned by the Germans during World War I in Ruhleben camp, near Berlin and in his absence, his wife, a teacher and pianist, ran the school. Some 4,000 of his fellow-countrymen found themselves interred at Ruhleben and as war had broken out between academic terms, the number included teachers and students. Bainton organised a madrigal choir and, having managed to obtain a copy of Stanford's *Songs of the Sea,* put on a concert for the German high command.
After emigrating to Australia, he served as director of the New South Wales Conservatory of Music (1933-1947).
Henry Wood expressed surprise that Bainton was not more prominent as a composer, and he selected Bainton's *Pompilia* (in 1903) and *Celtic Sketches* (in 1912) for his Promenade Concerts. Within the realm of church music his best known compositions are

the anthems 'And I saw a new Heaven' - a work that is universally sung - and 'Open Thy gates'.

BAIRNSFATHER, Thomas Henry (1859-1944)
Born in 1859; died in Haslemere, Surrey on 31 December 1944. Composed hymn tunes, and songs including 'Many waters'.

BAIRSTOW, Sir Edward Cuthbert (1874-1946)
Born in Huddersfield, Yorkshire on 22 August 1874; died in York on 1 May 1946.
Educated at Nottingham High School until 1889 when he moved to the Grocers' Company School in Hackney, London. Also had private tuition, and received organ lessons from either **John Farmer** (of Harrow School) or **Henry Farmer** (of Nottingham, where Bairstow attended school) - each alternative is feasible. A pupil of Henry L. Parratt, brother of the more famous **Walter Parratt** at Huddersfield Parish Church before being articled to **Frederick Bridge** at Westminster Abbey from 1893 to 1899.
Graduated B.Mus. (1894) and D.Mus. (1900) at the University of Durham. Accorded the honorary degrees of D.Litt. (Leeds, 1936) and D.Mus. (Oxford, 1945).
Knighted in 1932.
Organist of the Churches of All Saints, Norfolk Square, Paddington, West London (1893-1899); Wigan Parish Church, Lancashire (1899-1906) and Leeds Parish Church (1906-1913). The Leeds position enabled him, in his additional capacity as organist to the Leeds Festival, to become acquainted with **Edward Elgar** and **C.V. Stanford**. It is said that he read of the Leeds vacancy in the evening paper after attending the final day's play in the England v Australia test match at The Oval. Frederick Bridge, whom he consulted, did not rate Bairstow's chances highly, having wrongly concluded that the preferment would go instead to another former pupil, **Herbert Fricker**.
When **Tertius Noble** resigned and took up a position in the U.S.A., Bairstow succeeded him as organist of York Minster, where he served from 1913 to 1946. On radio, when asked whether he would like to follow his predecessor and go to the U.S.A., Bairstow replied that he would sooner go to the devil.
During his tenure, he dropped the anthems and services of some Victorian composers including **John Stainer, George Garrett** and **E.J. Hopkins** in favour of older works, and compositions of the 20th century.
From the death of **J.C. Bridge** he was professor of music at the University of Durham (1929-1946). From 1940 he was Ferens Fine Art Lecturer at University College, Hull. A series of lectures was later edited and published as *The Evolution of Musical Form* (1943).
He was also active in the newly-established College of St. Nicolas (later to become the Royal School of Church Music). Among those he influenced at Chislehurst was **Christopher Le Fleming**, who said of him that he could take an unexceptional anthem or motet and recapture the inspiration of the composer during its performance. **Ernest Bullock**, his former pupil, described him as a born teacher. He was said to be forthright yet sympathetic and sincere.
He wrote songs, a total of 12 pieces of organ music and church music of various kinds. He wrote many chants, 17 of which are found in *York Minster Chant Book*, and with **P.C. Buck** and **Charles Macpherson** he was co-editor of *The English Psalter*. He wrote the gradual 'Let my prayer come up into Thy presence' for the 1937 Coronation of George VI in Westminster Abbey.

Among his compositions are the hymn tunes 'Clamavi' and 'Minster Court', which were used in the Standard Edition (1916) of *Hymns Ancient and Modern*, and a Service in D. Of his 29 anthems, 'Blessed City, heavenly Salem' - where Bairstow's treatment of the plainsong melody has subsequently proved very influential - 'Save us, O Lord', 'Lord, Thou hast been our Refuge' and 'Let all mortal flesh keep silence' are among the most familiar today.
His later works are said to display a haunting and more concise musical style - principal among these are the Evening Service in G, often considered as finely-wrought and a chant setting sometimes described as 'remarkable' of *The Lamentations of Jeremiah* selected by Dean Milner White for use as an alternative Canticle during Lent and Passiontide.

BAKER, A.S. (1868-1896)
Graduated B.A. Organist of the Church of St. James, New York. Composed the anthems 'Be ye therefore followers' and 'O God, who hast prepared'.

BAKER, Albert Edward (1875-1945)
Born in Windsor, Berkshire in 1875; died in Brixham, Devon on 11 February 1945.
A chorister in the chapel of Eton College, and later, assistant organist there. Attended Guildhall School of Music; graduated B.Mus. (1903) at Queen's College, Oxford.
The first of Albert Baker's Berkshire organistships was at the Church of St. Laurence, Upton (1892). He moved to St. Andrew's, Clewer, near Windsor a year later and in 1895 he was appointed to Stoke Parish Church. Between 1897 and 1914 he was organist and choirmaster of Eton Parish Church, and choirmaster of Uxbridge Parish Church (1907-1908).
He taught piano at Cranford College (1896-1908) and he was on the music staff at Eton College (1914-1935). When he retired from Eton he severed a connection with the College that had lasted for 52 years as pupil, music teacher, and organist of the lower chapel. He was singing master of Windsor Boys' County School.
Author of a textbook on the theory and practice of scales, arpeggios and tonality.
Composed the anthem 'At the Cross' (1921). Also wrote anthems for boys' voices, songs and descants, plus works for piano and for violin.   Arranged, as an anthem for treble voices, the French carol melody 'Whence is the goodly fragrance flowing?'. 'This joyful Easter-tide' is for two trebles.

BAKER, David (b.1940)
Born in Nottingham in 1940, the son of **Reginald Baker**. Attended Nottingham High School and the Royal Academy of Music, where he studied piano and cello. Has composed hymn tunes, and a Sonata for Cello and Piano (1978).

BAKER, Frederick George (1839-1919)
Born in Shorwell, Isle of Wight on 19 May 1839; died in Shanklin, Isle of Wight on 10 March 1919.
A chorister of Winchester Cathedral. Later returned to the Isle of Wight and earned his living as a watch-maker and jeweller. Organist of Sandown Parish Church (1864-1871) before moving to St. Saviour's Church, Shanklin, where he held office for almost 30 years.

Composed music for local town bands. His hymn tunes include 'St. Saviour', which is still sung today with 'I sing the almighty power of God' from *Hymns and Psalms* (1983).

BAKER, Dr. George (c1773-1847)
Born in Exeter, Devon, probably in 1773; died in Rugeley, Staffordshire on 19 February 1847.
An aunt taught him to play the harpsichord, on which he was proficient by the age of seven. An organ pupil of the Exeter musicians **Hugh Bond** and **William Jackson** of Exeter. In London he studied violin with Ward, piano with Dussek, and also with **John Baptist Cramer**. Graduated B.Mus. at the University of Oxford (1797). Some sources maintain that he proceeded D.Mus. around the year 1801.
Organist of the three Parish Churches of St. Mary, Stafford (1795-1800); All Saints, Derby - elevated to cathedral status in 1923 (from 1810) and Rugeley, Staffordshire (1824-1847).
Composed anthems for four, five and six parts, plus glees, songs, organ voluntaries and piano sonatas.

BAKER, Henry (1835-1910)
Born in Nuneham Courtenay, Oxfordshire on 16 June 1835, the son of the rector, Revd. James Baker; died in Wimbledon, London on 1 February 1910.
Educated at Winchester College and trained as a civil engineer at Cooper's Hill. Received some training in music from **J.B. Dykes**, graduating B.Mus. at Exeter College, Oxford (1867).
Worked for some time on the Indian Railways.
His Morning, Evening and Holy Communion Service in F was published, after his death, in 1921. Composed the anthem 'O hide Thou not Thy face' (1868). His hymn tune 'Elim' (1854), also known as 'Hesperus' and 'Whitburn', is used today with the hymn 'Jesus, thy wandering sheep behold'. His Single Chant in C was used with part of Psalm 119 in *Cathedral Psalter Chants* (1875). Several of his tunes are found in *Worship Song*, edited by Revd. Garrett Horder.

BAKER, Revd. Sir Henry Williams (1821-1877)
Born in Vauxhall, London on 27 May 1821, the eldest son of Vice-Admiral Sir Henry Loraine Baker; died in Monkland, Herefordshire on 12 February 1877.
Educated at Trinity College, Cambridge, both graduating B.A. and being ordained in 1844, the year in which he succeeded to the baronetcy. Proceeded M.A. in 1847.
In 1851 he was appointed vicar of Monkland. He was present at the momentous meeting of 1858 in the clergy house of St. Barnabas, Pimlico, London at which the decision was taken to publish a new hymnal. This was to become *Hymns Ancient and Modern*. Baker was on the text committee that published the first volume (1861), the Appendix (1868) and the Revised Edition (1875). He became its first chairman but it is not clear when this took place. In *Songs of Praise Discussed*, Percy Dearmer suggests that he held the position from the outset and retained it for almost 20 years.
He contributed 33 texts and translations and was effectively editor-in-chief of the publication. One prospective contributor had his work altered so radically that he said that the book's title should be *Hymns Asked for and Mutilated*.
When dying, his last words were from the third verse of 'The King of love my Shepherd is', beginning 'Perverse and foolish'. A number of his own hymn tunes were published, including 'St.

Timothy' and 'Stephanos', both of which were in the Standard Edition (1916) of *Hymns Ancient and Modern*.

BAKER, James Andrew (1824-1863)
Born in Birmingham on 8 November 1824; died in Birmingham on 17 November 1863. Studied in Germany at the Leipzig Conservatory. Organist of St. Luke's Church, Bristol Street, Birmingham from around 1849 to 1863. His wife was a local singer.
Composer of a small number of chants and hymn tunes.

BAKER, J. Percy (1859-1930)
Born in Islington, London on 4 March 1859; died on 12 December 1930.
Following a private education he attended the Royal Academy of Music (from 1881). Graduated B.Mus. (1896) at the University of Durham. Organist and choirmaster of Tooting Graveney Parish Church (from 1891) and of St. Matthew's Parish Church, Upper Clapton (from 1904). Appointed editor of *Musical News* in 1904. He had already written a number of articles and exercises for the use of students of music. Author of *The Choir Boy's Handy Book*. Composed a number of services.

BAKER, Percy (19th/20th century)
Percy Baker was born in Tewkesbury, Gloucestershire.
Educated privately and at the Royal College of Music.
Sub organist of St. James's Church, Piccadilly, London, and organist of St. Thomas's Church, Regent Street.
Taught music in several schools. Served in World War I and awarded the Military Cross. Well known in the 1930s and 1940s as a teacher of diploma paper work by correspondence.
Composed a Holy Communion Service in A, the anthems 'God be in my head' (1931) and 'I am the Living Bread' (1933), and *Three Expressive Pieces* (1922) for piano.

BAKER, Revd. Reginald (b.1904)
Born in Dover, Kent in 1904. The father of **David Baker**.
Worked in the motor trade until at the age of 27 he began training at Rawdon College, Leeds for the ministry of the Baptist Church. Following ordination he was appointed pastor of the congregations at Westoe Road, South Shields and Mansfield Road, Nottingham. In 1960 he became Minister of the College Street Baptist Church, Northampton.
On the music advisory committee for *Baptist Hymn Book* (1962). A composer of hymn tunes.

BAKER, Dr. Reginald Tustin (1900-1966)
Born in Gloucester on 4 July 1900; died in Sheffield Cathedral following Evensong on 18 December 1966.
A chorister (1911-1915) and pupil (1915-1918) of **A.H. Brewer** at Gloucester Cathedral. His education continued at King's School, Gloucester. Graduated B.Mus. (1924) and D.Mus. (1934) at the University of Durham.
Tustin Baker served in the army during World War I. Assistant organist at Gloucester Cathedral (1920-1926), becoming known as a recitalist and composer. Organist of St. Luke's Church, San Francisco (1926-1928); Hexham Abbey (1928-1929); Halifax Parish Church (1929-1937) and Sheffield Cathedral (1937-1966).
Wrote anthems of which examples are 'At the Lamb's high feast' and 'The Lord is my Shepherd', services including an Evening Service in D, part songs and carols.

BALDWIN (Baldwine, Baldwyn, Baudewyn, Bawdwine), John (c1550-1615)

Born around the year 1550; died in London on 28 August 1615.

A tenor lay clerk of St. George's Chapel, Windsor Castle in 1575. A musician of the Chapel Royal, unofficially from February 1594, and appointed formally in August 1598. Renowned in his day for his accuracy and perseverance as a music copyist.

Compositions comprise anthems, motets including *Pater Noster* and *Redime Me*, canons and an Agnus Dei.

BALFE, Michael William (1808-1870)

Born in Dublin on 15 May 1808; died in Rowney Abbey, Hertfordshire on 20 October 1870.

The son of a dancing master, he played violin for his father during lessons at a young age.

A pupil of Charles Horn for violin, Karl Horn for composition, and of Rooke and Alexander Lee.

Became a violinist, securing a position with the Drury Lane Theatre, London in 1824. Also sang in London and elsewhere in the country.

A year later he received the patronage of the Italian, Count Mazzara who took him to Italy. In Milan, studied singing with Federici and voice production with Filippo Galli.

Sang in Italy and from 1828, in Paris, at which time he was principal baritone of the Italian Opera. Returned to London in 1833. Chosen by the composer Rossini to play the part of Figaro in *The Barber of Seville* in Paris. Rossini also advised him to continue voice studies with Bordogni.

His career developed and flourished in London. Manager of the Lyceum Theatre (from 1839) and conductor of Her Majesty's Theatre (1845-1852). Directed the National Concerts at Drury Lane in 1850.

Although London was his home, he made occasional visits abroad, encompassing Vienna (1846), Berlin (1848), St. Petersburg and Trieste (between 1852 and 1856).

In 1864 he retired to the country where he lived as a farmer and continued to compose.

Two biographies were written of him, in 1875 by Charles Kenney and in 1882 by **W.A. Barrett**.

Composed the anthem 'Save me, O God' but he is remembered for his many operas and musical dramas including *Falstaff* (1838) and *The Bohemian Girl* (1843), and songs including 'Come into the garden, Maud'.

BALL, Dr. Michael (b.1946)

Born in Manchester on 10 November 1946.

Educated at the Royal College of Music with **Herbert Howells**, Humphrey Searle and John Lambert. Also studied in Italy with Franco Donatoni. Involved in the compilation of *Baptist Praise and Worship*. Has composed orchestral and major choral works as well as items for chamber ensembles. His church music includes the carol 'A Maide so bright'.

BALL, Timothy Matti (b.1960)

Born in London on 29 February 1960.

Organ scholar (1980-1983) of Lincoln Cathedral under **Philip Marshall**. Graduated B.Ed. in music at the University of Nottingham.

Assistant director of music, Bearwood College, Berkshire (1984-1986); director of music, Cardinal Vaughan Memorial School, Kensington (1986-1993) and of The Church of Our Lady of Grace and St. Edward, Chiswick (1990-1991), both in London. Composer in residence of Tormead School, Guildford, Surrey (from 1994).

Freelance conductor, organist, pianist, coach, writer, and reviewer of recordings for *The Gramophone*. A lecturer on a variety of topics, including the life and works of Leonard Bernstein as composer. Has conducted at the Royal Festival Hall and other major venues.

Church compositions include a Jubilate Deo (1983), Evening Canticles for Boys' Voices (1977), Preces and Responses (broadcast in 1983) and the anthem 'Christ's gifts' (1995). Has also composed songs and orchestral works.

BALY, William (1825-1891)

Born in Warwick on 18 June 1825; died in Exeter, Devon on 4 July 1891.

Studied under a Clayton of Warwick. Entered the Royal Academy of Music in 1843, where his tutors were **William Sterndale Bennett** for piano and Cipriani Potter for harmony.

Lived in London where he taught harmony at the Harley Street College for Ladies. In 1853 he moved to Exeter where he took over the teaching practice of **Kellow Pye**.

Composed a Symphony in E-flat. Two concert overtures were composed while he was a student at the R.A.M. Also composed part songs and hymn tunes.

BAMBRIDGE, George Edmund (1842-1916)

Born in Windsor, Berkshire on 19 April 1842; died on 2 February 1916. A cousin of **William Bambridge**.

A chorister of St. George's Chapel, Windsor Castle. Studied at the Royal Academy of Music (1860-1865) where his teachers were **Charles Lucas, George Macfarren, Walter Macfarren**, and **Charles Steggall**. His subjects were piano, organ, cello and composition. Graduated B.Mus. (1872) at the University of Oxford. Organist of St. Luke's Church, Westbourne Park, London (from 1864) where he remained for around 50 years. A professor and examiner (from 1881) of Trinity College, London, of which he later became vice dean.

Composed an Evening Service in F, and works for piano.

BAMBRIDGE, William Samuel (1842-1923)

Born in Waimate, New Zealand on 18 July 1842; died in Marlborough, Wiltshire on 10 January 1923. A cousin of **George Bambridge**.

Came to England at the age of six and attended St. George's School, Windsor. Studied in the Royal Academy of Music under **H.C. Banister, Charles Steggall, William Dorrell** and W.H. Aylward. Graduated B.Mus. (1872) at Magdalen College, Oxford.

Appointed organist at the nearby Parish Church of St. Agnes, Clewer when aged 10 (1853-1864). Organist and choirmaster at Marlborough College (1864-1911), and temporary organist and director of music of the Royal Naval College, Osborne, Isle of Wight (1916-1919).

A justice of the peace, an alderman, and mayor of Marlborough.

Composed the hymn tune 'St. Asaph', which was used in the Standard Edition (1916) of *Hymns Ancient and Modern*. Also used by **Arthur Sullivan** in conjunction with the hymn by **Sabine Baring-Gould** 'Through the night of doubt and sorrow', in his compilation *Church Hymns* (1874). Composed other hymn tunes, carols and songs.

BANCROFT, Dr. Hugh (b.1904)
Born in England in 1904. Spent some of his working life in Canada. Retired in 1980, having been a teacher, organist, recitalist and choirmaster. Served churches and cathedrals in Edmonton, Vancouver, Winnipeg, Sydney and Nassau.
Awarded the Lambeth D.Mus.(1977) and in 1980, the honorary LL.D. from the University of Alberta, Canada.
Among his hymn tunes is 'Ascension' (1938), composed for 'There's a Voice in the wilderness crying'.

BANESTER, Gilbert (c1445-1487)
Born, probably in London, around the year 1445; died in August or possibly on 1 September 1487.
Master of the children of the Chapel Royal (from 1478). Part of his responsibility was to compose choral interludes for performance at court.
Composed a carol, motets and music for pageants. His court entertainment compositions include *Legend of Sigismund* and *Miracle of St. Thomas*. His antiphon *O Maria et Elizabeth* is thought to have been written for the marriage of Henry VII and Elizabeth of York in 1486.

BANISTER, Henry Charles (1831-1897)
Born in London on 13 June 1831; died in 1897. Grandson of Charles Banister, whose collection *Twelve Psalm and Hymn Tunes* was published in 1792.
Trained in music by his father, Henry Banister. Sang in concerts as a boy. Studied at the Royal Academy of Music, where his main teacher was Cipriani Potter.
In 1851 he was appointed an assistant professor of the R.A.M. and in 1853 he became professor of harmony and counterpoint. He was also a professor of harmony at the Royal Normal College for the Blind and from 1880 he was a professor at Guildhall School of Music.
Biographer of **George Macfarren**.
Composed an anthem 'O satisfy us early', a String Quartet in F-sharp Minor, symphonies, overtures and part songs.

BANKS, Ralph (1762-1841)
Born in Durham in 1762; died on 20 September 1841.
A chorister of Durham Cathedral under **Thomas Ebdon**, whom he later served as assistant organist.
After becoming organist of the Parish Church, Houghton-le-Spring in 1789 he was appointed master of the choristers of Rochester Cathedral. In 1792 he was additionally appointed organist: both appointments were held until 1841. He was also voluntary organist for the evening services at St. John's Church, Chatham.
He later remarked that when he first arrived at Rochester the cathedral was at a low ebb musically. The prayers were said rather than chanted, daily services were chanted, only one lay clerk reported for duty each week and on Sundays throughout the previous 12 years, the total repertory had consisted of seven anthems and only two canticle settings: the Services in G by **Henry Aldrich** and the Service in D by **Benjamin Rogers**, sung in rotation.
Ralph Banks composed an anthem 'O sing unto the Lord' for the re-opening of the organ on 22 November 1840. His other anthems include 'Give ear, O Heavens'.

BAPTIE, David (1822-1906)
Born in Edinburgh or Glasgow on 30 November 1822; died in Glasgow on 26 March 1906.
Self-taught musically, he maintained a catalogue of some 23,000 songs, glees and chamber works. He compiled hymnals, chant books and biographical dictionaries including *Handbook of Musical Biography* (1883) and *Musicians of all Times* (second edition, 1897). His largest project was his *Descriptive Catalogue* (of part songs, glees and trios), which engaged him from 1846 until 1898. It is now housed at the British Library.
His compositions include 'Sing aloud unto God' and other anthems, glees and part songs.

BARCLAY, Arthur (1869-1943)
Born in London in 1869; died in 1943. Studied composition and orchestration at Guildhall School of Music under **Thomas Wingham**. Held two important positions in London: director of music at Brompton Oratory for more than 30 years, and, until 1911, a professorship at G.S.M. Compositions include a Symphony in C Minor, orchestral overtures, works for piano and for organ, choral and church music including the motet *Libera* for unaccompanied double chorus.

BARCROFT (Barcrofte), George (c1550-1610)
He is probably the person of that name who graduated B.A. in 1577 or 1578, who was ordained priest in 1590 and who was then appointed vicar of Dillington, Cambridgeshire. Organist (1579-1610), vicar choral and minor canon of Ely Cathedral. Composed two anthems. He composed the anthems 'O almighty God' and 'O Lord, we beseech Thee'.

BARCROFT (Barcrofte), Thomas (16th century)
Little is known of Thomas Barcroft, save that he was a church musician and composer of the 16th century and a lay vicar of Ely Cathedral. Composed a Te Deum and Benedictus in F. Two anthems by 'Barcroft' were at one time attributed to Thomas but could well have been the work of George. A Service in G (1532) is attributed to Thomas Barcroft.

Bardd Alaw
See **PARRY**, John.

BARHAM-GOULD, Revd. Arthur Cyril (1891-1953)
Born in 1891; died in Tunbridge Wells, Kent on 14 February 1953.
Educated for the ministry of the Church of England at Ridley Hall, Cambridge, where he was ordained in 1927.
Associated with three London churches. Curate of All Souls', Langham Place (1927-1929) and Holy Trinity, Brompton (1932-1936); vicar of St. Paul's Church, Onslow Square (1936-1953).
His hymn tune 'St. Leonards', named after the town in Sussex where he lived, was used in the hymnal *With One Voice* (1978) with the hymn 'May the mind of Christ my Saviour' by Katie Wilkinson, a combination that first appeared in *Golden Bells* (1925).

BARING-GOULD, Revd. Sabine (1834-1924)
Born in Exeter, Devon on 28 January 1834; died in Lew Trenchard, Devon, on 2 January 1924.
His early education took place abroad, mainly because of ill-health. Studied at Clare College, Cambridge (from 1853), graduating B.A.

(1854) and M.A. (1856). Subsequently ordained deacon (1864) and priest (1865).

Assistant master of the choir school at St. Barnabas, Pimlico, London (1857) and of Hurstpierpoint College, East Sussex (1857-1864).

Appointed curate of Horbury, Yorkshire in 1864. In 1866 he moved within the same county to the incumbency of Dalton and in 1871 to become rector of East Mersea, Essex. In 1872 he inherited the family estate at Lew Trenchard, becoming rector of the village in 1881. Although a high churchman, he was equally opposed to what he perceived as the extreme positions of Catholicism and Calvinism.

Wrote the hymn 'Onward, Christian soldiers' (1865), initially set to music by **J.B. Dykes** but made famous a little later by **Arthur Sullivan**'s 'St. Gertrude'. In 1884 he published a collection *Church Songs*, in collaboration with Revd. Henry Fleetwood Sheppard. 159 of his books were published, and he is said to have more catalogue entries in the British Museum than any of his contemporaries. Edited a collection of limericks, for which he had great enthusiasm. Baring-Gould composed a tune, 'Eudoxia', that was initially set to the hymn 'Now the day is over' in *Hymns Ancient and Modern*. He was also one of the earliest of the modern collectors of folk songs, collaborating with Sheppard and with **Frederick Bussell** in the publication of *Songs and Ballads of the West*, a set of 121 folk songs from Devon and Cornwall.

BARKER, (Hacket) Mrs. Elizabeth M. (1829-1916)
Born in Leicester in 1829. She married a Mr. Raymond Barker and subsequently composed under her married name; died in Haywards Heath, Sussex on 6 October 1916. The hymn tune 'St. John Damascene' by Elizabeth Barker is used with a Latin hymn translated as 'Those eternal bowers' in the compilation *Church Hymns* (1874). She also published a collection *Songs for our little Friends* (1867).

BARLEY, Peter (b.1969)
A chorister at New College, Oxford, winning a music scholarship to Winchester College where, in his final year, he led the school orchestra and was assistant organist. Read music as organ scholar at King's College, Cambridge under **Stephen Cleobury**, and accompanied the College Choir in many broadcasts, concerts, recordings and tours. Studied at the Royal Academy of Music with Patrick Russill for two years on the sacred music course. Graduated M.Mus. at the University of London.

Organist and director of music at St. Marylebone Church, London. Accompanist of the London Concert Choir under the leadership of **Gregory Rose**.

Has composed the anthems 'Author of life Divine' and 'Not everyone that saith unto me'.

BARNARD, (Pye), Charlotte Alington (1830-1869)
Born in Louth, Lincolnshire on 23 December 1830; died in Dover, Kent on 30 January 1869. Studied music under **W.H. Holmes.** Author of *Fireside Thoughts* (1865) and *Thoughts, Verses and Songs* (1877). Composed hymn tunes, songs including 'Come back to Erin', duets, about a hundred ballads, and works for piano, sometimes preferring the pseudonym *Claribel* when composing.

BARNARD, John (b.1948)
Born in Wealdstone, Middlesex on 20 April 1948. Educated at John Lyon School, Harrow and at Selwyn College, Cambridge.

Taught at Cheltenham School; since 1974 has been head of modern languages at John Lyon School. An organist, and director of music at the Church of St. Alban, North Harrow. Has composed and arranged a number of hymn tunes, including the acclaimed 'Guiting Power', found in *Hymns for Today's Church,* and composed the anthem 'Lord, I want to be a Christian'. He harmonised the 'Londonderry Air'.

BARNARD, Revd. John (17th century)
Lived in the early part of the 17th century and is known to have been alive between the years 1625 and 1641.

A minor canon of St. Paul's Cathedral at some time during the reign of Charles I.

In 1641 he published his 10-volume *The First Book of Selected Church Musick,* a set of part books which deliberately excluded works by living composers. In doing so he became the first person known to issue a collection of English cathedral music. That collection has served as a reference source for scholars of the period. A further set intended as Part II was never published and remains in manuscript at the Royal College of Music.

Composer of several sets of Preces and Responses.

BARNBY, Sir Joseph (1838-1896)
Born in York on 12 August 1838, the son of an organist; died in Pimlico, London on 28 January 1896.

A boy chorister at York Minster in 1845. Entered the Royal Academy of Music in 1854. In 1856, he competed unsuccessfully against the 14 year old **Arthur Sullivan** for the newly-established Mendelssohn scholarship.

Knighted in 1892.

Organist of Mitcham Parish Church, Surrey before moving north to York for four years. Later, he was organist in the London churches of St. Michael, Queenhithe and St. James the Less, Westminster.

Took up the position of organist at St. Andrew's, Wells Street, an Anglo-Catholic stronghold of congregational singing (1863-1871). Under Barnby's command the music involved the congregation less and less and became the prerogative of the choir. This was heightened by the introduction of adaptations by Barnby of Roman Catholic masses. In 1871 he moved the short distance to St. Anne's Church, Soho where the services became known as 'the Sunday opera'. He remained at St. Anne's until 1886.

Conducted the first British performance of Bach's *St. John Passion* in March 1872. From 1861 to 1876 he was musical adviser to the publisher Novello, in which capacity he turned down three songs submitted in 1872 by **Hubert Parry**.

Precentor of Eton College (1875-1892), and principal of Guildhall School of Music (1892-1896).

Appointed musical editor of *The Hymnary* in 1872, and edited three other hymn books. His contemporaries saw him as a vigorous conductor, composer and innovator but he tends to be among those composers dismissed pejoratively by name or in general by 20th century commentators such as **E.H. Fellowes**, **Henry Hadow**, **Ernest Walker** and Donald Tovey as typically Victorian.

In 1886, as head of the board of examiners of the Royal College of Music he furiously denounced Parry, who at the time was a professor of the College, in an attempt to force his dismissal. Barnby judged the other's methods of teaching composition unconventional and ill-disciplined.

Barnby introduced the music of Wagner and Dvorak to English audiences.

Said to have composed 256 hymn tunes in total. Nine of these were used in *Church Hymns* (1874) and 11 in the Revised Edition (1927) of *Church Hymnary*. Elsewhere, his 'Laudes Domini' is found with 'When morning gilds the skies'. 'Cantate Domino', which uncharacteristically uses the double long metre, was used in *Songs of Praise* and *English Hymnal*. He also composed services, anthems, chants and an oratorio *Rebekah*. Many of his chants were included in *Cathedral Psalter Chants* (1875). His anthem 'The Lord is King' was performed at the Leeds Festival of 1883.

BARNES, Dr. Archie Fairbairn (1878-1960)
Born in Bristol, Gloucestershire in 1878; died in Paignton, Devon on 6 June 1960.
Studied at Bristol Grammar School, the Royal College of Music as exhibitioner and Keble College, Oxford as organ scholar (from 1898), where he graduated B.Mus. (1911) and D.Mus. (1912): also M.A.
Music master of Llandovery College (from 1903) and of Farnborough School (1907-1914). His career as a music master was interrupted by World War I. On the outbreak in 1914, Archie Barnes joined the army and served with the British Expeditionary Force in France. A captain in the Gloucester Regiment. Awarded the Military Cross in 1916. Wounded and captured in 1918. In 1920 he transferred to the Army Educational Corps. Wrote a war history of the 2nd/5th Gloucester Battalion.
He then returned to civilian life and became headmaster of the Queen Victoria School, Dunblane, Scotland and, later, the senior music master at Bishop's Stortford College, Hertfordshire. At some point in his career he was assistant visiting music instructor of the Merchant Taylors' School. In 1943 he moved in semi-retirement to Paignton.
Organist and choirmaster of Christ Church, Hampstead, London (from 1904); Holy Trinity Church, Folkestone and St. Andrew's Church, Paignton.
The Revised Edition (1927) of *Church Hymnary* contains his tune 'Dunblane Cathedral' as a setting of 'Far round the world Thy children sing their song' by Basil Matthews. 'Montague' is combined with 'These things shall be' by J.A. Symonds. He also composed anthems, carols, part songs, songs and nursery rhymes.

BARNES, Bryan (b.1934)
Born in Accrington, Lancashire in 1934.
Studied at St. John's College, Cambridge (1955-1959) under Thurston Dart and **George Guest**. In a 30-year career in music education, he has taught all age groups from nursery to adults. Conducted amateur and professional choirs and orchestras throughout this time. Retired early from his position as senior lecturer (1966-1989) at the Colchester Institute, Essex, in order to concentrate on composition. In 1980 he was asked to write a secular cantata for children at music camp. *The Sword in the Stone* thus came into being, following the success of which, other commissions followed for children's works, including a Easter-tide cantata *The Way of the Cross*. Has also composed a number of SATB works including a setting of Psalm 134 'Come, bless the Lord', carols, and sacred works with orchestration such as a Magnificat.

BARNES, Edwin (1833-1901)
Born in St. Pancras, London, on 8 June 1833. died in London on 4 December 1901. Father of **F.E.L. Barnes**. A chorister of King's College, London. Studied piano under **William Rea** and organ and

musical theory under **John Brownsmith**. Professor of music to the London Society for Teaching the Blind. In addition he was organist of Hornsey Parish Church, the Church of St. George the Martyr, Bloomsbury and (from 1862) Holy Trinity Church, Paddington, all in London. Composed an anthem, songs, and works for piano.

BARNES, Frederick Edwin Lucy (1858-1880)
Born in London in 1858, died in Montreal, Canada on 21 September 1880. The son of **Edwin Barnes**.
Studied at the Royal Academy of Music from 1872 and at the Chapel Royal under **Thomas Helmore**.
Organist of All Saints' Church, Norfolk Square, London (from 1872); St. Margaret's, Princess Square, Liverpool (from 1876) and of Montreal Cathedral (1878-1879). Then became assistant organist of Trinity Church, New York City.
Compositions include an opera, operetta, a setting of Psalm 23 for Voices and Orchestra, songs, and items for piano and for organ.

BARNES, Gerald Linton (b.1935)
Born in Hampstead, London on 6 June 1935.
Educated at Kilburn Grammar School, London and at the Royal Academy of Music. Studied music privately with C.H. Trevor and **Eric Thiman**. Organ scholar of Hertford College, Oxford (1953-1955).
Director of music of the Foundation Grammar School, and visiting tutor of the Mary Datchelor Girls' School, Camberwell and of the Kingsdale School, Dulwich, all three London appointments commencing in 1960. Head of music of Christ's College, Finchley, London (from 1966). A lecturer in the music departments of the North East Essex Technical College and the School of Art, Colchester, Essex (from 1970).
Appointed organist and choirmaster of Shepherds Bush Baptist Church (1951-1953) and of Muswell Hill Congregational Church (1955-1956). Organist and music director of Bloomsbury Central Baptist Church in 1956, then, in 1981, of the American Church of London.
A hymnal editor. His hymn tune 'Tetherdown' to 'The Kingdom of God' by Bryn Rees is named after the United Reformed Church in Muswell Hill, North London where Barnes was organist and Rees, minister. 'Luckington' and 'Farmington' are found in *Praise for Today* (1974). His compositions include introits and anthems for church choirs, such as 'I was glad' (1975).

BARNETT, John Francis (1837-1916)
Born in London on 16 October 1837; died in St. John's Wood, London on 24 November 1916.The son of the tenor and singing teacher Joseph Alfred Barnett and the nephew of the composer John Barnett.
Studied piano from the age of six, initially with his mother. From 1849, at the age of 11 he took lessons from **Henry Wylde**. At 12 he won a Queen's Scholarship to the Royal Academy of Music (1850-1857) and he attended the Leipzig Conservatory, Germany for three years concurrently with **Arthur Sullivan** and the pianists Franklin Taylor and Walter Bache, studying under Julius Rietz, Moritz Hauptmann, Louis Plaidy and Ignaz Moscheles.
A pianist, piano teacher and composer. Held professorships at the Royal College of Music and Guildhall School of Music.
Composed anthems including 'Come Thou Holy Spirit' (1884) and 'Christ is risen today' (1899). The combination of Barnett's hymn tune 'Calvary' with the hymn by Thomas Powell, 'Lord, when

beside the grave we mourn' was used by Arthur Sullivan in his compilation *Church Hymns* (1874).

Compositions include choral, orchestral and chamber music. His cantata *The Ancient Mariner* was first performed at the Birmingham Festival of 1867, and his setting of Longfellow's *The Building of the Ship* was composed for the Leeds Festival of 1880. Other works include a Symphony (1864) and an oratorio *The Raising of Lazarus* (1873).

BARNETT, John Maugham (1867-1938)

Maugham Barnett was born in Warwick in 1867; died in New Zealand on 1 January 1938. Lived in Tunbridge Wells, Kent but was compelled to move to New Zealand through ill health. In the more congenial climate his career flourished; he gave concert performances on organ and piano. Composed hymn tunes and items for piano.

BARNICOTT, Olinthus Roberts (1842-1908)

Born in Taunton, Somerset on 2 November 1842; died in Stratton-le-Fosse, Somerset on 11 March 1908. Composed a Te Deum in D (1893), hymn tunes and an anthem 'The Heavens are the Lord's' (1892).

BARNICOTT, Reginald Slater (1876-1944)

Born in Taunton, Somerset in 1876; died in Taunton on 19 May 1944. Composed the anthems 'O worship the Lord' (1898) and 'Break forth into joy' (1907), hymn tunes and songs.

BARRA, Séamas de (b.1955)

Studied music at University College, Cork, Ireland under Aloys Fleischmann, graduating B.Mus. (1977) and M.A. (1980).

A high proportion of his compositions have been by way of a commission, and from a variety of bodies. His Magnificat (1983) and *Song of Pan* (1989) were commissioned for the Cork International Choral Festivals of those years, and his *Canticum in Laudibus* (1988) was for the Irish Youth Choir. *Tibi laus, Tibi gloria* (1993) was at the behest of the Choir of Christ Church Cathedral, Dublin. His orchestral works include *Pezzetto Brioso* (1989).

BARRELL, Bernard (b.1919)

Born in Sudbury, Suffolk on 15 August, 1919. His wife, **Joyce Barrell** was also a composer.

Educated at Woodbridge School, Suffolk (1928-1936).

Has held various teaching appointments, including tutorships for the Workers' Educational Association from 1949 to 1985. Since 1955 he has also taught privately in various aspects of music, including harmony, counterpoint and composition.

A council member of the Composers' Guild of Great Britain (from 1993), having represented East Anglia since 1965.

Bernard Barrell's church compositions reflect his philosophy that music need not necessarily be complex in order to be good, and that suitable material ought to be on offer to parish church choirs and other amateur forces. Examples are his five Masses, his *Two short Anthems* (1986) and the anthem 'Shew yourselves joyful', based on Psalm 98 and composed in 1993 in celebration of the renovation of the organ of Westerfield Church in his native county. Many but not all of his secular works are also for amateurs: they include his recent symphonic movement *From the Waveney Valley* for a local orchestra. More demanding are Symphony for Strings and some of his chamber music.

BARRELL (Gedye), Joyce Howard (1917-1989)

Born in Salisbury, Wiltshire on 26 November 1917; died on 6 December 1989. Wife of **Bernard Barrell**. Attended the Collegiate School, Leicester and studied music privately with Harold Craxton, at the University of Leicester under **Benjamin Burrows** for piano, organ and composition, and with Grace Burrows for violin. Worked as a teacher and composer. Her works include the carols 'A Child is born' and 'A Child of our time', and chamber works such as a Trio for Clarinet, Viola and Piano (1970).

BARRETT, Dr. William Alexander (1836-1891)

Born in Hackney, London on 15 October 1836; died in Hackney on 17 October 1891.

A chorister of St. Paul's Cathedral (1846-1849). Studied music under **George Cooper**, **William Bayley** and, for composition, **John Goss**. Graduated B.Mus (1871) at the University of Oxford and D.Mus at Trinity College, Toronto.

W.A. Barrett also had artistic talent. He drew pictures on wood and he illustrated Holt's *Chronicle of the Crimean War*. The printed word played a major part in his career: he was a journalist on *Morning Chronicle* (1855-1857) and music critic of the *Morning Post* (1869-1891), a book reviewer and translator. From 1856 he lectured on a variety of musical topics.

Barrett was the principal alto at the church of St. Andrew, Wells Street, London (from 1858). At some time he was a vicar choral of St. Paul's Cathedral. A lay vicar of Magdalen College, Oxford (from 1861). Organist of the church of St. John, Cowley, Oxford (1863-1866).

With **John Stainer** under whom he served as assistant inspector of music in training colleges and schools, he compiled *Dictionary of Musical Terms*.

Composed an oratorio *Christ before Pilate*, anthems, songs and madrigals.

BARRETT-WATSON, Robert (1877-?)

Born in Cowling, Yorkshire in 1877.

Following a private education, he graduated B.Mus. at the University of Durham (1904).

Taught at the Royal Scottish Academy of Music (from 1921).

Organist and choirmaster of St. Mary's Church, Carleton-in-Craven (from 1897); choirmaster of Cowling Parish Church (from 1900); organist and choirmaster of Giggleswick Parish Church (from 1904); choirmaster of Stainforth Church (from 1905); organist and choirmaster of Holy Trinity Church, Sunningdale, Berkshire (from 1907); of St. Thomas's Episcopal Church, Aboyne (from 1911) and of Kelvin Grove United Free Church, Glasgow (from 1920). A conductor of local choral societies.

Joint author of *The Academus Primer of Music* and *The Academus Question Book*. Composed church and organ music.

BARROW, Thomas (1712-1789)

Born in Westminster, London in 1712; died in Westminster on 13 August 1789. A chorister, and, later, a gentleman of the Chapel Royal. Sang in performances of Handel's oratorios. Composed church music, including hymn tunes and chants. *Church Hymnary* (Revised Edition, 1927) contains his Double Chant in F.

BARRY, Charles Ainslie (1830-1915)

Born in London on 10 June 1830; died in Sydenham, Surrey on 21 March 1915.

Educated at Rugby School, Warwickshire and at Trinity College, Cambridge under **Thomas Attwood Walmisley**, continuing his musical studies at the Universities of Cologne and Leipzig, and at Dresden. It had originally been intended that he should study for the ministry.

At Leipzig he studied under Ignaz Moscheles and Ernst Richter. At Cologne he was directed by F. Weber, E. Frank and Ferdinand Hiller. At Dresden he was taught by Carl Reissiger.

Returned from Germany in 1858 and in 1860 he became organist and choirmaster of Forest School, Leytonstone Hill, Essex. As a violinist he was compared with Corelli. In addition, for many years he wrote programme notes for concerts that were said to be a model of their kind.

Music critic of *The Guardian* (1863-1879), contributing to other publications including *The Athenaeum* and *Musical World*. Edited *Monthly Musical Record.*

His hymn tunes 'Macedon' and 'Annunciation' were used in the Revised Edition (1916) of *Hymns Ancient and Modern*. Also composed a symphony and other orchestral pieces and cantatas, plus *The Story of the Resurrection,* a cycle of hymns.

BARTHÉLEMON, François-Hippolyte (1741-1808)
Born in Bordeaux, France on 27 July 1741; died in London on 23 July 1808.

Married the former Mary Young, musician and composer, in 1766. They travelled and performed together.

Reputedly an officer in the Irish Brigade. Came to England in 1765, settling in London. When Haydn visited London on two occasions during the 1790s, Barthélemon struck up a friendship with him.

A London violinist and composer, in 1770 he became leader of the Marylebone Gardens Orchestra, for which he also composed.

Wrote operas, stage music, and violin music. Within the church he is famous for his tune 'Morning Hymn', (sometimes known as 'Hippolytus') and 'Magdalene' to the words of Bishop Ken's hymn 'Awake my soul and with the sun', which he composed at the request of Revd. Jacob Duché, chaplain of the Female Orphan Asylum and which was published in 1785.

BARTHOLOMEW (Mounsey), Ann Sheppard (1811-1891)
Born in London on 17 April 1811; died in London on 24 June 1891.

A pupil of Johann Logier from 1817. In 1820 she was discovered on a visit to Logier's Institute, by the composer Spohr, who noted in his diary that her talent was 'precious'. She also studied with **Samuel Wesley** and **Thomas Attwood**.

Organist of St. Michael's Church, Wood Street, Clapton, London (1828-1837) and of St. Vedast's, Foster Lane, London (1837-1891).

Gave concerts of sacred music, and introduced a number of the smaller works of Mendelssohn.

A collection of 34 of her hymn tunes was published in 1883. Her other works include the anthem 'Holy is the Lord of Hosts', an oratorio *The Nativity* (1855), the cantata *Supplication and Thanksgiving,* organ works, piano items and over a hundred songs.

BARTHOLOMEW, R. (?-1891)
Organist of Ludlow Parish Church, Shropshire. Composed a service setting, *Canticles Pointed for Chanting* (c1860) and the anthem 'O that man would praise the Lord' (1870).

BARTON, Revd. William (c1598-1678)
Born around the year 1598; died in Leicester in May 1678.

Vicar of Mayfield, Staffordshire and of St. Martin's Church, Leicester (elevated to cathedral status in 1927). A friend of the theologian, Revd. Richard Baxter.

Chiefly remembered for his *Book of Psalms in Metre*, an attempt to improve upon the standard metrical paraphrase of the time, the Sternhold and Hopkins Edition. It was re-published with amendments in 1645, 1646, 1651, 1654 and later.

There were moves from the House of Lords in 1645 and 1646 to adopt Barton's version as the authorised Psalter. However, the Westminster Assembly of Divines insisted on the version by Francis Rous and the House of Commons voted likewise. In Scotland, the Assembly of 1647 devised a composite version from five sources, but most material was taken from the works by Barton and Rous.

A pioneer of hymnody, he sought to achieve acceptance of hymns based on the New Testament. In 1659 he published *A Century of Select Hymns*, followed by a number of similar collections.

William Barton composed four settings of the metrical version of the Te Deum.

BASKEYFIELD, George (1878-1955)
Born in Tunstall, Staffordshire in 1878; died in Stoke on Trent, Staffordshire on 28 February 1955. Educated at the Birmingham and Midlands Institute. Organist of the Jubilee Methodist Church, Tunstall (from 1896). Lectured in music in the Extra Mural Delegacy of the University of Oxford (from 1920). An adjudicator at competitive music festivals. On the committee of the Methodist Church Music Society. Presented the Great Britain Gramophone Reference Library to the city corporation of Stoke on Trent in 1947. A composer of hymn tunes.

BATCHELOR, Chappell (1822-1884)
Born in Southwell, Nottinghamshire in June 1822 and baptised in Southwell Minster on 1 July 1822; died in Derby on 11 January 1884. The son of a local apothecary. King's Scholar at the Royal Academy of Music under **John Goss**, Cipriani Potter and **Vincent Novello**. At the age of 12 he acted as the temporary organist of Southwell Minster during the interregnum between **Edward Heathcote** and Frederick Gunton, performing impressively despite his tender years. Succeeded Gunton as organist of Southwell Minster (1841-1857). Thereafter he resigned and moved first to Belper, Derbyshire and then to Derby.

Known for his hymn tune 'Batchelor'.

BATCHELOR, John Arthur (1857-1938)
Born in Newington, Surrey in 1857; died in Isleworth, Middlesex on 1 July 1938. Organist of the Kentish churches of St. John the Evangelist, Bexley (from 1883); Lamorbey Parish Church, Sidcup (from 1886) and of Abbot's Langley Parish Church (from 1885) and St. Anne's Church, Gresham Street, London (from 1887). A composer of hymn tunes.

BATE, Horace Alfred J. (1899-1995)
Born in Chatham, Kent in 1899; died in Muswell Hill, London, on 2 June 1995.

Studied under **Charles Hylton Stewart** at Rochester Cathedral and with **H.G. Ley** and **C.H. Kitson** at the Royal College of Music.

Organist of St. Margaret's Church, Rochester (1921) and of St. James's, Muswell Hill (1923). His speciality was the training of organists.

Hymn tune 'Collingwood' (1934) was suggested for use with either 'Father, whatever of earthly bliss' or 'O for a thousand tongues to sing' in *Hymns Ancient and Modern*. In the New Standard Edition it is found with 'Father of mercies, in Thy Word'.

BATEMAN, Robert Bowness (19th/20th century)
Studied music privately; graduated B.Mus. at New College, Oxford (1887). Organist of Penrith Parish Church (1862, and 1898-1906). In the meantime he had been organist of Aylesbury Parish Church, Buckinghamshire, and of Queen's Cross Free Church, Aberdeen (from 1890). Taught piano at a college in Aberdeen (from 1893). Music master of Penrith Grammar School (from1898). A conductor of choral societies. He composed a Kyrie (1886), a Magnificat and Nunc Dimittis in C (1904), anthems including 'Truly, God is loving unto Israel' (1886), and piano music.

BATES, Dr. Francis (1856-1936)
Born on 13 January 1856 at March, Cambridgeshire; died on 11 May 1936.
Frank Bates attended March Grammar School and studied music privately. Graduated B.Mus. (1880) and D.Mus. (1882). at Trinity College Dublin.
Assistant organist at Holy Trinity Church, Leamington Spa, Warwickshire; organist at St. Baldred's Episcopal Church, North Berwick, Scotland (from 1874) and then of St. John's Episcopal Church, Edinburgh (1882-1885).
Organist of Norwich Cathedral (1886-1928) until his retirement, securing his appointment against a field of 167 fellow applicants. In his time at Norwich he persuaded the authorities to purchase a new organ from the firm of Norman and Beard (1899). He was also a local choral and orchestral society conductor.
Published an autobiography *Reminiscences of a Musician in Retirement*. Lectured on musical topics.
Compositions include church music and an oratorio, *Samuel.* He composed Morning and Evening Services in B-flat, an Evening Service in C and anthems including 'God is our Hope' and 'I will sing'.

BATES, George (1802-1881)
Born in Halifax, Yorkshire on 6 July 1802; died on 24 January 1881. Organist of Ripon Cathedral (1829-1873). Composed hymn tunes including 'Veni Creator', and other items of church music.

BATESON, Thomas (c1570-1630)
Born in Cheshire around the year 1570; died in Dublin on 11 March 1630.
Graduated B.Mus. (1615) and M.A. (1622) at Trinity College, Dublin. He may thus have been the first ever recipient of a Dublin B.Mus.
Organist of Chester Cathedral (1599-1608), later moving to Ireland under the patronage of Lord Chichester. An organistship ensued at Christ Church Cathedral, Dublin (at the time, known as the Cathedral of the Holy Trinity) from 1608 to 1630. He was also vicar choral from either 1608 or 1609 until 1630, and master of the choristers (1618-1630).
One of a large number of contemporary composers writing madrigals. Wrote several devotional songs and at least one anthem, 'Holie Lord God almightie', scored for seven voices. It may have

been with this piece that he supplicated for his B.Mus. A Service by him was in existence until the early part of the 19th century, when it disappeared.

BATHE, Humphrey (16th century)
Little is known of Humphrey Bathe except that he was a composer of church music before the year 1600. He wrote a book entitled *Introduction to the Skill of Song* which was published in 1597.

BATSON, Revd. Arthur Wellesley (19th/20th century)
Educated privately in music; graduated B.Mus. (1878) at St. Alban Hall (now Merton College), Oxford.
Taught Classics at Swansea Grammar School (from 1873). Headmaster of the Swansea Collegiate School (from 1876). Precentor of St. Anne's Church, Soho, London (1881-1887), and rector of Ringstead (1888-1902).
Composed a motet *I will glorify,* anthems, services, a cantata *The Vineyard,* songs, part songs and glees.

BATTEN, Adrian (1591-1637)
Born in Salisbury, Wiltshire and was baptised on 1 March 1591; died in London in 1637.
The son of a joiner. Probably a chorister under **John Holmes**, organist of Winchester Cathedral, whose pupil he later became.
Moved to London in March 1614 and became a lay vicar at Westminster Abbey (1614-1626), supplementing his income by working as a copyist. Subsequently joint organist (with **John Tomkins**) and vicar choral of St. Paul's Cathedral (1626-1637).
His *Organ Book* is a set of 16th century organ scores in manuscript form. A prolific composer, exclusively for the church. Composed some 50 anthems in long and short form, some of which appeared in *Cathedral Music*, a collection published by **William Boyce**, and also Preces, Litanies, a set of Festal Psalms, and Services.
Has been criticised as a composer by Burney as being unadventurous melodically, although this charge could be laid equally against many of his contemporaries.
Many of his compositions, including a number of Services, are lost. Those that remain are highly regarded. Among his surviving compositions are 47 anthems including 'O sing joyfully', 'Hear my prayer, O God', 'O Lord, Thou hast searched me out' and 'When the Lord turned'. Composed 15 Services of which his Third Verse Service is available in two separate publishers' editions today.

BATTEN, Revd. John Henry (19th/20th century)
Graduated B.Mus. (1901) and B.A. (1906) at the University of Durham. Organ scholar at Hatfield Hall, Durham (1904-1906) and ordained in the latter year.
Organist of St. Maurice's, Church, and honorary organist of Trinity College, Winchester, from 1892. From 1895 to 1908 he was organist and choirmaster of Broadstairs Parish Church, Kent. Curate of Holy Trinity Church, Dover (from 1909).
Composed a setting of the Communion, Morning and Evening services, organ music and part songs.

BATTISHILL, Jonathan (1738-1801)
Born in London in May 1738; died in Islington, London on 10 December 1801. Buried, in accordance with his dying wish, near **William Boyce** in St. Paul's Cathedral.
A chorister at St. Paul's (from 1747) under **William Savage**, whose pupil he later became. Possessed a remarkable memory, with

the benefit of which he could play a piece years after hearing it performed just once.

A London organist. From August 1765 to 1801 he was organist of the united parishes of St. Clement's, Eastcheap, London and St. Martin's, Ongar and, from 1767, of Christ Church, Newgate Street. A counter tenor singer, he was also harpsichord player and conductor of the Covent Garden Theatre (it was usual for the two appointments to be held by a single person). He was William Boyce's sometime deputy as organist of the Chapel Royal.

His reputed weakness for alcohol possibly cost him the appointment of organist of St. Paul's Cathedral in 1796 on the decease of **John Jones**; he would otherwise have been a strong candidate but **Thomas Attwood** was preferred.

Composed glees, songs for performance in public gardens and material for the theatre. Won the gold medal of the Noblemen's Catch Club in 1771.

Later in life turned his skills to the service of the church. His compositional style was that of the traditional cathedral school and of his anthems, 'Call to remembrance' and 'O Lord, look down from Heaven' are performed regularly today. Many of his chants were included in *Cathedral Psalter Chants* (1875). He composed virtually nothing after the year 1777, in which his wife deserted him.

Composed hymn tunes, including 'Battishill' and 'St. Pancras'. In all he composed 12 tunes for use with the hymns of Charles Wesley.

Sometimes seen as the bridge between Boyce and **S.S. Wesley**, at a time when it is acknowledged that few English composers were able to sustain the standards set in earlier times.

BATTYE, James (1803-1858)

Born in Huddersfield, Yorkshire in 1803; died in Huddersfield on 10 October 1858. Parish clerk of Huddersfield, a teacher and composer. In 1854 he published *Twelve Glees for four and five voices*. Composer of glees. His anthem 'My soul truly waiteth' collected the Gresham Prize of 1845.

BAUGHEN, Rt. Revd. Dr. Michael Alfred (b.1930)

Born in Borehamwood, Hertfordshire on 7 June 1930.

Attended the University of London and Oak Hill Theological College. Graduated B.D. (1955); ordained deacon (1956) and priest (1957).

Began a career in banking but following his ordination, served as curate to Hyson Green Church, Nottingham and St. Mary's Church, Reigate, Surrey. Thereafter worked for the Church Pastoral Aid Society. Rector of the Church of the Holy Trinity, Platt, near Manchester (1964-1970). Vicar (1970-1975) and Rector (1975-1982) of All Souls' Church, Langham Place, London. An Area Dean (1978-1982), a Prebendary of St. Paul's Cathedral (1979-1982) and Bishop of Chester (1982-1996). Retired in 1996.

A hymn writer and composer, whose work has appeared in hymnals including *Youth Praise, Youth Praise II, Psalm Praise* and *Hymns for Today's Church*.

At the time of his ordination there was little published material available for youth groups. The success of his new songs for this age group led to the setting up of a committee and the eventual appearance of *Youth Praise* (1966) in which around one half of the 150 items was new material. The combined sales of the two *Youth Praise* books eventually exceeded one million copies.

His hymn tune known as 'Go forth' was actually written for the hymn 'Tell out my soul' by Revd. Timothy Dudley-Smith. James

Seddon later wrote his hymn 'Go forth and tell! O Church of God awake!' which is based on the text of Matthew 28:19 with 'Go forth' specifically in mind. Dudley-Smith's 'Lord of the Years' was sung to another of Baughen's tunes at the Consecration in Canterbury Cathedral of Archbishop George Carey.

Composed the Psalm setting 'Blessed is the man', a prototype of a project that was to reach its fulfilment some years later as *Psalm Praise,* in which he sought to achieve metrical rhythm without rhyming, in order to retain the accuracy of the paraphrase. Conducted a large choir at the Albert Hall, London for the launch of Youth Praise II, and has been involved with *Prom Praise* at which the collection is presented, around the UK.

BAUMER, Henry (1835-1888)

Born in 1835; died in Watford, Hertfordshire on 29 July 1888. Organist of Dulwich College, London and headmaster of the Watford School of Music, retiring from the latter in 1886. Composed the anthems 'Lord, how are they increased' (1876) and 'If ye love me', a cantata *Triumph of Labour* (1875), songs, part songs, a String Quartet, and piano music.

BAX, Sir Arnold Edward Trevor (1883-1953)

Born in Streatham, London on 8 November 1883; died in Cork, Ireland on 3 October 1953. The older brother of Clifford Lea Bax, poet and playwright.

A pupil of Frederick Corder and Tobias Matthay at the Royal Academy of Music (1900-1905). Awarded honorary doctorates by the Universities of Oxford (1934) and Durham (1935).

Knighted in 1937, appointed Master of the King's Musick in 1942 and appointed K.C.V.O. in 1953.

His friends included **Ralph Vaughan Williams** who in 1935 dedicated his Fourth Symphony to him, and **Herbert Howells.** A friendship with **John Ireland** survived rivalry and some resentment and perhaps jealousy on the part of the other. Highly accomplished as a sight-reading pianist. Visited Russia in 1910.

His interest in folk lore and legend enticed him to set some of the words of W.B. Yeats to music and led him to travel extensively in Ireland. Published three books under the pseudonym of Dermot O'Byrne, one of which was a commemoration of the Dublin Rising of Easter Week, 1916. Had been a friend of Pearse and some of the other leaders of that insurrection.

A keen follower of the game, he was often to be seen at Lord's cricket ground. He was said to have been of private means and therefore never totally dependent on music for his living. However he did receive funds from the Patron's Fund of the Royal College of Music.

His autobiography *Farewell, my Youth* (1943) was at least partly responsible for fostering the superficial impression of **Hubert Parry** as a Conservative country squire, sportsman and churchman, and thus turning opinion against Parry's music. In fact, Parry was a radical, anti-Conservative who never shot and disliked the company of those who did, and was utterly disillusioned with the Anglican Church.

Arnold Bax wrote songs, choral music, piano pieces, chamber music, seven symphonies, symphonic poems, concertos for violin, for viola and for cello, and ballet music, plus a Nunc Dimittis and Te Deum (1944). His Magnificat (1948) and Nunc Dimittis (1945) are unconnected and the former does not use the words of the Book of Common Prayer. His large scale unaccompanied choral work *Mater, ora Filium* is well known. **Henry Wood** wrote that he was 'unpretentious, but then great men are'.

BAXTER, Frederic Nathaniel (1859-?)
Born in Risely, Bedfordshire in 1859. Educated privately, graduating B.Mus. at the University of Durham (1899).
Organist of Colerne Parish Church from 1871, and of St. Saviour's Church, Tetbury, Gloucestershire (1880-1925). He was the conductor of the local philharmonic and orchestral society.
Compositions include the anthem 'God our Refuge', a cantata *By the Cross,* other church music, a *Salutaris Hostia* for organ, and part songs including 'My lady sleeps'.

BAYLEY, William (1810-1858)
Born in Tetbury, Staffordshire on 7 January 1810; died in Shoreditch, London on 8 November 1858.
A vicar choral of St. Paul's Cathedral. Succeeded **William Hawes** as master of the choristers there and held the position from 1846 until his death in 1858.
Organist of St. John's Church, Horsleydown, Southwark, London (from 1848). A teacher of organ, his pupils included **W.A. Barrett, Henry Gadsby, Arthur Sullivan** and a future organist of St. Paul's Cathedral, **John Stainer**.
Composed anthems including 'Enter not into judgement' and 'To the Lord our God', hymn tunes, chants and songs.

BEALE, Charles James (1819-1882)
Born in 1819; died in London on 19 March 1882. Organist of St. Paul's Church, Covent Garden, London, composing the anthem 'Laudate Dominum' (1863) and other church music, plus some secular vocal works.

BEALE, William (1784-1854)
Born in Landrake, Cornwall on 1 January 1784; died in Stockwell, London on 3 May 1854.
A chorister at Westminster Abbey under Samuel Arnold and **Robert Cooke**.
When his voice broke, he went to sea as a midshipman on the 44-gun frigate *Révolutionnaire,* which had been captured from the French. At one point he nearly drowned when he fell overboard in Cork harbour. When his voice settled down into a good quality baritone, he left the navy and sought a career in music.
He was a gentleman of the Chapel Royal (1816-1820) and organist of the Cambridge Colleges of Trinity and St. John (1820-1821) before he returned to London and with the help of **Thomas Attwood,** secured organistships at two London parish churches: Wandsworth and St. John's, Clapham Rise.
Won prizes for his madrigals including 'Awake, sweet morn' (1813) and glees. A Double Chant in G Minor by Beale was included in *Cathedral Psalter Chants* (1875). He composed the anthem 'Bow down Thine ear'.

BEAUMONT, Revd. Geoffrey Phillips (1903-1970)
Born in Coggeshall, Essex in 1903; died in Cape Town, South Africa on 24 August 1970.
Appointed M.B.E. for his services in the Sicily Campaign during World War II.
On leaving school he started work with his father's firm of solicitors. Subsequently went up to Trinity College, Cambridge (1928) and attended Ely Theological College, being ordained in 1932.
Served two London curacies: at the South London Mission Church and at St. John's Church, Waterloo Road (?-1947). A chaplain in the Royal Navy Volunteer Reserve (1941-1946): servicemen recalled him playing piano through the night. Later, he was chaplain to Trinity College, Cambridge (1947-1956) and to the British Embassy in Madrid (1952-1956). Then served as vicar of St. George's, Camberwell, London (1957-1959).
In 1961 he was admitted to the Community of the Resurrection in Mirfield, Yorkshire where he assumed the name Father Gerard.
In his time at Trinity College, Cambridge he composed for revues in the West End. He saw no reason to adopt a different idiom when composing music for the church. The result was *Twentieth Century Folk Mass* (1956), which aroused much controversy.
In a B.B.C. television broadcast on 13 October 1957 at St. Augustine's Church, Highgate, London, the *Folk Mass* was performed during Holy Communion by saxophone, trumpets, guitar and percussion, plus a 25-piece orchestra and the Peter Knight Singers. Writing in *Radio Times,* Revd. Oliver Hunkin introduced the work and its perspective. It read, 'It is hoped that both the action and the music will combine to bring home the meaning and relevance of the rite to our modern situation. The priest will not be in the sanctuary remote from the congregation... The use of "catchy" tunes and short phrases helps them in their task... As Psalm 67 says, Let all the people praise Thee, O God, yea, let *all* the people praise Thee.' The composer himself remarked that he was emulating the 16th-century **John Marbeck** in setting the liturgy to the folk music of the day and that he regarded the event as an experiment, but one that was nevertheless sincerely offered to God.
Controversy was assured, and the newspaper headlines the following day showed signs of shock: 'Calypso at Communion, Swing Service Televised' *(Daily Telegraph)*; 'Holy Communion in Jazz' *(Daily Mail)*; 'The Lord's Prayer Jazzed Up' *(Daily Express).* The *Daily Express* continued, 'This disturbing racket... was one of the most incongruous things ever seen on television... The whole service was completely lacking in grace and dignity.' Seven viewers telephoned the B.B.C., the first six to complain and the seventh to congratulate. *Church Times* took a more tolerant view. 'Not all modern art is bad just because it is modern... experiments should be made so that this generation shall be able to contribute... to the glory of God'.
Three hymn tunes were taken from this work 'Gracias', 'Chesterton' and 'Dean Street'. The first of these is used today with the hymn 'Now thank we all our God', translated from the German hymn of Martin Rinkart. Also composed a pantomime, *Arabian Nightmare.*

BEAUMONT, John (1762-1822)
Born in Holmfirth, Yorkshire in 1762; died in Macclesfield, Cheshire in 1822. Brought up in Yorkshire and developed a love of Psalm tunes. Became one of the preachers of John Wesley.
In 1793 he published a book of anthems in which he avoided any hint of fugue: he wished to avoid offending those who held that sacred texts should be enhanced by the music and not obscured by it. One of his hymn tunes, 'St. Ignatius' (1801), was used in *Hymns Ancient and Modern* with the hymn by Alice Bode, 'Once pledged by the Cross'. In c1795 he published *Four Anthems for Public Worship... to which are added 16 Psalm or Hymn Tunes.*

BECK, Revd. Anthony (17th century)
A church musician and minor composer of the 17th century who was precentor of Norwich Cathedral. Composed the anthem 'Who can tell how oft he offendeth?'.

BECKWITH, Revd. Edward James (1772-1833)
Born in Norwich, Norfolk in 1772; died on 7 January 1833. Succentor of St. Paul's Cathedral. Composed hymn tunes and chants. A Double Chant by Edward Beckwith was included in *Cathedral Psalter Chants* (1875).

BECKWITH, John (1728-1800)
Born in 1728; died on 14 May 1800. The uncle of **Edward Beckwith** and of **John 'Christmas' Beckwith**. A lay clerk of Norwich Cathedral. Composed the anthems 'I will alway give thanks' and 'Lift up thy voice'.

BECKWITH, Dr. John 'Christmas' (c1750-1809)
Born in Norwich, Norfolk in 1750 or 1759; died in Norwich of paralysis on 3 June 1809.
His middle name, which suggests that he was born on Christmas Day, appears to have been a nickname, perhaps to distinguish him from his son John Charles Beckwith (1788-1819) who succeeded him as organist of Norwich Cathedral. He studied music at Magdalen College, Oxford under **Philip Hayes** and **William Hayes**. Later in life he graduated B.Mus. and D.Mus. in the same year (1803) at the University of Oxford.
Organist at the church of St. Peter Mancroft, Norwich (from 1794) where he succeeded his father, Edward Beckwith.
From 1808 until the year of his death he was organist of Norwich Cathedral, succeeding **Thomas Garland**. For some time he had already been master of the choristers.
A brilliant improvising organ player, he also composed anthems, including 'The Lord is very great', and music for organ and for harpsichord. In 1808 he published *The First Verse of Every Psalm of David with an Ancient and Modern Chant.* He also composed glees, songs and piano works and was an amateur painter.

BEDFORD, Gertrude Lilian (b.1912)
Born in Bletchley, Buckinghamshire in 1912. For many years she has been connected with the Spurgeon Memorial Baptist Church, where she was organist (from 1937) and choirmaster (from 1942). Has composed anthems, hymn tunes, sacred songs for children, and introits.

BEDSMORE, Thomas (1833-1881)
Born in Lichfield, Staffordshire on 26 December 1833; died in Lichfield on 9 June 1881.
A chorister of Lichfield Cathedral (from 1843); later articled to the Cathedral organist, **Samuel Spofforth.**
Assistant organist to Spofforth, whom he succeeded as organist (1864-1881).
Held other organist appointments in and around Lichfield including St. Chad's Church, Stow (from 1854). While in charge at Lichfield Cathedral he was also organist of St. Mary's Church, Lichfield and of Barton-under-Needlewood Parish Church, Staffordshire. A captain in the Staffordshire Rifle Volunteers.
Composed church music including the anthems 'Awake, thou that sleepest' and 'Lord, who shall dwell', songs and works for piano.

BEDWELL, James Kibble Douglas (1883-1944)
Born in Cambridge in 1883; died in Surrey in 1944. An amateur musician at Cambridge and organist at Oxted, Surrey. Composed the hymn 'To brave hearts' (1915), the tune 'St. Hilda', and songs.

BEECHAM, Sir Adrian Welles (1904-1982)
Born in Lucerne, Switzerland in 1904, the son of Thomas Beecham; died on 4 September 1982.
Studied music privately with **Charles Wood**, **Thomas Dunhill**, and Edward German. Attended Trinity College of Music; graduated B.Mus. at the University of Durham.
The hymnal *With One Voice* (1978) combines the words of 'See, Christ was wounded for our sake' by Brian Foley with Adrian Beecham's 'Yellow Bittern', which was first published in *Cambridge Hymnal.* Has also composed a sacred cantata *Ruth,* songs around 85 in number, and part songs.

BEECHEY, Dr. Gwilym Edward (b.1938)
Born in London on 12 January 1938.
Studied at the Royal College of Music and at Magdalene College, Cambridge (1956-1962), where he was John Stewart of Rannoch Scholar in sacred music (1958), and research student. Holds the Cambridge degrees of M.A., Mus.B., and Ph.D.
Has worked as a school teacher, university lecturer, organ recitalist, composer, editor and arranger. Many of his articles have appeared in music journals, and he contributed to the 1980 edition of the Grove *Dictionary of Music and Musicians.*
Editor (1986-1993) of *The Consort,* the journal of the Dolmetsch Foundation. Has edited and published many 17th and 18th century works.
Examples of his own compositions are a Magnificat and Nunc Dimittis in A (the *St. Woolos* Service), the anthem 'O Saviour, with protecting care', a Christmas lullaby 'Sleep, holy Babe', hymns and organ works including his recent Elegy *In Memory of Herbert Sumsion.*

BEECROFT, George Andus Beaumont (1845-1873)
Son of the Member of Parliament for Leeds. Attended the University of Oxford where he graduated B.Mus. (1867), B.A. (1868) and M.A. (1872). Contributed to *The Choir* and other journals. Composed a Magnificat and Nunc Dimittis, the anthem 'Turn Thy face from my sins', secular vocal music and items for piano.

BEER, Alfred (1874-1963)
Born in Great Barr, Birmingham, in 1874; died in Poole, Dorset on 13 October 1963. The son of a Methodist minister. Studied piano under Oscar Beringer. Music master of Kingswood School, Bath, Somerset (from 1904). The onset of blindness caused him to retire in 1928, although he later briefly served as organist and choirmaster at Minehead Baptist Church, Somerset and the Uxbridge Central Hall, Middlesex. W.P. Workman, his headmaster at Kingswood, encouraged him to compose tunes to Methodist hymns. His tune 'Anchor' (used today with 'Now I have found the ground wherein') and four others were used in *Methodist Hymn Book* (1933). Composed the hymn 'Lo! He comes' (1904) and the anthem 'Peace I leave with you' (1904).

BELCHER, William Edward (1864-?)
Born in Handsworth, Birmingham, in 1864, the son of **William Thomas Belcher**.
Following his studies at the Royal College of Music he became choral scholar of King's College, Cambridge where he graduated M.A.

Organist of Kingston on Thames Parish Church, Surrey (from 1891) and of St. Michael's Church, Headingley, Leeds (from 1893). From 1895 he was deputy organist to Leeds Corporation. Organist of St. Asaph Cathedral (1901-1917).
Composed church music, including settings of the Morning Service in Welsh and of the Evening Service in English, in F (1907), and the *St. Asaph* Litany (1909).

BELCHER, Dr. William Thomas (1827-1905)
Born in Birmingham on 8 March 1827; died in Birmingham on 6 May 1905.
The father of **William Edward Belcher**.
A pupil of **Charles Corfe** and **W.T. Best**, he graduated B.Mus. (1867) and D.Mus. (1872) at the University of Oxford.
Organist of Great Barr Church, Birmingham (from 1856), and of other churches in that area (from 1884), eventually being appointed organist of Holy Trinity Church, Bordesley.
Composed an oratorio *The Sea of Galilee*, cantatas, a Te Deum in C (1869), an anthem based on the words of Psalm 122, hymn tunes, chants, and piano works.

BELL, Revd. Dr. George (19th/20th century)
Graduated B.Mus. (1882) and D.Mus. (1888) at the University of Dublin, and M.A. at Queen's University, Belfast. Held appointments in the Govan region of Glasgow. Assistant minister of the Parish Church of Saint Constantine the King and minister of St. Kenneth's, Holmfauldhead, South Govan. Writer of articles on church music, and composer of hymn tunes.

BELL, Dr. John (19th century)
Born in Gourock, Renfrewshire, Scotland. Graduated D.Mus. at the University of Toronto. Was at some time organist of four churches in the Glasgow area - Westbourne Free Church, and the Parish Churches of Springburn, Anderston and St. Vincent. Conductor to a number of choral societies, and music critic of *North British Daily Mail*. Composed or arranged some 50 anthems and part songs.

BELL, John Montgomerie (1837-1910)
Born in Edinburgh on 28 May 1837; died in Edinburgh on 8 June 1910. Educated in Edinburgh at the Academy and later at the University, where he read music and law. A writer, botanist and musician. Served on the committee for the compilation of *Church Hymnary* (1896). Composed hymn tunes. Revised Edition (1927) of *Church Hymnary* uses John Bell's 'St. Giles' with 'We give Thee but Thine own' by William Walsham How. Composed anthems, a tune to the hymn, 'Just as I am' (1928), and songs.

BELL, Maurice Frederick (1862-1947)
Born in St. Giles, Middlesex on 26 September 1862; died in Henfield, Sussex on 6 April 1947. Composed hymn tunes, a carol 'The Gospel sang the angels bright' (1913), and songs.

BELL, William Henry (1873-1946)
Born in St. Albans, Hertfordshire on 20 August 1873; died in Cape Town, South Africa, on 13 April 1946.
A chorister of St. Albans Cathedral. Won a Goss scholarship in 1889 to study at the Royal Academy of Music. He was at the R.A.M. until 1893, directed by Frederick Corder, **Charles Steggall** for organ, Alfred Burnett for violin, and Izard for piano. Around the year 1901 he studied with **C.V. Stanford**.

He was later to contrast the teaching methods of the two: Corder left the student almost without guidance, while Stanford's pupils were compelled to imitate the styles of each of the great composers in turn. Bell drew the conclusion that a middle way between the two extremes was the best course of development for young composers.
Of necessity a church organist for 20 years, but he disliked both the instrument itself and the clergy with whom it brought him into contact. A professor of harmony at the R.A.M. (1903-1912).
In 1912 he emigrated to South Africa where he was initially principal of the South Africa College of Music, Cape Town, and then professor at the University of Cape Town. Retired in 1934 and returned to England, but soon went back to South Africa.
Wrote two operas including *Hippolytus* (1914); two symphonies, a Symphonic Prelude *A Song of Morning* for a Gloucester Three Choirs' Festival around 1900, plus hymn tunes commissioned by **Ralph Vaughan Williams** for *English Hymnal* which survived into *New English Hymnal*. His 'Cathcart' was used in the Revised Edition (1927) of *Church Hymnary*.

BELLAMY, Richard (1743-1813)
Born in 1743; died in London on 11 September 1813.
Graduated Mus.B. at the University of Cambridge (1775).
A bass singer of the Chapel Royal. Appointed gentleman in March 1771. A lay vicar of Westminster Abbey (from 1773) and vicar choral of St. Paul's Cathedral (1777). Almoner and master of the choristers of St. Paul's Cathedral (1793-1800), in which position he succeeded **Robert Hudson**. In 1784 he sang bass at the Handel Commemoration. In 1801 he resigned from all his appointments other than his job at St. Paul's.
Composed anthems, including 'Come, Holy Ghost' and 'I waited patiently'. A set of anthems was published in 1788. His other works include a Te Deum with orchestral accompaniment, glees and sonatas.

BELLERBY, Dr. Edward Johnson (1858-1940)
Born in Pickering, Yorkshire on 28 March 1858; died in Southborough, Kent on 2 April 1940.
Studied under **E.G. Monk** at York Minster (1876-1880), during the latter part of which he was Dr. Monk's assistant. Graduated B.Mus (1879) and D.Mus. (1895) at the University of Oxford.
An organist and pianist, he was the private organist to Lord Hotham (1877-1878) and organist of Margate Parish Church, Kent (1881); Selby Abbey Church (1881-1884) and Holy Trinity Church, Margate (1884-1914).
Composed a Holy Communion Service in F, anthems including 'Jesu, my Lord', orchestral works, and items for piano and for organ.

BENET, John (15th century)
A composer who is believed to have been alive between the years 1420 and 1450. Wrote a Mass, a Sanctus and three motets in a style suggesting that he was a contemporary of **John Dunstable**. Some of his music is to be found in Italian collections. Works include the motet *Lux fulget et anglia*.

BENNET, John (16th/17th century)
John Bennet was probably born between the years 1575 and 1580, and was known still to be alive in 1614. Probably a Lancastrian. A madrigal composer, he was famous for his verse anthem 'All creatures now are merry minded'. Five of his tunes were used in

Barley's *Whole Booke of Psalms* (1599). He was also represented in **Thomas Ravenscroft**'s *Psalter*, and in *The Triumphes of Oriana*. Composed anthems including 'O God of Gods', hymn tunes and organ pieces.

BENNETT, Alfred William (1805-1830)
Born in Chichester, Sussex in 1805; died on 12 September 1830 following an accident in which he fell from a stage coach, the *Aurora*, en route to the Worcester Festival.
The eldest son of **Thomas Bennett** and the elder brother of **Henry Bennett**.
Studied music under his father, Thomas; graduated B.Mus. at the University of Oxford (1825).
On the death of William Woodcock, Alfred Bennett became organist of New College, Oxford and of the University. On his own premature death he was succeeded by **Stephen Elvey**.
Composed a service, anthems including 'Grant we beseech Thee' and 'O praise the Lord of Heaven', and chants, which he also collected with **William Marshall** and which were published in 1829. A Double Chant in F by Alfred Bennett was included in *Cathedral Psalter Chants* (1875).

BENNETT, Frederick James Wentworth (1856-?)
Born in Cadbury, Somerset in 1856. Studied in the Royal Academy of Music, and under A.P. Vivian and W.S. Rockstro. A professor of flute at the Brighton School of Music (from 1895),. Contributed to a number of musical journals including *Musical Times*. Composed a Mass in C Minor (1889), cantatas, works for piano and for flute, over two hundred songs, and part songs.

BENNETT, Dr. George John (1863-1930)
Born in Andover, Hampshire on 5 May 1863; died in Lincoln on 20 August 1930.
A chorister at Winchester Cathedral from 1872 until 1878. His well-rounded musical education included a Balfe Scholarship to the Royal Academy of Music, where he studied from 1879 to 1884, principally under **George Macfarren** and **Charles Steggall**, and others. He was at this time organist of the Westminster Methodist Chapel.
He followed this with two years under Friedrich Kiel and Hans Barth at the Berlin *Hochschule*, sponsored by the firm of Novello, and then a further two years at Munich under Josef Rheinberger for composition and Harald Bussmeyer for piano. Returned to England in 1887. Awarded Mus.B. (1888) and Mus.D. (1893) at the University of Cambridge.
In 1925 he was Sheriff of Lincoln, a rare honour for a church musician.
At the relatively early age of 25 George Bennett was appointed a professor of harmony and composition at the R.A.M. He was organist of St. John's, Wilton Road, Pimlico, London (1890-1895) and of Lincoln Cathedral (1895-1930) where he succeeded **Matthew Young** and became known as a disciplinarian. Conducted the Lincoln Festivals of 1896, 1899, 1902, 1906 and 1910.
The author of the textbook *Combined and Florid Counterpoint*, and of *The Choirboy's Elements of Music*.
Composed church music, including a Mass in B-flat Minor, a Festival Te Deum, a Festival Evening Service in A, other services and anthems, organ music and part songs.

BENNETT, Henry Robert (c1807-1861)
A chorister of Magdalen College, Oxford and a pupil of his father. The youngest son of **Thomas Bennett** and the brother of **Alfred William Bennett**. In 1848 he was appointed organist of Chichester Cathedral, in succession to his father, on a probationary basis. Confirmed in the position in 1849; served there until 1860. In the latter year he exchanged appointments with **Philip Armes**, organist of St. Andrew's Church, Wells Street, London. A number of his anthems were once in use at Chichester Cathedral: they include 'Like as the hart' and 'O God, the Strength'.

BENNETT, Nicholas (1823-1899)
Born in Glan-yr-afon, Trefeglwys, Montgomeryshire, Wales on 8 May 1823; died on 18 August 1899. Collected and studied works of history, poetry and music. A justice of the peace at Glan-yr-afon. Well-known in Wales as a conductor and judge at music festivals. In 1896 he published a collection of 500 hymn tunes by various composers, entitled *Alawon fy Ngwlad* (Melodies of my Country). The hymn tune 'Trewen' is his. Also composed songs.

BENNETT, Richard Rodney (b.1936)
Born in Broadstairs, Kent on 29 March 1936. His mother, a gifted pianist, had been a pupil of **Gustav Holst**.
Attended Leighton Park School, Reading and studied at the Royal Academy of Music with **Lennox Berkeley** and Howard Ferguson. His music education continued in Paris for two years under Pierre Boulez (1957-1958).
Appointed C.B.E. in 1977.
A professor of piano at the R.A.M. (1963-1965) and visiting professor of the Peabody Conservatory, Baltimore, U.S.A. (1970-1971). Vice president of the Royal College of Music (from 1983).
Has written operas, orchestral works, chamber music, *Verses*, a set of short anthems of which 'Hear us, O Lord' is one; *Five Carols* (1967), for film (including *Far from the Madding Crowd*, 1967) and for radio.

BENNETT, Robert (1788-1819)
Born in Bakewell, Derbyshire and baptised there on 6 February 1788; died in Sheffield, Yorkshire on 3 November 1819. He is perhaps better known as the father of **William Sterndale Bennett** than in his own right. A former chorister of King's College, Cambridge, he was later articled to the college organist, **John Clarke-Whitfeld**. His connection with the city of Cambridge began when the family moved there, when he was a child. On leaving King's, he took lessons with Clarke-Whitfeld. In 1811 became organist of Sheffield Parish Church. Prominent in the musical life of Sheffield; became friendly with a Mr. William Sterndale, after whom he named his son. Composed songs and hymn tunes, among them 'Bennett', also known as 'Hensbury', 'Scotland' and 'Eastgate'.

BENNETT, Saunders (?-1809)
Born towards the end of the 18th century; died, apparently prematurely, in 1809. Organist of Woodstock Parish Church, Oxfordshire. Composed anthems, songs, glees and items for piano.

BENNETT, Thomas (1779-1848)
Born in Fonthill, Sussex in 1779. died in Chichester, Sussex on 21 March 1848. He was the father of **Alfred Bennett** and **Henry Bennett**. A chorister at Salisbury Cathedral under **Joseph Corfe**. Organist of St. John's Chapel, Chichester, and of Chichester

Cathedral from 1803 to 1848. Succeeded by his son, Henry Bennett. Composed songs, and published collection of the music that was sung at Chichester. His own works include the anthems 'O Lord, the very Heavens' and 'I will magnify Thee, O God'.

BENNETT, William (c1767-c1833)
Born in Comteinteignhead, near Teignmouth, Devon around the year 1767; believed to have died around 1833. Taught by **Hugh Bond** and **William Jackson** of Exeter. On moving to London he studied under J.C. Bach and then Johann Schroeter. A pianist, organist and composer. In 1793 he was appointed organist of the Church of St. Andrew, Plymouth, serving until at least 1833. Composed anthems, glees, songs, and music for piano and for organ.

BENNETT, Sir William Sterndale (1816-1875)
Born in Sheffield, Yorkshire on 13 April 1816, the son of **Robert Bennett**; died in London on 1 February 1875. Buried in Westminster Abbey.
By 1819 both his parents had died, and Sterndale Bennett went to Cambridge to live with his grandparents. In February 1824 he became a chorister at King's College, Cambridge.
Two years later and before his 10th birthday he entered the Royal Academy of Music studying composition initially under **William Crotch** then, from 1832, with Cipriani Potter. His other tutors included **W.H. Holmes** and **Charles Lucas.** Graduated Mus.D. (1856) and M.A. (1857) at the University of Cambridge. Received the Oxford D.C.L. in 1870.
Knighted in 1871.
Attending a performance by the 17-year old Sterndale Bennett of a Mendelssohn concerto, the composer invited him to Leipzig 'not as my pupil but as my friend', as a result of which Sterndale Bennett became part of the Mendelssohn/Schumann circle. Schumann referred to Sterndale Bennett musically in his composition *Proud England* and dedicated the work to him. While in Leipzig, Sterndale Bennett studied under Ignaz Moscheles.
Mendelssohn and Sterndale Bennett continued to correspond and meet from time to time following the latter's return to England. He visited Germany from 1841 to 1842. On his return to London he gave concerts of chamber music at various times from 1843 to 1856.
Organist at St. Anne's Chapel, Wandsworth (1834-1835).
Piano teacher at the R.A.M., where his pupils included **Arthur Sullivan** and **C.V. Stanford. Hubert Parry**, who appreciated Sterndale Bennett's kindness, was a private pupil at some time between 1870 and 1873, but found him too sensitive to offer the constructive criticism that was needed for his musical development.
In 1849 he founded the Bach Society, which held its inaugural meeting on 27 October of that year. Although conducting was not his speciality he was conductor of the Philharmonic Society of London (1856-1866). Occasionally he sang in the choir of St. Paul's Cathedral.
Appointed Professor of Music in the University of Cambridge (1856). Some of his predecessors and successors regarded the Cambridge professorship as a sinecure but Sterndale Bennett took the responsibility seriously. Became principal of the R.A.M. in 1866. As the years passed, his teaching and administrative workload increased and the time available for composing diminished correspondingly.

He did not find composition particularly easy and confided that 'my life has been spent rejecting ideas'. His anthems 'God is a Spirit' and 'Abide with me' from his oratorio *The Woman of Samaria* are still well-known. A Single Chant in G Minor by him was included in *Cathedral Psalter Chants* (1875). Also composed hymn tunes, including 'Boolcote' (1839) and 'Russell Place'.

BENSON, George (1814-1884)
Born in 1814; died in London on 9 August 1884. Graduated Mus.B. at the University of Cambridge in 1878. A gentleman of the Chapel Royal and a vicar choral of Westminster Abbey. His compositions include glees, of which 'If music be the food of love' is perhaps the best known, and anthems, examples of which are 'My God, look upon me' and 'I will arise'.

BENSON, Henry Ford (1859-1933)
Born in Islington, London in 1859; e died in Brixton, London, on 23 April 1933. Ford Benson was for 50 years organist of Upton Baptist Church, Lambeth, London. Composed an anthem, 'Thou wilt keep him in perfect peace' (?1914), a setting of the hymn 'The Coming of his Feet' (1920) and hymn tunes.

BENSON, John Allanson (1848-1931)
Born near Ripley, Yorkshire on 8 February 1848; died in Bromley, Kent on 17 April 1931. He was related to E.W. Benson, Archbishop of Canterbury.
Allanson Benson joined the parish church choir when as a child his family moved to Harrogate, Yorkshire.
It had been the wish of his father that the young John Benson become an architect. In the event, his career developed as an organist, teacher, lecturer and composer. An expert hymnologist, and an authority on **Handel**.
Music master of Ashville College, and organist of the Methodist Free Church, Bilton. His first wife, Eliza Place, was organist of Harrogate Parish Church for 25 years.
Retired to Bromley through ill-health in 1897. During World War I he deputised as organist of Hither Green Methodist Church, Kent.
Examples of his anthems are 'Consider the lilies' (1922) and 'Glory to God' (1922). Composed an oratorio *King Hezekiah* (1886). Other works include cantatas, hymn tunes and music for the organ. Conducted some of his own works at Crystal Palace and elsewhere.

BENTLEY, Dr. John Morgan (1837-?)
Born in Manchester on 3 September 1837. Graduated Mus.B. (1877) and Mus.D. (1879) at the University of Cambridge. Organist of a number of churches in the North West of England: St. Philip's, Salford (from 1855); St. Stephen's, Manchester (from 1860); St. Saviour's, Manchester (from 1866); Bowdon Parish Church, Cheshire, and Cheadle Abbey Church, Cheshire. Also conducted several choral societies. Composed an oratorio *What is Life?* (1879), vocal cantatas, Vesper Canticles, chants, a Symphony and other orchestral works, and songs.

BERENGER
See **LINEKAR,** Thomas Joseph.

BERKELEY, Sir Lennox Randal Francis (1903-1989)
Born in Boar's Hill, near Oxford of French descent on 12 May 1903; died in 1989. His son **Michael Berkeley** has also pursued a musical career.

At the age of six he moved with his family to the city of Oxford.

Educated at Gresham's School, Holt, Norfolk (which Benjamin Britten attended 10 years later) and Merton College, Oxford (1922-1926) where he read French and philology. Composed while studying at Oxford, with very little guidance. Studied organ at Oxford with **William Harris**. Graduated B.A. in 1926 and was awarded, honorarily, D.Mus. in 1970.

Had become bilingual through frequent visits to his mother's family and he continued his studies in Paris (1927-1932), where he was a pupil for counterpoint and ear training of Nadia Boulanger until 1932. Met, in 1927, and later received help from, Maurice Ravel. Other acquaintances were Darius Milhaud, Arthur Honegger, Albert Roussel, Igor Stravinsky and Francis Poulenc, the latter becoming a life-long friend.

In 1935 he returned to the U.K. and a year later, while in Barcelona for a composition festival he met **Benjamin Britten**. The two collaborated in the writing of *Mont Juic,* an orchestral suite based on Catalan dance melodies.

Appointed C.B.E. in 1957, followed by a knighthood in 1974.

On the music staff of the B.B.C. (1942-1945) where he compiled orchestral programmes. A professor of composition at the Royal Academy of Music (1945-1968).

His works include chamber music and a concerto for flute. His conversion to Catholicism in 1928 was marked by the subsequent composition of a Magnificat, Stabat Mater, and Missa Brevis. He is also known for his *Three Latin Motets* and his anthems such as 'Lord, when the sense of Thy sweet grace' and 'The Lord is my Shepherd'. Composed the hymn tunes 'Christ is the world's Redeemer' (1963) and 'Boar's Hill' (1967) for 'I sing of a Maiden'.

BERKELEY, Michael (b.1948)

Born in London on 29 May 1948. The eldest son of **Lennox Berkeley**. A chorister at Westminster Cathedral; studied at the Royal Academy of Music, and subsequently with **Richard Rodney Bennett**. Also influenced musically during his formative years by his father, Lennox. A presenter and announcer with the B.B.C., and associate composer to the Scottish Chamber Orchestra. Has written an organ concerto, concertos for oboe and for clarinet, songs and an oratorio *Or shall we die?* His *Hereford* Communion Service, composed for the Three Choirs' Festival of 1985, was rewritten in Latin with the addition of a Kyrie and entitled *Missa Lumen de Lumine.* There is a collection *Twelve Latin motets,* and he has composed the anthems 'Easter' and 'Love is strong as death', and two hymn tunes. His opera *Baa Baa Black Sheep* (1993) took as its subject the author Rudyard Kipling and was first performed at the Cheltenham Festival of that year.

BERRIDGE, Arthur (1855-1932)

Born in St. Pancras, London in 1855; died in St. Marylebone, London on 9 October 1932. Organist and choirmaster of Westbourne Gardens Baptist Church for 25 years. Gave an organ recital at St. Alban's (English) Church, Copenhagen while touring with a concert party. His part song 'Go, lovely rose' was sung at the 1894 Festival of the Nonconformist Choir Union. In 1896 he won a composition prize for the N.C.U. Festival with his part song 'Every sweet with sour is tempered'. In 1904 he was appointed secretary of the N.C.U., remaining in office for nearly 30 years. Composed hymn tunes and anthems including 'All things praise the Lord most high' (1911) and 'All the year is crowned with gladness' (1913).

BERTALOT, John (b.1931)

Born in Maidstone, Kent on 15 September 1931. Following his training at the Royal College of Music he won a major organ scholarship to Lincoln College, Oxford and he was then organ scholar at Corpus Christi College, Cambridge (1955-1958). Awarded M.A. in 1961. Organist at the Church of St. Matthew, Northampton (1958-1964) where he succeeded Robert Joyce, and also conductor of the Northampton Symphony and Bach Choir. Later became organist and master of the choristers of Blackburn Cathedral (1964-1983). Tutor at the Royal Manchester College of Music (from 1964), a lecturer in the extra-mural department of the University of Manchester (from 1966) and a special commissioner of the Royal School of Church Music (from 1963). He then emigrated to the U.S.A. where he was appointed director of music at Holy Trinity Church, Princeton, New Jersey. Compositions include the anthem 'When I survey the wondrous Cross', a Magnificat and Nunc Dimittis, and two sets of Preces and Responses.

BESLY, Edward Maurice (c1888-1945)

Maurice Besly died in 1945 at the age of 57. Organist of Queen's College, Oxford. From 1929 he was on the board of the Performing Rights Society. Composed anthems including 'In the hour of my distress' (1921) and 'O Lord, support us'; 'Crossing the bar', a song after Tennyson and piano music. 'The second minuet' is a popular duet in the Edwardian style.

BEST, William Thomas (1826-1897)

Born in Carlisle, Cumberland on 13 August 1826; died in Liverpool on 10 May 1897.

Studied under Kohn Norman and under a local teacher by the name of Young, although he was largely self-taught as an organist. W.T. Best by the age of 14 had decided against a career as a civil engineer and architect in favour of earning his living from music.

In the years prior to 1848 he served, as organist, several churches in the Liverpool area, including Pembroke Road Chapel (1840) and the Church for the Blind (1847). From 1852 to 1855 he lived in London and was briefly organist at the Royal Panoptican, Leicester Square (1852); Lincoln's Inn Chapel (1854) and St. Martin-in-the-Fields (1852).

In 1848 he was appointed organist to the Liverpool Philharmonic Society. Organist of St. George's Hall, Liverpool (1855-1894); Wallasey Parish Church (1860) and Holy Trinity, near Liverpool (1863).

Took part in the Handel Festivals in London (1871-1891) and had the honour of giving the first recital on the new organ at the Royal Albert Hall (1871); on a new instrument in the town hall of Sydney, Australia (August 1890) and on the restored organ of St. Anne's Cathedral, Belfast (January 1876). Possibly the greatest concert organist of his generation, although something of a temperamental genius who could be very scathing.

Arranged orchestral works for organ, and also composed for the instrument, with works including a set of chorale preludes. Published, in separate editions, collections of the organ works of Handel and Bach. Also composed orchestral and piano pieces.

His church music included services, of which a Morning and Evening Service in F - the latter consisting of the Cantate Domino and Deus Misereatur rather than the usual Magnificat and Nunc Dimittis - were written for Leeds Parish Church, hymns, anthems including 'The Lord is great in Zion', 'Behold, I bring you glad tidings' and 'O praise the Lord all ye heathen', and six sets of Responses to the Commandments.

BETTERIDGE, Leslie (b.1903)
Born in Lichfield, Staffordshire in 1903.
Educated privately and at Cheltenham Grammar School, Gloucestershire. Studied music with H.A. Hulbert, Ernest Dicker, and **A.H. Brewer**.
Organist of St. Mary's Church, Charlton Kings, Cheltenham (1918-1927), and organist and choirmaster of St. Barnabas's Church, Oxford (1924-1942). From 1942 until 1946 he worked at the War Office. Later he was organist and choirmaster of St. John's Church, Crystal Palace, London and of the Church of St. Michael and All Angels, Croydon, Surrey (1951-1964). Organist of Bermuda Cathedral (from 1964).
Contributed articles on organ and other musical matters to various publications.
Composed anthems, a Missa *Sancti Barnabae* and a Missa Brevis, organ works, a Fantasy for Strings and a Toccata for Violin and Piano.

BETTS, Edward (?-1767)
Died in Manchester on 18 April 1767. A singing man and master of the choristers of Manchester Cathedral (from 1706) and organist (from September 1714), succeeding Edward Edge. Retained both senior positions until 1767. A musician and writer, he compiled *An Introduction to the Skill of Music...* (1724). Is said to have composed the 'Cheetham Grace'.

BEVIN, Elway (c1554-1638)
Born possibly at Wells, Somerset around the year 1554; died in Bristol and was buried there on 19 October 1638. Possibly of Welsh descent.
Is said to have been a pupil of **Thomas Tallis**.
A vicar choral of Wells Cathedral (1575-1584). From 1585 he was master of the choristers at Bristol Cathedral and from 1589 he was also organist. Reputedly taught **William Child**, although Child was actually articled to Thomas Prince. At a visitation in 1634, Archbishop William Laud found the music of Bristol Cathedral in some disarray due to the infirmity of Bevin. He was finally dismissed in 1638.
A gentleman extraordinary of the Chapel Royal (1605-1637). Said to have been expelled from the Chapel Royal because of Catholic sympathies but there is no evidence to support this.
Wrote a book on the theory of music, *Brief and Short Introduction to the Art of Musicke and Canons* (1631), which contained by way of illustration a number of canons.
Wrote six anthems including 'Turn us, O God' and 'Praise the Lord', plus at least three services. His Service in the Dorian Mode was published in **William Boyce**'s *Cathedral Music* and it has been performed regularly ever since. Another is his Short Service in D Minor.

BEXFIELD, Dr. William Richard (1824-1853)
Born in Norwich on 27 April 1824; died in London on 29 October 1853.
A chorister at Norwich Cathedral under **Zechariah Buck**, who was so impressed with the boy's compositions that he took him as an articled pupil at the age of 14. The University of Oxford awarded him B.Mus (1846); the University of Cambridge conferred on him Mus.D. (1849).

A lecturer by profession, Bexfield became organist of Boston Parish Church in 1845, remaining there until February 1848 when he took up an appointment at St. Helen's, Bishopsgate, London (1848-1853). He played at the Great Exhibition at Crystal Palace (1851), being praised highly for his dexterity.
A gifted composer, he had composed an eight-part anthem at the age of 11. His church music included seven anthems published as a set plus two others. His anthems include 'Hear My Prayer' and 'Remember, O Lord'.
A Single Chant in A-flat was included in *Cathedral Psalter Chants* (1875). Also composed hymn tunes; two oratorios, one of which was *Israel Restored,* and some organ fugues. His untimely death removed the possibility that he would become, as had once seemed likely, a force in church music to compare with **Henry Purcell**.

BEYNON, Rosser (Asaph Glan Tâf: 1811-1876)
Born in Glyn Eithinog, Vale of Neath, Glamorgan, Wales in 1811; died on 3 January 1876 and was buried at Merthyr Tydfil.
In 1815 the family moved to Merthyr Tydfil. Rosser Beynon had little or no schooling, beginning full-time work at the local iron foundry at the age of eight, rising to become, eventually, a manager. Studied privately and at evening classes, by which means he became a proficient musician.
The Soar Congregational Chapel appointed him precentor in 1835. At about that time he founded a class for the teaching of the rudiments of music. An adjudicator at *eisteddfodau.*
In 1836 he contributed the first of many articles to the periodical *Y Diwyggiwr.* He was later that journal's editor of hymn tunes.
His book *Telyn Seion* (Zion's Harp), published between 1845 and 1848, is a collection by various composers of 130 hymn tunes, together with a quantity of anthems, choruses and short pieces suitable for Sunday Schools. He composed 20 of the items it contained.

BIELBY, Jonathan Leonard (b.1944)
Born in Oxford on 23 November 1944.
Attended Magdalen College School, Oxford. Studied with **Bernard Rose** before going up as organ student to St. John's College, Cambridge, under George Guest. Also studied with Peter le Huray. Graduated B.A. (1966), Mus.B. (1967) and M.A. (1970).
Assistant organist of Manchester Cathedral (1968-1970) before being appointed organist of Wakefield Cathedral (from 1970). The first borough organist of Kirklees Yorkshire (1974-1988), in the course of which he gave recitals at Huddersfield Town Hall and elsewhere. Senior lecturer at the City of Leeds College of Music (from 1979).
The collection *Twenty-five years at Wakefield* in three volumes (1995-1996) contains a selection of his works, including the *Wakefield* Service and the anthems 'Love's endeavour, love's expense' and 'Let the roaring organs loudly play'. Another collection is *Sequence for Christmas* (1980).

BIGGS, Walter Lyle (1857-?)
Born in Notting Hill, London on 16 September 1857. Early in life he was taught music by his uncle, Revd. Samuel Lillycrop. Later studied organ and harmony under George F. Geaussent. Organist in London of All Saints' Church, Child's Hill, Kilburn (1877-1881). Moved to the church of St. Peter le Bailey, Oxford in 1882. Known as an organ recitalist. Composed church music, including a Te Deum in E-flat (1903), the festival anthem, 'Behold the name of the Lord' (1904) and cantatas.

BILBY, Thomas (1794-1872)
Born in Southampton on 18 April 1794; died in Islington, London on 24 September 1872. Served in the army. On returning to civilian life he became a teacher, and he was parish clerk of St. Mary's, Islington, London for 28 years. Wrote hymns, and his tune 'Joyful' has been used with his own 'Here we suffer grief and pain'.

BILL, Charles Milton (19th/20th century)
A chorister of Llandaff Cathedral. Awarded B.Mus. at the University of Durham in 1898.
Acted as organist to Llandaff Cathedral in 1901 and he was appointed organist and choirmaster of Holy Trinity Church, Gosport, Hampshire (1902-1914). Organist and choirmaster of Holy Trinity Church, Tulse Hill (from 1914) and of St. Simon's Church, Southsea, Hampshire (from 1921). A local philharmonic society organist.
Composed a Benedicite in E-flat, a chant setting of the Magnificat and Nunc Dimittis (1887), an 'Easter Anthem' and hymn tunes.

BILLINGTON, Thomas (c1754-1832)
Born in Exeter around the year 1754; died in Tunis in 1832. A full-time arranger, composer and compiler. As well as services (including a Morning and Evening Service for three voices, written in 1785) he wrote music to elegies by Grey and Pope, and music for harpsichord. Also composed instrumental duos, trios, quartets and sonatas.

BILTCLIFFE, Florence (20th century)
Born in Yorkshire. Studied piano under Blanche Smith at Bristol, and at summer schools at Queen's University, Kingston, Ontario, Canada (1944 and 1945) and Chautangua, New York State (1946, 1947 and 1949). Has taught music in private schools in Canada and the U.K. Composed the anthem 'God is our Hope', carols, a piano sonata, and chamber works.

BIRCH, Edward Henry (19th century)
A pupil at the Cathedral Schools of Gloucester and Worcester. Graduated B.Mus. at the University of Oxford (1875).
Organist of St. Saviour's Church, Eastbourne, Sussex (from 1872). Moving to London, he took up successive organist appointments at St. Gabriel's, Warwick Square (1873); All Saints, Kensington Park (1874) and St. James, Notting Hill (1886). Also choirmaster of St. Columba's Church, Notting Hill.
Composed an Evening Service in F and other church music, a cantata, and works for organ.

BIRCH, William Henry (1826-1888)
Born in Uxbridge, Middlesex on 5 May 1826; died in Caversham, Berkshire on 18 July 1888.
Studied under **George Elvey**, Richard Blagrove and Robert Barnett. As a chorister of St. Paul's Cathedral he was a pupil of **William Hawes** and **Thomas Attwood**.
Organist of St. Mary's Church, Amersham, Buckinghamshire; taught music at Caversham.
Composed a cantata *The Wreck of the Argosy* (1879). His church music includes Canticle settings. A set of 12 anthems was published in 1879. His anthems include 'Enter not into judgement' and 'Ponder my words'.

BIRD, ? (17th century)
A 17th century church musician and composer about whom very little is known. A service by him was listed during an inventory at Chichester Cathedral in 1621.

BIRD, Henry Richard (1842-1915)
Born in Walthamstow, Essex on 14 November 1842; died in Kensington, London on 21 November 1915.
Studied under **James Turle**, organist of Westminster Abbey. At the age of eight he acted as organist of St. John's Church, Walthamstow (1851-1858): formally appointed organist in 1854. Became organist in London of St. Mark's, Clerkenwell (1858); Holy Trinity, Sloane Street (1860); St. Gabriel's, Pimlico (1866) and St. Mary Abbotts, Kensington (1872). He was unsuccessful however in his application for the vacant organistship in 1860 of St. Luke's Church, Chelsea, which was awarded instead to **George Carter**.
Famous as an accompanist, from 1891 he was permanent accompanist to the Monday and Saturday Popular Classical Concerts at St. James's Hall. He was also a professor of piano at the Royal College of Music and at Trinity College, London.
Composed hymn tunes and a Magnificat and Nunc Dimittis in E-flat (1916).

BIRKBECK, John Barrass (1831-1917)
Born in Shiney Row, County Durham in 1831; died in County Durham in 1917. Composed anthems including 'It is a good thing to give thanks' (1898) and 'Arise, shine O Zion' (1911), hymn tunes and songs.

BIRNEY, Anthony (b.1932)
Born in Felling-on -Tyne on 17 March 1932. Holds the degrees of B.A. in French with Spanish (University of Durham, 1955) and B.Sc. in economics (University of London, 1965). Apart from piano lessons, he is musically self-taught. A former lecturer and acting head of a university modern languages department, Anthony Birney is now retired. Composed a number of hymns, including 'Stand up for Christ'. His oratorio *St. Paul* was performed as part of the 800th anniversary celebrations of the town of Washington, County Durham. Has composed the opera *Jane Eyre* and a musical entitled *Mr. Churchill*.

BISHOP, Graham (b.1953)
Born in Stowmarket, Suffolk on 3 February 1953. Educated at Colchester Institute School of Music and Brentwood College of Education. A peripatetic school teacher in Suffolk. His tune 'Wilverton' is used with 'Shout it in the street'. The name, which is derived from those of his parents William and Veronica, was the name of his house.

BISHOP, Sir Henry Rowley (1782-1855)
Born in London on 18 November 1782; died in London on 30 April 1855.
Studied music with Francesco Bianchi. Graduated B.Mus. (1839) and D.Mus. (1853) at the University of Oxford.
Knighted in 1842.
A founder, in 1813, of the Philharmonic Society.
Professor of music at the University of Edinburgh (1841-1843) and at the University of Oxford (1848-1855) where he succeeded **William Crotch**.

Director of music in London of the Drury Lane Theatre (1810-1811), of the Vauxhall Gardens (from 1830) and of the Covent Garden Theatre (1810-1824). Conductor of the Drury Lane Theatre (from 1825) and of the Concerts of Ancient Music (1840-1848).

Composed the anthem 'I have kept Thy ways' for the funeral of Queen Charlotte (1818). His other works are operas and musical dramas totalling more than one hundred and including *Vintagers* (1809), glees and songs of which 'Home, sweet Home' is probably the most famous.

BISHOP, John (1665-1737)
Born in 1665; died in Winchester, Hampshire on 19 December 1737. He was buried in the cloisters of Winchester Cathedral.
A pupil of **Daniel Roseingrave**.
A musician by the name of Bishop was a lay clerk and temporary organist of King's College, Cambridge from 1687. In the following year that same person was appointed to teach the choristers of King's.
John Bishop was organist at Winchester College from 1695 until at least 1730, succeeding **Jeremiah Clarke**.
A lay clerk at Winchester Cathedral (from 1697), before succeeding **Vaughan Richardson** as organist of Winchester Cathedral (1729-1737). This appointment was controversial in that Kent, a competitor, was acknowledged to be the better organist but Bishop was preferred out of sympathy by the Dean and Chapter for his advanced years, amiable disposition and family circumstances.
Published *A Sett of New Psalm Tunes* in 1700 or 1710, plus a *Supplement* in 1725. Five of his hymn tunes have remained popular, including 'Illsley', which is found in *Hymns Ancient and Modern* (New Standard Edition) and 'Bishop', used in the Standard Edition (1916) of that publication with the hymn 'O Saviour, who for man has trod'. Another popular tune has been 'Bedford', also known as 'Leicester', which was used in his *Sett of New Psalm Tunes* in conjunction with Psalm 112.
Composed the anthems 'Blessed are they' and 'Call to remembrance'. Other church music survives in manuscript.

BISHOP, John (1818-1890)
Born in Cheltenham, Gloucestershire on 31 July 1818; died in Cheltenham on 3 February 1890.
Organist of St. Paul's Church, Cheltenham (from 1834). A short period as an organist in Blackburn, Lancashire was followed by a return to Gloucestershire and organistships in Cheltenham at St. James's Church, St. John's Church and the Roman Catholic Chapel.
Wrote a *Brief Biography of Handel*. A music editor, also translating foreign-language books on musical theory.
Composed anthems, a hymn of thanksgiving 'Thou, O God, has heard our prayer' (1872), organ music and songs.

BLACK, George (19th century)
Organist, probationarily, of Chester Cathedral (1823-1824). He was not confirmed in the post and his subsequent career is unknown.
Composed a Service in B-flat which was sung at Chester Cathedral.

BLACKALL, Dr. Allen Keet (1877-1963)
Born in Ryde, Isle of Wight, on 13 November 1877; died in Canterbury, Kent on 3 April 1963.
Studied at the Royal Academy of Music (1894-1897).
Assistant organist of St. Anne's, Soho, London (1897-1898).
Organist of St. Mary's Collegiate Church, Warwick (1898-1945),

and a lecturer in music at the University of Birmingham (1919-1945). Conductor of the Birmingham Bach Choir (1930-1933), chorus master and assistant conductor of the Birmingham Festival Choral Society (1905-1923) and sub warden of the College of St. Nicolas (now the Royal School of Church Music) from 1945. A lecturer in music at the University of Birmingham (1919-1945), and principal of the Birmingham and Midland Institute School of Music (1934-1945).
Composer of a hymn tune 'Swanmore' (1946).

BLACKHALL, Andrew (Andro) (1535/6-1609)
Born in 1535 or 1536; died on 31 January 1609.
A canon of Holyrood Abbey, Scotland until the Reformation, at which point he served as minister to a number of local churches. In 1574 he became Minister of Inveresk Parish Church, Musselburgh.
One of the anthems he wrote was 'Judge and revenge my cause'. Also known to have composed a set of arrangements to Psalm tunes.

BLACKWELL, Isaac (17th century)
A vicar choral of St. Paul's Cathedral from 1687, being appointed organist of St. Paul's later that year. Composed the anthems 'Behold how good and joyful', 'Let my complaint' and 'O Lord our Governour'. All three were included in the second set of works compiled by **Richard Dering**, *Cantica Sacra*. Also composed songs.

BLACKWELL, Thomas Kenneth (b.1915)
Born in Wells, Somerset on 29 November 1915.
Educated at Wells Cathedral School. Trained as a municipal engineer and surveyor, holding organistships within the Methodist Church. Has since retired and lives in Abingdon, Oxfordshire.
Composed items for piano, songs and other choral works, and hymn tunes. His 'Pro nobis' is the tune used with 'O love how deep, how broad, how high'.

BLACOW, Frederick William (1855-1936)
Born in Manchester in 1855; died in Torquay, Devon on 20 March 1936.
Trainined in music at Manchester.
Organist of Pendleton Parish Church and violin master to the Manchester School Board before taking up organistships in Bournemouth, Dorset of Immanuel Church, Southbourne (from 1917) and All Saints' Church, Branksome Park (from 1919).
Composed chant settings of the Holy Communion Service (1894) and of the Te Deum (1888), the anthem 'Teach me Thy way, O Lord' (1889) and hymn tunes.

BLAIR, Dr. Hugh (1864-1932)
Born in Worcester on 25 May 1864, the son of Revd. R.H. Blair, rector of St. Martin's Church, Worcester; died in Worthing, Sussex on 22 July 1932.
Educated in Yorkshire, at Worcester Cathedral under **William Done** and at King's School, Worcester. In 1883 he went up as organ scholar and organist to Christ's College, Cambridge. Studied under **George Garrett** and **George Macfarren**, graduating B.A. (1886), M.A. (1896), Mus.B. (1887) and Mus.D. (1906).
Deputy organist of Worcester Cathedral (from 1886) under William Done, who by this time was in his 70s. Blair soon had full charge. Before the age of thirty he played a major part in the Three Choirs' Festivals, conducting in 1893.

Acting organist (1889) and organist (1895-1897) of Worcester Cathedral, being succeeded in the latter year by **Ivor Atkins**.

Encouraged the musical development of **Edward Elgar**, with whom he played golf. Elgar's Organ Sonata in G was first performed by Blair, at a recital in July 1895.

Organist and choirmaster of Holy Trinity Church, Marylebone, London (from 1898). Director of music of the Borough of Battersea, London (1900-1904). Worked at some time for the publishing firm of Novello.

Composed a Service in B Minor (1887), a work upon which Ivor Atkins carried out minor revisions in 1933 and which is widely sung today. Also wrote the anthems 'Joy of the Lord', 'Come with high and Holy gladness', and 'Hail, gladdening Light' and, for harvest-tide, 'Joy of the Lord'. Also an *Advent Cantata*, first performed at the Three Choirs' Festival of 1896. Composed part songs, orchestral music, and works for organ and for violin.

BLAKE, Revd. Dr. Edward (1708-1765)

Born in Salisbury, Wiltshire in 1708; died on 11 June 1765.

Studied at Balliol College, Oxford where he graduated B.A. (1733), M.A. (1737), B.D. (1744) and D.D. (1755).

Incumbent of the Church of St. Thomas, Salisbury (from 1740) and vicar of St. Mary's Church, Oxford (from 1754). In 1757 he was appointed prebendary of Salisbury Cathedral and rector of Tortworth, Gloucestershire.

Composed duets for violin and viola, and anthems including 'Thou, O God art praised' and 'I have set God alway before me'.

BLAKE, Howard (b.1938)

Born in London on 28 October 1938.

Studied piano under Harold Craxton, and composition with Howard Ferguson, at the Royal Academy of Music.

Worked as a pianist, conductor, composer and orchestrator in London (1960-1970). Since 1971 he has concentrated on freelance composition but since 1992 he has additionally been visiting professor of composition at the R.A.M.

Among other works he has written a Benedictus for Choir and Orchestra, a Festival Mass for Unaccompanied Double Choir (1987), 'The song of the Nativity' (1976) and 'The song of St. Francis' (1976), as well as film scores, but he is famous for the song 'The Snowman' from the children's musical of the same name.

BLAKE, Leonard James (1907-1989)

Born in Hendon, London on 7 October 1907; died on 2 August 1989.

The early part of his education was in Hendon, where he attended the County School. Studied at the Royal College of Music. Graduated B.Mus. at the University of London.

Organist and choirmaster at the Church of All Saints, Child's Hill (1926-1929) and Holy Trinity, Marylebone (1929). Taught music at Twyford School, Winchester (1929-1935). Director of music at Worksop College, Nottinghamshire (1935-1945) and at Malvern School (1945-1968). From 1949 he was conductor of the Malvern Music Society.

Editor of *English Church Music* (1948-1958) and a special commissioner for the Royal School of Church Music.

His hymn tune 'Twyford' was first used as an anthem and was then reset for the 1950 edition of *Hymns Ancient and Modern*. His tune 'Remission' was set to the hymn 'Not for our sins alone'. Among his anthems are 'Sing to the Lord of harvest' and 'Lord of the

worlds above'. Has also composed a Communion Service and an Evening Service in D.

BLAKELEY, William (1852-?)

Born in Wakefield, Yorkshire on 12 February 1852.

Studied under **William Spark** and **Frederick Bridge**. Graduated B.Mus. at the University of Toronto, Canada.

In 1868 he became organist of Thornes Church, Wakefield, Yorkshire. Held similar appointments in Croydon, Surrey and in Scotland at the Morningside United Presbyterian Church, Edinburgh (1881-1890) and Queen's Park Parish Church, Glasgow (from 1890).

Composed an oratorio *Jonah,* anthems including 'I will magnify Thee, O God' (1912), songs and organ music.

BLANCHARD, George Frederic (1868-1926)

Born in Norfolk in 1868; died in Weston-super-Mare, Somerset on 9 May 1926. Composed a recessional hymn 'God of our fathers' (1916) and hymn tunes.

BLANCHET, Alfred Tom (1868-1926)

Born in Buckinghamshire in 1868; died in Hampstead, London on 19 April 1926. Studied in the Royal College of Music, and with **Walter Parratt** for organ. An accomplished organist, adept at improvisation. Organist of the Church of St. John, Richmond, Surrey for more than 20 years, and then of St. Mary's Church, Slough, Buckinghamshire. Composed a setting of the Holy Communion Service in A-flat (1904) and hymn tunes.

BLANKS (Blancks), Edward (c1550-?)

Born around the year 1550; the year of his death is unknown. A London wait between the years 1582 and 1594. One of his tunes appears more than 30 times in Thomas East's *The Whole Booke of Psalmes* (1592) and he also figured in **Thomas Ravenscroft**'s collection with the same title (1621). Contributed similarly to William Barley's Psalter (1599). Composed what are now known as the hymn tunes 'Canterbury' and 'Low Dutch', motets including the 12-part *Credo quod Redemptor,* and instrumental works.

BLISS, Sir Arthur Drummond (1891-1975)

Born in London on 2 August 1891; died in London on 27 March 1975.

Attended Rugby School. Studied counterpoint at Pembroke College, Cambridge under **Charles Wood,** culminating in the degrees of B.A. and Mus.B. (1912). Continued his studies at the Royal Academy of Music (1913-1914) under **C.V. Stanford, Ralph Vaughan Williams** and **Gustav Holst.**

Knighted in 1950 and appointed K.C.V.O. in 1969.

Throughout World War I he served in the Royal Fusiliers and the Grenadier Guards, suffering badly when coming under attack by gas in 1918. On returning to civilian life he took up a career as a composer and conductor. Director of music at the B.B.C. (1942-1944). In 1953 he was appointed Master of the Queen's Music in succession to **Arnold Bax**. Lived for a while in California, where he was professor of music at the University of California.

Following World War I he established a reputation as an avant garde composer. *Colour Symphony* was very well received at the Gloucester Festival of 1920. Also composed film scores, an opera, a piano concerto (1959), ballet music, the cantata *Mary of Magdala* and the anthems 'Seek ye the Lord' (1956) and 'Stand up and bless the Lord' (1960). His *Beatitudes* was sung at the

Consecration Festival of Coventry Cathedral (1962). *Morning Heroes*, a memorial piece containing a part for reciter, was written after World War I.

BLISS, Revd. William Henry (?-1919)
Graduated B.Mus. at Exeter College, Oxford (1863); also B.A. (1862) and M.A. (1871). Ordained deacon in 1862, priest in 1863.
Precentor of Exeter College, Oxford (1862-1863) and of King's School, Sherborne, Dorset (1863-1867) where he also taught music.
A minor canon of St. George's Chapel, Windsor Castle (1867-1874); rector of West Ilsley, Berkshire (1873-1881); curate of Wexham, Buckinghamshire (1882-1885) and vicar of Kew, Surrey (from 1885).
From 1874 to 1876 he was an honorary chaplain to Queen Victoria, to whom in 1876 he was appointed chaplain in ordinary. From 1901 he was an honorary chaplain to Edward VII.
Composed several chant settings of the Te Deum (1884), anthems including 'Praise the Lord, O Jerusalem' (1876), chants and hymn tunes; published the *Kew Supplement to any Hymnal*.

BLITHEMAN (Blithman), Dr. John (c1525-1591)
John Blitheman, whose Christian name is sometimes wrongly given as William, was born around the year 1525; died in London on 23 May 1591.
Graduated Mus.B. (1586) and Mus.D. at the University of Cambridge.
Had became a gentleman of the Chapel Royal during the reign of Mary and was named as one of those on duty at her funeral in 1558. In 1564 he was appointed master of the choristers at Christ Church, Oxford. Appointed organist of the Chapel Royal in 1585, following the death of **Thomas Tallis**, and remained in office until the year of his decease.
A very able keyboard player. Among his pupils was **John Bull**, later to become his friend and to succeed him as organist of the Chapel Royal. It is also likely that he knew **Orlando Gibbons**.
Composed music for the virginal and for the church. Among his sacred music was the anthem 'Gloria laus et honor', composed for use on Palm Sunday, and 'In Pace', a Responsory for Compline that is often sung as an anthem. His friend and colleague John Bull succeeded him at the Chapel Royal.

BLOCKLEY, John (1801-1882)
Born in St. Pancras, London in 1801; died in Hampstead, London on 24 December 1882. A music publisher in London, and a composer of songs and hymn tunes.

BLOCKLEY, T. (19th century)
The hymn tune composer T. Blockley may in fact be Thomas Blockley, who was born in London around the year 1830 and died in Oxford on 26 April 1904, and who was the son of **John Blockley**, composer and song publisher. His song 'Leaning on Thee' (c1863) gave rise to the hymn tune 'Blockley', which is used today with the hymn 'Happy the man that finds the grace'.

BLOOMFIELD, Isaac William (18th century)
Connected with the town of Hornington, near Bury St. Edmunds, Suffolk. Composed the anthems 'Behold, the Lord is my Salvation' and 'I am well pleased'.

BLOW, Dr. John (1649-1708)
Born in Newark, Nottinghamshire, being baptised there on 23 February 1649; died in Westminster, London on 1 October 1708. Some sources prefer that he was also born in Westminster.
One of the first boy choristers in the newly-restored Chapel Royal under **Henry Cooke**. He was awarded the first ever Lambeth D.Mus. in 1677. Studied organ under **Christopher Gibbons**.
His career centred around the Chapel Royal, Westminster Abbey and St. Paul's Cathedral. A gentleman of the Chapel Royal from March 1674, one of its three organists from 1676, and master of the children from July 1674 in succession to **Pelham Humfrey**.
At the age of 18, Blow was appointed master of the children of Westminster Abbey (December 1668-1680 and 1695-1708). From 1680 to 1695 he stood down in favour of **Henry Purcell**.
He paid similar tribute to **Jeremiah Clarke** at St. Paul's Cathedral, making way for him in 1703. He had succeeded **Michael Wise** as almoner and master of the choristers at St. Paul's Cathedral in September 1687. For a time he was also organist of St. Margaret's Church, Westminster.
From 1700 he was composer to the Chapel Royal. Composer in ordinary (1687-1693) to James II and William III, and joint tuner of the king's instruments with 'Father' Smith (from 1695).
He was known for his goodness, amiability, moral character and sound musicianship. The fact that he taught Purcell, once in doubt, is confirmed in the inscription on his monument in Westminster Abbey 'Master to the famous Henry Purcell'.
Composed songs and music for the harpsichord, services and anthems, some of the latter at an early age. In fact three anthems were published in a collection of 1664 when he was barely 15 years old. Also composed extensively for organ.
The most prolific writer of services of his period; at least 13 were composed. Many of his compositions were unpublished. Among his anthems, of which he composed more than a hundred are 'I beheld and Lo, a great multitude', 'Be merciful unto me', and 'My days are gone like a shadow'. His *Salvator Mundi*, the Latin setting of the Passiontide Respond 'O Saviour of the world, who by Thy Cross and precious Blood hast redeemed us' remains in common use.

BLOW, Revd. William (1819-1886)
Born in York in 1819, a descendant of **John Blow**; died in Layer Breton, Essex on 25 December 1886. Rector of Layer Breton, Essex and an amateur violinist with a valuable collection of violins. Composed hymn tunes.

BLUNT, Frederick William (1839-1921)
Born in Mayfair, London on 1 July 1839; died in Kensington, London on 25 November 1921. Practised as a solicitor in London.
An amateur musician and composer, his hymn tunes include 'Art thou weary' (1866) and 'Lyndhurst' (1871), the latter being used in the Revised Edition (1927) of *Church Hymnary* with 'Now the day is over' by **Sabine Baring-Gould**.

BLYTH, Dr. Benjamin (19th century)
Benjamin Blyth the elder was awarded D.Mus. at Magdalen College Oxford in 1833. His son was also named Benjamin and followed a musical career.
Organist of Richmond Parish Church, Surrey and connected with the firm of Blyth and Sons, organ builders. Composed church music including the anthem 'I will arise'.

BLYTON, Carey (b.1932)

Born in Beckenham, Kent, on 14 March 1932. Nephew of the writer Enid Blyton.

Attended Beckenham and Penge Grammar School. Initially he studied zoology at University College, London (from 1950) before opting for a musical training at Trinity College of Music (1953-1957). Won the Bantock Prize for composition in 1954 and graduated B.Mus. (1957). Then studied with Jørgen Jersild at the Copenhagen Conservatory (1957-1958).

Worked as editor for music publishers Mills Music Ltd. (1958-1972). In 1964 he was appointed music editor to the publishers Faber and Faber (now Faber Music Ltd.), where he remained until 1974. Was personally responsible between 1963 and 1971 for editing the works of **Benjamin Britten** from *Curlew River* to *Owen Wingrave*, and he worked on a number of items by **Gustav Holst**.

A professor of harmony, counterpoint and orchestration at Trinity College (1963-1973) and visiting professor of composition for films, television and radio at Guildhall School of Music (1972-1983). He was compelled through ill health to retire prematurely from the latter post, but continued to teach through the Open University.

Among his compositions are *Seven Polyphonic Amens* (1964) and a number of carols, including *A Lullaby* for Christmas and its companion piece for Easter *A Litany*, both dating from 1956. His other works include chamber items and music for schools. Has also composed some 30 television commercials, and scores for a number of television plays. Has collaborated with the Royal Society for the Protection of Birds in composing for the Society's *Kites are Flying*, and other films.

BOARDMAN, John George (1819-1898)

Organist of Clapham Grammar School, London (1845-1876) and of St. Mark's Church, Kensington, London (1866-1894).

Published *Sacred Music, a Collection of Psalm Tunes* (1844). Composed anthems including 'Behold, how good and joyful', written expressly for the opening of Clapham Grammar School and 'Lord, let me know mine end'.

BOGGETT, Richard (1797-1879)

Born in Kippax, Yorkshire in 1797; died in Kippax on 17 September 1879. A corn miller and farmer, and a self-taught musician. Played and composed hymn tunes. These include 'Dawson's adieu' and 'Eccles'. The latter was named after Revd. A. Eccles Farrar, the choirmaster of the Wesleyan Chapel, Kippax. Boggett was most gratified to hear the tune played at the festival at the Brunswick Chapel, Leeds by **S.S. Wesley**.

BONAVIA-HUNT, Revd. Noel Aubrey (1882-?)

Born in Primrose Hill, London, in 1882. Educated privately. Choirmaster of St. Matthew's Church, Willesden, London (1905-1912); precentor and master of the choristers of All Saints' Church, St. John's Wood, London (1922-1930) and vicar of Stagsden, Bedford (from 1937). Author of *The Church Organ* and *Modern Organ Stops*. Composed a Te Deum, the anthem, 'Lead, kindly Light', and organ works.

BOND, Ann (b.1931)

Born in Grays, Essex on 29 September 1931. Educated at The Queen's School, Chester and Girton College, Cambridge where she graduated B.A. in music (1952) and Mus.B. (1953).

Lecturer in music and university organist at the University of Manchester (1953-1963).

Freelance writer thereafter, contributing to *New Grove Dictionary of Music and Musicians* and reviewing regularly for *Musical Times*. A book on the harpsichord is to be published in 1997.

Some of her organ recitals have been broadcast. Latterly harpsichordist with her own ensemble. Teacher at the Royal School of Church Music and at the Guildhall School of Music and Drama. Director of Music, Lingfield Collegiate Church, Surrey (1974-1986).

Ann Bond has composed the Whitsun anthem 'Come, Holy Ghost' and a widely-used set of Responses for Lingfield Collegiate Church. For the Centenary Service of Celebration at Girton College she composed as an anthem a setting of the College motto 'Hucusque auxiliatus'.

BOND, Capel L. (1730-1790)

Born in Gloucester and baptised on 14 December 1730; died in Coventry, Warwickshire on 14 February 1790.

It is likely that Capel Bond attended the Crypt School under his uncle, Daniel Bond. Apprenticed to **Martin Smith**, organist of Gloucester Cathedral, from the age of 12.

Pursued a career as a conductor and organist, moving to Coventry in 1749 in order to take up the organistship of St. Michael's Church (which was elevated to cathedral status in 1918). He took on a similar position at Holy Trinity Church in the city, holding both positions concurrently until his death in 1790. Served as the first organist to the Birmingham Festival (1768). In general he did much for the musical life of the Midlands.

Composed anthems, of which his *Six Anthems in Score* (1769) ran into at least six editions. They included the works 'Blessed be the Lord God' and 'Praise the Lord ye servants'. In 1766 he published his *Six Concertos in Seven Parts*. Also composed glees and songs.

BOND, Frank Heddon (1875-1948)

Born in Manchester in 1875; died in Buckinghamshire in 1948. Graduated M.A. at the University of Cambridge. Music master of Truro College (1898-1900). Organist of the Wesleyan Churches of Exmouth, Devon (1900-1902) and Leamington, Warwickshire (1902-1906), and Wellingborough Congregational Church, Northamptonshire (from 1906) where he was also organist of the Corn Exchange Cinema. Composed an anthem 'The earth is the Lord's' (1913) and hymn tunes.

BOND, Hugh (c1710-1792)

Born in Exeter, Devon around the year 1710; died in 1792. A lay vicar of Exeter Cathedral from 1762, organist of the Exeter Church of St. Mary Arches and a local professor of music. A number of his pupils became famous. Published a collection *Twelve Hymns and Four Anthems*. The work was entirely his. His anthems include 'I will alway give thanks' and 'My lot is fallen'. Also composed glees and songs. One of a number of composers from the 18th and 19th centuries who adapted Mass movements and oratorio choruses for use as anthems by shortening and simplifying them.

BONNER, Carey (1859-1938)

Born in Southwark, London on 1 May 1859; died in Muswell Hill, London, on 16 June 1938. Son of a Baptist minister.

Attended Plaistow School and studied in the Rawdon Baptist College, Leeds, where he was ordained in 1884. Served as a minister of the Baptist Church at Sale, Cheshire (1884-1895) and in Hampshire at the Portland Chapel, Southampton (1895-1900).

Carey Bonner then became associated with the administration of the Sunday School movement at national level (1900-1932): he was secretary (from 1900) and president (1922-1923) of the National Sunday School Union, and president of the Baptist Union (1931-1932).

Edited *Sunday School Hymnary* and published *Some Baptist Hymnists* (1937). With W.T. Whitley he edited *A Handbook to the Baptist Church Hymnal Revised* (1935).

Composed hymn tunes, sacred songs, anthems and cantatas. His arrangement of the hymn tune 'Praise Him' is used today with the hymn 'Praise Him, praise Him, all His children praise Him'. He favoured the use pseudonyms, including 'E. Rawdon Bailey', 'A. Bryce' and 'Nora C.E. Byrne'.

BOODLE, Christopher (b.1952)
Born in Gloucester in 1952. Educated at New College, Oxford and at the Royal College of Music. Lived in Belfast for six years, where he was assistant organist of St. Anne's Cathedral. Returned to England in 1983. A teacher and composer. Has performed at the Three Choirs' Festival and at the Ross-on-Wye Festival. Has composed church music, the cantata *Death of a Martyr* and a symphony.

BOOTH, Josiah (1852-1929)
Born in Coventry, Warwickshire on 27 March 1852; died in Hornsey, London on 29 December 1929.

Studied under Edward Simms of Coventry and James Taylor of Oxford. Attended the Royal Academy of Music where his studies were directed by Brinley Richards and **George Macfarren**.

Organist of the Banbury Wesleyan Chapel, Oxfordshire (1868-1876); organist and choirmaster of the Park Chapel Congregational Church, Crouch End (1877-1918), where **Eric Thiman** later held those positions.

Edited Parts II and III of *Congregational Church Hymnal* (1888) and he was music adviser to the Revision Committee for the 1927 edition of *Church Hymnary*.

Composed more than a hundred hymn tunes. His 'Beechwood', 'Excelsior', 'Limpsfield' and 'Remembrance' are found in the Revised Edition (1927) of *Church Hymnary*. He also composed songs, chants including a Chant in E, services, anthems including 'Grant, we beseech Thee' and 'Thou crownest the year' and an oratorio *Nehemiah*.

BOOTH, Robert (1862-?)
Born in St. Andrews, Scotland on 29 December 1862.

Studied in the Madras School, St. Andrews and at the University. Organist, in Scotland, of Holy Trinity Church, Kilmarnock (1884-1887) and Coltness Memorial Church, Newmains (from 1887). Recital organist to the art galleries of Glasgow Corporation (1909-1915) and principal music master of Wishaw High School.

Composed a Festival Service in G and an anthem 'The Lord is my Shepherd' based on Psalm 23. An operetta was entitled *Sisters Three, or Britannia's Heroes*.

BORTON, Alice (19th century)
Composed anthems including 'Sing, O daughter of Zion' and 'Da nobis pacem', songs and piano works.

BOUGHEN, Robert Keith (b.1929)
The hymnal *With One Voice* (1978) uses 'Urquhart' with the hymn 'When God almighty came to be one of us' by Michael Hewlett. The same publication uses Boughen's 'Bramwell' with the hymn by Brian Wren, 'I come with joy to meet my Lord'.

BOUNDY, Kate (?-1913)
Died in Abergavenny, Wales on 7 August 1913. Studied at the Royal College of Music. Composed the anthem 'O Lord of hearts' and other items of church music.

BOWDLER, Dr. Cyril William (1839-1918)
Born in Yorkshire on 28 September 1839; died in Camberley, Surrey on 5 November 1918. The family was Welsh on his mother's side.

As a boy he studied music under **John Camidge** (1790-1859) and later under **R.P. Stewart**. He held a number of degrees from the University of Dublin: B.Mus., M.A. and LL.B. (1864), and LL.D. (1896). Organist of All Saints' Church, Aldershot, Hampshire (1877-1879).

Composed an opera *Imelda*, hymn tunes, the vesper hymns 'Love not the world' and 'Delight in the Lord', a Liturgy *of St. John Chrysostom* (1864), Services in E, in F, in G, in B-flat and in C, and anthems.

BOWER, Sir John Dykes (1905-1981)
Born in Gloucester on 13 August 1905; died in Orpington, Kent on 29 May 1981.

The son of a doctor of medicine and a descendant of **J.B. Dykes**. Educated at Cheltenham College, Gloucestershire and studied with **Herbert Brewer**. Attended Corpus Christi College, Cambridge as organ scholar (1922), reading music and classics. Graduated B.A. (1925), Mus.B. (1928) and M.A. (1929). His qualifications included the honorary D.Mus. from the University of Oxford (1944).

Appointed C.V.O. (1953); knighted in 1968.

Organist and master of the choristers at Truro Cathedral (1926-1929); at New College, Oxford (1929-1933); at Durham Cathedral (1933-1936) and at St. Paul's Cathedral (1936-1967).

During World War II he served in the R.A.F.

A professor of organ at the Royal College of Music (1936-1969). Known to be a railway enthusiast.

One of the music editors of the 1950 edition of *Hymns Ancient and Modern*, also contributing the three tunes, 'Amen Court', 'Standish' and 'Elton'.

BOWER, Neville C. (20th century)
Born in Allahabad, India. The son of a British cavalry officer who was later deputy registrar of the High Court, Allahabad. Educated at Sherwood College, Naini Tal. Came to England to complete his education. A student of the Royal College of Music, his studies being interrupted by National Service. His teachers included Kendall Taylor for piano and **Patrick Hadley** for composition. Graduated B.A.

A solo and duo concert pianist. An examiner and assessor for the University of London Examinations and Assessment Council (ULEAC).

Director of music at Ealing Grammar School, London, where he composed works for school use and beyond. Three of his early works (1963-1966) were choral settings of words by Hilaire Belloc, including *Our Lord and Our Lady*. Has composed orchestral works such as *Concertante* for oboe and orchestra, and chamber music such as the organ work *Eternal*, a String Quartet, and *Four Sound Pieces*, a set of duets each scored for piano and one other instrument. 'I will lift up mine eyes' (1994) is a setting of Psalm 121.

BOWES, Charles Frederick (1866-?)
Born in Newcastle-on-Tyne in 1866. Graduated B.Mus. at the University of Durham (1892). Chairman of the firm of John Bowes Ltd. Organist of Jesmond Wesleyan Church (1883-1891) and of the People's Hall, Newcastle (1897-1919). Taught at the Northern School of Music (1891-1893). Honorary secretary and organist of the Wesleyan Service of Song (1889-1911). Composed anthems including 'God is my Salvation' (1898) and 'The people that walk in darkness' (1900), and songs.

BOWLES, Revd. William Lisle (1762-1850)
A residentiary canon of Salisbury Cathedral. Rector of Bremhill, Wiltshire. Also a poet and writer of pamphlets. Composed the anthems 'Grant, we beseech Thee' and 'Haste Thee, O God'.

BOWMAN, John (?-1730)
Died in Cambridge in 1730. Organist of Trinity College, Cambridge from 1717 until the year of his decease. Composed the anthem 'Show yourselves joyful'.

BOYCE, Thomas (17th century)
A composer of the early part of the 17th century. Graduated B.Mus. at the University of Oxford (1603). Known to have composed a Te Deum and Evening Service.

BOYCE, Dr. William (1711-1779)
Born in London; baptised on 11 September 1711; died in Kensington, London on 7 February 1779, being buried nine days later in St. Paul's Cathedral.
A boy chorister at St. Paul's under **Charles King**. An articled pupil of **Maurice Greene** until 1734, and later became his friend. Graduated D.Mus. at the University of Oxford (1749).
Organist at the Oxford Chapel, Vere Street, London from 1734 and the Churches of St. Michael, Cornhill (1736-1768), where he succeeded **Thomas Kelway**, and All Hallows, Thames Street (1749-1764). One of the three organists at the Chapel Royal, taking up the place made vacant by the decease of **John Travers**.
Master of the orchestra of George III, and Master of the King's Musick. Conductor of the Three Choirs' Festival (from 1737). His hearing began to fail in his youth and when the problem worsened he set about completing the collection of church music begun by Maurice Greene and **John Alcock** (1715-1806), which was published in three volumes in 1760, 1768 and 1773 as *Cathedral Music*. The response was disappointing initially but a new edition in 1788 proved more successful, being reprinted in 1841, 1848 and 1849.
Charles Wesley, describing William Boyce, paid the tribute, 'A more modest man I never knew.'
A composer of music for the stage and church, succeeding **John Weldon** on his death as composer to the Chapel Royal. Wrote eight symphonies. Of his 46 anthems, 'I have surely built Thee an house', 'The Lord is King', 'O where shall wisdom be found?' and 'Turn Thee unto me' are well known, and from the latter piece the middle section 'The sorrows of my heart are enlarged' is used as

separate item for two trebles. His five services include settings in A (completed by **Samuel Arnold**) and in C.
Also remembered for settings to Psalms 1, 4 and 5 (c1765), published in *A Collection of Melodies*. They were later used as hymn tunes and known as 'Chapel Royal', 'Halton Holgate' and 'Portsea'.
Arthur Sullivan in his edition *Church Hymns* (1874) used two of Boyce's tunes with hymns by Charles Wesley, 'Jersey' with 'Lord, if Thou the grace impart', and 'Oxford' to 'O Thou, who hast our sorrows borne'. *Cathedral Psalter Chants* (1875) included a Double Chant in D. A composer of organ voluntaries.

BOYCE-TILLMAN, Dr. June (b.1943)
Born in Lyndhurst, Hampshire in 1943.
Read music at St. Hugh's College, Oxford and studied for a postgraduate certificate in education at the London University Institute of Education, where she was later awarded a Ph.D. for her work on the musical development of children. This dissertation has been translated into several languages, and established Dr. Boyce-Tillman as an expert in the field. Has travelled extensively, touring and leading workshops.
Directed the junior choir of St. Paul's Church, Furzedown for 10 years, and helped to train the children for the television programme 'Soundings by Swann' (**Donald Swann**), singing in the programme for three years and recording Swann's *Song of Caedmon* with her school choir.
Taught in primary and secondary schools in London, and at the Inner London Education Authority's Centre for Young Musicians.
Is currently reader and principal lecturer in music at King Alfred's College of Higher Education, Winchester. Her work includes the development of degree courses in world music and the supervision of research students in branches of the subject including music and ritual, and the effect of Vatican II on the music of the Roman Catholic Church.
A singer, specialising in religious music and folk songs.
Worked with the (Methodist) Notting Hill team ministry in the late 1960s, at a time when the 'folk in worship' movement, and the music of **Sydney Carter** in particular, were pervasive.
Has promoted, written, and spoken on women in music and in the church generally, and has worked for the use of inclusive language in worship.
Has composed for the church, her works including *In praise of all-encircling love* (1992), an edition of hymns and songs in inclusive language; a further edition was issued in 1995. In 1980 she edited *Galliard Book of Carols*.

BOYD, Revd. William (1845-1928)
Born in Montego Bay, Jamaica in 1845 of a Scottish family; died in Maida Vale, London on 16 February 1928.
Educated at Hurstpierpoint College, Sussex, and while at school he received lessons in music from **Sabine Baring-Gould**. Went up to St. Edmund's Hall and Worcester College, Oxford (where he was choral scholar). Graduated B.A. and M.A. in the same year: 1882. Ordained deacon in 1877, priest in 1882.
Assistant curate of Charlcombe, Somerset (1877-1882); vicar of Stoke Bishop, Gloucestershire (1882-1884); rector of Wiggonholt, Sussex (1884-1893) and vicar of All Saints', Norfolk Square, London (1893-1918) where his organist from 1894 was **Edward Bairstow**.
The hymn tune 'Pentecost' was written at the request of Sabine Baring-Gould for the words of 'Veni Creator' but was linked with

'Fight the good fight' for the 1874 edition of *Church Hymns*. The same combination was used in the Standard Edition (1916) of *Hymns Ancient and Modern*. 'Petrox' was also used in *Church Hymns* to 'Lord, Thy word abideth' by **Henry Williams Baker**.

BOYDELL, Dr. Brian (b.1917)
Born in Dublin on 17 March 1917.
Took B.A. in natural sciences at Clare College, Cambridge and then studied singing, piano, organ, oboe and composition at the Royal College of Music (1938-1939) where his teachers included **Patrick Hadley** and **Herbert Howells**.
Continued his musical education at the Royal Irish Academy of Music, Dublin. Graduated B.Mus. (1942) and D.Mus. (1959) at Trinity College, Dublin. In 1984 his achievements were recognised by the award of D.Mus. *honoris causa* by the National University of Ireland.
A professor of singing at the Royal Irish Academy of Music (1944-1952). Director of the Dowland Consort (1958-1969). Professor of music at the University of Dublin (1962-1982). Following his retirement from teaching he carried out musical research and composition. His writings include contributions to *New Grove Dictionary of Music and Musicians* (1980). Has also adjudicated at musical festivals and he has made more than 900 broadcasts on musical topics.
Composed orchestral, chamber and vocal music. His work includes the anthem 'I will hear what God the Lord will speak', to the text of Psalm 85, performed initially at the 1988 Dublin International Organ Festival.

BOYLE, Malcolm Courtenay (1902-1976)
Born in Windsor Castle, Berkshire on 30 January 1902; died on 3 April 1976. Son of a lay clerk of St. George's Chapel, Windsor Castle.
A chorister at Eton College. On completing his studies at Eton he studied at the Royal Academy of Music, where from 1918 he held the John Goss organ scholarship, and at Queen's College, Oxford, where he graduated B.Mus (1932). An organ pupil of **Walter Parratt**.
From the age of 13, Malcolm Boyle was assistant organist of Holy Trinity Church, Windsor (1915-1917 and 1918-1924). In the intervening years (1917-1918) he was organist of the nearby St. Mary's Church, Datchet.
Acting organist (from 1924) at St. George's Chapel until the appointment in 1927 of **Walford Davies**, to whom he became assistant organist.
Organist of Chester Cathedral (1932-1949).
Director of music at King's School, Canterbury (1951-1954) and of Nottingham High School (1954-1957). Organist of West Bridgford Parish Church, Nottingham (1957-1961) and of Sandiway Parish Church, Cheshire (from 1965).
Among his compositions are the anthems 'Thou, O God, art praised in Zion', 'Before Thy throne' and 'Daughters of Zion'.

BRABHAM, James (1834-1904)
Born in Poplar, London in 1834; died in Lambeth, London on 7 February 1904. Composed the anthem 'O Sing unto the Lord with the voice of melody', hymn tunes and songs.

BRADFORD, Dr. Jacob (1842-1898)
Born in Bow, London on 3 June 1842; died in 1898.

A chorister at St. Paul's Church, Walworth, London. Musically he was self-taught before taking lessons with **Charles Steggall** and **John Goss**. Graduated B.Mus (1873) and D.Mus. (1878) at the University of Oxford.
Assistant organist under **Scotson Clark** at the London church of St. Helen and St. Ethelburga, Bishopsgate. At the age of 20 he was appointed organist of St. Philip's Church, Kensington, London and he was later organist of St. James's Church, Hatcham (1868-1875) and St. Mary's, Newington (from 1892).
A teacher of music in London at the Royal Navy School, New Cross. Taught at West Kent Grammar School. Became principal of the South London College of Music. Contributed to *Musical News* and other periodicals.
Composed an oratorio *Judith*, anthems including 'If ye love Me' and 'I was glad', services and overtures.

BRADLEY, Charles (1846-1915)
Born in Wakefield, Yorkshire on 20 October 1846; died on 16 March 1915.
Taught by **Philip Armes**, R.S. Burton and F.W. Davenport.
Held the Yorkshire organistships of St. Michael's, Wakefield (1856-1866) and St. Paul's, Middlesbrough (1871-1882) before moving to Scotland and serving at St. George's, Edinburgh (1882-1885); Abbey Parish Church (1885-1887) and South Leith Parish Church (from 1887). Conductor of the Edinburgh Choral Union.
Composed anthems such as 'In the Lord have I put my trust' (1880) and 'Seek ye the Lord' (1893), other forms of church music, items for organ, and songs.

BRADLEY, Revd. Charles Lister (19th/20th century)
Born in Ashbourne, Derbyshire.
Studied under **Francis Bates** and **Haydn Keeton**. Graduated B.Mus. at Exeter College, Oxford (1914); later M.A. Ordained deacon in 1903, priest in 1904.
Organist of the Church of St. John the Baptist, Harlow, Essex (from 1902). A minor canon and precentor of Peterborough Cathedral (1906-1909), and precentor of Newcastle Cathedral, New South Wales, Australia (from 1909). Rector of Walkerston, Queensland until 1911 when he appears to have returned to England and to have been appointed to the Kensington School of Music, Norwich.
For a time, he was a duet whistler, appearing under the pseudonym R.C. Drayton.
Composed a setting of the Benedicite (1909), a Holy Communion Service in G (1908), a Magnificat and Nunc Dimittis in A, anthems including 'Rejoice in His holy Name' (1905) and 'What reward shall I give?', services and songs. Another of his works was the *Isaak Walton* Suite for Military Band.

BRADLEY, Dr. William (1877-?)
Born in Leeds in 1877. Privately educated, he graduated B.Mus. (1902) and D.Mus at the University of Durham. Organist and choirmaster of Temple Newsam (from 1893) and the Leeds Churches of St. Matthew (from 1896); Christ Church, Upper Armley (from 1902) and St. Aidan (until around 1936). Composed an Evening Service in A, hymn tunes, piano music and school songs.

BRADSHAW, Richard John (b.1951)
Born in Derby on 24 May 1951. Educated at Bemrose Grammar School, the University of Cambridge, and Wesley College, Bristol.

Ordained as a minister of the Methodist Church in 1975. Has served the Church in Yorkshire and the Midlands. A chant tune was used in *Hymns and Psalms* (1983).

BRAMMA, Harry Wakefield (b.1936)
Born in Shipley, West Yorkshire on 11 November 1936.
Harry Bramma took lessons in music with **Melville Cook,** organist of Leeds Parish Church. Educated at Pembroke College, Oxford as organ scholar (1955-1960). Graduated B.A. (1958) and M.A.
Director of music at the King Edward VI School, Retford, Nottinghamshire (1961-1963); assistant organist at Worcester Cathedral (1963-1976) and organist of Southwark Cathedral (1976-1989). Director of music at King's School, Worcester (1965-1976). In 1989 he became director of the Royal School of Church Music. Also organist and director of music of All Saints' Church, Margaret Street, London.
Has published a set of Preces and Responses, a carol 'People look East' and the anthems 'God is Light' and 'Be filled with the Spirit'.

BRAMSTON, Richard (16th century)
A chorister of Wells Cathedral. Having deputised for his predecessor, **Richard Hygons,** he was eventually appointed organist and master of the choristers (1507-1508). In the latter year he went to St. Augustine's Abbey, Bristol (now Bristol Cathedral) as master of the Lady Chapel. Returned to Wells as a vicar choral in 1515 and began another term as organist and master of the choristers there. For a while he was also keeper of the fabric. **Thomas Morley** referred to him as a 'practicioner' in music.
Composed church music, including a Marian antiphon 'Marie Virginis fecunda viscera' in five parts, and 'Recordare Domine', an antiphon for male voices in four parts.

BRANSCOMBE, Horatio Arthur (1856-1941)
Born in Chelsea, London in 1856; died in Prestatyn, Flint on 27 April 1941. Organist of St. Margaret's Church, Princes Park, Liverpool until his retirement in 1928. His 'Litany' was used with the hymn 'Father, whose love we have wronged by transgression' by Vincent Coles in the Standard Edition (1916) of *Hymns Ancient and Modern*.

BRAYTON, Coulthart
See **MOODY,** Charles Henry.

BRENNAN., Charles John (1876-1972)
Born in Gosport, Hampshire in 1876; died in Belfast on 8 May 1972.
Graduated B.Mus. at the University of Durham (1904). In 1949 he was appointed O.B.E. and at a later date he was honorarily awarded M.A. by Queen's University, Belfast.
Organist and choirmaster at All Saints' Parish Church, Clifton, Bedfordshire (from 1892).
On moving to Northern Ireland in 1897 he held the two successive church organist appointments of Strabane Parish Church, County Tyrone (from 1897) and Elmwood Presbyterian Church (from 1901). He then took up the organistship of Belfast's St. Anne's Cathedral (1904-1964). Belfast city organist (from 1908), giving weekly recitals. A teacher of music, a choral and orchestral conductor (his appointments included the Ulster Male Voice Choir) and an adjudicator at music festivals.
He built up in his 60 years at St. Anne's a choir of some 50 voices - including ladies, reflecting Brennan's dislike of the male alto voice,

and strengthening the treble line. Served as an officer in the army during World War I - 'Captain' became his nickname for the rest of his life.
Composed little church music but is remembered for 'The Virgin's hush song' and 'The Annunciation'.

BRENT-SMITH, Alexander (1889-1950)
Born in Brookthorpe, Gloucestershire in 1889; died in Gloucester on 3 July 1950.
Attended King's School, Gloucester. For two years he was an articled assistant to **Ivor Atkins,** organist of Worcester Cathedral. Director of music at Lancing College, Sussex (1913-1934), where he succeeded **W.H. Ferguson.**
A music critic and writer on musical topics. Contributed notes on Schubert's symphonies and chamber music to the *Musical Pilgrims* series published by Oxford University Press. Served on the committee of the Gloucester Three Choirs' Festival. Arranged hymns for Festival services: some descants and orchestrations are widely used today.
Wrote articles for *Musical Times* and for *Music and Letters*. Author of *Studies in Caprices* (1938).
Composed hymn tunes, including 'Lancing' and 'Cotswold'. Represented in *Broadcast Praise*. His other works include a Concerto for Two Violins and Two Pianos, a tune to George Herbert's *The Call* and light operas including *The gentle tyrant*.

BREWER, Sir Alfred Herbert (1865-1928)
Born in Gloucester on 21 June 1865; died in Gloucester on 1 March 1928.
A chorister of Gloucester Cathedral (1877-1880) under **C.H. Lloyd,** with whom he studied organ. Educated at the cathedral school, the Royal College of Music (as the first open organ scholar: 1882) under **Walter Parratt, Frederick Bridge** and **C.V. Stanford,** and Exeter College, Oxford (as organ scholar: 1883-1885).
Graduated B.Mus. (1897) at the University of Dublin. In 1905 the Lambeth D.Mus. was conferred on him in recognition of his services to church music. Wider acknowledgement followed when he was knighted in 1926.
Organist at St. Catherine's College, Gloucester (1881); St. Mary de Crypt, Gloucester (1881-1882) and St. Giles's Church, Oxford (1882-1885), succeeding Walter Parratt. These appointments were concurrent with his continuing education.
Appointed organist of Bristol Cathedral in 1885 but the previous incumbent, **George Riseley** who had been dismissed, won his court case for reinstatement. Brewer moved on as organist to St. Michael's Church, Coventry (1886-1892). Director of music at Tonbridge School (1892-1896).
Succeeded **Charles Lee Williams** as organist of Gloucester Cathedral (1897-1928). During his organistship at Gloucester, the Three Choirs' Festival was his responsibility eight times. Brewer was recognised as a sound choir trainer, having reorganised the Coventry Choral Society during his time at St. Michael's.
His pupils at Gloucester included **Tustin Baker, John Dykes Bower,** Ivor Gurney, **Herbert Howells,** Ivor Novello and **Ambrose Porter.**
Brewer's memoirs revealed him in a more humorous manner than he suggested outwardly. He took his wider musical responsibilities seriously, establishing recitals in Gloucester Cathedral for elementary school children.

Composed the oratorio *Emmaus* (1901) which was scored by **Edward Elgar** and performed at the 1901 festival, part songs, organ pieces, operettas, Services respectively in B, D and E-flat and four hymn tunes including 'Esther', 'Festubert' and 'Glovernia'. His anthem 'O Lord God, thou Strength of my health' is still performed today.

BREWER, Thomas (1611-?)
Educated at Christ's Hospital, for which he later composed 'Eternal King', a Psalm of Thanksgiving. A viol player. Composed a number of fantasias for the instrument.

BRIANT, Rowland (1861-1933)
Born in Lambeth, London in 1861; died in Epsom, Surrey on 26 December 1933. Studied in the Royal Academy of Music, where he was later appointed a professor of organ. Organist of the Ecclestone Square Church, the Westbourne Park Chapel and the New Court Chapel, Tollington Park. Also a local choral society conductor. His anthems include 'Hear my prayer' and 'Praise ye the Lord'. Composed hymn tunes.

BRIDGE, Sir John Frederick (1844-1924)
Born in Oldbury, Worcestershire on 5 December 1844; died in Westminster, London on 18 March 1924.
The son of a lay clerk of Rochester Cathedral and the older brother of **J.C. Bridge**.
A Rochester Cathedral chorister (1850-1859) under **John Larkin Hopkins**, cathedral organist until 1856 and under **John Hopkins** who succeeded him. Articled to John Hopkins (1859-1868).
When Frederick Bridge joined the choir, the solo boy was **Philip Armes**, subsequently organist of Chichester and Durham Cathedrals. Armes was succeeded as solo boy by **Edwin Crow**, who later became organist of Ripon Cathedral.
Bridge and Crow sometimes sang part songs with the officers of the Royal Engineers, whose barracks were at Rochester. Bridge sang at the opening of Crystal Palace in 1855, on which occasion another young performer was **Arthur Sullivan**.
Studied organ and composition with **John Goss** (1863-1867). Graduated B.Mus. (1868) and D.Mus. (1874), the latter on the strength of the oratorio *Mount Moriah,* submitted as his exercise at Queen's College, Oxford. His B.Mus. examiners were **F.A.G. Ouseley**, **Charles Corfe** and **John Stainer**. In 1905 he graduated M.A. at the University of Durham.
Awarded a Jubilee medal (1887) and a knighthood (1897), and appointed M.V.O (1901) and C.V.O. (1910).
In his teens he was organist at Shorne Church, Gravesend, Kent (1861) and St. Nicholas, Strood, Kent. Shorne was five miles away and there were no trains. Bridge used to walk to Shorne, playing morning and evening services and taking a packed lunch with him. His route took him past Gad's Hill Place, the residence of the novelist Charles Dickens, whom Bridge often observed taking his dog for a walk.
At the age of 15 or 16 he joined the band of the 9th Kent Volunteers, for whom he played second cornet.
Named organist at the age of 20 of Holy Trinity Church, Windsor (1865-1869) on the recommendation of **James Turle**, organist of Westminster Abbey, who had previously been impressed with Bridge's playing. Bridge was encouraged by the organist of St. George's Chapel, Windsor Castle, **George Elvey**, with whom he sat in the organ loft of St. George's, and by the author Mrs. Oliphant,

who praised his compositions. At this time he also studied with John Goss.
At Holy Trinity, the choristers were pupils of the local St. Mark's School, where Bridge and his choir put on concerts from time to time. On one occasion **Hubert Parry** sang the bass part of the Prophet in Mendelssohn's *Elijah*. Bridge, who taught at Eton College, prepared Parry's B.Mus. exercise, which he composed while still a pupil, for performance at the Lower School, Eton by the St. Mark's choristers.
Following unsuccessful applications for the vacancies at Queen's College, Oxford and Llandaff Cathedral (1867), Frederick Bridge succeeded **Joseph John Harris** as organist of Manchester Cathedral (1869-1875). As was typical of cathedral establishments of the time, Manchester had only four lay vicars for weekday services. **John Troutbeck** was precentor of Manchester Cathedral on his arrival.
Gave evening classes in harmony at Owen's College, Manchester, the forerunner of the faculty of music of the University of Manchester. Bridge was later a professor of harmony (1872-1875) at Owen's College.
Moving south, he became permanent deputy organist at Westminster Abbey (1875-1882), where Troutbeck was now a minor canon. Troutbeck saw to it that Bridge was among the candidates. There was no audition and the assessment of candidates' abilities took place on the basis of qualifications (Bridge had recently graduated D.Mus.) and references. Turle retained the title of Abbey organist, and continued to live in the precincts. Troutbeck was succeeded later by **Samuel Flood Jones**.
The state of the music at Westminster Abbey on his arrival was a source of concern. There was no practice for the full choir. The lay vicars were undisciplined and erratic attenders. Some were old and had fallen below the standard of singing required. It was considered acceptable for the men to belong also to the choir of the Chapel Royal, St. James's Palace. Those who did - and some of those who did not - used to exit discreetly as the sermon began during morning service.
In 1882, on the death of Turle, Bridge took on the title of organist, serving until 1918 when he retired. During his time at Westminster Abbey he was responsible for the music at the celebration of the golden (1887) and diamond (1897) anniversaries of Queen Victoria's accession, and the Coronation of Edward VII (1902) and George V (1911).
Westminster Abbey during Frederick Bridge's first 20 years had no formal position of assistant organist but in 1896, **Walter Alcock** was appointed, remaining until he became organist of Salisbury Cathedral in 1916. Bridge could also call upon the services of **Edward Bairstow**, his articled pupil from 1893 to 1899.
One of the first professors at the opening in 1876 of the National Training School of Music. Shortly after that institution was superseded by the Royal College of Music (1882), he became a professor of harmony (1883-1924). His pupils included Hubert Parry and **C.V. Stanford**.
Frederick Bridge was one of the four unsuccessful candidates in 1894 for the vacant directorship of the R.C.M. following the retirement of George Grove, Parry being preferred.
From 1890 he was the first professor of music at the University of London. He also taught at the Crystal Palace School of Music and was Gresham professor of music (from 1890).
Bridge once acted in John Stainer's place as inspector of music in schools and training colleges. He described it as 'the hardest week's work I have ever done.'

Founded the Organists' Benevolent League in 1909, determined to relieve 'the sad lot of the great body of organists whose pay is never at all commensurate with their responsibilities'. The League had no subscription: instead, the members were obliged to give at least one recital per annum for the relief of destitute organists and their dependents. The cause was later taken up by the Royal College of Organists.

A competent choir trainer, he was conductor of the Royal Choral Society (1896-1922). He was known for his genial style as a lecturer and for a light-hearted approach to life in general. He described to **Henry Wood** how he approached his interview for the post of conductor of the Royal Choral Society. 'I fired off a joke as soon as I entered the room. I kept 'em in roars of laughter all through the interview... and that, my boy, was how I got the job.'

He met the composers Grieg and Dvorak at the Birmingham Festival of 1885.

He was the first Abbey organist since **Purcell** to direct the music of a coronation, the occasion being the Coronation in 1902 of Edward VII. It may have been something of a surprise to readers of his autobiography to learn that security, then as now, was a great concern: it was feared that the Abbey would be a target of Fenian bombers.

Composed services, oratorios, cantatas, anthems and carols. Wrote a number of musical text books, in preparation for which he carried out a great deal of antiquarian research into music. Wrote material for provincial music festivals and choral societies. Corresponded with Kipling, and set some of his works to music.

He also composed hymn tunes, two of which were used in *Hymns Ancient and Modern*. 'St. Beatrice', a title he chose following the death of his daughter, Beatrice, is in the 1875 edition, and 'God made me' was used with the hymn 'God made me for Himself to serve Him here' by **Henry Williams Baker**, in the Standard Edition (1916). His tune 'Spean' is still used today with 'Brightest and best of the sons of the morning'. Editor of *Methodist Hymn Book* (1904) but he was disappointed not to be invited to undertake the revision of *Hymns Ancient and Modern*.

BRIDGE, Dr. Joseph Cox (1853-1929)
Born in Rochester, Kent on 16 August 1853; died in St. Albans, Hertfordshire on 29 March 1929.
Brother of **Frederick Bridge**.
A chorister at Rochester Cathedral (where his father John Bridge was a vicar choral) prior to becoming assistant organist. He was a pupil and assistant of **John Larkin Hopkins** and of his brother **John Hopkins**. Organ scholar of Exeter College, Oxford (from 1871) where he graduated B.A. (1875), B.Mus. (1876), M.A. (1878) and D.Mus. (1885). His D.Mus. exercise was an oratorio *Daniel*. Awarded D. Mus. at the University of Durham (1908).
Organist of Exeter College (1871-1876). He then served his brother, Frederick, as assistant organist for a brief time at Manchester Cathedral before moving on to Chester Cathedral, firstly as assistant organist (1876-1877) to Frederick Gunton, and then as organist (1877-1925). In his time at Chester he re-established the city's triennial music festival, in which he was actively involved until 1900.
An examiner to the Universities of Oxford and London. Professor of music at the University of Durham (from 1908). Retired from Chester in 1925 and became director of studies at Trinity College of Music, London.
Composed cantatas, symphonies, church music and part songs. His sacred works include a Magnificat and Nunc Dimittis for Voices,

Orchestra and Organ (1879) and an anthem for use at harvest festivals.

BRIDGER, John Henry (1869-?)
Born in Farnborough, Hampshire in 1869. After a private education he graduated B. Mus. at the University of Durham (1896). Organist of Farnborough Parish Church (1893-1910) and temporary organist of St. Matthew's Church, Redhill, Surrey (1917-1919). Composed items for piano, anthems, an Evening Service in B-flat (1889), the anthem 'O be joyful in the Lord' (1909), hymn tunes, chants and orchestral works. Author of a textbook *How to Harmonize Melodies*.

BRIDGEWATER, Thomas (?-1831)
Died on 6 January 1831. Organist of St. Saviour's Church, York. Composed the anthem 'I will give thanks unto Thee'.

BRIERLEY, Revd. John Michael (b.1932)
Born in Leicester on 29 July 1932.
Attended Bromsgrove School and the Lichfield Theological College (from 1957). Ordained deacon in 1960, priest in 1961. Graduated B.D. at the University of London (1971).
Curate of Lower Mitton, Worcestershire (1960-1962); priest-in-charge (1962-1968) and subsequently vicar (1969-1971) of Dines Green; rector of Eastham with Rochford, Tenbury Wells (1971-1979); priest-in-charge of Knighton-on-Team Church (1976-1979); priest-in-charge (1979-1981) and vicar (1981-1992) of St. Luke's Church, Reddal Hill.
His hymn tune 'Camberwell' has become the standard modern tune to 'At the Name of Jesus'. It was composed prior to Brierley's ordination and is dedicated to **Geoffrey Beaumont**, who at the time it was written was vicar of St. George's, Camberwell. Descants have been written for performance by, among others, a choir in Hong Kong and a brass band in Yorkshire. Other hymns and hymn tunes have been published. An anthem for the consecration of a new church at Dines Green remains in manuscript.

BRIERLEY, Dr. William Booth (1870-?)
Born in Chester in 1870.
A chorister of Chester Cathedral. Graduated B.Mus. (1895) and D.Mus. (1903) at Queen's College, Oxford. Organist and choirmaster of St. Mary's-without-the-walls, Chester (from 1890); organist to the Duke of Westminster at Eaton Hall (from 1895) and organist and choirmaster of West Kirby Parish Church (from 1900).
Taught music at Calday Grange Grammar School and Wallasey Grammar School, and violin at The Leas Preparatory School, Hoylake. His other teaching appointments included a post at Oldershaw Secondary School, Wallasey. A local choral society conductor.
Composed church music including a Magnificat and Nunc Dimittis in C (1912), works for organ, and other chamber music.

BRIGGS, Revd. George Wallace (1875-1959)
Born in Kirkby, Nottinghamshire on 14 December 1875; died in Hindhead, Surrey on 30 December 1959.
Attended Emmanuel College, Cambridge where he graduated in classics (1897).
A chaplain in the Royal Navy (1902-1909); vicar of St. Andrew's Church, Norwich (from 1909) and rector of Loughborough,

Leicestershire (from 1918). A canon of the Cathedrals of Leicester (1927-1934) and Worcester (from 1934).

He was mainly responsible for the collection *Prayers and Hymns for use in Schools* (1927), published by Leicestershire County Council and he was involved in similar assignments for other local authorities. Collaborated with Percy Dearmer in the publication of *Songs of Praise* (1925). A founder of the Hymn Society, and chairman of its executive committee.

He set a number of hymns, including 'Son of the Lord Most High' to music, and he composed hymn tunes including 'Loughborough'. Six are found in the New Standard Edition of *Hymns Ancient and Modern.*

BRIGHT, Dr. Percy Sibthorpe (1867-?)

Born in Southsea, Hampshire in 1867.

Attended the Royal College of Music, and educated privately and in Italy. Graduated B.Mus. at the University of London (1896).

Director of music at the Norwood Technical Institute (1924-1932). Organist and choirmaster of Christ Church, Battersea, London (1893-1896) and of St. Luke's, Norwood, London (1896-1924). A local choral and orchestral society conductor.

Composed an Evening Service and a Festival Te Deum.

BRIMLEY (Brimlei), John (c1502-1576)

Born in or around the year 1502; died in Durham on 13 October 1576. Lived and worked at Durham, being cantor, and also organist there from 1549 at the latest until 1576. A Roman Catholic.

Composed a Te Deum and Benedictus for four-part Choir, and a set of Responses.

BRIND, Richard (?-1718)

Born towards the end of the 17th century; died in March 1718. Buried in St. Paul's Cathedral.

A chorister of St. Paul's, probably under **Jeremiah Clarke.**

From March 1707 or 1708 he was, probationarily, a vicar choral of St. Paul's. Succeeded Clarke as organist of St. Paul's (c1707-1718). **Maurice Greene** was one of his articled pupils. **Handel** played organ at St. Paul's during Brind's time.

Composed anthems including 'Behold, God is my Salvation' and 'Let God arise'.

BRITTEN, Edward Benjamin (1913-1976)

Born in Lowestoft, Suffolk on 22 November 1913, St. Cecilia's Day; died in Aldeburgh, Suffolk on 4 December 1976.

Took piano lessons with Harold Samuel at the age of five and studied the viola with Audrey Alston. Attended South Lodge Preparatory School (1923-1927) where he became head boy. He made public early in life the strength of his feelings against violence by writing an essay that argued the case against hunting. It received a mark of nought.

A pupil of **Walter Greatorex** at Gresham's School, Holt, Norfolk, where **Lennox Berkeley** had been a pupil 10 years earlier. The school was known for its progressive attitude which his parents thought would be congenial to him, but he found the musical environment uninspiring. At the age of 13 he became a composition pupil of Frank Bridge, whom he had met at the Norwich Festival of 1924.

In 1930 he won a scholarship to the Royal College of Music where his teachers were Arthur Benjamin, **John Ireland** and Harold Samuel. The selection panel included Ireland and **Ralph Vaughan Williams**. Ireland immediately discerned 'the finest musical brain

that has entered this building for generations', convincing his colleagues to award the scholarship to Britten. One of the examiners, said by some to be Vaughan Williams and named by others as S.P. Waddington, required some convincing, remarking, 'It isn't decent for a boy of his age to be writing this sort of music.'

Awarded doctorates by the Universities of Oxford (1943) and Cambridge (1959), and received a total of nine other honorary degrees.

Made Companion of Honour (1952), received the Order of Merit (1965) and became a life peer (1976), the first musician so to be honoured.

His work with John Grierson at the G.P.O. Film Unit has become well known. In effect, he was musical editor, working with W.H. Auden from 1935 onwards in documentary films. He left for the U.S.A. in May 1939 with Peter Pears, returning in March 1942 in order to write what was to become the opera *Peter Grimes*. On his return he registered with the authorities as a conscientious objector. From 1947 onwards he lived at Aldeburgh.

He composed without guidance from the age of five. He wrote chamber music and operas, including a made-for-television opera, *Owen Wingrave* in 1970 at the behest of the B.B.C. Wrote his *War Requiem* for the consecration of the rebuilt Coventry Cathedral in 1962. From 1961 he composed music specifically for the Russian cellist Mstislav Rostropovich.

His church music includes a Missa Brevis in D for **George Malcolm** and his Westminster Cathedral Choir (1959); a setting of Psalm 150; a Te Deum in C (1934) for the choir of the Church of St. Mark, North Audley Street, London and a companion Jubilate (1961) at the request of the Duke of Edinburgh for St. George's Chapel, Windsor Castle; a *Hymn to St. Cecilia*, the cantatas *Rejoice in the Lamb* (1943) *Misericordium* and *St. Nicolas* (1948), and a canticle *Abraham and Isaac*, which he wrote for a performance by the tenor, Peter Pears, the contralto, Kathleen Ferrier and himself as accompanist. A Jubilate in E-flat (1934) has recently been re-published The macaronic early carol setting *A hymn to the Virgin* (1930) is also widely used.

The combination of great musical talent, worldly success and unorthodox views led to complex relationships with his contemporaries. For example **William Walton** admired him although there was professional rivalry between the two.

Britten became ill in 1973, undergoing open heart surgery, but he continued to compose. According to Thomas Beecham, Britten was 'the only English composer worth while that has emanated from one of our colleges of music'.

BRITTON, Donald (b.1919)

Born in Brixton, London on 2 November 1919.

After attending Wilson's Grammar School, he went up as organ scholar in 1948 to Emmanuel College, Cambridge where he graduated Mus.B. and M.A. Also attended the London Academy of Music.

Appointed assistant music master of Winchester College, Hampshire. Later he became director of music at Melbourne Grammar School, Australia.

He has composed items for piano, an Anthem for Choir and Organ (1958), a Mass for Choir and Organ (1975) and a Communion Service for Keyboard, Choir and Congregation (1978).

His hymn tunes include 'Joy', 'Omnipotens' and 'Aaronic Blessing'.

BROCK, Cameron William Harrison (1855-1913)
Born in Droxford, Hampshire in 1855; died in Croydon, Surrey on 23 November 1913. Composed an Evening Service in C (1911), chant settings of the Benedicite and Te Deum (1895), the anthem 'Search me, O God' (1907) and hymn tunes.

BROCKLESS, Brian (1926-1995)
Born in London on 21 January 1926; died on 18 December 1995. Attended the Stationers' Company School and he studied at the Royal College of Music under **Herbert Howells**. After graduating B.Mus. he studied privately with Matyas Seiber and at the Accadamia Musicale, Chigiana, Siena, Italy with Sergiu Celibidache. Won the Conducting Prize at Siena in 1963.
Toured with various orchestras as guest conductor, including a visit to Italy with the London Schubert Orchestra.
Taught music at Battersea College of Technology (from 1948), where he became head of music in 1958. His academic career developed as senior lecturer and subsequently director of music at the University of Surrey. Brian Brockless is recognised as the driving force behind the foundation of the university's degree course in music, which incorporates the Tonmeister course in music recording. A professor of the Royal Academy of Music.
Director of music at a number of North London churches and, later, the Priory Church of St. Bartholomew-the-Great, Smithfield, London (1961-1971; 1979-1995). Founded the St. Bartholomew's Singers, later renamed Pro Cantione Antiqua, then the New Festival Singers and, finally, the Priory Festival Choir. Was also organist of the London Church of St. Mary, Aldermary.
From 1954 he was conductor of the choir of Goldsmiths' College. A proficient counter tenor, he was a member of the choir and deputy organist of the Chapel Royal, Savoy Hill, London. Sang also with the Schola Polyphonica under Henry Washington.
Composed songs and organ works including a Prelude, Toccata and Chaconne. His church music includes an Evening Service in A Minor, the anthem 'Behold, now praise the Lord' for St. John's Episcopal Church, Wisconsin and a Missa Brevis for two voices.

BROCKLESS, Dr. George Frederick (1887-1957)
Born in Fritwell, Oxfordshire in 1887; died in Redhill, Surrey on 30 November 1957.
Educated in Oxford at New College School and Queen's College. Awarded D.Mus. at the University of Durham (1928).
In 1908 he embarked for South Africa to take up appointments as music master of Kingswood College and organist of the Commemoration Church, Grahamstown. He remained in South Africa for six years.
On his return to England he became organist and choirmaster of Hornsey Parish Church, London (1920-1928); St. Barnabas, Kensington, London (1928-1943) and the Central Hall, Westminster (1944-1957). Lecturer at Westminster Teacher Training College for six years. Director of music at Battersea Polytechnic for 30 years and music master of the Abbey School, Barking, Essex. From 1951 he was a joint editor of *The Choir* and a musical adviser to the committee for *Methodist Hymn Book*.
His hymn tune 'Grainger' is used today with 'Lord, who throughout these forty days'. It was named after his father-in-law, Revd. Grainger Hargreaves.

BRODERIP, Edmund (18th century)
Edmund Broderip, the son of **William Broderip** and the brother of **John Broderip** and **Robert Broderip**, was organist of Wells

Cathedral around the year 1720. He composed services, anthems and glees.

BRODERIP, John (1719-1770)
Born in Wells, Somerset on 2 February 1719; died in Wells on 31 January 1770. He was probably the son of **William Broderip**, whose sixth of nine children was named John, and therefore the brother of **Edmund Broderip** and **Robert Broderip**.
Succeeded **William Evans** as organist and master of the choristers of Wells Cathedral (1741-1770), following a church organistship at Minehead, Somerset. Had been a vicar choral of the cathedral from 1740. Towards the end of his life he was organist of Shepton Mallet Parish Church, Somerset.
Published *A Set of New Anthems and Psalm Tunes* (1745) and *A Second book of New Anthems and Psalm Tunes* around the year 1765. His own anthems include 'As pants the hart' and 'If the Lord Himself'. Also composed Psalms, songs and glees.

BRODERIP, Robert (1721-1808)
Born in 1721 and died, possibly in Bristol, Gloucestershire where he lived, on 14 May 1808. He was probably a son of **William Broderip** and brother of **John Broderip** and **Edmund Broderip**. Organist of a Bristol church. Composed Psalm tunes, anthems including 'Awake up, my glory' and 'Is there not an appointed time?', odes, concertos and glees. Edited a book of Psalms with John Broderip.

BRODERIP, William (1683-1727)
Born on 10 July 1683; died in Wells, Somerset on 31 January 1727. Two of his nine children were named John and Robert and it is believed that these were **John Broderip** and **Robert Broderip**, church musicians and composers. He succeeded John George as organist of Wells Cathedral (1713-1726), having been a vicar choral since April 1701. From 1716 he was also master of the choristers. Composed the anthem 'God is our Hope and Strength' (1713) in celebration of the Peace of Utrecht, a Service in D, other services and a chant.

BROOKES, Ernest Paulton (c1872-1945)
Died in Bromley, Kent in 1945 at the age of 73. Graduated B.Mus. at the University of Durham (1912). Organist and choirmaster of the Church of Hovingham Spa, Yorkshire (1900-1907); St. Alkelda's, Giggleswick (1907-1913) and St. Matthew's, Lightcliffe (from 1914). Choirmaster of St. John's Church, Longcliffe (from 1912). Taught music at Giggleswick Grammar School (from 1910) and at Heath Grammar School, Halifax (from 1914). From 1941 to 1945 he was temporary organist of Bromley Presbyterian Church. A composer of church music.

BROOKES, Harry (?-1919)
Graduated B.Mus. at the University of Durham (1900).
Organist of Regent Street Congregational Church (1891-1894), organist and choirmaster of St. Mark's Church, Heyside (1894-1898) and of St. Peter's Church, Ashton-under-Lyne (1898-1901). From the latter year he was organist and choirmaster of the church of St. John the Baptist, Hey, Oldham, Lancashire. Principal of the Lyceum School of Music, and held appointments as conductor of local choral and orchestral societies.
Composed anthems including 'Sing praises unto the Lord' (1902) and 'The Lord is in His holy temple' (1918), part-songs and piano pieces.

BROOKS, Frederic (1874-?)
Born in Sutton-in-Ashfield, Nottinghamshire, in 1874. Trained at Trinity College of Music and graduated B.Mus. at the University of Durham (1912). Organist and choirmaster of St. Mark's Church, Mansfield, Nottinghamshire (1900-1906) and organist of the Old Meeting House, Mansfield (from 1907). Toured as a clarinettist (1894-1900). Around the year 1920 he was a teacher at Oakleigh School, Wells, Somerset. Composed works for piano and for violin, and published *The Church Service*, a collection of music for the liturgy. His *Six Kyries* were published in 1910.

BROOKSBANK, Hugh (1854-1894)
Born in Peterborough, Cambridgeshire on 13 September 1854; died in Cardiff on 28 April 1894. Elder brother of **Oliver Brooksbank**.
A chorister at St. George's Chapel, Windsor Castle. An articled pupil of **Haydn Keeton**, organist of Peterborough Cathedral. Organist and organ scholar of Exeter College, Oxford where he graduated B.Mus. (1874).
Before going up to Oxford, Hugh Brooksbank had been organist of St. John's Church, Peterborough and of Trinity College, Glenalmond. In 1881 he became organist of St. Alban's Church, Birmingham.
Organist of Llandaff Cathedral (1882-1894), where he organised the first Cardiff Music Festival.
Composed an Evening Service in B-flat, chants and songs.

BROOKSBANK, Oliver Oldham (1859-?)
Born in Peterborough, Cambridgeshire on 17 May 1859. Younger brother of **Hugh Brooksbank**.
Like Hugh, Oliver was a chorister of St. George's Chapel, Windsor Castle and a pupil of **Haydn Keeton** of Peterborough Cathedral. Graduated B.Mus. at the University of Durham (1894).
Organist of Fletton Church (1877); Alton Parish Church, Hampshire (1880); St. Leonards Church, Sussex (1882); St. John's, Leatherhead, Surrey (1883); St. Martin's, Bedford (1893); Addlestone Parish Church, Surrey and St. John's, Torquay, Devon (1905).
Organist or music teacher of Chardstock School (1880); Highbury School, London; St. Leonards School; Trinity College, Glenalmond (1881); Leamington College, Warwickshire (1887) and Tonbridge School, Kent (1891).
Composed a Benedicite (1891), a hymn, 'Iter triumphi' (1892), hymn tunes, songs and items for organ.

BROOME, Edward C. (?-1932)
Born in North Wales; died in 1932. Organist and choirmaster of St. Mary's Church, Bangor, North Wales. Competed in *eisteddfodau* as composer and conductor. Later emigrated to Montreal, Canada where he earned his living as an organist and teacher of music. Organist of the Jarvis Street Baptist Church, Toronto (from 1906), and worked also in the town of Brookville.
Composed an anthem in memory of Robert Rees (Eos Morlais).

BROOMFIELD, William Robert (1826-1888)
Born in Inverary, Argyllshire, Scotland on 14 October 1826; died in Aberdeen on 17 October 1888.
Worked for a firm of accountants in Glasgow, where he studied music under **John Turnbull**. In 1850 he moved to Aberdeen where his circumstances deteriorated and where he died in poverty.
Author of the two short books *A Manual of Harmony* and *The Principles of Ancient and Modern Music*.

Composed hymn tunes. Revised Edition (1927) of *Church Hymnary* employs his 'St. Kilda' (c1850) with 'Who fathoms the eternal thought?' by John Greenleaf Whittier. His other tunes include 'Shandon' and 'Zion'. Some were popular in his lifetime. A memorial edition of 12 of his hymn tunes was published in 1892. He also composed songs.

BROTHERTON, John Henry (19th/20th century)
Graduated B.Mus. at the University of Durham (1898). Taught music at Bishop Auckland Grammar School, County Durham. Composer of duets for two violins, piano pieces, part songs, and anthems.

BROWN, Arthur Henry (1830-1926)
Born in Brentwood, Essex on 24 July 1830; died in Brentwood on 15 February 1926.
Began to play organ at the age of 10. Musically he was almost entirely self-taught, although he received some formal organ training.
He is known for his long service to church music in the county of Essex. He was organist of Brentwood Parish Church (1842-1853) and also from 1858, the five years in between having been spent as organist at St. Edward's, Romford. In total, he was organist of Brentwood Parish Church for 40 years. Organist of St. Peter's Church, South Weald (from 1889). He was, until he died, organist of Sir Anthony Browne's School, Brentwood. Thus he was active as an organist for 84 years.
He was strongly influenced by the Oxford Movement and supported the return of plainchant to Anglican worship. A committee member of the London Gregorian Association, preparing the Service Book for the annual festival in St. Paul's Cathedral. Edited various publications, including *Altar Hymnal*, bringing to bear his detailed knowledge of Gregorian music.
Composed settings of the Canticles and the Holy Communion Service, a Children's Festival Service, anthems including 'The day is past and over' and 'O love Divine', songs and part songs.
Wrote over 800 hymn tunes and carols, the most famous of which is probably the tune 'Saffron Walden', often sung to the words 'Just as I am, without one plea', and his others included 'Gerran' (which appeared in the 1889 Supplement to *Hymns Ancient and Modern*) and a collection of nine tunes published in November 1862. *Church Hymns* (1874) used Brown's tunes 'Holy Church' and 'St. Anatolius'. Composed the carols 'Sing we now the Christmas tiding' and 'When Christ was born of Mary free'.

BROWN, Dr. Edward (19th century)
Known to have been alive between the years 1878 and 1897. Graduated B.Mus. (1878) and D.Mus. (1883) at New College, Oxford. Organist and choirmaster of St. James's Church, Barrow-in-Furness and of St. Paul's Church, Grange-over-Sands. Conductor of choral societies. Composed church music, including a setting of Psalm 45 'My heart is inditing', and songs.

BROWN-BORTHWICK, Revd. Robert (1840-1894)
Robert Brown was born in Aberdeen, Scotland on 18 May 1840; died in St. Marylebone, London on 17 March 1894. Appended his bride's maiden name to his own on their marriage, at which **Arthur Sullivan** was best man, at Westminster Abbey in 1868.
Educated at St. Margaret's Hall, Oxford and was ordained deacon in 1865, priest in 1866.

Curate of Sudely, Gloucestershire (1865-1866) and of Evesham, Worcestershire (1866-1868). Assistant minister of the Quebec Chapel, London (1868-1869) and vicar of Holy Trinity, Grange, near Keswick (1869-1872). In 1872 he became vicar of All Saints', Scarborough, Yorkshire. A number of his sermons were published, including *Art In Worship*.

A keen composer. Compiler of *A Supplemental Hymn and Tune Book* (1867) to which Sullivan, **John Goss**, **E.J. Hopkins** and **Jean Baptiste Calkin** contributed. Sullivan in turn included six of Brown-Borthwick's tunes in his edition *Church Hymns* (1874), among them 'Grange' to J. Krause's 'Alleluia, fairest morning' and 'Gretton' to 'Great King of nations, hear our prayer' by John Gurney. Also composed 12 Kyries, chants and the anthem 'Blessed are the dead'.

BROWNE, John (c1452-?)
A church musician of the mid 15th century. His common name has hindered scholars in the task of defining his career. Sacred music bearing the name of this composer includes carols and services. The *Eton Choir Book* contains Magnificats and Antiphons by John Browne.

BROWNE, Richard (17th century)
Little is known about Richard Browne, a church musician and composer of the early part of the 17th century. From not later than March 1614 until at least 1619 he was a vicar choral and organist of Wells Cathedral. Five anthems including 'If the Lord Himselfe' and a Service by 'Richard Browne' are, according to expert opinion, likely to have been composed by him.

BROWNE, Revd. Richard (c1630-1664)
Born around the year 1630; died in Worcester, being buried there on 27 August 1664. However, if the details that follow relate to the career of a single person then the date of birth has to be earlier than that given.

Successively a chorister, lay clerk, sub deacon (from 1642) and a minor canon (from 1644) of Worcester Cathedral. From 1662 to 1664 he was organist and master of the choristers at Worcester and from 1660 he was rector of St. Clement's Church, Worcester. Anthems include 'Christ, rising from the dead' and 'Unto Him that loved us'.

BROWNE, Richard (?-1710)
Details of his early life are obscure. Died in Lambeth, London and was buried on 21 May 1710.

Organist of St. Lawrence's Church, Jewry, London from March 1686 until his death. From March 1688 he was music master at Christ's Hospital, London until he was dismissed for negligence in 1697. In 1689 he had been reprimanded for mistreating the children there. From July 1701 he was organist at the church of St. Mary's, Lambeth.

Composed a set of eight *Psalms of Thanksgiving*, which were sung by the children of Christ's Hospital on the Monday, Tuesday and Wednesday of Holy week. Also composed catches and songs.

BROWNSMITH, John Leman (1809-1866)
Born in Westminster, London in 1809; died on 14 September 1866. A chorister at Westminster Abbey under **George Ebenezer Williams** and **Thomas Greatorex**. Studied organ construction and built a small instrument himself.

Organist of several churches in London, succeeding **Benjamin Jacob** at St. John's, Waterloo Road (1829-1838) and serving at St. Gabriel's, Pimlico (from 1853). From March 1838 he was a lay vicar of Westminster Abbey. Organist of the Sacred Harmonic Society (from October 1848) in succession to **William Edward Miller**. Organist at the Crystal Palace Handel Festivals of 1857, 1859, 1862 and 1865.

Brownsmith's Double Chant in F Minor was included in *Cathedral Psalter Chants* (1875).

BRUCE-PAYNE, David Malcolm (b.1945)
Born in Banbury, Oxfordshire on 8 August 1945.
A chorister at King's College, Cambridge; educated at Bryanston School and the Royal College of Music where he was W.T. Best Scholar. Graduated B.Mus. (1969) at the University of London.

Second assistant organist of Westminster Abbey (1968-1974) and a teacher at the Abbey choir school prior to his appointment as organist of Birmingham Cathedral (1974-1977). Director of music at the King Edward School, Birmingham (1974-1976). Since 1976 he has held lectureships in music in the Birmingham area. Director of music at St. George's Church, Edgbaston, Birmingham (from 1978).

Composer of the anthems 'O fear the Lord', and 'O Lord, the very Heavens'.

BRYAN, Cornelius (1773-1840)
Born in Bristol, Gloucestershire in 1773; died in Bristol on 18 March 1840. Organist of the Churches of St. Mark and St. Mary Redcliffe, Bristol. Published a collection of Psalm tunes in 1830, in which his 'Serenity' appeared. Also composed the operetta *Lundy* (1840).

BRYCE, A.
See **BONNER**, Carey.

BRYNE (Bryan, Brian), Albertus (c1621-?1668)
A church musician and composer during the middle years of the 17th century. It is likely that he was born around the year 1621. The date of his death cannot be stated with certainty as there were a number of contemporary church musicians with similar names but it was probably around 1668 or 1669.

Received his musical education from **John Tomkins**, organist of St. Paul's Cathedral. He himself later held that same position from the age of 17 until the Civil War and it is likely that he was John Tomkins's immediate successor. At the Restoration, Bryne was given back the organistship of St. Paul's. Some years later, following the Great Fire of London, he was organist of Westminster Abbey (1666-1668).

He may have been organist of Dulwich College, London (1671-1677), or the organist could have been someone else with a similar name. Likewise there was a Bryan who was organist of the Church of All Hallows, Barking, Essex from 1676 onwards, who could perhaps have been the son of Albertus Bryne.

A person or persons of this name composed at least three anthems including 'Behold, how good' and 'I heard a voice', a Morning and Evening Service, and works for organ.

BUCK, Sir Percy Carter (1871-1947)
Born in West Ham, London on 25 March 1871; died in Hindhead, Surrey on 3 October 1947.

A chorister of West Ham Parish Church (1881-1888). Educated at the Merchant Taylors' School, Guildhall School of Music, the Royal College of Music and, from 1891, Worcester College, Oxford.

At various times and places his teachers in music were **Charles Frost, Walter Parratt, C.H. Lloyd** and **Hubert Parry**. Graduated at the University of Oxford with the degrees of B.A. (1891), M.A. (1897), B.Mus. (1892) and D.Mus. (1897).

Knighted in 1935.

Organist of Kingston on Thames Parish Church, Surrey and of Worcester College, Oxford (1891-1894). Taught music at Rugby School (1894-1896). Director of the music at the church of St. John, Wilton Road, London and the Cathedrals of Wells (1896-1899) in succession to **Charles Lavington** and Bristol (1899-1901). At the latter his unsuccessful competitors had been **A.H. Brewer** and **Mark Monk**.

Director of music at Harrow School (1901-1917) where he succeeded **Eaton Faning**. Professor of music at Trinity College, Dublin, succeeding **Ebenezer Prout**. King Edward VII professor of music at the University of London (1925-1937). From 1923 he was the first Cramb Lecturer in Music at the University of Glasgow. Taught also at the R.C.M.

Chairman of the Editorial Committee for the *Tudor Church Music* series. Music advisor to London County Council (1927-1936).

The author of *History of Music* (1929); also wrote on the subject of organ playing. Contributed articles to Grove's *Dictionary of Music and Musicians* (1927). He, **Edward Bairstow** and **Charles Macpherson** were joint editors of *English Psalter* (1925).

Composed for organ and for choirs. Wrote hymn tunes including 'St. Sebastian', which was one of his 14 hymn tunes published in 1914 and used in the Standard Edition (1916) of *Hymns Ancient and Modern*, 'Herga' and 'Gonfalon Royal', which is still used today as a setting of 'The royal banners forward go'. Also composed anthems such as 'O Lord God' for upper voices - a setting of the Collect for Sexagesima - and a set of four anthems for men's voices including 'Beloved, now we are the sons of God'.

BUCK, Dr. Zechariah (1798-1879)

Born in Norwich, Norfolk on 9 September 1798; died in Newport, Essex on 3 October 1879.

A chorister at Norwich Cathedral (1807-1815) under **Thomas Garland, John 'Christmas' Beckwith** and his son John Charles, to whom he later became an articled pupil. Awarded the Lambeth D.Mus. in 1853.

Succeeded John Charles Beckwith as organist and master of the choristers of Norwich Cathedral in 1819, remaining at Norwich until his retirement in 1877. He was famous, even notorious, as a choirmaster of uncompromising standards and unusual methods. He devised the probationer system for new choristers. Boys producing a spectacular 'shake' (vibrato) were rewarded with half a crown.

An organ teacher, many of his pupils subsequently pursuing successful careers. Two of these became cathedral organists: (Ely Cathedral 1831-1866) and (King's College, Cambridge 1876-1929). His pupils included **Frederic Atkinson, William Bexfield, George Gaffe, Alfred Gaul, Robert Janes** and **A.H. Mann**.

Composed six anthems, including 'I heard a voice from Heaven' and 'Come hither, angel tongues invite', five hymn tunes, 23 chants (of which 12 were published in 1824), an Evening Service in A, and a Sanctus and set of Responses in G.

BUCKLAND, Henry B. (c1825-1867)

Born in 1825 or 1826; died in London on 13 August 1867.

A tenor vicar choral, and master of the boys of St. Paul's Cathedral (from 1858). Also sang at concerts. Conducted the annual Festival of the Charity Children (1863-1867). Composed the anthems 'Keep, we beseech Thee' and 'Teach me O Lord'.

BUCKNALL, Cedric (1849-1921)

Born in Bath, Somerset in 1849; died in Bedminster, Gloucestershire on 12 December 1921. A pupil of **W.H. Monk**; his assistant from 1868 onwards. Graduated B.Mus. at Keble College, Oxford (1878). Organist of St. Thomas's Church, Clapton, London (from 1870). Organist of Southwell Minster (1872-1876) and of All Saints' Church, Clifton (from 1876). Lecturer in harmony and composition at the University of Bristol. Three hymn tunes, 'Communio', 'Compassio' and 'Gloria', were used in the Standard Edition (1916) of *Hymns Ancient and Modern*. Composed carols and part songs, and edited hymns and tunes for use in schools.

BUFFEY, Dr. Thomas Goodburn (1859-?)

Born in Hull, Yorkshire in 1859.

Graduated B.Mus. (1891) and D.Mus. (1904) at the University of Durham.

Organist and choirmaster of the Hull Churches of St. Mark (from 1878) and St. Matthew (from 1889), and choirmaster to St. Silas's Church (from 1886). Organist to the Hull Board of Guardians (from 1898).

Teacher of violin and harmony at Hull and East Riding College of Music and at Hull High School for Girls, and teacher of violin and singing at Ellerslie House School.

Composed anthems, items for piano and violin, and part songs.

BULL, Dr. Arthur James (1901-?)

Born in Hull, Yorkshire in 1901. Educated privately, and at Pocklington School. An articled pupil at Newcastle Cathedral. Attended the Royal College of Music. Organist of St. John's Church, Newcastle-on-Tyne (1923-1924), and St. Andrew's Church, Stockwell, London (1925-1926). Music master of Judd School, Tonbridge, Kent (1926-1927); Bloxham School (1927-1929); and of the Grammar School and High School, Richmond, Yorkshire (1929-1947). During the latter period he was organist of Richmond Parish Church. Music organiser to the North Riding (of Yorkshire) Education Committee (from 1947).

Composed church music, including services and anthems.

BULL, Dr. John (1562-1628)

Born, possibly at Old Radnor, in 1562; died in Antwerp, Belgium on 12 March 1628.

A chorister of the Chapel Royal at the time of Elizabeth I. A pupil of **John Blitheman**. Graduated B.Mus. (1586) and D.Mus. (1592) at the University of Oxford, and Mus.D. at the University of Cambridge (1589).

Remembered as a composer but to his contemporaries, he was best known as a keyboard performer.

Organist of Hereford Cathedral, at first (from December 1582) jointly with John Hodges. From January 1583 he was master of the choristers but relations between him and the authorities deteriorated, with Bull being first suspended then dismissed from this position in June 1585.

Joined the Chapel Royal in January 1586; organist (from 1592) in succession to **John Blitheman**.

The first Gresham professor of music (1597-1607), an appointment he was forced to resign on his marriage. An ordinance was passed, allowing him to deliver the annual lecture in English. In 1601 he won permission to appoint a deputy, Thomas Bird, and, for the sake of his health, travel on the continent. While abroad, he was among a group of people challenged to add a further part to a 40-part piece of music. When Bull added a further 40 parts, his challenger declared that he had encountered either the devil or John Bull.

Musician to Prince Henry (from 1611) but fled the country in 1613 amid allegations of adultery.

Settled in Brussels as one of the three organists of the Royal Chapel (1613-1614), and then in Antwerp, where he was cathedral organist (1617-1628). He was a friend, and musical influence upon Sweelinck, and he was organist to the Archduke of Austria.

Composed for the virginal. Wrote anthems for voices and viols, including nine verse anthems, five full anthems, and more than 12 devotional songs. He is particularly associated with the Epiphany anthem 'Almighty God, who by the leading of a star'.

BULLARD, Alan (b.1947)

Born in London on 4 August 1947.

Attended St. Olave's Grammar School, London (1958-1965), the Royal College of Music (1965-1968), where he was taught and influenced by **Herbert Howells**, and the University of Nottingham (1968-1969). Holds London B.Mus. and Nottingham M.A. in analysis of contemporary music.

After a number of lectureships at establishments including the London College of Music (1970-1975) and a freelance editorship with Oxford University Press (1970-1978), Alan Bullard was appointed senior lecturer in the Department of Music of the Colchester Institute, a regional college of Anglia Polytechnic University (1981). His responsibilities include teaching composition (of which he is head of department) and 20th-century music.

In 1991 he adjudicated at the Colchester Music Festival.

Has contributed to a number of music journals including *Choir and Organ*, for which he regularly reviews choral and sacred works. His writings have also appeared in daily newspapers and in the *Times Educational Supplement*.

Has won a number of prizes for composition, including the Llangollen International Eisteddfod Composer's Competition (1979) and the Harold Smart Memorial Prize (1994) for his 'Come, let us join our cheerful songs'. His 'Alleluia' was recently performed in Reims Cathedral. Other recent works include the anthem 'Come, Holy Ghost, our souls inspire' (1994). Has also composed a number of instrumental works.

BULLINGER, Revd. Dr. Ethelbert William (1837-1913)

Born in Kent on 15 December 1837; died in Hendon, London on 6 June 1913. A chorister of Canterbury Cathedral and a scholar of Greek and Hebrew. Awarded the Lambeth D.D. in 1881. Composed a hymn 'Jesu, Refuge of the weary' (1874) and hymn tunes.

BULLIS, Thomas (1627-1708)

Born in Ely, Cambridgeshire and baptised on 26 August 1627; died in Ely, being buried on 23 January 1708. Father of the younger **Thomas Bullis**. Probably a chorister of Ely Cathedral under **John Amner** and Robert Claxton. A lay clerk (from 1661) under **John Ferrabosco** and the first **James Hawkins**. At times he acted as choirmaster and organist. In addition he was bailiff of the manor of Ely Porta, a possession of the Dean and Chapter, and churchwarden of Holy Trinity, Ely. He also carried on the family business of cordwaining. Composed anthems including 'Holy, holy, holy' and 'O clap your hands', and a Service in G.

BULLIS, Thomas (1657-1712)

Born in Ely, Cambridgeshire and baptised on 8 November 1657; died in Ely and buried on 24 August 1712.

The third child of the elder **Thomas Bullis**. A chorister and lay clerk under **John Ferrabosco** and subsequently under **James Hawkins**. Served as organist for six months when, in 1682, Ferrabosco died. Like his father, he was a churchwarden of Holy Trinity Church, Ely. Composed three services and seven anthems including 'Blessed is the man' and 'I will magnify'.

BULLIVANT, Gerald (1883-1937)

Born in West Ham, London in 1883; died in Kent in 1937.

Deputy to **Walford Davies** at the Temple Church, London, and organist of the London Churches of St. Mary-le-Bow; Christ Church, Woburn Square (from 1904) and St. James, Piccadilly. Choirmaster of Westminster Abbey School.

Composed a Te Deum in E-flat and an anthem 'Grant us Thy Peace' (1919). His hymn tune 'Bow Church' was included in the 1916 Supplement to *Hymns Ancient and Modern* with the German hymn 'Jesus still lead on'.

BULLOCK, Sir Ernest (1890-1979)

Born in Wigan, Lancashire on 15 September 1890; died near Aylesbury, Buckinghamshire on 23 May 1979.

Educated at Wigan Grammar School. Graduated B.Mus. (1908) and D.Mus. (1914) at the University of Durham. Accorded an honorary LL.D. (1955) at the University of Glasgow.

Appointed C.V.O. in 1937; knighted in 1951.

Deputy organist to **Edward Bairstow**, by whom he was greatly influenced, at Leeds Parish Church (1908-1912). Organist of St. Mary's Church, Micklefield (from 1908) and of Adel Church (1910-1912); sub organist of Manchester Cathedral under **Sydney Nicholson** (1912-1915); captain and adjutant in H.M. Forces in France (1915-1919); organist at St. Michael's College, Tenbury, Worcestershire (1919) and Exeter Cathedral (1919-1927). Organist and master of the choristers of Westminster Abbey (1928-1941) in succession to Sydney Nicholson. His home, property and papers were destroyed during a bombing raid in 1940.

Held the two teaching positions in Scotland of principal of the Scottish Academy of Music (now designated 'Royal') and Gardiner professor of music at the University of Glasgow (1941-1952) concurrently. He then succeeded **George Dyson** as director of the Royal College of Music (1953-1960).

Joint director of music at the Coronation of George VI in 1937, a collaborative effort on the part of the leading musicians of the day which resulted in what was said to be the finest music ever heard in the Abbey. Some of the fanfares were composed for the occasion by Ernest Bullock.

His most public compositions were the fanfares that he wrote for the Coronations of 1937 and 1953, and the anthem composed for the wedding of the Duke and Duchess of Kent. Most of his output was for the church. This includes some 12 anthems, two of the best known of which are 'Give us the wings of faith' and 'O most merciful', two Te Deum settings and two of the Magnificat.

His early compositions show the influence of **C.V. Stanford** and **Hubert Parry**, but his work acquired a certain bleakness later in his career. His motet *Wherefore, O Father* is still popular. Composed Evening Services in C, in D and in G Minor.

BULLOCK, William Henry (19th/20th century)
Attended the Royal College of Music; graduated B.Mus. at the University of Durham (1904).
A bass lay vicar of Westminster Abbey (from 1908).
Organist and choirmaster of St. Andrew's Church, Halstead, Essex (from 1903). He taught singing and piano at Colchester School of Music, and taught music at Earl's Colne Grammar School. Conductor of local choral societies.
Composed a cantata for Lent *The Saviour of the World,* an Evening Service in F and a Magnificat and Nunc Dimittis in E-flat.

BULMAN (Bullman), Baruch (Barick) (17th century)
Baruch (or Barick) Bulman was a lute composer and church musician of the 17th century, who probably wrote the anthems 'Lord, Thou hast commanded' and 'I beseech Thee to give me grace'.

BULMER, Revd. John (19th/20th century)
Graduated B.D. at the University of Durham (1871) and B.Mus. at the University of Dublin (1880). Composed a sacred cantata *The Dial of Ahaz,* an anthem 'The prayer of Jonah', songs, part songs, hymns and chants.

BUNNETT, Dr. Edward (1834-1923)
Born in Shipdham, near Norwich, Norfolk on 26 June 1834; died in Norwich on 5 January 1923.
A chorister of Norwich Cathedral, being articled to **Zechariah Buck**, cathedral organist, from 1849. Graduated Mus.B. (1857) and Mus.D. (1869) at Corpus Christi College, Cambridge. As a chorister he once sang with Jenny Lind, the 'Swedish Nightingale', and Miss Dolby in a performance of Mendelssohn's *Lift Thine Eyes.*
Assistant organist of Norwich Cathedral (1855-1877) under Buck. From the latter year he was organist of the Norwich Church of St. Peter, Mancroft. From 1880 to 1908 he was borough organist of Norwich and from 1908 until 1919 he was nave service organist of Norwich Cathedral.
Composed a Magnificat and Nunc Dimittis in F (1867). His anthems include 'Blessed be Thou' and 'Out of the deep' (1880), the latter based on Psalm 130. He also composed 24 hymn tunes including 'Agnes' and 'Montrose', 10 Christmas carols, cantatas, part songs and pieces for organ.

BUNNEY, Dr. Allan Walter (b.1905)
Born in Leicester in 1905. Attended Wyggeston Grammar School, Leicester and the Royal College of Music. Graduated D.Mus. at the University of London. Organist and choirmaster of Christ Church, Hampstead, London (1927-1939). His teaching appointments included that of music master of Owen's Boys' School, Islington, London and of Westminster City School. Director of music at Tonbridge School (1941-1967). A local philharmonic society conductor and, from 1948, an external examiner for the Royal College of Music. A special commissioner of the Royal School of Church Music.
Composed the hymn tune 'Hillside' to the words 'Stand up and bless the Lord'.

BURDER, George (1752-1832)
Born in London on 5 June 1752; died in St. Pancras, London, on 29 May 1832.
An engraver. After following the Methodist preacher George Whitefield for some time, he became minister and pastor of a Congregational church in Lancashire. He visited other towns in the north west and he became well known in that area.
His services were often interrupted and in Preston he had to contend with a theatre downstairs in the same building. On one occasion, Romeo in full dress burst in and demanded that the service stop.
Moved to Coventry, Warwickshire, where he established the city's first Sunday School (1785), and where one of the first pupils was **John Eagleton**, later himself to be a preacher and church music composer.
For the last 30 years of his life he lived in London. He was active in founding the Religious Tract Society and the British and Foreign Bible Society. Secretary of the London Missionary Society.
Issued a collection of hymns that was often used by non-conformists.
Composed hymn tunes including 'Luton', also known as 'Newhaven'.

BURGHERSH, Lord
See **WESTMORLAND**, Earl of.

BURGON, Geoffrey Alan (b.1941)
Born in Hambledon, Hampshire on 15 July 1941.
Attended Pewley School, Guildford, Surrey. Taught himself to play jazz trumpet at the age of 15 and it was through jazz that he was to become involved in church music. Attended Guildhall School of Music, London where his tutors were **Lennox Berkeley** and **Peter Wishart**. Studied harmony and counterpoint privately with Peter Wishart and trumpet under Bernard Brown.
A freelance trumpeter, often playing at the Royal Opera House, Covent Garden.
Has composed for radio and television, including the programmes 'The life of Brian' and 'Tinker, tailor, soldier, spy'. His works include *This World From* to a 16th century text for the 1980 Chichester Festival, the anthem 'At the round earth's imagined corners' (1971), a Magnificat and Nunc Dimittis (1979) based on a television theme tune, and a Short Mass.

BURNEY, Dr. Charles (1726-1814)
Born in Shrewsbury, Shropshire on 7 April 1726; died in Chelsea, London on 12 April 1814. He was born Macburney, but discarded the prefix.
Attended the Free School, Shrewsbury and Chester School. Studied music under Edmund Baker, organist of Chester Cathedral and in London from 1744 to 1747 under **Thomas Arne**. Graduated B.Mus. and D.Mus. at the University of Oxford, both in 1769.
Organist of the Church of St. Dionis, Backchurch, London (1749-1751); Lynn Regis Parish Church, Norfolk (1751-1760); Oxford Chapel (from May 1768) and Chelsea Hospital, London (from 1783).
Known as a minor composer, astronomer, poet, and connoisseur of painting. A well-educated man, known for his genial companionship, his friends included Johnson, Garrick, Reynolds, Burke and others. A Fellow of the Royal Society.
Haydn is known to have spent much time with Burney during his visits to London between the years 1791 and 1805.

Burney published his authoritative *History of Music* in four volumes. Once critical of J.S. Bach, he recanted his criticism later in life.

His anthem 'I will love Thee, O Lord my strength', based on the text of Psalm 18, was submitted as his D.Mus exercise. Also composed organ voluntaries.

BURROWES, John Freckleton (1787-1852)
Born in London on 23 April 1787; died in London on 31 March 1852.

A pupil of **William Horsley**, the London organist.

Lived in London for nearly 40 years and was organist at the Church of St. James, Westminster. One of the founders of the Philharmonic Society.

Composed an overture that was used as the concluding item at the concerts of the Philharmonic Society, and piano works. His Single Chant in E was included in *Cathedral Psalter Chants* (1875). The author of the two widely-used textbooks *Pianoforte Primer* (1818) and *Thorough-Bass Primer* (1819).

BURROWS, Dr. Benjamin (1891-1966)
Born in Leicester on 20 October 1891; died in Leicester on 29 January 1966.

Educated at Alderman Newton Boys' School but due to the weakening of an eye muscle he had to be withdrawn and taught privately. His instruction in music was from H.B. Ellis, organist and choirmaster of the church of St. Mary de Castro, Leicester. With the guidance of **C.H. Kitson**, he graduated B.Mus. (1913) and D.Mus. (1921) at the University of London.

His father was a teacher of music, principally violin; his mother was a pianist.

Had a varied musical career as an organist, choirmaster, lecturer at the University of Leicester, postal tutor, and composer. From 1910 he was organist and choirmaster of St. Mary's Church, Leicester.

He developed a process for typing music but the Imperial Typewriter Co. of Leicester, for whom it was devised, later adopted a rival system. From 1939 he worked in a factory where flanges were made for tanks. Later he worked at Gents of Leicester, a firm specialising in ships' chronometers. He invented an adjustable spirit level for installing machinery.

Ran a small publishing company, Bodnant Press, which brought out five or six items per month by subscription. Leicester City Reference Library became a subscriber in 1942.

His teaching career, which began in 1914, was interrupted by war service. From 1917 he served in the Kite Balloon section of the army, having joined up as a private. He was stationed at Orford Ness, Suffolk.

Resumed music teaching in Leicester on being demobilised. Resigned in 1923. Temporary organist of Leicester Cathedral in 1929 following the departure of **Gordon Slater** to Lincoln Cathedral. Organist of Victoria Road Baptist Church, Leicester (1929-1956), succeeding Victor Thomas and followed by Harry Shaw.

Taught at University College, Leicester, where his sister Grace was also on the teaching staff (from 1924). The lecturer in charge of music was **Markham Lee**. Also a tutor by correspondence. His ability as a teacher is demonstrated by the successes gained by his pupils: 56 graduated B.Mus. and 24 D.Mus, while 104 attained F.R.C.O.

Continuo player for the Leicester Bach Choir, for whom he was organist (1935-1940). A talented watercolourist of miniatures.

His compositions were published from 1915 onwards. On one occasion the organist **Alfred Hollins** heard his *Four Lyrics* and included it in his recital that same evening. From 1930 he composed many sacred works.

His music includes works for organ and for piano, five Psalms for chorus and orchestra, and other church music including the anthems 'Out of the deep' and 'Blest are they'. His songs include 'Come ye by?'.

BURSTALL, Frederick Hampton (1851-1916)
Born in Liverpool on 29 January 1851; died in Liverpool on 2 August 1916. Studied under Dr. Röhner. Went into business as a young man, before working full-time in music. Organist of Childwall Parish Church (from 1870) and Wallasey Church (1876-1883). When Liverpool Cathedral was created in 1880, Burstall became the first organist and choirmaster. Well known as an organ recitalist. Composed a Festival Te Deum, anthems, motets, hymn tunes, an Anniversary Ode for the Liverpool Pageant of 1907, songs and piano music.

BURTON, Avery (c1470-1542 or 1547)
A gentleman of the Chapel Royal from around 1509 to 1542. He is known to have composed, at least, a Mass.

BURTON, Claud Peter Primrose (1916-1957)
Born in Shere, Surrey in 1916; died, following a swimming accident, at Hemel Hempstead, Hertfordshire on 6 July 1957.

Attended St. John's College, Oxford (1935-1939). Studied music with **W.H. Harris**. Graduated B.A., B.Mus. and, in 1943, M.A., his studies having been interrupted by army service during World War II.

Organist and master of the choristers of St. Paul's Church, King's Cross, Halifax, Yorkshire (1939-1940), and of St. Mary's Collegiate Church, Warwick and of Warwick School (1946-1950). He then held similar positions at St. Albans Cathedral (1950-1957), concurrently holding the position of music master at St. Albans School, for which he composed the hymn tune to 'Alban, high in glory shining'. His 'Warwick School' was used in *Public School Hymn Book* with 'Onward, Christian soldiers'.

His compositions include a Simple Communion Service in F (1959), a Magnificat and Nunc Dimittis in G Minor, and organ works.

BUSBY, Dr. Thomas (1754-1838)
Born in Westminster, London on 26 December 1754; died in Islington, London on 28 May 1838.

Articled to **Jonathan Battishill** (1769-1774). Graduated Mus.D. (1800) and LL.D. at the University of Cambridge.

Organist of the Church of St. Mary, Newington Butts, Surrey (from 1784) and of St. Mary Woolnoth, Lombard Street, London (1798-1829).

Author of books on musical topics, including *A Musical Manual, or technical directory* (1828). Composed an oratorio *The Prophecy,* and anthems including a work written for the funeral of Jonathan Battishill. An example is 'O God, Thou art merciful'.

BUSH, Dr. Geoffrey (b.1920)
Born in London on 23 March 1920.

Attended Salisbury Cathedral School, Wiltshire (1928-1933); Lancing College, Sussex (1933-1938) and, as Nettleship Scholar and Masefield Memorial Student, Balliol College, Oxford (1938-

1940 and 1945-1946) where he graduated M.A. in classics, and D.Mus. (1946).

Staff lecturer (1947-1952) at the University of Oxford, staff tutor (1952-1964) and senior tutor (1964-1980) at the University of London. Visiting professor in music at King's College, London (from 1969).

He has researched British music of the 19th century, especially that of **Sterndale Bennett**, **C.V. Stanford** and **Hubert Parry**, and been musical adviser to the John Ireland Trust since 1969. Succeeded **John Ireland** as organist of St. Luke's Church, Chelsea, London.

Composed operas, two symphonies, three overtures, operas, songs, and chamber music. His anthems include 'Praise the Lord, O my soul', 'O love how deep, how broad' and 'O loving Saviour'. An Evening Service was composed in 1976.

BUSSELL, Revd. Dr. Frederick William (1862-1944)
Born in Cadmore End, Oxfordshire to a Devonshire family on 23 April 1862; died in 1944. His early musical education was private. Attended Charterhouse (1876-1881) and Magdalen College, Oxford where he graduated B.A. (1885), M.A. (1889), B.Mus. (1891), B.D. (1892) and D.D. (1897). Ordained deacon in 1891 and priest a year later. A fellow, tutor, junior dean and chaplain of Brasenose College, Oxford. His church career encompassed the rectorships of Shelland, Suffolk; Baddesley-Clinton, Warwickshire and Sizeland, Norfolk. Composed a Magnificat for Five Voices in Latin and a Mass in G Minor. With **Sabine Baring-Gould** he arranged and published a collection of music *English Minstrelsy*. Author of *The School of Plato* (1892).

BUSWELL, Dr. John (18th century)
Graduated Mus.B. at the University of Cambridge (1757) and D.Mus. at the University of Oxford (1759). A gentleman of the Chapel Royal. Composed the anthems 'Lord, how are they increased' and 'The souls of the righteous'. Also composed songs.

BUTCHER, Frank Charles (19th/20th century)
A chorister of Canterbury Cathedral. Graduated B.Mus. at the University of Durham (1909). Assistant organist of Canterbury Cathedral (1899-1902), organist and music master of St. Columba's College, Rathfarnham, Dublin (1902) and organist and choirmaster of Birchington Parish Church, Kent (1903-1907). He then emigrated to the U.S.A. where he was organist and taught music at Hoosack School, New York. Organist and choirmaster of St. Stephen's Church, Pittfield, Massachusetts, (from 1916). Composed Communion services, anthems, part songs, songs and works for piano and for organ.

BUTLER, James Theobald Bagot (1852-1929)
Born in Kilkenny, Ireland on 24 August 1852; died in Bournemouth, Dorset on 16 June 1929. Composed hymn tunes, a collection of which, *Original Hymn Tunes*, was published in 1900.

BUTLER, Martin (b.1960)
Born in Romsey, Hampshire on 1 March 1960.
Attended Winchester School of Art (1976-1978), the University of Manchester (1978-1981), where he graduated B.Mus., and the Royal Northern College of Music (1978-1982).
In 1983 he was awarded a Fulbright Scholarship to study in the U.S.A. at Princeton University, New Jersey. In 1985 he graduated Master of Fine Arts. Remained at Princeton until 1987.

Returning to England, Martin Butler was appointed a lecturer at the University of Sussex. A year later he received a Mendelssohn Scholarship to study at an electronic music workshop in Florence. Composed a Christmas carol 'To see the beauties of the earth' (1987) to words by Charles Butler. His other works include orchestral and chamber music, and a Sonata for Piano (1982).

BUTLIN, Cyril Walter (1886-?)
Born in Rothwell, Northamptonshire in 1886. Educated privately with A.H. Essam, **Cuthbert Harris**, **Henry Middleton** and **Charles Wood**. Organist and choirmaster of Fuller Baptist Church, Kettering, Northamptonshire. A lecturer with the Workers' Educational Association. Composed hymn tunes and other items of church music.

BUTTLE (Prins-Buttle), Ida Mary (b.1908)
Born in Hoxton, London on 17 February 1908. Wrote a number of hymns, together with tunes and composed the anthem 'Emmanuel' (1975).

BUTTON, Henry Elliot (1861-1925)
Born in Clevedon, Somerset on 8 August 1861; died in Hampstead, London on 1 August 1925.
The son of Eustace Button, organist of Clevedon Congregational Church and a Justice of the Peace.
The family was able to function as both a string and a vocal quartet. Elliot, who was said to be able to sing from a tonic Sol-fa score before he could read, played piano, organ and violin. He sang alto at Holy Trinity Church, Upper Chelsea, London.
Studied harmony with Windeyer Clark, who served **George Macfarren** as amanuensis, a responsibility that the two subsequently shared.
Known for his immense knowledge of hymn tunes. He edited three editions of *Bristol Tune Book* and he transcribed some madrigals which are now lodged with the British Library.
For 40 years, Elliot Button worked in the publishing department of the firm of Novello where his duties included proof reading and revising. His other jobs included teaching at a school in Hastings, Sussex and a position in research and development with the Globe Telephone Company. He was also in business in Bristol. Choirmaster of the church of St. Mary Abbott, Kensington, London.
Author of *System of Musical Notation* (1920).
Composed anthems, chants, songs for children and organ works. *Church Hymnary* in its Revised Edition (1927) uses his 'Child Service' with 'O what can little hands do?'. The tune was originally sung at a Sunday School festival in 1886. 'Wilton' is another of his tunes.

BYERS, David (b.1947)
Born in Belfast in 1947.
Studied composition with Raymond Warren, who taught at Queen's University, Belfast. From 1968 he studied composition with James Iliff at the Royal Academy of Music under a Henry Manson Scholarship. In 1972 he received a Macauley Fellowship from the Irish Arts Council, enabling him to study further in Liège with Henri Pousseur.
Has composed in many forms. His church music includes a Magnificat (1985) and a partita 'Jesu, meine Freude'. His *Planxty For The Dancer* (1983) was commissioned by Belfast City Council.

BYRCHELEY (Byrchley), John (16th century)
A school master at the monastery in Chester which, at the Reformation, gave rise to the cathedral, of which he became organist (1541-1550). He is presumed to be the John Byrchley whose works are held in manuscript in the Baldwin collection in Buckingham Palace.

BYRD, Thomas (?-1561)
Composer and gentleman of the Chapel Royal. He may have been the father of **William Byrd**, and he may have been a chorister of the Chapel Royal.

BYRD, William (1542/3-1623)
Born probably at Lincoln in 1542 or 1543 and died in Stondon Massey, Essex, on 4 July 1623.
It is probably true that he was born in Lincoln, where he took up his first appointment at the age of 19 or 20. But the fact that he studied under **Thomas Tallis** in London may indicate that he was born further South.
Organist of Lincoln Cathedral (1563-1572) and joint organist of the Chapel Royal of Elizabeth I with Tallis from, at the latest, 1575. In 1570 he became a gentleman of the Chapel Royal, succeeding the unfortunate **Robert Parsons** who had drowned in the River Trent at Newark. His pupils included **Thomas Morley and Thomas Tomkins**, and, possibly, **Peter Philips**, **John Bull** and **Thomas Weelkes**.
The dedicatees of his works were powerful figures, from which it can be concluded that he was well-connected. His patrons included the Earl of Worcester and the Petre family. Some of his poem settings could only have resulted from direct contact with the poets themselves.
His *Psalmes, Sonets and Songs* (1588) is only the third known book of English songs. *Cantiones sacrae* was published in two volumes. The first, in 1589, was for five voices and the second was for five and six.
Byrd was involved in protracted legal tussles, lasting for many years, over the title to various pieces of land.
A practising Roman Catholic, living with his family at Harlington (1572-1592) and listed as a recusant. They suffered from the religious intolerance of the time: his wife was charged with seeking converts to the Catholic cause, and the family was excommunicated for seven years. Moved to Stondon Massey in 1593, where there was a Catholic community in which the Petre family was prominent, with clandestine Masses being celebrated at Ingatestone Hall. Showing no little courage, he published three Mass settings, separately, between and around the years 1593-1599. His music for the Catholic church was brought back into use by **Richard Terry** of Westminster Cathedral between 1901 and 1924, following years of neglect.
Enjoyed a monopoly with Tallis from 1575 onwards over the printing of music and paper ruled for music. The patent lapsed in 1596 and passed to Morley, as a result of which more material appeared on the market.
Byrd was a prolific and versatile composer. He had begun to write church music while still in his teens. He composed music for the keyboard and viol, as well as songs and consort music for use outside the church. He published five collections of motets in the years 1585 (jointly with Tallis), 1589, 1591, 1605 and 1607. Commencing in the 1580s he produced a series of pavans and galliards for keyboard.

Interest in his music for the Anglican Church revived in the 1880s and 1890s. Works that are familiar today include a Short Service; the Fauxbourdon, Second and Third Services; the Great Service; the anthems 'Civitas, sancti tui', 'Prevent us, O Lord', 'Teach me, O Lord', 'Haec Dies' and 'Justorum animae'; a set of Preces and Responses and a Litany.
E.H. Fellowes undertook a complete edition of Byrd's works between 1937 and 1950. It was undoubtedly advantageous to have all Byrd's works available in a single edition but the editorship has been described as 'unsophisticated', and a number of editors since 1962 have attempted to improve upon the result.

BYRNE, Nora C.E.
See **BONNER**, Carey.

BYTERRING, ? (14th/15th century)
The composer Byterring lived in the late 14th and early 15th centuries.
May have been in the Chapel Royal of Henry V. Composed the motet *En Katerine,* plus other motets and canons. Some Italian collections of music feature his work.

C

CADMAN, Reginald Mandeville (1878-?)
Born in Malton, Yorkshire in 1878. Studied at the Royal Academy of Music and at Worcester College, Oxford where he graduated B.A. (1902), M.A. (1908) and B.Mus. (1911). Organist, choirmaster and a teacher at the Imperial Services College (St. Mark's School), Windsor, Berkshire (1895-1898). His other recorded appointments are organist and teacher of Fontmill Preparatory School, East Grinstead, Sussex (1903-1907) and organist and director of music at Trent College, Derbyshire (from 1908). Composer of church music including a Te Deum in F (1906) and the anthem 'I will love Thee' (1897) and part songs.

CAESAR, Revd. Anthony Douglass (20th century)
Born in Southampton, Hampshire.
Appointed L.V.O. (1987) and C.V.O. (1991).
A chorister of Winchester Cathedral. Educated at Cranleigh School and, as music scholar, at Magdalene College, Cambridge where he graduated B.A. and Mus.B. (1947) and M.A. (1949). Trained for the ministry of the Church of England at St. Stephen's House, Oxford (from 1959). Ordained deacon in 1961, priest in 1962.
Served in the R.A.F. (1943-1946).
Assistant music master at Eton College (from 1948) and organist of Windsor Parish Church from the same year. Precentor of Radley College, Oxfordshire (1952-1959).
His church appointments include that of chaplain to the Royal School of Church Music, Addington, Surrey (1965-1970); curate of St. Peter's Church, Bournemouth, Dorset (1970-1973); precentor and sacrist (1974-1979), residentiary canon (1976 -1979) and honorary canon (1975-1976; 1979-1991) of Winchester Cathedral; sub dean of the Chapels Royal, St. James's Palace (1979-1991).
His published works include anthems, a Missa Brevis, part songs and a Piano Duet. He is a co-editor of *New English Hymnal*.

CALAH, John (1758/9-1798/9)
Born in 1758 or 1759; died in Peterborough, Cambridgeshire on 4 August 1798 or on the same date the following year.
A John Calah or Calab was a chorister of Southwell Minster from 1769; no firm evidence supports or refutes the suggestion that this person is the same.

Organist of Peterborough Cathedral (1785-1798), prior to which he had been organist of the Parish Church, Newark on Trent, Nottinghamshire (from 1782) and master of the Magnus Song School. At Peterborough he complained bitterly about the poor condition of the cathedral organ, the keys of which he likened to a set of ivory spoons.
Composer of services, the anthem 'Behold how good and joyful', a Kyrie in D, hymns, a double chant and items for piano.

CALDBECK, George Thomas (1852-1918)
Born in Waterford, Ireland in 1852; died in Epsom, Surrey on 29 January 1918.
Educated at the National Model School, Waterford. Travelled to London in 1873 and later attended Islington Theological College. He had intended to become a missionary but this was not possible due to his poor health. Instead, he returned to Cork and followed a career as a school teacher.
Came back to London in 1888. He was not able to find a place within the church establishment and he became an independent itinerant preacher. Arrested in 1912 for selling scripture cards from door to door without a licence. At the time he was living in a Church Army hostel in Edgware Road. The magistrate dismissed the charge on learning that Caldbeck was the composer of the hymn tune 'Pax tecum'.
This tune was harmonised by **Charles Vincent** and used with the hymn 'Peace, perfect peace'. It has been used in a number of modern hymnals.

CALDICOTT, Alfred James (1842-1897)
Born in Worcester on 26 November 1842; died in Gloucester on 24 October 1897.
Alfred and his seven brothers were choristers of Worcester Cathedral. On 29 September 1856 he was one of the trebles, including **Arthur Sullivan** who augmented the choir of St. Michael's College, Tenbury, Worcestershire at its consecration.
At the age of 14 he was articled to **William Done**, Worcester Cathedral organist. Studied at the Leipzig Conservatory under Ignaz Moscheles, Moritz Hauptmann and Ernst Richter. Later in life (1878) he graduated Mus.B. at the University of Cambridge.
In 1864 he settled in Worcester, where he became organist of St. Stephen's Church and of Worcester Corporation. His prominence

in the musical life of the city of Worcester brought him into contact with the young **Edward Elgar** who was beginning his career as a composer. In 1881 he conducted the first performance of Elgar's *Air de ballet*.

After a year or so living in Torquay, Devon, in 1883 he moved to London and he was subsequently a professor of harmony at the Royal College of Music. Director of music at the Albert Palace, Battersea (1885) and principal of the Education Department of the London College of Music (1892).

Composer of the anthems 'Behold, how good and joyful' and 'He is risen'; operettas including *Treasure Trove* (1883); songs and part songs.

CALKIN, Jean-Baptiste (1827-1905)
Born in London on 16 March 1827; died in Hornsey, London on 15 April 1905. His family was musical: his brother, George, his father, James, and his uncle, Joseph, were accomplished musicians.

Following early musical tuition from his father, Calkin held an organistship in Ireland at St. Columba's College (1846-1853). Until 1849, when it moved to Rathfarnham, the school was at Navan. His successor was **E.G. Monk.**

Was then organist of Woburn Chapel, London (1853-1857); Camden Road Chapel (1863-1868) and St. Thomas's, Camden Town (1870-1884). A teacher and composer, he became a professor of Trinity College of Music and of Guildhall School of Music (from 1883).

Composer of services including a Service in B-flat, a Morning and Evening Service in E-flat and a Holy Communion Service in C, anthems such as 'Behold, now praise the Lord', a hymn tune 'St. John the Baptist', a carol 'Let music break on this blest morn', solo songs and music for piano and organ.

Arthur Sullivan used two of Calkin's tunes in *Church Hymns* (1874): 'Bonar' to the hymn by **Robert Brown-Borthwick** 'Come O Jesu to Thy table' and 'Ramoth' with 'Lord, to Thee alone we turn' by Albert Evans. The Revised Edition (1927) of *Church Hymnary* employs 'Nox praecessit' and 'St. Joseph'.

CALLCOTT, John George (1821-1895)
Born in London on 9 July 1821; died in Teddington, Middlesex on 7 January 1895. Organist of the Eaton Episcopal Chapel, Eaton Square; St. Stephen's Church, Westminster - an appointment which he held for more than 30 years before resigning in 1881 - and of Teddington Parish Church (until 1895). Accompanied **Henry Leslie**'s Choir on the piano and pursued a career as a pianist and teacher. Composer of part songs.

CALLCOTT, Dr. John Wall (1766-1821)
Born in Kensington, London on 20 November 1766; died near Bristol, Gloucestershire on 15 May 1821 and was buried eight days later in Kensington. His son was **William Hutchins Callcott**, and a later descendant was the composer Norman O'Neill.

His early schooling was at an institution run by a William Young, which he attended for five years from the age of seven. He learned to play clarinet and oboe. He later studied anatomy but, on being present at an operation, discovered that he was unsuited to the medical profession. In July 1785 he graduated B.Mus. at the University of Oxford. The Oxford D.Mus. followed in 1800, following the submission of his anthem 'Propter Sion non tacebo'.

He had been able to spend time in the organ loft of Kensington Parish Church observing the organist, Henry Whitney. By attending the services at the Chapel Royal, he became acquainted with **Samuel Arnold** - with whom he later collaborated - **Benjamin Cooke** and John Sale the elder. In 1791, during the visit of Haydn to England, Callcott took lessons with him. John Wall Callcott sometimes played oboe in the Academy of Ancient Music (from 1782). He sang in the chorus of the Drury Lane Theatre for the performance of certain oratorios (1783-1785).

Deputy organist to Charles Reinhold at the church of St. George the Martyr, Bloomsbury (1783-1785) and he was joint organist with **Charles Evans** of the Church of St. Paul, Covent Garden (from 1788).

Another organistship was that of the Asylum for Female Orphans (1793-1802). One unsuccessful change that he brought about was the replacement of congregational hymn singing, which was generally good, by solo singing, which was not always successful.

One of the founders of the Glee Club (1787). Succeeded **William Crotch** as lecturer in music at the Royal Institution (1806). He spent the years from 1807 to 1812 in a mental institution following health problems which were said to be through working too hard on a dictionary of musicians. His condition appeared to have improved but from 1816 deterioration took hold and he never fully recovered.

He began to compose glees from around 1784 and became very successful. He also composed sacred trios, odes, anthems including 'And I heard a voice from Heaven' and 'If the Lord Himself', hymns and services. Some of this material was composed for use in the chapel of the Asylum for Female Orphans.

A *Musical Grammar* compiled by him and published in 1806 was very successful, continuing in use as a standard work for a long time after his death.

CALLCOTT, William Hutchins (1807-1882)
Born in Kensington, London on 28 September 1807; died in Kensington on 4 August 1882.

Learned music from his father **John Wall Callcott** and from his brother in law, **William Horsley**.

Organist of the Ely Place Chapel, London and of St. Barnabas's Church, Kensington. He followed a career as a teacher. In 1836 he abridged and re-published his father's *Musical Dictionary*. In 1840 he contributed a set of hymn and Psalm tunes to the collection *Christian Psalmody* edited by Bickersteth.

William Callcott is best known for his transcriptions and arrangements for piano, of which there are several hundred. Composer of songs, glees and anthems, among them 'Give peace in our time, O Lord'. His hymn tune 'Intercession' was used in the Revised Edition (1927) of *Church Hymnary* with the hymn by Horatius Bonar, 'When the weary seeking rest'.

CALVERT, Dr. Ian Spencer (b.1940)
Born in Nelson, Lancashire in 1940. A general practitioner in Gloucestershire. Composer of hymn tunes. Associated with **Geoffrey Ainger** and other members of the Methodist Group Ministry in Notting Hill, London, during the 1960s.

CAMBRIDGE, Frederick (1841-1914)
Born in South Runton, Norfolk on 29 March 1841; died in Croydon, Surrey on 17 December 1914.

A chorister of Norwich Cathedral under **Zechariah Buck**, later studying harmony with Wilhelm Molique. Graduated B.Mus. at the University of Durham (1893).

Organist and choirmaster of St. Columba's College, Rathfarnham, Dublin (1862-1865); St. Mary's Church, Leicester (1866) and at Croydon Parish Church, Surrey (1868).

Composer of a Communion Service in C, anthems including 'Not unto us' and 'I was in the Spirit', hymn tunes, chants and works for organ and for piano. The collection *Responses to the Commandments* (1875) uses Frederick Cambridge's setting in C.

CAMIDGE, John (1734-1803)
Baptised in York on 8 December 1734; died in York on 25 April 1803. A chorister at York Minster, where he was later articled to the organist, **James Nares**. Studied under **Maurice Greene**, whom Nares succeeded in 1756 as one of the organists of the Chapel Royal, and under **Handel**. Organist of Doncaster Parish Church, Yorkshire for a period of six months in 1755. He succeeded Nares as organist of York Minster (1756-1799), resigning presumably in order that his son **Matthew Camidge** could succeed him. Composer of the anthems 'O save Thy people' and 'Blessed are all they that fear', glees, works for the harpsichord, and songs.

CAMIDGE, Dr. John (1790-1859)
Born in York in 1790; died in York on 21 September 1859. Grandson of **John Camidge** and the son of **Matthew Camidge**, both of whom were organists at the Minster.

Early studies in music were under the direction of his father. Graduated Mus.B. (1812) and Mus.D. (1819) at the University of Cambridge. Awarded the Lambeth D.Mus. in 1855 by Archbishop Sumner.

A talented organist. At an early age he was paid a retainer by the Minster authorities. After assisting his father at York Minster and at local musical events, he eventually succeeded him as organist (1842-1859). Following a stroke in 1848 he remained paralysed and was never able to play organ thereafter. His son **Thomas Simpson Camidge** acted as deputy thereafter.

Many of his compositions were in his collection *Cathedral Music* (1828). His anthems include 'Holy, Holy, Holy' and 'I will cry unto God'. A Double Chant in E was included in *Cathedral Psalter Chants* (1875).

CAMIDGE, John (1853-1929)
Born in York in 1853; died in 1929. Son of **Thomas Simpson Camidge**, grandson and great-great-grandson respectively of the two composers also named **John Camidge**, and great-grandson of **Matthew Camidge**.

Received his training in music at Christ Church Cathedral, Oxford. Organist of Beverley Minster, Yorkshire (from 1876). Composer of a Kyrie, Creed, Sanctus and Gloria.

CAMIDGE, Matthew (1764-1844)
Born in York (some sources erroneously prefer 1758) and was baptised on 25 May 1764; died in York on 23 October 1844. Son and father respectively of his two namesakes, noticed above, both of whom were organists of York Minster.

A Chapel Royal chorister under **James Nares**, who had already taught his father. Learned to play organ and violin.

Organist of York Minster (1799-1842), having acted as assistant to his father and having been *de facto* organist for some time. It is said that he was the first choir trainer to teach his boy choristers to read music rather than learn it by ear. An active local musician, directing several of the local festivals, including those of 1823 and 1825.

His instrumental compositions were sonatas and concertos for keyboard. For the church he composed services, anthems including 'Blessed is he that considereth' and 'Teach me, O Lord', Psalm tunes and chants. His Double Chant in E Minor was used in *Cathedral Psalter Chants* (1875) and his Double Chant in D Minor in the Revised Edition (1927) of *Church Hymnary*. Also composed glees and songs.

CAMIDGE, Thomas Simpson. (1838-1912)
Son and father respectively of the two composers named **John Camidge**, and the grandson of **Matthew Camidge**. A deputy organist of York Minster. Composer of the anthem 'Be merciful after Thy power'.

CAMPBELL, John (1807-1860)
Born in Paisley, Renfrewshire, Scotland in 1807; died in Glasgow on 7 October 1860. A Glasgow businessman. Collected and published a set of Psalm and hymn tunes *The Sacred Psaltery...* (1848), and *Campbell's Selection of Anthems and Doxologies...* (also 1848). Composer of a number of anthems, which were popular at the time in and around Glasgow. His anthems include 'Rejoice in the Lord' (published 1901).

CAMPBELL, Dr. Sidney Scholfield (1909-1974)
Born in London on 7 June 1909; died in Windsor Castle, Berkshire on 4 June 1974.

Studied organ under **Harold Darke** and **Ernest Bullock**. Graduated B.Mus. (1940) and D.Mus. (1946) at the University of Durham.

Appointed M.V.O. in 1972.

Until the age of 26, Campbell worked full-time as a bank clerk. Organist of St. Margaret's Church, Leytonstone, Essex (from 1927); Chigwell Parish Church, Essex (from 1929); West Ham Parish Church, London (1931-1936); St. Peter's, Croydon, Surrey (1936-1943) and St. Peter's Collegiate Church, Wolverhampton (1943-1947).

Sub warden of the College of St. Nicolas, which is now the Royal School of Church Music (1947-1949), and later served part-time as its director of studies (1954-1956). Organist of Sandwich Parish Church, Kent.

Organist and master of the choristers of the Cathedrals of Ely (1949-1953), Southwark (1953-1956) and Canterbury (1956-1961). From 1961 to 1974 he was organist and master of the choristers at St. George's Chapel, Windsor Castle.

Composer of organ music, a Fanfare for Brass, and anthems including 'Sing we merrily unto God our strength' and 'Praise to God in the highest'. Also composed a Te Deum in B-flat, and organ pieces.

CAMPBELL, Thomas (1800-1876)
Born in Sheffield, Yorkshire in 1800; died in Sheffield in 1876. Composer of a number of hymn tunes, all of which were given botanical names. In 1825 he published a collection of 23 of these tunes which he named *The Bouquet*. His most famous tune is 'Sagina' (Pearlwort), usually sung to the hymn 'And can it be that I should gain?'.

CAMPION (Campian), Dr. Thomas (1567-1620)
Born in Witham, Essex and was baptised on 12 February 1567; died in London and was buried on 1 March 1620.

Attended the University of Cambridge (1581-1584) but did not graduate. He then studied law at Gray's Inn (from 1586 until some time before 1595) but did not qualify. He graduated M.D. following his studies in medicine at the University of Caen in 1605.

Known as a poet, musicologist and composer of a large number of lute songs, to which he also wrote the words. These activities took up most of his time although he practised as a physician to a small extent. A friend of the fourth Earl of Cumberland, at whose house many of Campion's ayres received their first performance. His other friends included **Anthony Holborne, John Dowland John Coprario** and Philip Rosseter.

All of his musical compositions are for voices, and his work includes some sacred songs, published in his *Two Bookes of Ayres* (1610). Third and fourth books followed. His hymn tune 'Babylon's streams' from the first book was used in *Hymns Ancient and Modern* as a setting to the hymn 'That day of wrath, that dreadful day'. In *Church Hymns* (1874) the same tune is known as 'Babylon' and is found with the hymn by F.W. Faber 'O come and mourn beside the Cross'. Edited versions of the tune are found in *Songs of Praise* and *English Hymnal*.

CAMPLING, Revd. Christopher (b.1925)
Graduated B.A. (1950) and M.A. (1954) at St. Edmund's Hall, Oxford. Studied for the ministry of the Church of England at Cuddesdon College (from 1950). Ordained deacon in 1951, priest in 1952.

Curate of Basingstoke, Hampshire (1952-1955). Chaplain of the King's School, Ely, Cambridgeshire and minor canon of Ely Cathedral (1955-1959); chaplain of Lancing College, Sussex (1960-1967). Vicar of Pershore with Pinvin and Wick, and priest-in-charge of Birlingham with Nafford in Worcester Diocese (1967-1976). Archdeacon of Dudley and director of religious education and priest-in-charge of Dodderhill (1976-1984). Chairman of the House of Clergy, Worcester Dioces (1982-1984). Dean of Ripon (1984-1995).

Editor of *Words for Worship* (1970). Author of *The Way, the Truth and the Life* (1965) in six volumes, and of *The Fourth Lesson* (1972/1973) in two volumes. Continues to write in retirement.

Christopher Campling has composed a setting of the Rite A Order of Holy Communion.

CANDLYN, Thomas Frederick Handel (1892-1964)
Received his early musical training at Doncaster Parish Church, Yorkshire. In 1911 he graduated B.Mus. at the University of Durham. Assistant organist of Doncaster Parish Church, Yorkshire (1908-1910). Composer of church music including settings of the Magnificat and Nunc Dimittis in D-flat (1914) and in F (1935), the anthem 'He that is down needs fear no fall' (1944) and items for organ.

CAPERN, James Alfred (1866-1955)
Born in Newington, Surrey in 1866; died in Esher, Surrey on 7 April 1955. Organist and choirmaster of Beechen Grove Baptist Church, Watford (from 1905) and a composer of hymn tunes.

CARBERY, Mary Emily (1861-1949)
Born in Liverpool in 1861; died in Leominster, Herefordshire on 6 February 1949. Composer of hymn tunes.

CAREY (Savile), Henry (1687-1743)
Born in Rothwell, Yorkshire in 1687; died, possibly by suicide when deeply in debt, at Clerkenwell, London on 4 October 1743.

A poet, teacher and composer; a friend and admirer of **John Stanley**, the blind organist and composer. Worked as a singer at the Drury Lane Theatre and as a Psalm raiser (parish clerk) at Lincoln's Inn Chapel (1714-1717).

Carey was able to afford lessons in composition from Linnert, Francesco Geminiani and **Thomas Roseingrave** following the success of his most famous song 'Sally in our alley' (c1715). Even afterwards, the appeal of his music lay in the simple effectiveness of his tunes rather than the deployment of his newly-acquired musical theory.

Although he was a highly effective librettist, sometimes using the pseudonyms Benjamin Bounce and Signor Carini, he was financially insecure. He taught in boarding schools and privately in order to supplement his income.

Composer of much music for the theatre, consisting of operas, musical entertainments and vocal works. Some of Carey's *libretti* were set by other composers, for example, **John Lampe**.

Although he composed very little church music he has remained known for the hymn tune 'Surrey' which was used in *Hymns Ancient and Modern* to the words 'The Lord my pasture shall prepare', and with 'The Lord is my Portion' in *English Hymnal* and *Songs of Praise*. Other tunes are found in *Wesley's Hymns* (1877) including 'Osborne' (1743).

CARLETON, Nicholas (c1570-1630)
Born between the years 1570 and 1575; died in Beoley, Worcestershire in 1630. Believed to have been a chorister at St. Paul's Cathedral in 1582. A friend of **Thomas Tomkins**, he composed church music, some of which was included in the *Mulliner Book*, a collection of works by 16th century composers. His pieces for keyboard include one of the earliest known organ duets - the 'Verse for two to play'.

CARLTON, Revd. Richard (16th/17th century)
Richard Carlton is represented in *The Triumphes of Oriana*, a collection of madrigals made by **Thomas Morley** in honour of Queen Elizabeth I. Composer of the anthem 'Let God Arise'.

CARNABY, Dr. William (1772-1839)
Born in London in 1772; died in London on 13 November 1839.

As a chorister of the Chapel Royal, he studied under **James Nares** and **Edmund Ayrton**. Graduated Mus.B. (1803) and Mus.D. (1808) at the University of Cambridge.

Held organistships at Eye, Suffolk and at Huntingdon. From 1823 he was organist to the Hanover Chapel, Regent Street, London.

Composer of anthems including 'O God, whose nature and property', glees and songs.

CARNALL, Arthur (1852-1904)
Born in Peterborough, Cambridgeshire on 7 May 1852; died in Penge, Kent on 30 June 1904. Son of John Carnall, an amateur musician who was choirmaster of St. Mary's Church, Peterborough.

A chorister of Peterborough Cathedral before the family moved to Ely, where he became a pupil of the Cathedral organist, **E.T. Chipp**. Graduated Mus.B. at the University of Cambridge (1873). Organist of Penge Parish Church, Kent for 31 years.

Composer of chamber music including Wind Quintets in D and in F, an Orchestral Overture, glees, madrigals and songs. His church music included the Christmas anthem 'Hail! Thou that art highly favoured', services and hymn tunes.

CARR, Benjamin (17th/18th century)
Born towards the end of the 17th century. Emigrated to Philadelphia, U.S.A. in the early years of the 18th century.
His compositions include the hymn tune 'Madrid', also known as 'Spanish Melody'.

CARR (Carre), George (17th century)
The anthems 'Let Thy loving mercy' and 'I have lifted up' were composed by a person named George Carr. The possibility exists that this composer is the George Carr who was organist of Llandaff Cathedral from 1629.

CARR, Paul d'Argaville (b.1961)
Born in Redruth, Cornwall on 13 August 1961.
Attended Rudolf Steiner School and Guildhall School of Music. Studied privately with Michael Hall in Sussex.
Opera stage manager, currently working for the New Israeli Opera, Tel Aviv. Previously worked with English National Opera (1984-1987) and Australian Opera (1987-1992).
Has been composing since the age of 15, with works published in the U.K., U.S.A. and Australia. His church music includes the anthem 'The Lamb' and carols 'Shout for joy' and 'There is a star that shines so bright'. Examples of his secular works are a Concerto for Two Saxophones and Orchestra, and a Violin Concerto, the latter receiving its first performance at the Brighton Festival (1995).

CARROLL, Dr. Benjamin Hobson (19th/20th century)
Graduated B.Mus. (1880) and D.Mus. (1884) at the University of Dublin. Followed a career as an organist, pianist and violinist. Organist of Christ Church, Belfast and organist and choirmaster of Dunfermline Abbey (from 1892). His compositions include a Te Deum in E-flat and other settings of the Canticles, a motet *Light and darkness,* carols, songs, part songs and works for violin.

CARROLL, Dr. Walter (1869-?)
Born in Manchester, Lancashire in 1869.
Graduated B.Mus. at the University of Durham in 1891; from Owen's College, Victoria University, Manchester (as it then was) he achieved B.Mus. (1896) after studying with **Henry Hiles**, and D.Mus. (1900).
Organist and choirmaster of St. Clement's Church, Greenheys, Manchester (1892-1895); honorary choirmaster of St. James's Church, Birch-in-Rusholme, Manchester (1916-1938).
Taught music at Manchester Training College (1892-1909) and was singing master of Ellerslie Ladies' College (1900-1903).
A lecturer in harmony (1893-1904) and professor (1904-1920) at the Manchester College of Music.
Lecturer in composition and examiner for degrees at the University of Manchester (1910-1920). Professor of the art of teaching at the Royal Manchester College (1909-1910). Music adviser to the City of Manchester Education Committee (1918-1934).
Author of *The Training of Children's Voices* and *Handbook of Music for Schools.*
Composer of Morning and Evening Services, a setting of Psalm 146 for Soloists, Chorus and Orchestra, and items for piano.

CARROTT, Livesey Kennington Read (1863-1900)
Born in Boston, Lincolnshire in 1863; died in Kensington, London on 12 October 1900. Studied at the Royal Academy of Music. Had a varied musical career as virtuoso pianist, teacher, composer, conductor and choir trainer. Organist and choirmaster of All Saints' Church, Highgate, London (from 1882). Four years later he was appointed to a similar position at St. Matthew's Church, Bayswater. Composer of a Te Deum and Jubilate in D (1891), an Evening Service in D (1898), the anthem 'O magnify the Lord' (1899), hymn tunes, a sacred cantata *Martha* (1896) and songs.

CARTER, Andrew (b.1939)
Born in Leicester on 13 December 1939. A student of James Brown and **Philip Wilby** at the University of Leeds.
A Winston Churchill fellow in 1981, studying the choral techniques and repertoire of Scandinavia and, in particular, the Swedish composer Eric Ericson.
Founded the Chapter House Choir at York during his time in the Choir of York Minster (from 1962). The Choir was named the outstanding Choir of the Year in 1979 in the B.B.C. 'Let the Peoples Sing' Competition.
Spent a year as a conductor in Auckland, New Zealand (1984).
His Benedicite for Chorus and Orchestra is said to show a fresh approach and a highly distinctive idiom. Has also composed a Missa Brevis (1988), the *Wakefield* Service (1988), the anthem 'Great joy and jollity', an Easter anthem 'The strife is o'er', and the carols 'Make we merry' and 'A Maiden most gentle' (1975).

CARTER, Arthur Norman (1882-1964)
Born in Hampstead, London in 1882; died in Hampstead on 8 August 1964.
Educated at Mill Hill School, London and at Magdalen College, Oxford where he was a pupil of **John Varley Roberts** and, for organ, **Tobias Matthay**.
President of the Leather and Hide Trades Provident and Benevolent Association (from 1939).
From 1903, Arthur Carter was honorary organist of Lyndhurst Road Congregational Church, Hampstead where at the age of 21 he succeeded James Macey. On the committee for the music of the hymnal *Congregational Praise* (1951). Composer of hymn tunes including 'Palm Sunday' and 'Hero'.

CARTER, Charles Thomas (1734-1804)
Born in Dublin in 1734, the son of a choir man of Christ Church Cathedral; died in London on 12 October 1804.
A chorister of Christ Church, Dublin. He is said to have been able to sight read harpsichord music even when it was placed upside down. He gave organ recitals from his early teens.
Organist at the church of St. Werburgh, Dublin (1751-1769).
He later became director of music at the Royalty Theatre, London and also of Lord Barrymore's private theatre at Wargrave, Berkshire.
Composer of a number of musical comedies, all of which were performed at the Drury Lane Theatre. Around the year 1800 he published a collection of fugues and full pieces for organ. Also composed songs and harpsichord sonatas. One of the songs was adapted as a hymn tune and named 'Guardian angels'. Composer of four anthems including 'I cried unto the Lord' and 'Sing unto God', and a Te Deum and Jubilate in C.

CARTER, Revd. Edmund Sardinson (1845-1923)

Born in New Malton, Yorkshire on 3 February 1845; died in Scarborough, Yorkshire on 23 May 1923.

Attended Worcester College, Oxford where he graduated B.A. and M.A. (1871). Ordained deacon in 1871, priest in 1872.

Curate of Christ Church, Ealing, Middlesex (1871 to 1875). From 1875 he was a vicar choral of York Minster and from 1877 to 1882 he was rector of the church of St. Martin, Micklegate, York. From 1882 he was vicar of the church of St. Michael-le-Belfry, York. *Church Hymns* (1874) employs Edmund Carter's 'Day by day' with 'Day by day, we magnify Thee' by John Ellerton, and 'Wreford' with 'Our blest Redeemer, ere He breathed' by Godfrey Thring.

CARTER, Frederick George (b.1913)

Born in Enfield, Middlesex on 5 March 1913.

Educated at the George Spicer School, Enfield, and studied under **Harold Darke** for organ and **Harold Watts** for organ, piano and composition.

Organist and choirmaster of St. Saviour's Church, Stroud Green (1938-1941); organist of St. Paul's Church, St. Albans (1941-1948); music master of Aylesford House (from 1947) and then assistant organist of St. Alban's Abbey and music master at Hitchin Grammar School, Hertfordshire (1948-1951). Music master of Bryanston Junior School (1946-1947).

Following these appointments he became organist and master of the choristers of St. Patrick's Cathedral, Armagh (1951-1966). He then emigrated to Vancouver, Canada where he was organist of St. John's Church, Shaughnessy (from 1966) and music master of St. George's School. His hymn tune 'Manor house' is used with the hymn by Joseph Scriven 'What a friend we have in Jesus'. He was on the Music Sub Committee of *Irish Church Hymnal.*

CARTER, George (1835-1890)

Born in London on 26 January 1835; died in Wandsworth, London on 17 November 1890.

He was the brother of **Henry Carter** and **William Carter**, and should not be confused with another George Carter, lay vicar of Westminster Abbey and tenor singer of repute of glees and ballads, who was probably born in 1834.

Studied under **John Goss**.

His first organ appointment was at the age of 12 in 1847. Organist in London of St. Thomas's Church, Stamford Hill (from 1848); Christ Church, Camberwell (from 1850); Trinity Church, Upper Chelsea (from 1853); St. Luke's Church, Chelsea (from 1860). Organist of the Albert Hall.

Organist of Montreal Cathedral (1861-1870).

Composer of operas including *Fair Rosamond,* a High Festival Communion Service (1883) and songs.

CARTER, Henry (1837-?)

Born on 6 March 1837. The brother of **George Carter** and **William Carter**. Another composer of the same name was active in the mid 19th century producing waltzes and other dance music. Organist of Quebec Cathedral, Canada and later of St. Leonard's Church, New York City, where, in 1882, he became organist of Revd. Henry Ward Beecher's Church. Composer of anthems including 'God, who at sundry times' (1876), songs and organ music.

CARTER, Sydney Bertram (b.1915)

Born in Camden Town, London on 6 May 1915.

Educated at Montem Street london County Council School, Christ's Hospital and Balliol College, Oxford.

His early career includes a teaching position at Frensham Heights School, Surrey and service with the Friends' Ambulance Unit (including two years in Greece) during World War II. Subsequently he became known as a folk song writer and performer. Now lives in retirement in Herne Hill, London.

He wrote the words and music of a number of popular modern hymns, which often had a radical social and political message. His hymns include 'The devil wore a crucifix', 'It was on a Friday morning', and 'One more step along the road I go'. At one time he denied that these writings should be regarded as hymns, professing that he had intended them as songs to arrest and challenge young people. He adapted an old Shaker tune to accompany his hymn 'Lord of the Dance'. His 'Every star shall sing a carol' is well-known. A five-volume *Songs of Sydney Carter in the Present Tense* was published between 1968 and 1982, containing both religious and review songs.

CARTER, Thomas (c1735-1804)

Organist of St. Werburgh's Church, Dublin. Composer of the anthems 'Hear my prayer O God' and 'Sing unto the Lord'.

CARTER, William (1838-?)

Born in London on 7 December 1838.

The brother of **George Carter** and **Henry Carter**.

A chorister of St. Giles's Church, Camberwell (from 1845) and later of the Chapel Royal and of King's College, London. Studied music with his father and under Ernst Pauer.

Appointed organist of Christ Church, Rotherhithe, London (1848); Little Stanmore Parish Church, Whitchurch (1850); St. Mary's Church, Newington (1854) and St. Helen's Bishopsgate, London (1856). From 1859 he deputised for his brother Henry at Quebec Cathedral before returning to London and taking up organistships at St. Stephen's Church, Westbourne Park (1860) and at St. Paul's Church, Onslow Square (1868).

Active as a choral conductor in London. Formed a large choir for the opening of the Royal Albert Hall in 1871 and in 1894 he began to stage choral concerts in the Queen's Hall.

Composer of a Cantate Domino in E (1891); anthems, including an anthem of thanksgiving for the recovery from illness of the Prince of Wales in 1872; songs and part songs.

CARTLEDGE, James (?-1864)

A senior chorister of Manchester Collegiate Church (which was elevated to cathedral status in 1848) from 1826. Composer of the anthems 'Bow down Thine ear' and 'Save me, O God'.

CARVER, Robert (1487-?)

Born, presumably in Scotland, in 1487. It is known that he was still alive in 1546. He is one of the only two Scottish composers and contemporaries of **Thomas Tallis** whose work has survived. A monk for 36 years, and canon at Scone Abbey. The most accomplished Scottish composer of the 16th century.

Composer of Masses including a version for 10 voices *Dum sacrem mysterium.* He also composed a motet in 19 parts *O bone Jesu* and other motets including *Gaude flore Virginali.*

CASHMORE, Donald (b.1926)
Born in London on 12 July 1926.
Attended Sir Walter St. John School, Westminster City School and St. Chad's College. Went on to the Royal College of Music and the University of London, graduating B.Mus. and B.Sc.
Was solo chorister of St. Margaret's Church, Westminster.
Various appointments in and around London: Christ Church, Rotherhithe (1942-1944); St. John's Church, Wimbledon (1947-1950); St. John the Divine, Kennington (1950-1952); Kingsway Hall, London (1952-1963) and St. James's Church, Gerrards Cross, Buckinghamshire (1968-1973).
Conductor of the City of London Choir (1963-1989) and of the London Concert Choir (1973-1987), giving regular performances with both at London's South Bank concert halls.
His compositions include a number of anthems such as 'The strife is o'er' and 'Jesus comes with all His grace', *Five Festal Introits*, the cantatas *This Child behold* and *Jerusalem* for Chorus and Orchestra, part songs, and carol arrangements.

CASSELS-BROWN, Dr. Alastair Kennedy (b.1927)
Born in Chiswick, London in 1927.
Educated in Oxford at All Saints' Choir School, St. John's School and Worcester College.
Assistant music master of Wellington College, Berkshire (1950-1952).
His career developed in the United States of America. He was director of music of St. George's School, Rhode Island (1952-1955); associate organist of New York Cathedral (1955-1957) and master of the choristers of Grace Church, Utica, New York. In 1975 he was professor of music and speech at the Episcopal Divinity School, Cambridge, Massachusetts.
He has written concert reviews.
Composer of a Te Deum, the anthem 'Praise the Lord, O my soul' and other items of church music. He was responsible for the harmony to the folk tune 'Charlestown', often used with 'All who love and serve your city', written by Erik Routley in 1966. His other works include a String Quartet and a Fantasia for Four Cellos.

CASSON, Dr. John Hornsey (1843-1926)
Born in Bakewell, Derbyshire in 1843; died in Brighton, Sussex on 8 June 1926.
A physician, devoting his spare time to composing hymns and other forms of church music. Assistant organist of St. Patrick's Church, Hove.
His hymn tune 'Semper aspectemus' was used in the Revised Edition (1916) of *Hymns Ancient and Modern* with the hymn by Allen Chatfield 'For ever we would gaze on Thee' and with 'Hail Father, whose creating call' by **Samuel Wesley**.

CATHERWOOD, David (b.1956)
Born in Belfast on 7 May 1956. Attended Queen's University, Belfast, graduating in 1978. Since 1981 he has been assistant director of music at Campbell College, Belfast. A conductor of bands and choirs. Has led summer music camps in the U.K. and the U.S.A. Composer of a number of anthems, including 'Come, pure hearts' and 'Into your loving care'.

CAUSTUN (Causton), Thomas (c1520-1569)
Born probably between the years 1520 and 1525; died in London on 28 October 1569. A gentleman of the Chapel Royal of Edward VI, Mary and Elizabeth I, from around 1550. He set to music the Canticles as laid down in the Prayer Books of 1549 and 1552. Contributed anthems and services to a compilation *Certaine Notes* (1565) by **John Day**, and some of his tunes are in Day's *The Whole Psalmes In Foure Parts*. He wrote several anthems including 'Let all the congregation' and 'O sacred and holy banquet'.

CAVENDISH, Michael (c1565-1628)
Born around the year 1565; died in Aldermanbury, London in 1628, possibly on 5 July. A cousin of Lady Arabella Stuart, and a member of a rich Suffolk family. A servant of Prince Charles. Composer of ayres and madrigals. Some of his Psalm tunes are in Thomas East's *The Whole Booke of Psalmes* (1592), composed to fit the meter of the Sternhold and Hopkins Psalter. Some tunes are in the compilation *The Whole Booke of Psalmes* by **Thomas Ravenscroft**.

CECIL, Brownlow Thomas Montagu (1827-1905)
Born on 27 February 1827; died in Reigate, Surrey on 22 May 1905. Composer of hymn tunes.

CECIL, Revd. Richard (1748-1810)
Born in London on 8 November 1748; died in Hampstead, London on 15 August 1810.
Educated at Queen's College, Oxford (from 1773). As a young man he dedicated the rest of his life to the Church. Ordained deacon in 1776, priest in 1777.
Richard Cecil wrote poetry and music, and he was keenly interested in painting. Following his ordination he briefly took charge of two parishes in Leicestershire whose incumbent had recently died. He was then appointed vicar of two parishes near Lewes, Sussex.
He destroyed his violin so that it would not distract him from his ministry, and he vowed never again to visit a picture gallery after having his attention diverted by a work of art while visiting a sick parishioner.
He was known for his stirring evangelical preaching and he spent an increasing amount of time addressing audiences in London. In 1780 he became minister of St. John's Chapel, Bedford Row, London, having resigned his two livings in Lewes in 1797 and 1798 respectively. He also had the living of the Orange Street Chapel, London. He became vicar of Chobham and Bisley, Surrey, in 1800.
Composer of an anthem 'I will arise and go to my Father' and the hymn tune 'St. Ambrose' which was used in *Hymns Ancient and Modern* with 'From the depths of sin and failure' by Timothy Rees. Another tune 'St. John' was used in *Wesley's Hymns* (1877) with the hymn 'Jesu, Shepherd of the sheep'.

CENTER, Ronald (1913-1973)
Born in Aberdeen, Scotland on 2 April 1913; died on 18 April 1973. Studied with Julien Rosetti and William Swainson, but in composition he was almost entirely self-taught. A piano recitalist in Scotland. He also accompanied his wife, Evelyn, a soprano. Later in his career he concentrated on composing and giving private tuition. Compositions include three string quartets, works for string orchestra, songs, part songs, motets and other forms of church music.

CHADWYCK-HEALEY, Hilary Philip (1888-1976)
Born in London on 11 January 1888; died in Harrow, Middlesex on 30 March 1976.
Educated at Eton College. Served in the Surrey Regiment during World War I.
His career was in the electrical manufacturing business. A director of the Royal Academy of Music.
Composer of anthems, services, and works for piano and organ. In 1940 he composed the hymn tune 'Radwell', originally for 'Brightest and best of the sons of the morning', but in *Hymns Ancient and Modern* it was set to 'O Father, we thank You for Jesus your Son'. It has also been used in *Praise for Today* (1974).

CHALLINOR, Dr. Frederic Arthur (1866-1952)
Born in Longton, Staffordshire on 12 November 1866; died in Paignton, Devon on 10 June 1952.
The son of a miner. From the age of 11 he had worked in the brick fields and in collieries. At 15 he took a job in a china factory. The availability of a piano at home was the result of an inheritance when Frederick was 15 years old. Was able to study harmony during his meal breaks at work. Graduated B.Mus. (1897) at the University of Durham and D.Mus. (1903) at London.
More than one thousand of his compositions were published: cantatas, including the Lenten Cantata *The Passion of the Cross*, services, anthems, hymn tunes, carols, operas, songs and part songs. He wrote all the words and music for the bicentenary celebrations of the firm of Josiah Wedgwood of Stoke-on-Trent, Staffordshire (1930). Retired to Paignton.
His hymn tune 'Stories of Jesus' was composed for the National Sunday School Union and was included in *Sunday School Hymnary* (1905).

CHAMBERLAIN, Thomas (1810-1892)
Born in Oxfordshire in 1810; died in Oxford on 20 January 1892.
Composer of hymn tunes.

CHAMBERS, Herbert Arthur (1880-1967)
Born on 3 July 1880; died on 11 July 1967. Retired in 1959 from the firm of Novello after 53 years, having joined the firm as a reader in 1906. Composer of a Te Deum in D (1910), anthems including 'Lord, we pray Thee' (1909) and 'Praise to the Holiest' (1929) and songs and arranged other works, all of which are said to be in a very musicianly style.

CHAMPNEYS, Sir Francis Henry (1848-1930)
Born on 25 March 1848; died in Nutley, East Sussex on 30 July 1930.
Educated at Winchester College and Brasenose College, Oxford where he graduated M.A. and M.D. He also studied medicine at St. Bartholomew's Hospital. His medical qualifications included the B.M. (1875) and D.M. (1888). An amateur musician, he studied under **John Goss** and, while at Winchester College, with **S.S. Wesley**.
Held various medical posts between 1880 and 1913 including assistant obstetric physician at St. George's Hospital and at the General Lying-in Hospital (both from 1880), obstetric physician to St. George's Hospital (from 1885), and physician-accoucher of St. Bartholomew's Hospital (1891-1913).
One of the promoters of the Midwives Act of 1902 which established the role and brought about the recognition and

registration of midwives. Chaired the Central Midwives Board, set up under the 1902 Act, from 1903 until 1930.
He became a baronet in 1910.
Founded a choir in the late 1870s to perform Locke's *Macbeth*. The choir flourished for 20 years, reviving other works from earlier periods.
A council member, and member of the executive committee of the Royal College of Music for 15 years.
Contributed to *Dictionary of Musical Terms* by **John Stainer** and **W.A. Barrett**.
Composer of a number of hymn tunes, no doubt with the aid of the organ which he had installed at home. The Standard Edition (1916) of *Hymns Ancient and Modern* includes his tunes 'Assisi', 'Sales', 'St. Jerome' and 'St. Veronica'. He also composed anthems, including 'O Praise the Lord'.

CHANTER, Richard John Charles (19th/20th century)
A chorister of Westminster Abbey. Graduated B.Mus. at the University of Durham in 1912.
Organist and choirmaster of St. John's Church, Drury Lane, London (from 1906) and organist also in central London at Christ Church, Woburn Square (from 1907). Assistant organist to the Danish community at the Chapel Royal, Marlborough House (1909) and of Buckingham Palace (from 1914).
Worked for the charity Bermondsey Settlement in South East London as director of music, and conductor and lecturer from 1914. Composer of the Easter hymn 'Sing with joyful exultation'.

CHAPIN, Lucius (1760-1842)
Composer of the hymn tune 'Woodbury', used in conjunction with 'Come O thou traveller unknown'.

CHAPLIN, Revd. Wyndham Allan (19th/20th century)
Educated at Brussels Training School. Graduated B.A. and B.Mus. (1894) and M.A. (1898) at Keble College, Oxford. He was vicar of Falfield, Gloucestershire. Composer of two settings of the Morning Service, and songs.

CHAPMAN, Albert Edward (b.1901)
Born in Burgess Hill, Sussex in 1901. Studied at Brighton School of Music with **Alfred King**, **Alfred Abdey** and Chastey Hector. Director of music at Brighton, Hove and Sussex Grammar School (from 1945), and visiting music master of Hurstpierpoint College, Sussex (from 1946) A local harmonic society conductor. Organist and choirmaster the Sussex Churches of St. Mary, East Grinstead (1923-1927); St. Augustine, Brighton (1927-1932); St. John, Burgess Hill (1932-1939) and St. Nicholas, Brighton (1939-1948). Composer of a Mass in D, anthems, a piano concerto in F-sharp Minor, and songs.

CHAPMAN, Edward Thomas (1902-1981)
Born in Blisworth, Northamptonshire on 7 October 1902; died on 6 March 1981. Educated at Northampton School and at Pembroke College, Cambridge where he was organist and choirmaster (1922-1926). Graduated B.A. and Mus.B at the University of Cambridge. Assistant master of Portsmouth School (1926-1928), where he taught music and mathematics, and director of music of Highgate School (1928-1968). Broadcaster and choral society conductor. Organist and choirmaster of Christ Church, Crouch End (from 1968). Composer of the carol 'Sleep, Mary's Son', anthems and part songs.

CHAPMAN, Eric.A. (19th/20th century)
Born in Cheltenham, Gloucestershire. A horn player. For a time he lived at Kenton, Middlesex. Composer of a Kyrie, published in 1893.

CHAPMAN, Shadrach (19th century)
Associated with the town of Draycott, near Wells, Somerset. Composer of the anthems 'Arise, shine' (1838) and 'O God, Thou hast been displeased'.

CHAPPLE, Dr. Frank Arthur (1881-?)
Born in Cardiff in 1881.
Graduated B.Mus. at the University of Durham in 1907, followed by the D.Mus.
Sub organist of Llandaff Cathedral, and organist and choirmaster of the Church of All Souls, Llandaff (1899-1902); organist of Avenue Church, Southampton, Hampshire (1902-1904) and of Monmouth Church (1904-1908). Taught music at Monmouth Grammar School (1907-1908). Choirmaster of Llangattock Church (1905-1908).
Organist of Holy Trinity Church, Broadstairs, Kent (1908); organist and choirmaster of Pontefract Parish Church, Yorkshire (1909); music teacher at Pontefract Grammar School (1909) and at Pontefract High School for Girls (1911). A choral society conductor.
Composer of a Christmas Anthem, other anthems, hymn tunes and madrigals for men's voices. Also composed part songs.

CHAPPLE, Samuel (1775-1833)
Born in Crediton, Devon on 20 July 1775; died in Ashburton, Devon on 3 October 1833. At the age of 10 an attack of smallpox left him permanently blind. His musical ability was known and the local townspeople decided to fund his musical education with a local teacher of music named Eames, who was himself blind. Also studied with another local musician, Thomas. He learned to play organ, violin and piano. Organist of Ashburton (1795-1833), and taught locally. Composer of 18 anthems including 'It is a good thing' and 'Rejoice in the Lord', songs, glees and piano pieces.

CHARD, Dr. George William (1765-1849)
Born in Winchester, Hampshire in 1765; died in Winchester on 23 May 1849.
A chorister of St. Paul's Cathedral under **Robert Hudson**. Graduated Mus.D. at the University of Cambridge (1812).
In 1791 he became a lay clerk of Winchester Cathedral, acting additionally as assistant organist to **Peter Fussell**. When the latter died, Chard succeeded him (1802-1849). Organist and master of the choristers of Winchester College (1832-1849), where he earned the reputation of a fine trainer of boys' choirs. Organist of the church of St. Maurice with St. Mary Kalendar, Winchester.
Had the reputation of one who was fond of hunting: his wife sometimes had to find excuses for his absence while he was thus engaged.
Mayor of Winchester for a year.
Composer of church music of various kinds. His 28 anthems include 'Happy is the man' and 'O Lord my God'. He also composed chants, services, a Kyrie in B-flat, glees and solo songs.

CHARDE, John (16th century)
John Charde is known to have been alive around the years 1518 and 1519, when he graduated B.Mus. at the University of Oxford on the strength of his submission, a Mass for Five Voices. This was the first time that a five part piece had been entered as an Oxford degree exercise. He composed other settings of the Mass.

CHARLESWORTH, John (20th century)
John Charlesworth is based in Lichfield, Staffordshire. He has composed a setting of the carol 'Ding dong merrily on high'.

CHATER, William (19th century)
Organist of the Holy Trinity Church, Coventry, Warwickshire (1866-1880). Composer of the anthems 'Blessed is he' (1863) and 'By the waters of Babylon'.

CHATFIELD, Alfred (1874-?)
An articled pupil of **Frederick Bridge**. Graduated B.Mus. at Queen's College, Oxford (1914). Organist and choirmaster of St. Paul's Church, Finchley, London (1898-1904) and of Kidderminster Parish Church, Worcestershire (from 1903). Composer of a Magnificat and Nunc Dimittis in E-flat.

CHAUNDY, Dr. Edred Martin (1871-1960)
Born in Oxford in 1871; died in 1960.
Attended the University of Oxford where he was the pupil of **C.H. Lloyd** and **Henry Plumridge**. Graduated B.A. (1892), M.A. (1898), B.Mus. (1890) and D.Mus. (1898) at the University of Oxford.
Organist of Christ Church, Streatham Hill, London (1892-1895); Enniskillen Parish Church, Ireland (1895-1898); Pershore Abbey, Worcestershire (1898-1899); Holy Trinity Church, Stroud, Gloucestershire (1899-1901) and St. George's Church, Kidderminster, Worcestershire (1901).
He returned to Ireland as organist of St. Mark's Church, Strand Town (1905-1913); St. George's Church, Belfast (1913-1919); Bangor Abbey (1919) and Armagh Cathedral (1920-1935). An accomplished organist whose particular skill lay in improvisation.
Composer of works for organ, and settings of the Te Deum and Jubilate in G, the latter works being published privately.

CHAWNER, C.F.Fox (1840-1867)
Fox Chawner was an adult chorister of St. Michael's College, Tenbury, Worcestershire (1863-1867). Composer of anthems including 'Devout men carried Stephen', 'Draw nigh unto God' and 'Praise the Lord, O my soul'.

CHEESE, Griffith James (1751-1804)
Born in 1751; died in Manchester on 2 November 1804.
A blind musician. From 1783 to 1804 he was organist of Manchester Collegiate Church (which in 1848 was elevated to cathedral status). He is sometimes identified as a person of the same or similar name who was an organist in Leominster, Herefordshire from 1771 and a teacher in London.
Composer of church music including the Sunday School anthem 'Teach me, O Lord' (c1785) and songs, and wrote a book on a method of training the blind in the techniques of teaching piano and organ.

CHETHAM (Cheatham, Cheetham), Revd. John (c1665-1746)
Possibly born or baptised at Ashton-under-Lyne, Staffordshire on 4 February 1665; said to have been buried in Skipton, Yorkshire on 26 June 1746. But this would indicate that he would have been close to 70 years old when appointed curate (1735), and therefore the date of his birth may be closer to 1700.

Educated at Duckinfield (now Dukinfield) School, Cheshire.

He lived at Skipton, where he was a curate, from February 1741. Had been a schoolmaster from July 1723.

Chetham's *A Book of Psalmody* (1718), which was reprinted a number of times until the end of the 19th century, included a setting by him of Psalm 50. This was later given the name 'Aylesbury' and used in *Hymns Ancient and Modern* with the hymn 'Breathe on me, breath of God'. Composer of three anthems 'I heard a voice', 'O give thanks' and 'Sing we merrily'.

Chetham's compositions are significant for the way in which they helped to establish a choral presence within the parish church, at a time when many clergy were against the idea of church choirs and complex music.

CHILD, Dr. William (1606/7-1697)

Born in Bristol, Gloucestershire in 1606 or 1607; died in Windsor, Berkshire on 23 March 1697. He is buried inside St. George's Chapel within the grounds of Windsor Castle.

Said to be a pupil of **Elway Bevin** at Bristol Cathedral, but this is disputed. In 1620 he was apprenticed at Bristol to Thomas Prince. Graduated B.Mus. (1631) and D.Mus. (1663) at the University of Oxford.

A singing man of Bristol Cathedral. His subsequent career was greatly affected by the civil war and the events surrounding it. Appointed one of the musicians of Charles I in April 1630. In the same year he became an alto lay clerk at St. George's Chapel, Windsor Castle. Organist there following the death of **John Mundy**. Held the position jointly with **Nathaniel Giles** from 1630 until Giles's death, following which no replacement was appointed. He was never formally appointed master of the choristers.

In 1643, during the civil war, it is claimed that he retired to a farm near Windsor where he composed music including the anthem 'O God, grant the King a long life', and, in 1644, an anthem based on part of the text of Psalm 79 'O Lord God, the heathen are come into thine inheritance'.

Child was organist at the coronation of Charles II (1661), James II (1685), and William and Mary (1689), and he became one of Charles's private musicians. A friend of Samuel Pepys.

At the Restoration he resumed his duties at Windsor and became one of the three organists of the Chapel Royal. He took up a number of appointments within the royal household, including a position from June 1673 as one of the musicians in ordinary for the wind instruments. As father, or senior gentleman of the Chapel Royal, he had the honour of leading the procession at the coronation of James II.

He gave £20 towards the cost of a new town hall in Windsor, and paved the choir at St. George's, according to some, the result of losing a wager with the clergy that he would never receive an arrears of salary. The work which he paid for is still in place.

In 1639 he published a set of 20 Psalms for trebles and bass. It was later renamed *Choise Musicke*. Composer of some 20 services, usually in short form, of which his Service in D was said to be a favourite of Charles I.

Also composed some 50 anthems, many of which remain in manuscript only. One that is still performed today is 'Praise the Lord, O my soul'. Wrote a set of Preces; three sets of Responses to the Commandments in D, F and in G were published as part of a 19th century collection. His work might be performed more widely today were it not for the disparaging treatment it received from **E.H. Fellowes**.

CHIPP, Dr. Edmund Thomas (1823-1886)

Born in London on 25 December 1823; died in Nice, France on 17 December 1886. The son of T.P. Chipp, a leading drum player of the day.

A chorister at the Chapel Royal under **William Hawes**. Graduated Mus.B. (1859) and Mus.D. (1860) at the University of Cambridge. Studied violin from 1832 to 1840 under W. Thomas, J.B. Nadaud and A. Tolbecque.

Held a succession of six church organistships in London. These were Albany Chapel, Regent's Park (honorarily, 1842-1843); St. John's Chapel, Hampstead (1843-1846); the Percy Chapel, Tottenham Court Road (1846-1847); in succession to **Henry Gauntlett** at St. Olave's, Southwark (1847-1852); St. Mary-at-Hill, Eastcheap (1852-1856) and Holy Trinity, Paddington (1856-1862).

A violinist in Queen Victoria's private band (1843-1845). Played violin in the Royal Italian Opera, Philharmonic Society and Sacred Harmonic Society. In 1855 he succeeded **W.T. Best** as organist of the Panopticon, Leicester Square. Mendelssohn praised him for his performance of the Organ Sonata number 3 in A.

Spent four years in Belfast (1862-1866), where he was organist of St. George's Church and of the Ulster Hall. In 1866 he moved to Scotland where he became organist at Kinnaird Hall, Dundee (February to November 1866) and of St. Paul's Church, Edinburgh (May to November 1866). A teacher of violin and piano.

Organist of Ely Cathedral (1866-1886).

Composer of organ and piano pieces, songs, two oratorios *Naomi* and *Job* and some church music including a Service in A and a Te Deum in D plus five sets of Responses to the Commandments, published within a collection in 1875. Also composed the anthems 'Seek ye the Lord' and 'Lord of all power and might'. His organ works include an organ variation on the hymn tune 'Austria'.

CHIRBURY (Chyrbury), Robert (?-c.1456)

A gentleman of the Chapel Royal from 1421. A chaplain at Windsor Castle from 1455. Composer of four three-part Masses. One of the composers featured in the *Old Hall Manuscript*, a collection of church music from around 1415-1430 that is now kept in the British Museum.

CHOPE, Revd. Richard Robert (1830-1928)

Born in Bideford, Devon on 21 September 1830; died in Wimbledon, London on 29 May 1928.

Attended Exeter College, Oxford where he graduated B.A. (1855) and M.A. (1857). Ordained deacon in 1856, priest in 1857.

Curate of the churches of Stapleton (1856-1858), Sherborne (1858-1859), Upton Scudamore (1859-1861) and Brompton (1861-1865). From 1865, Richard Chope was incumbent of St. Augustine's Church, Queen's Gate, London.

Edited the *Hymn and Tune Book* between 1857 and 1862.

Church Hymns (1874) uses Richard Chope's 'Faber' with 'O Thou, before the world began' by Charles Wesley. 'St. Cyprian' is linked with 'Jesu, meek and lowly' by Henry Collins.

CHOVEAUX, Nicholas (b.1904)

Born in Kent on 22 April 1904. Educated at Trent College, Derbyshire and at the Tobias Matthay School with R. Arnold Grevi.

Pursued a career as an organ teacher and composer. His organistships include those of Chealsea Old Church, London; St. John's Church, Wimbledon, London and St. Bartholomew the Great, Smithfield, London. His compositions include a setting of the Holy Communion Service, Three Pieces for Organ, and a Prelude and Improvisation on the hymn tune 'Caswall'.

CHRISTOPHER, Dr. Cyril Stanley (1897-1979)
Born in Oldbury, Worcestershire on 23 June 1897; died on 31 March 1979.
Studied with **C.H. Kitson**, **Edward Bairstow**, **Alfred Hollins**, G.D. Cunningham and Ambrose Coviello. Graduated D.Mus. at the University of Durham.
An adjudicator, conductor, lecturer and organist, and chorus master for B.B.C. Midlands. Senior tutor in the Adult Education Department of the University of Birmingham; taught harmony and counterpoint at Birmingham School of Music. Music master of King Edward Grammar School.
Organist and director of music of Carr's Lane Church, Birmingham (from 1930).
Composer of cantatas including *Via Crucis* and *A new Heaven* and other choral works, music for piano and for organ, motets, and anthems.

CHUBB, Richard (b.1945)
Born in Hornsey, London on 26 June 1945. Composer of hymn tunes.

CHURCH, John (1675-1741)
Born, possibly in Windsor, Berkshire in 1675; died in London on 6 January 1741. Buried in Westminster Abbey.
A chorister at St. John's College, Oxford.
From 1695 he was a tenor singer at the Theatre Royal, London. He became a gentleman of the Chapel Royal in 1697, having been gentleman extraordinary for about one year. In the same year he was appointed a lay vicar at Westminster Abbey. He was later master of the choristers (1704-1740), and the principal music copyist until around 1735. Appointed vicar choral at St. Paul's Cathedral in 1740.
Church wrote an *Introduction to Psalmody* (1723). His church music includes a Service in F and at least one other, 17 anthems including 'Blessed is the man' and 'I will lift up mine eyes', chants and three hymn tunes. Also composed songs and catches.

CHURCHILL, John (b.1920)
Born in London on 29 May 1920. Studied at the Royal College of Music (1938-1940 and 1946-1947). Graduated B.Mus. Master of the music of St. Martin-in-the-Fields, London (1948-1967) and one of the founders of the Academy of the same name.
Music master of Alleyn's School, Dulwich, London (1947-1948) and a professor of the R.C.M. (1947-1967). A professor of music, and head of music department of Carleton University, Ottawa, Canada (from 1967). A local choral society conductor. One of his anthems is 'An old man's prayer to Our Lady'. He published set of songs which he named *Three Songs from Eastern Canada*. Author of *Congregational Singing* (1962).

CLAPPERTON, Christopher Irving (1853-1915)
Born in Cumberland in 1853; died in the Isle of Wight in 1915. Composer of hymns including 'When His salvation bringing' (1901), a set of Responses to the Commandments, and the anthem 'O, Sovereign Lord of earth and heaven' (1902).

CLARE, Edward (?-1869)
Died in London on 9 April 1869. An author and composer. His writings include instructions on the technique of chanting the Psalms, and the use of the thorough-bass. Used the pseudonym Grenville Smart and, as well as composing ballads, he transcribed and arranged material by other musicians.

CLARK, Revd. Frederick Scotson (1840-1883)
Born in London on 16 November 1840; died in London on 5 July 1883.
His mother, who had been a pupil of Chopin, was Scotson Clark's first teacher of music. Attended school in Ewell, Surrey, where he played organ at the local parish church. At the age of 14, in 1854, he was appointed organist of Regent Street Church, London.
later studied harmony in Paris under Sergent, organist of Notre Dame Cathedral; studied privately with **E.J. Hopkins**; at the Royal Academy of Music under **William Sterndale Bennett**, **John Goss**, Carl Engel, Ciro Pinsuti and Pettit and, as organ scholar and exhibitioner, at Exeter College, Oxford where he was also organist until at least 1867.
Graduated B.Mus. at the University of Oxford in 1857. After training for the ministry, and subsequent ordination - deacon (1868), priest (1869) - he studied music for two terms at Leipzig under Carl Reinecke and Ernst Richter. In 1870 he continued his studies at Stuttgart.
His complex career saw him as a composer, pianist, organist, clergyman, principal of a secondary school and the founder of the London Organ School. He was known as an accomplished organist and for his particular skill of improvisation. In 1858, at the age of 18, he taught at the Royal Academy of Music. Following his ordination he became curate of St. Michael's Church, Lewes, Sussex and headmaster of St. Michael's Grammar School, Brighton. He represented English organists at the Paris Exhibition (1878).
Composer of a large amount of material for organ (including 48 voluntaries and 15 marches) and for piano, also for the harmonium. Composer of songs and church music.

CLARK, Richard (1780-1856)
Born in Datchet, Berkshire on 5 April 1780; died in Westminster on 5 October 1856.
A chorister at St. George's Chapel, Windsor Castle under **Theodore Aylward** and at Eton College under Stephen Heather.
He followed his grandfather, John Sale the elder, as lay clerk at St. George's Chapel, Windsor Castle and at Eton College (1802-1811). Around the year 1805 he was active as a deputy: for Bartleman at the Chapel Royal; for his uncle, John Sale at St. Paul's Cathedral; and for another uncle, **John Bernard Sale** at Westminster Abbey.
Richard Clark took up the place made vacant by **Joseph Corfe** as a gentleman of the Chapel Royal (1820). Other choral appointments were as a vicar choral of St. Paul's Cathedral (1827) and a lay clerk of Westminster Abbey (1828).
He worked to restore the statutory rights of those who served in cathedrals and collegiate churches. Published the words of his favourite glees, catches and other songs (1814).
Composer of anthems, chants, hymn tunes and glees.

CLARK, Robert Ernest (19th/20th century)
Graduated B.Mus. at Queen's College, Oxford (1902). Organist of Falmouth Parish Church, Cornwall (from 1900), later becoming organist and choirmaster of St. Paul's Church Manningham,

Bradford (1911). Composer of church music including a Magnificat and Nunc Dimittis in B-flat (1905), songs, part songs and items for piano.

CLARK (Clarke), Thomas (1775-1859)

Born in Canterbury, Kent and baptised on 5 February 1775; died in Canterbury on 30 May 1859.

A cobbler. A choir trainer, he led the singing of the Psalms at the Wesleyan Chapel, Canterbury and later in the Unitarian Church, also in Canterbury. It has been claimed however that he never actually joined the Unitarians, although he was in sympathy with them and he resigned from the Methodists.

Published *Union Harmonist* in 1841. He harmonised the Second Edition of the *Union Tune Book* for the Sunday School Union (1842).

Composer of anthems including 'Awake up, my glory', 'Daughter of Zion' and 'Since I have placed my trust'.

His hymn tune 'Greenland' was specially composed for use with the hymn by Reginald Heber 'From Greenland's icy mountains' and has been used with it regularly ever since. His other hymn tunes include 'Acton' and 'Crediton'; the melody 'Warsaw' is also attributed to him. He also published more than 20 sets of hymn tunes.

CLARKE, Charles Erlin Jackson (1795-1844)

Born in Worcester on 19 December 1795, the son of Thomas Clarke, Cathedral Sacrist; died in Worcester on 28 April 1844. A chorister of Worcester Cathedral from 1804. At the age of 15, in 1811 he was appointed organist of Durham Cathedral, where he remained until 1813. He was then organist of Worcester Cathedral (1814-1844). He conducted his first Worcester Festival in 1815 at the age of 19. Charles Clarke composed anthems including 'May the grace of Christ our Saviour' and 'Gather yourselves together', and a Double Chant in F.

CLARKE, James Hamilton Siree (1840-1912)

Born in Birmingham on 25 January 1840; died in Banstead, Surrey on 9 July 1912.

In 1852, by the age of 12 he was an accomplished organist and able to take on his first organistship, that of St. Matthew's Church, Duddeston. Graduated B.Mus. at the University of Oxford in 1867. He was however articled from the age of 15 to an analytical chemist (1855-1861). Resided in Ireland from 1862, where he became organist of Parsonstown Parish Church. In 1863 he transferred to the Zion Church, Rathgar, Dublin.

His career progressed quickly. He played the first violin in the Dublin Philharmonic Orchestra and he assisted R.P. Stewart at Christ Church Cathedral. Later he was organist of the Ceremony Church, Belfast and of Carnmony Church (1864).

Held the organistship at Llandaff Cathedral temporarily for a few months in 1866 and, being unsuccessful in his application for the permanent position, moved in the same year to Queen's College, Oxford (1866-1867). In 1871 he succeeded Arthur Sullivan as organist at the London church of St. Peter, South Kensington.

A professional conductor, firstly at a number of theatres in the West End of London and then as a touring operatic conductor, his charges including the prestigious D'Oyly Carte Company. For a while he lived in Australia. He was conductor of the Victorian National Orchestra there from 1889. Also served as an inspector of military bands, returning to England in 1891.

In all he had some 400 published works to his credit. He presented papers before the Musical Society in 1886 and 1887.

Composer of two symphonies, six overtures and music of various other kinds including pieces for organ, anthems including an eight-part anthem 'The Lord is my light', which won the prize of the College of Organists in 1864, and services. It is believed that he scored some of the works of Arthur Sullivan.

CLARKE, Jeremiah (c1670-1707)

Born around the year 1670; died in London on 1 December 1707. Said to have shot himself after an unsuccessful love affair.

A pupil of John Blow, being recorded as a chorister of the Chapel Royal at the coronation of James II. He had departed by 1691. Organist of Winchester College (1692-1695). From 1693, he may have been master of the children of St. Paul's Cathedral. From June 1699 he was appointed probationarily in succession to Isaac Blackwell as a vicar choral at St. Paul's. He was formally confirmed in the appointment in 1705. Blackwell had also been organist and by the end of 1699 Clarke had acquired this position also.

From 1704 he was joint organist at the Chapel Royal, where he had been a gentleman extraordinary since 1700, with William Croft. From January 1704 he had also been almoner and master of the children of St. Paul's. Music master to Queen Anne.

Composer of music for the church and for the theatre, and also songs and works for the harpsichord. Composer of three services and 21 anthems, including 'O Lord God of my salvation' and 'The Lord is my strength'. He probably wrote the hymn tune 'Nottingham' (also known as 'Birmingham' and 'Greenock') which is used with the hymn 'Take my life, and let it be'.

A number of hymn tunes were written around the year 1700, seven of which were included in Robert Bridges's *Yattendon Hymnal* of 1899. In the preface, Bridges credited Clarke with being the first person to compose a modern hymn tune, as distinct from a metrical Psalm setting. His tunes were also used in *Hymns Ancient and Modern* and in *Church Hymns* (1874), where 'Brockham' and 'St. Magnus' are used.

CLARKE, John Grey (1871-?)

Born in Wingham, Kent in 1871.

Studied at the Royal College of Music. Graduated B.A. (1894), M.A. (1899) and B.Mus. (1903) at St. John's College, Oxford.

Held a number of appointments early in his career within the county of Norfolk: organist, choirmaster and assistant master at All Saints' School, Bloxham (1896-1898); classics master at King's Lynn Grammar School (1898-1901) and acting organist and choirmaster at King's Lynn Parish Church (1898 and 1900).

Organist, choirmaster and assistant master of Warwick School (1901-1902); organist and choirmaster of the churches of St. Mary-le-Bow, Cheapside, London (1903-1907) and St. George, Cannes, France (1908).

In Ireland he was organist, choirmaster and assistant master of St. Columba's College, Rathfarnham, Dublin (1909-1911) and senior classics master at Galway Grammar School (from 1911). Organist of Llandovery College (from 1918).

Composer of an Evening Service in C Minor and a Te Deum in A Minor.

CLARKE, Rhona (b.1958)

Born in Dublin in 1958. Studied at Dublin College of Music and at University College, Dublin. For two years (from 1990) she carried out postgraduate studies at Queen's University, Belfast. She is a teacher at a Dublin secondary school. Composer of a number of vocal and choral works, including items for the church such as a Magnificat (1990), *A Song For St. Cecilia's Day 1687* (1991) and a setting of Psalm 148 (1988). Has won a number of composition prizes, including the Music for the Movies Award at the Dublin Film Festival of 1992 for her *Whaling Afloat and Ashore*, an electro-acoustic piece.

CLARKE-WHITFELD, Dr. John (1770-1836)

John Clarke was born in Gloucester on 13 December 1770; died in Holmer, near Hereford, on 22 February 1836. Appended his mother's maiden name to his surname in 1814 in an unsuccessful attempt to benefit from the estate of her late brother, H. Fotherley Whitfeld. Buried in the cloisters of Hereford Cathedral.

Studied at the University of Oxford under **Philip Hayes**, where he graduated B.Mus. (1793) and D.Mus. (1810). The Universities of Dublin (1795) and Cambridge (1799) awarded him doctorates in music.

A parish church appointment at Ludlow, Shropshire early in his career (1789-1794) was followed by the first of his cathedral and collegiate church responsibilities, at Armagh Cathedral (1795-1798), where he succeeded **Richard Langdon**.

Clarke-Whitfeld was master of the choristers at the Dublin Cathedrals of Christ Church and St. Patrick (1793-1794). At one time it was believed that he was also organist at the Dublin Cathedrals around the year 1798 but this is now thought to be unlikely.

Appointed to Trinity College and St. John's College, Cambridge (1799-1820) and to Hereford Cathedral (1820-1832) until his retirement, stating that he returned to England in order to escape from the Irish Rebellion. His years at Hereford were marked by declining health and the musical standard suffered accordingly until it was revived by his successor, **S.S. Wesley.**

Professor of music at the University of Cambridge (1821-1836) although not resident. He corresponded with Sir Walter Scott and set some of Scott's poems to music.

He was praised by the writer Bumpus as upholding the standard of church music at a time of poor standards. His anthems, of which he composed 27, include 'Behold, how good and joyful' and 'I will lift up mine eyes'. Most of these were published in four separate editions of his *Cathedral Music* between 1800 and 1837. Composer of some 50 chants, five Morning Services, six Communion Services and 10 Evening Services including a Service in E plus two oratorios including *The Crucifixion*.

He edited the collections *Favourite Anthems* (1805) and *Single and Double Chants* (1810).

CLAXTON, Revd. William (?-1933)

A probationer and chorister at St. Michael's College, Tenbury, Worcestershire (1862-1868). Graduated B.A. (1876), B.Mus. (1882) and M.A. (1895) at Trinity College, Oxford following his studies there. Ordained deacon in 1887, priest in 1888.

Organist of St. Michael's College from 1877 to 1886. He served two curacies in the county of Hampshire: Hartley Wintney (from 1887) and Woolston, Southampton (from 1893). From 1897 he was vicar of Navestock, near Romford, Essex. He retired in 1921.

Composer of anthems including 'Blessed be the people' and 'O Lord, we beseech Thee', services including a Morning, Communion and Evening Service in G (1884), songs and part songs.

CLAY, Frédéric Emes (1813-1889)

Born in Paris on 3 August 1813; died in Great Marlow, Buckinghamshire on 24 November 1889. Son of a Member of Parliament.

Studied music with Wilhelm Molique in Paris and Moritz Hauptmann in Leipzig.

He worked at the Treasury but resigned on the death of his father to concentrate on a musical career, in pursuit of which he lived in London as a teacher and composer.

He worked with both W.S. Gilbert and **Arthur Sullivan**, of whom he was said to be the closest friend among his fellow composers. Clay was responsible for introducing them. Sullivan compiled the notes on Clay in the first edition of Grove's *Dictionary of Music and Musicians*.

Clay's most famous composition is his song 'I'll sing thee songs of Araby'. Sullivan's compilation *Church Hymns* (1874) matches Clay's 'Litany' with the hymn 'Jesu, with Thy Church abide' by Thomas Pollock. He also composed many successful operettas including *Constance* (1865).

CLEALL, Charles (b.1927)

Born in Heston, Middlesex on 1 June 1927.

Educated at Ashford County School; Hampton Grammar School; Jordanhill College, Glasgow; Trinity College of Music, London and the University College of North Wales. He was choral scholar at Westminster Abbey (1949-1952). Graduated B.Mus. at the University of London (1952) and M.A. at the University of Wales (1967).

In a varied career he has been a teacher (at Bellahouston Academy from 1953 and at the Glyn Company School, Ewell, Surrey 1955-1966); academic (lecturer at the Froebel Institute, 1967-1968 and professor of singing and voice production, choral repertoire and ear training at Trinity College of Music, 1949-1952); conductor (of the Aldeburgh Festival Choir, 1957-1960 and of the Morley College Orchestra, 1949-1951); music adviser (to the Royal Navy at Plymouth, 1946-1948 and to the London Borough of Harrow, 1969-1972); examiner (for Trinity College of Music); school inspector (in Scotland, 1972-1987) and editor (of the Ernest George White Society - from 1983). Organist and choirmaster of the Glasgow Choral Union (1952-1954), and a music assistant to the BBC Midland Region (1954-1955).

Charles Cleall has held a number of London organistships: St. Luke's Church, Chelsea (1945-1946); Wesley's Chapel, City Road (1950-1952) and St. Paul's Church, Portman Square (1957-1961). These appointments were followed by that of Holy Trinity Church, Guildford, Surrey (1961-1965).

Author of *The Selection and Training of Mixed Choirs in Churches* (1960) and *Voice Production in Choral Technique* (1970), among other works.

His compositions include a Te Deum, which won a prize in 1947 at the Cathedral of St. John the Divine, New York. He has composed the anthems 'A song for the harvest' (1954) and 'Blessed city, heavenly Salem' (1966).

CLEGG, John Arthur (1868-?)

Born in Rochdale, Lancashire in 1868. Graduated B.Mus at Queen's College, Oxford (1896), following a private education. Organist and choirmaster of St. Stephen's Church, Rochdale (1892) and of the Cross Street Chapel, Manchester (from 1899). Lived for a time in Malvern, Worcestershire. Composer of church music including a Magnificat and Nunc Dimittis in G (1899), the anthems 'O come, let us worship' (1904) and 'Truly, the Light is sweet' (1925) and school songs.

CLEMENS, Theodore Liley (1859-1933)
Born in Bailden, Yorkshire in 1859; died in Eydon, Northamptonshire on 23 July 1933. Composer of hymns including 'Soldiers of the Cross' (1906), the hymn tune 'Bathford' and a carol 'Star of Bethlehem'. Also organ works, songs and part songs.

CLEMENTS, Robert George (1813-1883)
Born in 1813; died in Hackney, London on 20 July 1883. Composer of hymn tunes.

CLEOBURY, Stephen (b.1948)
Born 31 December 1948. Chorister of Worcester Cathedral. Held the Done Music Scholarship while at King's School, Worcester. Was subsequently organ student (1967-1971) of St. John's College, Cambridge where he read music. Graduated B.A. (1970), Mus.B. (1971) and M.A. Organist of St. Matthew's Church, Northampton and director of music of Northampton Grammar School (1974-1978); sub-organist of Westminster Abbey (1974-1978); master of the music of Westminster Cathedral (1979-1982) and organist of King's College, Cambridge (from 1982). Chief conductor of B.B.C. Singers (from 1995). Has composed various anthems and carols, and is said to be imaginative in his treatment of carol arrangements.

CLIFF, Alice Mary
See **PAGE**, Alice Mary.

CLIFFE, Frederic (1857-1931)
Born in Low Moor, near Bradford, Yorkshire on 2 May 1857; died in London on 19 November 1931.
A competent pianist at the age of six and by 11 he was organist of Wyke Parish Church. When 16, from July 1873, he was organist to the Bradford Festival Choral Society. Studied from 1876 at the National Training School of Music where his teachers were Franklin Taylor, **Ebenezer Prout**, **Arthur Sullivan** and **John Stainer**.
Organist of the Leeds Festival, taking part in the first peformance of *The Golden Legend*.
Travelled extensively as a soloist, accompanist and examiner, visiting Australia (1898), South Africa (1900 and 1903) and the U.S.A. Organist to the London-based Bach Choir.
The first professor of piano at the opening of the Royal College of Music (from 1883) where his pupils included **John Ireland** and Arthur Benjamin. Also a professor of the Royal Academy of Music (from 1901).
Composer of a Symphony in C Minor and another in E Minor - first performed at the Leeds Festival of 1892 - songs and a violin concerto, plus church music. From around the year 1905 he no longer composed but concentrated on teaching and performing.

CLIFFORD, Benjamin (1752-1811)
Born in 1752; died in April 1811. Composer of hymn tunes.

CLIFFORD, Revd. James (1622-1698)
Born in 1622; died in 1698. A chorister of Magdalen College, Oxford from 1632. In 1661 he was appointed a minor canon of St. Paul's Cathedral, where in 1682 he became a senior cardinal.

Famous for his edition *A Collection of Divine Services and Anthems...* (1632), which contained an item of his own work, 'Instruct me, O Lord'.

CLIFTON, John Charles (1781-1841)
Born in London on 7 November 1781; died in Hammersmith, London on 18 November 1841.
A chorister of St. Paul's Cathedral. Studied music under a relative, **Richard Bellamy**, for five years.
A merchant, pianist, conductor and teacher, he gave up a job that he had held for two years at the Stationery Office to concentrate on a career in music, which he pursued in Bath and Dublin (from 1802) before settling in London in 1816. Taught piano and the Logier notation of music. In Dublin, he and **John Stevenson** organised a concert in aid of famine relief.
Composer of the anthems 'As pants the heart' and 'Wash me thoroughly' (1823), an opera, glees, songs, and the hymn tune 'Clifton', first published in 1837 and used in *Church Hymnary* (Revised Edition 1927) with 'Jesus, these eyes have never seen' by Ray Palmer.

CLIPPINGDALE, Josiah (1834-1900)
Born in 1834; died in West Kensington, London, on 21 March 1900. Composer of the anthems 'If ye walk in my statutes' and 'Rend your heart'.

CLUCAS, Humphrey (b.1941)
Born on 16 November 1941. Read English at King's College, Cambridge, where he was a choral scholar of under **David Willcocks**. A lay vicar of Westminster Abbey. Self-taught as a composer. His early Preces and Responses (1964) are widely used, but most of his works date from within the last 15 years. Special canticle settings have been written for Salisbury Cathedral (1981); King's College, Cambridge (for men's voices, 1980) and others. Works include an unaccompanied Requiem (1989), two Masses and a variety of anthems and carols. Concert works based on religious texts have also been written, and items for organ.

CLULEY, John (1856-1940)
Born in Willenhall, Staffordshire in 1856; died in Willenhall on 25 January 1940. Organist and choirmaster of a number of churches in the Willenhall area for a total of more than 50 years, including Lichfield Street, Willenhall (from 1861); Little London Baptist Church, Little London (from 1893) and the Wesleyan Chapel, Union Street. Composer of hymn tunes including 'Llyfnant' and 'Willenhall', both found in *Methodist Hymn Book* (1933).

COBB, Gerard Francis (1838-1904)
Born in Nettlestead, Kent on 15 October 1838; died in Cambridge on 31 March 1904.
Educated at Marlborough College (1849-1857) and Trinity College, Cambridge where he graduated B.A. (1861) and M.A. (1864). Studied music at Dresden. A devout man, he considered becoming a candidate for ordination but decided against it.
Assisted the university professor, **George Macfarren** in reforming the musical curriculum at the University of Cambridge.
Composer of a Setting of Psalm 62 for Solo Voices, Chorus and Orchestra, commissioned for the North East Choirs Association Festival at Ripon Cathedral in 1892.
Composer of seven services, including the Service in C for Men's Voices, which was written for St. George's Chapel, Windsor

Castle; anthems; the motet *Surge Illuminare* and glees. He is known today for his hymn tune 'Hemsford' which is found in the Standard Edition (1916) of *Hymns Ancient and Modern* with the hymn by Revd. J.M. Neale, 'With Christ we share a mystic grave'. 'Harrogate' appeared in *Baptist Church Hymnary* (1900). A processional tune to 'Laud, O Sion, thy Salvation' is used widely at celebrations of the feast of Corpus Christi. His other works include some 20 settings of Kipling's *Barrack Room Ballads* and a Suite for Violin.

COBB (Cob), John (17th century)
A 17th century musician of the Chapel Royal, where he is documented as a gentleman from 1638 and is known to have served also as organist. He also taught organ and virginals. He may have been in the service of **William Laud**, and he was acquainted with **Henry Lawes** and **William Lawes**. Composer of the anthem 'Let God arise', ayres, catches, canons and some instrumental music. Some of his anthems are recorded in manuscript at the Chapel Royal.

COBBOLD (Cobbald, Cobhold), William (c1560-1639)
Baptised in Norwich, Norfolk on 5 January 1560; died in Beccles, Suffolk on 7 November 1639. Organist of Norwich Cathedral from 1595 until some time between 1609 and 1612, at which point he was succeeded by **William Inglott**. From that time he continued at Norwich as a singing man. Known to have written a number of madrigals. Several four-part settings by Cobbold are in the compilation by Thomas East, *Whole Booke of Psalmes* (1592 and 1611), and in the *Psalter* (1621) of **Thomas Ravenscroft**. He is known for his setting to Psalm 18 'O God, my Strength and Fortitude'. Another anthem by him is 'In Bethlehem towne'.

COCKER, Norman (1889-1953)
Born in Sowerby Bridge, Yorkshire on 30 November 1889; died in Dukinfield, Cheshire on 15 November 1953. Son of a local dentist.
A chorister of Magdalen College, Oxford. From 1907 to 1909 he was organ scholar of Merton College, Oxford but he was sent down without taking a degree. The University of Manchester awarded him the degree of M.A. honorarily in 1951.
Organist at the church of SS Philip and James,. Oxford (1909-1913). From 1912 to 1915 he was music master of Magdalen College School, Oxford, at which point he joined the army.
Sub organist (1919-1943) and organist (1943-1953) of Manchester Cathedral. In 1921 he resigned to became organist of St. Peter's Church, Eaton Square, London but in 1923 he resumed as sub organist of Manchester Cathedral. Organist of The Holy Innocents' Church, Fallowfield; also of the Gaumont Theatre at the Kingsway, Manchester; the Regal, Altrincham, Cheshire and the Art Theatre, Bury, Lancashire.
Composer of a Communion Service in F Minor. His hymn tunes 'Ryburn' and 'Ripponden' are used today in the New Standard Edition of *Hymns Ancient and Modern*. He also composed for organ, being particularly remembered for his *Tuba Tune*, dedicated to **William Eveleigh**.

COCKRAM, Henry T. (?-1878)
Died in 1878, a victim of the *Princess Alice* disaster at Woolwich, London in which he drowned. Attended the Royal Academy of Music. Composer of the anthem 'O, that men would praise'.

CODNER, D. John D. (1851- ?)
Organist of St. Bride's Church, Fleet Street, London and of St. David's Cathedral, Wales (1894-1896), being forced to retire through illness. Composer of church music including three Chant settings of the Te Deum (1895).

COGAN (Coogan), Dr. Philip (c1750-1833)
Born in Cork, Ireland around 1750; died in Dublin on 3 February 1833. Other sources have it that he was born in Doncaster, Yorkshire in 1757. A chorister and later a singing man of St. Finn Barre Cathedral, Cork. A stipendary of Christ Church Cathedral, Dublin (from 1771) but was dismissed in the following year. Held various church organistships, including that of St. John's Church, Dublin (from 1778). Organist of St. Patrick's Cathedral (1780-1806), being known also as a piano teacher and virtuoso piano performer. His speciality was improvising on traditional Irish melodies. Composer of anthems, songs and sonatas for piano and violin.

COLBECK, William Robert (1852-?)
Born in Bebington, Cheshire in 1852. Studied under **French Flowers** and **Frederick Hird**.
At the age of 11 he became organist of Gamston Parish Church, Nottinghamshire. Other appointments held by him were St. Peter's Church, Morley, Leeds; St. Mathias, Burley, Leeds (from 1869) and Folkestone Parish Church, Kent (from 1876). In 1876 he emigrated to British Guiana (now Guyana) where he was organist of St. Philip's Church, Georgetown and town hall organist of Georgetown. Composer of a Tropical Harvest Hymn (1884), songs and items for piano.

COLBORNE, Dr. Langdon (1835-1889)
Born in Hackney, London on 15 September 1835; died in Hereford on 16 September 1889.
Studied under **George Cooper**, and graduated Mus.B. (1864) at the University of Cambridge. Awarded the Lambeth D.Mus.(1883). Organist of St. Michael's College, Tenbury, Worcestershire (1860-1874); Beverley Minster, Yorkshire (1874-1875); Wigan Parish Church, Lancashire (1875-1877); Dorking Parish Church, Surrey (1877) and Hereford Cathedral (1877-1891). In 1876 he was one of the unsuccessful applicants for the vacant position of organist of Chichester Cathedral, for which **T.E. Aylward** was preferred.
Composer of a Service in C and settings of the Magnificat and Nunc Dimittis in D, in A and in B-flat. His anthems include 'O Lord our governor' and 'Out of the deep'. Composer of an oratorio *Samuel* (1889), songs and part songs.

COLDWELL, Henry James (1844-1922)
Born in St. Marylebone, London in 1844; died in Leeds, Yorkshire on 7 April 1922. Composer of hymn tunes.

COLE, Frederick G. (19th/20th century)
Organist of St. John's Church, Notting Hill, London (from 1905). Composer of an Evening Service in E Minor.

COLE, James Parry (19th century)
Born in Tarrington, Herefordshire. Taught to play violin by his father. At the age of eight he joined the choir of Hereford Cathedral, later becoming a pupil of **George Townshend Smith**. Entered the Royal Academy of Music at the age of 15, studying

under Benjamin Blagrove, **William Dorrell**, **Charles Lucas** and **George Macfarren**. Early in his career he lived for five years at Arundel, Sussex where he was parish church organist and taught music. He then moved to London. Composer of songs, items for violin, stage music, a cantata *By the waters of Babylon,* and services.

COLE, Joseph Andrew (1861-1937)
Born in Grosmont, Monmouthshire, Wales in 1861; died in Southampton, Hampshire on 21 June 1937. The cousin of Alfred Gilbert, creator of the Eros statue in London. Whereas his father had been a chorister of Hereford Cathedral, Joseph Cole became a member of the local Congregational Church. He followed a commercial career, living and serving as organist and choirmaster in Leominster, Cheltenham and Hereford. The hymn tune 'Grosmont' by Joseph Cole was used in the hymnals *Congregational Praise* (1951) and *With One Voice* (1978).

COLE, William (c1764-1848)
Born around the year 1764; died in Pimlico, London on 11 August 1848. An organist and teacher in Colchester, Essex and in London. Compiled *The Psalmist's Exercise* for the use of country choirs. Composer of a Morning and Evening Service and six anthems including 'Hear my prayer, O Lord' and 'Let my complaint'.

COLEMAN, Dr. Richard Henry Pinwell (1888-1965)
Born in Dartmouth, Devon on 3 April 1888; died in Dartmouth on 17 February 1965.
A chorister of St. George's Church, Ramsgate, Kent. Educated at Denstone College. An articled pupil of **Sydney Nicholson**, he also trained with R.J. Forbes, Francis Harford and Paul le Vallon. Graduated B.Mus. (1919) and D.Mus. (1924) at the University of Dublin.
Organist of St. Stephen's Church, Carlisle; sub organist of Manchester Cathedral (1908-1912) and organist of Blackburn Parish Church (1912-1914). Held two cathedral organist appointments: Derry (1914-1920) and Peterborough (1921-1944). On returning to England in 1920 he became director of music of the Chailey Heritage School, near Lewes, Sussex.
Henry Coleman was Staffordshire's county music adviser (1943-1946); organist of Hatfield Parish Church, Hertfordshire (1947-1948) and director of music of All Saints' Church, Eastbourne, Sussex (1949-1959) and of the Chapel Royal, Brighton (from 1959).
Published editions of the organ music of **Handel**, **John Stanley** and others. His text book *The Amateur Choir Trainer* (1932) was re-published in 1964 under the title *The Church Choir Trainer*.
Composer of anthems, Services including an Evening Service in D, and music for organ and piano.

COLERAINE, Lord Hugh Hare (c1606-1667)
Hugh, Lord Coleraine, was born around the year 1606; died in Totteridge, Hertfordshire on 2 October 1667. Became a student at the Inner Temple in November 1620. Succeeded to the baronetcy on 31 August 1625. A courtier of Charles I and reputedly rich and eccentric. A classical scholar, linguist and traveller. The Civil War was a financial disaster for him: he lost some £40,000. Composer of descants to 15 Psalms and he may also have written the hymn tune 'Vincenza'.

COLERIDGE-TAYLOR, Samuel (1875-1912)
Born in Holborn, London on 15 August 1875; died on 1 September 1912 of pneumonia, possibly brought on through overwork.
He was brought up by his mother when his father returned to Africa. They moved to Croydon, Surrey where he received free violin lessons from Joseph Beckwith. From the age of 10 he sang in the choir of St. George's Presbyterian Church and then when his voice broke, he joined the choir of St. Mary Magdalene as an alto. Colonel H.A. Walters, a local choirmaster, approached Sir George Grove to discuss an arrangement whereby the talented but impecunious Coleridge-Taylor could study at the Royal College of Music.
Fortunately arrangements were made and Coleridge-Taylor duly attended the R.C.M. (1890-1897), initially as a violin student and then (from 1892) as a composition pupil of **C.V. Stanford**, winning an Open Scholarship for composition in 1893. His fellow students were **Gustav Holst**, William Hurlestone and **Ralph Vaughan Williams**.
Famous as a composer, his output would have been greater but for his teaching commitments: his major appointments began in 1898 when he was appointed to teach violin at the Royal Academy of Music. A professor of composition at Trinity College of Music (from 1903). In addition he was a successful conductor, making tours of the U.S.A. in 1904, 1906 and 1910 to conduct his own works.
He taught at Guildhall School of Music (from 1910) and he was conductor of the London Handel Choir (1904-1912).
In 1903 he founded an amateur string orchestra in Croydon where he lived. This was successful, and professional woodwind and brass sections were later added to the ensemble.
Composer in various genres and perhaps his best known work is *Hiawatha's Wedding Feast* (1898). August J. Jaeger introduced him to **Edward Elgar**, who helped him win a commission for the Three Choirs' Festival of 1898. His music for the church began with a Te Deum (1890), an anthem 'In Thee, O Lord' (1891) and four other anthems (1892). His other church music included a Morning and Evening Service in F.

COLES, Sydney George Randolph (1852-?)
Born in Bristol, Gloucestershire in 1852.
A chorister of St. Paul's Church in Bristol and a pupil of Alfred Stone. In 1873 he became an articled pupil of **W.H. Monk**. Graduated B.Mus. *in absentia* at the University of Toronto, Canada in 1887.
At the age of 18 he was appointed organist of St. John's Church, Broad Street, Bristol.
Settled in Eastbourne, Sussex in 1881 as a pianist and teacher. Organist of the Parish Church for 10 years before moving to a similar position at Eastbourne Presbyterian Church. He strongly defended the concept and practice of *in absentia* degrees in the early 1890s when they caused a great controversy.
Composer of a setting of the Holy Communion Service and of the offertory Sentences, a carol *The Bellringers*, an *Imperial Hymn,* a *Triumphal March* and works for organ and for piano.

COLLET, Sophia Dobson (1822-1894)
Born in London in 1822; died in Highbury Park, London, on 27 March 1894. Composer of music that was used at the South Place Chapel, London.

COLLIGNON, Dr. Charles (1725-1785)
Born in 1725; died in Cambridge on 1 October 1785. Educated at the University of Cambridge where he graduated M.B. (1749) and M.D. (1754). After practising as a doctor in Cambridge he became professor of anatomy at the university (1753-1785). Author of medical treatises. The hymn tune 'University' which is attributed to him was used in *Hymns Ancient and Modern* and elsewhere to the words 'The God of love my Shepherd is'.

COLLINGWOOD, William Bertram (1878-1929)
Born in Chesterfield, Derbyshire in 1878; died in Grahamstown, South Africa on 8 March 1929.
At the age of 14 he was organist of Abingdon, Berkshire. He attended school in the town: his music teacher was **Frederick Iliffe**. At 19 he won a scholarship to Pembroke College, Oxford and at 21 he was awarded a music exhibition at Jesus College. Held the Oxford M.A.
Music master of St. Edmund's School, Canterbury, Kent (from 1902). Emigrated to South Africa in 1906, taking up and holding for 13 years an organistship in Grahamstown. He was then organist of Kimberley Cathedral, a position he was eventually forced through ill-health to resign, becoming organist of the Commemoration Church, Grahamstown. In 1923 he was a member of the music department of Rhodes University at its inauguration.
Composer of hymn tunes, *Three Kyries* (1905) and sacred songs.

COLLINS, Thomas (18th century)
Thomas Collins lived during the 18th century in Nuneaton, Warwickshire. Published *A Collection of Anthems and Psalms* around the year 1789. The Standard Edition (1924) of *Hymns Ancient and Modern* uses his tune 'Bromsgrove' with the hymn by Isaac Watts and William Cameron, 'How bright these glorious spirits shine'.

COLLINSON, Thomas Henry (1858-1928)
Born in Alnwick, Northumberland on 24 April 1858; died in Edinburgh in 1928.
A pupil of **Philip Armes** at Durham Cathedral where he also served as deputy organist. Graduated B.Mus. in 1887 at New College, Oxford.
Organist of St. Oswald's Church, Durham (from 1876). In 1878 he was appointed organist of St. Mary's Church, Edinburgh (which gained cathedral status the following year) where he remained for 50 years and in 1898, of the University of Edinburgh. Lectured in church music at the Episcopal Theological College (from 1880). Composer of anthems.

COLLISON, Valerie (b.1933)
Born in Bromley, Kent on 23 March 1933. Educated at Bromley Grammar School for Girls and at secretarial college. A medical secretary in Bromley, Salisbury and Exeter. Her hymn tune 'Celebrations' is used for the hymn 'Come and join the celebration', which she also wrote. Both first appeared in *Carols for Children* (1972).

COLVIN, Revd. Thomas Stevenson (b.1925)
Born in Glasgow on 16 April 1925.
Studied at Trinity College, University of Glasgow.
A lieutenant in the Royal Engineers, serving in Burma and Singapore. A retired minister of the Church of Scotland. A missionary in Malawi and northern Ghana (1954-1974). From 1974 he was warden and leader of ministry of the Grove Centre in Sydenham, Surrey, returning subsequently to Africa, and serving the church in Africa for a total of 26 years.
Composer of the hymn tune 'Chereponi', an arrangement of a Ghanaian folk song, to accompany the hymn which he also wrote 'Jesu, Jesu, fill us with your love'.

COMLEY, James (1818-1901)
Born in Corsham, Wiltshire in 1818; died in Cheltenham, Gloucestershire in 1901. Little is known about him, except that he contributed a tune 'Malmesbury Abbey' to the 1875 edition of *Hymns Ancient and Modern*.

CONGREVE, Benjamin (1836-1871)
Born in 1836; died in London on 3 March 1871.
Composer of the anthems 'I will greatly rejoice' and 'The Lord is risen indeed', songs and part songs.

CONINGSBY, Charles (19th century)
Organist of Hornsey Parish Church, London in 1859. Composer of the anthem 'Try me, O God'.

CONRAN, Michael (19th century)
Organist of St. Patrick's Church, Manchester. Composer of a Stabat Mater (1865) and published a collection of hymns and Gregorian chants.

CONWAY, Dr. Marmaduke Percy (1885-1961)
Born in Walthamstow, Essex in 1885; died in Douglas, Isle of Man on 22 March 1961.
Following his studies at Bedford Grammar School he was organ scholar at the Royal College of Music. Graduated B.Mus. (Oxford, 1907) and D.Mus. (Dublin, 1914).
In Eastbourne, Sussex he was organist of Upperton Congregational Church (1900-1902), assistant organist of St. Saviour's (1902-1909) and organist and choirmaster of All Saints' (1908-1917).
From 1917 until 1921 he was organist of St. Andrew's Church, Wells Street, London. He was then associated with three cathedrals: Wells (as sub organist 1921-1925) and, as organist, Chichester (1925-1931) and Ely (1931-1949). The author of books and articles on techniques of organ playing, the latter appearing in *The Organist* and in *Musical Opinion*.
Composer of an Evening Service in B-flat Minor, a song 'The radiant morn', hymn tunes and chants. He also composed sight reading tests for organ candidates.

COOK, Dr. Alfred Melville (1912-1994)
Born in Gloucester on 18 June 1912; died in 1994.
Educated at King's School, Gloucester. A chorister and, for a short period, a student with **A.H. Brewer**. Following Brewer's death in office, Cook continued his studies with **Herbert Sumsion**. Graduated B.Mus. (1934) and D.Mus. (1940) at the University of Durham.
Assistant organist of Gloucester Cathedral (1932-1937); organist of All Saints' Church, Cheltenham (1935-1937) and of Leeds Parish Church (1937-1956). Organist of the Leeds Musical Festival in 1947, 1950 and 1953. The youngest organist ever to be appointed to the Leeds post, from a field of nearly sixty candidates. During World War II he served with the Royal Artillery.

Organist of Hereford Cathedral (1956-1966) before emigrating to Winnipeg, Canada where he was organist of All Saints' Church (1966-1967). He then became organist and master of the choristers of the Metropolitan United Church, Toronto. Retired in 1986, returning to the U.K. and living in Cheltenham.
Composer of the hymn tune 'Metropolitan'.

COOK, Dr. Edgar Tom (1880-1953)
Born in Worcester on 18 March 1880; died in Chipstead, Surrey on 5 March 1953.
Studied at Worcester Royal Grammar School, with **Hugh Blair** and **Ivor Atkins**, successive organists of Worcester Cathedral. Graduated B.Mus. at Queen's College, Oxford (1905). Accorded the Lambeth D.Mus. (1934).
Appointed C.B.E. in 1949.
Organist of the church of St. Oswald, Worcester (from 1893); of St. Leonard's, Newland (which at the time had a choir school of its own); Malvern (1898-1908). Assistant organist of Worcester Cathedral (1904-1908).
Organist of Southwark Cathedral (1908-1953), and one of the first organists to broadcast regularly on the radio: his weekly mid-day recitals were a feature of the late 1920s and early 1930s.
Composer of at least one hymn tune (found in *New English Hymnal*) and an Evening Service in G. Author of *The Use of Plainsong* (1928).

COOK, John (b.1918)
Composer of a Morning and Evening Service in G, an Organ Fanfare and a Paean on 'Divinum Misericordium'.

COOKE, Dr. Arnold Atkinson (b.1906)
Born in Gomersal, near Leeds, Yorkshire on 4 November 1906.
Following his schooling at Repton, Derbyshire (1921-1925), he studied at the University of Cambridge (1925-1929) then became a pupil of Paul Hindemith at the Berlin Hochschule für Musik (1929-1932). Awarded the Cambridge M.A. and Mus.D.
For a short time, Cooke was director of music at the Festival Theatre, Cambridge. A professor of harmony and composition at the Royal Manchester College of Music (1933-1938). Following active service in the Royal Navy during World War II (1941-1945) he settled in London and taught at Trinity College of Music (1947-1978).
Composer of chamber music, symphonies, choral and solo vocal works, a cantata *Ode on St. Cecilia's Day*, part songs and anthems.

COOKE, Dr. Benjamin (1734-1793)
Born in Covent Garden, London in 1734; died in Westminster, London on 14 September 1793 and was buried at Westminster Abbey. Father of **Robert Cooke**.
A pupil of J.C. Pepusch. Graduated Mus.D. at the University of Cambridge (1775). Awarded, honorarily, the D.Mus. at the University of Oxford (1782).
Appointed librarian (1749), and later succeeded Pepusch as conductor (1752-1589), of the Academy of Ancient Music, for which he also composed. He resigned as conductor, affronted, following a disagreement over policy.
Having been assistant organist from the age of 12 to John Robinson at Westminster Abbey, he was Robinson's successor (1762-1793); he had in the meantime already been appointed master of the choristers (1757-1793) in succession to **Bernard Gates**, and lay vicar (1752). His choristers included **William Beale**, **Thomas**

Greatorex, John Hindle, William Knyvett, Reginald Spofforth and **Thomas Forbes Walmisley**.
In 1782 he was appointed organist of St. Martin-in-the-Fields, London.
Composer of secular cantatas, organ music, chamber music, glees, catches and canons. His church music includes two services (including a Service in G, specially written for the newly-installed pedal organ at Westminster Abbey) and around 20 anthems including 'Behold how good and joyful' which was his Mus.D. exercise.
Harmonised the hymn tune 'Westminster' for *Hymns Ancient and Modern* for use with 'O Trinity, most blessed Light', and composed others. He was represented in *Cathedral Psalter Chants* (1875) by a Single Chant in F and by Double Chants in B-flat and in A Minor.

COOKE, Revd. Greville Vaughan Turner (1894-1989)
Born in Ealing, London on 14 July 1894; died on 7 November 1989.
Studied at the Royal Academy of Music from the age of 11 under **Tobias Matthay**. Organ scholar at Christ's College, Cambridge (1914-1916). Graduated B.A. and Mus.B. (both 1916) and M.A. (1920).
Following studies at Ridley Hall, Cambridge he was ordained deacon in 1918 and priest in 1919.
His career combined music with the service of the church. His teaching career included the appointments of professor of piano at the R.A.M. (from 1925), and lecturer at the University of London. Also a B.B.C. lecturer in music.
Assistant curate of Tavistock, Devon (1918-1920); deputy minor canon of St. Paul's Cathedral (1920-1921); assistant curate of St. Mary's, Ealing, London (1921); vicar of Cransley, Kettering, Northamptonshire (1921); canon of Peterborough Cathedral (1955) and rector of Buxted, Sussex (1956-1971).
Published *A Theory of Music* (1935) and *Art and Reality* (1940).
Composer of a number of hymn tunes; three written in 1944 were published in *Hymns Ancient and Modern*. One of these is 'Golden grove', used with 'Stand up, stand up for Jesus'. 'Ivinghoe' is used with his own hymn 'Jesus Christ, my heart's true Captain'.

COOKE, Henry (1616-1672)
Born, probably in Lichfield, Staffordshire on 14 September 1616; died in Hampton Court, Surrey on 13 July 1672 and was buried in the cloisters of Westminster Abbey a few days later. It is likely that he was the son of John Cooke of Lichfield who sang bass in the Chapel Royal from around 1620.
Henry Cooke was a boy chorister at the Chapel Royal in the time of Charles I.
Around 1642, during the civil war, Cooke joined the Royalist forces and took part in the retreat from Newcastle to York. He was promoted to captain, a rank which served as his nickname for the rest of his life. During the period of the Commonwealth he lived as an actor and opera singer and it is believed that he studied singing in Italy. Around the year 1654 he was noted to be singing 'in the Italian style'.
Following the Restoration, at the Coronation of Charles II, Henry Cooke composed all the special music. Charles II appointed him master of the children of the Chapel Royal (September 1660). The choir had been dissolved. Henry Cooke was allowed to re-introduce the system of pressing, in the course of which he travelled as far afield as Newark and Lincoln. Even so, in the early days of the

Restoration, on occasions he was forced to substitute cornetts for boys' voices.

A number of his choristers went on to pursue distinguished musical careers, including **Pelham Humfrey, John Blow, Henry Purcell, Robert Smith, Thomas Tudway** and **Michael Wise.**

He made gifts of money, clothing and other items to a number of boys whose voices had broken and he helped to find them employment. For example, Thomas Edwards in 1664 became clerk to Samuel Pepys on the recommendation of Henry Cooke. According to Pepys, Henry Cooke's success made him conceited, although his diary for July 1664 expresses admiration for his prowess as a singer and a trainer of boy choristers. Cooke remained at the Chapel Royal until the year of his death.

Composer of works for the stage and the church, and in particular for various royal and festive occasions. At the coronation of Charles II, five of the nine items sung were composed by Henry Cooke. In all he composed 32 anthems plus a setting of the Nicene Creed and of the Burial Service.

COOKE, Henry (1769-1840)

The third son of **Benjamin Cooke**. Worked for the General Post Office. Composer of the anthems 'Blessed be the Lord God' and 'Give the king'.

COOKE (Cook), John (?-c1419)

Believed to have died before 25 July 1419. Clerk to the Chapel Royal of Henry V and Henry VI, from around the time of the former's accession to the throne (1413), though historians have noted that there were two persons with the same name at the Chapel Royal of the time. Composer of the motet *Ave proles regia.* Probably also composed other motets, and Masses.

COOKE, John (1930-1995)

A student at the Royal College of Music, where his instruments were piano, organ, violin and percussion.

Organ teacher in the R.C.M. Junior Department. Director of the Northern Cathedral Singers. Well known as a choir trainer.

Northern commissioner and regional director (1975-1993) of the Royal School of Church Music. An examiner for the Associated Board of the Royal Schools of Music (from 1975), in connection with which he undertook examination tours of Hong Kong and Singapore. Also toured extensively in giving choral workshops, seminars and courses.

Organist and choirmaster of three churches in the London area. A teacher in Sussex and a local choral society conductor.

Composer of the anthem 'Renew us, Lord' (1990) for the Millenium Celebrations of the Saxon tower of the Church of St. Mary the Virgin, Ovingham, and many descants for hymns.

COOKE, Nathaniel (1773-?)

Born in Bosham, near Chichester, Sussex in 1773; it is likely that he died after 1820. Nephew of Matthew Cooke, organist of St. George's Church, Bloomsbury, London, with whom he studied music. Nathaniel Cooke was organist of Brighton Parish Church, Sussex. A collection of Psalm and hymn tunes published by him included a number of his own. He also composed a canon 'I have set God always before me' and works for piano.

COOKE, Robert (1768-1814)

Born in Westminster, London in 1768; died by drowning on 22 or 23 August 1814 following the onset of insanity. The son of **Benjamin Cooke.**

In 1793 he became organist of the Church of St. Martin-in-the-Fields, London on the retirement of his father, Benjamin. Robert Cooke became organist (1802-1814) and master of the choristers (1806-1814), of Westminster Abbey in succession to **Richard Guise.**

His secular music includes an *Ode to Friendship,* songs and glees. Composer of an Evening Service in C. A Double Chant is found in *Cathedral Psalter Chants* (1875).

COOKE, William Henry (1820-1912)

Born in 1820; died in Bath, Somerset in 1912. Lived in Bath for most of his life; organist of the Argyll Congregational Church from 1856 to 1880. Honorary choirmaster of Bath Abbey. Composer of hymn tunes including 'Sanctissimus', which was included in the 1881 edition of *Bristol Tune Book*. Later it was used in *Baptist Hymn Book* with the hymn 'Worship the Lord' by J.S.B. Monsell.

COOMBES, George (?-c1769)

Died in Bristol, Gloucestershire around the year 1769. Someone of this name was organist of Bristol Cathedral (1756-1759); this person or another identically named was organist of Wimbourne Minster (1743). Coombes's tune 'Oxford new', published around 1775 is used today with the hymn 'O lift us up, strong Son of God' by Cyril Hambly.

COOMBS (Combs), James Morris (1769-1820)

Born in Salisbury, Wiltshire in 1769; died in Chippenham, Wiltshire on 7 March 1820. A chorister of Salisbury Cathedral from 1776 to 1784. He later studied under **John Stephens** and Robert Parry, organist of Salisbury Cathedral. Organist of Chippenham Parish Church (1789-1820). Composer of anthems including 'Blessed is the man that feareth' and 'Out of the deep'.

COOMBS, James Morris (1799-1873)

Organist of Chippenham Parish Church, Wiltshire and, from 1831, of Bowood Private Chapel. His *Dictionary of Musicians* went to a second edition in 1827. Composer of the anthem 'Give ear, O Lord'.

COOMBS, William (18th century)

William Coombs lived in Bristol at the end of the 18th century. The hymn tune 'Oxford', which he composed, is sometime misattributed to the elder **James Coombs**.

COONEY, Dr. Edward (1848-?)

Born in Dublin in 1848. Educated at Christ Church Cathedral, Dublin. Graduated B.Mus. (1885) and D.Mus. (1887) at the University of Dublin. Organist of the Parish Churches of Nenagh (from 1868) and Ballymena (St. Patrick's Church). Taught piano and singing at the Coleraine Academic Institute. Composer of services, anthems including 'God, be merciful unto us' (1898), songs and part songs.

COOPER, Alexander Samuel (1835-1900)

Born in London on 30 April 1835; died in London, at the Charterhouse, on 19 May 1900.

A pupil of **E.J. Hopkins** and of Charles Hallé (1819-1895) for piano.

Organist of Trinity College, Glenalmond, Perth (1855-1857) and of St. Columba's College, Rathfarnham, Dublin (1857-1859). From the latter date he served as organist of various churches in and around London including St. John's, Putney (until 1866) and St. Paul's, Covent Garden. Organist of Tonbridge Grammar School, Kent (1866-1868).

His hymn tune 'Charterhouse' was first used in *The Hymnary*, (1872), edited by **Joseph Barnby**. It is used today in *Hymns and Psalms* (1983) with 'Life and light and joy are found' by C.E. Mudie.

Composer of a setting of the Nicene Creed (1869), anthems including 'Come unto Me' and 'I will lay me down', settings of the service of Holy Communion, chants, songs and part songs. Editor of *Parochial Psalter* and *Parochial Chant Book*.

COOPER, George (1820-1876)

Born in Lambeth, London on 7 July 1820; died in St. Pancras, London on 2 October 1876. His funeral took place in St. Paul's Cathedral.

His father (c1750-1799) and grandfather (c1783-1843), both also named George, were organists of St. Sepulchre's Church, Holborn, London. The father was assistant organist of St. Paul's Cathedral under **Thomas Attwood**, who recognised George Cooper's talent and encouraged him. At the age of 11 he deputised for his father at St. Paul's. Attwood arranged for him to improvise publicly and among those whom he impressed was Mendelssohn.

Beginning at the age of 13 he held the posts in London of organist of St. Benet's Church, Paul's Wharf (1833-1844), SS Ann and Agnes (1836-1844) and, maintaining the family connection, St. Sepulchre, Holborn (1843-1876).

George Cooper succeeded **John Bernard Sale** as one of the two organists of the Chapel Royal in 1856. The other was **George Smart**, upon whose decease George Cooper continued as the sole organist. From 1844 to 1876 he was also singing master and organist at Christ's Hospital.

Assistant organist to **John Goss** at St. Paul's Cathedral from 1838 until his death in 1876. Among his pupils were **Arthur Sullivan** and **John Stainer**.

In 1872, when Goss tendered his resignation he suggested to Cooper that he should apply for the vacant organistship at St. Paul's. Some of the vicars choral also favoured Cooper, but Stainer was appointed instead with Cooper continuing as assistant organist. Between 1838 and 1936, this was the only instance at St. Paul's of the assistant organist failing to secure preferment when the position next fell vacant.

According to **Henry Wood**, 'No man I ever heard played Handel's choruses with the same dignity and breadth'.

In 1862 he revised the work by Revd. W. Windle, *Church and Home Metrical Psalter*; some of the tunes in the Revised Edition were George Cooper's. On the death of **H.J. Gauntlett**, he took on the task of completing the editorship of the *Wesleyan Tune Book*, a task which he completed shortly before his death.

Composer of the hymn tunes 'Dorking' and (in 1836) 'St. Sepulchre', used in *Hymns Ancient and Modern* in conjunction with 'Lord Jesus, when we stand afar' and in *Church Hymns* (1874) with 'Creator of the starry height', the words being a translation by Francis Pott. Today the tune is used in the New Standard Edition of *Hymns Ancient and Modern* with the hymn 'Jesu, Thou Joy of loving hearts'.

He also composed the anthem 'Teach me, O Lord', and chants.

COOPER, James (?-1721)

Died in Norwich, Norfolk on 26 January 1721. Organist of Norwich Cathedral from 1689 until 1720. Composer of the anthems 'Glory to God in the highest' and 'O give thanks'.

COOPER, Dr. John George (19th/20th century)

Graduated B.Mus. (1905) and D.Mus. at the University of Durham. Organist and choirmaster of Kibworth Parish Church (1888-1891); Biggleswade Parish Church, Bedfordshire (1891-1912) and St. Paul's Church, Weston-super-Mare, Somerset (from 1912). Composer of a setting of the Te Deum, and works for piano and organ.

COOPER, Joseph Thomas (1819-1879)

Born in London on 25 May 1819; died in Highbury, London on 17 November 1879.

A pupil of **W.H. Holmes** and of Ignaz Moscheles.

Held a number of organistships in London: St. Michael's, Queenhithe (1838-1844); St. Paul's, Ball's Pond Road (1844-?1866); Christ Church, Newgate Street (1866) and Christ's Hospital (1876).

Composer of hymn tunes. His Single Chant in A Minor was published in *Cathedral Psalter Chants* (1875). Other material composed by him includes orchestral works, songs, part songs and works for organ.

COPE, Cecil (b.1909)

Born in Lichfield, Staffordshire, on 30 May 1909.

A chorister of Lichfield Cathedral (1918-1924) under **John Lott**. Ada Lewis Scholar at the Royal Academy of Music; won a special scholarship to Trinity College of Music.

A lay clerk of Rochester Cathedral (1927-1929), a vicar choral of St. Paul's Cathedral (1929-1935) and a lay vicar of Westminster Abbey (1935-1940, and 1946). A member of the New English Singers (from 1940).

Music master of St. Marylebone Grammar School, and a professor of singing at Trinity College, London (1936-1940) and at Morley College.

Following active service in the army during World War II, Cecil Cope was music organiser for the County of Devon (1946-1949) and lecturer in music at St. Luke's College, Exeter (from 1949).

His compositions include the carol 'Our lady's lullaby' and the anthems 'Bread of the world' and 'How sweet the name of Jesus sounds'. A number of his anthems were published by the School of English Church Music in war-time. He also composed school songs.

COPLEY, Dr. Ian Alfred (1926-?)

Born in Dartford, Kent on 3 October 1926.

Educated at Dartford Grammar School and at the Royal College of Music.

Music master of Thornbury Grammar School (1950-1953) and of Southfield School, Oxford (1953-1958). Lecturer in music at Dartford College of Physical Education (1958-1961) and lecturer in musical appreciation at Stockwell College of Education (1958-1961). He was later a lecturer at Brighton Polytechnic, Sussex, where he became head of the music department.

Author of studies of several English composers including George Butterworth, **Robin Milford, Peter Warlock** and **Charles Wood**. Also contributed to *Music in Education*.

His hymn tune 'Falmer' was used for the first time in *Hymns and Psalms* (1983) with the hymn 'Now thank we all our God'. 'Great Wilkins' is used in the New Standard Edition (1983) of *Hymns Ancient and Modern* with the hymn 'Rise and hear! The Lord is Speaking'. Also composed solo songs.

COPRARIO (Cooper, Cooperario), John (Giovanni) (c1575-1626)

Born around the year 1575; died in London around June 1626. He changed his name to Giovanni Coprario during a visit to Italy in 1600 and retained it on his return to England.

Served James I as composer and player of the lute and viol da gamba (1606-1626). He also taught music: his pupils included Charles I and **William Lawes**. Acquainted with **Thomas Tomkins** and **John Dowland**.

Wrote chamber music, some of which was specifically for court masques, and two devotional part songs, one of which is 'O Lord, how doe my woes encrease'. He wrote an anthem 'Ile lie me downe to sleep'. Also published a book around the year 1610 *Rules how to Compose*.

CORBETT, Dr. Samuel (1852-1924)

Born in Wellington, Shropshire on 29 January 1852; died in 1924. From the age of three months he was blind.

Studied under **James Stimpson** of Birmingham, **George Macfarren** and **James Coward**. Graduated Mus.B. (1873) and Mus.D. (1879) at St. John's College, Cambridge.

Organist of Christ Church, Wellington (1867-1874); Orpington Parish Church, Kent (1874-1875); St. Mary's Church, Bridgnorth, Shropshire (1875-1885); All Saints' Church, Derby (1886-1892); Holy Trinity Church, Bournemouth, Dorset (1892-1897); Nantwich Parish Church, Cheshire (1898-1903) and St. Andrew's Church, Nottingham (1905-1908).

Teacher and choral conductor. A professor of music at the Royal Midland Institute for the Blind from 1905 to 1912. He attended the Birmingham Festival and other events as music correspondent.

Composer of an Evening Service in F, an anthem, songs and part songs.

CORFE, Arthur Thomas (1773-1863)

Born in Salisbury, Wiltshire on 9 April 1773; died in Salisbury on 28 January 1863 and was buried in the cloisters of the Cathedral.

Third son of **Joseph Corfe**, a composer, and organist of Salisbury Cathedral. His own sons, including **Charles Corfe** followed a career in church music. In all he had 14 children.

Studied music at Salisbury with Antram. Also a piano pupil of Muzio Clementi. In 1783 he joined the choir of Westminster Abbey under **Benjamin Cooke**.

In 1804, succeeded his father as organist of Salisbury Cathedral. In 1828 he organised a festival at Salisbury at which he was conductor and his son, John Davis Corfe, who was organist of Bristol Cathedral for more than 50 years, played the organ.

Composer of anthems including 'Lord, Thou art become gracious' and 'Teach me, O Lord', services, and piano pieces.

CORFE, Dr. Charles William (1814-1883)

Born in 1814; died on 16 December 1883. Son of **Arthur Corfe** and the grandson of **Joseph Corfe**. A pupil of his father.

Graduated B.Mus. (1847) and D.Mus. (1852) at the University of Oxford. Organist of Christ Church, Oxford (1846-1883), and appointed coryphaeus of the University in 1856, choragus in 1860. His conservative and unchanging use of the same set of organ stops for the playing of the Psalms was known throughout the College as the 'Corfe Mixture'. Composer of glees, part songs and anthems including 'Thou visiteth the earth'.

CORFE, Joseph (1740-1820)

Born in Salisbury, Wiltshire on 25 December 1740; died in Salisbury on 29 July 1820. The father and grandfather respectively of **Arthur Corfe** and **Charles Corfe**. Learned music as a chorister (1752-1753) and apprentice of **John Stephens**, cathedral organist of Salisbury. A teacher of singing. In February 1782 he was appointed gentleman of the Chapel Royal, having been a lay vicar (1759-1760) of Salisbury. In 1781 the vacant organistship of Salisbury Cathedral was contested by Joseph Corfe and Robert Parry. Following a bitter dispute that became public, Parry was successful: Corfe eventually succeeded him as organist and master of the choristers (1792-1804) until he in turn resigned in 1804. Principal tenor at the Handel Commemoration (1784). Composer of a sizeable amount of church music including services and a Service in B-flat and 11 anthems of which 'I will magnify Thee' (for trebles), 'Be Thou my Judge' and 'The King shall rejoice' are examples. In addition he composed 36 glees and other music. The author of *Treatise on singing* (1799) and *Thorough Bass Simplified*.

CORKINE, William (16th/17th century)

Very little is known about the musician (probably a lute player) and minor composer William Corkine, who lived during the late 16th and early 17th century. It is likely that he had a private patron. Compiled a *Book of Ayres* and is known to have composed an anthem 'Praise the Lord'.

CORNYSHE, William (c1465-1523)

Born around the year 1465 in East Greenwich, Kent; died in Hylden, Kent in 1523, possibly in the month of October.

Court composer to Henry VII, entering his service in 1492. Became a gentleman of the Chapel Royal in 1496. Succeeded William Newark as master of the children (1509-1523), having deputised for him on previous occasions.

In 1504 he was imprisoned in The Fleet over a political pamphlet but he returned to favour and had certainly been released by 1508.

Took 10 choirboys to perform a pageant at the Field of the Cloth of Gold (1520). As well as being a musician, he was a playwright, actor, pageant master, and a supplier of guttering, paving and sanitary ware.

Composer of music for the viol and for pageants, banquets and plays. He also composed antiphons and a *Magnificat Regale*. His *Pater Noster* is in a collection *XX Songes* (1530). 'Woefully arrayed' and the song 'Ah Robin' are other examples of his works.

COSTA, Sir Michael (Michele) Andrew Angus (1808-1884)

Born in Naples, Italy on 4 February 1808; died in Hove, Sussex on 29 April 1884.

Studied music initially under his maternal grandfather, Giacomo Tritto, his father Pasquale Costa, and Giovanni Furno. Continued his studies at the Naples Conservatory, Italy with Girolam Crescenti for singing and Nicola Zingarelli for composition. Knighted in 1869.

Zingarelli received a commission from the organisers of the Birmingham Festival to compose a setting of Psalm 137 'By the waters of Babylon' and despatched Costa to Birmingham to conduct it. The directors of the festival considered him too young for such a responsibility but allowed him to sing the tenor part in this and other works. It was, however, a disaster. Costa decided to remain in England, where he received encouragement from Muzio Clementi.

In 1832 he was the musical director of the King's Theatre, London. A year later he was appointed conductor.

In 1846 he became conductor of the Philharmonic Society and in the same year, conductor of the Royal Italian Opera. In 1849 he received the conductorship of the Sacred Harmonic Society and became the regular conductor of the Birmingham Festival. Conductor of the Handel Festival (1847-1880). Director of music of His Majesty's Opera at The Haymarket, London (1871-1881).

Composer of hymn tunes and of the anthems 'Lord, I have loved the habitation' and 'God, who cannot be unjust'.

COSYN (Cosin), Benjamin (c1570-1653)

Born around the year 1570; died probably in London, and was buried on 14 September 1653. Music master and organist in London at Dulwich College (1622-1624) and The Charterhouse (1626-1643). Composer of keyboard music, an anthem 'O praise God in His holiness'. Added a Venite for, and in the style of, the Short Service by **Orlando Gibbons**.

COSYN (Cosin), Revd. John (1594-1672)

Born in Norwich, Norfolk on 30 November 1594; died on 15 January 1672.

Educated at Gonville and Caius College, Cambridge.

Following his ordination he was appointed chaplain to the Bishop of Durham. He was later prebendary of Durham and archdeacon to the West Riding of Yorkshire. In 1640 he became chancellor of the University of Cambridge. He is said to have held other posts at Cambridge, namely dean and master of Peterhouse.

He fell foul of the Puritans, by introducing choral chapel services, and was driven out by them in 1641, settling in France. In 1660 at the Restoration, he returned to England. He became rector of Brancepeth, County Durham, being later appointed bishop of Durham. His term of office saw large sums of money invested in the cathedral, the library and in works of charity.

In 1661 he was one of the 24 commissioners appointed to advise upon and review *Book of Common Prayer*, a new version of which was sanctioned in 1662.

He translated the hymn 'Come Holy Ghost, our souls inspire'. This was one of the two versions of the only hymn that appeared in the 1662 *Book of Common Prayer* and it was specified for the ordering of priests.

COTES, Revd. Digby H. (18th century)

Digby Cotes was the author of a sermon, published in 1756 *Music, a Rational Assistant in the Duty of Praise*. Composer of the anthem 'In the beginning'.

COTTMAN, Arthur (1841-1879)

Born in Ringwood, Hampshire in 1841; died in Ealing, London on 3 June 1879. A solicitor by profession and an amateur composer. His *Ten Original Hymn Tunes* (1872) contained his 'Caterham'.

COUCHER, Frank (1872-1962)

Born in Lambeth, London in 1872; died in Tunbridge Wells, Kent on 15 May 1962. Composer of hymn tunes and a song 'The Reaper and the Flowers' (1893) to words by Longfellow.

COULDERY, Claudius Herbert (1842-?)

Born in Lewisham, London on 17 August 1842. Went into business before studying at the Royal Academy of Music under **John Goss** and **William Sterndale Bennett**. A professor of Guildhall School of Music. His compositions include a sacred cantata *Christ's entry into Jerusalem* (1843) which was first performed at the R.A.M., an overture, Richard I (1885) and works for piano.

COULES, Reginald Froude (1855-1926)

Froude Coules was born in Cirencester, Gloucestershire in 1855; died in Worsley, Lancashire on 1 May 1926. Organist and choirmaster of St. Mark's Church, Worsley. Composer of a Vesper Hymn (1891) and hymn tunes.

COULSON, Richard (b.1948)

Born in Gateshead, County Durham in 1948. Educated at Newcastle Cathedral, Newcastle School of Music, the Royal College of Music and, under a Churchill Fellowship, with Gustav Leonhardt in The Netherlands. His organ tutors include **Colin Ross** and **Richard Popplewell**. Sub organist of St. Jude's Church, Courtfield Gardens, London (1966-1968); organist of Esher Parish Church, Surrey (from 1969). Director of music of Reed's School, Cobham, Surrey (from 1989). Has performed as an organist at the Promenade Concerts and on B.B.C. Radio 3. Was the first conductor of the 'Voices for Hospices' movement, with which he has been involved since 1989. A former chorus master for the Young Musicians' Symphony Orchestra. Composer of the carols 'In freezing winter night' and 'Infant Holy' and of 'A Prayer of Andrew Reed'.

COURTEVILLE, Raphael (c1675-1772)

Born in 1675 or 1676; thought to have died in 1772, possibly in June. The year previously given for his death, 1735, is now believed to be incorrect.

A chorister of the Chapel Royal.

Organist at St. James's Church, Piccadilly, London, the building being completed only shortly before his appointment in September 1691 at a salary of £20 per annum. From 1753 he required the help of a permanent assistant following a deterioration in his health. It is said that he held the post for 81 years. A claim that a son of the same name succeeded him during this time without the fact being properly recorded is no more than possible.

Said to be the author of *The Gazetteer*, a paper that strongly defended the government of Walpole. His opponents parodied his surname as 'Court Evil'.

Composer of the hymn tune 'St. James' (1697); it was used in *Hymns Ancient and Modern* with the hymn by George Doane 'Thou art the Way, by Thee alone'. **Arthur Sullivan** used the same combination in *Church Hymns* (1874). Courteville collaborated with **Henry Purcell** in composing music for the opera *Don Quixote* by Thomas d'Urfey. His chamber music includes six sonatas and a number of songs.

COWARD, Sir Henry (1849-1944)

Born in Liverpool on 26 November 1849; died in Sheffield, Yorkshire on 10 June 1944.

His father died when Henry was seven years old, whereupon he moved with his mother to Sheffield. Circumstances caused him to change schools frequently.

From the age of nine he was apprenticed to a local cutlery maker for 12 years, making pen and pocket knives. His skill at his trade won him a prize at an exhibition.

He was involved in church activities and his aptitude for music became apparent when he mastered the Tonic Sol-fa system, studying firstly with Thomas Fox and then under Samuel Hadfield. A Sunday School teacher taught him violin and a fellow-lodger, the flute.

Graduated B.Mus. (1889) at the University of Oxford - for which the examiners in the *viva voce* were **Hubert Parry** and **F.A. Ouseley** - and D.Mus. (1894).

Knighted in 1926.

In February 1872 he became a pupil teacher and was able to give away the tools of his former trade. He progressed rapidly, remaining in the profession for 17 years.

Had a formidable reputation as a choir trainer, undertaking a world tour in 1911 with the Sheffield Musical Union in which the U.S.A., Canada, Australia and South Africa were visited. Has been described as 'the pioneer chorus master'. Collaborated with **Cuthbert Harris**, promoter of British composers, and gave 16 concerts in 11 days in Canada with a combined choir drawn from a number of choral societies in the North of England (1908).

In August 1880 he took charge of the Sunday School Centenary gathering in Norfolk Park, Sheffield where 30,000 singers and 500 instrumentalists took part, watched by a gathering of 100,000 people. In 1889 he was appointed lecturer in music at Firth College, which in 1905 became part of the University of Sheffield. Retired in 1933.

Composer of cantatas, glees, songs, hymn tunes, including 'Norfolk Park' for the hymn 'Jesu high and holy' and anthems such as 'I will sing of the mercies of the Lord'. He also composed a String Quartet, songs, an orchestral overture, a cantata *Magna Carta* and an oratorio *The Story of Bethany*. In 1877 he became editor of *Primitive Methodist Hymnal*, containing 1,108 hymns.

COWARD, James (1824-1880)
Born in London on 25 January 1824; died in London on 22 January 1880.

A chorister at Westminster Abbey, frequently called upon as soloist.

Organist of several London Churches including St. Mary's, Lambeth; St. George's, Bloomsbury (1806-1809) and St. Magnus the Martyr, London Bridge which, like his tenure of the first organistship at the Crystal Palace (1857-1880), he held until his death. Organist to the Sacred Harmonic Society.

Composer of the hymn tune 'Sydenham', used in *Hymns Ancient and Modern*, the canon 'Sing unto God' and anthems including 'O Lord, correct me'. In addition he wrote madrigals, glees and items for piano and for organ.

COWARD, James Munro (19th/20th century)
Believed to be connected with the Metzler company, organ manufacturers. A skilled improviser, he gave performances at the South Kensington Exhibition of 1885. Composer of a cantata *The Fishers* (1889) and a Jubilee Hymn for Chorus and Military Band. Editor of *American Organ Journal*.

COWEN, Sir Frederic Hymen (1852-1935)
Born in Kingston, Jamaica on 29 January 1852; died in Maida Vale, London on 6 October 1935.

Came to England as a child of four. By the age of six a waltz by him had been published and an operetta at the age of eight. From November 1860 he took lessons with **John Goss** and Julius Benedict. Learned to play piano.

In 1865 he studied at the Leipzig Conservatory, under Louis Plaidy, Ignaz Moscheles, Carl Reinecke, Ernst Richter and Moritz Hauptmann. He had been awarded a second Mendelssohn Scholarship, the first having been awarded already to **Arthur Sullivan**, but did not take it up, his parents declining for reasons connected with the terms of the award.

Returned to the U.K. in 1866, undertaking further study in Germany some years later at the Berlin Conservatory where he studied with Carl Tausig and, for composition, Friedrich Kiel. In the course of his travels he met Liszt and Brahms.

Awarded doctorates in music honorarily by the Universities of Cambridge (1900) and Edinburgh (1910).

Received a knighthood in 1911.

Assistant to **Michael Costa** at Her Majesty's Theatre. In 1871 he was pianist and accompanist to the Italian Opera.

In 1873 he toured Italy and in 1878, partly on account of his health, the U.S.A.

Succeeded Sullivan as conductor of the Philharmonic Society (1882-1892 and 1900-1907). At the age of 36 he undertook a six-month engagement as musical director of the Centennial Exhibition in Melbourne, Australia, for which he was paid the enormous fee of £800 per month.

Conductor of the Hallé Orchestra (1896-1899) and of the Scottish Orchestra (1900-1907), among others. He also conducted at one time or another at all the major musical festivals between 1876 and 1895.

His First Symphony, composed at the age of 17, was given at St. James's Hall, London, on 9 December 1869. In all he composed six symphonies, ballads, songs, operas including *Pauline,* cantatas, orchestral works, an oratorio *The Transfiguration* (1895) and at least one hymn tune, 'Hymn of praise'.

COX, Father Charles Austin (1853-1916)
Born in London in 1853; died in Hammersmith, London on 26 June 1916. Educated at St. Edmund's School and at Hammersmith. Ordained in 1879. Connected professionally with the Our Lady institution in Kensington for 31 years; incumbent of Holy Trinity Roman Catholic Church, Brook Green, London (from 1910). Composer of sacred music including 'God bless our Pope', and hymn tunes.

COX, Charles Henry William (1860-1920)
Born in East Stonehouse, Devon on 23 June 1860; died in Carlton, Nottinghamshire on 1 July 1920. Composer of hymn tunes.

COY, Dr. Harry (19th/20th century)
Received his early music training at Manchester Cathedral. Graduated B.Mus (1878) and D.Mus. (1885) at New College, Oxford. Organist and choirmaster at the church of St. John the Divine, Brookland, Manchester (1878-1906) and St. John's Church, Old Colwyn, Wales (1907-1908). A conductor of local choral societies. Composer of a sacred cantata *Esther,* and anthems.

CRACKEL, Harry (1876-?)
Born in Rotherham, Yorkshire in 1876. Graduated B.Mus. at the University of Durham (1912). Organist and choirmaster of St. John's Church, Masborough near Rotherham (from 1899) and in the same area, of Eastwood Parish Church (from 1901). Composer of anthems including 'Great and marvellous' and 'Now, Father, we commend', organ pieces and songs.

CRAMENT, John Maude (1845-1912)
Born in Bolton Percy, Yorkshire on 2 April 1845; died on 4 March 1912.
Studied under **George Macfarren** and at the Berlin Hochschule under Carl Haupt and Friedrich Kiel. Graduated B.Mus. at the University of Oxford in 1880.
A professor of music at the Church Education Society Training College, Dublin (1873-1875). Organist in London at Brompton Parish Church and St. Paul's Church, Kensington. A choral society conductor.
Composer of cantatas, anthems including 'Praise the Lord, ye servants' (1897), an Advent Litany (1899), carols, songs and part songs.

CRAMER, John Baptist (1771-1858)
Born in Mannheim, Germany on 24 February 1771; died in Middlesex on 16 April 1858. Composer of many works, including hymn tunes.

CRAMPTON, Thomas (1817-1885)
Born in Sheerness, Kent in 1817; died in Chiswick, London on 13 April 1885. Edited collections of choral music. From 1875 he was purchaser of music to the British Museum. Edited Pitman's *Musical Monthly*. Composer of anthems including 'Lord Jesus, receive my spirit' and 'The sacrifices of God', glees and instrumental works.

CRANFORD, Thomas (16th/17th century)
Probably a vicar choral of St. Paul's Cathedral. He may have composed items of church music but it has proved difficult to distinguish between his work and that of William Cranford.

CRANFORD (Cranforth), William (c1635-?)
Born around the year 1635; died probably some time before 1675. In 1650 he was a chorister of St. Paul's Cathedral. A lay vicar of St. Paul's Cathedral during the reign of Charles I. Composer of a number of anthems, one of which was included in Clifford's *The Divine Services and Anthems* (1664 edition). They include 'O Lord, grant the king a long life' and 'O Lord, make thy servant'. One of his Psalm settings was in the collection by **Thomas Ravenscroft**, *Whole Booke of Psalmes* (1621). Also composed an Evening Service, the hymn tune 'Ely', catches, and more than 20 compositions for viol.

CRANMER, Philip (b.1918)
Born in Acocks Green, Birmingham on 1 April 1918, the son of Arthur Cranmer, a professional baritone.
A chorister at All Saints' Church, Margaret Street, London under Walter Vale. After attending Wellington College, Berkshire, he won an organ scholarship to Christ Church, Oxford, where he graduated M.A. and B.Mus. Also studied at the Royal College of Music.

Assistant music master of Wellington College (1938-1940); accompanist to the B.B.C. Midland Region (1948-1950); director of music at the King Edward School, Birmingham (1946-1947) and a lecturer at the University of Birmingham (1950-1954). He was Hamilton Harty professor of music at Queen's University, Belfast (1954-1970) and held a similar position at the University of Manchester (1970-1975).
Composer of organ music and the anthem 'Teach us, good Lord'. His other works include Variations for Flute and Clarinet, songs, and part songs.

CRANMER, Revd. Dr. Thomas (1489-1556)
Born in Edwinstowe, Nottinghamshire on 2 July 1489; put to death at Oxford on 21 March 1556.
In 1503, at the age of 14 he went up to the University of Cambridge where he remained for eight years, studying philosophy and logic. Graduated B.A. (c1511), M.A. (1515) and D.D. Became a fellow in 1510. Forfeited the fellowship on his marriage, but re-appointed following her death.
During a plague in 1529, he left Cambridge for Waltham, where he became a royal chaplain and archdeacon of Taunton.
Appointed grand plenipotentiary of England by Pope Clement VII.
As Archbishop of Canterbury he was responsible for the pronouncement of the marriage between Henry VIII and Catherine of Aragon as void *ab initio* and of that between Henry and Ann Boleyn as valid, for the subsequent annulment of that marriage in 1536 and for the divorce of Henry from Anne of Cleves (1540).
He was occupied with reform of the liturgy, such the use of the vernacular and the possibility of compressing the Hours into single Morning and Evening Services. He proposed musical reforms at St. Paul's Cathedral.
Wrote a Preface to the Bible in 1540. Compiled the Prayer Book of 1548, in which the Holy Communion Service replaced the Mass; composed the 42 Articles (later reduced to 39) in 1553. Made certain further changes to the Prayer Book in 1552.
Erred politically in subscribing to the instrument divesting the succession from Mary in favour of Lady Jane Grey (1553), whose reign lasted only 12 days. Subsequently sent to the Tower of London and found guilty of treason. Also tried before a Papal Commission in Oxford. Said to be a humane man, but a number of dissidents were burned during his term of office.
Composer of plainsong versions of Latin processions which conformed to his rule preventing over-elaboration: one note per syllable.

CRAWFORD, Thomas James (c1877-1955)
Born in Barrhead, Scotland around 1877; died in Barrie, Ontario, Canada at the age of 78 in 1955.
Attended the Allen Glen School, Glasgow; the University of Durham and the Leipzig Conservatory. Trained in music at Westminster Abbey, the Glasgow Athanaeum and Leipzig Conservatory where he was a first prize winner. Graduated B.Mus. at the University of Durham in 1901.
Organist of All Saints' Church, Leipzig (1894-1898); Holy Trinity, Eltham (1898-1899) and, also in London, St. Paul's Church, Camden Square (1899-1902) and St. Michael's, Chester Square (1902-1922).
A professor of Trinity College of Music, London (1919-1922). Gave recitals in London and at the Crystal Palace. Official organist to the Japanese-British Exhibition on 1910.

Worked for a time under **Frederick Bridge**. Assisted at the Coronation of Edward VII (1902).

Emigrated to Canada. Organist of St. Paul's Church, Toronto (from 1932), of Holy Trinity Church, and of the Eaton Memorial Church until his retirement in 1946. A teacher and examiner at the Toronto Conservatory.

Composer of a setting of the Communion Service, four quadruple chants for the Te Deum (1905), songs and works for organ and for piano.

CRAWFORD, Thomas (1850-1925)

Born in Falkirk, Stirlingshire in 1850; died in Nantwich, Cheshire on 29 January 1925. Composer of hymn tunes.

CREED, Dr. John Edward Hodgson (1904-1974)

Born in Southampton, Hampshire on 28 March 1904; died in Reigate, Surrey on 12 January 1974.

Educated at Highgate School, London, at Reigate Grammar School, Surrey and the Royal College of Music. Studied with **Henry Coleman**. Held a London University doctorate in music.

Organist and choirmaster of St. Luke's Church, Battersea, London (1937-1957); St. John's Church, Redhill, Surrey (1957-1961) and, also in Surrey, St. Philip's Church, Reigate (from 1968). A professor and examiner at the London College of Music (from 1949).

Composer of a Short Holy Communion Service in the Lydian Mode, and hymn tunes. His other works include a Symphony in E Minor and a String Trio in F.

CRESER, Dr. William (1844-1933)

Born in York on 9 September 1844; died in London on 13 March 1933.

Studied with his father, choirmaster of the church of St. John's, York. At the age of eight he became a chorister of York Minster. Studied organ and composition with **George Macfarren** and **F.A.G. Ouseley**. Following his studies at Trinity College of Music, London, he graduated B.Mus. (1869) and D.Mus. (1880) at New College, Oxford.

From 1856 he deputised occasionally for **Joseph Barnby** at St. Paul's Church, Holgate Road, York.

In 1859, at the age of 15, he was appointed organist of Holy Trinity Church, Micklegate, York. His other church organistships were at St. Paul's, York (replacing Barnby in 1863); St. Andrews, Grinton, York (1863-1875); St. Martin's, Scarborough (1875-1881) and Leeds Parish Church (1881-1891).

Composer of the cantata *The Golden Legend* with the intention that it should be used at the Leeds Triennial Festival of 1886. Unfortunately, **Arthur Sullivan** had composed a much larger work with the same name. A deal was struck: Creser put aside his cantata and was rewarded when Sullivan used his influence to secure Creser the preferment some years later at the Chapel Royal, St. James's Palace (1891-1902). In his time at Leeds, among the problems that Creser had to contend with was the 'poaching' of choristers for lucrative, secular engagements. On the other hand, the Parish Church could hardly complain, since it was accused of the same practice.

A musical examiner for T.C.M. for 35 years, in the course of which he travelled extensively in Canada, Australia, New Zealand and India.

Composer of oratorios including *Micah,* a Mass in C, two Psalm settings, a motet for double choir based on Psalm 46 *God is our Hope and Strength*, cantatas, organ and other music.

CREYGHTON (Creighton), Revd. Dr. Robert (c1636/7-1734)

Born probably in 1636 or 1637; died in Wells, Somerset on 17 February 1734.

Son of Bishop Robert Creyghton of Bath and Wells, with whom he went into exile during the interrregnum.

Educated at Trinity College, Cambridge: graduated B.A. (1655), M.A. (1662) and D.D. (1678). Learned music at an early age.

Took holy orders and was prebendary (1662 onwards), canon (1667-1734) and precentor (1674-1734) of Wells Cathedral. From 1692 he was Regius professor of Greek at the University of Cambridge.

A powerful preacher, he held several church appointments, being prebendary of Timberscombe until 1667, and of Yatton from that year. In 1670 he added the incumbencies of Ashbrittle, Somerset and Uplowman, Devon, retaining all three appointments until his decease.

His church music consists of 11 anthems, of which examples are 'Behold now praise the Lord' and 'I will arise', nine services including Services in E-flat and in B-flat.

CROAGER, Edward George (1861 -1922)

Born in London on 20 June 1861; died in Vancouver, British Columbia, Canada on 30 June 1922 whilst on an examination tour for the Associated Board of the Royal Schools of Music.

A chorister and pupil-assistant of St. Andrew's, Wells Street, London, later studying at the Royal Academy of Music.

Sub organist at St. Andrew's (1877-1883) before becoming organist and choirmaster within London successively at the Quebec Chapel, later renamed the Church of the Annunciation (1884-1887); St. Mark's, North Audley Street (1888-1890); St. James's, West Hampstead (1891-1897); St. Paul's, South Hampstead (1898-1919) and Christ Church, Brondesbury (from 1919).

Music master of Clapham Common College and of St. Paul's School, Kensington.

A local choral society conductor. Organist to the Kyrie Choir (from 1904) and to the Handel Society.

Composer of anthems, a patriotic cantata *Our Watchword* (1888), hymn tunes and other forms of church music.

CROFT (Crofts), Dr. William (1678-1727)

Born in Nether Ettington, Warwickshire, baptised on 30 December 1678; died in Bath, Somerset on 14 August 1727 and was buried near **Henry Purcell** at Westminster Abbey. Related to the notorious Judge Jeffreys.

A chorister and a pupil of **John Blow** at the Chapel Royal, which he did not leave until the age of 20, long after his voice had broken. Graduated D.Mus. at Christ Church, Oxford (1713).

His career was devoted almost entirely to the music of the Church; he is known for three London organistships, namely of St. Anne's, Soho (1700-1711), where he was probably the first organist; the Chapel Royal, succeeding **Francis Pigott**, (from 1704), jointly at first with **Jeremiah Clarke,** and then exclusively (from 1707) on the death of Clarke; and Westminster Abbey (1708-1727). It was the death of John Blow that gave rise to the vacancy at Westminster Abbey and those of master of the choristers and composer to the Chapel Royal which Croft also filled.

Composer for the Drury Lane Theatre (1700-1703). Wrote a setting of the Burial Service and much other church music. He was called upon to compose for special occasions such as the funeral of Queen Anne, the Coronations of George I and George II and services of thanksgiving for the victories of the Duke of Marlborough.

His output of 76 anthems include 'Cry aloud and shout', 'We will rejoice', 'God is gone up', 'Out of the deep' and 'The Lord is King'. In 1724 he published 30 of his anthems plus a setting of the Burial Service in two volumes entitled *Musica Sacra*.

Wrote a number of Psalm or hymn tunes around the year 1700, some of which were included in *Yattendon Hymnal* (1899) and *Hymns Ancient and Modern*. It is maintained that his Psalm tunes were the first in the English style as opposed to the slower Genevan form.

A Chant in A Minor was included in *Cathedral Psalter Chants* (1875). He also composed chamber music for violin and recorders, and he wrote incidental music for plays by Steele and Farquhar plus works for the harpsichord and organ. Some organ voluntaries are found in a modern edition. He is seen as a link, with **Maurice Greene**, **William Boyce** and others, between **Henry Purcell** and **Samuel Sebastian Wesley**.

CROFTON, Edward Henry Churchill (1834-1912)
Born in London on 21 October 1834; died in Ahaseragh, County Galway, Ireland on 22 September 1912. Composer of hymn tunes.

CROSBIE, Revd. Howard Augustus (1844-1918)
Born in Liverpool on 21 September 1844; died in Lindfield, Sussex on 23 April 1918.
Graduated B.A. (1867) and M.A. (1870) at Trinity College, Cambridge; ordained priest in 1868.
His first curacy was at Habergham Eaves, Burnley, Lancashire (1867-1875); his second was at Birchin-in-Rusholme, Manchester (1875-1876). He became curate-in-charge of Bamber Bridge near Preston (1876-1878) and then vicar of Milnrow, near Rochdale (1878-1883), both in Lancashire.
Vicar of Trumpington, Cambridge (1878-1883) and of Builth, Llanfair-yn-Cwm (1891), Wales. Incumbent of Llanddewi'r-Cwm, Wales (1891). Retired to Lindfield, Sussex in 1914.
A keen amateur musician and composer. The Revised Edition (1927) of *Church Hymnary* uses his 'Sefton' with 'God of heaven, hear our singing' by Frances Ridley Havergal.

CROSS, William (1777-1825)
Born in Oxford 1777; died in Oxford on 20 June 1825. Graduated B.Mus. in 1823. Organist of Christ Church Cathedral, St. John's College, the University Church and St. Martin's Church, all at Oxford, the first three from 1807 to 1825. At St. Martin's he succeeded his father. Published a collection *Chants, Kyries and Sanctuses for the use of the Church of England* (1818). Composer of hymn tunes and a Chant in C Minor for the funeral of Revd. Dr. White, a canon of Christ Church Cathedral.

CROSSE, Gordon (b.1937)
Born in Bury, Lancashire on 1 December 1937.
Attended the Manchester Warehousemen's and Clerks' School and St. Edmund Hall, Oxford, where under Egon Wellesz he spent two years carrying out research in to the music of the 15th century. From 1962 he studied in Rome with Goffredo Petrassi at the Accademia di Sta. Cecilia.

In 1964 he was appointed to the staff of the University of Birmingham, working as an extra mural staff tutor (1964-1966). A Haywood Fellow from 1966 to 1969, in which year he joined the music faculty of the University of Essex.

For two years he was composer in residence at King's College, Cambridge. In 1976 he moved to the county of Suffolk in order to devote more time to composition. In 1977 he was appointed visiting professor of composition at the University of California, U.S.A.

Among his compositions are 'O Blessed Lord' (1968), a festival anthem 'The covenant of the rainbow' (1968), *Two Christmas Songs,* operas including *The Grace of Todd* (1969) and orchestral works including two symphonies. Has also composed chamber music.

CROSSE, William (17th century)
Few personal details are known of William Crosse. A member of the Chapel Royal in 1625 and a servant of the dean to the Chapel. Composer of at least six anthems, the words of which have survived but not the music.

CROSSLEY, Thomas Henry Hastings (1846-1926)
Hastings Crossley was born in Glenburn, County Antrim, Northern Ireland on 1 August 1846; died in Bordighera in 1926. Studied under **Berthold Tours**. Professor of Greek at Queen's College, Belfast. Composer of hymn tunes and songs including 'Light in Darkness' (1884).

CROSSLEY, William Thomas (1867-1941)
Born in Bradford, Yorkshire in 1867; died in Bradford on 25 April 1941. Studied under **William Creser**. Organist of Low Moor Wesleyan Church, Bradford (1889-1917) and of Windhill Methodist Church, Shipley (from 1919). Composer of the sacred cantata *Light and Truth,* anthems, hymn tunes, carols, marches, and *Fifteen Yorkshire Songs.*

CROTCH, Dr. William (1775-1847)
Born in Norwich, Norfolk on 5 July 1775; died in Taunton, Somerset on 29 December 1847. He was the son of a music-loving carpenter who had built an organ from components.
At two years old he could play 'God Save the King' on the organ. He played piano and violin at seven years and by the age of 14 had written an oratorio and had it performed in Cambridge. Studied formally with **John Randall** at Cambridge from the age of 11, serving as Randall's assistant.
In 1788 he moved to Oxford, intending to study for the ministry of the church but the plan foundered when his patron died. However he graduated B.Mus. there in 1794; D.Mus. in 1799.
At 15 he became organist of Christ Church Cathedral, Oxford (1790), succeeding **Thomas Norris.** In 1797 at the age of 22 he became Oxford professor of music and organist of St. John's College in succession to **Philip Hayes**; additionally he was appointed organist of St. Mary's Church, Oxford.
In 1807 he moved to London. Later he was the first principal of the Royal Academy of Music (1822-1832).
His career had progressed in the direction of musical education rather than virtuoso playing. He also wrote on musical history and theory, publishing a set of discourses *Lectures on Music* (1831). Also painted in water colours.

Composer of the hymn tune 'Crotch', which was used in *Hymns Ancient and Modern*. Another tune, 'Sidon', was used in the Revised Edition (1927) of *Church Hymnary*.

Composer of many chants, a skill that he took very seriously, to the point of including the subject in the curriculum at the R.A.M. He is represented in the collection *Cathedral Psalter Chants* (1875).

A set of 10 anthems by him was published in 1804. His anthem 'Lo star-led chiefs' (which is actually a quartet from his oratorio *Palestine*) has been used as an anthem for Epiphany, while few of his other anthems, except perhaps 'How dear are Thy counsels' and 'Be peace on earth', are performed today. *Palestine* (1812) was highly successful, being regularly performed for 50 years after it was published.

Composer of large and small secular vocal works, concertos and music for the keyboard. Being ambidextrous, he developed the skill of writing on two staves simultaneously when composing.

CROW, Dr. Edwin John (1841-1908)

Born in Sittingbourne, Kent on 17 September 1841; died in Harrogate, Yorkshire on 7 December 1908.

A chorister at Rochester Cathedral under **John Larkin Hopkins**, to whom he was later articled. When in 1856 Hopkins moved to Cambridge and was succeeded by his cousin, **John Hopkins**, the articles were transferred. During this time, Crow taught the boys of the choir. Graduated Mus.B. (1872) and Mus.D. (1882) at the University of Cambridge.

Studied with **George Löhr** in Leicester (from 1858). Organist of Holy Trinity Church, Leicester (from 1861), having been acting organist for three years. Later, organist of St. Andrew's Church and St. John's Church, both also in Leicester.

In 1873 he was appointed organist of Ripon Cathedral with effect from 1 January the following year. Taught at Ripon Grammar School; conductor of local music societies. Organist of the Parish Church, Skelton-cum-Hardy (1876-1881). An examiner for the Incorporated School of Music. Retired in 1902.

His compositions include hymn tunes, a setting of Psalm 146, a *Harvest Cantata,* a Communion Service in F, a Morning Service in C (commissioned for the opening of the organ in Ripon Cathedral in April 1878) and settings of the Evening Service in G, in A and in D. He also composed songs, and pieces for organ and piano.

CROWEST, Frederick J. (c1850-1927)

Born on 30 November 1850 or 1860; died in Birmingham on 14 June 1927.

He was educated in London and Italy, studying music and singing with **James Turle**, Tamplin, Sims Reeves, Lamperti and Varchetti.

A professional tenor singer, using the name Arthur Vitton, and teacher. Organist of Christ Church, Kilburn, London; organist and choirmaster of St. Mary's Church, Somers Town, London.

From 1886 he earned his living as a musical editor and writer, holding various positions within the firm of Cassells. Compiled *Dictionary of British Musicians* (1895); other writings include *The Great Tone Poets* (1874) and *Book of Musical Anecdotes* (1878). General manager of the publishers Walter Scott, retiring in 1917 but continuing as a singer.

Crowest encouraged amateur music making. He held the view that choral music was inappropriate in church, where the laity tended to be excluded.

Composer of an Easy Communion Service in A (1876).

CROWFOOT, William (1724-1783)

Born in Beccles, Lancashire on 15 December 1724; died in Beccles on 25 March 1783. He lived in his native town, where he worked as a tanner and served as parish organist. His hymn tune, originally written as a setting to Psalm 57 and subsequently named 'St. Mark', was used in *Hymns Ancient and Modern* to the words 'Almighty Father, Lord most high'.

CROWLEY (Crole, Croleus), Revd. Robert (c1515-1588)

Born in Gloucestershire around the year 1515; died on 15 June 1588.

Attended the University of Oxford from around the year 1534. Graduated B.A. no later than 1542. Ordained deacon in September 1551.

An author and printer, as well as musician and cleric. Resident in Frankfurt in 1554, returning to England on the death of Queen Mary. Archdeacon (1559-1567) and prebend (1560-1568) of Hereford Cathedral. Held several church appointments in London, being known for his eloquent preaching and his anti-popery views, not least his particular objection to elaborate vestments.

Composer of the anthem 'That man is happy'. In 1549 he published a set of Psalm tunes for four voices *The Psalter of David Newly Translated into English Metre*. Although unsuccessful it has historical significance, being the first set of tunes to each of the Psalms in English verse.

CRUFT, Adrian Francis (1921-1987)

Born in Mitcham, Surrey on 10 February 1921; died on 20 February 1987.

Educated at Westminster Abbey Choir School, where he was head boy, and at Westminster School. Boult Conducting Scholar at the Royal College of Music (1938-1940; 1946-1947), where he studied composition with **Edmund Rubbra** and **Gordon Jacob**. Served in the armed forces during World War II.

A double bass player, touring with several orchestras between 1947 and 1969. In 1962 he became a professor of theory and composition at the R.C.M. Also taught orchestration at Guildhall School of Music (1972-1975), and made recordings.

The co-founder and assistant conductor of the London Classical Orchestra (from 1951). Music adviser to the Scottish Children's Theatre (1951-1965).

Compositions include music for organ and for strings, two Masses, two settings of the Te Deum and two Evening Services, including the *King's College* Service for Men's Voices, and many anthems, such as 'These hours'. His 'Come, Holy Dove' was specially composed for the Cookham Festival of May 1971.

CRUICKSHANK, William Alexander Campbell (1854-1934)

Born in Greenlaw, Berwickshire, Scotland on 1 June 1854; died in 1934.

Attended Epsom College, Surrey. A pupil of **Thomas Hewlett**. In 1885 he graduated B.Mus. at Keble College, Oxford.

Taught music at Loretto School, Musselburgh, Scotland (1874-1875).

Organist and choirmaster of St. John's Church, Selkirk, Scotland (1875-1876); St. John's, Alloa, Scotland (1876-1880) and Burnley Parish Church, Lancashire (from 1880). A local choral society conductor.

Composer of anthems including 'Sing, O ye heavens'; services including a Magnificat and Nunc Dimittis in G for the Festival of the London Church Choirs' Association and first sung in St. Paul's

Cathedral in May 1889; a Communion Service, Responses to the Commandments in E-flat, hymn tunes, chants, songs, and works for piano and for organ.

CULLEY, Revd. Arnold Duncan (1867-1947)
Born in Great Yarmouth, Norfolk on 9 March 1867; died in Seipton, Ludlow, Shropshire on 3 December 1947.
Educated at Great Yarmouth Grammar School, the Royal College of Music as the first Norwich and Norfolk scholar, and Emmanuel College, Cambridge (organ scholar 1891-1894). Graduated B.A. and Mus.B. (both 1894) and M.A. (1898) at Cambridge; M.A. (1906) at the University of Durham. Ordained deacon in 1894, priest in 1895.
Organist and choirmaster of St. Peter's Church, Hammersmith, London (1884-1889); organist of Christ Church, Surbiton, Surrey (from 1889) and curate of the Chapel Royal, Brighton (1894-1897). Appointed to Exeter Cathedral (1897); became sub organist there in 1900.
Appointed minor canon and precentor at Durham Cathedral (1906) and organist and master of the choristers (1907). He retired in 1932, to be succeeded by **John Dykes Bower**, but continued his ministry as rector of Burwarton with Cleobury North, Shropshire (1932-1941) and rural dean of Stottesdon (1939-1941).
Composer of church music, including anthems, the hymn tunes 'Llyfnant' and 'Willenhall' for *Methodist Hymn Book* (1904), and songs.

CULWICK, Dr. James C. (1845-1907)
Born in West Bromwich, Staffordshire on 28 April 1845; died in Dublin on 5 October 1907. Son of a vicar choral of Lichfield Cathedral.
A chorister of Lichfield Cathedral and, from the age of 14; an articled pupil of **Thomas Bedsmore**. An honorary Dublin D.Mus. (1893).
Assistant organist of Lichfield Cathedral, later taking up church organistships including St. Chad's, Church, Lichfield; Parsonstown, Ireland (1866); Bray, Ireland (1868) and St. Anne's Church, Dublin (1870) before becoming organist of the Chapel Royal, Dublin (1881-1907). Also organist, and a professor of piano and theory at Alexandra College.
Conducted the Dublin Harmonic Society (1872-1892). His writings on musical and other topics include a pamphlet (1891) on the discovery of the original word book of Handel's *Messiah* and a paper on artistic landmarks.
Composer of a setting of Psalm 104 for Solo Voice, Chorus and Orchestra; anthems including 'Bless the Lord, O my soul' and 'O Lord, grant the Queen a long life'; services including a Benedictus and Te Deum for Men's Voices (1892) for the Choir of Lichfield Cathedral; songs and chamber music. Author on the theory of music and on the works of his friend **R.P. Stewart**.

CUMMINGS, Dr. William Hayman (1831-1915)
Born in Devon on 22 August 1831; died in London on 6 June 1915.
A chorister at St. Paul's Cathedral from 1838 but by 1842 his father considered that the master of the choristers, **William Hawes**, treated the boys harshly. He withdrew William and placed him instead in the choir of the Temple Church, London under **E.J. Hopkins** and John Hobbs, whose daughter he later married.

While at the Temple Church, he sang as an alto in the first performance of Mendelssohn's *Elijah* at Exeter Hall on 16 April 1847, conducted by the composer. He left the choir a year later.
As an adult he studied operatic singing with Randegger. Trinity College, Dublin awarded him the degree of D.Mus. honorarily in 1900.
Organist of Waltham Abbey (1847). He later held a number of singing appointments in London: permanent deputy lay vicar of Westminster Abbey (1851), and tenor singer in the choir of the Temple Church (from 1853) and of the Chapel Royal (1865-1871). Precentor of St. Anne's Church, Soho, London (1886-1888).
His association as a singer with the Three Choirs' Festival began at Gloucester in 1865 and ended at Hereford in 1879. He also made two concert tours of the U.S.A., one of which was in 1871. A professor of singing at the Royal Academy of Music (1879-1896) and then he succeeded **Joseph Barnby** as principal of Guildhall School of Music (1896-1910) until his retirement. Had joined the teaching staff of G.S.M. when it opened in 1880. A professor of the Royal Normal College for the Blind (from 1879).
Contributed to Grove's *Dictionary of Music and Musicians*, gave public lectures and contributed articles to musical periodicals. His own library contained some 4,500 titles, some of which were quite rare.
Cummings composed cantatas, glees, and songs. He adapted the theme from *Festgesang* by Mendelssohn to the words of 'Hark, the herald angels sing' in 1840. Composer of anthems including 'O Lord, give ear' and 'Who is like unto the Lord our God?', a Te Deum, a setting of the Responses to the Commandments in F Minor, chants and carols.

CUNDELL, Henry Edric Arnold (1893-1961)
Born in London on 29 January 1893; died in Ashwell, Hertfordshire on 19 March 1961.
Appointed C.B.E. in 1949.
After attending Haberdasher's Aske School he studied the horn under Friedrich Borsdorf at Trinity College of Music, London, to which he had won a piano scholarship.
Played the horn in the Covent Garden Orchestra. A professor of composition (from 1920) and an examiner (from 1922) at T.C.M. Spent the year 1937 on the music staff of Glyndebourne. Succeeded Landon Ronald as principal of Guildhall School of Music (1938-1959). Guest conductor of Sadlers Wells and other principal London orchestras, as well as being a local orchestral society conductor.
Chairman of the music panel of the Arts Council of Great Britain (from 1951). Served on the committee of the Ralph Vaughan Williams Trust, the Royal Philharmonic Society and the Royal Musical Association.
His String Quartet won a Daily Telegraph chamber music prize in 1932. He also composed a Symphony, Piano Concerto, other chamber music, and songs. His hymn tune 'Ashwell' was first published in *Cambridge Hymnal* (1967) and it is used in *Hymns and Psalms* (1983) with 'Lord, it belongs not to my care' by Richard Baxter.

CURRAH, Revd. Michael Ewart (b.1931)
Born in Bridport, Dorset in 1931. Attended Bridport Grammar School; Downing College, Cambridge and Salisbury Theological College. Ordained deacon in 1956, priest in 1957. Curate of Calne, Wiltshire (1956-1960) and vicar of St. James's Church, Southbroom, Devizes, Wiltshire (1960-1969). From 1970 he was

head of religious studies at Woodroffe School, Lyme Regis, Dorset. His hymn tune 'Brushnorth' is used in *Hymns and Psalms* (1983) to 'For Your holy book, we thank You' by Ruth Carter.

CURRIE, John (b.1934)
Born in Prestwick, Ayrshire, Scotland in 1934.
Attended the Ayr Academy, the Royal Scottish Academy of Music and the University of Glasgow, where he graduated M.A. Lecturer in music at the University of Glasgow (1964-1971). Concurrently chorus master of the Scottish National Chorus (from 1965) and of the Edinburgh Festival. Became director of music at the University of Leicester in 1971, and he served on the Revision Committee for the Third Edition (1973) of *Church Hymnary*. Composer of the hymn tune 'Orb' for *Church Hymnary*. His other works include a song cycle for baritone and orchestra, and music for films and plays.

CUSINS, Sir William George (1833-1893)
Born in London on 14 October 1833; died in Remonchamps, in the Ardennes region of Belgium, on 31 August 1893.
A chorister at the Chapel Royal (from 1843). Studied at the Brussels Conservatory as a pupil of François-Joseph Fétis, and he won a King's Scholarship to the Royal Academy of Music (1847) where he studied with **William Sterndale Bennett, Charles Lucas**, Cipriani Potter and Prosper Sainton.
Knighted in 1892.
A violinist, pianist, organist, conductor, academic and composer. In 1849 he was appointed organist of the private chapel of Queen Victoria and also a rank and file member of the Royal Italian Opera.
Conductor of the Philharmonic Society (1867-1883) following the retirement of William Sterndale Bennett. Master of the Queen's Musick (1870-1893).
Became an associate professor of the R.A.M. in 1851, and a professor of Guildhall School of Music in 1885.
Composer of an oratorio *Gideon* which was performed at the Gloucester Festival of 1871, anthems including 'Grant the Queen a long life' and 'I will receive the cup', hymn tunes, orchestral overtures, a piano concerto, marches and songs. His hymn tune 'Palmae' was used in *Church Hymns* (1874) with 'Ride on! Ride on in majesty' by Henry Milman.

CUSTARD, Walter Henry Goss
See **GOSS-CUSTARD**, Walter Henry.

CUTLAND, William Henry (1852-1928)
Born in Somerset in 1852; died in Taunton, Somerset on 27 June 1928. Composer of hymn tunes and a collection of temperance songs (1911).

CUTLER, Edward (1831-1916)
Born in Edgware, Middlesex on 4 May 1831; died in Westminster, London on 22 December 1916.
Educated at Eton, Oxford and Dresden.
Having been called to the bar in 1857, he became a Queen's Counsel in 1884. An expert in the law of music copyright, collaborating with F.E. Weatherley and Eustace Smith in bringing out *Treatise of Musical and Dramatic Copyright*. A church organist at Whitchurch, Edgware, and grand organist of the English Freemasons (1892-1893).

An amateur composer. His anthems include 'I was glad'. His Double Chant in G, which is sometimes misattributed to **William Henry Cutler**, was composed in 1853 while he was at Oxford. Also composed songs, items for full orchestra and for piano.

CUTLER, William Henry (1792-?)
Born in London on 14 January 1792. He was known still to be alive on 5 June 1824 but his movements since that time and details of his eventual decease are unknown.
He learned music from his father, and was taught to play spinet by J.H. Little, piano by G.E. Griffen. A chorister of St. Paul's Cathedral (from 1803). Studied at Cambridge with **Thomas Busby**.
At other times his teachers were **Samuel Arnold** and **William Russell**. His exercise for the Oxford B.Mus. was the anthem 'O praise the Lord' (1812).
Having given his first public recital as a pianist at the age of eight, William Cutler was organist of the church of St. Helen, Bishopsgate, London (1809-1819) and of the Quebec Chapel, Portman Square, London (later known as the Church of the Annunciation) from 1823. Taught in London; Yarmouth, Norfolk and Norwich, Norfolk. Undertook an engagement as an oratorio singer at the Drury Lane Theatre but stage fright marred his performance and curtailed his ambitions in that direction.
Composer of services, anthems including 'O praise the Lord' and items for piano.

CUTTS, John (17th century)
Known to be alive in 1665; died, probably at Lincoln, some time before November 1692. A junior vicar and poor clerk at Lincoln Cathedral from May 1665; later became master of the choristers there (1684-1689). He then taught instrumental music to the boy choristers. Composer of eight anthems including 'Almighty, everlasting God' and 'My days are gone', and nine solos for bass viol.

CUTTS, Peter Warwick (b.1937)
Born in Birmingham on 4 June 1937.
Educated at King Edward School, Birmingham; Clare College, Cambridge, where he graduated B.A. in music (1961) and M.A. (1965) and at Mansfield College, Oxford where he read theology, taking an M.A. (1963). Musically, he was influenced by Paul Hindemith.
Lecturer in music at Huddersfield Technical College, Yorkshire (1963-1965) and Oastler College, Huddersfield (1965-1968). A lecturer in music (1968-1989) and director of chapel music at Bretton Hall College of Higher Education, Wakefield, Yorkshire. He now lives in the U.S.A. Retired in 1989 but remains as director of music at Newton Highlands Congregational Church and at Andover Newton Theological College, Massachusetts.
Composer of the hymn tunes 'Shillingford' and 'Grand prairie', used in the 1982 version of *The Hymnal* (U.S.A.) to 'Christ, upon the mountain rock', and 'Look there! The Christ our Brother comes'. Three other tunes were used in the same publication and he has also had compositions published in *Methodist Hymnal* (U.S.A.).
Has also composed tunes to words by Fred Kaan. *Hymns Ancient and Modern* (New Standard Edition) features his tunes 'Bridegroom', 'Blackbird Leys' and others. 'Bridegroom' was composed at Erik Routley's home in Newcastle-on-Tyne for Routley's hymn 'As the bridegroom to his chosen'. In all, some 35

of his 100 or so hymn tunes have been published. Has collaborated with the hymn writer Brian Wren and the results can be found in a number of modern hymnals.

CUZENS, Benjamin (18th century)
An organist and composer of the 18th century, probably living in Portsmouth, Hampshire. Composer of anthems including 'Almighty and Everlasting' and 'I will magnify'.

CZAPEK
See **HATTON**, John Liptrot.

D

DAKERS, Dr. Lionel Frederick (b.1924)
Born in Rochester, Kent on 24 February 1924.
Educated at Rochester Cathedral School (1931-1938). Studied with the cathedral organists H.A. Bennett of Rochester (1933-1940) and **Edward Bairstow** of York (1943-1945). On his return from service with the Royal Army Education Corps (1943-1947) he attended the Royal Academy of Music (1947-1951). Graduated B.Mus. at the University of Durham (1951). The Lambeth D.Mus. (1979) was followed by the honorary D.Mus. (Exeter) in 1982.
Appointed O.B.E. in 1984.
Organist of All Saints' Church, Frindsbury, Rochester (1939-1942); Cairo Cathedral, Egypt (1945-1947) and Finchley Parish Church, London (1948-1950). Assistant organist of St. George's Chapel, Windsor Castle (1950-1954) and assistant master of Eton College (1952-1954).
Two more cathedral organistships then followed: Ripon (1954-1957) and Exeter (1957-1972).
A special commissioner of the Royal School of Church Music (from 1958), whose director he later became (1973-1989). Lectured in music at St. Luke's College, Exeter (1958-1970). Revived Ripon Choral Society and founded the Harrogate String Orchestra.
An examiner to the Associated Board of the Royal Schools of Music (1958-1994).
Lionel Dakers has written a number of books examining the role of music in worship. His church music compositions include a Missa *Exoniensis*, a Benedicite in A Minor and an Evening Service in D Minor.

DALBY, John Martin (b.1942)
Born in Aberdeen, Scotland on 25 April 1942.
Educated at Aberdeen Grammar School and as foundation scholar at the Royal College of Music (1960-1963) where he studied viola with Frederick Riddle and composition with **Herbert Howells**. This was followed by two years on an Octavia Scholarship and a Sir James Caird Travelling Scholarship in Italy (1963-1964). Graduated B.Mus. at the University of Durham.
Had been a viola player in the National Youth Orchestra for three years prior to his studies at the R.C.M. His first full-time position was as a chamber music producer for B.B.C., London (1965-1971). In 1971 he became Cramb research fellow in composition at the University of Glasgow; in the following year he was appointed

head of music with B.B.C., Scotland. Retired from the B.B.C. in 1991 in order to compose full-time. Among his achievements with the B.B.C. was a large-scale radio history *Scotland's Music*.
Has composed orchestral and chamber works plus a significant quantity of church music, including *Two Liturgical Canticles* (1962), a Shorter Benedicite (1964) and the motets *Mater salutaris* and *The Sower*. Three of his hymn tunes are found in the Third Edition (1973) of *Church Hymnary*. A number of works have been commissioned by the major British music festivals.

DALE, Dr. Alfred Stanley (?-1918)
Received his early musical training at Rochester Cathedral. Graduated B.Mus. (1889), D.Mus. (1894) and B.A. (1895) at Brasenose College, Oxford. Organist of Trinity Presbyterian Church, Claughton, and of West Malling Parish Church, Kent (from 1895). In 1889 he became organist and choirmaster of St. Saviour's Church, Birkenhead, Cheshire and of St. Aidan's College. A pianist. Composed a Service, and songs.

DALE, Benjamin James (1885-1943)
Born in Highbury, London on 17 July 1885; died in Kensington, London on 30 July 1943. His father, **Charles Dale** was an illustrator; his mother, Jessie, was a pianist and teacher.
Attended the Stationers' Company School in Hornsey, East London and Oakfield School, Crouch End.
From 1902, under a Sir Michael Costa Scholarship in composition, he studied at the Royal Academy of Music with **Frederick Corder,** Howard Jones, Herbert Lake and **Henry Richards**.
Before 1914 was organist of a number of churches in London. Interned for four years in Ruhleben, near Berlin, Germany during World War I. Upon his release, he travelled the world for two years (1919-1920), spending part of the time as a musical examiner in Australia and New Zealand.
Organist of the City Road Wesleyan Methodist Chapel (from 1901) and organist and choirmaster of St. Stephen's Church, Ealing, Middlesex. As well as serving on the B.B.C. Music Panel (1936-1943) he was a professor of harmony and composition at the R.A.M, of which he was later warden.
In 1919, the critic Edwin Evans, writing in *Musical Times* had noted his promise as a composer, but little was published over the

next 40 years. His lack of recognition can be attributed at least in part to a refusal to adapt his style to suit contemporary taste.

Composed the overture *Horatius* at the age of 14, chamber music including a Piano Sonata (1905) and a Fantasy in D (1911). Also composed choral works; his church music includes six carols and a festival anthem *A Song of Praise*. His hymn tune 'Sidmouth' was used in *Methodist Hymn Book* (1933).

DALE, Charles James (1842-1912)
Born in Longton, Staffordshire on 9 May 1842; died in St. Marylebone, London on 16 June 1912. The father of **Benjamin Dale**.
His family moved to the town of Denby, Derbyshire during his childhood. At the age of 18, he set up in business in London. He was self-taught in music and he became an amateur musician. In 1870 he founded the Finsbury Choral Association, serving as its conductor for 20 years. Also founded the Metropolitan College of Music, Holloway (1888), which was subsequently incorporated into the London Academy of Music. A composer of hymn tunes.

DALE, Lawford William Torriano (1826-1898)
Born in Beckenham, Kent on 20 January 1826; died in Chiswick, London on 3 May 1898. A composer of hymn tunes.

DALE, Revd. Reginald Francis (1845-1919)
Born in Sydenham, Surrey on 12 September 1845; died in Headington, Oxford on 14 November 1919. Son of the dean of Rochester.
Attended Queen's College, Oxford where he graduated B.A. and B.Mus. (both 1866). Ordained deacon (1870) and priest (1871).
Assistant master of Westminster School, London (1870-1886); rector of Bletchingdon, Oxfordshire (1885-1899) and of Hampton Poyle (1890-1895). Rural dean of Islip (1894-1899) and incumbent of Binsey (1905-1910). From 1899 he lectured in mathematics at Keble College, Oxford. During his retirement he continued to live in Oxford.
His hymn tunes 'St. Petrox' and 'St. Catherine' were used in *Hymns Ancient and Modern*. Editor, jointly with Revd. H.J. Poole, of *22 Original Hymn Tunes by two Oxford Graduates* (1867). Also composed carols, songs and chants. With **John Troutbeck** he compiled *A Musical Primer for Schools*.

DALGLISH, Robert (1806-1875)
Born in Pollokshaws, Renfrewshire, Scotland in July 1806; died in Pollokshaws on 5 August 1875. A weaver by trade; self-taught in music. Compositions include anthems such as 'Create in me a new heart' and 'Great and marvellous', Psalm settings and glees, which were popular locally.

DAMETT, Revd. Thomas (c1389-c1437)
Probably born in the year 1389 or 1390; died before 13 April 1437. Attended Winchester College, Hampshire until 1407. Upon leaving he probably studied at university, but no details are known.
Following ordination he became rector of Stockton, Wiltshire. Chaplain to the Chapel Royal of Henry V and Henry VI. Prebendary of St. Paul's Cathedral and of St. George's Chapel, Windsor Castle (from 1431).
Nine of his compositions have survived, including four Glorias, two Credos and a motet said to have been sung at the celebration of the victory at Agincourt.

DAMON (Daman), William (c1540-1591)
Born in Liège, Belgium around the year 1540; died in London in 1591.
Engaged as a servant and brought to London in 1565 by Lord Buckhurst, a patron of music. A musician of Elizabeth I from 1579 to 1591. Gentleman of the Chapel Royal.
Composed a number of anthems and lute works, most of which remained unpublished. In 1579 an unauthorised publication was made of his collection of metrical Psalm tunes. This embarrassed Damon, who had only intended to use these works privately. He therefore elaborated these compositions and in 1591, the set was published officially in two volumes. His was probably the first application of part music to the complete set of Psalms in English.

DANCEY, Harry (c1883-1929)
Born around 1883; died in Putney, London on 10 January 1929 at the age of 66. Educated at the Royal Academy of Music. Graduated B.Mus. at the University of Durham in 1895. Organist and choirmaster of All Saints' Church, Putney Common. Composed a Morning, Communion and Evening Service, and anthems.

DANIEL, Albert Edward (1862-?)
Born in Birmingham on 9 November 1862. Studied music privately. His career as a pianist and organist suffered as he became increasingly deaf, but he was able to continue his musical career through teaching and composing. Composed a harvest-tide cantata and other items of church music. Also wrote songs, orchestral works and items for the piano and for organ.

DANIEL, Richard Blackburne (1852-1909)
Born in Ulverstone, Lancashire in 1852; died in Harrogate, Yorkshire on 17 March 1909. A composer of hymn tunes.

DANIELL, John (1788-1866)
Born in Gloucester on 5 January 1788; died in Bristol, Gloucestershire on 21 April 1866. A draper and auctioneer. Choirmaster at the Broadmead Baptist Church, Bristol (1825-1861). His hymn tune 'Broadmead', also known as 'David's harp', first appeared in *The Psalmist* (1842). It has since been used with the hymn 'How blest is life if lived for Thee' in *Hymns and Psalms* (1983).

DARBY, Dr. Ernest (1873-?)
Born in Wolverhampton, Staffordshire in 1873.
Received his early training in music privately and at the Collegiate Church of St. Peter, Wolverhampton. Graduated B.Mus. (1901) and D.Mus. (1914) at the University of Durham.
Organist and choirmaster of Bushbury Parish Church (1896-1898); St. Mark's, Wolverhampton (from 1898), Cannock Parish Church, Staffordshire (from 1905) and Penkridge Parish Church, Staffordshire (from 1912). Conductor of a local choral society.
Principal of the Wolverhampton School of Music (from 1902). From 1904 he taught piano at Wolverhampton Grammar School. Composed an Evening Service.

DARE, Charles James (?-1820)
Assistant organist of Westminster Abbey until 1805. Organist of Hereford Cathedral (1805-1818). Conducted the Hereford Festival in each of the years 1807, 1810, 1813 and 1816. The termination of his position at Hereford was said to be the consequence of an excess of alcohol. Composed a Service in G which was used at

Hereford Cathedral on audit days. He also wrote an anthem 'I will call upon the Lord'.

DARKE, Dr. Harold Edwin (1888-1976)
Born in Highbury, London on 29 October 1888; died in Cambridge on 28 November 1976.
Attended Owen's School, Islington, London, worshipping with his family at the Highbury Hill Baptist Church. Subsequently organ scholar under **Walter Parratt** at the Royal College of Music (from 1903), where he later studied composition (1908-1910) under **C.V. Stanford**. Graduated B.Mus. (1914) and D.Mus. (1919) at Queen's College, Oxford. Received an honorary M.A. from the University of Cambridge.
Appointed C.B.E. in 1966.
Had been the assistant of **Henry Walford Davies** at the Temple Church, London. Organist in London of Stoke Newington Presbyterian Church (1904-1906); Emmanuel Church, West Hampstead (1906-1911) and St. James's Church, Paddington (1911-1916).
Organist for 50 years at the church of St. Michael's Cornhill, London (1916-1966) where he gave recitals in which the music of **Hubert Parry** and **Ralph Vaughan Williams** was regularly played.
Deputised for **Boris Ord** at King's College, Cambridge when the other was abroad on military service (1941-1945).
He has been assessed as the best organ teacher and player of his generation. A teacher at the R.C.M. for 50 years (1919-1969).
Composed a Communion Service in A Minor for the Choir of St. Paul's Cathedral, Buffalo, U.S.A.; a Magnificat and Nunc Dimittis in F; anthems (which were often for festivals) and other choral and organ works. A Service in E, the *Collegium Regale*, was dedicated to King's College, Cambridge. His tune 'Naphill' is used in the Revised Edition of *Hymns Ancient and Modern*, *Hymns and Psalms* (1983) and elsewhere. His carol-anthem 'In the bleak mid winter' continues to be widely performed.

DARLINGTON, Stephen Mark (b.1952)
Born in Lapworth, Warwickshire on 21 September 1952.
Attended King's School Worcester, and, as organ scholar, Christ Church, Oxford (1971-1974) where he graduated B.A. (1974) and M.A. (1976).
Assistant organist (1974-1978) at Canterbury Cathedral. Played at the enthronement as archbishop of Dr. Donald Coggan. Subsequently organist of St. Albans Cathedral (1978-1985) and of Christ Church, Oxford (from 1985). A lecturer of the University of Oxford, conductor, broadcaster and recitalist. Composes church music in the modern idiom.

DARLOW, Denys (b.1921)
Born in London on 13 May 1921.
His music education was with **Harold Darke** and **Arthur Pritchard,** conducting with Stanford Robinson, conductor of the B.B.C. Opera Orchestra, and composition with **Edmund Rubbra**
A professor of the Royal College of Music. Has conducted and broadcast in many parts of the world, and has appeared at the B.B.C. promenade concerts.
Organist of Brentwood Parish Church, Essex (1942-1944) and of St. John's Church, Holland Road, West Kensington (from 1944). Director of music of St. George's Church, Hanover Square, London (from 1971).

Founder of the Tilford Bach Festival (1952) and, in 1978, the London Handel Festival and London Handel Choir and Orchestra. The latter festival came into being to give authentic performances of the composer's works, well-known and neglected, together with that of his contemporaries.
Compositions include a Missa Brevis, a Service in C, anthems and a set of Responses, and settings of the Requiem, Te Deum and Stabat Mater, primarily for concert use and scored for Solo Voices, Choir and Orchestra.

DARNTON, Charles (1836-1933)
Born in Islington, London on 10 October 1836; died in Barnet, Hertfordshire on 21 April 1933. For many years he was organist of the Park Chapel, Camden Town, London. Composed sacred cantatas including *The Star of Bethlehem* (1893) and *Abraham* (1895), anthems and hymn tunes. Compiled *Comprehensive Psalmody*, a collection of church music (1866).

DART, Henry John Baker (1854-?)
Born in Torquay, Devon on 5 March 1854.
A chorister of St. Luke's Church, Torquay from 1866 to 1868. On moving to London in 1875, he took music lessons from Charles Fowler and T. Craddock. Studied at the London Academy of Music under **E.J. Hopkins**, **John Francis Barnett** and **E.H. Turpin**.
Organist of St. Michael's Mission Church (from 1868) and of Christ Church, Ellacombe (from 1873), both in the Torquay area. Moved to London where he was organist of St. John's Church, Waterloo Road (1879-1893) and of St. James's Church, Paddington (from 1893).
A professor of the London Academy of Music. As conductor of the North London Philharmonic Society he introduced to London some major new works.
Composed a Sonata for Organ and Trombone (1884), a setting of Psalm 84 for Soloists, Chorus and Organ (1893) and a Morning and Evening Service in D.

DARWALL, Revd. John (c1730-1789)
Born in Haughton, Staffordshire where he was baptised on 13 January 1730 or 1731; died in Walsall, Staffordshire on 18 December 1789. Son of the local rector; grandfather of **Leicester Darwall** (1813-1897).
Attended Manchester Grammar School (from 1745) and Brasenose College, Oxford (from 1752). Graduated B.A. in 1756.
Following his ordination he became assistant curate of the church of St. Matthew's, Walsall (1761), becoming vicar of the same church (1769) where he remained until he died.
Composed two volumes of piano sonatas. Composed tunes to each of the 150 Psalms which, when published, amounted to three volumes. These tunes were scored for treble and bass only. His tune 'Darwall', otherwise known as 'Darwall's 148th' is associated with the hymn 'Ye holy angels bright'.

DARWALL, Revd. Leicester (1813-1897)
Born in Walsall, Staffordshire on 10 January 1813; died in Tenby, Glamorgan, Wales on 22 July 1897. Grandson of **John Darwall**.
Educated at Trinity College, Cambridge; graduated B.A. (1835) and M.A. (1838). Ordained deacon in 1836 and priest in 1837.
Assistant curate of Blakeney, Norfolk (1836-1837) and vicar of Criggion, Montgomeryshire (1838-1890).
Composed the hymn tune 'St. Hubert', used in *Hymns Ancient and Modern* and in *Church Hymns* (1874).

DARWALL, Leicester John Theodore (1855-1918)
Born in Shrewsbury, Shropshire in 1855; died in Warrington, Cheshire on 24 May 1918. Composer of hymn tunes, a Holy Communion Service in D (1937), a Magnificat and Nunc Dimittis in C (1894) and the harvest-tide anthem 'Fear not, O Land' (1887).

DAVID, John Winter (1837-1902)
Born in Guernsey, Channel Islands in 1837; died in Guernsey on 7 September 1902.
Virtually self taught in music although he took some lessons with **W.H. Longhurst,** organist of Canterbury Cathedral.
Worked in the Receiver-General's Office, Guernsey and took an active part in local government.
From 1852 he played the harmonium at the village chapel. A year later he was playing for the local French Wesleyan Chapel, an appointment which he retained when in 1865 he became organist of the Ebenezer English Wesleyan Chapel. At the church of St. Barnabas, Guernsey, where he was organist from 1874 to 1902, he was responsible for introducing the first regular choral services in the island.
His hymn tune 'Marienlyst' was originally used at the French Wesleyan Chapel. Today it is found in *Hymns and Psalms* (1983) with 'Captain of Israel's host, and Guide' by Charles Wesley.

DAVIE, Dr.Cedric Thorpe (1913-1983)
Born in London on 30 May 1913 although he was of Scottish descent. He died on 18 January 1983.
Educated at Glasgow High School, the Royal Scottish Academy of Music, the Royal College of Music and the Royal Academy of Music. Also trained privately in Budapest and in Helsinki. He graduated LL.D.
He was appointed O.B.E.
On the teaching staff of the R.S.A.M. Subsequently appointed reader in music at the University of St. Andrews, where he became professor of music in 1948. He was a church organist in Glasgow.
Composed orchestral music including a Symphony in C, together with works for film, stage and radio. In addition he composed the anthems 'The Lord is He whose Strength doth make me strong' and 'Come, Holy Ghost, the Maker'.

DAVIE, James (c1783-1857)
Born around the year 1783; died in Aberdeen, Scotland on 29 November 1857.
A lute player and composer with a teaching practice in Aberdeen where he was a member of the theatre orchestra and conductor of a local choral society. He was choirmaster of St. Andrew's Church, Aberdeen. Published a collection of the music of the Church of Scotland, and collections of other material.

DAVIES, ? (16th/17th century)
Lived around the year 1600. Composer of a set of Preces, and settings to Psalms 24 and 136.

DAVIES, David Gwilym (1875-?)
Born in Llandilo, Brecknockshire, Wales in 1875. Graduated B.Mus. at the University of Oxford in 1914. Organist of the Bethania Welsh Congregational Church, Dowlais, Glamorgan (1906-1914). In the latter year he became organist of the Castle Street Welsh Baptist Church in Oxford Circus, London. Composed anthems in Welsh, and hymn tunes.

DAVIES, Evan Thomas (1878-1969)
Born at Dowlais, Glamorgan, Wales on 10 April 1878; died on 25 December 1969. Privately educated in music. In 1920 he became the first full-time director of music at the University College of North Wales, Bangor. Retired with the position of director emeritus in 1943. Organist and choirmaster of Christ Church, Cyfartha, near Merthyr Tydfil (1900-1903) and of Pontmorlais (1903-1917). Made a piano and organ recital tour of the U.S.A. in 1900. He adjudicated at the national *eisteddfodau* of 1915, 1916. A contributor to, and joint editor of, *Welsh Methodist Hymnal.* Wrote reviews for *Y Cerddor* (The musician) and for *Welsh Folk Song Journal.* Composed the hymn tune 'Michaelmas', arrangements of Welsh folk songs, part songs and piano works.

DAVIES, Gabriel (18th /19th century)
Gabriel Davies's life spanned the years from 1770 or so to at least 1824. He led the music at the Baptist Chapel, Portsea, Hampshire. His hymn tune 'Monmouth' is found in *Forty Psalm tunes...* (c1800), which he published.

DAVIES, Sir Henry Walford (1869-1941)
Born in Oswestry, Shropshire on 6 September 1869; died in Wrington, Somerset on 11 March 1941.
A chorister at St. George's Chapel, Windsor Castle (from 1882) under **George Elvey,** and under his successor **Walter Parratt,** one of whose assistant organists he later became (1885-1890). Organist of the Windsor Great Park Chapel.
In 1890 he took up an open scholarship in composition at the Royal College of Music under **Hubert Parry, C.V. Stanford** and W.S. Rockstro.
Graduated Mus.B. (1892) and Mus.D. (1898) at the University of Cambridge and thereafter received honorary degrees at Leeds (LL.D. 1904), Glasgow (LL.D. 1926), Dublin (D.Mus. 1930) and Oxford (D.Mus. 1935).
Appointed O.B.E. in 1919, knighted in 1922 and appointed C.V.O. in 1932.
Organist in London of St. George's, Campden Hill (1890); St. Anne's, Soho (1890-1891) and Christ Church, Hampstead (1891-1898) before moving in succession to **E.J. Hopkins** to the Temple Church, London (1898-1923). The former boy soprano Ernest Lough has recalled that Davies took pains to ensure that the boys understood the words of the Psalms that they were called upon to sing.
Taught at the R.C.M.(1895-1903), returning to the R.C.M. later (1910-1916) as teacher of choir training. During World War I he took up the cause of entertaining and educating the troops in music (1915-1918); in 1918 he became musical director of the R.A.F. with the rank of major.
From 1919 to 1926 he was professor of music at the University College of Aberystwyth, Wales. On one occasion following a concert at which he performed and then talked on the subject of Beethoven, the students acclaimed him, in accordance with the custom of the time, with a college yell and then proceeded to carry him shoulder-high around the quadrangle.
Gave a number of talks on B.B.C. Radio (1924-1939). Organist at St. George's Chapel, Windsor Castle (1927-1932) and Master of the King's Musick (1934-1941).
Published compilations of music, sometimes in collaboration with others. Author of books, lectures and essays. It is rumoured that he was the second choice of Percy Dearmer for the editorship of

English Hymnal and would have been offered the position had it been refused by **Ralph Vaughan Williams**.

Composed works for solo voices chorus and orchestra, a 'Solemn Melody', a symphony, overture and other orchestral works, chamber music, songs, part songs and works for organ. His church music includes services, anthems, motets, chants, hymns, carols and lullabies. His Service in G includes solos for treble and baritone. Known for the anthems 'God be in my head', 'King of Glory' from the collection *12 Introits for the Temple Choir* and his arrangement of the French Easter Processional 'O sons and daughters, let us sing'.

Hymn tunes include 'Auctor vitae', 'Maclure', 'Oswald's tree' and 'Hampstead'; these and others were used in *Hymns Ancient and Modern*. Composed the tune 'Wengen' to the carol 'O little town of Bethlehem'. Other works include the famous *R.A.F. March Past*.

DAVIES (Davies), Hugh (c1580-1644)

Born around the year 1580; died in Hereford in 1644. In 1605 he became a vicar choral of Hereford Cathedral. Later he was custos (warden) of the vicars choral. Also appointed organist there at some time before 1630. Composed eight anthems, including 'Awake up, my glory' and 'Rejoice in the Lord O ye righteous'. Another - or the same - Hugh Davies is recorded as graduating B.Mus. at the University of Oxford in 1623.

DAVIES, Hugh (Pencerdd Maelor: 1844-1907)

Born in Garth, Denbighshire, Wales on 1 September 1844; died in Swansea, Glamorganshire on 12 October 1907.

Left school at the age of eight, working in the brick fields of the firm of J.C. Edwards and Company, in which he rose to the position of deputy manager.

Was taught music by Joseph Owen, a school teacher of Rhos. Studied the system and graduated from the Tonic Sol-fa college. He then organised classes in the method. At festivals of music he was an adjudicator and conductor. He succeeded **John Roberts** (Ieuan Gwyllt) as editor of *Cerddor y Tonic Sol-fa*.

After some time as a lay preacher of the Methodist Church, he was ordained in 1895 and became minister of the Smyrna Chapel, Plasmarl, Swansea.

Composed some two hundred works, many of which were for children. His cantatas *Joseph* and *Charles of Bala* were sung at schools throughout Wales. Also composed hymn tunes.

DAVIES, John (1787-1855)

Born in Morriston, Glamorganshire, Wales on 13 November 1787; died at Llanelli, Carmarthen, Wales on 27 April 1855. Well educated, and from the age of 14, he was taught to play the dulcimer by a visitor from London who lodged with the family. Became a stonemason and also carved tombstones. At the age of 30 he began to study music formally. Composed many anthems, and hymn tunes of which 'Gethsemane' is an example.

DAVIES, Joseph (1844-1921)

Born in 1844; died in Buckley, Flintshire, Wales on 14 August 1921. A composer of hymn tunes.

DAVIES, Lewis (1863-1951)

Born in 1863, probably in Wales; died in Wales in 1951. A school teacher by profession, indulging in music and writing novels in his spare time. Also served the Congregational Church as an elder and secretary. In 1886 he moved to Cymer, near Port Talbot, where he remained until his death. Remembered for his hymn tune 'Cymer'.

DAVIES, Matthew William (1882-1947)

Born in Neath, Glamorganshire, Wales in 1882; died in Neath in 1947. Went to London in order to study with **David Evans**. When, in 1908, Evans became professor of music at University College, Cardiff, Matthew Davies followed him there. He then spent a further year's training in London. Graduated B.Mus. and M.A. Lived and worked at Neath, where he taught music and was organist and precentor of the Bethlehem Green Presbyterian Church. Conducted the Neath Operatic Society for 36 years. Composed anthems, hymn tunes and part songs.

DAVIES, Morris (1796-1876)

Born in Mallwyd, Merioneth, Wales and was baptised on 19 October 1796; died in Bangor, Wales on 10 September 1876.

Attended schools in the villages of Dinas Mawddwy and Mallwyd, and at Welshpool.

Having taken a dislike to farm work he decided to become a school teacher. For a period of six months in 1819 he taught at a school in Welshpool under William Owen. Subsequent appointments took him to Syston, Leicestershire and Llanfair Caereinion. At Syston he assisted the parson, Edward Morgan, in the compilation of a biography of Thomas Charles.

In 1836 he became a clerk in a legal firm in Llanllyfni, relocating with the firm to Portmadoc and Pwllheli. From 1844 to 1849 he returned to the teaching profession at Portmadoc and in 1849 he became a clerk at Bangor.

Translated religious booklets into Welsh and he contributed 40 articles to *Y Traethodydd*. His work appeared in other publications and he compiled biographies.

A composer of hymn tunes and he edited and wrote on the subject of music. The collection *Caniaudau Seion* (Songs of Sion) of 1840 contained tunes by him.

He had begun to collect hymn tunes in 1815. Some of these appeared in his own collections; later publications by **Richard Mills** and **Griffith Harris** also used these tunes. The publication *Jeduthun* (1860) by Morris Davies contained 106 tunes, 10 of which were by him. One that is still used today is 'Rhoslan'.

DAVIES, Revd. Owen Humphrey (Eos Llechyd: 1828-1898)

Born in Llanllechid, near Bangor, Wales in September 1828; died in Llechcynfarwy, Anglesey, Wales on 11 August 1898.

When young he read books on music and learned to read music. He took holy orders later in life, being ordained deacon in 1877, priest in 1883.

From 1845 to 1862 he worked in the Penrhyn quarries. From 1848 he was precentor of the Llanechid church choir. A local choral society conductor. In the years 1862, 1864, 1867 and 1871 he conducted the church choral festivals at Llandaff.

From 1869 he was a lay reader at Ysgoldy, Maes-y-groes. Tutor in music (1870-1878) at the North Wales Normal College, Caernarvon.

Following his ordination he was curate of the parishes of St. Anne, Bangor (1877-1878); Llanberis (1878-1889) and Pen-tir (1888). He was rector of Rhiw, Llyn (1888-1894) and minister of Llechcynfarwy (from 1895).

An eisteddfod competitor, winning composition prizes at the Bethesda events of 1851, 1852 and 1853. He worked to improve the standard of church music in Wales. Between the years 1886 and 1895 he compiled a series of biographies of Welsh musicians. From 1861 to 1898 a number of articles by him appeared in music magazines.

Composed anthems, a cantata *Gwarchae Harlech*, and airs.

DAVIES, Sir Peter Maxwell (b.1934)

Born in Manchester on 8 September 1934.

Attended Leigh Grammar School, the University of Manchester (1952-1957) and the Royal Manchester College of Music (1952-1956), where he was a contemporary of his fellow composer and knight, Harrison Birtwistle, the trumpeter Elgar Howarth, the pianist John Ogdon and the composer Alexander Goehr. He later studied for 18 months by means of an Italian government scholarship under Goffredo Petrassi in Rome.

His education continued with Milton Babbitt, Earl Kim and Roger Sessions at the University of Princeton, U.S.A. (1962-1964) under a Harkness Fellowship. Graduated B.Mus. at the University of Manchester (1956) and awarded, honorarily, the Edinburgh D.Mus. (1979).

Director of music at Cirencester Grammar School, Gloucestershire (1959-1962) before embarking on extended tours of Europe, the U.S.A., Canada, Australia and New Zealand. Composer in residence at the University of Adelaide, Australia (1966), returning to the U.K. in 1967 and becoming a professor of composition at the R.M.C.M. (to 1980).

Lives in The Orkneys, Scotland, which has been part of the inspiration for his compositions. In 1977 he organised the first St. Magnus Festival, with which he has been associated annually ever since. As a teacher he recognised the musical needs and potential of children, and composed accordingly.

Regarded as a member of the European avant garde movement. Commencing at an early age, he has written for stage, opera and orchestra, including four symphonies. Many of his works are vocal. His church music includes *Five Motets* (1959) and *O magnum mysterium*, a set of modal carols separated by orchestral interludes (1960).

DAVIES, Thomas (Trithyd: ?1810-?1873)

Born in Carmarthenshire, Wales around the year 1810; died in Aberavon, Glamorgan, Wales around the year 1873. For many years, a farmer in Llantrithyd, Glamorgan, travelling around that part of Wales as a teacher of singing. He then studied music formally and became a travelling singing teacher. Around the year 1853 he moved to Cwmavon, Glamorgan. Opened a shop but failed to establish himself financially, dying in great poverty. Collected hymn tunes by others, and composed a number himself. He was the editor of *Y Blwych Cerddord* - The Musical Casket (1854) which contained 84 tunes, all by Welsh composers. Composed many works: 89 hymn tunes, 16 anthems, 90 temperance pieces, six hymn tunes for private family worship and a duet.

DAVIES, Thomas (1851-1892)

Born in Ebbw Vale, Glamorgan, Wales in 1851; died in Ebbw Vale on 20 December 1892. One of the first Welsh exponents of the Tonic Sol-fa system of musical notation. A conductor and teacher. Composed six anthems including 'Dyddian dyn sydd fel glaswelltyn'.

DAVIES, Thomas (1853-?)

Born in Brecon, Wales in 1853. Graduated B.Mus. at the University of Durham in 1904. Organist and choirmaster of St.

Mary's Church, Cardiff, from 1889 until at least 1925. An examiner in Wales for scholarships to the Royal College of Music. Organist and choirmaster of St. Edmund's Church, Crickhowell, until 1889, and choir trainer to the Brecon Archdeaconry. Composed a carol 'The holly' and a Christmas anthem 'While shepherds'.

DAVIES (Davis), William (18th century)

Master of the choristers of Worcester Cathedral (1721-1745). It appears that he is the same person who was organist of York Minster from 1721 to 1722. Composed the anthems 'Help Lord, for the godly', and 'They that put their trust'.

DAVIES, W.J. (1866-1947)

One of the four musical editors of *Congregational Hymn Book* (1921). Remembered for his hymn tune 'Rhys'.

DAVIS, Gabriel C. (c1770-1824)

Born in Bath, Somerset around 1770; died in Portsea, Hampshire in 1824. Issued *Sacred Music* (c1800), a collection of works for the church, during the time when he was choirmaster of the Kent Street Baptist Church, Portsea. His hymn tune 'Monmouth' was first used in *Wesley's Hymns* (1877). More recently it has been used to accompany the hymn by Isaac Watts 'I'll praise my Maker while I've breath'. Composed around 40 other hymn and Psalm tunes.

DAVISON, Dr. Donald (b.1937)

Studied mathematics at Queen's University, Belfast where he graduated M.Sc. Later graduated Ph.D. (1962) at Gonville and Caius College, Cambridge. Lecturer and senior lecturer at Queen's University, where he is currently head of the Department of Statistics and Operational Research. Organist at the church of St. John, Malone, and Belfast city organist, in which capacity he gives regular recitals in the Ulster Hall. Has set the Communion Service (Alternative Service Book version), and has composed short anthems and a chant to Psalm 150. Has also written and arranged tunes in *Irish Church Praise*, the supplement to *Irish Church Hymnal*, of which he is joint musical editor.

DAVISON, John Armitage (1898-1972)

Born in Kidderminster, Worcestershire on 23 December 1898; died in Waltham Chase, Hampshire on 23 July 1972.

Attended King Charles Grammar School, Kidderminster, going up to Selwyn College, Cambridge to read history. Studied with **Charles Wood** and **E.W. Naylor**. From 1920 he was John Stewart of Rannoch scholar. Graduated B.A. (1920) and M.A. (1927) at the University of Cambridge.

Director of music of Dauntsey's School (1923-1928) and of Malvern College, Worcestershire (1928-1940). During World War II he served as an officer in the R.A.F.

Organist of Portsmouth Cathedral (1945-1959) and a teacher at Portsmouth Grammar School. Following his retirement he was briefly organist of Cirencester Parish Church, Gloucestershire and then of Shedfield Parish Church, Hampshire.

Composed church music including a setting of Psalm 139, first performed at the Portsmouth Festival.

DAVY, John (1763-1824)

Born in Upton Helions, near Crediton, Devon on 23 December 1763; died in St. Martin's Lane, London on 22 February 1824.

Before the age of five he was able to play simple tunes on the fife. Later in his childhood he also learned to play harpsichord and viola. At the age of 12, he was articled as a pupil to **William Jackson**, organist of Exeter Cathedral.

Having completed his studies with Jackson, he remained in the city and worked as an organist and teacher. On moving to London (around 1800), became a violin player in the Covent Garden Orchestra.

His church music includes an anthem 'Lord, who shall dwell in Thy tabernacle?'. Two double chants and four single chants were composed around the year 1812. Novello's collection *Cathedral Psalter Chants* (1875) contains his Double Chant in D. Composed a Kyrie in F.

Wrote music for the theatre, including incidental music for *The Tempest*, glees, songs such as *The Bay of Biscay* and an opera. He did not achieve his full potential as a composer, partly through unsuccessful collaborations but also, it appears, through an excess of alcohol.

DAVY (Davys), Richard (c1467-c1516)
Born around 1467; died, possibly at Blickling, Norfolk around 1516. Alternatively, may have died in Exeter around 1507.

It is likely that two contemporaries had the same name and it has proved difficult for historians to distinguish confidently between their separate careers. A musician of this name attended Magdalen College, Oxford from 1483, and was organist and joint choirmaster (1490-1492) of the College. He may also be the Richard Davy who was priest and vicar choral at Exeter Cathedral (1494-1507). Richard Davy's surviving church music includes seven antiphons, a passion, a Magnificat, the anthem 'Have mercy on me' and a carol. Other works for the church are lost. Also composed part songs.

DAWES, Dr. Francis Eric (1902-1974)
Born in Oldbury, Worcestershire, on 7 March 1902; died in Blaketown, Worcestershire on 28 April 1974.

Attended King Edward School, Birmingham and Trinity Hall, Cambridge. Studied at the Birmingham School of Music and under **Cyril Rootham, Charles Wood, C.W. Perkins,** and G.D. Cunningham. Graduated M.A., LL.B. and Mus.B. at the University of Cambridge, and was a Dublin D.Mus.

Became a solicitor of a practice in Oldbury. Organist and choirmaster of the King Street Congregational Church, Dudley, Worcestershire (1926-1941) and master of the music of the (Baptist) Church of the Redeemer, Birmingham (from 1941). Served on the Music Advisory Committee of *Baptist Hymn Book* (1962).

Composed and arranged hymn tunes, his own including 'Kilantringan' and 'Broome'. Also part songs.

DAWNEY, Dr. Michael William (b.1942)
Born in Romford, Essex on 10 August 1942.

Educated at St. Bonaventure's Grammar School, the University of Durham and Lincoln College, Oxford where he studied under Egon Wellesz and **Edmund Rubbra**. Holds the degrees of B.A. (Durham) and B.Litt. (Oxford). Also attended Dorset Institute of Higher Education.

Studied film music under Richard Arnell at the London International Film School. Has held appointments at Trinity and All Saints' College of Education, Leeds, Yorkshire; Huddersfield Polytechnic, Yorkshire and University College, Cork, Ireland.

Has edited three books of folk songs and written on various subjects.

His church music includes *Ten Hymns In Praise Of God* (1982) and the hymn tune 'Bay Hall' (1973), named after an area of Huddersfield and used in *Hymns and Psalms* (1983) with the hymn 'Reap me the earth as a harvest to God' by Peter Icarus, the alias of Luke Connaughton. Has also composed a Magnificat and Nunc Dimittis, carols, songs, and works for flute, for brass and for organ.

DAY, Edgar Frederick (1891-1983)
Born in Haselton, Gloucestershire on 6 May 1891; died in Worcester on 16 March 1983. An articled pupil of **Ivor Atkins**, cathedral organist of Worcester, where he later became assistant organist (1912-1962). Music master of King's School, Worcester and of the College for the Blind (1921-1941). Wounded on active service during World War I. Worked with Atkins on many of the latter's projects and was invariably and graciously thanked in all the prefaces of the publications that ensued. Composed church music including a Magnificat and Nunc Dimittis in B-flat and the anthems 'When I survey' and 'God that madest earth and heaven', and songs.

DAY, John (1522-1584)
Born in Dunwich, Suffolk in 1522; died in Walden, Essex on 23 July 1584.

By 1549 he was established as a printer and publisher in Holborn, London. He was one of the earliest printers of music. Day had two shops in London - at Aldersgate and St. Paul's Churchyard. His support for the Reformed Church led to his persecution and he was forced to live abroad for a time.

His *Certaine Notes...* (1560) is a collection of services and anthems. He also published books of Psalm tunes, including a set to the edition of Psalm paraphrases published by Sternhold and Hopkins (1562).

He can be credited with two publishing firsts - a book of church music to English texts, and an edition of a metrical Psalter with an individual ('proper', as distinct from 'common', or shared) tune for each. He may also have been responsible for the first Psalter containing harmonised proper tunes.

One of Day's own anthems was included in Clifford's *Divine Services and Anthems* (1664).

DAY, Thomas (?-c1654)
Musician to Prince Henry and to Charles I. Organist of Westminster Abbey (1625-1632) and master of the choristers of the Chapel Royal from 1636 until some time after the execution of Charles I. Composed the anthem 'By the waters of Babylon'.

DAY, Timothy (b.1950)
Born on 10 May 1950. Organ scholar of St. John's College, Oxford (1970-1973). Curator of Western art music at the National Sound Archive, London. Composer of the introit 'Thou shalt shew me the path of life' during his time at Oxford.

DAYMOND, Dr. Emily Rosa (1866-1949)
Born in Plomesgate, Suffolk in 1866; died in Eastbourne, Sussex on 10 October 1949.

Studied at the Royal College of Music under a piano scholarship from 1883 to 1887 in the first intake of students. She met the requirements for the degrees of B.Mus. (1896) and D.Mus. (1901) at the University of Oxford but was statute-barred from receiving them until 1921, in which year she was awarded both degrees at the same ceremony.

Resident lecturer in music and organ at the Royal Holloway College, Egham, Surrey (1887-1899). A professor of piano and harmony at the R.C.M. (1908-1921).

Wrote two books of score-reading exercises and composed hymn tunes, songs, and pieces for piano.

DEALE, Edgar Martin (b.1902)
Born on 1 August 1902. Composer of hymn tunes and songs. Also composed the anthem 'A Virgin unspotted' (1955).

DEAN, William Henry (19th /20th century)
Graduated B.Mus. in 1900 at the University of Oxford. Organist and choirmaster of the Holy Trinity Church, Llandrindod Wells, Wales, and music teacher at the County School. Composed a Magnificat and Nunc Dimittis in A, items for violin, and songs.

DEANE, John Horth (1824-1881)
Born in Shoreditch, London in 1824; died in Eastbourne, Sussex on 24 April 1881. A composer of hymn tunes and of two settings in chant form of the Te Deum - in E and in G. Also composed pieces for organ. Published *17 Original Tunes* (1875), a collection of hymn tunes.

DEANE, Dr. Thomas (c1670-?)
There were probably at least two church composers and musicians by this name in the first half of the 18th century. This subject graduated D.Mus. at the University of Oxford in July 1731. It is unlikely that the Thomas Deane associated with Worcester, and organist of Bristol Cathedral from 1640 to 1668 is the same.

A violinist, said to be the first in England to perform a sonata by Arcangelo Corelli, this event being in 1709. An organist at Warwick Parish Church (1719-1744) and, from 1733 to 1749, at St. Michael's Church, Coventry (since elevated to cathedral status), where he was succeeded by **Capel Bond.**

Composed church music, including a Service in A. Also composed items for violin.

DEAR, James Richard (1870-?)
Born in Ventnor, Isle of Wight in 1870. Trained at Westminster Abbey under **Frederick Bridge.** Graduated B.Mus. at the University of Durham in 1895. Organist of the Church of St. Giles, South Mimms, near Barnet, Hertfordshire (from 1889); St. Luke's, Uxbridge Road (from 1893); St. James, West Hampstead (from 1898) and St. Saviour, Eastbourne, Sussex (from 1899). A choral society conductor. Composed church music including a Service in F Minor, songs and part songs.

DEARLE, Duncan William (1893-1954)
Born in Upper Tooting, London on 21 February 1893; died in Tunbridge Wells, Kent on 27 March 1954. Attended St. Winifred's School, Kenley, and then studied music under H.D. Welton at the Foundling Hospital, London. Graduated B.Mus. at Christ Church, Oxford (1917). Organist at the Churches of St. Luke, Battersea (1916-1919 and 1922-1927) and St. Stephen, Westminster, London (1920-1922). Art director of Morris and Company (1932-1940), following which he designed painted glass windows. A composer of hymn tunes: 'David' is found in *Church and School Hymnal* (1926).

DEARLE, Dr. Edward (1806-1891)
Born in Cambridge on 2 March 1806; died in Camberwell, London on 20 March 1891.

A chorister of King's College, Trinity College and St. John's College, Cambridge. Graduated Mus.B. (1836) and Mus.D. (1842) at the University of Cambridge.

Organist of St. Paul's Church, Deptford, Kent (from 1827), the Parish Churches of Blackheath, Kent (from 1830); Wisbech, Cambridgeshire (from 1832) and St. Mary's Collegiate Church, Warwick (from 1833). From 1835 to 1864 he was organist of the Parish Church and master of the Song School of Newark, Nottinghamshire. In 1864 he moved to Camberwell. One of the founders of Trinity College, London.

Composed the oratorio *Israel in the Wilderness* (1879), a Morning and Evening Service in F (1832) plus at least one further setting of each (c1852), and an anthem 'Turn Thee again, Thou God of hosts' which won the Gresham Prize of 1837. Published a set of 36 chants in 1852.

Dearle's hymn tune 'Penitentia' was used with the hymn 'Father, again in Jesus' Name we meet' by Lady Lucy Whitmore in the compilation *Church Hymns* (1874) by **Arthur Sullivan.** Composed the anthem 'The desert shall rejoice'. Also wrote part songs, including 'Sigh no more, ladies' and organ works.

DEARNALEY, Irvine (1839-1894)
Born in Broadbottom, Chester on 29 September 1839; died in Ashton under Lyme, Staffordshire on 18 September 1894. His father, who also had a musical talent, worked as a spinner in a cotton mill and encouraged Irvine Dearnaley as best he could within limited financial means to become proficient in music. Organist of Stalybridge, Cheshire from the age of 17. Studied under **Joseph John Harris,** took piano lessons from Charles Hallé and learned harmony with **Henry Hiles.** Organist of Christ Church, Ashton under Lyme and, from 1864, of the Parish Church. Conductor of a local glee club and philharmonic society, with a reputation as an organ recitalist. Composed anthems such as 'What reward shall I give?' and works for the piano.

DEARNLEY, Dr. Christopher Hugh (b.1930)
Born in Wolverhampton, Staffordshire on 11 February 1930.

Educated at Cranleigh School, Surrey and at Worcester College, Oxford under **Herbert Kennedy Andrews** and **Edmund Rubbra** from 1948 to 1952 where he was organ scholar and graduated B.A. and B.Mus (1952), and M.A. (1955). Accorded the Lambeth D.Mus. (1987). A Doctor of Fine Arts (Westminster College, U.S.A. 1989).

Assistant organist and director of music at the choir school of Salisbury Cathedral in 1954.

Organist and master of the choristers of Salisbury Cathedral (1957-1968). Relinquished these positions to become organist of St. Paul's Cathedral (1967-1990), where he took steps to increase the proportion of 20th century music performed.

Acting director of music at Christ Church, St. Laurence, Sydney, Australia (1990-1991). A significant editor of late 17th and 18th century works.

Has written and edited various books on musical topics. Editor of *Treasury of English Church Music 1650-1760.* His hymn tune 'Finnion' was used with 'Praise the Spirit in Creation' in *English Praise,* the supplement to *English Hymnal* (1976). Hymn tunes by him are also found in *New English Hymnal.* He has composed various other kinds of church music. Now lives in Australia.

DELAMAINE (Delamain, De La Main), Henry (?-1796)
Died in Cork, Ireland on 19 December 1796. The son of a French refugee who had settled in Ireland during the French Revolution. Organist of Christ Church, Cork from not later than 1762 until 1782, and of the cathedral of St. Finn Barre (1782-1796). Active and well known in Cork musical circles during the 18th century. Composed music of various kinds including *Six New Psalm Tunes* (1781), a collection of chants.

DE LLOYD, Dr. David John
See **LLOYD**, Dr. David John de

DENIS BROWNE, William (?-1915)
Killed in action in the Gallipoli Campaign of World War I, on 7 June 1915. Of Irish descent, being related to the Marquess of Sligo, although born in England.
Educated at Rugby School. Classical scholar (from 1907) of Clare College, Cambridge, where he graduated B.A. and, in 1912, Mus.B. A pupil of **Charles Wood** and **Alan Gray** for composition and organ respectively; studied piano with Ursula Newton, who had been a pupil of Busoni.
From 1910 he was organist and choirmaster of Clare College. He was later organist of Guy's Hospital, London. In 1912 he was appointed music master of Repton School, Derbyshire. Conductor of a local choral society.
A friend of the poet Rupert Brooke: the two served in the armed forces together.
His essays appeared in *The Times* and *New Statesman*. His special interest was early English music.
Composed songs including 'To Grantiana dancing and singing', and a motet *God is our strength and song* (1912).

DENNIS, Henry (1818-1887)
Born in Tickenhall (Ticknall), Derbyshire in 1818; died in Hugglescote, Leicestershire on 4 December 1887.
A skilled violin player, and a member of his local Baptist Church, having been a chorister from an early age. From around the year 1847 he lived at Hugglescote on a farm which had been in the possession of his mother's family for more than two hundred years. A guardian of the poor and a Conservative, a firm believer in protectionism. Composed several hymn tunes, of which an example is 'Euphony' (also known as 'Euphonia') which was first published in the magazine *The Soul's Welfare* (1850). Used in *Methodist Hymn Book* (1933) with the hymn 'Victim Divine, Thy grace we claim' by Charles Wesley.

DERING (Deering), Richard (c1580-1630)
Born around the year 1580 into an old Kentish family; died in London in 1630 and buried on 22 March.
Graduated B.Mus at Christ Church, Oxford in 1610, having previously studied music in Italy.
A Roman Catholic, he lived abroad between 1612 and 1625, serving as organist to a convent of English nuns in Brussels. He returned to England to take up a position as organist to Henrietta Maria on her marriage to Charles I. Henrietta had a private chapel within Somerset House, London. From around 1626 he was also a musician of the king.
Composed 12 verse anthems and a full anthem, said to have been liked by Oliver Cromwell, and several motets (1617), probably in Rome. These items included *Unto Thee, O Lord* and the Latin works *Vox in rama* and *Isti sunt sancti*. The seasonal motets

Factum est silentium (Michaelmas) and *Quem vidistis, pastores* (for the Nativity) are still widely used. Wrote madrigals and other choral items, into some of which were incorporated street cries and tradesmen's songs of London. Also composed music for viol.

DEWBERRY, William Charles (1843-1899)
Born in Cambridge on 16 January 1843; died in Cambridge on 15 September 1899. A chorister, solo boy and assistant organist of King's College, Cambridge. At the Royal Academy of Music he studied under **William Sterndale Bennett**, **Charles Lucas**, **Charles Steggall** and **William Cusins**. Graduated Mus.B. at the University of Cambridge in 1867. Organist of Clare College and of St. Edward's Church, Cambridge. Composed an Evening Service in E-flat, anthems such as 'Behold, a Virgin', chants and part songs.

DEXTER, Harold (b.1920)
Born in Leicester on 7 October 1920.
A chorister of Leicester Cathedral and pupil of the cathedral organist, **G.C. Gray**. His education continued at Wyggeston Grammar School, Leicester and at Corpus Christi College, Cambridge (1939-1941 and 1946) where he was organ scholar (1939) and John Stewart of Rannoch scholar (1940). Graduated B.A. and Mus.B. in 1942, M.A. in 1946. His period at Cambridge was interrupted by war service with the Royal Naval Volunteer Reserve and the Royal Navy (1941-1946).
Organist of Louth Parish Church, Lincolnshire (1947-1949) and music master at King Edward VI School, Louth, Lincolnshire (1946-1949). Organist of Holy Trinity Church, Leamington Spa, Warwickshire (1949-1956) and music master of Bablake School, Coventry (1953-1956).
Organist of Southwark Cathedral (1956-1968), and a professor of Guildhall School of Music, where he was head of the general musicianship Department (1963-1988). Following his departure from Southwark he took up the organistship of St. Botolph's Church, Aldgate. Author of a *Dictionary of Composers*.
Has composed a Series II setting of the Holy Communion Service, an Evening Service for Boys' and Men's Voices, and a Te Deum for Choral Society and Orchestra.

DIBDIN, Henry Edward (1813-1866)
Born in Sadler's Wells, London on 8 September 1813; died in Edinburgh on 6 May 1866. Youngest son of Charles Dibdin the younger and the grandson of the Charles Dibdin of 'Tom Bowling' fame.
Studied harp with his eldest sister, Mary Anne, and with Nicolas Bochsa. He also learned viola and organ.
As harpist at Covent Garden, he played on the occasion of the last concert by Niccolo Paganini there on 3 August 1832.
A teacher in Edinburgh from 1833. Honorary organist of Trinity Chapel. A capable painter.
With **J.T. Surenne** he published *A Collection of Church Music* (1843). He compiled *Standard Psalm Tune Book* (1852), which contained items that had already been in existence for many years. Composed a number of hymn- and Psalm tunes, of which 'Morningside' is used in *Hymns Ancient and Modern* with the hymn 'Hark! 'Tis the watchman's cry'. Also composed songs, and works for the piano and for the harp.

DICKINSON, Charles John (1822-1883)
Born in Dublin, Ireland in 1822; died in Bodmin, Cornwall on 9 April 1883. A composer of hymn tunes, a Magnificat and Nunc Dimittis (1883) and a Te Deum (1883). Compiler of *Hymn Tunes, double and single...* (1861).

DICKINSON, Peter (b.1934)
Born in Lytham St. Annes, Lancashire on 15 November 1934.
A member of a musical family (his sister is the *mezzo* Meriel Dickinson), he attended The Leys School, Cambridge and was then organ scholar at Queens' College, Cambridge, where he studied under **Philip Radcliffe**. Also received assistance and encouragement from **Lennox Berkeley**. Holds the Cambridge M.A.
Carried out three years' postgraduate study in the U.S.A. (from 1958), by means of a fellowship of the Rotary Foundation, at the Juilliard School, New York, where he worked under Bernard Wagenaar and met John Cage. Before returning to England he was a pianist with the New York City Ballet.
A lecturer at the College of SS Mark and John, Chelsea, London (1962-1966). Taught at the University of Birmingham (1966-1970), initially in the extra mural department and then in the department of music. For the next four years he operated as a freelance performer and lecturer.
Became the first professor of music at the University of Keele (1974-1984). The University quickly became known as one of the best centres of study in the country for American music.
For many years he has studied the life and work of Erik Satie, Charles Ives and Lord Berners as the basis of broadcasts and recordings.
In 1988, Peter Dickinson was the subject of a one-hour documentary on the television programme 'The South Bank Show'.
In 1984 he moved to London in order to concentrate on composition. His style is jazz-influenced. His church music output includes the anthem 'Jesus Christ is risen today' (1955), *Two Motets* (1963) and a set of Canticles in B-flat. A Mass *of the Acopalypse* (1984) was commissioned to mark the 300th anniversary of St. James's Church, Piccadilly, London.
His other compositions include orchestral works, the sacred cantata *Judas Tree*, items for wind and other chamber ensembles, songs and works for keyboard.

DIEMER, Philip Henry (1839-1910)
Born in Bedford on 18 July 1839 to a family of German extraction; died in Bedford on 7 May 1910. He was the cousin of the French-born pianist, Louis Diemer.
Studied piano under **W.H. Holmes,** and harmony with **George Macfarren,** at the Royal Academy of Music.
For more than 30 years he was organist and choirmaster of Holy Trinity Church, Bedford and for longer than 35 years, director of music at Bedford Grammar School.
Composed a cantata *Bethany* (1881), anthems, hymn tunes, songs, part songs and items for the piano.

DIGGLE, Frederick (19th /20th century)
Fred Diggle received his early musical training at Norwich Cathedral and in 1908, he graduated B.Mus. at the University of Durham. Organist and choirmaster of Hingham Parish Church, Norfolk and choirmaster of St. Clement's Church, Norwich (from 1904). Organist and choirmaster of Brackley Parish Church, Northamptonshire (from 1905); Brampton Parish Church (from 1909) and Standish Parish Church (from 1911). At Brackley he taught music at Magdalen College School. Conductor of local choral societies. Composed a setting of the Te Deum and Benedicite, Kyries and songs.

DISTIN, Theodore (1823-1893)
Born in Brighton, Sussex in 1823; died on 12 April 1893.
Studied music under his father, John Distin, inventor of the keyed bugle, and later with Thomas Cooke and Negri. The family formed a band, with which he toured as a French horn player from 1836 to 1844.
Became an operatic baritone and a teacher of music in London. Sang bass in the choir of Lincoln's Inn Chapel.
Composed a Service in C and another in G, two Masses, the anthems 'Blessed is the man' and 'Hear me when I call', glees, part songs and songs.

DIX, Leopold McClintock Lancaster (1861-1935)
Born in Dublin, Ireland in 1861; died in Dublin on 9 March 1935. Educated privately and at Trinity College, Dublin, becoming a solicitor by profession and a keen amateur musician. Arranged melodies, particularly Irish ones, for *Irish Church Hymnal* (1919). One of his arrangements, of the traditional tune 'Fingal', was used in the Revised Edition (1927) of *Church Hymnary*. Composed chants, songs and items for piano.

DIXON, Alfred Capel (1889-1949)
Born in Islington, London in 1889; died in Dorking, Surrey on 2 October 1949. A bank clerk, self-taught in music. A chorister of the Temple Church (from 1900) under **Walford Davies,** he joined the ranks of the tenors immediately after his voice broke. Later succeeded **Gregory Hast** as principal tenor of the decani. A composer of hymn tunes.

DIXON, Dr. George (1820-1887)
Born in Norwich, Norfolk on 5 June 1820; died in Finchley, London on 8 June 1887.
A chorister of Norwich Cathedral and a private pupil of the cathedral organist, **Zechariah Buck** until 1835. Graduated B.Mus. (1852) and D.Mus.(1858) at the University of Oxford.
Assistant organist of Grantham Parish Church, Lincolnshire (1835-1845) and organist of the Parish Churches of Retford, Nottinghamshire (1845-1859); Louth, Lincolnshire (1859-1865) and Grantham (1865 1886). A musical examiner.
Composed anthems such as 'I heard a voice' and 'Unto Thee, O my Strength', hymn tunes, Psalms and chants.

DIXON, Richard William (c.1810-1880)
An amateur composer, who lived in Newcastle-on-Tyne. Composer of the hymn tunes 'Staincliffe' and 'Castle Eden', used in the *Burnley Tune Book* (1875).

DIXON, William (c1760-1825)
Born around the year 1760; died in London in 1825. For most of his life he lived in Liverpoool and London as a music engraver, teacher and writer. Published a collection of church music (1790), containing a setting of the Te Deum, anthems including 'Almighty God, give us grace' and 'Most gracious God', Psalm tunes and hymns. Composed glees and wrote a manual on singing.

DIXON, William Hubert (1846-1893)
Born in Bishopstone, Wiltshire on 1 August 1846; died in Kilmarnock, Ayrshire, Scotland on 31 July 1893. Organist of High Church, Kilmarnock (from 1869). Composed a sacred cantata *Jerusalem* (1887), songs and items for the piano.

DOBBS, Jack Percival Baker (b.1922)
Born in Newport, Gloucestershire on 22 July 1922.
Attended Dursley Grammar School. Graduated B.Mus. at the University of Wales and M.Phil (1972) at the University of London. Also holds the degrees of B.A. and M.Ed. Studied with Eve Kirsch and A.E.F. Dickenson at the University of Durham.
Organist of the Dursley Tabernacle (1936-1940).
Taught music in Durham at Stanley Grammar School (1944-1947). County music adviser (1947-1951); taught music at the University of Durham (from 1952).
Director of music of the Malayan Teachers' College, Brinford Lodge (1955-1959), and lecturer at the London University Institute of Education (1959-1967). Director of musical studies and deputy principal of the Dartington College of Arts (1967- 1987).
A composer of hymn tunes including 'Teilo Sant' and 'Dursley Tabernacle'.

DOBNEY, Michael (18th /19th century)
Was associated with the town of Maidstone, Kent (c1810). Composed the anthems 'Be merciful to me, O God' and 'Unto Thee, O Lord, will I lift up'.

DOBSON, Cyril Comyn (1879-1960)
Born in Kensington, London on 26 June 1879; died in Lymington, Hampshire on 27 May 1960. A composer of hymn tunes. Published the collection *New tunes to well-known hymns* (1926).

DOCKER, Frederick Arthur William (1852-?)
Born in London on 14 August 1852.
A chorister at the Church of St. Andrew, Wells Street, London under **Joseph Barnby**, whose articled pupil he became at the age of 12. He then studied at the Royal Academy of Music under **W.H. Holmes**, **Charles Steggall** and **Arthur Sullivan**.
Early in his career he was assistant to Joseph Barnby at St. Andrew's, Wells Street. From 1871 he was organist there.
Conductor of the Handel Society from its inauguration in 1882 until 1892. His direction of the oratorio *Saul* drew congratulations from the Prince of Wales, who attended a performance in 1884.
A professor of organ at Guildhall School of Music (from 1895) and a professor and examiner of the R.A.M. He lectured and conducted examinations at Trinity College of Music.
Choirmaster of St. Pancras Church, London (from 1905).
Succeeded **Malcolm Lawson** as conductor of the Kyrie Society.
Composed a setting of the Te Deum, an anthem 'O ye that love the Lord', and part songs.

DODDS, George Robert (1876-1946)
Born in Newcastle-on-Tyne in 1876; died in Penarth, Glamorgan, Wales on 2 October 1946.
Studied at the Royal College of Music under **C.V. Stanford**, **Walter Parratt**, **Frederick Bridge**, Visetti and **W.S. Hoyte**.
Graduated B.Mus. at the University of Durham (1898).
Organist and choirmaster of the Parish Church of Corbridge-on-Tyne (1892-1894); St. Paul's, Newcastle (1894-1900) and choirmaster of Benwell Parish Church (1898-1899). From 1900 to 1914 he was organist and choirmaster of the Elswick Road Wesleyan Church, Newcastle. The conductor of local choral and philharmonic societies.
Author of a number of books on music, including *Practical Hints for Singers*. A festival adjudicator throughout the British Isles and, on two occasions, in Canada.
Composed anthems, hymn tunes, songs, part songs and organ music.

DODDS, Dr. Tom William (1852-1938)
Born in Leeds on 22 September 1852; died in 1938.
At the age of nine he was a chorister of Leeds Parish Church; a year later he was appointed organist of Headingley. Attended Bury Grammar School, Lancashire. Graduated B.Mus (1876) and D.Mus. (1887) at Queen's College, Oxford.
Organist of St. Matthew's Church, Leeds (1863-1866); St. Wilfred's College Chapel, Leeds (1866-1872) and of Queen's College and St. Clement's Church, Oxford (from 1872). Held the organistship of Queen's College for almost 50 years. A music examiner.
Composed an oratorio *Hezekiah*, a setting of Psalm 8, chants, anthems, hymn tunes and items for the piano.

DON, Nigel (b.1954)
Born in South London on 16 April 1954.
Attended Homefield Preparatory School, Sutton, Surrey and Kings College School, Wimbledon where he studied harmony and composition. Read chemical engineering at Pembroke College, Cambridge. Founded the University Big Band, and sang in the college choir under Ian Little.
Worked in the detergents industry until 1989, when he became a freelance piano teacher and composer.
Has composed anthems, the hymn tunes 'Heronpark' and 'Londonderry Farm' to words by Paul Wigmore, a nativity musical for Sunday School 'Wise men follow the star', alternative theme songs for Scripture Union holiday clubs, and *Music for Reflection*, a set of 16 instrumental voluntaries arranged flexibly so as to be playable on different instruments. Has also composed chamber music, orchestral pieces and secular songs.

DONE, Dr. William (1815-1895)
Born in Worcester on 4 October 1815; died in Worcester on 17 August 1895.
A chorister of Worcester Cathedral from 1825, taking part in the Worcester Festival of 1827 as a member of the chorus. From 1828 to 1835 he was articled to **C.E.J. Clarke**, cathedral organist, whom he served as deputy and eventually succeeded in 1844.
Conducted at his first Worcester Festival in 1845, beginning an association which continued until 1890 and saw many changes and notable events such as the conducting by Antonin Dvorak of his own works (1884) and the presence of the young **Edward Elgar** as a rank and file violinist in the orchestra (1887). Conducted the Worcester Philharmonic Society until 1884.
His long tenure as organist of Worcester Cathedral was marked by a reform of the services, the formation and encouragement of a voluntary choir and the performance of major musical works on special occasions.
Done was accorded the Lambeth D.Mus. in 1894, the jubilee of his appointment, in recognition of his work in improving the standard of music at Worcester.
Composed church music.

DONIACH, Shula (b.1905)
Educated at the City of London School for Girls, at the Royal Academy of Music and at the Tobias Matthay School, London. Also studied in Berlin, Vienna and Budapest.
In 1946, she gave a series of eight recitals at the Central Hall, Westminster, in which she performed in chronological order the 22 Beethoven piano sonatas.
Founded in London, and organised, the Friends of Music Society (1934-1936) to promote the performance of rare works from all periods. Helped to devise a method of teaching, by means of visualisation, the memorising of music.
A lecturer, she gave three sets of lectures on music at the Univeristy of London Extension College on music and the piano from the 16th to the 20th century (1944-1945). Also lectured for the Workers' Educational Association. Broadcast in Hebrew on the subject of English music for the B.B.C. Hebrew Section.
Composed *Forest Carol* and *Christmas Lullaby,* also a Passover counting song for mixed choir.

DONKIN, William Fishburn (1815-1869)
A Fellow of the Royal Society. Savilian professor of astronomy at the University of Oxford. His *Acoustics, Theoretical*, published in 1870, was intended as the first of a series of volumes on the science of sound but the remainder never materialised. Composed the anthem 'Justorum animae'.

DORAN, Revd. John Wilberforce (1834-?)
Born in London in 1834.
From 1856 he attended St. John's College, Cambridge where he graduated B.A. (1857) and M.A. (1861). Ordained deacon in 1857; priest in 1858.
Served eight separate curacies at Stisted, Essex (1857-1858); the three London churches of St. Thomas, Bethnal Green (1859-1861); St. Matthias, Stoke Newington (1861-1862) and St. Alban, Holborn (1862-1864); in Lincolnshire at North Kelsey (1865-1866) and Grasby (1868-1870); at the Sussex church of St. John's, St. Leonards-on-Sea (1872-1875) and St. Matthias, West Brompton, London (1872-1875).
Vicar of Fen Stanton, Huntingdonshire (1883-1889) and of Soulderne in the Diocese of Oxford (from 1889).
With **Spenser Nottingham** he edited *The Choir Directory of Plainsong* (1868).

DORRELL, William (1810-1895)
Born in London on 5 September 1810; died in London on 13 December 1895. The son of Edmund Dorrell, watercolourist.
Studied in London under **William Crotch** and Cipriani Potter. In 1844 he travelled to Paris in order to study under Friedrich Kalkbrenner and Stephen Heller. A piano recitalist and a teacher in London, where he taught piano for 40 years at the Royal Academy of Music. He was in demand as a private teacher to noble families. Composed the hymn tunes 'Coventry' and 'Exeter' which were used in *Hymns Ancient and Modern*. Other works by him were used privately and never published. Composer of the anthem 'Hear me when I call'.

DORWARD, David Campbell (b.1933)
Born in Dundee, Scotland on 7 August 1933. Attended the Morgan Academy, Dundee; the University of St. Andrews and the Royal Academy of Music. Holds the degree of M.A. For a short time he was a teacher for Middlesex County Council (1960-1961), and then

a freelance teacher. From 1962 he was a music producer at Edinburgh for the B.B.C. Has composed hymn tunes, a Symphony, concertos for various instruments, chamber and piano music, songs, music for radio, television documentaries and films and the musical *A Christmas Carol.*

DOUGALL, Neil (1776-1862)
Born in Greenock, Scotland on 9 December 1776; died on 1 October 1862.
The son of a wheelwright who was conscripted and who died in Ceylon when Neil was aged four.
Remained at school until the age of 15, when he became an apprentice on board the *Britannia*. He lost an arm and his sight on 1 June 1794 accidentally during the firing of a salute to celebrate the victory of Lord Howe over the French.
Became a popular teacher of singing. Kept a tavern and then a boarding house. For 60 years (1800-1860) he put on an annual concert in Greenock.
Composed around one hundred Psalm and hymn tunes, including 'Naples' (1801), 'Patience' and 'New East Church'. His 'Kilmarnock' (1823) was instantly popular, especially with Presbyterian congregations and it was used in *Church Hymnary*, Revised Edition (1927). In 1854 he published *Poems and Songs*, which included 13 items of church music, some of which were composed by him.

DOWLAND, John (c1562-1626)
Born between 1562 and 1586; died in London and was buried on 16 February 1626. The place of birth is also uncertain: it is likely that he was born in Ireland (possibly in Dublin) and if not, in London.
In 1588 he graduated B.Mus. at Christ Church, Oxford. At some time after the year 1593 he studied with Luca Marenzio (in Italy. A Mus.B. graduate of the University of Cambridge.
Lived in London at the age of 15, where he worked in the household of Sir Henry Cobham until 1583. Some time thereafter he was employed by Sir Edward Stafford. After the year 1593 he travelled extensively in France, Germany and Italy. He was never a professional church musician. It is said that he forsook his country after failing to get an appointment at the court of Elizabeth I.
Dowland was said to be the greatest lutenist of his age. He was Court Lutenist to Charles IV of Denmark from 1598 until 1606 and later, to Charles I. William Shakespeare praises him in *The Passionate Pilgrim*.
Composed for the lute and for the voice and lute, his music being published widely on the continent. Of his church music, the motet *My spirit longs for Thee* is still performed today. He was one of the 10 composers featured in Thomas East's *Whole Booke of Psalmes...* (1592). Composed Psalm tunes and spiritual songs such as 'All people that on earth do dwell' (Psalm 100) for four voices and 'An heart that's broken and contrite'.

DOWNES, Father James F. (19th century)
Born in Yorkshire. Priest of the Roman Catholic Church of St. Patrick, Bedford. His compositions include the two sacred cantatas *The Parable of the Ten Virgins* (1882) and *The Prodigal Son* (1885).

DOWNING, Jaemus (b.1951)
Born in Plymouth, Devon on 16 January 1951. Studied at Goldsmiths' College, London (1969-1974) including composition

with Jeremy Dale-Roberts, and graduated with a London B.Mus. Since 1978 he has been head of the music department of Launceston College. His compositions include the two carols 'A Boy was born' and 'Most highly favoured lady' (1978) for a cappella four-part Choir.

DRAKE, Thomas (19th century)
A chorister of Bristol Cathedral in 1863. Composed the anthem 'Preserve me, O God'.

DRAYTON, Paul (b.1944)
Born in Redcar, Yorkshire on 28 December 1944.
Attended the Royal Grammar School, High Wycombe, Buckinghamshire and went up to Oxford University.
Director of music of the choir school of New College, Oxford. Currently on the music staff of Stowe School, Buckingham. Also teaches part-time for the Workers' Educational Association and at the Department of Continuing Education, University of Exeter.
A pianist, composer and adjudicator.
His *New College* Service (1968) has been widely performed. Other works were written for New College, Oxford including the unaccompanied motet *Jesu, dulcis memoria*. Published works include the carols 'Joys seven' (1989) and 'Corpus Christi carol' (1973). Anthems include 'The spacious firmament on high' (1971) and 'Ecce ancilla Domini' (1972). *Creeds and Canons* was written for the Norwich Triennial Festival of 1979.

DREWETT, Edwin (1850-1924)
Born in Islington, London in 1850; died in Tunbridge Wells, Kent on 26 October 1924.
Studied at the Royal Academy of Music.
Held a number of organistships in London. Organist of the Harecourt Congregational Chapel; the German Lutheran Church, Dalton (1893-1905) and the German Embassy Church, Brompton (1905-1914). From 1917 to 1924 he was organist of the Church of King Charles the Martyr, Tunbridge Wells, Kent.
The Revised Edition (1927) of *Church Hymnary* uses Drewett's 'Elmhurst' with 'O God of mercy, God of might' by Godfrey Thring.

DRIFFIELD, Edward Townshend (1851-?)
Born in Prescot, near Liverpool on 10 December 1851. Organist of Christ Church, Claughton, near Birkenhead, Cheshire. Composed a sacred cantata *My soul doth magnify the Lord,* hymn tunes, a Sonata in G for Organ, and glees including 'Come follow me'. Also a four-part song 'Ripening love' (1955).

DRUMMOND, George (1798-1839)
Blind from an early age. Studied under **William Crotch** and graduated B.Mus. at the University of Oxford. Published a collection of Psalm melodies arranged for piano or organ and entitled *Parochial Psalmody*. Composed the anthems 'Lord of all power and might' and 'O give thanks unto the Lord'.

DUCKWORTH, Francis (1862-1941)
Born in Rimington, Lancashire on 25 December 1862; died in Colne, Lancashire on 16 August 1941.
The son of a grocer, he left school at the age of 12 to work in a cousin's tobacconist shop in Burnley. He moved to Colne in 1882 to work in the printing firm of his brother Joshua. In 1889 he started a grocery business.

At 12, Duckworth was organist of the Wesleyan Chapel at Stopper Lane, near Rimington. Later (1894-1929) he held a similar position at the Albert Road Wesleyan Church, Colne. His hymn tune 'Duckworth', also known as 'Rimington', is often used with 'Jesus shall reign where'er the sun'.

DUCKWORTH, F. (?-1946)
Died in Blackburn, Lancashire on 25 November 1946. Organist and choirmaster in Blackburn of St. Luke's Church, St. Mark's Church, and, for 34 years, Holy Trinity Church.

DUDDLE, James (19th /20th century)
Graduated B.Mus. at the University of Durham in 1903. Organist and choirmaster in Lancashire of Golborne Parish Church (1876-1887); St. Catherine's Church, Wigan (1887-1890); Leigh Wesleyan Chapel (1892-1894) and the Presbyterian Church, Withrington, Manchester (1894-1896). A professor of the Manchester School of Music from 1892 to 1905. In the latter year he became director of the Manchester Conservatory of Music. A composer of hymn tunes, part songs and organ pieces.

DUDENEY, Thomas James (1854-?)
Born in Mayfield, Sussex on 29 November 1854. Studied under **George Macfarren**. Organist of Dunster Parish Church (from 1876). Later held appointments at the churches of St. James, Taunton, Somerset and St. Anne, Eastbourne, Sussex. A recitalist and principal of the Taunton College of Music from 1888. Composed cantatas, organ pieces, songs and part songs.

DUFFELL, Dr. John (c.1871-1915)
Born in Tipton, Staffordshire around 1871; died in Sheffield, Yorkshire on 20 October 1915 at the age of 44. Educated at Isleworth College. Graduated B.Mus. (1899) and D.Mus. (1915) at the University of London. Organist and choirmaster in Sheffield, where he set up home in 1892, at the Wesleyan Chapels of St. John (1892-1900) and Carver Street (from 1903). He taught music at the Central High School (1896-1902) and, specialising in singing and harmony, at the Eton House School for Girls. Music instructor of the Sheffield University Training College (from 1908). Music master of King Edward VII School, Sheffield. In addition he acted as conductor to local choral, operatic and musical societies. Composed church music, including a setting of Psalm 126, operettas including *Hypatia*, a choral ballad *Hohenlinden*, and songs.

DUGDALE, Louise Zillah (1872-1943)
Born in Lambeth, London in 1872; died in Ilford, Essex on 19 March 1943. Graduated B.Mus. in 1904 at the University of Durham. Organist of the Baptist Churches of Sidcup, Kent (1891-1907), Woodgrange, Forest Gate, East London (1907-c1920) and High Road, Lee, South East London (from c1920). Published *A handy book of Descants to well-known Hymn Tunes*. Composed anthems, hymn tunes, material for use in Sunday schools, songs, madrigals and pieces for organ.

DUNCALF, Henry (?-1762)
Died in London on 10 June 1762.
Organist of St. Bartholomew's Church, near the Royal Exchange, London (1732-1762) and of the Church of St. Mary-at-Hill, London (1730-1762).

His tune 'St. Bartholomew' was used in *Parochial Harmony* (1762) where, as a melody only, it was used with Psalm 18. The tune was later harmonised and used this century with the hymn by Isaac Watts 'My God, my King, Thy various praise', and elsewhere. Other tunes were included in **William Riley**'s *Parochial Music Corrected* (1762). Composed and published a number of songs around the year 1758.

DUNCAN, William Edmondstoune (1866-1920)
Born in Sale, Cheshire in 1866; died on 26 June 1920.
Won a scholarship to the newly-opened Royal College of Music in 1883, where he studied under **Hubert Parry**, **C.V. Stanford**, **Frederick Bridge**, **George Martin** and Ernst Pauer. On leaving the R.C.M. he continued his studies under **George Macfarren**.
Lived in London and worked mainly as a composer. On returning to Sale he continued to compose and became a professor of Oldham College of Music, Lancashire.
Music critic of *Daily News*, and the Manchester correspondent of *Musical Opinion*. Wrote many books, including *A History of Music* (1908) and *The Art of Piano Playing* (1913). Music critic of a London and a provincial daily paper.
Composed an opera *Perseus*, a Mass in F Minor, a Morning, Communion and Evening Service in G, songs, part songs, orchestral items and works for organ.

DUNHILL, Dr. Thomas Frederick (1877-1946)
Born in Hampstead, London on 1 February 1877; died in Scunthorpe, Lincolnshire on 13 March 1946.
Attended school in St. John's Wood, London, and Kent College, Canterbury. From 1897 he studied at the Royal College of Music under a composition scholarship with Franklin Taylor for piano and **C.V. Stanford** for theory. Graduated D.Mus. honorarily at the University of Durham.
An assistant music master at Eton College under **C.H. Lloyd**. His fellow assistants were Colin Taylor who is remembered for his influence on **Peter Warlock**, and **Edward Mason**, a concert promoter and choir trainer who was killed in action in World War I. Dunhill taught at Eton from 1899 to 1908, returning temporarily to teach during World War II.
A professor of the Royal Academy of Music (from 1905), and a professor of harmony at the R.C.M. (from 1905). As an examiner to the Associated Examining Board, he visited Australia and New Zealand.
In 1907 he founded the Concerts of British Chamber Music which he conducted until 1916, its object being to promote the work of contemporary British composers.
Author of *Chamber Music* (1912) and *Sir Edward Elgar* (1938).
A composer of hymn tunes, some of which were especially commissioned by **Ralph Vaughan Williams** for *English Hymnal* (1906). He also wrote operas including the popular *Tantivy Towers* (1931), ballet music such as *Gallimaufry*, chamber music and a song cycle *The Wind Among The Reeds*. His early works were performed at the R.C.M. by means of the Palmer Patron's Fund.

DUNKERLEY, William Arthur (1852-1941)
Born in Cheetham, near Manchester on 12 November 1852; died in Worthing, Sussex on 23 January 1941. Used the alias John Oxenham. Composer of hymn tunes and of the anthem 'In Christ there is no East or West'.

DUNMAN, Revd. Sidney Joseph Palmer (1843-1913)
Born in Bridgwater, Somerset in 1843; died in Bristol, Gloucestershire on 30 March 1913. Became a minister of the Methodist Church in 1864. A member of the committee that selected the tunes for the publication *Wesley's Hymns* (1877). Several were his, and tunes are also found in *Sunday School Tune Book* (1879) where his 'St. Winifred' was used with the hymn by George Rowe, 'Cradled in a manger, meanly'.

DUNN, Matthew Sinclair (1846-?)
Born in Glasgow on 3 August 1846.
As a young man he played the cornet in the local volunteer band. He pursued a career in business but retained a keen interest in music. Appointed precentor to a church in Ayrshire, and choirmaster to the church of Lady Elizabeth Pringle in Berwickshire.
Won a scholarship to the Tonic Sol-fa College (1879) and later studied at the Royal Academy of Music where his teachers were Ettore Fiori, **W.H. Cummings**, John Welch for singing and **George Macfarren** for harmony.
A professional singer, teacher and composer. In 1888 he was appointed conductor of the choral class and teacher of singing at Trinity College of Music, London. He was the author of books on the subject of singing technique.
Composed six anthems, 12 trios for ladies' voices, part songs and a set of easy organ voluntaries.

DUNNE, Dr. John (1834-1883)
Born in York in 1834; died in Ashton, Killiney, near Dublin on 7 June 1883. In 1850 he became a chorister of Worcester Cathedral and in 1854, a chorister of Cashel Cathedral, Ireland. Graduated B.Mus. (1866) and D.Mus. (1870) at the University of Dublin. Sang in the Dublin Cathedral Choirs of St. Patrick and Christ Church, and in the Trinity College Choir. A music examiner. Composed Services, anthems such as 'Gracious and Righteous' and 'The Wilderness', cantatas including *Myra*, glees and songs.

DUNSTABLE, John (c1370-1453)
Born probably in Dunstable, Bedfordshire around the year 1370; died in Walbrook, London on 24 December 1453. England's first noteworthy composer, who dominated his field for the first half of the 15th century. Travelled widely. His works have been discovered in Italian libraries and it seems that he was an influence on Dufay and his school. Later in life he was a musical member of the court of the Duke of Bedford, who was Regent in France. A canon of Hereford Cathedral (1419-1440) and a prebendary of Putson Manor. Pursued his other interests in astronomy and mathematics. Composed exclusively for the church. His 67 known items include Masses, motets including the 4-part *Veni Creator*, hymn settings and antiphons such as *Quam pulchra es*.

DUNSTAN, Dr. Ralph (1857-1933)
Born in Carnon Downs near Truro, Cornwall on 17 November 1857; died in Truro on 2 April 1933.
A pupil teacher of St. Mary's Wesleyan Day School in Truro, Cornwall (1871-1876). A graduate of Westminster Training College (1877-1882), where he studied with James Thomson, and was organist from 1880. Dunstan also graduated from the Tonic Sol-fa College, and held the Mus.B. (1882) and Mus.D. (1892) from the University of Cambridge.

From 1882 he taught music at Westminster College and, from 1885, at Southlands Training College for Schoolmistresses. Head of the Battersea Polytechnic Institute (1893-1903), and a member of the Council of the Tonic Sol-fa College.

He wrote teaching manuals and other books, including a *Cyclopaedic Dictionary of Music*. Collected and published Cornish folk songs.

Composed services including a Morning Service and a setting of the Benedicite for a Double Choir of Men's Voices, anthems, hymn tunes and school songs.

DUPUIS, Dr. Thomas Sanders (1733-1796)
Born of French descent in London on 5 November 1733; died in London on 17 July 1796 through an overdose of opium and was buried in Westminster Abbey.

A chorister of the Chapel Royal under **Bernard Gates** and **James Nares**. An organ pupil of **John Travers**. Graduated B.Mus. and D.Mus. at the University of Oxford (1790).

Worked in London as an organist and composer. From 1773 (and possibly before) he was organist of the Charlotte Street Chapel, later renamed St. Peter's Chapel, near Buckingham Palace. His last appointment was that of organist and composer to the Chapel Royal (1779-1796), following **William Boyce**. He was succeeded by **Thomas Attwood**. His skill at improvising on fugues impressed those who heard him, including the visiting Haydn.

He was one of a group of composers praised by J.S. Bumpus as maintaining high standards of composition at a time when mediocrity was the norm. Composed for various instruments including organ. John Spencer, his pupil, published three volumes of his church music after the death of Dupuis. Another famous pupil was **George Smart**.

His church music includes a large number of chants. Three sets of Single and Double Chants were published. Some were included in *Cathedral Psalter Chants* (1875). The Revised Edition (1927) of *Church Hymnary* contains his Double Chant in A. Composed anthems including 'If the Lord Himself 'and 'Ponder my words' and an organ voluntary.

DUSSEK, Ronald Walter (1891-1961)
Born in Greenwich, London in 1891; died in Hammersmith, London, on 30 December 1961. His family included the Czech composer Jan Dussek.

A pupil of **George Huntley** at St. Peter's Church, Eaton Square, London where he was a chorister. He later served Huntley as assistant organist at St. Peter's and was subsequently organist and choirmaster (1908-1911 and 1913-1915).

Organist of the Surrey Churches of St. Matthew, Surbiton (1911-1916); St. Mary, Oatland Park, Weybridge (1916-1919); St. Mark, Surbiton (from 1919) and Epsom Parish Church (from 1923).

Organist of St. Mary's Church, Southampton, Hampshire (from 1928) where he succeeded **Heathcote Statham** who had been appointed to Norwich Cathedral. Precentor of Radley College, Oxfordshire (from 1933).

Organist of Guildford Cathedral from 1951 to 1960, and director of music of the Royal Grammar School, Guildford.

An associate of the Royal Philharmonic Society and a local music society conductor.

A composer of hymn tunes and of the Advent anthem 'Take ye heed' (1911).

DYCE, William (1806-1864)
Born in Aberdeen, Scotland on 19 September 1806; died in Streatham, London on 14 February 1864.

Educated at Aberdeen Grammar School, where he taught himself to play the organ. Later attended Marischal College, Aberdeen, where he initially studied medicine but changed to theology. By this time he was a keen amateur painter.

In 1838, Dyce was appointed superintendent of the School of Design at Somerset House, London. In 1840 he became professor of theory of fine art at King's College, London.

From 1840 to 1844 he studied church music and he did much to re-establish the use of plainchant using English text. One of the founders of the Old Motet Society.

Dyce's Single Chant in F was included in *Cathedral Psalter Chants* (1875). Also composed the anthems 'In Thee, O Lord, have I trusted' and 'O God, Thou art my God', and other forms of music.

DYER, Dr. Arthur Edwin (1843-1902)
Born in Frome, Somerset on 20 February 1843; died in Cheltenham, Gloucestershire on 10 April 1902. Father of **Herbert Dyer**. Graduated B.Mus. (1873) and D.Mus. (1880) at the University of Oxford. Organist of the parish church, Weston-super-Mare, Somerset (1865-1875). From 1875 he was director of music of Cheltenham Ladies' College. A local music society conductor. Composed a sacred cantata *Salvator Mundi* as his D.Mus. exercise, an anthem, 'Except the Lord build the house' for the Jubilee in 1891 of Cheltenham College, an Evening Service, hymn tunes and songs.

DYER, Herbert Arthur (1878-1917)
Born in Cheltenham, Gloucestershire in 1878; died in France on 7 December 1917. Son of **Arthur Dyer**, with whom he studied music. Graduated B.Mus. at the University of Oxford. Served in the army during World War I, rising to the rank of lieutenant in the Royal Flying Corps. Killed in action. A composer of hymn tunes and songs including 'At rest' (1916). 'Bromsgrove' was written for *Public School Hymn Book* (1919) and was named after the School at which he taught. Also composed the widely-used *Encore Pieces for Piano*.

DYER, William Fear (19th century)
Organist of the Church of St. Nicholas, Bristol. Conducted at the festivals of the Bristol Church Choral Union. Composed a cantata *The Second Advent of the Redeemer* (1889) and anthems.

DYGON, John (?-1509)
It is believed that Dygon was Prior of the Convent of St. Augustine, Canterbury, Kent in 1497. It appears to be a contemporary namesake rather than the same person who graduated B.Mus. at the University of Oxford in 1512. A three-part motet *Ad lapidis positionem* has been attributed to him.

DYKE, Revd. William (?19th century)
Curate of Winster, Derbyshire. Composer of the anthem 'Come, Holy Ghost'.

DYKES, John Arthur St. Oswald (1863-1948)
Born in Durham on 27 October 1863; died in Kensington, London on 31 January 1948. The son of **J.B. Dykes**. A composer of hymn tunes.

DYKES, Revd. Dr. John Bacchus (1823-1876)
Born in Hull, Yorkshire on 10 March 1823; died in a mental institution at Ticehurst, East Sussex on 22 January 1876. The son of a banker, William Hoy Dykes and the grandson of Revd. Thomas Dykes whose church organ he played from the age of 10.

His early musical education had been under **George Skelton**, an organist of Hull. His formal education was at a private school in Wakefield, Yorkshire and at St. Catherine's College, Cambridge (from 1843) where he received lessons in music from **T.A. Walmisley**.

At Cambridge he helped to found the University Musical Society. A popular event was the singing by Dykes of humorous songs. He abandoned such frivolity on his ordination as deacon in 1847.

Graduated B.A. (1847) and M.A. (1850) at the University of Cambridge. In 1849 the University of Durham conferred the degree of D.Mus. on him honorarily.

Dykes became curate of Malton, Yorkshire in 1847. In 1849 he became a minor canon and precentor of Durham. In 1853 he was also appointed librarian, deputy organist and master of the boys. In 1862 he resigned the precentorship and became a parish priest at the church of St. Oswald, Durham. He did, however, remain as minor canon. A noted theologian.

Dykes was shy and modest but he is said to have served his parish effectively. He was known for the lucidity of his sermons and of his writings. He was deeply concerned with the proper use of music in worship: in a paper published in 1871 he favoured the use of anthems in church but held that the Communion Service was too solemn and important to run the risk of being turned into an occasion 'for sensuous and aesthetic gratification'.

A man of principle, he was eventually embroiled with his bishop in a dispute over churchmanship and the conduct of services at St. Oswald's. The bishop accepted the need for two curates in the busy parish but refused to license them unless three practices were discontinued: the wearing of coloured stoles, the burning of incense and the turning by the clergy away from the congregation during Holy Communion at times other than the breaking of bread.

Dykes refused to meet these conditions and appealed to the Court of the Queen's Bench for a writ of *mandamus* which would compel the bishop to issue the licences unconditionally. He lost the case and by the end of 1874 his mental and physical health had deteriorated greatly. He moved to St. Leonards, Sussex where he subsequently died. The bishop whom he had opposed created a fund for his widow and children which raised a total of £10,000.

Dykes composed around 300 hymn tunes. Many were used in *Hymns Ancient and Modern*, of which he was joint editor. He is said to have composed the tune 'Lux benigna' for use with the hymn by J.H. Newman 'Lead, kindly Light' as he walked past Charing Cross railway station in London. Other influential tunes are 'Nicaea'and 'Dominus regit me'. Composed a Service in F, other services, and anthems, of which 'These are they which came out of great tribulation' is an example.

Arthur Sullivan used 14 of Dykes's compositions in his *Church Hymns* (1874), including 'St. Godric', 'Dies irae' and 'Melita'. The Revised Edition (1927) of *Church Hymnary* used a total of 26 of his hymn tunes.

DYKES BOWER, Sir John
See **BOWER**, Sir John Dykes.

DYSON, Sir George (1883-1964)

Born in Halifax, Yorkshire on 28 May 1883; died in Winchester, Hampshire on 28 September 1964.

Grew up in a neighbourhood from which the famous Black Dyke Mills Band drew its members. Educated at the Royal College of Music (1900-1904), where he was open scholar. His teachers at the R.C.M. included **C.V. Stanford** and among his contemporaries were **Thomas Dunhill** and **John Ireland**. While there, he sometimes played the services at Greenwich Parish Church. Raised money by playing drums or sound effects at theatres and concert halls, there being no student grants in those days.

He later won a Mendelssohn Travelling Scholarship, Stanford's advice reportedly being, 'Go to Italy, my boy, and sit in the sun.' Spent some years of his scholarship in Germany and Italy and his tutors included Buonamici in Florence, Sgambati in Rome and Martucci in Naples.

Returned to England in 1907. **Hubert Parry** helped to secure his appointment as director of music at the Royal Naval College, Osborne, Isle of Wight (1908).

The University of Oxford awarded him the degrees of B.Mus. (1909), D.Mus. (1918) and M.A. (1940). He held the LL.D. from the University of Aberdeen.

He was knighted (1941) and appointed K.C.V.O. (1953).

A lieutenant in the Royal Fusiliers (1914-1917) and a major in the R.A.F. (1919-1920). Invalided home from active service during World War I. While convalescing he prepared cases for the Board of Referees under the 1915 Finance Act. He then worked in the Air Ministry (1918-1920) and it was at this time that he wrote *The Manual of Grenade Fighting*, published by the War Office. He did not realise it at first, but this military association alienated him from some of his students. In 1918 he became musical director of the R.A.F.

For many years he was a teacher of music in schools including Marlborough College, Wiltshire (1911-1914), Rugby School, Warwickshire (from 1914), Wellington College, Berkshire (1921-1924) and Winchester College (1924-1937). While at Wellington he began to lecture and write. From 1930 he gave talks on B.B.C. Radio in the *Music and the Ordinary Listener* Series, succeeding **Walford Davies**. Principal of the R.C.M. (1937-1952), the first former student of the college to hold the post. Retired in 1952. *The New Music* (1924) is his commentary on the music of the first quarter of the 20th century.

Composed a Symphony (1937), a Violin Concerto (1943), and The Canterbury Pilgrims (1931). His church music includes settings of the Morning and Evening Service in C Minor and a further set in D. His anthems include 'I will worship' and 'O praise God in His holiness'. His 'Confortare' was used at the Coronation of George VI (1937). *Songs of Courage* and *Songs of Praise* are each a short set of three songs.

DYSON, John Ormandy (19th /20th century)
Graduated B.Mus. at the University of Oxford in 1905.

Assistant organist of Sheffield Parish Church, Yorkshire (1900-1904), and organist and choirmaster of the city's Sale Memorial Church (1905-1908), Burngreave Wesleyan Chapel (1908-1911) and Thurgoland Wesleyan Chapel (from 1912).

Composed the anthem 'Through the day', and organ music.

E

EAGLETON, John (1785-1832)

Born in Coventry, Warwickshire on 31 October 1785; died in Huddersfield, Yorkshire in 1832.

Attended a Congregational Sunday School in Coventry run by **George Burder**. Leader of the chapel choir until his voice broke. Became a preacher of the Wesleyan Church. At the age of 21 he succeeded his father as pastor of the meeting house that later joined forces with the Vicar Lane Congregational Church, Coventry. He took charge of the united congregation. Pastor of the Congregational Church in Birmingham and at Ramsden Street, Huddersfield.

Published two collections of hymn tunes of which one was *Sacred Harmony* (1816). His tune 'Justification' has been used in more than one publication with the hymn 'Praise ye the Lord: 'Tis good to raise' by Isaac Watts.

EARLE (Watson), Ethel Leader (1871-1938)

Born in Wandsworth, London in 1871; died in Ongar, Essex on 19 July 1938. Composer of hymn tunes, including 'Hindhead', used in *Baptist Church Hymnal* (1935). Also composed a Kyrie in E-flat.

EARNSHAW, Dr. Robert Henry (1856-1929)

Born in Todmorden, Lancashire on 17 September 1856; died in Dumfries, Scotland on 30 March 1929.

Received most of his musical education in London, where he arrived in 1880. Graduated B.Mus. (1892) and D.Mus. (1893) at the University of Dublin.

Lived for most of his life in Lancashire. Served on Southport Town Council. Was involved with the cinema industry. Organist and choirmaster of Morecambe Parish Church (1882-1885); St. Philip's Church, Southport (1890 -1891; 1899-1902) and Christ Church, Preston (1891-1897). In retirement he lived at Southport and Preston.

Composed hymn tunes including 'Arizona', used with a hymn for travellers by Henry Burton and issued in leaflet form on transatlantic liners. Also composed anthems, items for piano, songs and part songs.

EASDALE, Brian (1909-1995)

Born on 10 August 1909; died on 30 October 1995.

A chorister of Westminster Abbey; attended the Royal College of Music. His early *Death March* (1928) and *Six Poems for Orchestra* (1936) had some success but it was as a composer for films that Easdale became known. A contemporary of W.H. Auden and **Benjamin Britten** at the G.P.O. Film Unit. Wrote the score for *Men in Danger*.

Music director of Archers Film Unit (from 1948); Group Theatre (1937-1939); the Public Relations Film Unit of India (1943-1945) and Information Films of India, Bombay (1945-1946).

Associated with the film makers Michael Powell and Emeric Pressburger, and composed the original music for most of their films in the period 1947 to 1951. His score for *The Red Shoes* (1948) won him an Oscar award. During World War II he worked for the Crown Film Unit, spending part of the time in India. There, he met the writer Rumer Godden whose book *The Black Narcissus* became a film project, with the score composed by Easdale.

Composed a Missa *Coventrensis* (1962) for the Service of Consecration of the new Coventry Cathedral.

EAST (Este), Michael (c1580-1648)

Born in Manchester around the year 1580; died in Lichfield, Staffordshire in 1648. He may have been related to the printer Thomas East but this is by no means certain.

In 1606 he graduated Mus.B. at the University of Cambridge.

A lay clerk of Ely Cathedral (1609-1614). At some time before 1618 he moved to Lichfield and took up the appointment of master of the choristers. A great deal of his compositional material was published. The bulk was in seven sets of books, of which the sixth contained church music almost exclusively.

In 1634, one Lieutenant Hammond made a survey of the music of 26 counties, noting that Lichfield (during East's term of office) was very well served both by its choir and by its organs.

Renowned in his own times as a composer, Michael East is mainly remembered today for his chamber music, including madrigals and consorts. His sacred items include a Verse Service in D Minor, a setting of the Burial Sentences and the anthems 'When David heard' (acclaimed by some as a more satisfying setting than those of **Thomas Weelkes** and **Thomas Tomkins**), 'When Israel came out of Egypt' and 'As they departed', the latter commissioned by St. John's College, Oxford and for which he was paid 44s (£2.20). He composed 10 other anthems that have survived.

EASTON, Revd. Edward William (19th/20th century)
Trained in music at Hereford Cathedral. Graduated B.Mus. at Trinity College Dublin (1901). Vicar of Ripponden, Halifax, Yorkshire. Composed five anthems including 'He maketh peace' (1891) and 'They that sow in tears' (1891), hymn tunes and Band of Hope melodies.

EAYRES, William Henry (1846-?)
Born in St. Marylebone, London in 1846. As a child he studied violin as a pupil of Henry Blagrove. Later, taught by Prosper Sainton and Henri Wieniawski. Organist of Limerick Cathedral, Ireland for four years. Led the second violin players in the orchestras of the Philharmonic Society, Leeds Festival and Three Choirs' Festival. Composed Services, anthems, songs including 'Beguiling Eyes,' an overture, two string quartets, and music for the play *Lesbia*.

EBDON, Thomas (1738-1811)
Born in Durham in 1738; died in Durham on 23 September 1811. A chorister under **James Heseltine** at Durham Cathedral, and, later, Heseltine's articled pupil. Organist of Durham Cathedral (1763-1811). Composed sonatas and glees. His *Church Music*, issued in two volumes in 1790 and 1810, was still being composed towards his death - the latest unpublished manuscript dates from June 1811. His Evening Service in C was popular for a time and his anthems include 'Deliver me from mine enemies' and 'Hear me when I call'.

ECCLES, John (c1668-1735)
Born, possibly in London, around the year 1668; died in Hampton Wick, Middlesex on 12 January 1735.
Son of Solomon Eccles, a musician.
Published several songs in the year 1691. In 1693 he began to compose for the theatre, continuing in this line of work until around 1707 when he retired to Hampton Wick and spent much time fishing. Succeeded Nicholas Staggins as Master of the King's Band (1700-1735) of which he had been a member since 1694. From around 1710 until his death, he was a court composer, submitting odes annually for New Year's Day and the birthday of the sovereign. An example of these is 'Inspire us, Genius of ye Day', written for Queen Anne.
Collaborated with **Henry Purcell** in the production of a score for the drama *Don Quixote*. His music for the theatre totalled three books. Composed very little church music but his 'Ode to St. Cecilia' can be considered as such.

EDGCUMBE
See **MOUNT-EDGCUMBE**.

EDWARDES (Edwards), Richard (c1523-1566)
Born in Somerset of Welsh extraction around the year 1523; died in London on 31 October 1566.
Educated at Christ Church, Oxford, graduating M.A. (1547). Studied music under **George Etheridge**. A gentleman of the Chapel Royal (1553-1561), and master of the choristers (1563-1566). His duties included training the choristers in singing and acting for interludes at court. Composed poems and madrigals, and harmonised some of the Psalm tunes found in the collection *The Whole Psalmes...* (c1563) by **John Day**. His most famous work is the madrigal 'In going to my naked bed'. Composed the anthem 'Deliver me, O God'.

EDWARDS, Dr. Albert Henry (c1870-1944)
Born around 1870; died at the age of 74 on 13 November 1944.
Trained at Trinity College, London. Graduated B.Mus. (1895) at Queen's College, Oxford and D.Mus. (1904) at Trinity College, Dublin.
His first three appointments were as organist of the Churches of All Saints, Writtle, near Chelmsford, Essex (1885); St. Mary's, West Malling, Kent (1886) and St. George's, Barrow-in-Furness (1891). Organist and choirmaster at St. Mary's Church, Brecon (from 1894). Subsequently organist of Doncaster Parish Church (from 1896), and then organist and choirmaster at St. Margaret's, Ilkley, Yorkshire (1898); St. Mary Magdalene, Bradford (1899); St. Mary's, West Kensington, London (from 1911) and Holy Trinity, Richmond, Surrey (1915-1935). In 1935 he retired from all forms of music activity.
Devised exercises for the use of examination candidates including a collection *Melodies for Harmonisation*, and he composed church music such as the anthems 'Saviour, breathe an evening blessing' (1907) and 'Hark! the notes' (1907), part songs, songs, and items for piano and for organ.

EDWARDS, Arthur Charles (1869-?)
Born in Peterborough, Cambridgeshire in 1869.
Trained in music at the Cathedrals of Llandaff and Southwark. Graduated B.Mus. (1891) at St. Edmund Hall, Oxford.
Organist of the Parish Church, Whitchurch, Glamorgan (from 1888); St. John's Church, Harlow, Essex (from 1890) and St. Neots Parish Church, Huntingdonshire (from 1892). Organist and teacher of music at Framlingham College and deputy organist of Llandaff Cathedral, both commencing in 1894.
Organist and choirmaster of Bridlington Priory Church, Yorkshire (from 1896); Ealing Parish Church, Middlesex (from 1901); St. Andrew's Church, Croydon, Surrey (from 1902) and Holy Trinity Church, Aberystwyth, Wales (from 1906).
Composed anthems including 'Except the Lord build the house' (1903), the carol - words and music - 'To faithful shepherds watching' (1900) and music for piano.

EDWARDS, Arthur Morris (1854-1928)
Born in Clifton, Gloucestershire in 1854; died in Clifton on 14 April 1928. Composer of hymn tunes.

EDWARDS, Edwin (1830-1907)
Born in Street, Somerset in 1830; died in Rugby, Warwickshire on 21 August 1907.
Private organist to the Duke of Buccleuch at Dalkeith Place, near Edinburgh. Moved to Rugby as a teacher of music around the year 1865. Music master and organist of Rugby School (1867-1886) and musical editor of *Rugby School Hymn Book* for the issues of 1876 and 1897. Assisted William Horder in the production of *Worship Song* (1905). Composed hymn tunes and an Organ March in G (1881).

EDWARDS, Frederick George (1853-1909)
Born in St. Marylebone, London on 11 October 1853; died in Potters Bar, Hertfordshire on 28 November 1909.

Attended boarding school in Brixton Hill; Dedham Grammar School; the Royal Academy of Music (from 1875), where he studied organ with **Charles Steggall** and King's College, London. Studied organ with William Bevan at St. Mary's School, Kilburn and with **Henry Frost** of the Chapel Royal, Savoy Hill. Began to deputise and to give recitals, and played at the Exeter Hall (from 1873). In 1869 he started in business in London but by 1875 he had abandoned it.

Organist in London of the Surrey Chapel, Blackfriars Road (from 1873); Christ Church, Westminster Bridge Road (1876-1881) and the Presbyterian Church, St. John's Wood Road (1881-1895). A local choral society conductor.

Contributed articles to *The Guardian* under the pseudonym *Diapason*, and wrote books on church music and general musical topics. His monograph on *Elijah* is a standard work. Editor of *Musical Times* from April 1897 until the time of his death, having contributed to the journal since 1891. Editor of *100 Psalms* (1906). Lectured on the role of praise in church services.

On 23 April 1888 he was elected organist of the Nonconformist Choir Union. He shared the conducting and accompanying with **Nathaniel Minshall**.

Composed anthems, hymn tunes and pieces for piano.

EDWARDS, Dr. Henry John (1854-1933)
Born in Barnstaple, Devon on 24 February 1854; died in Barnstaple, on 8 April 1933. Son of **John Edwards** of Crediton.

Studied music with his father. Later, his teachers were **William Sterndale Bennett** for piano and orchestration, **George Macfarren** for composition, **H.C. Banister** for harmony, and **George Cooper**. Graduated B.Mus (New College, 1876) and D.Mus. (Keble, 1885) at the University of Oxford.

Became an honorary member of the Royal Academy of Music (1908) and received the honorary freedom of Barnstaple (1908).

Succeeded his father as organist of Barnstaple Parish Church and, in 1886, conductor of the local festival society. Retained the parish church appointment for more than 50 years (from 1876). Much in demand as a pianist, he gave recitals throughout the country. An oratorio society conductor.

Composed a Service, a motet *Praise to the holiest*, anthems, oratorios including *The Ascension,* songs, part songs and works for piano.

EDWARDS, John (1808-1894)
Born in Crediton, Devon in 1808; died in Barnstaple, Devon in April 1894. The father of **Henry Edwards**. Studied under a teacher of music, Moxen, in Exeter. Around the year 1833 he moved to the town of Barnstaple, where he was appointed assistant to the organist of the parish church, Huxtable, whom he succeeded around 1886. Founded a choral society, played violin and built up a teaching practice locally. Composed Services, anthems, hymn tunes and chants.

EDWARDS, John (1878-1928)
Born in Penrhiwceiber, Glamorganshire, Wales in 1878; died in the U.S.A. in 1928. A coal miner who studied music in the evenings. Became a fellow of the Tonic Sol-fa College, London. Emigrated to the U.S.A. where he taught music but was forced through illness to retire prematurely. Composed hymn tunes; his 'Maesgwyn' was first published in *Y Caniedydd Cynulleidfaol* (1921).

EDWARDS, Revd. John David (1805-1885)
Born in Penderlwyngoch, Gwynnws, Cardiganshire, Wales on 19 December 1805; died in Llanddoget, Denbighshire, Wales on 24 November 1885.

Attended Ystrad Meurig School and was taught music by **Dafydd Morgan**. Graduated B.A. at the University of Oxford (1830) and was ordained deacon in 1832, priest in 1833.

Held curacies at Llansantffraid, Glyndyfrdwy, and Aberdovey, and in 1843, became rector of Rhosymedre, near Wrexham. An adjudicator at *eisteddfodau*.

In 1836 he published a collection of hymn tunes entitled *Original Sacred Music*. It was the first such collection for the established church in Wales. A second volume was added in 1843. Edwards believed strongly in, and encouraged, congregational singing in worship.

Composed a large quantity of church music. 'Rhosymedre', named after a place near Ruabon is used today with 'Author of life divine' and is his most durable hymn tune. It is also known as 'Lovely', and it was used by **Ralph Vaughan Williams** in his Prelude on the Welsh tune *'Lovely'*.

EDWARDS, Paul Christison (b.1955)
Born in Bedford on 19 March 1955. Attended St. Paul's Cathedral Choir School and Bedford Modern School. An alto lay clerk of Peterborough Cathedral (1978-1982). Organist of a number of churches in the area around Bedford: currently director of music at St. Paul's Church, Bedford. Has composed items for organ, and songs for solo voice and piano. His church music includes anthems including 'O dearest Lord' and' I heard a voice from heaven', a carol 'No small wonder', introits, services and hymn tunes. *In Memoriam*, a choral anthology, is a recent work.

EDWARDS, Robert (1797-1862)
Born in Mostyn, Flintshire, Wales in 1797; died in Liverpool in 1862.

After spending his childhood in Mostyn and beginning work as a miller at the nearby village of Melin Gwibnant, he moved to Liverpool while still a young man and found employment as a carter for the Bridgwater Trustees, who managed the stretches of canal between Liverpool, Manchester and Runcorn. Later became the superintendent of the carting department.

Succeeded **John Ellis** as precentor of the Bedford Street Calvinistic Methodist Chapel, Liverpool (1835-1859).

Church Hymnary's Revised Edition (1927) uses his tune 'Caersalem' (1824) with 'Guide me O Thou Great Jehovah' by William Williams.

The stories that surround hymns and their tunes can be unreliable, but it is said 'Caersalem' only came into use because the composer had inadvertently left the score on his desk when he went away on holiday. The choir rehearsed it in his absence, found it to their liking and used it. A modest man, Carter would never have asked the choir to use his own material, which consisted of a number of tunes and perhaps other forms of church music.

EDWARDS, Dr. Thomas David (1875-1930)
Born in Pittston, Pennsylvania, U.S.A. in 1875; died in 1930.

His parents had lived in Rhymney, Monmouthshire before emigrating to the U.S.A. Thomas Edwards returned to Wales, where he lived at Pontypridd and studied music.

Held positions as organist and choirmaster in the towns of Porth; Brynhyfryd, near Treharris (at the Baptist Church, from 1909);

Pontypridd and the Portmadoc Tabernacle, and gained a reputation as an organ recitalist. A choral and music society conductor and festival adjudicator.

Composed the hymn tune 'Rhyd-y-Groes' (1899), and anthems and songs for use at festivals.

ELDRIDGE, Guy Henry (b.1904)

Born in St. Leonards-on-Sea, Sussex in 1904. Studied music privately and at the Royal College of Music, and graduated B.Mus. at the University of Durham. A professor of the London College of Music (from 1949) and of Guildhall School of Music (from 1951). London organist and choirmaster of St. Luke's Church, Chelsea and of St. Michael's Church, Chester Square (from 1953). A local choral and orchestral society conductor. Has composed anthems including 'Before the ending of the day' (1953) and 'Here, O my Lord, I see Thee' (1955), and a carol 'Behold, a simple tender Babe' (1955).

ELFYN JONES, Dr. Richard (b.1944)

Born in Blaenau Ffestiniog, Wales on 11 April 1944.

Educated at University of Wales, Bangor, and King's College, Cambridge. Graduated B.A., M.Mus. and Ph.D. (Wales). Lecturer at the University of Wales, Cardiff, since 1971, becoming senior lecturer in 1994. Conductor of the Cardiff Polyphonic Choir (1977-1991). In 1996 became adviser on Classical Music for S4C (Welsh Fourth Channel).

Author of *The Early Operas of Michael Tippett* (1996). Composer of orchestral and chamber music, including a String Quintet, two piano sonatas, *Brangwyn* Overture, choral and vocal works, and a large output of music for television. For the church he has written 'Le Vermeil du Soleil', a carol arranged for treble voice(s) and organ or piano; 'Good King Wenceslas'; *St. Augustine Mass*; two hymn-anthems, 'I hear thy welcome voice' and 'Tyddewi', and two spirituals, 'My Lord what a morning' and 'Were you there?'.

ELGAR, Sir Edward William (1857-1934)

Born in Broadheath, near Worcester on 2 June 1857; died in Worcester on 23 February 1934.

Son of an organist and music-seller. Attended Catholic schools in the Worcester area, including the local dame school, Spetchley Park, and Littleton House (1868). Left school at the age of 15. Learned to play piano and violin, taking lessons in the latter instrument locally and in 1877 and 1878 with Adolphe Pollitzer in London. He later bitterly put the total cost of his music education at £56 10s (£56 50)

In 1880 he took the local examination of the Royal Academy of Music in violin and general musical knowledge, and passed with honours.

Knighted in 1904, received the Order of Merit in 1911 and was created baronet in 1931.

Worked in a solicitor's office (1872-1873) and at the age of 16 he decided to pursue a career as a freelance musician.

In 1883 he heard Reinecke conduct at the Leipzig Gewandhaus. In the same year he became engaged to Miss Helen Weaver of Worcester but the engagement was broken a year later. This was said to have been for reasons of religious incompatibility (she was a Unitarian) but it could also have been because she, knowing she was ill with tuberculosis and smallpox, did not wish to be a burden to Elgar.

Band master at the mental institution at Powick (1879-1884). Played violin, his assignments including the Three Choirs Festivals

of 1878, 1881 and 1884, the latter under Dvorak. A teacher, although he found teaching something of an ordeal.

During the 1880s, Elgar used to travel up to London for the day to promote his music and to listen to concerts at the Crystal Palace.

He had served his father as assistant organist at St. George's Catholic Church, Worcester, and in 1885 succeeded him (until 1889).

Failing to establish himself sufficiently well in London (1890-1891), he returned to Malvern and Hereford. He spent an increasing amount of time composing, encouraged by his success at music festivals.

Became Master of the King's Musick in 1924. In 1932 he recorded his Violin Concerto with the 16-year old Yehudi Menuhin as soloist.

Around the turn of the century his standing as a composer increased enormously, due to the quality of works such as the *Enigma* Variations (1899) and the *Dream of Gerontius* (1900).

His church music includes the hymn tune 'Drake's Broughton', *Four Litanies* (1888), *Ecce sacerdos magnus* (1888), *Ave verum corpus* (1902), a Te Deum and Benedictus in F for the Three Choirs' Festival of 1897 and the anthems 'Fear not, O land' (1914) for harvest-tide and 'Great is the Lord' to words from Psalm 48 (1912). 'Give unto the Lord (1914) is a setting of Psalm 29. 'O hearken thou' was composed for the Coronation of George V (1911). 'The Spirit of the Lord' (from *The Kingdom*, one of his two linked oratorios) is also used as an anthem. He composed double chants to Psalms 68 and 75, which are found in *New Cathedral Psalter* (1909).

ELLERTON, John Lodge (1801-1873)

Born John Lodge in Cheshire on 11 January 1801; died on 3 January 1873.

Of an ancient Irish family, adding Ellerton to his name in 1838 or 1839.

Attended Rugby School, Warwickshire and Brasenose College, Oxford, where he graduated B.A. (1821) and M.A. (1828). In his time as an undergraduate he studied composition, having learned to play piano. Went on to study counterpoint in Rome for two years under Pietro Terziani.

Composed, as an amateur, a Service in A and other settings in B-flat, in C and E-flat; six anthems including 'I am well pleased' and 'The Lord is King'; 17 motets; six Masses including settings in C and in B-flat; operas; 61 glees, 83 duets; five symphonies; chamber music and an oratorio *Paradise Lost*. His compositions won him Catch Club prizes in 1835 and 1838.

ELLIOTT, Dr. Graham John (b.1947)

Born in Abergavenny, Wales on 10 November 1947.

Educated at Henry VIII School, Abergavenny and was organist of the Priory Church while still at school. Organ pupil of **Melville Cook** at Hereford Cathedral. Studied at the Royal Academy of Music (1964-1965). Organ student at St. George's Chapel, Windsor Castle (1965-1967).

Graduated M.A. (1982) and Ph.D. (1985) at the University of Wales and B.Mus. (1970) at the University of London.

Sub organist of Llandaff Cathedral (1967-1970). Organist of St. Asaph's Cathedral (1970-1981) and director of music at Lowther College (1970-1981).

Since 1981 he has been master of the music of Chelmsford Cathedral. Founder and director of the Cathedral Festival.

A professor of the Guildhall School of Music and Drama, London and a lecturer at Anglia University.

Numerous items of choral and organ music have been published, including the carol 'There is no rose', and the *Chelmsford* Setting of the Rite A Eucharist.

ELLIOTT, James William (1833-1915)

Born in Warwick on 13 February 1833; died in St. John's Wood, London on 5 February 1915.

A chorister at Leamington Parish Church, Warwickshire (1846-1848), later studying under **George Macfarren**.

Held a number of church organistships, spanning a period of almost 50 years. The first of these was Leamington Episcopal Chapel (1847-1852); immediately afterwards he was organist to the Earl of Wilton at Heaton Hall (1852-1860). Subsequently organist of St. Mary's, Banbury, Oxfordshire (1860-1862) and London Churches of St. Mary-the-Boltons, Kensington (1862-1864); All Saints, St. John's Wood (1864-1874) and St. Mark, Hamilton Terrace (1874-1909).

Adviser to Ashdowns, the music publishers.

His hymn tunes include 'Church triumphant', first used in *Church Hymns* (1874) and also by *Hymns Ancient and Modern* with 'Again, the Lord's new own day is here'. 'Hosanna' is used also in *Ancient and Modern* with 'Hosanna to the living Lord'. Other tunes include 'Cross and crown', 'Day of rest', and 'Litany of the Holy Ghost'.

14 of his tunes were included by **Arthur Sullivan**, whom he assisted in the compilation of *Church Hymns* (1874). Also composed services, anthems, harmonium works, songs, a collection of settings of nursery rhymes and two operettas, one of which was *Romance and Reality*.

ELLIS, Revd. Dr. David Henry (19th/20th century)

Graduated B.Mus. (1872), B.A. (1875), LL.B. (1876), LL.D. (1880) and B.D. (1886) at Trinity College, Dublin. Ordained deacon in 1861, priest in 1862. Curate of Roydon, Norfolk (1861-1872) and chaplain of the Gayton Union, Norfolk (1871-1872). A minor canon of Bangor Cathedral (1872-1876) and precentor of Sydney Cathedral, Australia (1880-1884). Continued his career in Australia as precentor of St. Saviour's Cathedral and chaplain to the bishop of Goulburn (1885-1889). In 1891 he was appointed vicar of St. Botolph's Church, Lincoln. Composed a setting of the Holy Communion Service in F (1895), Evening Services, and anthems such as 'Behold, a virgin shall conceive' (1890).

ELLIS, John (1760-1839)

Born in Ty'n-y-Gwernannau, Denbighshire, Wales in 1760; died in Liverpool on 31 January 1839.

Apprenticed to a saddler in the Welsh village of Llanrwst, where he later opened a shop. Also learned to play the flute.

In 1800 he joined the Calvinistic Methodist Church and was appointed a travelling teacher of congregational singing. A set of hymn tunes, *Mawl Yr Arglwydd* (The Lord's Praise) that he published in 1816 was the first collection of its kind in Wales.

Moved to Llanfyllin and, around 1822, to Liverpool, where he became precentor of the Pall Mall Chapel. In 1827 he joined the Bedford Street Chapel where he was later appointed precentor.

Composed anthems including *'Molwch Yr Arglwydd'*, and hymn tunes, a number of which are still used today, including 'Eliot' (1923), named after a coal merchant in Liverpool.

ELLIS, Martin John (b.1943)

Born in London on 23 September 1943. A chorister at the Temple Church, London under **George Thalben-Ball**, he was educated at the City of London School and at the Royal College of Music. Holds the Archbishop's Diploma in Church Music.

Assistant director of music at Taunton School (1973-1986), Somerset. He then became director of music at Reigate Grammar School, Surrey and, at around the same time, organist of St. Martin's Church, Dorking. A composer, arranger and publisher of church music. His hymn tune 'Staplegrove' (1976), named after Staplegrove Road where he lived in Taunton, has been used with the hymn 'Come, Thou everlasting Spirit'.

ELLIS, Richard (1775-1855)

Born in Dolgellau, Wales in 1775; died on 11 February 1855. A shoemaker, he succeeded **John Williams**, from whom he had earlier learned music, as precentor of St. Mary's Church, Dolgellau. Composed anthems and hymn tunes of which the best remembered is 'Hyder' (1824).

ELLIS, William (?-1674)

Graduated B.Mus. at the University of Oxford in 1639. Organist of Eton College and, from an unknown date until around 1646, of St. John's College, Oxford. It is assumed that he was re-appointed around 1660 at the Restoration and continued in office until the year of his death. His university colleagues regularly joined him for sessions of music making, playing on violin, viol, lute and virginal, and singing. His compositions for the church include the anthems 'Almighty God' and 'This is the record of John', both of which were composed for the Patronal Festival of St. John's College.

ELLIS, Dr. William (1868-1947)

Born in Tow Law, County Durham on 13 October 1868; died in Hexham, County Durham on 26 November 1947.

Played organ at an early age. By 14 he was organist of the Old Elvet Wesleyan Chapel, Durham. Studied at Old Elvet School and at Durham Cathedral under **Philip Armes**. Graduated B.Mus. at the University of Durham (1893). Awarded the Lambeth D.Mus. (1929).

Organist of the Church of St. Nicholas, Durham (from 1887); Holy Trinity Church, Richmond, Yorkshire and Richmond Parish Church (1894-1903). Organist and choirmaster of Richmond Grammar School. His other teaching positions were in Durham city at St. Hild's Training College and High School for Girls and at the County School for Girls.

In 1894 he also became private choirmaster to the Marquess of Zetland at Aske. A local choral society conductor.

The first official sub organist of Durham Cathedral from 1903 to 1918, firstly to Philip Armes and, from 1907, under **Arnold Culley**.

Organist of Newcastle Cathedral (1918-1933).

His hymn tune 'St. Nicholas' was used in *Hymns Ancient and Modern* with 'To the name of our salvation'. Elsewhere it was known as 'Dunelm'. 'St. Hild' was used in the Revised Edition (1927) of *Church Hymnary* with the hymn 'Lord of mercy and of might' by Reginald Heber. Also composed an anthem.

ELLOR, James (1819-1899)

Born in Droylesden, Lancashire in 1819; died in Newburgh, New York on 27 September 1899. Musically self-taught. A hatmaker, he later worked on the building of the railways. Led the Wesleyan

Chapel Choir at Droylesden, near Manchester. Emigrated to the U.S.A. in 1843. Once there, he resumed his trade as a hatmaker. Some years before his death he became blind. His hymn tune 'Diadem' (1838) is used with 'All hail the power of Jesus' name'.

ELVEY, Sir George Job (1816-1893)
Born in Canterbury, Kent on 27 March 1816; died in Windlesham, Surrey on 9 December 1893. Younger brother of **Stephen Elvey.**
A chorister of Canterbury Cathedral under the elder **Highmore Skeats**, whose daughter he later married, until 1830, the year in which his brother Stephen was appointed organist of New College, Oxford. George Elvey followed his brother to New College and became his pupil. Thereafter he studied at the Royal Academy of Music under **William Crotch** and Cipriani Potter. Graduated B.Mus. (1838) and D.Mus. (1840) at the University of Oxford. Knighted in 1871.
In 1833 he became a lay clerk of Christ Church Cathedral, Oxford. Appointed organist of St. George's Chapel, Windsor Castle in 1835, in succession to the younger **Highmore Skeats**. Among the unsuccessful candidates were **S.S. Wesley**, **George Smart** and **Henry Bishop**. He was only 19 years old at the time, and although his musical prowess was not in question, his appointment was in doubt because of his youth. William IV is said to have intervened to insist that the best candidate be appointed, regardless of age. His tenure covered three marriages of great pomp at Windsor, namely those of the Prince of Wales (1863), Princess Louise (1871) and the Duke of Albany (1882).
He inherited a musical establishment at Windsor that was under strength and demoralised, and during his long term of office he improved the choir and widened its repertory. He also changed the specification of the organ although he felt that advances in organ construction generally had led to over indulgence in organ accompaniment, to the detriment of the music of the church.
He was offered the organistship of Exeter Cathedral in 1842 or 1843 but declined it. S.S. Wesley was appointed instead. When Elvey left St. George's Chapel in 1882 it was to go into retirement. He had also been a private organist to Queen Victoria.
Elvey prepared **Hubert Parry**, who at the time was studying at Eton College, for the Oxford B.Mus. Parry at the time greatly admired Elvey but the latter's early musical influence on Parry diminished over time. Himself a violinist, Elvey insisted that his articled pupils take up the instrument. He was among the violins at the Handel Festival of 1888.
In 1833, the committee headed by William Crotch had preferred Elvey's anthem 'Bow down Thine ear' to S.S. Wesley's 'The Wilderness' for the Gresham Prize. In all he composed some 45 anthems, plus Morning and Evening Services and oratorios which are generally not used today. His 'Wherewithal shall a young man cleanse his way' was written for the confirmation of Prince George of Cambridge in St. George's Chapel.
Also composed some 30 chants, plus part songs and songs, but he is particularly remembered for his hymn tunes. 'St. George' is inseparably associated with 'Come, ye thankful people, come' in *Hymns Ancient and Modern* and elsewhere. Other tunes used in *Ancient and Modern* are 'St. Edward' and 'Sunninghill'. Some of his chants were published in *Cathedral Psalter Chants* (1875).

ELVEY, Dr. Stephen (1805-1860)
Born in Canterbury, Kent on 27 June 1805; died in Oxford on 6 October 1860. Elder brother of **George Elvey**.

A Canterbury chorister under the elder **Highmore Skeats**, and later studied under him. Graduated B.Mus (1831) and D.Mus. (1838) at the University of Oxford. For the latter, he submitted as his exercise an anthem 'Great is the Lord'.
At the age of 17 he was compelled to have a leg amputated following a shooting accident. The replacement wooden leg appeared in no way to hinder him as an organist.
Succeeded **Alfred Bennett** in 1831 as organist of New College, Oxford. He was later also organist of St. John's College (1846-1860), choragus of the University (1848-1860) and organist of the University Church of St. Mary the Virgin (from 1845). While at Oxford, he taught composition and musical theory to **F.A.G. Ouseley**.
Around the year 1825, he wrote a continuation of the Service in A by **William Croft**. Also composed a Kyrie, Sanctus and Credo in E-flat and a Service in F, plus the anthems 'These as they change' and 'Great is the Lord'. His Single Chant in E-flat was included in *Cathedral Psalter Chants* (1875). In collaboration with Ouseley he published a Psalter, which took seven years to compile and was subsequently known as *Elvey's Psalter*.

ELY, Frederic Arthur (1872-1955)
Born in Westminster, London on 1 November 1872; died in Ayr, Scotland on 21 April 1955. Attended the Royal College of Music and awarded B.Mus. by the University of London in 1900. Organist and choirmaster of the churches of St. Catherine, Leytonstone, Essex (1897-1901); Holy Trinity, Sunningdale, Berkshire (1901-1903) and Holy Trinity, Ayr (from 1903). Organist of Ayr Town Hall, a professor of singing at the Ayr Academy and the conductor of local choral societies. Composed a Vesper Hymn (1913), the anthem 'Go with our soldiers Lord, we pray' (1896) and hymn tunes.

ELY, Dr. Thomas (19th/20th century)
Graduated B.Mus. (1891) and D.Mus. (1896) at the University of London. Held five organistships - at the Church of St. Barnabas, Sutton, Surrey (1889-1890); St. John's College, Leatherhead, Surrey (1890-1893); St. Thomas's Church, Belfast (1893-1897); Christ Church, Scarborough, Yorkshire (1897-1908) and All Saints' Church, Scarborough (from 1908). Conductor to local choral and music societies. Composed an Evening Service, a Holy Communion Service in A for Trebles (1910), a Single and Double Chant (c1855), anthems including 'Lead, kindly light' (1905) and songs.

EMMANS, Les (b.1929)
Born in Norwich, Norfolk in 1929. Studied music with **Geoffrey Bush**. Trained as an engineer but turned to teaching, establishing a college music department in Derby. Organist and choirmaster of Breadsall Parish Church, Derbyshire. Editor of *Composer News*, the journal of the Composers' Guild. Has composed for the church, schools and the stage. Church compositions include the Breadsall Psalms and Canticles, the cantata *A simple Passion* and the musical plays *The Gifts* and *A Strange Happening at Bethlehem*.

ENNIS, Dr. John Matthew (1864-?)
Born in Dover, Kent on 5 August 1864.
Graduated B.Mus. (1892) and D.Mus. (1894) at the University of London.
Organist of the Church of St. Barnabas, King Square, London (from 1878). Organist and Choirmaster in London of the Churches

of St. Philip, Clerkenwell (1883-1887); Holy Trinity, Knightsbridge (1887-1893) and St. Mary, Brookfield (from 1893).

In 1900 he was appointed to Christ Church, St. Lawrence, Sydney, Australia. Professor of music at the University of Adelaide.

Composed a Magnificat for Soloists, Chorus, Strings and Organ, and songs including 'Beautiful maiden'.

Eos Ebrill
See **REES**, Lewis.

Eos Llechyd
See **DAVIES**, Revd. Owen.

ESTE, Michael
See **EAST**, Michael.

EVANS, Charles Smart (1778-1849)
Born in London in 1778; died in London on 4 January 1849. A chorister at the Chapel Royal under **Edmund Ayrton**. From 1808 he was a gentleman of the Chapel Royal. Organist of the Church of St. Paul, Covent Garden, London. Composed glees and other vocal works, winning prizes from the Catch Club (1811, 1812) and the Glee Club (1817). Composed motets for the Portuguese Ambassador's Chapel, Grosvenor Square, of which he was a member, and in addition composed anthems including 'I will love Thee' and 'Teach me, O Lord'.

EVANS, Dr. David (1874-1948)
Born in Resolven, Glamorgan, Wales on 6 February 1874; died in Rhosllanerchrugog, near Wrexham, Denbighshire, Wales on 17 May 1948, the day after he had conducted a choir of some 4,000 voices at the Rhos Eisteddfod.

Studied at Arnold College, Swansea and under **Joseph Parry** at University College, Cardiff. Graduated B.Mus.(1895) and D.Mus (1914) at Queen's College, Oxford.

Organist of the New Jewin Street Presbyterian Chapel, London (1899-1903). Lecturer and head of music at University College, Cardiff (1903-1908). When that institution was raised to university status, he was the first holder of the chair of music (1908-1939). Organist of the Pembroke Terrace Presbyterian Church (from 1904).

Musical editor and Welsh representative on the committee for the Revised Edition (1927) of *Church Hymnary*, to which he contributed 12 hymn tunes under his own name and eight as Edward Arthur, a pseudonym which he sometimes preferred. He was musical editor of another hymnal *Llfyr Emynau a Thonau* (Book of Hymns and Tunes). Other collections of tunes appeared under the title *Moliant Cenedl*. A conductor, an enthusiast and proponent of congregational singing and a leading adjudicator of national *eisteddfodau*, at which his own works were used as test pieces. He continued the large-scale festivals of Psalmody that had been started by **John Roberts** (Ieuan Gwyllt).

His works include anthems, services, items for choir and string orchestra and the hymn tune 'Lucerna laudoniae'. His 'Lumetto' was and is used with 'Jesus bids us shine'. Arranged music and edited the journal *Y Cerddor* (The Musician).

EVANS, David Emlyn (1843-1913)
Born in Newcastle Emlyn, Carmarthenshire, Wales on 21 September 1843; died in Cemaes Machynlleth, Montgomeryshire, Wales on 19 April 1913.

Apprenticed to a draper in Bridgend, later practising his trade and travelling as a salesman. Self-taught musically, using the few text books that were available to him, and took lessons with **John Roberts** (Ieuan Gwyllt) in 1858.

Travelled frequently and lived at different times in Swansea; Cheltenham; Newton, Montgomeryshire; Shrewsbury, Hereford and Camaes, Montgomeryshire.

It was in his spare time that he made his mark in the musical world. Competed at local *eisteddfodau* from 1865 to 1867, winning a total of 70 prizes. He retired from competition and began to act as local adjudicator following the event at Wrexham in 1876 when he won all four prizes for vocal composition. From 1879 he officiated at the national events.

Later turned against the eisteddfod movement, concluding that it hindered the development of Welsh music. He deprecated the writing of glees in a manner calculated to win prizes rather than pursue artistic excellence.

Wrote weekly columns in *Cardiff Times* and *South Wales Weekly News*, always striving to improve musical standards, particularly in congregational hymn singing. Joint editor, with **David Jenkins** of *Y Cerddor* (The Musician) for more than 30 years (1880-1913). Wrote in *Musical Times* and compiled a biographical dictionary of Welsh composers.

In *Alawon fy Ngwlad* (1896), he edited and harmonised 500 Welsh melodies that had been collected by **Nicholas Bennett**.

Composed 48 hymn tunes, including 'Glanceri', 'Eirinwg', 'Tre-wen', 'Gorffwysfa' and 'Bryndioddef'. His other compositions include a sacred cantata *The Christian's Prayer* (1891). Won a prize of three Guineas (£3.15) from the Nonconformist Choir Union in 1894 for a secular part song.

EVANS, Revd. Evan (Ieuan Glan Geirionydd: 1795-1855)
Born in Trefriw, Caernarvonshire, Wales on 20 April 1795; died, probably in Trefriw, on 21 January 1855.

Attended school at Trefriw and at the free school at Llanrwst. He was forced to leave school and to work on the family farm due to financial difficulties.

In 1816, at the age of 21, became a school teacher at Talybont. He then moved to Chester and before the age of 26 he was appointed an elder of the Methodist Church.

Became an ordination candidate and read with Thomas Richards at the town of Aberriw, also known as Beriw, Montgomeryshire before studying at St. Bee's College. Ordained in 1826.

Licensed to preach in Welsh at St. Martin's Church, Chester and at Christleton (1826-1843). In the latter year he moved on to Ince. He served at Trefriw (1852-1854) and in July 1854 he was appointed curate at Rhyl.

Helped Revd. John Parry to edit the monthly journal *Goleuad Gwynedd*. Appreciating the power of the written word, he wrote to the bishops to ask them to fund periodicals similar in style and tone to *Saturday Magazine*. The project came to fruition in 1833 in the form of *Y Gwladgarwr*. Evan Evans was editor for three years.

He was said to be the most versatile poet of the nineteenth century, influenced, but not unduly so, by the English 'graveyard school'. In addition he was an eisteddfod participant, hymn writer and translator. His hymns show the influence of a number of other writers including Isaac Watts.

In 1838 he published *Y Seraph* (The Seraph), a collection of sacred hymn tunes. Composed some hymn tunes, which were usually harmonised by others. His most enduring tune is 'Glan geirionydd', still used today with Welsh and English hymn texts. His compositions won prizes at *eisteddfodau*.

EVANS, Harry (1873-1914)
Born in Dowlais, Glamorgan, Wales on 24 May 1873; died in Liverpool on 23 July 1914.
The son of John Evans, a choral conductor and bass singer.
His sister taught him the rudiments of Tonic Sol-fa notation. At the age of nine he became organist of Gwernllwyn Congregational Chapel, Dowlais. The Chapel arranged for him to receive lessons in music from Edward Laurence of Merthyr Tydfil, who had himself been a pupil of Ignaz Moscheles. Achieved success in the Associated Board examinations. Wanted to pursue an education and career in music, while his father urged him to seek a more general education.
In 1887, he became organist of the Bethania Congregational Chapel in Dowlais, a position he retained until 1906. At the age of 14 he became a pupil-teacher of Abermorlais Boys' School and would have attended teacher training college but for a breakdown in health. From 1893 he concentrated exclusively on a musical career.
Regarded as an able and perceptive adjudicator at festivals. In 1898 he formed a ladies' choir at Merthyr Tydfil and a male voice choir at Dowlais, which won an eisteddfod prize at Liverpool in 1900, only two years after its formation. Continued to compete at *eisteddfodau* until 1903.
Moved in 1906 to Liverpool, where he became organist of the Great George Street Congregational Chapel. Conductor of the Liverpool Welsh Choral Union and (from 1913), director of music of University College, Bangor.
He died before a hymnal under his editorship was completed. Another unrealized ambition was to found a college of music in Wales. Granville Bantock dedicated *Vanity of Vanities* to him.
Composed anthems and hymn tunes. His dramatic cantata *Dafydd ap Gwilym* was performed at the National Eisteddfod of 1908.

EVANS, Dr. T. Hopkin (1879-1940)
Born in Resolven, Glamorgan, Wales in 1879; died in 1940. Graduated B.Mus. (1914) and D.Mus. at the University of Oxford. Organist, conductor and festival adjudicator. Conductor of the Liverpool Welsh Choral Union (1919-1940). In 1927 he was an adjudicator at the National Eisteddfod, U.S.A. Conducted a national song festival in Cleveland, Ohio in 1934. Composer of *The Triumph Song*, a hymn of thanksgiving (1934) and the hymn 'Deus omnipotens' (1941).

EVANS, William (c1693-1740)
Died on 22 September 1740 at the age of 47. Organist of Wells Cathedral from 1727 to 1740 and, from around the same time, vicar choral - probationarily - and master of the choristers. Composed the anthem 'In Thee, O Lord', and a Service for the use of Wells Cathedral around the year 1729, when the theft of services by **Henry Aldrich** and **Robert Creyghton** left the music library badly depleted.

EVANS, William John (1866-1947)
Born in Aberdare, Glamorgan, Wales in 1866; died at Aberystwyth, Cardiganshire, Wales on 29 December 1947. Lived in Aberdare all his life although he travelled throughout Wales conducting festivals of singing. Succeeded his father as conductor of the Aberdare Choral Society. Composed hymn tunes, including 'Rhys' which

was named after his father and is found in *Caniedydd Cynulleidfaol* (1921), of which he was co-editor.

EVELEIGH, Dr. William George (1868-1950)
Born in Meerit, India in 1868; died in 1950.
Studied music with **George Bambridge**, Julius Benedict, **John Hopkins** and **Joseph Cox Bridge**. Graduated B.Mus. (1890) and D.Mus. (1895) at Queen's College, Oxford.
Organist of Holywell Parish Church (from 1888) and organist and choirmaster of the Holy Trinity Episcopal Church, Ayr (from 1889). The dedicatee of *Tuba Tune* by **Norman Cocker**.
Organist of the cathedral of St. Fin Barre, Cork, Ireland (1903-1922). Taught music at the High School and at the Rochelle Seminary. Conducted local examinations for the Royal College of Music. Composed services, a cantata *In Domino confido*, an opera *Valkyriur*, pieces for violin, organ and piano, and songs.

EVERITT, James (19th/20th century)
Graduated B.Mus. at the University of Durham (1898). Organist and choirmaster of Christ Church, Southwark, London (from 1874); Cheam Parish Church, Surrey (from 1880) and Alton Parish Church, Hampshire (from 1892). A local choral society conductor. Composed a festival anthem 'I will greatly rejoice' (1901) and an Evening Service in D (1902).

EVERY, Dr. William (1883-1953)
Born in Lambeth, London in 1883; died in Carshalton, Surrey on 23 May 1953. Graduated D.Mus., having been educated privately in music. Organist and choirmaster of Balham Congregational Church, London (from 1901), and of the George Street Congregational Church, Croydon. Surrey. A teacher of singing, voice production, piano, harmony, counterpoint and composition. Coached students for degree examinations at Guildhall School of Music. Composer of the vesper hymn 'Save us, O Lord' (1933), and hymn tunes.

EVILL, William Ernest (1852-1935)
Born in Wandsworth, London on 27 July 1852; died in Canterbury, Kent on 22 August 1935. Composer of hymn tunes.

EWEN, William Hugh (19th/20th century)
Attended the University of Edinburgh, graduating B.Mus. in 1906. Organist and choirmaster in Haddington (from 1901); St. John's, Dalkeith (from 1902); Fountainhill Road Church, Edinburgh (from 1904) and Haddington Parish Church (from 1906). A local choral society conductor. Composed anthems, a song, and an Introduction and Fugue for organ.

EWING, Alexander (1830-1895)
Born in Old Machar, Aberdeen on 3 January 1830; died in Taunton, Somerset on 11 July 1895. Studied law at Marischal College, Aberdeen but without qualifying. Subsequently studied German and music at the University of Heidelberg, Germany.
Was associated with the Harmonic Choir of Aberdeen, which specialised in singing madrigals and anthems and at the time was directed by William Carnie. Following one choir practice, Ewing approached Carnie with a hymn tune in score and asked if he would be prepared to rehearse it. Carnie obliged and the tune 'Ewing' received its first public performance.

Enlisted in 1855, during the Crimean War. Rose to the rank of lieutenant-colonel, retiring from the army in 1889 after serving with distinction in the Crimea and China.

Composed, as an amateur, a large amount of music. His hymn tune 'Ewing' (1853), also known as 'Argyle', 'Bernard' and 'St. Bede's' was adapted without his consent while he was serving in China by the editors of *Hymns Ancient and Modern* in order to fit the hymn 'Jerusalem, the golden'. Other material remained undiscovered until 1954, at which time some of his work was published. In particular, some of his anthems and part songs became popular.

EYLAND, H. (?19th century)

Composer of the anthem 'Behold the eye of the Lord', published in 1851.

EYRE, Alfred James (1853-1919)

Born in Lambeth, London on 24 October 1853; died in Lower Norwood, Surrey on 11 October 1919.

Studied at the Royal Academy of Music under **George Macfarren**, **Frederick Westlake** and **George Cooper**.

Organist of the London Churches of St. Peter, Vauxhall (1867-1872; 1874-1881); St. Ethelburga, Bishopsgate (1872-1874) and St. John, Upper Norwood (1881). Organist of the Crystal Palace (1880-1894).

A professor of organ at the Royal Normal College for the Blind.

Composed services, one of which was written for the Salisbury Diocesan Choral Association. A Communion Service in E-flat remains in use. There is a hymn 'Angels of God' (1910): hymn tunes include 'St. Clare' and 'Selby', the latter being found in *Hymns Ancient and Modern* with 'O, for a thousand tongues to sing'. Evening Services including a Magnificat and Nunc Dimittis in D (1897). Also composed items for piano.

EYRE, Revd. Charles George (b.1925)

Born in Belfast on 2 June 1925. Educated at Portstewart and Coleraine, County Londonderry. Trained for the ministry of the Methodist Church at Edge Hill Theological College. His ministry began in 1947. Later, he served in Jamaica, where he became acquainted with the hymn writer Hugh Sherlock, for whose hymns he composed tunes. Served on the committee of the hymnal *Hymns and Psalms*, published in 1983.

The hymn tune 'Carlisle Memorial', named after a church in Belfast which he served for nine years, is used in *Hymns and Psalms* with the hymn 'Sweet is the work of God and King' by Isaac Watts. His cantata *Abraham*, composed especially for children, has been widely performed in Ireland.

F

FACER, Thomas (1857-1921)
Born in Stratford on Avon, Warwickshire in 1857; died in Birmingham on 21 October 1921. Held various organistships in the Birmingham area. Taught singing at the King Edward Foundation grammar schools. Conductor of the Birmingham Choral Union, and a teacher of singing. Composed hymn tunes, cantatas including *Noeltide* (1892) and *The Maid of Lorne* (1896), part songs and music for schools.

FAIRFAX (Fayrfax), Dr. Robert (1464-1521)
Born at Deeping Gate, Lincolnshire on 23 April 1464; died in St. Albans, Hertfordshire on 24 October 1521. Of an ancient Yorkshire family.
Graduated Mus.B. (1501) and Mus.D. (1504) at the University of Cambridge, the doctorate being awarded on the strength of the Mass *O Quam Glorifica* which he submitted as his exercise. Supplicated successfully for his D.Mus. at the University of Oxford (1511) with a *Gloria.*
Fairfax was probably organist of the Abbey Church of St. Alban from around 1500. He may also have been chanter there.
A gentleman of the Chapel Royal around 1497, a position which he probably held for the rest of his life. One of the singing men in attendance on Henry VIII at the Field of the Cloth of Gold. Also derived some additional income as a copyist. In September 1514 he was appointed a poor knight of Windsor.
Composed motets including *O bone Jesu,* Masses, two Magnificats, a Nunc Dimittis, antiphons and part songs. The *Eton College Choirbook* of around 1500 contained a Magnificat and two antiphons by Robert Fairfax.

FALCONER, Alexander Croil (1850-1903)
Born in 1850; died in Islington, London on 10 March 1903. Composed hymn tunes. Editor of *Anthems for use with Church Praise* (1883).

FANING, Dr. Joseph Eaton (1850-1927)
Born in Helston, Cornwall on 20 May 1850; died in Brighton, Sussex on 28 October 1927.
Taught to play piano and violin by his mother and father, a professor of music. Attended the Royal Academy of Music (1870) and won a Mendelssohn Scholarship to study in Leipzig (1873). His tutors included **William Sterndale Bennett, Charles Steggall,**

Arthur Sullivan, Frederick Jewson, William Aylward, Ciabatta and Pettitt. Graduated Mus.B. (1894) and Mus.D. (1900) at Trinity College, Cambridge.
Organist of Holbrook Parish Church, near Ipswich, from the age of 12.
Held appointments on the teaching staff of the R.A.M. where he was sub professor of harmony (from 1874), an assistant professor of piano, and a professor of piano (from 1878). A professor of piano and harmony at the National Training School of Music and at its successor, the Royal College of Music, (until 1885), and Guildhall School of Music.
Succeeded **John Farmer** as director of music of Harrow School (1885-1901); succeeded by **Percy Buck.** A music examiner to the University of Cambridge (1904-1909) and a member of the Board of Studies of the University of London.
Composed a quantity of church music including anthems, a Te Deum in C, sets of Responses to the Commandments in C and in F in a collection published around 1875. A Magnificat and Nunc Dimittis were composed for the Festival of the Sons of the Clergy in St. Paul's Cathedral. His other compositions include the song 'Moonlight'; operettas, one of which was *The two Majors*; a symphony; songs; part songs; duets and two cantatas.

FANSHAWE, David Arthur (b. 1942)
Born at Paignton, Devon on 19 April 1942.
Educated at St. George's School, Windsor and Stowe School. A foundation scholar at the Royal College of Music, studying composition with John Lambert. Prior to the R.C.M. he had worked in the film industry in the field of documentaries, where he gained experience as an editor. Has worked as a composer for the B.B.C. and for Independent Television; also for the film industry. His music has been heard with such programmes as B.B.C.'s 'When the Boat comes in'.
Founder of the Fanshawe Pacific Collections, for which he has spent considerable time in amassing materials that record the music and oral traditions of that region.
A pianist, he has made recordings and he has contributed articles to magazines. In a wide and varied career he has combined the role of composer with that of explorer and photographer. His compositions include *African Sanctus*, a Requiem *for the Children of Aberfan,*

the carol 'Ring out the bells' and the anthems 'Sing Christians, sing' and 'Sing Alleluia'.

FAREBROTHER, Bernard (?-1888)
A pupil of **Zechariah Buck**, organist of Norwich Cathedral. Organist of St. Paul's Church, Birmingham. Composer of the anthems 'Lo, the winter is past' and 'O give thanks unto the Lord'.

FARJEON, Henry (1878-1948)
Born at Hohokus, New Jersey, U.S.A. on 6 May 1878; died in Hampstead, London on 29 December 1948. Studied with **Battison Haynes**, **Frederick Corder** and Septimus Webbe. Awarded a Goring Thomas scholarship to the Royal Academy of Music. A professor of composition and harmony at the Blackheath Conservatory (from 1902), and he taught at the R.A.M. (from 1903). One of the original founders of the Society of British Composers. Contributed to *The Daily Telegraph* and to *Musical Times*. Composed a Mass *of St. Dominic*, with which he won the Carnegie Award of 1925, hymn tunes, concertos, sonatas, and piano music.

FARMER, Henry (1819-1891)
Born in Nottingham on 13 May 1819; died on 25 June 1891, two days after his retirement. Mainly self taught in music but he received lessons from John Thirlwall. A violinist, and a member of the orchestra of the Birmingham Festival. Organist of the High Pavement Chapel, Nottingham, for more than 40 years. Earned, literally, a fortune from a music business which he ran for 50 years, serving also as a volunteer in the Robin Hood Rifles, where he rose to the rank of captain. Composed a Mass in B-flat and supplied a set of Responses to the Commandments in F for a collection published around the year 1875. Also composed items for violin.

FARMER (Fermer, Fermor), John (c1570-after 1601)
Worked for a time in Ireland but it is likely that he was born in England.
Organist and master of the children of Christ Church Cathedral, Dublin (1595-1599). From 1596 he was also a vicar choral at Christ Church. At some other time he lived in London and he is probably the John Farmer, madrigal writer, known to be living in Bread Street, London in 1599.
Composed madrigals. Of his church music, the most enduring example is his setting of The Lord's Prayer, and he is also known for his anthem 'O Lord, on whom I do depend'. One of the 10 composers who supplied harmonisations for the collection *Whole Booke of Psalmes...* (1592) by Thomas East.

FARMER, John A. (1836-1901)
Born in Nottingham on 16 August 1836; died in Oxford on 17 July 1901.
Nephew and a piano pupil of Henry Farmer. His higher musical education took place in Germany, at the Leipzig Conservatory (from 1851) and, under Andreas Späth, at Saxe-Coburg.
For a while he taught music in Zürich before becoming music master of Harrow School (1862-1885) and organist of Balliol College, Oxford (from 1885).
Composed songs for the boys of Harrow School. His other compositions include an oratorio *Christ and His Soldiers* (1878) and a Requiem *in memory of departed Harrow friends*.
Edited the publication *Hymns and Hymn Tunes for High Schools*. *Church Hymnary*'s Revised Edition (1927) includes his tune 'In

the field' with 'In the field with their flocks abiding' by Frederic Farrar. Also composed two Septets for Piano, Flute and Strings.

FARNABY, Giles (c1560-1640)
Born in Truro, Cornwall around the year 1560; died in London and was buried on 25 November 1640.
One of a musical family. Graduated B.Mus. at the University of Oxford in July 1592, having studied music for 12 years.
A joiner by trade and a keen spinet player, Farnaby lived for a time in Lincolnshire but spent most of his life in Sevenoaks, Kent and London. From 1602 to 1608 he was employed as a household musician of Sir Nicholas Sanderson.
Composed music for virginals, and madrigals. He harmonised nine Psalm tunes for the collection *Whole Booke of Psalmes...* (1592) by Thomas East. Some of these tunes are found in a collection of the same title by **Thomas Ravenscroft**, published in 1621. Also composed a six part anthem 'O my soune Absolon'.

FARRANT, John (16th/17th century)
Scholars have had difficulty distinguishing between the careers of an unknown number of 16th and 17th century composers with the surname Farrant.
A John Farrant was master of the choristers of Salisbury Cathedral by October 1571. In 1587 was organist also; he had been a lay clerk at Salisbury from 1571.
Dismissed in 1592 after he had almost killed the dean - who was also his wife's uncle - in an altercation, having attacked him with a knife. He then went to Hereford Cathedral as organist and vicar choral, resigning both positions in 1593.
Other organistships held by a John Farrant are at the Cathedrals of Ely (1566-1568) and Bristol (1570-1571), and at Christ's Hospital, London (from 1607). Wells Cathedral had a vicar choral of the same name from around 1593 to 1599, who was probably rector of Allerton from 1594.
The John Farrant of Ely composed a Service in D Minor, and the anthems 'God be merciful' and 'O Lord almighty'.

FARRANT, Revd. Richard (c1540-1580)
Born around the year 1540, although some scholars put the year of his birth at 1530; died, probably in Windsor, Berkshire on 30 November 1580.
A gentleman of the Chapel Royal for two periods. The first of these lasted until his resignation in 1564. His re-appointment took place on the death of **Thomas Caustun**. Took part in the funeral of Edward VI and the Coronations of Mary and Elizabeth I.
Organist of St. George's Chapel, Windsor Castle (1564-1580), where he served jointly with **John Marbeck** and for which he had resigned his position at the Chapel Royal. At St. George's he was also lay vicar and master of the children. Owned houses in Blackfriars and Greenwich.
Involved from February 1567 in the production of court theatricals, which were very popular with the public and in which the evening opened with a selection of music. These were initially performed by the boys of St. George's. Later the choristers of the Chapel Royal also took part.
Organist of the Cathedrals of Bristol (1570-1571), Hereford (1592-1593) and Salisbury (1598-1602).
Between Hereford and Salisbury he was organist of Christ Church, Newgate Street, London.
Composed settings of the Morning and Evening Services in A Minor and in F, a Magnificat and Nunc Dimittis in Mode X - and

probably others, since lost. Known for his anthems 'Call to remembrance' and 'Hide Thou not Thy face', which were intended for use on Maundy Thursday, and 'When as we sat in Babylon'.

FARRANT, William (?-1580)
His hymn tune Farrant was used in *Church Hymns* (1875), edited by **Arthur Sullivan**, as a setting of the hymn 'O help us, Lord! Each hour of need' by Henry Milman.

FARRAR, Ernest Bristow (1885-1918)
Born in Blackheath, Kent on 7 July 1885; died in Le Cateau, Cambrai on 18 September 1918; killed in action.
Graduated in Durham then studied at the Royal College of Music with **C.V. Stanford** and **Walter Parratt**. Organist at the English Church in Dresden, then in South Shields and in Harrogate, where he was at Christ Church from 1912.
Until comparatively recently, he was remembered principally as the teacher of the young **Gerald Finzi** (from 1914), though Farrar's work as a composer is (like that of his older contemporary and friend, Frank Bridge) becoming increasingly valued. His organ works include Fantasy-Prelude (1908) and three Chorale Preludes (1920). Among his anthems are 'Almighty God, the fountain of wisdom'.
Frank Bridge dedicated his Piano Sonata as a memorial to Farrar, and a composition prize at the Royal College of Music was established in his memory.

FARRER, John Downing (1829-1919)
Born in Lowestoft, Suffolk on 31 March 1829; died in Boscombe, Dorset on 22 February 1919.
A businessman. Following his retirement he lived firstly in Norwich, Norfolk and then in Lowestoft. Worked in support of the Church Colonial and Continental Society and the Mission to Seamen, and it was mainly due to his efforts that a Seamen's Institute, subsequently known as 'Farrer's Cathedral' was built in Lowestoft.
Although he was unable to play any musical instrument, Farrer was a keen amateur musician. Composed many hymn tunes: a set of 85 was published under the title *The Lowestoft Tune Book. Church Hymnary*'s Revised Edition (1927) uses Farrer's 'New Calabar' with 'Lord, this day Thy children meet' by William Walsham How.

FAWCETT, John (1789-1867)
Born in Wennington, Lancashire on 8 December 1789, died in Bolton, Lancashire on 26 October 1867. Father of the 19th century **John Fawcett**.
Musically self-taught. Learned the Lancashire Sol-fa system and reinforced his knowledge by copying out the Psalm and hymn tunes that he encountered. A clarinet player, he was band master of the local militia at the age of 17.
A shoemaker until 1825, when he settled in Bolton as organist of the Bridge Street Wesleyan Chapel, professor of music and composer of sacred songs. Taught various musical instruments. Held various chapel organistships in Farnworth and Bolton, including the Maudsley Street Congregational Church, Bolton, declining offers of similar positions in Manchester.
Said to have composed 2,000 musical items, many of which were Psalm or hymn tunes. Three sets of these were published. His anthem 'Now is Christ risen' also became known. His hymn tune 'Relief' was used with 'O Thou in all Thy might so far'; 'Melling',

named after a town near his birthplace, served 'Children of the Heavenly God'. Also composed an oratorio *Paradise*.

FAWCETT, John (c1825-1857)
Born around the year 1825; died in Manchester on 1 July 1857.
Studied music under his father, **John Fawcett** of Wennington. Succeeded an elder brother as organist of Bolton Parish Church, Lancashire. In turn, his sister deputised for him when he moved to London to study at the Royal Academy of Music, in 1845, under **William Sterndale Bennett**. This period of study lasted about a year.
Graduated B.Mus. at the University of Oxford in November 1852, having submitted a sacred cantata *Supplication and Thanksgiving*, which was later published.
Organist of St. John's Church, Farnworth, Lancashire from the age of 10 (1835-1842). Resumed his duties at Bolton Parish Church after completing his studies, serving until his death. During his time in London he was organist of Earl Howe's Church at Curzon Street.
In addition to his cantata exercise, he composed anthems including 'All they that hope' and 'When the wicked man,' the hymn tune 'Bolton-le-Moors', songs, glees and items for piano.

FAWKYNER, Revd. John (15th/16th century)
Incumbent of Horncastle, Lincolnshire in the 1490s. Two items composed by him are the motets *Gaude virgo salutata* and *Gaude rose sine spina*.

FEARNSIDE, Frederick (c1836-1888)
Born around the year 1836; died in Bradford, Yorkshire in October 1888. A chorister of Norwich Cathedral under **Zechariah Buck**, to whom he was later articled. Wrote on diverse subjects. One of his published works was *The Systematic and Comprehensive Singing Manual* (1887). Composer of the anthem 'The Lord is gracious'.

FEILDEN, Revd. Oswald Mosley (1837-1924)
Born in Canterbury, Kent on 16 September 1837; died in Oswestry, Shropshire on 19 June 1924.
Educated at Eton College and Christ Church, Oxford. Graduated B.A. in 1859 and ordained deacon in 1861; priest in 1862.
Assistant curate of Whittington, Shropshire under William Walsham How (1861-1865) and incumbent of Welsh Frankton (from 1865).
His hymn tune 'Eden' was used with 'Lord, be Thy word my rule' in *Hymns Ancient and Modern*; in *Church Hymns* (1875) it is used with the hymn by Horatius Bonar, 'Thy way, not mine O Lord'. The collection also uses Feilden's 'St. John the Baptist', also known as 'Enon', with 'O let Him whose sorrow'.

FELLOWES, Revd. Dr. Edmund Horace (1870-1951)
Born in Paddington, London on 11 November 1870; died in Windsor, Berkshire on 20 December 1951.
His mother was a musician and watercolourist; his father died when Horace was 11 years old.
Educated at a preparatory school in Bickley, Kent (where his contemporaries included the cabinet minister H.A.L. Fisher), Winchester College and Oriel College, Oxford where he read theology (1889-1892) and remained for a fourth year (1893) in order to study for a degree in music. His Oxford contemporaries included **Ernest Walker** and **P.C. Buck**, and the cricketer Pelham Warner.

At the age of seven, he met Joachim and at an early age he heard performances by Lizst and Clara Schumann.

A violinist, he studied music with Fletcher and L. Straus. Graduated B.Mus. (1896) B.A. (1892) and M.A. (1896) at the University of Oxford, followed by honorary doctorates from the Universities of Dublin (1917), Oxford (1939) and Cambridge (1950). Ordained deacon (1894) at Rochester Cathedral by Bishop Randall Davidson, following a year's preparation at Llandaff; priest in 1895.

Appointed M.V.O. (1931) and became a Companion of Honour (1944).

Assistant curate in Wandsworth, London (1894-1897).

Wanted to become a cathedral minor canon immediately. A vacancy arose at Bristol, and **John Stainer** was called upon by the Dean and Chapter for advice. Knowing of the deep rift that existed between the organist, **George Riseley,** and the retiring precentor, William Mann, Stainer was reluctant for Fellowes to become embroiled. Mann had inflexible views about the prerogative of the precentor on matters of cathedral music (described under the entry for Riseley.)

Became precentor of Bristol Cathedral on 1 March 1897. Remained until 1900, from which time he was a minor canon of St. George's Chapel, Windsor Castle for a period of more than 50 years until his death.

Two major events witnessed by Fellowes shortly after his arrival at St. George's were the marriage of Clara Butt (1900) and the Funeral of Queen Victoria (1901). Some myths have grown up about the drawing of the gun carriage at the Queen's funeral, and Fellowes gave his account in an autobiography. One of the horses was restive. He was calmed but as soon as the procession started off from the station he was again unsettled. It was decided to unharness the horses. A detachment of Bluejackets from *H.M.S. Excellent* provided the guard, and they pulled the gun carriage along its route. Thus a precedent was established, which was followed in the funeral processions of Edward VII (1910) and George V (1936).

Fellowes took charge of the St. George's choir temporarily between the death of **Walter Parratt** and the appointment of **Henry Walford Davies** in 1927. According to Fellowes, Walford Davies declined the job in 1924. Instead, Fellowes became master of the choristers. Shortly after Fellowes's appointment, **Malcolm Boyle** was appointed to play organ.

Pioneering gramophone recordings were made by the Choir of St. George's Chapel (from 1925).

Walter Parratt's assistant had been **Martin Akerman**, who resigned through ill health. G.S. Kitchingman was persuaded to act as assistant organist. The main organ was out of use at that time, and a small temporary organ had been installed in the nave.

Toured Canada in 1927 with **Sydney Nicholson**, 12 boys from Westminster Abbey and eight lay clerks from St. George's Chapel. Honorary Librarian of St. Michael's College, Tenbury, Worcestershire (1918-1948). Lectured on early English music at many institutions, including the Universities of Liverpool (1932-1933) and Glasgow (1937-1938).

Achieved prominence in his field as an editor of the works of the early English madrigalists and lutenists, as well as the Tudor school of church music, in connection with which he edited the works of **William Byrd** in 20 volumes. Carried out the considerable task of editing the complete series of English madrigal and lute-song music, amounting to 68 volumes. Contributed 50 or so articles to Grove's *Dictionary of Music and Musicians,* and his writings

include *English Cathedral Music from Edward VI to Edward VII* (1942), which was revised in 1969 under the new title *English Cathedral Music.*

Composed a Morning and Evening Service in D, anthems, songs, part songs and a String Quartet.

FELTON, Revd. William (1715-1769)
Born in Drayton, Shropshire in 1715; died in Hereford on 6 December 1769.

Attended Manchester Grammar School. Graduated B.A. (1738) and M.A. (1743) at St. John's College, Cambridge. Ordained priest in August 1742.

Pursued a career within the Church of England, being associated with Hereford Cathedral from his mid 20s until his death. A keen amateur organist and harpsichordist. A steward at the Three Choirs' Festivals of 1744 and 1745.

Appointed vicar choral and sub chanter (succentor) in 1741, minor canon (1760) and *custos* of the college of vicars (1769).

Held various parish church appointments within the Hereford diocese from 1744, one of which was as vicar of Norton Canon (1751-1769).

Composed the hymn tune 'Fabian', and is represented in *Cathedral Psalter Chants* (1875). His Chant in C Minor is strongly associated with Psalm 130, a link that was maintained by **John Stainer** in *St. Paul's Cathedral Chant Book.* Composed a total of 32 concertos for organ or piano.

FERGUSON, Barry William Cammack (b.1942)
Born in London on 18 July 1942.

A chorister of Exeter Cathedral. From 1956 to 1960 he attended Clifton College, Bristol, going up as organ scholar to Peterhouse, Cambridge. Graduated B.A. (1963) and M.A. Performed postgraduate study at the Royal College of Music.

Assistant organist of Peterborough Cathedral (1964-1971) and organist of Wimborne Minster (1971-1977) before becoming organist of Rochester Cathedral (1977-1994). Subsequently organist of Shaftesbury Church, Dorset.

Has composed songs, music for piano and organ, two hymn tunes, the anthem 'All, my dear Lord' and a setting to the Rite A version of the Communion Service entitled the *Kent* Service. Also composed *Six Organ Pieces.*

FERGUSON, Revd. William Harold (1874-1950)
Born in Leeds on 1 January 1874; died in Littlehampton, Sussex on 18 October 1950.

Educated at Magdalen College School and Keble College, Oxford, graduating B.A. (1897) and M.A. (1906). Trained for the ministry of the Church of England at Cuddesdon College (from 1901), being ordained deacon (1902) and priest (1904).

Assistant master of St. Edward's School, Oxford (from 1896), and of Bilton Grange, Rugby, Warwickshire (from 1899). From 1902 onwards he taught at Lancing College, Sussex, of which he was also chaplain. From 1913 he was warden of St. Edward's School, Oxford and from 1925 he was warden of St. Peter's College, Radley. Canon and precentor of Salisbury Cathedral (1937-1947).

A member of a committee set up by the Headmasters' Conference to prepare *Public School Hymn Book.* Ferguson and **Geoffrey Shaw** were joint editors and the collection appeared in 1919.

In his time at Lancing College he composed the hymn tune 'Wolvercote'. Since then, it has become the preferred tune in many publications for the hymn 'O Jesus, I have promised'. His tunes 'Ladywell' and 'Cuddesdon' have also been popular.

FERRABOSCO (Ferabosco), Alphonso (1543-1588)
Born in Bologna, Italy and was baptised on 18 January 1543; died in Bologna on 12 August 1588. Father of the younger musician of the same name.
From 1560 to around 1578 he was in the service of Elizabeth I as a musician and possibly even as a secret agent, although there is little evidence of the latter. Became entangled in a murder case and failed to return punctually from leave of absence in Italy. Broke his pledge of lifelong service and returned to Italy around 1578.
Composed madrigals, motets, the six-part anthem 'O, remember not our old sins' and music for viol, and he was a friendly compositional rival of **William Byrd**.

FERRABOSCO, Alphonso (c1575-1628)
Born in Greenwich, London around the year 1575; died in Greenwich and was buried on 11 March 1628. Son of **Alphonso Ferrabosco** of Bologna.
May have lived in Italy for some time between 1578 and the first part of the 17th century. His father Alphonso is said to have abandoned his son in his haste to return to Italy.
Appointed to the court of James I as viol player (1604). In 1605 he became an extraordinary groom of the Privy Chamber and musical instructor to Prince Henry. Later served Charles I as composer in ordinary, following the death of **John Coprario**.
Composed instrumental music, including fantasias and pavans for viol, and songs. Collaborated with Ben Jonson and Inigo Jones in the production of masques (1605-1611). The anthems 'In death no man remembreth Thee' and 'In Thee, O Lord' are examples of works for the church by him.

FERRABOSCO, Dr. John (1626-1682)
Born in Greenwich, London and was baptised on 9 October 1626; died, probably in Ely, Cambridgeshire and was buried on 15 October 1682. He may have been the grandson of **Alphonso Ferrrabosco** of Bologna.
Graduated Mus.B. at the University of Cambridge on letters patent from Charles II. In 1671 he received the Cambridge Mus.D.
Organist of Ely Cathedral (1662-1682), the last five years of his tenure being marked by deteriorating health and the use of a deputy. At Ely his duties included those of cook but this was almost certainly simply a means of increasing his salary by £6 per annum and it is unlikely that he actually did much cooking.
Composed church music, including services, anthems including 'Like as the hart' and 'By the waters of Babylon', and music for harpsichord.

FIDO (Fidoe, Fidow, Fidor), Revd. John (c1570-c1640)
Born around the year 1570; died, possibly in Worcester, in about 1640.
His rather turbulent career centred around the Cathedrals of Hereford and Worcester.
Organist of Hereford Cathedral from 1591 to 1592 and from 1593 to 1594 or 1595, being dismissed in the February of the last year of his second period following a dispute with his colleagues. Reappointed organist of Hereford in 1597 but left in the same year.
Organist of Worcester Cathedral on the death of **Nathaniel Patrick**. Served until 1597 but for a month or so towards the end of 1596 there was a break in this employment. Later returned to Worcester as assistant to the organist, **Thomas Tomkins**. In 1610 he became a minor canon of Worcester Cathedral. Incumbent of the church of St. Nicholas, Worcester (1615-1636).
Other composers of the same name were active elsewhere in the early 17th century but there is insufficient evidence to determine how many there were and how their careers progressed.
One or more persons of the name John Fido composed a number of verse anthems, including 'Hear me, O Lord'.

FIELD, John Thomas (1850-?)
Born near Manchester on 4 February 1850.
Studied under **Frederick Bridge** and **John Stainer**.
Organist and choirmaster at Holywell Parish Church, North Wales (from 1868); Christ Church, Southport, Lancashire (from 1870); St. German's Church, Blackheath, Kent (from 1872) and Christ Church, Lee Park, London (from 1874), an appointment which he held for at least 20 years.
Composed a Morning and Evening Service in D, a Benedictus and Agnus Dei in F, a Magnificat and Nunc Dimittis in G, chants, anthems including 'Send out Thy light' and 'Hail, gladenning Light', carols, works for piano and for organ, songs and part songs.

FIELDEN, Dr. Thomas Perceval (1882-1974)
Born in Chichester, Sussex on 14 November 1882; died in Gloucester on 19 September 1974.
Educated at the Prebendal School, Chichester; Oxford University and the Royal College of Music. Graduated M.A. and B.Mus. (Oxford), and D.Mus. (Edinburgh).
Director of music at Hurstpierpoint College, Sussex (1903-1905) and Fettes College, Edinburgh (1908-1912). Director of the piano teaching department of Cheltenham Ladies' College, Gloucestershire (1912-1920). A professor of piano at the R.C.M. (1921-1947), and director of music of Charterhouse, Surrey (1928-1948). Director of the Rhodesian Academy of Music, Bulawayo (1952-1958).
On active service in World War I; a reservist in World War II.
Author of *Science of Pianoforte Technique*. Composed a Rigadoon for Piano (1913), hymn tunes, songs including 'The sea' and part songs.

FILBY, William Charles (1836-1913)
Born at Hammersmith, London on 18 December 1836; died in Richmond, Surrey on 22 June 1913.
Studied in France.
Recorded as holding eight organistships, namely St. Peter's Church, Hammersmith, London (from 1849); Bromley Parish Church, Kent (1853); the London Churches of St. Peter, Walworth; St. Matthew, Bayswater and St. Luke, Westbourne Park; Holy Trinity, Margate, Kent; Holy Trinity, Stepney, London and St. Paul, West Greenwich, London (1884). Organist at the International Exhibitions of 1882 and of 1885.
Author and lecturer on church music, opera and musical education. His many compositions include choral and congregational music: settings of the Mass in E and in E-flat, together with other music for the Roman Catholic Church, anthems and the hymn tune 'Hammersmith' which was used by *Hymns Ancient and Modern* with the hymn 'Far down the ages, now' by Horatius Bonar. Also composed organ voluntaries, operettas, songs, part songs and choruses.

FINCH, Revd. Edward (c1664-1738)
Born in the year 1664 or 1665; died in York on 14 February 1738. Prebendary of York Minster in 1704. Fifth son of the first Earl of Nottingham and the brother of Dean Finch. His church music compositions include a Te Deum and the anthems 'Grant, we beseech Thee' and 'By the waters of Babylon'. His works are found in the collection of **Thomas Tudway**.

FINLAY, Kenneth George (1882-1974)
Born in St. Marylebone, London on 3 February 1882; died in Glasgow on 15 April 1974. Son of professor D.W. Finlay of Aberdeen.
Educated at Robert Gordon's College, Aberdeen and at Merchiston Castle School, Edinburgh. Qualified as a Member of the Royal Institute of Naval Architects but in 1928 he decided upon a change in career, studying at the Royal College of Music for a year and then at the Jordanhill Teacher Training College, Glasgow.
On qualifying as a teacher he was appointed teacher of class singing at Irvine, Ayrshire. Retired in 1947.
Known for his cantatas *The Saviour's Birth* (1928) and *Before the Dawn* (1938), and for his hymn tunes 'Ardgowan' (1920) and 'Glenfinlas' (1926) that are still used in hymn books today. His 'Helensburg' was used in the Revised Edition (1927) of *Church Hymnary* with the hymn 'O ye who taste' by Christina Rossetti.

FINZI, Gerald Raphael (1901-1956)
Born in London on 14 July 1901; died in Oxford on 28 September 1956.
Studied with Ernest Farrar in Harrogate from (1914-1916). At this point Farrar joined the armed forces and in September 1918 he was killed in action in France. Finzi continued his studies with **Edward Bairstow** at York (1917-1922) and, for counterpoint, **R.O. Morris** in London (from 1925).
From 1922 onwards he lived in Painswick, Gloucestershire, but in 1926 he moved to London. In 1937 he built a house at Ashmansworth, Hampshire, where he composed and built up a significant music library.
A teacher of counterpoint at the Royal Academy of Music (1930-1933).
From 1935 onwards he catalogued the music of Ivor Gurney, whom he never met but whose poetry and songs he admired. In 1946, Finzi argued for the exemption of musicians from conscription. Perhaps it was his knowledge of the tragic circumstances of Gurney's decline following active service in World War I that caused him to take up the campaign.
Worked for the Ministry of War Transport (1941-1945) in Berkshire, taking an active part during his spare time in local amateur music-making.
Was acquainted with the composers **Ralph Vaughan Williams, Gustav Holst, Robin Milford** and **Edmund Rubbra**.
Vaughan Williams, knowing that Finzi disliked London, offered him the use of The White Gates, the Vaughan Williams family home at Dorking, Surrey while absent. Vaughan Williams admired the other's great knowledge of English poetry to which, among other qualities, he referred in a tribute in *The Times* following Finzi's death.
Finzi did much to revive the English music of the 17th century, including that of **William Boyce**. It is said that he treated Thomas Hardy's poems particularly sensitively.
He is remembered for his Cello and Clarinet Concertos, songs, orchestral works including *Severn Rhapsody*, anthems 'Lo, the full

final Sacrifice', 'God is gone up', 'The brightness of this day' and the cantatas *In terra pax* and *Dies natalis* is also well-known. His 'Intimations of Immortality' was unfortunately misprinted in score as 'Intimations of Immorality'.

FIRTH, R.A. (18th/19th century)
Organist of St. John's Church, Hampstead, London. Compiler of collections of church music, and composer of hymn tunes and items for piano.

FISH, Adrian Vernon (b.1956)
Born in Bristol, Gloucestershire on 20 January 1956. Educated at Dartington College of Arts (1973-1974) and at the Royal College of Music (1975-1978). Organist of the Church of St. Andrew Buckland, Monachorm (1974-1975); Perivale Church, Middlesex (1976-1978) and in London (1977-1978). Since 1988 he has been a radio presenter and player in a dance band. Has composed symphonies, organ music, a *Veni, Sancte Spiritus* for chorus and organ and an anthem setting of Psalm 33 'Shout for joy before the Lord'.

FISH, William (1775-c1863)
Born in 1775; died in 1863 or 1864, or, according to one source, in Norwich, Norfolk on 15 March 1866. A violinist of the Norwich Theatre. Taught and composed in Norwich, his students including **Edward Taylor**, later to be one of the founders of the Norwich Festival and a winner of the Gresham Prize for composition, and **George Perry**. Composed the anthem 'The Lord that made the heavens'. His works include a Grand Sonata for Piano, glees and songs.

FISHER, Arthur Colborne (1864-1896)
Organist of St. George's Church, Cannes, France. Composer of the anthems 'Blessed city' and 'God that madest'.

FISHWICK, Charles (1878-1963)
Born in Croydon, Surrey on 21 September 1878; died in Shanklin, Isle of Wight on 24 January 1963. A composer of hymn tunes.

FITZGERALD, William (1814-1883)
Born in 1814; died in Beverley, Yorkshire in 1883. A composer of hymn tunes.

FITZHERBERT, Revd. William (1713-1797)
Born in 1713; died in London on 2 October 1797. A minor canon of St. Paul's Cathedral (from 1744). Rector of Hadlow, Kent (from 1753); Hornedon on the Hill, Essex (1756-1771) and of the Church of St. Gregory by St. Paul, London. Composed a Double Chant in F, and other church music.

FITZWILLIAM, Edward Francis (1824-1857)
Born in Deal, Kent on 1 August 1824; died in London on 20 January 1857. Educated with a view to a career in music, specialising in composition. In 1853 he became director of music of the Haymarket Theatre, London. In the same year he published a set of 12 songs. His church music includes a Te Deum and a hymn 'O incomprehensible Creator'.

FLEMING, Michael Paschal Marcon (b.1928)
Born in Oxford in 1928. Educated at St. Edmund's School, Canterbury, Kent; the Royal School of Church Music and

University College, Durham, where he graduated B.A. Organist of All Saints' Church, Margaret Street, London (1958-1968); Croydon Parish Church, Surrey (1968-1978) and St. Alban's, Holborn, London. Appointed conductor of the Croydon Bach Society in 1968. An examiner for the Associated Board of the Royal Schools of Music. A tutor at the Royal School of Church Music. Has composed an Evening Service in G for Treble Voices, a number of anthems and chants, and five hymn tunes, including 'Palace Green', composed for **Arthur Hutchings** at Durham.

FLETCHER, Andrew Illston (b.1950)
Born on 25 November 1950. Educated in Birmingham and, as organ scholar, at Keble College, Oxford. Organist and choirmaster of St. Mary's Church, Warwick; St. Mark's Church, Swindon, Wiltshire and St. Peter's Church, Hall Green, Birmingham. Master of the music of St. Thomas's Church, Stourbridge. An organ recitalist, teacher of music and composer, many of his works being choral or for organ. Has composed a setting of the Alternative Service Book (Church of England) Versicles and Responses for Morning and Evening Prayer.

FLINTOFT, Revd. Luke (c1680-1727)
Born, probably in Yorkshire or Worcester, around 1680; died in Westminster, London on 3 November 1727 and buried in Westminster Abbey.
In May 1698 he was a chorister of Trinity College, Cambridge but this appointment appears to have been made for monetary reasons and he was not required to sing. Graduated B.A. at Queens' College, Cambridge (1700).
A priest vicar of Lincoln Cathedral (1704-1714) and a gentleman of the Chapel Royal (from December 1715). From July 1719 he was a reader of Whitehall Chapel; a minor canon of Westminster Abbey (from 1719). In 1725 he was imprisoned for debt until the Chapter paid the necessary 15 Guineas (£15.75) for his release.
The Double Chant in G Minor attributed to him is one of the earliest, if not the earliest, of its kind. It was adapted from a setting of Psalm 125 'They that put their trust in the Lord' found in **Richard Alison**'s *Psalter* (1599). Rival claims have been advanced on behalf of **William Hine, William Morley and John Robinson**.

FLOOD, Dr. William Henry Grattan (1859-1928)
Born in Lismore, County Waterford, Ireland on 1 November 1859; died in Enniscorthy, Ireland on 6 August 1928.
Received his early musical education from his mother before attending Mount Milleray Roman Catholic University; All Hallows College, Dublin and Carlow College. Studied music with Dr. Kerbusch and with **R.P. Stewart**. Also studied theology. The National University of Ireland awarded him D.Mus. honorarily in 1907, and he received the Order of St. Gregory in 1922.
Organist of the Star of the Sea Church, Sandymount, Dublin (from 1877); Belfast pro-Cathedral (from 1878); Thurles Cathedral (from 1882); Clongowes Wood College, County Kildare (from 1884); Monaghan Cathedral (from 1888) and Enniscorthy Cathedral (1895-1928).
Taught music at St. McCartan's College, Monaghan; St. Kieran's College, Kilkenny and at the Jesuit Colleges at Clongowes Wood and Tullabeg, as well as at Belfast Ladies' College. Classics and music master of St. Wilfrid's College, Uttoxeter, Staffordshire.
Conductor of the d'Oyly Carte Opera Company. Bandmaster of the 104th Regiment - the last civilian to hold such a position in Ireland.

A local choral society conductor and festival adjudicator. Held the unusual position as demonstrator at Dublin Museum.
Wrote on aspects of Irish music and musicians, contributing to the third edition of Grove's *Dictionary of Music and Musicians* and to *Dictionary of National Biography*. His works include *History of Irish Music* and *Story of the Harp*. Irish correspondent of *Musical Times*.
Composed music for the Roman Catholic Church, including the Masses *of St. Aidan* and *of St. Carthage* and Benediction Services. His hymn tune 'Rex' was used in *With One Voice* (1978) with the hymn 'Hail Redeemer! King Divine' by Patrick Brennan. Other compositions include part songs and items for piano.

FLOOD JONES, Revd. Samuel (1826-1895)
Born at Southwark, London on 3 October 1826; died in London on 26 February 1895 and buried in Westminster Abbey.
Educated at Pembroke College, Oxford.
Curate of St. Martin-in-the-Fields, London (1852-1854). A deputy minor canon (from 1857) and a minor canon (from 1859) of Westminster Abbey. Precentor of Westminster Abbey (1868-1895). Vicar of the London Churches of St. Matthew, Spring Gardens (1854-1876) and St. Botolph's, Aldersgate (1876-1895). Priest in ordinary to Queen Victoria (1869-1895).
Editor of *Hymns of Prayer and Praise* (1860) and co-editor of *Cathedral Psalter Chants*. His hymn tune 'St. Catherine' was used in *Methodist Hymn Book* (1933).

FLOWER, Eliza (1803-1846)
Born in Harlow, Essex on 19 April 1803; died in Hurstpierpoint, Sussex on 12 December 1846. Sister of Sarah Flower, the hymn writer. Composed hymns and anthems for the Finsbury Chapel, South Place, London. Wrote part songs including 'Now pray we for our country'.

FLOWERS, Dr. George French (1811-1872)
Born in Boston, Lincolnshire in 1811; died in London on 14 June 1872.
Studied in Germany under Johann Rinck and Schnyder von Wartensee. Graduated B.Mus. (1839) and D.Mus. (1865) at the University of Oxford.
Organist of the English Chapel, Paris and of St. Mark's Church, Myddleton Square, Clerkenwell, London. A teacher of singing. Editor of *Literary Gazette*. Sought, unsuccessfully, the vacant musical professorships of Oxford University (1848) and Gresham College (1863), the preferment going to **Henry Bishop** and **Henry Wylde** respectively.
Composer of the anthem 'To God ascribe the power'.

FLOYD, Dr. Alfred Ernest (1877-1974)
Born in Birmingham on 5 January 1877; died in Melbourne, Australia on 13 January 1974.
The son of a Welsh minister. Attended Bradford Grammar School, Yorkshire and The Leys School, Cambridge. Graduated B.Mus. (1912) at Queen's College, Oxford.
Accorded the Lambeth D.Mus., and appointed O.B.E. in 1948
Deputy organist of Winchester Cathedral (from 1898). Organist and choirmaster of Llangollen Parish Church (from 1900) and Oswestry Parish Church, Shropshire (from 1904). Taught music at Oswestry Grammar School (from 1906) and at Oswestry Boys' High School (from 1914). A local choral society conductor.

In 1914 he emigrated to Australia, becoming music critic of the *Melbourne Argus* and organist and director of the choir of St. Paul's Cathedral, Melbourne.

Composed an Evening Service, anthems, hymn tunes including 'Land of our birth', composed for *Methodist School Hymn Book* (1910), organ works, and part songs for women's voices and for men's voices.

FOOTE, Francis J. (19th/20th century)

Born in Tunbridge Wells, Kent. Studied at the Royal Academy of Music, where his teachers were Hans Wessely for violin, Theo Lierhammer and Frederic King for singing, Izard for piano, P. Parker for cello, **Frederick Corder**, and **Stewart Macpherson** for harmony. Founded and conducted the Tunbridge Wells Choral Society (1904). Composer of a Mass for Solo Voices, Choir and Orchestra, String Quartets in D Minor and in E, and a tone poem *Elaine*.

FOOTE, Guthrie Herbert (1897-1972)

Born in Kent on 15 January 1897; died in Haywards Heath, Sussex on 11 January 1972.

Attended Skinner's School, Tunbridge Wells, Kent and studied violin at the Royal Academy of Music. His studies were interrupted by active service in World War I and when he returned he entered the Royal College of Music. Studied conducting under **Henry Wood**.

Conductor of the Carla Rosa Opera Company. Founded the Tunbridge Wells Symphony Orchestra. Worked in the Music Department of Oxford University Press (from 1944) and later had the responsibility for hymn and service books. Retired in 1962 but continued to act as adviser to O.U.P. for the rest of his life. Consultant for the third edition (1973) of *Church Hymnary*. Composed hymn tunes, including 'Tredegar' and 'Into Thy keeping', both of which are found in the Third Edition of *Church Hymnary*, as is 'Normandy' an arrangement of an old Normandy carol.

FORBES, Henry (1804-1859)

Born in London in 1804; died on 24 November 1859. Studied music under **George Smart**, Johann Hummel, Ignaz Moscheles and Heinrich Herz. A pianist and organist, he gave concerts with his brother, George. Organist of the Church of St. Luke, Chelsea, London. Edited a collection of Psalm tunes for four voices entitled *National Psalmody*. Composer of an oratorio *Ruth* (1847), songs and items for piano.

FORBES, Sebastian (b. 1941)

Born in Amersham, Buckinghamshire on 22 May 1941 of a Scottish family. His father, Watson Forbes, was a chamber musician.

A chorister at Hampstead Parish Church (1949-1956) under Sidwell. Studied at University College School, Hampstead and at the Royal Academy of Music (1958-1960) where he received instruction in composition from **Howard Ferguson**. Attended King's College, Cambridge (1960-1964) where he studied under Thurston Dart and **Philip Radcliffe**. Graduated M.A. and Mus.B. at the University of Cambridge.

A bass singer in the choir of King's College, Cambridge (1961-1964).

Assistant organist of the Church of St. Clement Danes, London (from 1960). Organist of St. Andrew's, Kingsbury, London (1964-

1965); St. Giles, Cripplegate (1966-1967), and, briefly, Trinity College, Cambridge (1968).

A B.B.C. Radio Producer within the Music Division (1964-1967). A lecturer at the University College of North Wales, Bangor (1968-1972). Subsequently a lecturer of music at the University of Surrey; professor from 1981.

Has composed various orchestral, chamber, organ, vocal and choral works including a piano trio, madrigals, *Four Psalms* for Soprano and Organ, anthems including 'Haec dies' (Psalm 118), two hymn tunes, *Sequence of Carols* (1967) and two chants. His works are written in an idiom that puts them beyond all but the most competent of amateur choirs.

FORBES, Thomas Lawrence (1833-1903)

Born in Newington, Surrey in 1833; died in Hampstead, London on 9 May 1903. An amateur organist and composer. Compiled *Church Tune and Chorale Book* (1858). Composer of the hymn tune 'Come sing', used in *Hymns Ancient and Modern* with the hymn, translated from Latin, 'Come sing, ye choirs exultant'.

FORD, Dr. Charles Edgar (1881-?)

Born in Penn Fields, Wolverhampton in 1881.

Trained in music at Southwark Cathedral. Studied with **C.H. Kitson**. Graduated B.Mus (1908) and D.Mus. (1913) at New College, Oxford.

Organist and choirmaster of Penn Fields Parish Church (1897-1901) and assistant organist of Southwark Cathedral (1901-1908). Organist and choirmaster of the London Churches of St. Clement, Arundel Square (1902-1906); Roehampton Parish Church (1906-1917) and St. Saviour, Ealing (from 1917). Lived in the suburb of Chiswick.

A lecturer and examiner for Trinity College of Music, a festival adjudicator and an organ recitalist, activities that took him to South Africa, Australia, New Zealand, Canada and India.

Composed an Evening Sevice in G, anthems, a Festal Hymn, a Fantasy for Organ, songs, part songs and items for piano and for organ.

FORD, Revd. David Everard (1797-1875)

Born in Long Melford, Suffolk on 13 September 1797; died in Bedford on 23 October 1875. Organist of Lymington Parish Church, Hampshire. A minister of the Congregational Church. Composed many hymn tunes, seven books of which were published between 1827 and 1836. Disillusioned by their lack of success and quoted as saying, 'Psalmody is the most unprofitable of labours', he turned instead to hymn writing. This activity was however no more successful. Some of his tunes were eventually popular for a while. Wrote a book on the elements of music. His song 'The negro slave', dedicated to William Wilberforce, was popular for a time.

FORD, Ernest A.C. (1858-1919)

Born in Warminster, Wiltshire on 17 February 1858; died in London on 2 June 1919.

Trained with **John Richardson**, organist of Salisbury Cathedral and with a Dr. Dyer of Weston-super-Mare, Somerset. He was the first Sir John Goss scholar (from 1875) at the Royal Academy of Music, where he studied under **Arthur Sullivan**. Later studied in Paris with Edouard Lalo.

A leading conductor of the time. His London conductorships included the Royal English Opera House, to which he was appointed by Richard D'Oyly Carte, and the Empire Theatre,

Leicester Square. Chosen by Sullivan to conduct the first performance of the opera *Ivanhoe* (1891).

From 1916 he was a professor of singing at Guildhall School of Music.

Author of *A Short History of Music in England* (1912).

Composed a motet *Domine Deus* as a commission from the University of Harvard, U.S.A. to celebrate its 250th anniversary. Also composed operas, a String Quartet in F Minor, and songs. His operetta *Jane Annie* was given at the Savoy Theatre, and *House of Lords* was put on at the Lyric Theatre. His Bacchanale for Orchestra was given at the Queen's Hall, London under the conductor **Henry Wood**.

FORD, Thomas (c1580-1648)

Born in London around the year 1580; died in November 1648 and buried at St. Margaret's Church, Westminster, London on 17 November.

A lute player, he was a musician to Henry, Prince of Wales, son of James I (from 1611). In 1626 he was one of the musicians of Charles I.

In 1607 he published a collection *Musicke of Sundry Kindes...* containing material composed by him and including songs and pavans. The songs that he composed were both sacred and secular and in the latter field his madrigal 'Since first I saw your face' is perhaps the best remembered.

Also known for a number of anthems including 'Almighty God, who hast me brought', 'Let God arise' and 'Not unto us'. The hymn tune 'Ford' was used in *Hymns Ancient and Modern* with the translation of the Latin hymn 'O merciful Creator, hear'.

FOREST, ?John (14th/15th century)

The composer Forest is probably John Forest, who was born probably between 1365 and 1370 and died on 25 March 1446. John Forest was a member of Lincoln College, Oxford and a canon of Lincoln Cathedral. From 1415 he was archdeacon of Surrey and he also served as dean of Wells (1425-1446). Composed a Credo and a number of motets. Other works are sometimes attributed to him but their authorship is uncertain. Compositions by him are found in a number of Italian collections.

FORREST, Charles Henry (1846-1925)

Born in Birmingham in 1846; died in Lancashire in 1925. Composer of the hymns 'Where hast thou gleaned today' (1897) and 'The sacrifice and the song' (1897), and hymn tunes.

FORSTER, J.F. (19th century)

An organist of Somerset who lived around the year 1850. Composer of the anthems 'Give peace in our time' and 'If we say we have no sin'.

FORSYTH, Cecil (1870-1941)

Born in Greenwich, London on 30 November 1870; died in New York on 7 December 1941. Studied at the University of Edinburgh, and under **C.V. Stanford** and **Hubert Parry**, at the Royal College of Music. A viola player, he became a member of the Queen's Hall Orchestra. Also played at the Savoy Opera, where two of his own comic operas *Westward Ho!* and *Cinderella*, were produced. Following the outbreak of World War I he took up residence in the U.S.A. His books include *Music and Nationalism*, *Orchestration* (1914) and, with C.V. Stanford, *A History of Music* (1916).

Composed sacred music, songs, a Viola Concerto and other instrumental works.

FORTAY, James Butler (1856-1924)

Born in Liverpool on 26 October 1856; died in Liverpool on 31 March 1924.

Studied under D.C. Browne and G.W. Rohner.

Organist of the Liverpool Churches of St. Columba; St. Ambrose (1874-1879); Emmanuel, Everton (1879-1891); St. Michael-in-the-Hamlet (1891-1898) and Trinity Presbyterian Church (from 1898).

Taught and lectured in the city of Liverpool; music lecturer to the Corporation of Liverpool.

Composed a number of hymn tunes and chants, some of which were used in contemporary collections such as *Church of England Hymnal* and *Chant Book Companion*. A Kyrie was published in 1893. Also composed songs including 'Night and morning' and piano pieces.

FOSS, Hubert James (1899-1953)

Born in Croydon, Surrey on 2 May 1899; died in Golders Green, London on 27 May 1953.

Educated at Bradfield College, Berkshire.

At the age of 25, in 1924, he was appointed music editor of Oxford University Press. Later became the head of the music department, (until 1941). Launched the compositional career of **William Walton** and took over exclusively the work of **Ralph Vaughan Williams**. Quickly built up the O.U.P. music catalogue. His advice and guidance proved helpful to a number of young composers, and Vaughan Williams often sought his opinion.

Married to the singer, Dora Stevens, and accompanied her on piano at recitals.

Author of *Ralph Vaughan Williams: a Study* (1950).

Hubert Foss was a versatile musician but his compositions are few. They include a hymn tune 'Croydon', which he wrote in his teens and which was used in *Songs of Praise* (1931). His other works include *Seven Poems of Thomas Hardy* (1925) for Solo Baritone, Male Chorus and Piano.

FOSTER, Anthony (b.1926)

Born in Gravesend, Kent on 11 April 1926.

Attended Gravesend Grammar School, and educated privately in music with Anne Collins and Arthur Tracy Robson for piano, the parish church organists John Cook (Holy Trinity, Stratford-on-Avon) and John Webster (St. Mary the Virgin, Oxford) and, for orchestration, Gordon Jacob and Richard Arnell.

Pursued a teaching career, with appointments at schools in Stratford-on-Avon, Oxford and Brighton between 1952 and 1977.

Organist and choirmaster (1948-1972) of the Churches of All Saints, Perry Street, Northfleet, Kent and, in Brighton, Sussex, All Souls, St. Matthias and St. Augustine of Canterbury.

His church music includes the *St. Richard* Evening Service (1981) and the unison *St. Wilfrid* Communion Service (1986), the anthems 'All people that on earth do dwell' (1964) and 'My song shall be alway' (1981), plus carols, hymns and a Chant in G to the Nunc Dimittis (1976).

His other works are items for organ, orchestral pieces and vocal music. Has composed music for the schools' programme 'Young Music Makers' (B.B.C. Radio Brighton).

FOSTER, Henry Joseph (1845-1910)
Born in Northampton on 11 October 1845; died in Southport, Lancashire on 9 June 1910. Composer of hymn tunes.

FOSTER, James (1807-1885)
Born in Bristol, Gloucestershire on 12 September 1807; died in Bristol on 7 June 1885. A builder, self-taught musically. Organist of the Tabernacle Congregational Church, Bristol. With Revd. J.J. Waite he published the collection *Hallelujah!* with the objective of improving the standard of congregational singing. It contained his own tune 'Pembroke'.

FOSTER, John (?-1677)
Died on 20 April 1677. Organist of Durham Cathedral from December 1660 until his death. Composer of a quantity of church music, including three services and 11 anthems including 'Glory be to God' and 'If the Lord Himself'.

FOSTER, John (1827-1915)
Born in Staines, Middlesex in August 1827; died in Hampstead, London on 25 March 1915.
A chorister at St. George's Chapel, Windsor Castle from the age of nine, and a pupil of the chapel organist, **George Elvey**.
A tenor singer, he was a gentleman of the Chapel Royal.
In 1862 he was appointed by Eton College to rehearse the Music Society, of which the young **Hubert Parry** was a member. He later became Eton's master of singing.
Succeeded **Richard Redhead** as organist at the Church of St. Andrew, Wells Street, London (1847-1856), where he established cathedral-style choral services. Upon his appointment as a lay vicar of Westminster Abbey he was succeeded by **Philip Armes**. Foster sang for 34 years in the Noblemen's and Gentlemen's Catch Club.
John Foster's *Ely Confession* was given its first performance by **Robert Janes**, organist of Ely Cathedral.
Composed chants, some of which are found in *Cathedral Psalter Chants* (1875). His glee 'Sweet queen of autumn' for Men's Voices won a prize in 1852.

FOSTER, Myles Birket (1851-1922)
Born in St. Marylebone, London on 29 November 1851; died in Acton, Middlesex on 18 December 1922. Son of the artist Birket Foster.
Educated in Brighton, Sussex and at Guildford Grammar School, Surrey, studying music privately with **Hamilton Clarke**.
Discouraged by his family from pursuing a career in music. Began work with a firm of stockbrokers from the age of 20. Eventually however he studied at the Royal Academy of Music under **Arthur Sullivan**, **Frederick Westlake** and **Ebenezer Prout**, his chosen instruments being oboe, cello and clarinet.
London organist of St. James's Church, Marylebone (1873-1875); St. George's Church, Notting Hill Gate (1875-1879); the Foundling Hospital (1880-1892) and St. Alban's, Holborn.
Worked for the publishers Boosey and Company, and as a musical examiner for Trinity College of Music, London. The latter appointment caused him to travel to Australia (1895), where he was the first visiting English examiner and remained six years, and South Africa.
In his book *Anthems and Anthem Composers* (1901, republished 1971), an authoritative book of reference, he criticised those composers whose motivation in writing sacred music was mainly financial, or who wrote in such a way as to court popularity.

In 1913, its centenary year, he compiled a history of the Philharmonic Society. Editor of *Methodist Free Church Hymns* (1889).
Composed an Evening Service in C for Men's Voices; a Service in A for the Festival of the Sons of the Clergy, St. Paul's Cathedral (1883); a setting of the Holy Communion Service in B-flat and anthems.
His hymn tune 'Crucis milites' was employed in *Hymns Ancient and Modern* with the hymn 'Soldiers of Christ, arise'. His 'Crucis victoria' was also used, in conjunction with the hymn 'Lift up your heads ye gates of brass'. 'Salvator' was used in the Revised Edition (1927) of *Church Hymnary* with the hymn 'When the Lord of love was here' by Stopford Brooke. Also composed instrumental works, cantatas and songs for children.

FOWLE, Dr. Thomas Lloyd (1827-?)
Born in Amesbury, Wiltshire on 16 October 1827, the son of a prebendary of Salisbury Cathedral.
Graduated with a doctorate in philosophy from the University of Giessen, Germany. Musically self-taught.
His involvement with the awarding of degrees *in absentia* by Trinity University, Toronto, Canada led to great concern and accusation of sham qualifications being issued. The Union of Graduates in Music was established in 1893 as a result in order to protect the position of graduates of British universities.
Organist of his father's church in Amesbury, and later at a church in Crawley, Sussex. Wrote on the lives of Dickens and **Handel**, and was the author of a novel, *Gentle Edith*. In 1856 he became an editor and publisher.
Published anthems and Services.

FOWLES, Dr. Leonard Nowell (1870-1939)
Born in Portsea, Hampshire in 1870; died in Isleworth, Middlesex in 1939.
Educated at Brussels Conservatory and studied viola at the Royal College of Music. Graduated B.Mus. (1899) and D.Mus. (1904) at the University of London.
Organist and choirmaster of the Presbyterian Church, St. John's Wood, London (from 1905). Also conducted for local choral and orchestral societies.
Composed a Lenten Cantata *Calvary*, hymn tunes including 'Golders Green', one of his nine tunes found in *Congregational Hymnary* (1916), and works for violin and for organ.

FOWLES, Margaret F. (1846-1907)
Born in Ryde, Isle of Wight in 1846; died on 6 August while visiting her sister in the American city of Detroit. The daughter of an artist.
Studied piano, harmony and counterpoint with W.J.C. Masters, organ with **E.J. Hopkins**, and voice production and singing under Emil Behnke, Alberto Randegger and William Shakespeare.
At the age of 15, Margaret Fowles became organist of the Church of St. James, Ryde, succeeding her father. In 1878 she succeeded her brother, Claude, as organist and choir director of St. Michael's Church, Swanmore, Ryde. Founded the Ryde Choral Union in 1874 and remained as conductor until 1894.
Composed anthems including 'If ye love me, keep my Commandments' (1880), hymn tunes and songs. Published *Six original hymn tunes* (c1870).

FOX, Arthur Makinson (1863-1949)
Born in Dorchester, Dorset in 1863; died in Teddington, Middlesex on 4 June 1949. Graduated B.Mus. at the University of London (1893). Organist of Christ Church, Teddington (1882-1886). Composer of anthems, hymn tunes, carols and songs. His works include the funeral motet *As we have borne* (1940) and the carol 'Chant we hymns of adoration' (1900).

FOX, Dr. Christopher (b.1955)
Born in York on 10 March 1955. Studied at Liverpool, Southampton and the University of York, and with **Jonathan Harvey**. Graduated D.Phil. in composition (1984). Composer of the anthem 'Jerusalem is builded' (1987), for the centenary of Southlands Methodist Church, York.

FOX, William (?-1579)
Died in Ely, Cambridgeshire in September 1579 and was buried on the 10th of that month. A church musician and composer about whom very little is known, except that he was associated with Ely Cathedral from 1572 to 1579. Composer of the anthem 'Teach me Thy way', republished in the 19th century.

FOXELL, Revd. William James (c1857-1933)
Died in 1933 at the age of 76.
Graduated B.A. (1877) B.Mus. (1882) and M.A. (1893) at the University of London. Ordained deacon in 1881, priest in 1882 at St. Albans Cathedral.
An assistant master at Chigwell Grammar School, Essex and curate of All Souls' Church, Chigwell Row (1881-1883). Headmaster of Amersham Grammar School, Buckinghamshire and chaplain of the Amersham Union (1883-1886).
A minor canon of Canterbury Cathedral, and rector of St. Swithin's, London Stone with St. Mary Bothaw, London (1903-1933). President of Sion College in 1917 and in 1921.
Composed a Service, songs for boys and hymn tunes.

FRANCIS, John (1789-1843)
Born on 20 March 1789; died on 19 August 1843. A miller by trade, he learned music and began to compose while quite young. Precentor of Pen-Lan Congregational Chapel, Pwllheli, Wales. The periodical *Seren Gomer* for November 1821 contained his hymn tunes 'Mwyneidd-dra' and 'Gomer'. The March 1823 issue contained 'Pwllheli', also known as 'Morwyddon'. Also composed an anthem on Psalm 39 'I said, I will take heed to my ways', used in worship in Caernarvonshire, Wales.

FRASER, Shena Eleanor (b.1910)
Born in Stirling, Scotland on 26 May 1910. Educated at Queen Margaret's School, Scarborough, Yorkshire and at the Royal College of Music. A piano recitalist and lecturer in the field of adult education. Has composed anthems, the chorale suite *To Him give praise* for women's voices, carols including 'A Boy was born', part songs and instrumental pieces. Her tutorial *Sing At Sight* was published in 1981.

FRICKER, Dr. Herbert Austin (1868-1943)
Born in Canterbury, Kent in 1868; died in 1943.
A chorister of Canterbury Cathedral and, at the age of 15, a deputy organist.
Graduated B.Mus. at the University of Durham in 1893. Awarded the honorary D.Mus. by the University of Toronto, Canada.

Organist and choirmaster of Holy Trinity Church, Eastbourne, Sussex for 10 years and deputy organist of Canterbury Cathedral (1884-1894).
His career then centred on the city of Leeds for 19 years: he was organist of the town hall (from 1898) and of the Churches of St. Aidan (from 1900) and St. Michael, Headingley (from 1902). In addition he was chorus master of the Leeds Music Festivals of 1907 and 1910; he conducted for local choral and orchestral societies and he was organist and choirmaster of the Chapel of Leeds Grammar School. In 1917 he moved to Torquay, Devon.
He then emigrated to Canada where he was organist and choirmaster of the Metropolitan Church, Toronto and founder and conductor of the Mendelssohn Choir.
Composed a Magnificat and Nunc Dimittis in G (1897), anthems including 'The king of love my Shepherd is' (1912), organ works, songs and part songs.

FRICKER, Dr. Peter Racine (1920-1990)
Born in London on 5 September 1920; died on 1 February 1990. Educated at St. Paul's School, London and at the Royal College of Music (1937-1941) where he studied theory and composition with **R.O. Morris**, organ with **Ernest Bullock** and piano with Wilson. From 1945 he studied at Morley College under Matyas Seiber. Received the Honorary D.Mus. from the University of Leeds in 1958.
Following war service as a radio operator in the R.A.F., Fricker was a copyist and arranger. Succeeded **Michael Tippett** as director of music at Morley College, London (1953-1964). A professor of the R.C.M. (1955-1964). From 1964 he was a professor of music at the University of California, Santa Barbara.
Composed five symphonies, concertos, chamber music, incidental music, songs, *Two Motets* (1955-1956), *Two Carols* (1956) and a Magnificat (1968). *Vision of Judgment* was commissioned for the Leeds Festival of 1958.

FRIPP, Edward Bowles (1787-1870)
Born in Kingsdown, Bristol on 29 January 1787; died in Teignmouth, Devon on 1 September 1870. Honorary organist of St. James's Church, Bristol and of the Parish Churches of Westbury, Gloucestershire and Hutton, Weston-super-Mare, Somerset. An editor of church music. Composer of a hymn tune 'Charmouth', and other items for the church.

FRITH, John (17th century)
Supplicated for his Oxford B.Mus. with a work in seven parts (1636). Organist of St. John's College, Oxford. Composer of a Service in G.

FROGGATT, James Anthony (b.1946)
Born in Stockport, Cheshire on 16 August 1946.
Learned to play piano from the age of six. Attended King's School, Macclesfield, later studying at the University of Manchester and the Royal Manchester College of Music and graduating B.Mus (1969). Studied organ with Eric Chadwick, Brian Runnett and **Noel Rawsthorne**, and piano with Hedwig Stein.
A percussionist with the B.B.C. Northern Symphony Orchestra and organist of the University Church, Manchester. Assistant organist of Guildford Cathedral (1970-1977).
Organist of Portsmouth Cathedral (1977-1990), and a teacher at Portsmouth Grammar School.

Has composed seasonal introits, descants, a congregational setting of the Mass and carol arrangements, one of which is 'What Child is this?'.

FROST, Dr. Charles Joseph (1848-1918)
Born in Westbury-on-Trym, Somerset on 20 June 1848; died in Greenwich, London on 13 October 1918.
As a child he moved to Tewkesbury, Gloucestershire where his father became a school teacher and organist of Trinity Church.
Studied with his father and with **George Cooper, Charles Steggall** and **John Goss**. Graduated Mus.B. (1877) and Mus.D. (1882) at Sidney Sussex College, Cambridge.
A talented organist and pianist. Organist of a number of churches in London and the south west, namely St. James's, Cheltenham, Gloucestershire; Holy Trinity Westbury-on-Trym (1867-1869); Holy Trinity, Weston-super-Mare, Somerset (1869-1873); Holy Trinity, Lee, London (1873-1876); St. Mary's, Haggerston (1876-1880); Christ Church, Newgate Street, London (1880-1884) and St. Peter's, Brockley, Kent (from 1884).
In 1880 he became a professor at Guildhall School of Music. An author and recitalist. Head of music at Goldsmiths' College, London (1894-1904) and conductor of the college choir and orchestra. Contributed articles to *Musical Opinion* and other periodicals.
Composer of a Festival Te Deum, services and anthems. His hymn tunes 'Barmouth', 'Dulwich' and 'Harvest' were used in *Hymns Ancient and Modern*, while 'Weston' is found in *Church Hymns* (1875) as an accompaniment to the hymn 'How blessed from the bonds of care'. A collection of Responses to the Commandments published around 1875 includes two settings by Charles Frost. Also composed an oratorio *Nathan's Parable* (1878), songs, organ voluntaries and works for piano.

FROST, Henry Frederick (1848-1901)
Born in London on 15 March 1848; died on 3 May 1901. Brother of **William Frost**.
In 1856, Frost became a chorister of St. George's Chapel, Windsor Castle. From 1865 he studied organ under Sebastian Hart of St. Peter's Church, Great Windmill Street, London.
Within three weeks of becoming Hart's pupil, Frost was appointed as his assistant. From December 1865, when he was 17, until 1891 he was organist of the Chapel Royal, Savoy Hill.
In 1874 he was appointed music critic of *Weekly Despatch*. Later, music critic of *The Academy, The Athanaeum* and *The Standard*. On the staff of *Musical Times* for many years.
A professor of harmony and sight singing of Madame Dolby's Academy and a professor of piano at Guildhall School of Music (from 1880). Resigned from both appointments in 1888. Gave public lectures and wrote a book on the life of Schubert.
His compositions include hymn tunes and chants for the use of the Chapel Royal, Savoy Hill.

FROST, Percy Hollingworth (1847-1918)
Born in Barnet, Hertfordshire on 8 June 1847; died in Buxton, Derbyshire on 2 September 1918. Composer of a Benedicite in A (1890), and hymn tunes.

FROST, William Alfred (1850-1929)
Born in London on 7 November 1850; died on Whit Sunday 1929. Brother of **Henry Frost**.
A chorister of St. George's Chapel, Windsor Castle (1859-1866).

Moved to London in 1869. Sang alto in a number of church choirs, namely Archbishop Tenison's Chapel - since renamed and known as St. Thomas's Church, Regent Street (1869-1870); St. Andrew's, Wells Street (1870-1872) and All Saints, Margaret Street (from 1872).
In March 1873 he became an assistant vicar choral of St. Paul's Cathedral. On the death of **W.A. Barrett**, Frost took up the vacant place as vicar choral. At St. Paul's he taught piano and singing at the choir school from 1888. Known as a successful trainer of alto singers.
His compositions include Morning, Holy Communion and Evening Services for Men's Voices, composed at the request of the Cathedral organist **John Stainer** for use in St. Paul's. His anthems include 'I will go unto the altar of God', and he composed songs and part songs.

FROST, William Lane (1847-1920)
Born in Somerset in 1847; died in Richmond, Surrey in 1920. Composer of the harvest-tide anthem 'His wonderful works' (1904), the anniversary anthem 'Victory! Alleluia!' (1918), and hymn tunes.

FRYE, Frederick Robert (1851-1942)
Born in Brook, near Ashford, Kent in 1851; died in August 1942.
A pupil of **Alfred Legge**, organist of his local parish church; **E.H. Turpin**; James Higgs; **F.E. Gladstone** and F.W. Davenport.
Graduated Mus. B. at the University of Cambridge (1887).
Organist and choirmaster of the Church of St. Nicholas, New Romney, Kent (from 1871) and of St. Mary's Church, Chelmsford, Essex (from 1876). The latter church was raised to cathedral status in 1914, whereupon Frye continued in his two positions and remained in office until his retirement in June 1942.
A local choral and orchestral society conductor.
Composed an Evening Service in B-flat (1898), songs, a madrigal, items for piano, and a Fantasia for Organ (1912).

FRYE (ffry, Frey, Frie), Walter (? -before 1475)
Died before 5 June 1475. A member of the Guild of St. Nicholas, London from 1457. Also associated with the Court of Burgundy.
His compositions include songs, a rondeau, motets including *Ave regina caelorum* and three Masses. His compositions were as popular in northern Europe as they were in England.

FULLER, Dr. Robert (?-1743)
Died in Cambridge in 1743.
Graduated Mus.D. at the University of Cambridge in 1724.
Thomas Tudway, organist of King's College, was suspended in 1706, from which time Robert Fuller, a lay clerk, served as acting organist.
Succeeded Tudway as organist of King's College, Cambridge (1727-1742). From 1730 he was also master of the choristers of King's and from 1731 he was organist to the University. It is likely that this person is the same Robert Fuller who was master of the choristers of Trinity College, Cambridge from 1717.
Composed seven anthems including 'Behold, I bring you' and 'I will always give thanks'.

FULLER MAITLAND, John Alexander (1856-1936)
Born in London on 7 April 1856; died in Carnforth, Lancashire on 30 March 1936.

Attended Westminster School and Trinity College, Cambridge, where he graduated B.A. His M.A. followed in 1882. Studied piano with Edward Dannreuther and W.S. Rockstro.

Music critic of *Pall Mall Gazette* (1882-1884), *The Times* (1889-1911) and *Manchester Guardian* (1884-1889). Lectured on the history of English music. Pianist of the Bach Choir, and was also known as a harpsichordist.

Associated with Grove's *Dictionary of Music and Musicians*. Contributed to the first edition (1879-1889) and edited the appendix. Editor in chief of the second edition (1904-1910). Author of the fourth volume of *Oxford History of Music*.

Other editorships include *English Carols of the 15th Century* (1887). Collaborated with **Ralph Vaughan Williams** in the collection and publication of *English Country Songs* (1893).

Author of many books, including *The Music of Stanford and Parry* (1934). Composer of vesper hymns, including 'The bells of Paradise' (1916).

FUSSELL, Peter (1750-1802)
Born in Winchester, Hampshire in 1750; died in Winchester in July 1802. A chorister of Winchester Cathedral under **James Kent**, whom he succeeded in 1774. Retained the appointment until the year of his death. A teacher of music. Among his pupils was Charles Dibdin the elder, composer of the song 'Tom Bowling'. His Single Chant in G was included in *Cathedral Psalter Chants* (1875) as a setting of Psalm 98. A Single Chant in F is found in the Revised Edition (1927) of *Church Hymnary*.

G

GABRIEL (March), Mary Ann Virginia (1825-1877)
Born in Banstead, Surrey on 7 February 1825; died in London on 7 August 1877, following a coach accident. Studied music with Pixis, Döhler, Thalberg and Wilhelm Molique. An accomplished ballad composer with compositions including 'Across the Sea' and 'Wake, my Beloved'. Composed the anthem 'The Lord is my Portion' (1858).

GADSBY, Henry Robert (1842-1907)
Born in Hackney, London on 15 December 1842; died in Putney, London on 11 November 1907.
A chorister of St. Paul's Cathedral (1849-1858); almost an exact contemporary of **John Stainer**. Both boys were identified as having superior musical ability. They learned harmony with the master of the boys, **William Bayley**. Also received lessons from **George Cooper**.
Early in his career he was organist in London of St. Ann's Church, Blackfriars, and of Camden Church, Camberwell. Organist at the Church of St. Peter, Brockley, London (until 1884). In that year he succeeded **John Hullah** as professor of harmony at Queen's College, London. One of the original professors of Guildhall School of Music, London (founded in 1880).
Sang in the choir at the open-air service at St. Paul's Cathedral celebrating the Diamond Jubilee of Queen Victoria on 22 June 1897, and involved in the Handel Commemorations.
A member of the Philharmonic Society.
Wrote on harmony and sight singing. A talented artist, producing sketches and watercolours.
Composed Services, two of which were for the annual Festival of the Sons of the Clergy at St. Paul's Cathedral: 'Gadsby in C' was popular in Victorian times. There are some 10 anthems; a musical scene 'The Forest of Arden'; cantatas including *The Lord of the Isles* (1879); songs; part songs, services and a set of Responses to the Commandments. His anthems include a setting of Psalm 130 'Out of the deep' for eight voices (1872).
His Symphonies in C and in A were performed at the Crystal Palace during the 1870s.
Gadsby's hymn tune 'St. Boniface' was used in the Standard Edition (1916) of *Hymns Ancient and Modern* with the hymn 'Forward! Be our watchword' by Henry Alford.

GAFFE, George (1849-1907)
Born in Cawston, Norfolk on 27 July 1849; died in 1907.
From the age of nine he was a chorister of Norwich Cathedral. For seven years he was a pupil of the cathedral organist, **Zechariah Buck,** to whom he was later assistant.
Organist of Oswestry Parish Church, Shropshire (from 1874). Founded a music school in the town with **Henry Leslie**. Also set up a choral society.
Organist of St. Albans Cathedral (1880-1907).
Founded, and was principal of, the St. Albans College of Music.
Composed an Evening Service (1878) a hymn 'O father, whose Almighty hand' (1897) and a setting of the Offertory Sentences (1893).

GALE, Clement Rowland (19th/20th century)
Graduated B.A. (1883) and B.Mus. (1889) at Exeter College, Oxford.
Organist of Reading School, Berkshire (1883-1885), moving to Scotland in the latter year and becoming organist of Craigmount School, Edinburgh (1885-1890) and a music teacher at the John Watson Institute.
In 1890 he emigrated to the U.S.A. where he was organist and precentor of the Calvary Episcopal Church, New York and was associated with the Church of All Angels. Choirmaster of St. George's Church, Newburgh, New York State. A choral society conductor.
Composed a Benedicite in D (1900) and settings of the Magnificat and Nunc Dimittis in D (1893) and in F (1899) and anthems such as 'I heard a Voice from Heaven' (1895).

GALL, C. (17th century)
The composer Gall is known to have been alive in 1625. *Hymns Ancient and Modern*, Standard Edition (1924) employs his tune 'Beccles' with 'The great forerunner of the morn', a translation of a Latin hymn.

GALL, Revd. James (1808-?)
Born in Edinburgh on 27 September 1808. A member of the family firm of publishers, James Gall & Sons, which later became Gall & Inglis. It was the firm's policy to make selected hymn books available cheaply. An invention by James Gall helped to reduce the

costs of printing in general. Also known for his work within the Sunday School movement. Composer of hymn tunes.

GARBUTT, Clarkson (1827-1906)
Born in Hull, Yorkshire in 1827; died in Hornsey, London on 2 March 1906. His work is found in *Hymns and Psalms* (1983).

GARDINER, Henry Balfour (1877-1950)
Born in London on 7 November 1877; died in Salisbury, Wiltshire on 28 June, 1950.
Attended school in Eltham, London and studied organ under T.S. Guyer of Bexhill. Attended private schools in Margate and Folkestone, Kent and Temple Gate School, East Sheen, Surrey. Learned to play piano from the age of five and began to compose at nine. It was his ambition to be a concert pianist but when problems later developed with his left hand he was unable to fulfil his aim.
In 1891 he entered Charterhouse on a senior scholarship. Later attended Frankfurt Conservatory (1894-1896), studying composition under Iwan Knorr and piano with Lazzaro Uzielli. Influenced musically by Wagner and Tchaikovsky. Later became a friend and biographer of the latter.
His British contemporaries at Frankfurt included the composers Percy Grainger, Cyril Scott, **Roger Quilter** and Norman O'Neill.
Returned to England in 1896 as a student at New College, Oxford where he read and graduated in classics, and became friendly with (subsequently professor) Donald Tovey. Continued to visit Frankfurt, and studied conducting at Sonderhausen Conservatory.
The early part of his career was almost entirely devoted to composition, apart from a term on the music staff of Winchester College (1907) and for a period spent collecting folk songs in Hampshire (1905-1906).
Between March 1912 and March 1913, he backed eight concerts of British contemporary music, featuring his former fellow-students at Frankfurt and helping to establish their careers. A man of private means, Balfour Gardiner assisted **Gustav Holst** and Frederick Delius financially as well as promoting their works.
Joined the army in 1916 as a private. Like his fellow-composer Ivor Gurney, he came to admire the character and resilience of his comrades in arms. Later promoted to sub-lieutenant, and subsequently given the task of guarding prisoners of war in Wales, acting also as interpreter. The detainees worked as woodcutters, and the job of guarding them entailed long walks through the woods.
Balfour Gardiner found the work agreeable and in 1925, by which time he had come to feel out of sympathy with prevailing tastes in new music, he became involved with an afforestation project in Dorset.
Composed works for stage, songs, and pieces for piano. His short orchestral item 'Shepherd Fennel's Dance' (1911) was a success. In the realm of church music his most enduring work is his Evening Hymn (1908), a setting of the Latin hymn 'Te lucis ante terminum'. It has been suggested that his independent means took away some of the drive to compose that motivated his contemporaries.

GARDINER, William (1770-1853)
Born in Leicester on 15 March 1770; died in Leicester on 16 November 1853.
In a varied career he was a hosiery manufacturer, choirmaster, writer, musical editor and minor composer. His business often took him to mainland Europe, where he became familiar with the music of the day, particularly that of Germany. Built up an extensive knowledge, particularly of the works of Beethoven.
Trained a chorus of some hundred voices for the Leicester Festival of 1827. Sang as a member of the semichorus at the Coronation of Queen Victoria (1838).
Arranged and adapted works by Haydn, Mozart and Beethoven, in some cases considerably out of their original context and sometimes in questionable taste. He justified this treatment on the grounds that the church music of the day was very dry. Some of these works were extremely popular, especially in the Midlands.
His *Sacred Melodies from Haydn, Mozart and Beethoven...* (1812-1815) sold well. Two tunes from *Sacred Melodies*, 'Fulda' and 'Belmont' may have been composed by him.
A writer, whose works include *The Music of Nature* and *Music and Friends*.
Composed songs, glees, an oratorio *Judah* (which was actually a musical compilation from the works of Haydn, Mozart and Beethoven) and duets, sometimes under the pseudonym of W.G. Leicester. Composed a number of anthems, including 'One thing have I desired' (1843) and 'Holy, Holy, Holy'. A Psalm tune by him is under the pen name of Paxton.

GARDNER, Revd. George Lawrence Harter (1850-1925)
Born in Cheltenham, Gloucestershire on 1 December 1850; died in Marlow, Buckinghamshire on 20 September 1925.
Graduated B.Mus. at Christ Church College, Oxford (1875); B.A. (1873) and M.A. (1876) at Corpus Christi College, Cambridge. Ordained deacon in 1875 and priest a year later.
Following a curacy at St. Mary's Church, Nottingham (1875-1884) he was curate (1884-1886) and vicar (from 1886) of All Saints' Church, Cheltenham and an honorary canon of Gloucester Cathedral. Archdeacon of Cheltenham for four years, and of Aston. An honorary canon of Birmingham Cathedral.
Author of *Musical Worship* (1918), and co-editor, with **S.H. Nicholson** of *English Church Music* (1923). A member of the Archbishops' Committee on Church Music, and of the Church Music Society.
Encouraged by Granville Bantock, he composed a Te Deum (1915), an Evening Service and three settings of the Holy Communion Service. Composed anthems and provided tunes for *Hymns Ancient and Modern* (new Standard Edition).

GARDNER, John Linton (b.1917)
Born in Manchester on 2 March 1917.
Educated at Eagle House School and Wellington College, Berkshire. While still at school, he took lessons in counterpoint from **Gordon Jacob**. In 1935 he became organ scholar of Exeter College, Oxford where he studied under **Ernest Walker**, **H.P. Allen** and **Thomas Armstrong**. Graduated B.Mus. in 1939.
Appointed C.B.E. in 1976.
Chief music master of Repton School (1939-1940). Joined the Royal Air Force in 1940 as an aircraft-hand/musician, being promoted to bandmaster (1941-1943) and, finally, navigator. Répétiteur and assistant conductor of the Covent Garden Opera Company (1946-1952).
From 1952 until 1976 he taught music at Morley College, London, where he was director of music (1965-1969). From 1956 until 1986 he taught at the Royal Academy of Music, becoming a professor of harmony and composition in 1956.

In 1965 he succeeded **Herbert Howells** as director of music of St. Paul's School, Hammersmith, remaining until his retirement in 1975.

Contributed to periodicals including *The Listener* and *Musical Times*.

Composed a Stabat Mater, two Masses, some 30 motets and anthems, and the hymn collections *Five Hymns in Popular Style* (1963) and *Six American Hymns in Free Style* (1978). 'Tomorrow shall be my dancing day', a rhythmically-infectious carol, is one of a number also composed in a popular style. His hymn tunes are found in various publications. Secular works include *The Moon and Sixpence* (1957), three other operas, songs, three symphonies, three string quartets, three piano sonatas, a flute concerto and various chamber works.

GARLAND, Thomas (?1731-1808)

Thomas Garland was baptised in Norwich, Norfolk on 5 July 1731; died in Norwich on 23 February 1808. A pupil of **Maurice Greene**. In 1749, at the age of 18 he became organist of Norwich Cathedral. He held the position for 59 years and was responsible for the training of a number of musicians who later became famous. Composed the ordination hymn 'Come, Holy Ghost, our souls inspire', and anthems including 'Save me, O God'.

GARLAND, William Henry (1852-1897)

Born in York in June 1852; died in Halifax, Yorkshire on 13 February 1897.

At the age of seven he became a chorister of York Minster, later being articled to the cathedral organist, **E.G. Monk**. In 1878 he graduated B.Mus. at the University of Oxford.

Held an organistship at St. Paul's Church, Rome for three years before being forced by poor health to return to England. Organist of Reading Parish Church, Berkshire for a further three years, also acting as deputy to E.G. Monk in his absence through illness. Organist of Halifax Parish Church (from 1884). A local choral society conductor.

Composed church music including a Benedicite in E-flat (1891) and six settings of the Kyrie Eleison (1886).

GARRATT, Charles A. (19th century)

Born in England, but spent most of his life in the U.S.A.

Organist of the Immanuel Church, Milwaukee, Wisconsin. Later moved to Canada where, in the province of Ontario, he worked in the towns of Brantford and Hamilton, in the latter as organist of the Presbyterian Church.

Church Hymnary's Revised Edition (1927) uses Charles Garratt's tune 'Comfort' with 'Rescue the perishing, care for the dying' by Frances Austen (Fanny Crosby).

GARRETT, Charles (1823-1900)

Born in Shaftesbury, Dorset on 22 November 1823; died in Liverpool on 21 October 1900. Composer of hymn tunes.

GARRETT, Dr. George Mursell (1834-1897)

Born in Winchester, Hampshire on 8 June 1834; died in Cambridge on 8 April 1897. The son of a lay clerk of Winchester Cathedral.

Chorister of New College, Oxford (1844-1848) under **Stephen Elvey**. Associated with **S.S. Wesley** as a pupil (1847-1854) and assistant (1851-1854). Graduated Mus.B. (1857), Mus.D. (1867), and M.A. (1878) at the University of Cambridge.

Organist of the Winchester Churches of St. Thomas (from 1848) and Holy Trinity (from 1852).

Organist of Madras Cathedral, India (1854-1857) and St. John's College, Cambridge (1856-1897). At the University of Cambridge he succeeded **J.L. Hopkins** as organist (from 1873) and was a lecturer in harmony and counterpoint (from 1883). A musical examiner for a number of institutions.

Edited the Evening Service in E of S.S. Wesley, identifying and eradicating errors that had been present in the edition from which he worked and using his knowledge of Wesley's musical style to restore the work to a better rendering of the original.

George Garrett composed an oratorio *The Shunammite* (1882), performed at the Hereford Festival of that year; chants including a Double Chant in G; four Evening Services in the keys of D, E, E-flat and F and a number of settings of the Responses to the Commandments. His anthems include 'Prepare ye the way of the Lord' and 'Come, and let us return'.

His hymn tunes 'Beulah' - often used with the hymn 'There is a Land of pure delight' - 'Genesis' and 'St. Croix' were used in the Standard Edition (1916) of *Hymns Ancient and Modern*. Also composed songs and part songs.

GARTH, John (c1722-c1810)

Believed to have been born in Durham in 1722 and to have died in London in 1810.

Organist of Sedgefield. A friend of **Charles Avison**, he organised a series of Gentlemen's Subscription Concerts in Durham (1759).

Composed keyboard sonatas and cello concertos with string accompaniment. His compilation *The First 50 Psalms Of Marcello* (1757) was a matching of these tunes to English versions of the original texts. *Music to 30 Collects* was published around 1794.

Also composed six voluntaries for organ and six cello concertos, plus other works.

GARTH, Richard Machill (1860-1899)

Born in Pudsey, near Leeds, Yorkshire on 15 October 1860; died on 10 January 1899.

Attended Batley Grammar School, Yorkshire. A chorister of his parish church. Studied under James Broughton of Leeds for piano and also with J.H. Collinson and Gustav Schreck.

Active in Scotland as assistant organist of St. Mary's Cathedral, Edinburgh (from 1882). Private organist to Sir Michael Shaw Stewart and others. Organist of the Clark Memorial Church, Largs (from 1893) and choirmaster of St. Columba's Episcopal Church. An organ recitalist and choral society conductor.

Author of a textbook on arranging music for military bands.

Composed an oratorio *Ezekiel* (1888), a Service in E-flat (1888), anthems, hymn tunes, chants, songs and organ works.

GATER, Dr. William Henry (1849-1928)

Born in Dublin on 8 August 1849; died in Dublin on 21 June 1928. A blind musician. Studied organ under **R.P. Stewart** and graduated B.Mus. (1876), B.A. (1881) and D.Mus. (1886) at Trinity College, Dublin.

A professor of piano at Wesley College, Dublin, and a local choral society conductor.

Organist of Christ Church, Bray (1871-1873); organist to the Exhibition Palace, Dublin (1872-1873) and of the Dublin Churches of St. Andrew (1873-1876) and, for more than 50 years, St. Stephen (from 1876).

Composed two services and a tune, which won a prize at the Wrexham Eisteddfod of 1888, for use with the hymn 'From Greenland's icy mountains' by Reginald Heber. Composed a setting of Psalm 66 'God is our Hope and Strength'. Also a cantata *The Passions*, and items for organ.

GATES, Bernard (1685-1773)

Born in 1685; died in North Aston, near Oxford on 15 November 1773. A child (1702), gentleman (from 1708), and master of the children (1727-1757) of the Chapel Royal. Also master of the choristers of Westminster Abbey (1741-1757). Composed a Service in F and the anthems 'How long wilt Thou?' and 'O be joyful in the Lord'.

GATTY, Dr. Nicholas Comyn (1874-1946)

Born in Bradfield, Yorkshire on 13 September 1874; died in Paddington, London on 10 November 1946. The son of a vicar.

Educated at Downing College, Cambridge where he graduated B.A. (1896), Mus.B. (1898) and Mus.D. Also studied at the Royal College of Music under **C.V. Stanford**.

A friend of **Ralph Vaughan Williams**, with whom and with **Gustav Holst** he played in a quartet. Taught composition and played a part in the editing of two editions of Grove's *Dictionary of Music and Musicians*.

Pursued a career in music in London. Organist of the Duke of York's Royal Military School, Chelsea. Music critic of *Pall Mall Gazette* (1907-1914). Assistant conductor of the Royal Opera House, Covent Garden.

Composer of hymn tunes, some of which were commissioned by Vaughan Williams for *English Hymnal* (1906). They include 'Tugwood'. His other works consist of operas, examples of which are *The Tempest* and *Macbeth*. Wrote one-act operas including *Duke or Devil* (1908), songs and a piano trio.

GAUDRY, Richard Otto (1800-1825)

Born in Dublin in 1800; died in Dublin in August 1825. A chorister of the Chapel Royal, Dublin Castle. Composed anthems and songs including 'Away, away, ye notes of woe' (?1830).

GAUL, Alfred Robert (1837-1913)

Born in Norwich, Norfolk on 30 April 1837; died in King's Norton, Birmingham on 13 September 1913.

A chorister at Norwich Cathedral from 1846 and afterwards, a pupil and articled assistant to **Zechariah Buck**. Graduated Mus.B. at St. John's College, Cambridge (1863).

From the age of 17 he was organist of Fakenham, Norfolk, where he remained until 1859. Moved to Birmingham where he was organist of St. John's Church, Ladywood and, on its opening in 1868, St. Augustine's, Edgbaston. Taught harmony and counterpoint at the Birmingham and Midland Institute, where he was later appointed a professor of orchestration and composition. Taught harmony and singing at King Edward High School for Girls, Birmingham. A conductor of philharmonic societies.

Composed piano pieces, part songs, an oratorio and cantatas, including *Ruth* (1881), and *The Holy City* for the Birmingham Festival of 1882. Both were popular for a time in the U.S.A. His church music includes anthems, chants, hymn tunes and Psalm settings, including a version of Psalm 98 'O Sing unto the Lord' for eight-part Chorus.

GAUNTLETT, Dr. Henry John (1805-1876)

Born in Wellington, Shropshire on 9 July 1805; died in Kensington, London on 21 February 1876.

His father, Henry, formerly curate of Wellington, was curate (from 1811) and vicar (from 1815) of Olney Parish Church, Buckinghamshire.

The younger Henry was his father's organist for 10 years from the age of 10 in fulfilment of his father's pledge to his parishioners that if they were to raise the money for an organ, he would appoint one of his children as organist. Four sons helped meet the obligation, including Henry.

His early education was for a career in the ministry. **Thomas Attwood**, who had heard Gauntlett play organ at the age of 16, and had him in mind as a possible successor as organist of St. Paul's Cathedral, had offered to take him as a pupil. However, Gauntlett was prevailed upon by his father to pursue a legal career instead. Apprenticed to a firm of solicitors (from 1826). Qualified in 1831. Established a partnership with one of his brothers and practised law until 1846.

Archbishop Howley awarded him the Lambeth D.Mus. in 1842, the first such honour to be bestowed in two hundred years.

Organist in London of a church at or near Gray's Inn and then of St. Olave's, Southwark (1827-1846), during which time he took lessons with **Samuel Wesley**. Evening organist of Christ Church, Newgate Street (1836-1846).

From 1846 he took up various organistships. While organist of the Union Chapel, Islington (1853-1861) he collaborated with **Henry Allon** in the compilation of *The Congregational Psalmist* (1856). Organist of the Church of All Saints, Notting Hill (1861-1863) and St. Bartholomew-the-Less, Smithfield (1872-1876).

Mendelssohn admired his musical knowledge and his ability as an organist, and selected him in 1846 to play organ in the first performance of *Elijah* at Birmingham. An organ consultant. One of the earliest advocates (from 1850) of the use of electricity in organ design. Shortly thereafter he patented a design for an electrical action (1852).

A musical theorist, lecturer, pioneer of congregational singing, and critic. Founded *Church Musician* (1850) and edited *Musical World*, which he partly owned and in which (5 August 1836) he identified five categories of contemporary church compositional style. His own stated aim was to achieve expression, dignity and solemnity. He denounced the treatment of church music writing as an opportunity to demonstrate the secular values of sophistication and ingenuity.

In 1856 he wrote text and musical illustrations for *The Encyclopaedia of the Chant* (1885), compiled by Revd. J.J. Waite. Advocated the use of Gregorian plainchant in worship.

Composed anthems such as 'If ye love Me' and 'This is the day' and carols, but he is chiefly remembered for his hymn tunes, of which he composed a great many. The most famous and enduring of these is 'Irby' (1849), used then and now as the preferred tune to 'Once in royal David's city'.

Some were named after saints, including 'St. Chrysostom', 'St. Albinus', 'St. George' and 'St. Alphege'. Many are still in use today. A Single Chant in D Minor is found in the Revised Edition (1927) of *Church Hymnary*.

GAWTHORN, Nathaniel (18th century)
Conductor of Psalmody at The Friday Lecture in Eastcheap, London in the early part of the 18th century. *Harmonica Perfecta* (1730), which he compiled, contains a melody by him. It was later harmonised by **S.S. Wesley**. It is known as 'Eltham' and used in *Hymns and Psalms* (1983) and elsewhere.

GAY, George (1771-1833)
Born possibly in Corsham, Wiltshire on 17 November 1771; died by suicide in Corsham on 26 July 1833. A stonemason, verse writer, organ builder and musician. Built Melksham Bridge, Wiltshire. Organist of the Independent Chapel, Corsham. Compiled *Sacred Music*, published in 1827. His own compositions included anthems in three, five and eight parts.

GAZE, Nigel (b.1943)
Born in Leamington Spa, Warwickshire on 11 February 1943.
Educated at Prescot Grammar School, Lancashire and at the Universities of Liverpool and London. Trained privately in music with Caleb Jarvis and **Noel Rawsthorne** for organ and with Gordon Green and Douglas Miller for piano. His degrees include B.Mus. Trained as a doctor and now practises as a plastic surgeon at Preston and Blackpool Hospitals.
Active musically in Preston as organist of Fishergate Baptist Church and musical director of the Elizabethan Singers.
Has composed the anthem 'O Master, let me walk with Thee', commissioned by Liverpool Cathedral and 'O Lord, I beseech Thee' for a festival in Cumbria, other anthems, carols, and a set of Responses in A. Has also composed for organ in items of varying length and style, including a short Valediction and a longer Nocturne.

GEAR, Henry Handel (1805-1884)
Born in London on 28 October 1805; died in London on 16 October 1884. His father was a painter in the service of the Duke of Sussex.
A chorister of the Chapel Royal and of St. Paul's Cathedral.
A tenor singer and composer of London until, in 1822, he emigrated to the U.S.A. Appointed organist of Grace Church, New York.
In 1828 he moved to Italy, where he studied singing with Nozzari and others. Later sang in Frankfort, Germany and in Paris. Eventually returned to London, where he taught singing. For more than 17 years he was organist of the Quebec Chapel, Bryanston Street (later renamed the Church of the Annunciation).
Composed services, anthems including 'Christ, our Passover' and songs.

GEERES, John (?-1642)
Died in Durham and was buried on 4 March 1642. He may have been related to Gabriel Geeres, lay clerk of Christ Church, Oxford in 1670.
Graduated Mus.B. at the University of Cambridge (1623).
A lay clerk of King's College, Cambridge (1623-1626). Moved to Durham before 1630. From not later than 1630 until his death, he was a lay clerk of Durham Cathedral.

Composed at least three anthems, including 'Merciful Lord, we beseech Thee' and 'The eyes of all wait'. May have composed a five-part antiphon *In manus tuas*.

GEIKIE, James Stewart (1811-1883)
Born in Edinburgh on 12 January 1811; died in Ormiston, Haddington on 14 August 1883. Wrote on musical topics in *The Scotsman*. A conductor of local choral societies. Led the singing of the Psalms at St. Augustine's Church, Edinburgh (1843-1880). His compilations include *Songs of the Sanctuary* (1863). Composed Psalm tunes and other forms of church music, and songs.

GENGE, Robert Sealy (1862-1920)
Born in Limington, Somerset in 1862; died in Stratford on Avon, Warwickshire on 15 April 1920. Composer of a Ferial Holy Communion in G (1894), settings of the Benedictus Qui Venit and Agnus Dei (1895), and hymn tunes.

GEORGE, Graham (b.1912)
Born in Norwich, Norfolk on 11 April 1912. Composer of the Palm Sunday anthem 'Ride on! Ride on' (1970), the anthem 'In God's Commands' (1964) and hymn tunes.

GERARD, Alexander (?-1738)
Died in St. Asaph, Wales in March 1738. He is probably the person of that name who was a chorister of the Chapel Royal under **John Blow** until around 1694. Organist of St. Asaph Cathedral from (1694-1738) and succeeded by his son, John. Composed church music.

GIBBONS (**Gibbins**), Dr. Christopher (1615-1676)
Born in Westminster, London and baptised on 22 August 1615; died in Westminster on 20 October 1676 and buried in the cloisters of Westminster Abbey. The second oldest of **Orlando Gibbons**'s surviving sons.
A chorister in the Chapel Royal of Charles I. When his father died (1625), Christopher went to live with his uncle, Edward Gibbons, succentor of Exeter Cathedral. It is believed that Christopher remained at Exeter until his early twenties. In July 1664 he graduated D.Mus. at the University of Oxford at the instigation of Charles II.
Better known as an organist than as a composer. One of his organ pupils was **John Blow**. In 1638, he succeeded **Thomas Holmes** as organist of Winchester Cathedral. The appointment ended formally on 23 June 1661 but in effect when Parliamentarian forces destroyed the organ (1642).
Enlisted as a Royalist soldier (1644) during the interregnum. Played virginal as a recitalist and teacher.
At the Restoration, Christopher Gibbons became private organist to Charles II, and was appointed organist of the Chapel Royal (1660-1676) and of Westminster Abbey (1660-1666). Master of the choristers of Westminster Abbey (1664-1666).
Composed Latin sacred works, anthems including 'Sing unto the Lord, O ye saints' (1674), masque and consort music, and works for keyboard.

GIBBONS (Gibbins), Revd. Edward (c1568-c1650)
Born in Cambridge around the year 1568; died in Exeter, Devon around 1650. The eldest of the brothers of **Orlando Gibbons**.
Graduated B.Mus. at the University of Oxford (July 1592), and Mus.B. at about the same time at the University of Cambridge.
A lay clerk, and (from mid 1592 to 1599) master of the choristers of King's College, Cambridge, succeeding Thomas Hammond.
One of several differing accounts of his career from this point is that he went to Bristol Cathedral around 1600 as organist, priest vicar, sub chanter (succentor) and master of the choristers, before becoming organist and custos (warden) of the College of Priest Vicars of Exeter Cathedral (1611-1644), his Exeter period coming to a premature end with the destruction by Parliamentary forces of the organ there.
Said to have loaned £1,000 to Charles I, an action for which he was deprived of his estates and made homeless at the age of 79.
Composed a verse anthem 'How hath the city sate solitary?' and a Kyrie and Credo to the Short Service by **William Munday**.

GIBBONS (Gibbins), Dr. Orlando (1583-1625)
Born in Oxford in 1583 and baptised on 25 December; died in Canterbury, Kent on 5 June 1625, while awaiting with Charles I and his entourage the arrival of Henrietta Maria. Buried in Canterbury Cathedral, where a monument was erected to him. Brother of **Edward Gibbons** and father of **Christopher Gibbons**.
His father was a wait of Oxford. The family moved to Cambridge around the year 1590. A chorister of King's College, Cambridge under his brother, Edward (1596-1598). Studied at the University of Cambridge (from 1559), graduating Mus.B. (1606). An Oxford D.Mus. (1622): the anthem he submitted as his exercise was 'O clap your hands'.
By 1603, Orlando Gibbons was a member of the Chapel Royal, possibly as a gentleman extraordinary. One of the organists of the Chapel Royal of James I for the whole of his reign, and responsible for the music at James's funeral. At the time of the death of Orlando Gibbons the junior Chapel Royal organist was **Thomas Tomkins**.
In 1619 he was appointed to play virginals in the Privy Chamber of Charles I.
For the last two years of his life (1623-1625), Orlando Gibbons was also organist of Westminster Abbey, having succeeded **John Parsons**.
A compilation of hymn tunes by him was published in 1623. He also set the Responses to the Commandments and the Morning and Evening Service, including a Service in F.
All his choral works were in English. The anthems include 'This is the Record of John', 'Hosanna to the Son of David', 'Almighty and everlasting God', and 'See, see the Word is Incarnate'. They were different in style from those of other contemporary composers and have been characterised as more expressive and emotional, with less use of counterpoint.
Composed madrigals, including 'The Silver Swan'. A collection was published in 1622. Also composed works for solo keyboard and for ensembles.

GIBBS, Alan Trevor (b.1932)
Born in Chipping Norton, Oxfordshire on 21 April 1932.
Inspired to compose by Edwin C. Rose. Took organ lessons with John Webster; studied with Norman Barnes for theory and John McKinnell for piano. Won a music scholarship to the University of Durham, where the music professor was **Arthur Hutchings**.

Continued his organ studies at Durham Cathedral under Conrad Eden.
Taught at Archbishop Tenison's School, Kennington, London (1957-1986), during the early part of which he continued his studies with Mátyás Seiber.
Has contributed articles to journals on organs, their music, and on **Gustav Holst.**
His compositions are largely for organ or for the church. They include services such as an Evening Service for Boys' Voices, for Durham Cathedral, and the *St. Margaret* Setting of the Rite A Communion Service. The anthem 'I will lift up mine eyes' is one of 35 anthems and motets. 'Viewpoints' and 'Celebration' are two of some 16 organ works.

GIBBS, Dr. Cecil Armstrong (1889-1960)
Born in Great Baddow, near Chelmsford, Essex on 10 August 1889; died in Chelmsford on 12 May 1960.
Attended Winchester School before going up to Trinity College, Cambridge to read history and music. Graduated B.A. (1911), Mus.B. (1913) and Mus.D. His teachers included E.J. Dent and **Charles Wood**. Studied at the Royal College of Music (1919-1920) under **Ralph Vaughan Williams** for composition and Adrian Boult for conducting.
Taught in Sussex at Copthorne School, East Grinstead and at The Wick School, Hove (from 1915). Attempted to enlist during World War I but was rejected on medical grounds. At around this time he met the poet Walter de la Mare and the two became friends. Lived in the Danbury area of Essex (1921-1939) while on the staff of the R.C.M.
One of the adjudicators at the Carlisle Festival of April 1939. Their choice of best soloist was the rising young contralto, Kathleen Ferrier. Vice-chairman of the British Federation of Festivals.
Composed Psalm settings, carols, motets and anthems including 'Most glorious Lord of lyfe!' and 'O praise God in His Holiness'. Some of his hymn tunes are found in *Songs of Praise*. Also composed some attractive organ pieces, operas including *The Blue Peter* (1924), and orchestral and chamber works. Set some of the works of Walter de la Mare to music. Won the Cobbett Prize for composition (1920), and a Cobbett Gold Medal for his chamber music (1934).

GIBBS, John (16th/17th century)
A 17th century church musician and composer. Master of the choristers of Westminster Abbey (1605-1613). It may have been John Gibbs who actually composed some of the works attributed to **Richard Gibbs**.

GIBBS (Gibbes), Richard (17th century)
Organist of Norwich Cathedral from 1622 until at least 1642, and possibly to 1644, when Parliamentary forces silenced choral worship. Organist of Christ Church, Norwich. Composed works for keyboard, and catches. His 'Have mercy upon me' (1635) and his anthem for Good Friday 'See, sinful soul' were included in the collection *Divine Services* (1663), by **James Clifford**. Another anthem, 'Lord, in Thy wrath' is credited to Richard Gibbs but there is a possibility that this and other works were actually the compositions of **John Gibbs**.

GIBSON (Scott), Mrs. Isabella Mary (1786-1838)
Born in Edinburgh in 1786; died in Edinburgh on 28 November 1838. A distant relative of the novelist Sir Walter Scott. Kept a

girls' boarding school in Edinburgh. An amateur harpist. Composed Psalm or hymn tunes, a number of which were included in the compilation *Sacred Harmony* (1820) by **Andrew Thomson**. Also composed a song 'Loch na gar'.

GICK, Dr. Thomas (1837-?)
Born in Liverpool on 22 February 1837. Graduated B.Mus. (1880) and D.Mus. (1882) at the University of Dublin. A lay clerk of York Minster (from 1859); a vicar choral of the Dublin Cathedrals of Christ Church and St. Patrick (from 1864). An examiner in music. Compositions include a Morning and Evening Service in B-flat, the anthems 'O come, let us worship' and 'Hear Thou, O Shepherd', and a cantata *The Bard* (1882).

GILBERT, Alfred (1826-1902)
Born in Salisbury, Wiltshire on 21 October 1826; died in Paddington, London on 6 February 1902.
Studied music from the age of six. Taught by **Charles Corfe** and Alexander Lucas. Entered the Royal Academy of Music (1845).
Became assistant to his former teacher, Alexander Lucas, at the church of St. Thomas, Salisbury. Held organ appointments at St. Matthew's Church, Spring Gardens, Chepstow; in Mitcham, Surrey; at Kentish Town and at St. Mark's, Hamilton Terrace, London. Assistant organist of the Hanover Chapel, Regent Street.
A piano recitalist, lecturer, composer and the director of the Philharmonic Society.
Composer of hymn tunes, songs, operettas including *Outwitted* and works for piano.

GILBERT, Ernest Thomas Bennett (1833-1885)
Born in Salisbury, Wiltshire on 22 October 1833; died in Upper Norwood, London on 11 May 1885.
A student of the Royal Academy of Music (from 1847) and under Ignaz Moscheles, Moritz Hauptmann and Ernst Richter in Leipzig (from 1852).
Appointed to a number of organistships, including the Isle of Man Churches of St. George (1853) and St. Barnabas (1854); St. Paul's, Newport, Monmouthshire, Wales (1856); Abergavenny Parish Church (1857); and in London at St. Peter's, Walworth (1861); St. George's, Southwark (1864) and St. Matthew's, Southwark (1867). A tutor of singing in London.
Composed the anthem 'Come unto Me', hymn tunes, operettas including *Night in Fairyland* (1861), String Quartets in E-flat and in C, pieces for piano, songs and part songs.

GILBERT, Dr. Walter Bond (1829-1910)
Born in Exeter, Devon on 21 April 1829; died in Oxford on 2 March 1910.
Studied music at Exeter Cathedral and under **Alfred Angel**, **S.S. Wesley** and **Henry Bishop**. Graduated B.Mus (1854) and D.Mus. (1888) at New College, Oxford and D.Mus. At the University of Toronto, Canada (1888).
Held organistships in Devon at Topsham (1847) and Bideford (1849); in Kent at Tonbridge (1854), the Old Collegiate Church, Maidstone (1859) and Lee (1866); and at Boston, Lincolnshire (1868). A teacher at Tonbridge School.
Organist of the Episcopal Chapel, New York (1869-1897).
One of the founders of the College of Organists.

Editor of *The Episcopal Hymnal*, U.S.A. and author of a number of monographs including *Antiquities of Maidstone*.
At the age of 17 he composed a Cathedral Service. Continued to compose church music, producing works including other Services, and anthems, of which around 60 were written for his church in New York. A chant by Walter Gilbert was included in *Cathedral Psalter Chants* (1875).
His hymn tune 'Maidstone' was used in *Church Hymns* (1874) and *Hymns Ancient and Modern*. 'Maidstone' and 'Thanksgiving' were used in the Revised Edition (1927) of *Church Hymnary*.
Composed oratorios including *The Restoration of Israel* and *St. John* (1857), and organ works.

GILDING, Edmund (?-1782)
Died in London on 5 August 1782.
Held three London organist appointments, with some overlap, until his death, these being the Churches of St. Martin, Ludgate (from April 1745) and St. Edmund the King and Martyr (from November 1753), and of the Parish Clerks' Company (from July 1766).
His Psalm or hymn tune 'Dedication' (1762) was used in the Standard Edition (1916) of *Hymns Ancient and Modern* with the translation of the Latin hymn 'O word of God above'. 'St. Edmund' appeared in the compilation *Parochial Harmony Corrected* by **William Riley**. It is also to be found in the Revised Edition (1927) of *Church Hymnary* with the hymn 'My times are in Thy hand' by William Lloyd.

GILES (Gyles), Dr. Nathaniel (1558-1634)
Born in or near Worcester around the year 1558; died in Windsor, Berkshire on 24 January 1634 and buried at St. George's Chapel, Windsor Castle.
Son of William Giles, organist of St. Paul's Cathedral. Nathaniel Giles's son of the same name was a canon of St. George's Chapel, Windsor Castle and a prebendary of Worcester Cathedral.
Probably a pupil of John Golden, organist and master of the choristers of Worcester Cathedral. Graduated B.Mus. (June 1585) and D.Mus.(1622) at the University of Oxford.
Succeeded Golden as organist and master of the choristers of Worcester Cathedral (1581-1585). May also have been a lay clerk of Magdalen College, Oxford (1577). Appointed lay clerk, organist and master of the choristers of St. George's Chapel, Windsor Castle (1585). A gentleman, and master of the choristers (from 1597) of the Chapel Royal. Retained the appointments at St. George's Chapel and the Chapel Royal until his death. Responsible for producing choirboy plays at court (1600-1602).
Composed six Full Services. His anthems amount to between 20 and 30 and include 'God, which at this time' and 'Out of the deep'. Six motets, a set of Preces, two madrigals and sacred songs are also believed to be composed by him.

GILL, William Henry (1839-1923)
Born in Marsala, Sicily on 24 October 1839; died in Worthing, Sussex on 27 June 1923. Composed works published collectively as *Easy Anthems for Village Choirs* (1888-1891), part songs including *Three merry Maids*, and songs.

GILLESPIE, James (b.1929)
Born in Leeds, Yorkshire in 1929. Composer of hymn tunes.

GLADSTONE, Dr. Francis Edward (1845-1928)
Born in Summertown, near Oxford on 2 March 1845; died in Hereford on 5 September 1928.
His father, Revd. J.E. Gladstone, was a cousin of the Prime Minister, W.E. Gladstone.
Educated privately near Torquay, Devon. An articled pupil of **S.S. Wesley** (1859-1864). Graduated Mus.B. (1876) and Mus.D. (1879) at the University of Cambridge.
Organist of Holy Trinity Church, Weston-super-Mare, Somerset (1864-1866).
Organist of the Cathedrals of Llandaff (1866-1870), Chichester (1870-1873) and Norwich (1877-1881).
Organist in Sussex of the Churches of St. Patrick, Hove (1873-1875); St. Francis Xavier, Hove and St. Peter, Brighton (1875-1876). Moved to London where he was, briefly, organist of St. Mark's Church, Lewisham (1876).
Organist of Christ Church, Lancaster Gate (1881-1886). Following his conversion to Roman Catholicism in 1887 he became director of the choir of St. Mary of the Angels, Bayswater (until 1894).
A professor of Trinity College of Music (from 1881) and a professor of harmony and composition at the Royal College of Music (1883-1910), where one of his theory pupils (1890) was **Ralph Vaughan Williams**. An examiner in music for the Universities of Cambridge, Durham and London. Later moved to Hereford.
Author of *Treatise on Strict Counterpoint* (1906).
Composed a Morning and Evening Service in F; anthems including 'Almighty and everlasting God'; a Mass in E Minor for the Brompton Oratory, London; a Chant in C and hymn tunes. His cantatas include *Philippi* (for Newcastle Cathedral in July 1873), organ and chamber works.

GLADSTONE, Robertson (?19th century)
Robertson Gladstone composed a set of Responses to the Commandments in G, published around the year 1875 and a part song 'The gay birds are carolling' (1877).

GLADSTONE, William Henry (1840-1891)
Born in Hawarden, Flintshire, Wales on 3 June 1840; died in Westminster, London on 4 July 1891. Eldest son of W.E. Gladstone, Prime Minister.
Attended Eton College and read Greek and Latin at Christ Church, Oxford.
A Member of Parliament for a total of 20 years, representing Chester for three, Whitby, Yorkshire for 12 and East Worcestershire for five.
A singer and organist, and he was well versed in musical history especially the development of Anglican church music. He wrote on musical topics, and one of the views he expressed was that choral church services were to be deplored because 'the choirs often discourage the congregations from singing'. Disapproved of the practice of adapting Masses by foreign composers for use as Canticle settings in cathedrals and churches.
Compiled a hymn book *A Selection of Hymns and Tunes* (1882) on which **Walter Parratt** commented that it contained not a single bad tune, uniquely in his experience. Composed the anthems 'Gracious and Righteous' and 'Withdraw not Thou.' Of his 10 or so hymn tunes, 'Erskine', 'Hammersmith' and 'Ombersley' were used in the Revised Edition (1927) of *Church Hymnary*. The last of these was named after a village in his East Worcestershire

constituency. Also composed chants, anthems, introits and organ voluntaries.

GLASSER, Stanley (b.1926)
Born in Johannesburg, South Africa on 28 February 1926.
Attended King Edward VII School, Johannesburg and Witwatersrand University, where he took a degree in Economics (1950). Studied composition with Benjamin Frankel and Mátyás Seiber (1950-1954); read music at King's College, Cambridge (1955-1958).
A senior lecturer of Cape Town University (1959-1961). Held the first chair of music at Goldsmiths' College. Currently emeritus professor of music, University of London, and presenter for the radio station Classic FM. Compiler of *The A-Z of Classical Music* (1994).
Composed *Lamentations* for unaccompanied voices in five parts (1994) and a Magnificat and Nunc Dimittis, commissioned by St. George's Chapel, Windsor Castle (1995). Secular works include a one-act comic opera *The Gift* (1976), *Beat Music* for large orchestra (1986), and a Concerto for Piano and Orchestra (1993).

GLENDINING, Richard Rashleigh (1872-?)
Born in Tiverton, Devon in 1872.
Trained in music at the Church of St. Andrew, Plymouth. Graduated B.Mus. at Pembroke College, Oxford (1910).
Organist and choirmaster of St. German's Parish Church (1896-1910); Bodmin Parish Church, Cornwall (from 1910); Oswestry Parish Church, Shropshire (from 1915); Nuneaton Parish Church, Warwickshire (from around 1920); Holy Trinity Church, South Shore, Blackpool, Lancashire (from 1921) and St. Margaret's Church, Ilkley, Yorkshire (from around 1925).
Taught music at King Edward VI Grammar School, Nuneaton, Warwickshire.
Composed a Te Deum in D and an anthem 'Brightest and best'.

GLOVER, J.H.L. (19th century)
A musician and composer of the 19th century. Compiled *Concise Organ Tutor* and composed a Te Deum, songs and piano music.

GLOVER, John William (1815-?)
Born in Dublin on 19 June 1815. Composer of *Six Masses* (c1860-1872), an Offertorium 'O Jesu, bone Pastor' (1865), the motet *Ecce, Sacerdos magnus* and organ voluntaries.

GLOVER, William (1822-?)
Born in London in 1822. A chorister of Trinity College, Cambridge (1829-1838) and a pupil of **T.A. Walmisley**. Organist of Christ Church, Cambridge (1841-1842) and of St. Matthew's, Manchester. Organist of St. Luke's, Cheetham, Manchester (from 1846). In 1847 he met Mendelssohn in Manchester. Worked on the development of weaving mechanisms. Published *The Complete Daily Service of the Church...* (1847). Composed an oratorio *Jerusalem* (1847), a cantata *The Corsair*, piano trios, quartets and quintets.

GODDARD, Joseph (1833-1910)
Born in 1833; died in Hampstead, London on 9 December 1910.
Author and composer. Writings include *Moral Theory of Music* (1857) and *Philosophy of Music*. Contributed to *Musical Times* (1885). Composed the anthems 'I do set my bow' and 'These things I command', songs and piano music.

GODFREY, Arthur Eugene (1868-1939)
Born in Westminster, London on 28 September 1868; died in Hampstead, London on 23 February 1939. Son of Charles Godfrey, director of music of the Royal Horse Guards.
A chorister of St. Paul's Cathedral. Studied at the Royal Academy of Music.
A leading accompanist of his day. Organist in London of St. John's Church, Wapping (1883-1886); All Saints', Finchley (1886-1897); St. Mary the Virgin, Primrose Hill (1897-1900); and St. Andrew's Presbyterian Church, Frognal (from 1903).
Composer of hymn tunes and a light opera *Little Miss Nobody*, which enjoyed a long run at the Lyric Theatre.

GODFREY, Nathaniel Stedman (1817-1883)
Born in London in 1817; died in Southsea, Hampshire on 26 October 1883. Composer of hymn tunes. Published the collection *Original Tunes... for the Choir of St. Bartholomew, Southsea* (1874). Wrote the words and music of 'The battle prayer' (1855).

GOLDSCHMIDT, Otto Moritz David (1829-1907)
Born in Hamburg, Germany on 21 August 1829; died in London on 24 February 1907. Husband of the soprano Jenny Lind, whom he married in 1852 in Boston, U.S.A.
Studied piano and harmony with Friedrich Grund and Jakob Schmitt in Hamburg. In 1843 he was one of the first students of the new Leipzig Conservatory under Mendelssohn, Hans von Bülow, Louis Plaidy and Moritz Hauptmann.
Played music and taught at Leipzig (1846-1848). Went to Paris with the intention of studying with Chopin but the plan did not materialise and he moved instead to London, where he was accompanist to Jenny Lind. They lived in Dresden (1852-1853) before setting permanently in England from 1858. Both were friends of **Arthur Sullivan**.
Organist of St. John's Church, Putney. Worked with **William Sterndale Bennett** on *The Chorale Book for England* (1862-1864).
A teacher of piano (from 1863) and vice principal (from 1866) at the Royal Academy of Music. Helped to organise the teaching of music at Rugby School (1864-1869). An editor, chiefly of foreign polyphony such as the works of Eccard.
In 1875 he founded the London Bach Choir, serving as conductor for 10 years and being succeeded eventually by **C.V. Stanford**. The choir revived works by **Handel**.
Composed the oratorio *Ruth* (1867) and conducted the work at the Three Choirs' Festival of that year in Hereford. Also composed hymn tunes, songs, chamber music and a piano concerto. His unaccompanied motet carol *A tender shoot hath started up from a root of grace* is often broadcast.

GOLDSMITH, Edmund William (1860-1934)
Born in Duntisbourne Rouse, Gloucestershire in 1860; died in Torquay, Devon on 29 July 1934. Composer of hymn tunes. Editor of Missa *Deus Semperiterne*.

GOLDWIN (**Golding**), John (c1667-1719)
Born, probably in Windsor, Berkshire around the year 1667; died in Windsor on 7 November 1719.

A chorister and pupil of **William Child** at St. George's Chapel, Windsor Castle.
Assistant to William Child, organist, and Green, master of the choristers (from 1685). Took over these positions in April 1697 and in 1704 respectively. A Windsor lay clerk from 1689.
Composed the two motets *Libera me* and *O sapientia*. He composed more than 30 anthems including 'I will sing unto the Lord' and 'I have set God alway before me'. His Morning and Evening Service in F were included in the edition *Cathedral Music* (1790) by **Samuel Arnold**. There was a corresponding Communion Service.

GOOCH, Frederick (1804-1887)
Born in Saxlingham, Norfolk on 10 April 1804; died in Baginton, Warwickshire on 29 October 1887. *Church Hymnary*'s Revised Edition (1927) contains Gooch's tune 'Baginton' with the hymn 'Dear Shepherd of Thy people, hear' by John Newton.

GOODALL, David Stanton (b.1922)
Born in Hampstead, London on 30 December 1922. The hymn tune 'Montgomery' was used in *With One Voice* (1978) with the hymn 'Stand up and bless the Lord' by James Montgomery.

GOODENOUGH, Revd. Robert Philip (1775-1826)
Born in Ealing, London on 19 October 1775; died in Beelsby, Lincolnshire on 20 April 1826. *Cathedral Psalter Chants* (1875) contains a Double Chant in F Minor and another in F. Composer of hymn tunes.

GOODGROOME, John (1630-1704)
Born in 1630; died in June 1704. A chorister of St. George's Chapel, Windsor Castle. From 1660 he was a gentleman of the Chapel Royal. From 1664 he was a musician in ordinary to Charles II. Composed church music and songs.

GOODHART, Arthur Murray (1866-1941)
Born in Wimbledon, London on 14 June 1866; died in Oxford on 2 July 1941.
Studied with **Joseph Barnby**, **Frederick Bridge**, **George Garrett** and C.W. Pearce.
Graduated B.A. (1888), Mus.B. (1892) and M.A. (1894) at King's College, Cambridge.
An assistant classics master (from 1889), master (from 1894) and house master (1904-1924) at Eton College.
Composed a Holy Communion Service in E-flat, anthems, hymn tunes, carols, choral ballads, songs including 'Flower Crowns', part songs, orchestral works including an elegy, and works for military bands and for piano and for organ.

GOODSON, Richard (c1655-1718)
Born around 1655; died in Oxford on 13 January 1718 and was buried in a chapel within Christ Church Cathedral. A chorister of St. Paul's Cathedral. Graduated B.Mus. at the University of Oxford (1682). Organist at Oxford of New College (1682-1692) and Christ Church (1692-1718),, during the deanship of **Henry Aldrich**. From July 1682 he was professor of music of the University. Composed the anthem 'I am the Resurrection'. Three songs have been credited to him although one or more of these may actually be

the work of his son **Richard Goodson**. Also composed odes and church music.

GOODSON, Richard (c1685-1741)
Born around 1685; died in Oxford on 9 June 1741. Buried in Christ Church Cathedral near his father **Richard Goodson**.
Graduated B.Mus. at the University of Oxford in March 1716.
From August 1709 he was organist of Newbury Parish Church, Berkshire. On the death of his father (1718), he became organist of Christ Church Cathedral and New College, Oxford and professor of music of Oxford University. Held these positions concurrently until his death.
Composed church music and odes. Either he or his father composed single chants which were included in *Cathedral Psalter Chants* (1875), a Service and four anthems. The further possibility that father and son each composed part of the total output cannot be ruled out.

GOODWORTH, William George Waller (c1859-1938)
Died at the age of 79 in 1938.
Attended Trinity College of Music, London and was a B.Mus. graduate of the University of Durham (1905).
Worked as a local government officer. An examiner for theory and a professor of sight singing at Trinity College, and a fellow and examiner of the London Tonic Sol-fa College. Also taught at the Northern Polytechnic Institute and at St. Leonards College of Music, Sussex.
A solo singer and choir trainer.
Choirmaster of St. Augustine's Church, Highbury, London and a local choral society director. From 1910 he was musical editor of *The Schoolmistress*. Author of a number of books, including *Musicians of All Times*.
Composed anthems including 'Rejoice today with one accord' (1888) and 'Come out from among them' (1906), a glee and a part song.

GOOLD, Revd. Ebenezer (19th/20th century)
Graduate B.Mus. and M.A. (1883) at the University of Dublin.
Composed a setting of Psalm 46 'God is our Hope and Strength' for Solo Voices, Chorus and Orchestra.

GORDON, Revd. George (1776-1856)
Born in Fochabers, Elgin, Scotland on 27 March 1776; died in Dufftown on 10 May 1856. Studied at Valladolid for the ministry of the Roman Catholic Church. An amateur musician and violinist.
Produced a compilation of music for church choirs in two volumes.

GOSS, Sir John (1800-1880)
Born in Fareham, Hampshire on 27 December 1800; died in Brixton, London on 10 May 1880.
His father, Joseph, was organist of the local parish church. His uncle, John Jeremiah Goss, an alto singer, was a vicar choral of St. Paul's Cathedral, lay vicar of Westminster Abbey and gentleman of the Chapel Royal.
John Goss was a chorister of the Chapel Royal (1811-c1815) under **John Stafford Smith**. On leaving he became a composition pupil of **Thomas Attwood**. Graduated Mus.D. honorarily at the University of Cambridge (1876).
Knighted in 1872 shortly after a Service of Thanksgiving in St. Paul's Cathedral, of which he was organist, for the recovery from illness of the Prince of Wales.

Applied unsuccessfully in 1819 for the vacant organistship of the Old Chelsea Church, London. Having sung tenor - briefly - in the chorus of the Covent Garden Theatre, he had established his credentials for the post at St. Paul's with organist appointments at Stockwell Chapel (1821) and St. Luke's Chelsea, a new church (1824-1838). While at St. Luke's he composed church music, having already written a number of glees. Compiled *Parochial Psalmody* (1826), a tune book of Psalms and hymns which included his own tune 'Waterstock'.
Organist of St. Paul's Cathedral (1838-1872) in succession to Thomas Attwood.
His arrival was at a turbulent time. The succentor, Revd. E.G.A. Beckwith was at odds with the master of the choristers, **William Hawes**, and legal proceedings were threatened. Life at St. Paul's had, however, its lighter moments. Revd. Sydney Smith, a canon, was something of a wit. Soon after he arrived, Goss decided that the organ needed some new stops. Smith's response was, 'Mr. Goss, what a strange set of creatures you organists are! First you want the 'bull' stop. Then you want the 'tom tit' stop; in fact you are like a jaded old cab horse, always longing for another stop.'
A professor of harmony of the Royal Academy of Music (from 1827) where his pupils included **Frederick Bridge**, **Arthur Sullivan** and **Frederic Cowen**. On the death of **William Knyvett** he became a composer to the Chapel Royal.
Music editor of *Church Psalter and Hymn Book* (1854), edited by Revd. W. Mercer. The first edition did not contain any of his own tunes, but later editions did. Contributed the tune 'Bevan' to Maurice's *Choral Harmony* (1854).
Goss collaborated with **James Turle** of Westminster Abbey to publish a collection of established anthems and services. These were issued from 1843 in the form of 40 instalments, making up three volumes.
Early in his career, Goss composed two overtures, glees and incidental music for Banim's play *The Serjeant's Wife*. Although he composed an anthem in 1823, most of his church music was composed after 1850. In 1842 he composed the anthem 'Blessed is the Man,' based on the words of Psalm 1, which was intended as the first of a complete set of 150 Psalm-based anthems. However it was so badly received by the choir of St. Paul's that he was discouraged for the next 10 years from serious composition.
Among his best-known anthems are 'If we believe' (1852), composed for the funeral of the Duke of Wellington, the harvest-tide 'Fear not, O land', and 'I heard a Voice'. Also composed a number of chants, and hymn tunes including 'St. Hilary', 'Rothley' and 'Bevan'. Goss's tune to the hymn by **H.W. Baker** 'Praise my soul, the King of Heaven' is still much sung.

GOSS-CUSTARD, Dr. Walter Henry (1871-1964)
Born in St. Leonards on Sea, Sussex on 7 February 1871; died in St. Leonards on 6 July 1964.
The great-nephew of **John Goss** and the brother of a well-known London organist, Reginald Goss-Custard.
Educated privately. A pupil of **Edwin Lemare**, taking an Oxford B.Mus in 1895. Honoured with the Lambeth D.Mus. in 1953.
Organist of the Sussex Churches of Christ Church, Blacklands, Hastings (1887) and Holy Trinity, Hastings (1891). Appointments followed in London at St. John's, Lewisham High Road (1902) and St. Saviour's, West Ealing (1904-1917).
Organist of Liverpool Cathedral from 1917 until his retirement in 1953.

Organist of St. Mary's Church for the Blind, Liverpool (from 1917). Honorary organist to the Royal Philharmonic Society (1914-1917). In 1928 he visited the U.S.A. in order to lecture and give recitals before the Conference of the American Association of Organists.

Composed a setting of Psalm 68 'Let God arise', chants and a Communion Service in D.

GOSTELOW, Frederick James (1866-1942)
Born in Dunstable, Bedfordshire in 1866; died in Luton, Bedfordshire on 27 June 1942.

Educated at the Royal Academy of Music under **Frederick Bridge**, Frits Hartvigson, **Tobias Matthay** and C.W. Pearce. Organist of Dunstable Congregational Church at the age of 13, followed by a number of chapels in and around London. Organist of St. Mary's Church, Luton (1889-1942) and of the private chapel of Luton Hoo Manor (from 1900).

A professor, and examiner, and subsequently a member of the board of governors of Trinity College of Music. Toured Australia as an examiner for T.C.M., giving recitals there also.

Winner of the gold medal for piano playing at the International Music Trades Exhibition in 1896.

Composer of a Magnificat and Nunc Dimittis in A-flat (1894), a Te Deum in B-flat (1896), the anthem 'As Moses lifted up the serpent' (1895), and hymn tunes.

GOULD, Revd. Arthur Cyril Barham
See **BARHAM-GOULD**, Revd. Arthur Cyril.

GOULD, Revd. Sabine Baring
See **BARING-GOULD**, Revd. Sabine.

GOWER, Dr. John Henry (1855-1922)
Born in Rugby, Warwickshire on 25 May 1855; died in Denver, Colorado, U.S.A. on 30 July 1922.

Graduated B.Mus. (1876) and D.Mus. (1883) at Balliol College, Oxford.

At the age of 12 he was assistant organist of St. George's Chapel, Windsor Castle.

From 1874 he was organist and choirmaster of St. Paul's Church, Tunbridge Wells, Kent. Two years later he became organist and a teacher of music at Trent College, Derbyshire (1876-1887). During those years he was a local philharmonic society conductor and he was known as an organ recitalist. As a volunteer in the 1st Derbyshire Regiment he rose to the rank of captain.

In 1887 he emigrated to the U.S.A. as precentor and organist of St. John's Cathedral, Denver.

Composed a cantata *The Good Shepherd*, hymn tunes, songs and part songs.

GRAHAM, George Farquhar (1789-1867)
Born in Edinburgh on 29 December 1789; died in Edinburgh on 12 March 1867. Educated in Edinburgh at the High School and the University. Lived in Italy for a while. Wrote accounts of the Edinburgh Festivals of the time. Composer of hymn tunes, songs including 'While hours of bliss are fleeting' (1820) and glees.

GRAHAM, Thomas (1800-1867)
Organist of the chapel for the deaf and dumb, Old Trafford, Manchester, and of Wigan Parish Church, Lancashire (1844-1867). Conductor of Wigan Choral Society. The hymnal *Church Hymns* (1874) combined the hymn 'Giver of the perfect Gift' with his tune 'Wigan'.

GRANT, David (1833-1893)
Born in Aberdeen, Scotland on 19 September 1833; died in Forest Hill, London on 30 July 1893. A tobacconist of Union Street, Aberdeen with an interest in music. A member of the church and choir in the district of Footdie, he scored music for bands and he arranged tunes for use in *The Northern Psalter*, edited by William Carnie. The hymn tune 'Crimond' was at one time attributed to David Grant, but it is thought that he did no more than arrange it. The tune 'Raleigh' was composed by him.

GRAVES, Henry (19th/20th century)
Graduated B.Mus.(1903) at the University of Durham. A song man of York Minster (from 1880). Organist and choirmaster of the Scottish Parish Churches of Talgarth (from 1883); Woodside, Glasgow (from 1886); Dumfries (1890) and Ayr (from 1899).

A local choral society conductor. From June 1913 he was associated in Montreal, Canada with McGill University and the Crescent Street Presbyterian Church. Composed anthems and songs. Caprice Nocturne for Piano (1888).

GRAY, Dr. Alan (1855-1935)
Born in York on 23 December 1855; died in Cambridge on 27 September 1935.

Attended St. Peter's School, York. Trained as a solicitor, qualifying in 1881. Graduated LL.B. (1877) and LL.M. (1883). Studied music under **E.G. Monk** at York, and at Trinity College, Cambridge (from 1873) where he graduated Mus.B. (1886) and Mus.D. (1889).

Alan Gray was the first director of music at Wellington College, Berkshire (1883-1892), a member of a strong music staff that included A.H. Fox-Strangways, **H.P. Allen** and Walter Ford. Succeeded **C.V. Stanford** as organist of Trinity College, Cambridge (1892-1930). One of his organ pupils at Trinity was **Ralph Vaughan Williams**.

One of the leading organists and composers of the day who each contributed an item to the collection *For the little Organ Book* in memory of **Hubert Parry**.

President of the Royal College of Organists, and an editor of the Purcell Society.

Composed cantatas and organ sonatas. His church music includes six service settings, including Evening Services in A Minor and, for double choir, in F Minor; a Te Deum and Benedictus in G, and the anthem 'What are these that glow from afar?' (1928). The latter was a setting of words by Christina Rossetti and was composed in response to the loss of two sons in World War I. For a time it was often sung on Armistice Day. His hymn tune 'Battle Cry' was used in *Hymns Ancient and Modern* with the hymn by Ada Greenway, 'Rise at the cry of battle. Editor of a book of descants.

GRAY, Dr. George Charles (1897-1981)
Born in Nutfield, Surrey on 7 October 1897; died in Leicester on 24 March 1981. Buried in Leicester Cathedral.
Won a scholarship to Rotherham Grammar School, Yorkshire. During World War I he served in the Oxfordshire and Buckinghamshire Light Infantry. When it was discovered that he was under age, he was brought back from active service in Flanders. Took part in concert parties in 1918.
With the assistance of an army grant, he studied under **Edward Bairstow** and graduated B.Mus. at the University of Durham (1928). Received an honorary M.Mus. from the University of Leicester (1968), and the Lambeth D.Mus. (1969).
Organist of the Churches of St. Michael-le-Belfry, York (1920); St. Martin, Leeds (1923); All Saints', Alnwick (1925) and St. Mary-le-Tower, Ipswich (1927).
Organist of Leicester Cathedral (1931-1969).
A lecturer in music at the University of Leicester (1931-1946) and senior lecturer at Leicester College of Education (1945-1976). An extra-mural lecturer in music appreciation at Vaughan College (1931-1951), and an examiner for Trinity College of Music. Two of his pupils, **Stanley Vann** and **Harold Dexter** became English cathedral organists. **Jonathan Gregory** was organist of St. Anne's, Cathedral, Belfast and another pupil, **Jack Hawes,** became a composer of church music.
Composed chants and Responses. Author of *Notes on Choir Training* (1941).

GREATHEED, Revd. Samuel Stephenson (1813-1887)
Born near Weston-Super-Mare, Somerset on 22 February 1813; died in Corringham, Essex on 19 January 1887. A B.A. (1835) and M.A. (1838) graduate of the University of Cambridge. Ordained in 1838. Rector of Corringham, Essex. Composed an oratorio *Enoch's Prophecy* (1852), anthems including 'Blessed is the man' and 'Ye that fear the Lord', and hymn tunes. Published a collection of plainsong chants for use during Holy Communion on non-festival days.

GREATOREX, Revd. Edward (1820-1899)
Master of the choristers (from 1849) and precentor (1862-1872) of Durham Cathedral. Rector of Croxdale, County Durham from 1872. Composer of the anthem 'O Saviour of the World'.

GREATOREX, Thomas (1758-1831)
Born in North Wingfield near Chesterfield, Derbyshire on 5 October 1758; died in Hampton, Middlesex on 18 July 1831. Buried near **Benjamin Cooke** at Westminster Abbey.
His father, Anthony, was an organist of Burton-on-Trent, Staffordshire. Thomas's son Henry, who emigrated to the U.S.A., was a composer of hymn tunes.
The family moved to Leicester when Greatorex was eight years old (1767). Became a pupil of Benjamin Cooke in London (1772). Took lessons in singing with Santarelli in Rome and with Ignaz Pleyel in Strasbourg (from 1786). Made the acquaintance of Charles Edward, the Young Pretender, and acquired some music manuscripts from him. In 1788 he returned to London.
Became acquainted with the Earl of Sandwich and with Joah Bates, his secretary, while in Leicester. The Earl produced oratorios at Christmas at his seat of Hinchinbrook House, near Huntingdon; Greatorex took part in these from 1774 to 1776 inclusive. Bates, whom he succeeded on the latter's retirement in 1793, was

conductor of the Concerts of Ancient Music, having sung in the chorus.
Organist of Carlisle Cathedral (1781-1784).
Lived for a time in Newcastle-on-Tyne and travelled in the Netherlands, Italy and France. It was during this period that he took lessons in Strasbourg with Ignaz Pleyel. Taught singing and music from 1789.
Succeeded **George Ebenezer Williams** as organist of Westminster Abbey (1819 -1831).
In 1822 he became a professor of organ at the Royal Academy of Music.
Conducted the triennial music festivals at Birmingham, and those at York, Derby and other places.
His other interests included botany, mathematics and astronomy. A Fellow of the Royal Society.
His *Parochial Psalmody* (1825) was a set of existing Psalm tunes, harmonised by him for congregational singing.
Composer and arranger of glees, anthems, Psalm tunes and chants.

GREATOREX, Walter (1877-1949)
Born in Southwell, Nottinghamshire on 30 March 1877; died in Bournemouth, Dorset on 29 December 1949.
A chorister of King's College, Cambridge (1888-1893). Attended Derby School before going up to St. John's College, Cambridge, where he took an M.A.
Assistant music master at Uppingham School (1900-1910), where his pupils included **H.G. Ley**, and music master of Gresham's School, Holt, Norfolk (from 1911). His pupils at Gresham's included **Benjamin Britten** and W.H. Auden.
His hymn tune 'Woodlands' is widely used today with the hymn 'Tell out, my soul'.

GREAVES, Bernard (b.1936)
Born in Lancashire in 1936. Composer of hymn tunes.

GREAVES, Thomas (16th/17th century)
A lute player who lived and worked round 1600. Said to have been an old man in 1604. Lutenist to Sir Henry Pierrepoint of Holm, Nottinghamshire. Composed the anthem 'How long wilt Thou forget?', songs and madrigals. In 1604 his *Songs of Sundrie Kindes* was published, containing airs, songs of sadness and madrigals.

GREEN, Dr. Christie (1871-1939)
Born in Farnhill, near Keighley, Yorkshire in 1871; died in 1939.
Educated at Leeds Parish Church. Graduated B.Mus. (1895) and D.Mus. (1906) at Queen's College, Oxford.
Organist at the age of 11 of St. Thomas's Church, Sutton-in-Craven, Yorkshire (1883-1891). Assistant organist of Leeds Parish Church and organist and choirmaster of Emmanuel Church, Leeds (1891-1900). Organist and choirmaster of Blackburn Parish Church, Lancashire (1900-1912); Holy Trinity Church, Coventry, Warwickshire (1912-1918) and St. Margaret's Church, Dunham Massey, near Altrincham, Cheshire (1918-1926). A teacher of music for the Manchester Education Authority. A local choral society conductor. Composed a setting of the Holy Communion Service, anthems, songs, part songs for female voices and organ items.

GREEN, Harold (1871-1930)
Born in Helme, Yorkshire on 23 October 1871; died in Umzimkulu, Cape Province, South Africa on 20 December 1930. Composer of hymn tunes.

GREEN, James (c1690-c1750)
Organist of Hull Parish Church, Yorkshire in the first half of the 18th century.
In 1734 he published *A Book Of Psalmody containing Chanting Tunes...* which ran into 18 editions. His anthems include 'Behold, I bring you' and 'Lift up your hearts'. Also composed hymn tunes and was represented in the new Standard Edition of *Hymns Ancient and Modern*.

GREEN, Revd. Dr. John Edward (19th/20th century)
Born in London. Educated privately and at Shrewsbury School. Graduated B.Mus. and D.Mus. in the same year (1886) at Trinity College, Dublin, and B.A. (1890) and M.A. (1894) at St. John's College, Cambridge. Graduated LL.B. and M.A. from the University of Dublin, and was ordained deacon in 1894 priest in 1895.
A sub-lieutenant of the Royal Naval Volunteers (from 1888). Curate of St. Paul's Church, Grangetown, Diocese of York; Canton and St. Mary's Church, Cardiff (1894-1895). He was vicar of Farmcote and Lower Guiting (1895-1904), both in Gloucestershire.
Contributed articles on the Greek version of the New Testament to *The Churchman*, and composed an anthem 'Cry aloud' for saints' days.

GREEN, Dr. Joseph Ernst (19th/20th century)
Born in London. Educated privately, and graduated D.Mus. at the University of Durham (1910).
Organist (1893-1895) and choirmaster (from 1897) of the Rye Lane Baptist Church, Peckham, London. Lectured in music to special classes organised by London County Council (1900-1907). Organist and choirmaster of Spurgeon's Metropolitan Tabernacle and of the Stockwell Orphanage, London. Trained a choir of some 800 voices for the Spurgeon Centenary Meeting at the Royal Albert Hall (1934) and in charge of similar forces at the Baptist Forward Meeting (1936).
Composed anthems including 'Come unto Me' (1913), hymn tunes including 'Hadney' (1903) and a setting of the office of Vespers.

GREENE, Dr. Maurice (1696-1755)
Born in London on 12 August 1696; died in London on 1 December 1755.
Buried in the churchyard of St. Olave's, Jewry, at which Church his father had been minister. In 1888 on the demolition of St. Olave's, Maurice Greene's remains were removed to St. Paul's Cathedral, where he was reburied.
A chorister of St. Paul's Cathedral under **Jeremiah Clarke**, **Charles King** and **Richard Brind**, to whom he was articled (from 1710). Graduated Mus.D. at the University of Cambridge (1730). Greene's wife was related to both King and Clarke.
An organ recitalist, pioneering the imaginative use of solo stops. Organist of the Church of St. Dunstan-in-the-West, Fleet Street, London (1713/4-1718). Succeeded Daniel Purcell at St. Andrew's Church, Holborn but served only until April 1818. Brind had died

in the meantime and Greene succeeded him as organist of St. Paul's. Greene and **Handel** were at one time considered friends, and the latter was given the use of the organ at St. Paul's. The relationship later soured over the support given by Greene to the disgraced Giovanni Buononcini, Handel's rival.
Following the death of **William Croft**, Greene became organist and composer of the Chapel Royal. Greene was appointed professor of music at the University of Cambridge (1730) in succession to **Thomas Tudway**.
Appointed Master of the King's Musick in January 1735 on the death of **John Eccles**. In 1738 he was one of the founders of the Society of Musicians.
Towards the end of his life he inherited Bois Hall, Essex, from a cousin. This gave him the financial security and thus the opportunity to work (from 1750) on an ambitious project to publish a collection of church music. He intended to distribute the collection to every cathedral in the country. On hearing of Greene's scheme, the first **John Alcock** handed over his own collection. Greene's death delayed the publication but **William Boyce** promised Greene when the latter's health began to fail that he would take up the project and he saw the collection through to its eventual appearance.
Besides William Boyce, Greene's pupils included **John Travers** and **John Stanley**.
Composed keyboard music, two operas including *Florimel, or Love's Revenge* (1734) which was performed at the Three Choirs' Festival of 1745, oratorios and songs but he is remembered for his church music.
His anthems 'Lord, let me know mine end', 'God is our Hope' and the less well-known 'O God of my righteousness' are examples of at least 40 that he composed. 'Thou visiteth the earth', an extract from 'Thou, O God, art praised in Zion', is used extensively at Harvest-tide as is 'O clap your hands' at Ascensiontide. Other works include services, among which is a setting in C. His Te Deum in D for Choir and Orchestra is believed to have been written in celebration of the suppression of the Scottish rebellion in 1745. A Single Chant in B-flat was included in *Cathedral Psalter Chants* (1875).

GREENING, Anthony (1940-1996)
Born on 10 December 1940; died in March 1996. Assistant Organist of Ely Cathedral and later, a tutor at the Royal School of Church Music. A prolific editor of Tudor and other early church music. His published work includes 'Nativity' and A People's Eucharist (a setting of the Rite A form of Holy Communion from the *Alternative Service Book*).

GREENISH, Dr. Arthur James (1860-1935)
Born in Haverfordwest, Pembrokeshire, Wales on 26 January 1860; died in 1935. Brother of **Frederick Greenish.**
His mother was organist of the local village church and from the age of 11, Arthur Greenish acted as her assistant. Two years later he joined the choir of St. Saviour's Church, South Hampstead, London where, from 1877, he was articled to the organist.
In 1875 he went into his father's business in Haverfordwest, studying music theory privately. Later studied at the Royal Academy of Music for two years with **Charles Steggall** for organ, Fitton for piano and Lunn for harmony but he was forced through

ill-health to quit after two years. Graduated Mus.B. (1885) and Mus.D. (1892) at the University of Cambridge.

Organist of St. Mary's Church, Battersea, London (1880-1882), where the choirmaster was **Alfred Scott-Gatty**, Garter King-at-Arms.

Organist and choirmaster of St. Saviour's, South Hampstead (from 1882). A local musical society conductor. An examiner in music for Trinity College of Music. In 1899 he became a professor of harmony at the Royal Academy of Music, with which he was connected in one capacity or another for a total of 57 years.

Composed an Evening Service, songs, and pieces for violin.

GREENISH, Dr. Frederick Robert (?-1923)
Born in Haverfordwest, Pembrokeshire, the brother of **Arthur Greenish**; died in Warlingham, Surrey, on 11 November 1923.

Graduated B.Mus (1883) and D.Mus. (1891) at New College, Oxford. Organist and choirmaster of St. Martin's Church, Haverfordwest (1881-1887) and of St. Mary's Church, Haverfordwest (1888-1909). An adjudicator at the national eisteddfod in 1906. A justice of the peace in Haverfordwest, and high sheriff. Composed cantatas including *The Church Triumphant*, Services, anthems and songs.

GREENWOOD, Edward Norman (1902-1962)
Born in Hampstead, London on 16 December 1902; died in Klagenfurt, Austria on 16 September 1962. A professor of the Royal College of Music (from 1948), where he had earlier been a student (1919-1925). Composer of hymn tunes including 'Lansdowne', found in *Hymns and Songs* (1969).

GREENWOOD, James (1837-1894)
Invented the Lancashire Sol-fa method of musical notation. A voice trainer and composer. Among his compositions are a Magnificat and Nunc Dimittis in C (1882), a Jubilate (1860), the anthems 'The Lord loveth the gates of Zion' (1863) and 'Lord, we pray Thee'.

GREENWOOD, John (1795-1837)
Born in Shibden, Lancashire (or Sowerby Bridge, Yorkshire) on 17 June 1795; died, probably in Leeds, on 14 February 1837.

Took organ lessons with Stopforth, organist of Halifax Parish Church, Yorkshire.

Organist of Keighley Parish Church, Yorkshire from the age of 16 until the position at Leeds Parish Church fell vacant in 1821. A parochial election was held, an event that was conducted in the manner of a Parliamentary election, with three candidates and over 4,000 votes cast. Greenwood was successful.

Organist of Leeds Parish Church for six years and then spent two years each in France, London and the U.S.A. On his return he settled in Halifax, where he became organist of the South Parade Methodist Chapel. Retired through ill health in 1835.

Published collections of Psalmody, and an edition entitled *Modulus Sanctus*. A tune is found in *English Hymnal*.

GREGGS, William (c1652-1710)
Born either around the year 1652 or later - in 1661 or 1662; died in Durham and was buried on 16 October 1710. Organist and master of the choristers of Durham Cathedral from April 1682 until his death. In 1686 he was given three months' leave to take further tuition in music in London. In 1691 he purchased the Langley Song School, Durham. Composed six anthems including 'My heart is inditing'.

GREGOR, Revd. Christian (18th/19th century)
Bishop of the Unitas Fratrum (from 1802). Composed the anthems 'Glory to God in the highest' and 'Hosanna, blessed is He'.

GREGORY, Arthur Stephen (b.1890)
Born in Uppingham, Rutland in 1890. Educated privately and at Trinity College of Music. Organist and choirmaster of All Hallows Church, Seaton; organist of St. Andrew's Church, Great Easton (1913-1915) and sub organist of Uppingham Parish Church (1910-1930). Served in the armed forces for a period of three years during World War I. Composed a Magnificat and Nunc Dimittis in A, chants to the Canticles, anthems including 'Blest are the departed', carols, and hymn tunes.

GREGORY, George Herbert (1853-?)
Born in Clewer, near Windsor, Berkshire on 6 December 1853, the elder brother of **James Gregory**.

A graduate of New College, Oxford. Studied under **Samuel Reay**.

Organist of the Trinity Episcopal Church, Melrose, Scotland (1872-1874); Tamworth Parish Church, Staffordshire (1874-1875) and Boston Parish Church, Lincolnshire (from 1876). A tenor singer and a local choral society conductor.

Composed a Magnificat and Nunc Dimittis in E-flat (1878), a Te Deum (1885), anthems including 'God, who at this time' and other items of church music, songs, and part songs.

GREGORY, James Lively (1860-1916)
Born in Old Windsor, Berkshire on 27 March 1860; died on 13 October 1916.

Received training in music from his brother **George Gregory**. Graduated B.Mus. (1892) at the University of Durham.

Succeeded his brother George as organist of Holy Trinity Church, Melrose, Scotland (1875-1876). Organist of the Parish Churches of Welford, Hertfordshire (1877-1879); Ware, Hertfordshire (from 1880) and Hertford (from 1901). A teacher in Ware and organist and music teacher at Christ's Hospital, Hertford (from 1901). A local music society conductor.

Composed a Magnificat and Nunc Dimittis in A-flat in chant form (1898), the anthem 'O how amiable are Thy dwellings' (1911), songs, part songs and works for piano and for organ.

GREGORY, Jonathan (20th century)
An organist and composer of the 20th century. A chorister of Leicester Cathedral under **G.C. Gray**. Studied at the Royal Academy of Music and was organ scholar of Clare College, Cambridge where he studied under Gillian Weir. Organist of St. Anne's Cathedral, Belfast (1975-1983). Composer of the anthems 'O, Sweetest Jesu' and 'Easter Day'.

GREGORY, Revd. Stephen Herbert (1869-1950)
Born in Howden, Yorkshire in 1869; died in Ashbourne, Derbyshire on 28 September 1950. Educated at Didsbury College, Manchester for the ministry of the Methodist Church. A Methodist missionary in India (1892-1915). Composer of hymn tunes including 'Wendell' for *Methodist Hymn Book* (1933).

GREGORY, Theophilus Cyril (b.1901)
Born in Thorne, Yorkshire on 3 February 1901. Educated at Pembroke College, Oxford; the Royal College of Music, and privately. Assistant master of Guildford Royal Grammar School,

Surrey (1925-1928) and music master of Rydal School, Colwyn Bay, North Wales (from 1929). Composer of hymn tunes.

GREGORY, William (?-1663)
William Gregory's biographical details are not entirely clear but he is believed to have died in August or September 1663. A violinist and wind instrument maker to Charles I (1626) and Charles II from (1661-1663). Composed a coranto, sarabande and jigge for the edition *Court Ayres* (1655) by John Playford. Two anthems identified as Gregory's are 'Out of the deep' and 'O Lord, Thou hast cast us out'.

GREIG, William Sydney (1910-1983)
Born in Dublin on 25 November 1910; died in Dublin on 6 March 1983. A chorister under **George Hewson** at St. Patrick's Cathedral, Dublin. Organ scholar (1928-1931) of the Royal Irish Academy of Music. Graduated B.Mus (1934) at the University of Dublin. A professor of organ at the Municipal School of Music, Dublin (from 1955). Organist of Stillorgan Church, Dublin (1928-1929). Organist and choirmaster of the Abbey Presbyterian Church, Dublin (1929-1960).
Assistant organist of both Dublin cathedrals, Christ Church (1934-1943) and St. Patrick's (1943-1960).
Organist of St. Patrick's Cathedral (1960-1976), retiring in the latter year. Composed Evening Canticles in E Minor and another set in E-flat, and the anthem 'Let all the world in ev'ry corner sing' (1938).

GREVILLE, Revd. Robert (18th century)
Composed the prize glee 'Now the Bright Morning Star' (1787) and the anthem 'Turn Thee, O Lord'.

GREY, Revd. Francis Richard (1813-1890)
Born in St. Marylebone, London on 31 March 1813; died in Morpeth, County Durham on 22 March 1890. Rector of Morpeth Parish Church and an honorary canon of Durham Cathedral. Composer of hymn tunes. His 'St. Aidan' first appeared in *Bristol Tune Book* (1863).

GRIER, Francis John Roy (b.1955)
Born in Kotakinabalu, Sabah, Borneo, where his father worked for the Colonial Service, on 29 July 1955.
A chorister of St. George's Chapel, Windsor Castle (1963-1968) under **Sidney Campbell** and became the first music scholar of Eton College (1969-1973). Organ scholar of King's College, Cambridge (1973-1976) where he read music, worked with **David Willcocks** and **Philip Ledger** and graduated B.A. Studied music also with Joseph Cooper, Fanny Waterman, Bernard Roberts and, for organ, Gillian Weir.
Assistant organist of Christ Church Cathedral, Oxford (1977-1981) under **Simon Preston** and, for the following four years, organist (1981-1985), an appointment that he won at the age of 25. In his time at Christ Church he performed and recorded extensively, and commissioned works by the composers **William Matthias**, **Giles Swayne** and **John Tavener.**
In 1985 he resigned from Christ Church in order to pursue a number of options that were unavailable to him as a full-time musician. Studied theology and meditation in India, and worked with people with learning difficulties in London and Bangalore. Returned to England in 1989 and became a psychodynamic counsellor and marital psychotherapist, as well as composing extensively and performing.
Began to compose as a young boy. His works include a set of Advent Responsories for the choir of King's College, Cambridge (1990), the *Corpus Christi* Carol and the anthem 'Proclaim His triumph, heaven and earth'. In 1993, first performances were given of three newly-commissioned compositions for major choirs, namely 'Thou, O God, art praised in Sion' (Durham Cathedral), 'Let us invoke Christ' (St. Paul's Cathedral) and 'Salve Regina' (for the Border Choirs Festival). His other works include an opera *St. Francis*, and a setting of poems by Tagore for singer and chamber ensemble, written for the B.B.C. Television series *The Cry*.

GRIERSON, Hubert.
See **FOOTE**, Guthrie Herbert.

GRIESBACH, John Henry (1798-1875)
Born in Windsor, Berkshire, of German parents, on 20 June 1798; died in London on 9 January 1875. Studied under Friedrich Kalkbrenner. A pianist, and director of the Philharmonic Society. Composed anthems including 'I shall see Him, but not now', an operetta *James I or The Royal Captive*, an overture, and songs.

GRIEVE, John Charles (1842-?)
Born in Edinburgh on 29 August 1842. Lecturer in musical theory at Heriot-Watt College, Edinburgh, and choirmaster of Lady Yester's Church. Taught singing in schools and was a conductor. Editor of *Musical Star*. Composed an oratorio *Benjamin* (1877), cantatas, songs, and *The Sower and The Seed*, a Scripture parable for Solo Voices and Chorus. Published *Christian Songs of Praise*, a collection of 24 hymns for four voices.

GRIFFIN, George (b.1816)
Born in Wingrave, Buckinghamshire on 1 April 1816. Compiled *New Sacred Music* (1840) and *The Buckinghamshire Harmonist*. Funeral anthem 'I heard a Voice from Heaven' (c1865).

GRIFFITH, William (1867-1929)
Born in Syresham, Northamptonshire in 1867; died in Leicester on 21 August 1929.
Educated at Magdalen School, Brackley, Northamptonshire. In 1888 he qualified as a pharmacist. Graduated B.Mus. at the University of Durham (1894).
Following his pharmacy qualification he was in business in Lancashire until 1895, the year in which he took up a career in music. From that year until 1901 he was organist and choirmaster of the Church of the Holy Sepulchre, Northampton.
Held appointments in Scotland at the King Street United Free Church, Kilmarnock (1901-1909); Kilbarchan Parish Church, Renfrewshire (from 1909) and St. Ninian's Church, Stranraer. At some time in his career he was organist of the Church of SS Paul and Mary, Barrow-in-Furness.
Taught music at the Kilmarnock Academy (from 1906) and Athanaeum School of Music, Glasgow (1902-1908). A local operatic society conductor.

Composed anthems and hymn tunes. *Church Hymnary*'s Revised Edition (1927) uses 'Cuttle Mills' with 'Jesus, friend of little children' by Walter Mathams. Also composed songs and part songs.

GRIFFITHS, John Robert (1857-1936)
Born in Buckley, Flintshire, Wales in 1857; died in Buckley on 2 March 1936.
Graduated B.Mus. (1901) from the University of Durham.
Organist and choirmaster in London of Greville Place Congregational Church, St. John's Wood (from 1876); Highgate Congregational Church (from 1877) and Christ Church, Westminster Bridge Road (from 1881), and Cliff Town Congregational Church, Southend, Essex (from 1905).
Shared the organ playing duties at the 1889 Festival of the Nonconformist Choir Union at the Crystal Palace, London with E.W. Blandford. He continued as organist in 1890 and 1891. Editor of *The Bible Christian Sunday School Hymnal* (1898).

GRIFFITHS, Richard (c1789-1850)
Born around the year 1789; died in London on 18 July 1850.
Compiled *Psalm Tunes and Chants, Original and Selected* (1846).
Composed instrumental works.

GRIFFITHS, Robert (1824-1903)
Born in Carmarthen, Wales on 21 May 1824; died in Ilford, Essex on 1 January 1903.
While still very young, he moved with his family to Bristol. Precentor of the Sunday School of the Broadmead Chapel.
On the death of his father he went to live in London. Became precentor of the Baptist Chapel, Islington Green.
In 1851 he attended a lecture by John Curwen on the Tonic Sol-fa method of musical notation. This inspired him to take up the study of music by this means and two years later, in 1853, he became Secretary of the Tonic Sol-fa Society on its inception.
In 1854 he moved to Manchester, where he taught the method at Sunday Schools. Such was the success that by the time he left Manchester in 1865 to become secretary to John Curwen there were some 200 teachers and 2,000 pupils of the Tonic Sol-fa method.
Became secretary of the Tonic Sol-fa College when it was founded in 1875. Continued to lecture throughout England and Wales until his retirement to Ilford in 1900.
Composer of hymn tunes and other items of church music.

GRIFFITHS, Thomas Vernon (1894-1985)
Born in West Kirby, Cheshire on 22 June 1894; died in 1985. Graduated Mus.B. (1922) at Pembroke College, Cambridge. Senior music teacher, organist and choirmaster of St. Edmund's School, Canterbury. Composer of the anthem 'Jesu, grant me this, I pray' (1966), a Missa *Innocentium* (1938) for Boys' Voices, and hymn tunes.

GRIGG, Revd.?Jacob (18th/19th century)
A minister and amateur musician of the late 18th and probably the early 19th century. A Revd. Joseph Grigg (1722-1768) could be this person. Composed at least three hymn tunes. 'Tiverton' (c1791) was used with a translation of the Latin hymn 'Behold, the Messengers of Christ' in the Standard Edition (1916) of *Hymns Ancient and Modern*.

GRIMSHAW, Arthur Edmund (1864-1913)
Born in Leeds in 1864; died on 1 August 1913. Received his musical training in Leeds. Organist and choirmaster of St. Anne's Roman Catholic Cathedral, Leeds (from 1883). Composed a setting of Psalm 141 'Lord, I call upon Thee' for Solo Voices and Chorus (1885), other items of church music, operettas, songs and part songs including 'El Escribano' (1891).

GRIMSHAW, John (1765-1819)
Born in 1765; died in Lancashire on 18 February 1819. Organist of St. John's Church, Manchester. Composed at least 24 hymn tunes, including 'Heaton Norris', which was used in the Revised Edition (1927) of *Church Hymnary* with the hymn 'O happy day, that fixed my choice' by Philip Doddridge. Also composed songs.

GRINDLE, Dr. William Henry (20th century)
Born in Bangor, County Down, Northern Ireland.
A chorister of the Abbey Church, Bangor. Attended Regent House Grammar School, Newtownwards before taking up a place at Queen's University, Belfast, where he studied French language and literature.
Taught in London, where he also studied harmony and counterpoint with **Eric Thiman**, organ with Douglas Hawkridge and conducting with Adrian Boult. Also studied organ with Flor Peeters in Belgium, and orchestral conducting with Igor Markevitch at summer school in Monte Carlo.
His degrees include the B.Mus and Ph.D. from Trinity College, Dublin, and a master's degree from Queen's, Belfast.
Organist and master of the choristers at St. Anne's Cathedral, Belfast (1964-1975) where he succeeded **Charles Brennan**. In 1975 he was appointed lecturer in music at Stranmillis College of Education where he is now head of the music department.
Author of *Irish Cathedral Music* (1989) and music editor of the hymnal *Sing and Pray* (1990).
Composer of the carol-anthem 'What is that Light?', an Improvisation on 'University' for Organ, a set of Responses, hymn tunes and chants.

GROOME, Robert Hindes (1810-1889)
Born in Framlingham, Suffolk on 18 January 1810; died in Monk Soham, Suffolk on 19 March 1889. Composer of hymn tunes, and 'The song of the bells' (1884).

GROSVENOR, Symeon (1816-1866)
Born in Dudley, Worcestershire on 11 January 1816; died in Dudley on 7 July 1866. A pupil of Ignaz Moscheles and a Thomas Adams. Graduated B.Mus. (1852) at the University of Oxford. Organist of St. Thomas's Parish Church, Dudley (1836-1854). Composed and edited church music, including the thanksgiving anthem 'In Te, Domine, speravi' (1853).

GROVES, Cecil Tom (1888-1955)
Born in Leicester in 1888; died in Leicester on 27 October 1955. Served as a missionary of the Methodist church in India. Composer of hymn tunes including 'Hardwicke', found in *Methodist Hymn Book* (1933).

GRUNDY, David Heywood (b.1934)
Born in Haslingden, Lancashire in 1934. Composer of hymn tunes.

GUERNSEY, Wellington (1817-1885)

Born in Mullingar, Ireland on 8 June 1817; died in London on 13 November 1885. He wrote the words of many songs, including 'Mary Blane'. Composed a Mass in B-flat and other items of church music.

GUEST, Dr. Douglas Albert (b.1916)

Born in Mortomley, Yorkshire on 9 May 1916.

Educated at Reading School, Berkshire (1929-1933), the Royal College of Music (1933-1935) and King's College, Cambridge (1935-1939). At King's he was successively organ scholar and John Stewart of Rannoch scholar. Graduated Mus.B. (1938) and M.A. (1942) at Cambridge. Awarded the Lambeth D.Mus. in 1977. Appointed C.V.O. in 1975.

A major in the Royal Artillery during World War II, Douglas Guest was mentioned in despatches from Normandy in 1944. Director of music at Uppingham School (1945-1950).

Organist of the Cathedrals of Salisbury (1950-1957) and Worcester (1957-1963), and of Westminster Abbey (1963-1981). A professor of the R.C.M. (1963-1981).

During his time at Westminster Abbey, he composed items of music for use on special occasions, including the anthem 'For the fallen'. Also composed a Missa Brevis for his Salisbury Choir.

GUEST, George (1771-1831)

Born in Bury St. Edmunds in 1771; died in Wisbech, Cambridgeshire on 10 September 1831.

Learned music with his father, **Ralph Guest**, and as a chorister of the Chapel Royal under **James Nares** and **Edmund Ayrton**.

In 1787 he was appointed organist of the Parish Church of Eye, Suffolk. Remained there until 1789 when he became organist of Wisbech Parish Church, a position he held until his death.

Composed anthems, hymns, glees, duets, songs, organ pieces and music for military band.

GUEST, George Howell (b. 1924)

Born in Bangor, Wales in 1924. Educated locally and at Chester Cathedral with **Malcolm Boyle**, whose assistant he became.

His entire professional life has, unusually, been centred on one musical foundation. He was successively organ scholar and organist (1951-1990) of St. John's College, Cambridge, bringing the choir to world-wide prominence. Cambridge University organist (1974-1991) and University lecturer in music (1956-1982). President of the Royal College of Organists and the Incorporated Association of Organists. Closely associated with some American choirs including Berkshire Boys and Gloria Dei Cantores.

His published compositions include several carols, a number written for the St. John's College Advent Carol Service, held annually on the evening of Advent Sunday and broadcast by the B.B.C.

GUEST, Ralph (1742-1830)

Born in Basely, Shropshire in 1742; died in Bury St. Edmunds in June 1830. Father of **George Guest**.

As a young boy he sang in the choir of the parish church.

At the age of 21 he went to London, where he sang in the choir of the Portland Chapel. Five years later he moved to Bury St. Edmunds where he set up in business. He learned to play organ from Ford, the parish church organist.

In 1805, the year which marked his total commitment to music he was appointed choir master of St. James's, Bury St. Edmunds. When, in 1822, the church acquired an organ, Ralph Guest became the first organist.

Published *The Psalms of David...* A supplement, *Hymns and Psalms*, consisted of music adapted and composed by him. Also composed glees and songs.

GUISE, Richard (1740-1808)

Born in 1740; died on 10 March 1808.

A B.Mus. graduate, but the details are unknown.

A gentleman of the Chapel Royal (from 1779) and a lay clerk of St. George's Chapel, Windsor Castle (1756-1794) and of Eton College (1760-1773).

A lay vicar and master of the choristers (from 1793) of Westminster Abbey. **Samuel Arnold** accepted the organistship of Westminster Abbey in 1793 on condition that he was not required to take charge of the choir. Richard Guise took on that responsibility.

Composed a Service in E, the anthems 'Hear me, O Lord' and 'Wherewithal shall a young man cleanse his way?' and three single chants.

GUNDRY, Inglis (b.1905)

Born in Wimbledon, London on 8 May 1905.

Attended Mill Hill School; Balliol College, Oxford, where he read law; the Middle Temple; and the Royal College of Music (from 1935) under **Ralph Vaughan Williams**. Graduated M.A. and qualified as a barrister.

In 1942 he was appointed school master to the Royal Marines. Music adviser to the director of the Admiralty Education Department and a music tutor in the extra-mural department of London University (from 1947). In 1960 he was appointed director of the Sacred Music Drama Society.

A lecturer for the Workers' Educational Association at the University of London (from 1949).

Editor of *Naval Song Book*.

Composer of hymn tunes. Other works include operas, to his own libretti, including *Avon* (1949).

GUNN, Barnabas (?-1753)

Died in Birmingham on 6 February 1753.

The first organist (1715-1730) of the Church of St. Philip, Birmingham, which was later elevated to cathedral status.

Organist of Gloucester Cathedral (1730-1740).

Thereafter, he returned to Birmingham. Organised series of summer concerts at the Duddleston Gardens (1748-1753) along the lines of those at the Vauxhall Gardens, London.

Although he was nominally organist of Chelsea Hospital, London (1730-1753) his duties were permanently carried out by a deputy. Barnabas Gunn was said to be a brilliant organ player, particularly adept at improvisation.

Composed a Te Deum and Jubilate. **Handel** was among the subscribers to his *Two Cantatas and Six Songs*. Also composed sonatas for harpsichord.

GUTHRIE, Mrs. T.A.
See **AUSTEN**, Augusta A.

Gutyn Arfon
See **JONES**, Griffith Hugh.

GWILT, David William (b.1932)
Born in Edinburgh on 3 November 1932. Educated at Sedburgh School and St. John's College, Cambridge, where he graduated Mus.B. Composer of hymn tunes and a Suite for Woodwind and Brass instruments (1966).

Gwilym Gwent
See **WILLIAMS**, William Aubrey.

GWYNNETH (Guinneth), Revd. Dr. John (16th century)
John Gwynneth is known to have been alive between the years 1531 and 1533 and he was possibly born in Caernarvonshire, Wales.
He was probably educated at local monasteries. His studies at the University of Oxford are likely to have been made possible through one or more patrons. Graduated D.Mus. (1531) at the University of Oxford.
Rector of St. Peter's Church, Westcheap, London and described by **Thomas Morley** as an eminent musician. Also held a living in Luton, Bedfordshire. Henry VIII provided him with a sinecure, the rectorship of Clynnog-Fawr, Caernarvonshire, which he held until his death.
Author of works on Roman Catholicism. He may have been imprisoned during the reign of Elizabeth I for refusing to accept the Act of Uniformity of 1559.
Composed Masses and songs.

GWYTHER, H.M. (19th century)
In *Church Hymns* (1874), Gwyther's 'Daughters of Galilee' was used as a setting of 'O daughters blest of Galilee' by William Walsham How.

H

HABYNGTON
See **ABYNGDON**.

HACKETT, Charles Danvers (1812-1858)
Born in 1812; died in London in 1858. Graduated B.Mus. at the University of Oxford (1850). Organist of Rotherham Parish Church, Yorkshire. Edited *The National Psalmist* (1839), a collection of Psalm and hymn tunes. Composed church music, including the anthems 'I will arise' and 'The Lord is my strength', and a sacred cantata *Zion* (1853).

HADLEY, Dr. Patrick Arthur Sheldon (1899-1973)
Born in Cambridge on 5 March 1899; died in King's Lynn, Norfolk on 17 December 1973. Son of the master of Pembroke College and university professor of music.
Served in the armed forces in France during World War I. He lost a leg in action and his brother was killed.
Studied at Winchester College, Hampshire and at Pembroke College, Cambridge. Graduated M.A. and Mus.D. Also attended the Royal College of Music under **Ralph Vaughan Williams** for composition and Adrian Boult for conducting.
Taught at the R.C.M. (1925-1938). A Cambridge academic. Precentor, a fellow of Gonville and Caius College and a university lecturer (from 1938). Cambridge professor of music (1946- 1963).
Also remembered as a conductor and as a composer whose output was limited in quantity but of a high quality. A friend of the composer Constant Lambert.
The Trees so High (1932) was a symphonic ballad for Baritone, Chorus and Orchestra based on an old folk song. *The Hills* (1946) was inspired by the Peak District, while the cantata *Fen and Flood* was inspired by his experience of flooding in East Anglia during 1953, and sought to illustrate how men's wit and resource can overcome danger.
The anthem 'My beloved spake' (1936) and the carol 'I sing of a Maiden' (1936) represent his church music.

HADOW, Sir William Henry (1859-1937)
Born in Ebrington, Gloucestershire on 27 December 1859; died in London on 9 April 1937.
Said to be something of a musical prodigy, with a compositional style similar to that of Brahms.

Educated at Malvern College, Worcestershire (1871-1878) and at Worcester College, Oxford (1878-1882) where he graduated B.A. (1882), MA (1885) and, following study with **C.H. Lloyd** for composition, B.Mus. (1890) and D.Mus. (1909). Also studied at Darmstadt, Germany. Later he was awarded honorary doctorates in music by the Universities of Durham and Wales.
Appointed C.B.E., and subsequently knighted (1918).
He married the elder daughter of **John Troutbeck**.
A fellow, lecturer and tutor (from 1885) of his old college. A specialist in classics. Although music was not his principal subject, he lectured on occasions on behalf of the Oxford professor, **John Stainer**.
In 1898 it was proposed that the B.Mus. should only be awarded to students who had completed three years' study and residence at the University. In common with the Universities of Dublin, Durham and London, Oxford awarded musical degrees on the strength of compositions submitted. Oxford had no structure for teaching music at the time. Proponents of the reform argued that it would lead to the raising of standards, while those against it cited the difficulty in persuading professional musicians to study for three more years before earning their living.
Hadow, **Hubert Parry**, **Walter Parratt** and **C.V. Stanford** were in favour. John Stainer, **Ebenezer Prout** and **Frederick Bridge** opposed the idea. The Hebdomadal Council of the University rejected the proposal and it was not until 1944 that the University of Oxford put into place a formal scheme for the study of music on which the award of a degree would depend.
In 1896 Henry Hadow was general editor of *Oxford History of Music*. Lectured and wrote on musical topics, his publications including a work on Haydn. He collaborated with **Walford Davies** and David Lloyd George in the production of *Hymns of Western Europe*, published around 1924.
In 1910 Henry Hadow was appointed principal of Armstrong College, Newcastle-on-Tyne, part of the University of Durham. He was later vice chancellor of the Universities of Durham (1916-1919) and Sheffield (1919-1930), where he established a music department.
The Hadow Committee on Education, of which he was chairman, reported in 1926.

Played a principal part in the early days of the Church Music Society (founded 1906), serving as chairman from its inception until he was succeeded by **Sydney Nicholson** in 1919.

Hadow's hymn tune 'South Cerney' was used in the Revised Edition of *Church Hymnary* (1927) with the German hymn 'O Love, who formedst me'. Also composed an anthem 'When I was in trouble', songs and a String Quartet in E-flat.

HAGUE, Dr. Charles (1769-1821)
Born in Tadcaster on 4 May 1769; died in Cambridge on 18 June 1821.
Studied violin at Cambridge under Manini from 1779 to 1785, when he moved to London. His studies continued under Johann Salomon and **Benjamin Cooke**. Graduated Mus.B. (1794) and Mus.D. (1801) at Trinity Hall, Cambridge.
Succeeded **John Randall** as Cambridge professor of music (1799-1821). Among his pupils was the second **John Camidge**.
Charles Hague's compositions include a Psalm 'By the waters of Babylon', glees and piano music.

HAIGH, Dr. Tom (?-1927)
Organ scholar at the Royal College of Music (1894-1898). Graduated B.Mus. (1898) and D.Mus. (1907) at the University of Durham.
Organist and choirmaster of the Church of St. Mary, Boltons, South Kensington, London (from 1896) and of Ramsgate Parish Church, Kent (1898).
Emigrated to Australia in March 1927 as organist of St. Andrew's Cathedral, Adelaide and as principal of the Sydney Conservatory. Toured the world five times in connection with his work as an examiner for the Associated Board of the Royal Schools of Music.
Composed anthems, the Christmas carol 'O sing and rejoice' (1917), the morning hymn 'Darkly, in the verge of morning' (1909), songs, piano music, a Canon in A-flat (1911) and other items for the organ.

HAKE, John (16th century)
A church musician and composer of the 16th century. This composer may be the same John Hake who was master of the choristers of St. George's Chapel, Windsor Castle from or before 1558 until 1559 or later. Contributed harmonisations of 18 Psalm tunes to a collection by **John Day**, *The Whole Psalmes...* (1562). Also composed a Latin Kyrie.

HAKING, Revd. Dr. Richard (1830-1894)
Born in Bury, Lancashire in 1830; died in Southacre, Norfolk on 6 September 1894.
Graduated B.Mus. (1855) and D.Mus. (1864) at the University of Oxford. Ordained in 1861.
Rector of Eaton Gray, Malmesbury, Wiltshire (from 1763) and of Congham, Norfolk (from 1882).
Composed anthems including 'Doth not wisdom cry?' and 'Lord, let me know mine end'. *Church Hymns* (1874) links his tune 'Rodbourne' with the hymn by George Rawson, 'Come to our poor nature's night'. His other compositions include glees and songs.

HALAHAN, Guy Frederick Crosby (20th century)
Attended Westminster School and Trinity College, Cambridge where he graduated M.A. A double bass player and composer whose works include the anthem 'Let us all rejoice' (1963), the opera *Elanda and Eclipse* (1957) and *Songs from the Madhouse*.

HALFORD, George John (1858-?)
Born in Chilvers Coton, Warwickshire on 13 February 1858.
His organ studies were directed by William Chater, organist of Holy Trinity Church, Coventry, Warwickshire. In 1875 he moved to Birmingham where he studied piano and composition under **Charles Swinnerton Heap**. Graduated B.Mus. at the University of Durham in 1892.
Held the West Midlands organistships of SS Mary and George, Birmingham (1876-1880); St. John's, Wolverhampton (from 1881); St. Michael's, Handsworth (from 1886) and Handsworth Parish Church (from 1891). A choral and musical society conductor.
Composed a Te Deum in D (1915), anthems including 'Remember not, Lord, our offences' (1886) and 'The souls of the righteous' (1915), a cantata *The Paraclete* (1891), part songs, a concert overture and organ music.

HALL, Charles King (1845-1895)
Born in London in 1845; died in London on 1 September 1895.
Organist of the London churches of St. Paul's, Camden Square and Christ Church, Brondesbury. Reader to the music publishers Chappells.
Composed an Evening Service in E-flat, performed in St. Paul's Cathedral by the London Church Choirs' Association (1891), and other items of church music including anthems such as 'And the angel said unto her' and 'O Lord, my trust'. Also composed operas, a cantata *Beauty and the Beast*, songs and piano music. Author of manuals for harmonium and organ.

HALL, Revd. Edward Vine (1837-1909)
Born in Maidstone, Kent on 11 June 1837; died in Oxford on 7 July 1909. Son of the printer to the University of Oxford
A chorister of Magdalen College, Oxford (1844-1855), and a Magdalen lay clerk (from 1855). Graduated B.A. (1859) and M.A. (1862). Ordained deacon in 1861, priest in 1863.
Assistant organist of Magdalen College (1858-1859).
Curate of Hurst, Berkshire (1861-1863) and of Brighton Parish Church, Sussex (1863-1866). Incumbent of the Holy Trinity Chapel, Brighton (1866-1870); vicar of Spring Grove, Middlesex (1870-1878); a minor canon and sacrist of Worcester Cathedral (1877-1890) and vicar of Bromsgrove, Worcestershire (from 1890). A conductor, tenor singer, organ recitalist and a lecturer in music.
On 7 May 1888, he conducted **Edward Elgar**'s Three Pieces for String Orchestra, which Elgar later revised and issued as Serenade for Strings. Edward Vine published a book containing 'The waiting Saviour' and others of his sermons.
Composed two settings of the Holy Communion Service and two of the Magnificat and Nunc Dimittis, one of which was used at the conclusion of the Three Choirs' Festival at Worcester in 1881. His anthems include 'Praise the Lord' and 'O Jerusalem'. Also composed part songs.

HALL, Revd. Henry (1655-1707)
Born in New Windsor, Berkshire in 1655; died in Hereford on 30 March 1707 and was buried in the cathedral.
In 1698 he was ordained deacon.
A Chapel Royal chorister under **Henry Cooke**. Left the choir around the end of 1672 and was thus one of the last of Cooke's choristers. At this point he may have studied composition with **Pelham Humphrey**. It is known that he and **Henry Purcell** were pupils of **John Blow**.

A Henry Hall, who may or may not be the same person, was acting organist of Wells Cathedral in 1674.

From 1674 until 1679, Henry Hall was organist of Exeter Cathedral, succeeding Theodore Coleby. Prior to his formal departure he had been absent for some time.

In 1679 he was appointed vicar choral of Hereford Cathedral. His other responsibilities included assisting the organist and teaching the choristers.

Organist of Hereford Cathedral (1688-1707). Following his death his son, also named Henry, succeeded him.

A poet, and author of an *Ode to Purcell*.

A collection by **Thomas Tudway** contains a number of works by Henry Hall, these being a Te Deum in E-flat, a Benedicite in C Minor, a Cantate Domino, a Deus Misereatur in B-flat, and five anthems. Composed 11 anthems in all including 'Let God arise' and 'O clap your hands', two chants, songs, dialogues and catches.

HALL, Richard (b.1903)

Born in York on 16 September 1903. Educated at Loretto School, Edinburgh and, as organ scholar, Peterhouse, Cambridge. Organist of All Souls' Church, Leeds. Precentor of Leeds Parish Church. A professor of composition at the Royal Manchester College of Music (1938-1956), where his pupils included Ronald Stevenson, Alexander Goehr, Peter Maxwell Davies, Harrison Birtwistle and John Ogdon - a group of musicians sometimes styled the 'Manchester New Music Group'. Director of music at Dartington Hall, Devon (1956-1967). A minister of the Unitarian Church thereafter. Composer of the anthem 'Bread of the world' (1931).

HALL, Dr. William Alfred (1877-?)

Born in London in 1877.

Graduated B.Mus. (1903) and D.Mus. (1909) at Queen's College, Oxford.

Organist and choirmaster at the London Churches of St. Paul, Tottenham (1896-1898) and St. James, Garlick Hill (1899-1917), and then All Saints' Church, Eastbourne, Sussex (from 1917). Organist of Newark Parish Church, Nottinghamshire (from 1928), music master of Newark Grammar School and High School (from 1929), and organist of Claypole Parish Church (from 1934). A lecturer in music at Newark Technical College.

Composed a sacred cantata '*The Presentation in the Temple*' (1905), and anthems. Some of his organ music was published in *The Anglican Organist*.

HALLACK, Edith Sarah (1866-1957)

Born in Clerkenwell, London in 1866; died in Somerset on 8 April 1957. Composer of hymn tunes.

HALLAM, Edwin Percy (1887-1957)

Born in Nottingham on 4 September 1887; died in Bury St. Edmunds on 12 October 1957.

After serving articles under **James Kendrick Pyne** at Manchester Cathedral he graduated B.Mus. at the University of Durham (1907).

Gave his first organ recital at the age of 10, at St. Bartholomew's Church, Nottingham.

Assistant organist of the Churches of St. Thomas and St. Bartholomew, Nottingham, and of the Church of St. Chad, Ladyburn, Manchester (from 1907).

Appointed organist of St. Chad's, and subsequently organist and choirmaster of St. Mary's Church, Bury St. Edmunds (from 1909).

Organist of Ely Cathedral (1937-1957). Taught at Ely Grammar School. Conductor of local choral and operatic societies.

Composed a Magnificat and Nunc Dimittis in A-flat and an anthem.

HALSEY, Louis Arthur Owen (b.1929)

Born in London in 1929.

Educated at the resident choir school of All Saints' Church, Margaret Street, London; at King's School, Canterbury (where he was a music scholar) and, as choral scholar, at King's College, Cambridge. Has worked as a music producer for B.B.C. Radio. Founded and made broadcasts, tours, festival appearances and recordings with the Elizabethan Singers and the Louis Halsey singers. Has toured Europe, Australia, Hong Kong, Malaysia, Canada and the U.S.A. as a conductor, lecturer and examiner.

Professor of music and head of the choral department at the University of Illinois, U.S.A. (1982-1985). Since his return to the U.K. he has been guest chorus master of the Royal Liverpool Philharmonic Choir, and conductor of the Allegri Singers, a chamber choir specialising in the music of the 20th century. Director of Music at Regent's College, London, dealing specially with many visiting American students on 'study abroad' programmes.

A joint editor with Basil Ramsey of *Sing Nowell*, a collection of carols.

Has composed church music including the anthems 'O Lux, beata Trinitas' and 'O quam gloriosum' and, for Epiphany, 'Magi veniunt ab oriente'.

HAM, Dr. Albert (c1858-1940)

Born around 1858; died in Brighton, Sussex, at the age of 82 in 1940.

Graduated B.Mus. (1891) and D.Mus. (1894) at the University of Dublin. Awarded a doctorate in music honorarily by the University of Toronto.

A pupil of **James Kendrick Pyne**.

Organist of St. John's Church, Taunton, Somerset and the conductor of a local choral society. He held three further organistships briefly in the West of England, those of All Saints', Park Street, Bath (from 1879); Ilminster Parish Church (from 1880) and St. John the Evangelist, Taunton (1893).

In 1897 he emigrated to Canada where he became organist of St. James's Cathedral, Toronto (1897-1935); conductor of the National Chorus and professor of voice culture at the Toronto Conservatory. A lecturer of Trinity College of Music and an examiner and lecturer of the University of Toronto.

Founded the Canadian Guild of Organists and the National Chorus of Toronto, of which he was conductor for 25 years.

Author of text books on the rudiments of music, the training of boys' voices, and musical form.

Returned to England in 1935, living in retirement in Brighton.

Composed church music including a Benedicite in E-flat (1907), anthems such as 'The souls of the righteous' (1916) and 'In my Father's house' (1879), and part songs.

HAMAND, Dr. Louis Arthur (?-1955)

Graduated B.Mus. (1899) and D.Mus. (1906) at Queen's College, Oxford.

Sub organist of the Church of St. Mary Magdalene, Paddington, London (from 1894). His other organ appointments were organist of the Churches of St. John the Baptist, Hillingdon, Middlesex (from 1895) and St. Anne's, Eastbourne, Sussex (from 1907) and organist and choirmaster of Malvern Priory (1910-1945), Worcestershire.

From 1897 he' taught music at Clayesmore School, Enfield, London. In 1901 he became a professor of the London Organ School. Conductor of local choral and orchestral societies.

Author of *An Organist Remembers*.

Composed a Magnificat and Nunc Dimittis in B-flat (1905), the anthem 'The valleys are clothed with flocks' (?1905), songs and school songs.

HAMER, Norman Stanley (19th/20th century)
Educated in Manchester at Owen's College and Victoria University. Graduated B.Mus. (1905). Deputy organist of the Bridge Street Wesleyan Church, Bolton, Lancashire (from 1907). In 1912 he was appointed music master of Altrincham High School for Boys, Cheshire. Correspondence tutor for degrees in music at the Southern Counties' School of Music, Littlehampton, Sussex (from 1914). Composer of hymn tunes.

HAMERTON, Samuel Collingwood (1833-1872)
Born in Ellerton, Yorkshire in 1833; died in Shanklin, Isle of Wight on 6 January 1872. Composer of hymn tunes and the anthem 'Waken, Christian children' (1861).

HAMERTON, William Henry (1795-?)
Born in Nottingham in 1795; died possibly in India.
A chorister of Christ Church Cathedral, Dublin.
In 1812 he travelled to London where he studied music under Thomas Vaughan.
Returned to Dublin in 1814, where he taught music. In 1815 he succeeded John Elliott as master of the choristers of Christ Church Cathedral, Dublin. In 1823 he was appointed a gentleman of the Chapel Royal, Dublin.
In 1829 he resigned each of these appointments and went to Calcutta where he lived possibly for the rest of his life.
Composed anthems, chants, an opera *St. Alban* (1877), glees, songs, including 'The warrior's return', and duets.

HAMILTON, Sir Edward Walter (1847-1908)
Born in Salisbury, Wiltshire on 7 July 1847, the son of the bishop of Salisbury; died on 2 September 1908.
Appointed K.C.B. and K.C.V.O.
A cousin and life-long friend of **Hubert Parry**, acting as a go-between for Parry and Maude Herbert, whose mother disapproved of Parry's courtship.
Attended Eton College and Christ Church, Oxford where he graduated B.Mus. (1867) after studying with **John Stainer**.
From 1870 he was a clerk at the Treasury. Private Secretary (1873-1874) to W.E. Gladstone, assistant financial secretary (from 1892) and assistant secretary to the Treasury (from 1894). A member of the Council of the Royal College of Music.
Composed a hymn 'Great God, whose throne eternal stands' (1901) for the Accession of Edward VII, an anthem 'Mine eyes are ever looking unto the Lord' (1912), a sacred cantata *Praise the Lord, O my soul*, songs, quadrilles and piano music.

HAMILTON-GELL, Fielding Arthur Wolfe (19th century)
(formerly **HAMILTON**, F.A.W.)

Attended Trinity College, Dublin where he graduated B.A. and B.Mus. (1869), and M.A. (1874); passed the divinity examinations in 1874. Ordained deacon in 1870, priest in 1871.
Curate of Kimberworth, Yorkshire (1870-1872); incumbent of Wincobank, Yorkshire (1872-1875), vicar of Stanton-in-Peak (1875-1880), rector of Dry Drayton, Cambridgeshire (1881-1887) and of Clyst in the Diocese of Exeter (from 1894).
Composed a Jubilate, Te Deum, Magnificat and Nunc Dimittis in E-flat (1891); the hymn 'Emmanuel, God with us' (1919); songs and part songs.

HAMMOND, Mary Jane (1878-1964)
Born in 1878; died in St. Albans, Hertfordshire on 23 January 1964. Her hymn tune 'Spiritus vitae' was used in *With One Voice* (1978) with the hymn 'O Breath Of Life' by Bessie Head.

HAMMOND, Philip (b.1951)
Born on 5 May 1951. A composer from Northern Ireland whose church music has been sung at St. Anne's Cathedral, Belfast.

HAMPTON, John (c1455-c1521)
Born around 1455; died in or after 1521.
Master and organist of the Lady Chapel Choir of Worcester Cathedral (1484-1521). Also responsible for teaching plainsong and polyphony to the choristers.
Composed a Salve Regina, to be sung at Lady Mass during Lent. This work was included in the *Eton Choirbook*, a collection of church music made during the reign of Henry VII. Composed ballads of which none have survived.

HAMPTON, Revd. John (1834-1922).
Born in London on 7 February 1834; died on 4 December 1922.
A chorister at the London Churches of St. Paul, Knightsbridge, where the clergy included **F.A.G. Ouseley**, and St. Barnabas, Pimlico. Educated privately at Knightsbridge, and at Queens' College, Cambridge (from 1859). Ordained deacon in 1862, priest in 1863.
In 1856 he was appointed choirmaster of St. Michael's College, Tenbury, Worcestershire. Went up to Cambridge in 1859 but he retained his connections with St. Michael's, returning regularly during the vacations. In 1862 he became assistant curate and sub warden at the College. Hampton took a major responsibility in its running. One of his charges at Tenbury was **Heathcote Statham** who later became organist of Norwich Cathedral.
As a young man **Edward Elgar** played at the Tenbury Music Festival and began a friendship with Hampton, who was the dedicatee of Elgar's 'My Love dwelt in a Northern land'.
In 1889 he succeeded Ouseley as vicar and warden. In 1916, after 30 years of being in charge of the day-to-day operations of the College he retired and was succeeded, albeit briefly, by **Geoffrey Ryley**. He had declined several offers of prestigious appointments, including, according to rumour, the precentorship of Westminster Abbey. He did however accept the precentorship of Hereford Cathedral (1890).
His hymn tune 'St. Cecilia' is used in the Standard Edition of *Hymns Ancient and Modern* (1916) with 'The Royal banners forward go', translated from Latin.

HANBY, Benjamin Russell (1833-1867)
Educated for a career in the church but worked in the field of music. Collaborated with George Root in the editing of a musical

quarterly and the publication of *Chapel Gems* (1866), a collection of church music drawn from these journals. Composed the tune 'Lowliness' for his hymn 'Who is He in yonder stall?'. The combination was used in the Revised Edition (1927) of *Church Hymnary*. Also composed Sunday School and secular songs, including 'Darling Nellie Gray'.

HANCOCK, Benjamin John (1862-1937)
Born in Greenwich, London in 1862; died in Godalming, Surrey on 12 December 1937.
Graduated B.Mus. at Queen's College, Oxford (1905).
Organist and choirmaster in South London of St. Thomas's Church, Charlton (1893-1903) and Holy Trinity Church, Eltham (1903-1916), and of the Chapel of the Royal Military Academy, Woolwich (from 1916).
Composed church music, including hymn tunes. Also children's songs, school songs and piano music. His 'Easter time' was later arranged as a hymn tune by **Eric Thiman**.

HANCOCK, Charles (1852-1927)
Born in Islington, London on 4 January 1852; died in Leicester on 6 February 1927.
A chorister at the London Church of St. Michael, Cornhill (from 1859) under Richard Limpus. A chorister of St. George's Chapel, Windsor Castle (from 1861). Articled to the organist of St. George's Chapel, **George Elvey** (from 1867). Took piano lessons with **Haydn Keeton**. In 1874 he graduated B.Mus. at Magdalen Hall, Oxford.
While still in articles he was organist of the Parish Church of St. Mary, Datchet, Berkshire and St. Andrew's Church, Uxbridge, Middlesex. He was Elvey's assistant organist at St. George's Chapel (until 1875).
In 1875 he took up the organistship of St. Martin's Church, Leicester. St. Martin's later was elevated to collegiate church (1922-1926) and cathedral status (1927). Charles Hancock became a teacher and a conductor of musical and choral societies in the area. A local examiner for the Associated Board of the Royal Schools of Music.
Composed a setting of Psalm 18 'I will love Thee, O Lord my strength' for Solo Voices, Chorus and Orchestra; hymn tunes, organ music and songs.

HANCOCK, James (18th/19th century)
A musician and composer of the late 18th and early 19th century. In 1800 he published a collection of hymn tunes and sacred odes for three, four and five voices. Composed anthems and canons.

HANDEL, George Frederick (1685-1759)
Born in Halle, Germany on 23 February 1685; died in London on 14 April 1759. Son of the surgeon to the Duke of Saxony.
Handel's father intended him to follow a legal career but after the death of his father, Handel abandoned legal studies and concentrated on music. Studied in his home town of Halle under Friedrich Zachau, at Hamburg and in Italy (from 1706) where he met Arcangelo Corelli, and Alessandro and Domenico Scarlatti.
In 1710 he became Kapellmeister to the Elector of Saxony, later to be King George I of England. Handel first visited Britain in the same year, taking up permanent residence in 1713 and becoming a British subject in 1726.
Master of the chapel to the Duke of Chandos, London (from 1718). Continued to compose: his earlier works had included *Dixit*

Dominus and two other Latin Psalm settings, and Italian operas, which he continued to write until 1741. Not only did he write opera but he was also an impresario, first gaining and then losing a fortune in the process. By 1753 he was blind.
Enjoyed a more steady income through his oratorios. Composed his first English oratorio in 1720. There were seven in all of which the most enduringly popular has been The *Messiah* (1742).
Handel's church music includes hymn tunes, usually taken and adapted from his other works. The tune known as 'Maccabeus' and commonly used with the hymn 'Thine be the glory' is based on the tune of 'See the conquering hero comes' from the oratorio *Joshua*. The hymn tune 'Gopsal' is an adaptation made by **William Havergal** of a melody by Handel and named after Gopsal Hall, the home near Ashby-de-la-Zouche, Leicestershire of his librettist Jennens. It is used with the hymn 'Rejoice, the Lord is King'. The hymn tune 'Theodora' is taken from an oratorio of the same name and from 1877 it was used in conjunction with a paraphrase of Psalm 148 'O praise the Lord of Heaven'.

HANDS, John Dawson (1878-1963)
Born in Newark, Nottinghamshire in 1878; died in Clacton, Essex on 10 January 1963.
Educated with W.H.J. Keech, **H.A. Harding**, **Cuthbert Harris** and **C.H. Kitson**, and at the Royal College of Music. Graduated B.Mus. at the University of Dublin.
Resident music master of Shebbear College, North Devon (1906-1912) and organist and choirmaster of Dodbrook Parish Church, South Devon (1912-1916). Assistant master and music master of Liverpool Collegiate School (1919-1921).
Organist and choirmaster of Christ Church (1922-1929) and St. James's Church (1940-1945), Clacton, Essex.
Composer of the vesper hymn 'Lord, keep us safe' (1904), hymn tunes, songs and piano works.

HANFORTH, Thomas William (1867-1948)
Born in Hunslet, near Leeds on 6 March 1867; died in York on 5 June 1948.
A chorister at Leeds Parish Church, and at York Minster under R.S. Burton. Attended York Commercial College. A pupil of **William Garland** and **John Naylor**. Graduated B.Mus. at the University of Durham (1892).
Organist to Archbishop Thomson (1885-1888), and deputy organist to John Naylor at York Minster (1887-1892). Organist at the Church of St. Martin-le-Grand, York (1888-1892), where he succeeded **Edwin Lemare**, and of the Parish Church of Sheffield, St. Paul's (from 1892). Hanforth continued as organist through the elevation to cathedral status in 1914 until his retirement in 1937.
A professor of music at the Yorkshire School for the Blind (1888-1892). City organist of Sheffield (from 1932), and prominent in other local musical activities. Known as a choral conductor. Bandmaster of the 4th West Riding of Yorkshire Volunteer Artillery (1900-1903). Organist to the Grand Lodge of England (1923-1924 and 1937-1938).
Composed church music including a Magnificat and Nunc Dimittis in A (1894), a further setting in G (1894), anthems such as 'Saviour, abide with us' (1876), hymn tunes, songs, and works for piano and for organ.

HANN, Sidney Herbert (1867-1921)
Born in Lambeth, London in 1867; died in Wandsworth, London on 6 December 1921. A second cousin of **E.J. Hopkins**,

Sidney Hann was a chorister of the Chapel Royal. Studied piano at the Royal Academy of Music, where he won a medal.

Organist of the three London Churches of St. James, Clapham Park (1886-1888); St. Mary, Islington (1888-1907) and Brixton Independent Church (1907-1921). Grand organist of the English Freemasons (1915-1916).

Taught music at various schools including Queenswood School (then, at Clapham; now at Hatfield, Hertfordshire). A concert accompanist.

Composer of hymn tunes. *Congregational Praise* (1950) uses his 'Yuletide' with the hymn 'Love came down at Christmas' by Christina Rossetti.

HARCOURT, Ernest (1860-?)
Born in Norwich, Norfolk on 25 January 1860, the younger brother of **J. Arthur Harcourt**.

Solo chorister at the church of St. Peter Mancroft, Norwich.

Remained in Norwich, where he lived as a composer, conductor, violinist and cellist. Founded the Norwich Orchestral Union (1893).

Composed an oratorio *The Deluge*, an anthem 'And in the sixth month', cantatas including *The Chapel Bell*, a part song, a Quintet for Woodwind, and music for violin and for piano.

HARCOURT, James Arthur (1852-?)
Born in Norwich, Norfolk on 2 January 1852. The older brother of **Ernest Harcourt**. Trained in music by his father, James. Organist and choirmaster of the Roman Catholic Church, Norwich (from 1894). Composed Services, an operetta *The Science of Love*, a cantata, duets, and music for organ and for piano.

HARDESTY, George Alfred (1868-1933)
Born in Ashwellthorpe, Norfolk in 1868; died on 25 April 1933.

Graduated B.Mus. at St. John's College, Cambridge (1900).

Organist of St. Michael's Church, Norwich (from 1883). Organist and choirmaster of St. George's, Sevenoaks Weald, Kent (from 1887); Leighton Buzzard Parish Church, Bedfordshire (from 1902) and St. Stephen's, Hampstead, London (from 1904).

Organist of St. Martin's Church, Gospel Oak, London (from 1907), and organist and choirmaster of the Church of St. Michael and All Angels, Paddington (from 1919).

Composed a Magnificat and Nunc Dimittis in D (1892), a Festal March for Organ, and vocal music.

HARDING, Dr. Harry Alfred (1855-1930)
Born in Salisbury, Wiltshire on 25 July 1855; died in Goldington, Bedfordshire on 29 October 1930.

Studied under **Thomas Spinney, John Abram, Haydn Keeton** and **Charles Corfe**. Graduated B.Mus. (1877) and D.Mus. (1882) at New College, Oxford.

At the age of 14 he was accompanist to a travelling pantomime company.

Organist of Fisherton-de-la-Mere, near Salisbury, and at the age of 17, of Sidmouth Parish Church, Devon, where he remained for 16 years and became the conductor of a local choral society.

Organist and choirmaster of Bedford Parish Church, organist of Bedford School (1899-1926) and corporation organist of Bedford, having declined the organistship of All Saints' Church, Eastbourne. Similarly, he declined the offer of a job in Philadelphia, U.S.A. Taught at Bedford High School for Girls. Started a local

competitive music festival in Bedford (1920). Author of a number of books on the theory of music.

Honorary secretary of the Royal College of Organists for 22 years.

Composed a Morning Service in D, hymn tunes, an oratorio *St. Thomas*, songs, and piano music.

HARDING, James Procktor (1850-1911)
Born in Clerkenwell, London in 1850; died in Islington, London on 21 February 1911. For 35 years he was organist of St. Andrew's Church, Islington. Worked for the Civil Service. Composer of hymn tunes. *Congregational Praise* (1950) uses his Double Chant in A. Composed also for children's festivals at the Gifford Hall Mission, Islington.

HARDING, R.Y.
See **BONNER,** Carey.

HARDY, Benjamin Edward (1897-1962)
Born in Huddersfield, Yorkshire in 1897; died in Swindon, Wiltshire on 22 February 1962. His career as an organist began in 1917. Composer of hymn tunes including 'Wheeler', named after Revd. F. Wheeler and also known as 'Blessings bestow', and anthems.

HARDY, Joseph Naylor (?-1939)
A pupil of J. Emmerson of Wakefield, **William Spark, William Creser** and **Samuel Corbett**. Graduated B.Mus. at the University of Durham (1895). Held a number of organ appointments in Wakefield, and the conductorship of a local operatic society. Organist of the Roman Catholic Chapel (from 1875), the West Parade Chapel (from 1878) and the Parish Church of All Saints (from 1886). When All Saints' Church was elevated to cathedral status in 1888, Joseph Hardy was confirmed in the position of organist. Composed anthems and piano music.

HARDYMAN, Sandy (b.c1950)
Born in Bristol. The date of his birth is not known but it is likely to be before or around 1950. Joined the Community of the Celebration (1974), and travelled as a member of the team carrying out pastoral work. He wrote the hymn 'Lord, give us Your Spirit' and composed a tune for it which he gave the same name.

HARE, Ian Christopher (b.1949)
Born in Hull, Humberside on 26 December 1949.

Organ scholar of King's College, Cambridge (1968-1972) where he was John Stewart of Rannoch scholar (1969-1972) and where he graduated Mus.B. and M.A.

Lectured in music at the University of Lancaster (from 1974). Organist and master of the choristers of Cartmel Priory (1981-1989). Organist of the University of Lancaster (from 1983). Sub organist of Carlisle Cathedral (1989-1995)

His compositions include the anthems 'Thou, O God, art praised in Sion' (1973) and 'Sing praises unto The Lord' (1993), and the carol 'A Child is born' (1987).

HARFORD, Revd. Frederick Kill (1832-1891)
Born in Clifton, Bristol in 1832; died in 1891.

Educated at Rugby School, Warwickshire and Christ Church, Oxford where he graduated B.A. (1855) and M.A. (1858). Ordained deacon in 1856, priest in 1857.

A curate in Croydon, Surrey (1856-1858) and chaplain to the bishop of Gibraltar (from 1858). In 1861 he was appointed a minor canon of Westminster Abbey.

A pioneer in the use of music as a form of therapy in the treatment of illness, being associated with the Guild of St. Cecilia, which gave an experimental concert at the Westminster Palace Hotel, London on 14 September 1891.

Composed an Evening Service, anthems, a cantata *Haroun al Raschid* (1884), songs and orchestral works.

HARGREAVES, George (1799-1869)
Born in Liverpool in 1799; died in Liscard, Cornwall in 1869. Son of Thomas Hargreaves, a famous painter of miniatures. Composed the anthems 'Let God arise' and 'The earth is the Lord's', Masses, songs and prize glees.

HARINGTON (Harrington), Dr. Henry (1727-1816)
Born in Kelston, Somerset on 29 September 1727; died in Bath, Somerset on 15 January 1816. Buried in Bath Abbey.

Studied at Queen's College, Oxford (1745-1753), graduating B.A. (1749) and M.A. (1752). Had originally intended to become a priest but decided to pursue a career in medicine instead. In 1762 he graduated M.B. and M.D. at the University of Oxford.

At Oxford he joined an amateur music society organised by **William Hayes** to which entry was restricted to those who could sing or play at sight.

In 1771, qualified as a medical doctor, he moved to Bath, building up a practice locally to replace the one he had established in Wells (1753-1771). Physician to the Duke of York. Held the civic positions of alderman, magistrate and mayor of Bath. An amateur poet.

His hymn tune 'Lansdowne', also known variously as 'Harington', 'Orlingbury', 'Bath' and 'Retirement', is used with the hymn 'When all Thy mercies, O my God' by Joseph Addison in the hymnal *With One Voice* (1978), and is an adaptation of the glee 'Beneath the silent rural call' (c1775) for three voices. Harington's hymn 'Eloi! Eloi!' was sung in Bath Abbey on Good Friday for many years. Also composed anthems including 'O render thanks' and 'There was darkness' (Easter 1793), and glees.

HARKER, Arthur Clifford (b.1912)
Born in Newcastle-on-Tyne on 5 February 1912.

Educated at Dame Allan's School, Newcastle, privately with J.E. Hutchinson and **E.L. Bainton**, and at the Royal College of Music. Graduated B.Mus. at the University of Durham (1947); awarded the M.Mus. honorarily at the University of Bristol (1975).

Assistant organist of Newcastle Cathedral (from 1935), and organist of Rugby Parish Church, Warwickshire (1946-1949).

Organist and master of the choristers of Bristol Cathedral (1949-1983).

Following his retirement, from 1984, Clifford Harker has been organist of the Lord Mayor's Chapel, Bristol.

Composer of organ music. His works for the church include Evening Canticles in D and the anthems 'Bread of the world' and 'Come, my Way, my Truth' (both 1958).

HARKNESS, Robert (1880-1961)
Born in 1880; died in St. Marylebone, London in 1961. Composer of the hymn 'Never lose sight of Jesus' (1913), hymn tunes and choruses. Published a hymn collection in 1915.

HARLEY, E. Daker (20th century)
An electrician in Ealing, London. Has composed the carol 'Blessed art thou, Mary'.

HARPER, Dr. Edward Emanuel (19th/20th century)
Graduated B.Mus. (1892) and D.Mus. (1897) at the University of Dublin, and B.Mus. at the University of Durham.

Organist and choirmaster of the Church of the Holy Sepulchre, Halifax, Yorkshire (from 1895), and of the Emmanuel Church, Southport, Lancashire (from 1898). A local choral and operatic society conductor.

Lived and worked in Scotland shortly after the turn of the century. Principal of the Athanaeum Music School, Glasgow (from 1902). Organist and choirmaster of Kilbarchan Parish Church, Renfrewshire (from 1904) and conductor of the Arthur Balfour Choir (from 1905). A lecturer and choral adjudicator.

Composed Services, anthems, ballads, music for piano and for organ and an operetta *The Ladies' Chance*.

HARPER, Edward James (b.1941)
Born in Taunton, Somerset on 17 March 1941.

Attended the Royal Grammar Schol, Guildford, Surrey. Studied music at Christ Church, Oxford (1959-1963) and at the Royal College of Music (1963-1964) under **Gordon Jacob** for composition. Studied composition for a further year (1968) in Milan under Franco Donatoni. Graduated M.A. and M.Mus.

In 1964 he became lecturer in music at the University of Edinburgh. In 1975 he took up the position of director of the New Music Group of Scotland. Currently reader in music at the University of Edinburgh, a pianist and conductor.

Has composed two masses: the *Chester* Mass for choir and orchestra and *Qui creavit coelum* (1987) for unaccompanied choir. There is also a carol 'The universe'. Other works comprise three operas including *Fanny Robin* (1975), symphonic and chamber works.

HARPER, Dr. John Martin (b.1947)
Born in Wednesbury, Staffordshire on 11 July 1947.

A chorister of King's College, Cambridge (1956-1961) Studied at Clifton College, Bristol (1961-1966); Selwyn College, Cambridge as organ scholar (1966-1970); and at the University of Birmingham where he graduated Ph.D. in 1975. His earlier degrees included the B.A. (Cambridge, 1970), M.A. (Cambridge, 1972) and M.A. (Oxford, 1981). He has also been honoured with a Papal Award for services to church music (1978).

Organist and director of music at St. Chad's Cathedral, Birmingham (1972-1978). Lectured at the University of Birmingham (1974-1981) and was assistant director of music at King Edward School, Birmingham (1975-1976). Organist and master of the choristers at Magdalen College, Oxford (from 1981).

The author of *A History of Music in the English Church* (1990) and articles on musical matters, and has contributed to Grove's *Dictionary of Music and Musicians*.

His church music compositions include 'The Lord's prayer' and 'Ubi Caritas'.

HARPER, William Henry (1845-1933)
Born in Clerkenwell, London on 28 August 1845; died in Fulham, London on 4 February 1933. Composer of hymn tunes, an Allegro and Sarabande for Piano, and songs.

HARRIES, David (1747-1834)
Born in Nantllymystyn, Llansantffraid, Radnorshire, Wales on 16 September 1747; died in Carno on 6 January 1834. His hymn tune 'Babell' was unsuccessful at the Welshpool Eisteddfod of 1824 but it was included in the collection *Caniadau Seion.* His carol tune to the words *Cyduned pob Cristion* was published in *Ceryddor y Cymry* (The Welsh Musician). Composed an anthem 'Par i mi wybod dy ffyrdd', which was arranged for him by **John Roberts** (Ieuan Gwyllt) and remained popular until the early years of this century.

HARRIS, Charles (1865-1936)
Born in Islington, London on 20 July 1865; died in Oxford on 30 July 1936. Composer of hymn tunes.

HARRIS, Dr. Cuthbert (c1856-1932)
Born around 1856; died at the age of 76 in Gorleston on Sea on 17 June 1932.
Attended the London Organ School. Graduated B.Mus. (1894) and D.Mus. (1899) at the University of Durham.
Organist of the Presbyterian Church, Haverstock Hill, London (1889-1891), Welwyn Parish Church, Hertfordshire (1891-1893) and the London Churches of St. Andrew, Streatham (from 1893) and St. Leonard, Streatham (from 1903). A professor of harmony and song at the London Academy of Music. Conductor of a local choral society. Taught music by correspondence. Contributed articles to music periodicals. Author of *Examination Questions, and how to answer them.*
Composed a Magnificat and Nunc Dimittis in A (1896) and a further setting in C (1926), anthems such as 'I saw the Lord' (1912) and 'The Lord is my Strength and Song' (1915), songs, a cantata *The golden lily* and works for piano and violin and for organ.

HARRIS, Griffith (1813-1892)
Born in Carmarthen, Wales in 1813; died on 1 November 1892.
Kept a clothes shop in Carmarthen. His musical activities included the precentorship of the Walter Street Calvinistic Methodist Chapel, Carmarthen; choral conducting and collecting and publishing hymn tunes. The first of two volumes, *Haleluwia,* was issued with 260 tunes in 1849: the second, *Haleluwia Drachefn* (1855) contained 200. They are significant collections in that they document the early tunes from the Welsh revival movement of the 18th century.

HARRIS, Joseph John (1799-1869)
Born in London in 1799; died in Manchester on 10 February 1869. Father of **Joseph Thorne Harris.**
A chorister in the Chapel Royal for seven years under **John Stafford Smith.**
Organist of the Church of St. Olave, Southwark, London (1823-1828). Organist of Blackburn Parish Church, Lancashire (from 1828).
From 1831 he was associated with Manchester Collegiate Church. The Church functioned also as a parish church, and Joseph Harris was appointed parish singing master (April 1831) and parish organist (January 1834).
The Collegiate Church organist was **William Sudlow**, who was in office when in 1848 the Collegiate Church was elevated to the Cathedral Church of the newly-created Manchester Diocese. In March 1848, Joseph Harris succeeded Sudlow as organist and

master of the choristers of Manchester Cathedral. Harris remained in office until 1869, the year of his death.
Belonged to a glee club and other musical societies in Manchester. Composed Services, that remain unpublished, for use in the Cathedral. He also wrote the anthems 'I will arise' and 'The Lord is my Strength'. Six chants and three settings of the Responses to the Commandments were included in a collection by **Benjamin Joule**. Also composed songs, and works for piano. In 1827 he published *A Selection of Psalms and Hymn Tunes.*

HARRIS, Joseph Thorne (1827-1868)
Born in Bow, London in 1827; died in Broughton, Lancashire in 1868. Son of **Joseph John Harris**. Famous as a pianist in the Manchester area. Composed the anthems 'Blessed be the Lord God' and 'By the waters of Babylon'. *Congregational Praise* (1950) uses his Double Chant in E-flat. Also a composer of hymn tunes.

HARRIS, Joseph Macdonald (1789-1860)
Born in 1789; died in May 1860, having been confined to a mental institution since 1843. A chorister at Westminster Abbey under **Richard Guise**, and a pupil of **Robert Cooke**. A teacher and conductor. Composed songs, vocal duets including 'Adieu, fond youth' (1819), trios and works for piano. He arranged metrical Psalms, hymns and Psalm tunes by other composers.

HARRIS, Philip (b.1934)
Born in Hinckley, Leicestershire, on 10 February 1934. Attended Hinckley Grammar School (1945-1950); studied piano and organ privately. Finance director of an engineering company. Organist (from 1965) and choirmaster (from 1970) of Hinckley United Reformed Church. Has composed anthems; worship songs including 'O Father, let me walk with you' and carols such as 'Ring out, you bells!', a setting of his own words. Other works include a light musical *Benjamin*, and *Good Friday Paean* - an Easter story in the composer's words containing musical reflections of the life of Christ. Has expressed the intention to raise the quality of the music and especially the words of worship songs.

HARRIS, Richard (19th/20th century)
Graduated B.Mus. (1896) at Christ Church, Oxford, having studied music privately. Organist of Iffley Church, Oxford (from 1877). Music master of Cranleigh School, Surrey (from 1882). Composed an Evening Service and a sacred cantata *I saw the Lord.*

HARRIS, Sir William Henry (1883-1973)
Born in Tulse Hill, London on 28 March 1883; died in Petersfield, Hampshire on 6 September 1973.
A chorister of Holy Trinity Church, Tulse Hill where he was also a pupil of the organist, **Walmsley Little**. Pupil and assistant to Herbert Morris at St. David's Cathedral, Wales.
In 1899 he became Lord Charles Bruce scholar at the Royal College of Music, where his studies were directed by **Walter Parratt** for organ, and by **Henry Walford Davies** and **Charles Wood** for composition. Also studied at New College, Oxford, graduating B.Mus. (1904), D.Mus. (1910) and M.A. (1923).
Appointed C.V.O. (1942) and K.C.V.O. (1954).
His early musical career consisted of several organ positions in and around London. Assistant organist of the Temple Church. and organist of the Church of St. John the Baptist, Kensington;

Wimbledon Parish Church, London (from 1903) and Ewell Parish Church, Surrey (1906-1911).

From 1911 he was assistant organist at Lichfield Cathedral to **John Lott**.

A lecturer at the University of Birmingham, and organist of the Church of St. Augustine, Edgbaston (from 1913). A professor of harmony and counterpoint at the Birmingham and Midland Institute (from 1914).

Served in the 28th London Regiment during World War I.

Succeeded **H.P. Allen** as organist of New College, Oxford (1919-1928). Organist of Christ Church Cathedral, Oxford (1929-1933), in succession to Noel Ponsonby, and organist of St. George's Chapel, Windsor Castle (1933-1961), retiring in the latter year.

He was one of the two sub-conductors on each occasion at the Coronation of George VI (1937) and of Elizabeth II (1953).

A professor of organ and harmony at the R.C.M. (1923-1953). Director of music studies at the Royal School of Church Music, Croydon, Surrey (1956-1961).

Music editor of *Emynaur's Eglwys* (1952), the hymn book of the Church in Wales.

His compositions include works for organ and a considerable amount of church music, such as a setting of Psalm 103 for Double Choir. His hymn tune 'Alberta' was composed during a railway journey through Canada as part of an examining tour in 1924, for the hymn 'Lead, kindly Light' by J.H. Newman. He is also known for his tunes 'Petersfield', 'Sennen Cove' and 'Stoner Hill', found today in *Hymns and Psalms* (1983).

Composed a Communion Service in C and Evening services in A, in B-flat and in E, the latter being in eight parts. Perhaps his best known anthem is 'Faire is the Heaven' (1925). In a similar vein is 'Bring us, O Lord God'. Others include 'Holy is the true Light', 'Behold, now praise the Lord', 'O give thanks' and 'Behold, the Tabernacle'.

HARRISON, John (1808-1871)

Born in Canterbury, Kent in 1808; died in Deal, Kent on 21 February 1871, suffering a fatal heart attack during a concert. Learned to play piano, organ, violin and cello. A pupil of Thomas Goodban and of Field. Moved to Deal in 1835, taught music in the town and was organist of St. Andrew's Church (1852-1871). A member of the town council for five years. Composed the hymn tune 'Guilton', used in an early edition of *Hymns Ancient and Modern*, and published a collection of chants arranged for four voices.

HARRISON, John 'of Malton' (19th century)

Little is known of John Harrison except that he was connected with the Yorkshire town of Malton. Published a collection *Original Sacred Melodies* (1865).

HARRISON, Julius Allen Greenway (1885-1963)

Born in Stourport, Worcestershire on 26 March 1885; died in Harpenden, Hertfordshire on 5 April 1963.

Studied at Queen Elizabeth School, Hartlebury and at the Birmingham and Midland Institute under Granville Bantock.

A conductor of opera and orchestral music. In 1925 he succeeded Eugene Goossens as conductor of the Handel Society. He conducted for the Beecham Opera Company, the British National Opera Company (1922-1927), the Scottish Orchestra and, as director of music, the Borough of Hastings (1930-1940), where he succeeded Basil Cameron. Following the onset of deafness, he was forced to retire in 1940. A professor of composition at the Royal Academy of Music.

Contributed to *Musical Companion*. His books included a monograph on Brahms and his four symphonies.

His compositions include orchestral works, among them *Worcestershire Suite* and *Breedon Hill*. In lighter vein were his variations on the traditional drinking song, 'Down among the dead men'. His Mass in C (1949) and Requiem (1957) were written for Solo Voices, Choir and Orchestra. Also composed a Double Chant in D-flat, used in *Congregational Praise* (1950).

HARRISON, Revd. Ralph (1748-1810)

Born in Chinley, Derbyshire on 10 September 1748; died in Manchester on 4 November 1810.

Educated at the Unitarian Warrington Academy (1763-1767) and taught classics there for two years immediately afterwards.

His father, William, was minister of the Unitarian Church, Chinley for 27 years. Ralph also followed a career in the church, being assistant minister of the Presbyterian Chapel, Shrewsbury (1769-1771) and Pastor of the Cross Street Chapel, Manchester (1771-1809). He helped to found the Manchester Academy (1786), where he taught classics.

Published, two volumes of *Sacred Harmony* (1784 and 1791), in which his own work was represented by the hymn tunes 'Warrington', 'Ridley' and 'Peterborough'. 'Warrington' (1734) and 'Cambridge' have subsequently been used in various hymnals.

HARRISS, Dr. Charles Albert Edwin (1862-1929)

Born in London on 15 December 1862; died in Ottawa, Canada, on 31 July 1929. The son of Edwin Harriss, organist of St. Mark's Church, Wrexham, Wales.

A chorister from the age of eight at St. Mark's. In 1875 at the age of 12 he won an Ouseley Scholarship to St. Michael's College, Tenbury, Worcestershire.

Awarded the Lambeth D.Mus. and an honorary D.Mus. at McGill University, Canada.

In 1880 he was appointed assistant organist of St. Giles's Parish Church, Reading, Berkshire. A year later he became organist of Welshpool Parish Church, and private organist to the Earl of Powis.

In 1883 he emigrated with his father to Montreal, Canada, where he became organist and master of the choristers of Christ Church Cathedral. Finding the salary inadequate, he supplemented his income by teaching the children of the mechanics of the Grand Trunk Railway. Founded a choral union. Later held an organistship at the Church of St. James the Apostle.

In 1897 he married Ella Schönberger (née Batty), a wealthy widow. This enabled him to realise his ambitions of composing and promoting the works of Bristish composers by means of recital tours, among others. Directed the first cycle of music festivals in Canada devoted specifically to British composers (1903). In 1904 he was appointed director of the McGill University Conservatory of Music. Established glee and madrigal societies. In 1908, **Henry Coward** and his combined choir of some 200 voices toured Canada, an event which Harriss helped to organise.

In 1913 Harriss's Imperial Choir of London, some 2,000 voices strong, sang at the Ghent Exhibition in Belgium. Organised the Empire Peace Festival in Hyde Park, London (1919), featuring a huge choir assembled for the occasion. Arranged a concert tour of Canada by the Scots Guards to raise funds for veterans of World War I.

In 1906 he visited England in order to arrange for a tour of the leading musicians of the day to Canada. While in London he mounted a concert at the Queen's Hall in which **Edward Elgar, Hubert Parry, C.V. Stanford, Alexander Mackenzie** and **Frederic Cowen** each conducted his own work. Harriss's choral idyll, *Pan*, was also performed and the concert was attended by Edward VII and Princess Louise.

Composed many anthems, a cantata *Daniel before the King*, an opera *Torquil* (1896), songs, and organ and piano music.

HART, Charles (1797-1859)

Born on 19 May 1797; died in London on 29 March 1859.

A pupil at the Royal Academy of Music under **William Crotch**.

Organist in London of the Essex Street Chapel; St. Dunstan's Church, Stepney (1829-1833) and Trinity Church, Mile End and St. George's Church, Beckenham, Kent.

Published *Congregational Singing*, a collection of tunes harmonised and arranged for piano or organ.

Composed three anthems in 1830. In 1832 he was the first recipient of the Gresham Prize, introduced in order to encourage the improvement of church music, for his setting of the Jubilate and Te Deum in C. Around 1840 he composed a motet *Blessed are the dead*. Also composed an oratorio *Omnipotence*.

HART, Philip (c1674-1749)

Born, probably in London, around 1674; died in Bloomsbury, London on 17 July 1749.

Organist of churches in London for more than 50 years. Joint organist (1696-1697) with William Goodgroome and sole organist (1697-1749) of St. Andrew's, Undershaft. Organist of St. Michael's, Cornhill (1704-1723) and St. Dionis, Backchurch (1724-1749).

Some sources place the date of Philip Hart's birth at least 20 years previously to that given above and suggest that he was a gentleman of the Chapel Royal (1670-1718) and lay vicar of Westminster Abbey (1670-1718). It has also been put forward that he was a bass singer in the choir of York Minster.

Famous as an organ recitalist but his vibrato or shaking style was somewhat controversial.

Composed the anthems 'Praise the Lord, ye servants' (before 1718) and 'I will give thanks'. *Ode to Harmony* (1703) was probably written for St. Cecilia's Day.

His hymn tune 'Hilderstone' was used in *Church Hymns* (1874) with the hymn 'Jesus shall reign where'er the sun' by Isaac Watts, and in the Standard Edition (1916) of *Hymns Ancient and Modern* with 'Praise to our God, whose bounteous hand' by John Ellerton.

Also composed songs and items for the keyboard.

HART, William Henry (1826-1888)

Born in Southwark, London in 1826; died in Fulham, London in 1888. Composer of a setting of the Prayer of Jeremias, for the Mattins for Holy Saturday (1878), and hymn tunes.

HARTLAND, Timothy (1810-1891)

Born in 1810; died in West Bromwich, Staffordshire on 16 February 1891. His musical career centred around the town of West Bromwich, where he was organist of the Parish Church and, for 50 years, organist and choirmaster of the Ebenezer Church. A tenor singer and a flute player, and one of the first people in the Midlands to teach the **John Hullah** (fixed doh) notation as a means of learning music. Composed a great deal of church music

including anthems and hymn tunes, much of which was popular in the U.S.A. and in Australia.

HARTLESS, Revd. Gordon Frederick James (b.1913)

Born in Swindon, Wiltshire in 1913.

Attended local schools, the University of Leeds (1933-1936) and Worcester Ordination College (from 1954); ordained deacon (1955) and priest (1956).

Assistant master at Manley Hall College, Staffordshire (1936-1948) and at Shaftesbury Grammar School, Dorset (1948-1954). Organist and lay reader at Shaftesbury Parish Church.

Priest-in-charge of St. Peter's Church, Dorset (1959-1962) where he inaugurated the Monday Recitals series of classical organ and piano music with the assistance of a local organist, H. Mortimer. On the staff of the Church of England Children's Society (1962-1969). Then held a number of appointments in the Diocese of York: priest-in-charge of Hawnby with Old Byland (from 1969) and of Bilsdale Midcable (from 1975), and rector of Scawton with Cold Kirby (from 1969). Held these appointments concurrently until 1978, when he retired.

Began composing hymn tunes in 1957 by the influence of **Geoffrey Beaumont**, whom Hartless cites as the inaugurator of the composition of modern hymn tunes. His hymn tune 'Tersanctus' is used in *With One Voice* (1978) with 'Holy, Holy, Holy! Lord God almighty' by Reginald Heber. Has given many recitals of his own hymn tunes and has accompanied the singing of them in church services.

HARVEY, Dr. Jonathan Dean (b.1939)

Born in Sutton Coldfield, Warwickshire on 3 May 1939.

A chorister at St. Michael's College, Tenbury, Worcestershire (1949-1952). Attended Repton School. Studied privately; at St. John's College, Cambridge and at the Universities of Glasgow (where he graduated Ph.D.) and Princeton, New Jersey. His teachers have included Erwin Stein, Hans Keller, Milton Babbitt and, at Darmstadt, Karl-Heinz Stockhausen.

A lecturer at the University of Southampton (1964-1977). Reader (1977-1980) and professor of music (from 1980) at the University of Sussex. Was Harkness fellow of the University of Princeton, New Jersey (1969-1970).

Associated with Winchester Cathedral, where his son was a chorister.

His father, a businessman in Walsall, was also an amateur composer, who inspired Jonathan Harvey to compose from an early age. He has written music of various kinds, including vocal, instrumental and electronic.

Author of *The music of Stockhausen: An Introduction* (1974). Invited by the composer Pierre Boulez (b.1925) to work at the Ircam experimental contemporary music centre in France.

His church music includes The *Winchester* Litany, a Magnificat for Choir and Organ (1978), and the anthems 'The tree' to words from the book of Job, 'Come, Holy Ghost', written for the Southern Cathedrals' Festival of 1984, and 'I love the Lord' (1975). His other works include a symphony (1966).

HARVEY, Patrick Eugene Lawrence (b. 1910)

Born in Holborn, London in 1910. Composer of hymn tunes and a *Salute to Samuel Pepys* for piano (1964).

HARWOOD, Dr. Basil (1859-1949)

Born in Woodhouse, near Olveston, Gloucestershire on 11 April 1859; died in London on 3 April 1949.

Educated at Charterhouse, Surrey and Trinity College, Oxford, where **Charles Corfe** was his teacher in musical theory. Graduated B.Mus. (1880), B.A. (1881), M.A. (1884) and D.Mus (1896).

Studied organ under **George Riseley**, organist of Bristol Cathedral. Took lessons from Carl Carsten, Carl Reinecke and Salomon Jadassohn at the Leipzig Conservatory. A pupil of Joseph Roeckel.

Organist of Trinity College, Oxford (1878-1881) and St. Barnabas, Pimlico, London (1883-1887)

Organist of Ely Cathedral (1887-1892) and of Christ Church Cathedral, Oxford (1892-1909).

Precentor of Keble College, Oxford (1892-1903), choragus of the University (1900-1909), and the first conductor of the Oxford Bach Choir.

Music editor of *Oxford Hymn Book* (1908). His own 'Luckington' was included in the collection. His hymn tunes, many of which are named after places in Gloucestershire, have been extensively used and include 'Elberton', 'Berkeley' and 'Thornbury'. The latter was composed at the request of **George Martin**, organist of St. Paul's Cathedral, for a festival in 1898 as a setting of the hymn 'Thy hand, O God, has guided' by Edward Plumptre.

Retired in 1909 to Woodhouse, Gloucestershire, in order to concentrate on composition. His works include songs and an Organ Sonata in C-sharp Minor plus music for the church, which is said to reveal high church sympathies, subtly expressed. Composed the motets *O sacred banquet, Sacrifice triumphant* and *With angels' food*, the anthem 'O how glorious is the Kingdom', and a Morning, Evening and Communion Service in A-flat. Some of his works were performed at the Three Choirs' Festival, including the motet *Ye choirs of new Jerusalem* (Gloucester, 1928). The cantata *Sacrifice triumphant* is well-known.

HARWOOD, Edmund (1707-1787)

Born in Hoddesdon, near Darwen, Lancashire in the year 1707; died in Liverpool in 1787. A weaver and a member of the choir of the Higher Chapel, Darwen. Later in life, he took up music as a profession in Liverpool, where he was an alto in the choir of St. Peter's Church. Composed songs, anthems including 'Have mercy upon me' and 'Vital spark of heavenly flame' and two books of hymn tunes. The second (1786) contained his own 'Grosvenor', which is found today in *Hymns and Psalms* (1983).

HASKINS, Charles William (19th/20th century)

Graduated B.Mus. at the University of Durham (1900). The author of *Hugh Carrington's Ordeal* and articles on musical topics. Composed a Magnificat for Solo Treble, Quartet, Chorus and Strings; carols and hymn tunes.

HAST, Harry Edwin (Gregory Hast: 1862-1944)

Born in Westminster, London on 21 November 1862; died in Hampstead, London on 12 September 1944.

Studied under Sims Reeves.

A famous singer and teacher of music, undertaking tours of the U.S.A. and Europe. During the 1890s he was one of the Meister Glee Singers and sang before Queen Victoria at Windsor. His first appointment was at St. James's Hall, London (1898). Soon afterwards, he toured as a solo performer and with Adelina Patti.

Taught at Guildhall School of Music, and built up a strong private teaching practice. An examiner in vocal training at the University

of London. Chairman of the board for awarding music scholarships to the Royal Academy of Music. Author of *The Singer's Art* (1925).

A member of the Choir of Westminster Abbey, and of the Temple Church under **Walford Davies**. Sang at the Coronations of 1911 and 1937. Continued to sing at the Temple Church after his retirement in 1912, being renowned for his fine diction.

Composer of hymn tunes, sometimes using the pseudonym Gregory Hast.

HASTINGS, John Patrick (b.1927)

Born in Norwich, Norfolk in 1927. Educated at the Hartley Victoria College, Manchester. Ordained as a minister of the Methodist Church in 1952. Has spent much time working in India and Bangladesh. His tune 'Creation' is used in *Hymns and Psalms* (1983) with the hymn 'Lord, bring the day to pass' by Ian Fraser.

HATELY, Thomas Legerwood (1815-1867)

Born in Greenlaw, Berwickshire, Scotland on 26 September 1815; died in Edinburgh on 22 March 1867. Father of **Walter Hately**.

Apprenticed as a boy to Ballantyne & Company, a firm of printers, where he remained for 11 years. Among those to whom he carried proofs was Sir Walter Scott. Later worked for the printing firm of Thomas Constable, where he became a manager.

Musically self taught, although he came under the influence of **Robert Archibald Smith**.

Precentor of North Leith Church (from 1836) and St. Mary's Parish Church, Edinburgh.

Shortly afterwards came the events known as the Disruption, at which Hately was one of the few precentors to side with the dissidents. Led the singing at the first General Assembly of the Free Church of Scotland at Tanfield (1843), and he later became official precentor of the Free Church Assembly and of the Free High Church.

The singing of Psalms in Scotland at that time was dull and drawn out, due partly to the practice of 'lining out' or having each line sung first by the precentor and then repeated by the congregation, and also to the narrow selection of tunes available, some of which were overly intricate and contained repeats.

Hately worked to enliven the singing by composing new tunes and producing new collections of Psalm music such as *Free Church Psalmody* (1844). From 1846 he organised congregational singing practices and from 1850 he travelled through Scotland, training teachers and leading classes in church music as the representative of the Free Church Assembly.

Hately's Psalm tune 'Nenthorn' has been used recently with the hymn 'Nearer, my God, to Thee'. His other tunes include 'Leuchars', 'Glencairn' and 'Submission'.

HATELY, Walter (1843-1907)

Born in Edinburgh on 29 January 1843; died in Edinburgh on 25 January 1907. Son of **Thomas Hately**.

Educated at Edinburgh High School and Leipzig Conservatory (1861-1864), where he studied under Louis Plaidy, Ignaz Moscheles, Carl Reinecke, Moritz Hauptmann, Ernst Richter and Raimund Dreyschock. Went on to study with Julius Schulhoff in Dresden.

Returned to Edinburgh in 1865, where he taught piano at the Ladies' College, the schools of the Merchant Company and the Church of Scotland Training College. Precentor of the Free St. George Church.

Edited *Church of Scotland Hymnal* (1868). Composer of hymn tunes, songs and piano music. His tune 'St. Helen' was used in the Revised Edition (1927) of *Church Hymnary* with the German hymn, 'Be still, my soul'.

HATHAWAY, Dr. Joseph William George (1870-1956)
Born in Lydney, Gloucestershire in 1870; died on 18 February 1956.
Educated at the Royal College of Music. Graduated B.Mus. (1901) and D.Mus. (1906) at Queen's College, Oxford.
Organist and choirmaster of Wincanton Parish Church (1889-1895), Tonbridge Parish Church, Kent (1895-1914) and St. James's Church, Kidbroke, London (from 1914).
A professor of the R.C.M. and an examiner for the Associated Board of the Royal Schools of Music, in connection with which he toured Canada, Australia, New Zealand, South Africa, and India. In all he travelled around the world six times.
Author of *An Analysis of Mendelssohn's Organ Works*. Composed Services; anthems, including a setting of Psalm 5 'Ponder my words, O Lord' cantatas including *Among the trees*, songs and part songs.

HATHERLY, Very Revd. Dr. Stephen Georgeson (1827-?)
Born in Bristol on 14 February 1827.
Studied music with **William Havergal**, graduating B.Mus. (Oxford, 1856) and D.Mus. (St. Andrews, 1893). Ordained deacon and priest of the Greek Church in Constantinople (1871).
Organist of the Darlaston Parish Church (from 1844); Solihull Parish Church, Warwickshire (from 1847); St. James's Church, Wednesbury, Staffordshire (from 1855); and Tettenhall Parish Church, Staffordshire (1863-1868).
Musical conductor of the Greek Church in Liverpool and at some time he was involved in mission work among the Greek and Slavonic seamen in the Bristol Channel ports. In 1875 he was appointed protopresbyter of the Patriarchial Ecumenical Throne of Constantinople. Became an authority on the music of the Greek church, on which he wrote and lectured.
Composed a Te Deum and Jubilate (1853), a Service of the Greek Church in English (1860) and an Oratoriette Baptism (1860).

HATTERSLEY, Frederick Kilvington (1861-?)
Born in Wortley Grove, Leeds on 11 June 1861.
Studied with **John Naylor** of York Minster. Won a Balfe scholarship to the Royal Academy of Music (1881) and subsequently studied at Munich Conservatory under Josef Rheinburger. Graduated Mus.B. at the University of Cambridge (1887).
Organist and choirmaster of the Church of St. John the Evangelist, Leeds (from 1896). A teacher, choral society conductor and composer. Chorus master of the Bradford contingent of the Leeds Music Festival (1898) and of the Leeds Philharmonic Society (from 1898).
Composed an Evening Service in E-flat and other Services, a cantata *Robert of Sicily* (1894), songs, part songs, orchestral works and piano music. Composed an Orchestral Overture for the Leeds Festival of 1886.

HATTON, John (?-1793)
Born in St. Helens, Lancashire; died in Windle, St. Helens in 1793 and a funeral sermon was preached in his memory on 13 December of that year. He lived at Duke Street, Windle where he attended the local church. His hymn tune 'Duke Street', also known as 'Honiton', has been used in many hymnals with 'Fight the Good Fight'.

HATTON, John Liptrot (1808-1886)
Born in Liverpool on 12 October 1808; died in Margate, Kent on 20 September 1886.
J.L. Hatton's father and grandfather were professional violinists. A theatre conductor, composer, organist, pianist, actor and concert party member nationally and internationally.
Virtually self-taught in music. Organist of the local Churches of Woolton; Childwall and St. Nicholas, Chapel Street; organist of the Roman Catholic Cathedral, Liverpool.
In 1832 he moved to London where he acted in the Drury Lane Theatre production of *Othello*. In 1842 he became conductor of the Drury Lane Theatre. Director of music to the actor Charles Kean.
Commissioned by T. Staudigl, a member of the opera company at Drury Lane to compose an opera *Pasqal Bruno*. This was performed under the composer's supervision in Vienna (March 1844) with Staudigl taking the principal part. 'Revenge', an extract from the opera, later became popular as a song in England. Hatton made an equal impact in Vienna when he played his piano transpositions of the Preludes and Fugues of J.S. Bach. While in Vienna he took lessons in counterpoint from Simon Sechter.
Took part in the Three Choirs' Festival at Hereford in 1846, showing his versatility by appearing both as a vocalist and as the soloist in a Mozart Piano Concerto.
Toured the U.S.A. as a solo pianist, accompanist and singer (1848-1850). An adaptable performer, he dealt appropriately with all *genres* from comic to sacred.
Director of music of the Princess's Theatre (1853-1859) and he was a musical editor for the firm of Boosey.
From about the year 1877 he lived in Margate, Kent, although around 1880 he lived for a while in Aldeburgh, Suffolk.
His church music includes services including the *Aldeburgh* Te Deum (c1880) and 26 anthems. Composed a Morning and Evening Service in E and anthems including 'Blessed be the Lord of Israel' and 'Come, Holy Ghost'. Composed a sacred cantata *Hezekiah* (1877), oratorios and piano works. He sometimes used the pseudonym Czapek, the genitive plural form of the Hungarian word for 'hat'.
Composed over 300 solo songs plus part songs. 'Simon the celIerer' and 'To Anthea' are perhaps the best known, the latter being made especially popular by the singer Charles Santley.

HAUGHTON, Frederick Albert (b.1910)
Born in Belfast in 1910.
Attended Trinity College of Music, London.
A teacher of music. Contributed articles on music to the local press.
He was honorary music adviser to the Churches for Youth Welfare Council, Northern Ireland. A member of the B.B.C. Chorus in Belfast (1934-1939).
Organist and choirmaster of First Dromore Presbyterian Church (1936-1939) and of Holy Trinity Church, County Down (1946-1948), and organist and director of the Choir of All Saints' Parish Church, Belfast (from 1949).

HAVERFIELD, Revd. Thomas Tunstall (19th century)
Lived in the middle years of the 19th century. His book *Feriae Sacrae* dealt with the great festivals of the church and their liturgy,

and it included chants and hymns for suggested use on those occasions. Composed Collect settings, including 'Almighty God, to Whom all hearts be open' (c1830).

HAVERGAL, Miss Frances Ridley (1836-1879)

Born in Astley, Worcestershire on 14 December 1836; died in Oystermouth, Glamorgan, Wales on 3 June 1879. Her father, William Henry Havergal, was rector of Astley.

In 1852 she travelled with her father and stepmother to Germany. Attended school in Düsseldorf and studied privately with a German family, returning to England in 1853. Her tutors included **William Marshall** and Albert Randegger.

An accomplished linguist, she was fluent in French, German, Italian, Latin, Greek and Hebrew. Known for the strength of her faith and for her works as a philanthropist.

Wrote hymns, beginning at the age of seven, and composed hymn tunes. Probably her best known hymn is 'There is a green hill far away', universally sung to the eponymous 'Horsley' (**William Horsley**). Her hymn 'Who is on the Lord's side?' is sometimes sung to her tune 'Hermas'. Her other hymn tunes include 'Eirene', 'Claudia' and 'Tryphena'.

HAVERGAL, Revd. Henry East (1820-1875)

Born in 1820; died on 12 January 1875. Son of **William Havergal** and brother of **Frances Havergal**. Educated at Oxford. Rector of Cople, Bedfordshire (from 1847). Composed the anthem 'Hosanna to the Son of David', hymn tunes and chants. Edited *Hymns of the Church* (1846).

HAVERGAL, Revd. William Henry (1793-1870)

Born in High Wycombe, Buckinghamshire on 18 January 1793; died in Leamington Spa, Warwickshire on 19 April 1870. Father of **Frances Havergal** and **Henry Havergal**.

Attended school in Princes Risborough, Buckinghamshire before entering the Merchant Taylors' School, London (July 1806). Attended St. Edmund's Hall, Oxford where he graduated B.A. (1815) and M.A. (1819). Ordained deacon in 1816, priest in 1817.

From about the age of 14 he frequently played organ at the local parish church. Assistant curate at St. James's, Bristol; curate of Coaley, Gloucestershire (in 1820) and Astley, Worcestershire (1822). Became rector of Astley in 1829.

Suffered head injuries when he was thrown from his carriage shortly after the birth of his daughter Frances Havergal. Lost his sight temporarily, following which he had to resign his living as rector of Astley. Later able to resume his ministry elsewhere although his sight deteriorated later to the point of near blindness.

Appointed rector of the Church of St. Nicholas, Worcester (1845) and an honorary canon of Worcester Cathedral (1845). Vicar of Shareshill, Wolverhampton (from 1860). Retired and moved to Leamington in 1867.

Wrote a hundred or so hymns and composed about a hundred hymn tunes and chants. *Church Hymns* (1874) contains five hymn tunes by him, including 'Gennesaret' with the words 'Jesu! The very thought is sweet', translated from the Latin. The Revised Edition (1927) of *Church Hymnary* features 'Evan' and 'Patmos', while the Standard Edition of *Hymns Ancient and Modern* (1916) uses 'Zoan'. Arranged German chorale melodies for use as hymn tunes.

Composed two Evening Services, one in A (which won him the Gresham Prize in 1836) and the other in E-flat, plus an anthem 'Give thanks' (1841), which took a further Gresham Prize. A Single Chant in B-flat and a Double Chant in E are found in

Cathedral Psalter Chants (1875). Also composed catches, songs and rounds, and compiled *English Church Psalmody* (1847).

HAWDON, Matthias (?-1787)

Known to have been alive in the year 1776; died and was buried at Newcastle-on-Tyne on 22 March 1787. In his day and locality he was a famous organist and composer. Organist of Beverley Minster, and in 1776 he became organist of the Church of St. Nicholas, Newcastle (elevated to Newcastle Cathedral in 1882). Composed the hymn tune 'Beverley', songs, organ music and sonatas for harpsichord.

HAWEIS, Revd. Dr. Thomas (1734-1820)

Born in Redruth, Cornwall on 1 January 1734; died in Bath, Somerset on 11 February 1820.

Attended Truro Grammar School, Cornwall and was apprenticed to a local surgeon and apothecary. Profoundly influenced by the preaching of the Revd. Samuel Walker and sought ordination. Studied at Christ Church (1755-1757) and at Magdalen Hall, Oxford. Ordained in 1757. Graduated LL.B. at Cambridge (1772) and at around the same time, M.D. at a Scottish university.

Chaplain to the Earl of Peterborough, and curate of the church of St. Mary Magdalene, Oxford (from 1757). However he was dismissed from St. Mary's because of his ambivalence towards Methodism. He was then assistant to **Martin Madan** at the Locke Hospital Chapel, London. Vicar of All Saints', Aldwinkle, Northamptonshire (1764-1820).

In 1768 he became chaplain to Selina, Lady Huntingdon. Manager of the preachers' college sponsored by her at the religious community of Trevecca, Breconshire, Wales. The most musical of her ministers, he was her trustee and executor, becoming responsible on her death for managing all her chapels. The college at Trevecca was the forerunner of Cheshunt Congregational College, Cambridge.

A friend of John Newton, whose autobiography he edited.

Thomas Haweis was aware of the need to send out missionaries, and was willing to cooperate with other denominations to achieve this. In 1787 he offered to send two Trevecca-trained men to the South Sea Islands, but the bishops of the established church refused to ordain men who lacked a university education. At a meeting in the Castle and Falcon Hotel, the motion was proposed 'that the establishment of a society for sending missionaries to heathen countries is highly desirable.' As a result, the London Missionary Society was formed (1794).

Published *Carmina Christo* (Hymns to the Saviour), a collection of tunes designed to be used in conjunction by her congregations with Lady Huntingdon's *Select Collection of Hymns*.

Wrote hymns and composed hymn tunes. 'Richmond' (1792), otherwise known as 'Haweis', and 'Spa Fields Chapel' has long been associated with the hymn 'Praise to the Holiest in the height' by J.H. Newman. *With One Voice* (1978) employs his tune 'University' with Charles Wesley's 'O, for a thousand tongues to sing'.

HAWES, Jack Richards (b.1916)

Born in Ipswich, Suffolk on 18 May 1916.

Studied piano from the age of five, and at 10, was a chorister and organ pupil under **George Gray** at the Church of St. Mary-le-Tower, Ipswich. Attended Northgate School, Ipswich. Studied harmony, counterpoint and, with Alfred Earnshw, the cello at the Ipswich Conservatory.

Served in the Middle East, the Western Desert, Libya, Italy and Austria during World War II.

Worked in the insurance business from 16 until the age of 55, while involved musically as a piano accompanist to vocalists and choirs. Church organist and cellist in local orchestras. Associated with the Ipswich Orchestral Society, for which he later composed a number of works. Taking early retirement enabled him to compose full-time (from 1971).

Encouraged as a pianist by Stanley Wilson, himself a local pianist and composer.

Has composed works for brass, for woodwind, for organ and for piano. His church music includes the anthems 'O sing unto the Lord a new song' for the opening service at the 1989 Three Choirs' Festival, Gloucester and 'Stir up, we beseech Thee O Lord' (1987); Evening services in D and in B-flat; a carol 'Christ is born'; a setting for Rite A of the Holy Communion; and a Psalm Trilogy.

HAWES, Revd. Thomas Henry (1806-1888)
Chaplain of New College, Oxford. A minor canon of Wells Cathedral. Vicar of Burgh Castle, Suffolk. Composed anthems including 'Blessed are the people' and 'How doth the city'.

HAWES, William (1785-1846)
Born in London on 21 June 1785; died in London on 18 February 1846. His daughter was the contralto singer Maria Hawes.

A chorister of the Chapel Royal (1793-1801) under **Edmund Ayrton**.

From 1802, William Hawes was a violinist in the Covent Garden Orchestra. A deputy lay vicar (from 1803) and lay vicar (1817-1820) of Westminster Abbey, where he also taught singing. A gentleman of the Chapel Royal (from 1805). A vicar choral, and the almoner and master of the choristers of St. Paul's Cathedral (1814-1846). Master of the choristers and lutenist of the Chapel Royal (1817-1846).

He treated the boys harshly. A former chorister, **W.H. Cummings** later recalled, 'Mistakes in the rendering of the services were generally corrected by the master... aided by a charming little riding whip which he applied to their backs with benevolent impartiality.'

Also an organist, music publisher, director of opera at the Covent Garden and conductor of the Madrigal Society. From 1804 a high proportion of his compositions consisted of adaptations of foreign material for the English stage. One of the original associates of the Philharmonic Society (1813).

Composed glees and madrigals, Psalm tunes and other church music including chants. His Double Chant in E was published in *Cathedral Psalter Chants* (1875).

HAWKINS, Cecil Gordon (b.1911)
Born in Barnet, Hertfordshire on 23 August 1911.
Educated at Highgate School.

Organist of the Congregational Churches of Hendon (1934-1935) and Ealing (1935-1939 and 1946-1947). From the latter year he was bursar of the Royal Hospital School, Holbrook, Ipswich, Suffolk, where he was also organist of the Tacket Street Congregational Church (from 1948).

During World War II he joined the Royal Navy, later becoming a commander of the Royal Naval Volunteer Reserve.

Composer of hymn tunes. *Congregational Praise* (1950) uses his 'Ballards Lane' with John Cennick's 'Ere I sleep, for every favour'.

HAWKINS, Revd. Ernest (1802-1868)
Born in Lawrence End, Hertfordshire on 25 January 1802; died in Westminster, London on 5 October 1868 and was buried in Westminster Abbey.

Educated at Bedford and at Balliol College, Oxford where he graduated B.A. (1824), M.A. (1827) and B.D. (1839).

Following his ordination he was curate of Burwash, Sussex. A fellow of Exeter College, Oxford (1831-1852) and for a time, under-librarian of the Bodleian Library and curate of the Church of St. Aldate.

Moved to London around 1835, becoming curate of St. George's Church, Bloomsbury. In 1844 he was appointed prebendary of St. Paul's Cathedral and assistant preacher at Lincoln's Inn. Minister of the Curzon Chapel, Mayfair (1850-1868) and a canon of Westminster Abbey (1864-1868).

Secretary of the Society for the Propogation of the Gospel (1843-1864) and vice president of Bishop's College, Cape Town, South Africa (from 1859). Author of several books on church history.

Published *The Psalmist*, a collection of hymn tunes of which four were composed by him. One of these was an adaptation by him taken from the last part of the anthem by **Henry Purcell**, 'O God, Thou art my God', named 'Westminster Abbey'.

HAWKINS, James (c1662-1729)
Born in 1662 or 1663; died in Ely on 18 October 1729; buried in Ely Cathedral. His son was also named **James Hawkins**.

May have been a chorister of St. John's College, Cambridge or of Worcester Cathedral. Graduated B.Mus. (1719) at St. John's College.

In 1681 and 1682, James Hawkins was paid for his part in training the choristers of Ely Cathedral.

In 1682 he became the single holder of two positions at Ely Cathedral. The organistship had fallen vacant with the death of **John Ferrabosco**. At the same time he succeeded Robert Robinson, master of the choristers.

While at Ely, he arranged the manuscript voice parts that were in current use into volumes, adding works that he had composed.

Taught at Bury St. Edmunds and elsewhere.

Composed some 17 Services including two in A and around 75 anthems including 'The Lord is risen' and 'Behold, O God our defender' (1719).

HAWKINS, James (?-c1750)
Son of the first **James Hawkins**. Organist of Peterborough Cathedral (1714-1750). Towards the end of his term of office he was additionally surveyor of the works. In 1728 he was threatened with dismissal unless he ceased to be rude to members of the Chapter. Composed church music. An anthem 'O praise the Lord' is in the collection published by **Thomas Tudway**.

HAWKINS, John (17th/18th century)
Organist of Ripon Cathedral (1682-c1690). Anthems by him are in the collection published by **Thomas Tudway**.

HAWKINS, Malcolm (b.1944)
Born in Oporto, Portugal in 1944. Studied at the Royal Academy of Music and at the Salzburg Mozarteum, Austria, with Cesar Bresgen. A double-bass player who has performed with the London Symphony Orchestra. Teacher of piano. Formerly a teacher at Wells Cathedral School, before moving to the U.S.A. His many compositions include a setting of Psalm 49 'O hear this, all ye

people' (1991) and a Missa *Sancta Sophia* for Boys' Voices and Organ. In 1975, he won a composition prize for his songs from Austrian Radio.

HAY, Dr. Edward Norman (1889-1943)
Born in Faversham, Kent in 1889; died in Portstewart, Belfast on 10 September 1943.
His parents were from Ulster and the family moved to Coleraine following the premature death of his mother.
Virtually an invalid as a child. Studied with Francis Koeller, **Charles Brennan, Edred Chaundry, Lawrence Walker** and Arthur Hull. Graduated B.Mus. at Pembroke College, Oxford (1911). Later became D.Mus.
A member of the Belfast Philharmonic Orchestra (from 1905). In Coleraine he was conductor of the Madrigal Society (from 1911) and organist and choirmaster of both the Parish Church of St. Patrick (1914-1916), and of Bangor Abbey. Organist and choirmaster of Belmont Presbyterian Church, Belfast. A lecturer in music at Queen's University, Belfast (1926-1942). Director of music of Belmont Presbyterian College, Belfast (from 1922) and an external examiner for degrees in music for the University of Dublin (1923-1924). Contributed musical criticism under the pseudonym Rathcol to *Belfast Telegraph* (from 1926).
Some of his unpublished church music is lost. Among his published works are the anthems 'Behold, what manner of love' (1923) and 'Thou, O God, hast taught me' (1927). The anthem 'The life consecrated' won a prize. The first of these three anthems was for a time regularly used in St. Anne's Cathedral, Belfast. Also composed a vesper hymn, a song 'The Silent Land', and music for organ, including the voluntary *Wohin, geistliche Traume*. His String Quartet earned him a prize in the Cobbett Competition (1917).

HAYDEN, Henry (?1774-1848)
Born around the year 1774; died in 1848; buried at Llanbelig, Wales. A chorister of Norwich Cathedral and a pupil of the Cathedral organist, presumably **John 'Christmas' Beckwith** (1808-1809). At the age of 20 he became organist and a singing Man of St. Asaph Cathedral. The records show that he held the organistship from 1794 until 1834, but in fact he may have departed in 1828. Composed church music.

HAYDOCK, Dr. Frederick William (19th century)
Studied music privately and under **Horton Allison**. Graduated B.Mus. (1880) and D.Mus. (1891) at the University of Dublin. Held appointments in the Manchester area as organist of St. Gabriels's Church and the Union Chapel (from 1880). Organist and choirmaster of St. Mary's Church, Disley. A local choral society conductor. Composed two sacred cantatas *O Magnify the Lord* and *Lazarus* for Solo Voices, Chorus and Orchestra. Also composed songs.

HAYES, Dr. Philip (1738-1797)
Born in Oxford, where he was baptised on 17 April 1738; died in London on 19 March 1797. Buried in St. Paul's Cathedral. Second son of the first **William Hayes** and elder brother of the second.
A chorister of the Chapel Royal under **Bernard Gates**. Studied at Magdalen College, Oxford; graduated B.Mus (1763) and D.Mus. (1777).
Carried out the duties of organist at Christ Church Cathedral, Oxford (1763-1765). This may only have been on a temporary

basis as **Thomas Norris** was formally appointed organist in 1765. Thereafter, Philip Hayes lived in London, becoming a gentleman of the Chapel Royal (1767) and formally retaining the appointment until his death.
In 1776 Philip Hayes took up the first of a number of major appointments at the University of Oxford, succeeding Richard Church as organist of New College.
In the following year his father died. Philip succeeded him as organist of Magdalen College and professor of music. In 1790, on the death of Thomas Norris, he became organist of St. John's College. Retained each of these appointments until his death.
Reputed to be one of the worst tempered men in England, but generous on occasions. A large man, his name Phil Hayes was sometimes parodied as 'Fill Chaise' and he was believed to weigh around 20 stone.
Transcribed a large amount of church music by earlier composers.
In *Cathedral Psalter Chants* (1875) are his Single Chants in F and Single Chant in E. Composed some 16 Psalm tunes around the year 1788, eight anthems including 'The Lord descended from above', plus Services, Canticles and Responses. A hymn tune 'New College' was used in *Hymns Ancient and Modern*. Composed an oratorio *Prophecy* (c1778).

HAYES, Dr. William (1706- 1777)
Born in Hanbury, Worcestershire in December 1706 and was baptised on 26 January 1707; died in Oxford on 27 July 1777. Father of **Philip Hayes** and of the younger **William Hayes**.
A chorister of Gloucester Cathedral under **William Hine**. A Mrs. Viney, hearing him sing in the Cathedral, taught him to play harpsichord and later arranged his articles with Hine. Graduated B.Mus. (1735) and D.Mus. (1749) at the University of Oxford.
Appointed organist of the church of St. Mary, Shrewsbury (1729-1731) and of Worcester Cathedral (1731-1734).
Succeeded Thomas Hecht as organist and master of the choristers of Magdalen College, Oxford (1734-1777). In 1735 he was a steward at the Three Choirs' Festival; in 1763, at Gloucester, he was a conductor. In 1742 he succeeded **Richard Goodson** the younger as Oxford professor of music. Admired and championed the music of **Handel**.
A co-editor of the compilation *Cathedral Music* by **William Boyce**.
Composed some 20 anthems, a Te Deum in D and a setting of the metrical version of Psalm 100 'O be joyful in the Lord, all ye Lands'. The hymn tunes 'Tranmere' and 'Magdalen College' are by him and were originally published in a collection of 16 (1774) and used with Psalms 47 and 122. Also composed ballads and cantatas, and a Chime in C Minor for the bells of Gloucester Cathedral.

HAYES, Revd. William (1741-1790)
Born in Oxford and was baptised on 11 June 1741; died, probably at Tillingham, Essex on 22 October 1790.
The third son of the elder **William Hayes** and the brother of **Philip Hayes**.
A chorister of Magdalen College, Oxford (1749-1754). Gaduated B.A. (1761) at Magdalen College and M.A. (1764) at New College. Subsequently ordained priest.
A minor canon of Worcester Cathedral (from 1765) and of St. Paul's Cathedral (from 1766). Vicar of Tillingham (1783-1790).
Composed glees, canons and catches. His hymn tune 'Tranmere' was used in the Standard Edition (1916) of *Hymns Ancient and Modern*. The Revised Edition (1927) of *Church Hymnary* uses his

'New 113th' with the German hymn 'Thee Will I Love'. *Congregational Praise* (1950) uses the latter tune with Charles Wesley's 'Give me the faith which can remove'.

Cathedral Psalter Chants (1875) includes Single Chants in A, in A Minor and in C by William Hayes.

HAYNE, Revd. Dr. Leighton George (1836-1883)

Born in Exeter, Devon on 28 February 1836; died in Bradfield, near Harwich, Essex on 3 March 1883.

Educated at Eton College and Queen's College, Oxford; graduated B.Mus. (1856) and D.Mus. (1860). Ordained deacon in 1861, priest in 1862.

Precentor (1860-1866) and organist (1857-1861) of Queen's College, Oxford. Assistant curate of the Church of St. John the Baptist, Oxford (1864-1866); vicar of Helston, Cornwall (1866-1868) and succentor and organist of Eton College (1868-1871).

In 1863 he was appointed coryphaeus (precentor) of the University of Oxford and in 1871 he succeeded his father as rector of Mistley-with-Bradfield.

An amateur organ builder and theorist. Edited *The Merton Tune Book* (1863) with Revd. H.W. Sergeant, which includes 'St. Cecilia' and other tunes composed by him.

He felt strongly that church music should be kept in context and not become an art form rather than part of an act of worship. During the Church Congress at Bristol (1864), he argued that single chants were preferable to double because they offered less scope to the composer for the display of technique.

Composed many hymn tunes. His 'Buckland' and 'Compline' were used in *Hymns Ancient and Modern*. Other tunes by Hayne in the Standard Edition (1916) are 'Chalvey' and 'St. Lawrence'. A book of Responses to the Commandments, published around 1875, contains a setting in G by Hayne. Composed the anthems 'Haste Thee, O God' and 'Ponder My Words'.

HAYNES, Walter Battison (1859-1900)

Born in Kempsey, Worcestershire on 21 November 1859; died in St. Marylebone, London on 4 February 1900. Nephew of **William Haynes.**

Educated at Hanley Castle Grammar School. His early musical training was with his uncle, William Haynes, for whom he sometimes deputised at Malvern Priory, where Battison Haynes was a chorister. With the benefit of a Mozart Scholarship, he studied at the Leipzig Conservatory under Salomon Jadassohn and Carl Reinecke (from 1878).

On his return he lived in Boulogne for six months in order to improve his French, occasionally playing organ at Boulogne Cathedral. Continued his studies for piano under Franklin Taylor and for harmony under **Ebenezer Prout** at the School for the Higher Development of Piano Playing.

Organist of the Church of St. Philip, Upper Sydenham, Surrey (from 1884). Director of music at the Borough Polytechnic, London. In 1891 he succeeded **Henry Frost** as organist and director of the Choir of the Chapel Royal, Savoy Hill (1891-1900).

From 1890 he was a professor of harmony and composition at the Royal Academy of Music. Held both appointments until his premature death in 1900.

Composed Services, including three settings of the Magnificat and Nunc Dimittis, anthems including 'The sun is careering in glory and might', and hymn tunes. *Congregational Praise* (1951) employs his Single Chant in C. Also composed two cantatas for female voices, songs, duets, and music for violin and for piano.

HAYNES, William (1829-1901)

Born in Worcester on 19 September 1829; died in Malvern, Worcestershire on 26 April 1901. Uncle of **Battison Haynes.** An articled pupil of **William Done,** organist of Worcester Cathedral. Organist of Malvern Priory Church, Worcestershire (1850 -1893). In 1858 he established a music business in the town. Composed church music including a Festival Te Deum and Jubilate (1887), a Magnificat and Nunc Dimittis in A (1885), hymn tunes, songs and organ music.

HAYTER, Aaron Upjohn (1799-1873)

Born in Gillingham, Dorset on 16 December 1799; died in Boston, U.S.A. in 1873.

A chorister of Salisbury Cathedral. A pupil and later, assistant, of the cathedral organist, **Arthur Corfe.**

Succeeded **Charles Dare** as organist of Hereford Cathedral (1818), remaining at Hereford for two years before becoming organist of the Collegiate Church, Brecon, Wales.

Emigrated to the U.S.A. in 1835 and became organist of the Grace Church, New York; the Trinity Church, Boston (1837); and organist and musical adviser of the Handel and Haydn Society (1838).

Composed a Service in E-flat and an anthem 'Withdraw Thou not'.

HAYTER, Samuel (18th/19th century)

An organist of Mere, Wiltshire. Composed Services and anthems.

HEAD, Brian David (b.1936)

Born in Walthamstow, Essex in 1936. Educated at Christ's Hospital, Horsham, Sussex and King's College, Cambridge, where he was a choral scholar. Director of music of the Edinburgh Academy (from 1965). A local choral society conductor. Has composed Canticle settings, hymn tunes, and songs.

HEAD, Michael Dewar (1900-1976)

Born in Eastbourne, Sussex on 28 January 1900; died in Cape Town, South Africa on 24 August 1976.

Educated privately and at the Royal Academy of Music (1919-1925) where he studied composition under **Frederick Corder.** Also trained as a mechanical engineer.

A professor of piano at the R.A.M. (1927-1975), and an examiner for the Associated Board of the Royal Schools of Music. A festival adjudicator at events including the Jamaica Festivals of 1931 and 1934. Toured Australia and New Zealand as an adjudicator in 1936.

Composed some 85 songs that have been described as deft and delicate, some of which he sometimes recited with himself as accompanist. His works include the carol 'The little road to Bethlehem'.

HEALE, Helene (1855-?)

Born in London on 14 February 1855.

Attended Queen's College, Harley Street, London before attending the National Training School of Music (later, the Royal College of Music) under Ernst Pauer, **John Francis Barnett, Ebenezer Prout** and **Arthur Sullivan.**

Lived and worked in London as a teacher and composer of music. Performed before Queen Victoria at Windsor Castle (1880).

Composed eight Christmas carols, a madrigal, a cantata for female voices, a Jubilee Ode For Chorus and Orchestra (1887), and music for violin and for piano.

HEAP, Dr. Charles Swinnerton (1847-1900)
Born in Birmingham on 10 April 1847; died in Edgbaston, Birmingham on 11 June 1900. His untimely death in office as chorus master of the Birmingham Festival is given as one of the reasons for the poor first performance a few months later (3 October 1900) of **Edward Elgar**'s *Dream of Gerontius*.
Attended King Edward Grammar School, Birmingham and received musical training from Walter Brooks. Articled to **E.G. Monk** at York Minster.
In 1865 he was the second recipient of the newly-founded Mendelssohn Scholarship, the first being **Arthur Sullivan**. Studied at Leipzig under Ignaz Moscheles, Moritz Hauptmann, Ernst Richter and Carl Reinecke. Deputised on occasions for Reinecke at the Gewandhaus Concerts.
In 1867 he returned to Birmingham where he resumed his organ studies under **W.T. Best**. Graduated Mus.B. (1870) and Mus.D. (1871) at the University of Cambridge.
Conductor of the Birmingham Philharmonic Union (1870-1886) and held a number of organistships and musical society appointments in and around Birmingham between the years 1869 and 1886. One of the foremost choral conductors in the Midlands, founding the North Staffordshire Festival at Hanley and persuading Edward Elgar to conduct the first performance of his *King Olaf* there.
A musical examiner for the University of Cambridge (from 1884).
Composed anthems including 'I cried unto the Lord' and 'If ye love Me', choral cantatas, songs, part songs, chamber music and pieces for organ.

HEATH, John (16th century)
A church musician and minor composer who lived during the early part of the second half of the 16th century. The collection *Certain Notes...* (1565) by **John Day** contains a Service for Men's Voices by a John Heath, who could well be this same person. Also composed at least one part song. His Communion Service is found in the *Wanley Books* whose origin is unknown but which probably date from 1549-1552. Composed the anthem 'Almighty God, whose kingdom is Everlasting'.

HEATH, John (c1589-c1668)
A lay clerk of Rochester Cathedral, Kent until at least 1672. From 1614 until 1663 (and possibly before 1614) he was cathedral organist. It is possible that for a time he held the organistship jointly with his father, Philip. Composed some church music, including an Evening Service and the anthem 'When Israel came out of Egypt'.

HEATH-GRACIE, George Handel (1892-1987)
Born in Gosport, Hampshire in 1892; died in Devon on 20 April 1987.
Educated at Bristol Grammar School and received training in music from Hubert Hunt, organist of Bristol Cathedral. Graduated B.Mus. at the University of Durham (1932).
Between 1909 and 1904, George Heath-Gracie held organistships at a number of churches in and around Bristol. He was then organist of the Church of St. John, Frome, Somerset (1914-1915) before serving in H.M. Forces (1915-1919).
Organist of the Church of St. Peter, Brockley, London (1918-1933) and at the same time, music master of the Mercers' School, Holborn.

Organist of Derby Cathedral (1933-1958) following the resignation of Alfred Wilcock.
Director of music at Derby School (1938-1944) and a member of the extra-mural teaching staff of the University of Nottingham. Toured the U.S.A. and Canada in 1949 and 1953 as adjudicator, lecturer and recitalist.
A controversial figure, who resigned from his cathedral organistship on Christmas Day and about whom many anecdotes exist.

HEATHCOTE, Edward (c1797-1835)
Born around the year 1797; died in Southwell, Nottinghamshire in 1835 and was buried on 28 January. Organist of Bakewell Church, Derbyshire and Southwell Minster (1818-1835). His church music includes a Service in B-flat and a setting of the ordination hymn 'Come Holy Ghost, eternal God'.

HEATHCOTE, Revd. Gilbert (1765-1829)
A fellow of New College, Oxford and of Winchester College, Hampshire. Vicar of Hursley, Hampshire and archdeacon of Westminster. Composed anthems including 'Blessed are the people' and 'Save me, O God'. *Cathedral Psalter Chants* (1875) contains his Single Chant in B-flat. A Double Chant in A is associated with Psalm 23 in *St. Paul's Cathedral Chant Book* and elsewhere.

HECHT (Heicht, Height, Hight), Andrew (?-1693)
Born in Holland; died in Lincoln in 1693 and was buried on 31 March. Succeeded **Thomas Mudds** as organist of Lincoln Cathedral (1663-1693). Composed anthems including 'God is our Hope' and 'Out of the deep'.

HEDGES, Dr. Anthony John (b.1931)
Born in Bicester, Oxfordshire on 5 March 1931.
Attended Bicester Grammar School. Received violin tuition from his father, and took lessons in piano between the age of five and six.
Organist of Bicester Methodist Church while still in his teens.
Went up to Keble College, Oxford, spending a total of six years studying at the University, including post graduate work. His tutors were **Herbert Kennedy Andrews** for orchestration and **Thomas Armstrong** for harmony and counterpoint. Received no specialised undergraduate training in composition. Graduated B.Mus. and M.A. Awarded D.Mus. honorarily by the University of Hull (1986). National Service followed. After basic training at Catterick Camp, Yorkshire, Anthony Hedges joined the Band of the Royal Signals Regiment, which was nicknamed 'The Circus', as a pianist. He remained in the Band for two years and was obliged by the regulations to learn also to play the clarinet. His contemporaries included **Harrison Oxley**.
Taught counterpoint and musical history at the Royal Scottish Academy of Music (1957-1963). A church organist. His music reviews for *Glasgow Herald* developed into a significant part of his career. *Glasgow Herald* commissioned book reviews and feature articles. Further material appeared in *The Times*, *The Scotsman*, *The Guardian*, *The Daily Telegraph* and *Musical Times*.
Lecturer (from 1963), senior lecturer (from 1968) and reader in composition at the University of Hull.
While still a student he was editor of *Sunday School Praise* (1958) and during the decade that followed a number of anthems and carols were published. Other church music includes his Magnificat

and Nunc Dimittis (1976) and his Advent motet 'Gabriel's Message' (1989).

A Symphony (1975) and oratorio *The Temple of Solomon* (1979) represent his large-scale works. Other compositions include a Piano Trio (1977), film and theatre music, and works for amateurs and children.

HEIGHINGTON, Dr. Musgrave (1680-1774)
Born in 1680; died in Dundee, Scotland in 1774. A D.Mus. Held organistships in Yarmouth, Norfolk (1738) and Leicester (1739). For a time he lived in Dublin. Psalm or hymn melodies by Musgrave Heighington are found in the collection by the elder **John Alcock**, *Harmony of Jerusalem* (1801). Composer of the song 'Fast by the margin of the sea' (?1760).

HEINS, Nicholas (1839-1910)
Born in St. Pancras, London in 1839; died in Hereford on 8 May 1910. Composer of a Magnificat and Nunc Dimittis in D (1875) and a further setting in chant form (1881), and a number of quadruple chants and hymn tunes. A Kyrie was published in 1893.

HELE, John (1846-1899)
Born in Plymouth, Devon on 24 May 1846; died in Plymouth on 28 April 1899. Studied at the Royal Academy of Music. Graduated B.Mus. at the University of Oxford (1871). Organist of Pennycross Church, Plymouth (from 1860). Organist of the Devonport Churches of Christ Church (1863), St. Mary (1864) and St. Peter (1872). Held appointments in Morden, Surrey (1865-1867) and at Bodmin Parish Church (1868-1872). In 1894 he took up an organistship in Compton Giford. In 1883 he was appointed borough organist of Plymouth. A local choral society conductor.
Composed church music and items for organ.

HELE, John Calvert (19th century)
Graduated B.Mus. at New College, Oxford (1898). Held a succession of organist appointments in the West of England, at St. Saviour's, Plymouth (1873); Egg, Buckland (1874); All Saints', Plymouth (1875); Holy Trinity, Plymouth (1876); St. James the Great, Devonport (1878); St. George's, Stonehouse (1880); and St. Peter, Plymouth (1880). Composed a setting of Psalm 67 'Deus Misereatur'.

HELMORE, Revd. Thomas (1811-1890)
Born in Kidderminster, Worcestershire on 7 May 1811; died in London on 6 July 1890. The son of a minister of the Congregational Church.
Learned to play flute and cello. Trained his father's church choir while still in his teens. He then taught at Stratford-on-Avon, Warwickshire. Went up to Magdalen Hall, Oxford, graduating B.A. and being ordained in the same year (1840); M.A. (1845).
In 1840, Helmore was appointed curate of St. Michael's Church, Lichfield, Staffordshire, where he remained for two years. A priest vicar of Lichfield Cathedral.
He was instrumental in the revival in the Church of England of Gregorian plainchant as part of the worship. Vice principal and precentor of St. Mark's College Chelsea (from 1842), a new teacher training college for Church of England schools. A model school was attached to the college so that it was possible to form a choir to lead the daily unaccompanied services in the college chapel. There was no chapel organ until 1861. St. Mark's soon became famous for its chanting by the choir and congregation.

Master of the children of the Chapel Royal (1846-1886) in succession to **William Hawes**. One of his choristers was the young **Arthur Sullivan** (from 1854). A priest in ordinary of the Chapel Royal (from 1847).
Resigned as vice principal of St. Mark's but remained as precentor there until 1877. The two choirs sometimes combined and sang at St. Mark's.
In 1849 he published *The Psalter Noted*, a Gregorian Psalter. He urged that all adaptations of non-church music such as opera should be excluded from church music, and that items that had been written for the church but had become associated with use outside it should be abandoned. This was to mark church music as special and distinctive, more worthy for an act of worship. He presented papers at sessions of Church Congress in Wolverhampton (1867), Swansea (1879) and London (1880).
Published two collections of carols with J.M. Neale.
Composed the anthem 'Jesus said, let the little children.' He is represented in *Cathedral Psalter Chants* (1875) by a Single Chant in F. Adapted the hymn tune 'Veni Immanuel' for congregational singing. Composed a setting of the Benedictus and Agnus Dei for Two Trebles and Alto, and composed and arranged other music for the church.

HEMINGWAY, Roger (b.1951)
Born in London on 12 July 1951. Has composed the anthem 'Consider and hear me, O Lord my God' (1976) for boys' voices, and the anthem 'The sea of faith' (1978).

HEMPEL, Dr. Charles Frederick (1811-1867)
Born in Truro, Cornwall on 7 September 1811; died in Perth, Scotland on 25 April 1867. A son of **Charles William Hempel.** Studied music with his father. Graduated B.Mus. (1855) and D.Mus. (1862) at the University of Oxford. In 1844 he succeeded his father as organist of St. Mary's Church, Truro. Appointed organist of St. John's Episcopal Church, Perth in 1857. Composed anthems including 'Almighty and everlasting God' and 'Let God arise', an oratorio *The Seventh Seal*, songs and piano music.

HEMPEL, Charles William (1777-1855)
Father of **Charles Hempel.** Organist of St. Mary's Church, Truro until 1844, when succeeded by his son. Composed anthems including 'Like as the hart' and 'Unto Thee, O God'.

HEMSLEY, John (1838-?)
Born in Arnold, Nottinghamshire in 1838. A chorister of Lichfield Cathedral. Took up an organ appointment in Merevale, Warwickshire in 1857. A lay clerk of Ely Cathedral (from 1860). A stipendiary choir man of the Dublin Cathedrals of Christ Church and St. Patrick (from 1864). Composed anthems and songs.

HEMSTOCK, Arthur (1845-?)
Born in Bingham, Nottinghamshire in 1845. Organist of the Parish Churches of Bingham and of Diss, Norfolk. A local choral society conductor. Composed church music, including a setting of Psalm 145 'I will magnify Thee, O Lord my King' (1885).

HEMY, Henri Friedrich (1818-1888)
Born in Newcastle-on-Tyne on 12 November 1818; died in West Hartlepool, County Durham on 10 June 1888. His parents were German; his son was the marine painter Charles Napier Hemy.

Organist of St. Andrew's Roman Catholic Church, Newcastle. Taught music at Tynemouth and at St. Cuthbert's Theological College, Ushaw, Durham.

Author of a piano tutor and other works, and published a collection of hymn tunes *Easy Hymn Tunes for Catholic Schools* (1851-1853). His own hymn tune 'St. Catherine', also known as 'Tynemouth', was first published anonymously in his collection *The Crown of Jesus' Music* (1864), a publication and a tune (one of many) that were popular with Roman Catholic congregations. The tune is still in use today in *Hymns and Psalms* (1983).

HENDERSON, Revd. Andrew (1825-?)
Born in Kirkwall, Orkney, Scotland on 4 January 1825. Educated at St. Andrews, and ordained as Minister of Coldingham in 1847. Appointed to Abbey Close United Presbyterian Church, Paisley, in 1855. Composer of hymn tunes, but better known as a hymnal editor. Secretary to the Hymnal Committee of the United Presbyterian Church. Edited *Church Melodies* for the versions of 1858, 1860 and 1862. *New Scottish Psalter* (1870), also edited by him, contained some of his tunes.

HENDERSON, Thomas (?-1940)
Graduated B.Mus. at the University of Durham (1893), following a private education in music. Organist of Yarm Parish Church (1889-1896) and of St. Hilda's, Darlington (from 1896). Taught music at the local grammar school and girls' high school. His other teaching commitments in Darlington were at Polam Hall School for Girls and Thornbeck House School. A conductor of local choral and orchestral societies. Critic on the staff of *Northern Echo* for more than 50 years. An adjudicator and examiner. Composed a festival anthem 'Not unto us, O Lord', and marching tunes.

HENDRIE, Dr. Gerald Mills (b.1935)
Born in Westcliff on Sea, Essex on 28 October 1935.

Foundation scholar of Framlingham College, Suffolk (1949-1952). Studied as piano scholar at the Royal College of Music with Geoffrey Tankard for piano, **William Harris** and **Herbert Howells** for theory and **Harold Darke** for organ. Organ scholar and research student of Selwyn College, Cambridge (1954-1962) with Nigel Fortune and Thurston Dart. Graduated M.A., Mus. B. and Ph.D. Also received organ tuition from André Marchal, Ralph Downes and **John Dykes Bower**.

Director of music of Homerton College, Cambridge (1962-1963); lecturer in the music at the University of Manchester (1963-1967); professor and chairman of the Department of Music of the University of Victoria, British Columbia (1967-1969); and professor at the Open University (1969-1990), taking early retirement in the latter year in order to devote more time to composition. Supervisor of studies in music at St. John's College, Cambridge (1959-1962 and 1977-1985), the last four years of which were as director of studies.

As acting assistant organist of Canterbury Cathedral (1954) he took part in the first-ever Eurovision Outside Broadcast by the B.B.C., 'Carols from Canterbury'. Acting Assistant Organist of Ely Cathedral (1958) and, for six months, acting organist of Norwich Cathedral (1960-1961).

Former chairman of the Handel Institute, and an editor of Handel's church music.

Carried out major editions of the keyboard works of **Orlando Gibbons** for the collection *Musica Britannica* (1962). Has presented papers at conference and written for professional

journals, made recordings and composed. His works for the church include Services, of which examples are the *St. Paul's* Service for Boys' Voices (for the choir of St. Paul's Cathedral, 1988) and the *Canterbury* Service (1993), carols such as 'Sweet was the song the Virgin sang' (1964), and *Ave verum corpus* (1978). A carol 'As I outrode this enderyes night' has achieved recognition. His *In praise of Reconciliation* in four movements celebrates the 50th anniversary of the end of World War II. Other works have been composed for piano, for wind and for orchestra.

HENLEY, Revd. Phocian (1728-1764)
Born in Abbots Wootton, Wiltshire in 1728; died in London on 29 August 1764 of a fever which he contracted while visiting a sick parishioner. Graduated B.A. and M.A. from Wadham College, Oxford (1749), his undergraduate studies including music. Rector of the London Churches of St. Andrew-by-the-Wardrobe and St. Anne, Blackfriars (from 1759). His *Divine Harmony* (published some years after his death, in 1798) was a collection of hymn tunes composed or arranged by him. One such composition was the tune known as 'Henley'. Composed anthems including 'Hear my prayer' and 'The cure of Saul'. *Cathedral Psalter Chants* (1875) contains a Double Chant in E-flat.

Henllan
See **ROBERTS,** John.

HENMAN, Richard (?-1741)
The composer of this name may or may not be the same Richard Henman who was a chorister of the Chapel Royal and who took part in the Coronation of James II. Organist of Exeter Cathedral (1694-1741), being dismissed on 27 June 1741 for 'long absence and a disorderly life'. Is believed to have composed the anthem 'Have Mercy'.

HENNIKER, Dr. Henry Faulkner (1839-?)
Born in Chatham, Kent in 1839. Studied at the Royal Academy of Music under **William Sterndale Bennett** and Prosper Sainton. Awarded the Lambeth D.Mus. in 1889. Organist of the Church of Holy Trinity, Maidstone, Kent (from 1864). Conductor of the town's choral society (from 1866). Principal of the Kent County School of Music, Maidstone. Composed anthems, an oratorio *The Martyrdom of Stephen*, operas, songs, choruses and organ works.

HENRY VIII (1491-1547)
Born in Greenwich, London on 28 June 1491; died in Westminster, London on 28 January 1547. As the second son he did not expect to inherit the throne but his older brother, Arthur, died in 1502. As Henry VIII he reigned from 1509 to 1547. As a child he was trained in music. He played various musical instruments including lute and virginals. At court there was a great deal of formal and informal music, requiring, by the year 1547, a force totalling 58 musicians. Composed two Masses and works for voices and viols. Also composed part songs. Some five four-part and 12 three-part songs are documented, an example of the latter being 'Pastyme with good companye'.

HENSCHEL, Sir Isador Georg (1850-1934)
Born in Breslau, Germany on 18 February 1850; died in Aviemore, Scotland on 10 September 1934. Known as Sir George Henschel.

Belonged to a Jewish family living in Poland. Converted to Christianity when he was very young.

Studied with Julius Schäffer at St. Magdalene's College, Breslau; and at the Leipzig Conservatory (1867-1870) under Ignaz Moscheles for piano, Götze for singing and Carl Reinecke for theory.

Continued his studies in composition with Friedrick Kieland and in singing with Adolf Schulze. Awarded the honorary D.Mus. by the University of Edinburgh in 1910.

Knighted in 1914, retiring from his singing career in the same year. As a boy he had performed as a soprano soloist. His adult singing career commenced as a tenor but his voice deepened and by 1914 he was able to sing *basso profundo*. Made tours several times as a singer, and performed in the U.S.A. at Boston and New York.

The first conductor of the Boston Symphony Orchestra (1881-1884). Founded (1886) and conducted (1886-1897) the London Symphony Concerts. First conductor of the Scottish Orchestra (1893-1895).

A teacher of singing at the Royal College of Music (1886-1888). Professor of singing at the Institute of Musical Art, New York (1905-1908). As a singer he was a leading performer of the songs of Brahms, whom he knew personally.

Composed a Te Deum in C, a Stabat Mater, a Requiem Mass, operas including *A Sea Change*, songs, duets, quartets and chamber music.

HENSHAW, Dr. William (1791-?)
Born in 1791 in Marylebone, London. Organist of Durham Cathedral (1813-1862); awarded D.Mus. at the University of Durham in 1860. Composer of hymn tunes and chants.

HENSTRIDGE, Daniel (?-1736)
Known to have been alive in 1700; died in Canterbury, Kent in June 1736.

Organist successively of the Cathedrals of Gloucester (1666-1673), Rochester (1673-1698) and Canterbury 1698-1736).

Although these appointments cover 70 consecutive years it is both feasible and likely that they were held by one person rather than more than one with the same name.

By December 1718 his health had deteriorated and he was no longer capable of performing his duties at Canterbury. Accordingly, **William Raylton** was appointed master of the choristers. Henstridge remained nominally as organist.

Composed a Service in D, anthems including 'Blessed is the man' and 'The Lord is King', and other items of church music.

HERBERT, Edward (1830-1872)
Born in 1830; died in Wimborne, Dorset in 1872. Graduated B.Mus. at the University of Oxford (1862). Held organ appointments at Perth, Scotland; Sherborne Abbey Church, Dorset; and at Wimborne Minster, Dorset. Author of *Manual Of The Rudiments of Music*. Composed anthems including 'I saw the Lord' and 'Thou art gone up'.

HERBERT, George (1817-1906)
Born in 1817; died in Kensington, London on 14 June 1906. Organist of the Church of the Jesuit Fathers, Farm Street, London. Composer of hymn tunes. His 'Sunset', also known as 'St. Philip', was included in *Church Hymns* (1874).

HERON, Henry (?-1795)
Died around 20 June 1795. Organist of the Church of St. Magnus the Martyr, London (1768-1795). An organist of Ewell, Surrey named Henry Heron was probably the same person. Contributed Psalm tunes to the collection *Parochial Music Corrected* by **William Riley**. Composed voluntaries for organ or harpsichord.

HERSCHEL, Sir Friedrich Wilhelm (1738-1822)
Born in Hanover, Germany on 15 November 1738; died in Slough, Buckinghamshire on 25 August 1822.

He held the D.C.L. A Fellow of the Royal Society.

His father and brother were oboe players in the Hanoverian Guard, and he followed suit. Posted to England during the Seven Years' War. Returning to Germany in 1756, he resolved to return and eventually did, working as a copyist.

In 1760 he trained the Durham Militia Band and then settled in Leeds as a director of concerts (1762). In the North East he became acquainted with **Charles Avison** and **John Garth**.

He taught, and following a brief period of three months as the organist of Halifax Parish Church, Yorkshire (1766), in November 1766 he was appointed to the Octagon Chapel, Bath, Somerset, remaining there until June 1782.

His continuing studies helped to bring about a change in career. His knowledge of harmony gave him an understanding of mathematics, which he then studied further. Similarly, mathematics took him into astronomy. He discovered the planet Uranus (1781) and became court astronomer to George III. The king put up the sum of £2000 for him to build the world's largest telescope of the time.

Composed church music, including a Service in A and a Te Deum and Jubilate. There were also anthems including 'O come, loud anthems' (1789), most of which are lost. Also composed a symphony and two Concertos for Military Band.

HERVEY, Revd. Frederick Alfred John (1846-1910)
Born in St. James, Middlesex on 18 May 1846; died in Norwich, Norfolk on 8 August 1910.

Attended Marlborough School and Trinity Hall, Cambridge where he studied under **George Garrett**. During the vacations, he studied with **E.J. Hopkins**. Graduated B.A. (1868) and M.A. (1872). Ordained deacon (1869) and priest (1870).

Curate of Putney, London (1869-1876) and rector of Upton Pyne, Devon (1876-1878). Domestic chaplain to Baroness North (from 1873) and to the Prince of Wales (from 1878). Chaplain in ordinary to Queen Victoria (from 1886). An honorary canon of Norwich Cathedral (from 1891), domestic chaplain to Edward VII (from 1901) and rector of Sandringham, Norfolk (1878-1907). A governor of the Royal College of Music.

His Single Chants in D Minor and in F were used in *Cathedral Psalter Chants* (1875), but he is better known for his hymn tunes. The Standard Edition (1916) of *Hymns Ancient and Modern* contains 'Putney Hill' and 'Harting', while *Church Hymns* (1874) uses 'Lonsdale' three times and combines 'The roseate hues of early dawn' by Cecil Frances Alexander with 'Castle Rising'.

HESELTINE, James (c1692-1763)
Born around the year 1692; died in Durham on 20 June 1763. As a chorister of the Chapel Royal until 1707, he was one of the last in the charge of **John Blow**. Organist of the Church of St. Katherine-by-the-Tower, near the Tower of London (1709-1763). Retained this appointment throughout his long absence as organist of Durham Cathedral (1711-1763). Composed anthems, a number of which he is said to have destroyed following a disagreement with

the Dean and Chapter. His anthems include 'Unto Thee will I cry' and 'Praise the Lord'.

HESELTINE, Philip (1894-1930)

Born in the Savoy Hotel, London on 30 October 1894; died in London on 17 December 1930 from gas poisoning upon which a coroner's jury recorded an open verdict.

Lived for the first few years of his life in a house in Hans Road, Chelsea, bought later by Harrods.

From the age of five, Philip Heseltine went to school in Clieveden Place, Eaton Square. In 1903 his mother remarried and from a year later, Philip attended Stone House Preparatory School, Broadstairs, Kent. Athough he was easily top of his form within two weeks of arriving at the school, he received no formal musical education, a perceived disadvantage that he felt keenly during his musical career. From around 1906 he began to compose hymns.

Attended Eton College (1908-1911) and spent a year studying classics at the University of Oxford. At Eton, the Music Society was run by **C.H. Lloyd** but his musical mentor was another member of the music staff, Colin Taylor, who gave him clarinet lessons. In 1910, during his time at Eton, he met Frederick Delius in France.

He joined the Officer Training Corps at Eton and camped out on Farnborough Common, Hampshire in 1910, but strongly disliked the experience.

As early as September 1912, before his 18th birthday, an article on the composer Arnold Schönberg was published in *Musical Standard*. His piece *Some Reflections on Modern Day Criticism* was accepted by *Musical Times* in July 1913.

In October 1913 he went up to Christ Church, Oxford but after a year he abandoned his place. From October 1914 he studied at University College, London. However, his studies left him insufficient time as a writer and he abandoned the former. He worked for *Daily Mail* between February and June 1915.

A conscientious objector during World War I. Lived in Ireland from 1917 to 1918. Thereafter he lived in London. As a composer he was influenced by Delius and Bernard Van Dieren, both of whom he admired greatly. Others of his friends included the composers Cecil Gray, Constant Lambert and **E.J. Moeran**. He met, and for a time was a friend of, the author D.H. Lawrence.

He was openly hostile to Rutland Boughton and others. Somewhat mischievous, he was known to have written rude rhymes about some of his fellow composers and then to have sent the rhymes on a postcard to their subjects.

Transcribed 17th century songs from manuscript and edited Elizabethan lute songs. Wrote on Delius and other composers. Founded the periodical *The Sackbut* (1920). In 1923 he collected folk songs with E.J.Moeran in the East of England.

In 1930, the will of his late uncle Evelyn was published. Many of the family received sums of money from the £639,366 distributed, but Philip Heseltine received none. By this time he was extremely short of money.

From 1917, following poor critical reception of some of his early works, he adopted the pseudonym 'Peter Warlock', although he made no serious attempt to cloak his true identity. To his bitter amusement he was hailed as a promising new composer of songs and chamber music. In all he composed some hundred songs, describing himself as a tune trundler.

The carols 'Benedicamus Domino' (1918) and 'Adam lay Ybounden' (1922) were early successes.

Collaborated successfully but on a small scale with the writer Bruce Blunt. In December 1927 Blunt wrote the words of a carol, 'Bethlehem Down' - according to him, while walking from one country public house to another. Within a few days, Heseltine had set it to music and it was published in *Daily Telegraph* of 24 December 1927.

Two years later another successful collaboration resulted in 'The frostbound wood' being published in the Christmas edition of *Radio Times*. Blunt later suspected that if he had been able to produce the words of an equally-promising carol in 1930, Heseltine's premature and probably self-inflicted death might have been averted.

HESFORD, Dr. Bryan (1930-1996)

Born in Eccles, Manchester in July 1930; died in 1996.

Educated in Manchester, and studied music with W.H. Selby and the French organists Marcel Dupré and Jean Langlais. Held the degrees of Ph.D and D.Mus.

Organist of Prescot Parish Church, Manchester and assistant organist of Newcastle Cathedral.

Organist of Wymondham Abbey (1960-1963); Brecon Cathedral (1963-1966); St. Margaret's Priory Church, King's Lynn, Norfolk (1966-1970); Lancaster Priory (1970-1972); Melton Mowbray Parish Church, Leicestershire (1973-1978); Etne Parish Church, Norway (1985-1986); the Collegiate Church of St. Nicholas, Galway, Ireland (1990-1995) and Tuam Cathedral, Ireland (1995-1996).

An examiner for Trinity College of Music (1966-1985).

Composed a quantity of music for the church, including a Magnificat and Nunc Dimittis in E Minor for Boys' Voices (1960) for Newcastle Cathedral; a set of Responses (1966) for the King's Lynn Festival; anthems, of which examples are 'O Praise God in His holiness' (1976) for a Royal School of Church Music festival in Southwark Cathedral and 'Shew us, O Lord' (1991), the *Kiev Requiem* for Organ, Solo Voices, Strings and Choir for the city of Kiev (1994), and a set of three chants, two of which have been since been republished in the collections *Manchester Cathedral Chant Book* and *New Cathedral Psalter*. Other works include items and arrangements for organ.

HESTER, Charles Edward (1866-1946)

Born in Buckinghamshire in 1866; died in Princes Risborough, Buckinghamshire on 6 January 1946. Composer of hymn tunes.

HEWARD, Leslie Hays (1897-1943)

Born in Liversedge, Yorkshire on 8 December 1897; died in Birmingham on 3 May 1943. The son of an organist.

Received lessons in music from his father. A chorister of Manchester Cathedral under **S.H. Nicholson** and a pupil of Manchester Grammar School. Studied under **C.V. Stanford** and **Ralph Vaughan Williams** under a composition scholarship at the Royal College of Music (from 1917).

Assistant organist of Manchester Cathedral and organist of the Church of St. Andrew, Ancoats, Manchester (both from 1914). Music master of Eton College (from 1917) and organist of Holy Trinity Church, Windsor, Berkshire (from 1917). His other early appointments included playing a cinema organ in Brighton, Sussex. Director of music at Westminster School, London (from 1920).

Musical director of the South African Broadcasting Corporation (1924-1927). Acknowledged as a fine conductor. Succeeded Adrian Boult as conductor of the City of Birmingham Symphony

Orchestra (1930-1943). Appeared frequently in Leeds during the early war years. Conductor of the British National Opera Company. His hymn tune 'Wyke' is used with G. Matheson's hymn 'O Love that wilt not let me go' in the Standard Edition (1916) of *Hymns Ancient and· Modern.* He destroyed many of his other compositions, the earliest of which dated back to his time as a chorister at Manchester Cathedral.

HEWITT, John (?-1848)
Organist of St. Michael's Church, Staffordshire. Composed the anthem 'O praise the Lord of Heaven'.

HEWITT-JONES, Tony (1926-1989)
Born in. Ealing, London, on 27 January 1926; died on 30 September 1989. Attended Westminster School and went up to Christ Church, Oxford, where he studied with **Bernard Rose.** Also studied with Nadia Boulanger. Director of music of Dean Close Junior School, Cheltenham (1953-1957) and music adviser to Gloucestershire County (from 1958). A choral conductor and accompanist. A number of published compositions include a Te Deum, a set of Responses, the anthems 'Rejoice and be merry' and 'At the round earth's imagined corners'.

HEWLETT, Thomas (1845-1874)
Born in Oxford on 16 March 1845; died in Edinburgh on 10 April 1874. A pupil of **Leighton Hayne;** satisfied the technical requirements of the Oxford B.Mus. at the age of 14.
Organist to the Duke of Buccleuch (1865-1871), and, in Edinburgh, of the Church of St. Peter, Lutton Place (1868-1869); St. Mary's Roman Catholic Church and Newington Parish Church (1873-1874). Conductor of the Edinburgh Choral Union. Composed the anthem 'I am the Resurrection'.
His hymn tune 'Dalkeith' was used in the Standard Edition (1916) of *Hymns Ancient and Modern* with the hymn 'Weary of earth and laden with my sin' by S.J. Stone. The same tune was used in the Revised Edition (1927) of *Church Hymnary* with the hymn 'Not what I am, Lord, but what Thou art' by Horatius Bonar. Also composed organ and piano music, songs and part songs.

HEWSON, Dr. George Henry Phillips (1881-1972)
Born in Dublin on 19 November 1881; died in Dublin in November 1972.
A chorister of St. Patrick's Cathedral, Dublin (from 1889). Attended St. Patrick's Cathedral Grammar School and Trinity College, Dublin where he graduated B.Mus. (1903), B.A. (1905), D.Mus. (1914) and M.A. (1928).
Organist of Stillorgan Church (from 1898), Clontarf Church (from 1900) and the Zion Church (from 1901). Sub organist of St. Patrick's Cathedral, Dublin (from 1902).
Organist and master of the choristers of the Chapel Royal, Dublin Castle (from 1907); Armagh Cathedral (1916-1920) and St. Patrick's Cathedral, Dublin, where he succeeded **Charles Marchant** (from 1920). Remained in office at St. Patrick's until 1960, when he was succeeded by **William Greig,** who had been a chorister at St. Patrick's and who had served as Hewson's assistant for 18 years. Hewson was professor of music of Trinity College, Dublin (1935-1962).
At St. Patrick's Cathedral, he found difficulty in recruiting adult choir members of the required quality, and the low salary of £140 meant that some of the English applicants insisted on being free to supplement their income with outside engagements.

Composed church music. His works include at least three anthems, a Te Deum in E, a Communion Service in G Minor and three settings of the Magnificat and Nunc Dimittis, two of which are for men's voices.

HEYWOOD, John (1841-1915)
Born in Birmingham in 1841; died in Birmingham on 16 May 1915.
Studied piano and organ under John Chapman, organist of St. Thomas's Church, Birmingham. Continued his education at the Royal Academy of Music under **Charles Steggall, Walter Macfarren** and H. Regaldi.
Organist of the Churches of St. Jude, Birmingham (from 1863); St. Mary, Aston Brook (1864-1865); St. Margaret, Ward End (from 1865) and St. Paul, Balsall Heath (from 1866). Organist and choirmaster of the Plainsong Choir, Holy Trinity Church, Bordesley (1864-1865). A regional choir organiser.
Wrote on church music and contributed regularly to *The Choir, Saturday Musical Review* and *Monthly Musical Record.*
Composed anthems including 'Try me, O God' and 'I am the Lord'. A Single Chant in E-flat was published in *Cathedral Psalter Chants* (1875).
The Standard Edition (1916) of *Hymns Ancient and Modern* uses his tune 'Aston' with 'Out of the deep I call' by **H.W. Baker,** and 'St. Luke' with 'O God of Truth, whose living word' by Thomas Hughes. Editor of *Anglican Psalter Noted* (1864).

HICHENS, Frederick Harrison (1836-1921)
Born in Dulwich, London on 22 April 1836; died in Falmouth, Cornwall on 13 October 1921. Composer of hymn tunes.

HICKOX, Dr. Walter Herbert (1872-1931)
Born in Kensington, London on 23 June 1872; died on 7 August 1931.
Attended St. Mark's College, Chelsea, London. Trained at the Royal College of Music with **Walter Parratt, Hubert Parry, Frederick Bridge** and **F.E. Gladstone,** and at Guildhall School of Music under **Warwick Jordan.** Graduated B.Mus. at Queen's College, Oxford (1907), and D.Mus. at the University of Dublin (1909).
Having played at his first Service at the age of nine, Walter Hickox was organist concurrently of the two Kensington Churches of St. Elizabeth (from 1887) and St. Philip (from 1889). Gave more than a thousand organ recitals
A professor of organ at G.S.M. (from 1909). Taught piano and organ at Battersea Polytechnic, London (from 1911). A professor of the R.C.M.
Composed services, including two Masses, a Communion Service in E-flat for Women's Voices, an Ascension anthem 'Thou art gone up on high' and a Brigade Hymn for the Church Lads' Brigade.

HIGGINS, Edward (?-1769)
May have been the Edward Higgins who was organist of Bristol Cathedral (1759-1765). A vicar choral of the Dublin Cathedrals of Christ Church and St. Patrick (1765). Composer of chants. A Chant in F is attributed to him.

HIGGINSON, Gary Michael (b.1952)
Born in West Bromwich, Staffordshire on 29 December 1952.
Attended Dartmouth Grammar School, Walsall (1964-1971).
Studied at Guildhall School of Music, London (1971-1975) where

he specialised in singing, keyboard and, under **Edmund Rubbra**, composition. Graduated M.A. at the University of Birmingham (1982) following two years' study there.

Director of music at Bredon School, Upton on Severn (1975-1980). Assistant director of music at St. Helen's School, Abingdon, Berkshire (1983-1990) and director of music at Sion School, Worthing, Sussex (from 1990) and of St. Margaret's School, Exeter, Devon (1993-1995). Since then he has worked as a composer and freelance musician.

Assistant organist of St. Margaret's Church, Streatham Hill, London under Colin Nicholls, who was subsequently organist of Cork Cathedral. Organist and choirmaster of St. Peter's Church, West Bromwich (1968-1971); St. Mary Magdalene, Lyminster, West Sussex (1990-1993) and, since then, a freelance organist and director of music at local churches.

A member of the New London Consort and John Alldis Choir (1971-1975). Sang in the Tewkesbury Abbey Choir (1975-1983) and during the same period, with the all-male choir, The Tallismen. Has contributed to music journals. Reviews concerts and recordings for the British Music Society.

He has composed a version of the carol 'Away in a manger' and the Evening Hymn (1973). *Alleluja Psallite* (1978, revised 1991) was composed for Eton College Chapel. Other works include *Messages of Hope* (1987), a song cycle to words by Christopher Wordsworth and Colin Pedley.

HIGGS, Henry Marcellus (1855-1929)

Born in Hanover Square, London in 1855; died in Putney, London, on 28 October 1929. A son of Marcellus Higgs, an organist and composer. An organist. Chief Music Editor of the publishing firm of Chappell for 22 years, having previously worked for the firm of Metzler. Composer of hymn tunes, a *Suite de Ballet* for Orchestra, and music for organ, for violin and for piano.

HILES, Dr. Henry (1826-1904)

Born in Shrewsbury, Shropshire on 31 December 1826; died in Worthing, West Sussex on 20 October 1904. The younger brother of **John Hiles**.

Studied with his brother. Graduated B.Mus. (1862) and D.Mus. (1867) at the University of Oxford.

An organist by the age of 13 and held later appointments in London and the North West, these being at Bury (from 1846); Bishopwearmouth (from 1847); St. Michael's, Wood Street, London (from 1859); the Blind Asylum, Manchester (from 1860) and Bowdon, Cheshire (from 1861). From 1852 to 1859 he travelled round the world following serious illness. In 1864 he settled in Manchester, where he became the conductor of several music societies and organist of St. Paul's Church, Hulme (1864-1867).

Became lecturer in music at Owen's College, Manchester (from 1867) and at Victoria University. In 1893 he became a professor of harmony of the Royal Manchester College of Music. He worked to promote the Incorporated Society of Musicians, which was founded in 1882 and incorporated in 1892.

Author of an instruction book on the French harmonium (1877) and works on musical theory. Edited and contributed to *Quarterly Musical Review* (1885-1888); wrote for *Musical Opinion* and other journals. Presented papers at meetings of the Musical Association and at the Incorporated Society of Musicians.

Cathedral Psalter Chants (1875) contains Single Chants in A-flat and in B-flat. A collection of Responses to the Commandments of around the same year includes a setting by him in G.

The Standard Edition (1916) of *Hymns Ancient and Modern* uses his tune 'Haslingden' for the hymn 'O Christ our Joy gone up on high'. Composed Services, the anthem 'Blessed are the merciful', cantatas, oratorios and glees.

HILES, John (1810-1882)

Born in 1810; died in London on 4 February 1882. The brother of **Henry Hiles**. Held organistships in the towns of Shrewsbury, Shropshire; Portsmouth, Hampshire; Brighton, Sussex and London. Organist of the Shrewsbury Festival (1840-1841). Compiled a dictionary of some 12,500 musical terms (1871). Composed the anthem 'I am the Resurrection'. Other works include organ voluntaries, piano pieces and songs.

HILL, Berkeley (20th century)

A lecturer at Wye College, Kent. Composed a number of items including the anthem 'Glorious the Day'.

HILL, Claud Henry (19th/20th century)

Attended the Royal Academy of Music. Graduated B.Mus. at the University of Oxford (1908). Organist at Grange-over-Sands, and Jesmond Parish Church, Newcastle-on-Tyne (1894-1898). Director of music at King Edward's School, Wisley, Surrey (from 1898). Composed church music including a Benedicite in D (1907), songs and violin pieces.

HILL, Dr. Horace (c1822-1900)

Born in Norwich, Norfolk in 1822 or 1823; died on 16 March 1900.

Graduated Mus.B. (1869) and Mus.D. (1878) at the University of Cambridge. Conductor of the Norwich Festival Choir and of other local choral and musical societies. Composed a setting of the Benedictus, a cantata *A Song of Praise* performed at the Norwich Festival (1869), an oratorio *Nehemiah*, overtures and a part song.

HILL, John (1797-1846)

Born in Norwich, Norfolk on 5 April 1797; died in Norwich on 28 July 1846. Founded the Norwich Choral Society with Edward Taylor. Chorus master of the Norwich Festival (1826 -1846). Editor, with his son, James, of *Norwich Tune Book,* in which some tunes were composed by him.

HILL, Thomas (18th/19th century)

Organist of Carlisle Cathedral (1785-1833). In 1817 he was reprimanded for 'tipling and frequenting the cock pit'. Composed a chant.

HILL, Thomas Henry Weist (1828-1891)

Born in Islington, London on 3 January 1828; died in South Kensington, London on 26 December 1891.

Attended the Royal Academy of Music.

A violin recitalist, he toured the U.S.A. and Europe. He was involved with the orchestras of the Opera Society, the Philharmonic Society and the Sacred Harmonic Society. When the Alexandra Palace opened in 1873, Thomas Hill was its first conductor. Principal of Guildhall School of Music (1880 -1891).

His compositions were few. They include a Civic Anthem, performed at the Guildhall, London (December 1887), and works for violin and for cello.

HILTON, John (c1560-c1608)
Born around 1560; died in Cambridge before 20 March 1608. Father of **John Hilton** the younger.
May have been a pupil of **Thomas Tallis**. Said to have graduated B.Mus.
Sang counter tenor as a poor clerk, a status lower than that of a junior vicar choral, in the choir of Lincoln Cathedral. During his time at Lincoln he may have acted as deputy to the Cathedral organist, Thomas Butler. Taught the choristers of Lincoln. Helped to produce two comedies mounted by the choristers and other children.
He left Lincoln in 1594 to become organist of Trinity Hall, Cambridge.
The anthems 'Call to Remembrance' and 'Lord, for Thy tender mercies' sake' are assumed to be his rather than his son's. 'Teach me, O Lord' is still sung today. Composed the madrigal 'Fair Oriana, beauty's Queen'.

HILTON, John (1599-1657)
Born, probably in Cambridge, in 1599; died in Westminster, London and was buried on 21 March 1657. Son of the elder **John Hilton.**
Graduated Mus.B. (1626) at Trinity Hall, Cambridge.
Organist and parish clerk of St. Margaret's Church, Westminster (from 1628), probably retaining the latter appointment when, around 1644, the organ was suppressed.
Composed five full anthems, and 12 verse anthems. Also madrigals, catches, and music for viols. His *Catch that catch can* (1652) was a collection of catches, rounds and canons. His hymn tune 'Donne' may well have been commissioned by John Donne for his hymn or lute song 'Wilt thou forgive?'.

HINDE, Henry (?-1641)
Died in 1641, possibly on 6 August. Organist of Lichfield Cathedral from around 1630 to 1641. Composed the anthem 'Sing praises'.

HINDE, Richard (17th century)
A prebendary of Lichfield Cathedral at some time before 1700. Composed the anthem 'O sing unto the Lord' (1652)

HINDLE, John (1761-1796)
Born in Westminster, London in 1761; died in London in 1796. Graduated B.Mus. at Magdalen College, Oxford (1791). A counter-tenor singer. A lay vicar of Westminster Abbey (from 1785). While taking part in the Worcester Three Choirs' Festival of 1778, he sang in front of members of the Royal Family. *Cathedral Psalter Chants* (1875) included Single Chants in B-flat and in G. Composed songs and a glee 'Queen of the silver bow'.

HINDLEY, David Gallaway (b. 1933)
Born in Leeds in 1933. Composer of hymn tunes.

HINDMARSH, Clifford (1892-1974)
Born in Alnwick, Northumberland on 13 January 1892; died in Newcastle-on-Tyne on 12 August 1974. Composer of hymn tunes.

HINE (Hind, Hyne), William (1687-1730)
The details that follow assume that the Oxford and Gloucester details relate to the same person.
Born in Brightwell, Oxfordshire in 1687; died in Gloucester on 28 August 1730 and buried in the cathedral cloisters.
A chorister of Magdalen College, Oxford (1694-1705). Studied under Thomas Hecht and **Jeremiah Clarke.**
Appointed lay clerk of Magdalen College (1705) but dismissed in the same year. Served unofficially as deputy organist of Gloucester Cathedral until the organistship, promised to him when it next became available, fell vacant by the death of **Stephen Jeffries** and was duly awarded to him.
Organist of Gloucester Cathedral (1713-1730) his pupils including the elder **William Hayes.**
A singer and teacher of singing.
It was once said that he was one of the possible inventors of the double chant, following the chance juxtaposition of two single chants played by one of his pupils. However, rival claims have been advanced on behalf of **Luke Flintoft**, **John Robinson** and **William Morley.**
His Single Chant in D was included in *Cathedral Psalter Chants* (1875). Some of his anthems were published after his death by his widow under the title *Harmonia Sacra Gloucestriensis* (1730). Among those he wrote were a Jubilate and Te Deum and the anthems 'Save me' and 'Rejoice in the Lord, O ye righteous'.
With Henry Hall the younger he composed a Morning Service that was subsequently known as *'Hall and Hine in E Minor'.*

HINGSTON, Evelyn Mary (1876-1941)
Born in Totnes, Devon in 1876; died in Totnes on 7 July 1941. Composer of hymn tunes.

HINGSTON (Hinckson, Hingeston, Hinkstone), John (?-1683)
Believed to have been born in York in the early part of the 17th century; died in 1683 and buried on 17 December.
A chorister of York Minster in July 1618. Said to have been a pupil of **Orlando Gibbons.**
Musician to Charles I. State organist and private musician to Oliver Cromwell at Hampton Court (1654-1658), to where the organ of Magdalen College, Oxford had been removed. Taught music to Cromwell's daughters. It is likely that he ran a music society around this time.
Following the Restoration, in June 1660 he was appointed as a court viol player. A gentleman of the Chapel Royal (1661-1666). A deputy marshall of the City of London (from 1663).
Composed fantasies and dances for viols, plus organ music, and the anthems 'Blessed be the Lord my Strength' and 'Withdraw not Thy mercy'.

HINTON, Dr. John William (1849-?)
Born in Edmonton, Middlesex on 26 April 1849.
Studied at the Paris Conservatory. Graduated B.Mus. (1871), B.A. (1872), D.Mus. (1874) and M.A. (1876) at Trinity College, Dublin.
Organist of St. Mary's Church, Charing Cross Road, London (from 1876); St. Stephen's Church (1877-1885), and Holy Trinity Church (1885-1890), Guernsey; St. Michael's, Woolwich Dockyard, London (1891-1909) and the Church of the Ascension, Blackheath, London (1909-1912).
Secretary (1876-1878) and a professor of organ and singing at Trinity College of Music, London.

Wrote on topics connected with organ and on the harmonisation of Gregorian tones.

Composed church music including anthems, an oratorio *Pharaoh*, an opera *Mazeppa*, and organ music.

HINTON, Joseph Harold (1862-?)

Born in Claydon, Buckinghamshire on 1 January 1862. Studied under **Frederick Bridge**. Organist of Hyndland Church, Hillhead, Glasgow (from 1885). Composed a Requiem *Man Goeth Forth* for Voices and Orchestra, the anthem 'Out of the Deep have I called unto Thee, O Lord' (1887) and a cantata.

HIRD, Frederick William (1826-1887)

Born in Leeds in 1826; died in Leeds on 9 November 1887. Organist of All Souls' Church, Leeds. A pianist, musician and teacher. Gave chamber concerts in 1851 and 1852 with the Leeds violinist George Haddock. Composed anthems including 'O, ye priests of the Lord' and 'O God, our Defender' (1887), introits, Kyries, hymn tunes, chants, and music for piano and for organ.

HIRST, Dr. Alfred Livingstone (1874-?)

Born in Batley, Yorkshire in 1874. Trained in music at the Chapel Royal, St. James's Palace. Graduated D.Mus. at the University of Durham (1897). Organist of Gomersal (from 1891) and assistant organist of the Chapels Royal (from 1893). Organist and director of the choir of St. Stephen's Church, East Twickenham, Middlesex (1894-1917) and All Saints', Fulham, London (from 1917). Author of a manual on counterpoint, and magazine articles. Composed church music including anthems, songs and organ music.

HOARE, Revd. Brian Richard (b.1935)

Born in Upminster, Essex on 9 December 1935. Attended Southwell Minster School, Nottinghamshire; Westminster College, London and Richmond College. Ordained as a Minister of the Methodist Church. Allocated to the Hill Mission circuit (1974-1977). New Testament tutor at Cliff College, Derbyshire (1977-1986). A member of the committee for the hymnal *Hymns and Psalms* (1983), which contained his four tunes 'Cliff Lane,' 'Ridgeway' (1978), 'Curbar Edge' and 'Chatsworth'.

HODDINOTT, Dr. Alun (b.1929)

Born in Bargoed, Glamorgan on 11 August 1929.
Educated at Gowerton Grammar School. Learned to play violin. Studied under Arthur Benjamin in London. Graduated B.Mus. (1949) and D.Mus. (1960) at University College, Cardiff.
Appointed C.B.E.
A tutor at Cardiff College of Music and Drama (1951-1959). Joined the staff of his former college as a lecturer, progressing to reader (1965) and in succession to Joseph Morgan, professor of music (1967).
Organised the annual Cardiff Music Festival.
Composed six symphonies between 1955 and 1977. In all he has written five operas including *The Race of Adam* and 10 concertos for instruments including piano, organ, viola, clarinet and harp. His church music includes a setting of the Te Deum (1981), the anthems 'Great art Thou, O God' (1961) and 'Every man's work shall be made manifest' (1964), and the carol 'What tidings?' (1964).

HODGES, Dr. Edward (1796-1867)

Born in Bristol, Gloucestershire on 20 July 1796; died in Clifton, Bristol on 1 September 1867. Father of **Johann Sebastian Hodges**. Self-taught in music. Graduated Mus.D. at the University of Cambridge (1825).

The expenses that he incurred in obtaining his doctorate were substantial and by no means untypical. The total was £208 13s 8d (£208.68) of which the performance of the work itself cost £83 6s (£83.30)

Had a mechanical aptitude and from the age of 15 his inventions, which improved the design of organ bellows, helped to advance organ technology.

Organist of Clifton Church and of the Churches of St. James (1819-1838) and St. Nicholas (1821-1838), Bristol.

In 1838 he emigrated to Canada, taking up an organistship in Toronto. The following year he moved to New York, where he was director of music of Trinity Parish. Retired in 1859 and returned to England in 1863.

Author of *An Essay on the Cultivation of Church Music* (1841) and other works on musical topics.

Composed Services and anthems while at Bristol and during his time in New York. These include Services in C, in E and in F and the anthem 'I was glad'. His hymn tune 'Gloucester' is used in the Standard Edition (1916) of *Hymns Ancient and Modern* with the hymn 'Look down upon us, God of Grace' by Arthur Mason.

HODGES, Dr. Johann Sebastian Bach (1830-1915)

Born in Bristol, Gloucestershire in 1830; died in Baltimore, U.S.A. on 1 May 1915. A son of **Edward Hodges**. Held the D.D. Rector of the Church of St. Paul, Baltimore (1870-1905). Published a collection of sermons. Composed 12 Services and anthems including 'Grant, we beseech Thee' (1910), O Pray for the peace of Jerusalem' (1910); Kyries and chants.

HODSON, Revd. Henry Edward (1842-1917)

Born in Lichfield, Staffordshire in 1842; died in Churchdown, Gloucestershire on 18 February 1917.

Educated at Worcester College, Oxford, graduating B.A. (1866) and M.A. (1870).

Ordained deacon in 1867, priest in 1868, and held appointments at St. Andrew's Church, Chardstock (1867-1869); Landinabo, Herefordshire (1869-1870); Denstone, Staffordshire (1870-1876); Stoke-on-Terne (1876-1882); Eastnor, Herefordshire (1882-1883); Lyneal with Colemer, Shropshire (1883-1889) and The Lea, Gloucestershire (1892-1899).

Composed Services. His hymn tune 'Urbs caelestis' was used in the Standard Edition (1916) of *Hymns Ancient and Modern* with the hymn 'Blessed city, heavenly Salem'. The tune was written one evening beside the River Dove in the Peak District of Derbyshire. Also composed a dramatic cantata *The golden legend* (1865).

HOECK, William Thomson (1859-?)

Born in Paisley on 14 June 1859. Taught music by his father, Louis, a teacher of music in Paisley. Also studied with **Albert Peace**. Organist and choirmaster of Renfrew Parish Church, Glasgow (from 1874) and Queen's Park United Presbyterian Church, Glasgow (from 1880). A local music society conductor. Composed a setting of the Te Deum, hymn tunes and songs.

HOGAN, Revd. Frederick William (1845-1921)
Born in Richhill, County Armagh, Northern Ireland on 23 August 1845; died in Bournemouth, Dorset on 1 December 1921.
A pupil of **Robert Turle** (1804-1877) and **J.C. Marks** at the Cathedrals of Armagh and Cork.
Educated at Trinity College, Dublin where he graduated B.A. (1867) and M.A. (1881). Ordained deacon in 1869, priest in 1870.
Choirmaster of the Llandaff Diocesan Choral Union (from 1866).
Organist of St. Columba's College, Rathfarnham, County Dublin (1866-1868).
Held the County Derry curacies of Tamlaght Finlagan (1869-1870) and Killowen (1870-1873).
Chaplain of Boyd Church, Ballycastle (1873) and to the Earl of Erne.
Minister of Holy Trinity, Kinawley, County Fermanagh (1873-1882). Vicar of All Saints', Eglantine, County Down (1883-1915).
His hymn tune 'St. Patrick' was used in the Standard Edition (1916) of *Hymns Ancient and Modern* with the hymn 'How blest the Maiden who endued'.

HOGGETT, Thomas James (1864-?)
Born in Darlington, County Durham in 1864. Trained in music at Durham Cathedral. Graduated B.Mus. at the University of Durham (1892).
Organist and choirmaster of St. Ninian's Church, Whitby, Yorkshire (1886-1896) and of All Souls' Church, Leeds (1896-1901). For a period around the year 1937 he was organist of Northam Parish Church, Devon.
Conductor of local choral and orchestral societies.
Director of music at the Marquis of Normanby's School, Mulgrave Castle (1892-1904). Taught at Harrogate High School for Girls (1896-1906), Chapel Allerton and Ilkley Girls' High Schools and St. Mary's Catholic College.
Lectured in music and declamation at the University of Leeds and taught harmony, composition and the art of teaching at the Leeds City School of Music. Lectured on the theory of music and singing at the West Riding Training College for Women, Bingley.
Composed a setting of Psalm 100 'O Be Joyful' for Solo Voices, Chorus and Orchestra, and introits for organ.

HOLDEN, George (1800-1856)
Born in 1800; died in Liverpool on 5 December 1856. Organist of St. George's Church, Liverpool. Taught music and was conductor of the Apollo Glee Club, Liverpool. Composed church music, including anthems, and songs. Arranged the anthem 'Grant, O Lord' from Mozart.

HOLDER, Joseph William (1764-1832)
Born in Clerkenwell, London in 1764; died in 1832. He claimed to be descended through his father from Cardinal Wolsey. A chorister of the Chapel Royal under **James Nares**. Graduated B.Mus. at the University of Oxford (1792). Assistant to Charles Reinhold, organist of the church of St. George the Martyr, Queen Street, London. Organist of St. Mary's Church, Bungay before he moved to or near Chelmsford, Essex. Composed a Mass, anthems including 'Great is the Lord' and 'Out of the deep', glees, canons and songs.

HOLDER, Revd. Dr. William (1616-1697)
Born in Southwell, Nottinghamshire in 1616; died in Hertford on 24 January 1697. Buried in the crypt of St. Paul's Cathedral.

Attended Pembroke College, Cambridge (from 1633), graduating B.A. (1636) and M.A. (1640) at Cambridge, and M.A. (1643) and D.D. (1660) at Oxford. Ordained deacon in Lincoln Cathedral (1640).
Married Susanna, the sister of Christopher Wren.
Moved to Oxford during the Civil War. In 1642 he became rector of Blechindon, Oxfordshire. Although appointed canon of Ely Cathedral during this period, he did not take up the position until the Restoration. In January 1662 he became rector of Northwold, Norfolk and of Tidd St. Giles, Isle of Ely.
A prebendary, and shortly afterwards, a canon (from 1672) of St. Paul's Cathedral. Sub dean of the Chapel Royal (1674-1689) but lost this position before the end of 1689, possibly around December 1687. In May 1687 he was appointed rector of Therfield, Hertfordshire.
His book *Treatise on the Natural Grounds and Principles of Harmony* (1694) gives a valuable insight into the musical philosophy of the period.
Composed 10 anthems including settings of Psalms 64 'Arise, O Lord' and 130 'Out of the Deep', and an Evening Service in C.

HOLDROYD, Israel (18th century)
A musician and composer of the first half of the 18th century.
Published a collection *Chants and Anthems* (1733) under the pseudonym Philo-Musicae. Also compiled *The Spiritual Man's Companion* (1753), a history of church music. Composed anthems and chants.

HOLDSTOCK, Janice Mary (b.1941)
Born in Ipswich, Suffolk, in 1941. Educated at Lady Margaret Hall, Oxford, where she graduated M.A.
Senior lecturer in music at Leeds Metropolitan University, having taught in the Bahamas. Widely acknowledged as a leading figure in musical education, specialising as an author for children of junior school age, and known for her plays with music in association with Pat Belford *The Miracle Squad* and *The People's King*. Her carol 'Tell out the news' (a *quodlibet*) was composed for the Lord Mayor's Carol Concert for children with special educational needs, held annually at her instigation in association with the Yorkshire and Humberside Association for Music in Special Education, at Leeds Town Hall.

HOLLINS, Dr. Alfred (1865-1942)
Born in Hull, Yorkshire on 11 September 1865; died in Edinburgh on 17 May 1942. Totally blind from birth.
Studied at the Yorkshire School for the Blind and at the Royal Normal College for the Blind, Norwood, London. Studied organ under **E.J. Hopkins**, piano under Frits Hartvigson and Hans von Bülow in Berlin and Frankfort, and with Max Schwartz.
In 1922 he was awarded an honorary doctorate in music at the University of Edinburgh.
He played to Charles-Marie Widor with a view to becoming his pupil but Widor felt that he was not suitably equipped. Hollins took lessons instead with Félix Guilmant.
Toured as a solo piano and organ recitalist (from 1882), and gave performances in the U.S.A. in 1886 and 1888. Played privately on at least one occasion for Queen Victoria at Windsor Castle. Further recital tours were made to Australia (1904), South Africa (1907, 1909 and 1916) and the U.S.A. (1925).
Organist of St. John's Church, Redhill, Surrey (1884-1888) and St. Andrew's, Upper Norwood, London (1888-1897). The first

organist of the People's Palace, East London (1888-1889). Organist and choirmaster of the St. George's West Church, Edinburgh (1894-1942), where beside the organ there is a memorial tablet to him, which some visitors feel moved to touch in homage. A professor of piano and organ at the Royal Normal College (1886-1894). Having studied organ construction, he was an expert in the field.

Wrote an autobiography, published after his 70th birthday, *A Blind Organist looks back* (1936).

Composed anthems including 'The earth is the Lord's' and 'O worship the Lord', songs and works for piano and for organ.

HOLLINS, George (1809-1841)
Born in Birmingham on 16 March 1809; died in Birmingham on 16 December 1841. A pupil of Thomas Munden, whom he succeeded as organist of St. Paul's Church, Birmingham. Organist of Birmingham Town Hall (c1837). An organ and piano recitalist and baritone singer. Few of his compositions were published and they include a setting of the Benedicite, hymn tunes, chants and a song 'Sabbath Bell'.

HOLLOWAY, Dr. Arthur Stephen (c1849-1919)
Died on 23 March 1919 at the age of 70. Graduated B.Mus. (1875) and D.Mus. (1894) at Worcester College, Oxford. Musical editor of *Hymns on the Deeper Life* and *The Choir Companion*. Author of a text book on singing. An examiner for the London College of Music. His compositions include a Mass in B-flat, anthems, hymn tunes, a choral cantata for Advent and Christmas *The Promised King*, songs and music for piano and for organ.

HOLLOWAY, Dr. Henry (1871-?)
Born in Worcester in 1871.
Received his early music training at Worcester Cathedral. Graduated B.Mus. (1895) and D.Mus. (1902) at the University of Oxford.
Deputy organist of Worcester Cathedral (1889-1893). Organist of All Saints' Church, Worcester (1889-1893); organist and choirmaster of St. Stephen's Church, Bournemouth, Dorset (1893-1930). Precentor, organist and choirmaster of the Priory Church, Christchurch, Hampshire (from 1934). Choirmaster of Longfleet Parish Church, Poole, Dorset (1901-1902).
Chorus master of the Bournemouth Municipal Choir.
Composed Services, anthems, a ballad 'The Challenge' for Chorus and Orchestra, Symphony no. 1 in E Minor, Symphony no. 2 in D Minor, and music for piano and for organ.

HOLMAN, Dr. Derek (b.1931)
Born in Redruth, Cornwall in 1931.
Attended Truro School, Cornwall and the Royal Academy of Music. Graduated D.Mus. at the University of London.
An organist and tutor. Music master of the choir school of Westminster Abbey (1954-1955); organist and choirmaster of St. Stephen's Church, Westminster (1954-1955); a tutor (1956-1965), sub warden (1957-1964) and warden (1964-1965) at the Royal School of Church Music; assistant sub organist of St. Paul's Cathedral (1956-1958) and organist of Croydon Parish Church, Surrey (1958-1965). A choral society conductor.
Organist of Grace-Church-on-the-hill, Toronto, Canada (from 1965), and assistant professor of the faculty of music of the University of Toronto (from 1967). Choirmaster of the Bishop Strachan School, Toronto (1965-1970).

Has composed anthems including 'O God, my heart is ready' (1960) and, for Easter-tide 'Away with gloom' (1962) and songs.

HOLMES, George (c1680-1720)
Born around 1680; died in Lincoln in 1720. He may have been the son of **Thomas Holmes** and the grandson of **John Holmes**.
He may also be the Holmes who was organist to Nathaniel, Lord Crewe, Bishop of Durham, around the year 1698.
Organist of Lincoln Cathedral on the death of **Thomas Allinson** (1705-1720). A junior vicar of Lincoln Cathedral (from 1707). A master of the Company of Bellringers.
His compositions include the anthems 'Arise, Shine' (1707) in celebration of the Act of Union with Scotland, and 'I will love Thee, O Lord'. Composed an Ode for St. Cecilia's Day, two Magnificats for Five Voices and a setting of the Burial Sentences. Also composed songs and catches.

HOLMES, Revd. George Sydenham (1884-?)
Born near Gosport, Hampshire in 1884.
Organ scholar of Brasenose College, Oxford (1903-1907), where he graduated B.A. (1906) and B.Mus. (1907).
At Oxford he was music critic of the magazine *Isis*, and subsequently contributed articles to the main musical journals.
Assistant priest of the Church of St. John the Evangelist, Upper Norwood, London (1909-1915). Precentor of the Church of St. Andrew, Wells Street, London (1915-1916).
After four years as Diocesan missioner of Gloucester (1916-1920) he returned to St. John's, Upper Norwood, as organist and choirmaster.
Composed anthems including 'O Zion, that bringest good tidings' (1914) and other items of church music and a string quartet.

HOLMES, Henry (1839-1905)
Born in London on 7 November 1839; died in San Francisco, U.S.A. on 9 December 1905.
Studied music with his father. A chorister at the London Oratory.
He and his brother made their first appearance jointly as musicians at the Haymarket Theatre, London (July 1847) while still very young. They toured Europe giving recitals in 1855 and 1856, taking part in the Gewandhaus Concerts in Leipzig (1856). They were introduced to the composer Louis Spohr.
Gave concerts of chamber music in London (from 1868), which were very popular. In 1883 he was appointed a professor of violin at the Royal College of Music. 10 years later he was dismissed following allegations of advances towards female students. Moved to San Francisco, where he continued to teach violin.
Composed two sacred cantatas *Praise ye the Lord* and *Christmas Day*, the latter receiving its first performance at the Three Choirs' Festival, Gloucester (1880). Also composed a symphony, a violin concerto and other chamber works.

HOLMES, Henry James Ernest (1852-1938)
Born in Burnley, Lancashire in 1852; died in Burnley on 10 October 1938. Continued the family tradition of law. Attended Clitheroe Grammar School. Admitted solicitor of the High Court of Chancery (1875). Practised in the Burnley area for more than 60 years. Composed over 250 hymn tunes. His 'Pater omnium' was first published in *Burnley Hymn Book* (1875) with the hymn 'Onward through life Thy children stray' by William Whiting, and is used today in *Hymns and Psalms* (1983).

HOLMES, John (?-1629)
Died in Salisbury, Wiltshire on 30 January 1629. Father of **Thomas Holmes**, and possibly of **George Holmes**. Organist of Winchester Cathedral (1599-1621). A lay vicar of Salisbury Cathedral (from 1621); succeeded **John Bartlett** as master of the choristers (from 1629) and was a teacher of the choristers (from c1621), but was never organist of Salisbury. Composed a set of Preces and Responses, anthems including 'All laud and praise' and 'O, heavenly Father', a Christmas Evensong and a Magnificat. Contributed one of his madrigals to *The Triumphes of Oriana*.

HOLMES, Thomas (?1606-1638)
Thomas Holmes was baptised on 11 April 1606; died in Salisbury on 25 March 1638. A son of **John Holmes**. Organist of Winchester Cathedral (1631-1638), and a gentleman of the Chapel Royal (from 1633). Composed five anthems including 'I will magnify Thee' and 'The Lord hear thee'.

HOLMES, Thomas Barton (1865-1960)
Born in Hull, Yorkshire on 12 November 1865; died in Guildford, Surrey on 9 April 1960. Composer of hymn tunes.

HOLMES, William (1764-1829)
Leader of the Choir of Teignmouth Parish Church, Devon. Composed the anthem 'O Lord, Thou hast searched'.

HOLST, Gustav Theodore (1874-1934)
Born in Cheltenham, Gloucestershire on 21 September 1874; died in London on 25 May 1934. His ashes were interred in Chichester Cathedral.
Descended from a Baltic family. Attended Cheltenham Grammar School. From the age of 17 he led village choirs. In his late teens he was organist of Wyck Church, Gloucestershire.
After two months studying counterpoint in Oxford, he entered the Royal College of Music (1893-1898) where he learned composition with **C.V. Stanford** and took as his second subject the trombone. Studied organ with **W.S. Hoyte**.
A fellow student, **Ralph Vaughan Williams**, became a life-long friend and cited Holst as 'the greatest influence on my music'.
Holst had begun to compose, it was said, as soon as he was able to hold a pen. He struggled to make his mark as a composer in the early part of his career. Sustained himself during the summer holidays by playing the trombone on seaside piers.
Around the year 1907 he took several lessons with Maurice Ravel in Paris.
It was as a musician and then teacher that he established himself initially. Pianist and répétiteur with the Carl Rosa Opera Company (from 1898). Played the trombone in theatre orchestras and, for five years, with the Scottish Orchestra. In 1903 he gave up professional playing although he continued to be a church organist.
Following two years teaching at the James Allen Girls' School, Dulwich (1903-1905), he became director of music at St. Paul's Girls' School, Hammersmith, London (1905-1934) and of Morley College, London (1907-1924).
During World War I, Gustav Holst was determined to see active service. He was eventually given a job, in 1918, with the Educational Department of the Young Men's Christian Association, organising music among the troops in Turkey waiting to be demobilised, arriving in Salonika in October 1918.

Returned to England in June 1919. Took on further teaching appointments at the R.C.M. and, until 1923, at University College, Reading, Berkshire.
His war duties had caused him to miss the first public performance, under the conductor Adrian Boult, of his *Planets Suite* (February 1919). He had commenced this work prior to 1914.
In 1923 and 1932 he visited the U.S.A. as a lecturer and conductor.
His unorthodox teaching methods were based on the principle of learning by doing. He disliked textbooks and examinations. Following health problems, he gave up all teaching appointments in 1925 except for a reduced workload at St. Paul's Girls' School, thus allowing himself more time for composition.
Many of his works were written at his cottage in the Essex village of Thaxted, where he organised informal amateur music festivals each Whitsun (from 1916). Although demanding high standards of professional musicians, he was willing to work with and encourage amateurs provided that they made sufficient effort.
He extracted and arranged part of the music from 'Jupiter' for use as a hymn tune, which he named 'Thaxted'. It has been associated ever since with the hymn 'I vow to thee, my country' by Cecil Spring-Rice, whose daughter had attended St. Paul's Girls' School and had recently died. 'Cranham' is often used with Christina Rossetti's hymn 'In the bleak mid winter'. 'Essex' has been used with Harriet Auber's hymn 'Our blest Redeemer, ere He breathed'. *Four Old English Carols* (1907) were derived from medieval texts. Other sacred music includes the cantata *The hymn of Jesus* and *Two Psalms for Choir and Strings*. One of his more widely-known anthems is 'Turn back, O man', a setting of words by Clifford Bax to a melody from the *Genevan Psalter*, a work widely used in November at Remembrance-tide. Other works include *Choral Fantasia* (1930) to words by Robert Bridges and *Egdon Heath* (1927), an orchestral work inspired by the writing of the same name by Thomas Hardy. There were also operas, other orchestral and chamber works, and items designed to be played and sung by his pupils.

HONE, Timothy Graham (b.1957)
Born in Hinckley, Leicestershire on 27 August 1957. Studied at the John Cleveland College, Hinckley, and as organ scholar, Peterhouse, Cambridge (1976-1980) where he read music and graduated B.A. (1979), Mus.B. (1980) and M.A. (1982). Sub organist of Leeds Parish Church (1980-1981) and of Coventry Cathedral (1982-1987). Organist of Newcastle Cathedral (from 1987). Composer of the Advent carol 'Gabriel's message does away'.

HOOK, Revd. Walter (19th century)
A son of Walter Hook, dean of Chichester. Succentor of Chichester Cathedral, and rector of Lavington. Composed the anthems 'Blessed is the man that trusteth' (1868) and 'Mine eyes are ever looking' (1868).

HOOPER, Dr. Charles (1896-1963)
Born in Plymouth, Devon on 28 December 1896; died in Baildon, near Shipley, Yorkshire in 1963. Attended Plymouth Grammar School and took music lessons with **Harry Moreton**, organist of Plymouth Parish Church; **C.H. Kitson** and D.F. Tovey. Graduated M.A. (Leeds, 1942), B.Mus. (Dublin, 1935) and D.Mus. (Manchester, 1940). A teacher. Music adviser to Bradford Education Committee (from 1936) and music adviser and inspector

of schools to Leeds Education Committee (1947-1961). Organist of Bradford Cathedral (1938-1963). Composer of many anthems.

HOOPER, Edmund (c1553-1621)

Born in North Halberton near Tiverton, Devon around 1553; died in London on 14 July 1621 and buried in the cloisters of Westminster Abbey.

Probably a chorister of Exeter Cathedral. It follows that he must have moved to London during his childhood since he is said to have attended school in Greenwich.

In 1582 he was a member of the choir of Westminster Abbey and in December 1588 he became master of the choristers. It appears that he was also the first regular organist (from 1606).

.A gentleman of the Chapel Royal, succeeding William Randoll in March 1604. He shared the responsibility of playing organ with two others initially but by 1615 he and **Orlando Gibbons**, whom he is said to have influenced musically, were in effect joint organists, with Hooper regarded as the more senior.

Retained his positions at the Chapel Royal and Westminster Abbey until his death.

His full and verse anthems number some 20, including 'Behold, it is Christ'. Some anthems use viol rather than organ to accompany the voices. Psalms, Preces and Responses, and at least two Services were composed. He wrote at least one item for keyboard, and two sacred songs.

HOOPER, Revd. W. Nixon (19th century)

Precentor of Winchester Cathedral in 1848. Composer of the anthem 'Teach me, O Lord' (1849).

HOPE, John Ernest (19th/20th century)

Trained at Guildhall School of Music. Graduated B.Mus. at the University of Oxford (1909). Organist of St. Paul's Church, Clerkenwell, London (from 1911); organist and choirmaster of St. Botolph's Church, Aldersgate, London (from 1912). Lived in the London suburb of Holloway. Composed a hymn tune, and songs.

HOPKINS, Antony J. (b.1921)

Born in London on 21 March 1921.

Attended Berkhamstead School, Hertfordshire. Studied piano with Cyril Smith and composition with Gordon Jacob at the Royal College of Music (1939-1942), where he won the Chappell Gold Medal for piano playing.

Appointed C.B.E. in 1976.

A teacher at Morley College, South London. A piano recitalist, composer, conductor, writer and broadcaster, being particularly associated with the radio programme 'Talking about Music', on which he appeared for more than 20 years.

Formerly Gresham professor of music at the City University, London.

Composed a Magnificat and Nunc Dimittis for Female Voices and Organ (1961), a setting of Psalm 42 'Like as the hart' (1954), the carol 'Carillon' (1948), piano sonatas, chamber music, songs, a one-act opera *Lady Rohesia* (1948), and music for stage and radio.

HOPKINS, Dr. Douglas Edward (1902-1993)

Born in Dulwich, London on 23 December 1902; died in 1993.

A chorister of St. Paul's Cathedral, later studying at Dulwich College, the Guildhall School of Music, London and the Royal Academy of Music. Graduated B.Mus. (1932) and D.Mus. (1936) at the University of London

Organist of Christ Church, Greyfriars, London (1921-1927) and sub organist of St. Paul's Cathedral (1927-1946) to **Stanley Marchant** and **John Dykes Bower**. Deputised for the latter during World War II while he served with the Royal Air Force.

Taught at the R.A.M. (from 1935), being appointed a professor two years later (1937) and remaining there for more than 40 years (until 1978). A special commissioner of the Royal School of Church Music.

Master of the music of Peterborough Cathedral (1946-1952) and organist of Canterbury Cathedral (1952-1955).

Left Canterbury in order to concentrate on his teaching work at the R.A.M. Held appointments as director of music of St. Felix School, Southwold (1956-1965); St. Marylebone Parish Church, London (1965-1971) and the Chapel at the Royal Military Academy, Sandhurst (1971-1976).

Composed the hymn tune 'Buffham', used in *Hymns Ancient and Modern* with 'Let us thank the Christ' by John Crum.

HOPKINS, Dr. Edward John (1818-1901)

Born in Westminster, London on 30 June 1818; died in St. Pancras, London on 4 February 1901.

The older brother of **John Hopkins** and the cousin of **John Larkin Hopkins**.

A chorister in the Chapel Royal (1826-1833) under **William Hawes**. On leaving he became a pupil of **Thomas Forbes Walmisley**. Awarded the Lambeth D.Mus. (1882). Graduated D.Mus. at Trinity College, Toronto (1886).

Organist of Mitcham Parish Church, London from the age of 16 (1834-1838) but even prior to this, he had played organ at services in Westminster Abbey. At Mitcham there was some hesitation in appointing one so young, even though he was clearly the most proficient candidate. **James Turle**, organist of Westminster Abbey, intervened on Hopkins's behalf, 'Tell them, with my compliments, that if they fear to trust Hopkins to accompany chants and hymns at Mitcham Church, Mr. Turle does not hesitate to trust him to play Services and anthems at Westminster Abbey.'

Two further London Parish Church appointments were St. Peter's, Islington (1838-1841) and St. Luke's, Berwick Street (1841-1843). A professor of organ at the Royal Normal College for the Blind, Norwood, Surrey.

In 1842 the Temple Church in London had been restored and the decision was taken to have the services sung along the lines of cathedral worship. The organist, **George Warne** was not equipped for this change and he was retired on full pay in 1843. He was replaced by Edward Hopkins, who went on to serve for 55 years (1843-1898).

Known for his skill at improvising on organ. On Sunday, 12 March 1898, Edward Hopkins's final day in charge of the Temple Church before handing over to **Henry Walford Davies**, all the Chants, Canticle settings and anthems were his work. Gave organ recitals until his 78th birthday, in 1896.

An authority on the design of organs. Edited collections of madrigals and wrote on the subject of the organ in Grove's *Dictionary of Music and Musicians*.

One of the founders of the College of Organists (1864).

A hymnal editor. Published collections of hymns for the Wesleyan and Congregational Churches, the Free Church of Scotland and the Presbyterian Churches of England and Canada. Collected and published *The Psalter with Chants* and *The Temple Church Hymn Book*.

A prolific writer of hymn tunes, of which he composed more than 150. His work featured in most of the major hymnals of his time, and beyond. One of his enduring tunes is 'Ellers,' used with 'Father, again to Thy dear Name we raise' in *Hymns Ancient and Modern*, the *English Hymnal* and elsewhere. Others of his hymn tunes are 'St. Hugh', 'Shropshire', 'Wildersmouth' and 'St. Brannock'.

Composed Services in A and in F, each containing a set of Responses to the Commandments, and anthems including 'Out of the deep' and 'God is gone up', which won the Gresham prize of 1838 and 1840. *Cathedral Psalter Chants* (1875) contains single and double chants. Also composed for organ.

HOPKINS, Evan Henry (1837-1919)
Born in 1837; died in Surrey on 10 March 1919. Composer of hymn tunes.

HOPKINS, John (1822-1900)
Born in Westminster, London on 30 April 1822; died in Rochester, Kent on 27 August 1900. The younger brother of **E.J. Hopkins** and a cousin of **John Larkin Hopkins**.
A chorister of St. Paul's Cathedral under **Thomas Attwood** (1831-1838).
Succeeded his brother E.J. Hopkins as organist of Mitcham Parish Curch (1838). Held a series of organistship appointments in London at St. Stephen's Islington (from June 1839); St. Benet's, Paul's Wharf (from July 1841) and Holy Trinity, Islington (from May 1843). Organist of St. Mark's Church, Jersey (from February 1845), St. Michael's, Chester Square, London (from 1846) and Epsom Parish Church, Surrey (1854).
In May 1854 he succeeded his cousin John Larkin Hopkins as organist of Rochester Cathedral, where he remained in office until 1900. The selection process was devised by **John Goss** and it was a demanding one. Candidates had to audition and then write a paper containing a chorale melody to harmonise and a subject to be worked into a fugue. The unsuccessful candidates included **W.B. Gilbert, Philip Armes** and **James Coward**. John Hopkins became known at Rochester as a shy and retiring man.
Four of the Rochester pupils of John Hopkins became cathedral organists, namely **Frederick Bridge** (Westminster Abbey) and his brother **J.C. Bridge** (Chester), **E.J. Crow** (Ripon) and **D.J. Wood** (Exeter).
Composed Services, including a Thanksgiving Te Deum in E (1894), anthems of which an example is 'Haste Thee, O Lord, to deliver me', chants, and hymn tunes such as 'Sydney', 'Whitwell' and 'Allington'.

HOPKINS, Dr. John Larkin (1819-1873)
Born in Westminster, London on 25 November 1819; died in Ventnor, Isle of Wight on 25 April 1873. A cousin of the brothers **E.J. Hopkins** and **John Hopkins**.
A chorister at Westminster Abbey and subsequently a pupil of **James Turle**, Abbey organist. Graduated Mus.B. (1842) and Mus.D. (1867) at the University of Cambridge.
Organist of St. Paul's Chapel, Portman Street, London. An assistant organist of Westminster Abbey.
Organist of Rochester Cathedral (1841-1856) from the age of 22 in succession to **Ralph Banks**. Organist of Trinity College, Cambridge and of the University of Cambridge (1856-1873).
The collection *Responses to the Commandments* (c1875) contained two sets in C and a further set in E-flat by John Larkin Hopkins.

Also composed a Double Chant in D-flat; Services, among others, in C-flat and in E-flat; anthems including 'Be merciful' and 'Save me, O God'; carols; songs and glees.

HORAN, George Frederick (1858-1898)
A son of **John Horan**. Organist of the Dublin Churches of SS Thomas (from 1876 and from 1881) and Mary (from 1877), and Rathmines Church, Dublin (1886-1895). Composed the anthems 'A king shall reign and prosper' and 'Surely the Lord is in this place'. His works include songs such as 'A Voice in the Gloaming'.

HORAN, John (1831-1908)
Born in Drogheda, Ireland on 26 February 1831; died in Dublin on 31 January 1908. Father of **George Horan**.
A pupil of his father and a chorister of Christ Church Cathedral, Dublin (from 1841), where at the age of 16, he deputised for the organist, **Robert Prescott Stewart** for one day per week. Apprenticed to the organ building firm of Telford and Telford.
Organist of Booterstown Church; St. John's Church, Sandymount; St. Andrew's Church, Dublin and Adare Parish Church, Tuam, County Derry. Sang bass in the choir of St. Mary's Cathedral, Limerick.
Organist of the Cathedrals of Tuam (1857-1862) and Derry (1862-1873). Assistant organist (from 1873) under Robert Prescott Stewart at Christ Church Cathedral, Dublin. Succeeded Stewart as organist and choirmaster (1894-1906) of Christ Church Cathedral. From 1904 to 1906 he held the position jointly with James Ferrier Fitzgerald.
Composed Services, anthems and organ music.

HORDER, Mervyn (b.1910)
Born in London in 1910.
Son of Lord Horder, physician to five successive English monarchs.
Educated at Winchester College, Hampshire; Trinity College, Cambridge and Guildhall School of Music. Among his music teachers were **George Dyson, Hubert Middleton** and **Arthur Pritchard**. Graduated M.A. at the University of Cambridge
Has sung in church choirs continuously for 70 years.
Editor of *The Orange Carol Book* (1972) and *The Easter Carol Book* (1982). Own works include the carols 'And is it true?' and 'Carol for St. Martin' (1993), anthems, hymns and sacred songs. Has also composed voice and piano song cycles to words by William Shakespeare, John Betjeman, Dorothy Parker and others.

HORNABROOK, Mary Jane (1849-1930)
Born in Darlington, County Durham in 1849; died in Southport, Lancashire on 23 September 1930. Composer of hymn tunes.

HORNCASTLE, Frederick William (c1790-1850)
Born in London around 1790; died in 1850. A chorister of the Chapel Royal. Held the London organistships of Stamford Hill Chapel and Berkeley Chapel. Organist of Armagh Cathedral (1816-1823) until dismissed. A gentleman of the Chapel Royal from 1826. Composed a Mass, a glee, songs and items for piano.

HORNER, Dr. Egbert Foster (1864-1928)
Born in Greenwich, London on 11 February 1864; died in London on 10 October 1928.

A pupil of **Frederick Bridge**, graduating B.Mus. (1895) and D.Mus. (1900) at the University of Durham.

Organist of the Churches of St. Alphege, Southwark (1884-1886); St. Barnabas, Tunbridge Wells (1886-1890) and St. John, Westminster (1890-1919). Choirmaster of the Churches of St. Matthias, Upper Tulse Hill (1894-1910) and Holy Trinity Church, Bessborough Gardens (from 1910). A teacher of counterpoint at Trinity College of Music, London.

Examiner for several universities. Governor of the Royal Society of Musicians (from 1907) and honorary secretary of the Union of Graduates in Music. A recognised teacher in music, a member of the board of studies in music and a member of the faculty of music, of which he became dean, of the University of London.

Contributed seven tunes to *Methodist Hymn Book* (1904) and his 'Aldersgate Street' is used today in *Hymns and Psalms* (1983). Composed a prize canon, and an Andante in A for Organ.

HOROVITZ, Joseph (b.1926)
Born in Vienna, Austria on 26 May 1926.

Came to England in 1938. Attended the City of Oxford High School and studied music at New College, Oxford where graduated B.Mus. and M.A., and at the Royal College of Music. Studied with Nadia Boulanger in Paris.

Director of music of the Old Vic, Bristol (1950-1951); conductor of the Festival Gardens Orchestra and Open-Air Ballet (1951) and co-conductor of Ballets-Russes (1952). Associate director of the Intimate Opera Company (1952-1963).

Assistant conductor and continuo of Glyndebourne Opera (1956). In 1961 he was appointed a professor of composition at the R.C.M. His 'Sing unto the Lord a new song' was commissioned for the 317th Festival of the Sons of the Clergy in St. Paul's Cathedral at the instigation of Dean Sullivan, as a link betwen the Jewish and Christian faiths. Has composed an oratorio *Samson*, operas including *Gentleman's Island* (1959), and a Trumpet Concerto (1965). Also, many scores for theatre, for radio plays and for television programmes, perhaps the most famous of which is 'Rumpole of the Bailey'.

HORSLEY (Horsleye),? (17th century)
Nothing is known about the church musician and minor composer Horsley, who lived during the 17th century. A manuscript version of the anthem 'O Lord, on whome I doe depend' is held at Durham Cathedral.

HORSLEY, Charles Edward (1822-1876)
Born in London on 16 December 1822; died in New York City, U.S.A. on 2 May 1876. A son of **William Horsley**. Studied music under his father, with Ignaz Moscheles, and at Leipzig under Mendelssohn and Moritz Hauptmann. Organist of St. John's Church, Notting Hill, London. Emigrated to Australia in 1868 and then to the U.S.A. Author of a textbook on harmony. Composed anthems including 'I was glad', composed for the consecration of Fairfield Church, Liverpool and 'Thou art my Portion', oratorios *David* and *Joseph*, songs, part songs and chamber music.

HORSLEY, William (1774-1858)
Born in London on 15 November 1774; died in Kensington, London on 12 June 1858. Son-in-law of the church musician and composer **John Wall Callcott**, and father of **Charles Horsley** and the painter, J.C. Horsley, R.A.

From the age of 16, William Horsley was articled for five years to Theodore Smith, the pianist and composer. It seems that Smith treated him badly and gave him little useful instruction. He was then a pupil of John Wall Callcott, Pring, and of **William Gardiner**.

Graduated B.Mus (1800) at the University of Oxford having supplicated with his anthem 'When Israel came out of Egypt'.

A bass singer in the theatre. Held a number of organistships in London. Organist of the Ely Chapel, Holborn (1794-1798); assistant to John Wall Callcott at the Female Orphan Asylum (1798-1802), succeeding him as organist there (1802-1854). Organist of the Belgrave Chapel, Halkin Street (1812-1837) and the Charter House (1838-1858). One of the founders of the Philharmonic Society (1813).

Became friendly with several famous musicians during their visits to London, among them Mendelssohn, Chopin and Joachim. His daughter, Mary, married the engineer I.K. Brunel.

Served on the Gresham Committee chaired by **William Crotch**, which awarded a prize annually for church compositions. The winners conformed to a narrow style to which **S.S. Wesley** strongly and publicly objected.

Author of works on the theory of music.

His hymn tune 'Belgrave', which appeared originally in *National Psalmody* with Psalm 16 'Preserve me, O God' was arranged for hymn singing and used in the Revised Edition (1927) of *Church Hymnary* as the setting of the hymn 'When all thy mercies, O my God' by Joseph Addison. However his fame chiefly rests on his tune 'Horsley', long associated with Cecil Frances Alexander's hymn 'There is a green hill far away'. Also composed nine anthems including 'Come, Holy Spirit' and 'When Israel came out of Egypt', 24 Psalm tunes, and two motets. Composed glees, canons, songs and ballads.

HORWOOD, William (?-1484)
A member of the Fraternity of St. Nicholas, a guild of parish clerks based in London, from not later than 1459. Master of the Fraternity in 1474. By 1476, William Horwood was a vicar choral of Lincoln Cathedral, where he was later master of the choristers. His compositions include a Salve Regina, a Kyrie 'O Rex clemens' and a Magnificat for five voices.

HOTHBY (**Octobi, Otteby, Ottobi, Octobri**), John (c1410-1487)
Born, possibly abroad, around the year 1410; died in England in 1487. May have been a graduate of the University of Oxford. Travelled and lived in Italy, becoming a Carmelite monk. Taught music and other subjects while living in the monastery at Lucca (1468-1486). In the latter year he was recalled to England by Henry VII. Author of works on music. Composed for the church and for the secular world. His works include a Kyrie, settings of the Magnificat, and motets including *Ora pro nobis*.

HOUGHTON, William (1844-1871)
Born in Dublin in 1844; died in Dublin in 1871. A chorister and deputy organist of Christ Church Cathedral, Dublin. Organist of St. Ann's Church, Dublin. Composed anthems including 'Lord, we pray Thee', songs and organ music.

HOULDSWORTH, John (18th/19th century)
An organist, violinist and composer who died some time after 1836. Played in the first violins at the Yorkshire Festivals of 1823 and 1825. Composer of hymn tunes and chants.

HOW, Martin John Richard (b.1931)
Born in Liverpool, Lancashire on 3 April 1931.
Won a music scholarship to Repton School, Derbyshire (1945-1949). Organ scholar at Clare College, Cambridge (1949-1952) where he read music and theology and graduated M.A. Also attended Trinity College of Music, London.
Served in the army. Choirmaster and commissioner and special adviser of the Royal School of Church Music at its headquarters at Croydon, (and subsequently, Dorking) Surrey (from 1965). Has been organist of Grimsby Parish Church, Lincolnshire (1962-1965) and of a number of churches in the area around Croydon, Surrey. Has travelled widely as an accompanist, adjudicator, choral conductor and lecturer.
Has made broadcasts on radio and television, conducting choirs of the Royal School of Church Music in 'Choral Evensong'.
His compositions include the *Sanderstead* Mass, the *St. Nicholas* Mass and the anthems 'Day by day', 'Praise O praise' and 'Bless, O Lord'. A specialist in works for limited choral resources.

HOWARD, Brian Stanley (b.1930)
Born in Hendon, Middlesex in 1930. Composer of hymn tunes.

HOWARD, Cuthbert (1856-1927)
Born in Manchester in 1856; died in Manchester on 26 May 1927. Composer of hymn tunes.

HOWARD, Michael Stockwin (b.1922)
Born in London of a Derbyshire family on 14 September 1922.
Educated privately, at Ellesmere College and at the Royal Academy of Music where he was organ and composition scholar and worked under William Alwyn. Studied privately with G.D. Cunningham, Ralph Downes and Marcel Dupré.
Organist of Tewkesbury Abbey (1943-1944) and Christ Church, Woburn Square, London (1945-1950).
Organist of Ely Cathedral (1953-1958).
Director of music of St. Marylebone Parish Church, London (1971-1979) where he succeeded **Douglas Hopkins**. Organist to the Franciscans of Rye, Sussex (1979-1983) and organist and master of the choristers of Farnborough Abbey (1984-1986).
Director of music of St. George's School, Harpenden, Hertfordshire (1959-1961) and assistant in music preparation at the B.B.C. (1968-1978). A celebrated interpreter of the polyphony of the 16th century.
Has also been a freelance organist, harpsichordist and conductor. The author of articles and books on musical topics, on which he has also broadcast.
He has composed church music, including *Prayer Book Canticles* (1946 and 1949), a Mass (1961), anthems and organ music.

HOWARD, Dr. Samuel (1710-1782)
Born in London in 1710; died in London on 13 July 1782.
A chorister and pupil of **William Croft** at the Chapel Royal. Took lessons with J.C. Pepusch. Graduated Mus.D. at the University of Cambridge (1769).
Organist of the London Churches of St. Clement Dane (1769-1782) and St. Bride, Fleet Street (1736-1782).
Composed music for the gardens and for the theatre, cantatas solos and duets. Assisted **William Boyce** with in the compilation of *English Cathedral Music* (1760-1773).

His output of church music consists of hymn tunes and a number of anthems including 'This is the day' for choir and orchestra, and 'Wherewithal shall a young man'.
Church Hymns (1874) uses the hymn tunes 'Stafford' and 'St. Bride'; the Revised Edition (1927) of *Church Hymnary* includes 'Isleworth', 'Lancaster' and 'St. Bride'. 'Dublin' was attributed to him and used twice in *Congregational Praise* (1950).

HOWELL, Clifford Walter (b.1902)
An Antiphon by Clifford Howell was used in the hymnal *With One Voice* (1978) with Psalm 2 'Why do the heathen?'.

HOWELL, Francis (1834-1882)
Born in 1834; died on 28 October 1882. A son of James Howell, a double-bass player. Organist of Penkridge Church, Staffordshire. Composed anthems including 'By the word of the Lord' and 'We have heard with our own ears'. His two oratorios include *The Land of Promise*.

HOWELLS, Dr. Herbert Norman (1892-1983)
Born in Lydney, Gloucestershire on 17 October 1892; died in Putney, London on 23 February 1983. One of a family of eight children of a builder and decorator. His daughter is the actress Ursula Howells.
Following piano lessons from a sister, Herbert Howells was formally articled to **A.H. Brewer** of Gloucester Cathedral (1910-1912) at the same time as the poet and composer Ivor Gurney, and Ivor Novello.
Studied composition under **C.V. Stanford**, whose favourite pupil he was said to be, and counterpoint with **Charles Wood**, by means of an open scholarship at the Royal College of Music (from 1912). His other tutors at the College included **Hubert Parry** and **Walford Davies**. Held doctorates in music at the Universities of Oxford and Cambridge.
Appointed C.B.E. in 1953 and C.H. in 1972.
He has been variously described as a small, dapper and sociable figure, urbane, debonair and very English and on the other hand, too clever, conservative and elaborate, with a tendency to illustrate points of music with examples drawn excessively from his own work.
Appointed sub organist of Salisbury Cathedral (1917) to **W.G. Alcock** but within weeks he became seriously ill and had to relinquish the position.
Having recovered from his illness, he taught at the R.C.M. for over 50 years (1920-1972), travelling by bus from his home in Barnes even in old age. His many pupils included the composer **Thomas Armstrong** and the pianist Hilary Macnamara. Succeeded **Gustav Holst** as director of music of St. Paul's Girls' School, London (1934-1960). King Edward VII professor of music at the University of London (1955-1965).
Another sphere in which he did much to develop individuals' musicianship was at music festivals, in which he was an adjudicator throughout the U.K. His colleagues included **David Willcocks** and Keith Faulkner. Herbert Howells summed up in a way that was both concise and encouraging. He enjoyed this work, where he felt himself among ordinary lovers of music rather than as part of an elite. His Brass Band Suite of around 1930 was sometimes used as a test piece.
His chamber music included a Second Piano Concerto (1924), at the first performance of which, at the Queen's Hall in London, the work was heckled by a man said to be a friend of **Philip Heseltine**.

This may have discouraged Howells for a time. His other works include a Rhapsodic Quintet, said to evoke the Malvern Hills, and songs.

Composed items for organ but is known particularly for his church music. In fact, during the period 1939-1948, most of the material he composed was for the church.

His tune 'Michael' (1935), written specifically for the hymn 'All my hope in God is founded' by Robert Bridges, was named in memory of his son who had died at the age of nine. Michael Howells was buried at Twigworth, Gloucestershire, where his father's friend from adolescence and fellow-composer, Ivor Gurney, was buried not long afterwards. The tragedy of Michael's death haunted the whole family: his mother, Dorothy, had what almost amounted to a nervous breakdown and there was no composition of any kind from Herbert Howells for several years.

Hymnus Paradisi was completed in 1938. It was composed mainly at weekends, and although it was memorial in nature it ended in a mood of hope. The first performance of the work was not given until some years afterwards. The first performance (at the Three Choirs' Festival of 1950) was at Gloucester Cathedral, three miles from Michael's place of burial and on the day following the 15th anniversary of Michael's death. *Hymnus Paradisi* is generally acknowledged as Howells's finest composition.

In similarly tragic circumstances, Herbert Howells was invited in 1963 to compose a work in Washington, U.S.A. in memory of the assassinated president whom Herbert Howells had greatly admired, John Fitzgerald Kennedy. 'Take him, earth, for cherishing' was a setting of words by Prudentius, who lived in the fourth century.

There was an early Magnificat and Nunc Dimittis in G (1920). Although he had not played a service since 1917, Herbert Howells deputised for **Robin Orr** at St. John's College, Cambridge (1941) when the latter joined the R.A.F. The responsibility for the choir inspired him once more and he began to compose Canticle settings. He later remarked that he wrote with the building principally in mind, aiming to be in sympathy with the atmosphere where 'something of mine was going to be sung'. There followed many other services known principally by the venue of the choral foundation for which they were composed - including King's College, Cambridge (1945); Gloucester Cathedral (1946); Canterbury Cathedral (1946); St. Paul's Cathedral (1951); Worcester Cathedral (1951); St. John's College, Cambridge (1957); Chichester Cathedral (1967); York Minster (1973) and New College, Oxford. The Mass *in the Dorian Mode* (1912) and other early Latin church music recently re-discovered and published was devised specifically for **Richard Terry** and his Westminster Cathedral Choir. A Stabat Mater (1963) is for Chorus and Orchestra. His *Three Carol-Anthems* have been described as masterpieces of this miniature genre. ('A spotless rose is blowing' is that most performed.) 'Like as the hart desireth the waterbrooks' from *Four Anthems* (1941) occupies a highly-regarded place in the repertoire of countless choirs, as does the carol 'Here is the little door'. His output for organ was extensive, including two sets of *Psalm Preludes*, a large scale Sonata, a Partita (1970) and the significant and highly characteristic *Six Pieces* (1940), dedicated to **Herbert Sumsion**. Among the solo songs, 'King David', to a text by Walter de la Mare, is said to be of almost unbearable pathos.

HOWGATE, John (18th/19th century)
Nothing is known of the composer of church music, John Howgate. Around the year 1820 two volumes of hymn tunes were published in Manchester with the title *Sacred Music*, published by

subscription. Out of gratitude, Howgate named some of the tunes after certain of the subscribers. Perhaps 'Worsley' was one of them.

HOWGILL, William (18th/19th century)
William Howgill was an organist of Whitehaven in 1794 and was later active as an organist in London. Composed the anthems 'My song shall be alway' (c1800) and 'The righteous Souls', a piano sonata, and organ voluntaries. Published a collection of Psalm tunes.

HOYLAND, John (1783-1827)
Born, possibly in Sheffield, in 1783; died on 18 January 1827. A pupil of **William Mather**, organist of St. James's Church, Sheffield, whom he succeeded in 1808. In 1819 he moved to Louth, Lincolnshire where he taught music and eventually became organist of the parish church. Composed anthems and other sacred music, including a setting of Psalm 150 'O praise God in His Holiness' plus songs and items for piano.

HOYTE, Dr. William Stevenson (1844-1917)
Born in Sidmouth, Devon on 22 September 1844; died in Ealing, London on 27 July 1917.
Educated in Devon at Ottery St. Mary. Studied under **John Goss** and **George Cooper**. Awarded the Lambeth D.Mus. (1904).
He held a number of Church organistships, all except one of which were in London, these being St. Paul's, Hampstead; All Saints', King's Lynn, Norfolk; St. Paul's, Bow Common (from 1862); St. Matthew's, City Road (from 1864); Holy Trinity, Westminster (from 1865) and All Saints', Margaret Street (1867-1907), where his choristers included Dalton Baker who later became an opera singer. On his retirement he remained honorary organist until his death in 1917.
One of his organ pupils was the composer **Gustav Holst**.
An organ and piano recitalist. Held professorships of organ and choir training at the Royal College of Music (from 1888), of organ at the Royal Academy of Music (from 1893) and of piano at Guildhall School of Music (from 1888). A lifelong friend of **Frederick Bridge**. Retired from teaching through ill-health in 1910.
Composed a Holy Communion Service for Voices and Orchestra, other Services, anthems and songs.
The Standard Edition (1916) of *Hymns Ancient and Modern* uses his hymn tunes 'St. Edmund', 'St. Nicolas' and 'St. Columb', the last of these with 'From glory unto glory' by Frances Havergal. His Responses to the Commandments in D were used in a collection published around 1875.

HUDSON, Charles M. (?-1896)
Composer of the anthem 'I will extol Thee'.

HUDSON, Mary (c1758-1801)
Born around the year 1758; died in London on 28 March 1801. The first organist of St. Olave's Church, Hart Street, London (1781-1801). Organist of St. Gregory's Church, Old Fish Street (1785-1801). Composed a number of hymn tunes including 'Llandaff', although it is not entirely clear that they were by Mary and not by her father **Robert Hudson**.

HUDSON, Robert (1732-1815)
Born in London on 25 February 1732; died in Eton, Berkshire on 19 December 1815 and buried at St. Paul's Cathedral. Father of

Mary Hudson. One of the last pupils of **Charles King** at St. Paul's Cathedral. Sang in the Ranelagh and Marylebone Gardens, London as a young man. By 1755 he was assistant organist of the Church of St. Mildred, Bread Street, London. A vicar-choral of St. Paul's Cathedral (from 1756) for almost 60 years. Almoner and master of the choristers of St. Paul's (1773-1793). A gentleman of the Chapel Royal (from 1758). Taught music at Christ's Hospital (1762-1808). Compositions include a Psalm of Thanksgiving, a service, anthems, chants and hymn tunes. One of these is 'St. Olave', used in the Revised Edition (1927) of *Church Hymnary*. Also composed songs.

HUDSON, Thomas Charlton (1868-1937)
Born in Sheffield, Yorkshire on 10 June 1868; died in Saffron Walden, Essex on 19 May 1937. Composer of hymn tunes.

HUGELY, J. de
See **MATTHEWS**, John Henry.

HUGHES, Arwel (1909-1988)
Born in Rhosllanerchrugog, Denbighshire, Wales on 25 August 1909; died on 23 September 1988. Brother of **John Hughes**.
Educated at Ruabon Grammar School and at the Royal College of Music where he studied under **C.H. Kitson** and **Ralph Vaughan Williams**.
Organist of the church of SS Philip and James, Oxford (1933-1935).
In 1935, he returned to Wales to work in the B.B.C. Music Department, where his activities included conducting. On a number of occasions he conducted the B.B.C. Welsh Orchestra in first performances of pieces by Welsh composers including **Alun Hoddinott**. Arwel Hughes finished his career with the B.B.C. as head of the Music Department in Wales (1965-1971). Organist of the Tabernacle Chapel, The Hayes, Cardiff.
Composed orchestral works, oratorios including *Dewi Sant* (St. David), and a setting for the devotional poem *Tydi a Roddaist* ('Tis Thou didst give the dawn its hue). *In Memoriam* (1969), for Chorus and Organ was based on Psalm 121.

HUGHES, Dom Anselm (1889-1974)
Born in London on 15 April 1889; died in Nashdom Abbey, Burnham, Buckinghamshire on 8 October 1974.
Studied at Weam School; Keble College, Oxford, graduating B.A. (1911) and M.A. (1915) and Ely Theological College.
Undertook lecture tours on medieval church music in the U.S.A. and Canada in each of the years 1932, 1934, 1939 and 1940. Director of music (1922-1945) and prior (1936-1945) of Nashdom Abbey.
Contributed articles to Grove's *Dictionary of Music and Musicians*. An editor of the *New Oxford History of Music*.
With Revd. A. Ramsbotham and H.B. Collins, he edited the *Old Hall Manuscripts* (1933-1938) for the Plainsong and Medieval Music Society, of which he was honorary secretary and treasurer (1926-1936). These are a collection of copies made in the first half of the 15th century of works of church music composed in or around the period 1415 to 1430. They are so named following their presentation to Old Hall College near Ware, Hertfordshire in 1893 and they were bought by the British Museum in 1973.
His writings include the work *Early English Harmony*.
Composed the Missa *Sancti Benedicti* (1918) and a small quantity of other music for the church.

HUGHES, Griffith William (1861-1941)
Born in Wrexham, Wales in 1861; died in Prestatyn, Flintshire, Wales on 29 September 1941. Spent most of his life in Cefnmawr, Rhos, near Wrexham before living in retirement at Prestatyn. Composer of hymn tunes including 'Buddugoliaeth'. This was widely sung at festivals before it was published in 1929 in the collection *Llyfr, Emynan a Thonau y Methodstiad Calfinaidd a Wesleaidd*.

HUGHES, Humphrey Vaughan (1889-1974)
Born in Wandsworth, London on 15 April 1889; died in Burnham, Buckinghamshire on 8 October 1974. Composer of hymn tunes.

HUGHES, John (Glandwr: 1872-1914)
Born in Penbryn, near Cardigan in 1872; died in Swansea on 16 June 1914. At the age of two, he moved with his family to Swansea. His father died when John was 10 years old and he was obliged to leave school and become an errand boy at the Duffryn Steel and Tinplate Works at Morriston, near Swansea. His career prospered there and he eventually became commercial manager. A member of the Philadelphia Welsh Baptist Church, Hafod, for which he composed hymn tunes. 'Calon Lân' was used at revivalist meetings in Wales from around 1904. It was included in the collection *Y Cynulleidfaol Newydd* (1921) and also in some English hymnals.

HUGHES, John (1873-1932)
Born in Dowlais, Wales on 22 November 1873; died in Tonteg, Llantwit Fardre, Glamorgan on 14 May 1932.
The family moved in 1874 to Llantwit Fardre. From the age of 12 he worked at the Glyn Colliery in Llanilltyd Faerdref as a door boy. In 1905 he was employed as a clerk in the traffic department of the Great Western Railway in Pontypridd, for which he worked for over 40 years. Precentor and a deacon of the Salem Baptist Church, Llantwit.
His hymn tune 'Cwm Rhondda' was composed for the town's Baptist *Cymanfa Ganu* (song festival) in 1905. The hymn 'Guide me, O Thou great Redeemer' by William Williams (Pantecelyn) has maintained enormous popularity ever since, almost entirely through its association with this tune. John Hughes also composed other hymn tunes, anthems and songs but none of these has achieved anywhere near the same success as 'Cwm Rhondda'.

HUGHES, John (1896-1968)
Born in Rhosllanerchrugog, Denbighshire, Wales on 16 June 1896; died in Cardiff on 14 November 1968. Brother of **Arwel Hughes**. A miner by trade, working at the Hafod Colliery, Denbighshire. Studied music in his spare time, had lessons with **J.C. Bridge** at the age of 18; studied and graduated at University College, Aberystwyth (1921-1924). Choirmaster of the Nodffa Baptist Church, Treorchi and (from 1942) music organiser for Merionethshire Education Authority. Edited *Y Llawlyfr Moliant Newydd* (The New Handbook of Praise, 1956) and served on the music committee of *Baptist Hymn Book* (1962). Among his hymn tunes are 'Maelor' and 'Arwelfa'.

HUGHES, John Thomas (c1866-1934)
Born in Chester in 1866 or 1867; died in Chester on 27 February 1934. A chorister under Frederick Gunton at Chester Cathedral and was later articled to **J.C. Bridge**. Organist of Holy Trinity Church, Chester and of West Derby Parish Church, Liverpool (1885-1909)

where he succeeded **W.T. Best**. Assistant organist of Chester Cathedral (1909-1925). Given the title of nave organist, with the responsibility for the music of the congregational worship that took place in the nave of the cathedral. Organist of Chester Cathedral (1925-1930) in succession to Bridge. Composed church music, songs and items for organ.

HUGHES, Percy Edward (19th/20th century)
Trained at Ely Cathedral. Graduated B.Mus. at the University of Durham (1895) and B.Mus. at Queen's College, Oxford (1899).
Organist of St. Mary's Church, Ely (1890-1897) and deputy organist of Ely Cathedral (1893-1898). Organist and choirmaster of Cromer Parish Church, Norfolk (1897-1902) and a teacher of music at St. Laurence School, Suffield Park and at Sheringham Ladies' College. A choir trainer and honorary inspector of choirs for the Norwich Diocesan Choral Association. Conductor of a local choral society. Organist and choirmaster of Holy Trinity Church, and choirmaster of St. Peter's Church, Coventry, Warwickshire (from 1902). Composed an Evening Service and a setting of the Holy Communion Service, an anthem, hymn tunes, and music for violin and for piano.

HULLAH, Dr. John Pyke (1812-1884)
Born in Worcester on 27 June 1812; died in Westminster, London on 21 February 1884.
Studied music under **William Horsley** (from 1829) and under Gaetano Crivelli (from 1832) and at the Royal Academy of Music (1833-1835). In 1876 he was awarded the honorary LL.D. by the University of Edinburgh.
Organist of Croydon Parish Church, Surrey (from 1837). In 1839 he visited Paris in order to learn more about the teaching methods of **Joseph Mainzer**. The classes had been discontinued and the visitors spent time instead with another famous teacher of singing, Guillaume Wilhelm.
On his return to England, Hullah taught Wilhelm's *fixed doh* methods to singing teachers at St. John's College, Battersea, London (from 1840); at Exeter Hall (from 1841) and later at St. Mark's College, Chelsea.
Fixed doh sight reading involved a combination of singing and physical actions. The disadvantage was that *doh* always represented the same note, no matter what the key. Although the more flexible approach of John Curwen and his Tonic Sol-fa method, which Hullah loathed, eventually superseded it, some 25,000 pupils learned music through Hullah's methods in the space of 20 years.
Hullah advocated the raising of musical standards in church through awareness by the congregation of their duty to learn and practise music. By seating the congregation by parts, he achieved an effect similar to that of a small choral festival.
A conductor, Hullah later became a government inspector of colleges (1872-1883), organist of the Charter House (1858-1884) and a professor music at King's (1844-1874) and Queen's College, London. Also a professor of Bedford College, London. An examiner for the Society of Arts. Said to have been constantly trying to improve his students' knowledge of musical history and their awareness of the subject.
In 1865, W.E. Gladstone, prime minister and rector of the University of Edinburgh, used his casting vote to prevent John Hullah being elected professor of music.
Author of works on composition and on musical history. Edited Psalters, including *Book of Praise Hymnal* (1868), and collections of songs.

Composed songs, and an opera *The Village Coquettes* (1836) to words by Charles Dickens, whose sister, Fanny, he knew as a fellow pupil at the R.A.M.
His hymn tune 'The foe behind' was used in *Church Hymns* (1874) with the hymn 'The foe behind, the deep before'. The Revised Edition (1927) of *Church Hymnary* and *Congregational Praise* (1950) used his tune 'Bentley' with William Cowper's hymn 'Sometimes, a light surprises'. Composed anthems including 'I will magnify Thee' and 'The day is past'.

HULTON, Francis Everard William (1845-1922)
Born in King's Lynn, Norfolk in 1845; died in Putney, London on 24 December 1922. Studied at Cologne Conservatory and at the University of Oxford, graduating B.Mus. (1868) at New College. Director of music at Princess Helena College, Ealing and organist of St. Luke's Church, Chelsea, London (1870-1904). Composed a number of hymn tunes, of which 'For all the Saints', 'God of the living', and others were used in *Hymns Ancient and Modern*.

HUME, Revd. Francis Glyne (19th/20th century)
Graduated B.A. (1869) and M.A. (1881) at Queen's College, Oxford. Ordained deacon in 1870, priest in 1871. Curate of the Church of St. Mary Magdalene, St. Leonards-on-Sea, Sussex (1870-1887) and rector of Church Oakley in Winchester Diocese (from 1887).

HUME, William (1830-?)
Born in Edinburgh on 25 September 1830. Lived in Glasgow, where he taught violin and singing. Musical editor for the three music publishers Hamilton of Glasgow; Gall and Inglis, Edinburgh and Parlane of Edinburgh. Music critic of *The Bailie*, Glasgow (from 1872), and contributed to other contemporary journals. Editor of *Union Sacred Tune Book* and *Westminster Wesleyan Tune Book*. Composed a motet for soloists and chorus, anthems, cantatas, songs and part songs.

HUMFREY (Humphrey, Humphrys), Pelham (1647-1674)
Born in 1647; died in Windsor on 14 July 1674; buried in the cloisters of Westminster Abbey.
One of the first choristers of the newly-restored Chapel Royal under **Henry Cooke**.
Left the Chapel Royal in 1664 and went to study in France under Lully, and in Italy.
Appointed a gentleman of the Chapel Royal during his absence. Samuel Pepys later wrote disparagingly in a passage often quoted from his diary entry for 15th November 1667, 'little Pelham Humphreys (sic)... an absolute monsieur... disparages everything and everybody's skill but his own'.
Succeeded Henry Cooke in his various appointments at the Chapel Royal from 1672. In the same year he and **Thomas Purcell** were jointly appointed composers in ordinary for the violins to Charles II. Humfrey held these appointments for only two years before his premature death.
He had composed anthems by the age of 17, and seen them in use. Composed a Service in E Minor; anthems including 'Rejoice in the Lord, O ye righteous', based on Psalm 33. A chant known as *The Grand Chant* is one of the earliest known. Also composed songs and court odes.

HUMPHRIS, Ian William (b.1927)
Born in Clacton-on-Sea, Essex on 29 November 1927. Studied at the Royal Academy of Music. Director of music of South East Essex Technical College (1956-1959). A choral and orchestral conductor. Composer of hymn tunes.

HUNN, William Richard (1879-?)
Born in Great Yarmouth, Norfolk in 1879. Educated under Haydon Hare and **Cuthbert Harris**. Graduated B.Mus. at the University of Durham (1912). Organist and choirmaster of St. Mary's Church, Southtown, Great Yarmouth (1897-1904) and director of music at the Britannia Pier (from 1919). Conductor of the Norfolk Military Band. Organist of St. Peter's Parish Church, St. Albans, and music master of St. Albans Grammar School. A teacher of singing and piano. Composed two settings of the Te Deum, pageant music, songs, and works for military band.

HUNNIS, William (?-1597)
Lived during the 16th century; died in London on 6 June 1597. A gentleman of the Chapel Royal of Edward VI. A devout Protestant, he was imprisoned in 1555 or 1556 but he was restored to the Chapel by Elizabeth I and became master of the choristers there (1566-1597) in succession to Richard Edwards. Produced musical dramas at court, featuring the Chapel choristers. Custodian of the gardens and orchards at Greenwich, London (from 1562).
Some of his music exists in manuscript in the Music School at the University of Oxford.. His texts were used by **Thomas Morley**, **Thomas Weelkes** and **William Mundy**.

HUNT, Dr. Donald Frederick (b.1930)
Born in Gloucester on 26 July 1930.
Educated at King's School, Gloucester and a pupil of **Herbert Sumsion**. Holds the honorary D.Mus. (1975) from the University of Leeds.
Appointed O.B.E. in 1993.
Assistant organist to Sumsion at Gloucester Cathedral (1947-1954) before performing National Service. Took part in the Gloucester Three Choirs' Festivals of 1950 and 1953.
Organist of St. John's Church, Torquay, Devon (1954-1957) and of Leeds Parish Church (1957-1975). While at Torquay he was music master of the grammar school, and during his time at Leeds he was on the staff of the Leeds Music Centre (now the City of Leeds College of Music). Chorus master of the Leeds Festival. Conductor of the Halifax Choral Society (1957-1987) - a position that he retained after his move to Worcester - and of Leeds Philharmonic Society (1961-1975) as successor to Sir Malcolm Sargent. Instrumental in founding the Yorkshire Sinfonia.
Appointed organist of Worcester Cathedral in 1975, following the departure of **Christopher Robinson** to St. George's Chapel, Windsor Castle. Has conducted on many occasions at Three Choirs' Festivals, and made recordings.
Compiled a biography of one of his predecessors as organist of Leeds Parish Church, **S.S. Wesley**.
His compositions include a Magnificat and Nunc Dimittis in G Minor, a set of the Versicles and Responses, a Missa Brevis, a Missa Nova, Services, the carol 'Christmas night', the anthem 'God be gracious' and a set of motets *My God and King*. Also composed a song cycle *Strings in the Earth and Air*, a Suite for Organ, and the Cantatas *Hymnus Paschalis, A Song of Celebration* and *A Man for Others*.

HUNT, Revd. Dr. Henry George Bonavia (1847-1917)
Born in Malta on 30 June 1847; died in Brighton, Sussex on 4 October 1917.
Educated privately in music and graduated B.Mus. at Christ Church, Oxford (1876). Graduated B.Mus. and D.Mus. (1887) at Trinity College, Dublin. Ordained deacon in 1878, priest in 1879.
Choirmaster of South Hackney Parish Church, London (1872-1875). Curate of Esher Parish Church, Surrey (1878-1880) and in London, lecturer at St. Philip's Church, Regent Street (1882-1883); Evening Preacher at St. James's Church, Piccadilly (1884-1887); incumbent (from 1887) and vicar (from 1897) of St. Paul's, Kilburn. Vicar of Burgess Hill, Sussex (from 1905).
Had a long connection with Trinity College of Music, London, as founder, its first warden (1872-1892), professor of musical history (1876-1887) and chaplain (1880-1890). A recognised teacher at the University of London (1900-1907) where his subject was musical history.
The author of *A Concise History of Music* (1878). Published a number of his sermons. He edited the periodical *Quiver* for 40 years, *Little Folks* (from 1876) and *Cassell's Magazine* (1874-1896), and contributed to *The Manchester Guardian*.
Composed an Evening Service, and anthems.

HUNT, John (1806-1842)
Born in Marnhull, Dorset on 30 December 1806; died in Hereford on 17 November 1842. A chorister of Salisbury Cathedral and a pupil of **Arthur Corfe**. A lay vicar of Lichfield Cathedral (from 1827). Organist of the church attached to the St. John's Almshouses, Lichfield, Staffordshire. Succeeded **S.S. Wesley** as organist of Hereford Cathedral (1835-1842). His premature death ensued from a collision with a dinner trolley laden with crockery and glasses following an audit dinner at the cathedral. The tragedy had further consequences when John Hunt's adoptive nephew, a chorister, failed to recover from the shock and died. Composed a double chant, the hymn tune 'Hereford', glees and songs.

HUNT, John Eric (1903-1958)
Born in Islington, London in 1903; died in Shrewsbury, Shropshire on 12 November 1958.
Attended Worcester College for the Blind and studied under G.D. Cunningham.
Organist of the Church of St. Mark, Hamilton Terrace, London; Bickley Parish Church, Kent (1927-1943) and St. Mary's Church, Shrewsbury (1943-1958). Director of music at the Royal Normal College for the Blind at Rowton Castle, Shropshire (1951-1958) and he taught at the Royal School of Church Music.
Author of a handbook for blind teachers of music and a history of the Collegiate Church of St. Mary, Shrewsbury.
Composed Services, including an Evening Service in E-flat, and hymn tunes of which 'Shrewsbury' is an example. 'Adoration' was first used in *Christian Praise* (1957) and subsequently in the Revised Edition of *Hymns Ancient and Modern* and in *Hymns and Psalms* (1983). Both are acknowledged as fine tunes, and commentators have found their exclusion from modern hymnals somewhat perplexing.

HUNT, Thomas (16th/17th century)
Thomas Hunt was a church musician and minor composer who lived around 1600. Said to have been B.Mus. May have been the same Thomas Hunt who was organist of Wells Cathedral.

Composed a set of Preces, a Short Service, anthems including 'Put me not to rebuke', and at least one madrigal.

HUNT, Dr. William Henry (1852-1894)
Born in London in 1852; died in Birkenhead, Cheshire on 6 December 1894. Attended Cooper's School, Ratcliffe. Studied music from the age of 12, largely unsupervised. One of the first two B.Mus. graduates (1880) at the University of London, proceeding D.Mus. in 1886. After spending the early part of his career teaching various subjects at a number of schools, he settled permanently in Birkenhead, Cheshire, where he continued to teach. Paralysed in 1894. Composed Services; a Stabat Mater for Solo Voices, Chorus and Orchestra; anthems; two comic operas; songs, and exercises for piano.

HUNTLEY, Dr. George Frederic (1859-1913)
Born in Datchet, Berkshire on 31 May 1859; died in Hemel Hempstead, Hertfordshire on 4 August 1913. A son of the former headmaster of Datchet School.
A chorister of Datchet Parish Church. Attended Datchet School and, from the age of 13, St. Mark's School, Windsor. Studied under **Haydn Keeton** and **Charles Hancock** and with **George Elvey** (from 1874). Graduated Mus.B. (1888) and Mus.D. (1894) at Trinity College, Cambridge.
Organist and choirmaster of St. Mary's Church, Datchet, (from 1879) and the London Churches of St. George, Kensington (from 1880) and St. Andrew, Westminster (from 1890).
Organist and choirmaster of Newcastle Cathedral (1894-1895).
Returned to London as organist and choirmaster of St. Peter's Church, Eaton Square where he remained in office for the rest of his life
A professor of music at the Royal Academy of Music, an examiner for the Royal College of Organists, and the conductor of local choral and orchestral societies. Music adviser to the Borough Polytechnic Institute (from 1911).
Composed a Service in E-flat and another in G, both of which were composed for festivals in St. Paul's Cathedral; a Festival Te Deum; anthems, an oratorio *Dies Domini*, cantatas including *O Lord, I will praise Thee*, hymn tunes and operettas.

HURD, Michael (b.1928)
Born in Gloucester on 19 December 1928.
Attended the Crypt Grammar School, Gloucester and Pembroke College, Oxford (1950-1953) where he studied music under **Thomas Armstrong** and **Bernard Rose** and graduated B.A. (1953) and M.A. (1958). Continued his music studies with **Lennox Berkeley** (1953-1959).
A professor of theory at the Royal Marines' School of Music (1953-1959), working thereafter as a freelance composer and author. His writings include contributions to Grove's *Dictionary of Music and Musicians, The New Oxford Companion to Music,* biographies of Rutland Boughton and Ivor Gurney, *The Oxford Junior Companion to Music* and *An Outline of European Music*.
His church compositions include a Missa Brevis and seven anthems including 'It is a good thing to give thanks' and 'Rejoice with us'. Has composed two operas, numerous works for chorus and orchestra, and a series of popular cantatas such as *Jonah-man Jazz*.

HURFORD, Peter John (b.1930)
Born in Minehead, Somerset on 22 November 1930.

Attended Blundell's School (until 1948); the Royal College of Music as foundation scholar (1948-1949), studying under **Harold Darke**; and as organ scholar, Jesus College, Cambridge (1949-1953), where he graduated in law (B.A. 1953; M.A. 1956) and music (Mus.B. 1958). For a short time he studied under André Marchal in Paris.
Appointed O.B.E. in 1984, and has received many academic honours.
Organist of the Church of Holy Trinity, Leamington Spa, Warwickshire (1956-1957), succeeding **Harold Dexter**, and music master of Bablake School, Coventry.
Organist and master of the choristers of St. Albans Abbey (1958-1978), during which time he established the International Organ Festival, first held in 1963. He has served as President both of the Royal College of Organists and of the Incorporated Association of Organists.
Visiting professor at the University of Cincinnati (1967-1978) and the University of Western Ontario (1976-1977). Artist in residence at Sydney Opera House (1980-1982). A professor at the Royal Academy of Music (1982-1988).
He has acted internationally as an adjudicator and is well known as an organ theorist and designer. He has made over 60 recordings, including the complete organ works of J.S. Bach for the Decca recording company and for the B.B.C.
His writings include *Making Music on the Organ* (1988).
His compositions embrace organ music, anthems (including 'Litany to the Holy Spirit'), and Masses for Series III, and Rite II and III of the American Episcopal Church.

HURLEY, Donal (b.1950)
Born in Dublin in 1950. Studied music at University College, Dublin. A lecturer in music at the Mater Dei Institute, Dublin. His compositions for the church include a Magnificat (1982) and a Mass *for Mater Dei* (1984), and the anthem 'Let the peoples praise You, O Lord' (1985). His other works include a chamber opera *The Devil* (1992) amd a number of electro-acoustic works such as *Portraits* (1990) and *Lifescapes* (1992).

HURNDALL, Dr. William Flavel (1830-1888)
Born in Basingstoke, Hampshire on 10 July 1830; died in Scarborough, Yorkshire on 19 August 1888. Composer of hymn tunes. Published the collection *Tunes and Chants* (1878).

HURST, Revd. John (19th/20th century)
Graduated B.Mus. at Queen's College, Oxford (1896). Composed church music including a Benedicite in F (1889), the anthems 'Teach me, O Lord, the way of Thy statutes' (1891-1892) and 'O Come let us sing unto the Lord' (1892), items for organ and music for children.

HURST, William (1849-1934)
Born in Leicester in 1849; died in Coalville, Leicestershire in 1934. Lived for most of his life in Coalville. Did not hold a regular church organistship, but often deputised. His hymn tune 'Leicester' was used in the Revised Edition (1927) of *Church Hymnary*, with the hymn 'I am not worthy, Holy Lord' by **H.W. Baker**. Composed other forms of church music, and works for organ.

HUSBAND, Revd. Edward (1843-1908)
Born in Hampshire in 1843; died in Folkestone, Kent on 3 January 1908. Attended St. Aidan's Theological College, Birkenhead,

Cheshire. Ordained deacon in 1866, priest in 1867. Curate of Atherstone, Warwickshire (1866-1872) and of Folkestone (1872-1878). Vicar of the Church of St. Michael and All Angels, Folkestone (from 1878) where he was both incumbent and organist. Gave many organ recitals and his 'Sunday afternoons for the people,' at which an organ recital was combined with an address, proved popular. The 250th such event was reached in 1907. Edited *Supplemental Tunes to Popular Hymns* (published 1882). Composed an Evening Service, an anthem and hymn tunes.

HUSBAND, John Jenkins (1760-1825)
Born in Plymouth, Devon in 1760; died in Philadelphia, U.S.A. on 19 May 1825. Precentor of the Surrey Chapel, Plymouth. In 1809 he emigrated to the U.S.A. Taught singing in Philadelphia, where he was also clerk to St. Paul's Episcopal Church. Composer of hymn tunes and anthems. His 'Rejoice and be glad' was first used in the U.S.A. with Horatius Bonar's, 'Rejoice and be glad; the Redeemer hath come'. In 1933 the same combination was adopted for *Methodist Hymn Book* in the U.K.

HUSSEY, Matthew (?-1766)
Died, probably in London, around 1 April 1766. A chorister at St. Paul's Cathedral under **Charles King**. Organist of St. Alban's Church, Wood Street, London (1736-1766). Around 1763 he was also organist of Newington Butts. Contributed Psalm tunes to **William Riley**'s collection, *Parochial Music Corrected* (1762).

HUTCHESON, Charles (1792-1860)
Born in Glasgow in 1792; died in Glasgow on 20 January 1860. A merchant in the city of Glasgow, where he lived all his life. In his spare time he studied and practised music, especially Psalmody. In 1832 he published *Christian Vespers*, a collection of harmonised Psalm or hymn tunes. At least one tune, 'Stracathro', named after a village on the banks of the River Esk was by Charles Hutcheson himself. It was written in the late 1840s for the Church of St. George, Glasgow, where he worshipped, and is associated with the hymn 'O for a closer walk with God'.

HUTCHINGS, Dr. Arthur James Bramwell (1906-1989)
Born in Sunbury-on-Thames, Middlesex on 14 July 1906; died in Colyton, Devon in 1989.
Gained his early knowledge of music through playing violin and by singing church music as a chorister. Graduated B.A. and B.Mus., D.Mus.(1953) and Ph.D.
A school teacher. Served in the R.A.F. before becoming professor of music at the University of Durham (1947-1968) and at the University of Exeter (1968-1971), where he was the first holder of the chair.
Has written articles as a critic and reviewer, and biographies of composers including Delius and Schubert. Author also of *Church Music in the 19th Century* (1967). Somewhat controversial in his views. Was on the Editorial Committee of *English Praise* and *New English Hymnal*.
Composed the anthems 'Grant them rest', 'God is gone up' and 'Victim Divine, Thy grace we claim'. His hymn tune 'Fudgie' was used in the Revised Edition (1927) of *Church Hymnary* with the hymn 'O Thou who camest from above'. Composed a comic opera and works for strings.

HUTCHINSON, John (c1615-?)
Baptised in Durham on 2 July 1615. A son of **Richard Hutchinson**. Organist of Southwell Minster (c1622-c1634). He may be the person of that name who was organist of York Minster from March 1634. A minor composer whose output included anthems, one of which, 'Of mortall man', was known as the 'Southwell' anthem. Also composed a setting of Psalm 130 'Out of the deep'.

HUTCHINSON (Hutcheson), Richard (?-1646)
Died in Durham on 7 June 1646. Father of **John Hutchinson**.
Organist of Durham Cathedral (1613-1644), succeeding **Edward Smith**, until the Cathedral organ was suppressed. From around 1614 he was also a lay clerk of Durham Cathedral.
The years 1626 to 1628 had been turbulent. He went to gaol, fell into debt, frequented ale houses, set upon and wounded a lay clerk, Toby Broking, with a candlestick and was suspended from his position as a teacher of the choristers. It seems remarkable that he should have been allowed to continue in office but it was recognised that Richard Hutchinson had achieved a high musical standard at Durham Cathedral.
A lay clerk, Henry Palmer, was put in charge of the choristers but Richard Hutchinson was required to teach the virginals and organ three times per week. In return, a debt of £10 was written off.
William Smith (composer of the famous Preces and Responses) deputised for Richard Hutchinson during the time he was in gaol.
A minor composer. his anthems include 'Lord, I am not high minded' and 'O Lord, let my complaint'.

HUTCHINSON, Dr. Thomas (1854-1917)
Born in Hendon, County Durham on 23 April 1854; died in Darlington, County Durham on 4 February 1917.
His early musical education was at Durham Cathedral. Studied under **Philip Armes** and **Samuel Reay**. Graduated B.Mus. (1879) and D.Mus. (1894) at the University of Oxford. Received an honorary doctorate in music from the University of Durham (1897).
A teacher, composer and examiner. Author of *Dr. Hutchinson's Singing Tutor*. A freemason.
At the age of 17, Thomas Hutchinson was organist and choirmaster of St. Paul's Church, Hendon (from 1871); organist of St. Cuthbert's Church, Darlington (1896-1917). Organist of Silksworth Parish Church for 20 years, and of Darlington Parish Church (from 1896).
Composed Services, a Te Deum and Jubilate in E-flat, anthems, hymn tunes, choral cantatas including *The Redeemer*, songs, and music for piano and for organ.

HUTTON, Laura Josephine (1852-1888)
Born in Spridlington, Lincolnshire on 17 July 1852; died in Spridlington on 17 June 1888. For a time she acted as housekeeper to her brother, Revd. Vernon Woolaston Hutton, vicar of Sneinton, Nottinghamshire and a prebendary of Lincoln Cathedral. On his retirement, Laura Huton went to live with him in Lincoln. When he died, she took up residence with her brother-in-law, who the incumbent of Spridlington. Her tune 'Eternity' was used in the Revised Edition (1927) of *Church Hymnary* with the hymn 'Every morning the red sun' by Cecil Frances Alexander. After a serious illness, Laura Hutton composed tunes for a number of Miss Alexander's hymns for children, some of which were published privately in 1880.

HYDE, Dr. Derek (b.1931)
Born in Gloucestershire on 1 November 1931. Studied at the University of Durham (1950-1953), graduating B.A. and B.Mus. Studied further at St. John's College, Cambridge (1955-1956) and at Trinity College of Music (1986-1987). Awarded the M.Phil. (1973) and Ph.D. (1979) at the University of Reading. Director of music of Woodbridge School (1956-1961). Head of music and performing arts at Nonington College, Canterbury (1961-1986). Senior lecturer at Christ Church College, Canterbury (from 1987). A tutor of the Open University since 1973 and an examiner for Trinity College of Music since 1988. His compositions include a 'Psalm of Celebration' and a 'Carol for Today'.

HYGONS, Richard (?-1509)
Studied under **Abyngdon**, succentor of Wells Cathedral. A vicar-choral of Wells (from 1458). Joint organist (1461-1462), master of the choristers (1479-1507) and organist (1497-1507) of Wells Cathedral. A fragment exists in the library of Wells Cathedral of a Marian antiphon *Virgo, mater Christi*. There is a Salve Regina in the *Eton College Choir Book*.

HYLTON STEWART, Arthur Charles Lestoc (1884-1932)
Born in Chester on 21 March 1884; died in Windsor, Berkshire on 14 November 1932.
The son of Revd. C.H. Hylton-Stewart, vicar of New Brighton and canon of Chester and former organist of Chichester Cathedral.
A pupil of **J.C. Bridge**, organist of Chester Cathedral.. Educated at Magdalen College School, Oxford and at Peterhouse, Cambridge (1903-1907) where he was Stewart of Rannoch scholar in sacred music. Graduated B.A. (1906), Mus.B. (1907) and M.A. (1910) at the University of Cambridge.
Assistant organist (1906-1907) to A.H. Mann, organist of King's College, Cambridge. Organist of Emmanuel Church, New Brighton (1901-1903); organist and music master of Sedbergh School, Cumbria (from 1907) and organist and choirmaster of St. Martin's Church, Scarborough, Yorkshire (1908-1914). Organist of Blackburn Parish Church, Lancashire (1914-1916), since elevated to cathedral status. A local choral society conductor.
Organist and master of the choristers of Rochester Cathedral (1916-1930) and of Chester Cathedral (1930-1932). He took office as organist and master of the choristers of St. George's Chapel, Windsor Castle on 1 September 1933 but died only 12 weeks afterwards.
One of the editors, with **H.G. Ley** and Edgar Stanley Roper, organists of Christ Church Cathedral, Oxford and of the Chapel Royal, of *Oxford Psalter*.
Composed settings of the Magnificat and Nunc Dimittis in the First Mode, in A-flat (1912), in C (1925) and in F (1921). There are other services, including a setting in unison. 'Christ, being raised from the dead' (1935) is an example of his anthems, and he composed hymn tunes including 'Rochester', found in *New English Hymnal*, and 'Corona' (1927)

I

Ieuan Glan Alarch
See **MILLS**, Revd. John.

Ieuan Gwyllt
See **ROBERTS**, Revd. John

IGGULDEN, Dr. Athelstan Glover (19th/20th century)
Graduated B.Mus.(1894) and D.Mus. (1901) at the University of Durham. Music master of Farnborough School, Hampshire (from 1900), organist and choirmaster of Hawarden Parish Church and organist and music master of St. David's Church, Reigate, Surrey (from 1895). A local choral society conductor. A teacher of music by correspondence (from 1937). Composed church music, and pieces for piano and for violin.

ILIFFE, Dr. Frederick (1847-1928)
Born in Smeeton, near Westerby, Leicestershire on 21 February 1847; died in Oxford on 2 February 1928.
Educated at Kibworth Grammar School, and privately. Graduated B.Mus. (1873) and D.Mus. (1879) at New College, Oxford. Also held the Oxford M.A.
Organist of St. Wilfred's Church, Kibworth, Leicestershire and held appointments in Oxford at St. Barnabas's Church (1879-1883), St. John's College (from 1883), St. Mary's Church (from 1900) and the University (1900-1925). Examiner for musical degrees at the University of Oxford (from 1908).
Composed services, including a Magnificat and Nunc Dimittis for Male Voices (1885), and published a series of collections of anthems suitable for parish church choirs (1876 to 1899). Included his own 'I will magnify Thee O Lord, my King'. An eight-part motet *Sweet Echo* was composed for the Cheltenham Festival Society (1898). Also composed an oratorio *The Vision of St. John the Divine*, a Passion cantata *Vox Crucis*, and part songs. His hymn tune 'Autumn' featured in *Church Hymns* (1874); 'Warnborough' was used in the Standard Edition (1916) of *Hymns Ancient and Modern*.

ILLSLEY, Dr. Percival John (1864/5-1924)
Born in Leek, Staffordshire around 1864; died in Montreal, Canada, on 14 October 1924. Received his early musical training at Lichfield Cathedral. Awarded the Lambeth D.Mus. in 1912.

Assistant organist of Lichfield Cathedral (from 1887), and organist to the Marchioness of Hastings at Grendon, Warwickshire (from 1888). Organist and choirmaster of Queensbury Parish Church, Yorkshire (from 1889). The following year he emigrated to Montreal and became organist and choirmaster of St. George's Church. President of the Canadian College of Organists (1922-1923). Composed anthems including 'There is joy' and 'Angels from the realms', a cantata *Ruth*, a part song 'Ye mariners of England' and songs.

INGHAM, Percival Arthur (b.1895)
Born in Bradford, Yorkshire, in 1895. Attended Bradford Grammar School and studied music with **Walter Hickox** and **Albert Tysoe**. Organist and choirmaster of Cawood Parish Church, near Selby (from 1924). Composed a hymn 'Bless, Lord, the Saints who worship Thee'.

INGHAM, Richard (1804-1841)
Born in 1804; died in June 1841. Organist of St. Mary's Church, Gateshead, County Durham prior to becoming organist of Carlisle Cathedral (1833-1841). Composed the anthem 'O clap your hands together', and secular vocal music.

INGRAM, Thomas (19th century)
Active as a musician in the 19th century. Organist of All Souls' Church, Langham Place, London, and secretary of the Motett Society. Composed the anthem 'Rend your hearts'.

INGRAM, Thomas Herbert (1873-1948)
Born in Wigan, Lancashire in 1873; died at Southport, Lancashire on 27 July 1948. Composer of hymn tunes.

IONS, Dr. Thomas (1817-1857)
Born, possibly in Newcastle-on-Tyne, on 19 August 1817; died in Gateshead on 25 September 1857.
A brother of **William Ions**.
Studied locally under Munro, Marr, **Richard Ingham** and Thomas Thompson, and later under Ignaz Moscheles. Graduated B.Mus. (1848) and D.Mus. (1854) at the University of Oxford.
Succeeded Richard Ingham as organist of St. Mary's Church, Gateshead (1833). The appointment was decided by a contest but

when the judges observed the youthful demeanour of the 16 year old Ions they insisted that he repeated the Bach fugue and Handel chorus that had been the test pieces. To their admiration he did so most competently.

He succeeded Thomas Thompson as organist of the church of St. Nicholas, Newcastle-on-Tyne on Thompson's death, retaining the position until 1857. A local choral society conductor. Established a glee club.

Chorus master and assistant conductor of the Newcastle Festival under **George Smart** (1842).

Editor of *Cantica Ecclesiastica* (1849), a volume of congregational music which included tunes and chants by himself. Composed Services in A, in C and in E-flat; anthems; motets; a setting of Psalm 137 'By the waters of Babylon' for Six Voices and Orchestra; a cantata *Prayer and Thanksgiving* for Eight-Part Chorus and Orchestra; and a Christmas Madrigal (1849). Also composed songs, part songs and piano music.

IONS, William Jamson (1833-1906)
Born in Newcastle-on-Tyne on 3 November 1833; died in Newcastle on 30 March 1906.
A brother of **Thomas Ions**.
A chorister, an articled pupil (from 1849) and assistant (from 1850) under his brother, Thomas, at the Church of St. Nicholas, Newcastle. Studied in Germany (1852 -1854), the subjects including the construction of large organs.

Succeeded Thomas Ions, on his death in 1857, as organist of St. Nicholas's Church. St. Nicholas's was elevated to cathedral status in 1882: William Ions continued as organist until his retirement, following the onset of deafness, in 1894. He specified the design of a new organ, which was opened in 1891.

William Ions worked with **J.B. Dykes** to compile and improve the liturgy and music of the diocesan choral festivals. Became life governor of the Northern Counties' Orphanage (1864) in recognition of his efforts in improving the music there.

Composed Services, anthems, and other forms of church music.

IRELAND, Dr. John Nicholson (1879-1962)
Born in Bowdon, Cheshire on 13 August 1879; died in Washington, Sussex on 12 June 1962.
Educated privately at Colwyn Bay and at Leeds Grammar School, where he remained until the age of 13. He had run away from boarding school at the age of seven.

Won a place at the Royal College of Music (1893) where he initially studied piano under **Frederick Cliffe** and later became a composition scholar (1897-1901) under **C.V. Stanford**, whose methods were rigorous and demanding but, as Ireland later acknowledged, of great benefit to him. Graduated B.Mus. (1908) at the University of Durham and later received the honorary D.Mus. (1932).

One of a number of contemporaries at the R.C.M. who struck up a friendship and met regularly at a tea shop in Kensington to discuss matters of musical interest. The group included **Ralph Vaughan Williams**, **Thomas Dunhill**, Evlyn Howard-Jones, Fritz Hart and **Gustav Holst**. Vaughan Williams remarked afterwards that he learned more about music from these discussions than from attending lessons. In order to help fund his studies, Ireland used to accompany singers at smoking concerts for 5s (£0.25) per appearance.

A professor of composition at the R.C.M. (1923- 1939). His pupils included Richard Arnell, **Benjamin Britten**, Alan Bush, **E.J. Moeran** and Humphrey Searle.

Held organ positions at various London churches. Assistant organist to **Walter Alcock** from the age of 17 at Holy Trinity, Sloane Street (1896-1902); organist of All Saints', Tufnell Park (1897-1899) and of the Chelsea Churches of St. Jude (1899-1904) and St. Luke (1904-1926). He had hoped to succeed Alcock at Holy Trinity when Alcock was appointed deputy organist of Westminster Abbey, but it was decided that he was too young, St. Jude's being considered a more suitable appointment for him.

In 1940, having retired to the island of Guernsey, he was - briefly - organist of the Church of St. Stephen, St. Peter Port but he was forced to flee the island almost immediately as the threat of Nazi occupation loomed large. He then settled in West Sussex.

Active as a composer for more than 50 years. A Sextet and the anthem 'Vexilla regis' (both 1898) marked the start of his compositional career while the carol 'Adam lay ybounden' (1956) was one of his last works. In between were some 90 songs, chamber music and Services in C and in F. The anthem 'Greater love hath no man' (1912) remains most popular today: in 1986 it was sung in more cathedrals and collegiate churches in the British Isles than any other anthem. Less well known is 'It is a thing most wonderful'.

Composed eight hymn tunes including 'Irene', 'Sampford' and 'Chelsea'. By far the most popular is 'Love Unknown', universally found with the poem by Samuel Crossman, 'My song is love unknown'. In a letter to the Daily Telegraph in April 1950 it was claimed that the latter tune was written in 15 minutes at the behest of **Geoffrey Shaw**.

IRONS, Herbert Stephen (1834-1905)
Born in Canterbury, Kent on 19 January 1834; died in Nottingham on 29 June 1905. His father was a lay vicar of Canterbury Cathedral, and he was a nephew of **George Elvey** and **Stephen Elvey.**
A chorister of Canterbury Cathedral (1844-1849) and a pupil of Stephen Elvey at the University of Oxford.
Precentor and master of the choristers of St. Columba's College, Rathfarnham, Ireland (1856-1857).
Organist of Southwell Minster (1857-1872).
Assistant organist of Chester Cathedral (from 1872) and organist of St. Andrew's Church, Nottingham (1876-1905).
Composed a Magnificat and Nunc Dimittis in B-flat (1888), settings of the Te Deum and Jubilate, and anthems including 'Praise the Lord, ye Servants' (1900). Composer of the hymn tunes 'Manifestation', 'St. Osmund', 'St. Columba' and 'Southwell', each of which was used in *Hymns Ancient and Modern*, and works for organ.

IRVINE, Jessie Seymour (1836-1887)
Born in Dunnottar, Kincardineshire, Scotland on 26 July 1836; died in Aberdeen on 2 September 1887.
The daughter of a church minister. The family moved to Peterhead and then to Crimond. According to her sister, Annie, Jessie wrote the melody known as 'Crimond' (1871) and sent it to William Carnie, editor of *The Northern Psalter* (1872), where it was credited to **David Grant** who had harmonised the tune. The tune continued to be attributed to Grant until 1911.

ISAAC, B. (17th century)
Composer of the anthem 'Come unto Me'.

ISAAC, Elias (1725-1793)
Born in Tormanton, Gloucestershire in 1725; died in Worcester on 14 July 1793. A pupil of **Maurice Greene**. A lay clerk of Gloucester Cathedral (from 1743). Organist of Worcester Cathedral (1747-1793). A number of his anthems including 'O Lord, grant the king' were in use at Durham Cathedral. Also composed a cantata *The Blackbirds*.

Isalaw
See **RICHARDS**, John.

ISHAM (Isum), John (1685-1726)
Born in 1685; died in London and was buried on 12 June 1726. Graduated B.Mus. (1713). Deputy to **William Croft** at St. Anne's Church, Soho, London; succeeded him as organist (1713). Held the position concurrently with the organistship of St. Andrew's Holborn (from April 1718). Later, he was organist of St. Margaret's Church, Westminster. Composed Services, anthems such as 'O sing unto the Lord', two of which were included in Croft's *Divine Harmony*, songs and catches.

ISHERWOOD, James Wright (1812-1854)
Born in Manchester on 2 March 1812; died in Manchester on 30 October 1854. Organist of St. Anne's Church, Manchester.
Composed the anthems 'As the hart desireth' and 'How long wilt Thou forget?', and glees.

IVE (Ives), Simon (1600-1662)
Born in 1600; baptised at Ware, Hertfordshire on 20 July 1600; died in London on 1 July 1662.
Lived at Earl's Colne, Essex around the year 1626. Some four or so years later he was a countertenor vicar choral of St. Paul's Cathedral. A London Wait (from 1637) and a minor prebendary of St. Paul's Cathedral (from 1661). Also said to have held an organistship in Newgate, London. It is known that he was an accomplished player of the viol and the theorbo, and a teacher of music.
With **William Lawes** he composed *The Triumph of Peace* (1633-1634) for the masque by James Shirley, a substantial work which, among other things, mocked the system of monopolies. Composed the anthem 'Almighty and everlasting God', the hymn 'Lift up your hearts' (1658), songs, rounds, catches including 'Come, honest friends', pavans and works for viol.

IVES, Grayston (b.1948)
Has composed a setting of the Jubilate, the anthems 'O be joyful in the Lord' (1975) and 'Let all the world in every corner sing' (1978), the latter to words by George Herbert, the hymn tune 'Gracious Spirit' - found in *Broadcast Praise* - and songs in folk tune idiom.

IVES, Joshua (1854-?)
Born in Hyde, Cheshire in 1854. Studied under **Frederick Bridge** and **E.T. Chipp**. Graduated Mus.B. at the University of Cambridge (1884). Organist of Anderton Parish Church, Glasgow, and lectured at the Athanaeum School of Music. In 1884 he emigrated to Adelaide, Australia as university professor of music and city organist. Lectured on music and wrote a text book on harmony. Composed church music and works for organ.

IVIMEY, Dr. John William (1868-1961)
Born in West Ham, London on 12 September 1868; died in Marlborough, Wiltshire on 16 April 1961.
Educated at Herne Bay College, Kent, and privately. Studied music with his parents, Ella and Joseph Ivimey, the latter being organist of St. Paul's Church, Stratford, London. A pupil of **Henry Gadsby**. Attended Guildhall School of Music as an exhibitioner (1886-1889). Graduated B.Mus. at the University of Oxford (1911). Later, an Oxford D.Mus.
Assistant music master of Wellington College, Berkshire (1888-1890) and of Harrow School (1890-1894). Director of music of Chelsea Polytechnic, London; Cheltenham College, Gloucestershire and Marlborough College, Wiltshire.
Musical director of the South West Polytechnic (1896-1902). Lecturer in music to the London County Council (from 1913). A member of the Royal Philharmonic Society. A freemason, and grand organist of the Grand Lodge.
Organist and choirmaster of the Church of St. Peter, Norbiton, Surrey from the age of 15 (1883-1890); also St. Paul's, Onslow Square, Kensington (1891-1906) and Dulwich College (1906-1910). Organist and director of music of All Souls' Church, Langham Place, London. Advised on the reconstruction of organs for Londonderry Cathedral and St. Paul's Church, Onslow Square.
Composed anthems, hymn tunes, comic operas including *Fairy Genesta*, and a Trio for Strings (1889).

J

JACKSON, Arthur Herbert (1852-1881)
Born in 1852; died in London on 27 September 1881. A student at the Royal Academy of Music (from 1872); returned to the R.A.M. in 1878 as a professor of harmony and composition. His compositions include a Magnificat for Chorus and Orchestra, two Masses, and sets of Responses to the Commandments in C and in F. Also composed works for piano (around 1880) and a number of songs, including 'Twas when the seas were roaring' (1882) to words by George Gay.

JACKSON, Dr. Francis Alan (b.1917)
Born in Malton, Yorkshire on 2 October 1917.
A chorister of York Minster (1929-1933) where he studied under **Edward Bairstow**, cathedral organist. Graduated B.Mus. (1937) and D.Mus. (1957) at the University of Durham; received the honorary D.Univ. (1983) at the University of York.
Appointed O.B.E. in 1978.
Organist of Malton Parish Church (1933-1940).
During World War II, he served with the 9th Lancers in Italy, Egypt and North Africa.
After being appointed assistant organist of York Minster in 1946, he succeeded Edward Bairstow as organist in the same year and held the position until his retirement in 1982.
A former president of the Royal College of Organists and of the Incorporated Association of Organists.
As well as being an organ recitalist, his practical knowledge of the instrument led to commissions as a design consultant.
A recent commission is the anthem 'I will extol Thee' for the Southern Cathedrals' Festival at Winchester. Among his existing 40 anthems are 'Blow ye the trumpet in Zion', 'Daughters of Zion', 'How bright these glorious spirits' and 'Remember for good, O Father'.
Has composed a number of Services, many of which were commissioned. These include a Te Deum and Jubilate in G (Leeds Festival, 1964) and a number of settings of the Magnificat and Nunc Dimittis: in D (Birmingham Cathedral), D Minor (ATB, for Guildford Cathedral and Caius College), in E-flat (Clayesmore School), another in E-flat (St. Bride's Church, Fleet Street, London), in F-sharp Minor (Hereford Cathedral), Fauxbourdon (St. Margaret's Church, Ilkley, Yorkshire). Also Composed a setting in G Minor and a complete service provision (Te Deum, Jubilate,

Benedicite, Holy Communion, Magnificat and Nunc Dimittis) in G.
There are five settings of the Holy Communion Services, including those written for Toronto Cathedral, Leeds Parish Church and Blackburn Cathedral. A Missa *Matris Dei* was written for Farm Street, London.
Sets of Responses were commissioned for the West Riding Cathedral Festival (1976) and for St. Bride's Church, Fleet Street (1984).
His 'East Acklam' (1957), named after the small village near Malton where he now lives, was written as a replacement tune for the hymn 'God that madest earth and heaven'. Subsequently, Fred Pratt Green wrote 'For the fruits of His creation' to fit the tune.
Collaborated with the actor and director John Stuart Anderson as librettist in writing the monodramas with music *Daniel in Babylon* (1962) for the festival celebrating the consecration of Coventry Cathedral and *A Time of Fire*, giving an account of the life and work of William Tyndale.
Has also composed a Symphony in D Minor (1957), in which year his very characteristic Toccata, Chorale and Fugue for organ appeared. For organ there are in total some 30 pieces including four sonatas. The organ also features in a Concerto with Strings and Percussion and a Recitative and Allegro with trombone.

JACKSON, Gabriel (b.1962)
Born in Bermuda in 1962.
A chorister of Canterbury Cathedral for three years. Studied composition at the Royal College of Music, firstly in the Junior Department with Richard Blackford, and later with John Lambert. As well as graduating B.Mus. (1983), he won the R.O. Morris Prize for Composition in 1981 and 1983.
Commissions have been received for works to be performed at a number of festivals including those of Belfast, Copenhagen and Norwich and by a number of artists including the Chamber Group of Scotland, Capella Nova and the New Danish Saxophone Quartet. His works reflect his involvement with the visual arts. Black and White Trio (1988-1989) is based on a work by the conceptual artist Richard Long, and a trilogy has recently been completed derived from works by the controversial Scottish artist Ian Hamilton Finlay. Compositions for the church include the anthems 'Ah, mine heart' (1987) and 'O nata lux' (1989-1990), first performed respectively

by the Choirs of Canterbury Cathedral and St. Paul's Cathedral. 'Tomorrow go ye forth' (1992), based on the words of the Vesper Respond for Advent Sunday, was commissioned by the Choir of Norwich Cathedral.

JACKSON, John (?-1688)

Died in Wells, Somerset in March 1688.

Organist and vicar choral of Wells Cathedral (1674-1688). From 1680 until at least 1681 he was also master of the choristers.

A number of chants in the library of the Royal College of Music are attributed to John Jackson, but may be the work of another. A Service in C, a Burial Service and a number of anthems by him were in regular use at one time at Wells Cathedral. It is also known that he was paid £2 by the Dean and Chapter (1681) for composing a Service.

There may or may not have been a contemporary church musician who was a namesake, for a John Jackson was master of the choristers of Ely Cathedral (1669-1670), and composer of the anthem 'The Lord said unto my Lord'.

JACKSON, Dr. John William (19th/20th century)

Graduated B.Mus. (1886) and D.Mus. (1891), the latter at Dublin. Organist and choirmaster of the Wesleyan Church, Macclesfield, Cheshire and of St. George's Church, Macclesfield. Conductor of local choral and philharmonic societies. His compositions include a setting of Psalm 77 'I will cry unto God with my voice', anthems and piano music.

JACKSON, Robert (1840-1914)

Born in Oldham, Lancashire in May 1840; died in Royton, Oldham on 12 July 1914.

Studied at the Royal Academy of Music.

Organist of the Church of St. Mark, North Audley Street, London (1866-1868), then succeeded his father as organist of St. Peter's Church, Oldham (1868-1914). Father (48 years) and son (46 years) together accumulated 94 years' service to St. Peter's Church.

Robert Jackson published *Choral Songs for School and Home* (1876) and *Hymns suitable for School Festivals* (1876). Composed a number of songs, a carol 'There came a little Child' (1894) to words by Emily Elliott, and hymn tunes including 'Niagara' (1887) and 'Trentham', both of which continue to be found in modern hymnals.

JACKSON, Thomas (c1715-1781)

Born around the year 1715, died in Newark, Nottinghamshire on 11 November 1781. Organist and master of the Song School of the Parish Church of St. Mary Magdalene, Newark (from 1768), where he succeeded **John Alcock** the younger. In 1780 he published a collection of 12 Psalm tunes and 18 Chants. One of these tunes, known as 'Byzantium' or 'Jackson', has appeared in many hymnals over the past three hundred years. In the Standard Edition (1916) of *Hymns Ancient and Modern* it is used with the hymn 'Behold Us Lord' by John Ellerton.

JACKSON, William (1730-1803)

'Jackson of Exeter' was born in Exeter, Devon on 29 May 1730; he died in Exeter on 5 July 1803.

Studied at Exeter under the Cathedral organist, John Silvester, and in London (1746-1748) under **John Travers**, organist of the Chapel Royal. Jackson was forced to return to Exeter prematurely owing to a shortage of funds.

On his return to Exeter he took up performing and teaching music until he became sub chanter, organist, lay vicar and master of the choristers of Exeter Cathedral (1777-1803) in succession to **Richard Langdon**.

With a number of friends, he founded a library in Exeter. He had a certain talent as a painter and in 1771, he was accorded an exhibition at the Royal Academy. His friends included Thomas Gainsborough and Joshua Reynolds. His literary works, which included prefaces and essays, brought about friendships with Oliver Goldsmith and the Sheridans.

William Jackson's published writings include *Observations on the Present State of Music in London* (1791). Contributed to *History of Music*, compiled and published in 1776 by **Charles Burney**.

An apparently unremarkable Te Deum has become famous. His other compositions include Services in C, in E, in E-flat and in F; anthems such as 'I beheld, and lo!' (1793) and 'O be joyful'; a musical drama based on the work *Lycidas* (1767) by John Milton; a comic opera *Lord of the Manor* (1780); odes; instrumental works and songs. His pupil James Peddon published a number of anthems and services by William Jackson in 1819.

JACKSON, William (1815-1866)

'Jackson of Masham' was born in Masham, Yorkshire on 9 January 1815; died in Bradford, Yorkshire on 15 April 1866. Unrelated to his namesake of Exeter. Father of the younger **William Jackson**.

His father was a miller, and William left school at the age of 13 to work in the mill and bakery.

There was a barrel organ in the West gallery of Masham Parish Church. While still young, William Jackson made a copy of it at home, a device which was able to play 10 tunes. He borrowed books on music, learned musical theory in his spare time, and gained knowledge on how to build and repair organs. Took music lessons in Ripon. Organist of Masham Parish Church (from 1832).

In business as a tallow chandler (1839-1852). Moved to Bradford (1852), where he sold music. Organist of St. John's Church (1852-1856) and of Horton Lane Independent Church (from 1856). Became a skilled choral conductor. Chorus master to the Bradford Musical Festivals of 1853, 1856 and 1859. Took a choir to Buckingham Palace to perform before Queen Victoria (1858).

While at Horton Lane, he was one of the compilers of *Congregational Psalmody*.

His earliest composition, an anthem, dates from 1839. Among his first compositions were 12 short anthems. There followed a Mass in E, a Canticle setting known as 'Jackson's' Te Deum and a version of Psalm 103 'Praise the Lord, O my soul' (1841), scored for Double Choir and Orchestra, for the Huddersfield Choral Society.

The hymn tune 'Evening Hymn', also known as 'Bradford', has been used in the hymnals *Methodist Hymn Book* (1933) and, in its Revised Edition (1927), *Church Hymnary*.

His other works include an oratorio *The Deliverance of Israel from Babylon* (1844), a glee 'Sisters of the Lea' (1840), which won a prize offered by the Huddersfield Glee Club in preference to entries by **William Horsley** and **Samuel Webbe** the younger. Also composed items for military band, and songs.

JACKSON, William (1853-1877)

Born in Bradford, Yorkshire in 1853; died in Ripon, Yorkshire on 10 September 1877. The son of **William Jackson** of Masham, from whom he learned music. Organist of Morningside Parish Church, Edinburgh. Composed the anthem 'O give thanks', and part songs.

JACOB, Benjamin (1778-1829)

Born in London on 15 May 1778; died in London on 24 August 1829.

Learned basic musical theory from his father. At the age of seven (1786) he took singing lessons from Robert Willoughby and joined the choir of the Portland Chapel, London. A chorister at the Handel Commemoration of 1791. Studied harpsichord and organ with **William Shrubsole**, organist of the Spa Fields Chapel and Matthew Cooke, organist of St. George's Church Bloomsbury. Later, learned harmony from **Samuel Arnold**.

Organist of a number of churches in London, beginning with the Salem Chapel, Soho at the age of 10 (from 1788). Organist of the Carlisle Chapel, Kennington Lane (from 1790) and in the same year, Bentinck Chapel, Lisson Grove (1790-1794). His last two organistships were at the Surrey Chapel (1794-1825), where he succeeded John Immyns, and St. John's, Waterloo Road (from 1823).

Conducted the Lenten oratorios at the Covent Garden Theatre (1818).

Gave a number of recitals in London, both solo and with other eminent recitalists such as **William Crotch**, Johann Salomon and **Samuel Wesley**. The works of J.S. Bach featured prominently.

In 1815 he published a collection of harmonised hymn tunes and Canticle Chants entitled *National Psalmody* and containing 12 items of his own. It was republished three times in the next 40 years. His hymn tune 'Halstead' was used in the Standard Edition (1916) of *Hymns Ancient and Modern* with the hymn 'Come, Holy Spirit come' by Joseph Hart. Also composed glees and incidental music for the play *Macbeth*.

JACOB, Dr. Gordon Percival Septimus (1895-1984)

Born in Norwood, London on 5 July 1895; died in Saffron Walden, Essex on 8 June 1984.

Educated at Dulwich College, London and, soon after the end of World War I, at the Royal College of Music under **C.V. Stanford**, **Herbert Howells** and **Ralph Vaughan Williams**. A D.Mus. graduate. During World War I he was taken prisoner while serving with the armed forces (from 1914).

Appointed C.B.E. in 1968.

Taught theory and composition in London at Birkbeck College, Morley College and the R.C.M. (1924-1967), where his pupils included Malcolm Arnold, Imogen Holst and **Antony Hopkins**. An examiner to the Universities of Oxford, Cambridge, London, and Wales, and to the Associated Board of the Royal Schools of Music. Known as an expert on orchestration, he wrote a textbook on scoring and transcription. From 1948 onwards he edited scores for the publishing house of Penguin.

Composed two symphonies, organ pieces, works for wind instruments, and film scores. His church compositions include the anthem 'To my humble supplication' and a setting of Sidney Gray's carol 'The Babe so sweet' (1952).

JACOB, William (1777-1845)

Born near Carmarthen, Wales in 1777; died, possibly in Holywell, Wales on 27 October 1845. Lived in Manchester until around 1818, when he moved to Holywell, where he was a singer and precentor of the Wesleyan Chapel. In 1844 he published *Eos Cymru*, a collection of hymn tunes, chants and anthems. The publication included four hymn tunes and one anthem composed by him.

JACOBS, William (1796-1872)

Born in Eton, Berkshire in 1796; died in Oxford on 20 December 1872. Composer of a Benedicite in Chant form (1866) and hymn tunes.

JACQUES, Dr. Thomas Reginald (1894-1969)

Born in Ashby de la Zouche, Leicestershire on 13 January 1894; died in Stowmarket, Suffolk on 2 June 1969.

Attended Ashby Grammar School and Queen's College, Oxford, where he graduated B.Mus. and M.A. Also awarded the Lambeth D.Mus.

Appointed C.B.E. in 1954.

Served in the 2nd Battalion of the West Yorkshire Regiment in France and in Flanders during World War I. Wounded and returned to England, never being fully restored to health. During his recuperation he met **H.P. Allen** at Oxford, who encouraged him to study music at Queen's College.

Conductor of the National Youth Orchestra of Great Britain (from 1948) and of the Edinburgh Festival (from 1947).

Adviser to the publishers Novello and Company.

Organist at the church of SS Philip and James, Oxford (1918-1922). Organist and director of music of Queen's College, Oxford (1926-1936); director of music at the University of Reading, Berkshire (1937-1938); music adviser to the London County Council (1936-1942) and a professor of the Royal College of Music (from 1937). He was the first director of C.E.M.A. (1940-1945), which is now the Arts Council of Great Britain.

A choral and orchestral conductor. As well as taking charge of the London-based Bach Choir (1937-1961), he conducted each of the main British orchestras at some time. Founded and conducted The Jacques Orchestra. Retired from conducting in 1961. As an adjudicator, the tactful delivery of his assessments was well received by the competitors.

His textbook *Voice Training and Conducting in Schools* (1934) was followed by the first (1961) of a number of book of *Carols for Choirs*, produced in collaboration with **David Willcocks.**

Composed songs, carols and a setting of the processional hymn 'Christ Is The Foundation' (1906) by John Monsell.

JACQUET, Richard H. (b.1947)

Born in Staines, Middlesex in 1947. Composer of hymn tunes.

JAGGER, Dr. Ernest (19th/20th century)

Graduated B.Mus. at the University of Durham (1897). Held a number of musical appointments in and around the town of Pontefract, Yorkshire. Organist of the Church of St. John the Evangelist, Wentbridge (from 1888); organist and choirmaster of Ackworth Parish Church; and of All Saints' Church, Ackworth (from 1896) and music master of King's School, Pontefract. Composed a setting of Psalm 46 'God is our Hope and Strength'.

JAMES, David John (1743-1841)

A Welsh composer. The compilation *Caniadau y Cyssegr* (Hymns of the Sanctuary) issued in 1839 by **John Roberts** contains David James's hymn tunes by 'Dorcas' and 'Priscilla'.

JAMES, Frederic (1858-1922)

Born in Masborough, near Rotherham, Yorkshire in 1858; died in Bradford, Yorkshire on 18 January 1922.

Attended Westminster Teacher Training College (from 1877), where he was organist. Even earlier, from the age of 11, he had served as deputy to his father, organist of the Wesleyan Chapel in Masborough. Taught at the Ellesmere Wesleyan School, Sheffield (1878-1884) and at Woodhouse Grove School, Bradford (1884-1912).

The hymn tune 'Noricum' has remained popular, particularly with Baptist and Methodist congregations. Also composed a work which he described as a 'hymn anthem' to the well known 'Abide with me' by H.F. Lyte. His other works include *Three Evening Hymns set to Music* (1891), a part song, choral cantatas and works for piano and for organ.

JAMES, George Eric (1894-?)
Born in Apperley Bridge, Yorkshire, in 1894. Music master of Woodhouse Grove School, Bradford. Composed an anthem, published in 1936 to words by Charles Wesley 'Glory be to God on high'.

JAMIESON, Augustus Grant (1844-1888)
Born in Edinburgh on 20 December 1844; died in Edinburgh in 1888. Studied music under J.C. Kieser, **J.T. Surenne** and John Donaldson. Later studied in Stuttgart, Germany. Organist of St. Paul's Episcopal Church, Edinburgh (1872-1888). A local orchestral society conductor. His hymn tunes include 'Brierley' and 'St. Sulpice'. Also composed piano music.

JAMONEAU, Arthur James (1865-1927)
Born in Guernsey, Channel Isles in 1865; died in Yorkshire on 7 December 1927. Composer of a Magnificat and Nunc Dimittis in E-flat (1905), the anthems 'I will lift up mine eyes' (1899) and 'Blessed be the Lord' (1917), the festival anthem 'Awake! Awake! Put on thy strength' (1922) and hymn tunes. Also composed the sacred cantata *The Cross of Life* (1905) and the festival hymn 'Give praise' (1921).

JANES, Robert (1806-1866)
Born on 3 February 1806; died in Ely, Suffolk on 10 June 1866. Educated at Dulwich College, London, where he was a 'Sol-fa scholar' (chorister). An articled pupil of **Zechariah Buck**, organist of Norwich Cathedral. Organist of Ely Cathedral (1830-1866). An amateur printer, he was able to typeset and print music for use at Ely on his own press. Built up a thriving and lucrative teaching practice in the counties of Norfolk and Suffolk. A Psalter editor. Said to have composed the 'Ely Confession' (1864) as well as other items of church music. Also composed songs.

JARMAN, Robert Francis (1874-?)
Born in Stockton-on-Tees, County Durham in 1874.
Educated privately in music. Graduated B.Mus. at the University of Durham (1909).
A lecturer at Sunderland Training College.
Held a number of musical positions at churches in the North East of England. Organist of St. Stephen's, Ayres Quay, Sunderland (1890-1894) and St. Peter's, Bishopwearmouth (1897-1904). Organist and choirmaster of St. Peter's, Monkwearmouth (1904-1918). Organist of St. Gabriel's Church, Bishopwearmouth (1918-1919) and St. George's Presbyterian Church, Sunderland (from 1919). Teacher of music at Sunderland Bede Collegiate School.

Composed a vocal quartet 'The Lord is gracious' and, as his degree exercise, the anthem 'Sing unto the Lord'. Composed other anthems.

JARMAN, Thomas (1782-1861)
Born in Clipston, Northamptonshire in 1782; died in Clipston in January 1861.
Joined the choir of his local Baptist chapel, of which he later became choirmaster. Thomas Jarman, like his father, was a tailor. A teacher of singing and harmony, and a choir trainer and organiser. It was largely through his efforts that the successful village choir festival at Naseby of 1837 took place.
He is associated mainly with his native village of Clipston, although he spent some six or seven years at Leamington Spa, Warwickshire, where he became acquainted with C. Rider, a wealthy Methodist church musician.
Published *Sacred Music* (c1800), a set of books of church music.
Composed a number of Services, including a Magnificat for Dr. Marsh's Episcopal Chapel, Leamington and anthems, some of which were for special occasions. They include 'An anthem for Christmas Day' (1812) and 'Enrobed in light the Holy One' (1869). Of 600 or so hymn tunes, the best remembered is 'Lyngham', which is known within *Salvation Army Tune Book* as 'Nativity'. It was initially used with the hymn 'O for a thousand tongues to sing' by Charles Wesley. His other tunes include 'Fuguing tune', which is the only tune currently in use.

JARVIS, Samuel (?-c1785)
Blind for at least part of his life. Took organ lessons with **John Worgan**. Organist of the Foundling Hospital, London and of the Church of St. Sepulchre. His pupils included **William Russell**. Composed the hymn tune 'Montgomery', songs and an ode in honour of The Albion's Society (1780).

JEATER, William (1858-1919)
Born in Reigate, Surrey in 1858; died in Wandsworth, London on 16 February 1919. Composer of hymn tunes.

JEBOULT, Harold Arthur (1871-1925)
Born in Taunton, Somerset in 1871; died in Taunton on 16 July 1925. A pupil of **Albert Ham**. Organist and choirmaster of the Churches of Holy Trinity (1889-1897) and St. Mary Magdalene (1897-1925), Taunton. His book *Somerset Composers, Musicians and Music* was one in a series of works by a number of authors about various aspects of that area. A local examiner for the Royal College of Music. Composed a setting of the Benedicite, a Quadruple Chant (1903) and the anthem 'Come unto Me ye weary' (1907) for Men's Voices to words by William Chatterton Dix, songs and organ works. The hymn tune 'St. Mary Magdalene' was used in the Revised Edition (1927) of *Church Hymnary*.

JEFFERSON, George Leonard (1887-1955)
Born in Sheffield, Yorkshire in 1887; died in Whitby, Yorkshire on 21 January 1955. Composer of hymn tunes.

JEFFERSON, William Arthur (1854-1929)
Born in Leeds, Yorkshire in 1854; died in Leeds on 4 March 1929. An organist. Published *The National Book of Hymn Tunes, Chants and Kyries* (1885) and composed hymn tunes.

JEFFREYS (Jeffries), George (c1610-1685)
Born, possibly in Worcestershire, around the year 1610; died in Weldon, Northamptonshire on 12 July 1685. He may have been the son of **Matthew Jeffreys**. Joint organist with **John Wilson** of the court of Charles I at Oxford. Part of that time was spent in Italy. During the Civil War, Jeffreys was organist to Charles I at Oxford. Lived in Little Weldon, Northamptonshire (from 1648). Steward to Sir Christopher Hatton at Kirkby.
Through the advocacy of **Peter Aston**, Jeffreys has achieved recognition in modern times. Composed string fantasias and music for plays, but most of his compositional work was for the church. Composed Morning and Evening Services, a Jubilate in C, a Gloria, a set of Responses to the Commandments, some 60 Latin motets, and 35 English anthems. The latter include 'How wretched is the state', 'The Lord, in thy adversity' (based on the words of Psalm 20) and 'Turn Thee, again' (1648).

JEFFREYS (Jeffries), Matthew (16th/17th century)
May have been the father of **George Jeffreys**. Graduated B.Mus. at the University of Oxford (1593). A vicar choral of Wells Cathedral. Those compositions that have come to light were for the church. They include three services, seven full anthems and five verse anthems, all in either five or six parts. 'Rejoice in the Lord' is perhaps the best known, and his others include 'My soul shall be alway'.

JEFFRIES, John (c1718-1798)
Born at Llanynys, Denbighshire, Wales around 1718; died in 1798. A contemporary of John Williams (Ioan Rhagfyr) who was probably influential upon him. Lived in Denbighshire at Llanynys and Ruthin. The hymn tunes 'Dyfrdwy' and 'Llangoedmor' are attributed to him. The latter has been used by a number of English compilations including *English Hymnal* and *Songs of Praise*. 'Hero' and 'Traethdon' (a chant) were included in the publication *Y Cerddor Cymrieg* (The Welsh Musician).

JEFFRIES, John Edward (1863-1918)
Born in Walsall, Staffordshire on 18 October 1863; died in Walsall on 11 May 1918.
A chorister of the Church of St. Paul, Walsall where his father was organist. Studied at the Royal College of Music under **George Martin** for organ, **Frederick Bridge** for counterpoint, **F.E. Gladstone** for harmony and Franklin Taylor for piano.
Having been assistant organist at St. Paul's, Walsall, from the age of 17, he became organist of the Parish Church, and, later, choirmaster. Conductor and choral inspector for the Lichfield Diocesan Festivals of that time. Conductor of local philharmonic and amateur vocal societies.
Organist and choirmaster of Newcastle Cathedral. (1895-1918)
Composed church music including a Communion Service in A-flat (1892) and a Magnificat and Nunc Dimittis in E-flat (1900). There is also an oratorio *The Life and Death of Christ*.

JEKYLL, Charles Sherwood (1842-1914)
Born in Westminster, London on 29 November 1842; died in Camberwell, London on 7 November 1914.
A chorister of Westminster Abbey, later studying under **James Coward** and **George Macfarren**.
Organist in London of the temporary Church of St. Paul, Kensington (from 1857); assistant organist of Westminster Abbey

(1860-1875); organist of Acton Parish Church (1860-1861) and St. George's Church, Hanover Square (1861-1877).
Organist and composer to the Chapel Royal, St. James's Palace (1876-1891).
Composed services, including a Magnificat and Nunc Dimittis in C (1901). Other music for the church includes the Jubilee anthem 'Go forth, ye daughters of Zion' (1887) and the anthem 'Blessed is he that considereth the poor and needy' (1878).
His hymn tune 'Stoneleigh' was used with the hymn 'Through the day Thy love hast spared us' by Thomas Kelly in the compilation *Church Hymns* (1874) by **Arthur Sullivan**. 'St. Omer' was used in the Standard Edition (1916) of *Hymns Ancient and Modern*. His works include songs, part songs and pieces for organ, including a march for the wedding of Princess Louise of Wales (1889).

JENKINS, David (1848-1915)
Born at Trecastell, Brecknock, Wales on 31 December 1848; died in Aberystwyth, Wales on 10 December 1915.
Following the premature death of his father he was apprenticed to a tailor and, like many of his local contemporaries, learned music through the Tonic Sol-fa method. Later studied music at the University College of Wales, Aberystwyth (from 1874) with **Joseph Parry**. Graduated Mus.B. at St. John's College, Cambridge (1878).
Taught at University College, Aberystwyth. In 1893 the College became incorporated in the University of Wales. David Jenkins was appointed as an instructor (from 1892), later becoming a lecturer (1899) and professor and head of the Music Department (1910-1915). An examiner for the Tonic Sol-fa College and the Royal College of Music.
Precentor of the English Presbyterian Church, Aberystwyth. Conductor at music festivals; adjudicator at *eisteddfodau* including the national eisteddfod. Joint editor of the monthly *Y Cerddor* (The Musician) with **David Emlyn Evans**.
Composed extensively for the church. His work includes anthems and hymn tunes of which examples are 'Penlan', widely used in English publications, 'Builth', 'Gnoll Avenue' and 'Bod Alwyn'. *Gemau Mawl* was a set of his hymn tunes. *The Psalm of Life* was composed for the Cardiff Festival of 1895, following which it was performed by a choir of some 2,000 voices at the Crystal Palace. Also composed oratorios including *David and Saul*, songs, part songs, works for male voice choirs, glees, cantatas, an opera *The Enchanted Island*.

JENKINS, John (1592-1678)
Born in Maidstone, Kent in 1592; died in Kimberley, Norfolk on 27 October 1678. His career was spent in service at court during the reign of Charles I and Charles II. During the interregnum and continuing into the reign of Charles II he served a number of wealthy families in the county of Norfolk as a teacher of music. In February 1634, John Jenkins was one of those taking part in the masque *The Triumph of Peace*. Later became one of Charles I's viol players. A court musician (1660-1678), being formally appointed musician in ordinary to Charles II in 1662. Composed some 800 instrumental works, many of which were fancies for viol. Also songs. His music for the church includes a number of anthems which include 'Turn me, O Lord'.

JENKINS, Thomas Llewellyn (19th/20th century)
Born in Rhydyfelin, Glamorgan, Wales. Studied with **Thomas Edwards**, Ap Tafonwy Mills, G.G. Beale, **Caradog Roberts** and

John Owen Jones. Organist of Moriah Welsh Congregational Church, Cilfynydd (1908-1924; Saron, Ynyshir, Rhondda (1924-1932); St. Peter's Church, Lampeter (1922-1926) and the Aberystwyth Tabernacle (from 1936). A choral conductor and eisteddfod adjudicator. One of the founders of the Three Valleys Festival. Music organiser to the National Council of Music (1929-1930). Composed hymn tunes for Welsh Congregational hymnals.

JENNER, Revd. Dr. Henry Lascelles (1820-1898)
Born in Chislehurst, Kent on 6 June 1820; died in Preston-next-Wingham, Kent on 18 September 1898.
Educated at Harrow School and Trinity Hall, Cambridge where he graduated LL.B. (1841) and D.D. (1867). Ordained deacon in 1843, priest in 1844. At Cambridge he was in the cricket XI of 1840.
Curate of Chevening, Kent (1843-1846); the Cornwall parishes of St. Columb (1846-1849) and Antony (1849-1851); Leigh, Essex and Brasted, Kent (1852). A minor canon of Canterbury Cathedral (1852-1854) before becoming vicar of Preston (1854). He retained this position until 1898 and it was apparently held open for him during his time in New Zealand as Bishop of Dunedin (1866-1871) and as Bishop of the Église Catholique in Gallicane, Paris (1882-1893).
He found among his fellow-students at Cambridge a number who shared his views on the importance of congregational singing, ancient hymnology and plainsong, and who as a group acted to revive these.
Jenner composed a carol for Ascension Day 'The birds are singing' (1873). Of his hymn tunes, 'Quam dilecta' is found in *Church Hymns* (1874) and other hymnals, while 'Preston', 'Unitas' and 'Jenner' are found in *Hymns Ancient and Modern*.

JENNER, Henry (1848-1934)
Born in Sevenoaks, Kent in 1848; died in Bospowes, Cornwall on 8 May 1934. Composer of hymn tunes.

JENNISON (?18th century)
Lived in Malton, Yorkshire. Composed the hymn tune 'Daisy Hill'.

JESSON, Dr. Roy Hart (1926-1972)
Born in Friern Barnet, Hertfordshire on 5 February 1926; died in Haringey, London on 8 October 1972.
A chorister locally, he was educated at Queen Elizabeth School, Barnet and at the Royal College of Music (1942-1944). Served in the army (1944-1947) before resuming his studies at Christ Church, Oxford (1947-1950), where he graduated B.Mus. and M.A. From 1950 he studied at the University of Indiana, U.S.A. and graduated M.A. and Ph.D.
Roy Jesson began a teaching career in the U.S.A. An instructor at the North Illinois State College (1952-1953) before becoming associate professor of music at Longwood College, Virginia (1953-1955) and at the University of Richmond, Virginia (1956-1961). A professor of the Royal Academy of Music (from 1961). Associated with Glyndebourne Opera, Sussex (1965-1967).
His hymn tune 'Barnet', composed in or around 1942, was written for a competition and it was subsequently used in the Revised Edition (1950) of *Hymns Ancient and Modern*. The carol 'A virgin most pure' was published in 1963. Composed a song 'The hag' (1942).

JEWETT (**Juet**), Revd. Randolph (Randal) (c1603-1675)
Born, probably in Chester, around the year 1603; died in Winchester, Hampshire on 3 July 1675. His father was mayor of Winchester in 1578.
A chorister of Chester Cathedral. May have studied subsequently with **Orlando Gibbons.** Graduated B.Mus. at Trinity College, Dublin, which may have been awarded honorarily. In or around 1638 he was ordained deacon.
From 1631 or earlier Jewett was organist of both Dublin Cathedrals, Christ Church and St. Patrick's A vicar choral at Christ Church (from 1638) and St. Patrick's (from 1639). In 1639 he was dismissed following a number of offences including rudeness to the Archbishop of Dublin. Jewett appealed successfully for reinstatement at St. Patrick's. **Benjamin Rogers** succeeded him at Christ Church.
Organist of Chester Cathedral, (164-1644) at the time of the Siege of Chester.
It is believed that he was organist for a second time of the Dublin Cathedrals, St. Patrick's (from 1644) and Christ Church (from 1646). It is reasonably certain that he was a vicar choral at both Cathedrals at this time. He returned to London not later than 1649.
During the interregnum his organistship at St. Patrick's had been held open for him and at the Restoration he was expected to return to Dublin from London, where he had become a minor canon of St. Paul's Cathedral at some time before 1649. He failed to return and he was replaced by John Hawkshaw, who deputised during his absence.
In fact Jewett had become almoner (1660) and minor canon (1661) of St. Paul's Cathedral. He was later organist and master of the choristers of Winchester Cathedral (1666-1675).
Composed an Evening Service in the short form, and six verse anthems including 'Bow down thine ear, O Lord' and 'I heard a voice from Heaven'.

JEWSON, James Pentland (1825-1889)
Born in Scarborough, Yorkshire in 1825; died in Coatham, Yorkshire on 24 June 1889. An organist in the town of Sedgefield and then, for 30 years, organist of the Parish Church, Stockton-on-Tees. A teacher of music, and a music and orchestral society conductor. Composed hymn tunes including 'Tudor', which appeared in *Bristol Tune Book* (1876).

JOHNSON, Edward (16th/17th century)
Graduated Mus.B. (1594) at Gonville and Caius College, Cambridge. In 1572 he was known to be working for the Kitson family in Suffolk. He remained there until at least 1575. His compositions were admired by **Thomas Morley** and **William Byrd**. Three Psalm settings of 1592 were included in the edition *A Whole Booke of Psalmes* by Thomas East. Also composed songs and a madrigal for six voices 'Come, blessed bird' (1601).

JOHNSON, John Barham (1890-?)
Born in Welbourne, Norfolk in 1890.
Educated at the choir school of St. George's Chapel, Windsor Castle, and at Selwyn College, Cambridge.
Assistant music master of Uppingham School (from 1913), and director of music of the Nevill Holt School (1920) and of Oakham School (from 1923). A teacher of piano at Leicester School of Music. Director of music, organist and choirmaster of Shrewsbury School (from 1933).

Organist of Oakham Parish Church, and a local choral society conductor.

Composed hymn tunes for *Fellowship Hymn Book*, and anthems including 'The way, the truth, the life'.

JOHNSON, Norman Frederick Byng (20th century)

Graduated B.Mus. at the University of Durham. Assistant music master of Denstone College, Staffordshire and director of music of Ellesmere College, Shropshire. Composed anthems, and a Melody in D-flat for Organ and Strings.

JOHNSON, Robert (c1500-c1560)

Born in Duns, Scotland around the year 1500; died around 1560.

He may have been a priest and it is sometimes claimed that he was chaplain to Anne Boleyn. Fled to England when accused of heresy and he may have lived in York for some time around 1530. After returning temporarily to Scotland he settled in England from around 1535.

Composed Services, a votive antiphon *Ave Dei patris filia* for five voices, and motets including *Benedicam Domino*, based on the words of Psalm 34. The anthem 'O eternal God almighty', dating from before 1550, was one of the first to be written to an English text. Also composed songs, part songs and works for virginal.

Contributed two items to the collection *Certaine Notes* by **John Day**, including the anthem 'I give you a new Commandment'.

JOHNSON, Robert (c1583-1633)

Born, probably in London, around the year 1583; died in London shortly before 26 November 1633.

Indentured to the Lord Chamberlain, Sir George Carney (from 1596), with whom he studied music and who introduced him to a number of people in the theatrical world, for a period of seven years.

A court lutenist and musician (1604-1633) to James I, Prince Henry and Charles I. Succeeded **Thomas Lupo** the elder as composer for lute and voices from Lupo's death until his own.

His church music includes the anthem for five voices 'Save me, O Lord' (1614). Other anthems include 'This is my Commandment'. From 1607 onwards, Robert Johnson composed songs for London theatrical productions including *Cymbeline* (c1609). Composed some 20 pieces for lute, and consort songs.

JOHNSON, Robert Sherlaw.
See **SHERLAW JOHNSON**, Robert.

JOHNSON, William (1853-1928)

Born in Warrington, Cheshire on 23 September 1853; died in Altrincham, Cheshire on 19 March 1928. Studied piano under T. Standish, organ with **Thomas Pattison** and harmony with **Horton Allison**. Organist at the age of 15 of St. Anne's Church, Warrington (from 1868). It is likely but not certain that he is the W. Johnson who was appointed organist of St. George's Church, Altrincham in 1903. A local musical society produced his cantata *Ecce Homo*. Also composed a number of anthems.

JOHNSON, William George Bernard (1868-1935)

Born in Norfolk on 1 December 1868; died in Horning, Norfolk on 16 May 1935.

Graduated B.A. (1889) and Mus.B. (1897) at Selwyn College, Cambridge.

Organist, choirmaster and music master of Framlingham College, Suffolk (1888-1891), following which he was appointed assistant master, organist and choirmaster of Leeds Grammar School (1891-1905). He lectured on music in Leeds at the Day Training College and at Yorkshire College.

Moving to Bridlington, East Yorkshire in 1905, he became organist of the Priory Church and music master of the Grammar School.. Organist and director of music at the Albert Hall, Nottingham (from 1910).

His anthem 'Christ is risen' was published in 1908. In addition he composed a Magnificat and Nunc Dimittis (1913), a Service in A for Mixed Voices (1921), hymn tunes, songs, and works for piano and for organ.

JOHNSTON, Agnes (19th/20th century)

Attended the University of Edinburgh (1893-1899); graduated B.Mus. in 1899. Composed an anthem 'Grant us such grace'.

JOLLEY, Dr. Charles Edward (1860-1949)

Born in Higham Ferrers, Northamptonshire in 1860; died in 1949. Graduated B.Mus. (1888) and D.Mus. (1889) at New College, Oxford. Organist of Holy Trinity Church, Twickenham, Middlesex (1886-1892) and St. George's, Hanover Square, London (1892-1947). A teacher of music at Richmond County School, Surrey (from 1900) and at the Strand School (from 1913). A local choral and philharmonic society conductor. Retired in 1947. Composed a Missa Solemnis.

JOLLY, John (1794-1838)

Born in Knutsford, Cheshire in 1794; died in London in April 1838. Organist of St. Philip's Chapel, London. Published various collections, including *Devotional Music for the use of Families and Schools* (c1835). Also composed glees and songs.

JONES, Cadwaladr (1794-1883)

Born in Talgruffydd, near Castell Prysor, Trawsfynydd, Merioneth, Wales in 1794; died in Brynrwy, Trawsfynydd, Wales on 3 January 1883. Walked regularly from Trarwsfynydd to Bangor for music lessons with **Joseph Pring**, organist of Bangor Cathedral. A stonemason by trade and, for 50 years, precentor at Trawsfynydd Church, where he ran a choir and held classes in music. When his singing voice began to fail he used a violin to lead the congregation in singing. Towards the end of his life he was blind. Composed anthems and hymn tunes.

JONES, Dafydd (1743-1831)

Born in Llandanwg, Merionethshire, Wales in 1743 and baptised on 5 May; died, possibly in Ponrhyndendraeth, Wales on 30 March 1831. As well as running a school at Beddgelert he was a bookbinder, musician and poet. His works in the latter sphere are said to show a transition form the style prevalent at the end of the 18th century to that of the early 19th. He was in charge of the singing at Llanfrothen Church until he left to join the Calvinistic Methodists, and was given a similar responsibility at Ponrhyndendraeth Chapel. He wrote elegies on the death of his two wives. Author of many carols and hymns, seven of which are preserved in manuscript in the National Library of Wales. His hymn tunes 'Iago' and 'Digonolrwydd' were published in *Caiadau y Cysegr*. He may also have composed the hymn tune 'Priscilla'.

JONES, Dr. Daniel C. (1857-?)
Born in Tamworth, Staffordshire on 20 November 1857. Educated at Lichfield Cathedral under **Thomas Bedsmore**. Graduated B.Mus. (1887) and D.Mus. (1894) at Trinity College, Toronto, Canada. Organist and choirmaster of Londonderry Cathedral, Ireland (1878-1911). Composed anthems and other items of church music. One of his works is the anthem 'Thus saith the Lord concerning the king of Assyria', written for the service in Londonderry Cathedral on 18 December 1888 to commemorate the bicentenary of the closing of the city gates of Londonderry by the apprentice boys.

JONES, Edward (1749-1779)
Born near Criccieth, Caernarvonshire, Wales in 1749; died probably in Lland-Wrog, Wales in 1779. A number of anthems and hymn tunes composed by him remain in manuscript. However his anthem 'Arglwydd, Chwiliaist ac adnabuost fi' was very popular and was later arranged by William Owen (Tremadoc) and **John Roberts** (Ieuan Gwyllt).

JONES (Stephen), Revd. Edward (Tanymarian: 1822-1885)
Born in Maentwrog, Merionethshire, Wales, where he was baptised on 15 December 1822; died in Llanllechid, Wales on 10 May 1885. He was born Edward Jones but while at college used his grandfather's surname, Stephen, instead of his own in order to distinguish between himself and a namesake among the students. Better known as 'Tanymarian'.
Both his parents were singers and his father was a harp player.
Apprenticed to a tailor, he attended the Congregational College, Bala (from 1843) and studied theology and music. Preached at the Saron Congregational Chapel, Ffestiniog from the age of 18. Ordained in 1847.
Minister of Horeb Chapel, Dywgyfylchi, North Wales (from 1847). Held the post for 10 years, during which time he became known throughout the principality not only for his preaching but also for his musical and teaching ability. Minister of the Welsh Independent Church, Dwygfylchi (from 1856) and, later that year, of churches of Bethlehem and Carmel, Llanllechid, near Bangor. Moved into a house named Tanymarian. Supported the presence of choirs in Welsh chapels, in the face of opposition from those who believed that any singing during worship should be strictly congregational.
Editor of *Cerddor y Cysegr* - Musician of the Sanctuary - (from 1859), a collection of hymns and tunes published together rather than as separate volumes for the first time. Some of the tunes were harmonised by him, in a manner that sought to achieve effective part writing, but none of his own original tunes were included in the collection.
Editor with **Joseph Jones** of the first edition (1869) of *Llyfr Tonau ac Emynau* (The Book of Tunes and Hymns). Sole editor of the second edition (1879). The first book contained two hymn tunes by him; the second, nine plus some well-received arrangements of some earlier Welsh tunes.
His oratorio *Y Storm Tiberias* (The Storm on the Sea of Tiberias) of May 1852 was the first such to be written by a Welshman. Its choruses were often used as test pieces at subsequent *eisteddfodau*. Also composed anthems; hymn tunes including 'Gwalchmai', used extensively in English hymnals with the hymn 'King of glory, King of peace' by George Herbert, 'Tanymarian' and 'Glan Dwyryd'; glees, songs and part songs.

JONES, George Edward (b.1911)
Born in Forest Gate, London on 6 June 1911. Composer of hymn tunes.

JONES, Griffith Hugh (Gutyn Arfon: 1849-1919)
Born in Llanberis, Caernarvonshire, Wales in January 1849; died in Rhiwddolion, Caernarvonshire on 26 July 1919.
His father was precentor of Capel Goch, Llanberis for 60 years. The minister there was **John Roberts** (Ieuan Gwyllt), who was quick to recognise and develop Griffith Jones's musical ability. At the age of 14 he became assistant to his father.
A pupil-teacher of Dolbadarn School. Assistant master at the British School, Aberystwyth. At the age of 20 he became a teacher at the Rhiwddolion Elementary School (from 1869), where he remained for 50 years.
A poet, musician and conductor, travelling extensively within the district from event to event. Founded music classes in Capel Curig, Betws-y-Coed (where he also set up a music society), Penmachno, Ysbyty Ifan, Capel Garmon and Dolwyddelan.
Taught music by means of the Tonic Sol-fa method. Trained choirs and conducted brass bands and festivals of singing. Adjudicated at *eisteddfodau*.
By installing an organ at Rhiwddolion, he was probably the first person to introduce a musical instrument into the worship of a North Wales chapel.
Composed anthems, and the hymn tunes 'Dagrau Lesu' (published in 1923) and 'Llef' (A cry), used in a number of English publications including *Methodist Hymn Book* (1933). The tune was a memorial to his late brother, David H. Jones (Dewi Arfon), whose poems he collected and published. Also arranged operettas for school children.
The anthem 'Pwy a'n gwahana ni?' (1892) is by Griffith Jones.

JONES, Dr. Henry William (c1866-1953)
Died aged 87 on 27 February 1953.
Attended the London Organ School. Graduated B.Mus. (1893) and D.Mus. (1899) at the University of London.
Organist and choirmaster at the South East London Churches of All Saints, Shooters' Hill (from 1888); St. John's, Plumstead (from 1892); St. John's, Woolwich (from 1893) and St. Mary's Parish Church, Woolwich (from 1912). A professor of organ and composition at the London Organ School.
Composed the anthems 'O Lord our Governour' (which he submitted as his B.Mus. exercise), 'O Lord, rebuke me not' and 'Blest Creator of light'. Composed a sacred cantata *A Song of Deliverance* for his D.Mus. supplication. Also composed the part song 'A song on May morning' for male voices.

JONES, Revd. Dr. Ivor Harold (b.1934)
Born in Bradford, Yorkshire on 31 January 1934. Son of the minister of the Wesleyan Reform Church, Bradford.
Educated at King Edward VII School, Sheffield. Heberden organ scholar of Brasenose College, Oxford. Studied at Wesley House, Cambridge and at the University and Cantor School of Heidelberg, Germany. Graduated M.A. (Oxford) and B.A. (Cambridge).
Became a minister of the Methodist Church in 1958, serving various circuits and colleges before he became principal of Wesley House.
Author of hymn texts. He both composed and arranged hymn tunes, examples of his compositions being 'Muff Field' and

'Sharrow Vale'. Both of these appeared in *Hymns and Psalms* (1983).

JONES, John (1728-1796)

Born in London in 1728; died in London on 17 February 1796.

A chorister of St. Paul's Cathedral under **Maurice Greene**.

Organist of St. Paul's Cathedral (1755-1796), continuing to hold concurrently until his death the other London organistships of the Middle Temple (from 1749) and Charter House (from 1753).

Composed songs, plus a number of single and double chants. Published a collection of 60 single and double chants (1785).

The composer Haydn, who heard his Double Chant in D at a Festival of the Charity Children at St. Paul's Cathedral (1791) said of it,'In all my life, nothing has moved me so deeply as this pious and innocent music.' **William Crotch** took the melody from another chant in the collection as a fugue subject (1836). Two Services were composed for use in St. Paul's Cathedral and his anthems include 'Arise, O Lord' and 'Blessed is he that considereth'.

JONES, John 'of Talysarn' (1796-1857)

Born in Tan-y-Castell, Dolwyddelan, Caernarvonshire, Wales on 1 March 1796; died in Talysarn, Caernarvonshire on 17 August 1857.

Received no formal education, his father having died when John was 12 years old. The boy was faced with the task of supporting his mother and eight younger siblings. He learned to read at home, and he received some teaching from **Evan Evans** (Ieuan Glan Geirionydd).

Worked on building the main road from Capel Curig to Lake Ogwen, and subsequently at the Trefriw Quarry. From 1823 he worked in the quarries at Tal-y-Sarn and Llanllyfni. Later worked in the shop owned by his wife. Around 1850 he became part owner of the Dorothea Quarry, Tal-y-Sarn.

Joined the local congregation at Llangernyw during the Beddgelert Revival of 1819. Began to preach (from 1821) and came under increasing pressure as a lay reader to seek ordination. In 1822 he began to attend the Merioneth Monthly Meeting.

Ordained locally into the Calvinistic Methodist Church (1829). An independent thinker and powerful orator, he helped to sway the argument against the asceticism of the absolute Calvinists, who were a powerful force in Wales. His open air meetings, at which he preached a more practical message than many of his counterparts, attracted congregations of thousands of people at a time. He sustained this ministry for 28 years.

Composed around 50 hymn tunes. 'Llanllyfni' is perhaps the best known, appearing in *Songs of Praise* (1925) and in a number of other hymnals but he may have done no more than harmonise this particular tune. 'Tan-y-Castell' has also been popular.

JONES, John (Eos Bradwen: 1831-1899)

Born near Tal-y-Llyn, Merionethshire, Wales on 16 October 1831; died on 29 May 1899 and was buried at Llanbeblig, Wales. Lived for a time at Tregororwyr before moving to Dolgellau, where he published *Y Seraph neu Gyfaill Y Cerddor Ieuanc*, a collection of hymn tunes and airs. In 1858 he moved to Aberystwyth. Leader of the Choir of St. Asaph Cathedral (from 1863), an appointment he held for 15 years. Later lived in Rhyl and in Caernarvon. An *eisteddfodwr*, winning prizes for his poems. His cantata *Owain Glyndwr* was very popular.

JONES, John Jeremiah (?-1856)

Graduated B.Mus. at the University of Oxford. Organist of St. Paul's Church, Manchester. Composed the anthem 'When the wicked man'.

JONES, John Owen (1876-1962)

Born on 20 May 1876; died on 6 March 1962. A pupil of Walter Williams, graduating B.Mus. at the University of Durham. Served with the Royal Engineers during World War I. He taught music, his pupils including Ivor Novello. Organist of the Tredegarville Baptist Church, Cardiff. Composed songs and choruses, test pieces for *eisteddfodau*, and a setting of Percy Bysshe Shelley's 'Spirit of Delight'.

JONES, Joseph David (1827-1870)

Born in Bryngrugog, Llanfair-Caereinon, Montgomeryshire, Wales in 1827; died in Ruthin, Denbighshire, Wales on 17 September 1870. The father of Sir H. Haydn Jones, Member of Parliament for Merioneth.

Son of a weaver and lay preacher of the Wesleyan Church. Received only one year's formal schooling. At the age of 14, against the wishes of his father, he attended a class in singing at Dolannog, two miles from the family home.

When the family moved to Pant-Gwyn near Llanfair Caereinion, the facilities for learning music were better. He learned to play cello.

Published *Y Perganiedydd* (1847), a small collection of hymn tunes, before the age of 20 and on the proceeds he was able to finance six months' study at the Borough Road Training College, London. Eventually qualified as a teacher in 1851.

Following the death of his mother, Joseph Jones went to Towyn, Merionethshire to take care of a fellow pupil. A number of friends asked him to remain there and open a school offering music, which he did. Music was taught and evening classes were set up, at Towyn and at Bryn-Crug, Llanegryn and Aberdovey.

Master of the British School, Towyn (from 1851-1865). Resigned in order to open a small grammar school at Clwyd Bank, Ruthin which he presided over until the year of his death.

Partly under Joseph Jones's influence, the music of worship in Wales moved away from the ballads of the 18th century towards the music of **Joseph Parry** and other contemporary Welsh composers.

In addition to his early *Y Perganieddyd* he published other collections of hymns and tunes including *Tonau ac Emynau* (1868) and *Y Cerub*. Editor with **Edward Jones** (Tanymarian) of *Llyfr Tonau ac Emynau*. Joseph Jones was responsible for collecting, selecting and harmonising the hymn tunes. Arranged a hymnal for the Welsh Wesleyan Church, published in 1872 after his death.

One of his anthems, 'Ymddyrcha, O Dduw' won a prize at the Bethesda Eisteddfod (1853).

JONES (**Owen**), Morfydd Llwyn (1891-1918)

Born in Treforest, Glamorgan, Wales in 1891; died in Swansea on 7 September 1918. Educated at Pontypridd County School and subsequently (as Caradog music scholar 1909-1912) at the University College of South Wales and Monmouthshire where she graduated B.Mus. (1912). Studied under a Goring Thomas scholarship for composition (1913-1917) at the Royal Academy of Music. A singer and pianist. Composer of hymn tunes including 'Richard', 'William' and 'Penucha'; songs; choral works and orchestral music. Her compositions are said to show an awareness of Welsh musical culture.

JONES, Moses Owen (1842-1908)
Born in Gallt-y-Foel, Dinorwig, Caernarvonshire, Wales on 31 October 1842; died on 27 July 1908.
A pupil teacher at the British School, Deiniolen. Studied at the Borough Road Training College, London (from 1861), where he also learned the Tonic Sol-fa system of musical notation.
An assistant master of Carneddi School, Bethesda (from 1862) and headmaster of a school in Treherbert, Glamorganshire (from 1863). Precentor of the Carmel Congregational Chapel, Treherbert (from 1868).
A conductor of singing festivals, winning prizes at *eisteddfodau* with his choir. An adjudicator. One of the editors of the hymnal *Y Caniedydd Cynulleidfaol* (1895), in which some hymn tunes were his own.
A local historian and essayist in Welsh. One of the subjects he took up was the folk lore of Wales. Some texts were written in English.
Produced a set of biographies of Welsh musicians for the Aberdare Eisteddfod of 1885. Compiled a list of 19th century *eisteddfodau* and a handbook on the most notable of these for the Chicago World Fair (1893), and a bibliography of Welsh musicians up to the year 1896 for the Cardiff Eisteddfod of 1899.

JONES, Nancy (Nancy Crug-y-Bar: 1760-1833)
Around 1800 she was famous for her religious fervour and her leading of hymn singing. It is possible that she composed the hymn tune 'Crugybar', but by no means certain.

JONES, Philip William (b.1949)
Born in Preston, Lancashire on 28 October 1949. Educated at the Royal Northern College of Music. Organist of the Guttridge Memorial Methodist Church (1966-1970, 1973-1983). Composer of motets, anthems, hymn tunes and pieces for guitar. His hymn tunes include 'Darwen' and St. Clair', which were included in his collection of 22 hymn tunes (1981).

JONES, Richard Elfyn
see **ELFYN JONES**, Richard

JONES, Robert (16th century)
Known to have been a gentleman of the Royal Household Chapel in 1520, and to have attended the ceremonies and celebrations of the Field of the Cloth of Gold. He may earlier have been a chorister and (from 1512), a gentleman of the Chapel, possibly travelling to France with the Chapel in 1513. Composed the five-part Mass *Spes nostra* and a five-part Magnificat, plus a song 'Who shall have my fayr lady?'.

JONES (**Jonys**), Dr. Robert (16th/17th century)
Born towards the end of the 16th century and lived into the 17th.
Graduated B.Mus. at the University of Oxford (1597), and D.Mus. at some time afterwards.
In January 1610, Robert Jones, Philip Rosseter, Philip Kingham and Ralph Reeve were jointly granted a patent for teaching music to certain children, known as the children of the Revels of the Queen within Whitefriars.
Contributed a madrigal to *The Triumphes of Oriana*, a collection of 29 madrigals by 26 composers, edited by **Thomas Morley** (1601). Robert Jones subsequently published a collection of madrigals

(1607). Three of his anthems were published in 1614. His anthems include 'Let Thy salvation' and 'What shall I render?'.

JONES, Roger (b.1948)
Born in Birmingham on 15 May 1948. He has composed, among other works, the musical *A Grain of Mustard Seed*, a celebration of the life of Robert Raikes, founder of the Sunday School movement (1979).

JONES, Revd. Samuel Flood
See **FLOOD JONES**, Revd. Samuel.

JONES, Thomas (Canrhawdfardd: 1823-1904)
Born in Bwlch-y-Creigiau, near Nannerch, Flintshire, Wales on 2 July 1823; died on 26 October 1904 and was buried at Coed-Poerth, near Wrexham, Wales.
Learned to read music when young and at the age of 16, he was appointed to lead the singing in the local Wesleyan Chapel. Conducted music classes locally.
In 1849 he began to preach the Wesleyan cause. He moved to Holywell (1851) and to Lixwm. Lived at Coedpoerth, near Wrexham (from 1864), where he ran a printing and book selling business.
Musical editor of *Cydymaith yr Addolydd* (The Worshipper's Companion: 1852), compiled by Revd. Robert Williams for the Wesleyan Methodist Movement in Wales.
A prize winning composer and writer who produced a great deal of material. His anthems were especially popular.

JONES, Thomas Evance (1805-1872)
Born in 1805; died in Canterbury, Kent in 1872. A chorister of Canterbury Cathedral from 1813, and a pupil of **Highmore Skeats** the elder. A lay clerk (from 1822), master of the choristers (from 1830) and organist (from 1831) of Canterbury Cathedral. Composed anthems including 'Blessed is he that considereth' and 'Unto Him that loved us'. His hymn tune 'Quinquagesima' was used in the Methodist Church's *School Hymn Book* (1950).

JONES, Thomas Gruffydd (Tafalaw Bencerdd: 1832-1898)
Born in Pen-y-Cae, Monmouthshire, Wales on 6 January 1832; died in the U.S.A. on 17 March 1898.
Apprenticed to a carpenter, and an amateur musician. Took lessons with **Rosser Beynon**.
At the age of 16 he became precentor of Sardis Church, Pontypridd where his father was the minister.
Competed at *eisteddfodau* (from 1850), winning a composition prize at the Bethesda Eisteddfod with an anthem. Subsequently became an adjudicator.
Published *Y Drysorfa Gorawl* (1858), a collection of anthems and choral pieces.
His travels took him to Cardiff, Kenfig Hill, Cwmavon and, in 1860, to North Wales. Here he remained for a time as private secretary to Thomas Gee, a Denbigh Calvinist minister and politician.
Moved to Aberdare (1863). Three years later he emigrated to the U.S.A. where he became Minister of the Congregational Church at Salem, Massachusetts (1867). A teacher of fine arts at Emporia College (from 1869).
His cantata *Gwarchae Harlech* was first performed in 1865.

JONES, Revd. William (1726-1800)

Born in Lowick, Northamptonshire and was baptised on 20 July 1726; died in Stoke-by-Nayland, Suffolk on 6 January 1800.

A descendant of Colonel John Jones, one of those who had signed the death warrant of Charles I. He was deeply ashamed of this connection and he kept 30 January, the anniversary of Charles's execution, as a day of personal humiliation. His long connection with the Suffolk village led to his being known as 'Jones of Nayland'.

Educated at Charter House, London and at University College, Oxford where he studied science and music. Graduated B.A. (1749). Ordained in 1751. An Oxford M.A. was later withdrawn following a controversial essay by him on natural philosophy.

Studied in London under James Oswald and **J.C. Pepusch**. In 1782, while a pensioner of Sidney Sussex College, Cambridge, he graduated M.A.

Vicar of Bethersden, Kent (from 1764) and later, of Pluckley, Kent. Vicar of Paston, Northamptonshire. In 1776 he travelled on the continent. Incumbent of Nayland, near Colchester (1777-1798). Rector of Hollingbourne, Kent (from 1798).

He took the view that whereas the performance of music was a skill which could be improved through practice, composition was a God-given gift which, accordingly, could not be taught.

His *Treatise on the Art of Music* was published in 1784.

The hymn tune 'St. Stephen', also known as 'Newington', has been used in many 20th century hymnals. Also composed a double chant, four anthems (1789) including 'From Thy seat' and 'Thou, Lord, in the beginning', rounds and items for organ.

JONES, William (19th century)

Organist at some time of the Church of St. Alban, Blackburn, Lancashire. Composed a hymn for four voices 'Hail! Queen of Heaven' (1869), and two Litany settings.

JORDAN, Dr. Charles Warwick (1840-1909)

Born in Clifton, Bristol on 28 December 1840; died by his own hand at Haywards Heath, Sussex on 30 August 1909.

A chorister of Bristol Cathedral and St. Paul's Cathedral. Graduated B.Mus. at the University of Oxford (1869). Accorded the Lambeth D.Mus. in 1886.

Organist of the London Churches of St. Paul, Bunhill Row (from 1857); St. Luke, West Holloway (from 1860) and St. Stephen, Lewisham (from 1866 until at least 1897).

A professor of organ and harmony at Guildhall School of Music and a musical examiner for the Royal College of Organists and for Trinity College of Music, London.

Honorary organist of the London Gregorian Association, his duties included playing at the annual festival in St. Paul's Cathedral. An honorary fellow, examiner and treasurer of the R.C.O. He opened the organ, newly rebuilt by Lewis & Co., at Leavesden Church, near Watford, Hertfordshire on 7 November 1908.

Composed a Festival Te Deum for Organ, Trumpets, Drums and Choir which was performed by some 4,000 voices at the Crystal Palace on 16 June 1895. Also composed a Festival Jubilate in C (1897), a Holy Communion Service in E, anthems, harmonies for Gregorian chants (on the subject of which he wrote a book), a cantata *Blow ye the trumpet in Zion* for Solo Voices, Chorus and Orchestra, hymn tunes and an overture *Pray and Praise* for Organ, Trumpet and Trombones.

JOSEPH, Jane Marian (1894-1929)

Born in Kensington, London in 1894; died in Kensington on 9 March 1929. Attended St. Paul's Girls' School, Hammersmith, where her music teacher was **Gustav Holst**. Composed a Hymn for Whitsuntide for unaccompanied mixed voices (1924), hymn tunes, a Festival Venite for Choir and Orchestra (1922), *Three old carols* (1925) and a Carol for Unison Voices (1925).

JOUBERT, John Pierre Herman (b.1927)

Born in Cape Town, South Africa on 20 March 1927.

Attended the Diocesan College, Rondebusch (1934-1944) and the South African College of Music, Cape Town (1944-1946), where he studied under **W.H. Bell**. Attended the Royal Academy of Music, London (1946-1950) where his teachers included Holland and Howard Ferguson. Graduated B.Mus. at the University of Durham.

A lecturer in music at the University of Hull (1950-1962), and reader in music at the University of Birmingham. Visiting professor of the University of Otago, New Zealand (1979).

President of the Midlands Section of the Free Church Choir Union.

Began to compose while still at school. His first catalogued work was a String Quartet (1950), but much of his subsequent work has been, in one form or another, for voices.

He won Novello's anthem competition in 1952 with his entry 'O Lorde, the Maker of al thing'. His other anthems include 'All wisdom cometh from the Lord', 'Christ is risen' and 'Let me rejoice'. As well as a Te Deum he has composed the carols 'There is no rose' (1954) and 'Torches' (1952).

His hymn tune 'Moseley' was used in the Third Edition (1973) of *Church Hymnary*, and elsewhere. His work is said to show the musical influence of **William Walton** and **Benjamin Britten**.

JOULE, Anthony (b.c1960)

Studied at the Royal Northern College of Music. A lay clerk of St. George's Chapel, Windsor Castle (c1982), of Lichfield Cathedral (1983-1986) and, briefly, of York Minster. Organist of St. James's Church, Grimsby, Lincolnshire. Composed the anthems 'Beloved, let us love one another' and 'Drop, drop slow tears'.

JOULE, Benjamin St. John Baptist (1817-1895)

Born in Salford, Lancashire on 8 November 1817; died in Rothesay, Inverness-shire, Scotland on 21 May 1895.

Studied violin under Richard Cudmore, and singing and musical theory under **Joseph John Harris**, organist of the Collegiate Church, Manchester.

Organist and master of the choristers at the Church of the Holy Trinity, Hulme, Lancashire (1846-1853) and of St. Margaret's, Whalley Range, Manchester (1849-1852).

Honorary organist of St. Peter's Church, Manchester (from 1853). During his time at St. Peter's, the Church became famous for its recitals, often featuring distinguished visiting organists including **R.P. Stewart** and **W.T. Best**.

Lectured on topics relating to church music. Music critic of *Manchester Courier* (1850-1870). Contributed to a number of musical journals and served as a Justice of the Peace.

Published a collection of chants in 1861. Composed a setting of the Holy Communion Service, based on the harmonisation of a monotone. His anthems include 'The Lord is my Shepherd' and 'Vital spark'. Also composed music for piano, and for organ.

JOWETT, Revd. Joseph (1784-1856)
Born in London on 22 February 1784; died in Silk Willoughby, near Sleaford, Lincolnshire on 13 May 1856. Graduated at Queen's College, Oxford (1806). Rector of Silk Willoughby (1813-1856). Published collections of church music, and devotional music designed for use at home. Adapted and harmonised a number of Psalm and hymn tunes. His tune 'Thanet' was first found in *Musae Solitariae* (1823), a publication consisting entirely of his own compositions and intended for private use, but it has been used in a number of hymnals this century including *Congregational Praise* (1950).

JOZÉ, Dr. Thomas Richard Gonzalvez (1853-1924)
Born in Dublin on 26 September 1853; died in Dublin on 20 March 1924. A chorister (from 1861) and deputy organist (from 1869) of Christ Church Cathedral, Dublin,. Graduated D.Mus. at the University of Dublin (1877). Organist of St. Paul's Church, Glengarry (from 1870) and Christ Church, Leeson Park, Dublin. A professor of organ and harmony at the Royal Irish Academy of Music. Musical examiner for several institutions. Composed a prize festival hymn 'St. Patrick's breastplate', two cantatas, a glee, part songs and piano music.

JUDD, Roger Langley (b.1944)
Born in Chichester, West Sussex on 23 October 1944. Organ scholar at Pembroke College, Cambridge (1963-1966). Director of music of St. George's School, Windsor Castle (1967-1968) and assistant organist of Ely Cathedral (1968-1972). Master of the music of St. Michael's College, Tenbury, Worcestershire (1973-1985). Assistant organist of St. George's Chapel, Windsor Castle (from 1985). Has composed two sets of Responses for Boys' Voices, a Magnificat and Nunc Dimittis for Boys' Voices and Organ, and a number of carol arrangements.

JUDE, William Herbert (1851-1922)
Born in Westleton, Suffolk in 1851; died in Willesden, London on 8 August 1922. Received training in music from his uncle, D.C. Browne, organist of the Church for the Blind, Liverpool. Organist of the Blue Coat Hospital, Liverpool. Founder of the Purcell Society. Established his career as a recitalist when he gave a series of 15 performances during the absence in Rome of **W.T. Best**. A lecturer. Organist of Stretford Town Hall, near Manchester (from 1889). Composed hymn tunes, an operetta *Innocents Abroad* (1882) and songs such as 'The Skipper'.

JUGLOTT, William
See **INGLOTT**, William.

JULIAN, Hubert (b.1923)
Born in Newquay, Cornwall on 12 September 1923. Attended St. Austell Grammar School, Cornwall. Following war service he went into banking, being active in his spare time with local choral societies and choirs. His tune 'Porwhele' was used in *Hymns and Psalms* (1983) with the hymn 'How wonderful this world of Thine' by Fred Pratt Green.

JUTSON, Revd. Charles Bentley (1870-1930)
Born in Canterbury, Kent on 28 June 1870; died in Reigate, Surrey on 18 September 1930. Ordained as a minister of the Congregational Church after studying at Cheshunt, Hertfordshire. Served at Forest Hill, London; Clemont, Brighton, Sussex and Reigate, Surrey. His hymn tune 'The Story of Jesus' was used in *School Worship* (1926), for the publication of which he was a committee member.

JUXON, George (17th century)
A younger contemporary of **William Byrd**. A vicar choral of Canterbury Cathedral from 1590 or before, until 1599. Organist of Canterbury Cathedral from 1589 until at least 1590. Composed a set of Preces and the Easter anthem 'Christ rising'.

JUXON, Revd. William (1582-1668)
As Bishop of London he attended Charles I at his execution in 1649. At the Restoration, William Juxon became Archbishop of Canterbury (1660-1663), and it was his more pleasant duty to carry out the Coronation of Charles II. Composed the anthem 'Come, Holy Ghost'.

K

KEAY, Louis Harold (19th/20th century)
Graduated B.Mus. at the University of Durham (1893). Organist and choirmaster of the Churches of St. Bride, Stretford, Manchester (from 1878) and St. Luke's Heywood, Lancashire (from 1894). Composed a cantata based on Psalm 145 *I will magnify Thee, O God* for Solo Voices, Chorus and Strings.

KEECH, William John (19th/20th century)
Born in Gosport, Hampshire. Educated privately, and graduated B.Mus. at the University of Durham (1910). Organist and choirmaster of St. Mary's Church, Bedford (1894-1903) and of Faversham Parish Church, Kent (from 1903). A local philharmonic society conductor, and a teacher of music and singing in Faversham at the Queen Elizabeth Grammar School, Wright's School and William Gibbs School for Girls. Singing master of Borden Grammar School, Sittingbourne, Kent. Composed an Evening Service in E-flat and a setting of Psalm 42 'Like as the hart' for Solo Voices, Chorus and Strings.

KEETON, Dr. Haydn (1847-1921)
Born in Mosborough, near Chesterfield, Derbyshire on 26 October 1847; died on 27 May 1921.
His father, Edwin Keeton, was organist of Eckington Parish Church, Derbyshire.
A chorister at St. George's Chapel, Windsor Castle and an articled pupil (1862-1868) of the chapel organist, **George Elvey**. Graduated B.Mus (1869) and D.Mus (1877) at New College, Oxford.
Held a number of musical appointments near Windsor. Organist of Datchet Church (1867-1869); assistant music master of Eton College (from 1868) and organist of Aldin House Preparatory School, Slough (1869-1870).
Organist of Peterborough Cathedral for more than 50 years (1870-1921). His articled pupils included **Thomas Armstrong** (from 1913) and the conductor, Malcolm Sargent (from 1911). A musical examiner to the Universities of Oxford and Durham.
Composed services, chants, anthems including 'I will alway give thanks', hymn tunes, organ voluntaries, a symphony, pieces for piano, and part songs.

KEIGHLEY, Dr. Thomas (1869-1936)
Born in Stalybridge in 1869; died in Cheadle, Cheshire on 13 November 1936.
As a boy he worked in the local cotton mill. Studied at the Royal Manchester College of Music (from 1895) and at Owen's College, Victoria University of Manchester (1896-1898) where he graduated B.Mus. (1898) and D.Mus. (1901). His teachers included **Henry Hiles** and **James Kendrick Pyne**.
Organist of Christ Church, Stalybridge (from 1887) and organist and choirmaster of St. John's Church, Dukinfield (1887-1889); Albion Congregational Church, Ashton-under-Lyne (1897-1911 and 1913-1932) and the Holy Innocents' Church, Fallowfield (from 1932).
Taught at the R.M.C.M. (from 1898), his special subjects being theory, sight singing and musical dictation. He also took the choral class. Later, he taught teacher training. An examiner. Taught history of music at the Day Training College, Victoria University of Manchester. A local choral society conductor.
Author of books and musical exercises. The composition submitted for his B.Mus. exercise was a setting of Psalm 90 'Lord, Thou hast been our Refuge', for Solo Voices, Chorus, Strings and Woodwind. Composed for brass band.

KELLY, Bryan George (b.1934)
Born in Oxford on 3 January 1934.
Studied at the Royal College of Music (1951-1955) under **Gordon Jacob** and **Herbert Howells**, and privately with Nadia Boulanger in Paris.
Taught at the Royal Scottish Academy of Music (1958-1961). A professor of theory and composition at the R.C.M. (1963-1984), during which time he spent a year teaching at the American University in Washington D.C., U.S.A.
His compositions include orchestral and band pieces. Noted for his original approach to the service repertoire using Latin-American rhythms, typified by his Evening Canticles for John Birch and the Southern Cathedrals Festival (1965). Has also composed an Evening Service in C (1968), a Te Deum and Jubilate (1979) for the Choir of Leeds Parish Church, a Missa Brevis and Evening Service for Peterborough Cathedral, a setting of Psalm 150 'O praise God in His holiness' and the anthem 'O, sweet Jesu'. Composer of *Veni, Sancte Spiritus* and other large-scale motets.

Has collaborated with the poet John Fuller in composing items for children, including the cantata *Half a Fortnight* (1972).

KELLY, Katharine Agnes May (1869-1942)
Born in Croydon, Surrey in 1869; died in Tunbridge Wells, Kent on 4 August 1942. Composer of hymn tunes.

KELWAY, Thomas (1695-1744)
Born in Chichester, Sussex in August 1695; died in Chichester on 21 May 1744. His tombstone erroneously shows the year of his decease as 1749.
One of the five sons of a vicar choral of Chichester Cathedral, Thomas Kelway. His younger brother, Joseph, was also a church musician.
A chorister of Chichester Cathedral (from 1704). He may also have studied under **John Weldon** as his compositions are said to exhibit signs of Weldon's influence.
Organist of Chichester Cathedral, probationarily, from 1720. It appears that he was not formally confirmed as organist until 1733. In office until 1744.
Composed church music, including some seven services, of which his Service in B Minor is still performed today, and nine anthems including 'Teach me, O Lord' and 'I will give thanks'.
Cathedral Psalter Chants (1874) contains Single Chants in D and in G Minor. Also composed hymn tunes.

KEMP, Dr. Joseph (1778-1824)
Born in Exeter, Devon in 1778; died in London on 22 May 1824.
A chorister of Exeter Cathedral under **William Jackson**, whose pupil he became on leaving the choir. Graduated Mus.B. (1808) and Mus.D. (1809) at Sydney Sussex College, Cambridge, the works submitted being a war anthem 'A sound of battle is in the land' (Mus.B.) and a cantata *The Crucifixion* (Mus.D.).
Organist of Bristol Cathedral (1802-1807).
He must have had an immediate impact, for in 1803 the Dean and Chapter awarded him a gold medal for his 'unremitting attention to the improvement of the choir of this Church'.
Lived in London (1807-1813), where he was active as a teacher of music from around 1809. Founded a college of music at Exeter (1814). Apart from a three year period in France (1818-1821), he lived in Exeter for the remainder of his life.
His book *A New System of Musical Education* (c1810-1819) described what was probably the first formal method of teaching music to groups of people.
His compositions include works for the theatre, songs, glees, anthems including 'I am Alpha and Omega', and 20 double chants, dating from around 1800.

KEMPTON, Thomas (1702-1762)
Baptised in Ely, Cambridgeshire on 3 May 1702; died in Ely on 16 June 1762. A pupil of the elder **James Hawkins**. Organist of Ely Cathedral (1729-1762). His descendants sang in the choir of the Cathedral until the 19th century. Composed anthems including 'Behold, it is Christ' and 'Shew me Thy ways'. His Single Chant in B-flat was included in *Cathedral Psalter Chants* (1874). A Service in B-flat was published in a collection by **F.A.G. Ouseley**.

KENNEDY, Arnold (1852-1938)
Born in Stepney, London in 1852; died in Hampstead, London on 5 March 1938.

Educated in Edinburgh, where he attended the High School and the University, graduating M.A. As a boy he learned music under the Tonic Sol-fa notation. Attended the Royal Academy of Music and graduated B.Mus. at the University of Oxford (1893). Lived in London as a teacher and composer. Composed a Magnificat and Nunc Dimittis (1936), hymn tunes, songs and an operetta for children *Prince Ferdinand*.

KENT, James (1700-1776)
Born in Winchester, Hampshire on 13 March 1700; died in Winchester on 6 May 1776.
A chorister at Winchester Cathedral (from 1711) for two years under **Vaughan Richardson**, and at the Chapel Royal (1714-1718) under **William Croft**, of whose music he was later said to be one of the best performers in the country.
Early in his career, Kent was organist of Finedon, Northamptonshire (1718-1731).
Organist of Trinity College, Cambridge (1731-1737) and of the Cathedral and College of Winchester (1738-1774), being succeeded in the latter year by his former pupil, **Peter Fussell**.
It is believed that he assisted **William Boyce** in the compilation of *Cathedral Music*. Composed Services in C and in D. A volume of 12 of his anthems was published during his lifetime (1773); a further eight, and some Morning and Evening Services were published posthumously. His anthems include 'Teach me, O Lord' and 'Hear my prayer'. Also composed hymn tunes.

KERBUSCH, Dr. Leo (1828-?)
A pupil of Louis Spohr and a D.Mus. graduate of Dublin. A writer and composer, whose works include the anthem 'Rise up, my love'.

KETTLE, Charles Edward (1833-1895)
Born in Bury St. Edmunds, Suffolk on 28 March 1833; died in Hove, Sussex on 2 March 1895.
Organist of the London Churches of St. Margaret, Plumstead; St. Nicholas, Plumstead and Holy Trinity, Woolwich. Held appointments in Sussex at Hove Parish Church and Queen's Square Congregational Church, Brighton. Composed chants, Sunday School hymns, hymn tunes, three operas and works for piano and for organ. *Congregational Church Hymnal* uses his tunes 'Blendon', 'Leyton', and 'Salvator amicus'.

KEY, Joseph (19th century)
Joseph Key was said to be 'of Nuneaton', Warwickshire, and active in the first half of the 19th century. Composed marches for organ, anthems including 'Arise, shine' and 'O clap your hands', and Psalm tunes.

KIDD, Malcolm Brown (19th/20th century)
Graduated B.Mus. at the University of Durham (1899). Active in Scotland. Organist and choirmaster of the United Presbyterian Church, Moffat (from 1894) and of the Parish Churches of Forfar (from 1900) and Kelso (from 1907). Composed anthems and songs.

KIDSON, James (19th/20th century)
Graduated B.Mus. at the University of Durham (1904). Organist of St. John's Church, Percy (from 1890); deputy organist of Tynemouth Parish Church (from 1894). Organist and choirmaster of Bream Parish Church (from 1897) and St. Paul's Church, Weymouth (from 1906). Composed a setting *The Lord's Prayer*

(1911) and of Psalm 145 'The Lord is loving', and an anthem 'Our soul waiteth for the Lord' (1902).

KILBURN, Dr. Nicholas (1843-1923)
Born in Bishop Auckland, County Durham on 7 February 1843; died in 1923.
Educated privately in music. Graduated Mus.B. at the University of Cambridge (1880) and, honorarily, D.Mus. at the University of Durham (1914).
Conductor a number of choral societies in the North East of England. An iron merchant in Sunderland. A friend and dedicatee of **Edward Elgar**, he performed all of the latter's major choral works. Author of a book on the management of choral societies.
Composed the sacred cantatas *The Lord is my Shepherd* (1892) and *By the Waters of Babylon* (1895) for Choir, Organ and Orchestra; Services; anthems including 'Hear my cry' (1915); an oratorio *St. Thomas;* songs; part songs and works for piano and for violin.

KILNER, Thomas (?-1876)
Died in London on 30 September 1876. Organist of Christ Church, Highbury, London (1848-1868). Published *Manual of Psalmody and Chanting*, and *Pocket Chant Book* (both 1850). Composed the anthem 'My voice shalt thou hear'.

KINDERSLEY (**Kennersley**), Robert (?-c1634)
A royal musician between 1628 and 1631, and possibly before and after these dates. Composed the anthems 'O God, to whom all hearts are seen' and 'Judge them, O Lord'. Both were used in the collection *Teares and Lamentaions of a Sorrowful Soule* (1614) published by **William Leighton**.

KING, Dr. Alfred (1837-1926)
Born in Shelley, Essex on 24 April 1837; died in Brighton, Sussex on 26 April 1926.
It was intended that he should seek ordination but he opted for a career in music instead. Studied organ under **Charles Steggall**, graduating B.Mus. (1872) and D.Mus. (1890) at Exeter College, Oxford.
Organist of Cuddesden Theological College (from 1856); Eastnor Castle, the seat of Earl Somers (1857-1864); the Church of St. Michael and All Angels, Brighton (1865-1877); Brighton Parish Church (1877-1887) and Brighton Corporation (1878). Director of the Brighton School of Music, where his pupils included **Christopher Le Fleming**.
Composed organ music, a choral cantata *Deliverance*, an oratorio *The Epiphany*, a Mass in B-flat, an Evening Service in B-flat, hymns and part songs.

KING, Charles (c1693-1748)
Baptised in Bury St. Edmunds, Suffolk on 5 June 1693; died in London on 17 March 1748. Some sources give the year of his birth as 1687.
A chorister of St. Paul's Cathedral under **John Blow** and **Jeremiah Clarke**, to whom he was later apprenticed. Graduated B.Mus. at the University of Oxford (1707).
A vicar choral of St. Paul's (1730-1748). In 1707 he succeeded Jeremiah Clarke (whose sister he married) as almoner and master of the children of St. Paul's, a position which he likewise retained until his death.
The organistship of St. Paul's was a separate appointment. Charles King worked alongside **Richard Brind** and **Maurice Greene**, his

former pupil. Organist of the Church of St. Benet Fink at the Royal Exchange, London (c1715- 1747).
His other famous pupils include **Jonathan Battishill**, the first **John Alcock** and **Robert Hudson.**
Composed Services, sets of Responses to the Commandments in B-flat, in C, and in F. *Cathedral Psalter Chants* (1874) contains a Single Chant in G. Also composed anthems including 'Rejoice in the Lord' and 'Wherewithal shall a young man cleanse his way'.

KING, Charles John (1859-1934)
Born in Portsea in 1859; died in Northampton on 16 February 1934.
A chorister of St. George's Chapel, Windsor Castle for six years, studying under **George Elvey**, Chapel organist.
Organist of Farnham Royal Church, Buckinghamshire (from 1877), Hinckley Parish Church, Leicestershire (from 1878), and of the Northampton Churches of St. Sepulchre (from 1890) and St. Matthew (1895-1934). Taught music in three Northampton schools.
His hymn tune 'Northampton' (1939), written during his time at St. Matthew's, has been used with James Montgomery's hymn 'Songs of praise the angels sang' for many years.

KING, Oliver Arthur (1855-1923)
Born in Islington, London in 1855; died in Hammersmith, London on 23 August 1923.
A chorister at St. Andrew's Church, Wells Street, London under **Joseph Barnby**, whose articled pupil he later became. Studied piano under **W.H. Holmes** and, at the Leipzig Conservatory (1874-1877), under Carl Reinecke and others.
Assistant organist of St. Anne's Church, Soho, London. In 1879 he became organist to Princess Louise, travelling with her to Canada (1880-1883) and giving a number of recitals there. Director of music of Marylebone Parish Church, London (1884-1886) and a professor of piano at the Royal Academy of Music (from 1893).
Composed Morning and Evening Services in D, some 50 anthems, duets, songs, part songs and items for violin. *Congregational Church Hymnal* uses his tune 'Westmeath' with the hymn 'O Sing to the Lord' by Richard Littledale.

KING, Robert (c1660-c1720)
Graduated Mus.B. at St. Catherine's College, Cambridge (1696).
Organist of St. Martin-in-the-Fields, London (1676-1713). One of the private musicians to Charles II (from 1680). Served four other monarchs. William and Mary appear to have held him in particularly high regard, appointing him composer in ordinary (1689). He was licensed to give private concerts.
Robert King and John Banister jointly sold printed music (1700-1702), including works by Arcangelo Corelli.
Composed the anthem 'I will alway give thanks'. Set the *Ode to St. Cecilia's Day. Church Hymns* (1874) uses his tune 'Lambeth' with John Ellerton's, 'God of the living'. 'David's harp' is used in a number of 20th century hymns. Also composed songs and instrumental works.

KING, Revd. William (1624-1680)
Born in Winchester, Hampshire in 1624; died in Oxford on 17 November 1680.
A son of George King, organist of Winchester Cathedral. A clerk of Magdalen College, Oxford (from 1648). Graduated B.Mus., B.A. (1649) and M.A. (1655).

A clerk (1648-1652) and chaplain (1652-1654) of Magdalen College; organist of New College (1664-1680) in succession to **Robert Pickaver**.

Composed church music and songs. His anthems include 'O be joyful in the Lord.' and 'Have mercy upon me'. Composed services, of which his set, with Litany, in B-flat is an example. Also composed songs.

KINGHAM, Millicent Douglas (1886-1927)

Organist of St. Andrew's Church, Hertford in the 1890s and of St. Thomas's Hospital, London, retiring in 1926.

Her hymn tune 'Benson' was used with the hymn 'God is working His purpose out' by Arthur Ainger, in the Standard Edition (1916) of *Hymns Ancient and Modern*. It was dedicated to E.W. Benson, Archbishop of Canterbury from 1882 to 1896.

KINGSTON, Matthew (19th/20th century)

Associated with the town of Bournemouth, Dorset. His anthem 'Bless the Lord, O my soul' won the composition prize at the Nonconformist Choir Union Festival of 1891. Other works include settings of the Benedictus in A-flat (1906) and in C (1897) and the Office of Holy Communion in A-flat (1902), a Short Festival Magnificat and Nunc Dimittis in D (1902), a Magnificat and Nunc Dimittis in A-flat (1907), the anthem 'God so loved the world' (1881) and the sacred song 'My prayer' (1928).

KINKEE, Frederick (1826-1899)

Born probably in London on 27 March 1826; died in 1899. A teacher of organ and piano in London. Organist of St. Paul's Church, Knightsbridge (1852) and St. Mary's Church, Lambeth (1868-1879).

KINROSS, John (1848-1890)

Born in Edinburgh on 16 October 1848; died in Hampstead, London on 30 December 1890.

Musically self taught. In his twenties, while living in Scotland, he studied during his holidays in London with **George Macfarren**.

His early career consisted of an apprenticeship to a music seller and a period working in a telegraph office in Ireland. Around the year 1865 he moved to Dundee, Scotland and in 1883 he settled in London. By this time he had become a music teacher and composer.

Composed songs, part songs and works for the harmonium. The 19th century *Congregational Church Hymnal* uses his anthems 'Almighty God unto whom' and 'O Wisdom' and his hymn tunes 'Pax' and 'Snaresbrook'. Also composed chants.

KINSEY, Thomas Hague (1858-?)

Born in Liverpool on 15 December 1858. Studied privately and at the Leipzig Conservatory under Oscar Paul, Ernst Richter and Salomon Jadassohn. Taught piano in and around Liverpool. Organist of Sefton Park Church. Composed orchestral works, songs, part songs and church music including the carol 'Hail sweet Babe, so pure and holy' (1895), the anthem 'It is a good thing to give thanks' (1897) and the sacred song 'The Christ Truth way' (1921).

KIRBY, William Edward (c1877-1953)

William Edward Kirby died aged 76 on 3 November 1953. Studied organ at Trinity College of Music, and under **A.H. Mann** at King's

College, Cambridge. Organist of All Saints' Church, Clifton, Gloucestershire for 27 years. Composed a Missa *Sancti Albani*.

KIRBY, William Rayment (19th/20th Century)

Born in Kennington, London. Studied music with **Frederick Bridge** and C.W. Pearce. Graduated B.Mus. at the University of Durham (1891).

Lived and worked in London. Organist and choirmaster in Camberwell of the Emmanuel Church (1877-1880) and of St. Philip's Church (1880-1882). Organist and choirmaster of St. Mary's Church, Newington (1882-1892), during which time he was also choirmaster for six years. Organist and choirmaster of the Church of St. George the Martyr, Southwark (1894-1896) before returning to St. Mary's Newington as organist (from 1897) and later, organist and choirmaster (from 1907).

Lived in Streatham. Taught music at Balham Grammar School. A professor of singing at the West Newington Literary and Scientific Institution (1881-1882) and conductor of the choral society.

Composed a setting of Psalm 18 'I will love the Lord' for Solo Voices, Chorus and Strings, which was submitted as his degree exercise.

KIRBYE (Kirby), George (?c1565-1634)

Born in Suffolk, possibly around 1565; died in Bury St. Edmunds, Suffolk and was buried on 6 October 1634.

Employed by Sir Robert Jermyn of Rushbrooke Hall, Suffolk as a domestic musician. His contemporary and fellow church musician **John Wilbye** lived no more than a few miles away and it is likely that the two were acquainted. May have been a churchwarden of St. Mary's Church, Bury St. Edmunds.

Composed madrigals and anthems including 'O Jesu, look'. The madrigal 'With angel's face' was included in the collection *The Triumphs of Oriana* (1601). *Church Hymns* (1874) uses his tune 'Winchester Old' with John Newton's hymn 'Great Shepherd of Thy people, hear'. The tune is used in many hymnals of this century for 'While shepherds watched'. His other church music includes the motet *Vox in Rama*.

KITCHEN, Dr. John P. (20th century)

Senior lecturer and university organist at the University of Edinburgh, and formerly of the University of St. Andrews. Organist of Old St. Paul's Episcopal Church, Edinburgh. Two anthems are 'Look how the dawn' and 'Lord, by Thy Spirit'.

KITSON, Dr. Charles Herbert (1874-1944)

Born in Leyburn, Yorkshire on 13 September 1874; died in Kensington, London on 13 May 1944.

Educated at Ripon School. Organ scholar (1894-1897) at Selwyn College, Cambridge, where he read divinity, winning a prize and graduating B.A. (1896) and M.A. (1903). Also graduated B.Mus. (1897) and D.Mus. (1902) at St. Edmund Hall, Oxford.

Assistant music master of Haileybury School (1897-1898) and St. Edmund's School, Canterbury, Kent (1898-1901).

Organist of the Church of St. John the Baptist, Leicester (1901-1913). Held four major musical appointments in Dublin. Organist of Christ Church Cathedral (1913-1920); senior theory professor at the Royal Irish Academy of Music (1918-1920). A professor of music at University College (1915-1920) and, later, Trinity College (1920-1935). Witnessed and later wrote an account of the Irish Rebellion of 1916.

The post at Trinity College was non-residential and Kitson held the position concurrently with a teaching position at the Royal College of Music (from 1920). Also taught at Trinity College of Music, London. Musical examiner to a number of universities. Co-editor, with **C.G. Marchant** of the (Irish) *Church Hymnal* (1919). Among his students for composition was **Michael Tippett**. Author of works on the theory of composition, including *The Art of Counterpoint*.

Composed services including settings of the Magnificat and Nunc Dimittis in D (1896), in E-flat (1918) and in F (1929); a Benedictus in F (1929); settings of the Mass in D (1931), in C Minor (1934) and in D Minor (1936); anthems such as 'Jesu, grant me this, I pray' (1933); the motets *God be in my head* (1911) and *Panis angelicus* (1933); the carol 'O leave your sheep' (1931); hymn tunes; works for organ and part songs.

KNAPP, William (c1698-1768)

Born in Wareham, Dorset in 1698 or 1699; died in Poole, Dorset and was buried on 26 September 1768.

A glover by trade, he was parish clerk of St. James's Church, Poole for 39 years (1729-1768). He trained the choirs of a number of Dorset churches and it is believed that he was the organist of churches in Wareham and Poole.

Published several collections of church music, including *A Sett of new Psalm Tunes and Anthems*, which went to eight editions between 1738 and 1770 and included some of his own compositions.

His tune 'Wareham', a slight revision of which is known as 'Blandford', was formerly used with 'Rejoice, O land' but is associated today with 'Jesus, where'er thy people meet'. This tune and 'Spetisbury' (1736) are found in the Revised Edition (1916) of *Hymns Ancient and Modern*. Composed the anthem 'Blessed are all they'.

KNIFTON, Thomas William (1887-?)

Born in Coalville, Leicestershire in 1887. Attended Trinity College of Music. Music director, pianist and organist of a number of cinemas, including The Square, Walsall; The Palace, Berwick on Tweed; The Dorking Palace; The Bideford Palace and The Theatre of Variety, Holloway Road, London. Organist and choirmaster of Hugglescote Parish Church, Leicestershire. Composed the anthem 'Awake! Thou that sleepest'.

KNIGHT, Dr. Gerald Hocken (1908-1979)

Born in Par, Cornwall on 27 July 1908; died in Paddington, London on 16 September 1979.

Appointed C.B.E. in 1971.

A chorister at Truro Cathedral. Choral exhibitioner (1926-1929) of Peterhouse, Cambridge, where he graduated B.A. (1930), M.A. (1933) and B.Mus. (1932). Also studied at the School of English Church Music (now the Royal School of Church Music). Articled to **H.S. Middleton** at Truro (from 1922). Studied at the Royal College of Music (1929-1931). Awarded the Lambeth D.Mus. (1961).

At an early age he had been assistant organist (1922-1926) at Truro Cathedral. A tutor in plainsong in the School of English Church Music at Chislehurst, Kent (1931-1936). Organist of St. Augustine's Church, Queen's Gate, London (1931-1937). Organist of Canterbury Cathedral (1937- 1952) from the age of 28. During World War II he served in the R.A.F. as an airman (1942 - 1943) and education officer (1943-1945). A local posting enabled him to spend part of his time at Canterbury Cathedral. The choir school had been evacuated to Cornwall in 1940 and the organ, which had been dismantled, was not reassembled until 1949. Services were held in the eastern crypt.

From 1945 to 1952, Gerald Knight was a fellow and warden of the College of St. Nicolas, later incorporated into the Royal School of Church Music. On the death of **S.H. Nicholson**, Gerald Knight was one of the three associate directors appointed. Appointed director of the R.S.C.M. in 1952, upon which he resigned his cathedral appointment. The College moved to Addington, near Croydon, Surrey in 1954. Knight served until 1972 and continued in the capacity of overseas commissioner until 1978.

Visited Westminster Choir College in Princeton, New Jersey, U.S.A. in 1965 as an honorary fellow. An editor of hymnals and Psalters, being best known for his work as joint editor of the 1950 Revision of *Hymns Ancient and Modern,* which contains his 'Veryan' and 'Valley'. He was on the Committee for *100 Hymns for Today* (1969) and *100 More Hymns for Today* (1980).

His chant to Psalm 61 remains popular. The anthem 'Now the God of peace', composed for the enthronement of Archbishop Geoffrey Fisher in 1945, is still widely sung. Other compositions include incidental music for two plays *The Zeal of thy House* and *The Devil to Pay* (1939) by Dorothy L. Sayers.

KNIGHT, Timothy John (b.1959)

Born in Northallerton, Yorkshire on 10 September 1959.

A chorister of York Minster (1969-1973) under **Francis Jackson**.

Entered a career in administration but turned to music and especially composition following his success at competitive festivals. Also active as a conductor.

Director of music at Studio la Pointe Performing Arts College, Leeds. Organist and choirmaster of St. Mary's Parish Church, Middleton, Leeds.

Writes for forces that he considers neglected, namely those churches with limited vocal resources, for whom the range of music available is unnecessarily restricted. His 'May the Grace of God ' and 'According to Thy gracious word' are scored accordingly for soprano and bass. There are also organ pieces and items for woodwind, including the quartet Short Woodwind Suite.

KNOTT, John (?-1837)

John Knott died in Edinburgh in 1837. Composed hymn tunes and other devotional music. His *Sacred Harmony* (1814) is a collection of Psalm and hymn tunes.

KNOWLES, Charles Edgar (1887-1973)

Born in Luton, Bedfordshire on 15 May 1887; died in Luton on 25 August 1973. Educated at Bedford School. Studied music with **Stanley Marchant**. Became a solicitor, living in London. From 1904 he was organist and choirmaster of the King Street Congregational Church, Luton. *Congregational Praise* (1951) uses his tune 'Mahon' with 'Jesus calls us o'er the tumult' by Cecil Frances Alexander. The tune was named after Revd. E.B. Mahon, minister of the King Street Church from 1909 to 1923.

KNOWLES, Francis William (19th/20th century)

Graduated B.Mus. at the University of Durham (1903). Submitted as his degree exercise a setting of Psalm 48 'Great is the Lord'.

KNOWLES, George J. (1749-1789)
Born in 1749; died in Birse, Aberdeen on 29 March 1789.
Educated at Marischal College, Aberdeen. In 1771 he was licensed
to preach. Minister of Birse (1778-1779). An amateur musician and
composer. Composed a Psalm tune 'Birse', also known as
'Balfour', included in the New Edition (1933) of *English Hymnal*
and the Enlarged Edition (1931) of *Songs of Praise*. Remembered
more for his poem *On Deeside* (1814).

KNYVETT, William (1779-1856)
Born on 21 April 1779; died in Ryde, Isle of Wight on 17
November 1856.
A son of Charles Knyvett the elder, a singer and organist. Studied
music with his father and with the elder **Samuel Webbe.**
A lay vicar of Westminster Abbey (from c1797). A gentleman
(from 1797) and composer (1808-1856) of the Chapel Royal where
he succeeded his father.
Sang in the Concerts of Ancient Music as a treble (from 1788) and
as an alto (from 1795). Also a concert singer, specialising in glees.
Conductor of the Concerts of Ancient Music (1832-1840).
Conducted at music festivals in Birmingham and York.
Composed anthems, including those used at the Coronations of
George IV (1821) 'The King shall rejoice' and Victoria (1838)
'This is the day'; 46 glees including 'When the fair rose', and
songs.

L

LACK, Graham Anthony (b.1954)

Born in Epsom, Surrey on 18 August 1954.

Attended Bishop Otter College, Chichester, Sussex (until 1975); Goldsmiths' College (to 1980), where he graduated B.Mus. and King's College, London (to 1980), where he worked for the M.Mus. Studied composition with **Anthony Milner** and historical musicology with Brian Trowell.

Lived and worked for 15 years in Germany in the cities of Munich and Cologne, from where he made radio broadcasts of church music. His radio career developed in 1995 when he became involved in a number of freelance activities for the B.B.C. including studio productions and being a member of the editorial team for the German language version of *B.B.C. Music Magazine.*

As conductor of the Cambridge Consort of Voices he toured Germany (1992) and took part in the Festival of European Church Music.

Has lectured in music at various colleges from 1981, including the University of Maryland, U.S.A. and Cricklade College, Andover, Hampshire where he was head of music.

Has composed Single Chant and Double Chant settings of Psalms 68 and 128-130, a Kyrie (1975), Sanctus (1986) and Gloria (1980), and the anthem 'The song of Zechariah'.

LACY, Frederick St. John (1862-1935)

Born in Blackrock, County Cork, Ireland on 27 March 1862; died in 1935.

Educated at Castlerock College, County Dublin with the aim of a career in law. Turned to music instead, studying at the Cork School of Music (1880-1883), privately under H.C. Swertz, and at the Royal Academy of Music in London under **George Macfarren, Ebenezer Prout, W.H. Cummings** and others.

A teacher in London (1886-1900). Returned to Cork in the latter year. Lecturer in music at Queen's College, Cork (from 1906); lecturer (from 1908) and a professor (1910-1933) at University College, Cork. Remained for a further year temporarily; retired and appointed emeritus professor in 1935.

Director of the choir of St. Augustine's Church, Ramsgate, Kent (1893-1894).

Promoted recitals of chamber music and served as a musical examiner. Author of works including *Notes on Irish Music.*

Composed a Mass in C, a Benediction Service in B-flat, songs, part songs and incidental music.

LAHEE, Henry (1826-1912)

Born in Chelsea, London on 11 April 1826; died in Croydon, Surrey on 29 April 1912.

Educated privately. A pupil of **William Sterndale Bennett, John Goss** for composition and Cipriani Potter for piano.

A London teacher and organist from the age of 17. Organist of St. Swithin's Church, London Stone (1843-1847). For the next 27 years he was organist of Holy Trinity Church, Brompton (1847-1874) where in collaboration with the vicar, Revd. William Irons he produced *The Metrical Psalter* (1855) and *One Hundred Hymn Tunes* (1857). Irons and Lahee were determined to improve the standard of music at Holy Trinity. Services for choir and orchestra, conducted by **Arthur Sullivan** were introduced.

Moved to Croydon, Surrey, where he taught music, performed as a concert pianist, and composed..

His hymn tune 'Nativity', composed for Philip Doddrige's 'High let us swell our tuneful notes' appeared in *The Metrical Psalter.* The tune has since been used in almost all major modern hymnals with 'Come, let us join our cheerful song' by Isaac Watts.

His works include cantatas, anthems such as 'Grant, we beseech Thee' and 'Praise the Lord', songs, instrumental works, glees including 'Hark, how the birds', and madrigals.

LAKE, George Ernest (1854-1893)

Born in London on 29 May 1854; died in London on 15 November 1893. Son of the musician George Handy Lake. Organist and music master of St. George's School, Brampton, Hertfordshire (from 1876) and an examiner for Trinity College of Music, London. He held church organistships at St. John's Episcopal Church, Edinburgh; Weybridge Parish Church, Surrey and All Saints', North Kensington, London (from 1885). Composed anthems including 'O Lamb of God', hymn tunes, chants, organ works and part songs, and the musical comedy *Sweepstakes.*

LAKE, Dr. Harold Charles (19th/20th century)

Graduated B.Mus. (1903) and D.Mus. (1912) at Queen's College, Oxford. A lecturer employed by Plymouth Education Authority, Devon. Organist of Plymouth Presbyterian Church (from 1894), and organist and choirmaster of Mutley Baptist Church, Plymouth (from 1897). A local choral society conductor. For his B.Mus. exercise he composed the anthem 'A shepherd's song of thanksgiving'.

LAMB, Benjamin (c1674-c1733)
A chorister of St. George's Chapel, Windsor Castle (from 1683). Succeeded **John Walter** as teacher of the choristers (from 1704) and organist (1703-1733) of Eton College, where was also copyist. After 1733 he is no longer mentioned in the College accounts. Deputy to **John Golding** and John Pigott at St. George's Chapel, Windsor Castle, where, from around 1715, he was verger. Composed a Service in E Minor, an Evening Service in B Minor, the anthem 'Unto Thee have I cried', and a Single Chant in F. Also songs.

LAMB, Revd. James (1835-1904)
Educated at the University of Edinburgh, where his course of study in the arts included music. Minister of the United Presbyterian Church, Old Kilpatrick, Dumbartonshire, Scotland (from 1867) and remained there for the rest of his life. Clerk to the committee of *Presbyterian Hymnal* and *Presbyterian Psalter* for the United Presbyterian Church. A member of the music committee for *Church Hymnary* (1898). Composed a hymn tune 'Invermay'.

LAMB, William (17th/18th century)
Succeeded his father and namesake as organist of Lichfield Cathedral. The records show that he still held the position in 1694. Composed the anthem 'Lord, who shall dwell'. It is said that he dishonestly claimed to have composed a Service actually written by Berchinshaw.

LAMBE, Walter (c1450-c1499)
Born in 1450 or 1451; died after 29 September, 1499.
May be the same Walter Lambe who was born in Salisbury, Wiltshire and entered Eton College at the age of 15 in July 1467.
Clerk of St. George's Chapel, Windsor Castle (from 1479). At some time he relinquished this position but he was re-appointed in July 1492.
At Michaelmas 1479, he and William Edmunds became joint masters of the Eton choristers, replacing Thomas Gossyp who had died of the plague. Lambe held the post exclusively from December 1479 until 1484 or 1485.
Composed a Magnificat and a number of motets. Some of his works are preserved in the *Eton Choirbook*, a major collection of contemporary church music dating from around the end of the 15th century.

LAMPE, John Frederick (c1703-1751)
Born in Saxony, Germany around the year 1703; died in Edinburgh on 25 July 1751.
Arrived in London around 1724. A skilled bassoon player, he found work almost immediately playing for the theatre. In 1748 or 1749 he moved to Dublin, where was a conductor of concerts and of incidental music for theatre. In November 1750 he settled in Edinburgh, where he found work in the Canongate Theatre.
Author of *The Art of Music* (1740), a work on harmony.
Composed operas that were said to be in the Italian style, and pantomimes. Lampe was a friend of Charles Wesley, for whose hymns he composed a number of tunes including 'Richmond', not

to be confused with a very popular tune of the same name by **Thomas Haweis**. Another tune by Lampe is 'Kent'.

LAMPLOUGH, Edmund Sykes (1860-?)
Born in Islington, London in 1860. Attended school in Tulse Hill, London. A member of the Committee for the *Methodist Hymn Book* (1904). Assisted in the compilation of *Methodist School Hymnal*, to which he contributed his tune 'Edinburgh'. At the invitation of **Frederick Bridge**, he sang in the Choir at the Coronation of George V in Westminster Abbey (1911).

LANCASTER, Joseph (1833-1880)
Organist of the Mill Hill Chapel, Leeds. Edited *Leeds Tune Book* (1868). Composed hymn tunes and other forms of church music. His 'St. Silas' appeared in *Bristol Tune Book* (1876). Also composed ballads and dance music.

LANCASTER, Walter James (1860-1952)
Born in Canterbury, Kent in 1860; died on 26 January 1952.
A chorister of St. George's Chapel, Windsor Castle for six months. Later studied under **E.J. Hopkins**, **Thomas Evance Jones** and **W.H. Longhurst**. Graduated B.Mus. at Owen's College, Victoria University of Manchester (1897).
Organist of St. Mary's Church, Dover, Kent (from 1878) and of All Saints' Church, Kingston-on-Thames, Surrey (from 1883). Organist and music master of St. Michael's College, Tenbury, Worcestershire (1886-1889). Organist and choirmaster of Bolton Parish Church, Lancashire (1889-1947), having been appointed on the advice of **John Stainer**.
Composed as his degree exercise a setting of Psalm 84 'O how amiable are Thy dwellings', an Evening Service, and songs.

LANE, Elihu Burritt (1849-1927)
Born in Christchurch, Hampshire in 1849; died in 1927.
Studied at Trinity College of Music, London. Graduated B.Mus. at the University of Durham (1891).
A teacher of organ at Bromley College of Music, Kent and an examiner for T.C.M., London. Teacher of music at Steyning Grammar School, Sussex (from 1913).
Organist and choirmaster of a number of churches in London and South East England. The first three were the Congregational Churches of Surbiton, Surrey (1868-1874); the King's Weigh House, London (1874-1879) and Anerley, Surrey (1879-1883). Organist of Holy Trinity Church, Twickenham, Middlesex (1883-1885) and Abney Congregional Church, Stoke Newington (1886-1891). Appointed to Bromley Parish Church, Kent (1891-1895) and subsequently to the Congregational Churches of Clifton and Peckham (1896), and restored to his previous position at the King's Weigh House (1896-1901).
Organist and choirmaster of Redhill Congregational Church, Surrey (1902-1910) and of Steyning Parish Church, Worthing (from 1910). A councillor, and a governor of Steyning Grammar School.
Composed a Te Deum, a Kyrie, hymn tunes and songs. Author of magazine articles for such publications as *Academic Gazette* and *Musical News*.

LANG, Craig Sellar (1891-1971)
Born in Hastings, near Napier, New Zealand in 1891; died in London on 24 November 1971.

Educated at Clifton College, Gloucestershire and, with piano and organ scholarships, at the Royal College of Music under **Walter Parratt** and **C.V. Stanford**.

Assistant music master of the Royal Naval College, Osborne, Isle of Wight (from 1913); Banstead Hall Preparatory School (1914-1920) and Clifton College (1920-1929) before becoming director of music of Christ's Hospital (1929-1945).

Resigned in 1945 in order to concentrate on examining and composition. Produced the Revised Edition (1949) of *Public School Hymn Book*. From around 1953 he lived at Polzeath, Cornwall.

Composed a Service in E-flat for Men's Voices and another, similarly scored, in C-sharp Minor. Also anthems such as 'Sing Alleluia' and hymn and carol tunes. These include a tune for the Epiphany carol 'Eastern monarchs, sages three'. His 'St. Enodoc' (1929), composed for Christ's Hospital to accompany the hymn 'O Jesu, strong and pure and true' by William Walsham How, is one of a number of tunes named after places in Cornwall. His tunes and descants are found in *Public School Hymn Book*. Composed a violin concerto, oratorios and works for piano and for organ.

LANGDON, Richard (c1729-1803)
Born in Exeter, Devon around the year 1729; died in Exeter on 8 September 1803. Probably the grandson of Tobias Langdon, a vicar choral of Exeter. Graduated B.Mus. at Exeter College, Oxford (1761). A lay vicar and organist of Exeter Cathedral (1753-1777); master of the choristers from 1762. Subsequently organist of the Cathedrals of Ely (1777), Bristol (1777-1781) and Armagh (1782-1794). Left Armagh in poor health and retired, probably to Exeter. A Richard Langdon was appointed organist of Peterborough Cathedral in June 1784 but did not take up the position. Whether or not this was the same person is conjectural. Published *Divine Harmony* (1794), a collection of Psalms and anthems. Composed anthems including 'Blessed is he that considereth' and 'O Lord, our Governour'. *Cathedral Psalter Chants* (1874) contains his Double Chant in F, first published in 1774. A Double Chant in E has been used in modern times. Also composed cantatas and songs.

LANGRAN, James (1835-1909)
Born in St. Pancras, London on 10 November 1835; died in Tottenham, London on 8 June 1909. A pupil of **Jean-Baptiste Calkin** and **Frederick Bridge**. Graduated B.Mus. at the University of Oxford (1884). Organist of the London Churches of St. Michael, Wood Green (1856-1859); Holy Trinity, Tottenham (1859-1870) and All Hallows, Tottenham (1870-1909). Taught at St. Katherine's Training College, Tottenham, (1878-1909). Musical editor of *New Mitre Hymnal* (1875). Composed a Morning and Evening Service, and some 50 hymn tunes. His 'St. Agnes' (1861), also known as 'Evensong', was composed for the hymn 'Abide with me' by H.F. Lyte. Others include 'Deerhurst', named after a village near Tewkesbury, Gloucestershire, 'St. Philip' and 'St. James'.

LANGSHAW, John (1763-after 1798)
Studied with Charles Wesley. A concert pianist. Taught music in London. Succeeded his father, John, as organist of Lancaster Parish Church (1798). Composed hymns, chants, songs and concertos for piano.

LANIER (Laniere, Laneare, Lanyer, Lenear), Nicholas (1588-1666)
Born in London and baptised on 10 September 1588; died in London and buried on 24 February 1666. Indentured to the Earl of Salisbury until 1607. Worked for the Cecil family at Hatfield House, Hertfordshire (1605-1613). Musician to the Princes Henry and Charles, and master of the music to the latter (from 1618). A lutenist of the king's music (from 1616). On the accession of Charles I to the throne (1625), Lanier became master of the king's music in all but name. He bought paintings on Charles's behalf in Venice and elsewhere. His arrest in 1629 for disorderly behaviour in the street caused a scandal. He sought exile during the period of the Protectorate, living for a while in France and the Low Countries. Composed ayres, works for the stage, a funeral hymn for Charles I and the motet *O amantissime Domine*.

LARDNER, Thomas William (19th/20th century)
Educated privately and at the Royal Academy of Music. His training in church music was at the Church of St. Matthias, Earl's Court, London. Graduated B.Mus. at Queen's College, Oxford (1913). Organist and choirmaster of the three Churches of St. John the Divine, Balham, London (from 1896); Marlow Parish Church, Buckinghamshire (1897-1903) All Saints, Upper Norwood, Surrey (1903-1918). Lived in the London suburb of Wandsworth. Composed an anthem 'Exultate te, Deus', and songs.

LATHAM, Morton (c.1843-1931)
Born around 1843; died at the age of 88 on 5 November 1931. Educated at Trinity College, Cambridge where he graduated B.A. (1865), M.A. and Mus.B. (1882). A lecturer and Justice of the Peace. Honorary secretary of the Bach Choir (1886-1900) and honorary conductor of Farnham Orchestral Society. Composed a Te Deum, and songs.

LATHAM, Richard Oskatel (1906-?)
Born in London in 1906. A chorister of St. George's Chapel, Windsor Castle, continuing his education at Cheltenham College, Gloucestershire and at the Royal College of Music. Organist of the London Churches of St. Matthew, Ealing (1924-1930); St. John the Baptist, Holland Road (1930-1933); and St. Paul, Knightsbridge. A professor of the R.C.M. (from 1934), where he taught organ and directed the choir-training class. Principal and director of music of the London College for Choristers. Director of music of the Madrigal Society. Composed a motet *O God of Truth*, settings of the Magnificat and Nunc Dimittis in F and in E-flat, anthems, and songs.

LATROBE, Revd. Christian Ignatius (1758-1836)
Born in Fulneck, Leeds on 12 February 1758; died in Fairfield, near Liverpool on 6 May 1836. Father of **Peter Latrobe**.
Studied for the ministry of the Moravian Church: ordained in 1784. Taught at a high school in Upper Lusatia, returning to England in 1784. Became secretary to the Society for the Furtherance of the Gospel (1787), and to the Unity of Brethren in England (1795). Visited South Africa (1815 -1816).
Never a professional musician, but edited and composed a significant amount of material. Editor of the first edition of *Moravian Hymn Book*. Published selections of sacred music by German and Italian composers (1806-1825).
His own works include anthems such as 'Make a joyful noise' and 'O be joyful', chorales, hymn tunes - some of which are found in

Methodist Hymn Book (1933) - a Morning and Evening Service in G (1817), a *Dies Irae* (1799) and various instrumental works.

LATROBE, Revd. Peter (1795-1863)
Born in London on 15 February 1795; died in Bertheldorf, near Herrnhut, Germany in 1863. The son of **Christian Latrobe**. Became a minister of the Moravian Church. Secretary of the Moravian Mission. Compiled a brief history of Church Psalmody as an introduction to a collection of Moravian hymn tunes. His own compositions include hymn tunes and chants.

LAVINGTON, Charles Williams (1819-1895)
Born in Wells, Somerset on 20 February 1819; died in Wells on 27 October 1895.
A chorister of Wells Cathedral, where he was also a pupil of the cathedral organist, **William Perkins**. Studied under **James Turle** of Westminster Abbey.
Although nominally assistant organist of Wells Cathedral (from 1843), he was actually given day-to-day responsibility for the music at once. Eventually appointed organist of Wells Cathedral (1860-1895), following the death of William Perkins.
Made history by being the first Wells organist not to be a vicar choral. Established a reputation very quickly as a martinet, expelling two boys from the choir immediately following a single instance of unauthorised absence. Also organist of Wells Theological College. During a long illness, T.H. Davis (a lay vicar) and **C.H. Moody** deputised for him.
Composed anthems including 'Fear thou not' and 'O almighty God', and chants.

LAW, John
See **LEECH-WILKINSON**, Arthur.

LAWES, Henry (1596-1662)
Born in Dinton, Wiltshire on 5 January 1596; died in London on 21 October 1662. Buried in the cloisters of Westminster Abbey. Elder brother of **William Lawes**.
May have been a chorister at Salisbury Cathedral, where his father was a vicar-choral from 1602. A pupil of **John Coprario**.
In 1626 he was employed at the Chapel Royal as epistolar (one who reads the Epistle during Holy Communion). Later that year he became a gentleman of the Chapel Royal and some time afterwards, clerk of the cheque. A royal musician to Charles I 'for the lutes and voices'(from 1631). A teacher of singing and viol. At some time before the Commonwealth period he taught music to the daughters of the Earl of Bridgwater. Became known for his fashionable music parties.
The Civil War interrupted his career at the Chapel Royal. At the Restoration he returned to his previous positions at the Chapel Royal, but his task was made difficult by the fact that tastes had progressed in the intervening years, and he found himself to some extent out of touch. Worse still, the lack of experienced boy trebles made it necessary to have the top part sung falsetto by men, or played by cornetts.
Known to have composed music for the theatre and other forms of public entertainment, amounting to some 434 songs. A friend of John Milton, for whose *Comus* (1637) Henry Lawes composed incidental music. In 1646 Milton dedicated a sonnet to Henry Lawes which began 'Harry, whose tuneful and well-measured song.'

Composed 'Zadok the priest' as a Coronation anthem for Charles II, and other anthems including 'When the mountains were brought forth' and 'The Lord, in thy adversity'. Of his Psalm tunes, two have been adapted for hymn singing. 'Farley Castle' was composed for Psalm 72 and 'Whitehall' for Psalm 8. Both are found in *Songs of Praise* and many other hymnals. Lawes is credited with taking great care to bring out the meaning of the texts in his compositions.

LAWES, William (1602-1645)
Born in Salisbury, Wiltshire and baptised on 1 May 1602; died on 24 September 1645 while fighting on the Royalist side at the Siege of Chester. The younger brother of **Henry Lawes**. Probably educated at Salisbury Grammar School. A pupil of **John Coprario**. A musician to Charles I and on the death of John Lawrence (1635), succeeded him as a member of the King's Music, for lutes and voices. Moved with Charles to Oxford in 1642. Unlike his brother, Henry, William had no connection with the Chapel Royal. His most famous composition of all is the song 'Gather ye rosebuds while ye may', one of a number of items of consort music. Composed at least four anthems, one of which is 'The Lord is my Light'.

LAWRANCE, Edward (1836-1900)
Born in Weymouth, Dorset on 28 March 1836; died in Merthyr Tydfil, Wales on 10 June 1900. Studied locally under Ricardo Linter and at the Leipzig Conservatory under Ignaz Moscheles, Louis Plaidy, Ernst Richter, Moritz Hauptmann and others (1856-1858). Organist of Sidmouth Parish Church, Devon (from 1859) and of St. David's Church, Merthyr Tydfil (from 1860). He held both appointments until 1891 when he resigned as a matter of principle over the spread of ritualistic practices at each. Organist of Christ Church, Cyfartha (from 1892). Composed a trio for piano and strings, an opera *Conradine*, anthems, services, chants, hymn tunes and songs. His cantata *The Siege of Harlech* won a prize at the National Eisteddfod of 1863.

LAWRENCE, Elizabeth S. (19th century)
Elizabeth Lawrence and her daughter **Emily Lawrence** were church musicians and composers from the middle years of the 19th century. Elizabeth Lawrence was organist of Rugby Parish Church, Warwickshire (1842-1877). She compiled a book of Psalm tunes, and composed hymn tunes and chants.

LAWRENCE, Emily M. (1854-?)
Born in Rugby, Warwickshire in 1854. Studied privately with her mother, **Elizabeth Lawrence** and for three years at the Royal Academy of Music under **William Sterndale Bennett**, Manuel Garcia and **Charles Steggall**. Organist of St. John's Church, Wembley, Middlesex (from 1889). Composed anthems, two cantatas for ladies' voices, songs, part songs and duets.

LAWRIE, Alexander (1818-1880)
Born in Edinburgh on 26 June 1818; died in Edinburgh on 9 December 1880. A blind musician. Organist of St. James's Episcopal Chapel, Edinburgh and of Revd. John Kirk's Chapel, Edinburgh. Composed songs and hymn tunes, and arranged music for piano.

LAWSON, Gordon (b.1931)
Born near Glasgow on 22 December 1931. Studied at Glasgow Academy; Rydal School, North Wales and St. John's College, Cambridge. Assistant director of music at Ellesmere College,

Shropshire and Malvern College, Worcestershire. Director of music of Brighton College, Sussex and director of chapel music. A local choral society conductor. Organist of Ringmer Parish Church, Sussex (1991-1996). Has composed a Magnificat and Nunc Dimittis in F, carols such as 'When Christ was born', an arrangement of 'How far is it to Bethlehem?' and settings of Psalms 23 and 121.

LAWSON, Malcolm Leonard (1849-?)
Born in London in 1849. Studied in London and in France, Italy and Germany. Helped to revive the popularity of works by Christoph Gluck, Leonardo Leo, Giovanni Pergolesi and **Henry Purcell**. Organist and choirmaster of the Catholic Apostolic Church, London (from 1876), for which he composed Festival Services in D and in F. Also composed six anthems, motets for ladies' voices and music for the play *Olivia* (1877).

LAYCOCK, Geoffrey Newton Stephen (1927-1986)
Born in York on 27 January 1927; died in Norwich, Norfolk on 21 May 1986.
A chorister at York Minster under **Edward Bairstow** before studying at York Grammar School and at the Royal College of Music.
A teacher. Principal lecturer at Keswick Hall College, Norwich (1961-1981). Musical editor for the 1971 Edition of *New Catholic Hymnal*. Organist of St. George's Roman Catholic Church, Norwich.
Two of his own tunes that he included in his 1971 compilation are 'Niamryl' (an anagram of Marilyn) and 'Harvest'. The latter was also used in *100 More Hymns for Today* (1980). His tunes are also found in *New Celebration Hymnal*. Widely recognised as influential upon the hymnody of the Roman Catholic Church.

LAYLAND, John (19th/20th century)
Graduated B.Mus. at the University of Durham (1907). Organist of St. Mary's Church, Shroton, Dorset. As his degree exercise he composed the anthem 'Praise the Lord, O Jerusalem', the words taken from Psalms 145-147.

LEACH, James (1762-1798)
Born in Wardle, near Rochdale, Lancashire in 1762; died in Blackley, near Manchester on 8 February 1798 following a stage coach accident.
Had little musical training except for some tuition on violin.
A hand loom weaver by trade, he eventually joined the King's Band and became known as a singer, choir trainer and teacher in London, Rochdale (from 1789) and Salford (from 1796). Took part in the Handel Festivals in Westminster Abbey.
Director of the Union Street Methodist Chapel, Rochdale.
In 1788, John Wesley preached at Wandle at the Methodist meeting house of which James Leach was a member. Wesley asked whose tunes were being sung and was told by Leach's uncle that they were by James Leach. They were introduced and Wesley, who was in his 85th year, gave Leach words of encouragement.
Published two compilations of hymn tunes (1789 and 1798). He included his own 'Watchman', which is found in modern hymnals including *Hymns and Psalms* (1983). Other tunes include 'Penn', 'Egypt' and 'Mount Pleasant'. His hymn tunes were particularly popular in the U.S.A. Also composed anthems, and trios for two violins and bass viol. His 'Pastoral' was composed at the age of 18.

LEAH, John Edward (1870-1949)
Born in Eastwood, Yorkshire in 1870; died in 1949. Educated privately. Organist of St. John's Congregational Church, West Hartlepool (from 1904). Organist and choirmaster of Hillcrest Road Congregational Church, Bournemouth, Dorset, around 1937. Held similar positions at the Congregational Churches of Richmond Hill, Bournemouth and Guildford, Surrey, where he taught music at the County Secondary School for Girls. A teacher of piano and organ at the University College of Wales, Aberystwyth (1900-1903). Composed choral music.

LEAKE, George (1859-1928)
Born in Derby in 1859; died on 8 May 1928.
Trained in music privately and at Lichfield Cathedral. Graduated B.Mus. at the University of Durham (1900).
Organist and choirmaster of Holy Trinity Church, Halstead, Essex (1880-1899); St. Mark's Church (1899-1919) and St. Mary's Church (from 1917), Southampton. A local choral and philharmonic society conductor.
Lectured in music at Hartley University College, Southampton. A musical examiner for the Associated Board of the Royal Schools of Music. Head of the department of music of Southampton University from its inception. Appointed professor in 1920.
Composed a setting of Psalm 130 'Out of the deep' for Solo Voices, Chorus and Strings.

LEAVER, Wiliam John (19th century)
Studied at the Royal Academy of Music. Graduated Mus.B. at the University of Cambridge (1884). Organist and choirmaster of the Church of St. John, Blackheath, London. Composed a setting of Psalm 146 'Praise the Lord, O my soul' for Solo Voices, Chorus and Orchestra; anthems; songs; part songs and items for piano.

LEDGER, Dr. Philip Stevens (b.1937)
Born in Bexhill-on-Sea, Sussex on 12 December 1937.
Studied at Bexhill Grammar School and at King's College, Cambridge where he graduated M.A. and Mus.B. The University of Strathclyde created him LL.D. honorarily in 1987.
Appointed C.B.E. in 1985.
On his appointment at Chelmsford, Philip Ledger became the youngest cathedral organist in the country, (1962-1965). Director of music at the University of East Anglia (1965-1973), and dean of the School of Fine Arts and Music (1968-1971).
Organist of King's College, Cambridge (1974-1982).
Artistic director (from 1968) and later a vice-president of the Aldeburgh Festival, Suffolk.
Principal of the Royal Scottish Academy of Music and Drama, Glasgow (from 1982).
Editor of arrangements of *Anthems For Choirs* (1973), and *The Oxford Book of English Madrigals*.
His own arrangements include the carols 'I saw three ships', 'Still, still, still' and 'On Christmas night'. Compositions include the anthem 'O Master, let me walk with Thee'.

LE FLEMING, Christopher Kaye (1908-1985)
Born in Wimborne Minster, Dorset in 1908; died in 1985.
Studied at Down House School, Rottingdean, Sussex, and at the nearby Brighton School of Music where he learned to play organ under **Alfred King**. Also studied with George Reeves and **S.H. Nicholson**. Aspired to a place at the Royal College of Music but an eye specialist forbade it as a further threat to his already-weak

eyesight. He did however study piano under Evlyn Howard Jones, a fashionable teacher whose other pupils included **Edmund Rubbra**. Studied at the Royal School of Church Music.

Pursued a career as a musician, critic and composer and is particularly remembered for his work with the Rural Music Schools' Association. A critic on the staff of the Columbia Company (1928-1931).

Called up for active service during World War II but soon discharged because of his poor eyesight.

Director of music of St. Mary's Church, Calne (1943-1946) and of the Wiltshire Rural Music School (1943-1945). Assistant director of the Rural Music Schools' Association (1945-1952) and music master of Sutton Valence School, Kent (1957-1958).

Published an autobiography *Journey into Music* (1982).

His compositions include an Evening Service in D (1953), a Cradle Song for Christmas (1929), a *Christmas Triptych* (1966), a motet *Since we stay not here*, songs and pieces for piano.

LEE, Dr. Ernest Markham (1874-1956)
Born in Cambridge on 8 June 1874; died in Eastbourne, Sussex on 13 November 1956.

A chorister of Clare College, Cambridge from the age of nine, and a pupil of the college organist, **William Dewberry**. Attended Perse School, Cambridge. Graduated B.A. (1894), Mus.B. (1894) M.A. (1899) and Mus.D. (1899) at Emmanuel College, Cambridge, where he was organ scholar, and organist (1894-1896).

Organist of the Churches of St. Matthew, Cambridge (from 1890) and All Saints, Woodford Green, Essex (1896-1911).

A professor at Guildhall School of Music (from 1905) and an extension lecturer at the universities of Oxford, Cambridge and London. A musical examiner for the University of London (1913-1917) and elsewhere, undertaking examination tours of Canada and New Zealand (1929-1930), Jamaica and Canada (1933) and India (1934).

Adjudicated at competitive music festivals.

Author of works including *On Listening to Music*, biographies of Tchaikovsky and Grieg and books on the subject of opera.

Began to compose at the age of 14. His works comprise services, anthems including 'Blessed be the Lord, my Strength' (1956), carols, an *Ode to Prince Edward*, cantatas, organ music, the light opera *Paris in Spring*, songs and part songs.

LEE, J.S. (1831-?)
Born on 14 February 1831. Bandmaster of the 20th Hussars for many years. At one time he was one of the oldest bandmasters in the British Army. Composed church music for military choirs, works for military bands, and songs.

LEE, James Vernon (1892-1959)
Born in Hove, Sussex on 7 February 1892; died in Southampton, Hampshire on 6 November 1959.

Awarded the Military Cross in World War I, serving in France.

Bursar of Caterham School, Surrey (1919-1939) and entertainments officer in South Wales during World War II. Accomplished both as a musician and as a magician, he combined these gifts as a professional entertainer. Gave a Command Performance at Windsor Castle (1937). Awarded the Gold Star of the Magic Circle (1940).

From around 1953 he lived in Ditchling, Sussex.

An organist, also devoting much of his spare time to youth work and in particular the Boys' Brigade, for whom he was an officer of the Brighton Battalion (1910-1914).

Composed several hymn tunes. 'Eastview', composed for 'Rejoice! The Lord is King!' by Charles Wesley on the occasion of the eightieth birthday of Lee's mother, was used in *Congregational Praise* (1951) and has been used in a number of hymnals since.

LEE, Thomas (19th/20th century)
Graduated Mus.B. at the University of Cambridge (1885). Organist and choirmaster of St. Peter's Church, Finchley, London and of Formby Parish Church, near Liverpool. Taught vocal and theoretical music at Southport Municipal School, Lancashire. Music master of Southport University School. As his university exercise he composed a setting of Psalm 126 'When the Lord' for Solo Voices, Chorus and Orchestra.

LEE, William (?-1754)
Organist of Southwell Minster (1718-1754). Composed the anthems 'O do well unto Thy servants' and 'They that put their trust'. *Cathedral Psalter Chants* (1875) contains his Single Chant in G.

LEEDS, Frederic (1866-1961)
Born in Lee, London in 1866; died in Reigate, Surrey on 4 May 1961.

Educated at the Royal College of Music and at the University of Cambridge, where graduated Mus.B. (1888). His teachers in music were **C.V. Stanford**, **Hubert Parry**, **Walter Parratt** and George Grove.

Master of singing in London at Colfe's Grammar School, Lewisham (1896-1920); Blackheath School and Eltham College. Sang at Queen Victoria's Golden Jubilee Service (1897) in Westminster Abbey, and at the Coronations of Edward VII and George V.

Organist of St. Mark's Church, Lewisham (from 1886). Organist and choirmaster to a number of Churches in and around London, namely Christ Church, Brondesbury (1890); St. Luke's Parish Church, Charlton (from 1893) and the Parish Churches of St. Mary, Lewisham (1895); and St. Margaret, Lee (1899-1934). He then moved to Sussex and was organist and choirmaster of St. Mary's Church, Battle (1935) and St. Matthew's Church, St. Leonard's (1936). A local orchestral society conductor.

Joint editor, with **Walford Davies**, of *The Psalter Newly Pointed*.

Composed an Evening Service for Male Voices and a choral setting of the Evening Canticles which was included in *Bristol Service Book*. Also composed songs and a dramatic poem *Home and Liberty* for accompanied Male Voices.

LEEVES, Revd. William (1748-1828)
Born on 11 June 1748; died in Wrington, Somerset on 25 May 1828. A soldier, minister of the church, poet and composer of church and other music. Joined the army (1764); promoted to ensign (1769), lieutenant, and captain (1772) of the 1st Regiment of Foot Guards. Ordained priest in 1779. Rector of Wrington (1779-1828). A cellist and poet. Composed the song 'Auld Robin Gray' (1770), and church music.

LEFFLER, Adam (1808-1857)
Born in 1808; died in London on 28 March 1857. A chorister of Westminster Abbey. A bass opera and concert singer. Composed the anthem 'Try me, O God'.

LEGGE, Alfred (1843-1919)
Born in Cambridge in 1843; died in Ashford, Kent in 1919.
At the age of nine he became a chorister of Trinity College, Cambridge, where he became assistant organist. Studied under **T.A. Walmisley** and **J.L. Hopkins**.
Organist of St. Clement's Church, Cambridge; Wickham Parish Church, Berkshire and All Saints' Church, Cambridge. Subsequently organist of Ashford Parish Church for more than 50 years.
A teacher of music. His pupils included Queen Marie of Rumania and Grand Duchess Cyril of Russia.
His hymn tune 'Theodora' was composed for the Choir of Ashford Parish Church to accompany the hymn 'Rest of the Weary' by John Monsell. It was published in *Congregational Psalmist* (1875).

LEIGH, Arthur George (1846-1904)
Born in Ashton in Makerfield, Lancashire on 22 August 1846; died in 1904. Studied music under **Thomas Graham** (1860-1866). Organist and choirmaster of Chorley Parish Church (1866-1868) and St. George's Church, Chorley (1877-1896). A councillor at Chorley; mayor in 1887, 1888 and 1889. Composed 10 sets of Responses, chants, hymn tunes, and songs. A Kyrie by him was first published in 1893.

LEIGHTON, Dr. Kenneth (1929-1988)
Born in Wakefield, Yorkshire on 2 October 1929; died in Edinburgh on 24 August 1988.
A chorister of Wakefield Cathedral. Attended Queen Elizabeth Grammar School, Wakefield. Studied classics (1947-1950) and music (1950-1951) at Queen's College, Oxford, where his tutor for composition was **Bernard Rose** and where he was awarded the D.Mus. honorarily. Won a Mendelssohn Scholarship to Rome (1951), studying under Goffredo Petrassi.
A professor of theory at the Royal Northern College of Music (1952-1953). A lecturer in musical composition and Gregory fellow at the University of Leeds (1953-1955). Lecturer in composition at the University of Edinburgh (1955-1968); lecturer in music at Worcester College, Oxford (from 1968).
Reid professor of music at the University of Edinburgh (from 1970).
A pianist, and composer of more than one hundred works. Musical consultant to the Revision Committee for the Third Edition (1973) of *Church Hymnary*.
Composed orchestral works, and chamber and instrumental music. His compositions for the church include a set of Responses, a Te Deum, the *Magdalen College* Service and the anthems 'Let all the world', 'Sequence for all Saints', 'Solus ad victimam' ('Alone to sacrifice, Thou goest, Lord'), 'Give me the wings of faith' and 'Alleluia, Amen'. Also composed much important organ music, including a Prelude, Scherzo and Passacaglia; a Paean and an organ duet 'Martyrs'.

LEIGHTON, Sir William (c1565-1622)
Born, probably in Plash, Shropshire around 1565; died in 1622 and was buried in London on 31 July.
Attended Shrewsbury School (from 1758).

Member of Parliament for Much Wenlock (from 1601). A member of the Honourable Band of Gentleman Pensioners of James I (from 1602).
Wrote a poem in honour of James I (1603), in which year he received a knighthood.
In 1609 he was imprisoned for debt. During his detention he wrote metrical paraphrases of the Psalms and devotional poems. These he later published, set to music by the leading composers of the day, as *The Teares or Lamentations of a Sorrowful Soule* (1613). By 1615 he had been released from prison.
An amateur composer. His works include the anthem 'Thou art my God'. Eight of the 17 consort songs in *Lamentations* were his.

LEMARE, Dr. William (1839-1917)
Born in Godalming, Surrey in 1839; died in Chingford, Essex, on 29 March 1917.
Attended Dr. Watson's College, Guildford. Received lessons in music from his father, and studied further with **Henry Gauntlett**. The Lambeth D.Mus. was conferred upon him in 1888.
Active musically in and around London. Gave concerts at the Gresham Hall, Brixton; the Crystal Palace and the Brighton Aquarium, Surrey.
A conductor for choral societies. Director of the Bournemouth Music Festival, Dorset. Trained the chorus for the 1880 series of promenade concerts at Covent Garden.
Organist of St. Jude's Church, East London (from 1860); St. Andrew's, Stockwell (from 1865); Brixton Parish Church (from 1872); St. Saviour's, Herne Hill (from 1876); St. Mary's, Newington (from 1880); St. Mary's, Longfleet, Kent (from 1888); St. Nathaniel, Westbourne (from 1894) and All Saints', Leyton (from 1897). Choirmaster of Ringwood Parish Church, Hampshire.
Ill through overwork. Compelled to rest and recuperate for three years. Eventually he leased the Bournemouth Winter Gardens and gave daily concerts there, as well as establishing a school of music in the town.
Composed services, anthems, operettas including *A calm sea* (1882), and songs.

LEMON, John (1754-1814)
Born in Truro, Cornwall and baptised on 29 November 1754; died at Polvellen, Cornwall on 5 April 1814. His grandfather had become wealthy through his copper mining business. Lemon became a lieutenant-colonel in the Horse Guards. Later became Member of Parliament for West Looe, Saltash and Truro (1796-1814). An amateur musician and composer. *Cathedral Psalter Chants* (1874) included his Double Chant in G: there is also a Chant in D.

LESLIE, Ernest B. (19th/20th century)
Lived and worked in London in the early part of the present century. Little else is known about him. Composed the hymn tunes 'Greenwell', first published in *Sunday School Hymnary* (1905) and 'Adsum'.

LESLIE, Henry David (1822-1896)
Born in London on 18 June 1822; died in Llansaintfraid, near Oswestry on 4 February 1896.
A pupil of **Charles Lucas**.
Very well known in his day through 'Leslie's Choir of London'. It had been founded by Joseph Heming. Leslie was conductor from 1855 to 1880 and from 1885 to 1887. The choir had a wide range

of works by English composers in the repertoire and won first prize in an international contest held in Paris in 1878.

An advocate of choral singing, doing much to promote it when he moved to Oswestry. A trainer of various village choirs. Founded the Oswestry School of Music and the Oswestry Festival (1879). Noticed the young **Walford Davies**, whose talent he recognised and whom he encouraged accordingly.

A cellist, editor and administrator. Edited Cassell's *Choral Music* (1867). Principal of the National College of Music from 1864 until its dissolution in 1866.

His works include a Morning Service in D, the anthems 'Blow ye the trumpet' and 'O have mercy', oratorios, a Symphony in F, and songs.

LESLIE, Henry Temple (c1825-1876)

Born around the year 1825; died in Sandown, Isle of Wight on 5 May 1876. Organist of the Church of St. Mary le Port, Bristol. A musical editor and teacher of music. May also have been involved with the temperance movement. Joint editor of *Clifton Conference Hymns*, which included his own 'Ephraim'. *Cathedral Psalter Chants* (1874) contains his Single Chant in F Minor. Also composed songs.

LEWIS, David (1828-1908)

Born in Llanrwrytd, Cardiganshire, Wales on 12 November 1828; died on 6 October 1908. The older brother of **John Lewis**.

Studied music with his father, Lewis Lewis and under Thomas Jenkins, who also taught **John Roberts** (Ieuan Gwyllt).

Both sons started work in the tailoring trade. David Lewis conducted singing classes and became a musical adjudicator throughout Wales. Researched into the lives and works of the Welsh hymn writers and composers.

Like his father, he collected Welsh melodies. A number of these were later edited and published by **J.T. Rees**.

Composed from the age of 15. His hymn tunes won prizes at *eisteddfodau* in the 1860s, following an early success when the adjudicator had been **Edward Jones** (Tanymarian). Many were published in periodicals such as *Y Cerddor Cymreig*.

Joint musical editor, with **William Williams** (Gwilym Gwent), of *Llwybraur Moliant* (The Paths of Praise), a hymnal used in Welsh Baptist Churches.

LEWIS, David William (1845-1920)

Born in Brynaman, Carmarthenshire, Wales on 15 April 1845; died on 20 January 1920. From the age of nine he worked in a colliery, studying music in his leisure time using books by **John Mills** (Ieuan Glan Alarch) and Eleazar Roberts. Learned the Tonic Sol-fa method of notation and passed his examinations in Bristol (1870). Became the first fellow of the Tonic Sol-fa College in Wales. Carried on music classes in Carmarthenshire and conducted festivals of hymn singing. Published *Odlau Mawl* and *Llawlyfy y Llais* and, in collaboration with others, edited similar publications. A Justice of the Peace for Carmarthenshire (from 1919). Composed anthems and hymn tunes, some of which were written specifically for children.

LEWIS, Jeffrey (b.1942)

Born in Port Talbot, South Wales, on 28 November 1942.

Awarded a Welsh Arts Council Bursary (1967-1968), enabling him to travel and study at Darmstadt with Karl-Heinz Stockhausen and György Ligeti, and at Krakow with Bogusław Schäffer. Graduated

B.Mus. (1965) and M.Mus. (1967) at University College, Cardiff, and awarded the Ph.D. in composition (1977) at the University of Wales. Has also studied electronic composition with Don Banks in London.

A pianist with the Paris Chamber Ensemble (1967-1968). Lecturer in 20th century compositional techniques and experimental music at the City of Leeds College of Music (1969-1972). Lecturer (1973-1987) and senior lecturer (1987-1992) at the University of Wales, Bangor, taking early retirement in order to devote more time to composition.

Has lectured publicly on 'Contemporary music for the cathedral repertoire: a composer's viewpoint', and 'Change and challenge: the current state of British cathedral music', the latter being published in *Choir and Organ*.

Has won a number of composition prizes, including awards at the International organist/composer Competition in Zwolle, Holland and at the Stroud Festival International Composers' Competition.

His works include the *Westminster* Mass (1996), commissioned by Westminster Abbey, three settings of the Magnificat and Nunc Dimittis, and the anthem 'Lux perpetua', commissioned by the Hillyard Ensemble. Organ works comprise Mutations II; Esultante; Momentum; Antiphon for Trumpet and Organ, and others.

LEWIS, John (1836-1892)

Born in Wales on 6 April 1836; died on 2 November 1892. The brother of **David Lewis**. Both sons, like their father, were tailors. John is better known as a poet than a musician, winning eisteddfod prizes for his works. He did however compose some hymn tunes, one of which, 'Adgyfodiad' (1896), was included in a collection by William Harries (Heolyfelin). Also composed part songs.

LEWIS, Joseph Rhys (1860-1920)

Born in Penderyn, Brecknock, Wales on 15 June 1860; died in Ferndale, Wales on 17 June 1920. As a child his health was poor and he received little formal education. Took piano lessons with **Joseph Parry**, and with **David Evans** in Cardiff. Organist of the Penuel Chapel, Ferndale and of the Bethania Chapel, Maerdy. His hymn tune 'Nazareth' was popular during the Welsh religious revival of 1904-1905. Also composed the two operas *Caradog* and *Resurrected Life*.

LEWIS, Rees (Eos Ebrill: 1828-1880)

Born in Twyn Cynordy near Bryn-Mawr, Brecknock, Wales in 1828; died on 14 December 1880. Son of the precentor of the Nebo Chapel, Pen-y-Cal. Studied music with his father and with a musician from Pembrokeshire who lived in the area. Spent two years at Borough Road Training College, London. Taught at Blaina, Monmouthshire and in Cardiff. A conductor and violin player, he strove to improve musical tastes and standards in Cardiff. Formed the Cardiff Philharmonic Society and played violin in a band which he led. Edited a hymnal intended for the use of Baptist congregations in Wales but it was never published. Composed an anthem 'Arglwydd, gollwng' which was published in *Y Gerddorfa*, and many other works.

LEY, Dr. Henry George (1887-1962)

Born in Chagford, Devon on 30 December 1887; died near Ottery, Devon on 24 August 1962. His father, Revd. G.L.H. Ley, was rector of Chagford.

A chorister of St. George's Chapel, Windsor Castle (from 1896), where he was allowed to play an organ voluntary at the age of 10 and an entire Service at 12. Attended Uppingham School and the Royal College of Music (from 1904) where his teachers were **Walter Parratt**, **C.V. Stanford** and **Charles Wood**. Organ scholar of Keble College, Oxford (1906-1909). Graduated B.Mus. (1911, at Christ Church), M.A. (1913) and D.Mus. (1919).

Had been organist of St. Mary's Church, Farnham Royal, Buckinghamshire (1905-1906) prior to Oxford. On completing his studies he became organist of Christ Church Cathedral, Oxford (1909-1926), where one of his choristers was the young **William Walton**. Later became choragus of the university (1923-1926). Precentor of Radley College, Oxfordshire (1916-1918) and of Eton College (1926-1945). Teacher of organ at the R.C.M. (1919-1945). One of the editors of *Oxford Psalter* (1932), *Church Anthem Book* (1933) and *Oxford Chant Book Number Two* (1934). Contributed articles on **Walford Davies** and **Basil Harwood** to *Dictionary of National Biography*.

A railway enthusiast. While precentor at Eton he was able to indulge in his hobby of train-spotting, and he became acquainted with a number of engine drivers at the Royal Oak Depot, West London.

Composed services including a Morning and Evening Service in C, settings of the Holy Comunion in B-flat and in E Minor, anthems such as 'Lo round the throne' and 'The strife is o'er', songs, organ music and the children's operetta *Savernake*. The hymn tune 'Ad Astra' was used in the Revised Edition (1950) of *Hymns Ancient and Modern* and in *Hymns and Psalms* (1983). Other tunes include 'Rushford' and 'Ottery St. Mary'. Composed Chants in C and in E. The Prayer of King Henry VI, a motet, is widely sung.

LIDDLE, John Shepherd (?-1921)
Died on 30 March 1921. A chorister of St. George's Chapel, Windsor Castle. Graduated Mus.B. at St. John's College, Cambridge (1876). A teacher at University College, Reading. Played viola, violin and piano. Organist of the Parish Churches of Clewer, near Windsor (from 1872), Halifax, Yorkshire (from 1883) and Newbury, Berkshire (from 1884). A local choral and orchestral society conductor, and conductor of the English Ladies' Orchestral Society. In 1896 he succeeded Augustus Manns as conductor of the Handel Society in London.

LIDDLE, Robert William (1864-1917)
Born in Durham on 14 March 1864; died in Southwell, Nottinghamshire on 23 December 1917. A chorister at St. Oswald's Church, Durham and subsequently at Durham Cathedral where he studied under **Philip Armes**. Organist of St. Baldred's Church, North Berwick (from 1885). Organist and choirmaster of Southwell Minster (1888-1917) and of St. Peter's Church, Mansfield, Nottinghamshire (from 1904). A violinist, he formed a quartet. His compositions include services, hymn tunes, chants and the anthem 'O, send out Thy light' (1909).

LIMPUS, Revd. F. Henry (?-1893)
Brother of Richard D. Limpus, one of the founders of the College of Organists. A minor canon of St. George's Chapel, Windsor Castle and vicar of Twickenham, Middlesex. Composed the anthems 'Bring unto the Lord' and 'The Lord is my Shepherd', and the oratorio *The Prodigal Son* (1870).

LINDLEY, Simon Geoffrey (b. 1948)
Born in Barnhurst, Kent on 10 October 1948, a grandson of the Belgian poet, Emile Cammaerts.

Educated at Magdalen College School, Oxford and, as an exhibitioner, the Royal College of Music where he studied organ with John Birch. While at the R.C.M. he held organistships at various London churches and was deputy organist at Westminster Cathedral.

Assistant organist at St. Albans Cathedral and director of music at St. Albans School (1971-1975). Organist of Leeds Parish Church (from April 1975) and Leeds City organist (from January 1976). For 12 years he was a senior lecturer at Leeds Metropolitan University and was senior assistant music officer for Leeds City Council (from 1988). An international organ recitalist, he has toured countries including South Africa and Russia.

Among his compositions are short pieces for upper voices (mostly in unison), including a Litany for Mary (Ave Maria), the Evening Prayer 'Matthew, Mark, Luke and John', and the anthem 'O God, my heart is ready'. Other liturgical pieces include descants, chants and arrangements, among which are carol settings and chorales by Bach and Bourgeois.

LINDOP, Ernest (19th/20th century)
Graduated B.Mus. at the University of Durham (1897). Organist and choirmaster of Hednesford Parish Church, Staffordshire (1884-1893); Wigton Parish Church (1893-1898); St. Cuthbert's Church, Carlisle (1898-1901) and St. John's Episcopal Church, Dumfries (1901-1906). Composed a setting of the Te Deum and Jubilate, and an *Andante Cantabile* for organ.

LINEKAR, Thomas Joseph (c1858-1918)
Born in 1858 or 1859; died in Colwyn Bay, Wales on 8 February 1918. Organist of Haylake Parish Church for 10 years (1874-1884) and of St. John's Wesleyan Church, Colwyn Bay, in which town he was a prominent freemason, for 30. A local choral society conductor. Composed services and hymn tunes, some of which can be found in *Methodist Tune Book* under the pseudonym of Berenger.

LINGARD, Frederick (1811-1847)
Born in Manchester in 1811; died in Durham on 4 July 1847. Studied music under **Joseph John Harris**. Organist of St. George's Church, Hulme, where his brother, Joshua Lingard, was vicar. A lay vicar of Durham Cathedral (1835-1847). Teacher of music. Composed chants, anthems, songs and duets.

LINLEY, Revd. Ozias Thurston (1765-1831)
Born in Bath, Somerset in August 1765; died in London on 6 March 1831. The son of the elder **Thomas Linley**. Studied with his father, and at Corpus Christi College, Oxford, where he graduated B.A. (1789). Also studied astronomy under **Friedrich Herschel**. A minor canon of Norwich Cathedral (from 1790). Organist of Dulwich College, London (1816-1831). Composed songs and other vocal music. During his time at Dulwich, he composed anthems and chants, the manuscripts of some of which are preserved at the Royal College of Music. His anthems include 'Lord, let me know mine end'.

LINLEY, Thomas (1733-1795)
Born in Badminton, Gloucestershire on 17 January 1733; died in London on 19 November 1795. Buried at Wells Cathedral.

A carpenter, as was his father. Decided to become a musician on hearing the playing and singing of Thomas Chilcot while he was working at the home of the Duke of Beaufort at Badminton.

Studied under Chilcot; also with Pietro Paradies in Naples and **William Boyce** in London.

Taught singing and promoted concerts in Bath. In 1774 he became joint manager, with **John Stanley** of the Drury Lane Oratorios. When Stanley died, **Samuel Arnold** succeeded him.

Richard Sheridan, Thomas Linley's son-in-law, became manager of the Drury Lane Theatre in 1776, upon which Linley took charge of the music there. He mounted performances of oratorios during Lent, at which time plays were prohibited.

Composed the anthems 'O how amiable' and 'Bow down Thine ear', and music for the stage.

LINLEY, Thomas (1756-1778)
Born in Bath, Somerset on 5 May 1756; died at Grimsthorpe, Lincolnshire on 7 August 1778 following a boating accident. A member of a musical family, including his father **Thomas Linley** and brothers **Ozias Linley** and **William Linley**. Studied under his father, Thomas and under **William Boyce**. Studied for about three years in Florence under Pietro Nardini,. At the age of 14 he became acquainted with Mozart. A violinist, he was a leader and soloist of the Bath Concerts and of those at Drury Lane in London. Composed anthems including 'Let God arise' for the Three Choirs' Festival, Worcester (1773), glees, songs and an oratorio *The Song of Moses*.

LINLEY, William (1771-1835)
Born in Bath in February 1771; died in London on 6 May 1835. Attended St. Paul's School, London and Harrow School, studying music also with his father, **Thomas Linley**, and Karl Abel. Worked for the East India Company until his late thirties. In 1790 travelled to Madras, where he was deputy secretary to the Military Board (from 1793). Returned to England in 1796, but by 1800 he was back in Madras. Paymaster of Nellore (from 1801); in 1805 he was appointed sub treasurer and mint master to the Presidency at Fort St. George. Finally returned to London in 1806. Associated with his brother-in-law, Sheridan, in operating the Drury Lane Theatre.

Composed anthems including 'God be merciful' and 'I called upon The Lord'. Wrote services, songs, operas, glees, verses and novels. Winner of a Glee Club prize in 1821.

LISTER, Henry Joseph (19th/20th century)
Graduated B.Mus. at New College, Oxford in 1879. Organist of the Parish Churches of Whitechapel, London and Bromley, Kent and of St. Peter's, Islington, London. Composed as his degree exercise a setting of Psalm 147 ' Praise the Lord, O Jerusalem'.

LITHGOW, William Hume (1806-1874)
Born in Leith on 15 February 1806; died in Glasgow on 22 August 1874. Studied in London and Edinburgh. Precentor of St. Enoch's Parish Church, Glasgow and music master of Glasgow High School (from 1842). Composed songs and some 50 Psalm or hymn tunes. Compiled *Parochial Sacred Music* (c1845).

LITTLE, Dr. Henry Walmsley (1853-1913)
Born in London on 12 September 1853; died in West Norwood. Surrey, on 28 July 1913.
Studied at the Royal Academy of Music under **George Macfarren**, **Charles Steggall**, **H.C. Banister** and Frederick Jewson (1872-1878). Graduated B.Mus. (1877) and D.Mus. (1885) at New College, Oxford.

Organist of All Saints' Church, Surrey Square, London (1869-1871); the Church of the Annunciation, Chislehurst, Kent (1871-1874); Christ Church, Woburn Square, London (1874-1880); St. Matthew's, Denmark Hill (1880-1881); St. Giles-in-the-Fields (1881-1887) and Holy Trinity, Tulse Hill (1886).

A musical examiner and corporate board member of Trinity College of Music, London, and a member of the Council of the Union of Graduates in Music and of the Royal College of Organists.

Composed cantatas, services, anthems, part songs and works for orchestra.

LITTLEJOHN, A.H. (19th century)
A.H. Littlejohn is represented in *Cathedral Psalter Chants* (1875) by Single Chants in F and in G.

LITTLEJOHN, Charles Edward Scott (1879-?1959)
Born in Broughty Ferry, Dundee, Scotland in 1879. A 'David C.E.S. Littlejohn' is recorded as having died, aged 80, in Winchester, Hampshire in 1959.

Attended the Royal College of Music. Graduated B.Mus. at Queen's College, Oxford (1907).

Organist of Holy Trinity Church, Latimer Road, London (from 1899). Organist and choirmaster of St. Saviour's, Sunbury Common, Middlesex (1899-1901); St. John's Episcopal Church, Coatbridge, Scotland (1912-1916); St. Barnabas, Paisley (from 1916) and Christ Church, Falkirk (1919-1931). Temporary acting organist and choirmaster of St. Mary's Cathedral, Glasgow (1916-1917).

Organist and choirmaster of St. Paul's Church, Knightsbridge, London (1931-1934); Beckenham Parish Church, Kent (1934-1935); Great Warley Parish Church (from around 1937) and Brentwood Parish Church, Essex.

Assistant music master of Repton School, Derbyshire (1901-1912), and a tutor of the College of St. Nicolas, Chislehurst, Kent - now the Royal School of Church Music (1934-1935).

Served in the armed forces (1917-1918) during World War I.

Composed services, an anthem and part songs. A number of his works were published by the School of English Church Music, now known as the Royal School of Church Music.

LIVINGSTONE, James R. (19th century)
James Livingstone lived in Glasgow (from 1844). He was the author of *Organ Defended*. Composed anthems including 'Turn ye unto Me' and songs.

LLEWELLYN, William Benjamin James (b.1925)
Born in Widnes, Lancashire in 1925.

Went to school at Rydal, Colwyn Bay and Conway, then read natural sciences at Emmanuel College, Cambridge.

While in the army (1944-1948) he ran a choir. Studied composition at the Royal Academy of Music under William Alwyn and **Eric Thiman**.

Appointed M.B.E. in 1987.

Assistant music master at Charterhouse, Surrey, where he became director of music in 1965. For the last three years, he was also second master.

Music adviser for the National Federation of Women's Institutes for six years. Appointed president of the Incorporated Society of Musicians in 1978, travelling all over the country for meetings and discussions with professional musicians.

Has adjudicated widely in Great Britain, also visiting Hong Kong (1990). Conducted at the music festivals of Leith Hill, Surrey (1982-1995) and Petersfield, Hampshire (1990-1995).

Compiled and edited *Novello Book of Carols* (1986) containing various arrangements and compositions, *Sing with all my Soul* (1993), and *Fifty-two Worship Songs Arranged for Choirs*.

A Mass setting for the 150th anniversary of the Sisters of the Presentation of Mary in Exeter, Devon was first sung in February 1966. His hymns first appeared in *The Anglican Hymn book* (1965). The tune 'Westron Wynde' appears in *More Hymns for Today* (1980) and elsewhere. 'The Beautitudes', written for Charterhouse, appears in *New Church Praise* (1975*)* and *Songs of Worship* (1980). The anthems 'Simple gifts' and 'Love is your name' appear in collections.

Other compositions include *Flying Colours*, commissioned by Farnham Festival, Surrey (1994). His *Lincolnshire Voices* has been performed several times in the county by various choral societies.

LLOYD, Charles Francis (1852-1917)
Born in Chester on 7 October 1852; died in Newcastle-on-Tyne on 12 October 1917.

The son of **John Ambrose Lloyd** senior and the brother of **John Ambrose Lloyd** junior. At 13, attended a school run by **Joseph David Jones** at Ruthin, Wales. Took piano lessons there with W. Argent (possibly William Ignatius Argent). Attended school at Tattenhall, near Chester for two years, sometimes deputising for the organist of the parish church. Graduated B.Mus. at New College, Oxford (1878).

At 16 he became organist of Beaumaris Parish Church; organist of Tynemouth Parish Church four years later.

A banker by profession, he was a conductor for choral societies, and an adjudicator at *eisteddfodau* including the national events. A music critic for *Newcastle Daily Chronicle*. Compiled a biography of his father, John Ambrose Lloyd.

In 1891 he resigned his appointments in order to devote his time to composition. His works include services, anthems, songs, part songs and a Festival Overture, composed for the Pontypridd National Eisteddfod (1893).

Five hymn tunes by him were included in *Aberth Moliant* (1873). 'Ravensworth' was included in *Welsh Congregational Hymnary* (1921).

LLOYD, Dr. Charles Harford (1849-1919)
Born in Thornbury, Gloucestershire on 16 October 1849; died in Slough, Berkshire, on 16 October 1919, his 70th birthday. A memorial window to him was placed in Gloucester Cathedral.

Played services at Rangeworthy Church and Falfield Church at the age of 10. Attended Thornbury Grammar School; Rossall School (1865-1868), where he studied organ with Charles Handel Tovey, and, as open scholar, Magdalen Hall (now Hertford College), Oxford where he studied music and theology. Among his contemporaries at Oxford were **Hubert Parry** and **Walter Parratt**. Took a term's lessons in harmony with **John Stainer**, from whom 'I gained an experience of untold value to me in watching him as he played the organ'. Considered offering himself as an ordination candidate while at Oxford. Had studied music regularly from the age of 13, with lessons from John Barrett of Bristol in piano and harmony. Graduated B.Mus (1871), B.A. (1872), M.A. (1875) and D.Mus. (1891).

Around 1875 he engaged in private tutoring.

Impressed **S.S. Welsey** when he played piano and organ to him at Gloucester. Wesley said of him, 'I haven't heard such playing as this for years'. In fact, he was to succeed S.S. Wesley as organist of Gloucester Cathedral (1876-1882), the appointment being a controversial one as Lloyd was so young. His pupils at Gloucester included **G.R. Sinclair** who later became organist of Hereford Cathedral. Later succeeded **C.W. Corfe** as organist of Christ Church Cathedral, Oxford (1882-1892). Taught organ and composition at the Royal College of Music (1887-1892) and in the latter year he was appointed precentor of Eton College (1892-1914) in succession to **Joseph Barnby**.

Organist and composer to the Chapel Royal, St. James's Palace (from 1914-1919). Musical editor of a revision of *Church Hymns*, which appeared in 1903.

Composed songs and cantatas, a number of which specifically for Three Choirs' Festivals, including *Hero and Leander* (Worcester, 1884); *Song of Balder* (Hereford, 1885) and *The Souls of the Righteous* (Gloucester, 1901). His church music includes anthems and various services, the Service in E-flat (1880) being best known. Hymn tunes by him include 'Credo Domine', 'Lundy' and 'Dayspring'.

LLOYD, Dr. David John de (1883-1948)
Born in Skewen, Wales on 30 April 1883; died in Aberystwyth, Wales on 20 August 1948.

Studied at the University College of Wales, Aberystwyth, graduating B.A. (1903) and B.Mus. (1905). Also graduated D.Mus. (1915) and B.A. at the University of Dublin. His music degree was one of the first to be awarded at the University of Wales. Studied further at the Leipzig Conservatory (1906-1907).

Appointed organist of the Zion Baptist Church, Llanelli (1911), one of the best attended Congregational Churches in Wales.

Taught music at Woolwich Polytechnic, London (1908-1911), at the Llanelli Intermediate County School (1914-1919) and at his former college at Aberystwyth where he became lecturer (1919-1926) and, succeeding **Walford Davies**, professor (1926-1948).

Composed two operas, choral works and a Service for St. David's Day (1946). Compiled a hymnal in collaboration with Ifor Leslie Evans, which was published in 1951. His tune 'Richmond Hill' was composed for the publication *Can â Moliant* in 1915. Additionally he composed part songs, and arrangements of Welsh folk songs. *Fy mugail yw yr Arglwydd* ('The Lord is my Shepherd') was published in 1919, the carol *Ffarwel Gŵyr Aberffraw* in 1934.

LLOYD (Floyd, Flude), Revd. John (c1475-1523)
Born probably in Caerlon, Montgomeryshire, Wales around the year 1475; died in London on 3 April 1523. Graduated B.Mus. at the University of Oxford. A priest (from 1505) and a gentleman (from c1510) of the Chapel Royal. Parish priest of Munslow, Herefordshire (from 1506). In February 1518 he was one of those who received livery for the funeral of Prince Henry, and it is believed that he made a pilgrimage to Jerusalem in the same year. Attended Henry VIII at the Field of the Cloth of Gold in 1520. Composed an antiphon *Ave Regina* and a Mass *O Quam Suavis*. Either or both may have been a degree exercise.

LLOYD, John Ambrose (1815-1874)
Born in Mold, Flintshire, Wales on 14 June 1815; died in Liverpool on 14 November 1874.

In 1830 his father was ordained minister of the High Cliffe Chapel, Warrington, Cheshire. John Lloyd went to live in Liverpool with his brother, Isaac, a schoolteacher.

His brother became editor of *Blackburn Standard* and left Liverpool. John Lloyd remained there as assistant master of a private school. Took up a similar appointment at Picton School, Cheshire. Taught at the Liverpool Mechanics' Institute (from 1838) but in 1849 he was forced to retire from teaching due to ill-health. With a friend he established a lithography business, but it failed to prosper. A commercial traveller in North Wales for the firm of Firth and Company (from 1851) and, on the death of the proprietor, for Woodall and Jones, who took over the business. Lived initially at Bwlch Bach, two miles from Conway but for the sake of his children's education, the family moved to Chester a year later. In 1864 he moved to Rhyl where he lived for the rest of his life. Deteriorating health finally forced him to retire in 1871.

He and his brother Isaac attended the Welsh Church of Dewi Sant, Liverpool, until 1835. In that year, following the departure of Isaac to Blackburn, John joined the Tabernacle Congregational Church, where his cousin William Ambrose was already a member. John became precentor soon after joining.

Took on the precentorship of the newly-opened New Chapel at Salem, Brownlow Hill (from 1841).

A founder of the Welsh choral Union of Liverpool and an eisteddfod adjudicator. His work as a choir trainer involved using a version of the Tonic Sol-fa notation.

His first hymn tune, 'Liverpool' was composed in 1830 at the age of 16. Within the collection *Y Gwladgarwr* (1835) the tune is known as 'Wyddgrug'. From 1841 he regularly collected and composed hymn tunes. He published two collections: *Casgliad O Donau* (1843) and jointly, with Ebenezer Rees, *Aberth Moliant* (1873).

The first of these collections contained 229 tunes of which 27 plus two anthems were by him. Musical critics have dismissed *Casgliad O Donau* as lacking in taste and a sense of devotion, and added what is perhaps the ultimate insult by describing it as a poor imitation of English taste. *Aberth Moliant* has fared better at the hands of the critics. Only 'Wyddgrug' and 'Eifionydd' of his 27 hymn tunes in his earlier compilation were included. His church compositions from 1843 onwards are said to show a better sense of dignity and devotion.

One hymn tune, 'Groeswen' was included in *Hymns and Psalms* (1983) and a few other recent English hymnals. Other tunes include 'Abergele', 'Cromer' and 'Downing'.

As well as 790 hymn tunes, he composed part songs, three cantatas including *The prayer of Habakkuk* and 28 anthems. 'The Kingdom of the earth' which won an eisteddfod prize in 1852, was said to be the most popular anthem in Wales at the time. While living at Bwlch Bach he composed the anthem 'Teyrnasoedd y Ddaear'.

LLOYD, John Ambrose (1840-1914)
Born in Liverpool in 1840; died in Bootle, Lancashire on 6 September 1914. Educated at the Liverpool Institute. Followed a business career in Chester with the firm of Frost and Company before moving to Liverpool and joining the corn merchants, Lloyd and Thomas. A keen amateur musician. Organist of the Queen Street Congregational Church, Chester. Composed a number of hymn tunes including 'Kilmorey', which was included in the second supplement to the publication *Llyfr Tonau Cynulleidfaol* of which **John Roberts** (Ieuan Gwyllt) was editor.

LLOYD, Dr. John Morgan (Pentre Rhondda: 1880-1960)
Born in Ystradyfodwg, Wales in 1880; died in Barry, South Wales on 30 June 1960.
Studied at Pengam Grammar School and at University College Cardiff. His teachers in music were C.H. Kitson and Eaglefield Hull. Graduated B.Mus. and D.Mus. at Trinity College, Dublin.
On active service during and after World War I (1915-1920).
Lecturer in music at his former college (from 1920), where he was appointed professor in 1949. A lecturer in music for Glamorgan County Council and an adjudicator for the national eisteddfod. An examiner in music for the Associated Board of the Royal Schools of Music.
Welsh representative on the Committee for the Revised Edition (1927) of *Church Hymnary*.
Music editor of *The Treasury* and of *Yy Athro*.
Organist and choirmaster of the Trinity Presbyterian Church, Barry and of the Cathedral Road Presbyterian Church, Cardiff.
Composed anthems, songs and part songs. His hymn tunes include 'Benediction', 'Nadolig', 'Colwinstone', 'Porthkerry' and Pro Nostris Liberis'. Also a Festival Te Deum for Chorus and Orchestra.

LLOYD, Richard Francis (1871-1943)
Born in Liverpool in 1871; died in Wandsworth, London on 11 April 1943.
Attended the Liverpool College of Music and graduated B.Mus. at the University of London (1893).
Pursued a musical career in and around Liverpool. A professor of the Liverpool College of Music (1894-1900), principal of the Liverpool Academy of Music (from 1901) and musical editor of *The Free Methodist* (1898-1900). Organist and choirmaster of St. Simon's Parish Church (from 1889) and organist of the UMF Church, Grove Street (from 1890). Organist and choirmaster of Brunswick Church (from 1891); St. John's Wesleyan Church, Prince's Park (1893-1895) and the Presbyterian Churches at Canning Street (from 1897) and Sefton Park (1903-1934).
Composed anthems including 'Let the righteous be glad' and the harvest-tide 'Fear not, O land', part songs and piano music. Won a composition prize of five guineas (£5.25) at the Festival of the Nonconformist Choir Union in 1895 with an anthem.

LLOYD, Richard Hey (b.1933)
Born near Stockport, Cheshire on 25 June 1933.
A chorister of Lichfield Cathedral (1942-1947). Attended Rugby School, Warwickshire (1947-1951) and, as organ scholar, Jesus College, Cambridge (1952-1955), where he graduated M.A.
Assistant organist of Salisbury Cathedral (1957-1966).
Organist of the Cathedrals of Hereford (1966-1974) and Durham (1974-1985).
In 1985 he became deputy head of Salisbury Cathedral School but retired through ill-health in 1988.
Has composed numerous Service settings for individual Cathedrals including Hereford and Salisbury, and Responses for Hereford and Durham. There are carols and anthems of which examples are 'God is love' and 'All so still'. His early works include the unaccompanied anthem 'View me, Lord' to words by Thomas Campion..

LLOYD, William (1786-1852)
Born in Rhos Goch, Llaniestyn, Caernarvonshire, Wales in 1786; died in Rhos Goch on 7 June 1852. Entirely self-educated. A

farmer and cattle drover, his travels enabling him to observe the singing of English congregations. He led singing classes in Llaniestyn, Merionydd, travelling through the district of Lleyn to hold meetings of singing and to teach the subject. Composed the hymn tune 'Merionydd', also known as 'Berth' under which name it appeared in *Songs of Praise*, and many others.

LLOYD WEBBER, Dr. William Southcombe (1914-1982)
Born in Chelsea, London on 11 March 1914; died in London on 29 October 1982. The father of Sir Andrew Lloyd Webber and Julian Lloyd Webber.
William Lloyd Webber's father took a keen interest in the organ, and he would often take his son to organ recitals. Subsequently, William himself learned to play the organ and by the age of 14 he had become known as a recitalist. At the age of 13, he made a broadcast from the Church of St. Mary le Bow, London. Won an organ scholarship to Mercers' School, and, at the age of 14, a Sir John Goss scholarship to the Royal College of Music, where he studied composition with **Ralph Vaughan Williams.**
In a successful career in music, he was director of the London College of Music (from 1964) and professor of theory and composition at the R.C.M. An examiner for the Associated Board of the Royal Schools of Music (1946-1964)
Organist of the Central Hall, Westminster (from 1958) and of the London Churches of Christ Church, Newgate Street (1929-1932); St. Cyprian, Clarence Gate and All Saints, Margaret Street (1932-1939).
His compositions for the church include Communion Services in D Minor, E-flat and E Minor; Masses *The Prince of Peace* (1962) and *of St. Mary Magdalene* (1978) and the anthems 'Beneath the glory of the skies', 'A Child my choice', 'O for a closer walk' and 'Most gracious Lord of life'. It has been suggested that prejudice against him in Anglican circles has prevented his works from being more widely known and performed. His secular pieces include a Fantasy Trio (1936). His output increased after the end of World War II and included the orchestral tone-poem *Aurora* (1951). Feeling out of step towards the end of his life with contemporary tastes and styles in music, and refusing to compromise his own style, he devoted most of his energies to the academic and administrative aspects of music.

LLWYD, Stephen (1794-1854)
Born in Llystyn-Bach near Nevern, Pembrokeshire, Wales some time after March 1794; died in April 1854. Like his father, he became a tailor. Learned music under **Dafydd Siencyn Morgan.** Lived at Fishguard, where he became precentor of the Baptist Chapel and was well known as a musician. In 1840 he moved to Pontypridd and became precentor of the Carmel Baptist Chapel. Conducted music classes in the town. His hymn tune 'Caerllyngoed' was published in 1822. Other tunes include 'Abergwaun', 'Taf' and 'Rhondda'. Also composed a carol.

LOCKE (Lock), Matthew (1621/2-1677)
Born, probably in Devon, in 1621 or 1622; died in London in August 1677.
A chorister of Exeter Cathedral in 1638. It is likely that he studied composition with **Edward Gibbons**, violin with William Wake and organ with **John Lugge**.
During the Interregnum, he spent time studying.

Appointed composer-in-ordinary to Charles II, and Locke composed band music for the pre-Coronation progress through London on 22 April 1661.
He may have been, secretly, a Roman Catholic. Organist to Queen Catherine, who had a Roman Catholic Chapel at Somerset House, London.
Knew **Henry Purcell** and his family.
Composed with **Christopher Gibbons** for the theatre. In addition he composed songs, stage and instrumental works, services, motets, Latin hymns and about 60 anthems, including 'O Lord hear my prayer' and 'When the son of man' (a setting of Matthew 25).
His Responses to the Commandments were unconventional, each Response varying slightly. They were clearly not to the taste of the Choir of the Chapel Royal whose performance of them on 1 April 1666 in front of Charles II and Samuel Pepys led to an accusation by Locke that the choir had sabotaged the Responses deliberately. Locke composed no further works for the Chapel Royal thereafter.

LOCKETT, William (1835-1893)
Born in Manchester in 1835; died in 1893. Deputy assistant organist of Manchester Cathedral. Organist of St. John's Church, Higher Broughton (1855-1861); St. Mark's Church, Cheetham; the Union Chapel (1877) and Cross Street Chapel, Manchester.
Composed anthems including 'Praised be the Lord' and 'Watch and pray', and songs.

LOCKHART, Charles (c1745-1815)
Born in London around the year 1745; died in Lambeth, London on 9 February 1815. Blind from infancy and possibly from birth. A skilled musician. In particular he was known for his ability as a trainer of children's choirs. A tenor singer. Organist in London of the Church of St. Katherine Cree (1766-1815); Lock Hospital Chapel (1772 and 1790-1797); St. Mary's Church, Lambeth (1780) and the Orange Street Chapel (of the Congregational Church) until 1797. Composed songs and anthems, and is remembered for his one hymn tune 'Carlisle', also known as 'Invocation', which has since been used in most of the major hymnals of this century with the hymn 'Stand up and bless the Lord' by James Montgomery.

LODGE, John.
See **ELLERTON,** John Lodge.

LOFTHOUSE, Dr. Benjamin (1867-?)
Born in Tadcaster, Yorkshire in 1867. Educated at York Minster. Graduated B.Mus. (1898) at Queen's College, Oxford and D.Mus. (1914) at the University of Dublin. Graduated at the Tonic Sol-fa College (1905). Organist and choirmaster of Tadcaster Parish Church (from 1882); St. Martin's Church, Coney Street (from 1892) and St. Andrew's Church, Southport, Lancashire (1897-1917). Taught music in Southport at St. Andrew's Hall (from 1908), Bickerton House and Sunnybrae House School. Also a local music society director. Composed as his B.Mus. exercise the anthem 'Jesus, lover of my soul' for Solo Voices, Chorus and Orchestra.

LÖHR, Frederick Nicholls (1844-1888)
Born in Norwich, Norfolk in January 1844; died in Plymouth, Devon on 18 December 1888. A pupil of **Zechariah Buck**, organist of Norwich Cathedral. An organist of Sherwell Chapel, Plymouth, and a local teacher and concert performer. Composed

the anthem 'The Lord is my Shepherd', songs, and orchestral and piano music.

LÖHR, George Augustus (1821-1897)
Born in Norwich, Norfolk in 1821; died in Leicester in 1897. The father of **Richard Löhr**. A chorister of Magdalen College, Oxford. Assistant organist of Norwich Cathedral under **Zechariah Buck**. Organist of St. Margaret's Church, Leicester (from 1845-1885), and for much of that time he was also choirmaster. Pioneered choral services in Leicester. Composed the hymn tune 'St. Francis'.

LÖHR, Richard Harvey (1856-1927)
Born in Leicester on 13 June 1856; died in 1927. The son of **George Löhr**. Harvey Löhr was educated at home and at the Royal Academy of Music under **Arthur Sullivan**, **Ebenezer Prout** and **W.H. Holmes**. An organist from the age of 10, Löhr was appointed to St. James's Church, Marylebone, London around 1897. Gave concerts in London (from 1882) and recitals of chamber music in Leicester. A teacher and accompanist. His compositions include an oratorio *The Queen of Sheba*, the anthem, 'God who madest Earth and Heaven', a Morning and Evening Service in C, songs and part songs.

LOLE, Simon (b.1957)
A chorister, and later, organ scholar, of St. Paul's Cathedral. Studied at King's College, University of London and Guildhall School of Music. Organist of Croydon Parish Church, Surrey (1980-1985); director of music of the Collegiate Choir of St. Mary, Warwick (1985-1994). Master of the music of Sheffield Cathedral (from 1994). Composer of a number of anthems, settings and carols including 'The Journey', 'The Father's love' and 'Shall we not love Thee?'.

LOMAS, George (1834-1884)
Born in Birch Hall, Bolton, Lancashire on 30 November 1834; died on 18 October 1884. Studied under **Charles Steggall**, **William Sterndale Bennett** and **Frederick Bridge**. Graduated B.Mus. at New College, Oxford (1876). For seven years he was organist of Didsbury Parish Church and for many years he served similarly the Emmanuel Church, Barlow Moor, Manchester (1858-1884). Composed church music, including the hymn tune 'Submission', used in *Methodist Hymn Book* (1933). His other hymn tunes include 'Pentecost' and 'Sursum Corda'. Some tunes are found in the 1876 edition of *Bristol Tune Book*. Composed the anthems 'Praised be the Lord daily' and 'Whoso dwelleth'.

LONG, James Charles (19th/20th century)
Graduated B.Mus. at Queen's College, Oxford (1901).
Organist and choirmaster of St. Stephen's Church (from 1896) and Christ Church (from 1897), both in Cheltenham, Gloucestershire. His remaining appointments were in London as organist and choirmaster of St. James's Church, Westmorland Street, Marylebone (from 1901); master of the choristers of All Saints' Church, Norfolk Square (from 1907) and choirmaster of St. Alban's Church, Holborn (from 1908).
Organist to the Honourable Society of Gray's Inn (from 1904), and principal of the organ Branch of the London College for Choristers (from 1905). A professor of organ and harmony at the Incorporated London Academy of Music (from 1914). Taught organ, harmony, counterpoint, rudiments of music, and theory at Trinity College of Music. A glee society conductor.

Composed an Evening Service, anthems, part songs and music for piano.

LONG, Kenneth (1926-1975)
Spent most of his childhood in Canterbury, Kent, where he studied music theory and organ under the Cathedral organist, **Gerald Knight**.
Bass choral scholar at King's College, Cambridge under **'Boris' Ord** (1946-1949). Graduated in music and English.
Organist of the Church of St. Mary Redcliffe, Bristol.
Organist and master of the choristers of St. Andrew's Cathedral, Sydney, Australia (from 1953). In Australia he became known as a recitalist and conductor through appearances in the concert hall, on radio and on television.
Returned to England and became a lecturer at the University of Manchester. Organist of Altrincham Parish Church, Cheshire.
His book *The Music of the English Church*, (1972, reprinted in 1991) bitterly denounced some of the later Victorian composers and their church music.

LONG, Samuel (?-1764)
Died on 7 August 1764. A chorister of St. Paul's Cathedral under **Charles King**. An organist, composer and teacher of harpsichord. Organist of the Church of St. Peter le Poer. Some of his Psalm tunes were used in the collection *Parish Music Corrected* (1762) by **William Riley**. Won a prize for his glee 'Hush the God of love' (1764). Composed Psalm tunes, some of which were in Riley's collection.

LONGMIRE, John Basil Hugh (1902-?)
Born in Gainsborough, Lincolnshire in 1902.
Educated at Benjamin Allard's School and at the Royal College of Music, to which he won a Gervase Elwes Memorial Scholarship.
A pianist and composer. Music master of Tonbridge School, Kent (1925-1926) and of Sevenoaks School (1927-1936). Around the time of World War II he was assistant master of Bromsgrove County High School, Worcestershire. Thereafter he taught at Epsom College, Surrey (1946-1947), and was music master of Guernsey Ladies' College, Gloucestershire (1948-1950) and of Northcote College, New Zealand (1951-1954). An examiner for Trinity College of Music (from 1958). A choral conductor. Author of a biography of **John Ireland**, and of a set of sight-reading books used at T.C.M. Composed school songs and the two-act operettas *The Bells of Bruges* and *Pedro, the Gipsy Boy*.

LONGHURST, Dr. William Henry (1819-1904)
Born in Lambeth, London on 6 October 1819; died in Canterbury, Kent on 17 February 1904.
Awarded the Lambeth D.Mus.(1875).
The son of an organ builder. When two years old, his family moved to Canterbury. Shortly afterwards, the boy began an association with the local cathedral that lasted for 70 years.
A chorister under **Highmore Skeats** the elder (from 1828). Studied under Skeats's successor, **Thomas Evance Jones** and with **Stephen Elvey**. Assistant organist, lay clerk and master of the choristers (from 1836). Succeeded Jones as organist in 1873, continuing in office until his retirement in 1898. Lectured in music locally at St. Augustine's College. It is said that he was offered the organistship of Carlisle Cathedral in 1842, but declined it.

Composed services including a Service in E, an oratorio *David and Absalom*, cantatas, anthems including 'Blessed is He', chants, part songs and duets for violin and piano.

LONSDALE, William (1773-1833)

Born in Bolton, Lancashire in 1773; died in Bolton in 1833. Blind from birth. A proficient player of several musical instruments. In addition it was said that he could play tunes on a set of glasses and he gave passable vocal imitations of the French horn and bassoon. Appointed organist of Bolton Parish Church at the age of 36. In a fit of absent mindedness he once played a jig during a Service and was immediately dismissed by Canon Slade. His hymn tunes include 'Moab'.

LOOSEMORE, Dr. George (?-1682)

Born in Devon; died in Cambridge in 1682. Probably the son of **Henry Loosemore**. His brother John built the organ of Exeter Cathedral. Graduated Mus.D. at the University of Cambridge (1665). Organist of Jesus College, Cambridge (from 1635) and of Trinity College (1660-1682). Composed sacred music, including the anthems 'Glory be to God' and 'Hear my crying'. Also composed for harpsichord and for viols.

LOOSEMORE, Henry (c1600-1670)

Born, possibly in Devon, around the year 1600; died in Cambridge in 1670.

Probably the father of **George Loosemore** and of John Loosemore.

Graduated Mus.B. at the University of Cambridge (1640).

Organist of King's College, Cambridge (1627-1670), retaining the position even during the period of the Commonwealth.

Had connections with the North family of Kirtling, whose children he taught.

Composed some 30 anthems including 'Put me not to rebuke' and 'Why art thou so heavy, O my soul?'. In addition he composed two Services, a Litany in D Minor which remained popular long after his death, a Gloria and some instrumental works. Compositions have been misattributed between Henry and John, while Henry Loosemore's 'O Lord, increase my faith' was formerly attributed to **Orlando Gibbons**.

LORD, Revd. Austin E. (19th/20th century)

Some doubt exists as to whether Austin Lord was actually the composer of the hymn tune known as 'St. Austin' or 'Hotham'.

LORD, David (b.1944)

Born in Oxford on 3 October 1944.

The son of a leading designer of medical rehabilitation equipment who was based at the Radcliffe Infirmary, Oxford.

Attended the Salesian College, Cowley, Oxford and the Royal Academy of Music (1963-1967), where he studied composition with **Richard Rodney Bennett**.

Lived in London (1967-1970) as a performer, conductor and freelance composer. Worked extensively at this time for the B.B.C. Schools Music Department as a scriptwriter, composer and programme presenter. Became producer of 'Music Session One'. Arranged nursery rhymes for 'Listen with Mother', and composed the jingle played between schools' programmes on television as the clock ticked round.

Head of music at Laban Art of Movement Studio, a part of the University of London, in Addlestone, Surrey (1971-1975); visiting lecturer in composition, Bath College of Higher Education (1974-

1978) and co-director of Crescent Records (1976-1978). Heavily involved in the musical life of the area around Bath, Somerset, in activities ranging from entertaining patients in local homes and hospitals to major festival events.

Developed a career as a record producer and engineer, with 'top ten' hits in England, the U.S.A., Australia and elsewhere, and working with major international artists such as Peter Gabriel, Kate Bush and Tears for Fears.

Composed in the classical idiom for a variety of individuals and organisations, including the London Symphony Orchestra and the Academy of St. Martin-in-the-Fields. His church music includes contributions to the 1973 collection, *Sing the Mass*, and anthems such as 'A prayer for peace' (1966) and 'Most Glorious Lord of Lyfe' (1969).

LORIMER, John (1812-1878)

Born in Paisley, Scotland on 9 June 1812; died in Paisley on 13 October 1878. An artist and a poet, living for most of his life in Paisley. His Psalm tunes include 'Crookston'. An example of his songs is 'I'm ower auld to marry noo'.

LORING, Revd. John Henry (1906-1995)

Born in 1906; died in Wantage, Berkshire on 6 June 1995 at the age of 88. Educated at Eton College; King's College, Cambridge, where he graduated M.A. (1932); and at Cuddesdon College, where he trained for the ministry. Ordained deacon in 1931, priest in 1932. Assistant curate of Knebworth Parish Church (1932-1934) and curate of St. Peter's Church, Swansea (1934-1945). Vicar of Foxfield, near Petersfield, Hampshire (from 1945) and of Edmondsham, Dorset. A composer of hymn tunes.

LOTT, Dr. Edwin Matthew (1836-?)

Born in St. Helier, Jersey on 31 January 1836.

Studied with **W.T. Best**, (1851-1852) and graduated D.Mus. honorarily at the University of Toronto, Canada.

From the age of 10 he was organist of St. Matthew's Church. Other appointments in Jersey followed. Organist of St. Clement Danes and a number of other London Churches (1860-1864). His pupils included **Henry Wood**.

Returned to Jersey in 1865 where he became professor of music at Victoria College, and bandmaster to three regiments.

Organist of the St. Peter's Church, Bayswater, London (from 1870), St. Ethelburga's, Bishopsgate (from 1880) and St. Sepulchre, Holborn (from 1883). A professor and examiner in music at Trinity College of Music. Author of works on music.

In 1891 he was appointed professor of music at the University of Toronto.

Composed some 300 works for piano. There are compositions for organ, cantatas and songs. His church music consists of anthems and services.

LOTT, John Browning (1849-1924)

Born in Faversham, Kent in 1849; died in Buxted, Sussex on 29 September 1924.

A chorister at Canterbury Cathedral under **W.H. Longhurst**, studying music with Longhurst and with **Thomas Evance Jones**. Graduated B.Mus. at the University of Oxford (1876).

Organist of the Canterbury Churches of St. Dunstan and St. Paul, the latter until 1873. In that year he became assistant organist of Canterbury Cathedral; two years later he was organist of Margate Parish Church.

Organist of Lichfield Cathedral (1881-1925). A local musical society conductor.
Composed church music and part songs.

LOWE, Albert Henry (1842-1886)
Born in 1842; died in 1886. His anthems include 'Hosanna!' and 'The Lord is my Strength'.

LOWE, Edward (c1610-1682)
Born in Salisbury, Wiltshire around the year 1610; died in Oxford on 11 July 1682.
A chorister at Salisbury Cathedral under **John Holmes**.
Organist of Christ Church Cathedral, Oxford (1630-1656), succeeding **William Stonard**. Some sources believe that he retained the position until he died, except for the period of the Protectorate.
From 1660 he was one of the three organists of the Chapel Royal, his colleagues initially being **William Child** and **Christopher Gibbons**. In 1662 he succeeded **John Wilson** as professor of music at the University of Oxford.
His *Short Directions for the Performance of the Cathedral Service* (1661) contained instructions on the art of singing the Liturgy, that had been lost during the Interregnum. The other problem he faced was coming to terms with the change in musical taste that had taken place in the intervening period.
Composed four part songs and 10 anthems including 'If the Lord Himself' and 'O how amiable', plus a chant.

LOWE, Richard (1810-1853)
Born in Llandidloes, Montgomeryshire, Wales in 1810; died in Newtown, Wales in 1853. A weaver by trade, he studied music with **James Mills** and the elder **Richard Mills**. Precentor of Llandidloes Parish Church. Composed hymn tunes including 'Pererindod' and 'Diwygiad'.

LUARD-SELBY, Bertram (1853-1918)
Born in Ightham, Kent on 12 February 1853; died in Glanford Brigg, Lincolnshire on 26 December 1918.
Studied at the Leipzig Conservatory under Carl Reinecke and Salomon Jadassohn.
Organist in London of St. Barnabas's Church, Marylebone; Highgate School (from 1876) and the Church of St. Barnabas, Marylebone.
Organist of Salisbury Cathedral (1881-1883).
Organist of St. John's Church, Torquay, Devon (1884); St. Barnabas, Pimlico, London (1887).
Succeeded **John Hopkins** as organist of Rochester Cathedral (1900-1916).
At other times in his career he was organist of the London Churches of St. Andrew, Willesden Green and All Saints, Norfolk Square. Director of music of Bradfield College, Berkshire (from 1916).
Musical editor of the 1904 edition of *Hymns Ancient and Modern*.
Composed two unpublished operas including *The Ring* (1886), works for piano and organ, and incidental music for the play *Helena in Troas* (1886). His compositions include Morning, Evening and Holy Communion Services in C and sets of Responses to the Commandments in D and in E-flat. His hymn tunes include 'Adoration', 'Innocence', 'Supplication' and 'Eccles'. Also composed organ pieces, an Idyll for Orchestra, and chamber works.

LUCAS, Charles (1808-1869)
Born in Salisbury, Wiltshire on 28 July 1808; died in London on 23 March 1869.
A chorister (1815-1823) and pupil of **A.T. Corfe** at Salisbury Cathedral. Attended the Royal Academy of Music (1823-1830), where his instructors included **William Crotch**.
He returned to the R.A.M. as a conductor (from 1832) and principal (1859-1866), succeeding Cipriani Potter.
Organist of the Hanover Chapel, Regent Street, London (from 1839).
An opera cellist, and a cellist in the private band of Queen Adelaide. Occasionally (in the years 1840-1843) he conducted the Ancient Concerts.
A member of the firm of music publishers, Addison, Hollier and Lucas (1856-1865).
His Magnificat for Four Voices in Canon was awarded the Gresham Prize of 1836. Composed an opera *The Regicide*, three symphonies, quartets, anthems including 'Blessed be the Lord' and 'O Lord, open Thou', overtures, and songs such as 'Homeward thoughts'.

LUDFORD, Nicholas (c1485-c1557)
Born around the year 1485; died in Westminster, London in or after 1557. Verger of St. Stephen's Church, Westminster.
Composed a Mass and a Magnificat.

LUGGE (Lugg), John (c1587-after 1647)
Born in Exeter, Devon around the year 1587; died in Exeter some time after 1647. Probably the son of Thomas Lugge, lay clerk.
Organist (from 1602) and a lay vicar-choral (from 1605) of Exeter Cathedral. Known as a virtuoso organist. Suspected by the Privy Council of being a Roman Catholic, and his bishop, William Cotton, interviewed him. Cotton recommended that Lugge should be excused on grounds of youth. His anthems include 'It is a good thing' and 'Let my complaint'. Composed services, including a setting in C. Also wrote fantasias for organ.

LUGGE, Robert (1620-?)
Graduated B.Mus. at St. John's College, Oxford (1638). Brought up in Lisbon, Portugal, where he had developed a sympathy for the Catholic cause that caused him problems as a young man. It has proved difficult to distinguish with certainty between the compositions of Robert Lugge and those of other composers similarly named. A Litany, a Service in G and three anthems are likely to have been the work of Robert Lugge.

LUMSDEN, Sir David James (b.1928)
Born in Newcastle-on-Tyne on 19 March 1928. The father of Andrew Lumsden, organist of Lichfield Cathedral.
Attended Dame Allan's School, Newcastle-on-Tyne. Studied as organ scholar with **'Boris' Ord** and Thurston Dart at Selwyn College, Cambridge, where he graduated Mus.B. (1951), M.A. (1955) and D.Phil (1957). Received a musical doctorate at the University of Oxford (1959). Holds doctorates in philosophy from the Universities of Oxford and Cambridge.
Knighted in 1985.
Assistant organist of St. John's College, Cambridge (1954-1956); rector chori of Southwell Minster (1956-1959); organist of the University of Nottingham and of Nottingham Parish Church (1956-1959) and director of music at University College of North Staffordshire, Keele (1958-1959).

A professor of harmony at the Royal Academy of Music (1959-1961. Organist (from 1966), lecturer and fellow of New College, Oxford and music lecturer at the university (1959-1976). Visiting professor at Yale University (1974-1975).

Principal of the Royal Scottish Academy of Music and Drama, Glasgow (1976-1982), and a board member of the Scottish Opera (1977-1983) and of the English National Opera (1983-1988). Since 1982 he has been principal of the R.A.M.

He has written books and magazine articles. Has composed a set of Responses for Boys' or Men's Voices.

LUPI, Eduardi (c1530-?)
Born, of Portuguese extraction, around the year 1530. Composer of the anthem 'Now it is high time'.

LUPO, Thomas (?-1628)
Known to have been alive from 1579; died in March 1628. **Thomas Lupo** (below) was his cousin. Probably the first member of this family to be born in England. A musician to Charles I, he was probably a viol player or violinist. A member of the Royal Band (from 1579). Composer to the Lutes and Voices (1621-1628). It is unclear whether the Thomas Lupo who composed the anthems 'O Lord, give ear' and 'Out of the deep', and whose works featured in the compilation *Teares* or *Lamentations of a Sorrowful Soule* (1613) by **William Leighton**, is the first or the second composer of that name, or even if they are by one and the same composer.

LUPO, Thomas (?-1642)
Active between 1598 and 1642. The cousin of **Thomas Lupo**. By 1598 he was one of the violinists of Elizabeth I. A member of the Band of Musicians of Prince Henry (from 1610), and a musician to Charles I. Either or both of the composers named Thomas Lupo could have composed the anthems 'O Lord, give ear' and 'Out of the deep', and could be the composer of works featured in the compilation *Teares* or *Lamentations of a Sorrowful Soule* (1613) by **William Leighton**.

LUPTON, Revd. James (1799-1873)
Born in York in 1799; died in London on 21 December 1873. A chorister at York Minster. Ordained in 1824. A minor canon of St. Paul's Cathedral and of Westminster Abbey. He sought to improve the status of vicars-choral. Composed church and secular music.

LUTTMAN, Willie Lewis (1874-1930)
Born in High Wycombe, Buckinghamshire on 20 February 1874; died on 2 February 1930. A pupil of and assistant to **J.G. Wrigley**, Parish Church organist. Attended the Royal Grammar School, High Wycombe; the Royal College of Music for 10 terms from July 1893 and, as organ scholar (1894-1898) Peterhouse, Cambridge, where he graduated Mus.B. and M.A. At the age of 14 he was appointed organist and master of the choristers of Tyler's Green Church, Buckinghamshire (1888-1891). Organist of Hughenden Parish Church (January to September 1894) and Banbury Parish Church, Oxfordshire (1898-1907).

Organist and master of the choristers of St. Albans Cathedral (from 1907). A sub-lieutenant in the Royal Naval Volunteer Reserve (1918-1919). Principal of St. Albans School of Music. Composed songs, anthems and services.

LUTZ, Wilhelm Meyer (c1822-1903)
Born in Männerstadt, near Kissingen, Germany in 1822 or 1830; died in Kensington, London on 31 January 1903. Studied in Würzburg at the *Gymnasium* and the university, where his tutors in music were Eisenhofer and Keller. Moved to England in 1848. Had performed as a pianist with an orchestra at the age of 12, and sought a career in music. Obtained work as a manager of opera tours and as a theatre conductor, his major appointments being at the Surrey Theatre (1851-1855) and the Gaiety Theatre (1869-1896). Organist of the Churches of St. Chad, Birmingham and St. Ann, Leeds before becoming choirmaster and organist of St. George's Roman Catholic Cathedral, London. A grand organist of the Freemasons. A significant composer whose works includes music for St. George's Cathedral, operas, cantatas, orchestral and chamber works, and motets.

LYLE, George Edwin (c1842-1900)
Born in Sheffield, Yorkshire; died in the age of 57 on 3 January 1900. Organist of Pitsmoor Church, Mold Parish Church, Flintshire and of Sherborne Abbey for nearly 22 years in the latter part of the 19th century. At Sherborne he was also district choirmaster of the Salisbury Diocesan choral Association, and directed many choral festivals. Composed cantatas including *St. Philip*. Composed a Festival Te Deum for the dedication of the organ at Sherborne Abbey, for Chorus Organ and Military Band, first performed on 9 November 1887.

LYNE, Arthur (1870-?)
Born in Manchester in 1870. Graduated B.Mus. at the University of Durham (1897). Organist and choirmaster of St. Kohn's Church, Lindow (from 1892), Ramsgate Congregational Church, Kent (from 1899) and West Kilbride Parish Church, Scotland (from 1904). From 1901 he was music master at Truro College, Cornwall. For his degree exercise he submitted a setting of Psalm 85: 'Lord, Thou art become gracious'.

LYNE, Frederick Edward (19th/20th century)
Graduated B.Mus. at the University of London in 1890. Organist of the Church of St. Paul, Brentford, Middlesex (from 1888). His degree exercise was a cantata *Early life of Samuel* for Solo Voices, Chorus and Orchestra.

LYON, Dr. James (1872-1949)
Born in Manchester on 25 October 1872; died in Australia in August 1949.

A pupil of **Tom Dodds** and Herbert Botting. Graduated B.Mus. (1900) and D.Mus. (1905) at Queen's College, Oxford.

Sub organist of Bangor Cathedral (from 1892). A year later he was appointed organist and music master of St. Michael's College, Tenbury, Worcestershire (1893-1896). He taught at the Birmingham and Midland Institute (until 1938) and at Trinity College of Music.

His later posts were organist and choirmaster of St. Mark's Church, Surbiton, Surrey (1896), organist and director of music at King Edward School, Warwick (1897) and organist of Wallasey Parish Church, Cheshire (1899). Also a philharmonic and operatic society conductor, and a festival adjudicator, undertaking tours of Canada (1924-1925), South Africa (1931), and Canada and New Zealand (1933). Music master of Harrow School.

Author of *Primer on the Modern Orchestra*, and books of score-reading exercises.

Composed Services, anthems, songs, piano music, items for organ and for strings, and exercises for candidates for the examinations of the Royal College of Organists.

LYTE, Revd. Henry Francis (1793-1847)
Born in Ednam, near Kelso, Scotland on 1 June 1793; died in Nice, France on 20 November 1847.
Lyte was educated at Portora, the Royal School of Enniskillen and Trinity College, Dublin where he won the poetry prize on three occasions. Ordained in 1815, having intended originally to pursue a career in the medical profession.
Curate of a number of parishes in Ireland and the West of England including Taghmon, near Wexford (1815) and Marazion, Cornwall (1817). Further curacies followed: Lymington, Hampshire; Charlton, Devon; and Dittisham. In 1823 he became the incumbent of Lower Brixham, Devon, retaining the position until the year of his death.
His preaching took on a more urgent tone following the death of a neighbouring colleague whose children Lyte then cared for. Eventually his health began to fail and he went to the continent in order to recuperate.
Took a number of private pupils, including a future Prime Minister, Lord Salisbury.
His collection *Poems; chiefly religious*, was published in 1833. Another collection, *Spirit of the Psalms*, followed a year later. It contained two hymns that remain popular today: 'God of mercy, God of grace' and 'Praise my soul, the King of heaven'.
Wrote the hymn 'Abide with me' and composed a tune for it, and he was known for a number of other sacred poems and hymns.

M

MACALISTER, Dr. Robert Alexander Stewart (1870-1950)
Born in Dublin on 8 July 1870; died in Cambridge on 26 April 1950.
Educated at Rathmines School, Dublin; privately in Germany and at the University of Cambridge. His qualifications included the doctorates Litt.D. and LL.D.
An archaeologist, he became professor of Celtic Archaeology in University College, Dublin and published a number of books on his subject. Director of excavations to the Palestine Exploration Fund, (1900-1909), later taking part in expeditions to the Holy Land (1923-1924). It was in the latter phase that his team discovered part of the walls of the Jesubite fortress Millo within a particularly ancient part of Jerusalem.
Wrote about his experiences and findings, and also on aspects of ancient Irish history.
Organist and choirmaster of the Adelaide Road Presbyterian Church, Dublin, serving on the Revision Committee and the Music Sub Committee for the Revised Edition (1927) of *Church Hymnary*, to which he contributed several tunes.
Translated ancient hymns. Among the hymn tunes he composed are 'New Grange' and 'St. Darerca'.

MACBURNEY, Charles
See **BURNEY,** Charles

MCBURNEY, Dr. Samuel (19th/20th century)
Educated privately in music. Graduated B.Mus. (1890) and D.Mus. (1896) at the University of Dublin, and awarded a further D.Mus. at the University of Melbourne (1900). Inspector of music in Australia for the State of Victoria (1892-1893) and examiner in music for the Universities of Tasmania (1896-1901) and Melbourne (1898-1899). Settings of the Psalms were submitted as his degree exercises at Dublin - Psalm 23 'The Lord is my Shepherd' for Solo Voices and Chorus (B.Mus.), and Psalm 103 'Praise the Lord, O my soul' for Soprano, Double Chorus and Orchestra (D.Mus.). Also composed the cantatas *Christmas Greeting, Victoria* and *Children's Festival.*

MCCABE, John (b.1939)
Born in Huyton, Lancashire on 21 April 1939. The family was Scottish and Irish on his father's side, and on his mother's, German, Scandinavian and Spanish.
Educated at the Liverpool Institute High School for Boys; the University of Manchester, where he graduated B.Mus. (1960); the Royal Manchester College of Music under Thomas Pittfield and the Hochschule, Munich, with Harald Genzmer.
Appointed C.B.E. in 1985.
Appointments include pianist in residence, University College, Cardiff (1965-1968); director of the London College of Music (1983-1990) and visiting professor of composition at the Royal Academy of Music (from 1995).
A piano recitalist, he has recorded all of the Haydn Sonatas. Frequently visits the U.S.A. and Australia as both pianist and composer. Author of a short biography *Rachmaninov* (1974).
Church compositions include 'Canticles for Salisbury' (1966) and 'Norwich Canticles' (1970), the anthem 'Great Lord of Lords' and the well-known carols 'Coventry Carol' and 'A lute-book lullaby'. Composed a Stabat Mater for Soprano, Chorus and Orchestra (1976); a ballet, *Mary, Queen of Scots*, and four symphonies, the fourth being styled *of Time and the River.*

MCCARTHY, David Wyn (b.1931)
Born in Pentre Broughton, Flintshire, Wales on 2 April 1931.
Educated at Newcastle-under-Lyme High School, Staffordshire; Queen Elizabeth Grammar School, Wakefield, Yorkshire and Downing College, Cambridge, where he was also organist (1952-1953). Graduated M.A. Taught at Woodhouse Grove School, Yorkshire (from 1960). He has directed, on behalf of the Methodist Church Music Society, a number of the 'Youth Makes Music' courses (since 1969). Has composed a Magnificat and Nunc Dimittis and hymn tunes, among which is 'Ruach'.

MACE, Thomas (1619-1709)
Born, possibly in York, in 1619; died in 1709. A lutenist and a lay clerk of Trinity College, Cambridge. Although deaf, he designed a 50-string lute, the dyphone, which he invented (1672). A clerk of Trinity College, Cambridge. He lived, London (from 1690). *Musick's Monument* (1676) was a manual on the subjects of church

music, and on playing the lute and viol. Composed the anthem 'I heard a Voice'.

MACEY, James Douglas (1860-1933)

Born in Maidstone, Kent on 10 March 1860; died in Canada in 1933. Organist of the Lyndhurst Road Congregational Church, Hampstead, London (1881-1903). Emigrated in 1903 to British Columbia, Canada and was succeeded by **Arthur Carter**. Published several hymn tunes, one of which, 'Mayfield', was included in *Baptist Church Hymnal* (1900). His others include 'Elsenham' and 'Lyndhurst Road'.

MACFARLANE, John Reid (1800-1841)

Born in 1800; died in London on 10 June 1841. Precentor of the Outer High Church, Glasgow (1824-1828). Later worked in London as a teacher and composer. Editor of *Harmonica Sacra* (c1835), a collection of church music. His own compositions included Psalm tunes and glees.

MACFARREN, Sir George Alexander (1813-1887)

Born in Westminster, London on 2 March 1813; died in St. Marylebone, London on 31 October 1887. The brother of **Walter Macfarren** and the son of George M. Macfarren, the dramatist, theatrical manager and amateur musician.

Knighted at Windsor Castle (1883) to honour his achievements as principal of the Royal Academy of Music. At the same ceremony, his counterpart at the National Training School of Music, **Arthur Sullivan** and at the new Royal College of Music, George Grove, were also honoured. It is said that Macfarren was reluctant to accept the honour but was persuaded by Sullivan.

Studied under his father, George Macfarren and at the R.A.M. (1829-1836) under **Charles Lucas** and Cipriani Potter. Graduated Mus.B. and Mus.D. at the University of Cambridge (1875).

A professor of harmony and composition at the R.A.M. (1837-1846 and 1851-1875), succeeding **William Sterndale Bennett** as principal (1875-1887). During this period he was also Cambridge professor of music. The opportunity to create a new, unified institution from the National Training School of Music and the R.A.M. arose (1879) but Macfarren was against the idea.

The onset of blindness (1860) did not appear to hinder him unduly. He wrote books on musical theory, covering such topics as harmony and counterpoint.

He held and expressed strong views on the subject of the composition of church music and the selection of church organists. He argued that solo writing in anthems and services ought to be discouraged as there was a danger that their performance would be taken more seriously than the act of worship of which they were part.

In a similar vein he held that anthems should be composed in such a way as to highlight the words, while greater musical creativity could be employed in services, of which the words were more frequently used and therefore thoroughly familiar. In his opinion, church organist appointments should not be selected on the basis of technical skill, a criterion more appropriate only to secular organistships.

As a composer his early works were for the stage and for the concert hall, his compositional efforts later being devoted to church music. He also edited collections of songs.

Arthur Jacobs has expressed the view that Macfarren's *Jessy Lea* (1853) was one of the two major influences under which Arthur Sullivan began to compose operettas, the work incorporating a light hearted approach and a fast-moving plot but employing elegant musical techniques.

Composed services, including a Service in E-flat and a unison version in G; anthems including 'Behold', 'To obey is better' and 'Let us not be weary'; Responses to the Commandments; chants, including a Single Chant in A-flat which was contained in the Revised Edition (1927) of *Church Hymnary*, and hymn tunes, of which 'Their life was given', 'Father, let me dedicate' and 'Macfarren' were included in the Standard Edition of *Hymns Ancient and Modern*.

Among his oratorios was *St. John the Baptist*, performed at the Bristol Festival on 23 October 1873.

There were operas including *The Devil's Opera* (1838) and it was always Macfarren's intention to write an opera that fully expressed this country's spirit.

MACFARREN, Walter Cecil (1826-1905)

Born in Westminster, London on 28 August 1826; died in St. Pancras, London on 2 September 1905. Brother of **George Macfarren**.

A chorister at Westminster Abbey from the age of nine (1836-1841) under **James Turle**, and sang at King's College, London where **W.H. Monk** was organist. A student at the Royal Academy of Music (from 1842) under his brother (who paid his fees) for composition and with **W.H. Holmes** and Cipriani Potter. He met Mendelssohn at the age of 15.

Took a job in a music shop selling pianos for three months, aged 15, in Brighton, Sussex. Organist of Harrow School (1848-1850). A pianist. An assistant professor (1846-1848), professor of piano (1846-1903) and a member of the Management Committee (from 1870) of the R.A.M. In 1873 he took over from **John Hullah** the running of the choir and orchestra, resigning through failing eyesight in 1880. He declined to seek the vacant principalship when his brother died in 1887.

A director, and treasurer, of the Philharmonic Society.

Author of an autobiography *Musical Memories* (1905).

Composed three services, hymn tunes including 'Barmouth' and 'Heri Mundus Exultavit', both of which were used in *Hymns Ancient and Modern*, a Symphony, 10 Overtures, piano music, some 36 part songs and madrigals, and overtures on Shakespearian subjects.

MCGLYNN, Michael (b.1964)

Born in Dublin in 1964. Attended the National University of Ireland, where he graduated in 1986. As well as being a tenor recitalist specialising in early music, is also active as a composer. Won a number of awards, including the Dublin Millenium Young composers' Competition. His works include a Mass (1992), anthems such as 'Good people all' (1990) and 'Come, let us sing' (1988), and chamber works of which 'Rince' (1984) for Piano and Trumpet is an example.

MCINTYRE, Daniel (19th/20th century)

Trained privately in music. Graduated B.Mus. (1909) at the University of Durham. Organist and choirmaster in Edinburgh of St. Columba's Episcopal Church (1878-1879), the Wesleyan Church (1889-1891), Corstophine Parish Church (1892-1895), Mayfield Parish Church (1895-1907) and All Saints' Episcopal Church (1907-1908). Also organist and choirmaster of Dufftown Parish Church, Banffshire. A teacher, he conducted for local choral and orchestral societies. Assistant director and professor of organ and piano at Mount Allison Conservatory of Music in Sackville, Canada (from 1912).

His degree exercise was the anthem 'Praise and prayer' for Solo Voices, Chorus, Strings and Piano. Also composed a Festal March and a sacred song 'Lead, kindly Light'.

MACIRONE, Clara Angela (1821-1914)
Born in London on 21 January 1821; died on 19 August 1914. Her father was a tenor singer and her mother, a pianist. Studied at the Royal Academy of Music (1839-1844) under Cipriani Potter and from 1842 under **W.H. Holmes** and **Charles Lucas**. A professor of piano at the R.A.M. Head of music at Aske's School for Girls, Hatcham, London (1872-1878) and at the Church of England School for Girls, Baker Street, London. Contributed articles to *Girls' Own Paper*. Her setting of the Benedictus (1846) was praised by Mendelssohn. Her other works include a Te Deum and Jubilate (which was the first Service by a woman composer to be used at the Hanover Chapel, London), the anthem 'By the rivers of Babylon', sacred songs, duets and piano music. Her part songs include 'The Battle of the Baltic' and 'Ragged, torn and true'.

MACKENDRICK, William (c1840-1908)
Born around 1840; died in Hackney, London in 1908. Composed hymn tunes, and his part song for the 1895 Festival of the Nonconformist Choir Union won a prize of 5 guineas (£5.25).

MACKENZIE, Sir Alexander Campbell (1847-1935)
Born in Edinburgh on 22 August 1847; died in St. Pancras, London on 28 April 1935.
His great-grandfather had been a member of a military band and his grandfather, a drummer boy with Wolfe at Quebec. His father and grandfather had been violinists.
Learned the rudiments of music from his father, Alexander Mackenzie, and from the age of 10, he studied in Germany. Initially he was directed by K.W. Uhlrich for violin and then at Schwarzenburg-Sonderhausen (1857-1862) by Eduard Stein for composition. At 11 he became an orchestral player, returning to England (1862) to take up a scholarship at the Royal Academy of Music, where his tutors were Prosper Sainton for theory, Frederick Jewson for piano, and **Charles Lucas**. So long had been his absence from this country that he had to re-learn English on his return.
He earned many degrees: among his seven honorary doctorates in music were those awarded at the universities of St. Andrews (1886), Cambridge (1890), Edinburgh (1896) and Oxford (1922). Awarded the LL.D. at the Universities of Glasgow (1901) and Leeds (1904). The Canadian Universities of McGill, Montreal (D.C.L., 1903) and Toronto (D.Mus.) also honoured him.
Awarded the Goldene Verdienstmedaille (Hessen, 1886), the Ordre Pour La Mérite (Saxe Coburg Gotha, 1894) and he became a member of the Royal Swedish Academy (1897).
Knighted (1895) and appointed K.C.V.O. (1922).
In Edinburgh (1866-1881), he earned his living as a violinist, pianist, organist and conductor. Lived in Florence (1881-1888), returning in the latter year as principal of the R.A.M., in which capacity he served until 1924. Conductor of the Concerts of the Philharmonic Society, London (1892-1899).
His autobiography *A Musician's Narrative* was published in 1927.
As a composer his admirers included Liszt and **Edward Elgar**. Compositions for the church include settings of the Responses to the Commandments in A and in F.

His secular music includes *A Scottish Concerto*, of which the first performance was given (1897) with the Philharmonic Society of London by the pianist Paderewski. His operas include *Colomba* (1883), and *Rose of Sharon* (1884). Much of his music is said to have a Scottish flavour to it.

MCKIE, Sir William Neil (1901-1984)
Born in Melbourne, Australia on 22 May 1901; died on 1 December 1984.
Educated at Melbourne Grammar School; the Royal College of Music and Worcester College, Oxford (1921-1924). In Australia he was a music pupil of Arthur Nickson, who himself had been a pupil of **Walter Parratt**. A composition pupil of **Gustav Holst**. His other teachers included **H.G. Ley**. Graduated M.A. and D.Mus., the latter honorarily from both the Universities of Oxford and Melbourne.
Directed the music at the Coronation in 1953 of the present Queen, for which he received a knighthood. Also appointed M.V.O.
An assistant music master at Radley College, Oxfordshire (1923-1926) and director of music at Clifton College, Gloucestershire (1926-1930). In Australia he was city organist of Melbourne (1931-1938) and director of music at Geelong Grammar School (1934-1938). Organist of the Sheldonian Theatre (1939-1941) and an organ professor of the Royal Academy of Music (1946-1963). He retired to Ottawa, Canada.
As a church organist his appointments were at the Church of St. Agnes, Kennington Park, London (1920-1921); Magdalen College, Oxford (1938-1941) and Westminster Abbey (1941-1953). He did not actually take up the latter appointment until 1946 as he was away serving with the R.A.F. Volunteer Reserve (1941-1946).
His liturgical music includes an anthem for the Royal Wedding of 1947,'We wait for Thy loving-kindness, O God', which was sung at the Wedding of Prince Andrew and Sarah Ferguson (1985). Other important ceremonial music includes Fauxbourdon harmonies for plainsong Psalms. Arranged **William Walton's** 1953 Coronation March *Orb and Sceptre* for organ.

MACKINTOSH, Dr. Alfred Alexander (1860-?)
Born in Lowestoft, Suffolk in 1860.
Educated privately in music, studying with **Frederick Mann, Francis Gladstone, Arthur Mann, C.H. Kitson** and **A.W. Marchant**. Graduated B.Mus. (1913) at the University of Oxford, and D.Mus. at the University of Dublin (1921).
Organist and choirmaster at St. Peter's Church, Lowestoft, Suffolk (1880-1881); St. Mary's Church, Kippington, near Sevenoaks, Kent (1881-1885); All Saints' Church, Huntingdon (1885-1890); Godalming Parish Church, Surrey (from 1890) and Shackleford Parish Church. A music master in Godalming at Hillside, Branksome, Killcott and Holloway House Schools, and a local choral society conductor. His B.Mus. exercise was the motet *Morte Aequalis*.

MCKORKELL, Charles (1809-1879)
Born in 1809; died in Northampton on 10 January 1879. Studied at the Royal Academy of Music. Organist of the Church of All Saints, Northampton for 40 years. Compiled *The Sacred Music Book*. His compositions include anthems and piano music.

MACLAGAN, Revd. William Dalrymple (1826-1910)
Born in Edinburgh on 18 June 1826; died in Kensington, London on 19 September 1910.

Studied law at the University of Edinburgh. Following service with the 51st Regiment of the Madras Native Infantry (1847-1849), he graduated B.A. at St. Peter's College (later renamed Peterhouse), Cambridge (1857), having been ordained the previous year.

In the early part of his career he was curate of the London Churches of St. Saviour, Paddington and St. Stephen, Marylebone. He was later curate of Enfield Parish Church, Middlesex, and prebendary of Reculverland in St. Paul's Cathedral.

Rector of Newington (1869-1875) and of St. Mary's, Kensington (1875-1878). Bishop of Lichfield (1878-1891) and Archbishop of York (1891-1908), in which capacity he crowned Queen Alexandra (1902).

Established a theological college at York.

Author of hymns and composer of hymn tunes. Six of the latter appeared in *Hymns Ancient and Modern* including 'Troas', 'Newington' and 'Palms of glory'.

MACLEAN, Dr. Charles Donald (1843-1916)

Born in Cambridge on 27 March 1843; died in London on 23 June 1916.

Attended Shrewsbury School. Went up to Exeter College, Oxford as an exhibitioner, graduating B.Mus. (1862), D.Mus. (1865) and M.A. (1875). A pupil in Cologne of Ferdinand Hiller.

Organist of Exeter College, Oxford (1863-1865). Director of music at Eton College (1872-1875). Served in the Indian Civil Service for almost a quarter of a century, mainly in the city of Madras, before returning, at the age of 55 in 1898, to London. He was General Secretary of the Internationale Musikgesellschaft, a Leipzig-based international music society.

A solo organist, performing in many venues including St. George's Hall, Liverpool. Runner-up in the contest for the vacant organistship of the Crystal Palace (1880). Unsuccessfully contested the vacant position of principal of Guildhall School of Music (1892), the appointment going instead to **Joseph Barnby**.

Composed a Requiem Mass, an oratorio *Noah*, a Symphony in G, songs and a Piano Trio in B.

MCLEAN, Revd. Col. William Richard James (19th/20th century)

Educated privately in music. Graduated B.Mus. at the University of Durham (1894). Also graduated T.D.

Appointed C.B.E.

An army officer and civil servant, he was later ordained into the Church of England.

Senior staff officer and head of the Registry Section at the Board of Education, and assistant examiner of music papers (1896-1904).

lieutenant-colonel (commanding) of the 13th (Kensington) Battalion of the London Regiment, and assistant adjutant general and inspecting officer of the Transport Workers' Battalions.

Organist and choirmaster of St. James's Church, Clerkenwell, London (1896-1898) and of Christ Church, Fulham (1905-1910). Organist of a number of Masonic lodges, and a choral and music society conductor. Grand organist to the Royal Arch Masons (from 1905).

Wrote articles in *Year's Music* and other journals, and published an essay on strict counterpoint.

Around the year 1920 he became curate of Heston Church, Middlesex.

His B.Mus. exercise was a setting of Psalm 48 'Magnus Dominus' for Solo Voices, Chorus and String Orchestra; also composed hymn tunes, carols, songs, marches for military band and piano music.

MACMEIKAN, John Alexander (1849-1932)

Born in West Ham, London on 8 February 1849; died in Deal, Kent on 21 February 1932. Attended Repton School, Derbyshire and St. John's College, Oxford (1867). Graduated B.A. (1871) and M.A. (1876). Pursued a career in law. Admitted to Lincoln's Inn (May 1870) and called to the bar (June 1873). Designed and carved decorations in a number of churches in Kent. His other accomplishments included learning to drive a car at the age of 82. His compositions include the hymn tune 'St. Columba', a sacred song 'I am the Shepherd true' and the instrumental work *The March of The Paladine*.

MACMILLAN, James (b.1959)

Born in Kilwinning, Ayrshire, Scotland in 1959. Studied at the Universities of Edinburgh and Durham, later teaching in the music department of each. A lecturer at the Royal Scottish Academy of Music and Dance. A prolific composer whose works include *Beatus Vir* for Chorus and Organ (1983), an anthem for St. Cecilia's Day (1994), first performed at St. Paul's Cathedral, and *The Seven Last Words from the Cross* (first performed on B.B.C. Television in Easter, 1994).

MACMURDIE, Joseph (1793-1878)

Born in London on 19 March 1793; died in Merton, Surrey on 23 December 1878. Studied under **William Crotch** and graduated B.Mus. at the University of Oxford (1814). A pianist, violinist, and director of the Philharmonic Society. Organist of Brixton Parish Church, London. Composed a motet *De profundis clamavi* based on Psalm 130, the anthem 'O Give Thanks', glees, canons and trios.

MCPHEE, George (b.1937)

Born in Glasgow in 1937.

Studied at the Royal Scottish Academy of Music and Drama and at the University of Edinburgh, also studying organ privately with Herrick Bunney and, in Italy, Fernando Germani.

Appointed M.B.E. (1995) for services to music.

Assistant organist of St. Giles' Cathedral, Edinburgh (to 1963). Director of music of Paisley Abbey (from 1963), joining the staff of the R.S.A.M.D. in the same year, where he now teaches organ and composition. Visiting professor of organ at St. Andrews University.

Organ recitalist and broadcaster, having toured the U.S.A. and Canada a number of times, and participated at a number of major festivals including the Aldeburgh Festival. Chairman of the Paisley International Organ Festival. Has been soloist and conductor with the B.B.C. Scottish Orchestra and Scottish National Symphony Orchestra.

A festival adjudicator, local choral society conductor, and conductor of the Scottish Chamber Choir.

Joint editor of *New Scottish Song Book*.

His compositions include a number of works for the church, such as a Service in A for Boys' Voices, a Magnificat and Nunc Dimittis, a Missa Brevis, a Jubilate Deo, the anthem 'Make we joy' and carol arrangements including 'Whence is that goodly fragrance'.

MACPHERSON, Dr. Charles (1870-1927)

Born in Edinburgh on 10 May 1870; died in Westminster, London on 28 May 1927.

A chorister of St. Paul's Cathedral (from 1879); studied at the Royal Academy of Music. Awarded the honorary D.Mus. at the University of Durham.

Choirmaster of St. Clement's Church, Eastcheap, London.

Organist of St. David's Church, Weem, Aberfeldy, Wales (1879-1889) and private organist to Sir Robert Menzies. Organist to the Private Chapel of Madame de Falbu at Luton Hoo Park, Bedfordshire (1889-1895). Sub organist (from 1895) and organist (1916-1927) of St. Paul's Cathedral.

A professor of harmony at the R.A.M. Author of *A Short History of Harmony* and editor of *New Cathedral Psalter Chant Book* (Village Church Edition).

The Holy Communion Service in E-flat has a demanding top C-flat in the treble line. His hymn tunes 'Exsurgat Deus' and 'Stonypath' were used in *Hymns Ancient and Modern*. Composed the anthem 'O praise God in His holiness', part songs, arrangements of Scottish music, an Orchestral Overture and two suites for orchestra.

MACPHERSON, Charles Stewart (1865-1941)

Born in Liverpool on 29 March 1865; died in London in 1941.

Educated at the City of London School and won a Sterndale Bennett scholarship to the Royal Academy of Music (1880). Studied piano with **Walter Macfarren**.

Appointed a professor of harmony and composition at the R.A.M. (1889).

External examiner for university degrees for the University of Ireland, in connection with which he visited Canada, Australia and New Zealand (1900), and South Africa (1905).

From 1903 he was a professor of composition at the Royal Normal College for the Blind. Director of the Royal Philharmonic Society (1913-1914).

One of the founders of the Music Teachers' Association (1908). This body was one of the first to recognise the value of aural training in formal music education.

Organist and choirmaster of Immanuel Church, Streatham Common, London (from 1885).

Author of *Practical Harmony: a Concise Treatise* (1894).

As a student he composed prolifically. His work includes church music, a Symphony in C (1888), songs and duets.

MCQUAID, Dr. John Stephen (b.1909)

Born in Lochgelly, Fife, Scotland on 14 March 1909.

Graduated M.A. in modern languages (1932), M.Ed (1952) and Ph.D. (1949) at the Universities of Glasgow and Edinburgh. Studied privately with Erik Chisholm (1938-1940).

Taught languages (1935-1941) before serving in World War II with the Intelligence Corps (1941-1946) in West Africa, India and South-East Asia. Resumed teaching after the war (1946-1954) before practising as a psychologist (1954-1977).

After making an initial music transmission in India (1944), he has broadcast widely (from 1948).

Composed liturgical music and hymn tunes, including 'Chapman', found in *St. Andrew Hymnal*. Won a competition with his secular piece *Three little Waltzes*, since broadcast and published.

MCWILLIAM, Clement Charles (b.1934)

Born in Greenwich, London on 19 January 1934. Composed hymn tunes.

MADAN, Revd. Martin (c1725-1790)

Born in Hertingfordbury, Hertfordshire in 1725 or 1726; died in Epsom, Surrey on 2 May 1790. His brother Spencer was Bishop of Peterborough; the poet William Cowper was a cousin.

Educated at Westminster School, London and at Christ Church, Oxford where he graduated B.A. (1746).

Became a barrister (1748).

On hearing the preaching of Charles Wesley he took up the Methodist cause. One version of this event has it that his fellow members of a convivial club encouraged him to attend one of Wesley's meetings simply to ridicule him but instead he came away profoundly affected by what he heard. Offered himself as an ordination candidate shortly afterwards.

Chaplain of the Lock Hospital, London (1750-1780), which he founded. His preaching was so powerful and popular that a larger chapel had to be built.

His book *Thelyphthora* (1780) advocated polygamy as an answer to the social conditions of the time, drawing on items from the Old Testament to argue his case. A great scandal and controversy ensued, as a result of which Madan retired to Epsom, Surrey.

A hymnal editor, publishing a collection of hymns without tunes in 1760. A further collection with tunes (1769) became known as the *Lock Hospital Collection*. Later enlarged and republished (1792).

Composed hymn tunes including 'Wandsworth' and 'Huddersfield'. Arranged a tune by **Thomas Oliviers** and named it 'Helmsley': it was said to be a favourite of Queen Victoria. Composed a Sonata for Harpsichord (c1785).

MAHAFFY, Revd. Dr. John Pentland (1839-1919)

Born in Chapponnani, near Vevey, Switzerland on 26 February 1839; died on 30 April 1919. Of an Irish family. Educated at Trinity College, Dublin, with which he was associated for some 55 years. Vice provost (1913), provost (1915) and precentor of the College Chapel. It is said that he raised the standard of the degrees. **Ebenezer Prout** (1894), and **Percy Buck** (1910) were appointed to Trinity College on the strength of his recommendation. Appointed C.V.O. Held a doctorate in divinity from the University of Dublin. Various honorary degrees were awarded, including D.C.L. (Oxford), LL.D. (St. Andrews), Litt.D. (Louvain), Ph.D. (Athens) and D.Mus. (Dublin: 1891). Senior fellow of Queen's College, Oxford and professor of ancient history at the University of Oxford.

MAHER, Dom William Joseph (1823-1877)

Born in Bristol, Gloucestershire on 30 March 1823; died in Paris on 19 July 1877 while en route to Lourdes, suffering from cancer. Attended Stoneyhurst College before entering a Jesuit order (1841). Returned to Stoneyhurst College as a teacher (1846-1849). Studied at the Jesuit College, Malta (1849-1853). Read theology at St. Benno's College, North Wales, where he was ordained priest (1856). Devoted the remainder of his life to mission work in London. Composed Masses and services, and edited Francis Trappe's *Liturgical Hymns for the Chief Festivals of the Year* (1865).

MAHON, Dr. Herbert (1871-1943)

Born in Leigh-on-Mendip, Somerset in 1871; died in Saffron Walden, Essex on 3 May 1943.

Trained at Westminster Abbey, and privately. Graduated B.Mus. (1903) and D.Mus. (1923) at the University of Durham.

Music master of Honiton School (from 1893), Newport Grammar School, Essex (from 1911), Saffron Walden Grammar School and at the Bishop Stortford School. Also taught music at the Cambridge House Girls' School, Saffron Walden.

Organist of Holy Trinity Church, Lambeth, London (1896). Organist and choirmaster of All Hallows Church, Southwark (from 1897) and of Saffron Walden Parish Church (from 1898). A conductor of choral and music societies.

Composed an anthem 'In my distress' based upon Psalm 120, which he submitted successfully as his B.Mus. exercise. Also composed three settings of the Benedicite.

MAINE, Revd. Basil Stephen (1894-1972)
Born in Norwich, Norfolk on 4 March 1894; died in Sheringham, Norfolk, on 13 October 1972.

Attended City of Norwich School. Assistant organist of the Church of St. Peter Mancroft, Norwich (1910-1913), before going up as organ scholar to Queens' College, Cambridge (1913-1917) under **C.V. Stanford**, Edward Dent and **Cyril Rootham**. Graduated M.A. Ordained priest in 1939, prior to which he had been a schoolteacher, author, actor, musical director, and music critic of *Daily Telegraph* and *The Spectator*.

Assistant organist of Durham Cathedral (from 1919). In the same year he became music and mathematics master of Durnford School, Langton Matravers, Somerset.

Author of a biography of **Edward Elgar**, published in two volumes (1933), followed by a collection of essays entitled *The Glory of English Music* (1937).

Narrator in the first performance of *Morning Heroes* by **Arthur Bliss** at the Norwich Music Festival of 1930.

Composed choral and organ works, a Te Deum for Chorus and Orchestra, anthems including 'O Lord our Governour' and 'Praise to God', carols, and songs.

MAINWARING, Townshend (c1809-1883)
Born around the year 1809; died in Galltfaenan, near Denbigh, Wales in December 1883. Member of Parliament for Denbigh (1841-1847; 1857-1868). Composed hymn tunes including the advent hymn 'Emyn ail ddfodid Crist' (1890).

MAITLAND, J.A. Fuller
See **FULLER-MAITLAND,** J.A.

MAKER, Frederick Charles (1844-1927)
Born in Bristol, Gloucestershire in 1844; died in Bristol on 1 January 1927. A chorister at Bristol Cathedral and a pupil of Alfred Stone. Lived in Bristol all his life. Organist of the Milk Street Methodist Free Church, the Clifton Downs Congregational Church and the Redland Park Congregational Church where he remained for almost 30 years (1882-1910). Conducted the Bristol Free Church Choir Association. Visiting music Teacher at Clifton College, Gloucestershire. Composed anthems, hymn tunes, including the popular 'Rest', found in *Methodist Hymn Book* (1933) and elsewhere, and 'St. Christopher' and 'Wentworth', both of which featured in the Revised Edition (1927) of *Church Hymnary*. Also a cantata *Moses in the Bullrushes*.

MALAN (de Mérindol), Revd. Dr. Caesar (1787-1864)
Born in 1787; died in 1864. A pastor of Geneva. Composed the anthems 'Lord my God' and 'Unto Him that loved us'.

MALCOLM, Dr. George John (b.1917)
Born in London in 1917.

Educated at Wimbledon College, London; Balliol College, Oxford, and the Royal College of Music. Graduated M.A. and B.Mus. at Oxford. Became an honorary fellow of Balliol College in 1966. Appointed C.B.E. in 1965, Papal Knight of the Order of St. Gregory the Great in 1970, and awarded honorary D.Mus. (Sheffield) in 1978.

Master of music at Westminster Cathedral (1947-1959). It was for his choir that **Benjamin Britten** composed his Missa Brevis. His work in other musical spheres, as conductor and harpsichordist, includes long connections with the Aldeburgh Festival, English Chamber Orchestra, Philomusica of London and the Northern Sinfonia Orchestra.

His compositions include motets such as *Veritas mea*, and works for Christmas, a set of Responsories 'Christus factus est', and a Missa *ad praesepe*. As an editor of polyphonic music he has done work for the Westminster Series.

MALET, Guilbert Edward Wyndham (1839-1918)
Born in Taunton, Somerset on 12 July 1839; died in Worle, Axbridge, Somerset on 15 October 1918. Composer of hymn tunes.

MALONE, Dr. Robert (?1851-1911)
Born around 1851; died in 1911 at the age of 60. Graduated B.Mus. (1882) and D.Mus. (1885) at the University of Dublin. Organist and choirmaster in Ireland of St. Michael's, Church, Dublin (from 1866); Roscrea Church (from 1869) and Carlow Church (from 1880). A music society conductor. Wrote and lectured on musical topics. His B.Mus. exercise was an anthem 'Praise the Lord' for Solo Voices, Choir and Orchestra. Also composed services, Kyries, hymns, chants and piano music.

MANDER, Dr. Richard Yates (19th/20th century)
Trained privately in music. Graduated B.Mus. (1896) and D.Mus. (1902) at Queen's College, Oxford. Organist and choirmaster of the Churches of St. John, Leamington Spa, Warwickshire (from 1879); St. Philip, Birmingham (from 1888) and Ryde Parish Church, Isle of Wight (from 1898).

Music master of the College for the Blind, Worcester (1892-1897) and of the Royal Naval College, Osborne, Isle of Wight (1904-1908). Teacher and organist of the Birmingham and Midland Institute School of Music (1892-1895). Organist to Ryde Corporation (from 1899).

His anthem 'Glory to Thee, my God, this night' was submitted as his B.Mus. exercise. For his doctorate he tendered a sacred cantata, *Noah*, for Solo Voices, Choir and Orchestra.

MANN, Dr. Arthur Henry (1850-1929)
Born in Norwich, Norfolk on 16 May 1850; died in Cambridge on 19 November 1929. The younger brother of the church musician Frederick Mann.

A chorister of Norwich Cathedral under **Zechariah Buck**, to whom he was assistant organist. Graduated B.Mus. (1874) and D.Mus. (1882) at New College, Oxford, and M.A. at the University of Cambridge.

Organist of St. Peter's Church, Wolverhampton (1870-1871); Tettenhall Parish Church, Staffordshire (1871-1875) and Beverley Minster (1875-1876).

Organist of King's College, Cambridge (1876-1929), where he is credited with raising musical standards greatly. This he achieved partly by establishing a choir school and by using as his adult singers choral scholars instead of lay clerks.

Organist to the University of Cambridge (1897-1929). For much of his time in Cambridge he was music master of The Leys School (1894-1922).

Musical editor of *Church of England Hymnal* (1895). Edited the motet *Spem in alium* for 40 voices by **Thomas Tallis**. One of the compilers of the catalogue of the music contents of the Fitzwilliam Museum, Cambridge. An authority on the works of **Handel**.

A man who expressed his views forthrightly, yet somehow usually managed to avoid giving offence.

Composed much church music, including an Evening Service in E, a Te Deum (1887) and anthems. His hymn tune 'Wilton' was used in the First Edition (1898) of *Church Hymnary* with the hymn 'Light of the world! For ever, ever shining' by Horatius Bonar. His re-harmonisation of **Henry Gauntlett**'s tune 'Irby', universally sung to 'Once in Royal David's City', first used at King's College and sung since at the opening of countless carol services, has been described as 'magically deft'. Also composed an oratorio, a quantity of part songs and some organ music.

MANN, Lionel Frederic (b.1927)
Born in Norwich, Norfolk in 1927. Educated at the City of Norwich School and at the Royal College of Music. Organist and choirmaster of St. Leonard's Church, Norwich (1942-1948) and of Church House, British Army on the Rhine, Hanover District (1946-1948). Assistant organist of Wembley Parish Church, Middlesex (1948-1950); organist and choirmaster of St. Mary-the-Boltons, South Kensington, London (1950-1953); Tokyngton Parish Church, Wembley (1953-1958); Hampton Parish Church, Surrey (1958-1963). Organist of St. Mark's Church, Wellington, New Zealand (1965-1968). Music master of William Penn School, Slough, Berkshire (1952-1955) and music master of Latymer Foundation School, Hammersnith, London (1955-1958). Organist and master of the choristers of Napier Cathedral, New Zealand (from 1968); and principal of St. Mildred's School, Napier (from 1969). Composer of anthems, and other items of church music.

MANN, Richard (1837-1869)
Born in 1837; died in Chichester, Sussex in 1869. Lived in Chichester as a teacher and organist. Composer of anthems and author of *A Manual of singing* (1866). Composed the anthem 'Grant, we beseech Thee'.

MANNIN, John (1802-1865)
Born in Ireland in 1802; died in St. Marylebone, London on 25 December 1865. His biographical details are incomplete but it is known that in 1851 he was living in Newman Street, London and working as a teacher of music. Later moved to the nearby Berners Street. Composer of hymn tunes.

MANSELL, David John (b.1936)
Born in South London in 1936. Educated at King's College, London where he graduated in physics. Worked initially in engineering before going into business. Eventually became an evangelist. Wrote the words and tune of the hymn 'Jesus is Lord', first published in the collection *Sound of Living Waters* (1970) and subsequently used in *Hymns and Psalms* (1983).

MANSFELDT, Edgar.
See **PIERSON,** Henry Hugo.

MANSFIELD, Dr. Orlando Augustine (1863-1936)
Born in Horningsham, Wiltshire on 28 November 1863; died in Cheltenham, Gloucestershire on 6 July 1936. The son of a clergyman and the father of **Purcell Mansfield**

Studied music privately. Graduated B.Mus. (1887) and D.Mus. (1890) at Trinity College, Toronto, Canada.

Organist of the Manvers Street Wesleyan Chapel, Trowbridge, Wiltshire (from 1883). Organist of Holy Trinity Church (1885-1895) and of Belgrave Church, Torquay, Devon (1890-1912). Professor of theory and composition at Gainesville College, Georgia, U.S.A. (from 1919). In the same year he was appointed dean of the School of Music at Lincoln-Jefferson University, Chicago.

A lecturer and writer, he contributed articles to *Musical Standard*. Editor of the organ department of *Musical Observer* (from 1920).

His compositions number some six hundred and they include anthems, hymn tunes and organ music. In 1896 he won the Anthem Prize at the Festival of the Nonconformist Choir Union at the Crystal Palace, London, for his 'There shall come forth a star'.

MANSFIELD, Purcell James (1889-1968)
Born in Torquay, Devon on 24 May 1889; died in Glasgow on 24 September 1968. The son of **Orlando A. Mansfield**. Organist of the Wesleyan Church, Paignton (1905-1908); Bideford (1908-1910) and of Park Parish Church, Glasgow (1910-1919). Organist and choirmaster of Paisley Abbey (1919-1923). Organist of Clark Town Hall, Paisley and St. Kentigern's Parish Church, Pollokshields, Glasgow (from 1923). A renowned recitalist. A choral society conductor. Composed hymn tunes such as a Fauxbourdon setting that was included in the Revised Edition (1927) of *Church Hymnary*. Also composed choral and orchestral works; an opera *The Hawaiian Maid;* two comic operas, including *The Duke's Dilemma* and five concert overtures for organ.

MARBECK (Marbecke, Merbecke), John (1523-1585)
Born possibly in Windsor, Berkshire in 1523; died in 1585. Graduated B.Mus. at the University of Oxford (1550).

A chorister (from 1531), a lay clerk, and organist (c1541-c1585) of St. George's Chapel, Windsor Castle. For at least part of his term as organist he probably shared the post with George Thexton.

Studied the works of John Calvin at an early age and found himself in sympathy with the Protestant Reformation. Discreetly annotated his Bible, and began to compile a Concordance (March 1542 or 1543). Arrested by commissioners who had searched Windsor for heretical books. Arrested with four others including two lay clerks of St. George's Chapel, charged with copying a letter of Calvin against the Mass, found guilty and condemned to be burned at the stake.

He was spared on the intervention of Gardiner, Bishop of Winchester, and allowed to resume his duties as organist but it was not until the reign of Edward VI that he felt safe in making his views public. Escaped persecution during the reign of Mary.

Completed the compilation of the Concordance, and published it in 1574 as *The Lives of the Holy Sainctes, Prophets, Patriarchs and others Contained in Holy Scripture*. The work was dedicated to Edward VI and in the dedication Marbeck described himself as 'destitute of learnyng and eloquence', going on to express his regret that he 'consumed vainly the greatest part of my life' studying music and playing organ.

Famous for his *Book of Common Prayer Noted* (1550), a matching of ancient plainsong to the then new vernacular services of the

Church of England, that is still in use today. The aim was to fit a single note to each syllable and to make the melody clear and dignified. Also composed a set of Preces and Responses, and motets.

MARCH, Mrs. G. E.
See **GABRIEL,** Miss M.A.V.

MARCH, John (?1752-1828)
Born around the year 1752; died in 1828. Composed the anthem 'O Lord, who hast taught us'.

MARCHANT, Dr. Arthur William (1850-?)
Born in London on 18 October 1850.
Educated privately in music, graduating B.Mus. (1879) and D.Mus. (1898) at New College, Oxford.
Organist of St. John's Church, Mansfield, Nottinghamshire (1870-1877); Streatham Parish Church, Surrey (from 1876) and St. Luke's, Kentish Town, London (1878-1880).
Organist and choirmaster of St. John's Cathedral, Denver, U.S.A. (from 1880). Returned to England two years later and became organist and choirmaster of All Saints' Church, Sevenoaks, Kent; All Saints' Church, Huntingdon (1895) and St. John's Episcopal Church, Dumfries, Scotland (from 1901). Organist and choirmaster of Holy Trinity Church, Stirling, Scotland. A local choral society conductor.
Composed a Morning and Evening Service, the anthems 'This is the day' and 'Hail to the Lord', a short oratorio *Jehosaphat*, songs, part songs and organ music. Author of a number of books on aspects of the teaching of music.

MARCHANT, Dr. Charles George (1857-1920)
Born to a Huguenot family in Dublin in 1857; died on 16 January 1920.
A chorister of St. Patrick's Cathedral, Dublin under Frank Robinson (1865-1873), and during his last five years as chorister he was principal treble soloist. An organ pupil of William Murphy (1861-1879), Cathedral organist. Studied piano at the Royal Irish Academy of Music under George Sproule. Graduated D.Mus. (1906).
Organist of the Holy Trinity Church, Rathmines, Dublin and Christ Church, Bray, Ireland (from 1876). For one week he was organist of St. Matthias's Church, Dublin before being appointed organist and choirmaster of St. Patrick's Cathedral, Dublin (1879-1920).
Marchant faced a long and constant struggle to set and maintain high musical standards. A new succentor, Revd. William Stillman who arrived from Beverley Minster (January 1885-1890), helped to improve attendance of the adult choir members at services and rehearsals. When he left, the situation deteriorated.
Matters came to a head (March 1896) when a Mr. Kelly refused to sing the solo part in an anthem. A sub committee of the cathedral was set up and drafted what today would be a job description. It covered attendance at services and rehearsals, holidays and the use of deputies. A schedule of fines for non-compliance was included, and each choirman was expected to sign a pledge to abide by it.
The succentor (from 1899) and warden of the Cathedral Grammar School was Revd. D.F.R. Wilson, who tried to raise standards by such methods as introducing a choral scholarship (1902). Difficulties remained: choirmen's salaries were low, forcing them to augment their incomes elsewhere and World War I made it even harder to find suitable adult singers.

Organist and conductor of the choral society of the University of Dublin. Professor of organ at the Royal Irish Academy of Music.
With **C.H. Kitson** he was joint editor of the Revised Edition of *Irish Church Hymnal*.
Composed a Service in A, and other items of church music.

MARCHANT, Sir Stanley Robert (1883-1949)
Born in London on 15 May 1883; died in London on 28 February 1949.
Goss Scholar at the Royal Academy of Music (1900). Graduated B.Mus (1909) and D.Mus. (1914) at Pembroke College, Oxford. Also awarded, honorarily, an Oxford M.A.
Knighted (1943) and appointed C.V.O. (1935).
Organist and choirmaster of the Churches of St. Mary, Kensington, London (1899-1903); Christ Church, Newgate Street (1903-1913) and St. Peter, Eaton Square (1913-1921). Sub organist of St. Paul's Cathedral (from 1916), a position which he held for 11 years until his appointment as organist (1927-1936). One of his choristers was (Sir) Charles Groves, the famous conductor.
During and immediately after World War I he served in Europe (1917-1919).
A professor of organ (1914-1936), warden (1934-1946) and principal (1936-1949) of the R.A.M. King Edward professor of music at the University of London (1937-1948); visiting music master at Wycombe Abbey School, Buckinghamshire (1926-1936) and lecturer in music at the University of Liverpool (1936-1937).
With Revd. M.F. Foxell he edited *St. Paul's Cathedral Psalter* (1934).
Composed services, anthems including 'Very bread' and his B.Mus. exercise 'The Lord is King'. His Double Chant in F was included in the Third Edition (1973) of *Church Hymnary*.
A special Te Deum in D by Stanley Marchant was sung at a Service of Thanksgiving in St. Paul's Cathedral (June 1930), attended by the King and Queen.
Also composed songs and organ music, and was a talented amateur watercolourist.

MARKS, David (1788-1871)
Born in Cilrhedyn, Carmarthenshire, Wales in 1788; died in Ffynnondrain, Newchurch, near Carmarthen on 3 October 1871. A stonemason by trade. Also a teacher of music. Two hymn tunes, 'Cannon Street' and 'Manchester', were included in the publication *Haleliwia Drachefyn* (1855).

MARKS, Dr. James Christopher (1835-1903)
Born in Armagh, Ireland on 4 May 1835; died in Clifton, Gloucestershire on 17 July 1903. His son was also named **James Marks**.
A chorister of Armagh Cathedral (from 1842), where other members of his family had previously served, under Robert Turle. A pupil of F. Hart for violin. Graduated B.Mus. (1863) and D.Mus. (1868) at the University of Oxford.
A choirman and assistant organist (1852-1860) of Armagh Cathedral.
Organist and choirmaster of St. Fin Barre Cathedral, Cork (1860-1903).
The last service was held in Cork Cathedral prior to rebuilding in November 1864. The Psalms were chanted to compositions by Marks himself. The new cathedral was completed and consecrated in November 1870, when Marks was presented with a

commemorative gold medal by the dean. Full choral services were resumed after an absence of almost two hundred years.

Had the honour of being organist at the reopening of Cloyne Cathedral, following restoration (29 May 1894). Marks had been the conductor of the first annual Cloyne Choral Festival (1879).

Faced the same problems as his cathedral colleagues in other parts of Ireland in finding and retaining suitable adult choir members. **R.P. Stewart** was outraged when, attending a service in the Cathedral (January 1880) he heard the chorus 'For unto us' from Handel's *Messiah* attempted without any altos.

Conductor of harmonic societies and of the Cork Musical Festival (1862).

Composed an anthem 'If we believe', an oratorio *Gideon* (his degree exercise), songs and piano music.

MARKS, James Christopher (1863-1946)
Born in Cork on 29 July 1863; died in New York City on 14 October 1946. The son of **James Marks** and the step-brother of **Thomas Marks**. A chorister of Cork Cathedral, in his father's choir (from 1871). Appointed organist and choirmaster of St. Luke's Church, Cork (1883-1902), subsequently emigrating to the U.S.A. An organist in the cities of Pittsburgh and New York. Composed Evening Services in A, in B-flat and in D, anthems including 'The day is past and over' and 'The souls of the righteous', and vocal and piano music.

MARKS, Dr. Thomas Osborne (1845-1916)
Born in Armagh, Ireland on 6 February 1845; died on 11 September 1916. Step-brother of the younger **James Marks**. At the age of six he became a chorister of Armagh Cathedral. Graduated B.Mus. (Oxford, 1870) and D.Mus. (Dublin, 1874). At 15, appointed assistant organist to Robert Turle. Organist of St. Patrick's Cathedral, Armagh (1872-1916), succeeding Turle. His pupils included **Charles Wood**, later a professor of the Royal College of Music. Also held the position of organist of St. Mark's Church, Armagh. Composed church music including a setting of Psalm 95 'O come let us sing unto the Lord', a cantata *St. John the Baptist*, and songs.

MARLOW, Dr. Richard Kenneth (b.1939)
Born in Banstead, Surrey on 26 July 1939.

Attended St. Olave's Grammar School, London and Selwyn College, Cambridge (1958-1962) where he was Stewart of Rannoch Scholar. Graduated B.A. (1961), Mus.B. (1962), M.A. (1965) and Ph.D. (1965).

Lecturer in music at the University of Southampton (1965-1968) and at the University of Cambridge (from 1968), in which year he was also appointed fellow, lecturer, organist and director of music of Trinity College. A research fellow of Selwyn College (1963-1965).

Master of the music of St. Mary's Church, Southampton (1967-1968).

Composed the Whitsun-tide anthem 'Veni, Creator Spiritus'. Other works include an Advent Responsory, an Epiphany Responsory, and a set of Preces and Responses *E quinque notis*. Has also composed choral descants.

MARSDEN, Dr. George (1843-?)
Born in Stalybridge, Cheshire on 11 April 1843. Studied at the Cologne Conservatory under Ferdinand Hiller and others. Graduated Mus.B. (1876) and Mus.D. (1882) at the University of

Cambridge. A teacher in Manchester. Organist of St. Thomas's Church, Werneth, near Oldham and principal of the Oldham School of Music. His church music compositions included settings of Psalms 23 'The Lord is my Shepherd' and 46 'God is our Hope and Strength'. Also wrote part songs and orchestral works.

MARSH, John (1752-1828)
Born in Dorking, Surrey in 1752; died in Chichester, Sussex in 1828. Older brother of **William Marsh**. Articled to a solicitor in Romsey, Hampshire (from 1768). Lived in Salisbury, Wiltshire (from 1776), Canterbury, Kent (from 1785) and Chichester (1787-1828). In each of these places he directed concerts and deputised for the cathedral organist. Composed and published six anthems (1790). Issued collections of chants and hymns. His anthems include 'O Lord, Thou hast taught us' and 'O praise the Lord', and his other compositions include glees, songs and orchestral works.

MARSH, William (1757-1818)
Born in Liverpool in 1757; died in 1818. Younger brother of **John Marsh**. Commissioned lieutenant in the Royal Navy (1778). A pianist, organist and composer. His works include cantatas and other forms of church music. His Double Chant in A was included in *Baptist Hymn Book* (1962).

MARSHALL, Frederick (c1790-1857)
Born in Northampton around the year 1790; died near Olney, Buckinghamshire in July 1857. Organist of Rugby School, Warwickshire; Christ Church, Leamington Spa, Warwickshire and of Banbury Parish Church, Oxfordshire. Composer of hymn tunes.

MARSHALL, Dr. Philip (b.1921)
Born in Brighouse, Yorkshire in 1921.

His early life was spent at Alford, Lincolnshire where he studied music under Frank Graves. Graduated B.Mus. at the University of Durham (1950), and D.Mus. (1955), following study with **Francis Jackson**, organist of York Minster.

Served in the army, in the R.A.S.C. His civilian career began in Yorkshire. Taught music at Keighley Grammar School and was sub organist to **Melville Cook** at Leeds Parish Church. Organist of All Souls' Church, Haley Hill, Halifax.

Organist of St. Botolph's Church, Boston (1951-1957) and of Ripon Cathedral (1957-1966). Organist of Lincoln Cathedral (1966-1986), also teaching music at the Cathedral School. A local music society conductor and a renowned improviser on the organ. Helped to establish a regular joint festival with the Cathedrals of Peterborough and Southwell (1982).

Composed a setting of the Litany (1982) for a visit to Lincoln Cathedral of the Conference of North American Deans. His other compositions include a setting of the Benedicite, anthems, chants, organ music and songs.

MARSHALL, Dr. William (1806-1875)
Born in Oxford in 1806; died in Handsworth, Birmingham on 17 August 1875. A chorister of the Chapel Royal under **John Smith** and **William Hawes**. A pupil of John Braham, Charles Neate and **William Horsley**. Joined the choir of St. John's College, Oxford (1823). Graduated B.Mus. (1826) and D.Mus. (1840) at the University. Organist of Christ Church Cathedral, Oxford; St. John's College (1825-1846); All Saints' Church, Oxford (from 1839) and St. Mary's Church, Kidderminster, Worcestershire (from 1846). Edited a collection of chants with **Alfred Bennett**.

Composed anthems and other items of church music. Author of a work entitled *The Art of Reading Church Music.*

MARSHALL, Worth (18th century)
A lay clerk of Ely Cathedral in 1759. Composed the anthem 'O my son, despise thou not'.

MARSON (Mason), Revd. George (c1570-1632)
Born around the year 1570; died in Canterbury, Kent in 1632 and was buried on 5 February of that year. **James Clifford** refers to this composer as 'Mason'. Was said to hold B.Mus. but the circumstances of the award are not known. A minor canon and organist and master of the choristers of Canterbury Cathedral. Composed a set of Preces and a setting of Psalm 16: 'Preserve Me O God'. Anthems include 'Judge me O God' and 'O gracious God'. His madrigal *The Nimphes and Shepherdes* was included in the collection *The Triumphes of Oriana* (1601) by **Thomas Morley.**

MART, Samuel (1811-1884)
Born in 1811; died in Sutton-at-Hone, Kent on 16 July 1884. Composer of hymn tunes.

MARTIN, Donald (c1897-c1972)
Died around 1972 at the age of 75. A pupil of **Haydn Keeton** at Peterborough Cathedral. His first organistship was at Middlesbrough Parish Church, Yorkshire. Organist of St. Margaret's Church, Ilkley for more than 20 years. Composed five settings of the Holy Communion Service, and other items.

MARTIN, Sir George Clement (1844-1916)
Born in Lambourn, Berkshire on 11 September 1844; died in London on 23 February 1916.
As a child he heard **Herbert Oakeley** play Bach fugues on the organ of Lambourn Parish Church, while visiting the local squire. This inspired him to pursue a similar career. Three months later he had made sufficient progress to play the service at the parish church.
Studied under **J. Pearson** and **John Stainer.** Twice a week he travelled more than 20 miles by horse to Oxford for lessons with Stainer, who at the time was organist of Magdalen College.
Graduated B.Mus. at New College, Oxford (1869). Received an honorary doctorate from the University of Oxford (1912), and was awarded the Lambeth D.Mus. (1883).
Received a knighthood (1897), following his direction from the West Steps of St. Paul's Cathedral of the Thanksgiving Service for the Diamond Jubilee of Queen Victoria. For that occasion he had composed a special anthem, in which the Great Paul Bell was part of the orchestra. He was also appointed M.V.O.
Private organist to the Duke of Buccleuch at Dalkeith, Scotland (from 1871). The Duke provided for daily cathedral-style services. From that year he was also organist of St. Peter's Episcopal Church, Lutton Place, Edinburgh.
Three years later he began his long association with St. Paul's Cathedral as master of song at the Choir School (from 1874), sub organist (from 1876) under John Stainer and, following Stainer's retirement, organist (1888-1916).
Professor of organ at the Royal College of Music (from 1883) and at the Royal Academy of Music (from 1895). Said to be a shy and retiring man, but of strong character.
Editor of a collection of Responses to the Commandments. With **C.H. Lloyd** and others he edited *The New Cathedral Psalter* and

the *St. Paul's* Edition of the *New Cathedral Psalter Chant Book.* Author of the work *The Art of Training Choirboys,* which soon became a standard work.
Composed Morning and Evening Services, a setting of the Te Deum for the Diamond Jubilee of Queen Victoria on 22 June 1897, the anthems 'Rejoice in the Lord' and 'Come my soul' and part songs. Chants composed by him include Double Chants in A-flat, in D-flat and in G.
Three of his hymn tunes featured in *Hymns Ancient and Modern* and elsewhere: 'Lambourn', 'St. Faith' and 'St. Helen'. The Revised Edition (1927) of *Church Hymnary* uses 'Chilton foliat' and 'Israel' while 'Ashbury' has been popular with Baptist congregations.

MARTIN, George Walter (1828-1881)
Born on 8 March 1828; died in Wandsworth, London on 16 April 1881, having been homeless for some time and thus weakened by poverty and exposure. Some sources give his second Christian name as William. A chorister of St. Paul's Cathedral under **William Hawes.** A professor of music in the Normal College for Army Schoolmasters, and music master of St. John's Training College, Battersea, London (1845-1853). Organist of Christ Church, Battersea (from 1849). A choral conductor, he edited *Journal of Parts Music* (1861-1862) and contributed to other musical journals. Conducted the Concerts of the Metropolitan Schools' Choir Association and the National Choral Society. Alcoholism dogged the latter stages of his career. Composed anthems of which examples are 'Forsake me not' and 'O sing unto the Lord', hymn tunes including 'Leominster', glees and songs.

MARTYN, Samuel Symons (19th/20th century)
Trained privately in music. Graduated B.Mus. (1888) at Keble College, Oxford. Organist and choirmaster of the London Churches of St. Andrew, Stockwell (1891-1918) and All Saints, Upper Norwood (from 1893). Reappointed to his previous positions at St. Andrew's (1899). Composed as his B.Mus. exercise a setting of Psalm 37 'The Lord is my Light' for Solo Voices, Chorus and Strings.

MASON, George
See **MARSON,** George.

MASON, Dr. Edward (1864-?)
Born in Newcastle-under-Lyme, Staffordshire on 4 July 1864 into an old Staffordshire family who had settled in the town in the 16th century.
His musical training was at St. John's College, Battersea, under **Edward Mills** and at the Tonic Sol-fa College under William McNaught and Leonard Venables. Graduated B.Mus. (1892) at the University of Durham and D.Mus. (1915) at the University of Manchester.
A teacher of singing at schools in Arbroath, Scotland (1892-1901). A local choral society conductor. Choirmaster of St. Mary's Episcopal Church, Arbroath (1892-1901).
Headmaster of Rye Croft Council School, Newcastle-under-Lyme, Staffordshire (from 1907) and of Hassell Street Evening School (1901-1909). Choirmaster of St. George's Church (from 1908). Organist of Colne Parish Church, Lancashire (from 1913).
Wrote newspaper articles and was the author of a number of books on sight reading and the teaching of music.

Composed an Evening Service, a cantata for Good Friday *The Man of Sorrows* (1896), and a series of 12 anthems and part songs.

MASON, Sir John (?-c1548)
Graduated B.Mus.(1508), probably at the University of Oxford. Referred to by **Thomas Morley** as 'a famous musician'. Master of the choristers of Magdalen College, Oxford (from 1508). Composed the anthems 'God is our Hope' and 'O clap your hands'.

MASON, Revd. William (1725-1797)
Born in Hull, Yorkshire in 1725; died in Aston, Yorkshire on 5 April 1797.
Ordained (1755) and graduated M.A.
Prebendary and precentor (from 1763) of York Minster, holding the latter position for 35 years. A poet; a friend and the literary editor of Thomas Grey. A writer; his observations on church music were published collectively in the form of *Four Essays* (1795). One of his arguments was that church music ought to be simple in order to facilitate devotion: secular music on the other hand could be allowed to be amusing and ornate.
Famous locally for his preaching, his training of the singers and his introduction of the barrel-organ (1782), one of the first instances of the instrument being used in an English church.
One of the first Englishmen to own a piano. He took an interest in the internal workings of keyboard instruments and he invented the celestinette.
His dramatic poem 'Elfrida' was set to music by **Thomas Arne.** Among his friends were **Charles Avison**, **Charles Burney** and the **Camidge** family.
Composed anthems including 'If ye love me' and 'Lord of all power and might', hymns, a Kyrie in D and a set of Responses.

MASON, William Wright (1853-1932)
Born in Spilsby, Lincolnshire in 1853; died in Louth, Lincolnshire on 11 August 1932. Composer of hymn tunes.

MASSER, John Thornton (1855-1929)
Born in Bradford, Yorkshire in 1855; died in Nottingham on 23 January 1929. Trained at Bramham College, Tadcaster, Yorkshire. Organist of Bramham College; Hornton Lane Church, Bradford; and the Addison Street Church, Nottingham. Composer of hymn tunes.

MASSEY, Bernard Stanford (b.1927)
Born in Rickmansworth, Hertfordshire on 22 June 1927. Educated at Watford Grammar School, Hertfordshire, and at Queen Mary College, London. Member of the Department of Mechanical Engineering (from 1952); reader emeritus and an honorary research fellow (from 1984) of University College, London. Editor of the supplementary hymnal *New Songs* (1962). A member the respective music committees for the publications *Hymns and Psalms* (1983), which includes three of his own hymn tunes, and *Rejoice and Sing* (1991), which includes four tunes and several arrangements. Joint author of *Companion to Rejoice and Sing* (1996). Editor of the *Bulletin* of the Hymn Society of Great Britain and Ireland (from 1975). His hymn tunes include 'Gatton Park', 'Living Bread' and 'Mansfield College'.

MASSEY, Richard (1798-1883)
Born in 1798; died in London on 21 April 1883. Another musician of the same name who was active at the same time may have been his father. Organist of the Chapel Royal, Whitehall, London (1837-

1877). *Cathedral Psalter Chants* (1874) contains a Double Chant in E.

MATHER, Dr. George (?-1854)
A D.Mus. graduate. A blind organist whose appointments included St. Bride's Church, Fleet Street, London (1821-1854). A teacher of music. Published *The Calcutta Melodies* (1844), a set of 36 Psalm and hymn tunes. Composed songs and wrote a manual on singing.

MATHER, Samuel (1783-1824)
Born in Sheffield in 1783; died in Edinburgh on 26 May 1824. Son of **William Mather**. Organist, in Sheffield, of the Churches of St. James (from 1799) and St. Paul (from 1808). Bandmaster of the Sheffield Volunteers (from 1805). Compiled a book of Psalm tunes and assisted Thomas Cotterill in compiling *Christian Psalmody* (1834). Composed a Te Deum, hymn tunes, glees and songs.

MATHER, William (1756-1808)
Born in Sheffield in 1756; died in Sheffield in 1808. Father of **Samuel Mather**. Organist in Sheffield, where he had a music shop, at the Churches of St. Paul and St. James. Compiled and sold by subscription a collection of his hymn and Psalm tunes, *Sacred music...* (1806) which was intended to be a complete edition of his own works. His hymn tunes include 'Sheffield', also known as 'Attercliffe'.

MATHIAS, Dr. William James (1934-1992)
Born in Whitland, Carmarthenshire, Wales on 1 November 1934; died on 29 July 1992.
Educated at Whitland Grammar School; University College, Aberystwyth where he graduated B.Mus and at the Royal Academy of Music with an Open Scholarship in Composition. His studies at the R.A.M. were directed by Peter Katin for piano and **Lennox Berkeley** for composition.
Graduated D.Mus. at the University of Wales (1966). Westminster Choir College, Princeton, New Jersey, U.S.A. accorded him the honorary D.Mus in 1987.
Appointed C.B.E. (1985).
Pursued an academic career, being lecturer in music at Bangor College (1959-1968) and senior lecturer in music at the University of Edinburgh (1968-1970). Professor of music at University College, Bangor, University of Wales (from 1970).
Artistic director of the North Wales Music Festival, held annually at St. Asaph.
Composed from an early age and his works vary from church music to items for the theatre, television and radio.
The most widely heard of his compositions for the church is the anthem 'Let the people praise thee, O God', commissioned for the wedding of H.R.H. Prince Charles and Lady Diana Spencer (1981). Also composed services including the *Jesus College* Service, a Festival Te Deum (1965) and two settings of the Mass.
His hymn tune 'Barnton' was used in the Third Edition (1973) of *Church Hymnary* with the poem by Shillito, 'Away with gloom, away with doubt', from the latter's collection *Jesus of the Scars* (1919). His carols include 'Sweet was the song' (1988).
Has been assessed as a major contributor to the repertory and direction of 20th century organ music. His Clarinet Sonatina was performed at the Cheltenham Festival (1957).

MATTHAY, Tobias Augustus (1858-1945)

Born in Clapham, London on 19 February 1858; died in Haslemere, Surrey in 1945.

Attended Miss Brown's Preparatory School, Clapham and the Royal Academy of Music (from 1871), becoming Sterndale Bennett Scholar a year later. For composition his teachers were **William Sterndale Bennett**, **Arthur Sullivan** and **Ebenezer Prout**. Studied piano under **William Dorrell** and **Walter Macfarren**. Another teacher was Edwin Hurst, who had been a pupil of Ignaz Moscheles. Also studied at the London Academy of Music under **Henry Wylde**.

Sub professor of harmony (from 1876) and professor of piano (1880) at the R.A.M. A concert pianist, giving his first recital in 1880.

Developed a system of teaching piano using principles of the sciences of physics and psychology. Later founded his own school, which at one time employed 18 senior teachers, each of whom he himself trained. Some famous pupils include York Bowen, George Aitken, Amy Grinson and Myra Hess. *The Art of Touch* (1903) was a publication of the results of his research.

Began composing as a student. His works include a setting of Psalm 126 'When the Lord turned against the captivity of Sion' and orchestral items.

MATTHEWS, John (1856-1938)

Born in Liskeard, Cornwall on 27 March 1856; died in 1938. Studied with **S. Weeks** and at the Dresden Conservatory under Gustav Merkel and Felix Draeske. Organist of St. James's Church, Swansea (1882-1885) and of Saint Austell Parish Church, Cornwall (1886-1889). Lived in Guernsey (from 1889) as a teacher and recitalist. Organist of St. Stephen's Church (1889-1931). He wrote a number of books, including *The Organ Described*. His Evening Service in D was composed for the St. Austell Deanery Choir Festival (1888). Also composed a Te Deum in F, anthems, songs, part songs, organ works including a Sonata in C Minor, and violin music.

MATTHEWS, Revd. John Henry (1859-1953)

Born in Chesham, Buckinghamshire on 11 December 1859; died in Parkstone, Dorset on 27 November 1953. Educated at St. John's College, Cambridge where he graduated B.A. (1882) and M.A. (1887). Ordained deacon (1882), priest (1884). Assistant curate of Chedgrave with Langley, Norfolk (from 1882), Beverley Minster (from 1885) and Knaresborough, Yorkshire (from 1888). Rector of Hedgerley with Hedgerley Dean (from 1890) and chaplain at Biarritz, France (1917-1927). Rector of St. Thomas's Church, Arcachon (1927-1929). His hymn tune 'Belfry Praise' (1904 or 1905) appeared initially under the pseudonym of J. de Hugely and was included in *Hymns Ancient and Modern*.

MATTHEWS, Richard Northon (1860-1942)

Born in North Coates, Lincolnshire in 1860; died in Leamington, Warwickshire on 18 February 1942. Composer of hymn tunes.

MATTHEWS, Samuel (1769-1832)

Born in 1769; died on 9 December 1832. A chorister of Westminster Abbey. Graduated Mus.B. at the University of Cambridge (1828). A lay clerk of Winchester Cathedral. Organist of Trinity College and St. John's College, Cambridge (both 1821-1832).

Composed a Service in D. Arranged and published anthems from works by a number of famous composers. His anthems include 'Behold', 'Now praise' and 'Is there not an appointed time?' *Cathedral Psalter Chants* (1874) contains a Double Chant in E by him.

MATTHEWS, Revd. Timothy Richard (1826-1910)

Born in Colmworth, near Bedford on 4 November 1826; died in Tetney, Lincolnshire on 5 January 1910. Son of the rector of Colmworth.

Attended Bedford Grammar School and graduated Mus.B. at Gonville and Caius College, Cambridge (1853). Ordained in the same year.

Became the private tutor to the family of Revd. Lord Wriothesley Russell, a canon of St. George's Chapel, Windsor Castle, where he studied under the organist, **George Elvey**, subsequently a life-long friend.

Curate (1853-1859) and curate-in-charge (1859-1869) of St. Mary's Church, Nottingham. In his time at Nottingham he founded the city's Working Men's Institute.

Rector to North Coates, Lincolnshire (from 1869). He retired in 1907 to live with his eldest son at Tetney Vicarage.

He was editor of the *North Coates Supplemental Tune Book* and *The Village Organist*.

Composed Morning and Evening Services, chants and responses, also earning a reputation for simple but effective hymn tunes with over 100 hymn tunes including 'North Coates', 'Ludborough', 'Chenies' and 'Winthorpe'. William Howard requested six such items from him for a children's hymn book. Matthews responded and completed the work within a day. Also composed a Christmas carol and a few songs.

MATTHEWS, William (1759-1830)

Born in Ilkeston, Derbyshire in 1759; died in Nottingham in 1830. A manufacturer of hosiery in Nottingham. A choirmaster and teacher of music. Later, he owned a music shop in the city's Houndsgate. Composed many anthems and hymn tunes. His 'Madrid' is said to be a good example of Methodist hymn tunes of the period, and it was used in *Baptist Hymn Book* (1962) with the hymn 'Now I have found the ground' by Johann Rothe. Others include 'Tranquillity', which was written to celebrate the restoration of tranquillity to the hosiery trade around Nottingham following the Luddite disturbances (around 1811).

MAUDE (Ogle), Caroline Anna Mary (1848-1930)

Born in Warwick in 1848; died in Wimbledon, London on 15 March 1930. She composed hymn tunes.

MAUNDER, John Henry (1858-1920)

Born in Chelsea, London on 21 February 1858; died in Brighton, Sussex on 25 January 1920.

A student of the Royal Academy of Music.

Organist of the South London Churches of St. Matthew Sydenham (1876-1877) and St. Paul Forest Hill (1878-1879). Organist of St. Michael's Church, Blackheath Park, Kent (from 1906) and Christ Church, Sutton, Surrey. Choir trainer to the Lyceum Theatre.

In demand as an accompanist. Became associated with the singer Sims Reeves. Reeves was accompanied by Maunder, as usual, in his final performance at the Royal Albert Hall (11 May 1891). Conductor of the Civil Service Choral Union.

Maunder concentrated on sacred music towards the end of his career. Composed two Evening Services, a Te Deum and Benedicite, cantatas including *Olivet to Calvary* and *Penitence, Pardon and Peace*, anthems, carols and songs.

His hymn tune 'Martham' first appeared in the *Westminster Abbey Hymn Book* (1883) and has often since been used with 'O Love, O God' by Horatius Bonar in Baptist Churches. 'The whole wide world' was written for 'The whole wide world for Jesus!' by Catherine Johnson. Composed an oratorio *The Martyrs* (1894) and an opera *Daisy Dingle* (1885).

MAURICE, Revd. Dr. Peter (1803-1878)
Born in Greenwich, London on 29 June 1803; died in Yarnton, Woodstock, Oxfordshire on 30 March 1878.

Educated at Bangor Grammar School and at Jesus College, Oxford where he graduated B.A. (1826). Graduated M.A. (1829) at New College, Oxford. Ordained in 1827. Also graduated B.D. (1837) and D.D. (1840).

His curacies were at Llanwrst and at Kennington, Oxford (1829-1854). Vicar of Yarnton, Oxford (1854-1878) and chaplain of All Souls' College (from 1837), and New College (from 1858), Oxford. Composed an Evening Service, the anthem 'With angels and archangels' (1836), and hymn tunes including 'Springfield'. Published a collection of hymn tunes entitled *Choral Harmony* (1854).

MAW, Nicholas (b.1935)
Born in Grantham, Lincolnshire on 5 November 1935. Learned to play clarinet and piano. Attended Wennington School, Yorkshire. A pupil of **Lennox Berkeley** and Paul Steinitz (1955-1958) at the Royal Academy of Music. Studied in Paris with Nadia Boulanger and Max Deutsch (1958-1959). Composer-in-residence and fellow-commoner in creative arts at Trinity College, Cambridge (1966-1969). A friend of **William Walton**. Composed the anthem 'Our Lady's song' (1961) for Unaccompanied Voices; *Three Hymns* (1989), first performed at the Lichfield Festival of that year and a Te Deum for Soprano, Tenor, Chorus and Organ (1975). His secular works include the comic opera *One Man Show* (1964) and a Sinfonia for Chamber Orchestra (1966).

MAWBY, Colin John Beverley (b.1936)
Born in Plymouth, Devon on 9 May 1936. Master of the music of Westminster Cathedral before taking up the position of choral director of Radio Telefis Eireann, the Irish national broadcasting station (1991-1996). A performing musician, appearing at a number of U.K. festivals including the City of London Festival, and broadcasting in many countries. Former conductor of the B.B.C. Singers. Has also conducted the London Mozart Players and the Nash Ensemble. Composed 17 Masses, and more than a hundred works for choir and/or congregation, including the anthems 'I will lift up my eyes' and 'By the rivers of Babylon'. His other works include the important set of *Ten Psalms with Antiphons* in the *Grail Translation*, the through-composed rhythms of which have been found more serviceable and enduring than those of the pioneering Joseph Gelineau. There are also song cycles and organ works.

MAXFIELD, William Henry (1849-?)
Born in North Somercotes, Lincolnshire on 27 April 1849. A chorister of St. Paul's Church, Hulme, Manchester (1860-1865) and a pupil of Frederick Pugh and **Henry Hiles**. Graduated B.Mus.

at the University of Toronto, Canada (1889). Organist and choirmaster of St. Peter's Church, Levenshulme, Manchester (from 1866); St. Thomas's Church, Norbury, Surrey (from 1872) and in Altricham, Cheshire at the Churches of St. George (from 1879) and St. John (from 1884). A choral society conductor and a lecturer on musical topics. Composed anthems, cantatas including *The Lord Is Risen* (1890), and music for piano and for organ.

MAXTED, Walter (19th/20th century)
Received his early musical training at Canterbury Cathedral. Graduated B.Mus. at the University of Durham (1898). Assistant organist of Canterbury Cathedral. Organist and choirmaster of St. Andrew's Church, Derby (from 1884) and in Dover, Kent at the Churches of St. James (from 1886; and 1908) and St. Barnabas (from 1902). His B.Mus. exercise was an anthem 'The mercy of God'.

MAXWELL DAVIES, Peter
See **DAVIES,** Peter Maxwell.

MAY, Charles John (1871-1945)
Born in Lewisham, Kent in 1871; died in Bromley in the same county on 18 January 1945. Organist and choirmaster of St. James's Church, Hatcham (from 1918). Composer of hymn tunes.

MAYBRICK, Michael (1799-1846)
Born in 1799; died in Liverpool in May 1846. A pupil of **Richard Wainwright**. Organist of St. Peter's Church, Liverpool. Composed chants and organ music.

MAYNE, Frederick Kimbell (1845-1909)
Born in Braunstone, Northamptonshire in 1845; died in Bradford, Yorkshire on 10 May 1909. Composer of hymn tunes.

MAYNE, Dr. Thomas Robert (19th/20th century)
Trained privately in music. Graduated B.Mus. (1906), D.Mus. (1912), B.A. (in classics: 1909) and, honorarily, M.A. (1920) at the Royal University of Ireland. Organist of All Saints' Church, Newbridge-on-Wye (1900-1902). A professor of music at the Borough Polytechnic Institute, London, where he deputised at a number of churches. Organist and choirmaster of Lambeth Parish Church. Taught woodwind instruments for the London County Council, also organising and training a number of violin classes. Also worked for Willesden Education Committee. A first lieutenant in the 12th Royal Warwickshire Regiment (1914).

His B.Mus. exercise was a Festal Anthem 'Awake thou North wind' for Solo Voices, Chorus and Organ. Composed other anthems, a setting of the *Recessional* by Rudyard Kipling, and dance music.

MEACHAM, Charles John Blood (19th/20th century)
Received his early musical training at Ely Cathedral. Graduated Mus.B. at the University of Cambridge (1871). Organist in Birmingham of St. Philip's Church (1871-1878) and of St. George's Church, Edgbaston (from 1888). His Mus.B. exercise was a setting of Psalm 65 for Tenor Solo, Chorus and Organ 'Thou, O God, art praised in Zion'. Also composed services, anthems and songs.

MEADOWCROFT, John (1827-1873)
Born in 1827; died in Scarborough, Yorkshire on 28 August 1873. A chorister of Manchester Cathedral and subsequently honorary organist for afternoon services. A Psalter editor. Composer of chants.

MEDLEY, John (1804-1892)
Bishop of Frederickton, Canada (from 1845) and Metropolitan of Canada (from 1879). Composed a Single Chant in G which was included in *Cathedral Psalter Chants* (1874). His other works include the anthems 'Blessed are the dead' and 'Like as the hart'.

MEE, Revd. Dr. John Henry (1852-1918)
Born in Riddings, Derbyshire on 16 August 1852; died on 15 January 1918.
Studied classics at Merton College, Oxford where he graduated B.A. (1875), B.Mus. (1882) and D.Mus. (1888). For the statutory performance of his D.Mus. at the Sheldonian Theatre, Oxford, he engaged a choir from Leeds and a number of London orchestral players.
Ordained deacon (1876) and priest (1877), and received the Oxford M.A. at Worcester College (1878).
Succentor of Queen's College, Oxford (1876) and precentor of Chichester Cathedral (1889). Served on West Sussex County Council (from 1890) and was coryphaeus of the University of Oxford (1890-1900).
One of the founders of the Musicians' Union (1884). An honorary fellow of St. Michael's College, Tenbury, Worcestershire (1886).
Published *10 years of University Music in Oxford* (1894) and *10 More Years of University Music in Oxford* (1904).
Contributed an article on 'The oldest music room in Europe' to Grove's *Dictionary of Music and Musicians*.
Composed a Mass, anthems including 'God, who at sundry times', a String Quartet, and ballads for men's voices.

MEEN, Josiah Fountain (1846-1909)
Born in Hackney, London on 14 September 1846; died in Islington, London on 11 October 1909. Self-taught in music. Organist (from around 1891) and treasurer (from 1900) of the Nonconformist Choir Union, and organist in London of the Clapton Wesleyan Chapel; St. Mary's Church, Stoke Newington and of the Union Chapel, Islington (from 1880). A professor of organ at Guildhall School of Music (from 1886). Organist to the Sacred Harmonic Society, accompanying most of the leading singers of his day. Composer of hymn tunes.

MEERS, Ernest George (c1848-1928)
Born near Ashford, Kent around 1848; died in York on 20 August 1928 at the age of 80. Attended Faversham Grammar School, Kent and was trained privately in music with F.E. Gladstone, **Frederick Bridge** and **Walter Parratt**. Graduated B.Mus. at Queen's College, Oxford (1878). Founded the firm of Watts Ltd. (1871), of which he was chairman and managing director until his death. An athlete (amateur tennis champion of England in the late 1880s) and traveller. A patron of music, he sponsored students, organs and organ playing. He gave the organs of the Kent Parish Churches of Maidstone and Borden. Organist of Wimbledon Parish Church, London (from 1871) and of St. Mark's Church, Lewisham, Kent (1878-1890). His degree exercise was an anthem 'I will extol Thee' for Five Voices, Strings and Organ.

MELLERS, Dr. Wilfrid Howard (b.1914)
Born in Leamington Spa, Warwickshire on 26 April 1914. Studied at Leamington College and at the University of Cambridge under Egon Wellesz and **Edmund Rubbra**, both for composition, (1933-1938). Graduated M.A. (Cambridge) and D.Mus. (Birmingham). Taught at Dartington Hall (1938-1940) and was supervisor at Downing College, Cambridge (1945-1948). On the staff of the University of Birmingham (1948-1960) as staff tutor in the extra-mural department. Andrew W. Mellon professor of music at the University of Pittsburg, U.S.A (1960-1963). Appointed professor of music at the University of York (1964).
His writings include *Studies in Contemporary Music* (1947). His sacred compositions include a *Missa Brevis*; his secular works include operas, of which *The Ancient Wound* (1970) is one.

MELLOR, Richard (1816-1889)
Born in Huddersfield, Yorkshire on 23 March 1816; died in St. Leonards, Sussex on 22 June 1889. Organist of the Zion Chapel, Lindley at the age of 18. Organist of Linthwaite Church; Honley Wesleyan Chapel and St. Patrick's Roman Catholic Church, Huddersfield, Yorkshire. His next appointment, at the Ramsden Street Independent Chapel, lasted for 33 years. Retired around 1874 from a large music and piano business. Made a major contribution to the musical life of Huddersfield. His hymn tune 'Elevation' was composed for a Sunday School Anniversary and it was sung, in Whitsun 1861, outside Leeds Town Hall.

MELVILLE, Derek (20th century)
Studied piano with Cyril Smith at the Royal College of Music and with Harold Craxton at the Royal Academy of Music, where he also worked on composition with Theodore Holland. Continued his studies in composition with **Lennox Berkeley**, whose guidance subsequently proved particularly helpful. Has composed a number of anthems and carols, of which an example is 'Swete Jesu, King of bliss'. Recent works include *24 Preludes for Piano* (Aldeburgh Festival, 1994) and *24 studies for Piano* (Cheltenham Festival, 1995), each using all the keys.

MERRICK, Dr. Frank (1886-1981)
Born in Clifton, Bristol on 30 April 1886; died in 1981. Trained privately in music, including a course of study with Leschetizky in Vienna. Graduated B.Mus. (1888) and D.Mus. (1890) at the University of Dublin. A pianist, making his first concert appearance (1895) in Bristol and his first London performance in 1903, in which some of the works played were his own. Lived in Manchester, and was a professor of piano at the Royal Manchester College of Music (from 1929). His B.Mus. exercise was a hymnal anthem 'To God be praise and glory' for Solo Voices, Chorus, Organ and Orchestra. Also composed a Piano Concerto and Piano Trio.

MERRICK, Revd. George Purnell (1842-1918)
Born in Bedminster, Somerset in 1842; died in Westminster, London on 31 October 1918. Educated at Exeter College, Oxford where he was organist (1867-1871). Curate of Knightsbridge, London and the incumbent of St. Stephen's Church, Westminster. A London prison chaplain. Composed the hymn tune 'Aldersgate'.

MERRICOCKE, Robert
See **MORECOCKE,** Robert.

MERRYLEES, James (1824-1891)
Born in Paisley, Scotland on 10 April 1824; died in Dullatur, Dumbartonshire, Scotland on 31 October 1891. Studied music under John Curwen and Colin Brown. An editor and arranger. Composed anthems and hymn tunes including 'Atlantic' and 'Formosa', winning a prize in a competition (1871-1872). Also composed part songs.

METCALFE, Richard Daniel (19th/20th century)
Born in Stepney, London. Trained at the Royal Academy of Music and the Tonic Sol-fa College. Graduated B.Mus. at the University of Durham (1891). Organist of the Stepney Meeting Congregational Church (1881-1887; 1891-1898) and of the Children's Home, Victoria Park (1887-1890). Organist of the Church of St. Michael and All Angels, Stoke Newington (1898-1903) and St. Alban, Wood Street London (from 1903). Composed as his B.Mus. exercise a setting of Jeremiah 23 'Ah, Lord God' for Tenor Soloist, Chorus, Quartet and Strings. Also composed anthems, part songs and an operetta *Prince Ferdinand.*

MICHELL, Guy (1876-?)
Born in Horsham, Sussex in 1876. Studied music with **Edwin Lemare** and **Henry Richards.** An organ recitalist, and honorary organist of St. Margaret's Church, Brighton. Composed an anthem 'The Lord is my Strength', a Te Deum in E, a Benedicite in A, a sacred song: 'The path of life', an Advent oratorio, hymns, and chamber works such as the Piano Quartet in F.

MICKLEM, Thomas Caryl (b.1925)
Born in Oxford on 1 August 1925, the son of Revd. E.R. Micklem who at the time was chaplain of Mansfield College, Oxford.
Attended Mill Hill School, London and New College, Oxford where he graduated (1948). Trained at Mansfield College, Oxford for the ministry of the Congregational Church. Minister of the Congregational Churches of Oundle, Northamptonshire (1949-1953); Banstead, Surrey (1953-1958) and Allen Street, Kensington, London (from 1958). Has been Minister of the St. Columba United Reformed Church, Oxford. One of the four prominent hymn writers this century to have studied at Mansfield College, the others being Albert Bayly, **Erik Routley** and Brian Wren. Was the Free Church Adviser to the Associated Television network, and represented the Free Churches on the Council of the Royal School of Church Music. Cited as an outstanding hymnodist whose words and tunes are much admired.

MIDDLETON, Dr. Hubert Stanley (1890-1959)
Born in Windsor, Berkshire on 11 May 1890; died on 13 August 1959.
Educated at the Imperial Service College, Windsor. After private study with **Walter Parratt** he attended the Royal Academy of Music and Peterhouse, Cambridge where he graduated Mus.B. (1920) and M.A. (1920). Achieved doctorates in music at the Universities of Oxford and Cambridge.
Organist and master of the choristers of the Cathedrals of Truro (1920-1926) and Ely (1926-1931).
Lectured in music at the University of Cambridge, and was a conductor of choral and orchestral societies.
A professor of composition at the R.A.M. (from 1920), director of studies in music at Trinity College of Music (from 1931), director of music at Peterhouse (from 1933) and Cambridge University

lecturer in music (from 1938). Compiled the syllabus for the tripos examination (introduced 1945).
A member of the council of the Royal College of Organists.
Composed church music and items for organ.

MIDDLETON, Dr. James Roland (b.1896)
Born in Ringwood, Hampshire in 1896. Educated privately and graduated D.Mus. at the University of Durham. Sub organist of Chester Cathedral. Organist of Christchurch Priory, Hampshire; Kinson Parish Church (1914-1915), Ringwood Parish Church (from 1915) and Mold Parish Church, Flintshire, Wales (1923-1944). On active service during World War I. Organist of the Cathedrals of Chelmsford (1944-1949), Chester (1949-1963) and St. Asaph (1963-1970). An examiner for Trinity College of Music (from 1944) and for the Royal College of Organists (from 1957). Composed the anthem 'Sanctify O Lord'.

MILES, R.E. (1857-1929)
Born in Rochester, Kent on 24 May 1857; died in Ovingdean, Sussex on 13 September 1929.
His father was a lay clerk and later the dean's verger of Rochester Cathedral, and was the person on whom Charles Dickens based the character Mr. Tope in the novel *Edwin Drood.*
For five years from the age of nine he was a chorister of Rochester Cathedral, later studying at the Royal Academy of Music under Alberto Randegger, E. Morton and **Charles Steggall.**
As a young man (1875) he sang the part of Elijah in a performance of Mendelssohn's oratorio at Rochester Cathedral. Choirmaster of St. Mark's Church, Lewisham, London (from 1881). Sang in the Choir of St. Paul's Cathedral for 33 years as an assistant vicar choral (from 1886) and vicar choral (from 1901).
Sang in the celebrations at St. Paul's of the Jubilee (1887) and Diamond Jubilee (1897) of the reign of Queen Victoria. Also sang at Westminster Abbey at the Coronations of Edward VII (1902) and George V (1911).
A professor of singing at the R.A.M. (1886-1899) and at Guildhall School of Music (from 1896).
Composed services and songs, including 'The language of the heart'.

MILFORD, Robin Humphrey (1903-1959)
Born in Oxford on 22 January 1903; died in Lyme Regis, Dorset on 29 December 1959. The son of Sir Humphrey Milford, publisher to the University of Oxford.
The family moved to Surrey (1906), initially to the town of Ashtead and then to Epsom.
Attended West Downs Preparatory School and Rugby School, Warwickshire, where his instruction in music was under Peppin. Learned to play flute and piano. Studied at the Royal College of Music (1921-1926), where his teachers were **Ralph Vaughan Williams, Gustav Holst, H.G. Ley** and **R.O. Morris.**
Took a part time job with the Aeolian Company, editing pianola rolls (1920-1930). Became a schoolteacher, initially at Ludgrove School, Cockfosters, Middlesex. Moved to Newbury, Berkshire (1932) but continued to teach at Ludgrove for another four years. Acquainted with, and patronised by, **Henry Balfour Gardiner** who provided him with a small car and advanced some money for the education of his son Barnaby who died tragically at the age of five in a road accident while fetching some music for his father. A year later, Robin Milford attempted suicide, and a further attempt was the cause of his death.

Milford was also acquainted with the Berkshire-based composer **Gerald Finzi** whom he first met in 1929.

Joined the army as a volunteer (1939), serving with the Pioneer Corps, but after only one week he suffered a nervous breakdown. He was sent to Guernsey to recuperate. Moved to Butcombe, near Bristol (1946). Taught at Badminton School and was appointed organist of Butcombe Church (1948). Taught also at Parrott Hill, a preparatory school in Somerset (from 1956). Organist and choirmaster of Uplyme Parish Church.

Milford began broadcasting in 1946; joined the B.B.C. West of England Auditioning Panel (1950) and the West Regional Listening Panel (1955).

His depression continued and he began to receive shock therapy (1953).

His works, which began to be published around 1924, include a Mass, hymn tunes, 'A Litany to the Holy Spirit' (1947), and oratorios *The Pilgrim's Progress* (1932) and *A Prophet in the Land* (1931) for the Three Choirs' Festival of that year. Also composed a Violin Concerto (1937).

MILGROVE, Benjamin (c1731-1810)

Born, probably in Bath, Somerset around the year 1731; died in Bath in 1810. Precentor and then organist at the Countess of Huntingdon's Church in Bath. He owned a shop in Bath and is described in a directory of the time as a 'toyman'. One of the proprietors, or those responsible for the financial affairs, of the New King Street Chapel of John Wesley, Bath. Composed church music, including the hymn tunes 'Harts', 'Mount Ephraim', 'Hartford' and 'Loughton'. Published a collection *16 Hymns As They Are Sung at the Right Honourable Countess of Huntingdon's Chapel in Bath* (c1769). Two further sets each of 12 were published later. 'Mount Ephraim' was one of the original 16 and was used in *Baptist Hymn Book* (1962).

MILLER, Charles Edward (1856-1933)

Born in Croydon, Surrey on 30 December 1856; died in Gunnersbury, Middlesex on 8 September 1933. Grandson of Thomas Miller, fellow of Trinity College, Cambridge who founded the Cambridge University Music Society. A solicitor, and organist of Lambeth Parish Church, London, and the Church of SS Augustine and Faith, Watling Street, London (1883-1893). Composed Masses and motets including *Justorum animae* for Westminster Cathedral, services and anthems. **R.R. Terry** said of him that if he had chosen to be a professional musician, he would have been a top composer of the late Victorian/Edwardian era. He twice won a prize from the Madrigal Society, an example of his work in this genre being the eight-part 'Charm me asleep'.

MILLER, Dr. Edward (1735-1807)

Born in Norwich, Norfolk on 30 October 1735; died in Doncaster, Yorkshire on 12 September 1807. The son of a stone mason and the father of **William Miller.**

Apprenticed to a stone mason but absconded. Later studied music at King's Lynn under **Charles Burney**. Graduated Mus.D. at the University of Cambridge (1786).

Organist of Doncaster Parish Church (1751-1807), an appointment he secured on the recommendation of **James Nares**, organist of the Chapel Royal. His knowledge of the locality inspired him to write a *History of Doncaster* (1804). He also wrote on antiquarian and other topics.

Played the German flute in Handel's Orchestra.

Editor of *The Psalms of David For The Use of Parish Churches* (1790), a collection that was successful immediately. George III sent him £25 in appreciation. He also edited *Psalms and Hymns Set to New music* (1801) and other similar publications. Author of many articles on Psalmody and on collections of Psalm tunes.

Composed Psalm and hymn tunes including 'Galway'. A group of people in the Isle of Man commissioned a barrel organ to play Edward Miller's hymn tunes. Also composed songs and items for flute and for harpsichord.

MILLER, Henry Walter (1843-?)

Born in London on 15 June 1843. Studied with **Frederick Bridge** and graduated B.Mus. (1865), B.A. (1868) and M.A. (1875) at the University of Oxford. Taught harmony at an academy in Glasgow, and gave a number of Ewing Lectures, one of which was on 'The Influence of Italy on Classical music'. Appointed organist of Hobart Cathedral, Tasmania, Australia (1885) and examiner to the Government of Tasmania where he was also a choral society conductor. Organist of the American Episcopal Church in Nice, France (from 1894). Wrote magazine articles and composed anthems, cantatas, songs and works for piano and for organ.

MILLER, Revd. William Edward (1766-1839)

Born in Doncaster, Yorkshire in 1766; died in Sheffield, Yorkshire in 1839.

The son of **Edward Miller.**

A pupil of his father and of **J.B. Cramer.**

Spent six years in India before settling in Sheffield as a professional musician. A violin player.

Attended the Norfolk Street Chapel, which was famous for its singing. He started to preach and to write hymns and hymn tunes, many of which were during a major revival (around 1796).

Entered the ministry of the Wesleyan Church (1799). Never played his violin again. A man of strong religious beliefs, he also felt uneasy at travelling by horse when Jesus had been content to use an ass.

Editor of *David's Harp* (1805), which is said to be the most important Methodist hymn book of that period. The Preface carried a stern judgement on the congregational tunes of the day: 'Among the Methodists, a light, indecorous style of music has frequently been introduced. Many persons... think themselves qualified to compose hymns... but these compositions expose their authors to ridicule... A number of these effusions have lately been brought over from America.' The book contains nearly 300 tunes, some hundred of which were composed by William Miller or by his father. None of the tunes by William Miller have survived into current use.

MILLER, William F.(?-1863)

Composed the anthems 'O Lord rebuke me not' and 'O pray for the peace'.

MILLINGTON, Andrew Thomas Seager (b.1952)

Born in Willenhall, Staffordshire on 2 May 1952. Educated at Hanley Castle Grammar School and King's School, Worcester. Studied organ at Worcester Cathedral under **Harry Bramma** and **Christopher Robinson**. Won an Organ Scholarship to Downing College, Cambridge (1971); graduated B.A. (1974) and M.A. (1978). Assistant organist of Gloucester Cathedral (from 1975) where he took part in the Three Choirs' Festivals of 1977 and 1980. Organist and master of the choristers of Guildford Cathedral (from 1983). A local choral society conductor. Has composed sets of Preces and Responses, anthems, chants, and other items of church music.

MILLS, James (1790-1844)

Perhaps his most important musical achievement was his conductorship of the Bethel Music Society (founded 1834). It met on Sundays and during the week, with the objectives of teaching the rudiments of music and raising the standards of congregational singing, and it attracted a regular attendance of 60 to 70 young people. Composed anthems and hymn tunes, including 'Hosanna'.

MILLS, Richard (1809-1844)

Born in Tynewydd, near Llanidloes, Wales in March 1809; died in September 1844.

Father of the younger **Richard Mills**.

Left school at the age of 11 and was apprenticed to a weaver.

By the age of 15 he was a member of the local music society, was known locally as a musician and had seen his hymn tune 'Maes-y-llan' published in *Seren Gomer*. His hymn tunes won prizes at *eisteddfodau* in 1838 and 1840.

Delivered an address entitled 'Music' to the Llanidloes Welsh Society at the age of 26, following which he was frequently called upon as a lecturer on musical topics, including hymn singing.

Published a collection of hymns and tunes *Caniadau Seion* (Songs of Sion) in 1840. In the Introduction he regretted having to include some tunes from outside Wales, which he denounced as unsuitable and ineffective. The collection contained 214 hymns and 13 anthems, and it was followed two years later by a Supplement.

These publications are said to have made possible a major improvement in the standard of Welsh congregational singing. They included tunes by **Rosser Beynon** and by himself, and anthems by **Handel** and Haydn. Some of the hymn tunes had been collected in Wales and published by **Morris Davies**, a schoolteacher, editor and writer.

Yr Arweinydd Cerddoral (The Musical Guide) broadened the choice of available church music. It was published in three parts (1842-1845), the third part after his death.

Part One embraced the elements of music, voice exercises and hints on composition. Part Two (1843) contained anthems and hymn tunes and marked a notable first: 'Mannheim' by J.S. Bach was the first German tune to be featured in a Welsh publication. Part Three was a further collection of anthems and hymn tunes.

His anthems continued to be sung for some time after his death but subsequently their use diminished.

MILLS, Richard (1840-1903)

Born in 1840; died on 18 May 1903. Son of **Richard Mills** the elder.

His father died while the second Richard was still a child, causing him to live with his mother's family at Newtown. Later returned to the town of Llanidloes as a compositor, using staff notation, in the printing firm of his stepfather, John Pryse.

Studied music in his spare time and became an accomplished composer of hymn tunes, winning eisteddfod prizes for his 'Pendref' and for a three-part cantata (1864).

Moved to Wrexham in order to work as supervisor for the publishers Hughes and Company. He conducted choirs in the town and elsewhere. Started a printing firm at Rhosllannerchrugog (1878) and founded *Rhos Herald* (1894), a newspaper which he edited until his death. He conducted a choir at Rhos.

Composed anthems, hymn tunes of which 'Arweiniad' was widely used, and songs. Arranged many hymn tunes.

He and John Mills published *Cerddor Eglwysig* (The Church Musician), containing 101 tunes of which six of Welsh origin (1846). A Supplement followed (1847) with a further 55 tunes.

MILLS, Robert Heath (1837-1900)

Born in St. Pancras, London in 1837; died in Sandy, Bedfordshire on 18 May 1900. Director of music of the West London Mission. Composer of hymn tunes.

MILNER, Dr. Anthony Francis Dominic (b.1925)

Born in Bristol, Gloucestershire on 13 May 1925 into a Roman Catholic family: his four siblings include a priest and a nun.

Between the ages of 4 and 14 he studied piano, harmony and violin. His instructor was Nora Ford, a violinist. Won a scholarship to Douai School, Woolhampton, Berkshire (1939-1943).

Studied at the Royal College of Music (1945-1947), his teachers being George Fryer for piano, **George Thalben-Ball** for organ and **R.O. Morris** for theory. Additionally he studied with Matyas Seiber (1944-1948). His other teachers include Charles Wilkinson and Oscar Beringer.

Graduated B.Mus. (1950) and D.Mus. (1967) at the University of London.

Tutor in theory, harpsichord and the history of music at Morley College, London (1949-1965). Extension lecturer of the University of London (1954-1965); also worked in the extra-mural department of the University of Durham and of King's College, Newcastle.

Lecturer at King's College London (1965-1971); senior lecturer (1971-1974) and principal lecturer (1974-1980) at Goldsmiths' College. Taught at the R.C.M. for some time prior to his appointment as principal lecturer (1980). He has also been an examiner in music.

Composer-in-residence at the Summer School of Liturgical Music, Loyola University, New Orleans, U.S.A. (1964-1966).

Has composed for the changing liturgy of the Roman Catholic Church. Also composed the anthem 'Praise the Lord of Heaven' (1959), which draws from the text of Psalms 148 and 150. His other compositions include hymn tunes, an oratorio *The Water and the Fire*, a Wind Quintet, and organ music.

MILNER, Dr. Arthur Frederick (1894-1972)

Born in Manchester on 22 October 1894; died in Newcastle-on-Tyne on 11 September 1972. Educated at Dame Allen's School, Newcastle. Studied with **Harold Watts** and **Edgar Bainton**. Graduated D.Mus. at the University of Durham. Director of music of the Royal Grammar School, Newcastle (1926-1948) and master of the music of St. George's Church, Newcastle (1931-1934). Senior music critic of the *Newcastle Journal* (1950-1967). Reviewed church and organ music in *Musical Times*. Published a biography of **Charles Avison** (1954), which appeared in *Musical Times*. Composed anthems and organ works.

MILNES, Ian (b.1943)

Born in Leeds, Yorkshire on 15 December 1943.

Learned violin and viola with Eta Cohen, author of well-known tutor books. Achieved the highest mark ever recorded by Leeds' schools in his General Certificate of Education Ordinary Level paper in music, but did not continue his studies in the subject and remains largely self-taught. Graduated in science at the University of Leeds (1968).

Worked as librarian of the Leeds Music Centre (now the City of Leeds College of Music). Has also worked in the music trade and as a private teacher of music as well as composing. Assistant choirmaster of Hamilton Street Methodist Church, Hoole, Cheshire.

Began to compose at the age of 13. Works include a Magnificat and Nunc Dimittis, commissioned by the Chester St. Cecilia Singers (1987) and a setting of Psalm 122 'I was glad' (1982). Among his chamber works is his Viola Sonata (1991).

MILTON, John (c1563-1647)

Born in Stanton St. John, near Oxford around the year 1563; died in London and was buried on 15 March 1647.

His son John Milton was the author of *Paradise Lost*.

Became a Protestant while living in Oxford, and in consequence he was disinherited by his father and went to live in London. A member of the Scriveners' Company (of which he was master from 1634), living and working in Bread Street, Cheapside (from 1600).

During his time in London he held weekly meetings at his house at which his compositions were performed. He had become a wealthy man and an organ was installed at his home.

Retired to Horton, Buckinghamshire (1632). On the death of his wife (around 1640) he moved to Reading, Berkshire, but subsequently moved back to London and lived with his son (1643).

Composed anthems including 'When David heard', motets, songs and madrigals including 'Fayre Oriana in the Morne'. It is believed that he received a gold medal from a Polish count for composing a 40-part setting of *In Nomine*.

His Psalm tune 'York' was used in *Hymns Ancient and Modern*, having been used as a common tune in the Scottish Psalter (1615) where it was known as 'The Stilt'. Contributed two harmonisations to the *Whole Book of Psalmes* by **Thomas Ravenscroft**.

MINSHALL, Nathaniel Ebenezer (1845-1933)

Born in Oswestry, Shropshire in 1845; died in Folkestone, Kent on 27 April 1933.

Studied for a career in law but earned his living as a musician, lecturer, editor and author. Editor of *Musical Journal*.

At the age of 16 he was appointed organist at Leatherhead Congregational Church, Surrey. Later, an organist in Oswestry, Shropshire. Organist of the Uxbridge Road Chapel, London (from 1874). Organist and director of music at the City Temple, London (1876-1893).

Chairman and conductor of the new Nonconformist Choir Union (from 1888). At its Festival at the City Temple of that year he shared the duties of conducting and accompanying with Frederick Edwards. In its Festival at the Crystal Palace in June of the following year he was joint conductor (with T.R. Croger), presiding over some hundred choirs comprising in total around 2,000 voices. The Handel Orchestra accompanied. Sole conductor for the Festival of 1890. At this time there was still some resistance within the Free Church to the use of choirs in worship. The 1900 Festival was sung by some 1,700 voices, the railway companies having withdrawn the concessionary tickets under which many singers had travelled in previous years. Minshall established a series of regional rehearsals for these festivals.

Composed anthems and hymn tunes.

MISTOWSKI, Dr. Alfred (1872-?)

Born in Torquay, Devon in 1872. Educated privately and at Trinity College of Music, London. Graduated B.Mus. (1898) and D.Mus. (1921) at the University of Oxford. Organist of the German Church, Forest Hill, London and musical director of the Richmond Theatre (1898-1901). Examiner in music for T.C.M. (from 1901). Composed services, part songs and items for violin and for piano.

MOBERLY, Revd. Charles Edward (c1820-1893)

Born in Islington, London in 1820 or 1821; died in Oxford on 19 July 1893.

Elected to Balliol College, Oxford (1837) at the age of 16. Graduated B.A. (1840) and M.A. (1843). Ordained deacon (1846) and priest (1848). Incumbent of Beeston, Yorkshire (1855-1857). Assistant master of Rugby School, Warwickshire (1859-1879) and rector of Coln-Rogers, Gloucestershire (1879-1883). Books written by Charles Moberley include *Stories From Herodotus* (1847) and *The Early Tudors* (1877). Composed the hymn tune 'Charnwood'.

MOERAN, Ernest John (1894-1950)

Born in Heston, Middlesex on 31 December 1894; died in Kenmare, County Kerry in Ireland on 1 December 1950. Of Irish descent. His father was the vicar of a parish in Norfolk.

Learned music from hymn books at an early age.

Entered the Royal College of Music shortly before World War I. Fought and was wounded in the war when a piece of shrapnel lodged in his head. Studied with **John Ireland** (1920-1923), whose friend he later became.

Collected Norfolk folk songs, living in the county for a while. His interest in the genre had come about before World War I through being turned away from a Bach recital, which was sold out, at St. Paul's Cathedral. Seeking musical entertainment of one sort or another, Moeran attended one of the concerts at the Queen's Hall sponsored by **Henry Balfour Gardiner** to encourage a number of emerging young British composers of the time: **Gustav Holst**, **Ralph Vaughan Williams**, **Arnold Bax** and the Australian, Percy Grainger.

One of the works performed was a Vaughan Williams Rhapsody based on a Norfolk folk song. It was the first time that Moeran had heard such a work and it captivated him, embodying the spirit of the English countryside. Moeran resolved to seek out and preserve as many as possible of any Norfolk folk songs that had not yet been set down.

He frequently travelled with Arnold Bax to Ireland where they enjoyed the tranquillity of County Kerry.

Composed an Evening Service in D - a work in which, he reported to **Philip Heseltine**, he inserted what he described as some 'luscious Stainerisms' - a Te Deum and Jubilate in E-flat and a Symphony in G Minor.

MOFFAT, Dr. James (1870-1944)

Born in Glasgow in 1870; died in New York City on 27 June 1944. Educated in Glasgow at the Academy, the University and at the Free Church College, following which he was ordained (1896) as a minister of the Free Church of Scotland (later, the United Free Church of Scotland). Held ministries at Dundonald, Ayrshire and at East Church, Broughty Ferry, following which his career developed as an academic. He was Lowett lecturer in London (from 1907); Yates professor of Greek at Mansfield College, Oxford (1911-1915) and professor of church history in the United Free Church College, Glasgow (1915-1927). Was later Washburn professor of Church history at the Union Theological Seminary, New York. On the Revision Committee of *Church Hymnary*: the Revised Edition was published (1927) and included his own tune 'Ultima'.

MOIR, Frank Lewis (1852-1904)
Born in Market Harborough, Leicestershire on 22 April 1852; died in 1904.
It had been assumed that, like his father, he would become an artist and he studied art in South Kensington. However he sought and won a scholarship to the National Training School of Music at its opening (1876). A song recitalist. Composed services, comic operas and songs.

MOLD, Simon Peter (b.1957)
Born in Buxton, Derbyshire on 3 November 1957.
Received his early training in music from his father, Peter. Attended King's School, Peterborough, Cambridgeshire (1969-1976).
A chorister and subsequently acting lay clerk of Peterborough Cathedral (1969-1972 and 1974-1976). Choral scholar of Durham Cathedral (1977-1979). Graduated B.A. in English language and medieval literature at the University of Durham.
A deputy lay clerk of Canterbury Cathedral (from 1980) and a lay clerk of Rochester Cathedral (1982-1990 and from 1992). Sang with the choir of St. John's Metropolitan Cathedral, Cardiff (1990-1991).
A counter tenor singer, who has been engaged by various organisations and choral societies. Has also sung with the London Handel Choir and Orchestra. Manager of an unaccompanied sextet, Six in a Bar. A broadcaster on radio and television.
Has written descriptive inserts to accompany compact disc recordings, and has contributed articles to *Church Music Quarterly*, *Musical Times* and other journals, and is a regular reviewer with *Organists' Review*.
He cites **Stanley Vann**, as influential in the development of his own compositional style. While still a cathedral chorister, at the age of 14, he conducted a performance in Peterborough Cathedral of an item of his own work. Other works include the anthem 'My soul, within the bed of Heaven' (1983), a hymn 'On the nativity of my Saviour' (1996) and a Prelude on *Rendez à Dieu* and other organ works.

MOLLE, Henry (17th century)
Public orator to the University of Cambridge. Organist of Peterhouse from early in the 17th century. Composed a setting of the Latin and English Version of the Litany. Also composed the anthems 'God the Protector' and 'Thou art my portion'.

MONK, Dr. Edwin George (1819-1900)
Born in Frome, Somerset on 13 December 1819; died in Radley near Oxford on 3 January 1900. Brother of **Henry Monk** and the uncle of **Mark Monk**.
A pupil of Henry and George Field. Studied the Tonic Sol-fa notation with **John Hullah**, singing with Henry Phillips and composition under **George Macfarren**. Graduated B.Mus. (1848) and D.Mus. (1856) at the University of Oxford.
Organist of Midsomer Norton Parish Church and at Christ Church, Frome and then spent two years in Ireland (1844-1846) as organist of St. Columba's College which at that time was sited at Stackallan, Lord Boyne's mansion near Navan, but was later moved to Rathfarnham, near Dublin.
On his return he became the first organist and music master of St. Peter's College, Radley where he remained from the opening of the school (1848) until 1859. Full cathedral services were established and maintained on Sundays and certain weekdays. Monk grew fond of the town of Radley, and later retired there.
Organist of York Minster (1859-1883), succeeding **John Camidge**. An examiner for musical degrees with **F.A.G. Ouseley** for the University of Oxford.
His hobby was astronomy; he became a Fellow of the Royal Astronomical Society (1871).
An editor of church music. He produced the *Anglican Chant Book* and the *Anglican Choral Service Book*, the *Anglican Hymn Book* with Revd. R. Singleton and *The Psalter and Canticles Pointed for Chanting* and *Anglican Psalter Chants* with Ouseley.
Composed services, including a Unison Setting in A; anthems of which examples are 'God so loved the world' and 'My soul truly waiteth', a setting in A of the Responses to the Commandments, hymn tunes and songs. In *Cathedral Psalter Chants* (1875) he was represented by Single Chants, in A Minor, A-flat, D, E-flat and G Minor.
He held strong views on hymn tunes, which he felt should be 'devout, unsecular and soul-stirring', consisting of sober melodies underlaid by masculine, dignified and untheatrical harmonies.
His hymn tunes include 'St. Dionysius', 'St. Ninian' and 'Angel voices', the latter being written at the request of Revd. W.K. Macrorie, who later became bishop of Maritzburg, to accompany the hymn 'Angel voices ever singing' by Francis Pott at the celebration of the opening of the organ at Wingate Church, Lancashire (February 1861). All three tunes were included in *Hymns Ancient and Modern*.

MONK, Henry Theophilus (1831-1857)
Born in Frome, Somerset on 6 March 1831; drowned while swimming in North Wales on 23 July 1857. Brother of **Edwin Monk**. Studied under **Charles Lavington** and **George Macfarren**. Taught music at Forest School, Walthamstow, Essex where he was also organist. His other organistships were in Wells, Radley, Berkshire and at St. Philip's Church, Sheffield. Composed chants, and other vocal music.

MONK, James Jonathan (1846-1900)
Born in Bolton-le-Moors on 20 February 1846; died in 1900. Studied under James Thomson and **William Westbrook**. Lived and worked in the Liverpool area as an organist, recitalist, teacher and music critic for a local paper. Composed a Te Deum, the anthem 'Let your light', the festival anthem 'O be joyful in the Lord', and songs.

MONK, Dr. Mark James (1858-1929)
Born in Hunmanby, Yorkshire on 16 March 1858; died in Blackheath, Kent on 5 May 1929.
His early musical training was at York Minster (1867-1878) under his uncle, **Edwin Monk**. Graduated B.Mus. (1878) and D.Mus. (1888) at New College, Oxford.
After early organistships in York including the position of assistant organist at York Minster, he was appointed to the Church of St. John, Ladywood, Birmingham (1879); Ashby de la Zouche Parish Church, Leicestershire (1880) and Banbury, Oxfordshire (1883).
Organist of Truro Cathedral (1890-1920) until his retirement and subsequent move to Bournemouth, Dorset. A local choral and philharmonic society conductor.
Composed as his D.Mus. exercise a Festival Te Deum for Solo Voices, Eight-Part Chorus, Organ and Full Orchestra. His other

works include services, anthems, the hymn tune 'Give light', sacred songs, a Wind Quintet, and music for piano and for organ.

MONK, Dr. William Henry (1823-1889)
Born in Brompton, London on 16 March 1823; died in Stoke Newington, London on 1 March 1889.
Studied under **Thomas Adams**, James Hamilton and **G.A. Griesbach**. Graduated D.Mus. honorarily at the University of Durham (1882).
Organist in London of Eaton Chapel, Pimlico (1841-1843); St. George's Chapel, Albermarle Street (1843-1845); Portman Chapel, Marylebone (1845-1847) and St. Mathias's Church, Stoke Newington, where he introduced and continued daily cathedral-style choral services with a voluntary choir (from 1852).
Long associated with King's College London, of which he was choirmaster (from 1847), organist (from 1849) and professor of vocal music (from 1874). A professor of music at the School for the Indigent Blind (from 1851) and a professor of the National Training School of Music (from 1876).
Particularly remembered for his work as musical editor of *Hymns Ancient and Modern* where he reigned supreme musically. It was he who suggested the collection's title. In its early days it was known as 'Monk's Book.' His own 'Eventide' was among the 15 tunes selected for the 1861 Edition, in which there were also 60 arrangements by him; he died after the Supplement had gone to press but before it was published.
A deeply religious man who was devoted to the music of congregational worship. He had a strong dislike for tunes that displayed 'a sweet melody and an effeminate harmony' and to him, the purpose of the organ in church was to reach people's souls, not to serve as the vehicle for a display of skill. He recognised the importance of congregational hymn singing in public worship and did much to strengthen it.
Composed settings of the Responses to the Commandments in E-flat and in F, chants, Kyries, settings of the Te Deum, and anthems including 'In God's Word will I rejoice' and 'And the angel Gabriel'. Composed a secular song.

MONTGOMERY, William Augustus (1872-1949)
Born in Hawick, Scotland on 25 November 1872; died on 18 December 1949.
Trained privately in music in Scarborough, Yorkshire with Owen Williams and Henry Hill. Attended Scarborough Grammar School. Graduated B.Mus. at the University of Durham (1897).
Organist of the Church of St. Madoc, Doune, Scotland (from 1889). Organist of St. Andrew's Church, Pau, France (from 1890). Returning to Scotland in 1894, he became music master of Wallace Hall Academy, and organist of the Parish Churches of Closeburn (from 1894) and Jedburgh (from 1897).
Organist of St. Edmund's Church, Hunstanton, Norfolk (from 1898); SS Philip and James, Ilfracombe, Devon (from 1899) and Gainsborough Parish Church, Lincolnshire (from 1906).
Organist of St. Peter's Church, Sherbrooke, Quebec (1914) and of All Saints' Cathedral, Halifax, Nova Scotia (1918-1940).
Composed as his B.Mus. exercise a setting of Psalm 23: 'The Lord is my Shepherd' for Solo Voices, Chorus and Strings. Also composed anthems, songs, organ works and items for piano.

MOODIE, William (1833-?)
Born in Bonhill, Dumbarton, Scotland on 19 April 1833. Conductor of the Psalmody at the Dumbarton Episcopal Church;

Lansdowne United Presbyterian Church, Glasgow (1864-1877); Barony Church (1877-1879) and East Pollokshields Free Church (1889-1892). A choral society conductor. Composed anthems, part songs, cantatas and piano music.

MOODY, Dr. Charles Harry (1874-1965)
Born in Stourbridge, Worcestershire on 22 March 1874; died on 10 May 1965.
An articled pupil of **Tom Morgan** at Bangor Cathedral.
Appointed C.B.E. (1920), and awarded the Lambeth D.Mus (1923).
Acting organist of St. Michael's College, Tenbury, Worcestershire (1894). Deputy organist and, later, acting organist of Wells Cathedral. Private organist to the bishop of Bath and Wells (from 1894). Organist of Wigan Parish Church, Lancashire at the instigation of **John Stainer** (from 1895), and of Holy Trinity Church, Coventry, Warwickshire (from 1899). Choirmaster of Christ Church, Harrogate, Yorkshire (from 1904).
Organist of Ripon Cathedral (1902-1954).
Music master to the Duchess of Leeds at Hornby Castle, Yorkshire (from 1903).
Involved in a High Court action (1943) against the Dean and Chapter of Ripon Cathedral when the authorities attempted to dispense with the choral setting of the Canticles at Sunday services. He was backed by the Bishop of Ripon and by **Ralph Vaughan Williams**.
Lectured in music at Ripon and Wakefield Diocesan Training College (1902-1952). A local choral and madrigal society conductor.
Author of articles in *The Times* and *The Manchester Guardian*, books including *A Choral Elegy* and *A Choirboy in the Making*, and composer of church music and other items. These included a Magnificat for each of two local celebrations: the Festival of North-Eastern Cathedral Choirs at York Minster (1902) and the 800th anniversary of Fountains Abbey (1932). Composed anthems. Some songs composed under the pseudonym of Coulthard Brayton.

MOODY, Marie (19th century)
Composed the anthem 'Great Lord of lords', overtures and chamber works.

MOONIE, James Anderson (1853-1923)
Born in Edinburgh in 1853; died in 1923. Studied under Alberto Randegger, Cottell and John Welch. Taught at schools in Edinburgh, where he was also active as an organist. Composed a short cantata *Jerusalem, my happy home*.

MOORE, James (b.1909)
Born in Ramelton, County Donegal, Ireland on 10 April 1909.
A pupil of Ernest Hay, **Ernest Bullock** and John Vine.
Associated with Sir Hamilton Harty, conductor of the Hallé Orchestra.
Organist and choirmaster of the Presbyterian Churches of First Ballymoney (1928-1934) and First Coleraine (1934-1945 and from 1956), where he was also an elder of the church.
Lectured in church music at Magee Theological College, Derry (1948-1962). Director of music of Coleraine Academical Institute (from 1950). President of the Professional Musicians' Society of Ulster.
Composed the hymn tunes 'Ramelton' and 'Culrathain', both based on Irish melodies, which were included in the Third Edition (1973)

of *Church Hymnary*. Composed two piano pieces and arranged Irish folk songs.

MOORE, Philip (b.1943)
Born in London on 30 September 1943.
Studied piano, organ, composition and conducting at the Royal College of Music, during which time he was organist of St. Gabriel's Church, Cricklewood, London. Graduated B.Mus. at the University of Durham.
Taught music at Eton College (from 1965). Assistant organist of Canterbury Cathedral (1968-1974).
Organist and master of the choristers of Guildford Cathedral (1974-1983), and organist and master of the music of York Minster (from 1983).
Has composed nearly 100 anthems, 10 settings of the Evening Canticles, six settings of the Mass/Communion Service, and six settings of the Preces and Responses. Representative works include the anthem 'All wisdom cometh from the Lord', *Three Prayers of Dietrich Bonhöffer* and a double choir unaccompanied setting of the Alternative Service Book Communion Service. Has also written chamber music, organ music, orchestral works and three cantatas for chorus and orchestra.

MOORE, Thomas (1710-c1792)
Born, possibly in Manchester, in 1710; died in Glasgow around 1792. Lived and worked as a music teacher in Manchester for 10 years (from around 1740). Moved to Glasgow where he became precentor of Blackfriars Parish Church (from 1855). Taught music at Hutcheson's Hospital (1756-1787). A bookseller in Princes Street and Stockwell Street. A compiler of Psalters. Published *The Psalm Singer's Divine Companion* in two volumes (c1750). This work was followed by *The Psalm Singer's Compleat Tutor and Divine Companion* (1750) and *The Psalm Singer's Pocket Companion* (1756). The hymn tune 'Glasgow' was published in one of his collections. Also composed the tune 'Burgess' (1759).

MOORE, William (1811-1880)
Born in Manchester in 1811; died in Manchester in 1880. Composer of hymn tunes.

MOORE, William (1841-1930)
Born in 1841; died in Leamington, Warwickshire on 15 January 1930. Lived in Reading, Berkshire (until 1901), where he was a member of the Trinity Congregational Church and an amateur musician. He then moved to Leamington. Involved with the Leamington and County Music Festival, serving as vice-chairman of the Festival Committee. Towards the end of his life he was both deaf and blind. Composer of hymn tunes, including 'Barford'.

MORECOCKE (Merricocke), Robert (?-1581)
A composer of the Chapel Royal. Composed settings of the Te Deum, Magnificat and Nunc Dimittis.

MORETON, Frederick William (19th/20th century)
Trained privately in music, graduating B.Mus. at the University of Durham (1894). Organist and choirmaster of Yealmpton Parish Church, Devon (from 1887); St. Mark's Church, Ford (from 1888) and the Church of St. James the Great, Devonport (from 1889). His B.Mus. exercise was a setting of Psalm 96 'O sing unto the Lord a new song' for Solo Voices, Five-Part Choir and Strings. Also

composed a setting of the Service of Holy Communion, a carol and a children's operetta.

MORETON, Dr. George Harry (1865-1961)
Born in Devonport in 1865; died in Plympton, Devon in September 1961.
Trained in music at Winchester Cathedral. Graduated B.Mus. at the University of Durham (1897). Later accorded the Lambeth D.Mus.
Organist of Stoke Damaral Parish Church (from 1876). Assistant organist of Winchester Cathedral (from 1879) and organist of St. Michael's Church, Winchester (from 1879). Organist and choirmaster of St. George's Church, East Stonehouse, Plymouth (from 1882) and of East Stonehouse Parish Church, (1885-1959).
Also a local choral society conductor. Town organist of East Stonehouse (from 1894) and borough organist of Plymouth (from 1899).
Submitted as his B.Mus. exercise a setting of Psalm 103 'Praise the Lord O my soul'. Also composed services, a Te Deum, anthems, a set of Preces and Responses, chants and hymn tunes.

MORETON, John (1764-1804)
Born in Birmingham in 1764; died in Birmingham in 1804. Leader of singing at the King Street Chapel of Lady Huntingdon's Connexion. Lived in Summer Lane, Birmingham. Composer of hymn tunes including 'Eglon', found in *Sacred Melody*, a tune book that he compiled for the King Street Chapel. This and other tunes were popular in the Midlands.

MORGAN, Alfred Phillips (1857-1942)
Born in Builth Wells, Breconshire, Wales in 1857; died in Builth on 8 February 1942. Director of music of the Presbyterian Church of Wales, Builth Wells, where he set and maintained a high standard of music. Served on the Welsh Book Committee for the Revised Edition (1927) of *Church Hymnary*, and was honoured at the national *eisteddfodau* of 1897 and 1898. Composed church music including the hymn tune 'St. Appollos', and part songs.

MORGAN, Dafydd Siencyn (David Jenkin: 1752-1844)
Born in Penshingrug, Llangrannog, Cardiganshire, Wales in 1752; died in Penllwyn-du, near Cardigan on 18 November 1844.
Learned music with his father, a parish sexton.
At the age of 20 he joined the Pembrokeshire Volunteers, which gave him the opportunity to develop his knowledge of music and to play the clarinet.
When he returned to Llangrannog he studied music from a textbook by **William Tans'ur**, there being no similar publications available in Welsh. Became precentor of the Parish Church and held music classes.
Eventually gave up the precentorship and toured North Wales, giving classes in singing for several months, following which he travelled through Glamorgan and Monmouthshire. Dafydd Morgan worked with all denominations including the established church, where the best voices were said to be found at the time. He taught the elements of music and trained his choirs to sing in a more disciplined manner. Owing to a lack of suitable materials there was much copying by hand and teaching by ear.
Became a member of the Capel Isaf Congregational Chapel, Llechryd, Cardiganshire, where he was later appointed precentor.
A work by him that closely resembles a glee has, through the arrangements of **David Evans** and **John Lloyd**, seen use as the anthem 'Teyrnasa Iesu Mawr' (Reign, great Jesus) and the hymn

tune 'Mercurial'. His hymn tunes began to be published in musical journals following his success at a competition in Welshpool. They include 'Horeb', also known as 'Penllyn', which has been used into the present century.

MORGAN, David C. (b. 1932)
Born on 18 May 1932. David Morgan has composed a Palm Sunday Antiphon, and the carol 'All Bethlehem a-blazing'.

MORGAN, Evan (1846-1920)
Born in Tyn-dre, Morfa Bycham, near Portmadoc, Wales on 27 March 1846; died on 1 November 1920. A furniture maker. Had musical ability with a good singing voice, and was a poet. His interest in music developed when young. Sang at venues around Portmadoc. His hymn tunes won prizes at competitions organised by the Congregational Church in Carmarthenshire. His first, 'Llanerch', was named after the neighbouring farm. 'Salem' was well known, and his other tunes include 'Tyddyn' and 'Llwyn'.

MORGAN, Revd. George Arthur (1892-1957)
Born in Derby in 1892; died in Thornbury, Yorkshire on 1 September 1957. Studied theology at Hartley College, where as a student he was college organist. Ordained as a minister of the Methodist Church (1915). Served a number of Methodist circuits.
A gifted musician. Served on the committee of *School Hymn Book of the Methodist Church* (1950). His own hymn tune 'Ashbourne Road' featured in that collection with the hymn by Alice Pulle 'For men's unceasing quest for God'.

MORGAN, George Washbourne (1823-1892)
Born in Gloucester on 9 April 1823; died in Tacoma, Washington, U.S.A. in July 1892. An articled pupil of **John Amott**. Held an organ appointment in Cheltenham (from 1844). Organist of Christ Church, Gloucester; St. James's Church, Gloucester and St. Olave's, Southwark, London. An unsuccessful candidate for the vacant organist's post at Worcester Cathedral (1845). Organist of South Hackney, London. Emigrated to the U.S.A. (1853) and was organist in New York City of St. Thomas's Episcopal Church, Grace Church and St. Stephen's, before commencing 12 years' service at the Brooklyn Tabernacle. Composed church music, including the anthem 'Ponder my words' and the carol 'There were shepherds', vocal items and music for piano and for orchestra.

MORGAN, Robert Orlando (1865-1956)
Born in Manchester on 16 March 1865; died in 1956. Won a Merchant Taylors' Scholarship to the Guildhall School of Music where he studied piano and composition. His tutors were **John Francis Barnett**, **Henry Gadsby** and **Charles Jordan**. A professor of piano and composition at G.S.M. (from 1887). An examiner in music. Made his first appearance as a solo pianist in 1878. His six books include *Modern School of Pianoforte Technique*.
Won 50 guineas (£52.50) in a competition for anthem writing (1893). His compositions won a gold medal and first prize at the Grand Concours International de Composition Musicale, Brussels (1894). Other works include the church cantata *The Crown of Thorns*, a comic opera *Two Merry Monarchs*, some two hundred songs and part songs, orchestral works and piano music.

MORGAN, Tom Westlake (1869-?)
Born in Congresbury, Somerset on 6 August 1869.

A chorister of King's College, Cambridge (from 1879) and later, pupil-assistant to the cathedral organist, **A.H. Mann**. A pupil of **Boyton Smith** in Dorchester, Dorset. Studied at St. Catherine's College, Cambridge, where he was organist, and at the Royal College of Music (from 1890) under **Walter Parratt** and **Francis Gladstone**.
Organist of St. George's Anglican Church, Paris (from 1889); St. John's Church, Wilton Road, London (from 1890); St. David's Church, Merthyr Tydfil (from 1891) and St. Bride's Church, Fleet Street.
Organist of Bangor Cathedral (1892-1906).
Editor of *The Church Musician*.
Music master at the North Wales Training College, Bangor (1895-1897). Instrumental in raising funds for the new organ (commissioned 1897).
Composed church music including anthems in Welsh for diocesan festivals at Bangor Cathedral, and for festivals at St. Paul's Cathedral.

MORI, Nicholas (1822-?)
Born on 14 January 1822. Studied under his father, Frank Mori, with **Charles Lucas**, and in Paris. Composed a setting of Psalm 137 'By the waters of Babylon'. His other works include a setting of 'The wicked world' by W.S. Gilbert.

MORICE, Revd. Francis David (1849-1926)
Born in St. Marylebone, London in 1849; died in Woking, Surrey on 21 September 1926. Educated at Uppingham School, Leicestershire and Winchester College, Hampshire. Went up to New College, Oxford, where he graduated B.A. and M.A. Assistant music master (from 1874) and house master (1884-1894) of Rugby School, Warwickshire. Author of *Stories in Attic Greek* and *Pindar for English Readers*. Composer of hymn tunes; arranged the hymn tune 'Ascendit'.

MORLEY, Felix Wilson (1855-?)
Born in Bassingbourne, Cambridgeshire on 20 November 1855. Attended Pembroke College, Cambridge (from 1873) as organ scholar. Graduated B.A. (1878), and remained at the college as organist. Also graduated M.A. (1883) and Mus.B. (1885). Honorary organist of Bassingbourne Parish Church (1868-1873). A composer, choral society conductor and musical inspector for the Diocese of Ely. Composed a Magnificat and Nunc Dimittis and other services, a setting of Psalm 150 'O praise God in His holiness', songs, part songs, works for cello and piano music.

MORLEY, Henry Litchfield (1830-1916)
Born in 1830; died in Greenwich, Kent on 20 October 1916. Composed the hymn tune 'Newcastle' (1876) which appeared with the hymn 'Eternal Light' by Thomas Binney in *London Tunebook* (1877), for which it was commissioned.

MORLEY, Thomas (c1557-1602)
Born in Norwich, Norfolk in 1557 or 1558; died in London in October 1602.
His father was a brewer who may also have been a verger of Norwich Cathedral.
Studied under **William Byrd**. A chorister of St. Paul's Cathedral. Graduated B.Mus. at the University of Oxford (1588).

Organist and master of the choristers of Norwich Cathedral (1583-1587) but shared the salary and probably the duties of the position of master of the choristers with Edmund Inglott.

Organist of St. Paul's Cathedral (from around 1591), a position he resigned on becoming a gentleman of the Chapel Royal (1592-1602) where he was later epistler and, later still, gospeller.

Held a patent for the printing of music manuscript paper (from 1598).

Set about improving the standards of church music, noting that most choirmen were careless and made no attempt to improve their singing. A book *A Plaine and Easie Introduction to Practicall Musicke...* (1597) was dedicated to William Byrd. It was used as a textbook for two hundred years and is still of value as an insight into the musical ways of the 16th century.

Edited, arranged and published works by other composers. He may have been acquainted with William Shakespeare, for whose plays he composed songs.

His enduring works include a Short Service and a large-scale First Verse Service, a setting of the Preces, the fine verse anthem 'Out of the deep have I called unto Thee, O Lord' and a number of Latin pieces including 'Nolo mortem peccatoris'. His collection *The Triumphes of Oriana* (1601) featured the secular works of a number of contemporary composers.

MORLEY, William (?-1731)
Died in Westminster, London on 29 October 1731. Graduated B.Mus. at Merton College, Oxford (1713). A gentleman of the Chapel Royal (from 1715). With his example in D Minor he is one of the possible inventors of the double chant - but see the rival claims of **Luke Flintoft**, **William Hine** and John Robinson. Also composed songs.

MORNINGTON, Earl of (Garret Colley Wellesley: 1735-1781)
Born in Dangan, Ireland on 19 July 1735; died in Kensington, London on 22 May 1781. Father of the 'Soldier Duke'.

As a child he learned to play violin, harpsichord and organ. May have been a pupil of **Ralph Roseingrave**. Graduated B.A. (1754) and D.Mus. and became the first professor of music (1764-1774) at the University of Dublin.

Succeeded to the family title in 1758, and became Viscount Wellesley (1760). His private chapel at Dangan Castle, County Meath had regular cathedral-style services.

The Wellesley and Wesley families were related and there was regular contact between them.

Composed chants including a Double Chant in D and other items of church music such as the anthems 'O Lord, hear the prayer of thy servants' and 'Rejoice in the Lord alway', madrigals, glees and catches. His glee 'Here in a cool grot' won a prize in 1779.

MORRIS, Herbert C. (1873-?)
Born in Coventry, Warwickshire on 18 June 1873. A pupil of **Frank Spinney** at Leamington Spa, of **A.H. Brewer** at Coventry and of **Walter Parratt** and others at the Royal College of Music, where he was exhibitioner (1891-1894). Organist of Kenilworth Parish Church, Warwickshire, the Boscombe Pavilion, Dorset and various churches in the London area. Appointed assistant organist of Manchester Cathedral (1895-1896). Organist of St. Andrew's Church, Bath, Somerset (from 1896). In the same year he was appointed organist of St. David's Cathedral, where he was also a lay vicar. Composed services and anthems.

MORRIS, Reginald Owen (1886-1948)
Born in York on 3 March 1886; died in Kensington, London on 15 December 1948.

Studied at Harrow School, New College, Oxford and, under **Charles Wood**, at the Royal College of Music.

One of the rising group of musicians and composers who served in the army during World War I: others included George Butterworth and **Ralph Vaughan Williams**, who became his brother-in-law. At the end of the war he worked as a journalist.

Visited and worked in the U.S.A. (1921-1931) where his appointments included the teaching of musical theory at the Curtis Institute of Music, Philadelphia (1926-1928). His work in the U.S.A. interrupted his teaching at the R.C.M. (1920-1926; 1928-1948).

A shy man with a fondness for cats and a delicate appetite who compiled crossword puzzles for *The Times*.

His text book *Contrapuntal Technique in the 16th Century* (1922) became a standard text.

Composed motets, songs, part songs, and symphonies. His hymn tune 'Hermitage' was composed for *Songs of Praise* (1925) where it was coupled with the hymn by Christina Rossetti 'Love came down at Christmas'.

MOSELEY, Lucy (18th century)
Composed the anthem 'Blessed are all they' (1793).

MOSS, Edwin (1838-1919)
Born in London on 4 January 1838; died in Hackney, London on 16 February 1919. A teacher in Cardiff and Wantage, Berkshire. Possessed a fine tenor voice and was precentor of Poultry Chapel, London (1866-1875). Sang at the Foundling Chapel, London (from 1877). Composer of hymn tunes. Editor of *London Tune Book* (1877).

MOTE, Arnold Rudolph (19th/20th century)
Educated privately in music. Graduated B.A. at the University of Sydney (1902), B.Mus. at Queen's College, Oxford (1906) and B.Mus. at the University of Durham (1906).

Organist of the Centenary Hall, Sydney, Australia (1894-1904), the University of Sydney (1898-1904) and Sydney Town Hall (1900-1901). Accompanied the Sydney Liedertafel (1901-1904). A professor of piano and theory at Rivière College, Sydney.

Organist and choirmaster of Catford Parish Church, Kent (1905-1906) and of Sherborne Abbey, Dorset (1907).

Composed anthems, hymn tunes, carols, part songs and organ voluntaries.

MOULE, Handley Carr Glynn (1841-1920)
Born in Fordington, Dorset on 23 December 1841; died in Cambridge on 8 May 1920. Composer of hymn tunes.

MOULTON, William Fiddian (1866-1929)
Born in Richmond, Surrey on 5 August 1866; died in Sunderland on 17 September 1929. Composer of hymn tunes.

MOUNSEY, Ann Sheppard
See **BARTHOLOMEW**, Ann Sheppard.

MOUNT-EDGCUMBE, Richard, Second Earl of (1764-1839)
Born on 13 September 1764; died in Richmond, Surrey on 26 September 1839. Member of Parliament for Lostwithiel, Cornwall

(1790-1791) and for Fowey (1791-1795). His autobiography *Musical Reminiscences* ran to a fourth edition (1834). Composed a Service in A, and the anthem 'I will take heed unto my ways' (1851). Other works include the opera *Zenobia* (1800).

MOUNTAIN, Dr. James (1844-1933)
Born in New Wortley, Leeds on 16 July 1844; died in Tunbridge Wells, Kent on 27 June 1933.
Educated at Cheshunt College, Hertfordshire for the ministry of the church of the Countess of Huntingdon's Connexion. He then studied in Germany at the Universities of Heidelberg and Tübingen. Ordained at Great Marlow, Buckinghamshire and later graduated D.D. at Ewing College, Illinois, U.S.A.
His ministry was interrupted by a deterioration in his health, forcing him to live in Switzerland for two years. Inspired by the Sankey and Moody Revival, he undertook extensive evangelistic tours of the U.K. (for eight years) and throughout the world (for seven years). Minister of the Emmanuel Church and St. John's Free Church, Tunbridge Wells, Kent (1878-1898).
Set the hymn 'Jesus I am resting' by Jean Pigott, naming the tune after the title. This and many other of his tunes were contained in *Hymns of Consecration and Faith* (1876), which he compiled. 'Like a river' was used in the Revised Edition (1927) of *Church Hymnary*.

MUDDS (Mudd, Muds), John (1555-1631)
Born in London in 1555; buried in Peterborough, Cambridgeshire on 16 December 1631. Organist, vicar choral and epistolar of Peterborough Cathedral, jointly with Richard Tiller (1583-1592) and exclusively thereafter (1592-1631). Composed a service and four anthems including 'O God, who hast prepared'.

MUDDS (Mudd, Mudde, Muds), Thomas (c1560-c1619)
Born in London around the year 1560; died in or after the year 1619. Composed anthems including 'Bow down Thine ear' and 'O clap your hands'.

MUDIE, Thomas Molleson (1809-1876)
Born in Chelsea, London on 30 November 1809; died in Westminster, London on 24 July 1876. Studied at the Royal Academy of Music under **William Crotch** and Cipriani Potter. Returned as a professor of piano (1832-1844). An organist at Gatton, Surrey (1833-1844). Taught for a while in Edinburgh and returned to London in 1863. Composed anthems including 'Blessed be Thy name for ever', songs, Symphonies in B-flat, in C, in D and in F, and chamber works.

MULLEN, Joseph (1826-1896)
Born in Dublin in 1826; died in 1896. Chorister of Christ Church Cathedral in Dublin. Possibly, organist of Tuam Cathedral. Succentor of Limerick Cathedral. Organist of the Dublin Churches of St. Mary and St. Catherine, and Christ Church, Leeson Park. Composed the anthem 'O give thanks unto the Lord'.

MULLER, Hermann von
See **BONNER,** Carey.

MULLINAR, Thomas Michael (1895-1973)
Born in Bangor, Wales on 25 October 1895; died in Richmond, Surrey on 16 June 1973. Studied with **Roland Rogers** and at the Royal College of Music. Accompanist to the City of Birmingham

Municipal Orchestra. Composed three carols, 'The vagrant song' for Voice and Piano, and solo works for piano.

MUNDELLA, Emma (1858-1896)
Born in Nottingham in 1858; died on 20 February 1896. Studied music with her parents and with **Arthur Page**, winning a Nottingham Scholarship to the National Training School of Music at its inception (1876). Director of music at St. Elphin's Clergy Daughters' School, Warrington, Cheshire and of Wimbledon High School, Surrey (from 1880). Editor of *The Day School Hymn Book*. Composed anthems including 'Blessed be the Lord' and 'Our God is Lord of the harvest', and songs.

MUNDY, Dr. John (c1555-1630)
Born around the year 1555; died in Windsor, Berkshire on 29 June 1630. The son of **William Mundy**. Studied music under his father. Graduated B.Mus. (1586) and D.Mus. (1624) at the University of Oxford. Organist of Eton College, and of St. George's Chapel, Windsor Castle (from 1585), where it is believed that he succeeded **John Marbecke**. In the same year, **Nathaniel Giles** was appointed master of the choristers at St. George's Chapel. Composed Psalms, anthems including 'Sing joyfully' and 'Give laud unto the Lord', songs, and madrigals including 'Lightly she tripped', published in the collection;*The Triumphes of Oriana* (1601) by **Thomas Morley**. Published a collection of music *Songs and Psalmes* (1594).

MUNDY, William (c1529-c1591)
Born, possibly in London, where he spent most of his life, around the year 1529; died, possibly in London, around 1591. Father of **John Mundy**. Chorister head boy (1543) of Westminster Abbey. A member of the Choir of the London Church of St. Mary-at-Hill, a vicar choral of St. Paul's Cathedral and a gentleman of the Chapel Royal (1563-1591) of Elizabeth I. Composed Services for men's voices and for full choir, and anthems including 'Teach me, O Lord' and 'O Lord, the Maker of all things'. Some of the compositions attributed to William Mundy could have been the work of his father, Thomas, who was sexton of the Church of St. Mary-at-Hill (1527-1558).

MURGATROYD, Charles (?-1741)
Died on 4 September 1741. Organist, and a junior vicar, of Lincoln Cathedral (1721-1741). Unusually, the Choir was consulted in the appointment. Instructed to play a short organ voluntary immediately before the Second Lesson (20 June 1731), a practice that continued until the time of **Matthew Young**. Suspended for negligence on 24 March 1733 and replaced temporarily by Samuel Wise. Composed chants.

MURRAY, Dom Anthony Gregory (1905-1992)
Born in Fulham, London on 27 February 1905; died in January 1992.
Educated at Westminster Cathedral Choir School, during which time he was assistant organist to **Richard Terry**. Attended Ealing Priory School and Christ's College, Cambridge.
Organist and director of music of Downside Abbey (1932-1940), which he had entered as a novice (1922). Ordained in 1932. Gave organ recitals from Downside, which were broadcast on the radio from time to time.
His ministry as a parish priest took him coincidentally to Churches named after St. Benedict: at Church Hindley, Wigan, Lancashire

(1948-1952) and Stratton-on-the-Fosse, Bath, Somerset (from 1952). Later returned to the religious community of Downside Abbey.

An authority on Gregorian Chant. Editor of *Music and Liturgy*. His *Gregorian Chant according to the Manuscripts* successfully challenged some conventional wisdom that had grown up on interpretation.

Composed settings of the Mass for congregational use, including A People's Mass, and hymn tunes, 22 of which appeared in *Westminster Hymnal* (1940) together with some of his harmonisations of tunes by other composers. One of the 22 was 'Angelorum Apostolus', composed on 13 May 1935 for a Latin hymn in honour of St. Gregory, the Patron Saint of Downside Abbey. 'Trysagion' and 'Reproaches' were contained in the Third Edition (1973) of *Church Hymnary*. His tunes also appeared in *Praise The Lord* (1966, Revised 1971) and *New Catholic Hymnal* (1971). 'Ubi Caritas' has been popular. In addition, he composed antiphons, chants, part songs, organ interludes and an orchestral work *Homage to Delius*.

MURRAY, James (19th/20th century)
Born in Newmachar, Aberdeenshire. Educated at the Tonic Sol-fa College, and with **George Oakey**, F.C. Hyde-Field and Charles Soutar. A festival adjudicator. A music master (1913-1917) and teacher of vocal music (1914-1927) for Aberdeen Education Committee, and director of music for Inverness-shire Education Committee of the Badeizock Strathspey area (from 1927). A teacher of Grantown Grammar School (from 1933). Author of *Handbook for Class Teachers on Teaching of Singing in Schools with Sight Singing*. Composed anthems, songs, and part songs.

MURRAY, James Robertson (1836-1885)
Born in Westminster, London in 1836; died in Islington, London on 3 September 1885. Organist of St. Botolph's Church, Aldersgate, London. Founded the London Church Choir Association and conductor of its annual services in St. Paul's Cathedral (from 1890). Composer of hymn tunes.

MURRILL, Herbert Henry John (1909-1952)
Born in Wandsworth, London on 11 May 1909; died in St. Marylebone, London on 25 July 1952.

Studied at Aske's School, Hatcham and at the Royal Academy of Music (1925-1928). Organ scholar of Worcester College, Oxford (from 1928), studying with **William Harris** and **Hugh Allen**. Graduated B.Mus. and M.A.

His wife was the cellist Vera Canning, for whom he composed a number of works.

Returned to the R.A.M. as a teacher of composition, and was later a professor (1933-1952). Associated with the B.B.C. (from 1936), becoming assistant director of music (1948-1950) and director of music (1950-1952).

Organist of Christ Church, Lancaster Gate and of St. Thomas's Church, Regent Street.

Little of the music that he composed was for the church, but it includes an Evening Service in E and a Double Chant in G which was used in the *Baptist Hymn Book* (1962). The hymn tune 'Carolyn' is also his.

While he was an undergraduate, his opera *Man in Cage* (1930) ran for eight weeks. Also composed a String Quartet (1939).

MUSGRAVE, John Thomas (1851-1920)
Born in 1851; died in Kilburn, London in 1920. Organist of a number of Anglican and Methodist Churches in London. Composer of hymn tunes. 'St. John's Park' was used in Congregational Praise (1951).

MUTLOW, William (1761-1832)
Born in 1761; died in Gloucester in 1832. A chorister of Gloucester Cathedral. As a boy he was very fat and a story circulated that he fell from the triforium into the quire, bounced like a rubber ball and rose to his feet unhurt. Organist of Gloucester Cathedral (1782-1832). Conducted the Three Choirs' Festivals in Gloucester (1790-1832). Composed anthems including 'Unto Thee, O Lord'. A Chant was included in a collection published by **John 'Christmas' Beckwith**.

N

NATTRASS, James Conder (1852-1925)
Born in Weardale, Yorkshire on 1 August 1852; died in Gosforth, Cumberland on 6 August 1925. Composer of hymn tunes.

NAYLOR, Bernard James (1907-1986)
Born in Cambridge on 22 November 1907; died on 19 May 1986.
Studied as open scholar in composition at the Royal College of Music (1924-1927) under **Ralph Vaughan Williams**, **Gustav Holst** and **John Ireland**. Organ scholar of Exeter College, Oxford (1927-1931); graduated B.Mus. and M.A.
Conductor of the Oxford University Opera Club (1927-1931), after which his career alternated between England and Canada.
In 1932 he emigrated to Canada, where he became conductor of the Winnipeg Symphony Orchestra. In 1936 he returned to England as organist and director of music of Queen's College, Oxford (1936-1939).
In 1939 he travelled once again to Canada and became conductor of the Little Symphony Orchestra, Montreal (1942-1947). In 1950, now back in England, he taught at the Universities of Oxford (1950-1952) and Reading (1953-1959). In 1959 he emigrated finally to Canada.
Composed a set of nine motets, and other items of church music including a Holy Communion Service in D, and anthems including 'God that madest' and 'Lead, kindly Light'. Also part songs for male voices.

NAYLOR, Charles Legh (1869-1945)
Born in Scarborough, Yorkshire on 14 October 1869; died in Harrogate, Yorkshire on 22 November 1945. A son of **John Naylor**; brother of **Edward Naylor**. Attended St. Peter's School, York and Emmanuel College, Cambridge, where he was organist from 1888.
Assistant organist of York Minster (from 1891), and organist of St. Peter's Church, Harrogate for two periods (1892-1902, 1917-1935). Taught music at a number of schools in the town and was a local orchestral society conductor. Conductor of the Harrogate Kursaal Orchestra (1902-1906). Organist of the Hook Memorial Church, Leeds (from 1911).
Music editor of *Methodist School Hymnal* (1911), to which he contributed 41 tunes of his own, including 'Derwent', later used in *Hymns and Psalms* (1983).

NAYLOR, Dr. Edward Woodall (1867-1934)
Born in Scarborough, Yorkshire on 9 February 1867; died in Cambridge on 7 May 1934. A son of **John Naylor** and brother of **Charles Naylor**.
A chorister at York Minster under his father. Studied at the Royal College of Music and, as organ scholar, at Emmanuel College, Cambridge (1884-1888). Graduated B.A. (1887), Mus.B. (1891), M.A. (1891) and Mus.D.
Organist of the London Churches of St. Michael, Chester Square (1889-1896) and St. Mary, Kilburn (1896-1897).
Organist of Emmanuel College, Cambridge (from 1897). Assistant music master of The Leys School, Cambridge (1897-1902) and a lecturer in music at Emmanuel College (from 1902). University lecturer in music history (1926-1932).
Author of a *Shakespeare and Music* (1896), it being his aim to bring the arts of music and literature closer together.
Composed a Magnificat and Nunc Dimittis in A for Double Choir unaccompanied. Like settings by Charles Wood and Herbert Howells it is styled *Collegium Regale* on account of being composed for King's College, Cambridge. Other works include a Requiem *Pax Dei* and hymn tunes including 'From strength to strength', first published in *Public School Hymn Book* (1919). The large-scale motet *Vox dicentis, clama* is much sung during Advent and at Feasts of St. John Baptist. An early Benedicite in G achieved popularity in schools and churches. Also composed an opera *The Angelus* (1909), a cantata, part songs, and a piano trio.

NAYLOR, Dr. John (1838-1897)
Born in Stanningley, near Leeds on 8 June 1838; died on 15 May 1897 at sea, en route to Australia.
Father of **Charles Naylor** and of **Edward Naylor**.
A chorister of Leeds Parish Church, where he was a pupil and assistant of R.S. Burton. Graduated B.Mus. (1863) and D.Mus. (1872) at the University of Oxford.
Organist of St. Mary's Church (from 1856), and St. Michael's Church (from 1873), Scarborough. At St. Michael's the incumbent was **Robert Brown-Borthwick**.
Organist of York Minster (1883-1897), succeeding **E.G. Monk**. Retired through ill-health.
A local music society conductor.

Composed a Service in G, anthems including 'Out of the deep' and 'O ye that love the Lord', works for choir and military band for the annual military services held in York Minster, festival cantatas including *Jeremiah*, and hymn tunes.

NAYLOR, Kenneth Nicholson (1931-1993)
Born in Sunderland, County Durham in 1931; died in 1993. Educated at Kingswood School, Bath, Somerset Attended Magdalene College, Cambridge, graduating M.A. and Mus.B. Director of Music of The Leys School, Cambridge (from 1953); taught music at Christ's Hospital, Horsham, Sussex (1980-1986). A local orchestral society conductor. President of the Music Masters' Association (1971-1972). Composer of church music in various forms, including hymn tunes.

NAYLOR, Sydney (1841-1895)
A chorister of the Temple Church, London under **E.J. Hopkins**. Organist of St. George's Church, Bloomsbury, London; St. Michael's Church, Bassishaw and St. Mary's Church, Newington. An accompanist, pianist, conductor and composer: his works include the anthem 'Blessed are all they that fear'.

NEALE, Revd. Dr. John Mason (1818-1866)
Born in Bloomsbury, London on 24 January 1818; died in East Grinstead, Sussex on 6 August 1866.
Educated at Sherborne Grammar School, Dorset and at Trinity College, Cambridge (from 1836). Graduated B.A. (1840), ordained in 1841, and later received an honorary doctorate in divinity from an American university.
Briefly a fellow and chaplain of Downing College, Cambridge, and curate of St. Michael's Church, Guildford, Surrey.
In 1843 he was appointed curate of Crawley Parish Church, Sussex but before he could take up the appointment, a lung complaint badly affected his health and he was forced to take a long recuperation in Madeira. The congenial climate and the availability of an excellent library enabled him to continue his research and translations.
In 1846 he was appointed warden of Sackville College, East Grinstead, a position he held until the end of his life. Already a controversial figure due to his high church sympathies, the situation continued through his association with the Oxford Movement. He was constantly at odds with his bishop and he was attacked by a mob in Liverpool. At one point he was offered the position of provost of St. Ninian's Cathedral, Perth but he had to decline it, fearing that his health was too delicate for the rigours of the Scottish climate.
A leading member of the Ecclesiological Society, a body that concerned itself with what it perceived as correctness in church architecture, furnishings, vestments, ritual, historical integrity and - eventually - church music.
Set up a number of relief agencies, even though he had to overcome some bitter local opposition. The most prolific was the Sisterhood of St. Margaret (1854), which spread to other parts of the country and abroad. Its aims were to minister to the bodily and spiritual needs of the sick. Also founded an orphanage, a girls' school and, in the garrison town of Aldershot, Hampshire, a prostitutes' refuge. The latter however was forced to close in the face of local hostility.
Author of works on the subject of the Eastern Church, enhancing its understanding in this country.
Translated a hundred or so hymn texts and wrote original hymns; about an eighth of the material in *Hymns Ancient and Modern*

consisted of hymns or translations by him. His efforts made available and comprehensible some inspiring but obscure texts that were held privately in monasteries and cathedral libraries abroad. He claimed no right to his work, preferring to offer it freely to the worship of God.
Composed hymn tunes, an Easter Carol (1849) and other church music. His collections *Carols for Christmas-tide* and *Carols for Easter-tide* were both edited in 1854 by his friend and fellow-ecclesiologist **Thomas Helmore**.

NEARY, Martin Gerard James (b.1940)
Born in London on 28 March 1940.
A chorister of the Chapel Royal, St. James's Palace and was thus entitled to sing at the Coronation of Queen Elizabeth (1953). Attended the City of London School. Organ scholar of Gonville and Caius College, Cambridge (1958-1963), where he graduated M.A. in theology and music. Won a conducting scholarship to the Berkshire Music Center, Tanglewood, U.S.A. (1963).
His organ playing brought a prize at the International Organ Festival, St. Albans, in 1963 and a diploma at the Third International J.S. Bach Competition in Leipzig, Germany, in the same year.
Organist of St. Mary's Church, Hornsey Rise, London (1958). Assistant organist (1963-1965), and organist and master of the music (1965-1971) of St. Margaret's Church, Westminster. Founded the St. Margaret's Singers (1966). Conductor of the Twickenham Musical Society, Middlesex (1966-1972) and of the Waynflete Singers (1972-1988). Has toured world-wide as a recitalist, and made many recordings.
Organist and master of the music of Winchester Cathedral (1972-1987) and organist and master of the choristers of Westminster Abbey (from 1988).
Artist in residence at the University of California, Davis, U.S.A. (1984).
A professor of organ at Trinity College of Music (1963- 1972) and has been a local music society conductor. Has given national and international organ recitals and made a number of choral and organ recordings. Editor of organ music.
Has composed a set of Preces and Responses, an anthem 'What is man?', carol arrangements, and many descants.

NEEDHAM (Montgomery), Alicia Adelaide (1864-1945)
Born in Oldcastle, County Meath, Ireland on 31 October 1864; died in York on 24 December 1945.
Attended Victoria College, Londonderry and the Royal Academy of Music, where her tutors included **Ebenezer Prout**, Arthur O'Leary for piano and Davenport for harmony.
An accomplished composer, based in Clapham, London. For six consecutive years she was awarded the first prize for original songs at the Irish Music Festival. In a song competition as part of the celebrations for the Coronation of Edward VII (1902), she was awarded first prize of £100.
Composed a Service and hymn tunes. Her other works include some six hundred songs, duets and quartets; and an Irish song cycle *A Bunch of Shamrocks*.

NELSON, Dr. Havelock (b.1917)
Born in Cork, Ireland on 25 May 1917. Educated in Dublin at St. Andrew's College, Trinity College, the University of Dublin and the Irish Academy of Music. Studied privately with Jean Martinon, with Gerald Moore for piano and with Wilem Tausky for

conducting. A member of the B.B.C. Music Department, Belfast (from 1947); conductor of the Studio Symphony Orchestra (from 1948), the Studio Opera Group (from 1950) and the Ulster Singers (from 1955). Associate conductor of the B.B.C. Northern Ireland Orchestra (from 1965). A festival adjudicator at home and abroad. Composer of the three-part 'Come down, O Love divine' and 'They that wait upon the Lord', many songs and a small number of other chamber works.

NEWBOULT, Henry (19th/20th century)
Educated at the National Training School of Music. Graduated Mus.B. at the University of Cambridge (1888). Recorded as organist and choirmaster of a number of Churches that are possibly in and around Pretoria: St. John's Wesleyan Church (1881-1888), St. Andrew's (1889-1890), St. Barnabas (1890-1894) and Greenfield Congregational Church (1900-1904). Organist and choirmaster of the Wesley Church, Pretoria (from 1904). Composed as his Mus.B. exercise the anthem 'Praise the Lord, O my Soul' for Solo Voices, five-part Chorus and Strings. Composed other anthems, and part songs.

NEWELL, Joseph Edward (1843-?)
Born in Hunslet, near Leeds on 11 October 1843. Studied under **Frederick Hird**. Held a number of musical appointments in Leeds (1859-1892). Organist of St. Philip's Church, and St. Michael's, Headingley (1866-1885). Organist and singing master of Leeds Grammar School, and of St. Wilfred's Chapel. In 1892 he moved to London, where he worked as a music arranger in the publishing business. Composed a cantata *The Christian Pilgrim* which was first performed at Trinity Church, Leeds in March 1889. Also composed anthems. Used the pseudonyms Carlo Murretti and Nicola Podesta when composing works for guitar and mandolin.

NEWEY, William F. (c1850-1922)
Born between 1850 and 1860; died in Middlesex in 1922. Composer of hymn tunes.

NEWMAN, Richard Stinson (1850-1927)
Born in Wednesbury, Staffordshire in 1850; died in Abergele, Denbighshire, Wales in 1927. Organist of the Trinity Wesleyan Chapel, Wolverhampton from around 1870 for 35 years. Composed hymn tunes. His 'Companion', also known as 'A hymn for evening', was one of his 22 in *Hymns for School Festivals, Harvest Thanksgiving and other Services*.

NEWPORT, Doreen (b.1927)
Born in Manchester on 24 February 1927. Attended Somerville College, Oxford, where she read French and music. Studied for a postgraduate diploma in education at the University of Manchester. A teacher in the county of Norfolk, and leader of the Emmanuel Congregational Church, Cambridge. Married Revd. J.E. Newport, President of Cheshunt College (1951), after which she taught in Winchester, Hampshire, where her husband was a Congregational minister. Has composed hymn tunes including 'We thank You, Lord'.

NEWTON, Frank Ernest
See **BONNER**, Carey.

NEWTON, Revd. John (17th century)
Rector of Ross, Scotland from 1677. Composed the anthems 'Be merciful unto me' and 'Rejoice in the Lord'.

NEWTON, John (1802-1886)
Born in Nottingham in 1802; died in Nottingham on 4 December 1886. Attended the Castle Gate Congregational Chapel, Nottingham as a child. Around 1824, he joined the Nottingham Zion Chapel and reorganised the choir. A lace maker by trade. Due to a depression in the industry he moved to the nearby town of Beeston around 1830. There, he became choirmaster of the Wesleyan Chapel. Eventually returned to Notttingham and was choirmaster of the Parliament Street Chapel (1834-1842). Also involved with the Nottingham Choral Society. Composed hymn tunes. 'Sovereignty' was one of 28 by him in a collection *The Pilgrim*, published at some time before 1839.

NICHOL, Henry Ernest (1862-1926)
Born in Hull, Yorkshire on 10 December 1862; died in Aldborough, Skirlaugh, Yorkshire on 30 August 1926.
Apprenticed to a firm of civil engineers (from 1877) but in 1885 he decided to pursue a career in music, graduating B.Mus. at New College, Oxford in 1888.
Lived and worked in Hull as a teacher and performer of music. Music master of Hull Grammar School; organist of St. Andrew's Church, Kirk Ella, and a local choral society conductor.
The author of works on choir training and on transposition.
Composed an Evening Service in F, anthems including his B.Mus. exercise 'The Lord is my Light', other anthems, carols, cantatas such as *The Holy Grail* and *Day and Night*, part songs and piano works.
Composed hymn tunes, his 'Message' being included in the *Baptist Hymn Book* (1962). Also wrote the words and music of a number of Sunday School hymns.

NICHOLAS, John Morgan (1895-1963)
Born in Port Talbot, Glamorgan, Wales in 1895; died in Cardiff on 12 August 1963.
Studied at Eton College and, as open piano scholar, at the Royal College of Music.
Organist of the Chapel Royal, Windsor Great Park, Berkshire, deputising on occasions for **Walter Parratt**, organist of St. George's Chapel, Windsor Castle. Music master of Shrewsbury (from 1936) and Oswestry Schools, and organist of Oswestry Parish Church, Shropshire.
Director of music for Montgomeryshire, Wales (1920-1924) and chief officer of the Council of Music of the University of Wales (1947-1960). Known to radio listeners as a piano recitalist and through his talks.
Performed with the London Symphony Orchestra and with the National Orchestra of Wales. Active as a conductor at many of the major Welsh festivals.
Composed the hymn tune 'Bryn Myrddin', and an Evening Hymn for Semi Chorus, Chorus and Orchestra. His other works include songs to Welsh words, children's songs, and chamber works for oboe with piano.

NICHOLAS, Dr. Michael Bernard (b.1938)
Born in Isleworth, Middlesex on 31 August 1938.
A junior exhibitioner of Trinity College of Music (1950-1956) and organ scholar of Jesus College, Oxford (1957-1960). Studied organ

privately with John Webster and C.H. Trevor. Graduated M.A. at the University of Oxford.

Organist and choirmaster of Louth Parish Church, Lincolnshire (1960-1964) and St. Matthew's Church, Northampton (1965-1971).

Organist and master of the choristers of Norwich Cathedral, part-time lecturer in music at the University of East Anglia and conductor of Norwich Philharmonic Chorus (1971-1994).

Since 1994, chief executive of the Royal College of Organists. Director of the Allegri Singers. Well known as a recitalist and recording artist.

Has composed chants, carol arrangements and a cantata *From the Rising of the Sun*.

NICHOLDS, Joseph (?-1860)

Born in Sedgley, Staffordshire; died in poverty in Dudley, Staffordshire on 18 February 1860. Director of Wombwell's Band and a teacher of music. Composed Psalm and hymn tunes, oratorios including *Babylon* (1844), and songs.

NICHOLL, Horace Wadham (1848-1922)

Born in West Bromwich, Staffordshire on 17 March 1848; died in New York, U.S.A. in 1922. Son of a local musician. Studied with Samuel Prince. Held organistships in Staffordshire. Emigrated in his early twenties to the U.S.A., where he took jobs in Pittsburg and New York, including reader for the firm of Schirmer. Composed a Mass, anthems, four oratorios, songs, works for organ, 12 symphonic preludes, piano music and other chamber works.

NICHOLSON, Sir Sydney Hugo (1875-1947)

Born in London on 9 February 1875; died in Ashford, Kent on 30 May 1947. A son of Sir Charles Nicholson, one of the founders of the University of Sydney and its first chancellor.

Educated at Rugby School, Warwickshire; the Royal College of Music under **C.V. Stanford**, **Walter Parratt**, **Walford Davies**, and New College, Oxford. Graduated B.Mus. (1902) and M.A.

Appointed M.V.O. (1926) and knighted in 1938, in recognition of his services to church music.

Organist and choirmaster of Barnet Parish Church, Hertfordshire (from 1898) while still a student. Organist of the Lower Chapel, Eton College (from 1903). Acting organist and master of the boys of Carlisle Cathedral (1904-1908).

Organist and master of the choristers of Manchester Cathedral (1909-1918) and Westminster Abbey (1918-1927).

In 1927 he resigned his position at Westminster Abbey in order to work full-time on the establishment of the School of English Church Music and the related College of St. Nicolas at Chislehurst, Kent. The project had begun in earnest following a resolution adopted in London on St. Nicolas's Day of that year, and as a result of a survey culminating in a report *Choirs and Places*. Nicholson put up some of his personal fortune for the project, and other finances were to be derived from affiliation fees paid by choirs at home and abroad. Sydney Nicholson, who was said to be a born organiser and administrator, toured the country, lecturing and canvassing for membership. By 1950, some 3,000 choirs were affiliated. The philosophy of the S.E.C.M. was the same as his own as regards church music, and his ideals can still be recognised in the institution of today.

Organists and choristers were trained at the College, which provided a choir to sing the Morning Eucharist at St. Sepulchre's Church, Holborn, London. Annual festivals of church music were

mounted at Crystal Palace and the Royal Albert Hall. The School and College became the Royal School of Church Music in 1945.

Chairman of the Church Music Society (1919-1930). A famed organ improviser and a choir trainer with an informal approach.

Music editor (from 1913) and chief musical adviser (from 1916) to *Hymns Ancient and Modern*, and was engaged on the Revised Edition (published in 1950) when he died. In 1928 he was the first layman to become a proprietor of *Hymns Ancient and Modern*.

Compiled *A Manual of English Church Music* with **George Gardner.**

Composed an Evening Service in D-flat and another in A-flat and anthems including 'Teach us, good Lord' and 'Be strong in the Lord'. His hymn tunes include 'Barnet', 'Boston', 'Cosmos' and 'Trafalgar', all of which were included in *Hymns Ancient and Modern*, and 'Bow Brickhill'. Composed a choral ballad *Ivy* for Female Voices.

NICOLSON, Ludovick (c1770-1852)

Born in Paisley, Scotland around the year 1770; died in Paisley on 3 August 1852. A weaver by trade. Acquainted with local celebrities of the day such as the musician **Robert Archibald Smith** and the poet Tannahill. Compiled a collection of Psalm and hymn tunes. His own compositions include the hymn tunes 'Paisley' and 'Low Church'.

NICOLSON (**Nicholson**), Richard (c1570-1639)

Born around the year 1570; died in Oxford in 1639. Instructor of the choristers and, probably, organist of Magdalen College, Oxford (1595-1639). Choragus and first Heather professor of music at the University of Oxford (1626-1639). Composed the anthems 'Come, Holy Ghost' and 'O pray for the peace' and madrigals, contributing to the collection *The Triumphes of Oriana* (1601) of **Thomas Morley**. A setting by Nicolson for three voices of a poem 'The Wooing of Joan and John', which is divided in 11 sections, has been seen as the first song cycle ever composed.

NIECKS, Dr. Frederick (1845-1924)

Born in Dusseldorf, Germany on 3 February 1845; died in Edinburgh on 24 June 1924.

Educated privately, studying violin under Langhans, Grünewald and Leopold Auer, and piano with J. Tausch. Spent two terms at the University of Leipzig in 1877.

Graduated D.Mus. honorarily at the University of Dublin (1896) and awarded the LL.D. at the University of Edinburgh (1915).

A violinist in Dusseldorf (from 1857), where he was an orchestral player until 1867. By the end of this period he was also concert master. In 1868 he moved to Dumfries, Scotland where he was an organist, and played viola in a quartet that included **Alexander Mackenzie**.

After further study in Leipzig in 1877, he travelled in Italy before taking up residence in London as a critic for *Monthly Musical Record* and *Musical Times*.

Professor of music and dean of the Faculty of Music at the University of Edinburgh (1891-1914). Among his reforms were the admission of women students and a comprehensive plan for courses and examinations. Established a regular series of chamber music concerts.

Author of a number of works, including *A Concise Dictionary of Musical Terms* and *Frederick Chopin as a Man and a Musician*.

NIGHTINGALE, John Charles (1785-1837)
Organist of the Foundling Hospital. Composed the anthem 'Arise, shine!'.

NISBET, John MacDonnell (1857-1935)
Born in West Derby, Liverpool in 1857; died in Aberdeen on 9 March 1935. Educated in Liverpool. Organist of St. John's Episcopal Church, Selkirk, Scotland (from 1876) and, for a time, organist of Heatherlie Park Church. In 1878 he moved to Rothesay and became organist of New Rothesay Parish Church. Organist of St. Nicholas's Parish Church, Aberdeen (from 1890) and of Marischal College, University of Aberdeen. Taught piano at Rothesay Academy, the Church of Scotland College, Blair's College and the Convent of the Sacred Heart. A lecturer in music at Aberdeen Training College (from 1907). A member of the Music Sub Committee for the Revised Edition (1927) of *Church Hymnary*. Composed a hymn tune 'Carden Place'.

NIXON, Henry Cotter (1842-1907)
Born in London on 17 May 1842; died in Bromley, Kent on 25 December 1907.
The fourth son of **Henry George Nixon**. His maternal grandfather was the glee composer John Danby.
Studied under Harry Deval, **Henry Smart**, **Charles Macfarren** and **George Macfarren**. Graduated Mus.B. at the University of Cambridge (1876).
Organist of St. Peter's Church, Woolwich, London (1864-1868); St. James's, Spanish Place (from 1870); St. Mary's, St. Leonards-on-Sea, Sussex (1872-1877) and St. Patrick's Roman Catholic Church, Soho Square, London.
A local orchestral society conductor.
Won prizes for a piano music composition (1880), a madrigal (1889) and a two-part song (1893).
Composed a setting of Psalm 95 'O come let us sing unto the Lord' for Solo Voices, Chorus and Orchestra. His other works include a symphonic poem, *Four Concert Overtures*, a piano concerto, songs, part songs and madrigals.

NIXON, Henry George (1796-1849)
Born in Winchester, Hampshire on 20 February 1796; died in London in 1849. The father of **Henry Cotter Nixon**. Organist of St. George's Chapel, London Road (1817-1820); Warwick Street Chapel (1820-1836), St. Andrew's Roman Catholic Chapel, Glasgow (1836-1839) and St. George's Roman Catholic Cathedral, London (1839-1849). Composed five settings of the Mass and other items of music for the Roman Catholic Church, songs and piano works.

NOBLE, Harold (b.1903)
Born in Blackpool, Lancashire on 3 June 1903. A chorister of All Saints' Church, Blackpool, of which he was later director of music. Attended Blackpool Grammar School, where he was later music master. Studied music privately with Vivian Jackson, Robert Thompson and Dr. Fittwood. A baritone singer, and singing tutor. Has adjudicated at festivals of music. Conductor and Chorus Master of the B.B.C., London. Part of his responsibility was to audition the choirs of universities, cathedrals and parish churches wishing to take part in broadcast worship. Conductor of hundreds of services broadcast on radio. Has composed a Te Deum and Jubilate; Evening Canticles; a Mass *Novella Omnium Temporum*;

the anthems 'Lift up your hearts', 'God be in my head' and 'Sweet Spirit, comfort me'; chants and hymn tunes.

NOBLE, Dr. Thomas Tertius (1867-1953)
Born in Bath, Somerset on 5 May 1867; died in Rockport, Massachusetts, U.S.A. on 4 May 1953.
The uncle of Ray Noble, band leader.
Took private tuition with Revd. C. Everitt in Colchester, Essex (from 1881) and was appointed organist of All Saints' Church, Colchester at the age of 14.
Exhibitioner and scholar at the Royal College of Music under **Walter Parratt** for organ, and **C.V. Stanford** and **Frederick Bridge** for theory. Also a pupil of **Edwin Nunn**.
Graduated M.A. at Columbia University, U.S.A. (1918) and D.Mus. at Trinity College Hartford, U.S.A. Accorded the Lambeth D.Mus in 1932.
Organist of St. John's Church, Wilton Road, London (from 1889) and assistant organist at Trinity College, Cambridge (1890-1892) to Stanford.
Organist and master of the choristers of Ely Cathedral (1892-1898) and of York Minster (1898-1913).
Organist (from 1898) and conductor (until 1912) of the York Symphony Orchestra, which he founded.
Resigned the organistship of York Minster in order to take up the position of organist of St. Thomas's Episcopal Church, New York. He remained there until his retirement in 1947, which was marked on 26 February by a recital of his own works. Founded a choir school at St. Thomas's (1919).
Author of *The Training of the Boy Chorister* (1943).
Composed Morning and Evening Services in A and in A Minor; his famous Evening Service in B Minor was written at the instigation of Walter Parratt, who challenged him to produce a work similar in style to the D Minor Evening Service of **T.A. Walmisley**. Composed anthems including 'Grieve not the Holy Spirit'; the hymn tunes 'York Minster' and 'Eastwick', both of which were used in *Hymns Ancient and Modern*; chamber music, pieces for violin; a comic opera and orchestral and organ works. The hymn tune 'Ora labora', much sung in the U.S.A., was composed for the school hymn of the Choir School of Saint Thomas 5th Avenue 'Come labour on: who dares stand idle on the harvest-plain?'.

NORRIS, Thomas (c1675-c1710)
A chorister and gentleman of the Chapel Royal. A lay vicar of Lincoln Cathedral (from 1686). Steward of the choristers (from 1693) and may have been master of the choristers. Some church music by him remains in manuscript. Among his published works is a Chant in A-flat, found in *Congregational Praise* (1951).

NORRIS, Thomas (1741-1790)
Born in Mere, near Salisbury, Wiltshire in about August 1741; died in Himley Hall, Staffordshire on 3 September 1790. His death was said to be at least partly due to overwork in connection with the Birmingham Festival.
A chorister of Salisbury Cathedral under **John Stephens**. Graduated B.Mus. at St. John's College, Oxford (1865).
Organist of Christ Church Cathedral, Oxford (1776-1790) and St. John's College, Oxford (1776-1790). A lay clerk of the two Oxford Colleges of Christ Church (from 1767) and Magdalen (from 1771). A tenor soloist, he sang at the Three Choirs' Festivals of 1761 and 1762 at Hereford and Worcester, at the Handel Commemoration of 1784 and at the Drury Lane Theatre.

Unfortunately, his career was marked by excessive drinking, and it was said that at a festival in Westminster Abbey in 1789 he was barely able to hold the book from which he was singing.

Composed anthems including 'Hear my prayer, O Lord' and 'The Lord is King', hymns, glees, songs and six symphonies.

NORRIS, William (1676-1710)
A chorister of the Chapel Royal in 1685. Master of the choristers of Lincoln Cathedral. Composed anthems including 'Behold, now praise' and 'My heart rejoiceth'.

NORTH, John William Allen (1869-1937)
Born in Wakefield, Yorkshire in 1869; died in Birkdale, Southport, Lancashire on 15 August 1937. Composer of hymn tunes.

NORTHROP, Abraham (1863-1938)
Born in Hartlepool, County Durham in 1863; died in Hartlepool on 30 August 1938. Organist and choirmaster of Burbank Church, West Hartlepool (from 1886). Composer of hymn tunes.

NOTTINGHAM, Spenser (1822-1908)
Born in 1822; died in Bedford Park, Chiswick, West London on 17 December 1908. Precentor of the Church of St. Matthias, Stoke Newington, London (1852-1856), where **W.H. Monk** was organist from the same year. Honorary choirmaster of St. Mary's Church, Chiswick (1868-1872). It is said that he played a part in the revival of plainsong, for which, with **John Doran** he compiled a *Directory* (1908). Composed hymn tunes including 'Bride of Christ', used in *Hymns Ancient and Modern*.

NOVELLO, Francis Vincent (1781-1861)
Born in London on 6 September 1781; died in Nice, France on 9 August 1861.
Educated at Huitmille, near Boulogne, France. A chorister under **Samuel Webbe** the elder at the Sardinian Embassy Chapel, Duke Street, London.
Deputy to Samuel Webbe, and to John Danby at the chapel of the Spanish Embassy, Manchester Square.
Organist of the Portuguese Chapel (1797-1822) and of the Roman Catholic Chapel at Moorfields, London (1840-1843).
Founded Novello and Company (1811), the first publication being *A Collection of Sacred Music* in two volumes. Other editions that followed included the collected works of **William Croft** and of **Maurice Greene**.
Pianist to the Italian Opera in London (1812). One of the founders of the Philharmonic Society (1812), and sometimes conductor of the concerts.
A Purcell enthusiast, he wrote a biography of the composer in 1832. In 1849 he retired to Nice. A collection *The Psalmist* was published in four individual volumes between 1835 and 1843. Most of the harmonies were written by him.
His compositions include anthems of which examples are 'Like as the hart', 'God be merciful' and 'Rejoice in the Lord', hymn tunes including 'Albano' and 'Penshurst', both of which were used in *Hymns Ancient and Modern*, other items of church music, songs, glees and organ works. *Cathedral Psalter Chants* (1875) contains a Single Chant in A.

NUNN, Edward Cuthbert (?1869-1915)
Died on 26 November 1915 at the age of 46. Studied at the Royal Academy of Music as Sterndale Bennett Scholar, winning the Lucas Prize. Lived in Leytonstone, Essex, where he was organist of St. John's Church for 25 years. A piano recitalist, a teacher and a composer of church music. Composed an Evening Service, a setting of Psalm 100 'O be joyful in the Lord' for Solo Voices and Chorus, songs, operettas, organ works and cantatas including *Everyman*.

NUNN, Elizabeth Annie (1860-1894)
Born in 1860; died in Fallowfield, Manchester on 7 January 1894. Composed a Mass in C for Solo Voices, Chorus and Orchestra, and other church music.

NUNN, John Hopkins (1827-1905)
Born in Bury St. Edmunds on 10 November 1827; died in Penzance, Cornwall on 17 October 1905. Studied at the Royal Academy of Music (1848-1851). He held an organistship in Sherborne, Dorset in 1852. Moved to Penzance two years later, where he was organist of St. Mary's Church for 35 years (from 1859). A local choral and philharmonic society conductor. Composed a Te Deum setting, and anthems.

O

OAKELEY, Sir Herbert Stanley (1830-1903)

Born in Ealing, London on 20 July 1830; died in Eastbourne, Sussex on 26 October 1903.

The son of Revd. Sir Herbert Oakeley, vicar of Ealing and later Archdeacon of Colchester.

Attended Rugby School, Warwickshire before going up to Christ Church, Oxford where he graduated B.A. (1853) and M.A. (1856). Learned harmony under **Stephen Elvey**, following which he studied in Leipzig under Louis Plaidy, Ignaz Moscheles and Papperitz, at Dresden with Johann Schneider and in Bonn under H. Karl Breidenstein.

Awarded the Lambeth D.Mus. and nine university doctorates in music including those of Cambridge (1871) and Oxford (1879). Also held the law degrees of LL.D. and D.C.L.

In 1876 Herbert Oakeley was knighted by Queen Victoria following his services as composer and director of music at the inauguration of the Scottish National Monument to Prince Albert.

A lecturer and organ recitalist. In 1865 he succeeded John Donaldson as Reid professor of music at the University of Edinburgh, a controversial appointment in that he was not a professional musician. He retained the professorship until 1891, and he was organist of the Episcopal Church of St. Paul.

At Edinburgh he also had the responsibility of conducting the Reid Concerts. Part of the achievement of his 26 years as professor was the introduction of formal examinations for musical degrees. A more general achievement in Scottish music was to help win the acceptance of the organ in the services of the Scottish Church. In 1892 he was named Emeritus professor.

Composer to the Queen in Scotland (from 1881). A reporter on music festivals and concerts to *The Manchester Guardian*, for whom he was music critic (1858-1868).

Composed a Service in E-flat, an anthem 'Behold, now praise the Lord', Psalms, and hymn tunes including 'Abends', 'Edina' and 'Dominica'. *Cathedral Psalter Chants* (1875) contains a Double Chant in D and a Quadruple Chant in F by Herbert Oakeley. Also composed songs, duets, instrumental works and works for organ.

OAKEY, George (1841-1927)

Born in St. Pancras, London on 14 October 1841; died in Goodmayes, Romford, Essex on 9 June 1927. Self-taught musically, graduating Mus.B. at the University of Cambridge

(1877). An examiner in harmony and composition at the Tonic Sol-fa College and a professor in the same subjects at the City of London College. Author of text books on music. Composed anthems including 'Blessed be the Lord', hymns, chants and part songs including 'The daisies peep'.

OBERTHUR, Charles (1819-1895)

A pupil of G.V. Röder. A harpist, who worked at the Zurich Theatre and the Wiesbaden Court Theatre, and in Mannheim. Moved to London (1844) and worked for the Italian Theatre. A teacher and composer, whose works include the anthem 'Give ear, O Lord'.

O'CONNOR-MORRIS, Geoffrey (1886-1964)

Born in Thun, Switzerland in 1886; died in 1964. Educated in Dublin and at the Royal College of Music. Assistant organist of Carlisle Cathedral (from 1903) and organist of St. Cuthbert's Church, Carlisle. Organist of St. John's Church, Wilton Square, London and of St. Paul's, Onslow Square (1910-1918). At some time after World War I he was conductor of the Carl Rosa Opera Company. An accompanist and opera coach. Also known to have worked for the B.B.C. During World War II he was a professor at Guildhall School of Music. An examiner for Trinity College of Music. Composed a Communion Service in E-flat (1922); orchestral works, some of which were performed at the Promenade Concerts; and organ works.

OKELAND, Christopher (16th century)

A contemporary of **Thomas Tallis**. Composed anthems including 'Grant, we beseech Thee' and 'The King shall rejoice'.

OKELAND, Robert (16th century)

An adult member of the choir of the Chapel Royal, joining after 1526 and still a member in 1547. Composed the anthems 'Praise the Lord, O our souls' and 'Praise we the Father'.

OKEOVER (Oker), John (17th century)

Graduated B.Mus. at the University of Oxford (1633).

Probably employed at Ingatestone Hall, Essex, in 1616. His name is also carved in the organ loft of Winchester College Chapel.

From 1619 or 1620 until 1640 he was a vicar choral and organist of Wells Cathedral. Additionally master of the choristers (from 1625), replacing William Tailer.

From time to time he was in dispute with the cathedral authorities: at Archbishop Laud's visitation of 1634 it was said that the choristers were unruly.

Organist of Gloucester Cathedral (1640-1644) and, following the period of the Commonwealth, he was reappointed organist of Wells Cathedral (1660-1663). However, it is possible that there may be more than one person of this name at that time - possibly father and son - and that the Gloucester position was held by the namesake.

Composed anthems including 'The King shall rejoice' and 'God shall send forth His mercy and truth', and works for viol.

OLDEN, George Ronaldson Cuming (c1870-1952)
Born some time between 1870 and 1880; died in Rostrevor, County Down, Ireland on 7 May 1952. A composer of hymn tunes and the carol 'The Light of man' (1915).

OLDHAM, Arthur William (b.1926)
Born in Wandsworth, London on 6 September 1926.

Educated at Wallington County Grammar School, Surrey and at the Royal College of Music.

Director of music of the Ballet Rambert (1946-1947) and of the Mercury Theatre (from 1949). Chorus master of the Edinburgh Festival, Scottish Opera (from 1966) and London Symphony Orchestra. Director of the Scottish Festival Chorus (from 1965). Director of music of the Mercury Theatre (1945-1946).

Director of music of St. Mary's Roman Catholic Cathedral (from 1957).

Composed a setting of the Mass, anthems, and the hymn tunes 'Laudes creaturarum' and 'In nomine Jesu'. In addition he composed incidental music for films and radio, and ballets including *Mr. Punch*.

OLDROYD, Dr. George (1886-1951)
Born in Healey, Yorkshire in 1886; died on 26 February 1951.

Trained privately in music with A. Eaglefield Hull. For violin, he studied with Johann Rasch and Frank Arnold. Graduated B.Mus. (1912) and D.Mus. (1917) at the University of London. Awarded the Lambeth D.Mus. (1951).

A professor of organ, solo singing, voice production, harmony, theory, counterpoint and the rudiments of music at Trinity College of Music.

Assistant organist of Huddersfield Parish Church, Yorkshire. Organist and choirmaster of the Churches of St. Andrew, Halstead, Essex (from 1909); St. George, Paris; St. Alban, Holborn, London and St. Michael, Croydon, Surrey. Taught violin at Earl's Colne Grammar School and was a professor and examiner of T.C.M., where he served on the board of governors.

King Edward professor of music at the University of London (from 1951).

Author of *The Technique and Spirit of Fugue*, a subject on which he was an authority.

Composed a Stabat Mater, a setting of the Magnificat and Nunc Dimittis in A and of the Holy Comunion Service in D: the Mass *Of the Quiet Hour* (1928), dedicated to the Archbishop of Canterbury. On a larger scale there are also a highly-regarded *Stabat Mater* and *A Spiritual Rhapsody*. Composer of a part song 'Lute book lullaby', organ works including a Liturgical Prelude, and pieces for piano and for violin.

O'LEARY, Arthur (1834-1919)
Born in Tralee, County Kerry, Ireland on 15 May 1834; died on 13 March 1919.

His grandfather was a teacher of music, his father was organist of Tralee Parish Church and his uncle was organist of Killarney Cathedral. His father was the first cousin of **Arthur Sullivan**'s grandfather.

Able to study due to the patronage of Wyndham Gould, firstly in Dublin (1844-1846) and at Leipzig Conservatory (from 1847) under Louis Plaidy, Ernst Richter, Ignaz Moscheles, Moritz Hauptmann and Julius Rietz. Took part in Mendelssohn's funeral procession (1847). Attended the Royal Academy of Music (from 1852) and studied under Cipriani Potter and **William Sterndale Bennett**.

A professor of the R.A.M. (1852-1903), his pupils including Arthur Sullivan and **C.V. Stanford**. Taught at the National Training School of Music (from 1876) and, from its opening in 1880, at Guildhall School of Music. A recitalist, lecturer and writer.

Composed a Mass *of St. John* and edited settings of the Mass by other composers. Also composed orchestral works, including a Symphony in C, songs, and pieces for piano.

OLIVERS, Thomas (1725-1799)
Born in Tregynon, Montgomeryshire, Wales in 1725; died in London in March 1799.

Orphaned at the age of four and had little formal education. Apprenticed to a shoemaker (from 1743) and worked as a cobbler.

In 1753, on hearing George Whitfield preach in Bristol, Thomas Olivers was converted to the Methodist cause. He paid off his debts and became a travelling preacher. For 22 years he roamed through England, Scotland and Ireland.

Appointed supervisor of the Methodist Press (1775), but was removed in 1789 following some problems of quality.

Issued many controversial pamphlets. A writer of hymns, of which the most enduring is 'The God of Abraham praise', inspired by the singing of the *Yigdal*, the Hebrew Confession.

His hymn tune 'Olivers', also known as 'Helmsley' (1765) was said later to be a favourite of Queen Victoria.

ORCHARD, Edwin John (1834-1914)
Born in Bristol, Gloucestershire in 1834; died in Salisbury, Wiltshire on 5 November 1914. A composer of hymn tunes.

ORCHARD, William Arundel (c1868-1961)
Died at sea at the age of 93 on 7 April 1961.

Trained privately in music. Graduated B.Mus. (1893) at the University of Durham.

Held the two organistships of St. Paul's, Finchley (from 1889) and St. Jude's, Gray's Inn Road (from 1891) in London before emigrating to Australia around 1892.

Organist of the Cathedrals of St. George, Perth, Western Australia (from 1895) and St. David, Hobart, Tasmania (from 1897).

Organist of St. Stephen's Church, Colorado Springs, U.S.A. (from 1900) before returning to Australia. Music master of Craven College and the conductor of musical and orchestral societies including the Sydney Liedertafel (from 1903) and the Sydney Symphony Orchestra (1908-1909). Director of the New South Wales State Conservatory (1923-1934).

Composed as his B.Mus. exercise a setting of Psalm 100 'O be joyful in the Lord'. Also composed an oratorio *Easter Morn*

(1892), a Three-Act opera *A Picture of Dorian Gray,* and works for piano and for string orchestra.

ORD, Dr. Bernhard 'Boris' (1897-1961)

Born in Clifton, Gloucestershire on 9 July 1897; died in Cambridge on 30 December 1961.

His teachers in music included **Walter Parratt**. Educated at Clifton College and at Corpus Christi College, Cambridge, where he was organ scholar (from 1919) and John Stewart of Rannoch scholar in sacred music (1920). Graduated M.A., Mus.B. and, honorarily, D.Mus. (1960). Received the honorary D.Mus. at the University of Durham (1955).

Appointed C.B.E. in 1958.

Served in World War I as a pilot and was wounded twice. Worked for a year at the Cologne Opera (1927).

Organist of King's College, Cambridge (1929-1958). In World War II he was a flight lieutenant (1941-1945), taking part in the Normandy Landings. During his absence on active service, **Harold Darke** acted as his deputy. A lecturer in music at Cambridge University (1936-1958); university organist (1929-1958). A conductor and a harpsichordist, specialising in continuo playing. An adjudicator at festivals of music.

Composed the carol 'Adam lay ybounden'.

ORD-HUME, Ian Donald (b.1948)

Born in Bromley, Kent on 28 November 1948. Grandson of John Ord-Hume, and great-grandson of James Ord-Hume: both were composers for military brass band. A solicitor, practising in Wokingham, Berkshire. Organist of the Berkshire Churches of St. John the Evangelist, Woodley (1975-1983) and St. Paul, Wokingham (from 1983). Composer of the anthems 'We have a King who came to earth' and 'Christ is now risen again'. A number of unpublished works exist, all of which were written for a specific choir, group or occasion. These include the Missa *Sancti Pauli,* a setting of the Rite B Anglican Mass for the Choir of St. Paul's, Wokingham; the unaccompanied motet *Sweet the Moments* for Holy Week, and numerous Psalm chants and hymn descants.

ORR, Dr. Robin Kemsley (b.1909)

Born in Brechin, Angus, Scotland on 2 June 1909.

Educated at Loretto School, the Royal College of Music, Pembroke College, Cambridge (as organ scholar) and at the Accademia Musicale Chigiana, Siena, Italy. Also studied privately with Alfredo Casella, Nadia Boulanger and E.J. Dent.

Graduated M.A. and Mus.D. at the University of Cambridge. Received the honorary doctorates of D.Mus (Glasgow, 1972) and LL.D. (Dundee, 1976). A fellow of St. John's College, Cambridge (1948-1956; 1965-1976); an honorary fellow of St. John's College (1987) and Pembroke College (1988), Cambridge.

Appointed C.B.E. in 1972.

Director of music of Sidcot School, Somerset (1933-1936) and assistant lecturer in music at the University of Leeds (1936-1938). Organist and director of studies in music at St. John's College, Cambridge (1938-1951).

During World War II he was a flight lieutenant in the Royal Air Force Volunteer Reserve, serving in the Photographic Intelligence Unit.

A lecturer in music at the University of Cambridge (1947-1956). A professor of theory and composition at the R.C.M. (1950-1956). A liveryman of the musicians' company, London.

Gardiner professor of music at the University of Glasgow (1956-1965), and professor of music at the University of Cambridge (1965-1976).

Chairman of Scottish Opera (1962-1976), a director of the Arts Theatre, Cambridge (1970-1975) and a director of Welsh National Opera (1977-1983).

Composed a Te Deum and Jubilate in C (1953), a Festival Te Deum (1950), a Magnificat and Nunc Dimittis in C (1967), and the anthems 'I was glad' and 'Sing aloud unto God'.

His hymn tune 'Lochwinnoch' was used in the Third Edition (1973) of *Church Hymnary* with 'From glory to glory advancing', a paraphrase of the Litany of Dismissal in the fifth century Liturgy of St. James. His secular works include an opera *On the Razzle,* a Rhapsody for String Orchestra, songs, organ works, three symphonies including the Symphony in One Movement (1963), and operas such as *Full Circle* (1968).

OSBORNE, George Alexander (1806-1893)

Born in Limerick, Ireland in 1806; died in 1893. A pupil of Johann Pixis, François-Joseph Fétis and Friedrich Kalkbrennner in Paris. Moved to London (1843) and worked as a pianist, teacher and composer of chamber music. A friend of Berlioz and Chopin. Composed the anthems 'Hail! Thou that art highly favoured' and 'The Lord is my Shepherd'.

OSBORNE, Nigel (b.1948)

Born on 23 June 1948.

Studied at the University of Oxford. Studied composition with **Kenneth Leighton** and serial techniques with Egon Wellesz. Continued his studies at the Warsaw Academy and at the Polish Radio Experimental Studio.

A lecturer in music at the University of Nottingham (1978-1986); professor of music at the University of Edinburgh (from 1990).

Has composed a setting of the Rite A version of Holy Communion. His other works include the operas *The Electrification of the Soviet Union* (1987) and *Terrible mouth,* and Sinfonia I, commissioned for the Promenade Concerts of 1982.

OSMOND, Harold Bartrum (1869-?)

Born in Southampton, Hampshire on 19 January 1869.

Studied at Guildhall School of Music under D. Beardswell and **Henry Gadsby**.

Organist of the churches of St. Peter, Bethnal Green, London (from 1884); St. Barnabas, Homerton (from 1886) and St. Peter's-in-Thanet, Broadstairs, Kent (from 1889). Organist and choirmaster of Holy Trinity Church, Coventry, Warwickshire (from 1918).

A choral society conductor.

Composed a setting of Holy Communion in E, anthems, a sacred cantata *The Ascension* (1886) and orchestral works.

OUSELEY, Revd. Sir Frederick Arthur Gore (1825-1889)

Born in London on 12 August 1825; died in Hereford on 6 April 1889.

His father was Sir Gore Ouseley, an oriental scholar who was Ambassador to Persia and, later, to St. Petersburg. Sir Gore was also one of the founders of the Royal Academy of Music (1822). His Godparents were the Duke of York and the Duke of Wellington.

He did not attend school, being privately educated at home. Until 1832 he lived at Woolmer's, Hertingfordbury, Hertfordshire and thereafter at Hall Barn Park near Beaconsfield, Buckinghamshire.

A number of youthful musical exploits are documented. He played duets with Queen Victoria and entertained her as Princess Victoria at Kensington Palace with his singing, playing and composing. He claimed to have played a duet with Mendelssohn at the age of six when the latter visited the family home. A duet by Ouseley was published in 1834.

Studied with Revd. James Joyce, vicar of Dorking, Surrey (from 1840). Went up to Christ Church, Oxford as a gentleman commoner (1843). Something of a practical joker (see **Charles Corfe**), he may perhaps have neglected his studies.

Active musically as an undergraduate. Organised concerts and glee singing, and acted as organist for a few months between the resignation of **William Marshall** and the appointment of Charles Corfe (1846). He took lessons in theory and composition with **Stephen Elvey**. Some claim to detect the influence of **William Crotch**, university professor, in Ouseley's compositions but by that time, Crotch was professionally inactive and the two men may never have met.

Unlike other prominent 19th century composers of church music, Ouseley was never a boy chorister of a cathedral or collegiate church. He may not even have known the standard cathedral music repertory when he went up to Christ Church, and when he arrived there he encountered a cathedral choir that was one of the worst in the country. During his undergraduate days he composed some church music, including Services in G and in A. At this time he may also have recognised the need to improve cathedral music standards and possibly the desirability of an institution where this could be encouraged.

Performed poorly in the finals of his B.A. examination although he passed. He had been expected to do well in mathematics. His later degrees were the Oxford M.A. (1849), B.Mus. (1850) and D.Mus. (1854), the Durham M.A. and D.Mus. (1856) and the Cambridge Mus.D. (1862). The Universities of Cambridge and Edinburgh each conferred the LL.D. upon him

Lived in London following his graduation. He did some of his reading for ordination with Revd. James Wayland Joyce, rector of Burford and the son of Ouseley's former tutor, Revd. James Joyce. This involved visiting Joyce on the Herefordshire/Worcestershire border near Tenbury. While in London he sang in the choir of his local Parish Church of St. Paul, Knightsbridge.

This time excelling in his examinations, he was ordained deacon in 1849. Became an honorary curate in his home parish of St. Paul's, Knightsbridge, within which was being built the daughter church of St. Barnabas, Pimlico. The new church was actually part of a college community to consist of a parish school, and living accommodation for the clergy and for 12 chorister boys.

The new church with its immediate reputation for ritual aroused angry passions in the neighbourhood. On Saturday 9 November 1850, Ouseley was confronted in the street. The following day, Evening Service was cancelled as a precaution when trouble threatened.

A week later, a hundred police kept an angry mob at bay during the service and there were disturbances for the next three Sundays. Later that year, the vicar, Revd. W.J.E. Bennett, Ouseley and his two fellow curates resigned. Ouseley, suffering from nervous exhaustion, set off on a tour of Europe, having made provision for the nine remaining resident choristers whose services were no longer required at St. Barnabas. The boys were boarded at Langley House, near Langley, Berkshire.

Ouseley's European journey took in Portugal, Spain, Rome, Venice and Germany, where he was very impressed with the singing of the boy trebles in Leipzig and Dresden. Being a wealthy man he was able to add to his growing library of valuable music manuscripts. The trip decided Ouseley against any ideas he may have had of going over to the Roman Catholic Church.

By September 1851 Ouseley had clarified his objectives, which were the setting up of a place of daily choral worship, the provision of a liberal and classical education to sons of the clergy and the raising of standards of adult singing and chanting, with a view to improving choral cathedral services. Following a short search for a suitable location he established the Church and College of St. Michael, Tenbury, Worcestershire. Land was purchased in June 1852 and the foundation stone was laid on 3 May 1854.

The small community at Lovehill House had thrived in the meantime. Two of the original 12 boys of 1850 sang as adults at the consecration of St. Michael's on 29 September 1856. Ouseley was the College's first warden. The second organist was **John Stainer**. St. Michael's College continued in existence until 1985. It surely achieved and exceeded the aims of its founder. Ouseley's collection of music and manuscripts was preserved there until its removal to Oriel College, Oxford.

Ouseley had delayed his ordination to the priesthood until 1855. In the same year he was appointed precentor of Hereford Cathedral, a position that carried no financial reward and continued in existence largely through the determination of the bishop. Ouseley's sole duty was to preach a sermon on Christmas Day: a succentor was responsible for the day-to-day musical activity. Ouseley was appointed a canon residentiary of Hereford Cathedral in 1886.

When, following the death of **Henry Bishop**, the Oxford professorship of music fell vacant (1855), Ouseley was appointed. The salary was only £100 per annum but the duties were minimal. There were no student lectures, no form of teaching and no curriculum. All he was required to do was conduct examinations for music degrees and give public lectures.

Ouseley carried out a number of reforms along the lines of those already instituted at the Universities of Cambridge and Dublin. There had only been 35 graduations in music between 1800 and 1849 at Oxford and in Ouseley's time the numbers increased slightly. Music still lacked the prestige of other Oxford degrees; there was still no teaching of undergraduates and no requirement of residence at the end of Ouseley's term in office.

Ouseley had been associated with high churchmanship in his days at St. Barnabas, Pimlico but in fact this was only true to a degree and he opposed what he perceived as extreme ritualism and the restrictiveness of its musical manifestation, congregational Gregorian Chant. In 1876 he deplored the growing use in church of music more suited to the concert hall. He urged church music composers to become thoroughly familiar with strict counterpoint in order to be aware of the proper style.

Author of works on harmony, counterpoint, musical form and composition. He made a valuable collection of antiquarian music (both printed and in manuscript) and musical literature which he bequeathed to St. Michael's College, almost the whole of which is now in the Bodleian Library, Oxford.

Ouseley revised and approved the music of the original version of *Hymns Ancient and Modern* (1861) in collaboration with **W.H. Monk**, with whom he collaborated in *Anglican Psalter Chants* (1876). His view was that hymns should have "strong, healthy, hearty tunes", avoiding the mawkish, the sentimental and the secular. He canvassed his contemporary composers including - unsuccessfully - **S.S. Wesley** to contribute items to his collection

Special Anthems for Certain Seasons, which was published in 1861.

Composed Services in A, in E and in G, and a hundred or so anthems, including 'It came to pass' and 'How goodly are Thy tents', which was inspired by the sight of the plain of Lombardy in bright sunshine, causing him to recall the words of Numbers 24 vv5-6: As the valleys are they spread forth, as gardens by the riverside... and as cedar trees beside the waters. 'Is it nothing to you?' was composed for Good Friday. 'From the rising of the sun' is widely performed. Also known for his eight-part motet *O Saviour of the world*.

Cathedral Psalter Chants (1875) featured Single Chants by him and a set of Responses to the Commandments published around the same time contained five settings by him in A, in B Minor, in C, in E-flat and in E.

His hymn tunes include 'Aberystwyth', 'Brightness' and 'Christchurch' which, with six others, were included in *Hymns Ancient and Modern*. 'Woolmer's' was composed for the consecration of St. Michael's, Tenbury in September 1856. His other works include operas, oratorios, organ works, two string quartets, songs and part songs.

OVERTON, James Ingham (1864-1927)

Born in Burnley, Lancashire in 1864; died in Bradford, Yorkshire on 23 January 1927. A composer of hymn tunes.

OWEN, John (Owain Alaw: 1821-1883)

Born in Chester of Welsh parents on 14 November 1821; died in Chester on 30 January 1883. The father of **William Henry Owen**.

Apprenticed to the firm of Powell and Edwards, cutlers of Chester. Studied music with Edward Peters of Chester and with C. Lucas (presumably Charles Lucas) of London.

A manual worker until 1844, when he took up a career in music. While young, he was organist of the Countess of Huntingdon's Chapel, probably in Chester. Organist of St. Paul's Church, Broughton; St. Bride's Church, Chester and St. Mary's Welsh Church, Chester. A strong believer in the value of musical education. A baritone singer.

He was given the name Owain Alaw at the Rhuddlan Eisteddfod (1851), at which he won a prize for his anthem 'Deborah a balac'. A prize winner at other *eisteddfodau* for his compositions. Issued *Gems of Welsh Melodies* (1860), a collection of tunes. Editor of the music series *Y Gyfres Gerddoral*. An accompanist and adjudicator throughout Wales.

Composed anthems including 'Pa fodd y glanha' and 'Gwyn fyd ystyria wrth y tlawd', an oratorio *Jeremiah* (1878), cantatas including *The Prince of Wales*, said to be the first secular cantata in the Welsh language (but see the rival claim of **J.A. Lloyd**), glees and songs. Published collections of hymns for use in Sunday Schools. One of his hymn tunes is 'Calfari'.

OWEN, John (Ap Glaslyn: 1857-1934)

Born in Beddgelert, Wales on 6 May 1857; died, possibly in Llanbradach, Wales on 16 April 1934. Educated at the local school. Became a pupil teacher and then worked in slate quarries at Ffestiniog and Llanberis. An actor and singer. Worked for the temperance movement and for the Good Templars during the religious revival of 1904-1905, during and for which he composed the words and music of songs. Subsequently became a preacher, serving as a minister of the Calvinistic Methodist Church. Was associated with the Forward Movement of South Wales in Geli,

Rhondda and Llanbradach. Published the book *Y Llenor Ieunae* (1876).

OWEN, Morfydd Llwyn

See **JONES**, Morfydd Llwyn.

OWEN, Richard Griffith (Pencerdd Llyfnwy: 1869-1930)

Born in Tal-y-Sarn, Caernarvonshire, Wales on 1 April 1869; died on 24 May 1930. Played cello and clarinet. Published a collection of hymn tunes *Llais y Durtur*. Arranged works for orchestra to accompany the singing at festivals held by the Calvinistic Methodists and Congregationalists in the county of Caernarvonshire and elsewhere. Won a prize at the Corwen National Eisteddfod (1919) for his orchestral arrangement of Welsh airs. Also won prizes for a temperance cantata and for anthems. His tunes are also found in *Llyfr Tonau y Methodistaid Calfinaidd a Wesleyaidd* and *Perorydd yr Ysgol Sul*.

OWEN, William (1830-1865)

Born in Tremadoc, Caernarvonshire, Wales on 11 May 1830; died on 2 August 1865. Attended the British School at Pont-y-nys-Galch, Portmadoc. Also studied with Owen Griffith (Garn Dolbenmaen) and took organ lessons with a Mrs. Coventry, the niece of the Earl of Coventry. Worked in the timber trade. An accomplished amateur composer. His anthem 'Cân Moses a chân yr oen' won a prize at the Besthesda Eisteddfod (1851), and won composition prizes at other *eisteddfodau*. Composed the hymn tune 'Porthmadog', and carols.

OWEN, William (Gwilym Ddu Glan Hafren: 1788-1838)

Born in Brynhafod, Clynnog, Caernarvonshire, Wales in 1788; died on 8 October 1838. Around the year 1815 he moved to Welshpool, where he worked as a school teacher. He then moved to Newtown. A bard, musician, Calvinist Methodist preacher and contributor to periodicals. He dedicated a book to John Jenkins (Ifor Keri), incumbent of Kerry, Montgomeryshire. Issued *Y Caniedydd Crefyddor* (The Sacred Songbook) in 1828. It contained articles on the principles of music, essays by various writers on music, and a collection of tunes. The articles have been condemned as poorly written and riddled with errors and some of the tunes are said to be weak.

OWEN, William 'of Prysgol' (1813-1893)

William Owen of Prysgol was born in Bangor, Caernarvonshire, Wales on 12 December 1813; died in Caernarvon on 20 July 1893. The son of a quarryman.

Grew up in Bethesda, North Wales. Worked in a slate quarry from the age of 10. Lived near St. Anne's Church and he took every opportunity to hear the organ played. Attended music classes given by **Robert Williams** (Cae Aseth) at Carneddi and by **William Roberts** (Tyn-y-Mais), composer of the hymn tune 'Andalusia'. He himself became a good musician and began to compose at an early age. When the family moved to Bangor, William Owen formed a temperance choir there. Later moved to Prysgol, near Caernarvon. Choirmaster of Caethraw Chapel.

In 1852 he published *Y Perl Cerddorol* (The musical Pearl), in which were a number of his own hymn tunes and anthems. It sold some 3,000 copies before being brought out in a Tonic Sol-fa edition (1886), which sold 4,000 copies.

His first hymn tune was composed at the age of 18 and published in the June 1841 issue of *Y Drysorfa*. Many of his hymn tunes were specifically for the temperance movement.

He is now remembered for 'Bryn Calfaria' in particular. It was included in *English Hymnal* (1906) whose editor, **Ralph Vaughan Williams** also wrote an organ prelude based on the tune.

OWEN, William Henry (1845-1868)
Born in Chester in 1845; died in Abergele, Wales on 20 August 1868 in a railway accident. The son of **John Owen** (Owain Alaw). An organist in Dublin. Composed a setting of the Magnificat, and anthems in Welsh.

OXENHAM, John
See **DUNKERLEY**, William Arthur.

OXLEY, Thomas Frederick Harrison (b.1933)
Born in Sheffield on 3 April 1933. Harrison Oxley was foundation scholar at King Edward School, Birmingham. Organ scholar of Christ Church, Oxford (1951-1955), where he graduated M.A. and B.Mus. Assistant organist of Birmingham Cathedral (1950-1951) and of Christ Church Cathedral, Oxford (1953-1955). Served in the Royal Signals Orchestra (1956-1957). Organist and master of the choristers of St. Edmundsbury Cathedral (1958-1984) at the age of 24. Conductor of St. Edmundsbury Bach Choir and Orchestra (from 1958). Now a freelance organist, examiner, conductor and composer. He has composed carols, the anthem 'The eternal Spirit' and the collection of Psalm settings *Ring out your joy*. His arrangement of 'Mater, ora Filium' is widely sung. More recently, many of his editions and arrangements of choral and organ music have been published.

P

PAGE (Cliff), Alice Mary (19th/20th century)
Graduated B.Mus. (1904) at the University of Durham. Lived in Leeds. Composed as her degree exercise the anthem 'Great is our Lord' for Soprano, Chorus and Strings. Also composed the anthem 'Out of the deep' (1887).

PAGE, Arthur James (1846-1916)
Born in Ipswich, Suffolk on 3 March 1846; died in 1916.
From the age of seven he was a chorister of Norwich Cathedral. At 14 he was articled to the cathedral organist, **Zechariah Buck** for seven years. His teacher for counterpoint was **Edward Bunnett**, another prominent Norwich church musician. Buck later offered Page a partnership, which he declined.
Organist and choirmaster of St. Mary's Church, Nottingham (from 1867) where he built up and maintained a choir. A music master of Trent College, Derbyshire and a contributor to the music press.
Composed services and anthems. His cantatas, the words for many of which were supplied by his son, Arthur Bernard Page, include *Snow Queen*. Also composed operettas for treble voices, songs, and works for organ or harmonium.

PAGE, Edward Osmund (?-1883)
Died on 23 December 1883. Lived in Manchester as an organist and teacher. Composed a setting of the Mass, and other music for voices.

PAINE, Robert Parker (1823-1900)
Born in Sandgate, Kent on 15 November 1823; died in Clewer, Berkshire on 28 March 1900. Self-taught in composition. Received encouragement from his friend **Charles Purday** who lived locally. Paine contributed to Purday's collection of rounds.
On moving to Windsor, Berkshire, Paine received further encouragement from the organist of St. George's Chapel, **George Elvey**. Composed a setting of the Te Deum (1884); an oratorio *The Prodigal Son* (1884); a setting of Psalm 93 'The Lord is King' for Bass Solo, Chorus and Orchestra (1887); other anthems; chants; hymn tunes and songs.

PALMER, Dr. Clement Charlton (1871-1944)
Born in Barton-under-Needlewood, Staffordshire on 26 April 1871; died in Canterbury, Kent on 13 August 1944.

Educated at Derby School of Music and Repton College, Derbyshire. Graduated B.Mus. (1891) and D.Mus. (1896) at the University of Oxford.
Organist and choirmaster of the Church of St. Leonard, Wichnor, Berkshire (1887-1888) and organist of St. Andrew's Church, Pau, France (1888-1891).
On his return to England he was assistant organist of Lichfield Cathedral (1891-1897); organist and choirmaster of Holy Trinity Church, Burton on Trent, Staffordshire (1891-1897) and of Ludlow Parish Church, Shropshire (1897-1908).
Organist and master of the choristers of Canterbury Cathedral (1908-1936). On one occasion, in the course of giving the choristers a lesson on transition and modulation he played on the organ a short item which changed key in the middle and finished with a long arpeggio. He asked what the piece illustrated, expecting the answer 'transition'. Instead, he received the response, 'swank, sir'.
Submitted as his B.Mus. exercise the anthem 'Prayer and praise' for Solo Voices, Choir and Strings; for his doctorate, a setting of Psalm 7 'O Lord, my God' for Baritone Solo, Quartet, eight-part Chorus and Orchestra.
Composed a Service in E-flat, and a setting of the Evening Service in F for Men's Voices. In addition he composed hymn tunes, a chant to Psalm 70, the ballad *Cassabianca* for Chorus and Orchestra, and organ works. His tunes are found in a number of modern Free Church hymnals such as *Hymns and Psalms*.

PALMER, Florence Mary Spencer (b.1900)
Born in Thornbury, Gloucestershire on 27 July 1900. Composer of hymn tunes, the motet *Except the Lord build the house* (1956) from Psalm 127 and *Like as a father* (1948) from Psalm 103.

PALMER, Revd. George Herbert (1846-1926)
Born in Grantchester, Cambridgeshire on 9 August 1846; died in Oxford on 20 June 1926. Educated at Trinity College, Cambridge. Curate of St. Margaret's Church, Toxteth Park, Liverpool. Published *The Antiphoner and Grail* (1881), *Harmonies of the Office Hymn Book* (1891) and *Sarum Psalter* (1894). His compositions include hymn tunes.

PALMER, Henry (c1590-c1660)
Born between the years 1590 and 1600; died in Durham between 1660 and 1670. Associated with Durham Cathedral. Contributed tunes to **Thomas Ravenscroft**'s *Psalter*. Composed of a set of Preces and a setting of Psalm 118 'O give thanks unto the Lord'. His other works include the anthems 'Blow up the trumpet' and 'Lord, what is man?'.

PALMER, Horatio Richmond (1834-1907)
Studied in Berlin and in Florence. A teacher in New York and Chicago. Director of the Church Choral Union (1884), which grew to some 4,000 voices. Probably a member of the Baptist Church. Published collections of songs. Author of the hymn 'Yield not to temptation' and composer of the tune 'Fortitude' to accompany it.

PALMER (Dibdin), Isabella Perkins (1828-?)
Born in Southwold, Suffolk on 19 January 1828. A soprano singer and composer of hymn tunes.

PALMER, Mary (1839-1903)
Born in 1839; died in Clapham, London on 25 February 1903. A composer of hymn tunes.

PALMER, Thomas (19th/20th century)
Graduated B.Mus. at the University of Oxford (1879). Organist of the Church of All Saints, Londonderry (from 1873); Alton Parish Church, Hampshire (from 1876), Omagh Parish Church, County Tyrone, Northern Ireland (from 1877) and St. Matthew's Church, Ipswich, Suffolk (from 1880). A local choral society conductor. Composed a setting of Psalm 108 for Solo Voices, Chorus and Orchestra; an Evening Service in F; the anthem 'O sing unto the Lord'; part songs and piano works.

PARDY, Ptolemy S.T. (19th/20th century)
Trained privately in music. Graduated B.Mus. at the University of Durham (1908). Organist and choirmaster of the Churches of St. Paul, Kingston, Surrey; St. Paul, Finsbury, London; Ewell Parish Church, Surrey and St. Peter, Norbiton, Surrey. A local orchestral society conductor. Composed anthems, songs, and works for piano, for organ and for violin.

PARISH, Frank Wilson (1869-1945)
Born in London in 1869; died in Maidstone, Kent in 1945. Educated with **Frederick Bridge** and with **Edouard Silas**. Organist and choirmaster of St. Paul's Church (for three years) and All Saints' Church (for 53 years) at Maidstone, Kent. Composed services including an Evening Service in E-flat, anthems and songs.

PARKER, Handel (1854-1928)
Born in Oxenhope, Yorkshire on 29 January 1854; died in Shipley, Yorkshire on 30 January 1928. A member of a large musical family in which most of the children were named after musicians. Two of his siblings were Haydn and Jubal. Something of a child prodigy. A member of the Oxenhope Drum and Fife Band from the age of seven. At around the age of 10 he was organist of Hawksbridge Baptist Church, moving to the Parish Church at 14. A performer and teacher of music. A pianist, trombonist, violinist, conductor and adjudicator. Organist of Nassau Cathedral, The Bahamas. Published a collection of church music *The Deep Harmony Hymnary*, a North-country classic, which included his Four-Fold

Amen and 16 hymns. His 'Bodmin' was used in the Revised Edition (1927) of *Church Hymnary*.

PARKER, Leonard (19th/20th century)
Trained privately in music. Graduated B.Mus. at the University of Durham (1898). Organist of the Trinity Wesleyan Church, Oldham, Lancashire and organist and choirmaster of the Plymouth Grove Valley Wesleyan Chapel, Manchester (from 1914). Composed as his B.Mus. exercise the anthem 'The Majesty of God'. Also composed hymn tunes, songs, and works for piano and for organ.

PARKER, Septimus (1824-1886)
Born in London on 10 June 1824; died in Aberdeen on 27 April 1886. Lived in London at North Bank, Regent's Park (1843) and Bedford Street, Strand (1844). Organist of the Surrey Parish Churches of Ashtead (1844-1859 and 1874-1877), Epsom (1859-1861) and Godalming (1864-1874). Held a number of appointments in Aberdeen, including St. Paul's Episcopal Church (1877-1879 and 1880-1882); St. John's, Longside and St. Mary's (1885-1886). Editor of *A Selection of Church Tunes and Cathedral Chants...* (1850). Composed Services, anthems, hymn tunes and part songs.

PARKES, David (19th/20th century)
Born in Blackheath, Staffordshire. Trained privately in music with **C. Swinnerton Heap**. Graduated B.Mus. (1901) at Queen's College, Oxford. Organist and choirmaster of the Ebenezer Wesleyan Church, Plymouth, Devon and a local choral society conductor. Organist of Plymouth Central Hall. Local representative of the Royal Academy of Music. Composed a setting of the Benedictus for Solo Voices, Chorus, Strings and Organ as his degree exercise. His other works include anthems such as 'What are these?', a part song 'When twilight dews', and items for piano.

PARKINSON, Bernard Robert (1872-1952)
Born in Islington, London in 1872; died in Worthing, Sussex on 27 September 1952. Composer of the Sunday School Anniversary hymn 'Hark, Hark my soul' (1901) and hymn tunes. Published *A Collection of Original Hymn Tunes* (1893).

PARKYN, William George (1881-1957)
Born in St. Pancras, London in 1881; died in Berkhamstead, Hertfordshire on 24 September 1957. Organist and choirmaster of the Congregational Church, East Finchley High Road, London (from 1902). Composer of the hymn 'Jesus is our loving Saviour' (1905), hymn tunes, and the anthems 'O taste and see' (1909) and 'Thou, O God, art praised in Zion' (1909).

PARNELL, Revd. Claude William (1872-?)
Born in Burton on Trent, Staffordshire in 1872.
Educated privately with **Henry Richards**, **W.G. Alcock** and George Miller, and at the University of Cambridge. Graduated M.A. (1901) and Mus.B. (1911) at Queens' College.
Organist and choirmaster of St. Saviour's Church, Brixton Hill, London. Also lived at Ruardean Rectory, Gloucestershire.
Acting organist and choirmaster of Ross Parish Church and of Tewkesbury Abbey.
Composed a Morning Holy Communion and Evening Service in E-flat, an Evening Service in B-flat, six anthems, piano works and a Prelude and Fugue in G for Organ.

PARR, Revd. Henry (1815-1905)

Born in Lythwood Hall, Shropshire on 16 August 1815; died in Blackheath, Kent on 4 May 1905. Educated at the University of Oxford and ordained in 1845. Vicar of Taunton, Somerset (1849-1858); curate of Tonbridge, Kent (1859-1861); incumbent of Ash, Gloucestershire (1861-1862) and of Yoxford Parish Church, Suffolk (from 1867). His bibliographical article *Collections of Chants* appeared in *Musical Times* (June 1879). Compiler of *Church of England Psalmody...* which ran into eight editions. His own works include chants and hymn tunes.

PARRATT, Sir Walter (1841-1924)

Born in Huddersfield, Yorkshire on 10 February 1841; died in Windsor, Berkshire on 27 August 1924, the date on which his father, Thomas Parratt, had died in 1862.

A pupil of his father, and of **George Cooper** at St. Sepulchre's Church, Holborn.

Played his first service at the age of seven at Armitage Bridge Church where, four years later (1852-1853) he succeeded his brother, Henry L. Parratt, as organist at an annual salary of £10.

At the age of 10 he had been able to play all 48 of Bach's Preludes and Fugues from memory. Another musical gift was that of perfect pitch.

On one occasion, Parratt played anthems in St. Paul's Cathedral during the time that **John Stainer** was a chorister, and he met **John Goss**, organist of St. Paul's. **F.A.G. Ouseley** was a friend of the family.

Attended the choir school of St. Peter's Chapel, Charlotte Street, London and the College School, Huddersfield. Went up to Magdalen College, Oxford in 1868. Graduated B.Mus. (1873), and received an honorary musical doctorate (1894).

Knighted in 1892, and appointed M.V.O. (1901) and K.C.V.O. (1921). Knighthoods were also awarded in 1892 to his fellow musicians **Joseph Barnby** and **William Cusins**, Master of the Queen's Music, who resigned a year later and was succeeded by Parratt.

After his Armitage Bridge appointment (1852) he became organist of St. Paul's Church, Huddersfield (1854-1861), where again he succeeded his brother, Henry. Organist to Lord Dudley at Witley Court, Worcestershire; Great Witley Church (1861-1868) and Wigan Parish Church, Lancashire (from 1868). Witley Court had a good library and Parratt was able to read many of the classics. Tenbury, where Ouseley had established St. Michael's College, was some 15 miles away and Parratt used to walk there and back to visit him.

In 1860 he competed unsuccessfully for the town organistships of Newcastle-on-Tyne, where he finished third out of 22 finalists, and Leeds, where he came second to **William Spark**.

In 1872 he succeeded John Stainer as organist of Magdalen College, Oxford on the latter's recommendation, although Parratt was reluctant initially to leave Wigan. He remained at Magdalen until 1882, when he was appointed to succeed **George Elvey** at St. George's Chapel, Windsor Castle on Elvey's retirement. The Dean of Windsor intimated that if suitable terms could be negotiated the post was his, despite the large number of candidates. His first assistant at Windsor was Hubert Hunt, subsequently organist of Bristol Cathedral. In 1882 **Walford Davies** was a senior chorister.

In 1875 the organistship of Westminster Abbey had fallen vacant. The precentor, **Samuel Flood Jones**, and Ouseley both urged Parratt to compete but Dean Stanley would not agree to the reform of the choir and the refurbishment of organ, both of which were in decline. Parratt withdrew, and he decided not to apply for the vacancy at Christ Church Cathedral, Oxford, that arose in the same year. In 1881 he was offered the post of organist of Salisbury Cathedral, but declined it.

Organist of St. Giles's Church, Oxford concurrently with Magdalen College. Inherited problems at Magdalen, where some of the choirmen were apt to miss practices and turn up for services the worse for drink.

At Wigan and at St. Giles's, Oxford he used to hold congregational practices after Sunday Evensong for the music of the following week. He was in favour of women in choirs, congregational practices, less music and more speech during services, and putting the choir among the congregation.

Professor of music at the University of Oxford (1908-1918), where he succeeded **Hubert Parry**; dean of the Faculty of Music of the University of London (1916-1920). The first professor of organ at the Royal College of Music (1883-1924), where he also conducted the choral class. Master of music to successive sovereigns from 1893 until 1924.

His daily routine, combining the duties at St. George's Chapel and the R.C.M., was to take choir practice at 8:30, run down Castle Hill to Windsor Station in order to catch the 9.05 train to London, carry out his teaching duties at the R.C.M. from 10 a.m. and return to St. George's in time for Evening Service.

He updated the repertory of the Chapel, introducing new music and ensuring that each decade of the four hundred years of English choral writing was adequately represented, taking pains also to improve the sight reading abilities of the choristers. Famous as an organ recitalist as well as an academic and a writer. Contributed articles to Grove's *Dictionary of Music and Musicians*, and lectured on organ and ancient music.

A number of his pupils later held important positions, including **Thomas Armstrong**, principal of the Royal Academy of Music; **George Thalben Ball**, organist of the Temple Church, London; **A.H. Brewer**, organist of Gloucester Cathedral; **P.C. Buck**, cathedral organist, and professor of music at Trinity College, Dublin; **Marmaduke Conway**, organist of the Cathedrals of Wells, Chichester and Ely; **Harold Darke**, organist of St. Michael's Church, Cornhill and professor of the R.C.M.; **Henry Walford Davies**, composer, broadcaster and organist of St. George's Chapel, Windsor Castle; **William Harris**, composer and organist of St. George's Chapel, Windsor Castle; **Herbert Howells**, composer and professor of the R.C.M.; **John Ireland**, composer and professor of the R.C.M.; **Basil Johnson**, precentor of Eton College; **H.G. Ley**, organist of Christ Church Cathedral, Oxford; **S.H. Nicholson**, organist of Manchester Cathedral and of Westminster Abbey; **Tertius Noble**, organist of York Minster; **Boris Ord**, organist of King's College, Cambridge; **Noel Ponsonby**, organist of Christ Church Cathedral, Oxford; **Harold Rhodes**, organist of Coventry Cathedral; **Arthur Somervell**, conductor, composer and professor of the Royal College of Music; **Heathcote Statham**, organist of Norwich Cathedral; **Ralph Vaughan Williams**, composer; **Archibald Wilson**, organist of the Cathedrals of Ely and Manchester.

The hymn tune 'Huddersfield' was one of a number of tunes which appeared in *English Hymnal* (1906). Also composed anthems, songs, works for organ and for piano and a March for the Royal Wedding at St. George's Chapel, Windsor Castle (7 July 1891). His other works include anthems, songs, dramatic works, and organ pieces.

PARRY, Sir Charles Hubert Hastings (1848-1918)
Born in Bournemouth, Dorset on 27 February 1848; died in Rustington, Sussex on 7 October 1918. A son of **Thomas Parry**.
Educated at Twyford School near Winchester, Hampshire; Eton College and Exeter College, Oxford (from 1867). Having satisfied the academic requirements of the Oxford B.Mus. while still at Eton he was awarded the degree in 1867.
Graduated Mus.D. honorarily at the University of Cambridge (1883) and, by decree, D.Mus. (1864) at the University of Oxford, from which he also graduated M.A. and D.C.L. (1899).
His teachers in music were **George Elvey**, organist of St. George's Chapel, Windsor Castle, with whom Parry studied while at Eton; **William Sterndale Bennett** and **George Macfarren**. Took piano lessons with Edward Dannreuther. Studied in Stuttgart, Germany with **H.H. Pierson**.
Hubert Parry was knighted in 1898 and was created baronet in 1905.
For three years, Parry was a member of Lloyds but resigned in order to concentrate on a career in music. A professor of composition (from 1883), lecturer in musical history, and director (1894-1918) of the Royal College of Music
Choragus (from 1883) and professor of music (1900-1908) of the University of Oxford.
Parry's pupils include **Arthur Somervell**, **Walford Davies**, **Samuel Coleridge-Taylor**, **Ralph Vaughan Williams** and **George Thalben-Ball**. Vaughan Williams knew of Parry's reputation and was determined to become his composition pupil, having detected in Parry's music a unique English quality.
Parry was the author of a number of works including *Short Studies of Great Composers, Summary of Musical History* and *Music of the 17th Century.*
Parry's compositional efforts were limited by his teaching and administrative duties. Had these been less onerous, Parry's compositions might have been more prolific and influential. His *Prometheus Unbound* (1880) is seen by some as one of the items marking the revival of English composition.
His music includes the oratorios *Judith* (1888), *King Saul* (1894) and *Job* (1898) Services include a setting in D (1881). Composed the hymn tunes 'Intercessor' (1904) 'Jerusalem' and 'Laudate Dominum' (1915), the latter being an extract from his anthem 'Hear my words, O ye people' which was composed for the Salisbury Diocesan Festival of 1894.
'Jerusalem' was sung at a meeting in March 1918 to celebrate the granting of the vote to women. *Student Hymnal* (1923) was the first to publish the now famous combination of the tune with the words by William Blake. His other works include four symphonies, orchestral suites, string quartets and other chamber works.
At Parry's funeral in St. Paul's Cathedral in 1918, the composers **C.V. Stanford**, **Frederick Bridge**, Henry Walford Davies, **Harold Darke**, **W.G. Alcock**, **Charles Wood** and George Thalben-Ball each composed a section of a musical tribute. It was later enlarged and published as *A Little Organ Book* (1924).

PARRY, Dr. Joseph (1841-1903)
Born in Merthyr Tydfil, Wales on 21 May 1841; died in Penarth, Wales on 17 February 1903.
Graduated Mus.B. (1871) and Mus.D. (1878) at the University of Cambridge.
It appears that he went to work at 10, either in a colliery for two years and then at an iron works, or at a puddling furnace.
Sang alto in oratorios conducted by **Rosser Beynon**.

In 1854 he moved with his family to Dannville, Pennsylvania, U.S.A. where he worked in a rolling mill until 1865. Studied music at classes organised by his fellow Welsh immigrants. In 1860 he won a prize for composition and his colleagues raised funds for him to study music in Genesco, New York. His family had been too poor to afford music lessons for him.
Returned temporarily to Wales in 1862. He won prizes at the national *eisteddfodau* of 1863, 1864 and 1866. In 1865 he was nominated *Pencerdd* of the U.S.A. Gave concerts in the U.S.A. (1866-1867), the proceeds from which, together with funds collected by friends, financed his studies at the Royal Academy of Music (1868-1871).
Brinley Richards, an adjudicator at the Swansea Eisteddfod of 1865, at which Parry won a prize, was instrumental in persuading Parry to study at the R.A.M. His teachers included **William Sterndale Bennett**, Manuel Garcia and **Charles Steggall**.
Returned to Dannville (1871), where he founded a music school.
Three years later he was back in Wales as head of music at the new University College, Aberystwyth (1874-1879). He then ran a private college of music in the town for two years before moving it to Swansea (1881) and continuing to run it until 1888. Organist of the Ebenezer Chapel, Swansea (1881-1888).
A lecturer in music at the University College of South Wales, Cardiff (from 1888). An adjudicator and concert promoter. The first Welsh composer to have a thorough academic training in music. As a teacher, he was influential upon the rising generation of Welsh musicians.
Edited *Cambrian Minstrelsie,* collections of Welsh songs.
His hymn tunes number some 400, including 'Aberystwyth' (1876) used widely in English hymnals. Among his other hymn tunes are 'Dies Irae', also known as 'Merthyr Tydfil', and 'Llangristiolus'. He is said to have written a hymn tune each week for many years.
Also composed anthems, oratorios including *Emmanuel* (1880), cantatas including *The Prodigal Son*, five operas of which *Blodwen* (1878) is an example, songs, orchestral overtures and instrumental works.

PARRY, Thomas Gambier (1816-1888)
Born in Highnam, Gloucestershire on 22 February 1816; died in Highnam on 28 September 1888. The father of **Hubert Parry**. Attended Eton College and studied at Trinity College, Cambridge, graduating B.A. (1837) and M.A. (1848). An amateur painter, he invented a process named spirit fresco. Also a linguist and musician. His hymn tune 'St. Agatha' was used in *Hymns Ancient and Modern.*

PARSLEY (Parslie, Persley), Osbert (1511-1585)
Born in 1511; died in Norwich, Norfolk in 1585. A lay clerk of Norwich Cathedral for around 50 years. Composed two Morning Services, motets and works for viol.

PARSONS, Alfred William (1853-?)
Born in Salisbury, Wiltshire on 31 December 1853.
A chorister of Salisbury Cathedral. Graduated B.Mus. at the University of Durham (1891).
Organist of St. John's Church, Leicester (1878-1889); Aberystwyth Parish Church, Wales (1889-1897); St. George's Church, Kendal (1897-1903) and St. Denys's Parish Church, Sleaford, Lincolnshire (from 1903). A lecturer in music at St. David's College, Lampeter, North Wales (1894-1896) and music master of Carre's Grammar School (from 1903).

Composed as his degree exercise a setting of Psalm 18 'I will love Thee'. Also composed two settings of the Te Deum and a sacred song 'Story of the Cross'.

PARSONS, Charles (19th century)
A chorister of Wells Cathedral. Composed the anthems 'Grant to us, Lord' and 'I will give thanks'.

PARSONS, George Collison Tuting (1849-1929)
Born in Stourbridge, Worcestershire in 1849; died in Sutton Coldfield, Warwickshire on 21 January 1929. Composer of hymn tunes.

PARSONS, John (1563-1623)
Born in 1563; died in July 1623. A son of **Robert Parsons**. A parish clerk of St. Margaret's Church, Westminster, London in 1616. Organist of Westminster Abbey (1621-1623). Composed a setting of the Burial Service and anthems including 'Man that is born' and 'All people clap your hands'.

PARSONS, Robert (c1530-1570)
Born in Exeter, Devon around the year 1530; died by drowning in the River Trent at Newark, Nottinghamshire on 25 January 1570. Father of **John Parsons**. A gentleman of the Chapel Royal (from 1563). Composed settings of the Morning, Holy Communion and Evening Services, the anthem 'Deliver me from mine enemies', and madrigals.

PARSONS, William (c1515-after 1561)
The accounts of Wells Cathedral of around 1550 contain entries indicating payments made to William Parsons for compositions and for making musical copies. Organist of Wells Cathedral (1550-1560). Composed the anthems 'Almighty God, whose kingdom' and 'Remember not O Lord'.

PARTRIDGE, James (1850-?)
Born in Staffordshire in 1850. Studied at Saltley College for two years with the intention of becoming a teacher. Organist of the college, unusually for a student. He held organistships in various places before travelling to London. Studied at the Royal Academy of Music (from 1875) under **Charles Steggall** and Brinley Richards. The latter and he became friends. Partridge was Richards's deputy as a teacher at Guildhall School of Music and succeeded him. A reader for several publishing firms. Organist of St. Andrew's Church, Hammersmith, London. Composed church music, songs, and pieces for organ.

PASFIELD, Dr. William Reginald (b.1909)
Born in Dudley, Worcestershire on 20 June 1909.
Educated at Lichfield Cathedral, Dudley Grammar School, the University of Birmingham and the Birmingham School of Music. His tutors included **Ambrose Porter**, G.D. Cunningham and Granville Bantock. Graduated B.A. and B.Mus. at the University of Birmingham.
A lecturer in music. Taught at the Kent Music School. Music adviser to the firm of Ashdown Ltd.
Organist and choirmaster of St. Agnes' Church, Moseley, Birmingham (1931-1938).
Director of music of Strathallan School, Perthshire, Scotland (1939-1943); King's School, Canterbury, Kent (1944-1945) and St. Lawrence College, Ramsgate, Kent (1946-1949). Director of music

of The Heritage Craft Schools, Chailey, Sussex (from 1949). A professor and examiner of the London College of Music (from 1950). Head of music of Brownhills School, Staffordshire (1955-1957). Head of graduate diplomas, and of the junior department of the L.C.M. (from 1958).
Author of works on a number of subjects, with titles including *An Introduction to Counterpoint in the style of J.S. Bach*.
Composed the cantata *A Song of Wisdom* for Solo Voices, Chorus and Orchestra; songs; part songs and carols.

PATRICK, Nathaniel (?-1595)
Died at Worcester and was buried in March 1595, possibly on the 23rd. Organist of Worcester Cathedral (1590-1595). Succeeded by **Thomas Tomkins**, who married his widow. Composed Evening Services in G Minor and in B-flat, the anthems 'Prepare to dye' and 'Send forth Thy sighes', and a number of madrigals which are lost. His *Songs of Sundry Natures* was published in 1597.

PATRICK, Richard (17th century)
A lay vicar of Westminster Abbey (1616-c1625). Composed a set of Responses to the Commandments, published in a collection around 1875. His other works include the anthems 'I will lift up mine eyes' and 'O clap your hands'.

PATTEN, William (1804-1863)
Born in Fareham, Hampshire in 1804; died in 1863. Organist of St. Cross, Winchester, Hampshire. Published a number of compilations including *Congregational Melodies, Original and Selected...* and *Six Anthems for Large or Small Choirs*. His compositions include three settings of the Sanctus for four voices, anthems such as 'The Lord is in His holy temple' and 'Thou shalt open my lips', hymn tunes and songs.

PATTERSON, Dr. Annie Wilson (1868-1934)
Born in Lurgan, County Armagh, Northern Ireland on 27 October 1868; died in Cork, ireland on 17 February 1934.
Of French Huguenot descent.
Received private musical training and attended the Royal Irish Academy of Music, Dublin. Graduated B.Mus. (1887) and D.Mus. (1889) at the National University of Ireland.
Organist of a number of churches in and around Dublin (1883-1896). Organist of St. Anne's Church, Shandon, County Cork (from 1909). A local choral and harmonic society conductor, and music examiner for Cork Municipal School of Music. Cork Corporation lecturer on Irish music at University College, Cork. A music journalist and author, her writings include *The Story of Oratorio*.
Established the Irish Music Festival (1897).
Her compositions include the anthems 'Meta tanta' (St. John's vision of Heaven) and 'In memoriam'. Her B.Mus. exercise was a sacred drametta *The Raising of Lazarus* for Solo Voices, Chorus and Organ. Also wrote songs to Gaelic words.

PATTERSON, Paul Leslie (b.1947)
Born in Chesterfield, Derbyshire on 15 June 1947.
Educated in Exeter and at the Royal Academy of Music.
Became a brass teacher in 1967.
Director of the Manson Trust for Contemporary Music at the R.A.M. (from 1968) and in the same year he joined the Executive Committee of the Composers' Guild. Composer in residence to English Sinfonia (1969-1970) and to the South East Arts

Association (1980-1982). Director of contemporary music at the University of Warwick (1974-1980). Director of music of Bedford School (1984-1985). Has been on the staff of the R.A.M. since 1970, as a professor and head of composition, and head of 20th century music (from 1985).

Has been associated with the Exeter Festival as composer-in-residence (1990-1991) and as artistic director (from 1991).

A freelance composer since 1968. Has composed a Te Deum for the 1989 Three Choirs' Festival at Hereford, a Magnificat (1994) and a Mass *of the Sea*, for the Three Choirs' Festival of 1988. His other works include a Symphony (1990), and music for the opening of the Channel Tunnel (1994).

PATTISON, Thomas Mee (1845-?)

Born in Warrington, Cheshire on 27 January 1845. Organist of St. Paul's Church, Warrington (from 1869). A local choral society conductor. Moved to London around 1886. Author of *Rudiments of Vocal Music*. Composed anthems including 'There were shepherds' and 'O praise the Lord', cantatas both sacred such as *A day with our Lord* and secular, of which an example is *The Ancient Mariner*. Also composed organ works, items for piano and a comic opera *The Happy Valley*.

PATTON, Arthur St.George (1853-1892)

Born in Belfast on 23 April 1853; died in Bayswater, London on 20 October 1892. Educated at Trinity College, Dublin. Organist of All Saints' Church, Blackrock (from 1875); Trinity Church, Rathmines (from 1877) and St. Anne's Church, Dublin (from 1881). Composed hymn tunes including 'Lyra', found in *Hymns Ancient and Modern*.

PAVIOR, Paul (b.1931)

Born in Birmingham on 14 April 1931. Has composed a Threnody for Good Friday and a setting of the work 'And there is joy in Heaven' by Edmund Spenser.

PAXTON

See **GARDINER**, William.

PAYTON, William Henry (19th/20th century)

Educated at Owen's College, Victoria University of Manchester, where he graduated B.Mus. (1898). Organist and choirmaster of Wycliff Church, Warrington, Cheshire, where he was also a music master at the People's College and a music society conductor. Composed a setting of Psalm 96 'O sing unto the Lord' for Solo Voices, Chorus, Strings and Woodwind as his degree exercise.

PEACE, Dr. Albert Lister (1844-1912)

Born in Huddersfield, Yorkshire on 26 January 1844; died in Liverpool on 14 March 1912.

Studied with Henry Horn and Henry Parratt. Graduated B.Mus. (1870) and D.Mus. (1875) at the University of Oxford.

His first four church organistships were in Yorkshire, from the age of nine. These were Holmfirth Parish Church (from 1853); Dewsbury Parish Church; St. Thomas's, Huddersfield; and Providence Place Chapel, Cleckheaton.

Held appointments in Glasgow at Trinity Congregational Church (from 1865), the University of Glasgow (from 1870), St. John's Episcopal Church (from 1873), Maxwell Parish Church (from 1875), Hillhead Episcopal Church (from 1876) and St. Andrew's Halls (from 1877).

Organist of Glasgow Cathedral (1879-1897).

In the latter year he succeeded **W.T. Best** as organist of St. George's Hall, Liverpool, an appointment he retained until 1912.

His Scottish appointments followed the acceptance of the use of organ in the congregational worship of the Church of Scotland. A ban existed until 1865. Many church organs were built and opened in the country over a period of some 25 years and Albert Peace is said to have opened about two thirds of these. He also had the honour of opening the new organ of Canterbury Cathedral (1886).

Music editor of *Scottish Hymnal* (1885). Compiled works of Psalmody for the Church of Scotland.

His B.Mus. exercise was 'I will give thanks unto Thee, O Lord', a setting of Psalm 138 for Solo Voices, Chorus and Orchestra. For his D.Mus. he submitted a cantata *St. John the Baptist*. Composed Morning, Holy Communion and Evening Services. His other anthems include 'God be merciful' and 'Awake up, my glory'. Composed hymn tunes including 'Guild' and 'St. Margaret', and organ sonatas.

PEACE, Frederick William (1883-?)

Born in Thornhill, Dewsbury, Yorkshire in 1883. Organist and choirmaster of the Church of the Good Shepherd, Thornhill for 15 years, and of Edge Road Methodist Church for 12 years. Composed music for use in Church and Sunday School, including 25 sacred cantatas for mixed choir, 50 song services, and more than 200 anthems for festival and general use. Also composed songs and part songs.

PEACE, Lister Radcliffe (1885-1969)

Born in Glasgow on 5 November 1885; died in Hove, Sussex on 7 March 1969. Composer of hymn tunes. Editor, with **Hugh Blair**, of *The Church Hymnal for the Christian Year*.

PEAKE, John Daulby (19th/20th century)

Born in Codnor, Derbyshire. Studied at the Royal Academy of Music and in Berlin, and graduated B.A. at the University of London. Organist and director of the music of the Park Church, Elmira, New York State (1903-1910). Music master of Derby School (from 1910). Composed anthems including 'Hide Thou not Thy face far from me' and 'I will lift up mine eyes', a carol Christ the Babe was born', and a part song 'Ring out, wild bells'.

PEARCE, Dr. Charles William (1856-1928)

Born in Salisbury, Wiltshire on 5 December 1856; died in Wimborne, Dorset on 2 December 1928.

Trained privately in music. For harmony and composition he studied with **C.J. Read**, **E.J. Hopkins** and **Ebenezer Prout**. His organ teachers were Theodore Aylward, **W.S. Hoyte**, and E.J. Hopkins. Articled to **Charles Verrinder** in London. Graduated Mus.B. (1881) and Mus.D. (1884) at the University of Cambridge. Organist of St. Martin's, Salisbury from the age of 14 (1871-1873), and of the London Churches of St. Luke, Old Street (1874-1885) and St. Clement, Eastcheap (1885-after 1897).

A professor of organ and composition (from 1882), dean (from 1891) and Queen Victoria lecturer and director of examinations (from 1902) of Trinity College of Music, London. A professor of harmony at Guildhall School of Music (1898-1912) and dean of the Faculty of Music, University of London (1908-1912).

An examiner for a number of other musical bodies including the University of Cambridge (1888-1891) and the Royal College of Music (from 1902). Candidates feared his ruthless exposure of their inadequacies and among those to provoke his scorn was **Walford Davies**, supplicating for his Cambridge Mus.D. in 1898 and receiving back his piece annotated with comments including 'ocean of ugliness'. Director of the Philharmonic Society (from 1902).

Author of a number of books on musical theory published by T.C.M.. His other works include *Notes on Old London Churches*. Co-editor with **Charles Vincent** of *The Organist and Choirmaster*. One of the editors of *The Anglican Choir Series of Church Music*. Composed as his B.Mus. exercise a Cantata for All Saints' Day and for his doctorate, an oratorio *Lux benigna*. Composed Services, anthems, a Passion Cantata *The Man of Sorrows*, hymn tunes including 'Midsomer Norton' and 'St. Martin Ongar', both of which were used in *Hymns Ancient and Modern*. His other works include songs and items for organ.

PEARCE, Dr. William Henry Vivian (19th/20th century)
Trained privately in music. Graduated B.Mus. (1893) and D.Mus. (1917) at the University of London. Organist and choirmaster of Cambourne Wesleyan Church, Cornwall and of East Cliff Congregational Church, Bournemouth, Dorset. Conductor of local choral and musical societies. Composed anthems based on Psalm 8 'O Lord, our Governor' and Psalm 139 'O Lord, Thou hast searched me out'. Also composed works for organ.

PEARMAN, James (c1818-1880)
Born in Winchester, Hampshire around the year 1818; died in Dundee, Scotland on 3 April 1880. Studied under **George Chard**. Lived and worked in Dundee as an organist and a teacher of music. Composed a setting of the Mass, songs and piano music.

PEARSALL (de Pearsall), Robert Lucas (1795-1856)
Born in Clifton, Gloucestershire on 14 March 1795; died in Wartensee, Switzerland on 5 August 1856.
The son of an army officer.
Studied law and music; called to the bar in 1821 and practised law until 1825. Then studied music at the University of Mainz under Panny, and church music at Munich under Caspar Ett.
Following a year in England (1829) he lived in Karlsruhe, Germany and from time to time made extended visits to London (1836). Bought a castle at Mayence, Lake Constance (1832 or 1842) from the proceeds from the sale of some property he inherited in Willsbridge, Gloucestershire.
Translated the works of Goethe and Schiller into English and had essays published entitled *Consecutive Fifths* and *Octaves in Counterpoint*. One of the editors of the *St. Gall Gesangbuch* which was eventually published in 1863.
Converted to the Roman Catholic Church and changed his name to de Pearsall. He was received by the bishop of St. Gall.
Had composed a cantata *Saul and the Witch of Endor* (1808) at the age of 13. Later in life he composed for the Roman Catholic Church and for the Church of England. His hymn tunes include 'Pearsall'. Composed a setting of *In dulci jubilo*. Examples of his anthems are 'Blessed word of God incarnate' and 'Therefore we before Him bending'.
Of his madrigals, in many cases he wrote both words and the music. Composed part songs, including 'Sir Patrick Spens'.

PEARSON, Arthur (1866-?)
Born in Stanningley, near Leeds on 22 April 1866. Graduated B.Mus. (1899) at Queen's College, Oxford. Organist and choirmaster of St. Paul's Church, Huddersfield (from 1884) and organist to Huddersfield Corporation (from 1891). A local choral and orchestral society conductor. Editor of *The Yorkshire Musician*. Composed as his B.Mus. exercise *Veni, Creator* for Baritone Solo, Chorus, Quartet and Strings. Composer of a cantata *The Promised Land* (1885) and the anthems 'By the rivers of Babylon' (1916) and 'Arise, shine' (1926).

PEARSON, John Ena (19th/20th century)
Trained privately in music. Graduated B.Mus. (1907) at the University of Durham. Organist and choirmaster of Avenue Congregational Church, Southampton. Composed as his degree exercise a setting of the words of Wisdom 3: 'The souls of the righteous'. Also composed an anthem, hymn tunes, songs and part songs.

PEARSON, Louis (19th/20th century)
Received his training in music privately and at Durham Cathedral. Graduated B.Mus. (1907) at the University of Durham.
Organist and choirmaster of Holy Trinity Church, South Shields and of Tynemouth Parish Church. Composed as his B.Mus. exercise the cantata *Praise The Lord O Jerusalem* for Solo, Chorus, Piano, Quartet and Strings. Also composed an anthem 'There, the wicked', hymn tunes, organ pieces and a song 'Beauty, wit and gold'.

PEARSON, William Dean (20th century)
Studied with **Edward Bairstow**, **George Gray** and with T.E. Pearson. Graduated B.Mus. at the University of Durham, and B.Sc. Assistant organist of Halifax Parish Church, Yorkshire (1924-1929). Organist and choirmaster of Todmorden Parish Church, Yorkshire (1926-1930) and Melton Mowbray Parish Church, Leicestershire (from 1930). Music master of Melton Mowbray Grammar School (from 1930). A lecturer in music at the Adult Education Department of Loughborough College (from 1931). A local choral society conductor. Composed a Sevenfold Amen for female voices (1957); services, including a unison setting of the Te Deum (1963) and anthems.

PEARSON, William Webster (1839-1913)
Born in Bishop Auckland, County Durham on 17 September 1839; died in South Walsham, Norfolk on 5 December 1913.
A chorister of York Minster under **John Camidge** (1790-1859). Musically self-taught. Organist and choirmaster of Elmhurst Parish Church, Norfolk (from 1935). Master of music and art at Watts' Naval College, North Elmham and teacher of violin at Norfolk County School, Dereham. A local orchestral society conductor. Author of publications including *Nation Method of Vocal Music for Elementary Schools* (1874). Inventor of a system of sight singing. Composed church music including anthems, organ works, piano pieces, songs, dance music, the Cantata *Voice of the Flowers* for Female Voices, and part songs. Many of his works remain unpublished.

PEEBLES (Peblis, Pables), David (?-1579)
Died in St. Andrews, Fifeshire, Scotland in 1579. A brother of the Abbey of St. Andrew, he was also a competent musician. Arranged the canticle *Si quis diligit me* (around 1530) and presented it to James V of Scotland. Asked by the prior to harmonise the Psalms and hymns of the Reformed Church. Composed a four-part motet *Quam multi Domine sunt*.

PEEL, Revd. Frederick (19th century)
Graduated B.Mus. at the University of Oxford in 1872. Music master and organist of Reading School, Berkshire (1871-1875) and vicar of Heslington, near York. Composed a setting of Psalm 145 'I will magnify Thee O God my King' for Solo Voices, Chorus and Orchestra; Services; anthems; hymn tunes; songs and works for organ and for piano.

PEERSON (Pearson, Pierson), Martin (c1571-1651)
Born, possibly at March, Cambridgeshire between 1571 and 1573; died in London and was buried on 15 January 1651. Master of the children of St. Paul's Cathedral, and almoner (from 1613). His *Motets, or Grave Chamber Music* was published in 1630. Composed around 20 anthems including 'Plead Thou my cause', 'O let me at Thy footstall fall' and 'Blow ye the trumpet', airs and instrumental music.

PENNY, Alfred Samuel (1831-1909)
Born in 1831; died in London on 25 July 1909. Composer of hymn tunes.

PEPUSCH, Dr. John Christopher (1667-1752)
Graduated D.Mus. at the University of Oxford. Organist to the Duke of Chandos (from 1712), and to the Charter House (from 1737). His works include the anthems 'I will give thanks' (1826) and 'O God, thou art my God' (1749).

PERCIVAL, Dr. Allen Dain (1925-1992)
Born in Bradford, Yorkshire on 25 April 1925; died in London on 19 September 1992.
Attended Bradford Grammar School and studied under John Brayshaw at the University of Cambridge. Graduated Mus.B. at Magdalene College, Cambridge.
Appointed C.B.E.
Formed a dance band. At other times he was a member of an orchestra, a cinema organist, pianist, conductor, scholar, teacher, writer, editor and publisher.
Served in the Royal Navy during World War II. Following a post as music officer at the British Council in Paris (1948-1950), he taught at Haileybury School (1950-1951). He met Thurston Dart, who persuaded him to return to the University of Cambridge as an administrator. Senior lecturer in music at Homerton College, Cambridge (1951-1962). Conductor of the Cambridge University Music Society (1954-1958) and of the Cambridgeshire Opera Group (1952-1954).
Director of musical studies at Guildhall School of Music (1962-1965). As principal of the G.S.M. (1965-1978) he was responsible for moving the school to new premises at The Barbican. He worked voluntarily for the Musicians' Benevolent Fund and for 30 years he was a director of the publishers, Stainer and Bell, where he was executive chairman (1978-1990).
Joint editor of *Partners in Praise* (1978) and edited *Galliard Book of Carols* (1980). He also published *The Orchestra* (1956) and *The Teach Yourself History of Music* (1961).
Composed 'The donkey's carol' to words by Fred Pratt Green.

PERCIVAL, Samuel (1824-1876)
Born in 1824; died in Liverpool on 7 November 1876. Studied at the Royal Academy of Music. Organist of Wallasey Parish Church and of the School for the Blind, Liverpool, in which city he held other teaching positions. Composed a Magnificat and Nunc

Dimittis in F (1866), a setting of the Nicene Creed for four voices (1906), the anthem 'Teach me, O Lord' (1860), a cantata *The Lyre*, works for flute and for piano, and songs.

PERCIVALL,? (17th century)
The composer Percivall's works include the anthems 'Bow down thine ear' and 'O be Joyful'.

PERKINS, Charles William (1855-1927)
Born in Birmingham on 4 October 1855; died in Bromley, Kent on 2 August 1927.
Studied organ under Andrew Deakin and piano and composition under **Charles Swinnerton Heap**.
Organist of Wretham Road Church, Handsworth, Birmingham (?-1884) and an assistant to **Frederick Bridge**, with whom he studied, at Westminster Abbey (from 1884).
Organist in London of Immanuel Church, Streatham Common and St. Michael's Church, Paddington. Organist of Birmingham Town Hall (from June 1888). A prominent organ recitalist, he performed at major venues including the Crystal Palace and St. George's Hall, Liverpool. Organist to the Bimingham Festival (from 1888), Blenheim Palace, Oxfordshire and the University of Birmingham. Composer of hymn tunes.

PERKINS, William (?-1860)
Died on 11 November 1860. Organist of Wells Cathedral from 1820 until 1860, succeeding his father, Dodd Perkins, having been a vicar choral of Wells since 1804. **Charles Lavington** became his deputy (1843), and took over the running of the music. Composed the anthems 'I cried unto the Lord' and 'O Lord, our Governour'.

PERRIN, Dr. Harry Crane (1865-?)
Born in Wellingborough, Northamptonshire in 1865.
A pupil of **R.P. Stewart**, graduating B.Mus. (1890) and D.Mus. (1901) at Trinity College, Dublin.
Organist of St. Columba's College, Rathfarnham, Dublin (1886-1888) and of St. John's Church, Lowestoft, Suffolk (from 1888). Organist and choirmaster of St. Michael's Church, Coventry, Warwickshire (1892-1898). A local choral and orchestral society conductor.
Organist and master of the Choristers of Canterbury Cathedral (1898-1908). He resigned when appointed professor of music in the University of Montreal, Canada, and director of the university's Conservatory of Music.
Submitted as his B.Mus. exercise a cantata *Blind Bartimaeus*. His doctorate was awarded on the strength of a setting of Psalm 122, 'I was glad' for Solo Voices, Chorus and Orchestra. His other cantatas include *Abode of Worship*. In addition he wrote Morning and Evening Services, anthems, songs and items for piano.

PERRIN, Ronald Edward (b.1931)
Born in Enfield, Middlesex on 13 April 1931. Won an organ scholarship to Christ Church, Oxford (1949), taking an honours degree in music. Following National Service in Berlin, was sub organist and later acting organist of Leeds Parish Church during the interregnum between the departure of **Melville Cook** and the arrival of **Donald Hunt**. Sub organist of York Minster prior to his appointment as organist of Ripon Cathedral (1966). Has composed hymn tunes; the *Ripon* Setting to the Rite A version of Holy Communion; the Missa *Sancti Petri* and anthems for treble voices

including 'Jacob's ladder', 'All creatures of our God and King' and 'Angel voices'.

PERRONET, Revd. Edward (1726-1792)
Born in Sundridge, Kent in 1726; died in Canterbury, Kent on 8 January 1792.
His father, Vincent Perronet, was vicar of Shoreham, Kent for 57 years and was sometimes called 'the archbishop of Methodism'. His grandfather had fled to England at the time of the persecution of the Huguenots. The Wesleys were family friends.
Perronet visited the North of England with John Wesley (1749) and shortly afterwards became an itinerant Methodist preacher. The two men quarrelled following an article by Perronet in *The Mitre* (1757) in which he denounced certain abuses within the church. Other differences in opinion had surfaced over the questions of separation from the Church of England and the licensing of itinerant preachers to administer the sacraments.
Had severed his association with the Wesleys completely by 1771. Joined the Countess of Huntingdon's Connexion but in time the Countess and Perronet parted company over the latter's fierce denunciation of the Church of England.
Perronet, who had preached for the Connexion in Canterbury, continued in that city as an independent preacher. Although of violent temper and lacking in patience his religious faith was a strong one. He had a talent for poetry and he is well known for his hymn 'All hail the power of Jesus' name'. A composer of hymn tunes.

PERROT, Clement Hamill (1842-1910)
Born in Jersey, Channel Islands in 1842; died in Sheffield, Yorkshire on 16 July 1910. Composed hymn tunes and anthems including 'Happy is the man that findeth wisdom' (1879) and 'I acknowledge my transgressions' (1879).

PERRY, Edwin Cooper (1856-1938)
Born in Castle Bromwich, Staffordshire on 10 September 1856; died in Worthing, Sussex on 17 December 1938. Composed hymn tunes.

PERRY, George (1793-1862)
Born in Norwich, Norfolk in 1793; died in London on 4 March 1862. A pupil of **William Fish** and 'of Beckwith'. Conductor of the Haymarket Theatre, London and organist of the Quebec Chapel and of Trinity Church, Gray's Inn Road. Composed anthems including 'I will arise' and 'The Queen shall rejoice', oratorios and operas.

PERRY, Revd. Michael Arnold (b.1942)
Born in Beckenham, Kent on 8 March 1942. Educated at Ridley Hall, Cambridge. A parish priest in the cities of Liverpool and Southampton. He became rector of Eversleigh, Hampshire and chaplain to the National Staff Police College. On the Executive Committee for the collection *Hymns for Today's Church* (1982), an edition that contains his 'Calypso Carol'.

PETERSON, Franklin Sievewright (1861-1914)
Born in Edinburgh on 24 February 1861; died on 21June 1914.
Educated in Edinburgh and Dresden, where he was an organ pupil of Carl Fischer. Graduated B.Mus. at New College, Oxford (1892). A lecturer in music history at Dundee University College and at the extension centres of Edinburgh and St. Andrews. Music master of Edinburgh Ladies' College (from 1893) and of Fettes College (from 1894). Professor of music at the University of Melbourne (from 1901). Examined candidates for scholarships in music to the University of Edinburgh.
Organist and choirmaster of Palmerston Place Church, Edinburgh (from 1884).
Author of *Elements of Music* (1896) and of articles for the music journals. Contributed entries on musical topics to *Chambers Encyclopaedia*.
Composed as his B.Mus. exercise a setting of the Kyrie Eleison, Benedictus and Agnus Dei for Solo Voices, Chorus, Strings and Orchestra. Also composed anthems, songs and part songs.

PETTET, Alfred (1790-1837)
Born in 1790; died in Norwich, Norfolk on 16 March 1837. Articled to **John 'Christmas' Beckwith**. Organist of the Church of St. Peter Mancroft, Norwich (1810-1837). Suffered from a spinal disease which restricted him physically. Compiled *Original Sacred Music...* (published 1826). Composed hymn tunes including 'Domine, Probasti' which was used in *Hymns Ancient and Modern*. Also composed duettinos, trios and waltzes for piano.

PETTMAN, Charles Edgar (1866-1943)
Born in Dunkirk, near Faversham, Kent on 20 April 1866; died in Battersea, London on 20 January 1943. Educated at the Royal Academy of Music (1882-1886). Organist in London of the Churches of St. Matthew, New Kent Road and St. James, Piccadilly.
One of those responsible for the reawakening interest in carols. He arranged a large number of French and Spanish carols. Many of these arrangements appeared in *The University Carol Book* and *Sunday School Praise*. Composed a cantata *The Nativity* (1885) and other items of church music. His hymn tunes include 'Love Incarnate', which was used in *Baptist Hymn Book* (1962).

PHILIP AP PRYS (16th century)
A number of variants of the name exist. Known to have been alive in and around the year 1530. Three of his works survive and are found in the British Library. Probably one of the group of Welsh musicians referred to in **Thomas Morley**'s *A Plain and Easy Introduction*. Is said to have been 'of St. Paul's Cathedral', and thus he would have been acquainted with such musicians and composers as **Robert Redford** and **William Whitebroke**.
Author of an Organ Mass in a style that was common between around 1425 and 1700 in France, Germany and Italy but in which no other British composer is believed to have written. The Kyrie, Gloria, Offertory, Sanctus, Benedictus and Agnus Dei are all provided, and the work appears to have been composed specifically for use on Trinity Sunday. Other works include a setting of the antiphon *Miserere mihi, Domine* and the Offertory *Felix namque*.

PHILIPPS, Arthur (1605-?)
Graduated B.Mus. at the University of Oxford (1640). A clerk of New College, Oxford (from 1622). Organist of Bristol Cathedral (from 1638). Organist of Magdalen College, Oxford (from 1639) and choragus of Oxford University (from 1639). Organist to Queen Henrietta Maria of France. On his return to England he became the private organist to a Mr. Carlyle, a gentlemen of Essex. Composed 'The Requiem' or 'Liberty of An Imprisoned Royalist' (1641) and 'The Resurrection' (1649). Composed the anthem 'Blessed art thou'.

PHILIPS, Peter (Petrus Philippus) (c1560-c1625)
Born around the year 1560 or 1561; died according to some sources in April 1625 but others state that he died in Brussels, Belgium in 1628.
A member of a Catholic family. He may have been a chorister of St. Paul's Cathedral. It is known that he was acquainted with the cathedral almoner, Sebastian Westcote, who made provision for Philips in his will.
Left England in 1582; arriving in Douai, France on 18 August 1582, presenting himself at the English College, presumably in search of employment. Travelled on to Rome, where he was organist to the English College (1582-1585), and employed by Cardinal Farnese.
Entered the service of Lord Thomas Paget (1585), with whom he travelled to Spain, France and The Netherlands. Paget and his retinue visited Paris (1587-1588) and Antwerp (1588-1589), and settled in Brussels, where Paget then died. Philips returned to Antwerp as a teacher of keyboard instruments.
Travelled to Amsterdam (1593), where he met the composer Jan Sweelinck. During his return journey to Antwerp in 1593 year he was stopped at the town of Middelburgh and put on trial in The Hague for allegedly planning the assassination of Queen Elizabeth I. He was charged with having, with Paget, burned an effigy of Elizabeth in Paris. The case was dismissed because of lack of evidence. Philips continued his return journey to Antwerp, arriving late in 1593.
Moved to Brussels in 1597 and became organist of the Royal Chapel of Archduke Albert. Philips was named organist to their Supreme Highnesses the Archduke Albert and Isabella.
Appointed canon of Soignés (March 1610), although he continued to live in Brussels. Became chaplain of Tirlemont (January 1621). Still referred to as canon of Soignés (1623) and also known as canon of Bethune.
Composed motets including the still-popular *Ascendit Deus* for Ascension Day, anthems including 'Blessed art thou that fearest' and 'O give thanks', madrigals and works for virginal.

PHILLIPS, Alfred (1844-?)
Born in 1844 of Welsh descendants. Founded the firm of Alfred Phillips Ltd., piano and music dealers. Joined forces with Sydney Page (1883), trading as Phillips and Page. Corresponded with the French composer, Charles Gounod (from 1883) leading to the publication of a number of new songs after an absence of some 20 years. Retired to North Devon (1898). His hymn tune 'Rosehill' is found in *Church Hymns* (1874). Composed hymns for Sunday School Anniversaries, including 'Voces Angelorum', which were sung at gatherings that took place at the Crystal Palace. Composed piano works under the pseudonym Sarakowski and songs as Leigh Kingsmill.

PHILLIPS, John (Tegidon: 1810-1877)
Born in Bala, Wales on 12 April 1810; died in Portmadoc, Wales on 28 May 1877. Educated at Bala, where he was apprenticed to the printer Robert Sanderson. Moved to Chester, where he was the supervisor of the printing works owned by John Parry, publisher of *Y Drysorfa* and *Goleuad Cymru,* to which Phillips contributed many articles. Moved around 1850 to Portmadoc, where he became secretary of the Welsh Slate Company, and was later the chief agent for more than 20 years. Sub editor of *Y Gwyliedydd.* Editor of the poetry of *Goleuad Cymru* (1922-1938). A poet in free verse, and a public speaker. Composed hymns for special occasions, some

of which were published in *Welsh Congregational Hymn Book* and *Methodist Hymn Book* (1933). Also composed songs for children and young people.

PHILLIPS, John Charles (b.1921)
Born in Pershore, Worcestershire in 1921.
Educated at the Worcester Cathedral Choir School, at King's School, Worcester and at the Birmingham School of Music. Graduated B.Mus. at the University of Durham.
Organist of Wick Parish Church (from 1946); senior music master of Pershore County Modern School (1948-1956); director of music at King Charles I School, Kidderminster (1956-1963); senior lecturer in music and head of the Department of Music of Summerfield College of Education (1963-1971), and principal lecturer in music and head of the Department of Music of Shenstone New College, Staffordshire (from 1971).
His compositions include a Christmas anthem 'To welcome Christ'; a String Quartet in B; a cantata *A Song of Faith* for Soprano Solo, Choir and Orchestra and many songs.

PHILLIPS, John George (19th/20th century)
Graduated B.Mus. (1895) at the University of Durham. Organist and choirmaster of St. John's Parish Church, Seaham Harbour (from 1869). Lived in Sunderland. Phillips composed as his B.Mus. exercise a work based on texts from Psalm 34 and Isiah 26. Also composed a Magnificat and Nunc Dimittis.

PHILLIPS, Thomas (1735-1807)
Born in Bristol, Gloucestershire in 1735; died in Bristol on 15 June 1807. By trade he was a brushmaker. An obituary notice in the *Bristol Journal* (20 June 1807) describes him as one of the city's 'lovers of Psalmody'. His hymn tune 'Lydia' was used in *Baptist Hymn Book* (1962).

PHILLIPS, Thomas (1774-1841)
Born in London in 1774; died in Hartford, Cheshire on 27 October 1841 following a railway accident. The family was originally from Monmouthshire, Wales. A tenor singer, lecturer and composer. Made his first appearance at the Royal Opera House, Covent Garden (1796) as Philip in *Castle of Andalusia.* Author of *Elementary Principles and Practices for singing* (1830) and compiler of *Improved Psalmody for the Church and the Chamber.* Composed songs, part songs and glees.

PHILLIPS, Dr. William James (1873-1963)
Born in London on 17 February 1873; died on 2 February 1963.
Following training in music with **Basil Harwood** he was organ scholar at the Royal College of Music (1890-1894), where his teachers were **Walter Parratt, Frederick Bridge** and **Hubert Parry.** Graduated B.Mus. (1898) and D.Mus. (1907) at Queen's College, Oxford.
Appointed M.V.O. (1955).
Organist and choirmaster at the Church of SS Mary and John, Oxford (1894-1896); the London Churches of St. John, Hammersmith (1896-1902); St. Barnabas, Pimlico (1902-1917); St. Cuthbert, Philbeach Gardens and Holy Trinity, Clapham Common (1917-1924).
Organist and master of the choristers of the Chapel Royal, Hampton Court (1930-1956), where he won a reputation for his sympathetic treatment of Victorian church music.

A teacher of singing (1908-1910) at the Girls' High Schools of Kensington, Notting Hill, Wimbledon, East Putney and Streatham Hill.

Appointed lecturer in practical harmony at the London Day Training College (1917). A professor, lecturer and examiner in harmony, composition and music history at Guildhall School of Music (from 1921).

Author of *Carols and their Origin*.

Composed as his B.Mus. exercise a setting of Psalm 137 'By the waters of Babylon' for Solo Voices, Chorus and Strings. For his doctorate he submitted a Mass in E for Solo Voices, Double Choir and Orchestra.

Also composed anthems; hymn tunes including those used by *Hymns Ancient and Modern*: 'Cowley', 'St. John' and 'Gurney'; a prize part song (the prize awarded by *Musical News*) and songs.

PHILLIPS, William Lovell (1816-1860)

Born in Bristol, Gloucestershire on 26 December 1816; died in London on 19 March 1860. A chorister of Bristol Cathedral. Studied at the Royal Academy of Music under Cipriani Potter as a contemporary of **William Sterndale Bennett**. Also studied cello with Robert Lindley. In his short career, Phillips was a member of the Orchestras of Her Majesty's Theatre, the Philharmonic Society and the Sacred Harmonic Society. Conductor of the Olympic Theatre and the Princess Theatre. A professor of composition at the R.A.M., and organist of the Church of St. Catherine, Regent's Park. Composed a setting of the Offertory Sentences, a symphony, theatrical works and songs including 'Lady mine'.

PHILPOT, Stephen Rowland (1872-1950)

Born in London in 1872; died in 1950. Studied at Grosvenor College, Brixton, London and with **George Macfarren** at the Royal Academy of Music. Emigrated to Monte Carlo (1920), returning to England in 1940 at the German occupation of Monaco. Organist of St. James's Church, Taunton, Somerset. Composed a Mass in D Minor, which was performed several times in Monaco Cathedral; operas; a cantata; some two hundred songs and items for violin and for piano.

PHIPPS, Alexander James (1867-?)

Studied at the Royal Academy of Music under **W.H. Holmes** and **Charles Steggall**. A conductor of opera and oratorio societies. Organist of St. James's Church, Swansea (from 1866); St. John's Church, Bootle, Lancashire and Roby Church, Liverpool. Author of *Comprehensive Guide to the Study of Music* (1874). Composed *Meditation on the Passion* (1893) for Chorus and Orchestra, an oratorio *The Ten Virgins*, songs and other works.

PICKAVER (Peckover, Pickhaver), Robert (?-1678)

Organist of New College, Oxford (1662-1663) and of Winchester College, Hampshire (1665-1678). Composed the anthems 'Consider and hear me' and 'Sing unto the Lord'.

PICKERING, John (1792-1843)

Born in London on 23 May 1792; died in Manchester on 6 November 1843. Studied under Domenico Corri. A teacher in Preston, Lancashire (from 1812). From about five years later he lived and worked in Manchester as a teacher and pianist. Composed church music including the anthem 'Every day will I give thanks' (1848) and items for piano.

PIERACCINI, Emilio Vincenzio (1833-1902)

Born in Italy in 1833; died in Forest Gate, London on 16 July 1902. Composed hymn tunes.

PIERSON (Pearson), Henry Hugo (1816-1873)

Born in Oxford on 12 April 1816; died in Leipzig on 28 January 1873.

Son of the dean of Salisbury. Changed the spelling of his name while living in Germany, according to a sympathetic biographer to ensure that it was pronounced correctly. Other sources claim that it followed an unsuccessful love affair and to avoid what to his parents was the embarrassment of a career in music.

Educated at Harrow School and at Trinity College, Cambridge.

Travelled to Germany (1839) where he studied under Carl Reissiger, Johann Rinck, Johann Tomaschek and Ernst Wenzel.

In Leipzig he became a member of the circle of composers and musicians that had formed around Mendelssohn and Schumann, and met Louis Spohr.

It came as something of a surprise in the musical world when he was appointed professor of music at the University of Edinburgh (1844). He held the position only for a short time before returning to Germany where he afterwards married.

As a composer he used the pseudonym Edgar Mansfeldt. His secular works were highly regarded in Germany but never in England. His works include operas such as *Leila* (1848); oratorios including *Jerusalem*, composed for the Norwich Festival of 1852; the anthem 'Blessed are the dead' and settings of the Te Deum and the Service of Holy Communion (1870).

Published sets each of 30 hymn tunes (1870 and 1872). His other works include theatre music, orchestral overtures and instrumental pieces.

PIGGOTT, Francis (c1650-1704)

Born around the year 1650, or, according to one source, 1666; died on 15 May 1704.

A Francis Piggott - who may or may not be the same person - was a child of the Chapel Royal (1679-1683).

Graduated Mus.B. at the University of Cambridge (1698).

Organist of Magdalen College, Oxford (1686-1687), prior to which he may have been organist of St. John's College. His career then continued in London where he was organist of the Temple Church (1688-1704) and a gentleman (from 1695) and organist (1697-1704) of the Chapel Royal.

Composed anthems including 'I was glad', and published a collection of music for harpsichord.

PIGGOTT, Henry (?1839-1916)

Died on 29 March 1916 at the age of 77. Trained privately in music, studying under **Samuel Wesley** at Winchester Cathedral. Graduated Mus.B. (1887) at the University of Cambridge. Organist of All Saints' Church, Alton, Hampshire from its consecration (1874). Composed as his degree exercise a cantata *The Ascension* for Solo Voices, Chorus, Strings and Orchestra. Also composed other items of church music, and part songs.

PIKE, Henry Michael (1842-1916)

Born in Bishops Sutton, Derbyshire in 1842; died in Southampton on 5 December 1916. Composed hymn tunes.

PITCHER, Richard James (1870-1946)
Born in Devonport on 10 April 1870; died in West Hampstead in May 1946.
Attended Clifton Grammar School, Plymouth, Devon. Received his early music training at Westminster Abbey, and later, privately under **Frederick Bridge**, Ernst Pauer and **Frederick Cliffe**. Studied singing in Milan. Graduated B.Mus. at the University of Durham (1892).
Moved to London in 1902.
Organist of the Churches of St. Matthew, Stonehouse, Gloucestershire (1887-1889); Christ Church, Plymouth (1889-1891); St. John, Lowestoft, Suffolk (1892-1896) and Holy Trinity, Scarborough, Yorkshire (1896-1903).
In London he was organist of St. Swithin's Church, London Stone (1903-1906); St. Mary's, Kilburn (1906-1915); Christ Church, Chelsea (from 1915); St. Mark's, Hamilton Terrace and St. Mary's, West Hampstead for many years.
He was a professor of singing at Guildhall School of Music (1905-1915), a teacher at Trinity College of Music and a lecturer on music appreciation for London County Council. Author of works on the art of singing, and of teaching it.
Composed as his B.Mus. exercise an anthem based on words taken from Psalms 13, 138 and 149. Also composed songs and items for piano and a set of Festal Responses and Sevenfold Amen (1891).

PITT, Thomas (?-1806)
Died on 21 April 1806. A chorister of Worcester Cathedral, where he was later pupil/assistant to the Cathedral organist **Elias Isaac**. Organist of Worcester Cathedral (1793-1806). Published two volumes of church music (1788 and 1789), including settings of the Te Deum and Jubilate. His works include the anthem 'O Lord, I need not'.

PITTMAN, Josiah (1816-1886)
A pupil of **S.S. Wesley**, Ignaz Moscheles and Schnyder von Wartensee. Organist in London of Sydenham, (from 1831), Spitalfields (1835-1837) and Lincoln's Inn (1852-1864). Also worked at Her Majesty's Theatre (1865-1868) and Covent Garden Theatre (1868-1880). Composed, among others, the anthem 'The Lord is King' (1889). Made several piano arrangements.

PITTS, Antony Philip David (b.1969)
Born in Farnborough, Kent on 24 March 1969. Educated at Tiffin Boys' School, Kingston-on-Thames and New College, Oxford. Producer for B.B.C. Radio 3 and director of the ensemble Tonus Peregrinus. Has written operas including *The Book of the True Story*, and organ works including 'In the year that King Uzziah died'. His church compositions include a Sanctus and Benedictus; three Easter Anthems 'The Lord is risen', 'Thou knowest my lying down' and 'The bread which we break'; an Antiphon for Good Friday 'O my people' and the Advent Antiphon 'O wisdom of God'; and anthems including 'Why art thou cast down, O my soul?' and 'O Holy of Holies'.

PITTS, William John (1829-1903)
Born in Tansor, near Oundle, Northamptonshire on 17 April 1829; died in Kensington, London on 3 June 1903. The son of an organ builder. From the age of 14 he was organist of Elton Church, Huntingdonshire. Organist of Brompton Oratory, Kensington from its founding, for more than 50 years. Composed hymn tunes including 'Princethorpe', and other items of vocal music.

PLANT, Dr. Arthur Blurton (1853-1914)
Born in Lichfield, Staffordshire on 12 May 1853; died in 1914.
From the age of seven he was a chorister of Lichfield Cathedral. An articled pupil of the organist, **Thomas Bedsmore**. Graduated B.Mus. (1882) and D.Mus. (1896) at New College, Oxford.
For many years he was associated with the town of Burton on Trent, Staffordshire. Organist and choirmaster of St. Paul's Church (from 1874), organist and choirmaster of St. Margaret's Church, and organist to the Corporation (from 1895).
His degree exercises were a setting of Psalm 13 'How long wilt Thou forgive me' for Solo Voices, Chorus and Orchestra (B.Mus.) and of Psalm 72 'Give the King thy judgements' (D.Mus.). Also composed a setting of the Service of Holy Communion, part songs, glees, and arrangements for piano and for organ.

PLEASANTS, Thomas (1648-1689)
Born in 1648; died on 20 November 1689. Organist of Norwich Cathedral (1670-1689). Composed church music including the anthem 'O Praise the Lord' and other vocal items.

PLEASANTS, William (17th century)
Composer of the anthem 'O sing unto the Lord'.

PLUMRIDGE, Dr. Henry (19th/20th century)
Graduated B.Mus. at St. Mary Hall, Oxford (1871) and D.Mus. at Keble College, Oxford (1888). Organist and choirmaster of Hursley Church, Winchester, Hampshire (1866-1868) and of University College, Oxford (1868-1901). Held other appointments in Oxford as organist and choirmaster of the Churches of Holywell (1868-1870), St. Giles (1870-1875), the City Church (1875-1896) and St. Mary the Virgin, Monken Hadley (from 1902). Choirmaster of St. Ebbe's Church, Oxford (1890-1901). Composed as his B.Mus. exercise a setting of a text taken from Habak 3 'God came from Teman' for Solo Voices, Chorus and Strings. For his doctorate he submitted an oratorio *Daniel* for Solo Voices, Chorus, Organ and Orchestra. Also composed anthems.

POLE, Dr. William (1814-1900)
Born in Birmingham on 22 April 1814; died in London on 30 December 1900.
Graduated B.Mus. (1860) and D.Mus. (1867) at the University of Oxford. Fellow of the Royal Societies of London (1861) and Edinburgh (1877). A harmony pupil of Thomas Murden.
Civil engineer and a writer on scientific topics, as well as being an amateur musician. Organist of the Wesleyan Chapel, Birmingham, at age 17. Organist of St. Mark's Church, North Audley Street, London (1836-1844 and 1849-1866).
Professor of Civil Engineering at University College London (1859-1876), also holding appointments in India (1844-1849).
Examiner in music to the University of London (1878-1890). The first published paper by him on music was in *Musical World* (1836), dealing with the construction of organ pipes. Many others appeared in *Musical Times* and *The Athanaeum*. His book, *The Philosophy of Music* (1879) was republished in 1924. In addition he wrote programme notes for many of the New Philharmonic Concerts, and he contributed to Grove's *Dictionary of Music and Musicians*.
Composed, in cantata form, a setting of Psalm 100 *O be joyful in the Lord, O ye Lands* for the Tenbury Festival (October 1861). Other works include anthems such as 'All people that on Earth', motets, and items of organ music.

POLLITT, Dr. Arthur Wormald (c1879-1933)
Died in Liverpool at the age of 54 on 3 February 1933.
A chorister of Manchester Cathedral, and later, sub organist.
Educated at the Royal Manchester College of Music, Owen's
College and Manchester Cathedral, where he was sub organist.
Graduated B.Mus. (1899) and D.Mus. (1905) at the University of
Durham.
Taught music at St. Mary's College for the Blind, Liverpool, where
he was also organist and director of the choir, for 17 years.
Organist of the Hope Street Unitarian Church.
Held a number of academic appointments in Liverpool. A professor
of harmony at the German Institute of Music, and a lecturer and
examiner to the Extension Board of the University. Also lectured in
music at Liverpool University and at Edge Hill Training College.
Chorus master of the Liverpool Philharmonic Society (1918-1929).
Compiled *The Unison Chant Book* with E. Bryson.
Submitted as his B.Mus. exercise the cantata *Confitebor Tibi* for
Tenor Solo, five-part Chorus and Strings. For his doctorate he
composed *A Song of Solomon* for Soprano Solo, eight-part Chorus
and Orchestra. Other compositions of church music include
services and anthems. Wrote songs, part songs, organ works and
items for piano.

PONT, Kenneth H. (b.1934)
Born in Brighton, Sussex in 1934.
Educated at Varndean School. Studied organ with John Wills and
specialised in accompaniment. Member of staff of Oxford
University Press for over 25 years, working mainly in educational
music publishing. Began teaching at St. Leonards-Mayfield School
(1970); appointed director of music in 1983.Organist and director
of music at Mayfield Parish Church (from 1968). Co-founder of the
Mayfield Festival in 1970. Founder and conductor of the Gibbons
Consort of Voices. Has accompanied a number of well-known
artists following his debut at the Wigmore Hall, London in 1971.
His publications include the schools anthologies *Harvest Time* and
Angel Band, the latter being a collection of carols.
For the church he has written a Communion Service in F,
reconstructed from hymn tunes by **Orlando Gibbons**; chants;
hymn descants; a Te Deum in F; a Cantate Domino and the anthem
'God is gone up with a merry noise'.

POOLE, Clement William (1828-1924)
Born in Ealing, Middlesex on 7 June 1828; died in Ramsgate, Kent
on 10 July 1924. Studied music with **Joseph Cooper**. At the age of
18 he became a junior clerk in the Audit Office. He worked in the
Civil Service until his late fifties, when he ventured unsuccessfully,
into commerce. A deeply religious man, happy to serve the church
musically. Honorary organist of Kingston Parish Church, Surrey;
Christ Church, Ealing and Holy Trinity Church, Ramsgate.
Composed a setting of the Magnificat, some 30 hymn tunes
including 'Petersham', which was included in the Revised Edition
(1927) of *Church Hymnary*, 'Gibraltar' and 'Westenhanger'. Also
composed a setting of the Magnificat, marches, and vocal music.

POOLE, Revd. Henry James (1843-1897)
Born in Huntspill, Somerset on 8 March 1843; died in Stowell,
Somerset on 15 January 1897. Composed the hymn tune 'St. Lucy'
and an *Andante Cantabile* for Piano (1873).

POPE, George Alexander (1830-1893)
Born in 1830; died in Romford, Essex in 1893. Composed hymn
tunes.

POPPLE, Revd. Herbert (1891-1965)
Born in Berkhamstead, Hertfordshire in 1891; died in
Berkhamstead on 16 July 1965. Educated at Lichfield Theological
College and at University College Durham. Ordained in 1923.
Served with the armed forces during World War I. Curate of St.
Mary's Church, Blythe (1923-1930) and St. Peter's Church,
Streatham. Author of a nativity play. Composed hymn tunes
including 'St. Aidan', written for 'Thine are all the gifts, O God' in
Songs of Praise (1931). Also composed two settings of the Mass.

POPPLEWELL, Richard John (b.1935)
Born in Halifax, Yorkshire on 18 October 1935.
A chorister, and organ scholar (from 1955) of King's College,
Cambridge. Studied at Clifton College, Bristol and, with an open
scholarship, at the Royal College of Music (from 1953).
Appointed M.V.O. (1990).
An organ recitalist. Assistant organist of St. Paul's Cathedral
(1958-1966); director of music of St. Michael's Church, Cornhill,
London (1966-1979) and organist, choirmaster and composer to the
Chapel Royal, St. James's Palace (from 1979). A professor of
organ at the R.C.M. (from 1962).
His many church music compositions include an *Easter Hymn*
(1977) for Organ, two Final Amens (1989), the carol 'There is no
Rose' (1974) and the anthems 'O how amiable' (1992) and 'A vast
cloud of love' (1996).
Richard Popplewell has the distinction of having composed
anthems for three Royal Baptisms: 'Lord Jesus Christ, our Lord
most dear' (Frederick, son of Prince Michael of Kent: 1979),
'Blessed Jesus, here we stand' (Prince William, son of the Prince of
Wales: 1982) and 'To Thee, O Father, Lamp of all the living'
(Princess Beatrice, daughter of the Duke of York: 1988).

PORTER, Ambrose Probert (1885-1971)
Born in Coleford, Gloucestershire in 1885; died in May 1971.
A chorister of Gloucester Cathedral (1900-1907) under **A.H.
Brewer**. Attended Bell's Grammar School, Coleford. Suffered
from poor health as a child, and unable to attend school for long
periods. Studied with Brewer as an articled pupil (1907-1913) and
served as his assistant. Among his fellow students was **Herbert
Howells**. Graduated B.Mus. at the University of Oxford.
At the age of 10 he became organist of Coleford Parish Church.
Organist of Newland Church, Gloucestershire (1898-1904) and St.
Catherine's Church, Gloucester (1907-1913).
Organist and choirmaster of St. Matthias's Church, Richmond,
Surrey (1913). Choirmaster of Richmond Parish Church. For two
years he was a professor of harmony, form and aural training at the
Royal Military School of Music, Kneller Hall, Twickenham,
Middlesex. During World War I he served at the Admiralty.
Organist of Lichfield Cathedral (1925-1959), where his pupils
included **Richard H. Lloyd** and **Christopher Robinson**. A local
choral society conductor. On retiring (1959), moved to the South
coast but on the death of his wife he took up residence in
Alverstoke, Hampshire and was assistant organist of the parish
church.
Composed as his B.Mus. exercise a setting of Psalm 42 'Like as the
hart desireth the water brooks' for Soprano Solo, Chorus and
Orchestra. Much of his church music remained unpublished but his

work includes the anthem 'Almighty and most merciful Father' to words by Samuel Johnson of Lichfield, hymn tunes including 'Laus Deo', chants, songs and works for organ including a Fantasia *on St. Magnus*.

PORTER (Paterson), Dorothy de Bock (1873-1956)
Born in Greenwich, Kent on 6 November 1873; died in Hendon, Middlesex on 11 February 1956. Composer of hymn tunes including 'Kingsway' to words by H. de Bock Porter for the Coronation of George V (1911).

PORTER, Samuel (1733-1810)
Born in Norwich, Norfolk in 1733; died in Canterbury, Kent on 11 December 1810. Father of **Samuel Porter** the younger and of **William Porter**. A chorister of St. Paul's Cathedral under **Charles King** and later studied under **Maurice Greene**, organist of St. Paul's Cathedral. Organist of Canterbury Cathedral (1757-1803). A volume of Samuel Porter's works was published by his son, William Porter. His music includes the collection *Four Anthems and Two Psalm Tunes* (1800), a Service in D, a set of Responses to the Commandments in D, songs, glees and marches. His anthems include 'Save me, O God' and 'O be joyful in the Lord'.

PORTER, Samuel (c1750-1823)
The son of **Samuel Porter** the elder and the brother of **William Porter**. A member of the King's Band. Organist of Faversham, Kent for 37 years. Composed anthems including 'O where shall wisdom be found?'

PORTER, Walter (c1595-1659)
Born around the year 1595; died in London in October 1659. A chorister of Westminster Abbey. Said to have been a pupil of Monteverdi, he graduated B.Mus. at the University of Oxford (1600). A musician to James I (from 1603). A gentleman of the Chapel Royal (from 1616), a position he held until the Civil War. Master of the choristers of Westminster Abbey(1639). Published a collection *Madrigales and Ayres* (1632), forms of music in which he himself composed. He also wrote a setting of Psalm 121 'I will lift up mine eyes', other anthems including 'When Israel', and motets.

PORTER, Walter (1856-1935)
Born in Boston, Lincolnshire in May 1856; died in Hull, Yorkshire on 4 July 1935. At the age of eight he became a chorister of Boston Parish Church. Took lessons in music with **Walter Gilbert** (from 1868) and with **Daniel Wood**. Organist and choirmaster of Bourne Abbey Church, Lincolnshire (from 1874) and St. Mary's Church, Wallgate, Hull (from 1875). Composed a setting of the Service of Holy Communion, a Te Deum, hymn tunes, organ music, a string quartet and piano works.

PORTER, Revd. William James (?-1865)
The son of the elder, and brother of the younger **Samuel Porter**. Head master of Worcester College School and chaplain to Viscount Fitzwilliam. Vicar of Himbleton, Worcestershire (1815-1865). Composed the anthems 'Like as the hart' and 'Ponder my words'.

PORTMAN, Richard (c1610-1659)
Born around the year 1610; died in November 1659. A pupil of **Orlando Gibbons**. Organist of Westminster Abbey (1633-1648). A gentleman of the Chapel Royal (from 1638). Believed to have

lived for a time in France with a former dean of Westminster, Dr. Williams, a patron of music and musicians. Composed services, anthems including 'Behold, how good and joyful' and 'Rejoice in the Lord', and a Fantasia for Double Organ.

POSTON, Elizabeth (1905-1987)
Born in Highfield, Hertfordshire on 24 October 1905; died in Stevenage, Hertfordshire on 18 March 1987.
Educated privately, studying piano at the Royal Academy of Music, abroad, and under Harold Samuel.
Travelled abroad, collecting folk songs (1930-1939). In charge of the music of the European Service of the B.B.C. (1943-1945). It is said that messages were encoded in the music. Involved in the launch of the Third Programme.
An artist and a writer. Had published a set of seven poems including 'Sweet Suffolk Owl' (1925).
President of the Society of Women Musicians (1955-1961), and governor of the Hertfordshire Rural Music School (1957-1959).
Composed scores for many radio plays. Music editor of *Cambridge Hymnal* (1967) and of *Penguin Book of Christmas Carols* and *Second Penguin Book of Christmas Carols*. Her setting of the 18th century carol 'Jesus Christ the Apple Tree' is widely sung.
Composed a setting of Psalm 150 'O praise God in his holiness', an Antiphon and Psalm for St. Cecilia's Day, choral works and a Sonata for Piano and Violin.

POTT, Revd. Francis (1832-1909)
Born in Southwark, London in 1832; died in Speldhurst, Kent in 1909.
Educated at Brasenose College, Oxford, and ordained in 1856.
Curate of Bishopsworth, Somerset and of the Sussex Parish Churches of Ardingly and Ticehurst. Rector of Northill, Bedfordshire (1866-1891), being forced to retire with the onset of deafness. Spent his retirement at Speldhurst.
Had always taken an interest in hymnology. On the original Committee of *Hymns Ancient and Modern*. Published *Hymns Fitted to the Order of Common Prayer* (1861).
Another musical interest was the development of congregational chanting. Produced *The Free Rhythm Psalter* (1898) but most congregations found it beyond their capabilities.
Author of a pamphlet on the Athanasian Creed and a book on the Te Deum. Wrote a number of hymns including 'Forty Days and Forty Nights' and 'Angel voices ever singing'.
Composed the Christmas motet *Nunc natus est Altissimus*.

POTT, Francis John Dolben (b.1957)
Born in Wallingford, Oxfordshire on 25 August 1957.
A chorister of New College, Oxford, and music scholar of Winchester College, Hampshire and of Magdalene College, Cambridge. Studied composition with Robin Holloway and Hugh Wood, and, privately, piano with Hamish Milne. Graduated M.A. and Mus.B. at the University of Cambridge.
John Bennett lecturer in music at St. Hilda's College, Oxford (from 1991). A bass lay clerk of Winchester Cathedral (from 1991).
Composed *Christus,* a Passion Symphony in five movements, first performed by Iain Simcock at Westminster Cathedral (1991). At 2 hours 20 minutes it is one of the longest organ works in existence.
Has received awards for composition including the Gerald Finzi Trust Memorial Prize (1981) for 'Mosaici di Ravenna'. Has toured extensively in France and the U.S.A. as a recitalist.

Has written works for piano, and chamber music including a Piano Quintet. His church music includes a Magnificat and Nunc Dimittis for Double Choir and Organ (1992), a carol 'That yonge childe', and anthems including 'Almighty God, grant all go well with thee' and a Remembrance Day Anthem 'We who are left'. He cites as influential Nielsen, 15th/16th century polyphony, post-war jazz, the works of **Michael Tippett** prior to 1960, and Robert Simpson.

POWELL, Revd. Clement (1855-1934)
Born on 23 November 1855; died in Burgess Hill, Sussex on 16 July 1934. Educated at Bradfield College, Berkshire and Oriel College, Oxford where he graduated B.A. (1879) and M.A. (1882). Ordained deacon (1880) and priest (1881). Curate of Farnham, Surrey. Rector of Newick, Sussex (from 1885), retiring to Burgess Hill, Sussex in 1919. His hymn tunes 'Clapton', 'Dorking', 'Newick' and 'Light's abode' were used in *Hymns Ancient and Modern. Baptist Hymn Book* (1962) uses his tune 'What do I owe' with the hymn of the same name by **William Dunkerley**.

POWELL, Revd. James Baden
See **BADEN-POWELL**, Revd. James

POWELL, Revd. Thomas Edward (1823-1901)
Born in Hampstead, London on 22 August 1823; died in Whitley, Reading on 8 February 1901. Composed hymn tunes.

POWER, Lionel (?-1445)
Died in Canterbury on 5 June 1445. A contemporary of **John Dunstable**. His *Treatise on the Gamme* was an essay on musical theory. Composed church music. Some manuscripts are to be found in Bologna and in the British Library.

POWERS, Anthony (b.1953)
Born in London on 13 March 1953. Studied music with Nadia Boulanger in Paris, and with **David Blake** and Bernard Rands at York. He has been composer-in-residence to Southern Arts and to the University of Wales. Composed the carol 'This endless night' (1974).

PRATT, George Malcolm (b.1935)
Born in Cheshire on 11 February 1935. Educated at Birkenhead School, Cheshire and as organ scholar at St. Peter's College, Oxford (1956-1960) where he graduated B.Mus (1960) and M.A. Director of music of Abingdon School, Oxfordshire (1960-1964); a lecturer (1964-1974), senior lecturer (1974-1985) and head of department (1984-1985) of the University of Keele. Head of the Department of Music at Huddersfield Polytechnic (1985-1991). Director of the Unit for Research into Applied Musical Perception (R.A.M.P.). Has composed a number of anthems, including 'The earth is the Lord's' and 'O sing unto the Lord'.

PRATT, John (c1772-1855)
Born in 1772 or 1779; died in Cambridge on 9 March 1855. A chorister of King's College, Cambridge, where he studied under **John Randall**, whom he succeeded as organist of King's College (1799-1855) and of the University of Cambridge (from 1800). Appointed organist of St. Peter's College in 1813. Produced collections of church music, including *Psalmodia Cantabrigiensis* (1805), a number of ancient and modern Psalm tunes. Composed a Service in E-flat, four double chants, a Kyrie in E, anthems

including 'Almighty and everlasting' and 'Why art thou so vexed?' and a set of Responses to the Commandments.

PRENDERGAST, Arthur Hugh Dalrymple (1833-1910)
Born in St. Marylebone, London on 28 June 1833; died in Kensington, London on 13 July 1910. Studied music with **James Turle**, organist of Westminster Abbey. Trained as a solicitor, graduating M.A. at the University of Oxford. An amateur musician and a conductor of choral and musical societies. Secretary of the Bach Choir and a fellow of St. Michael's College Tenbury, Worcestershire. One of the first people to introduce the music of **Edward Elgar** to London audiences, putting on *The Black Knight* in May 1895. Composed a Festival Te Deum, settings of the Holy Communion and Evening Service, and anthems of which 'O Lord our Governour' and 'O God thou hast cast us out' are examples. His hymn tunes include 'Axbridge', found in *Hymns Ancient and Modern*. Also composed a sacred cantata *The Second Advent* and madrigals, winning Madrigal Society Prizes (1880 and 1889).

PRENDERGAST, Dr. William (1868-1933)
Born in Burneston, Yorkshire on 4 November 1868; died on 20 February 1933.
The son of an organist of Wem, Shropshire.
A chorister of Winchester Cathedral under **George Arnold**, and assistant organist at some time. Attended Wem Grammar School. Went up to Queen's College, Oxford where he graduated B.Mus. (1898) and D.Mus. (1904).
Organist and choirmaster of the Churches of St. Laurence, Winchester; St. Baldred, North Berwick (from 1888) and St. Paul, York Place, Edinburgh (from 1891).
In Edinburgh he was senior music master at the Royal Blind Asylum and School, and music master at Fettes College. Musical editor of *Scottish Guardian*. His articles on choir training appeared in *Scottish Standard Bearer*. A local musical society conductor.
Organist of Winchester Cathedral (1902-1933).
Composed as his B.Mus. exercise a setting of the Evening Hymn. For his doctorate his exercise consisted of an Overture in C and a Festival Te Deum. In addition he composed Evening and Holy Communion Services, part songs and songs.

PRENTICE, Thomas Ridley (1842-1895)
Born in Ongar, Essex on 6 July 1842; died in Hampstead, London on 15 July 1895.
Studied at the Royal Academy of Music under **George Macfarren** and **Walter Macfarren**.
Gave monthly piano recitals at Brixton, London over a period of several years (from 1869). Organist of Christ Church, Lee, Kent (from 1872) but ill health compelled him to resign and terminate the piano recitals.
A professor of piano at Guildhall School of Music (from 1880) and at the Blackheath Conservatory, Kent. Principal of the Beckenham School of Music (founded 1883). Successful and highly regarded as a teacher of music, and wrote books on piano technique.
Composed an Evening Service, anthems including 'I love the Lord' and 'The God of love my Shepherd is', works for ladies' voices including the cantata *Linda*, part songs and piano pieces.

PRESCOTT, Oliviera Louisa (1842-?)
Born in London on 3 September 1842. Studied privately with Lindsay Sloper, and for seven years at the Royal Academy of

Music under **George Macfarren**, Frederick Jewson, Folkes and Francis Ralph.

Taught harmony in London at the Church of England High School for Girls, Baker Street. At around the same time she was a lecturer in harmony and composition for Newnham College, Cambridge in their correspondence scheme.

Became the amanuensis to George Macfarren. Contributed to *Musical World* and was the author of *Form or Design in Music*.

Her compositions include a setting of Psalm 13 'How long wilt Thou forget me, O Lord?' for Soprano Solo, Chorus and Orchestra and of Psalm 126 'When the Lord turned against the captivity of Sion' for Unaccompanied Voices. Her anthems include 'The righteous live for evermore'. There were ballads and orchestral works including Symphonies in B-flat and in D Minor.

PRESTON, Simon (b.1938)
Born in Bournemouth, Dorset on 4 August 1938.

Educated at Canford School; the Royal Academy of Music and King's College, Cambridge where he graduated B.A. (1961), Mus.B. (1962) and M.A. (1964).

Sub organist of Westminster Abbey (1962-1967), acting organist of St. Albans Abbey (1968-1969), and organist and tutor in music at Christ Church, Oxford (1970-1981). C.U.F. lecturer in music at Oxford University (1972-1981).

Organist and master of the choristers of Westminster Abbey (1981-1987), since when he has concentrated on giving recitals, conducting and recording.

Composed a setting of the Jubilate for Chorus and Orchestra, a Missa Brevis for Choir and Organ, and an eight-part anthem 'God is our Hope and Strength'. Also *Alleluyas*, *Vox Dicentis* and a Fantasia *The Christmas Light* for Organ Solo.

PRESTON, Thomas (c1662-1730)
Born around the year 1662; died in Ripon, Yorkshire in October 1730. Organist of Ripon Cathedral (1690-1730). Composed the anthem 'Sing aloud unto God'.

PRICE, Addison (1871-?)
Studied with **Basil Harwood**. Organist of St. Mary's Catholic Church, Cadogan Gardens (1899-1914) and of the Servite Friars' St. Mary's Priory in Fulham Road, London (from 1919). Composed three Masses, a Stabat Mater, a Benedictus, services and motets. Also composed an opera *Don Quixote*, and songs.

PRICE, Edward Meredith (1816-1898)
Born in St. Harmon, Radnorshire, Wales in 1816; died in Builth, Wales on 5 March 1898.

Both parents died while he was still young. Acquainted with **Thomas Williams**, publisher of *Ceinon Cerddoriaeth* (1852) to which Price contributed six hymn tunes including 'St. Garmon'. Also composed 'Natalia' which appeared in **Griffith Harris**'s *Haleliwiah Drachefn*.

Emigrated to Australia following the death of his brother. Intending to return home, he booked his passage on the *Royal Charter* but to his good fortune, he missed the sailing - the vessel was wrecked off the coast of Anglesey on 20 October 1859 with great loss of life. Returned to St. Harmon but later moved to Builth, continuing to compose.

PRICE, John (Beulah: 1857-1930)
Born in Llangam March, Brecknockshire, Wales on 5 March 1857; died in Builth, Brecknockshire on 21 April 1930.

Moved while young with his family to Beulah, where he remained for the rest of his life. A chorister form the age of 10 at Beulah. At the age of 22 he graduated from the Tonic Sol-fa College. He held music classes in the counties of Brecknockshire, Radnorshire and Carmarthenshire. Conductor of a number of choirs, and an eisteddfod adjudicator.

For 40 years he was an active member of the Tonic Sol-fa Composition Club. His works include anthems such as 'Clyw, fienaid, clyw' and 'Dyma'r dydd', hymn tunes including 'Gwyneth' which was included in the Revised Edition (1927) of *Church Hymnary*, and glees. His compositions were published in the periodical *Y Cerddor*.

PRICE, Richard (17th century)
Composed the anthems 'Almighty and everlasting God' and 'O God, who through the preaching'.

PRICE, Dr. Richard Maldwyn (1890-1953)
Born in Welshpool, Montgomeryshire, Wales in 1890; died on 11 November 1953. Studied at the University College of Wales, Aberystwyth, where he was Open Music exhibitioner and the first student to graduate D.Mus. (Wales). Music master of St. Anne's School, Redhill, Surrey (from 1915) and of Wells House School, Malvern Wells, Worcestershire (from 1919). Organist and choirmaster of St. Mary's Church, Welshpool (from 1933). A local choral society conductor. Composed sacred choral works, part songs, and orchestral and chamber items including a string quartet. Also composed and arranged for brass band. Won first prize at the national eisteddfod of 1911 for his composition for small orchestra.

PRICE, Thomas (1809-1892)
Born in Builth, Brecknockshire, Wales on 17 May 1809; died in Hereford on 7 March 1892. Moved to Crickhowell as a young man, where he kept a shop. Clerk to the local board of guardians. Organist of Llangattock Parish Church for many years. Composer of a number of hymn tunes, of which 'Cysur' is best known. These featured in *Yr Arweinydd Cerddor* and *Caniadan Seion*.

PRICE, Tom (1857-1925)
Born in Rhymney, Monmouthshire, Wales in 1857; died in Merthyr Tydfil, Glamorganshire, Wales on 8 July 1925.

From the age of 10 he worked in a colliery. Musically self taught, acquiring practical knowledge from attending the performances of choirs at Rhymney and at the Three Choirs' Festival. Had a strong interest in Welsh literature. Joined a number of choirs. Worked on the railways, and as a commercial traveller for six years. Eventually became a professional musician and a visiting music master in the newly-established intermediate schools of Glamorganshire County Council (from 1896).

Precentor of Hope Presbyterian Church, Merthyr Tydfil. He adjudicated and conducted at festivals of Psalmody. A successful competitor at *eisteddfodau* between 1887 and 1891. Music editor of *Young Wales* and *Y Solffaydd*.

Composed anthems, hymn tunes, songs, part songs and dramatic cantatas including *The Prodigal Son* (1891). Many of his works were for children. His part song 'Hands all round' won a prize at the Wrexham Festival (1886).

PRINCE, Alfred (19th/20th century)
Trained privately in music. Graduated B.Mus. at the University of Durham (1912). Organist and choirmaster of Holy Trinity Church, Smethwick, Birmingham. Composed as his B.Mus. exercise a 'Song of Thanksgiving'. Also wrote a setting of the Service of Holy Communion, and items for piano.

PRING, Isaac (1777-1799)
Born in Kensington, London in 1777; died in Oxford on 18 October 1799. His brothers were **Jacob** and **Joseph** and he was the uncle of **James Sharpe Pring**. A chorister of St. Paul's Cathedral and later an assistant to **Philip Hayes**, organist of New College, Oxford, whom he succeeded in 1797. Graduated B.Mus. (1799) at the University of Oxford. Composed anthems and chants.

PRING, Jacob Cubitt (1771-1799)
Born in Lewisham, London in 1771 and baptised on 3 November 1771; died in 1799. Brother of **Isaac Pring** and **Joseph Pring** and the uncle of **James Pring**. Like his brother, Isaac, he was a chorister of St. Paul's Cathedral. Later a pupil of **Robert Hudson**. Graduated B.Mus. at the University of Oxford (1797). An organist and a teacher of singing and harpsichord. When the organistship of St. Botolph's Church, Aldersgate, London fell vacant (1786), the candidates included Jacob Pring and Elizabeth Goadby. So bitter was the dispute following the latter's success - by a single vote - that until 1790, the post was shared between the two (1787-1799). Cubitt took the morning services and taught the children, while Goadby played at the afternoon and evening services. Cubitt was the sole organist from 1790. Composed a Magnificat, songs, sonnets, glees, canons and catches.

PRING, James Sharpe (c1811-1868)
Born around the year 1811; died on 3 June 1868. Nephew of the brothers **Isaac Pring** and **Jacob Pring** and the son of **Joseph Pring**. A chorister of Bangor Cathedral, and later assistant to his father, the cathedral organist. Appointed organist of Bangor Cathedral (1842) but only for a period of one year, an arrangement that was repeated until his death (1868). Said to be a very obese man. On at least one occasion, **John Owen** (Owen Alaiw) was the conductor and James Pring the organist of a choral festival in the cathedral. He was the musical editor of the *Bangor Collection of Anthems* (1848). Composer of chants.

PRING, Dr. Joseph (1776-1842)
Born in Kensington, London on 15 January 1776; died in Bangor on 13 February 1842.
His brothers were **Isaac Pring** and **Jacob Pring** and his son was **James Pring**
A chorister of St. Paul's Cathedral (1785-1792). Graduated B.Mus. and D.Mus. at the University of Oxford (1808).
Became organist of Bangor Cathedral (1793-1842) when the incumbent, Edmund Olive resigned in his favour but he was not formally confirmed in the post until September 1810.
He took part, with three vicars choral, in a long and acrimonious dispute with the Dean and Chapter (1813-1819) over the restoration of tithes, alleged to have been misappropriated, for the maintenance of the cathedral choir. The case was heard by Lord Eldon, Lord Chancellor. The plaintiffs were only partly successful and the action was said to have impoverished Pring greatly. Wrote a book describing his experiences.

Compiled an edition of music *A Collection of Anthems used in Bangor Cathedral*. On becoming involved in traditional Welsh music making he was created a Welsh bardic Pencerdd and learned to speak Welsh.
Composed a Magnificat, anthems including 'If the Lord himself' (1798) and 'Ponder my words', and other items of church music.

PRINGUER, Dr. Henry Thomas (1852-1930)
Born in 1852; died on 26 October 1930.
A chorister of Canterbury Cathedral under **W.H. Longhurst**, and at St. Paul's Cathedral under **John Goss**, for whom he deputised occasionally. Graduated B.Mus. (1877) and D.Mus. (1883) at New College, Oxford.
Organist of St. Dunstan's Church, Canterbury (1866-1869); organist and choirmaster of St. Matthew's Church, Redhill, Surrey (1870-1881); organist of St. Mary's Church, Stoke Newington, London (1880-1920), and organist and choirmaster of All Saints' Church Lindfield, Sussex (1920-1930).
A professor of harmony at Trinity College, London and conductor of the choir. On the Board of Studies of the University of London, and a local examiner for the Royal College of Music.
His degree exercises were anthems based on the Book of Psalms. The B.Mus. submission was Psalm 107 'O give thanks unto the Lord' for Solo Voices, Chorus and Orchestra. and for his doctorate the work was from Psalm 48 'Great is the Lord' for the same forces. Also composed a Te Deum and Benedictus in A-flat, a carol 'In the Virgin's arms', an opera *Guinivere* (1890), songs and piano items.

PRINS-BUTTLE, Clara
See **BUTTLE**, Clara.

PRIOR, George (1830-1906)
Born in 1830; died in Battersea, Surrey on 30 April 1906. Composed 12 settings of the Benedicite (1883), a Holy Communion Service (1875), a Thanksgiving Te Deum for the Choir of St. George's Church, Ramsgate, Kent (1887), and hymn tunes.

PRITCHARD, Dr. Arthur John (b.1908)
Born in Gloucester in 1908. Educated at King's School, Gloucester, at the Royal College of Music, and privately under **Alfred Brewer**. Graduated D.Mus. at the University of Durham. Music master of King's School, Gloucester (1927-1931). Chorus accompanist to the Three Choirs' Festival (1927-1932). Director of music of Bartrum Gables, Broadstairs, Kent (from 1935). A professor of harmony and composition at the Royal Academy of Music (from 1947), master of the music of the St. John's Wood Choir (from 1947), and dean of the Faculty of Music of London University (from 1966). Assistant organist of Gloucester Cathedral (1927-1932) and director of music of Christ Church, Lancaster Gate, London (1932-1946). A special commissioner of the Royal School of Church Music. Composed Services, the anthems 'With a voice of singing', 'In heavenly love abiding' and 'O praise God in His Holiness', and organ music.

PRITCHARD, George (19th/20th century)
Born in Burton, near Chester.
Trained privately, at the Holy Trinity School, Runcorn, Cheshire and at Owen's College, Manchester, where he was Hargreaves scholar. Graduated B.Mus. at the University of Durham (1900).

Organist and choirmaster (1903-1906) and choirmaster (1906-1923) of St. Philip's Church, Bradford Road, Manchester. Choirmaster of St. Matthew's Church, Bolton (1914). Held subsequent appointments in and around the city of Manchester as organist and choirmaster of St. Bride's Church, Old Trafford (1906-1915), St. Margaret's Church, Whalley Range (1915-1918), Christ Church, Pendlebury (1918-1925), and St. Ann's Church (1925-1941). Choirmaster of All Saints' Church, Weaste (1918-1919).

Author of *A Course of Preparation in the Theory of Music*.

Composed as his degree exercise *A song of joy and praise* for Tenor Solo, five-part Chorus, Piano and Strings. Also composed a setting of the Te Deum, chants including a Single Chant in F for use with the Te Deum, hymn tunes, and organ works.

PRITCHARD, Revd. Roland Huw (1811-1887)

Born in Y Graienyn, near Bala, Wales on 14 January 1811; died in Holywell, Wales on 25 January 1887. Grandson of the bard Rowland Huw. Lived for most of his life in Bala, where he was a minister and the precentor of the annual Sasiwns y Bala. Moved to Holywell (1880). That year, at the age of 69, he was forced through poverty to take a job as a loom tender's assistant in the mills of the Welsh Flannel Manufacturing Company. Many of his hymn tunes were published in the periodicals of the time. 'Hyfrydol', his most enduring tune, was composed as a young man of 20 and achieved prominence following the harmonisation by **Ralph Vaughan Williams** for *English Hymnal* (1906). Published *Cyfaill y Cantorion* (The Singers Friend: 1824) in which most of the tunes were by him. Also published a booklet of hymns and tunes for children. Other notable tunes by him are 'Elizabeth' and 'Hiraeth y Cristion'. Composer of anthems.

PRITCHARDTS (Pritchard), Thomas Cuthbertson Leithead (1885-1960)

Born in Gorbals, Glasgow on 11 March 1885; died in Glasgow on 24 April 1960. Studied church music at York Minster. Graduated M.A. (University of Glasgow) and B.Mus. (University of Dublin). Organist and choirmaster of Fullarton Church, Irvine and the United Free Churches of St. Stephen, Glasgow, Bearsden, Sherbrooke and Bellhaven (from 1913), the last two named in Glasgow. A professor at the Athanaeum School of Music and a local education authority supervisor of music in schools. Lectured in church music for the training of organists for the Church of Scotland and the United Free Church. An organ recitalist, he wrote articles on various musical topics. He was on the Committee for the Revised Edition (1927) of *Church Hymnary*. Composed hymn tunes including 'Bellhaven', 'Gifford' and 'Leithead', each of which was used in that edition.

PROTHERO, Dr. Daniel (1866-1934)

Born in Ystradgynlais, Wales on 5 November 1866; died in Chicago, U.S.A. on 25 February 1934.

A pupil of **John Rees** (1857-1949). Graduated B.Mus. (1890) and D.Mus. at the University of Toronto.

With a good treble voice he was able to win prizes at the Swansea National Eisteddfod (1880) and at Merthyr Tydfil (1881). At the age of 16 conducted the Ystradgynlais Choir, wining the prize at the Llandeilo Eisteddfod. A year later he emigrated to Scranton, Pennsylvania, U.S.A. where he attended classes given by Parson Price, Dudley Buck and Hugo Karn.

Conductor of the Cymmrodorion Choral Society for 18 years. Moved to Milwaukee in 1892, and subsequently to Chicago. Taught at Sherwood Music School, and was director of music of the Central Church, Chicago. Conducted a number of famous American choirs. Often returned to Wales where he conducted choral festivals. Conductor of the Harlech Music Festival of 1931. Author of *Arwain Corau* (1914).

Composed vocal music, including the cantata *S. Pedr*; many hymn tunes, including 'Hiraeth' (longing); pieces for male voices, including the cantatas *Invictus* and *Nun of Nidaros*, and anthems.

PROTHERO, Henry Allen (1848-1906)

Born in Whippingham, Isle of Wight on 4 November 1848; died in Cheltenham, Gloucestershire on 25 November 1906. Composed hymn tunes.

PROUT, Dr. Ebenezer (1835-1909)

Born in Oundle, Northamptonshire on 1 March 1835; died in Hackney, London on 5 December 1909.

Son of a minister of the Congregational Church.

Attended Denmark Hill Grammar School. Had piano lessons as a boy and later with **Charles Salaman**.

Graduated B.A. at the University of London (1854), at the age of 19 and trained as a schoolteacher. Recipient of the honorary degree of D.Mus. at the Universities of Dublin and Edinburgh (1895): his was Edinburgh's first such award.

Taught at private schools in London and Leatherhead, Surrey (1852-1859) but in the latter year he decided to pursue a career in music.

A professor of piano at the Crystal Palace School of Art (1861-1885), a professor of harmony and counterpoint at the National Training School of Music from its inception (1876-1882) and a professor of piano at Guildhall School of Music (1884-1909). Succeeded **R.P. Stewart** as professor of music at the University of Dublin (1894-1909). Taught harmony and composition at the Royal Academy of Music (1879-1909).

Took over the classes of **Arthur Sullivan** (1899).

He held a number of church organistships in London including those of St. Thomas's Square Chapel, Islington; the Kentish Town Congregational Church; the New Tabernacle, Old Kent Road; St. Mary, Newington Butts and the Union Chapel, Islington (1861-1873).

Editor of the *Monthly Musical Record* (1871-1874) and a critic for *The Academy* (1874-1879) and *The Athanaeum* (1879-1889). As an author his works centred on music theory. They were well received and were translated into a number of languages. They include *Instrumentation* (1876) and *Harmony: Its Theory and Practice* (1889) but his text book on fugue has proved to be the most enduring.

Composed a Magnificat in C (1873), anthems including 'We give Thee thanks' and a setting of Psalm 100. His hymn tunes include 'Laus Sempiterna' and 'Raleigh', both of which were used in the Revised Edition (1927) of *Church Hymnary*.

His other works include three symphonies, 20 overtures, cantatas, string quartets, and organ music.

PRYS, Revd. Edmund (c1544-1624)

Born in Maen Twrog, Wales around the year 1544; died at Maen Twrog in 1624. Educated at St. John's College, Cambridge.

Rector of Ffestiniog (1572). Also rector of Llaneddwyn (from 1580) which carried the responsibility for a chapel at Llanddwywe.

Chaplain to Sir Henry Sydney (from 1567), Lord President of Wales. It was his aim to propagate the singing of church music in Welsh. Published *Llyfr y Psalmau*,(1621) a translation of the Book of Psalms into Welsh. It was included as an appendix to the *Book of Common Prayer* in Welsh. The hymn tunes 'Martyrs', 'Windsor' (also known as 'Dundee') and 'St. Mary', which are sometimes attributed to him, may in fact be English in origin.

PUGH, Arnold (b.1935)

Born, of British parentage, in Central Blissville, New Brunswick, Canada on 27 July 1935, on a large farm, in a small village.

Arrived in England and received his first formal training in music in 1951. Apprenticed and subsequently qualified as a printer but resigned at the age of 28 to study music, initially for three years with a local village organist. Subsequently moved to Rugby Parish Church, Warwickshire, for further study with Alfred Noyce, formerly assistant organist of Ely Cathedral under **Marmaduke Conway**. During National Service, studied with **Russell Missin** at St. Mary's Church, Nottingham. Received further tuition in the 1980s from **David Sanger**.

Organist and choirmaster of Dunchurch Church and Brownson Church, Warwickshire. Organist and director of music of Rugby Parish Church (from 1966). Under his direction, the choir has sung the services in a number of English cathedrals, has recorded music and has performed abroad.

His compositions include the anthem 'God be in my head'.

PUGH, William James Frederick (1887-?)

Born in Doncaster, Yorkshire in 1887. Educated privately, and at the Royal College of Music. Organist and choirmaster in London of St. Peter's Church, Walworth (1912-1914); Chiswick Parish Church (1915-1917) and St. Michael's Church, Sutton Court, Chiswick (from 1919). A local choral society conductor. Composed the anthems 'Crossing the bar' and 'Thanks to God', and organ works including a Rondo in B-flat.

PULLEIN, John (20th century)

Born in Lincoln. Studied with the cathedral organist, **George Bennett**. Organist and choirmaster of the churches of Willingham by Stow, St. Swithin, Lincoln and St. Peter, Harrogate. Organist of St. Mary's Roman Catholic Cathedral, Glasgow (from 1917). Composed church music and part songs.

PULLEIN, William Rose (1865-1945)

Born in Lincoln in 1865; died in Calne, Wiltshire on 8 November 1945. Trained in music at Lincoln Cathedral, where he was assistant organist. Organist to the Marquis of Lansdowne and to H.G. Harris at Calne, Wiltshire, where he was also organist and choirmaster of the Parish Church. A local music and orchestral society conductor. Composed a Benedicite in E-flat (1908), a Magnificat and Nunc Dimittis in B-flat (1909), in F (1909), in E-flat (1921) and a unison version in C (1927) and a setting of the evening hymn 'Before the ending of the day' (1909) and hymn tunes.

PULLON, Helen Robertson (19th/20th century)

Trained privately in music before studying at the University of Edinburgh, where she graduated B.Mus. She lived in Huddersfield, Yorkshire. Composed as her B.Mus. exercise a setting of a paraphrase of Psalm 42 'As pants the hart'. Also the hymn tune 'Edinburgh' to 'The night is come'.

PUNTER, William Harvey (1886-?)

Born in Staple Hill in 1886. Educated privately with **George Riseley**, W.E. Fowler and F. Merrick. Organist and choirmaster of the Bristol Churches of St. Mark (from 1901), St. Michael (from 1908), and Christ Church, Downend (from 1920), and deputy organist of All Saints' Church. Composed a setting of the Benedicite, Magnificat and Nunc Dimittis, a setting of the Holy Communion Service, and anthems including 'Seek ye the Lord' and 'The Lord is my Shepherd'.

PURCELL, Daniel (c1660-1717)

Born in London around the year 1660; died in London and was buried on 26 November 1717.

Brother of **Henry Purcell**.

Although competent musically his career was overshadowed by that of his brother Henry. It is believed that he came to London in May 1695, having previously been organist of Magdalen College, Oxford (1688-c1695). In London he composed for the theatre and he was organist of the Church of St. Dunstan-in-the-East (c1696-1717). Prior to his official appointment he may have served voluntarily.

Voluntary organist of St. Alban's Church, Holborn (c1713-1717).

His patrons included Anthony Henley of The Grange and Philip Norton of Southwick, both in the county of Hampshire.

Compositions include annual Odes to St. Cecilia's Day, a Single Chant in G, hymn tunes, incidental music for around 30 dramas and odes including a Funeral Ode to his brother, Henry. His Evening Service in E Minor was revived by **John Stainer** and newly edited this century by **Christopher Dearnley**.

PURCELL, Henry (1658-1695)

Born in Westminster, London in 1658; died in Westminster on 21 November 1695 and he was buried in Westminster Abbey.

Brother of **Daniel Purcell** and probably the nephew of **Thomas Purcell**.

Sources disagree as to whether his father was Henry Purcell, a gentleman of the Chapel Royal and master of the choristers of Westminster Abbey, or **Thomas Purcell**. One version of events is that the latter adopted Henry when his father, Henry senior, died. Henceforth, Thomas referred to Henry as his son.

Chorister of the Chapel Royal (from 1669), under **Henry Cooke** and **Pelham Humfrey**. Also taught by **John Blow**. Learned to play lute, viol and organ.

When his voice broke (1673), Henry Purcell became a distinguished bass and counter tenor singer. Apprenticed to **John Hingston**, principal keeper of the King's Instruments. Became keeper of the King's wind instruments (1683).

Purcell tuned the organ of Westminster Abbey from 1674 to 1678.

Following the death of Matthew Locke, Purcell became composer to the King's Violins (string band). Members of this ensemble were required, five or six at a time, to spend a month playing in the Chapel Royal while the king was in residence. James II neglected the Chapel Royal and used for his devotions a private Roman Catholic chapel that had been constructed for him at Whitehall.

Following the death of John Blow (1679), Purcell became organist of Westminster Abbey. Appointed a bass lay clerk and, jointly, organist of the Chapel Royal (1682), succeeding **Edward Lowe**.

Appointed composer-in-ordinary to Charles II (1683) and became harpsichordist (conductor) in the King's Private Music in 1685.

Although some sources dispute this he is believed to have been copyist of Westminster Abbey (1676-1678 and from 1688).

The famous Battle of the Organs occurred (1684) at the Temple Church, London. A contest was arranged between the two shortlisted suppliers of a new organ, Renatus Harris and 'Father' Bernard Smith. Harris's instrument was played by John Draghi while John Blow and Henry Purcell, remaining on friendly terms with Draghi, represented the opposition, in whose favour the choice was made.

A dispute took place (1689) between Purcell and the Dean and Chapter of Westminster Abbey. At the Coronation of William and Mary in the Abbey, Purcell had charged admission money to those wanting to sit in the organ loft during the ceremony. Purcell, who considered the practice a perquisite of the job of organist, was given two days to surrender the money. The manner in which the problem was resolved is not known but good relations continued between Purcell and the authorities.

Purcell had provided a temporary organ for the Coronation, around which was arranged the choir of the Chapel Royal while the Abbey choir were close to the main organ.

Worked in various capacities at Westminster Abbey and at the Chapel Royal, taught music to the gentry and the aristocracy and composed for church, court and theatre. He weakened himself through working long hours and premature death was probably contributed to by overwork.

Henry Purcell composed Services, anthems including 'I was glad'- composed for the Coronation of James II (1685) - chants, and sacred songs.

Purcell's Te Deum and Jubilate in D (1694) was set to an orchestral accompaniment, the first such scoring in this country. The Service was adopted by the Corporation of the Sons of the Clergy for their annual Festival and was so used (1697-1713).

The anthem 'They that go down to the sea in ships' was composed to a text from the Book of Psalms at the behest of his friend, the bass singer John Gostling who had been prevailed upon to accompany Charles II and others on a yachting expedition off the North Foreland of Kent which had nearly turned to disaster in adverse conditions.

Composed for the theatre (around 1680). The proportion of his output devoted to such work increased, especially when (from around 1690) he collaborated with the poet Dryden. His operas include **Dido and Aeneas**, and **King Arthur** (1691).

The anthems 'Blessed is the man that feareth the Lord' and 'Thou knowest, Lord, the secrets of our hearts' were composed for the funeral of Queen Mary that so poignantly anticipated his own imminent decease.

Purcell's anthems include a substantial corpus with accompaniment for strings - of these anthems, much the best known are 'Rejoice in the Lord alway' (the *Bell* anthem, on account of its descending scale figuration in the opening symphony) and 'My beloved spake', part of the central section of which was adapted by John Stainer as a double chant. Among simple anthem constructions are the penitential setting of 'Hear my prayer' in eight parts (possibly an opening of a more substantial piece never completed) and 'Remember not, Lord, our offences' for five voices.

PURCELL, Thomas (?-1682)
Born in Westminster, London; died in London on 31 July 1682. The probable uncle of **Daniel Purcell** and **Henry Purcell**. A gentleman of the Chapel Royal (from 1660). A year later he was a lay vicar and copyist of Westminster Abbey and lute player to Charles II (from 1662) in succession to **Henry Lawes**. Composer-

in-ordinary for the Violins (1672), with **Pelham Humfrey**, and marshal of the Corporation of Music in Westminster. Succeeded **John Wilson** (1674) as musician in ordinary. Composed chants.

PURDAY, Charles Henry (1799-1885)
Born in Folkestone, Kent on 11 January 1799; died in Kensington, London on 23 April 1885. The son of a bookseller, Purday was a singer who was one of the performers at the Coronation of Queen Victoria (1837). A lecturer on music in London and elsewhere, a pioneer in the compiling of programme notes for concerts and a reformer of the law on music copyright. He was conductor of Psalmody of the Church of Scotland, Covent Garden. His compilations include *Crown Court Psalmody* (1854), *Church and Home Tune Book* (1857), and, jointly with **William Havergal**, *Songs of Peace and Joy* (1879). His hymn tunes include 'Sandon' and 'Notting Hill'. Also composed many songs.

PYE, Kellow John (1812-1901)
Born in Exeter, Devon on 9 February 1812; died in Exmouth, Devon on 22 September 1901.
Studied at the Royal Academy of Music from its opening (1823-1829) and was the first person to receive a piano lesson (from Cipriani Potter) within the walls of the R.A.M. His other teacher was **William Crotch**. Graduated B.Mus. at the University of Oxford (1842). A teacher of music in Exeter (1830) and became well known in the West of England as a conductor, but handed over his practice (1853) and set himself up in London as a wine merchant. Continued to take an interest in music, being appointed director and chairman of the R.A.M. and serving on the council of the Royal College of Music and the Committee of the Bach Choir. He supported actively the Madrigal Society.
Composed a Te Deum, anthems, a Double Chant in E, madrigals and songs. His anthem 'Turn Thee again' won the Gresham Prize (1833).

PYGOTT,? (16th century)
One of the works of this composer is *Quid petis O Fili*.

PYMAR, Thomas (1775-1854)
Born in 1775; died in 1854. Organist of Beccles Parish Church, Lancashire for 49 years. Composed the anthem 'O God our Refuge' and a Single Chant in A.

PYNE, James Kendrick (1810-1898)
Born in London on 21 August 1810; died on 2 March 1898. Father of **James Kendrick Pyne**. Organist of Bath Abbey Church for 53 years. His anthem 'Proclaim ye this' gained the Gresham Prize of 1839.

PYNE, Dr. James Kendrick (1852-1938)
Born in Bath, Somerset on 5 February 1852; died in 1938.
Son of **James Kendrick Pyne**.
Trained at Bath Abbey and at the Cathedrals of Winchester and Gloucester. Awarded the Lambeth D.Mus. (1900) and the honorary D.Mus. at the University of London.
Assistant organist of the Cathedrals of Winchester, under **S.S. Wesley**, to whom he was articled, and Gloucester.
At the age of 11 he was appointed organist of All Saints' Church, Bath (1863). Other appointments followed at St. Mary's Church, Aylesbury, Buckinghamshire and Christ Church, Clifton, Gloucestershire (from 1873). Organist of St. Mark's Church,

Philadelphia, U.S.A. (1875-1876) and of Manchester Corporation (from 1877).

Lecturer in church music (from 1900) and dean of the Faculty of Music (from 1907) of the Victoria University of Manchester. A professor of organ at the Royal Manchester College of Music (from 1893) and an examiner for the Royal College of Music (1900-1901).

Organist and choirmaster of the Cathedrals of Chichester (1873-1874) and Manchester (1876-1908).

Acquainted with the composers Franck, Guilmant and Widor.

Composed Morning and Festival Holy Communion Services, organ works and piano music.

Q

QUAILE, Robert Newton (1867-1927)
Born in Rathkeale, County Limerick, Ireland on 22 March 1867; died in Mallow, County Cork, Ireland on 26 July 1927. The son of a minister of the Irish Methodist Church. Educated at Wesley College, Dublin. A businessman and amateur musician of Mallow. His home and possessions were destroyed by arson in 1920. His hymn tunes 'Athlone' and 'Oldbridge' were included in the Revised Edition (1927) of *Church Hymnary*.

QUARLES, Charles (?-1727)
Died in York in 1727. Graduated Mus. B. at the University of Cambridge (1698). May have been the son of Charles Quarles, an organ builder who supplied instruments to Pembroke College and Christ Church College in 1707. Organist of York Minster (1722-1727). A person of the same name, and probably a member of the same family, was organist of Trinity College, Cambridge (1688-1717). Composed church music and lessons for the harpsichord. His anthems include 'I will love Thee, O Lord', and 'We will go into His tabernacles'.

QUAYLE, John Edward (19th/20th century)
Born in Malew, Isle of Man. Graduated B.Mus. at the University of Durham (1912). Choirmaster of Rosemount Church, Douglas, Isle of Man. Composed as his degree exercise the anthem 'Domine refugium'. His other works include a setting of Psalm 23 for Solo Voices, Chorus and String Orchestra and orchestral and organ works such as his Prelude and Fugue in B Minor and Variations on a 17th Century Manx Chorale for Organ (1937).

QUILTER, Roger Cuthbert (1877-1953)
Born in Brighton, Sussex on 1 November 1877; died in London on 21 September 1953.
The son of Sir Cuthbert Quilter, Member of Parliament.
Led a sheltered childhood and suffered from poor health. Attended a preparatory school at Farnborough, Hampshire and then Eton College. For four years he studied at the Frankfurt Conservatory where his teachers for composition included Iwan Knorr.
Forged a friendship in Germany with a group of his contemporaries: Norman O'Neill, Cyril Scott, Percy Grainger and **Henry Balfour Gardiner**. Collectively, they showed the

characteristics of a distinct school of composition, and they became known as the 'Frankfurt Group'.
Lived in London at Marble Arch and St. John's Wood. Described as charming, witty, gentle and conservative. He refused to take pupils for formal musical appointments but he encouraged young singers.
His love of poetry was even greater than that of music, and he admired particularly the works of Herrick, Keats, Shakespeare and Shelley.
An operation failed to cure a stomach ailment and he was bed-ridden from time to time. Towards the end of his life he suffered from mental illness, accentuated by the death of a nephew, and he spent two prolonged periods, from 1936, in a mental institution. He died insane.
Remembered for a number of elegant songs, and for the incidental music he composed for the stage. Composed the song cycle *Julia* (1936). His church music includes the anthem 'Lead us, Heavenly Father' (1908).

R

RADCLIFFE, James (1751-1818)
A lay clerk of the Cathedrals of Worcester and Durham. Composed anthems including 'O be joyful in the Lord' and 'Thy Word is a lantern'.

RADCLIFFE, Philip Fitzhugh (1905-1985)
Born in Godalming, Surrey, in 1905; died on 2 September 1985. Attended Charterhouse, Surrey (1918-1924) and King's College, Cambridge, where he read classics and music with Moule and E.J. Dent, graduating B.A. (1928) and Mus.B. (1929). A fellow (1931-1937 and from 1948) and university lecturer in music (1947-1972). Books include *Mendelssohn*, published as part of the Dent *Master Musician* Series (1954, republished in 1967) and *Schubert Sonatas* (1967). Contributed to the fifth edition of Grove's *Dictionary of Music and Musicians*, and to *Criterion* and other journals. Also wrote a biography of **John Ireland** (1954).
Compositions include the anthems 'I will lift up mine eyes' (1931) for Male Voices and Organ, 'God be in my head' (1975) and *Three Introits* (1964). Also composed songs, and a string quartet.

RADIGER, Anton (1749-1817)
Born in Chatham, Kent in 1749 of German parents; died in Chatham in 1817. Compositions include Psalm tunes such as 'Praise', 'Compassion' and 'Denton's Green'. Also composed songs and piano music. Published three duets (1796).

RAMSEY, Benjamin Mansell (1849-1923)
Born in Surrey in 1849; died in West Wittering, Chichester, Sussex on 31 August 1923. An author of hymns and composer of hymn tunes.

RAMSEY, Robert (c1600-1664)
Graduated Mus.B. at the University of Cambridge (1616). A member of Trinity College, Cambridge, where he was master of the choristers (1637-1644). A number of services by him were published, including a Service in F. Also composed three settings of the Litany, anthems including 'Almighty and everlasting God' and 'How are the mighty fallen', and madrigals. His degree exercise was a Canticum, performed at St. Mary's Church, Cambridge.

RANDALL, Greenwood (17th/18th century)
Lived around the end of the 17th century. Composed a Short Service.

RANDALL, Dr. John (1717-1799)
Born on 26 February 1717; died in Cambridge on 18 March 1799. A chorister of the Chapel Royal under **Bernard Gates**.
Graduated Mus.B. (1744) and Mus.D. (1756) at the University of Cambridge, where he was organist of King's College (1742-1799), Trinity College (1777-1799), St. John's College and Pembroke Hall. Organist to the University of Cambridge and St. Mary's Church, Cambridge.
Professor of music of the University of Cambridge (1755-1799), succeeding **Maurice Greene**.
His friends included the poet Thomas Grey, some of whose odes he set to music.
His church music includes two famous Double Chants, Psalms, anthems including 'O Lord, grant the King' and 'Who hath believed?' and hymn tunes. *A Collection of Psalm and Hymn Tunes...* (1794) contained six of his own hymn tunes including 'Lewes' (c1774), subsequently used in *Hymns Ancient and Modern*.
Other compositions include songs such as 'Happy Swain'.

RANDALL (Randoll), William (?-c1604)
Died, possibly in Exeter, Devon around the year 1604. A chorister and a vicar choral of Exeter Cathedral. A gentleman (from 1584) and organist of the Chapel Royal (1592-1604). Took part in the Funeral of Elizabeth I and the Coronation of James I. Two years earlier he had enlisted Elizabeth's assistance in his attempt to claim back his vicar choralship at Exeter, claiming that he had been dismissed on being appointed to the Chapel Royal. The continuing absence of his name in the cathedral records of that time suggests that he was unsuccessful. Composed various items of church music.

RAPLEY, Edmund Felton (b.1907)
Born in Gosport, Hampshire in 1907. Educated at Winchester Cathedral School and with **William Prendergast**. Music editor of the publishing house of Chappell (1949-1967), and organist and choirmaster of Epsom Parish Church, Surrey (1948-1965).

Composed anthems and other items of church music, film music, and light orchestral works.

RATCLIFFE, Desmond (b.1917)
Born on 8 December 1917. His compositions include an Evening Service in F, the anthems 'Give us the wings of faith' and 'In salutation', and the organ piece *The Infant King* based on a Spanish carol. 'How long wilt Thou be angry?', written for the Choir of Leeds Parish Church, has been charactersied as in the style of Hindemith.

RATCLIFFE, James (1751-1818)
A lay vicar of Durham Cathedral. His composition of church music includes Psalms, chants and anthems.

RATHBONE, George (1874-?)
Born in Manchester in 1874. Educated privately and at the Royal College of Music, and graduated B.Mus. at the University of Durham. A pianist, and the chorus master of a choir whose members were drawn from a number of villages in Westmorland.
The anthem 'Rejoice in the Lord alway' is an example of his church music: he also composed services. Among his cantatas is *The Pied Piper*, and his other works include school songs and part songs.

RAVENSCROFT, Thomas (c1590-c1635)
Baptised either in 1590 or on 13 June 1592; died in London around 1635.
A chorister of St. Paul's Cathedral under Edmund Pearce or **Martin Peerson** and he attended lectures at Gresham College, London. Graduated Mus.B. at the University of Cambridge in 1605 or 1607.
Related to the poet John Milton, with whose father, **John Milton**, he collaborated. Music master of Christ's Hospital, London (1618-1622). Part of his working life was spent in Reading, Berkshire.
Famous for his *Whole Booke of Psalmes* (1621, corrected and enlarged in 1633) in which the Psalms were set to existing tunes that had been harmonised by 16 leading composers of the day, including **Thomas Ravenscroft, Richard Alison, Thomas Tallis** and **Thomas Tomkins.**
Published books of rounds and catches: his *Pammelia* is the earliest known collection of rounds and canons to be published in this country.
In addition to rounds and songs he composed some 11 anthems including 'O Jesu meek' and 'Ah, helpless wretch'. At least 11 of his anthems were composed for the boys of Christ's Hospital.
His hymn tunes include 'Durham' and 'Gloucester', and although he did not actually begin the practice of naming tunes after English place names, he made it popular.

RAWLE, George Daniel (19th/20th century)
Graduated B.Mus. at the University of London in 1897. Lived in Ealing, Middlesex. Composed as his degree exercise a setting of Psalm 24 'The earth is the Lord's' for Solo Voices, Chorus and Strings. Also composed a service, songs and piano music.

RAWSTHORNE, Christopher Noel (b.1929)
Born in Birkenhead, Cheshire on 24 December 1929.
Noel Rawsthorne was a chorister of Liverpool Cathedral. Attended the Liverpool Institute High School, winning a scholarship to the Royal Manchester College of Music. Studied with Germani at the

Chigiana Academia, Siena, Italy and with Marcel Dupré in France, both under a Gulbenkian scholarship.
Assistant organist (from 1949) and organist (1955-1980) of Liverpool Cathedral. Senior lecturer at St. Katharine's College of Education.
Composed the anthem 'O give thanks to the Lord' and a Rite A Festive Eucharist. His output and range of compositions has increased considerably since his retirement from Liverpool.

RAYLTON (Railton), William (?-1757)
Pobably a chorister of Canterbury Cathedral. Master of the choristers and acting organist of Canterbury Cathedral for Daniel Henstridge from December 1718; organist (1736-1757). Composed Sevices in A and in E-flat, and anthems including 'Behold, I bring you' and 'O give thanks'.

REA, Dr. William (1827-1903)
Born in London on 25 March 1827; died in Newcastle-on-Tyne in 1903.
An articled pupil of **Josiah Pittman**. Later studied under **William Sterndale Bennett**. In 1849 he studied at Leipzig and Prague under Raimund Dreyschock, Ignaz Moscheles and Ernst Richter.
Graduated D.Mus. honorarily at the University of Durham in 1886.
Having deputised as organist for Josiah Pittman, William Rea was organist of the London Churches of Christ Church, Watling Street (1843); St. Andrew, Undershaft (1847-1848) and St. Michael, Stockwell.
Organist at concerts of the Society of British Musicians and a performer at chamber concerts. Accompanist to the Harmonic Union.
His career progressed in North East England. Organist to the Corporation of Newcastle-on-Tyne (1860-1888). Organist of the Churches of SS Thomas, Andrew and Mary, North Shields between 1864 and 1878, and of St. Hilda's Church, South Shields. Founded music societies, promoted concerts (1867-1876) and introduced major new works.
Was introduced to Mendelssohn and became acquainted with other prominent composers of the period.
Composed anthems including 'Sing, O daughter of Zion' and 'O give thanks', a Jubilee Ode for the Newcastle Exhibition (1887), songs, and works for piano and for organ.

READ, Dr. Frederick John (1857-1925)
Born in Faversham, Kent in December 1857; died in Chichester, Sussex on 28 January 1925.
Graduated B.Mus. (1876) and D.Mus. (1891) at the University of Oxford.
A pupil of Robert Sloman, **C.W. Corfe** and **Frederick Bridge**.
Organist of Christ Church, Reading, Berkshire (1876-1886), where one of his pupils was **H.P. Allen.**
Organist of Chichester Cathedral for two terms of office (1887-1902 and 1921-1925).
Joined the Royal College of Music in 1886 as a professor of harmony. Also a member of the Council of the Royal College of Organists, for whom he was an examiner. His absence from Chichester in London on College and other business gave rise to disapproval among the cathedral authorities. Accordingly he resigned in 1902, but he was reappointed in 1921.
An examiner for the Associated Board of the Royal Schools of Music and to the Universities of Oxford (1903-1907) and London (1910-1914).

Dean of the Faculty of Music of the University of London (1912-1916).

Composed services, anthems including 'Let my complaint', madrigals such as 'My dearest love', part songs and items for organ.

READING, John (?-1692)

Died in Winchester, Hampshire in 1692.

A junior vicar, poor clerk (from 1667), and master of the choristers (from 1670) of Lincoln Cathedral.

Organist and master of the choristers of Winchester Cathedral (1675-1681) and of Winchester College (1681-1692) where he composed an Election Grace for the scholars.

Composed the anthems 'All people that on earth do dwell' and 'Thou knowest, Lord'.

READING, John (1677-1764)

Born in 1677; died in London on 2 September 1764.

A John Reading, possibly this person, was a child of the Chapel Royal until 1699 under **John Blow**, with whom he also studied.

He held four London organistships simultaneously until his death: St. Mary, Woolnoth (from 1727); St. Dunstan-in-the-West (from 1739); St. John's, Hackney (from 1707 or 1708) and St. Mary's, Woolchurchhaw. Organist of Dulwich College, London (1700-1702) and an original member of the Royal Society of Musicians.

A lay vicar (from 1702) and master of the choristers (from 1703) of Lincoln Cathedral.

Published *A Book of New Anthems...* (1715) and *A Book of New Songs...* (1720). His anthems include 'Be merciful unto me' and 'Unto Thee, O Lord'.

REAY, Samuel (1822-1905)

Born in Hexham on 17 March 1822; died in Newark, Nottinghamshire on 21 July 1905.

Son of George Agnew Reay, organist of Hexham Abbey Church.

At the age of eight, following the family's move to Ryton-on-Tyne, he became a chorister of Durham Cathedral. Studied under the cathedral organist, William Henshaw, and under the precentor, Revd. Peter Penson. Graduated B.Mus. at the University of Oxford in 1871.

Assistant organist of St. Andrew's Church, Newcastle-on-Tyne under James Stimpson. Organist of North Shields Roman Catholic Chapel; the Parish Churches of St. Hilda, South Shields and St. Michael, Houghton le Spring; and St. Andrew's, Newcastle (from 1841), where he took up the position made vacant by the departure of **James Stimpson** to Carlisle Cathedral.

Thereafter organist of the Churches of St. Thomas, Barras Bridge, Newcastle (from 1845); St. Peter, Tiverton (from 1847); St. John, Hampstead, London (from 1854); St. Saviour, Warwick Road (from 1856) and St. Stephen, Paddington.

Succeeded **E.G. Monk** as organist and precentor of Radley College, Oxfordshire (from 1859). In 1861 he became organist of Bury Parish Church, Lancashire and in 1864 he succeeded **Edward Dearle** as song schoolmaster of Newark Parish Church, where he was also organist (1864-1901).

On 27 October 1879, Samuel Reay performed Bach's *Peasant Cantata* and *Coffee Cantata* with the Newark Philharmonic Society at the Bromley and Bow Institute, London, the first person in England to give these works. He and a Mrs. Newton had edited the English text. Another Samuel Reay 'first' was his inaugural recital on the organ of Newcastle Cathedral (1891) and a probable

other was his playing of Mendelssohn's *Wedding March* - his performance at a wedding at Tiverton Parish Church on 2 June 1847 may have been the first in this country.

With **Henry Gauntlett** and (probably **Frederick**) **Bridge** editor of Dobson's *Tunes New and Old*.

Composed church music, including Morning, Holy Communion and Evening services in F; anthems such as 'I will go to the altar', 'O Lord, why sleepest Thou?' and 'O Sing unto the Lord'; hymn tunes including 'Stamford', found today in *Hymns and Psalms* (1983), chants, a set of Responses to the Commandments in F, and part songs including 'As it fell upon a day'.

REDFORD, John (c1485-1547)

Born around the year 1485; died late in 1547. A chorister and a vicar choral of St. Paul's Cathedral. Played organ sufficiently regularly at St. Paul's from 1525 to around 1540 to be described as 'organist', although organists were not formally appointed until the latter part of the 17th century. Almoner and master of the choristers, his duties including the preparation of the choir boys for plays. Author of a play for them. Composed a number of items for the Choir of St. Paul's Cathedral. 'Rejoice in the Lord alway' is attributed to him. Other items are found in manuscript within various private collections. He also composed organ works.

REDHEAD, Alfred Edward (1855-1937)

Born in Swaffham, Norfolk in 1855; died in Guildford, Surrey on 17 July 1937. The son of **Richard Redhead**. At the age of 12 he was organist of St. Mark's Church, North Audley Street, London. Organist of St. Augustine's Church, Kilburn, London (1878-1915); Bletchingley Parish Church, Surrey (1916-1922) and Ranmore Parish Church (1922-1936), giving a farewell organ recital on 1 November 1936. Organist of Lord Ascombe's private chapel at Ranmore Common. Composed more than 500 items. The hymn tune 'Petra' is often used with 'Rock of Ages'; another of his tunes is 'King Alfred', Composed Christmas carols for children, cantatas for female voices including *The Flower Pilgrims* and *Twelfth Night*, part songs and songs.

REDHEAD, Richard (1820-1901)

Born in Harrow, Middlesex on 1 March 1820; died in Hellingly, Sussex on 27 April 1901. Father of **Alfred Redhead**.

A chorister of Magdalen College, Oxford (from 1829), and a pupil of the College organist, Walter Vicary.

Organist in London of the Margaret Chapel (later renamed All Saints' Church, Margaret Street) from 1839 to 1864, where the incumbent was Revd. Frederick Oakeley. Daily choral services were introduced. For a short time during his term of office at All Saints' he held the position concurrently with that of St. Thomas's Church, Portman Square.

His other organistships were those of St. Andrew's Church, Wells Street (1847-1856) and, for 30 years, the Church of St. Mary Magdalene, Paddington (1864-1894).

A supporter of the Oxford Movement, and with Revd. Frederick Oakeley editor of the first Gregorian Psalter, entitled Laudes Diurnae (1843). Edited various collections of church music, including the *Parish Tune Book* and *Church Hymn Tunes* (1853).

Composed hymn tunes including 'Bright the Vision'. Other tunes have been misattributed to him. Also composed Masses, a Te Deum in C, and anthems.

REES, John Thomas (1858-1949)
Born in Ystradgynlais, Breconshire, Wales in 1858; died in Aberystwyth, Wales on 14 October 1949.
Received very little formal education before beginning work at the age of nine in the colliery at Cwm Rhondda. He learned the rudiments of music using the Tonic Sol-fa method through self study. Eventually he studied music under **Joseph Parry** at the University College of Wales, Aberystwyth. Graduated B.Mus. at the University of Toronto.
A lecturer in the School of Music, University College Aberystwyth. Led festivals of music in the town and acted as adjudicator at *eisteddfodau.* He is said to have conducted more *cymanfaoedd ganu* (festivals of congregational hymn singing) than any other Welsh musician.
For some years he was a teacher of music in the U.S.A. One of his pupils was **Daniel Prothero,** who was to become a conductor both in Wales and the U.S.A.
A member of the committee for *Methodist Hymn Book* of 1897 and of 1929. In the latter edition, 16 tunes plus 12 arrangements were by him. One of the 16 was 'Llwynbedw', named after the farmhouse where he was born. Another popular hymn tune by him was 'Dole'. Composed other works for voices, and some instrumental items.

REES, William Thomas (Alaw Ddu: 1838-1904)
Born near Bridgend, Glamorgan, Wales on 29 September 1838; died on 19 March 1904.
The family moved to Aberdare in 1851. Shortly thereafter the father died and the son began work in a colliery. Moved to Dinas (1861), where he composed the hymn tune 'Glanrhondda', and to Pontypridd (1864) where he became precentor of Pennel Calvinistic Methodist Chapel and later, of Lady Llanover's Chapel (from 1868). Moved again, this time to Llanelly (1870) and became precentor of the Trinity Calvinistic Methodist Chapel. Founded a philharmonic society, conducted at singing festivals and adjudicated at *eisteddfodau.*
Musically self-taught, and was influenced by **John Roberts** (Ieuan Gwyllt), whose biography he compiled, and by other musicians living around Aberdare.
An eisteddfod adjudicator, and prizewinner with his motet *Gweledigaetn Ioan* (Conway Eisteddfod: 1877) and for his dissertation on the subject of raising musical standards (London Eisteddfod: 1887). Contributed articles on music to various journals. Editor of *Y Gerddorfa* (1872-1879) and of other journals. Composed four Requiems, anthems, the oratorio *Ruth a Naomi,* an opera *Llewellyn* for children, cantatas, choruses, glees, songs and part songs.

REEVE, William (1757-1815)
Born on 4 March 1757; died in London on 22 June 1815. An alto singer, organist and composer, being elected to the Royal Society of Musicians in 1786. Held organ positions in Totnes, Devon (1781-1783) and in London at Astley's Circus, Covent Garden Theatre (from 1791) and Sadlers Wells (from 1794) of which he was a proprietor, and of the Church of St. Martin, Ludgate Hill (from 1792). Composed music for such plays as *Oscar and Malvina* (1791) and *Apparition* (1794). Also composed glees and songs.

REID, Eric James (1936-1970)
Born in Banff, Scotland on 24 February 1936; died in Aberdeen, Scotland in a car accident on 20 August 1970. Educated at the University of Aberdeen before carrying out postgraduate study in Germany, where he became interested in twelve-tone music. Lecturer in music at Turriff Academy (1961-1967) and at Dundee College of Education, Scotland (1967-1969). Spent a year as a teacher on an exchange programme at Tenton Street College, New Jersey, U.S.A. He took part in the Scottish Church's Consultation on Church music, Dunblane (from 1962). His hymn tune 'Trotting' was composed for his own hymn, 'Trotting through Jerusalem'. Composed a ballad opera *Tisty's Annie.*

REINAGLE, Alexander Robert (1756-1809)
Born in Portsmouth, Hampshire, where he was baptised on 23 April 1756; died in Baltimore, U.S.A. on 21 September 1809.
The uncle of **Alexander Reinagle.**
Studied in Edinburgh with Raynor Taylor, and in London.
Organist of St. Peter's Church, East Oxford. This connection has led to the attribution to him of the hymn tune 'St. Peter', which is also known as 'Christchurch'. It is more likely to be the work of his nephew, who later held the same office.
Visited Lisbon and other European cities. A friend of C.P.E. Bach.
In 1786 he travelled to New York. In the same year he settled in Philadelphia, where he taught, and managed subscription concerts. In New York he was also a concert promoter, as well as being a singer, pianist, conductor and composer.
Associated with the Old American Company, for whom he may have acted as harpsichordist, probably featuring in the company's 1788-1789 season in New York.
In 1793 he became director of music of a company incorporated for the production of plays and comic operas. The General director was Thomas Wignell. The New Theatre opened in New York in February 1793 with Reinagle as composer, singer and director. Later managed a company in Baltimore.
He is credited with being responsible for the introduction of four-hand piano music to the U.S.A.
Composed Single Chants in D and in F. His other works include piano sonatas, a Violin Sonata (c1780) and music for the theatre.

REINAGLE, Alexander Robert (1799-1877)
Born in Brighthelmstone (now Brighton), Sussex on 21 August 1799, died in Kidlington, Oxfordshire on 6 April 1877. The son of Joseph Reinagle, a cellist and composer whose family originated in Austria, and the nephew of **Alexander Reinagle.** His only musical appointment was that of St. Peter's Church, Oxford (1822-1853). A teacher of organ. Compiled tutors for violin and for cello. He published books of hymn tunes in 1836 and in 1840. Composed the hymn tunes 'St. Peter' (1830) and 'Beati immaculati', chants, organ introits and violin exercises.

REITH, Angela (b.1952)
Born in Somerset on 23 April 1952. Educated at the University of Birmingham; at Homerton College, Cambridge and, in theology, at St. John's College, Cambridge and the University of Nottingham. Became an audio-visual producer, working on a freelance basis for charities and religious groups such as the Scripture Union. A descant by Angela Reith is found in *Hymns and Psalms* (1983).

RENSHAW, William H. (1863-?)
Born in Sutton in Ashfield, Nottinghamshire in 1863. Studied music with C.H. Briggs. Music master of Barnsley Grammar School, and organist and choirmaster of Annesley Parish Church, Nottinghamshire. Composed anthems, songs, and marches.

REYNOLDS, Dr. Charles Tom (1865-?)
Born in Ross-on-Wye, Herefordshire on 1 October 1865. A chorister of Hereford Cathedral. Graduated B.Mus. (1890) and D.Mus. (1895) at New College, Oxford. Organist and choirmaster of Denstone College, Staffordshire (from 1882). Organist of Oswestry Parish Church, Shropshire (from 1885) and, in Birkenhead, Cheshire, of the Churches of St. Mark (1896 -1897) and Christ Church (from 1897). Also a local choral and philharmonic society conductor in the North West of England. His degree submissions were the anthem 'De profundis' (B.Mus.) and a cantata *The Childhood of Samuel* for Solo Voices, Chorus and Orchestra (D.Mus.). Also composed services, anthems and part songs.

REYNOLDS, Gordon (1921-1995)
Born in Hull, Yorkshire on 30 June 1921; died in Petersham, Surrey on 18 May 1995.
Appointed L.V.O. (1983).
A chorister of Holy Trinity Church, Hull. Pupil and assistant from the age of 15 to **Herbert Kennedy Andrews**, organist of Beverley Minster. Read English at University College, Hull. Studied at the Royal College of Music with **Harold Edwin Darke** and **Walter Alcock**. Learned the art of choir training under **E.T. Cook**.
Saw war service with the R.A.F. Second assistant organist of Bradford Cathedral (1946-1947) and taught at Hanson High School, Bradford. Organist of St. Martin's Church, Hull and taught at Kingston High School, Hull (from 1947).
From 1950-1958 he was a producer for the B.B.C. in the Schools' Music Department. His programme 'Music Box' became well known, as did 'Singing Together'. The first organist appointed to bomb-damaged St. Bride's Church, Fleet Street, London after World War II, serving from 1952-1965. The incumbent was Revd. Cyril Armitage, formerly precentor of Westminster Abbey for 17 years, who was in sympathy with Reynolds' desire to restore the music to its former glory of pre-war years.
He joined Whitelands College, Putney, the Anglican teacher training college, in 1958, as a member of the music department. In 1969 he became senior academic professor of music at the Royal Military College of Music, Kneller Hall, Twickenham, Middlesex. Retired in 1986 and was accorded the title of emeritus professor.
Organist of the Chapel Royal, Hampton Court Palace (from 1967), a position he held until his death. From 1987 he was chairman of the Church Music Society.
Author of a number of books on subjects relating to music and education, and on church music. He edited *the Oxford School Music Course* series. Consultant editor of the journal *Music in Education* and contributed as reviewer to a number of publications including *Gramophone*, and *Choir and Organ*. From 1962 he was an adviser to the publisher Novello & Co.
Composed the anthem 'Alleluia! God is gone up with a merry noise'.

REYNOLDS, John (?-?1770)
Died in Lambeth, London either in 1770 or in November 1778. A gentleman of the Chapel Royal (1765-1770). Composed the anthem 'My God, my God, look upon me'.

REYNOLDS, Simon (20th century)
Has composed a version of the carol 'Good King Wenceslas', and the anthems 'Like as the hart' and 'The Holy Son of God'.

RHODES, Dr. Harold William (1889-1956)
Born in Hanley, Staffordshire on 15 September 1889; died in Sanderstead, Surrey on 27 February 1956.
A chorister of St. George's Chapel, Windsor Castle, and subsequently trained at the Royal College of Music (from 1904) as open scholar in organ playing and composition, under **Walter Parratt**. Graduated B.Mus. (1911) and D.Mus. (1923) at the University of London.
In his 13th year he was appointed to an organistship in Worcester. Acting assistant to Walter Parratt at St. George's Chapel, Windsor Castle (1908-1910). Organist and choirmaster of the Chapel Royal, Windsor Great Park (1909-1910).
Music master and assistant organist of Lancing College, Sussex (1910-1912) and he was organist and choirmaster of St. John's Church, Torquay, Devon (1912-1928).
Appointed organist of Coventry Cathedral in July 1928. Not the authorities' initial choice, for **Herbert Sumsion** had been offered the job and accepted it. Sumsion asked to be released from his commitment when, following the death of **A.H. Brewer**, he was appointed organist of Gloucester Cathedral. Rhodes remained in office for five years, from where many of his organ recitals were broadcast on the radio.
Organist of Winchester Cathedral (1933-1948).
A professor of the Royal Academy of Music (from 1938), and an examiner for the Associated Board of the Royal Schools of Music and for the Royal College of Organists.
Composed services, anthems, a Single Chant in D which is found in *Baptist Hymn Book* (1962), part songs and items for piano.

RHODES, Keith Vernon (1930-1992)
Born in Bradford, Yorkshire on 4 March 1930; died in 1992.
Attended Grange Grammar School, Bradford and the University of Leeds where he graduated B.Mus. (1952). Studied music with **Melville Cook**, organist of Leeds Parish Church.
Returned to his former school as music master in 1955, remaining there until 1973. He taught at the Royal Manchester College of Music (1975-1984) and at Huddersfield Technical College.
Organist of Menston Parish Church, Yorkshire (1958-1960) and Heaton Parish Church, Bradford (1960-1963).
Organist and master of the choristers of Bradford Cathedral (1963-1981). On leaving Bradford Cathedral he was founder-director of the Bradford Choristers.
For 21 years he was deputy chorus master, organist and accompanist to the Huddersfield Choral Society. Appointed director of music at Ashville College, Harrogate in 1984.
An examiner in music with the Associated Board of the Royal Schools of Music, and a special commissioner of the Royal School of Church Music.
Author of *Musical Training for Choristers* (1969).
His compositions include a setting of the Alternative Service Book version of the Order of Holy Communion.

RICHARDS, Revd. David (1822-1900)
Born in Brynberian, Pembrokeshire, Wales in 1822; died on 1 March 1900.
The son of a ship's carpenter who was an amateur singer. Moved to Blaenau, Monmouthshire while young and worked in a colliery. Learned music through using *Gramadeg Cerddoriaeth*, a textbook on the elements of music by **John Mills** (Ieuan Glan Alarch). Became familiar with the (**John**) **Hullah** system of notation, which he then taught.
Led the singing in the Congregational Chapel, Berea. Moved to Brynberian, where he kept a school, and then to Cefn Cantref, near Brecon, where he did likewise. Studied at the Congregational College, Brecon (1851-1855) and was precentor of Plough Chapel. Upon ordination became minister of Siloam Congregational Church, Llanelli (1855-1862), where he collected hymn tunes as memorised and sung by some of the older members of the congregation. In 1862, when he moved to the Caerphilly area, he published this collection, which contains many Welsh airs, under the title of *Sŵn Addoli* (Sound of Worship).
Wrote articles, and lectured, on music. A music festival adjudicator. Composed hymn tunes, and duets.

RICHARDS, David (1835-1906)
Emigrated to Wilksbarre, Pennsylvania, U.S.A. Composed the hymn tune 'Dyffryn Baca' (The Valley of Baca) which was first published in *Y Blwch Cerddorol* (The Musical Casket) in 1854.

RICHARDS, Dr. Henry William (1865-1956)
Born in Notting Hill, London in 1865; died near Reading, Berkshire on 4 January 1956.
Trained at All Saints' Choir School, Notting Hill. Graduated B.Mus. (1895) and D.Mus. (1903) at the University of Durham.
Deputy organist in London at All Saints' Church, Notting Hill (1878-1880).
Henry Richards was organist and choirmaster of the London Churches of St. John, Kilburn (1880-1886) and Christ Church, Lancaster Gate (from 1886), where he remained for 35 years. A recitalist, in 1882 he performed before Queen Victoria in Windsor Castle. Became organist of the Queen's Hall Choral Society in 1897.
A professor of organ and choir training at the Royal Academy of Music, and a professor of organ at the London Music School. In each of the years 1909, 1910 and 1912 he was director of the Royal Philharmonic Society. An examiner for the Royal College of Organists and a member of the Committee of the R.A.M.
Warden of the R.A.M. (1924-1934) and president of the R.C.O.
Among his published writings was a series of lectures on choir training; he was the author of *Organ Accompaniment of the Church Services*.
Composed as his B.Mus. exercise a work taken from the text of Isaiah 23: *Song of Praise* and for the D.Mus., the cantata *The foe behind*. Composed anthems and organ works.

RICHARDS, Hubert J. (b.1921)
Born in Weilderstadt, Germany on 25 December 1921. At the age of six the family returned to England.
Educated at Finchley Grammar School, London; the Gregorian University, Rome and at the Biblical Institute, Rome. A lecturer in Scripture at St. Edmund's College, Ware, Hertfordshire (1949-1965).

Principal of Corpus Christi College, London (1965-1972) and senior lecturer in religious studies at Keswick Hall College, near Norwich (from 1975).
His hymn tune 'Go tell everyone' is found in the modern collection *Hymns and Psalms* (1983).

RICHARDS, John (Isalaw: 1843-1901)
Born in Bangor, Wales on 13 July 1843; died in Bangor on 15 September 1901.
Attended Garth British School, Bangor and, for two years, Shoreland Road School, Birmingham. Studied music in Birmingham with Andrew Deakin, although he lived for most of his life in Bangor.
Found work as a clerk. Mastered the Tonic Sol-fa notation and, with Thomas Williams, Precentor of Tabernacle Calvinistic Methodist Chapel, founded a class in Bangor - the first ever in the district. His ability to transcribe to and from staff notation brought him a steady supply of work, particularly when items were being prepared for publication. Also a maker of illuminated addresses. Author of the novel *Y Cymro*, which was serialised.
Wrote many articles for musical journals, and composed hymn tunes. One charming but possibly apocryphal story has it that he sometimes woke up in the night with a tune in his head, which he would set out in soap on the bedroom mirror if he did not have writing materials to hand.
As well as hymn tunes, of which his most famous is 'Sanctus', he composed glees and part songs. The latter were often to words by hymn writers. At the time of his death he was working on a commission for *The Task is Ended* from the Liverpool Philharmonic Choir, which was to have been performed in Easter 1902.

RICHARDSON, Dr. Alfred Madeley (1868-1949)
Born in Southend, Essex on 1 June 1868; died in New York on 23 July 1949.
Received training in music from William Haynes of Malvern, Worcestershire and at the Royal College of Music, from **Walter Parratt** and **Hubert Parry**. Organ scholar of Keble College, Oxford (1885-1889) where he graduated B.Mus (1888) B.A. (1890), M.A. (1892) and D.Mus. (1896).
Organist of the Emmanuel Church, Malvern; Hindlip Church, Worcester (1889-1891); the London Churches of Holy Trinity, Sloane Street (1891-1892) and St. Jude's, Gray's Inn Road (1892) and All Saints' Church, Scarborough, Yorkshire (from 1892).
Organist of St. Saviour's Church, Southwark, London (1897-1909). Richardson's period of office continued through two major changes: the elevation of the church to the status of collegiate church in 1898 and, seven years later, its consecration as a cathedral.
Emigrated to the U.S.A. in 1909, where the first of his appointments was that of organist of St. Paul's Church, Baltimore, Maryland. He held the position for about a year before moving to Trinity Church, Rhode Island. He also taught at the Juilliard School of Music, New York.
A novel feature of his rendering of the Psalms during services was his practice of illustrating changes in mood by means of short organ interludes between the appropriate verses.
Author of *The Psalms: their Structure and Musical Rendering* and other works. Editor of *Southwark Psalter*.
Composed services and part songs.

RICHARDSON, Arnold (1914-1973)
Born in Ely in 1914; died in London on 26 June 1973.
Attended Ely Cathedral Choir School and Paxton School, St. Neots.
A pupil of **'Boris' Ord** and of G.D. Cunningham. Studied with
Benjamin Dale at the Royal Academy of Music.
Organist of St. Luke's Church, Cambridge, and succeeded G.D.
Cunningham as organist of St. Alban's Church, Holborn, London.
Organist of the West London Synagogue (from 1949).
Borough organist of Wolverhampton (1938-1973), and conductor
of Wolverhampton Civic Choir (from 1948).
Made broadcasts for the B.B.C. (from 1938). Taught at the R.A.M.
(from 1953), where his stated aim was to encourage students to
think for themselves rather than absorb ideas handed down from
the past.
Composed a Mass in A for Choir and Organ, which was first
performed under **Henry Wood** at the Promenade Concerts of 1948,
piano items, and organ works.

RICHARDSON, John (1816-1879)
Born in Preston, Lancashire on 14 December 1816; died in Preston
in 1879, on either 13 April or 13 September.
Educated at the Catholic Day School, Preston and a chorister of the
Roman Catholic Church of St. Nicholas.
A house painter and decorator until 1836, when he took up music.
As his career developed he became a well-known teacher of music
in the area, acting privately and at St. Edward's College (1844-
1857). His other appointments were at Ushaw College, Durham
and in the town of Warrington, Cheshire.
Among his pupils were the subsequently-famous baritone singer,
Charles Santley and the virtuoso organist **W.T. Best** who later
achieved a grand reputation as an organist and testified to his
counterpoint training from John Richardson.
Became one of the foremost musicians of the Roman Catholic
Church in this country. Organist of St. Mary's Cathedral Church,
Liverpool (1835-1837) and of the Church of St. Nicholas,
Liverpool (1837-1857). As a young man he had a fine alto voice.
Received presentations from Cardinals Newman and Wiseman, and
from Pope Pius IX.
His wife and children died in an epidemic in 1857. Shortly
afterwards his own health deteriorated and he lived in Preston as an
invalid from 1860 until his death.
Composed Masses, the anthem 'The Lord reigneth', hymn tunes
including 'St. Bernard' and 'Titchfield', glees and music for the
Collins's *Ode to the Passions*.

RICHARDSON, John Elliott (19th century)
Born in Salisbury, Wiltshire. A chorister of Salisbury Cathedral
under **A.T. Corfe**, whom he served as assistant for 18 years and
eventually succeeded. Organist and master of the choristers of
Salisbury Cathedral (1863-1881) resigning through ill-health. At
some time thereafter he was organist of a Roman Catholic Church
in Bognor, Sussex. A local choral society conductor. Author of *The
Tour of a Cathedral Organist* (1870), and the editor of *Salisbury
Chant Book* (1859). Other works edited by him were collections of
anthems by composers including **Maurice Greene**, a number of
settings of the Kyrie and Sanctus, and a book of organ voluntaries.
His own works consist of a Service in F and anthems including 'I
will give thanks' and 'Turn Thee, O Lord'.

RICHARDSON, Stephen (1863-?)
Born in Low Fell, Durham, in 1863. Educated in Edinburgh.
Organist and choirmaster of Perth Cathedral (from 1891), and a
local choral society conductor. Composed services, anthems, songs
and part songs.

RICHARDSON, Thomas Bentick (1831-1893)
Born in 1831; died in Bury St. Edmunds, Suffolk in April 1893. A
chorister and assistant organist of Salisbury Cathedral. Organist of
St. Mary's Church, Bury St. Edmunds for nearly 30 years.
Composer of the anthem 'Thou, O God art praised'.

RICHARDSON, Vaughan (c1670-1729)
Born, possibly in London, around the year 1670; died in
Winchester, Hampshire in May 1729.
By 1678 he was a chorister of the Chapel Royal, where he studied
under **John Blow**.
Organist, master of the choristers and a lay vicar of Winchester
Cathedral (1692-1729). A person of the same name was temporary
organist of Worcester Cathedral (Christmas 1686-May 1688): the
two organists could well be one and the same.
Sang at the Coronation of James II in 1685.
Published a collection of songs in 1701.
His compositions include anthems including 'This is the day' and
'O how amiable are Thy dwellings', odes, cantatas and songs.

RICHARDSON, William (?-c1731)
A chorister of the Chapel Royal under **John Blow**. Organist of the
church of St. Nicholas, Deptford, London from 1697, following the
rebuilding of the organ. Published *Lessons for the Harpsichord or
Spinet* (1708) and his collection, *The Pious Recreation...* (1729)
contains the hymn tune 'Greenwich' composed by him.

RICHINGS, Revd. Richard Frederick Littledale (1849-1878)
Born in 1849; died on 28 January 1878. The son of F.H.R.
Richings of Atherstone, Warwickshire. Educated at St. Edmund's
Hall, Oxford and at Christ Church, Oxford. A minor canon of the
Cathedrals of Chester, where he was also librarian (1873-1874),
and of Canterbury (1874-1878). Composed the hymn tune
'Maidstone'.

RICHMOND, William Henry (19th century)
Studied music with James Rhodes and T.A. Marsh. Organist of
Holy Trinity Church, Knaresborough in Yorkshire, St. Paul's pro-
Cathedral in Dundee, Scotland (from 1870) and St. Michael's
Church, Exeter, Devon. Composed services, anthems, organ music,
items for piano and songs.

RIDEOUT, Dr. Percy Rodney (1868-?)
Open scholar at the Royal College of Music, where he studied
under **Hubert Parry** for three years. Thereafter he received a grant
to continue his studies in Germany. Graduated B.Mus. (1894) and
D.Mus. (1896) at the University of London.
Taught piano at the London Organ School. Held professorships in
London at the London Academy of Music, Guildhall School of
Music and the Hampstead Conservatory.
Organist and choirmaster of St. Paul's Church, Wokingham,
Berkshire (from 1896), the London Churches of St. Philip, Regent
Street (from 1899); St. Paul, Great Portland Street (from 1900) and
St. George, Bloomsbury (from 1904). Organist and choirmaster of
the West London Synagogue (from 1904) and of Wimbledon Parish

Church, London (from 1910). Composed an Evening Service in A, a setting of Psalm 115 'Not unto us, O Lord', and an orchestral symphonic poem on the work of Shelley, *Epipsychidion* (1891).

RIDLEY, Sebastian Claude (1853-?)
Born in West Derby, Liverpool on 31 December 1853. Claude Ridley was the son of **William Ridley**, with whom he studied. Attended the Royal Institution, Liverpool. His career centred upon the Liverpool area. Assistant organist of West Derby Parish Church (1865-1870). Organist of the Church of St. John the Baptist, Tue Brook (1870-1878); the Liverpool Seamen's Orphanage Church (1878-1891); the Renshaw Street Unitarian Chapel (1891-1894); the Great George Street Congregational Chapel (1894-1906) and Egremont Parish Church (from 1907). Choirmaster of the Churches of St. Cuthbert (from 1883) and St. Chad (from 1887). A local choral society conductor and organ recitalist. Composed a Unison Service in G, hymn tunes, and songs including 'The Wrecker'.

RIDLEY, William (1820-1886)
Born in Newark, Nottinghamshire in 1820; died in Liverpool on 5 October 1886. Father of **S. Claude Ridley**. An articled pupil of **Edward Dearle**. Organist of Swaffham Parish Church, Norfolk; Kingston Parish Church, Surrey; West Derby Parish Church, Liverpool (1853-1878) and the Church of St. John the Baptist, Liverpool, where he succeeded his son, Claude. Private organist to the Earl of Oxford. A local choral society conductor. Lived in Liverpool for 33 years, where he became a leading figure in musical circles and did much to improve the standard of music in church services. Compiled a collection of some 301 Chants, of varying antiquity, and composed many hymn tunes.

RIDOUT, Alan (1934-1996)
Born in West Wickham, Kent on 9 December 1934; died in 1996. Studied with Gordon Jacob and Herbert Howells at the Royal College of Music, and, privately, with **Michael Tippett**, Peter Racine Fricker and Herr Badings.
A teacher of composition at the Universities of London, Oxford, Cambridge and Oxford. A professor of the R.C.M. (1960-1984). Supervisor in composition at Birmingham (1961-1962) and a teacher of composition at the University of Cambridge (1963) and at Canterbury Cathedral Choir School (from 1964). An examiner for the Associated Board of the Royal Schools of Music (from 1966).
A broadcaster, especially between 1962 and 1966, during which he took part in two complete series of *Background to Music*.
Composer of a number of church operas including *Children's Crusade* (1968) and *Creation* (1973), first given at Canterbury and Ely Cathedrals respectively; a Magnificat and Nunc Dimittis in F; anthems including the Christmas 'It was the winter wild', 'Christus factus est', 'On this mountain' and 'A pure river of water of life'; a *St. Matthew Passion* for Solo Voices, Chorus, Boys' Choir and Orchestra; organ music such as the *Marche Joyeuse* and chamber works. Many items were composed for **Allan Wicks** and his Canterbury Cathedral Choir.

RIDSDALE, Revd. Charles Joseph (1840-1929)
Born in Stoke Newington, London in 1840; died in Dorking, Surrey on 20 June 1929. Educated at Gonville and Caius College, Cambridge, where he graduated M.A. Ordained in 1864. Curate of Whistable and Seasalter, Kent (1864-1866) and perpetual curate of St. Peter's Church, Folkestone (1868-1923). Composed a setting of

the order of Holy Communion *Cantio Dominica* (1882); three settings, with Fauxbourdons, of the Magnificat; a Benedicite with antiphons; a Festal Te Deum and a hymn tune 'None other Lamb'.

RIGBY, Dr. William (1877-?)
Born in Bury, Lancashire in 1877. Graduated B.Mus. (1897) and D.Mus. (1904). Organist and choirmaster of Ainsworth Presbyterian Church (from 1896); New Road Congregational Church, Bury (from 1899); Avenue Congregational Church, Southampton, Hampshire (from 1905); Bank Street Presbyterian Church, Bury (from 1908) and St. James's Church, Paisley, Scotland (from 1912). His B.Mus. submission was the anthem 'A song of prayer and praise'. For his doctorate he submitted 'The Love of Christ'. Composed other items of church music, plus some part songs.

RILEY, William (c1725-1784)
Born around the year 1725; died on 22 June 1784.
Singing master to the School of the Society of Ancient Britons, Clerkenwell Green, London (1764). Principal teacher of Psalmody to the Charity Schools in London, Westminster and the surrounding area. Took his duties very seriously and he was determined that the children in his charge should be properly trained in congregational singing.
His famous publication *Parochial Music Corrected...* (1762) complained that the Anglican admiration of the high standard of the Methodists' singing had allowed some questionable tunes to infiltrate the services. These he objected to on the grounds that they were light, trivial and associated with matters secular.
Other items of interest in the Introduction are a denunciation of 'fuguing' hymn tunes and a complaint that parish church lectureships had been instituted with the intention of providing religious education but had led to misuse and the playing and singing of unsuitable new tunes, with the clerk and organist being bribed to stay away from these meetings.
He proposed that the practice of lining out Psalm and hymn tunes, by which the clerk would sing a line at a time for repetition by the congregation, be abandoned. He also wanted to speed up the singing and abandon organ interludes that were sometimes played between lines. The book provided tunes that he considered suitable for congregational singing.
A compiler and composer of church music. His Psalm tunes are to be found in the collection by **John Alcock**, *Harmony of Jerusalem* (1801).

RIMBAULT, Dr. Edward Francis (1816-1876)
Born in Soho, London on 13 June 1816; died in London on 26 September 1876.
Son of Stephen Francis Rimbault, organist of the London Church of St. Giles-in-the-Fields, and church composer.
Studied music with his father, with **S.S. Wesley** and **William Crotch**. Awarded honorary doctorates at the Universities of Stockholm (Ph.D: 1842), Harvard (LLD: 1848) and Göttingen, Germany (D.Phil.).
Organist in London of the Swiss Church, Soho, London (from 1832); St. Peter's Church, Vere Street (1866-1871); St. John's Wood Presbyterian Church and St. Giles-in-the-Fields.
Developed a keen interest in English musical history and carried out a great deal of antiquarian research. Beginning in 1838 he lectured on the history of music. Founded the Musical Antiquarian Society (1840) with E. Taylor and W. Chappell.

A musical editor of the Motet Society, a group of Anglicans who met weekly to sing the music of the English Church from the 16th century and before. He took a great deal of interest in the standard of church music, writing scathingly to *Musical World* in November 1842 about the musicianship of the services of the Chapel Royal, St. James's Palace and St. Paul's Cathedral.

Contributed articles to Grove's *Dictionary of Music and Musicians* and to the *Imperial Dictionary of Biography* as well as to the journals of the time. He and **E.J. Hopkins** collaborated in what was to become the standard work of the 19th century on the organ.

Music editor of *Scottish Psalter* (1867), a publication that was used all over the British Empire.

Composed Single Chants in C Minor, in E-flat, in F and in G. His hymn tunes include 'Delhi' (1857) and his anthems 'In God the Lord' and 'The Lord is righteous'. Composed songs such as 'Happy Land'.

RIMMER, Dr. Frederick William (b.1914)
Born in Liverpool on 21 February 1914.
Educated Quarry Bank High School, the University of Durham and, as organ scholar, Selwyn College, Cambridge (1946-1948). Graduated M.A. at Cambridge and B.Mus (1939) at Durham. Awarded the D.Mus. honorarily by the University of Durham (1991).
Appointed C.B.E. in 1980.
Served with the Lancashire Fusiliers during World War II.
At the University of Cambridge he was senior lecturer in music at Homerton College (1948-1951), and honorary organist and adviser in musical studies at Selwyn College (1948-1951). Superviser in music studies of the University of Cambridge (1950-1951).
Cramb lecturer in music (1951-1956), acting head of the music department (1953-1956), senior lecturer (1956-1966), organist (1954-1966), Gardiner professor of music (1966-1980) and professor emeritus (from 1980) at the University of Glasgow.
Director of the Scottish Music Archives (1968-1980), a director of Scottish Opera (1966-1980) and chairman of the B.B.C. Scottish Music Advisory Committee.
Organist and choirmaster of All Hallows Church, Allerton, Liverpool (1938-1940) and St. Paul's Anglican Cathedral, Malta (1941-1944).
He has written many articles on the music of the 20th century and contributed chapters covering the years 1800-1970 *to History of Scottish Music*, published in 1973 by the B.B.C.
Has composed a Magnificat and Nunc Dimittis, *Five Carols of The Nativity*, the anthem 'Sing we merrily', Five Preludes for Organ on Scottish Psalm Tunes, and Five Tempers for Two Violins.

RISDALE, Charles Joseph
See **RIDSDALE,** Charles Joseph.

RISELEY, George (1845-1932)
Born in Bristol, Gloucestershire on 28 August 1845; died in Bristol on 12 April 1932.
From 1852, at the age of seven, he was a chorister of Bristol Cathedral. From 1862 he was articled to the Cathedral organist, John Davis Corfe, to whom he was assistant.
He held several church organistships prior to that of All Saints' Church, Clifton, a position he held until 1876 when he succeeded J.D. Corfe as organist of Bristol Cathedral. Remained in office until 1898 but in the previous year he had been dismissed. **A.H.**

Brewer was appointed to replace him but Riseley took the Dean and Chapter to court and won his case for reinstatement.
Riseley was at loggerheads with the precentor, William Mann, who claimed the prerogative of the precentor on matters of cathedral music. Riseley was charged by the Dean and Chapter with neglect, and dismissed at three months' notice. The Chancellor of the Diocese ruled in Riseley's favour on a technicality. Had Riseley been dismissed summarily, it would have been lawful. The story is told that the anthem sung at the Evensong of the first Sunday after his reestablishment was Handel's chorus 'Fixed in His everlasting Seat'.
Mann and Riseley continued to feud. On one occasion, Mann gave out an anthem and Riseley played something different.
After Riseley had seriously neglected his duties by spending much of his time in his teaching practice in Bristol, he was given a second admonition. Riseley appealed to the Cathedral Visitor to have his admonition quashed, and both sides employed counsel. The admonition was upheld, although the Dean and Chapter were also criticised by the Visitor, who drew particular attention to the tactlessness of Mann. The legal costs were very heavy and by coincidence, on the day that the judgement was announced, the anthem at Evensong was 'How dear are Thy counsels'. Both sides were ordered to contribute to the costs.
The Cathedral was now divided into two warring factions. Mann retired and was replaced by **E.H. Fellowes** but the situation did not improve. Riseley failed to keep his commitments to the Dean and Chapter and eventually, Riseley was called upon to show why he should not receive a third admonition, which would have led automatically to dismissal. Shortly afterwards he agreed to resign with an annuity, and was succeeded by **P.C. Buck**.
Since 1870 he had been organist of the Colston Hall, Bristol, and he continued to take an active part in local musical activities. In 1877 he began the Bristol Monday Popular Concerts (of orchestral music). A local teacher.
Conductor of the Bristol Orpheus Society (from 1878). In 1895 the choir performed before Queen Victoria at Windsor Castle, following which the Society was allowed to assume the title of 'Royal'.
Gave a series of recitals at the Royal Albert Hall, London in 1885 and conducted the Bristol Musical Festival of 1896.
A professor of organ at the Royal Academy of Music (from 1893). Director of music of the Alexandra Palace, London. Sheriff of the City of Bristol (1909-1911).
Composed a Christmas carol, a Jubilee Ode (1897), a part song for men's voices and a Jubilee March for Organ.

ROBERTON, Sir Hugh Stevenson (1874-1952)
Born in Glasgow in 1874; died in Glasgow in 1952.
Conductor of the Glasgow Orpheus Choir, which he founded in 1906 from an earlier choir that had disbanded. Tours were made to the U.S.A., Canada and many European countries. The Glasgow Phoenix Choir formed from the Orpheus Choir on Roberton's retirement in 1951.
Knighted in 1931.
Banned from broadcasting during World War II because of his pacifist views and his refusal to play the National Anthem. The ban was lifted following an intervention in the House of Commons.
Published an autobiography *A Prelude to Orpheus*. Author of articles and booklets.
A member of the Board of Governors of the Royal Scottish Academy of Music, and President of the Tonic Sol-fa College.

Self-taught as a composer, his works number more than 300 and include the anthem 'Be with us, Lord, this eventide' for Men's Voices, and part songs. His 'All in the April evening' is much used as an anthem. An arranger of Scottish folk songs.

ROBERTS, Arthur Owen (1869-1952)
Born in Liverpool in 1869; died in Hoylake, Cheshire on 1 September 1952. The son of Eleazar Roberts, the Welsh pioneer of the Tonic Sol-fa method of musical notation. Honorary organist of the Presbyterian Church of Wales in Hoylake, for more than 30 years (from 1890). An elder of the church. Secretary of the Music Section of the Welsh Presbyterian Church Committee for the Revised Edition (1927) of *Church Hymnary*, for which he was also a member of the Joint Revision Committee. Composed the hymn tunes 'Blodyn' and 'Hoylake'.

ROBERTS, Cadwaladr (?-c1708)
Died in 1708 or 1709 and was buried on 14 February. A poet of Pennant Melangell, Wales, and a contemporary of the poet Huw Morys, with whom a poem was jointly written on the subject of matrimony. Composed five Nativity carols, one of which was published by David Jones of Trefriw in *Bloden-Gerdd Cymry*. Published an anthology of works by himself, Huw Morys and Edward Morris.

ROBERTS, Dr. Caradog (1878-1935)
Born in Rhosllanerchrugog, Denbighshire, Wales on 30 October 1878; died in Wrexham, Denbighshire on 3 March 1935.
Trained privately in music before taking the Oxford degrees of B.Mus. (1906) and D.Mus. (1911). His doctorate made him the youngest ever Welshman to achieve this distinction, and the first from North Wales. Among those with whom he studied were **J.C. Bridge**, organist of Chester Cathedral and Johannes Weingartner, both for piano, Dan C. Owen of Rhos for organ, and Norton Bailey. Organist of Mynydd Seion Congregational Church, Ponkey, near Wrexham (from 1894) and of the Bethlehem Congregational Church, Rhosllanerchrugog (1904-1935). Officiated as precentor at festivals of Welsh Psalmody.
A student teacher in an elementary school and then a carpenter, serving his apprenticeship for three years. His musical skills included those of singer, pianist, organist and composer.
Director of music at the University College of North Wales, Bangor (1914-1920), and an adjudicator at provincial and national *eisteddfodau*.
Editor of *Y Caniedydd Cynulleidfaol Newydd*, the hymnal of the Welsh Independent Church, published in 1921. Also edited *Caniedydd yr Ysgol Sul*, that Church's Sunday School hymnal. An organ recitalist.
Composed hymn tunes, including 'Berwyn', 'Rachie' and 'In Memoriam', the last of which was named in memory of Harry Evans. Each of these first appeared in *Congregational Hymnary* (1916). His degree exercises were *A Hymn of Thanksgiving* (B.Mus.) and *The Resurrection of Christ* (D.Mus.).
There are important, and highly characteristic, harmonised settings of two traditional Welsh carol melodies in the 1928 *Oxford Book of Carols* at numbers 34 ('All poor men and humble') and 59 ('Awake were they only, those shepherds so lonely').

ROBERTS, David (Alawydd: 1820-1872)
Born in Llanllechid, Wales on 16 June 1820; died on 26 May 1872.

His father was a smith at Cae Braich-y-cafn Quarry, and the family moved to Bethesda so as to be closer to work. Educated at schools in Llandygài, Carneddi and Llanllechid. Attended evening school in Tregarth. Joined the Carneddi music society at the age of 13. A member of the choir of Bethesda Congregational Chapel.
Devised some lessons in order to start music classes. Showed the materials to **John Ambrose Lloyd** and **Edward Stephens** (Tanymarian) and was persuaded to publish them. They appeared in 1848 as *Gramadeg Cerddol* and were much in demand, leading to further editions.
Won prizes at the Bethesda Eisteddfod of 1852 and 1853 for his anthems. His 'Bendigedig fyddo'r Arglwydd' is found in the collection *Y Gyfres Gerddorol*. In 1867 he published the hymnal *Llyfr y Psalmau*. Some 60 out of 150 were tunes that he himself composed. His best-known hymn tune is 'Catherine'.

ROBERTS, John (Aberdar: 1806-1879)
Born near Bala, Wales in 1806; died in Aberystwyth on 18 November 1879. Worked on farms near his home, and moved as a young man to Aberystwyth. Learned the craft of bookbinding, and later, engraving. Studied music in his spare time and became well known locally. In 1855 he moved to Aberdare Composed hymn tunes and he was famous for 'Alexander' which he composed at the age of 18. This was published uncredited at first but later it appeared in his own collection: *Perorydd y Cysegr* (The musician of the Sanctuary: 1853).

ROBERTS, John (Henllan: 1807-1876)
Born in Henllan, near Denbigh, Wales on 30 March 1807; died on 4 April 1876.
Attended the village school until the age of 13. At 15, studied with Thomas Jones, Congregational minister of Denbigh. Also studied music with Thomas David of Henlan.
He took down a number of tunes that had been learned by rote and sung by two local leaders of singing, Moses Parry of Denbigh and John Peters of Henllan. Typically, these tunes had been composed or used during a time of religious revival. In collaboration with Revd. John Parry of Chester he jointly edited *Peroriaeth Hyfryd* (Sweet music: 1837), in which some of these tunes appeared. Published a collection of 55 Psalm tunes *Caniadau y Cysegr...* (Songs of the Sanctuary) in 1839, providing harmonies to a number of these tunes himself. Following his death, in 1876, two of his sons published a collection of 11 of his hymn tunes under the title *In memoriam*.

ROBERTS, Revd. John (Ieuan Gwyllt: 1822-1877)
Born in Tanrhiwfelen, near Aberystwyth on 27 December 1822; died in Vron, near Caernarvon, on 14 May 1877.
Styled himself Ieuan Gwyllt (John Wild) in a poetry competition as a young man. At this time in his life he wrote poetry, some of which was intended for use in Sunday School services.
The parents were both musical: his mother was a good singer and his father led the singing in chapel.
In 1823 the family moved to Aberystwyth, where John Roberts later attended the school run by Dr. Lewis Edwards. In 1829 the family moved again, this time to Pistyllgwyn in the Melindwr Valley.
Became a clerk in a pharmacy in Aberystwyth in 1842. A local school appointed him as a master in 1844 and a few months later he underwent teacher training at the Borough Road Normal School,

London. He did not leave with a certificate, possibly having failed to qualify through ill health.

Returned to Aberystwyth in 1845 and established the British School. However after only nine months he left and went to work for a firm of solicitors, whom he served for seven years. This was the period of his life when his musical development was at its most rapid. During these years he had contact with the Mills family of Llanidloes.

In 1852 he set up home in Liverpool as assistant editor of the Welsh language *Yr Amserau* (The Times). Almost immediately he became the driving force behind the paper, being a talented journalist himself. Travelled, sometimes to London, to attend and report on concerts and recitals. In these years he was also a judge and conductor at local festivals of music.

He first preached at Runcorn, Cheshire in 1856. Joined the Rose Place Church, where he led the singing for a time. At some time during his time in Liverpool he was an ordination candidate, but was not accepted.

He met, and worked with, Eleazar Roberts, the Welsh Tonic Sol-fa pioneer.

1858 he gave up *Yr Amserau* and took up an appointment in Aberdare as editor of *Y Gwladgarwr* (The Patriot). Carried on what to day would be styled campaigning journalism, denouncing in editorials the social evils of the time. Far from being universally popular, his radical views alienated him from some while simply being a journalist was sufficient to bring him into contention with others. It must have been almost with a sense of relief that he accepted an invitation in 1859 to become the minister of a Calvinistic Methodist Church in Merthyr Tydfil. He trained formally for the ministry from that year (1861), and was ordained.

In 1865 he became minister of the Welsh Calvinistic Methodist Church in Capel Coch, Llanberis. He remained there until his retirement in 1869, when he went to live at Llangfaglan, near Caernarvon.

He collected and edited collections of hymn tunes, many of which he wrote down while travelling as a preacher. Produced musical journals and he preached and lectured on the need to improve the musical standards of worship.

The outdoor singing associated with the Temperance Society, begun in 1835, led to the institution of the Cymanfa Gann or festival of hymn singing, of which John Roberts is acknowledged as the founder (1859). Proof sheets *of Llyfr Tonau Cynulleidfaol*, published that same year, were distributed at the early meetings. These events clearly met a great need in the country and by 1861 there were many unions of congregational singing throughout Wales, with many calls for John Roberts to lecture.

He admired the work of German composers. Contributed an article in 1857 on the life and works of Mendelssohn to *Traethodydd* (The Essayist). This was the first in a series, and he is also credited with the introduction to Welsh choirs of the works of Bach, Handel and Mendelssohn.

In 1852, he as editor and three friends set up a partnership and brought out a monthly journal *Blodau Cerdd* (Flowers of music). The first four issues were printed in Aberystwyth and the next three in Llanidloes. The aim of the publication, which contained hymns and hymn tunes, some of the latter being by the younger **John Ambrose Lloyd** was to give instruction in music and to improve the standard of music in church. In his view, hymns were to be sung to German chorale tunes and the like: simple, majestic and devotional as compared to some of the elaborate tunes in use at the time.

In 1859 he published *Llyfr Tonau Cynulleidfaol* (The Book of Congregational Tunes), which was intended to be interdenominational and was adopted by the Welsh Calvinistic Methodists. Initially it contained 220 tunes with a further 20 added later in the form of a supplement. 17,000 copies were sold in three years. In a preface he urged that meetings of singing be held in each church, with the entire congregation in attendance, learning and practising tunes for the forthcoming services. Ministers, he held, should be experts in the field of church music.

For two years (1859-1861), John Roberts and Revd. Thomas Levi published *Telyn y Plantt* (The children's harp). When the publication was incorporated into *Trysorfa'r Plant* (The children's treasury), John Roberts contributed a regular music section.

In March 1861 he brought out a new periodical: *Y Cerddor Cymraeg* (The Welsh musician). Responsible for the first four years of the publication, which contained, among other things, musical items by Welsh composers and instruction in Tonic Sol-fa notation.

The latter began to appear between 1861 and 1862 in the form of a series of letters by Eleazar Roberts, submitted with the blessing of John Roberts whose method it was. John Roberts was unconvinced initially, but by 1863 he had come to appreciate its value. *Y Cerddor* started to include compositions in Tonic Sol-fa notation. The journal was taken over by the Wrexham firm of Hughes & Co. in 1865 but John Roberts continued as editor.

Also around the year 1863 a Tonic Sol-fa version of *Llyfr Tonau Cynulleidfaol* appeared, and John Roberts introduced the journal *Cerddor y Tonic Sol-ffa* (The Tonic Sol-fa musician) and gave classes in the method: he had 150 students in Llanberis alone.

From 1871, John Roberts was editor of *Y Goleuad* (Illumination) but resigned after barely a year.

In 1874 the preachers Sankey and Moody campaigned through Great Britain. John Roberts travelled to Edinburgh to listen to them and was profoundly influenced, finding himself now possessed of a more fluent and urgent style of preaching. The music of Sankey and Moody was aimed at the industrial city underclasses. Previously, John Roberts would have denounced that style of music but now he acknowledged its appeal and to some extent he recanted his earlier views on musical propriety. In 1874 he published a translation of the Sankey and Moody material: *Swn Y Jiwbili* (The Sound of Jubilee) which was published in six parts. The take-up was slow but by 1934 it had sold around 500,000 copies and a single volume version was available.

John Roberts composed the hymn tune 'Hafila' at the age of less than 15: it was published in 1839. Other hymn tunes include 'Moab' - which, in the opinion of the musicologist **W.H. Hadow** was one of the six best hymn tunes ever written - 'Ardudwy', 'Bont-Newydd' and 'Liverpool'.

ROBERTS, John Dryhurst (1862-1907)
Born in Anglesey in 1862; died in Northwich, Cheshire in 1907. Organist of the Welsh Baptist Church, Castle Street, London for 19 years. Composed the hymn tune 'Caergybi', which first appeared in *Y Llawlyfr Moliant* (1890).

ROBERTS, John Henry (Pencerdd Gwynedd: 1848-1924)
Born in Mynydd Llandegai, Caernarvonshire, Wales on 31 March 1848; died in Liverpool on 6 August 1924.

Worked in a quarry when young. Received lessons from a local teacher of music. By the age of 12 he was able to play organ and at 14 he was organist of Seilo Wesleyan Methodist Chapel. At 19 he won a composition prize for his cantata *Y mab afradlon* at an eisteddfod near Chester.

Worked as a clerk at the Bryneglwys Quarry, Abergynolwyn, Merionethshire (from 1868), and formed a choir to take part in the Harlech Music Festival of 1868. By this time he had gained a reputation as an accompanist, and the Harlech Festival Committee together with a number of local people arranged for him to receive tuition. Studied with **S.S. Wesley** at Gloucester Cathedral. Trained at the Royal Academy of Music under **William Sterndale Bennett** and **Charles Steggall** (1870-1874). Graduated Mus. B. at the University of Cambridge (1882). Became a fellow of the Tonic Sol-fa College.

During his time at the R.A.M. he composed one of his most successful part songs, 'Cwsg, filwr, cwsg', which was sung at the Rhyl National Eisteddfod of 1892.

While living in Caernarvon he founded the publishing firm of J.H. Roberts (1874), which he later moved to Liverpool. Associated with Bethesda Congregational Church, Caernarvon until 1897 as organist (from 1874) and choirmaster (from 1878). Organist and choirmaster of Castle Street Presbyterian Church, Caernarvon (from 1878), where he worked as a teacher of music and a composer. In 1897 he was organist of the Chatham Street Calvinistic Methodist Chapel, Liverpool. Founded the Cambrian School of Music.

Music editor of *Handbook of Praise, Sunday School Handbook of Praise* and *Congregational Tune Book*. Edited an anthem book for Welsh choirs. Author of *Hand Book on the Elements of Music*.

Contributed to the journal *Y Cerddor*. Took all the prizes for composition at the Aberdare National Eisteddfod (1885) with an anthem, a six-part madrigal and a tenor song.

Composed as his Mus.B. exercise a cantata *Prayer and Praise* for Solo Voices, Chorus and Orchestra. Also composed a setting of Psalm 46 'God is our Hope' for the same forces. His compositions include many anthems, hymn tunes including 'O grant us light', a Chant in E-flat, part songs and an overture *Caractacus*. Editor of *Llawlyfr elfennan cerddoriaeth* (1890); *Llyfr anthemau* (1896); *Llawlfyr Moliant* for the Caernarvon Baptists (1880 and 1890) and *Hymnau yr eglwys* (selected and edited 1893).

ROBERTS, Dr. John Varley (1841-1920)

Born in Stanningley, near Leeds, Yorkshire on 25 September 1841; died in Oxford on 9 February 1920. Graduated B.Mus. (1871) and D.Mus. (1876) at Christ Church, Oxford. Awarded the honorary Oxford M.A. (1916).

At the age of 12 he was organist of St. John's Church, Farsley, near Leeds. Organist of St. Bartholomew's Church, Armley, Leeds (1862-1868) and of Halifax Parish Church (1868-1882) where he was also choirmaster.

Appointed organist of Magdalen College, Oxford (1882-1918) in succession to **Walter Parratt**, who had gone to St. George's Chapel, Windsor Castle.

A lecturer in harmony and counterpoint for the University professor of music, and organist of St. Giles's Church, Oxford (1885-1893). An examiner for musical degrees at Oxford University in each of the years 1883, 1886, 1889-1890 and 1899-1900. A local choral and philharmonic society conductor.

Author of *A Practical Method of Training Choristers* (1898). Editor of *Parish Church Chant Book*.

Composed as his B.Mus. exercise a setting of Psalm 103 'Praise the Lord, O my soul' for Chorus and Orchestra. His other compositions include hymn tunes, chants, around 50 anthems

including 'Lord, we pray', services, settings of the Offertory Sentences and other items of church music; an oratorio *Jonah*, part songs, songs and organ voluntaries. His anthem 'Seek ye the Lord while He may be found' for Solo Tenor and Choir, dedicated to the wife of his Halifax vicar, has recently been re-published and has enjoyed something of a revival.

ROBERTS, Lewis Jones (1866-1931)

Born in Aberaeyron, Cardiganshire, Wales on 29 May 1866; died in Aberaeyron on 20 December 1931.

Attended St. David's College, Lampeter, North Wales where he graduated B.A. An MA of Exeter College, Oxford, where he was a member of *Cymdeithas Dafydd ap Gwilym*.

A lecturer at St. David's, Lampeter. Inspector of Schools in Wales (1894-1921), being based in turn at Aberystwyth, Rhyl, Llandudno and Swansea.

Associated with the eisteddfod movement for more than 40 years, presiding at the Wrexham National Eisteddfod of 1910. His compositions were sung at *eisteddfodau*. Also involved with the Cambrian Archaeological Association.

Founded a number of *Cymmrodorion* societies in North Wales.

His book in Welsh on Owen Glyndwr (1904) became established as the standard work on the subject. Editor of *Awelon O Hiraethog* and contributed articles in Welsh to books and magazines. Music editor of the monthly *Cymru*, started in 1891 by Sir Owen Edwards, in which a new tune was published in each issue. For 30 years, he and J.M. Howell of Aberaeyron provided the music and the words respectively for a carol for the December issue. Contributed carols to other journals. Editor of *Awelon o hiraethog* - a selection of the poems of William Rees.

His hymn tunes are to be found in hymnals on both sides of the Atlantic. They include 'Nesta'.

ROBERTS, Robert (1840-1871)

Born in Llandegai, near Bangor, Wales on 24 May 1840; died on 9 February 1871.

His father died when Robert was 12, and he began work in a quarry. A chorister of St. Anne's Church, Llandegai and a pupil of Henry Hayden, organist of St. Mary's Church, Caernarvon and son of William Henry Hayden, sub organist of St. Asaph's Cathedral. Also trained in the rudiments of music by Owen Davies (Eos Llechid). Went on to study at the North Wales College for Schoolmasters.

He joined the staff of the College, initially as third master and music master.

Assistant organist (1865), probationary organist (1867-1868) and organist (1868-1871) of Bangor Cathedral. Compositions include 'Y gwlithyn', the cantata *Gwarchae Harlech* (The Siege of Harlech), and hymn tunes found in *Llyfr tonau ac Emynan* and *Llyfr y Psalmau*.

Composed a setting of the Burial Service in Welsh, a cantata, and part songs.

ROBERTS, Robert (1863-1941)

Born, of Welsh parents, in Liverpool in 1863; died in 1941. Educated in Liverpool. Virtually self-taught in music. In 1887 he became a teacher at Daffryn Board School, Merioneth, serving for 30 years before retiring through ill-health in 1917. Published *The Cambrian Song Book* (1889) for children. Participated in *eisteddfodau*, winning prizes for composition with his hymn tunes. These include 'Alice'.

ROBERTS, Revd. Robert Edwin (1878-1940)
Born in Llangerniew, Denbighshire, Wales on 6 December 1878; died in Ashwell, Oakham, Rutland on 18 June 1940. Attended Ellesmere College, Shropshire and the University of Durham. Ordained as a minister of the Church of England. Master of the Choir School of Westminster Abbey. Precentor of Peterborough Cathedral. A chaplain to H.M. Forces in France during World War I, after which he was vicar of Knighton, Leicestershire. Precentor of Leicester Cathedral, and subsequently dean. Compiled *The Transition Tune Book* (1924) and *Hymns for Home Missions* (1929). His own compositions include the hymn tune 'Philippine'.

ROBERTS, Thomas Osborne (1879-1948)
Born in Weston Rhyn, Shropshire in 1879; died in 1948. Moved to Ysbyty, North Wales at the age of 12. Worked in the office of a large estate until, around 1900, he moved to Llandudno and earned a living from music. An organist in Llandudno and Caernarvon, and a conductor and adjudicator in North Wales. Conducted the National Eisteddfod Choir. Composed the hymn tune 'Pennant', and songs.

ROBERTS, William Morgan (1853-1923)
Born near Llangynog, Montgomeryshire, Wales in October 1853; died on 26 May 1923.
His grandfather was the author of a text book on music; his father played in a brass band. Lived at Corwen and then at Wrexham. Won a prize with a part song 'Y Daran' at the Amlwch Eisteddfod of 1878. Another part song, 'Cwsg, fy Maban' was used as a test piece at the National Eisteddfod of Corwen and of Caernarvon. Moved to Liverpool and thence to Manchester before settling in Wrexham and joining the firm of Hughes & Co. It was he who suggested that the firm launch *Y Cerddor* under the editorship of David Jenkins and D. Emlyn Evans. Secretary of the Liverpool Eisteddfod (1884) and the Wrexham Eisteddfod (1888). Editor of the s   econd supplement to *Tonau cynulleidfaol* (Ieuan Gwyllt). Worked for the Ministry of Agriculture (from 1918). Composer of hymn tunes.

ROBERTSON, Henry Kinniburgh (1895-?)
Born in Edinburgh in 1895. Graduated B.Mus. at the University of Edinburgh. Studied with Thomas Collinson, Philip Halstead and C.E.S. Paterson. Music master of Edinburgh Ladies' College. Organist and choirmaster of Cramond Parish Church. Composed two Scottish Psalm tunes, an anthem for Advent 'O sapientia', songs and piano works.

ROBERTSON, John (1838-?)
Born in Edinburgh on 16 February 1838.
Studied music privately, at the University of Edinburgh with the University professor, John Donaldson, and in Berlin. Whilst reading music at Edinburgh he accepted a scholarship from the United Presbyterian Church but later resigned it, having decided to pursue a career in music. Graduated B.Mus. at St. John's College, Oxford (1884), where he was the first recorded Scotsman with this achievement.
Organist and director of the Choir of New Greyfriars Parish Church (1876-1894); St. Andrew's Episcopal Church, Edinburgh (1872-1894 or later) and Nicolson United Free Church (1898-1905). A local choral society conductor.
Contributed articles on harmony and counterpoint to *Musical Educator*.

His B.Mus. exercise was a setting of Psalm 122 'I was glad' for Solo Voices, Chorus, Organ and Orchestra. Also composed settings of the Te Deum in C and in F, an anthem 'Pray for the peace of Jerusalem' - also based on Psalm 122 - songs and part songs of which an example is 'Lull ye, my love, asleep'.

ROBINSON, Revd. Arthur Huw Rawlins (19th/20th century)
Arthur Robinson trained privately in music. Graduated Mus.B. at Clare College, Cambridge in 1901. Also graduated B.A. (1900) and M.A. (1904). Ordained deacon in 1909 and priest a year later. Organist and choirmaster to Lord Wimborne at Camborne, Dorset (from 1901) and of St. Simon's Church, Southsea, Hampshire (from 1904). Organist and music master of Wellington House School, Westgate-on-Sea, Kent (from 1904) and honorary curate of St. Saviour's, Westgate. Assistant curate of Lambeth Parish Church, London (from 1912). Around the year 1924 he was rector of Merstham, Surrey. A local madrigal and music society conductor. Composed a setting of the Service of Holy Communion in C (1902).

ROBINSON, Christopher John (b.1936)
Born in Peterborough, Cambridgeshire on 20 April 1936. Educated at St. Michael's College, Tenbury, Worcestershire and music scholar of Rugby School, Warwickshire, where he was organ scholar. Graduated B.A. (1957), B.Mus. (1958) and M.A. (1964) at Christ Church, Oxford. Graduated M.Mus. honorarily at the University of Birmingham (1987). Appointed L.V.O. in 1986 and C.V.O. in 1992. Assistant organist of Christ Church Cathedral, Oxford (1955-1958); New College, Oxford (1957-1958) and Worcester Cathedral (1962-1963). In the intervening years (1959-1962) he was music master of Oundle School, Northamptonshire. Organist and master of the choristers of Worcester Cathedral (1963-1974) and St. George's Chapel, Windsor Castle (1974-1991). Subsequently succeeded **George Guest** as organist of St. John's College, Cambridge. Composed a Magnificat and Nunc Dimittis in C for Boys' Voices and a setting of the Rite B version of the Holy Communion Service.

ROBINSON, Dr. Francis James (1799-1872)
Born in Dublin in 1799; died in Dublin on 21 October 1872. The older brother of **Joseph Robinson.** A chorister of Christ Church Cathedral. Graduated D.Mus. honorarily at Trinity College, Dublin (1852). Associated with both Dublin Anglican Cathedrals as an adult: at Christ Church he was assistant organist (1816-1841) and a vicar choral (from 1833); at St. Patrick's, master of the boys (1819-1844) and organist (not later than 1829 -1830). At St. Patrick's he shared a vicar choral's position (from 1830) and was a vicar choral (from 1843). One of the finest tenor singers of his generation. Composed church music and songs. Editor of *Irish Melodies*, a collection which appeared in 1866 with an introduction on the subject of Irish music by George Farquhar Graham.

ROBINSON, Dr. Hamilton (1861-?)
Born in Brighton, Sussex on 6 December 1861.
Trained at the Royal Academy of Music. Graduated B.Mus. (1891) and D.Mus. (1897) at the University of Durham.
A professor of harmony, composition and sight singing at Guildhall School of Music, London. A lecturer in harmony at the University of London (from 1893).

Organist and choirmaster of the Brunswick Chapel, Hyde Park (from 1897) and St. Stephen's Church, South Kensington (from 1885). A local choral society conductor.

He submitted as his B.Mus. exercise a setting of Psalm 126 *In convertendo* for Solo Voices, Chorus and Strings. Submitted a work with the same title for his doctorate, scored for Baritone Solo, Double Chorus and Orchestra.

Composed services, a setting of the Agnus Dei and Benedictus in E-flat, three Christmas carols, songs including 'Love's challenge', and works for piano and for organ.

ROBINSON, John (c1682-1762)

Born in Westminster, London in 1681 or 1682; died in Westminster on 30 April 1762.

A chorister of the Chapel Royal, where he studied under **John Blow**.

Organist of the London Churches of St. Lawrence, Jewry (1710-1762) and St. Magnus the Martyr, London Bridge (c1712-1762). His first wife, Anne Turner (?-1741) was a singer and Handel performer.

An accomplished organist and harpsichord player, and an original member of the Royal Society of Musicians.

Organist of Westminster Abbey (1727-1762), in succession to **William Croft,** having been Croft's deputy.

Composed Psalm tunes and a Double Chant in E-flat, said to be a particular favourite of George III. In fact he is one of the possible inventors of the double chant-but see **William Hine**, **Luke Flintoft**, and **William Morley**. A manuscript of the E-flat Double Chant at St. Paul's Cathedral bears the date 1706.

ROBINSON, Joseph (1816-1898)

Born in Dublin on 20 August 1816; died in Dublin in 1898.

Younger brother of **Francis Robinson**.

A chorister of St. Patrick's Cathedral, Dublin (1824). When his voice broke he was appointed organist of Sandford Church. When young he visited London and Paris, where he was able to meet the leading musicians of the day.

An accomplished baritone singer. The four brothers Francis, Joseph, John and William, a bass, formed a vocal quartet and introduced some German part songs of the time to Irish audiences.

A stipendary of Christ Church Cathedral, Dublin until 1843 when he resigned in order to become a vicar choral at St. Patrick's Cathedral.

A founder, in 1834, of the Ancient Concerts, of which he was conductor for nearly 30 years. A friend of another leading Dublin church musician, **R.P. Stewart**.

His wife, Fanny, was a pianist who had studied with **William Sterndale Bennett** and with Thalberg. He and his wife were professors at the Royal Irish Academy of Music.

Conductor at the Cork Exhibitions of 1852 and 1883; also, the Dublin Exhibition of 1853, for the opening of which he composed a march.

His other works include services such as a Magnificat and Nunc Dimittis in D and in D Minor (composed 1867, published 1895), a setting of Psalm 115 'Not unto us, O Lord (1869), other anthems including 'Bow down Thine ear' (1881), and songs.

ROBSON, Dr. Robert Walker (1878-?)

Born in Alnwick, Northumberland in 1878. Attended Rutherford College, Newcastle-on-Tyne; trained in music with **William Rea** and at the Royal College of Music. Graduated B.Mus. at Queen's

College, Oxford (1908) and D.Mus. at the University of Durham (1914). Organist and choirmaster of the churches of St. James, Pokesdown and Boscombe (1897-1899), Dorset; Prittlewell Parish Church (1899-1904) and, in London, Harlesden Parish Church (1904-1907) and Christ Church, Crouch End (1907-1947). Lived in Highgate, London. Wrote extensively on church music matters, chiefly in *Musical Opinion*. Composed services, anthems, a hymn, carols, a song and part songs.

ROBSON, William (20th century)

Born in Yarm, Yorkshire. Studied music with **H.A. Bennett** and with Arthur Kitson. Organist and choirmaster in Stockton-on-Tees at the Presbyterian Church of SS Andrew and George (1923-1926) and St. John the Baptist Church (1926-1929); St. Mary's Parish Church, Egglescliffe, Durham (from 1929) and at the Church of St. Michael and All Angels, Norton, Stockton-on-Tees, Yorkshire (from 1937). An adjudicator at festivals of music. Composed the anthem 'Before the ending of the day', organ works, and songs.

ROCKSTRO, William Smyth (1823-1895)

Born in North Cheam, Surrey on 5 January 1823; died in London on 2 July 1895. Changed to an earlier form and spelling of his name in 1846.

A pupil of **William Sterndale Bennett** and John Purkis. Studied in Germany (1845-1846 at the Leipzig Conservatory under Mendelssohn, who later became a friend, and with Moritz Hauptmann, and Louis Plaidy.

On his return to London he taught piano and singing. As his interest in church music developed he studied the subject further and he became an authority on plainchant.

Applied unsuccessfully for the organistships of a number of Churches in the City of London between 1840 and 1847.

Editor of operas from 1847 for the publishing firm of Novello, orchestrating and writing a historical narrative to accompany them. The works were published monthly and priced so as to make them as broadly available as possible.

Lived in Torquay, Devon and from 1867 he was organist and honorary precentor of All Saints' Church, Babbacombe.

In 1876 he converted to the Roman Catholic faith.

At the London Exhibition of 1885 William Rockstro conducted concerts of the 16th and 17th century sacred music of Italy and England.

From 1891 he lectured at the Royal Academy of Music and at the Royal College of Music, where he also took a class in plainsong. Among his pupils at the R.C.M. was **Walford Davies**.

Composed a sacred cantata *The Good Shepherd* for the Three Choirs' Festival at Gloucester in 1886. Harmonised Ambrosian tones into Chants for Psalms and the Te Deum.

Author of a number of books including *A History of Music for Young Students* (1879) and *A Practical Harmony* (1881). Also contributed articles to Grove's *Dictionary of Music and Musicians*, *Musical Times*, *Musical Society*, and other journals.

Composed the anthems 'O Lord, rebuke us not' and 'Woe unto us'. Composed piano works and a popular ballad 'Queen and huntress'.

RODGERS, Sarah (b.1953)

Born in Aylesbury, Buckinghamshire in 1953.

Educated at Walthamstow Hall School, Sevenoaks and the University of Nottingham where she graduated B.A. (1974) in music and archaeology.

Chairman of the Composers' Guild of Great Britain (1992-1995), and a director of the British Music Information Centre.

Took part for two years in the Voluntary Service Overseas programme in West Africa, as a result of which the music of other cultures attracted her attention and influenced her compositions. The results can be seen in *The Roaring Whirl* (1990) and *Saigyo* (1995). Her music for the church includes Mass *of St. Anne* (1982), four anthems and *Celebrating in Song*, a setting of the Communion Service of the Methodist Church.

ROE, John Edward (1838-1871)
Born in Middlesex in 1838; died in Brighton, Sussex in 1871. Composed hymn tunes.

ROGERS, Dr. Benjamin (1614-1698)
Born in Windsor, Berkshire and baptised on 2 June 1614; died in Oxford in June 1698.

The son of Peter Rogers, a singing man of St. George's Chapel, Windsor Castle.

A chorister of St. George's Chapel under **Nathaniel Giles**. Graduated Mus.B. (Cambridge: 1658) and D.Mus. (Oxford: 1669). The Cambridge degree was conferred following the intervention of Oliver Cromwell, who sent a mandate to the vice chancellor and Senate asking them to waive certain of the qualifications.

A lay clerk of St. George's Chapel, Windsor Castle for three distinct periods, the first of which was in the 1630s.

He then travelled to Ireland and was organist of Christ Church Cathedral, Dublin following the dismissal of Randal Jewett. Became organist officially in 1639 but held office for only two years, alarmed by the Irish Rebellion of 1841 and returning to England.

Reappointed as a lay clerk of St. George's Chapel, Windsor Castle in 1641. Remained until the Civil War, and taught music in the town of Windsor.

A clerk of Eton College (from 1653) and later, master of the choristers. Initially (from 1662) he shared this responsibility with a Mr. Tudaway but frm the following year he had sole charge. At that time, Eton College had no formal position of organist. Had it then existed, Benjamin Rogers would have held office.

In the early years of the 1660s, Benjamin Rogers resumed his connection with St. George's Chapel by taking up a lay clerkship. From 1662 he drew an extra £1 per month in salary for acting as deputy to **William Child**.

Organist and master of the choristers of Magdalen College, Oxford (from 1665). His tenure came to an abrupt end when in January 1686 he was dismissed for a combination of his unruly behaviour and the scandal of his daughter being made pregnant by a college porter. Granted a small pension on condition that he severed all connections with the College.

His *Hymnus Eucharisticus* (1660) is still sung on 1 May each year from the tower of Magdalen College. Also composed an Evening Service in G, sets of Responses to the Commandments in D and E Minor, and the anthems 'Behold, now praise the Lord' and 'Teach me, O Lord'. Also composed a set of airs in four parts for violins; songs; and other instrumental works.

ROGERS, Edmund (1851-1919)
Born in Salisbury, Wiltshire on 9 October 1851; died in St. Marylebone, London in 1919. A chorister of Salisbury Cathedral (1860-1865). Organist of Holy Trinity Church, Windsor, Berkshire (from 1869), and in London at the Churches of St. Alban, Holborn (from 1870); St. Thomas, Portman Square (from 1871) and St. Michael, Paddington (from 1888). A local choral society conductor. His works include a Mass in D, a setting of the Offertory Sentences, hymn tunes, anthems and sacred cantatas including *The Pilgrim's Progress* (1883). Other items include operettas such as *Elinor, or The Border Bride* (1887), songs, part songs and pieces for organ and piano.

ROGERS, Frederick F. (1846-?)
Born in Cheltenham, Gloucestershire in 1846. Organist and choirmaster of Highworth Parish Church (from 1863), and assistant organist of Great Malvern Parish Church, Worcestershire. Organist of Malvern College Chapel (from 1865) and St. Peter's Church, Malvern Wells (from 1869). Manager of the Steinway Hall in London (from 1893). Composed a setting of Psalm 69 'Save me, O God'; a Festival Te Deum in F; a setting of the Offertory Sentences; a sacred cantata *Deborah* for Solo Voices, Chorus and Orchestra, cantatas for female voices including *The Fairy Flower* (1884) and items for piano, such as the Minuet in A.

ROGERS (Rodgers), James (?-?1784)
Organist of Ely Cathedral (1774-1777), and probably the James Rodgers who was organist of Peterborough Cathedral (1777-1784). Composed an Evening Service in A. Three anthems by him were edited by his pupil, Henry Burdett. His anthems include 'Behold, I bring you' and 'Be light and glad'.

ROGERS, Sir John Leman (1780-1847)
Born on 18 April 1780; died in Ivybridge, Devon on 10 December 1847. Eldest son of Sir Frederick Leman Rogers, M.P., whom he succeeded to the baronetcy in 1797. A member (from 1819) and president (1820-1841) of the Madrigal Society. Admired the works of **Thomas Tallis** and set up an annual service in Westminster Abbey at which the music was by Tallis. Composed services, chants including a Double Chant in A, anthems such as 'Be Thou my Judge' and 'I will give thanks', hymn tunes and 16 glees.

ROGERS, Peter (17th century)
Lived in the early part of the 17th century. Said to be 'of Windsor'. Composed a Service in G.

ROGERS, Dr. Roland (1847-1927)
Born in West Bromwich, Staffordshire on 17 November 1847; died in Bangor, Wales on 30 July 1927.

Studied music with his father, a local violinist and teacher, and with other musicians. Graduated B.Mus. (1870) and D.Mus. (1875) at New College, Oxford.

From the age of 11 (in 1858), Roland Rogers played the harmonium of St. Peter's Church, Wolverhampton. Organist at the age of 15 at St. John's, Wolverhampton (1863-1868) and Tettenhall Parish Church, Staffordshire (1868-1871).

Organist of Bangor Cathedral for two periods: 1871-1892 and 1906-1927. The cathedral authorities looked askance at the extent of his outside activities and it was this that caused his departure in 1892. The Dean objected to his playing in Nonconformist chapels. However, the differences were resolved sufficiently for Rogers to be reappointed in 1902. His pupils include D. Ffrancon Davies, William Davies and R.S. Hughes.

An accomplished recitalist, choral society conductor and eisteddfod competitor. A lecturer in music at the University College of North Wales (from 1892). Taught music at Rydal Mount School, Colwyn

Bay. Conductor of the Bethesda Choir that won prizes at the successive National *Eisteddfodau* of Denbigh (1882), Cardiff (1883) and Liverpool (1884). Adjudicator at the Bangor National Eisteddfod of 1874.

Editor of Welsh Psalter and *Emyniadur yr eglwys*.

Composed as his B.Mus. exercise a setting of Psalm 130 'Out of the deep' for Solo Voices, five part chorus and Strings. Supplicated for his doctorate with the cantata *Prayer and Praise* for Solo Voices, eight-part Chorus and Orchestra.

Composed services including settings in A and in F, anthems of which an example is 'Lord, who shall dwell?', songs, part songs and organ marches. Won a prize for his cantata *The Garden* at the Llandudno National Eisteddfod.

ROGERS, Timothy J. (b.1961)
Born in Sheffield, Yorkshire in 1961. Won a music scholarship to St. Edward's School, Oxford and read music at University College, Cardiff. Studied violin with James Barton, was tutored by H.C. Robbins Landon and was strongly influenced by **Alun Hoddinott** and **William Mathias**. As well as composing he is the proprietor of a music publishing house. Has written music for organ including *Exultate* and *Majestas* and choral works including 'Now sing glory to God' and 'O Queen of Heaven'.

ROOPER, Jasper Bonfoy (1898-1981)
Born in Penkridge, Staffordshire on 30 June 1898; died on 31 August 1981.
Attended Lancing College, Sussex. George Carter scholar (1926-1927) at the Royal College of Music, and returned to the R.C.M. for further study (1932-1933). His teachers were **W.G. Alcock, George Thalben-Ball** and, for composition, **Ralph Vaughan Williams**. Assistant music master (from 1927) and director of music (1937-1948) of Lancing College. Staff music tutor in the Extra Mural Department of Oxford University (1951-1965). A part-time lecturer in the Department of Continuing Education at the University of Sussex. Composer of the Evening Office, *Three Psalms*, a Christmas Rhapsody, madrigals, part songs and piano music.

ROOTHAM, Dr. Cyril Bradley (1875-1938)
Born in Bristol, Gloucestershire on 5 October 1875; died in Cambridge on 18 March 1938.
Studied music with his father, Daniel W. Rootham, conductor of the Bristol Madrigal Society. Attended Bristol Grammar School and Clifton College under W.F. Trimnell and Cedric Bucknall.
At the age of 19 he went up to St. John's College, Cambridge where he studied classics. Graduated B.A. (1897), B.Mus. (1900), M.A. (1901) and D.Mus. (1910).
Studied at the Royal College of Music under **Walter Parratt** and **C.V. Stanford**.
Organist of Christ Church, Hampstead, London (1898-1901), where he succeeded **Walford Davies**.
Organist of St. Asaph's Cathedral for six months in 1901; organist of St. John's College, Cambridge (1901-1938).
University lecturer in form and analysis (1913-1918) and in harmony and counterpoint (from 1924). An examiner for musical degrees. Lecturer in music at St. John's College (from 1919).
Author of *Voice Training for Choirs and Schools*.
Cyril Rootham composed an Evening Service in E Minor, a setting of Psalm 103 'Praise the Lord, O my soul' for Chorus and

Orchestra, anthems, an opera *The Two Sisters*, songs, part songs, chamber music, and Irish miniatures for violin and orchestra.

ROSCOE, Revd. J.E. (1880-?)
Born in London in 1880. Studied at Pembroke College, Oxford. Composed a chant setting of the Holy Communion Service, and songs.

ROSE, Barry Michael (b.1934)
Born in Chingford, Essex on 24 May 1934.
Educated at St. George Monoux School, Walthamstow, London and the Royal Academy of Music (1958-1960), where he studied organ under C.H. Trevor.
Worked in insurance upon leaving school. Organist from the age of 11 of St. Anne's Church, Chingford (1946-1956). Sang bass in the Choir of Hampstead Parish Church (1956-1957) and organist of St. Andrew's Church, Kingsbury, London (1957-1960).
The first organist of the newly-built Guildford Cathedral (1960-1974), where he formed the professional choir and established daily choral services. Sub organist (from 1974) and master of the choir of St. Paul's Cathedral (1977-1984).
A teacher of music at King's School, Canterbury, Kent (1984-1988).
Master of the music of St. Albans Cathedral (from 1988).
Musical adviser (1971-1991) to Religious Broadcasting at the B.B.C., for whom he was for some time producer of the 'Choral Evensong' radio broadcasts. A lively and entertaining speaker, Barry Rose describes how he was able to judge the quality of the chanting during those services of the Psalms: if the radio engineers stopped work to listen then the standard was high.
Has made many recordings as organist and conductor, and co-founded the recording company Guild Records in 1967.
He has composed a hymn tune 'Cross Deep' which appeared in *Broadcast Praise* (1981) and a chant to Psalm 121. His other works include radio signature tunes such as 'The Grace Book' and that which introduced 'The Christian Centuries' on B.B.C. Radio 4. Other compositions include a setting of Psalm 121 for Her Majesty the Queen's Silver Jubilee Service in St. Paul's Cathedral in 1977. 'O Lord our Governor' (1994) was commissioned for a concert in St. Albans Cathedral.
Influential in the revival of notable examples of the Victorian church music repertoire.

ROSE, Dr. Bernard William George (b.1916)
Born in Little Hallingbury, Hertfordshire on 9 May 1916.
A chorister of Salisbury Cathedral, attending Salisbury Cathedral School (1925-1931). An exhibitioner at the Royal College of Music (1933-1935), where he studied under the organist from his days at Salisbury, **W.G. Alcock**.
Attended St. Catharine's College, Cambridge (1935-1939) as organ scholar and Stewart of Rannoch scholar. A pupil of **Hubert Middleton** and E.J. Dent. Graduated Mus.B. (1938), B.A. (1939) and M.A. (1944) at Cambridge, and M.A. (1946) and D.Mus. (1951) at the University of Oxford.
Appointed O.B.E. in 1980.
Organist of Queen's College, Oxford (1939-1957), and organist and informator choristarum of Magdalen College, Oxford (1957-1981).
His musical career was interrupted while he saw war service (1940-1941) with the 2nd Northamptonshire Yeomanry and with the Fourth County of London Yeomanry (Sharpshooters) from 1941 to

1945: he was made adjutant in 1942, and taken and held prisoner-of-war (1943-1944).

A tutor and lecturer in the Faculty of Music (from 1945), University lecturer in music (1950-1981) and choragus of Oxford University (1958-1963). A fellow of Queen's College, Oxford (1949-1957), and vice president of Magdalen College (1973-1975). He conducted the first performance, at Queen's College, of the Oxford Elegy (1952) by **Ralph Vaughan Williams**.

His work as an editor of music includes the *Complete Musica Deo Sacra* of **Thomas Tomkins**. Has contributed articles to the journals *Music and Letters* and *Musical Times*.

Has composed anthems including 'Praise ye the Lord' (1949) and 'O praise God in His Holiness' (1980); settings of the Evening Canticles in the form of a Short Service (1962), a Service in C Minor (1968) and the Chichester Service (1994) and the Missa *Voces Choristarum* for Four Sopranos and Organ (1974). A set of Versicles, Responses and the Lord's Prayer (1961) is significant in that it was the first to be published with a through-composed melodic line provided for the officiant, rather than merely the Anglican inflections derived from Plainchant models. The setting also includes thematic reference to the chimes of Magdalen College tower. Other works include a *Feast Song for St. Cecilia* (1975), an ode 'Catharine' (1973) and a setting of William Wordsworth's 'Upon Westminster Bridge' (1990). Also responsible for many editions of church music.

ROSE, John (b.1928)

Born in London in 1928 of Dutch parents. Began composing while at school in South Africa (1940-1946). Studied organ at the Royal Academy of Music and composition at Oxford with **Edmund Rubbra**. Lecturer in music at Langside College of Further Education, Glasgow. Founder of the St. Albans' Chamber Choir. Composer of a Prelude and Fugue and a Scherzo, Intermezzo and Toccata for Organ. His church music includes 'Sweet was the song', an arrangement of the *Coventry Carol*, and an anthem 'Hymn to the Father'.

ROSE, Dr. John Luke (b.1933)

Born in Northwood Hills, Middlesex on 19 July 1933. Attended Chislehurst and Sidcup Grammar School, Kent. Educated at the University of London, graduating B.Mus. (1957) and Ph.D. (1963), and at Trinity College of Music, London (1954-1958). Lecturer and examiner for T.C.M. (1960-1962). A lecturer in adult education at the University of Oxford (1962-1966). Staff lecturer in music at London University (from 1966). Compositions include a collection *Seven mystical anthems* and other anthems; a Magnificat, Sevenfold Amen and Nunc Dimittis; and a setting of Psalm 98. Also a musical play *St. Francis* (1985), symphonies and piano works.

ROSE, Peter Gregory (b.1948)

Born in Beaconsfield, Buckinghamshire on 18 April 1948. A chorister at Salisbury Cathedral (1957-1961) and an academical clerk at Magdalen College, Oxford (1967-1970). Teacher of music at Camrose Secondary School, Edgware, London (from 1970). He works principally as a conductor but has composed several sacred pieces, some of which have been published. They include the carol 'Everlasting Mary'; the *Camrose* Lord's Prayer; Vespers *for Mary Magdalen*, featuring 21 Solo Voices (1970); *God's strange ways* (1971) and several carols such as 'Shepherds' carol', 'Manger carol' and 'Bells carol'; also the motet *Dum transisset Sabbatum*.

ROSEINGRAVE (Rosingrave), Daniel (?-1727)

Died in Dublin in May 1727. Father of **Ralph Roseingrave** and **Thomas Roseingrave**.

Said to have been a chorister of the Chapel Royal under **John Blow** and **Henry Purcell**, but the records do not bear this out.

Organist and master of the choristers of Gloucester Cathedral (1679-1681). Organist and lay vicar of Winchester Cathedral (1681-1692). Organist of Salisbury Cathedral (1693-1698), competing successfully against **Stephen Jeffries**, organist of Gloucester Cathedral. **Vaughan Richardson**, another unsuccessful candidate, eventually succeeded him as organist of Winchester Cathedral.

From 1698 he was organist of the two Anglican Cathedrals in Dublin, St. Patrick's and Christ Church. Also a stipendary of Christ Church and a vicar choral of St. Patrick's, his four combined salaries making him one of the best-paid organists in the British Isles. Remained at St. Patrick's until February 1719 when he resigned due to ill-health and was replaced by his son, Ralph. Continued in office at Christ Church until his death.

At St. Patrick's he had succeeded Robert Hodge as organist. The two men operated together at Christ Church, where Hodge was master of the choristers. In 1699 the two men appeared before the dean of Christ Church, charged with swearing and brawling in a public house. Daniel Roseingrave had been in trouble with the authorities in Gloucester in 1679, where he was admonished for wounding a singing man, John Payn. In 1700 he complained to the dean of Christ Church of assault by Thomas Field, a vicar choral.

Seven anthems by Daniel Roseingrave have survived in manuscript form, including a setting of Psalm 85 'Lord, Thou art become gracious unto Thy land'. Is thought to have composed three Services and two settings of the Creed in 1698, for the use of the choir of Christ Church Cathedral. Doubts exists as to the true authorship: although the works were in Daniel Roseingrave's handwriting he was known to be a competent copyist and the works could have been written by someone else. Conversely, some of the works credited to his son Ralph could, in fact, be his.

ROSEINGRAVE, Ralph (c1695-1747)

Born in Salisbury, Wiltshire around the year 1695; died in Dublin and was buried on 7 December 1747.

The son of **Daniel Roseingrave** and the brother of **Thomas Roseingrave**.

Succeeded his father in 1719 as vicar choral (and in effect, as organist) of St. Patrick's Cathedral, Dublin and at Christ Church Cathedral, Dublin in October 1727. Retained both positions until his death. **The Earl of Mornington**, father of the 'Soldier Duke' (of Wellington), was one of his pupils.

Sang, as a vicar-choral of St. Patrick's Cathedral, in the chorus of the first performance, in Dublin on 13 April 1742, of **Handel**'s *Messiah*.

Composed services in C and in F, and some 22 anthems including a setting of Psalm 86 'Bow down Thine ear, O Lord'. Some of these compositions may actually be the work of his father, Daniel Roseingrave.

ROSEINGRAVE, Thomas (1691-1766)

Born in 1691; died in 1766. **Daniel Roseingrave** and **Ralph Roseingrave** were his father and brother.

Was seven years old when the family moved to Dublin in order for Daniel Roseingrave to take up his appointments at the two Dublin Anglican Cathedrals. Probably a chorister of St. Patrick's

Cathedral, as St. Patrick's granted him £10 to study abroad in 1709.

Studied in Trinity College, Dublin without taking a degree. Spent three years travelling and studying in Italy, where he was befriended by Alessandro and Domenico Scarlatti. Returned to Ireland around the year 1713 to work for two years as part of what was probably a gentlemen's agreement between him and the authorities of St. Patrick's Cathedral.

He went to live in London in 1717, by which time he had become a virtuoso organist. In 1725 he became the first organist of the fashionable St. George's, Hanover Square. Handel, a member of the congregation, set the seven candidates a fugue subject; the other contestants included **John Stanley**, **Thomas Arne** and Michael Festing, the founding secretary of the Society of Musicians. Thomas Roseingrave won the contest on the strength of his extemporary playing, even though his harmonisation was said to be crude and his modulations characterised as extravagant.

Eventually became insane, which was said to be the consequence of an unsuccessful love affair. In 1747 he returned to Dublin.

His compositions include the verse anthem 'Arise, shine', written in Venice in 1712 and a setting of Psalm 145 'Great is the Lord'. In 1739 he issued a collection of 42 of the harpsichord works of Domenico Scarlatti. Thomas Roseingrave is also remembered as a harpsichord composer.

ROSS, Colin Archibald Campbell (1911-1993)

Born in Brecon, South Wales on 7 December 1911; died in 1993.

Educated at Hereford Cathedral; Christ's College, Brecon and at the Royal College of Music, London (1941-1942). An articled pupil of the organist of Brecon Cathedral, J.H. Carden (1929-1930). Later articled to Percy Hull, organist of Hereford Cathedral (1930-1935).

Assistant organist of Hereford Cathedral (1935-1940).

A répétitieur of the Sadlers Wells Theatre, London (from 1942), and conductor of the Croydon Symphony Orchestra, Surrey (1942-1943). Organist of the Church of St. Barnabas, Tunbridge Wells, Kent (1945-1948). An examiner for the Associated Board of the Royal Schools of Music.

Emigrated to Australia in 1948. Organist and director of the choir of St. Paul's Cathedral, Melbourne (1948-1951). Principal study teacher of the Melbourne Conservatory of Music.

On his return to England he was organist of Worthing Parish Church, Sussex (1953-1956).

Master of the music of Newcastle Cathedral (1955-1966).

In 1966 he moved to Worthing, Sussex, where he was music master of the High School for Boys. Retired formally in 1969, but resumed teaching, in 1973, at Chichester College of Further Education.

Composed an anthem 'Let this mind', and other items of church music. His other works include a cantata *Hiawatha*, songs, organ works and a Rhapsody and Variations for Piano.

ROSS, George (19th/20th century)

Graduated B.Mus. in 1910 at the University of Durham. Lived and worked in Scotland. Organist and choirmaster of the West United Free Church, Coldstream (1900-1904). Private organist to the Marquis of Breadalbane at Taymouth Castle (1904-1910).

He was then organist and choirmaster of St. John's Presbyterian Church, Moncton. A composer of anthems.

ROSS, John (1763-1837)

Born in Newcastle-on-Tyne on 12 October 1763; died in Aberdeen, Scotland on 28 July 1837. Composed hymn tunes.

ROSS, Roger Rowson (1817-1894)

Born in Montrose, Scotland on 25 August 1817; died in Manchester on 19 June 1894. Lived in Manchester as a merchant and insurance agent. Founded two scholarships at the Royal Academy of Music, one for the study of church music and the other for the performance of wind instruments. Associated with St. Peter's Church, Manchester, where Benjamin St. Joule Baptiste was organist. Sang alto in the church choir, and was a warden (1859-1892). In 1861 he published a collection of chants. Composed the hymn tune 'Manchester', which is also known as 'St. Peter's'.

ROSS, Wallace Michael (b.1920)

Born in Yeovil, Somerset on 19 September 1920.

Attended Rugby School, Warwickshire until 1938, and the Royal College of Music. Organ scholar of Balliol College, Oxford (from 1939). His studies were interrupted by World War II, in which he served with the Royal Artillery. Graduated B.A. and M.A. and B.Mus. (1950). Articled to Horace Hawkins, organist of Chichester Cathedral (1947-1948).

Director of music of Pocklington School, York (from 1948), and assistant organist of Beverley Minster, Yorkshire (1948-1950).

Second assistant organist of Leicester Cathedral (1951-1954) and music master of Newton Boys' School, Leicester. Assistant organist of Gloucester Cathedral (1954-1958), and director of music at King's School, Gloucester.

Worked with brass bands, and conducted a male voice choir.

Organist of Derby Cathedral (1958-1983 and of Sturgess Boys' School, Derby.

Following his resignation from Derby Cathedral he became organist of Kegworth Parish Church.

Composed four carols.

ROSS, Dr. William Baird (1871-1950)

Born in Montrose, Scotland on 30 November 1871; died in Edinburgh on 10 August 1950.

Educated at Montrose Academy and in Edinburgh. Graduated B.Mus. (1896) and D.Mus. (1904) at Queen's College, Oxford.

A teacher of singing and piano at the George Watson Ladies' College, Edinburgh (from 1907). Taught at the New College Students' Music Society, Edinburgh (from 1909). A lecturer in Church Praise at New College (from 1911) and at the Divinity Colleges of the United Free Church in Glasgow and Aberdeen (from 1912). A lecturer in church music at New College, Edinburgh (1910-1930).

A piano recitalist in Edinburgh. Organist and choirmaster of Farnell Parish Church (from 1885); the Maisondieu, Brechin (1890); St. Luke's Church, Montrose (from 1890) and the Broughton Place Church, Edinburgh (1896-1936). Choirmaster of the Dublin Street Baptist Church, Edinburgh (1895-1903) and organist and choirmaster of the Ancient Church of the Holy Rood, Stirling.

Composed as his B.Mus. exercise the anthem 'Laus Deo' for Solo Voices, Chorus and Strings. Also composed hymn tunes.

ROUTLEY, Revd. Dr. Erik Reginald (1917-1982)
Born in Brighton, Sussex on 31 October 1917; died in Nashville, Tennessee on 8 October 1982.
Educated at Fonthill School; Lancing School, Sussex and Magdalen College, Oxford where he graduated in 1940. Studied at Mansfield College, Oxford for the ministry of the Congregational Church. Ordained at Trinity Congregational Church, Wednesbury, Staffordshire (1943). Graduated B.D. (1946) and D.Phil. (1952) at the University of Oxford, the latter degree for his thesis on the music of Christian hymnody.
Trinity Church was his first ministry and in 1945, he moved to Dartford Congregational Church, Kent. From 1948 he lectured in church history. at Mansfield College, Oxford and in 1959 he was appointed Minister of the Augustine-Bristo Congregational Church in Edinburgh. Moved on to St. James's Church, Newcastle-on-Tyne in 1967.
His last appointment was as professor of Church music and director of the Westminster Choir College of Princeton, New Jersey, U.S.A. (from 1975).
Author of 10 books on the subject of hymns, including *Church Music and Theology* (1959). Secretary to the Committee for the hymnal *Congregational Praise* (1953), and compiled the notes on the music for the hymnal companion which appeared two years later.
Continued to develop hymnals in the U.S.A. Edited *Westminster Praise* (1976). A consultant to the Standing Commission on Church Music, the body incorporated in the mid-1970s and responsible for *The Hymnal* (1982), which contained two texts and five tunes or arrangements by Erik Routley.
Edited the *Bulletin* of the Hymn Society of Great Britain and Ireland (1948-1974).
Far from reluctant to express controversial opinions. His denunciation of Victorian church music composers was unrestrained. Writing of **John Stainer**, whose Meditation *The Crucifixion* (1887) has inspired successive generations, his view was, 'Stainer at least once reached the top flight - in his Chant in E Minor'.
Wrote hymns and composed hymn tunes including 'Augustine', first used in *Hymns For Church and School* (1964). 'Abingdon' was composed in 1945.

ROWBOTHAM, John Frederick (1854-?)
Born in Edinburgh on 18 April 1854. The son of Revd. Frank Rowbotham, incumbent of St. James's Church.
Educated at Edinburgh Academy, Rossall School and the University of Oxford, winning a scholarship to Balliol College at the age of 18. Finished top in classics, and also studied Italian and music. Continued his music studies at the Stern Conservatory, Berlin for five years and then in Paris, Dresden and Vienna.
He resumed his travels on the continent in order to collect material for his *History of Music*, published in three volumes between 1885 and 1887. His other works included *How to Write Music Correctly* (1889), articles to *Chambers Encyclopaedia* and the journals *19th Century*, *National Review* and *Blackwood's Magazine*.
A poet, his works including *The Death of Rowland* (1886).
Composed a Mass for Double Choir and Orchestra, and three songs to words by Alfred Musset.

ROWDEN, Revd. Dr. George Croke (1820-1863)
Born in Highworth, Wiltshire in 1820; died on 17 April 1863. Educated at Winchester School, Hampshire and at New College,

Oxford where he graduated B.C.L. (1842) and D.C.L. (1848). Ordained deacon in 1843, priest in 1844. Headmaster of Temple Grove School, East Sheen, Surrey (from 1845), and precentor of Chichester Cathedral (from 1859). Chaplain to the Royal Scoiety of Musicians. Composed a Service in A, the anthem 'Come unto Me', the hymn tune 'Chantry', other items of church music, and glees including 'Return of May'.

ROWLANDS, William Penfro (1860-1937)
Born in Maenclochog, Pembrokeshire, Wales in 1860; died in Morriston, Swansea on 22 October 1937. A schoolteacher, and conductor of the Morriston United Choral Society, which was reputed to be one of the best in Wales. Precentor of the Morriston Tabernacle Congregational Church (from 1892). His compositions include the hymn tune 'Blaenwern', composed around the year 1904 during the Welsh Revival and named after a farm near Tufton, Pembrokeshire where he recuperated from serious illness as a boy. It was first published in *Cân a Moliant* (1916). There were other hymn tunes, and he composed anthems.

ROWLEY, Alec (1892-1958)
Born in Hammersmith, London on 13 March 1892; died in Weybridge, Surrey, on 12 January 1958.
Became an assistant organist at the age of 12, and was trained by Henry Gibson.
Studied at the Royal Academy of Music as Mary Maud scholar (1908-1911) and Henry Smart scholar (1911-1914). His teachers included Frederick Corder.
A sub professor at the R.A.M. (from 1914). A Reader for the firm of Winthrop Rogers (from 1918). In October 1918 he joined the R.A.F. In 1919 he joined the staff of Trinity College of Music, where he taught piano and composition. Later, vice principal of T.C.M. and, in the absence of Dr. Greenhouse Allt during 1947, he acted as principal.
Organist of the Churches of St. Mary Magdalene, Chiswick, London (1910-1912), St. John the Divine, Richmond, Surrey (1912-1921) and St. Alban, Teddington, Middlesex (from 1921).
On 31 July 1924 he gave a broadcast talk on 'Music that speaks to you in sound'. Articles by him began to be published by *Musical Mirror* (from 1927). Author of *Pocket Pronouncing Musical Dictionary*.
Composed several Masses for Churches of the Anglo-Catholic tradition, and the anthem 'Praise'. His other works include a pantomime *The princess who lost a tune*, two Piano Concertos, trios, chamber music and songs.

ROWLEY, Charles (c1870-1943)
Born around the year 1870; died in Middlesex on 26 February 1943. Choirmaster of the New Court Church, Tollington Park (from 1916). Composed hymn tunes.

ROWLEY, Christopher Edward (1840-?)
Born in Manchester on 5 January 1840. Studied piano and organ with George Grundy of Manchester, harmony and counterpoint with **H.C. Banister**. Organist and choirmaster at the age of 19 of Christ Church, Harpurley; and of St. Augustine's Church, Pendlebury (from 1885). Active in the Manchester area in setting up and conducting choirs. A professional voice trainer. Contributed articles on subjects of musical interest to local papers. Composed a Holy Communion Service in F, anthems, operas including *The*

Dragon of Wantley (1881), *Twelve Songs* (1891), part songs, duets and glees.

ROWTON, Revd. Dr. Samuel James (1844-1930)
Born in Hackney, London on 3 July 1844; died in West Runton, Norfolk on 18 March 1930.
Educated at University College, Durham where he graduated B.A. (1871), M.A. (1874), B.Mus. (1890) and D.Mus. (1891).
Ordained deacon in 1872, priest in 1873. Also graduated B.Mus. (1889) and D.Mus. (1890) at Trinity College, Dublin. Organist and director of music of the Royal Medical College, Epsom, Surrey (1872-1901) and of Bradfield College, Berkshire (1901-1907). Assistant priest and organist of Christ Church, Scarborough, Yorkshire (1907-1908), and of St. Michael's Church, Folkestone, Kent (1908-1915). Rector of Wicken Bonant (1915-1916) and of Fulletby, Horncastle, Lincolnshire (1916-1922). Priest-in-charge of Orby Church, near Burgh, Lincolnshire (1922-1927). Published *The Organist's Chantbook*. Composed the hymn tune 'Victory', songs, part songs and items for piano.

RUBBRA, Dr. Charles Edmund (1901-1986)
Born in Northampton on 23 May 1901; died on 14 February 1986. Both parents were musical: his mother taught him to play piano.
He left school in his early teens and was a railway clerk between the ages of 14 and 19. Involved in music in his spare time, composing and in 1918, organising concerts of works by his favourite composer, Cyril Scott, who later gave him piano lessons.
He won a composition scholarship at the University of Reading and another scholarship a year later at the Royal College of Music, where he was taught from 1919 by **Gustav Holst**. His studies at the R.C.M. were also directed by **John Ireland, R.O. Morris,** Eugene Goosens and **Ralph Vaughan Williams**. Studied privately with Evlyn Howard Jones. Graduated D.Mus. at the University of Durham and M.A. at Oxford.
Served in the Royal Artillery (1941-1945).
A senior lecturer in music at the University of Oxford (1947-1968), and a fellow of Worcester College (1963-1968). Taught at Guildhall School of Music (from 1961).
His Evening Service in A-flat contains a highly original organ part. There are also four unaccompanied Mass settings including the Missa *in honorem Sancti Dominici* and Missa *Cantuarensis*, an anthem 'The revival', three motets including *Let us now praise famous men*, three cantatas - *Te Deum, Song of the soul* and *The morning watch*, a Cello Sonata (1946) and various instrumental works.

RUDDLE, Valerie (b.1932)
Born in Halstead, Essex on 15 October 1932. Educated at the Royal Academy of Music. A teacher of music, initially in Scunthorpe, Lincolnshire and then in the West Indies. On her return to the U.K. she became a member of the Methodist Church Music Society and of the Hymn Society of Great Britain and Ireland. Has lived in Kent, at Sittingbourne and Sevenoaks. Director of Music at Sevenoaks Methodist Church. She has composed the anthem 'Isaiah's good news'. Her hymn tune 'Sittingbourne' (1977) was first sung at a harvest festival service in Sevenoaks Methodist Church. Her 'Foye' (1981) is an old spelling of the town of Fowey in Cornwall, the birthplace of her paternal grandmother.

RUSHBRIDGE (Rusbridge), Arthur Ewart (1917-1969)
Born in Reading, Berkshire in 1917; died in Bristol, Gloucestershire on 5 March 1969. Educated at Reading School and graduated M.A. at St. John's College, Oxford. A schoolteacher: at Monmouth School (1940-1944), Mill Hill School, Wales (1944-1948) and at Bristol Grammar School (from 1948). At the last two named he was director of music and at Bristol he also taught classics. A music tutor for the Workers' Educational Association in St. Bees, Cumberland (from 1945). A founder of the Baptist Music Society and a member of the Music Advisory Committee for the *Baptist Hymn Book* (1962). His hymn tunes include 'Horfield', named after the Baptist Church in Bristol where he was choirmaster.

RUSSE, Alfred William (19th/20th century)
Graduated B.Mus. at the University of Durham in 1896. Music master of Bournemouth Collegiate School for Girls, Dorset. Organist and choirmaster of the Church of St. Michael, Bournemouth and choirmaster of Christ Church, Westbourne. A local choral and philharmonic society conductor. Composed as his B.Mus. exercise a setting of Psalm 33 'Rejoice in the Lord' for Solo Voices, Chorus and Strings. His other works include services and anthems.

RUSSELL, Frederick George (1867-1929)
Born in Hoxton, London in 1867; died in Stoke Newington, London on 16 January 1929. Studied at the University of London and graduated B.A. (1889) in engineering, and B.Mus. (1894). Director of music of The Haberdashers' Aske's School, Cricklewood. Lived in Stoke Newington. Organist and choirmaster of the Holy Trinity Church, Hoxton (from 1893) and of St. Edmund's, Lombard Street (from 1895). Composed as his degree exercise a setting of the Magnificat for Solo Voices, Quartet, Chorus and Strings. Also composed anthems, hymn tunes, songs and items for piano.

RUSSELL, Dr. Studley Leslie Lane (1901-1978)
Born in Staines, Middlesex on 7 July 1901; died in Tehidy, Cambourne, Cornwall on 10 February 1978. A chorister of Christ Church Cathedral, Oxford. Studied at Clifton College, Gloucestershire. Returned to Christ Church as organ scholar and later attended the Royal College of Music, where his tutors included **Ralph Vaughan Williams** and Malcolm Sargent. Travelled on a scholarship to Vienna and Italy. Graduated M.A. and D.Mus at the University of Oxford. Director of music of Sutton Valence School, Kent. Music adviser to Buckinghamshire County Council and to the London County Council (1945-1961). Founded and conducted the London Schools' Symphony Orchestra. Compiled books of hymns and carols for schools, including *Kingsway Carol Book*. A composer of hymn tunes and these include 'Charing', which first appeared in *Songs of Praise* (1931).

RUSSELL, Vincent Stuart Harley (1900-1956)
Born in Staines, Middlesex on 16 February 1900; died in Godalming, Surrey on 6 July 1956. Taught classics at Charterhouse and was on the committee responsible for *Clarendon Hymn Book*, published in 1936. Composed a descant to the hymn tune 'Gerontius'.

RUSSELL, William (1777-1813)

Born in London on 6 October 1777; died in Clerkenwell, London on 21 November 1813. His father, Henry Russell, was an organ builder, and organist of St. Mary's Church, Aldermanbury, London. Studied under **William Shrubsole** and **Samuel Arnold.** Graduated B.Mus. at the University of Oxford (1808). Acted as deputy organist for his father at St. Mary's Church, Aldermanbury (1789-1793 and 1798). A pianist and piano teacher. Played at the Sadlers Wells Theatre (from 1800) and the Covent Garden Theatre (from 1801).

Organist of the Great Queen Street Chapel, Lincoln's Inn Fields, London (1793-1798). Organist, concurrently, of St. Anne's Church, Limehouse (from 1798) and the Foundling Hospital (from 1801); he held both positions until his death.

Editor of *Psalms, Hymns and Anthems for the Foundling Chapel* (1809).

Composed a Mass in C Minor for Four Voices, a Service in A, a Single Chant in F and a Double Chant in E, services, anthems such as 'Behold, the eye of the Lord' and 'O Lord God of Hosts', three oratorios including *Job* (1826), and organ voluntaries.

RUTTER, George (17th century)

A 17th century musician and composer. Composed the anthem 'Blessed is the Man'.

RUTTER, Dr. John (b.1945)

Born in London on 24 September 1945. Studied at Clare College, Cambridge, where he graduated M.A. and Mus.B. Holds the Lambeth Doctorate of Music. Director of music of Clare College (1975-1979) and a lecturer at the Open University (1975-1988). Founded, and is director of, the Cambridge Singers. Founded his own recording company, Collegium, in 1984. John Rutter is very well known internationally as a composer of choral music. The 'Shepherd's pipe' carol was composed in his undergraduate days at Cambridge. Has also composed a Magnificat, Requiem and Gloria and anthems including 'Lord, make me an instrument of Thy peace'. His *Psalmfest* (1996) is a suite comprising, in part, settings from other works. His Series III Holy Communion Service was one of the very first available, and achieved wide influence.

S

SADLER, Sydney Thomas (19th/20th century)
Graduated B.Mus. at the University of Durham (1901). Organist of Radbourne Church, Derby, where he lived and worked as a bandmaster and operatic society conductor. Composed the anthem 'Laus Deo' as his degree exercise. Other compositions include the hymn 'O Lord, be with us when we sail' (1916).

SAINT, David (b.1954)
Director of music of the Metropolitan Cathedral, Birmingham. Educated at the Universities of Hull (B.A., 1975) and Liverpool (B.Mus., 1976). Organist of St. Chad's Roman Catholic Cathedral, Birmingham (from 1978). Head of organ studies and director of the chamber choir of Birmingham Conservatory. David Saint has composed the Mass *of St. Chad* and much other music for the Roman Catholic liturgy, including Responses, Masses, Gospel acclamations, Psalms, and hymn arrangements.

SALAMAN, Charles Kensington (1814-1901)
Born in London on 3 March 1814; died in London on 23 June 1901. Learned to play violin at the age of seven. A year later he began to play piano, taking lessons with S.F. Rimbault. Awarded a place at the Royal Academy of Music (1824) but did not take it up. Studied piano under Charles Neate (1826-1831) and with Henri Herz in Paris (1828).
A piano recitalist and teacher, orchestral and choral society conductor, and composer.
Began teaching in 1831. Gave annual orchestral concerts in the Hanover Square Rooms, London (1833-1837). Organised the Concerti da Camera with Henry Blagrove, **Charles Lucas** and others.
In 1836 he visited continental Europe, giving recitals in Munich, Vienna and elsewhere. Became acquainted with composers including Schumann, Czerny and Thalberg. From 1846 to 1848 he lived in Rome.
Became a member of the Royal Society of Musicians (1837). An Associate of the Philharmonic Society (1837-1855).
Founded an amateur choral society in London (1849). Some six years later he began a series of lectures, which he continued for several years, in London and the provinces.
Jewish by birth but composed for both Church and Synagogue. His first published composition was a song 'O come, dear Louise', first performed in Blackheath, Kent in the summer of 1828. Other secular works include song settings including 'I will arise from dreams of thee' by Shelley, and an Overture in D.
Composed a hundred Jewish choral works, settings of Psalm 84 'O how amiable are Thy dwellings' and of Psalm 29 'Bring unto the Lord, O ye mighty' for Double Choir, and anthems including 'Preserve me, O God'. Also composed organ voluntaries.

SALSBURY, Dr. Janet Mary (1881-?)
Born in Pershore, Worcestershire on 13 May 1881. Graduated B.Mus. (1905) and D.Mus. (1910) at the University of Durham. Teacher of piano and harmony, and honorary organist at Cheltenham Ladies' College, Gloucestershire. A professor of music by correspondence, and an examiner in theory at Trinity College of Music. Author of *An Analysis of Mozart's 22 Piano Sonatas*. Published *Specimen Aural Tests* (1924-1926) for examination candidates. Composed Christmas carols, a festival anthem 'O sing unto the Lord', carols including 'Hark! The joyous bells' (1913), a part song and a song cycle *A Ballad of Evesham* (1907).

SALTER, Philip (?-1834)
A vicar choral of Exeter Cathedral. Composed the anthems 'Lord, how long wilt Thou?' and 'Almighty and everlasting God'.

SAMPSON, Brook (1848-1920)
Born in Leeds on 5 January 1848; died in Hove, Sussex on 2 February 1920. A chorister of the Episcopal Church of St. Saviour, Bridge of Allan, and a pupil of **William Spark**. Trained privately in music, graduating B.Mus. (1875) at Exeter College, Oxford. Lived in Bradford until 1868. Organist and choirmaster of St. Catherine's Church (from 1868), and St. Edmund's (from 1883), Kettering, Northamptonshire and All Saints', Northampton (1891-1914). A local choral society conductor. Author of works including *A Digest of the Analysis of J.S. Bach's 48 Fugues* (1905-1907), with the reputation of an authority on Bach. Composed church music including hymn tunes such as 'Vesper Hymn' (1904). His degree exercise was a setting of Psalm 147 'O praise the Lord' for Solo Voices, Chorus and Orchestra.

SAMPSON, George (1861-?)
Born in Clifton, Gloucestershire in 1861. Organist of St. James's Church, Bristol (from 1879), and organist and director of music of St. Alban's Holborn, London (from 1884). Music master and precentor of Brighton College (from 1888), for which he composed a Jubilee Hymn (1897) and a set of songs (1896 and 1897). An author and composer, his writings including *A Text Book on the Elements of Music* and a similar volume on piano, for use in schools. His compositions include a setting of the Holy Communion Service in D, Evening Services (1894), an O Salutaris in E-flat and an Ave Verum in D-flat for Baritone Solo and Men's Chorus. Also composed part songs.

SAMPSON, Godfrey (1902-1949)
Born in Gloucester in 1902; died in 1949. Attended Westminster School and, as Goring Thomas scholar (1924), the Royal Academy of Music. Also won a Mendelssohn Scholarship. A professor of composition at the R.A.M. His works include the anthems 'Come, my Way, my Truth, my Life' (1938), 'The God of love my Shepherd is' (1932) and 'My song shall be alway of the loving kindness of the Lord' (1937). Also composed a setting of the Benedicite (1940). His secular works include songs, part songs, and instrumental chamber music.

SAMPSON, William Herbert (19th/20th century)
Graduated B.A. (1882) and B.Mus. (1896) at the University of London. Organist and choirmaster of Bromsgrove School, Worcestershire (from 1885); St. George's Church, Worthing, Sussex (from 1887); St. Luke's Church, Redcliffe Square, London (from 1893); Herne Bay Parish Church, Kent (from 1893) and the Park Chapel, Chelsea, London (1896-1900). Lived for a time in the London suburb of Putney. Superintendent of examinations for the University of London (from 1901). Submitted a Mass in B-flat as his B.Mus. exercise. Composed a chant setting of the Benedicite (1892), a Morning and Evening Service in D (1882), the anthem 'God, who madest earth and Heaven' (1884) and a collection of 12 hymn tunes (1882).

SAMSON, Revd. Arthur Murray (1883-?)
Born in Reading, Berkshire in 1883. Organ scholar (1911-1913) of Queens' College, Cambridge. Graduated Mus.B. (1913), B.A. (1913) and M.A. Studied at Sarum Theological College. Music master of Rossall Preparatory School (1904-1908) and St. Christopher's School, Eastbourne, Sussex (1908-1910). Assistant curate of the Church of St. Peter-in-Eastgate, Lincoln (from 1914), and vicar of St. Peter's Church, Loughborough (from 1948). Composed church music including a Magnificat and Nunc Dimittis in D (1910) and the anthem 'The Lord hear thee in the day of trouble' (1909), and songs including the two-part 'Serenity' (1939).

SANDERS, Francis George (19th/20th century)
Trained privately and at the Royal College of Music, where he was Charlotte Holm exhibitioner (from 1893). Graduated B.Mus. at Queen's College, Oxford (1899). Organist and choirmaster of Chislehurst Parish Church, Kent (1894-1896) and of All Saints' Church, Ennismore Gardens, London (1896-1902). Lived in Clapham, London. Music master at the School of the Indigent Blind, Southwark (1899-1902). Submitted as his degree exercise the anthem 'O Lord, Thou art my God' for Soprano Solo, Quartet, Chorus and Strings. Also composed a setting of the Te Deum

(1908) and Benedicite in A-flat (1909), the anthem 'Keep innocency and take heed' (1915), and hymn tunes.

SANDERS, Dr. John Derek (b.1933)
Born in Woodford, Essex on 26 November 1933.
Won music scholarships to Felsted School, Essex and to the Royal College of Music (1950-1952). A pupil of **John Dykes Bower**, organist of St. Paul's Cathedral. Organ scholar of Gonville and Caius College, Cambridge (1952-1956). Graduated B.A. (1955), M.A. (1958) and Mus.B. (1956). In 1990 he was awarded the Lambeth D.Mus.
Appointed O.B.E. in 1994.
Assistant organist of Gloucester Cathedral (1958-1963) under **Herbert Sumsion**. Director of music of King's School, Gloucester and Cheltenham Ladies' College, Gloucestershire (from 1968). Organist and master of the choristers of Chester Cathedral (1964-1967), returning to Gloucester Cathedral to succeed Dr. Sumsion. Retired in 1994. Directed the 250th Three Choirs' Festival, in Gloucester (1977). A local choral society conductor.
Compositions include a Festival Te Deum (1962), settings of the Jubilate Deo and the Reproaches, two set of Preces and Responses and the carol 'Whence is that goodly fragrance flowing?' His Soliloquy for Organ dates from 1977.

SANDERSON, Wilfred Ernest (1878-1935)
Born in Ipswich, Suffolk on 23 December 1878; died in Nutfield, Surrey on 10 December 1935.
Trained in music at Westminster Abbey and attended St. Dunstan's College, Catford, Kent and the City of London School. Pupil-assistant to **Frederick Bridge**, organist of Westminster Abbey. Graduated B.Mus. at the University of Durham (1900).
After two years in business, Wilfred Sanderson made music his full-time career.
Organist and choirmaster of the Church of St. Stephen, Walthamstow, Essex (from 1896); the London Churches of All Hallows, Southwark (from 1898) and St. James, West Hampstead (from 1899); and St. George's Church, Doncaster, Yorkshire (from 1904).
An examiner for Trinity College of Music, London, and a local choral and operatic society conductor.
Composed as his degree exercise the anthem 'Praise to the Holiest' for Solo Voices, Chorus and Strings. His other works comprise hymn tunes including 'The fisherman's prayer' (1918), songs, Two Solos for Piano (1908), and organ works. Known as a composer of Edwardian ballads.

SANDYS, William (c1792-1874)
Born around 1792; died in London on 18 February 1874. A lawyer. Author of *A History of violin...* (1864). Published *Christmas Carols, Ancient and Modern...* (1833) and other collections. Composed a number of carols, including 'This day a Child is born'.

SANGER, David John (b.1947)
Born in London on 17 April 1947. Educated at Eltham College, Kent (1957-1963) and at the Royal Academy of Music (1963-1966). Organist for many years of the Church of St. Lawrence, Catford, Kent. A professor of the Royal Academy of Music. Has composed many works for use in Christian worship, including a Magnificat and Nunc Dimittis (The *St. Paul's* Service) for the Trebles of the Choir of St. Paul's Cathedral with a version for full choir. A Missa Brevis was for James O'Donnell and the Choristers

of Westminster Cathedral. Christmas carols include 'Christmas Day' and the unaccompanied 'Sweet was the song the Virgin sang'. *Spring Rising!* is a dramatic musical in the modern style, telling the story of the first Easter.

SANGSTER, Dr. Walter Hay (1835-1899)
Born in London on 17 September 1835; died in Eastbourne, Sussex on 2 March 1899.
Educated at the City of London School. Studied with **E.J. Hopkins**, under whom he was a chorister at the Temple Church, and with **W. Rea**. Studied in Berlin (1855), and was organist of the English Ambassador's Church. Graduated B.Mus. (1870) and D.Mus. (1877) at the University of Oxford.
His pupils include **Healey Willan**.
Organist of Christ Church, Ealing, London before going to Berlin. Organist of the London Churches of St. Michael, Chester Square (until 1861) and All Saints, St. John's Wood (1861-1864). Organist of the Parish Church of St. James, Weybridge, Surrey (1865-1872); St. Michael's Church, Paddington, London (1872-1878) and St. Saviour's Church, Eastbourne, Sussex (1880-1889).
Composer of hymn tunes, of which 'Ad Infernos' and 'Weybridge' were selected for *Hymns Ancient and Modern*. Also composed a Quadruple Chant setting of the Te Deum (1891), anthems including 'Lo! star led chiefs' (1888) and 'Blessed is the man', cantatas such as *The Lord is my Light*, part songs, an Overture, Prelude and Fugue for Organ, and other works for organ and for piano.

SANTLEY, Sir Charles (1834-1922)
Born in Liverpool on 28 February 1834; died in London in 1922. The son of William Santley, a local teacher of singing and piano.
A chorister of a number of churches in Liverpool.
Knighted in 1907. Received the papal award of Knight Commander of St. Gregory the Great (1887).
A famous baritone opera and oratorio singer. Began as an amateur, giving a farewell concert in Liverpool on 15 September 1855 before setting off for Italy to study under Gaetano Nava. Returned to England in October 1857 and took further lessons with Manuel Garcia.
His first two professional engagements were as Adam in Haydn's *Creation* (16 November 1857) and, exactly one month later, in Handel's *Messiah*, both at St. Martin's Hall, London. His first appearance at Covent Garden was in October 1859 as Hoel in *Dinorah*.
Sang at each of the Leeds Festivals from 1857 to 1886, except for that of 1880. Began a long association with the Norwich Festival in 1860. Sang at each of the Birmingham Festivals between the years 1861 and 1891 except for 1867. Sang at many Three Choirs' Festivals between 1863 and 1894 and at many of the Handel Festivals at Crystal Palace (from 1862).
Toured the U.S.A. (1871 and 1891) and Australia (1889-1890).
Converted to Roman Catholicism around the year 1880.
Composed a Mass in A-flat for Solo Voices, Chorus and Orchestra (1892). Other items of church music include a setting of the Offertory and an Ave Maria. Also composed a madrigal, and songs.

SAUNDERS, Dr. Joseph Gordon (c1837-1912)
Died at the age of 75 on 17 June 1912.
Graduated B.Mus. (1872) and D.Mus. (1878) at Hertford College, Oxford.

A professor of harmony and counterpoint at Trinity College of Music, London. An examiner and associate of the Royal Philharmonic Society. Lived in the London suburb of South Hampstead.
Author of the primer *Examples in Strict Counterpoint, Fingering and Phrasing,* and compiler of *A Set of Studies, Original and Selected, for the Pianoforte* (1896), which was published in four volumes.
Submitted the cantata *Domine, Dominus Noster* as his B.Mus. exercise and a cantata *Benedici, anima mea* for Solo Voices, Chorus and Orchestra for his doctorate. Also composed a Magnificat in F, anthems including 'The Lord is in His holy temple' (1876), chants, songs such as 'Memories' (1868), part songs, piano works and items for organ.

SAVAGE, William (c1720-1789)
Born around the year 1720; died in London on 27 July 1789. Studied under **J.C. Pepusch**. An organist of Finchley, London of this name who was active around the year 1743 may be the same person. A gentleman of the Chapel Royal (from 1744). A vicar choral, and almoner and master of the choristers of St. Paul's Cathedral (1748-1773), being removed from the latter 'on account of the great harshness with which he treated the boys committed to his charge'. Composed a Single Chant in C, and other items of church music.

SAVILLE (Sharpe), Evelyn Mary (1884-1969)
Born in Battersea, London on 2 September 1884; died in St. Marylebone, London on 15 August 1969. Educated privately. Composer of hymn tunes, light orchestral works, educational music, and settings of poems.

SAWYER, Dr. Frank Joseph (1857-1908)
Born on 19 June 1857 in Brighton, Sussex; died in Brighton on 29 April 1908.
Studied at the Leipzig Conservatory under Ernst Richter and others. A pupil/assistant of **Frederick Bridge**, organist of Westminster Abbey. Graduated B.Mus. (1877) and D.Mus. (1884) at the University of Oxford.
Organist and choirmaster of St. Patrick's Church, Hove, Sussex. A local choral and orchestral society conductor. A professor of sight singing at the Royal College of Music. Gave organ recitals at the Bow and Bromley Institute, and lectured on the subjects of organ music and the history of dance at various institutions.
A grand organist of the Freemasons.
Joint author, with Frederick Bridge, of *A Course of Harmony* (1899); his other published works include *A Primer of Extemporisation and Sight Reading.*
Composer of hymn tunes. His works include a harvest anthem 'All people that on earth do dwell' (1899) and other anthems, an oratorio *Mary the Virgin* (1884), sacred cantatas such as *Jerusalem* (1880), *Six Christmas Carols* (1880), part songs and instrumental works.

SCARISBRICK, Thomas (1805-1869)
Born in Prescot, Lancashire on 24 March 1805; died in Kendal on 26 February 1869. Organist of Kendal Parish Church. Composed anthems including 'O praise God in His holiness' (1908) and 'Sing and rejoice', and other items of church music.

SCHOLEFIELD, Revd. Clement Cotterill (1839-1904)

Born in Edgbaston, Birmingham on 22 June 1839; died in Godalming, Surrey on 10 September 1904.

The seventh and youngest son of William Scholefield, Member of Parliament for Birmingham (1847-1867)

Educated at Pocklington Grammar School, Yorkshire and at St. John's College, Cambridge where he graduated of B.A. (1864) and M.A. (1867). Admitted to the Inner Temple (1863). A pianist. Ordained deacon in 1867, priest in 1868.

Curate of Hove Parish Church, Sussex (1867-1869) and of St. Peter's Church, South Kensington, London (1871-1879), where he was a colleague of **Arthur Sullivan,** who was organist of St. Peter's from 1867 until 1872. Curate of St. Luke's Church, Chelsea (1879-1880).

Conduct (chaplain) of Eton College (1880-1890), and vicar of Holy Trinity Church, Knightsbridge (1890-1895). Retired to Godalming in 1895.

Scholefield composed a total of 41 hymn tunes including 'Fides' and 'St. Nicholas', published as a collection in 1902. Also a Wedding Hymn (1889), a setting of the Benedicite in G (1901) and songs.

His hymn tune 'St. Clement', which is now firmly associated with 'The day Thou gavest, Lord, is ended', first appeared in conjunction with these words in *Church Hymns* (1874), edited by Arthur Sullivan. Among others, those who condemned the tune as weak and mawkish were the composer **Ralph Vaughan Williams** and the Archbishop of Canterbury, Cosmo Gordon Lang, whose letter to *The Times* set off a series of correspondence.

SCOTT, James Kim (1839-1883)

Born in Urr, Kirkcudbrightshire, Scotland in 1839; died in Edinburgh on 15 March 1883. Composer of hymn tunes.

SCOTT, John (1776-1815)

Born in 1776; died in Jamaica in 1815. A chorister of St. George's Chapel, Windsor Castle and of Eton College, and a pupil of **Theodore Aylward** and **Samuel Webbe** the elder. Was deputy to **Samuel Arnold,** organist of Westminster Abbey. Organist of Spanish Town, Jamaica. Composed the anthem 'Praise the Lord, O Jerusalem'.

SCOTT, John Sebastian (1881-1960)

Born in Leicester on 17 March 1881; died in Scarborough, Yorkshire on 19 September 1960.

Educated at Oakham College, Rutland and Emmanuel College, Cambridge where he took the Classical Tripos in 1903. Studied organ with **E.W. Naylor** and composition with **Ivor Atkins.**

Assistant master of Giggleswick School (1904-1909). Music master of The Leys School, Hoylake (1909-1910).

Served in Salonika (1916-1919) during World War I.

Inspector to the Nottinghamshire Board of Education, with special responsibility for music and music courses (1919-1936) and to the Board of the East Riding of Yorkshire (1937-1946). Retired in 1946 and moved to Scarborough. Chairman of the Nottingham Music Festival (1929-1936).

Composer of hymn tunes including 'Northenden' (1911), and a Metrical Litany.

SCOTT, Walter (1842-?)

Born in Long Sutton, Lincolnshire on 10 October 1842. Studied music with Julius Benedict and, for violin, with a Mr. Holmes -

possibly **Henry Holmes.** Lived in Cardiff. A local examiner for the Royal College of Organists. Organist of St. Margaret's Church, Cardiff. Performed at Cardiff *eisteddfodau* as an organ soloist. Until around 1890 he trained the Cardiff-based contingent of the choirs of the Gloucester and Worcester Festivals. From that time, predominantly local people made up the choirs. Chorus master of the Cardiff Music Festival. Composed a setting of the Holy Communion Service, a Te Deum and Benedictus, songs, and works for violin and for piano.

SCOTT, William Herbert (1862-1932)

Born in Lichfield, Staffordshire in 1862; died in Roundhay on September 21st 1932. The son of a minister of the Congregational Church. As a boy he lived in Shropshire. Joined the staff of *Yorkshire Post* (1886). Served for 40 years, retiring in 1926. Rose to the position of chief reporter. Writer of hymns and poetry. His friend, the composer Edward German, set some of his works to music. Published a biography of German in 1932. Composer of hymn tunes, and of a Benedictus in chant form (1889).

SCOTT-GATTY, Sir Alfred (1847-1918)

Born in Ecclesfield, Yorkshire on 26 April 1847; died in St. Marylebone, London on 18 December 1918. The son of Revd. Dr. Alfred Gatty, sub dean of York Minster. Educated at Marlborough College, Wiltshire and Christ's College, Cambridge. Attached his mother's maiden name to his own by royal licence. Became an expert in heraldry, in which he built a career. Rouge dragon pursuivant of arms, York herald and acting registrar of the College of Arms, and garter principal king of arms (from 1904), for which he was appointed K.C.V.O. Published collections including *Little Songs for Little Voices,* and musical plays for children. Composer of hymn tunes including 'Welwyn', which first appeared in the Roman Catholic Church's *Arundel Hymns* (1902), and 'Bodmin'. Published hundreds of what have been characterised as drawing-room songs.

SCRIVENER, Percy Ravenscroft (1872-?)

Born in Lewisham, London in 1872. Educated in Asansol, India, and privately. A professor of the University of Reading, Berkshire. Singing master of Newbury Grammar School; Wallingford Grammar School; Kendrick Girls' School, Reading and Portway College, Reading. A local philharmonic society conductor. Organist and choirmaster of the Reading Churches of St. John, Caversham and St. Giles. Choirmaster of Holy Trinity Church, Reading. Composed a setting of the Holy Communion Service in E-flat, and a Holy Communion Service in A-flat for Men's Voices.

SCULL, Harold Thomas (1898-1971)

Born in London on 29 October 1898; died on 8 November 1971. Organist of the Queen's Park Congregational Church, Harrow Road, London; the Primitive Methodist Church, Kilburn Lane (for 14 years) and the Wesleyan Church, Calais (from 1919). Composer of the choral song 'Rise up, O men of God' (1938). His other works include the motet *Hosanna in the Highest* (1932), orchestral works, and songs. Published a total of more than 50 works.

SEAMAN, Barry (b.1946)

Born on 10 December 1946. Studied at York University (1969-1972), specialising in composition. Worked as a teacher until 1981. His compositions include *Three carols* (1986), 'Angels' for Two Voices and Keyboard, 'Gabriel's greeting' for Female Voice and

Organ and a Mass *The Cutty Wren*.

SEATON, Frank Richard Hayne (20th century)
Educated at Llandaff Cathedral School, and privately. Organist and choirmaster of St. Theodore's Parish Church, Port Talbot; an organ recitalist and a local choral society conductor. Composed a Holy Communion Service in F, hymn tunes, chants, and vesper hymns.

SEDDING, Edward Edmund (1835-1868)
Born in 1835; died in Penzance, Cornwall, on 11 June 1868. Brother of **John Sedding**, architect and church musician. A pupil of the architect G.E. Street, who built and restored a number of churches in the West of England. Organist of the Church of St. Mary the Virgin, Crown Street, Soho, London. Honorary precentor of the St. Raphael Homes, Bristol. An expert in plainsong. Published *Collection of English Carols, French Noels, etc.*, and *Collection of Ancient Christmas Carols Arranged for Four Voices*. Set hymn translations by **J.M. Neale** to music. Composed the cantata *Dives and Lazarus* (1867) and hymn tunes including 'Gibbons'.

SEDDING, John Dando (1838-1891)
Born in Eton, Berkshire on 13 April 1838; died in London (or possibly Winsford, Somerset) on 7 April 1891. Brother of **Edward Sedding**. An architect, organist and church musician. Organist of Beddington Parish Church, Surrey. Composer of hymn tunes.

SEIVEWRIGHT, Robert Andrew (b.1926)
Born in Plungar, Leicestershire on 22 April, 1926.
Educated at Stoneygate Preparatory School, Leicester; Denstone College, Staffordshire; King's College, Cambridge (1944 and 1948-1951) and Bretton Hall College of Education (1951-1952).
Studied organ with **Harold Darke**, **Boris Ord** and **Francis Jackson**. His composition tutors at Cambridge were **Patrick Hadley**, **Robin Orr** and **Philip Radcliffe**.
Served in the R.A.F. (1944-1948). Music master at Ermysted's Grammar School, Skipton (1952), and was also organist at Rylstone Parish Church and conductor of the Skipton Male Voice Choir at this time; from 1956 was music master at King's School, Pontefract, organist of St. Giles' Parish Church and conductor of the Pontefract Choral Society.
Master of the music at Carlisle Cathedral (1960-1991).
In 1962 he formed the Abbey Singers. Worked as an extra-mural lecturer for Glasgow and Newcastle Universities, and as a script-writer and presenter for Radio Cumbria and Border Television. Since his retirement in 1991 he has been freelance performer and composer. In 1995 he spent three months as organist and composer in residence at Southminster Presbyterian Church, Pittsburgh, Pennsylvania.
Composed *Celebration Overture* in 1992; his recent church compositions include the anthems Loving Shepherd' and 'Lullaby of the Madonna'.

SELBY, Bertram Luard
See **LUARD-SELBY**, Bertram.

SELBY, William (c1738-1798)
Born in England around 1738; died in Boston, U.S.A. on 12 December 1798.
Organist of All Hallows Church, Bread Street, London (1756-1773) and of Magdalen Hospital (1766-1769). Joint organist of the London Church of St. Sepulchre, Holborn (1760-1773), when the records show that he resigned 'to quit this kingdom'. In fact it was in order to emigrate to the U.S.A.
The organistships he held in the U.S.A. include King's Chapel, Boston; Trinity Church, Newport, Rhode Island (1773-1774); Trinity Church, Boston (1776) and Stone Chapel, the former King's Chapel (from 1778). Active in Boston as an organist and conductor. A concert manager and teacher of music. Said to have sold groceries and liquor at some time.
Psalm tunes by William Selby are found in the collection *Parochial Music Corrected...* (1762) by **William Riley**. Composed other items of church music, songs, and works for guitar and for organ. Increasingly prolific as a composer from 1782.

SELF, Adrian (b.1952)
Born on 1 August 1952.
Son of **Geoffrey Self**.
Educated at Redruth Grammar School, Cornwall; Southampton University, Hampshire; King Alfred's College, Winchester and Huddersfield University, Yorkshire. Graduated B.A. (1973), and M.A. in composition (1993). Has won several prizes including the Lennox Berkeley Cup for Composition (1982) and the Harold Smart Composition Award (1992).
A teacher of music in schools (1974-1984). A piano teacher at Dean Close School, Cheltenham (1984-1987) and Southern Area Representative for the music department of Oxford University Press (1987-1989). Director of music at Fareham Parish Church, Surrey (1972-1976) and All Saints', Cheltenham (1983-1988). Director of music at Cartmel Priory (from 1990), and conductor of Cartmel Choral Society. A director of Animus Music Publishing.
Has composed a large number of secular works including three piano concertos, chamber music and a rock opera. His organ compositions include two sets of variations, on 'Iste Confessor' and 'Veni, Emmanuel'. He has written several sets of the Magnificat and Nunc Dimittis; Preces and Responses; choral works including a Stabat Mater and a Missa Brevis; motets and anthems. Composed the *St. Barnabas* Mass (1978) and the anthems 'Jesus' prayer' (1980) and 'Ave verum corpus'.

SELF, Geoffrey (b.1930)
Born in Carshalton, Surrey on 23 January 1930. Father of **Adrian Self**. Graduated B.Mus. (London) and M.Phil. (Exeter). Honoured with the Gorsedd Shield for services to Cornish music (1981). Somerset County Music organiser (1959-1964) and head of music at Cornwall College (1964-1981). Conducted the Somerset County Orchestra (1959-1964) and the Cornwall Symphony Orchestra (1973-1981). His published works include *The Music of E.J. Moeran*. His religious compositions include the carol collection *A Nativity Triptych* and the carol 'O little one sweet'; a Magnificat; a setting of the Cantate Domino, and 'When Christ was born of Mary free'.

SEVERN, Charles (1805-1894)
Born in London in 1805; died in December 1894. The younger brother of **Thomas Severn**. The painter Joseph Severn was another brother; their father was Charles Severn, a music teacher of Hoxton, London. A cello and double bass player, performing with the main London orchestras. Took part in the first English performance of Mendelssohn's oratorio *Elijah* (1846). Organist of St. Mary's Church, Islington, London for 46 years. Editor of *Psalms and Hymn Tunes, Chants etc. for the use of the Parish*

Church of St. Mary, Islington (1853). His compositions include motets, a part song 'The Sunset' (1863) and others.

SEVERN, Thomas Henry (1801-1881)
Born in London on 5 November 1801; died in Wandsworth, London on 15 April 1881. Brother of **Charles Severn** and the painter Joseph Severn. Their father was a music teacher of Hoxton. A singer and composer, able to play organ, piano, cello, double bass, violin and viola. A teacher of music. Organist of the Lutheran German Church, Trinity Lane, London (1838). A member of the Royal Society of Musicians (from 1839). Composed a setting of the Te Deum in C (1865), duets, songs including 'Fill the goblet' (?1835) and piano music.

SEWELL, John (1832-1909)
Born in 1832 (an alternative year of 1822 is sometimes given.); died in Bridgnorth, Shropshire on 23 December 1909. Father of **William Sewell**. Was not the John Sewell who graduated B.Mus. (1848) and D.Mus. (1856) at the University of Oxford. A music seller in Bridgnorth and organist of St. Leonard's Church (1848-1907). Published *The Order of Service With Choral Responses* (1892). Composed the anthems 'Break forth into joy' (1866) and' Blessed are the undefiled in the way' (1864), and hymn tunes including 'Amesbury'.

SEWELL, William (19th century)
Born in Bridgnorth, Shropshire. Son of **John Sewell**. Studied at the Royal Academy of Music as Balfe scholar (1876) and Novello scholar (1879). Organist of Christ Church, Clapham, London (from 1882) and of The Oratory, Edgbaston, Birmingham (from 1886). From 1882 to 1885 he gave a series of organ recitals in the town of Bridgnorth. Composed the Mass *of St. Philp Neri*, a Magnificat, the anthems 'O salutaris hostia' and 'Tantum ergo', other items of church music, and chamber and instrumental works.

SEXTON, William (1764-1824)
Born in 1764; died in Windsor, Berkshire on 23 February 1824. Should not be confused with a namesake who was active musically in the second half of the 19th century. A chorister of St. George's Chapel, Windsor Castle (1773-1781) and of Eton College (from 1773). Studied under **Edward Webb**. Organist, master of the choristers and sub precentor of St. George's Chapel, Windsor Castle (1801-1824). Acted as organist of Eton College while the incumbent was ill. Composed anthems including 'Come, Holy Ghost', glees and songs.

SEYMOUR, Charles A. (1810-1875)
A violinist, and the leader of the Gentlemen's Concerts in Manchester (1845-1875). Composer of the anthem 'Fret not thyself'.

SEYMOUR, Joseph (1854-1922)
Born in Cork, Ireland on 14 May 1854; died on 2 December 1922. Studied at Malines under Nicolas Lemmens, and at Ratisbon under Franz Haberl. Graduated B.Mus. at Trinity College, Dublin (1892). Succeeded his father as organist of the Church of SS Peter and Paul, Cork (from 1878). Organist of St. Andrew's Church, Dublin (from 1881), a position he retained for nearly 20 years.
A professor of music at the Board of Education Training College, Drumcondra and an examiner for the Royal Irish Academy of Music. Editor of the Dublin *Lyra Ecclesiastica* (1884-1891), and

correspondent to a number of other musical journals. Edited Curwen's *Latin Series of Church Music*, and other collections.
Composed a Mass *Adeste Fideles* (1886), a Mass in A-flat (1888), a Missa *Trinitatis*, *Six Motets* and other items of church music. Also composed an Irish May Day children's operetta on Irish airs, and a part song 'Bells of Shandon'.

SHARPE, Ernest Newton (1867-1949)
Born in Hampstead, London on 19 April 1867; died in Tunbridge Wells, Kent on 20 January 1949. Composer of hymn tunes and a song 'Gleams of Sunshine' (1899).

SHARPE, Evelyn Mary
See **SAVILLE**, Evelyn Mary.

SHARPLEY, Arthur Edward (1858-1941)
Born in Lambeth, Surrey in 1858; died in Winkfield, Berkshire on 14 February 1941. Composed the anthem 'Blessed are they that dwell in Thy house' (1911) and hymn tunes.

SHAVE, Revd. Eric Charles Leach (b.1901)
Born in Cleckheaton, Yorkshire in 1901. His father, Revd. Charles Henry Shave, was a minister of the Congregational Church. Educated at Taunton School, Somerset; St. Catherine's College, Oxford and, for the ministry, at Mansfield College, Oxford. Graduated B.A. (1924) and M.A. (1927). Ordained at Eastwood Congregational Church, Nottinghamshire (1927). Minister of the Congregational Churches of Crosby, Liverpool (1930-1939) and Eastwood (from 1939). Author of *Prayer Time* and other works. Composer of hymn tunes including 'Crosby' and 'Eastwood' and anthems, examples of which are 'Teach us, good Lord' and 'I see His Blood upon the rose'. 'Hymn of Trust' was published in 1964.

SHAW, Alexander (?-c1681)
Organist of Durham Cathedral (1677-1681), where he married Eleanor, the widow of his predecessor, **John Foster**. Composed the anthems 'I will sing unto the Lord' and 'Lord, Thou art become gracious'.

SHAW, Dr. Geoffrey Turton (1879-1943)
Born in Clapham, London on 14 November 1879; died in Westminster, London on 14 April 1943.
Son of **James Shaw** and brother of **Martin Shaw**.
A chorister of St. Paul's Cathedral under **George Martin**. Studied at Derby School and at Gonville and Caius College, Cambridge where he was organ scholar (1899-1902) and Stewart of Rannoch scholar in music. A pupil of **C.V. Stanford** and **Charles Wood**, graduating B.A. and Mus.B. (1902). Also studied with Neville Cox and J.R. Sterndale Bennett.
Awarded the Lambeth D.Mus. (1932) with his brother, Martin.
Music master of Gresham's School, Holt, Norfolk (1902-1910). A local choral society conductor and organist of St. Andrew's Church.
Had a strong influence on policy as H.M. inspector of music to the Board of Education (from 1911).
Master of music of St. Mary's Church, Primrose Hill, Hampstead, London (from 1920), succeeding his brother, Martin. Chairman of the Schools' Music Committee of the B.B.C., and an adjudicator at festivals of music.
Composed a Magnificat and Nunc Dimittis, the anthem 'Lord, let me know my end' and hymn tunes including 'Gresham',

'Rockingham' and 'St. Magnus'. Also composed a part song, 'Honour, riches, marriage, blessing' and works for piano.

SHAW, James (1842-1907)

Born in Leeds in 1842; died in Ramsgate, Kent on 12 May 1907. Father of **Geoffrey Shaw** and **Martin Shaw**. A chorister of Leeds Parish Church under R. Senior Burton, with whom he studied music. Organist of St. John's Episcopal Chapel and St. Paul's Church, Edinburgh. Organist of Hampstead Parish Church, London (1874-1895), and of the Collegiate Chapel of St. John, Clapham. A local choral society conductor and an organ recitalist. Founder of the Middlesex Choral Union. Composed an Evening Service (1874) for the London Church Choirs' Association; other services; a setting of the Responses to the Commandments in G; a Thanksgiving Ode (1880) for Solo Voices, Chorus and Orchestra; anthems; songs including 'Break, break', part songs and organ works.

SHAW, Dr. Martin Edward Fallas (1875-1958)

Born in Kennington, London on 9 March 1875; died in Southwold, Suffolk on 24 October 1958.

The son of **James Shaw** and a brother of **Geoffrey Shaw**.

Studied at the Royal College of Music, where his tutors were **C.V. Stanford**, **Hubert Parry** and **Henry Walford Davies**.

Awarded the Lambeth D.Mus.in the same year as his brother Geoffrey (1932).

Appointed O.B.E. in 1955.

Martin Shaw was Ellen Terry's conductor, and toured Europe as conductor to Isadora Duncan (1906-1908).

Organist of St. Mary's Church, Primrose Hill, London (1908-1920) where the incumbent until 1915 was Revd. Percy Dearmer. Succeeded as organist by his brother, Geoffrey. Lecturer and music director of the Summer School of Church Music at Oxford (1913). Organist of the Church of St. Martin-in-the-Fields, London (1920-1924). Master of music at the Guildhouse, London (1924-1935). A lay canon of Liverpool Cathedral (from 1931). Director of music of the Diocese of Chelmsford (1935-1945).

One of the founders of the Plainsong and Medieval Music Society. Founded the Purcell Society (London, 1900). Promoted and encouraged community singing.

A friend of the composer **Ralph Vaughan Williams**. The two collaborated in the editing of *Songs of Praise* (1925 and 1931) and *The Oxford Book of Carols* (1928). Editor of *English Carol Book* and *Songs of Britain*. Known for his view that the works of the 19th century were typically 'stuffy'.

In 1955, on Martin Shaw's 80th birthday, a service of celebration took place at the church of St. Mary-le-Tower, Ipswich, Suffolk, at which Vaughan Williams gave the address.

Published an autobiography *Up to Now* (1929). His other writings include *The Principles of English Church Music Composition* (1921). His compositions include an Anglican Folk Mass, a Te Deum and the anthems 'Christ is our Corner Stone' and 'With a voice of singing'. *The Redeemer* is one of a number of oratorios.

Of his hymn tunes, 'Marching' and 'Little Cornard' are particularly well known, being long associated with the hymns 'Through The night of doubt and sorrow' and 'Hills of the North, rejoice'.

With Clifford Bax as librettist, Martin Shaw composed the opera *Mr. Pepys* (1926). Composed around 100 songs, and music for the theatre.

SHAW, Thomas (18th/19th century)

A violinist and composer To distinguish him from other composers of the same name he is sometimes referred to as 'of Drury Lane Theatre'. His works include an anthem on the death of Princess Charlotte (1817), songs of which 'The Stranger' (1798) is an example, a Trio for Two Violins and Cello, Concertos for Violin and Piano, a Solo for Flute, and songs.

SHEBBEARE, Fr. William George Alphege (1875-1958)

Born in Bromley, Kent in 1875; died in Twyford Abbey, Hampshire on 19 January 1958. Attended Blackheath School, Kent and studied music with **Warwick Jordan**. Organist and choirmaster of Cowley Fathers' Church, Oxford (1899-1905) and of Downside Abbey (from 1905). Music master of Downside School (1905-1908), for which he composed the school song. Converted to the Roman Catholic faith in 1905 and was ordained priest at Downside in 1914. An adjudicator of the entries in plain song at the Dublin *Feis Ceoil* of 1930-1931. Collaborated in *Cowley Carol Book*, edited by Revd. G.R. Woodward, and in *Westminster Hymnal*. Composed The *Hindley* Children's Mass (1923), hymn tunes, and *Three Songs* (1898).

SHEELES, John (17th/18th century)

A keyboard player and composer. A teacher of harpsichord in London around the year 1810. A member of the Society of Musicians from 1739 until at least 1755. Published *A Set of Lessons for Harpsichord or Spinet* (c1725). John Sheele's hymn tune 'Addison's' was a setting of the hymn 'The spacious Firmament on High' by Joseph Addison, editor of *The Spectator*. His other works include the anthems 'How dear are Thy counsels' and 'O Lord, Thou hast searched'. Also composed songs.

SHELDON, Robin Treeby (b.1932)

Born in Cheltenham, Gloucestershire in 1932. Music editor of *Anglican Hymn Book* (1965). Composer of hymn tunes and editor of the collection for the Children's Special Service Mission (1980).

SHENTON, Revd. Robert (1730-1798)

Born in 1730; died in Dublin in 1798. A chorister and a lay clerk of Magdalen College, Oxford. Graduated B.A. (1750) at the University of Oxford and M.A. (1757) at the University of Cambridge. A lay clerk at Hereford Cathedral. Dean's vicar of Christ Church Cathedral, Dublin (from 1757) and a vicar of St. Patrick's Anglican Cathedral, Dublin (from 1758). Composed four services, 17 anthems including 'I will magnify Thee' and 'Sing we merrily', and other items of church music.

SHENTON, William (20th century)

Studied music with **Arnold Culley** and **Thomas Hutchinson**. Organist and choirmaster of Houghton le Spring Parish Church. Composer of a Vesper and Six-fold Amen.

SHEPHARD, Richard (b.1949)

A chorister of Gloucester Cathedral under **Herbert Sumsion**. Read music at the University of Cambridge. After a number of teaching appointments in Salisbury, where he sang as a lay vicar in the cathedral choir, he was appointed to York as head master of the Minster School. Is also sub chamberlain of York Minster. A member of the Archbishops' Commission on Church Music ('In tune with Heaven') and the Archbishops' Commission on Cathedrals ('Heritage and Renewal'). His church compositions include the *Addington* Service, the *Wiltshire* Service and a Communion Service for Gloucester Cathedral, and the anthems 'Ye choirs of new Jerusalem' and 'The strife is o'er'. In addition to his church compositions he has written orchestral works, cantatas, oratorios, a setting of the Requiem and two operas.

SHEPHERD, Charles Henry (1847-1886)

Born in 1847; died in Newcastle-on-Tyne on 29 April 1886. Studied at the Royal Academy of Music and held a number of organistships in London before being appointed organist of St. Thomas's Church, Newcastle-on-Tyne (1876). His wife was a soprano singer who achieved fame in the North of England. Composed a setting of the Te Deum in F (1870), anthems including 'Hallelujah! what are these?' (1878) and 'O Praise the Lord' and songs including 'The lass I left ashore' (1878).

SHEPHERD, Revd. James Francis (1871-1963)

Born in Grimsby, Lincolnshire on 31 August 1871; died in Halifax, Yorkshire on 4 November 1963.
The son of Revd. Robert Shepherd, a minister of the Congregational Church. When James was three months old, the family moved to Beverley, Yorkshire.
Educated at Hull and East Riding College; Lincoln College, Oxford, where he read modern history and graduated B.A. (1893); and Mansfield College, Oxford (1893), where he was organist.
Between 1896 and his retirement in 1948 he was minister of a number of Congregational Churches: Haverhill (from 1896), Withrington, Manchester (from 1903), Belmont, Aberdeen (from 1914), Park Church, Halifax (from 1919) and Beverley (1946-1948).
A Fellow of the Royal Astronomical Society.
Composer of hymn tunes including 'Beverlac'. A member of the Committee and of the Music Advisory Committee of the hymnal *Congregational Praise* (from October 1944).

SHEPHERD, John (b.1899)

Born in Treherbert, Glamorganshire, Wales in 1899. A miner, studying piano in his spare time. Became organist of the Soar Welsh Baptist Church. In January 1926 he moved to Coventry, Warwickshire, where a year later he was one of the founders and the first conductor of a Welsh male voice choir. Choirmaster of the Queen's Road Baptist Church, Coventry (1928-1939). In 1934 John Shepherd established an annual festival of Welsh hymn singing, held in alternate years at Coventry and Rugby. Composer of hymn tunes, including 'Avondale'.

SHEPPARD, Revd. Henry Fleetwood (1824-1901)

Born on 5 February 1824; died in Oxford on 27 December 1901. A minor canon of Gloucester Cathedral and of St. George's Chapel, Windsor Castle. For 30 years he was rector of Thurnscoe, near Doncaster, Yorkshire. From 1884 he was sub dean of the Chapel Royal, Savoy Hill, London. With **Sabine Baring-Gould** he collected and arranged *Songs and Ballads of the West* (1891). His compositions include the anthems 'O Lord the very Heavens' and 'If the Lord Himself'. Arranged settings of the Te Deum, Benedictus, Magnificat and Nunc Dimittis. Composed hymn tunes.

SHEPPARD, James Hallett (1835-1879)

Born in 1835; died in Clapham, London on 11 January 1879. Gave piano recitals in London. Composed a Mass *of St. Anselm* (1869) and hymn tunes: two are found in *Wesley's Hymns* (1877) and one

of these, 'St. Martin', is also used in *Hymns and Psalms* (1983). Composed songs and part songs.

SHEPPARD (Shepherd), Dr. John (c1520-c1563)

A chorister of St. Paul's Cathedral under Thomas Mulliner.
Organist and instructor of the choristers (1542 or 1544-c1547), and a fellow (1549-1551) of Magdalen College, Oxford. One version of events has it that Sheppard was appointed in 1542 and resigned the following year, perhaps due to disagreement among the fellows on matters of politics and religion, and was later reappointed.
In 1554 he supplicated for the degree of D.Mus. at the University of Oxford, having already graduated B.Mus. The College records show that he was formally admonished on three separate occasions, one of which was for forcibly removing a chorister from Malmesbury, Somerset and bringing him to Oxford without a licence from the king.
Appointed a gentleman of the Chapel Royal some time between 1547 and 1553. Attended the Funeral of Edward VI (1553) and the Coronations of Queen Mary (1553) and Queen Elizabeth (1559). Left Magdalen College in 1556 or 1557.
His compositions reflect the changes in taste and liturgy following the Reformation, prior to which he composed five Masses, including a setting known as the *French* Mass, and motets. Thereafter he produced vernacular material including services, anthems of which examples are 'I give you a new Commandment' and 'O Lord of hosts', and Psalm settings. Some of his works are found in the collection by Clifford.

SHERLAW JOHNSON, Dr. Robert (b.1932)

Born in Sunderland on 21 May, 1932.
Educated at Gosforth Grammar School, Newcastle-on-Tyne; took his first degree in music at Durham University (1953). Studied at the Royal Academy of Music (1953-1957): piano with Max Pirani and composition with William Alwyn, Alan Bush and Howard Ferguson. Studied in Paris (1957-1958): composition with Nadia Boulanger and piano with Jacques Février. Attended classes with Olivier Messiaen at the Paris Conservatory. Returned to London and studied composition with Humphrey Searle. Graduated D.Mus. at the Universities of Leeds (1971) and Oxford (1990).
Assistant lecturer in music at Leeds University (from 1961); director of music at Bradford Girls' Grammar School (from 1963); lecturer in music at the University of York (from 1975). In 1970 elected a fellow of Worcester College and lecturer in music at the University of Oxford, and in 1985 appointed visiting professor of composition at the Eastman School of Music, University of Rochester, New York.
As a concert pianist has specialised in the music of Olivier Messiaen and other 20th century composers. His research interests include the problem of transcribing the 9th and 10th century rhythmic neums of Gregorian Chant for use in performance, in connection with which he directs the Gregorian Chant Group at the Oratory (St. Aloysius Church), Oxford.
For the church he has written choral music including an 'Anthem for the Trinity' (1971), a carol 'The manger', and a Missa *Aedis Christi* (1991). He has also written music for congregational use for the Roman Catholic Mass. Has written an opera *The Lambton Worm*, concertos for piano and for clarinet, and chamber music.

SHIELD, William (1748-1829)

Apprenticed to a boat builder in North Shields and he was a pupil of **Charles Avison**. Master of the Royal Music, succeeding **Robert**

Parsons (from 1817). Principal tenor player of the Covent Garden Opera. His compositions include the anthems 'How beautiful upon the mountains' and 'When I was a child', and his other works consist of ballad operas.

SHINN, George (1837-?)
Born in Clerkenwell, London on 6 March 1837. Graduated Mus. B. (1880) at the University of Cambridge. Organist of St. Peter,'s Church, Hackney Road, London (from 1859); St. Jude's, Whitechapel (from 1863); St. Paul's, Canonbury (from 1866); St. Matthew's, Brixton (from 1872); Christ Church, Upper Norwood (1887-1897) and St. Bartholomew's, Gray's Inn Road (1900-1915). Lived in Brixton. Composed an Evening Service in F (1890), a Te Deum, anthems, hymn tunes and chants. Also composed oratorios including *Lazarus of Bethany* (1892) and *The Captives of Babylon*, a cantata *Treasures of the Deep*, and part songs. His degree exercise was a setting of Psalm 145 'Great is the Lord, and marvellous' for Solo Voices, Chorus and Strings.

SHOEL, Thomas (1759-1823)
Born in Montacute, Somerset in 1759; died in 1823. Compiled collections of works including *Thirty Psalm Tunes,* a song 'Peace' for two parts, and other songs.

SHORE, William (1791-1877)
Born in Manchester on 21 November 1791; died in Buxton, Derbyshire on 16 January 1877. A founder and the director of music of the Manchester Madrigal Society. Editor of *Sacred Music, Selected and Arranged...* (1835). Composed anthems, hymn tunes, glees, a song 'O Willie brewed a peck o' malt', songs, and piano music.

SHORT, Joseph (1831-?)
Born in Caldmore, Walsall, Staffordshire on 22 May 1831.
A merchant and a self-taught amateur musician. A bass singer.
Organist of Wednesbury Roman Catholic Church, Staffordshire (from 1853) and of St. Mary's Church, Walsall, where he gave concert performances, with orchestra, of large-scale Masses. One of these was the Mass in F by Schubert, in 1873. Produced the same work at the Masonic Hall, Birmingham on 7 September 1875. These were the first two performances of the work in England.
Moved to Birmingham in 1861. Cantor of St. Chad's Roman Catholic Cathedral until 1867, when he moved to St. Joseph's Church, Nechells, Birmingham. In October 1872 he became choirmaster of St. Michael's Church, Moor Street.
Represented England at the Sacred Congregation of Rites in the Revision of Liturgical Rules for the Guidance of Composers for the Roman Catholic Church.
Composed two Masses: the *St. Joseph* (1880), which he dedicated to John Henry Newman and the *St. George* (1886). Also composed Offertoria, and Latin anthems and motets including *De profundis.*

SHOUBRIDGE, James (1804-1872)
Born in Canterbury, Kent in 1804; died in London in December 1872. A teacher in Canterbury, and a lay clerk of Canterbury Cathedral. A vicar choral of St. Paul's Cathedral (from 1847). Conductor of the Cecilian Society, London (from 1852). Published *Twenty-Four Original Psalm and Hymn Tunes for Four Voices* (?1840). His works include the anthem 'He Comes! He Comes!' (1834).

SHRUBSOLE, William (c1760-1806)
Born in Canterbury, Kent where he was baptised on 13 January 1759 or 1760; died in London on 18 January 1806 and was buried at Bunhill Fields. In 1892, a monument was erected there, funded by public subscription and raised by **F.G. Edwards**.
The son of a farrier.
A chorister of Canterbury Cathedral (1770-1777).
As a young man he taught music in London.
Organist of Bangor Cathedral (1782-1783).
His sympathies were with the Methodists and Dissenters and within a year of his appointment he had been in contention with the authorities for 'frequenting conventicles', for which he was eventually dismissed.
Returned to London and worked as a teacher of music: his pupils included **Benjamin Jacob** and **William Russell**. An alto singer at the Drury Lane Theatre and of Westminster Abbey.
Organist of the Spa Fields Chapel, London (1784-1806) and of the Church of St. Bartholomew-the-Less, London (1800-1806).
William Shrubsole's fame rests upon his hymn tune 'Miles Lane', also known as 'Scarborough,' which he composed around the age of 19. The tune first appeared in *The Gospel Magazine* (November 1779) and it has always been associated with the hymn 'All hail the power of Jesu's Name' by Edward Perronet. **Edward Elgar** pronounced the tune 'the finest in English hymnody.' Shrubsole and Perronet met in Canterbury while the latter was in charge of a local Congregational chapel. They became friends: Shrubsole was the executor of Perronet's will and was bequeathed some land in Wandsworth, London by him.

SIDEBOTHAM, Mary Ann (1833-1913)
Born in London in 1833; died in the Isle of Wight, Hampshire on 20 February 1913. Organist of the Church of St. Thomas-on-the-Bourne. Lived with her brother, who may have been vicar of St. Thomas's. A skilled pianist and musician, and a lifelong friend of the organist **Henry Smart**. Musical editor of *Children's Hymn Book* (1881), although not credited as such. The book was a collaboration between her and Carey Brock. Mary Sidebotham contributed 12 tunes to it. A further collaboration resulted in a collection of 12 Christmas carols (1894). Mary Sidebotham's hymn tunes include 'Europa' and her carols, 'The night is dark'.

SILAS, Edouard (1827-1909)
Born in Amsterdam, The Netherlands on 22 August 1827; died in West Kensington, London on 8 February 1909.
Studied under Neher of the Mannheim Court Orchestra, continuing his piano studies with Lacombe (from 1839) and, in Paris, with Kalkbrenner (from 1842). At the Paris Conservatory he studied with Beoist for organ and Halévy for composition. In 1849 he won first prize for organ playing. Settled in the U.K. in the following year.
Pianist to the Liverpool Philharmonic Society (from 1850). On 21 May 1851, he took part in one of Ellers's London Musical Matinées.
Organist of the Roman Catholic Chapel, Kingston-on-Thames, Surrey.
Author of a number of essays and monographs, many of which remain unpublished.
A lecturer in harmony at the Guildhall School of Music and at the Royal Academy of Music.
In 1866, he won the first prize in a Belgian competition for his Mass for Four Voices and Organ.

A prolific composer. His works include a set of Responses to the Commandments in F Minor, hymn tunes, an oratorio *Joash* (for the Norwich Music Festival of 1863), a Symphony in A (1863), piano and organ works.

SILVER, Dr. Alfred Jethro (1870-?)

Born in Windsor, Berkshire on 20 December 1870.

A chorister of St. George's Chapel, Windsor Castle under **Walter Parratt** and was assistant organist to him. Graduated B.Mus. (1902) and D.Mus. (1907) at the University of Durham.

Organist of Clewer Parish Church, Berkshire (from 1888); Ealing Parish Church, Middlesex (from 1889); St. David's Church, Merthyr Tydfil, Wales (from 1892); St. Peter's Church, Carmarthen (from 1897) and Handsworth Parish Church, Birmingham (from 1901).

Music master of Handsworth High School (from 1904), and Grammar School (from 1907), a cellist in the City of Birmingham Symphony Orchestra and a local choral and orchestral society conductor.

Composed church music including Masses such as the Mass *of St. Philip Neri* (1923) and the anthem 'Let us now praise famous men' (1909).

As his degree exercises he submitted a cantata *Praise the Lord, His glories show* for Soprano Solo, five-part Chorus and Strings (B.Mus.) and a fantasy 'Chronos' for Baritone and Tenor Solo Voices, eight-part Chorus and Orchestra (D.Mus.).

SILVER (Sylver), John (c1606-?)

A lay vicar and master of the choristers of Winchester Cathedral (from 1638), following the death of **Thomas Holmes**. May be the John Silver who was a lay clerk of Winchester Cathedral from 1626 to 1627 and organist of Dulwich College, London (1627-1631). The organist of Winchester Cathedral at the time, **Christopher Gibbons,** joined the Royalist forces in the Civil War. Silver remained at Winchester and may well have deputised for Gibbons. John Silver was appointed organist of Winchester Cathedral in succession to Gibbons in June 1661, retaining his appointment of master of the choristers. Left at some time after June 1666. Other church musicians of the same name cloud the picture. It is therefore unlikely that the Winchester organist was the same person who was organist of Wimborne Minster in 1663. Composed a Service in F, and the two anthems 'Lay not up' and 'Lord, Thou art become gracious'.

SIMMS, Arthur (1839-1914)

Born in Birmingham on 11 June 1839; died in Hythe, Kent on 4 February 1914. Nephew of **Henry Simms** and cousin of **Samuel Simms**. A chorister of Holy Trinity Church, Birmingham and pupil of Henry Simms, organist of St. Philip's Church, Birmingham.

Graduated B.Mus. at New College, Oxford (1874). Assistant organist of the Birmingham Churches of St. Philip and Holy Trinity (1856-1865). Organist and choirmaster of the Parish Churches of Shifnal (from 1866) and Wilmslow, Cheshire (from 1870); St. Mary's Episcopal Church, Glasgow (from 1875) and Hythe Parish Church, Kent (1893-1902). Organist and music master of Walthamstow Forest School, Essex (from 1880). A local philharmonic society conductor and correspondence tutor of the Queen Margaret College, Glasgow. Composed as his B.Mus. exercise a cantata based on Psalm 33 *Rejoice in the Lord* for Voices and Orchestra. Composed a setting of the Holy Communion Service and a series of five anthems for major events in the church

year: Christmas, Easter, Ascension, Annunciation and Harvest. Also composed an oratorio *Lazarus* and an Impromptu For Organ.

SIMMS, Henry (1804-1872)

Born in 1804; died on 1 May 1872. A piano pupil of Ignaz Moscheles. Organist of the Birmingham Churches of Holy Trinity, Bordesley (1825-1875) and St. Philip (1829- 1871). A teacher of singing and piano, on and famous as an improviser. Composed a setting of the Holy Communion Service, sacred and secular songs, and items designed to assist in the teaching of piano.

SIMMS, Samuel (1836-1885)

Born in Stourbridge, Worcestershire in 1836; died in Stourbridge on 22 February 1885. Succeeded his father, Samuel Simms, as organist of St. Thomas's Church, Stourbridge. Organist of the Birmingham Churches of St. John, Ladywood and St. Cyprian, Hay Mills. At St. Cyprian, the incumbent was his brother, Revd. G. Handel Simms. The services were ambitious musically. Samuel Simms was a local choral society conductor. Composed services, a Benedicite (1891), unpublished anthems and organ works.

SIMPER, Caleb (1856-1942)

Born in Barford St. Martin, Wiltshire on 12 September 1856; died in Barnstaple, Devon on 28 August 1942. Organist of the Church of St. Mary Magdalene, Worcester for 14 years. The manager of F.J. Spark. Eventually settled at Barnstaple and composed extensively. Many of his works are simple anthems and they include 'I will feed my flock' and 'He is risen'. A number of his hymn tunes won prizes.

SIMPSON, David (19th/20th century)

Born in Dundee, Scotland. Organist and choirmaster of Schoolwynd Church (1905-1907) and Lochee Parish Church (1907-1911), both in Dundee, and of Leslie Parish Church, Fife (1911-1920) and St. George's Church, Hawick (from 1920). A local choral society conductor. Composed anthems, hymn tunes, and songs including 'Reverie'.

SIMPSON, Lionel (b.1901)

Born in Streatham Hill, London on 7 December 1901. Educated at Forest School, Essex, where he learnt the organ, and at the Guildhall School of Music, London. For 20 years was organist and choir master at St. Edward's King and Martyr, Corfe Castle, Dorset. Has written music for three operettas, and organ works. For the church has written a setting of Rite A Eucharist Communion Service, a Magnificat and Nunc Dimittis in D, and a Christmas carol 'Sing happy child'. There are also a number of anthems.

SIMPSON, Robert (1790-1832)

Born in Glasgow on 4 November 1790; died in Greenock in July or August 1832. A weaver by trade, and self-educated. Led the singing at the Church in Glasgow of Dr. Ralph Wardlaw and at the Albion Street Congregational Chapel. Precentor and Session clerk of East Parish Church, Greenock (from 1823). Composer of hymn tunes. His 'Ballerma' was probably a copy or adaptation of a melody composed or arranged by **François Barthélémon**.

SINCLAIR, Dr. George Robertson (1863-1917)

Born in Croydon, Surrey on 28 October 1863; died in Birmingham on 7 February 1917.

The son of an employee of the Civil Service in India.

At the age of eight he studied at the Royal Irish Academy of Music under **R.P. Stewart**. From the age of nine, for six years he was a chorister of St. Michael's College, Tenbury, Worcestershire, acting as assistant organist for part of that period. A pupil of **C.H. Lloyd** (from 1879) and assistant to Lloyd at Gloucester Cathedral (from 1880).

Awarded the Lambeth D.Mus. in 1899.

Organist of the Church of St. Mary de Crypt, Gloucester (1881) and, later that year, organist of Truro pro-Cathedral. The Service of Consecration took place in November 1887: George Sinclair directed some 700 singers. Organist of Truro Cathedral until 1889. Organist of Hereford Cathedral (1889-1917). Introduced the music of Richard Wagner at the triennial Hereford Festival. A local music and choral society conductor, and a fellow of St. Michael's College, Tenbury.

A friend of **Edward Elgar**, who dedicated Pomp & Circumstance No. 4 to him. *G.R.S.*, the 11th Enigma Variation, is believed to be a musical characterisation of Sinclair's devoted bulldog, Dan. Another friend of Sinclair was **Hubert Parry**: the two liked to sail long distances in Parry's yacht.

Composer of hymn tunes. Some of his chants appear in most collections.

SKEATS, Highmore (1760-1831)

Born in 1760; died in Canterbury on 29 June 1831. A chorister of Exeter Cathedral. A vicar choral of Salisbury Cathedral. Organist of the Cathedrals of Ely (1778-1803) and Canterbury (1803-1831). Succeeded at Canterbury by his son **Highmore Skeats**. A traditionalist. The story is told that when, around the year 1825, pedals and 16' pipes were added to the Canterbury organ, Skeats refused to use them. When asked to demonstrate them, he passed the request on to his pupil, **Thomas Evance Jones,** saying that he never learned to dance. Compiled *A Collection of Songs* (1784) and was editor of Dr. J. Stephens's *Cathedral Music* (1805). Composed a Morning and Evening Service in C, anthems including 'Come unto Me', and hymn tunes. Also composed glees including 'All gracious freedom', and songs.

SKEATS, Highmore (c1785-1835)

Born in Canterbury, Kent around 1785; died in Windsor, Berkshire on 24 February 1835. A pupil of his father, **Highmore Skeats**. Organist of Ely Cathedral (1804-1830) in succession to his father on his appointment to Canterbury Cathedral. Organist of St. George's Chapel, Windsor Castle (1830-1835). Composed church music.

SKELTON, George James (19th century)

Organist of Holy Trinity Church, Hull, Yorkshire. Was the son of George Skelton, organist of Lincoln Cathedral (1794-1850). Composed a Chant Service, known as Skelton in D, a set of Responses to the Commandments, and songs.

SKILTON, Captain Edward (1773-1842)

A military knight of Windsor Castle, Berkshire. Composed a Sanctus and Kyrie in D.

SLATER, Dr. Ernest (1860-?)

Born in Taunton, Somerset in 1860.
The son of Revd. W.P. Slater, governor and chaplain of Queen's College, Taunton.

Studied at Queen's College and at the Royal Academy of Music under Harold Thomas, **Charles Steggall** and **Tobias Matthay**. Pupil of Julius Benedict and **D.J. Wood**.

Awarded the Lambeth D.Mus. in 1911.

Assistant organist of Exeter Cathedral (from 1881). Two years later, in 1883, he was appointed organist of Lampeter Parish Church, North Wales. A sub professor of the R.A.M.

Organist of Lambeth Parish Church (from 1917). Sometimes officiated as organist at the private chapel of Lambeth Palace.

On the recommendation of **John Stainer**, Ernest Slater was appointed organist of Calcutta Cathedral in 1885. Professor of music at La Martinière College, Calcutta and taught music to the families of three viceroys of India.

Composed a Chant Service, a Jubilee Anthem 'All the kings of the earth shall praise Thee' for the Golden Jubilee Service of Queen Victoria in Calcutta Cathedral; a Jubilate for St. George's Chapel, Windsor Castle; a Te Deum dedicated to the Prince of Wales; a Festival Overture (1885), an Organ Fugue and songs. Arranged certain Armenian melodies for three voices for use in the Armenian Church.

SLATER, Dr. Gordon Archbold (1896-1979)

Born in Harrogate, Yorkshire on 1 March 1896; died in Lincoln on 26 January 1979.

From 1914 to 1916 he was a pupil of **Edward Bairstow**, organist of York Minster. Graduated B.Mus. (1915) and D.Mus. (1923) at the University of Durham. Appointed O.B.E. in 1974.

At the age of 14 he was sub organist of St. Mark's Church, Harrogate. Served in the Royal Garrison Artillery during World War I, which broke out not long after his appointment.

Lived in Boston, Lincolnshire after the war. Taught at the local grammar school and was organist of St. Botolph's Parish Church (1919-1927).

Organist of the Cathedrals of Leicester (1927-1931) and Lincoln (1931-1966), retiring at the age of 70.

At Lincoln he increased the use of the works of **William Byrd**, who had been organist of Lincoln Cathedral from 1563 to 1562.

Gordon Slater had an extensive academic career. A lecturer in singing at Leicester University College, and lecturer in music in the extra-mural department of Leicester University College (1929-1930) and the Universities of Nottingham (1929-1959), Hull (1932-1972) and Sheffield (1972-1974). Ferens Fine Art lecturer at University College, Hull (from 1946). An external examiner in music to a total of five universities.

A teacher of piano, organ and singing. Formed and trained local choral societies. An organ recitalist and consultant. Adjudicated at festivals of music in Canada in 1935 and 1948.

Gordon Slater's hymn tunes include 'Bilsdale' and 'St. Botolph'. Composed as his B.Mus. exercise the cantata *Let God arise* and for his D.Mus. *From the night of forebeing*. Composed an Organ Voluntary on the Canticle *St. Fulbert,,* the anthem 'Grant O Lord, we beseech Thee' (1957) and *An Easter Alleluya* for organ.

SLATTER, Revd. George Maximillian (1790-1868)

Born in 1790; died on 27 April 1868. Rector of West Anstey, Devon and a priest-vicar of Exeter Cathedral. His collection *Ten Collects as Anthems* includes the works 'Almighty and everlasting God', and 'I will magnify Thee'. A further small collection of his compositions, consisting of three anthems, a Te Deum, three Psalm tunes and eight Chants, was published in 1854. Composed other chants, and songs.

SLEEMAN, Philip Rowling (1841-1917)
Born in Bristol, Gloucestershire in 1841; died in Clifton, Bristol on 12 November 1917. Composer of hymn tunes.

SLOANE-EVANS, Revd. William (1823-1899)
Born in Churstone Ferrers, Devon on 21 August 1823; died in Kingsbridge, Devon on 4 March 1899. Educated at Trinity College, Cambridge where he graduated B.A. (1845). Ordained deacon in 1847, priest in 1849. William Sloane-Evans's appointments were within his native county, except for the last. Assistant curate of St. David's Church, Exeter (from 1847); vicar of Holy Trinity Church, Barnstaple (1851-1852) and assistant curate of the Churches of Cornworthy (1852-1854), East Allington (1854-1856) and Sherford (1875-1877). Chaplain of the Kingsbridge Union. Vicar of Egloskerry, Cornwall (1877-1896). For the period 1856-1877 he is described as 'Lecturer of Kingsbridge'. Author of *Grammar of British Heraldry*, the Second Edition of which was published in 1880. Composer of hymn tunes including 'Clarion'.

SLOMAN, Dr. Robert (c1830-1895)
Born in Gloucester around 1830; died in West Norwood, Surrey on 2 July 1895. Studied under **John Amott, S.S. Wesley** and **Charles Lucas**. Graduated B.Mus. (1861) and D.Mus. (1867) at the University of Oxford.
Private organist to the Earl of Powis (from 1852). Organist of Welshpool Parish Church, St. Martin's Church, Scarborough, Yorkshire (from 1869) and of Lower Norwood Parish Church, Surrey (from 1877). Attended concerts at the Crystal Palace while writing notices for *Musical Standard*. Composed the cantatas *Supplication and Praise* and *Constantia*, songs, part songs, and piano works. *Sacred Strains* (?1860) was a collection of hymn tunes.

SLY, R.
An organist in Lynn (probably, Norfolk). Composed the anthem 'I will give thanks'.

SMALLMAN, Charles Stanley (1894-?)
Born in Fulham, London in 1894. Studied music at Trinity College London, where he was directed by **C.W. Peace** and others in organ, harmony and composition. On active service during World War I. Organist and choirmaster of the Haven Green Baptist Church, Ealing, London (1921-1965). Founded the West Middlesex Music Society (1922) and was conductor until 1965. Composed anthems, hymn tunes, a choral song: 'Land of joy and liberty' (1909) for Chorus and Orchestra, and a Fantasia *The Sea of Galilee* for Orchestra.

SMALLWOOD, William (1831-1897)
Born in Kendal on 31 December 1831; died in Kendal on 6 August 1897. Studied under **John Camidge** (1790-1859) and Henry Phillips. Organist of St. George's Church, Kendal from the age of 15 in 1847. Served there for more than 50 years. The author of *A Pianoforte Tutor*. Composed anthems including 'Awake! Awake!' and the Easter-tide anthem 'Thanks Be To God' (1887), hymn tunes including 'Antwerp' which was published in *Bristol Tune Book* (1876), songs, and piano works, many of them expressly written for teaching purposes.

SMART, Sir George Thomas (1776-1867)
Born in Westminster, London on 10 May 1776; died in Bloomsbury, London on 23 February 1867.
The son of George Smart, a music and instrument seller with premises in Hampstead Road, and the uncle of **Henry Smart**.
A chorister of the Chapel Royal (1783-1792) under **Edmund Ayrton**. Studied organ with **Thomas Dupuis**, piano with **J.B. Cramer** and composition with **Samuel Arnold**, organist of Westminster Abbey, for whom he sometimes acted as deputy.
Has been described as the most eminent professional musician of his time. Knighted by the Lord Lieutenant of Ireland in Dublin after conducting a series of concerts there.
At the age of 15, he was appointed organist of St. James's Church, Hampstead Road, London (1791). Organist of the Brunswick Chapel. Sang as a bass at the Italian Operas (1794) and at the Antient Concert. One of the organists of the Chapel Royal (1822-1867), succeeding **Thomas Attwood,** as composer (1838).
A violinist in the concerts given by Salomon.
Met and became acquainted with some of the most eminent of the international composers of the day including Haydn, for whom he once played drums in a concert at short notice. Visited Beethoven in Vienna. Weber was also a friend: he died in Smart's house.
Conducted at all the major music festivals and was prominent in many of the significant musical events of his time. An original member of the Philharmonic Society (from 1813), conducting the Society's concerts from 1818 until 1894.
Director of music of the Covent Garden Theatre, and conductor of the London oratorios (1813-1825). Conducted the first English performance of the oratorio *St. Paul* by Mendelssohn in Liverpool on 7 October 1836. Arranged and conducted the music at the Coronation of William IV (1831) and Victoria (1838).
A music academic and administrator, and a teacher of singing. One of his pupils was the 'Swedish Nightingale,' Jenny Lind. In 1823 he became one of the first members of the Board of Professors of the Royal Academy of Music. Active in setting up the Mendelssohn Scholarship, the first beneficiary of which was **Arthur Sullivan**.
Editor of *First Set of Madrigals* (1841) by **Orlando Gibbons** for the Music Antiquarian Society.
He published a set of anthems in 1860, containing his works 'Blessed is he that considereth' and 'O God, who art the author'. Editor of *Collection of Sacred Music* (1863) in which he included his own hymn tune 'Wiltshire', which he composed at the age of 19 to be sung with the metrical version of Psalm 48 'Great is the Lord'. Composed other hymn tunes, and glees.

SMART, Grenville
See **CLARE,** Edward.

SMART (Callow), Harriet Anne (1817-1883)
Born in London on 20 October 1817; died in London on 30 June 1883. Married William Callow, the watercolourist. An amateur composer whose works included hymn tunes and other vocal music.

SMART, Henry Thomas (1813-1879)
Born in St. Marylebone, London on 26 November 1813; died in Hampstead, London on 6 July 1879 and is buried in Hampstead Cemetery. Nephew of **George Thomas Smart**.
Attended Highgate School., London. Studied music with W.H. Kearns, leader of the Covent Garden Orchestra.

As a boy he often visited the organ factory of Robson and Flight, where he learned about the techniques of organ construction. Attended a number of meetings of the Royal Institution with his uncle, Captain Bagnold, in the course of which he met the inventors Humphrey Davy and Michael Faraday, as well as the reformer William Wilberforce. Met Nield, the organist of All Souls' Church, Langham Place, London who encouraged his interest in music.

Offered a commission in the Indian Army but declined it. Instead, largely through the pressure exerted on him by his family, he was articled to a solicitor for four years before deciding to pursue music as a full-time career.

Henry Smart spent some time in Great Yarmouth and at the town's Parish Church of St. Nicholas, and at Portsmouth, as a result of which he developed a love of the sea.

Organist of St. Mary's Church, Blackburn in Lancashire (which in 1927 was elevated to cathedral status) from 1831 until 1836. A Festival took place on 4 October 1835 to celebrate the 300th anniversary of the Reformation. He composed an anthem for the occasion, and his hymn tune 'Lancashire' was sung for the first time.

From 1836 he was organist of a number of churches in London, including St. Philip's, Regent Street (1838-1844); St. Luke's, Old Street (1844-1865), for which he edited *The Choral Book* (1858) and St. Pancras, Euston Road (1865-1879). Actually dismissed from St. Lukes, having been appointed out of some 30 candidates by a selection committee including the organists of Westminster Abbey, **James Turle** and St. Paul's Cathedral, **John Goss**, and Robert Topliff.

Lost his sight in 1864 but continued his career in music. His daughter Clara and later his pupil Thomas J. Bradbury acted as his amanuenses. His chief biographer was **William Spark**.

An organ authority, responsible for the specification of the instruments for Leeds Town Hall and in Glasgow, the City Hall and St. Andrew's Hall. Well known for his organ extemporisations.

Favoured unison congregational singing and a champion of traditional metrical Psalmody. Disapproved of the hymn tunes of **J.B. Dykes**, dismissing them as effeminate and he was equally scornful of tunes with 'a jigging motion in the rhythm,' such as 'Miles Lane' by **William Shrubsole**.

He is quoted as admonishing a young clergyman, who had innocently put forward the case for Gregorian Chant at a dinner party: 'Now look here! This won't do; who asked your opinion, sir, upon a musical question of which you evidently know absolutely nothing? You may rely on it, that some day when you and your friends are shouting those ugly Gregorian Chants, Heaven will punish you and rain down bags of crotchets upon your heads, and prevent you from ever singing them again!'

A critic for *The Atlas*. Editor of *Presbyterian Psalter and Hymnal* (1877-1878), the first ever tune book for the United Presbyterian Church.

Composed a Morning Service in F, Morning and Evening Services in F and in G (1871), an Evening Service in B-flat, Responses to the Commandments in F, Single Chants in A, D, E and G, and Double Chants in A, E and G. His anthems include 'The Lord is my Strength', 'O be joyful in the Lord' and 'The Lord is my Shepherd.'

Composer of hymn tunes including 'Heathlands', 'Lancashire' and 'Chebar', cantatas such as *The Fishermaidens*, the oratorio *Jacob*, two operas including *Bertha, or The Gnome of The Hartzberg*

(1855), around 140 part songs and trios, 167 songs, and organ works.

SMART, William Henry (19th/20th century)
Graduated B.Mus. at Dublin in 1880. Organist of Ascot Parish Church, Berkshire (from 1865); St. Paul's Church, Langlebury, Hertfordshire (1869-1873) and the London Churches of Sr. Mark, Old Street (1875-1878); St. Andrew, Queen Victoria Street (1878-1881) and St. Clement Danes, Strand (1884-1889). Editor of a collection of Dublin Kyries. Composed an Evening Service in B-flat (1897) and hymn tunes. His degree exercise was an Evening Service for Solo Voices, Chorus, Organ and Strings.

SMEE, Frederick (?-1879)
An employee of the Bank of England. Composed anthems including 'I will magnify Thee' and 'O Lord, we beseech Thee'.

SMEWENS, Thomas (17th century)
Composer of the anthem 'I Heard A Voice From Heaven'.

SMIETON, John More (1857-1904)
Born in Dundee, Scotland in 1857; died in the nearby village of Broughty Ferry on 13 July 1904. His brother, James Smieton, was a poet. A pupil of, among others, **H.S. Oakeley**, **John Frederick Bridge**, F.H.Cowen, and **Georg Henschel**. Followed a career in music at Broughty Ferry, and was active in the local jute business. Composed as his degree exercise a setting of Psalm 121 'I will lift up mine eyes' for Tenor Solo, Chorus and Orchestra. Composed the harvest or general anthem 'Lift up thy voice with strength' (1898), cantatas including *Pearl* (1880), and a string quartet. With his brother, James, as librettist, he composed a number of choral works including *Ariadne* (1884), *King Arthur* (1899) and *Connla* (1900).

SMITH, Albert George Warren (b.1894)
Born in Camberwell, London in 1894. A composer of hymn tunes.

SMITH, Alexander Brent
See **BRENT-SMITH,** Alexander

SMITH, Alfred Montem (1828-1891)
Born on 13 May 1828, the day of the year known as 'Montem Day'; died in 1891. A chorister of St. George's Chapel, Windsor Castle.
Tenor singer, and composer. A lay vicar of Westminster Abbey and a gentleman of the Chapel Royal (from 1858). A professor of singing of the Royal Academy of Music and Guildhall School of Music. Composed the anthems 'Be ye kind to one another' and 'The eyes of all wait'.

SMITH, Arthur Francis (?-1915)
An articled pupil of Edward Chadfield. Graduated B.Mus. at Queens' College, Cambridge (1883).
Organist of Tickenhall Parish Church (1869-1872) and of the Church of St. Werburgh (from 1872), where he remained for nearly 40 years. A local choral society conductor. Editor of the monthly journal of the Incorporated Society of Musicians, of which he was the honorary local representative and examiner, as well as for the Royal Academy of Music and the Royal College of Music. Lived in Derby and was joint founder and director of the Derby School of Music. Composed as his degree exercise a setting of Psalm 103

'Praise the Lord' for Five Voices, Strings and Orchestra. Composed other church music including a Te Deum in G (1894), songs, and items for piano.

SMITH, Boyton (1837-?)
Born in Dorchester, Dorset on 22 February 1837. A chorister, under **S.S. Wesley,** of the Cathedrals of Hereford and Winchester. Organist of Dorchester Parish Church. Composed a Service in D (1897), in E-flat (1898) and in G (1918), anthems including 'I will lay me down in peace' (1919), a set of Responses to the Commandments in E-flat, songs, piano works and organ music for use in church.

SMITH, Charles Edwin (1856-1932)
Born in London in 1856; died in Much Hadham, Hertfordshire on 25 September 1932. Organist of Downs Baptist Church, Clapton, London (1879-1896) and of Regent's Park Baptist Church (from 1896). Composer of hymn tunes including 'My thankful heart', to words by William Winks. Composed songs, of which one is 'Quiet ways are best' (1896).

SMITH, Dr. Clement (1760-1826)
Born in Richmond, Surrey in 1760; died in Richmond on 16 November 1826. Graduated B.Mus. (1791) and D.Mus. (1800) at the University of Oxford. A teacher in Richmond. Composed church music, glees, songs, piano duets and a Sonata Cappriciosa for Harpsichord (1790).

SMITH, Edward (?-c1612)
Edward Smith was buried in 1611 or 1612, on 4 February. A lay clerk and master of the choristers of Durham Cathedral (c1608-c1611). Three anthems are found in the 1664 edition of the collection by **James Clifford**, *The Divine Services and Anthems*. Composed four verse anthems, a set of Preces, and settings of Psalms 8 and 119. The anthems include 'If the Lord Himself' and 'O praise God in His Holiness'.

SMITH, Edward W. (19th century)
Said to be 'of Windsor'; lived in the second half of the 19th century. Could therefore be Edward Woodley Smith. Composed the anthems 'Hear my crying' and 'Try me, O God'.

SMITH, Elias (?-1620)
Died in Gloucester in 1620. Organist and master of the choristers of Gloucester Cathedral from 1605 or before until 1620. He may be the person of the same name who was a Gloucester lay clerk in 1594. Composed the anthem 'How is the golde become dim'.

SMITH, Ernest Harry (1862-?)
Born in Faversham, Kent in 1862. Studied music with W.H. Drake and with **A.W. Marchant**. Organist of St. Bede's Church, Liverpool, and of St. James's Church, New Brighton. Composed anthems including 'They that sow in tears' (1922) and 'There were shepherds' (1924), fantasias on various hymn tunes including 'Eventide' and 'Moscow', and part songs.

SMITH, Dr. George Henry (19th/20th century)
Born in Hull, Yorkshire. Graduated B.Mus. (1878) and D.Mus. (1895) at New College, Oxford.
Held a number of academic and administrative positions. Correspondence secretary of the Incorporated Staff Sight-singing College, lecturer in music of the Hull Municipal Training College, principal of the Hull and East Riding College of Music, and examiner in music to the Ministry of Education, Northern Ireland. An examiner for the Incorporated Society of Musicians.
Organist of Christ Church, Hull (1881-1883); organist and choirmaster of Sculcoates Parish Church (from 1883) and of All Saints' Church, Hull. Honorary organist of Patrington Parish Church (from 1892).
Choirmaster of the rural deaneries of Hedon (1892-1900) and Hornsea (1896-1902), and of Hornsea Parish Church (1899-1903). A local choral and orchestral society conductor.
Author of *History of Hull Organists and Organs*.
Composed as his B.Mus. exercise a Benedictus for Solo Voices, Chorus and Strings. For his D.Mus. he successfully submitted a setting of Psalm 46 'God is our Hope and Strength' for eight-part Chorus, Solo Voices and Full Orchestra.
Composed a Magnificat and Nunc Dimittis in G (1883), a Te Deum in E-flat (1900) a Benediction Service, school songs, a three-part song 'Spring' (1915), and piano works.

SMITH, George Montague (1843-?)
Born in Norwich, Norfolk in July 1843. Organist of the University of Glasgow, and conductor of the University Choral Society. A local examiner in music for the University. Organist of St. Silas's Episcopal Church and of Coats' Memorial Church, Paisley. A professor of harmony at Queen Margaret's College, Glasgow. Composed a Festival Te Deum, cantatas including *Blessed is the Man*, and an opera *The Killabag Shootings*, songs, part songs and a Concert Overture, composed expressly for the Gloucester Festival of 1877.

SMITH, George Townshend (1813-1877)
Born in Windsor, Berkshire on 14 November 1813; died in Hereford on 3 August 1877.
A brother of **Samuel Smith** and the son of Edward Woodley Smith, a lay-clerk of St. George's Chapel, Windsor Castle.
George Smith was himself a chorister of St. George's under **Highmore Skeats** the younger.
Studied music under **Samuel Wesley**.
Organist of Eastbourne Old Parish Church, Sussex and of St. Margaret's Church, Lynn.
Organist of Hereford Cathedral (1843-1877), applying successfully from a field of 43 candidates to replace the unfortunate **John Hunt** (1806-1842) who had died following an accident at the Cathedral. Conductor and honorary secretary of the Three Choirs' Festival. His tenure as organist coincided with a prolonged restoration project. The cathedral was out of action completely from 1842 until 1850, and services were held in All Saints' Church during this time. From 1850 to 1863, services took place in the nave and on 30 June 1863 the cathedral was reopened in its entirety.
Composed a Jubilate for the Three Choirs' Festival, Hereford in 1855. His anthems include 'Lord, I call upon Thee', and 'O how amiable' for the reopening of the Cathedral. Composed other vocal music, and light music for piano.

SMITH, Revd. Henry Percy (1825-1898)
Born in Malta in December 1825; died in Bournemouth, Dorset on 28 January 1898. Educated at Balliol College, Oxford, where he graduated B.A. (1848) and M.A. (1850). Curate of Eversley, Hampshire (1849-1851) under Charles Kingsley. Perpetual curate of St. Michael's Church, York Town, Farnborough, Hampshire

(1851-1868) and vicar of Great Barnton, Suffolk (1868-1882). Chaplain of Christ Church, Cannes, France (1882-1892) and canon of Gibraltar (from 1892). Compiled a *Glossary of Terms and Phrases* (1883). Composed a hymn tune 'Maryton', first published in 1874 in *Church Hymns* with 'Sun of my Soul'.

SMITH, Isaac (1734-1805)
Born in 1734; died in Walworth, London on 14 December 1805. Clerk (precentor) of the Alie Street Meeting House, Goodman's Fields, Whitechapel, London, which was a Baptist Church, and it is likely that he was the first dissentient precentor to draw a salary. It is believed that he was a linen draper in Cheapside, London. His *A Collection of Psalm Tunes in Three Parts...* (c1770) ran to at least five editions. The Fifth Edition (1788) contained a preface in which he advocated congregational hymn singing practice. The collection contained the tune 'Irish', which has been attributed to him, as well as 'St. Stephen', also known as 'Abridge'. Composed other Psalm tunes, some of which are found in the collection Universal Psalmist (1763 and 1770) by Aaron Williams. *Hymns and Psalms* (1983) uses 'Falcon Street'. Other popular tunes by him include 'Silver Street'.

SMITH, James Whitehead (1827-1912)
Born in Wells, Somerset in 1827; died in Sandown, Isle of Wight on 9 September 1912. Took lessons in music with Dix and Angel (possibly **Alfred Angel**). In 1843 he entered the Royal Academy of Music, where he earned a reputation as a pianist at the Academy's concerts. Also played violin in the students' orchestra. Assistant organist of St. Mary's Church, Paddington Green, London. Organist of Wimborne Minster for more than 30 years. Librarian and organist of Marlborough College, Wiltshire and a local examiner for the Royal College of Music. A composer of hymn tunes.

SMITH, Dr. John (1795-1861)
Born in Cambridge in 1795; died near Dublin on 12 November 1861.
As a boy he went to live with his uncle, Dr. John Spray, whose daughter he later married.
Graduated D.Mus. (1827) at the University of Dublin.
A counter tenor singer. A stipendary choirman of Christ Church Cathedral, Dublin (from 1815) and a vicar choral of St. Patrick's Cathedral, Dublin (from 1816). Was suspended from Christ Church for a time, following allegations that he failed to comply with its code of conduct: his transgression was to have sung at a 'public musical performance in the play house in Passion week.' He took legal proceedings against the Dean and Chapter to recover his position. Organist of the Chapel of Dublin Castle (1833-1835).
The position of professor of music at Trinity College, Dublin had been vacant since the death of Lord Mornington in 1774, until the appointment of John Smith in 1845. Served until the year of his death and he was succeeded by **R.P. Stewart.**
Editor of the collection *Cathedral Music in Vocal Score with Organ or Pianoforte Accompaniment* (1837) and *Lyra Masonica* (1847), a collection of Masonic songs.
Composed Services in A and in B-flat, Chants, a number of anthems including 'Blessed be Thou' and 'O Lord, grant the king', an oratorio *The Revelation*, glees and songs including 'Rememb'rest Thou'.

SMITH, John Stafford (1750-1836)
Born in Gloucester where he was baptised on 30 March 1750; died in London on 21 September 1836.
The son of Martin S. Smith, organist of Gloucester Cathedral (1740-1782).
A chorister of the Chapel Royal. Studied music with **William Boyce** and with his father.
A tenor singer. A gentleman of the Chapel Royal (from 1784) and a lay vicar of Westminster Abbey (from 1795). Succeeded **Samuel Arnold** as organist (1802-1836) and **Edmund Ayrton** as master of the children (1805-1817) of the Chapel Royal. Performed, as organist, at the Gloucester Festival of 1790.
Built up a large and valuable music library which was sold by auction in 1844 after his death. The manuscripts in his collection were used as a source of reference when he helped Hawkins with his compilation *General History of the Science and Practice of Music*, published between 1776 and 1789. Published collections of glees and songs, and edited *Musica Antiqua...* (1812), a two-volume work that covered the entire period from the 12th to 18th centuries.
Composer of hymn tunes, and anthems including 'Come unto Me all ye that labour' (1862) and 'Praise the Lord'. His Chants include a Double Chant in G and another in G Minor. A set of 12 chants by him was published in 1803. Also composed catches.

SMITH, Joseph (1800-1873)
Born in Halesowen, Staffordshire in 1800; died in Halesowen in 1873. An amateur musician with a good alto singing voice, but never took up music as a profession. Lived in Halesowen for most of his life. Composer of hymn tunes including 'Innocents' and other items of church music, often written especially for the Sunday School movement.

SMITH, Dr. Joseph (1856-?)
Born, of Irish parentage, in Dudley, Worcestershire in 1856. Graduated B.Mus. (1880) and D.Mus. (1881) at the University of Dublin and subsequently pursued a career in music in Ireland. At the age of 17 he was appointed organist of a church in Galway. Organist of Limerick Cathedral (1877-1882). In 1882 he moved to Dublin, where he became organist of the Church of the Three Patrons, Rathgar and a professor of music at the Convent School of Sacré Coeur, Annville. Director of music at the Dublin Artisan's Exhibition of 1885, composing an Inaugural Ode for the occasion. A local music society conductor. Editor of *Catholic Choir Music* (1891) and compiled a hymn book with tunes for the Roman Catholic Church. Composed three Masses including settings in C (1889) and D (1889), anthems, a motet *God be merciful* (1881) which won a prize at the Welsh National Eisteddfod of 1880, a cantata *St. Kevin* for the Hereford Festival of 1885, a Triumphal March (1885) for Orchestra, and part songs.

SMITH, Dr. Joseph Sutcliffe (c1869-?)
Born in Halifax, Yorkshire around 1869.
Trained at the Tonic Sol-fa College, where he won a prize in counterpoint. His tutors were **Walter Carroll, Athelstan Iggulden, Haydn Keeton** and F.W. Furnish. Graduated B.Mus. (1902) and D.Mus. (1917) at the University of Durham.
Organist of Friday Bridge Parish Church at the age of 13 (from 1883); and organist and choirmaster of Wisbech Parish Church, Cambridgeshire (1898-1918) and of Knaresborough Parish Church, Yorkshire (1918-1921).

A teacher of music at the Pupil-Teachers Centre, Wisbech, and music master at Wisbech Grammar School. Taught singing at March High School (from 1905), and was a local orchestral society conductor.

The author of *Orchestral Players' Guide, Choristers' Companion, The Music of the Yorkshire Dales*, and of magazine articles. *A Musical Pilgrimage in Yorkshire* is a valuable guide to the local music of the time.

During World War I he was deputy head of Wisbech Barton School, and was director of singing to the Y.M.C.A. at Ripon and Catterick Camps.

Composed as his degree exercise a setting of Psalm 86 'Bow down Thine ear, O Lord.' Also composed a setting of Psalm 104 'Praise the Lord O my soul' (1915), hymns, carols, piano works and songs. His 'Hail, mightiest Lord' (1912) was a hymn-anthem for Easter.

SMITH, Kenneth Donald (b.1928)
Born in Manchester on 28 September 1928. Educated at Long Eaton Grammar School, Nottingham and at Keble College, Oxford. Assistant director of music at Wrekin College, Shropshire (1953-1958); head of the Music Department of Sir Thomas Rich's School, Gloucester (1958-1963) and the St. Matthias College of Education, Bristol (from 1964). Has written articles on musical topics, including hymnody, for various journals. Associated with a number of modern hymnals, contributing to *Anglican Hymn Book* (1965) and *New Catholic Hymnal* (1971), and being joint musical editor for *Sunday School Praise* (1958) and *The School Assembly* (1958). Composer of hymn tunes including 'Longwall', and other items of church music. His *New Orbit* (1972) was a collection of songs and hymns for small children.

SMITH, Martin (?-1786)
Died in Churchdown, Gloucestershire on 13 April 1786. The father of **John Stafford Smith.** Is believed to have been a pupil of **Maurice Greene,** organist of St. Paul's Cathedral. Organist of Gloucester Cathedral from 1739 until 1781. Composed the anthems 'I will magnify Thee' and 'Praise the Lord'.

SMITH, Revd. Peter Donald (b.1938)
Born in Weybridge, Surrey on 26 April 1938. Educated at Farnham Grammar School, Surrey, and apprenticed into the aircraft industry. Trained as a classical pianist. A minister of the Methodist Church. Folk singer and guitarist. Editor of collections including *Faith, Folk and Clarity* (1968) and *Faith, Folk and Nativity* (1969). A hymn writer, composing the tune 'Healer' in sea-shanty form, for his own 'When Jesus the Healer passed through Galilee' (1975).

SMITH, Robert (17th century)
Composer of anthems including 'God be Merciful' and 'Sing unto the Lord'.

SMITH, Robert Archibald (1780-1829)
Born in Reading, Berkshire on 16 November 1780; died in Edinburgh on 3 January 1829.

The son of Robert Smith, a silk weaver of East Kilbride, Scotland who had travelled South when his trade in the Paisley area was depressed and settled in Reading in 1774.

Robert Smith had musical talents, learning to play violin at the age of 10 and later progressing to the viola and cello. Apprenticed in the weaving trade. Became a weaver, firstly in Reading, and then in Paisley (from 1800). Later earned his living from music (from 1803),. From 1807 he taught the subject in Paisley and in the same year he was appointed precentor at the Abbey Church. Played viola in the Glasgow Music Festival of 1821. A tenor singer.

Director of music of St. George's Church, Edinburgh (from 1823) under the minister, **Andrew Thomson,** himself a keen musician. The two collaborated in the publication of *Sacred Harmony for the use of St. George's Church, Edinburgh...* (1820).

As Robert Smith's career progressed he became a very influential figure in his field.

Published a number of collections, in which are found some of his own works. These editions include *Devotional Music, Original and Selected...* (1810) and *The Irish Minstrel... Vocal Melodies of Ireland, Ancient and Modern* (1825). *The Scottish Minstrel* was published in six volumes between 1820 and 1824. Author of *An Introduction to Singing...* (1826).

His Psalm tunes include 'Morven,' 'St. Mirren' and 'Invocation'. Among his anthems is 'How beautiful upon the mountains' (1868) and 'Give ear unto my Voice'. Composed songs including 'Bonnie Mary Hay'. A friend of the poet Robert Tannahill, some of whose works he set to music, an example being 'Jessie, the flow'r of Dunblane' (1816).

SMITH, Samuel (1821-1917)
Born in Eton, Berkshire on 29 August 1821; died in Windsor, Berkshire on 1 January 1917. The son of **Edward Woodley Smith,** a lay clerk of St. George's Chapel, Windsor Castle, and the brother of **George Townshend Smith** and **Alfred Montem Smith.**

At the age of 14, Samuel Smith became a chorister of the Chapel Royal, St. James's Palace, where he studied under the organist, **William Hawes** and where he sang at both the Coronation (1830) and Funeral (1837) of William IV. Also studied with **George Elvey,** organist of St. George's Chapel.

Organist of Hayes Church, Midlesex; Eton Parish Church; Egham Parish Church, Surrey (1846-1858); Organist of Holy Trinity Church, Windsor (1858-1861) and of Windsor Parish Church (1861-1895). Taught music at Beaumont College, Old Windsor (1861-1903).

His hymn tune 'Ruth' was first published in *Church Hymns* (1874) with the hymn 'Summer suns are glowing' by William Walsham How. His other tunes include 'Newton Ferns'. There are also Psalms, anthems and songs. Many were published within collections such as *Psalms and Chants* (1860).

SMITH, Sidney (1839-1889)
Studied in Leipzig under Ignaz Moscheles, Louis Plaidy, Moritz Hauptman and Ernst Richter (from 1855). He returned to London in 1859 where he settled as a pianist and composer. His works include the anthem 'The Lord is great.

SMITH, Thomas (1832-1905)
Born in Arnold, Nottinghamshire on 20 February 1832; died in Bury St. Edmunds, Suffolk on 10 September 1905. Studied piano with **Henry Farmer** and organ with Charles Noble. At the age of 15 he became organist of the Church of St. Stephen, Sneinton, Nottinghamshire. Organist of St. John's Church, Bury St. Edmunds (from 1873) and private organist to the Marquis of Bristol at his seat of Hozzinger (from 1880). Author of *A Concise and Practical Explanation of the Rules of Simple Harmony and Thorough Bass* and other works. His anthems include 'O worship the Lord' and 'Thou crownest the Year'.

SMITH, Thomas Roylands (1847-1927)
Born in Highgate, London on 28 October 1847; died in Torquay, Devon, in 1927. Studied music with **J.T. Cooper** and **F. Scotson Clark**. Music master of Abingdon Grammar School, Oxfordshire. Lived in Torquay and was organist of the Churches of St. John (until 1876), St. Mary (until 1892), and All Saints'. A teacher and a local choral society conductor. From 1875 he was conductor of the Plympton Deanery Choral Union and choirmaster of the Exeter Diocese, a position which entailed travelling into some remote parts of the diocese. Each organisation mounted up to 12 choral festivals per annum, with as many as 3,000 voices taking part at a time. Some of these festivals were held in Exeter Cathedral. Contributed articles on church and choral music to various journals. Composed a Te Deum, a Pater Noster, five Evening Services based upon Ambrosian and Gregorian melodies, and a carol 'The Child is born' (1918).

SMITH, Thomas Sydney (19th century)
Choirmaster and deputy organist of St. George's Cathedral, Southwark. Organist of the London Church of St. Mary, South Kensington. Author of a piano *Vade Mecum* (1879) and other works. Composed sacred music including the anthems 'Out of the south cometh the Whirlwind' (1892) and 'The Lord is great' (1887), songs and items for piano.

SMITH, Walter Ernest (19th/20th century)
A chorister of the Cathedrals of Wells and Bristol. Graduated B.Mus (1907) at Queen's College, Oxford. Organist and choirmaster of the Bristol Churches of St. Peter (1900-1910), Clifton Parish Church and St. Saviour, Woolcott Park. From 1902 he was piano master and co-director of music of Clifton College, and director of music of Redlands High School. Lived in Bristol. Composed as his degree exercise a setting of Psalm 130 'Out of the deep'. His other works include a Holy Communion Service in E-flat (1914), a Magnificat and Nunc Dimittis (1930) and *Six Little Pieces* (1907) for Piano.

SMITH, William (c1603-1645)
William Smith, popularly known as 'Smith of Durham' was baptised on 3 April 1603; died in Durham on 19 April 1645. Is often confused with the musician of the same name and period. A minor canon of Durham from 20 July 1627. Composed the famous set of Preces and Responses which bear his name. Also composed five sets of festal Psalms including a version of Psalm 67 'God be merciful', and seven verse anthems.

SMITH, Revd. William (16th century)
Priest-organist of Durham Cathedral (1588-1598). Composed anthems including 'Almighty and everlasting God' and 'I will wash my hands'.

SMITH, William Seymour (1836-1905)
Born in Marlow, Buckinghamshire on 20 August 1836; died in Brockley, Kent on 12 September 1905. A baritone singer, composer and organist. Studied singing with **Michael Balfe**, piano and composition with **C.E. Horsley**. Organist of Hampstead Parish Church, London (from 1862) and of Wimbledon Parish Church. Lecturer in music at the Royal Polytechnic and a professor of singing at the Royal College of Music and at the Goldsmiths' Institute. His Musical Sketches were popular in London and in other parts of the country. Composed sacred cantatas including

Joshua (1887), anthems such as 'Not unto us, O Lord' (1889), songs including *The Rovers* (1883), piano pieces and an Andante in C (1884) for organ.

SOAPER, John (c1743-1794)
Born in London around the year 1743; died in London on 5 June 1794 and was buried at St. Paul's Cathedral. A chorister of St. Paul's under **William Savage**, his treble voice remaining with him until the age of 18. A lay vicar of Westminster Abbey, a gentleman of the Chapel Royal (from May 1764) and a vicar choral of St. Paul's Cathedral (from 1764) on the departure of Robert Wass. An organist. Composed a Sanctus in C, Psalms and chants, including a Double Chant in D.

SOAR, Dr. Joseph (1878-1971)
Born in 1878; died in June 1971.
An exhibitioner at the Royal College of Music, and trained with **Walford Davies** at the Temple Church, London. Graduated B.Mus. (1910) at the University of Durham. Accorded the Lambeth D.Mus. in 1934.
Appointed M.B.E. in 1947.
Served with the armed forces (1915-1921)..
Organist and choirmaster of Chapeltown Parish Church, Sheffield, Yorkshire (from 1892), at the age of 14. Subsequently organist and choirmaster of St. John's Church, Clapham, London (from 1898); All Saints' Church, Derby (now elevated to cathedral status) from 1901; Barnsley Parish Church, Yorkshire (from 1904); Halifax Parish Church (from 1912); Burnham-on-Sea Parish Church, Somerset (from 1921). A music master of Barnsley Grammar School. Conductor of local choral and operatic societies.
Organist and choirmaster of St. David's Cathedral (1922-1954). A local magistrate and honorary secretary of the lifeboat station. As a member of the crew he won a bronze medal for gallantry in 1943 from the Royal National Lifeboat Institution.
Composed Holy Communion Service in F (1936), a Benedicite (1930), chants, Kyries, a card of two Final Amens (1907), songs and a part song. Author of a Lullaby for Piano. His degree exercise was a setting of Psalm 32 'Blessed is he'.

SOLOMON, Laban (1842-1903)
Born in West Bromwich, Staffordshire in 1842; died in Barnsley, Yorkshire on 29 April 1903. Composer of hymn tunes including 'Festal Day' (1891) to words by Marianne Farningham.

SOMERVELL, Sir Arthur (1863-1937)
Born in Windermere on 5 June 1863; died in St. Marylebone, London on 2 May 1937.
Attended Uppingham School and studied music privately with **Hubert Parry**. Studied with **C.V. Stanford** at King's College, Cambridge. Graduated B.A. (1883)) and studied further at the Berlin Hochschule under Friedrich Kiel (1883-1885), and at the Royal College of Music (1885-1887).
Knighted in 1929.
A professor of the R.C.M. (from 1894). In 1901 he became an inspector of music in schools. Principal inspector of music to the Board of Education (1920-1928) and to the Scottish Education Department. Chairman of the Council of the School of English Church Music, which is now the Royal School of Church Music.
Composed a Service in F; a Mass in C for Solo Voices, Chorus and Orchestra (1891); the sacred cantatas *A Song of Praise* (1891) and *The Passion of Christ*; hymn tunes including 'Rugby' - named

after the public school at which his son was educated - 'Windermere' and 'Langdale'; an Ode to the Sea, and song cycles including *The Broken Arc* (1923).

SORESBY, Roger William (19th/20th century)
Born in Derby. Trained in music at Lincoln Cathedral. Graduated B.Mus. (1914) at the University of Durham. Lived in the Nottinghamshire towns of Radcliffe-on-Trent, where he was music master of the Grammar School, and Retford. Organist and choirmaster of St. Leodgarius, Nottingham (from 1900); St. Mary, Radcliffe (from 1911) and East Retford (from 1915). Composed as his degree exercise 'Song of Praise' for Solo Voices, Chorus and Strings. Also wrote the anthem 'Praise the Lord, O my soul (1916), organ works, and items for piano.

SOUTH, Charles Frederick (1850-1916)
Born in London on 6 February 1850; died in Salisbury, Wiltshire on 12 August 1916. Received organ lessons from his brother, Henry J. South and with **George Cooper**, for whom he sometimes deputised. Organist, at the age of 16, of Aske's Hospital at Hoxton, London (from 1866). Organist of the London Church of St. Augustine with St. Faith, Watling Street (1868-1883). Organist of Salisbury Cathedral (1883-1916), having been recommended for the post by **John Stainer**. A local choral society conductor. His compositional output was small and it includes a Benedicite in D-flat (1882), chants and introits.

SOUTHGATE, Revd. Frederic (1824-1885)
Born in Gravesend, Kent on 7 October 1824; died in Northfleet, Kent on 30 January 1885. Educated at Ramsgate. Having decided upon a career in the church, he went up to Emmanuel College, Cambridge where he graduated B.A. in 1848. Ordained in 1849. Curate of Castle Headingham, Suffolk and minister of St. Mark's Church, Rosherville, and of Northfleet (from 1858). Publisher of a collection *Favourite Hymn Tunes... used at St. Botolph's Church, Northfleet* (1873). Composed church music including hymn tunes such as 'St. Agatha', which is found in the Revised Edition (1927) of *Church Hymnary*.

SOUTHGATE, Thomas Bishop (1814-1868)
Born in Hornsey, Middlesex on 8 June 1814; died in Highgate, London on 3 November 1868. A chorister of the Chapel Royal, St. James's Palace and from the age of 12 he deputised occasionally for the organist, **George Smart**. Studied harmony with **Thomas Attwood** and **John Goss**, and organ with **Samuel Wesley**. Organist of Leyton Parish Church, Essex; Hornsey Parish Church, London (for 19 years) and St. Anne's Church, Highgate Rise. A violinist. Composed sacred songs including 'Nearer, my God, to Thee' (1855) and 'Thy will be done' (1855), hymn tunes including 'Southgate', anthems, piano music, and exercises and scales for piano.

SOUTHWARD, Revd. Walter Thomas (19th/20th century)
Graduated Mus.B. (1888) at the University of Cambridge, where he was a fellow (from 1876), dean (from 1884) and tutor (from 1892) of St. Catherine's College. Composed as his degree exercise the sacred cantata *O Lord turn not Thy face* for Solo Voices, Chorus and Strings. His other works comprise an Evening Service in B-flat (1895), hymn tunes and sacred songs including *The good Shepherd* (1895).

SPARK, Dr. William (1825-1897)
Born in Exeter, Devon on 28 October 1825; died in Leeds on 16 June 1897.
The most famous member of a musical family. The family association with Exeter Cathedral lasted almost 60 years, and continued when William Spark became a chorister. An articled pupil of **S.S. Wesley** at Exeter Cathedral from 1834. When in 1842 Wesley moved to Leeds Parish Church, William Spark made the same journey and became his deputy.
Organist of the Church of St. Thomas, Exeter (from 1840). After his time as deputy to Wesley, William Spark was successively organist of Chapeltown Parish Church, Leeds; St. Paul's Church, Leeds; Tiverton Parish Church, Devon; Daventry Parish Church and St. George's Church, Leeds (1850).
Founded the Leeds Madrigal Society and the People's Concerts. Assisted **Henry Smart** in the design of the new organ for Leeds Town Hall. A lecturer and organ recitalist. Borough organist of Leeds (from 1859) and city organist (from 1893).
William Spark contributed articles to *Yorkshire Post* and to the musical press. Editor of *Organists' Quarterly Journal*.
A biographer of S.S. Wesley, of whom he noted that eccentric behaviour sometimes intruded on the services at Leeds Parish Church, but even so the musical standards were high and large congregations were drawn accordingly. Another biographical subject was Henry Smart. Completed his autobiography, *Musical Memories*, in 1888. His other books include *Musical Reminiscences* (1892).
Held strong views on the teaching of music and in 1870 in an essay he complained about the poor quality of some music teachers whose teaching methods and the lack of substance in the lessons they gave caused him concern.
Composed a Magnificat and Nunc Dimittis in D, anthems including 'All we like sheep', 'O God have mercy' and 'O Lord, our Governor', an oratorio *Immanuel* (1887), cantatas including *Trust and Triumph* (1861), glees, songs and organ works.

SPEARING, Robert (b.1950)
Born on 22 May 1950. Trained at the Royal College of Music, where he was a pupil of **Herbert Howells.** Studied conducting with Vernon Handley, and has since directed a wide range of music, especially from the 20th century repertoire. His works as a composer include the Christmas anthems 'A Hymn to the Virgin' (1973) and 'Jesu, Son most sweet and dear' (1990), other anthems, two symphonies, an Oboe Concerto, and music for the theatre including the burlesque *Commedia* (1996), performed at the Cheltenham Festival of the same year. His cantata *The Seagull* was commissioned and broadcast by B.B.C. Radio 3. Other Radio 3 broadcasts include his Second Symphony and his Oboe Sonata (1996).

SPEDDING, Alan John (b.1938)
Born in Wimbledon, London on 25 September 1938. Studied at the Royal College of Music. Organist of Kingston-on-Thames Parish Church, Surrey (1963-1966). Has been organist and master of the choristers of Beverley Minster since 1967. A local choral society conductor and part-time lecturer at the University of Hull (from 1989). Associate editor of *Organist's Review* (from 1990). Graduated D.Mus., honorarily, at the University of Hull (1994). Has given many recitals and taken part frequently in broadcasts on radio and television. A festival adjudicator. Has composed the carols 'Make we Joy', 'Out of the Orient, crystal skies' and 'All

and some' (a commission from Manchester Cathedral). Organ pieces include 'Variations on "Urbs beata"' and 'Toccata-Carillon'. A number of unpublished anthems, carols and chants exist.

SPEDDING, Dr. Frank Donald (b.1929)
Born in Liverpool on 21 August 1929. Educated at Nottingham High School and at the Royal College of Music. Taught by **R.O. Morris,** who was a strong influence on Spedding's church music. Graduated D.Mus. at the University of London. Music master of Quernmore School, Bromley, Kent (1952-1958). Associated with the Royal Scottish Academy of Music and Drama from 1957 to 1986, as lecturer in harmony and counterpoint (from 1958), and head of department (from 1962) and director of the school of music (from 1980). Has composed the hymn tune 'Mapperley', a Cello Concerto, a Piano Concerto, film scores and short choral works. Composed a setting of 'Venite, adoremus Domino' (1995).

SPEER, Charles Templeman (1859-1937)
Born in Cheltenham, Gloucestershire on 21 November 1859; died in 1937. Cousin of **William Speer.** Studied music in Dublin under **R.P. Stewart,** at the London Academy of Music under **Henry Wylde** and **George Cooper,** and at the Royal Academy of Music. Gave his first public organ recital at the Dublin Exhibition Palace in November 1868. Held a number of organistships in London. Assistant organist of St. Michael's Church, Paddington (from 1876); organist and choirmaster of All Souls' Church, St. John's Wood (from 1877) and of St. Paul's Church, Bow Common (from 1880). Organist and music director of St. Nicholas's Church, Sutton, Surrey (from 1899). Composed church music including a Magnificat and Nunc Dimittis in E-flat (1895), a set of *Twelve Double Chants* (c1870), a three-act opera *Helen,* an Overture in C for Full Orchestra, cantatas and songs.

SPEER, Dr. William Henry (1863-?)
Born in London on 9 November 1863. Cousin of **Charles Speer.** Studied at the Royal College of Music for three years and at Trinity College, Cambridge where he graduated M.A. (1890), Mus.B. (1890) and Mus.D. (1906). His teachers in music included **William Haynes, Walter Parratt, C.H. Lloyd, George Garrett** and **C.V. Stanford.** Organist of Christ Church, High Wycombe, Buckinghamshire (1902-1903). Then lived in Sussex at Balcombe and St. Leonard's-on-Sea. Organist and choirmaster of St. Peter's Church, Bexhill (1903-1910). An oratorio society conductor and an organ recitalist. Composed a Morning and Evening Service in E-flat (1906), a Holy Communion Service in G (1934), a string quartet, a Symphony in E-flat (his Mus.D. exercise), sonatas for piano and for violin and piano, a Nocturne for String Orchestra (1913), and songs. Composed as his first degree exercise a Credo for Solo Voices, Chorus, Strings and Organ.

SPENCER, Charles Child (1797-1869)
Born in London in 1797; died in London on 4 June 1869. Organist and choirmaster of St. James's Chapel, London. Author of *Elements of Practical Music* (1829), *Elements of Musical Composition* (1840) and other works. Composed *A Set of Short Anthems or Introits* (1847), glees including 'The beauteous rosebud' (c1840), and songs.

SPENCER, John (?18th/19th century)
A pupil of Thomas Sanders Dupuis and later became his son-in-law. Edited and published as *Cathedral Music,* in three volumes,

the work of Dupuis. Spencer composed carols, glees including 'Again, the balmy Zephyr blows' (1799), songs and piano music.

SPENCER-PALMER, Florence Margaret (b.1900)
Born in Thornbury, Gloucestershire on 27 July 1900. Attended Thornbury Grammar School. 'Peggy' Spencer-Palmer studied piano at the Tobias Matthay Piano School, London with Vivian Langrish. Took lessons in composition from B.J. Dale, **Ivor Atkins** and Norman Sprankling, graduating B.Mus. at the University of London. Director of music of Clarendon School, Malvern, Worcestershire (1929-1947). The school later moved to Abergele. Appointed visiting teacher of piano at Redlands High School, Bristol (1948-1958). Also taught at St. Brandon's School, Clevedon (1959-1961). Author of a number of books including the textbook *Simplified Sight Reading* (1970). Composer of anthems, and hymn tunes including 'Brynland', 'Duplock' and 'Ellasgarth', the latter being a unison setting with piano accompaniment for use at Clarendon School. Also composed songs.

SPICER, Harold William (1888-?)
Born in Banbury, Oxfordshire in 1888. The grandfather of **Paul Spicer.** Organist of Manchester College, Oxford (from 1916) and of Culham College (from 1949). Director of music of Southfield School, Oxford (1934-1949) and of the City of Oxford High School (1931-1934). Composer of hymn tunes and a sacred song 'The Birds' (1949).

SPICER, Paul (b.1952)
Born in Bowdon, Cheshire on 6 June 1952. The grandson of **Harold Spicer.**
A chorister of New College, Oxford (from 1959) and a music scholar at Oakham School, Rutland (1965-1970). Studied at the Royal College of Music, London (1970-1973) with, among many others, **Herbert Howells** (composition) and **Richard Popplewell** (organ), winning the Walford Davies Organ Prize.
From 1974 taught music for 10 years at Uppingham School, Leicestershire and Ellesmere College, Shropshire. In 1984 became a producer for B.B.C. Radio 3 and in 1986 became senior producer for the Midlands Region, based in Birmingham. An organist, a record producer and a radio presenter. In 1990 became artistic director of the Lichfield International Arts Festival and also director of the Abbotsholme Arts Society. An expert on Herbert Howells and his music.
Has conducted Bach Choirs in Chester, Leicester and Birmingham. Founder and conductor of the Finzi Singers. Principal conductor of the R.C.M. Chamber Choir and a guest conductor of The Netherlands Radio Choir.
Has written a song cycle *A song for birds,* a piano sonata, and organ music including *The Martyrdom of St. Oswald, Prelude in homage to Maurice Duruflé* and *Kiwi fireworks.* His music for the church includes several sets of Preces and Responses, a Magnificat and Nunc Dimittis, and the anthem 'Drop, drop slow tears' for initial performance at Lichfield Cathedral in March 1992.

SPINNEY, Frank (1850-1888)
Born in Dorset on 20 March 1850; died in Leamington, Warwickshire on 5 June 1888. Brother of **Thomas Herbert Spinney** and **Walter Spinney,** and the son of **Thomas Edward Spinney.** Articled to **L.G. Hayne** at Oxford. Organist of the Churches of St. Denys, Warminster (from 1869) and All Saints, Emscote, Warwick (from 1873). Organist of Leamington Parish

Church, where a stained glass window stands in his memory, (from 1878). A local music society conductor and organ recitalist. Composer of hymn tunes, the thanksgiving hymn 'Sing praise to God who reigns above' (1883), and organ music.

SPINNEY, Thomas Edward (1824-?)
Born on 24 June 1824. Father of **Frank Spinney, Thomas Herbert Spinney** and **Walter Spinney**. A pupil of **Henry Bishop**, professor of music at the Universities of Edinburgh and Oxford. Organist of Witney Parish Church, Oxfordshire. Organist and choirmaster of St. Edmund's Church, Salisbury, Wiltshire. A teacher (at one time the Duke of Albany was one of his pupils) and a local choral society conductor. Composed church music, including a set of Offertory Sentences (1882). Also a cantata *Village Bells* (1895) and songs.

SPINNEY, Revd. Thomas Herbert (1857-?)
Born on 13 January 1857. Brother of **Frank Spiney** and **Walter Spinney**, and the son of **Thomas Edward Spinney** (see above and below). Graduated M.A. at the University of Oxford (1884), having being ordained deacon in 1881 and priest in 1882. Studied music with **G.B. Arnold**, and with **Frederick Bridge**. Won a prize for composition at Trinity College, London in 1876.
At the age of 16 he held an organistship in Salisbury. A piano and organ recitalist, later becoming organist and assistant chaplain of Exeter College, Oxford. Curate of South Hinksey, Berkshire (1881-1882) and of Wallasey, Cheshire (from 1883). Vicar of Newborough, Burton-on-Trent, Staffordshire. Composed an Evening Service in E-flat (1890), a chant setting of the Magnificat and Nunc Dimittis (1892), anthems including 'Christ the first fruits', three series of carols, hymns, and organ pieces.

SPINNEY, Walter (1852-1894)
Born on 26 March 1852; died in Leamington, Warwickshire on 21 June 1894. Was the son of **Thomas Edward Spinney** and the brother of **Frank Spinney** and **Thomas Herbert Spinney**. Articled to John Elliot Richardson, organist of Salisbury Cathedral, to whom he was assistant. Organist of St. Edmund's Church, Sslisbury; of Dudley Parish Church, Worcestershire; Christ Church, Doncaster, Yorkshire and Leamington Parish Church (from 1888) where he succeeded his brother Frank. In Leamington Spa he earned his living in music as a teacher, performer, composer and editor. Produced the two organ editions *Vesper Bell* and *Organ Library*, in which were some pieces composed by him. Also composed services, anthems including 'Thou art worthy, O Lord' (1902) and 'Watch ye; stand fast' (1902), hymn tunes and songs.

SPOFFORTH, Reginald (1770-1827)
Born in Southwell, Nottinghamshire in 1770; died in Brompton, Yorkshire on 8 September 1827. The brother of **Samuel Spofforth** and the nephew of **Thomas Spofforth**. A chorister of Southwell Minster under his uncle, Thomas Spofforth, with whom he studied music. His other teacher was **Benjamin Cooke**, organist of Westminster Abbey. For a time, Regianld Spofforth was deputy organist of Lincoln Cathedral. He is known as a glee composer: he won two prizes awarded by the Noblemen's Catch Club. Composer of a Christmas glee *Hail, smiling morn* (c.1820) which has achieved quasi-carol status in the North of England, especially in the West Riding of Yorkshire, where it is much given by bands as well as choirs.

SPOFFORTH, Samuel (?1780-1864)
Born in Southwell, Nottinghamshire around the year 1780; died in Lichfield, Staffordshire on 6 June 1864 at the age of 84. Younger brother of **Reginald Spofforth** and the nephew of **Thomas Spofforth**. A chorister of Southwell Minster (1793-1798). Studied music with his uncle, Thomas Spofforth. Organist of the Cathedrals of Peterborough (1798-1807) and Lichfield (1807-1864). Composed church music, including a Double Chant in D.

SPOFFORTH, Thomas (c1742-1826)
Born around the year 1742; died in May 1826 when his age was believed to be 84. Uncle of **Reginald Spofforth** and **Samuel Spofforth**. Organist of Southwell Minster (1764-1818). His choristers included his two nephews. Known as a local benefactor, making gifts to the poor of coal at Christmas and bread at Easter and Christmas. Composed a Double Chant in F.

SPOONER-LILLINGSTON, Revd. Dr. Septimus Ernest Luke (1865-?)
Born in Edgbaston, Birmingham on 18 April 1865. Graduated B.Mus. (1888) and D.Mus. (1913) at Hertford College, Oxford. Also graduated B.A. (1886) and M.A. (1889). Curate of the Church of St. John the Baptist, North Marldon, Devon and St. Andrew's Church, North Paignton. Incumbent in London of St. Paul's, Knightsbridge (from 1894); St. Cuthbert's, South Kensington (from 1897); St. Augustine's, Kilburn and St. Thomas's, Regent Street (from 1904). Composed Mass setings in C and in G, anthems, hymn tunes and an overture 'Memories of Ceylon'. His B.Mus. exercise was a *Harvest Cantata* for Five Voices and Orchestra; for his D.Mus. he submitted *From Death to Life Eternal* for Soprano, Tenor and Bass Solo and eight-voice Chorus.

STAINER, Sir John (1840-1901).
Born in London on 6 June 1840; died in Verona, Italy on 31 March 1901, nine days after the death of Queen Victoria.
The eighth of nine children of whom seven survived. On his mother's side, the Collier family were Huguenots who settled in Spitalfield as silk weavers. His father, William Stainer, was vestry clerk, register of births and a teacher at St. Thomas's School, Southwark.
William was a sufficiently accomplished flautist to be able to play hymn tunes, and he gave the young John lessons on the family's chamber organ.
At the age of five, John Stainer lost an eye in an accident.
William often took his son to the Church of St. Olave, Southwark where the organist was the composer of hymn tunes, **H.J. Gauntlett**. His deputy was **William Pole**, with whom John Stainer became acquainted. Pole held singing parties to which John Stainer was invited on a number of occasions.
John Stainer was a chorister of St. Paul's Cathedral (1847-1856), occasionally playing organ during services towards the end of this period. As solo boy he was rewarded by members of the congregation with coins, with which he treated his fellow-choristers to tarts and lemonade.
Studied music with the Cathedral organist, **John Goss**; **William Bayley**, a vicar-choral of St. Paul's; **Charles Steggall**, a professor of the Royal Academy of Music and **George Cooper**, assistant organist to John Goss. Steggall used Stainer in 1851 for the performance in Cambridge of his D.Mus. exercise. The university professor, **T.A. Walmisley** was greatly impressed by Stainer's voice and personality.

As a treble, John Stainer sang at the first English performance, on 6 April 1854, of Bach's *St. Matthew Passion*, mounted by the Bach Society under their conductor, the academic and composer **William Sterndale Bennett**. Sang at St. Paul's on the occasion of the Funerals of the painter J.M.W. Turner (1851) and of the soldier, the Duke of Wellington. Among his childhood friends were **Arthur Sullivan** and **Henry Gadsby**, who was later a vicar choral under Stainer at St. Paul's.

Stainer and Sullivan were fellow organ pupils of George Cooper. Lessons were given in the church of St. Sepulchre, Holborn. Cooper predicted a bright musical future for both boys.

John Stainer later described the depth to which standards at St. Paul's had dropped: the vicars choral were poor attenders and at some services a complete vocal part could be missing. Handel's 'Hallelujah Chorus' was once sung by a handful of boys plus two men.

Stainer continued to play organ occasionally at St. Paul's after his departure, and continued to take lessons with George Cooper through funding from the benefactor Maria Hackett.

Matriculated at Christ Church, Oxford in 1859. In the same year he graduated B.Mus at the University of Oxford on the strength of his exercise based on Psalm 103 'Praise the Lord O my soul'; D.Mus. followed in 1865 following the submission of the oratorio *Gideon*. By this time he had established a reputation and the statutory performance of *Gideon* was moved to the Sheldonian Theatre to accommodate the many members of the university who wished to hear the statutory performance of the work which, because of its length, was given in extract only. Among those who presented Stainer with his doctor's robes was H.R. Bramley, the hymn writer who later collaborated with Stainer in publishing a collection of carols. His other degrees included the Oxford B.A. (1864) and M.A. (1866) from St. Edmund's Hall.

At the age of 14 he was appointed organist of the London Church of SS Benet and Peter, Paul's Wharf (1854-1857), succeeding George Cooper. The Revd. J.H. Coward, a minor canon of St. Paul's, was also rector of the church.

Frederick Ouseley encountered John Stainer when on an examining visit to St. Paul's. On a later visit in 1856, Stainer was playing the organ. Expecting to encounter Goss or Cooper, Ouseley went into the organ loft to see if either man could recommend a young organist for the new establishment, St. Michael's College, Tenbury, Worcestershire which he had founded. Stainer was offered the position and accepted it. Ouseley later officiated at Stainer's marriage, on 27th December 1865.

St. Michael's was founded in 1856. Its objectives were to offer a daily choral service, to train boys to the necessary standard in music and Christianity and to serve as a model for choral worship. Stainer was organist from Michaelmas 1857 until 1859. The partnership between Ouseley and Stainer was successful. Stainer was regarded as efficient and conscientious, while Ouseley made available his extensive library of musical manuscripts. Stainer began to compose around this time, his works from this period including the anthems 'I saw the Lord' and 'The righteous live'.

Organist of Magdalen College, Oxford from January 1860 until 1872, succeeding **Benjamin Blyth.** On the death of **Stephen Elvey**, John Stainer became organist of the University Church of St. Mary-the-Virgin and University organist and was succeeded at Magdalen College by **Walter Parratt**.

In 1867 he was appointed University examiner, and one of the first candidates he confronted was **Hubert Parry**. Parry was an undergraduate of Exeter College and the two men had known each other since 1866, when Stainer had advised Parry on acquiring his B.Mus. Parry was a member of the Exeter College Music Society, which Stainer had run since 1864. Stainer had conducted some of Parry's works.

In 1865 the Reid Professorship of Edinburgh University had fallen vacant. Stainer was one of 21 candidates and on this occasion he was unsuccessful, the position being awarded to **H.S. Oakeley**.

Organist of the Royal Choral Society (1873-1888).

Following the retirement of John Goss in 1872, John Stainer was appointed organist of St. Paul's Cathedral. He resigned in 1888, and was succeeded by his former pupil and sub organist, **George Martin**.

The situation at St. Paul's had not improved since Stainer's time as a chorister. According to *The Choir*, the singing was in a bad way: the choir 'cannot even sing the Amens with ordinary care and decency'. Stainer was aware that he was expected to remedy the situation. He asked for and was given a period of two years in which to carry out his reforms, during which any shortcomings would be overlooked but at the end of which the situation would be reviewed.

Prior to Stainer's appointment, the Dean and Chapter had changed completely within two years. Robert Gregory and H.P. Liddon were appointed canons residentiary in December 1868 and September 1870 respectively, and R.W. Church was appointed dean in 1871. Canon Lightfoot was also sympathetic to the move for reform. The Oxford Movement had helped to create a climate in which dignity could be brought back into worship.

Stainer intended to increase the size of the choir by a factor of three. A residential choir school was opened in 1875 with accommodation for up to 40 boys. The task of bringing the music up to standard took its toll on him: after only 18 months at St. Paul's he had a nervous breakdown and went to the Isle of Wight to recuperate. In 1875 he was further afflicted; playing fives with Ouseley he was struck by the ball in the eye and was off work for six weeks as a result.

Awarded the honorary D.Mus. (1885) and honorary D.C.L. (1895) at the University of Durham. In 1878 he was made Chevalier of the Legion of Honour of France, following his service on the jury for organ building at the Paris Exhibition of that year.

Knighted at Windsor Castle on 17 July 1888, following his retirement from the position of organist of St. Paul's Cathedral.

In 1889, following the death of Ouseley, the Oxford professorship fell vacant. Stainer was successful from a field of 24 applicants, holding the position until his resignation in June 1899 when he was succeeded by Parry. Stainer was a lively and popular lecturer. He delivered one lecture per term in addition to the three given by the choragus, Parry.

Stainer was keen to establish a School of Music at the University but the time was not yet right. A similar issue in connection with the reform of the teaching of music at Oxford was the reconsideration in 1898 of the suggestion of three years' compulsory residence for music students, culminating in a B.A. Stainer was against the idea, feeling that it would be a burden on those musicians who had already spent time and achieved proficiency at one of the colleges of music. **Frederick Bridge** and **Ebenezer Prout** sided with Stainer while the proposed reform was supported by Parry, **C.V. Stanford**, **W.H. Hadow** and **Walter Parratt**. Stainer's view prevailed.

Stainer held a number of other significant musical posts. He succeeded **John Hullah**, who had resigned in 1883, as national inspector of music in the training colleges and schols. His assistants were **W.A. Barrett,** with whom he was joint editor of *Dictionary of Musical Terms*, and W.G. McNaught.

Stainer retained this position until his death, and his partnership with McNaught was particularly successful. Stainer supplied the technical musical expertise, while McNaught was a very experienced teacher of the subject. The job entailed a considerable amount of travel around the country. Frederick Bridge took over temporarily from Stainer when in 1896 the latter was ill. The demands on Stainer can be judged from the following account from Bridge in his autobiography *A Westminster Pilgrim*: 'I accompanied the late Dr. McNaught for a week on one of those whirlwind examination tours in which his soul delighted. The genial doctor was Sir John's assistant, but I believe Sir John's physical make up could not support the fierce bouts of inspecting that seemed to be the breath of life to McNaught. My week with him is a nightmare, in which processions of candidates come and go endlessly; in which we seem always to be boarding trains by the smallest margin of safety; in which night brings no rest, for we have to sit far into the small hours making up returns and preparing for the morrow; and generally the whole things proceeds at breathless speed and the problem emerges in all its stupendous proportions. I remember telling my companion that it really had been the hardest week's work I had ever done, and I would not undertake his job for £5,000 a year.'.

John Stainer held other important positions in education and administration. He taught at Guildhall School of Music and at the Crystal Palace School of Music. In November 1875 he became one of five principal professors of the National Training School of Music, succeeding Arthur Sullivan as principal in 1881. With William Pole, whom he had known since boyhood, John Stainer was one of the first two examiners for music degrees at the University of London (1879-1889).

In 1893, John Stainer helped to establish the Union of Graduates in Music, an organisation set up to protect the holders of British degrees in music from what was perceived as unfair competition from those who had obtained degrees alleged to be of little merit from certain Commonwealth and foreign institutions.

In a paper delivered to the Church Congress of 1872, John Stainer argued that it was the duty of those responsible for the service music in cathedrals to include the best examples of all periods and styles. At St. Paul's Cathedral, he brought into the repertory some of the works of his contemporaries. In a paper at a later Church Congress (1874), he put forward the view that church music should enjoy a freedom of style but it must nevertheless retain a special, devotional character.

His treatise *A Theory of Harmony* (1871) became popular, and Stainer wrote widely on topics concerning church music, and on education. Is also known for his *Dufay and his Contemporaries*.

A member of the Tunes Committee (from 1870) under **Henry Williams Baker** for *Hymns Ancient and Modern*. Editor of the first edition (1898) of *Church Hymnary*, and of *St. Paul's Chant Book*. Composed Services in A, B-flat, D and E-flat.

His anthems fall into three distinct periods: the time prior to his St. Paul's appointment (eight, including 'I saw the Lord' and 'The righteous live for evermore', composed at Tenbury while he was still in his teens), his St. Paul's years (fourteen including 'I desired wisdom: 1876) and thereafter (thirteen, including 'Blessed is the man': c1896).

With the needs of the choir of St. Paul's specifically in mind, he composed 17 Single Chants, 15 Double Chants and five Triple Chants.

His hymn tunes are found in some 40 different collections, published or private. Many have featured *in Hymns Ancient and Modern*. The best known tunes are perhaps 'Love Divine' (1889) and 'Vesper' (1874), the latter being commonly used with 'Holy Father, cheer our way', by Richard Robinson. Others include 'Charity' and 'Sebaste'. It was a source of great satisfaction to him that his hymn tunes were popularly accepted. In a speech to his fellow-musicians on one occasion, he confessed, 'I was one Sunday morning walking at some seaside place and on turning a corner I heard a number of Sunday School children singing a tune I had composed. I thought to myself: I want no higher reward than this for all my work. I can only tell you that I would not exchange it for the very finest monument in Westminster Abbey.'.

John Stainer's most famous work, *The Crucifixion* (1887) is often mistakenly described as an oratorio and then unfairly derided as lightweight. In fact it was written as 'a Meditation on the Sacred Passion of the Holy Redeemer'. At least two of the fine hymn tunes enjoy an independent existence for other texts and have found their way into modern hymnals. He did in fact write an oratorio *The Daughter of Jairus* in addition to *Gideon*, his degree exercise, and other large-scale choral works. His other music includes madrigals such as *Like as a Ship* (1865), and organ items.

STAINER (Bridge), Rosalind Flora (1884-1966)

Born in Westminster, London on 2 February 1884; died in Farnham Common, Buckinghamshire on 1 July 1966. Daughter of **John Frederick Bridge**. Married Dr. Edward Stainer, the second son of **John Stainer** on 1 June 1907. Studied harmony with her father and violin with various teachers. Composer of hymn tunes. Her 'Bethsaida' is one of two tunes that are found in *Methodist Hymn Book*! (1904) of which her father was music editor.

STANDFORD, Patric John (b.1939)

Born in Barnsley, Yorkshire on 5 February 1939. Studied at the Guildhall School of Music, London with **Edmund Rubbra** and later as Mendelssohn Scholar (1964-1965) with Gianfrancesco Malipiero and Witold Lutoslawski. Graduated M.Mus. at London University.

Was a professor of composition at the Guildhall School of Music (1969-1980) and head of music at Bretton Hall University College, Yorkshire (1980-1993). His compositions include six symphonies and concertos for cello and for violin. His sacred music includes the oratorios *Christus Requiem* and *Messiah Reborn*, a Stabat Mater, settings of the mass including Mass *of Our Lady and St. Rochus*, motets, and an anthem 'How amiable are thy dwellings'.

STANFORD, Charles Villiers (1852-1924)

Born in Dublin on 30 September 1854; died in London on 29 March 1924, being buried in Westminster Abbey near **Henry Purcell**.

The son of John Stanford, examiner in the Court of Chancery, Dublin who was a keen amateur bass singer. His mother was a pianist.

The young Stanford attended H. Tilney Basset's School in Lower Mount Street, Dublin. Educated musically in Dublin and London, where he moved in 1862 at the age of 10 in order to study with Ernst Pauer. In Dublin he studied with **R.P. Stewart** for organ and with Michael Quarry for piano, having previously had piano lessons with the Misses Flynn and Meake, former pupils of Ignaz Moscheles. Also studied music with Joseph Robinson.

By the age of 16 he had decided to be a musician. In 1870 he went up to the University of Cambridge, graduating B.A. with honours in Classics (1874), and M.A. (1877): his father had insisted on him continuing his general education. At Cambridge he was a choral scholar of Queens' College (from 1870), and studied at Trinity College (from 1873). Had sought a scholarship for Trinity Hall but was unsuccessful.

Organist of Trinity College, Cambridge (1873-1892) and prior to his appointment he had deputised for the incumbent, **J.L. Hopkins** when in 1872 he fell ill. The college authorities gave Stanford leave of absence in order to study in Germany. During his absence, **Alan Gray** and **Gerard Cobb** deputised for him, while **Joseph Eaton Faning** took over temporarily the conductorship of the Cambridge University Music Society which Stanford had held since the age of 20.

Stanford spent the second half of each of the years 1874 to 1876 in Germany, giving him the opportunity to attend the inaugural season at Bayreuth in 1876. Sat behind Wagner and Liszt in the audience. Commented on Wagner that the music was the music of Jekyll but the face was the face of Hyde, and of Liszt that as soon as his fingers touched the keys, the immense gap between him and all other pianists became apparent. A friend and admirer of Brahms.

Studied in Leipzig with Carl Reinecke and shared a room with **Bertram Luard-Selby**, later to be organist of Rochester Cathedral. Thereafter he continued his studies in Berlin with Friedrich Kiel. Stanford found Reinecke 'dry', Papperitz better and Kiel better still. He felt that he learned more from Kiel in the space of three months than he had from the others in three years.

Honorary degrees followed from the Universities of Durham (D.C.L.,1893) Leeds (LL.D., 1904) and Oxford (D.Mus., 1883) and from Trinity College, Cambridge (Mus.D., 1887).

In 1892, Trinity College, Dublin invited Parry to become a D.Mus., and Stanford to be a guest at the ceremony. It was not until 1921 that Trinity College, Dublin offered Stanford a D.Mus. But by this time his health had deteriorated and he could not accept.

Stanford was knighted in 1902.

At the opening of the Royal College of Music he was a professor of composition (from 1883). While he was still in his thirties he was appointed professor of music at the University of Cambridge (from 1887). Retained both positions until the year of his decease, although relations between Stanford and the University had become greatly strained by that time.

He had been under increasing pressure to resign. In his later years at Cambridge he was said to travel up by train, give a lesson in the station waiting room and then return to London without actually setting foot in the University. In 1899 his four lectures of that year were shunned, with only E.J. Dent attending. The following year was equally contentious, and only **Cyril Rootham** was prepared to attend. **A.H. Mann** of King's College was deeply opposed to him.

With Hubert Parry he was one of the two most influential academic figures in British music for generations. He presided over something of a musical renaissance, of which he was a part. Stanford and Parry respected each other but their relationship was at risk from the Irishman's fiery temper. Parry as director of the R.C.M. was Stanford's superior and found him troublesome on a number of occasions.

In 1893, Stanford presided at the jubilee celebrations of the C.U.M.S. Distinguished international composers were invited each to receive an honorary degree and hear their own compositions played. Saint-Saens, Bruch, Tchaikovsky and Boito accepted but Verdi, Brahms and Grieg did not.

Stanford's pupils form a long and distinguished list of performers composers and teachers: **Edgar Bainton**, composer and administrator; Arthur Benjamin, pianist, teacher and composer; **W.H. Bell**, composer and administrator; **Arthur Bliss** Master of the Queen's Music; Rutland Boughton, composer; Frank Bridge, composer; George Butterworth of *Shropshire Lad* fame; **Samuel Coleridge-Taylor**, composer; **Harold Darke**, organist and academic; **Walford Davies**, church musician and broadcasting pioneer; **Thomas Dunhill**, composer and a professor of the Royal Academy of Music; **George Dyson**, composer, academic and administrator; Cecil Forsyth, viola player and composer, with whom Stanford later collaborated in the book *History of Music* (1916); James Friskin, American pianist and composer; **Nicholas Gatty**, music critic and composer; Eugene Goossens composer; Ivor Gurney, poet and composer, who of all Stanford's pupils came closest to his definition of genius; Leslie Heward, conductor; **Gustav Holst,** composer of *The Planets Suite*; **Herbert Howells**, academic and church music composer; William Hurlestone, composer; **John Ireland**, a professor of the R.C.M. and composer, **Gordon Jacob**, academic and composer; **C.S. Lang**, composer; **E.J. Moeran**, composer and collector of folk songs; **S.H. Nicholson**, cathedral organist, a founder of what is now the Royal School of Church Music and a proprietor of *Hymns Ancient and Modern*; **Cyril Rootham**, lecturer of Cambridge University; **Harold Samuel**, pianist; **Martin Shaw**, composer and writer; **George Thalben-Ball**, organist of the Temple Church, London; S.P. Waddington, academic; **Ralph Vaughan Williams**, composer and academic; **Charles Wood**, composer and a professor of the R.C.M. and the University of Cambridge, and Haydn Wood, composer of 'Roses of Picardy'.

His rigorous and uncompromising teaching methods, depending on the pupil's point of view, were either a valuable grounding in the art or a threat to originality. Was both famous and feared for his unique brand of breezy ruthlessness with those students who failed to follow his instructions. At the R.C.M. he tried to provide the facilities for his pupils to hear played their own compositions.

He was however unsuccessful on a number of occasions when competing for important teaching positions. A contender for the vacancy created at the R.C.M. in 1894 by the resignation of George Grove, but Parry was appointed. In the same year, in his native Dublin, following the death of R.P. Stewart, Trinity College sought a new professor of music and the preferment went to **Ebenezer Prout**.

Conductor of the Bach Choir (1885-1902); the Leeds Philharmonic Society (from 1897); the Leeds Festival (1901-1910), for which he composed his very popular Songs of The Sea (1904) and Songs of The Fleet (1910); and the Cambridge Music Society (from 1873) for 20 years. A member of the Philharmonic Society.

As well as being a conductor, composer and academic he was a pianist and a collector and editor of Irish folk tunes. Collaborated with Alfred Graves, a friend from childhood, in a set of arrangements of old Irish melodies.

Published an autobiography *Pages from an Unwritten Diary* (1914). Among other things it gives an insight into the state of music at the University of Cambridge in the early 1870s: 'Music in Cambridge was then in a disorganised state. There was plenty of talent but no means of concentrating it for useful purposes. The University Musical Society, which was one of the most ancient in England, was at low ebb.'

At the age of eight, Stanford composed a march which two or three years later was used in a pantomime: *Puss in Boots* at the Theatre

Royal, Dublin. Composed some songs at Cambridge but his career as a composer accelerated when he won second prize at the Alexandra Palace, London in 1876 for a symphony. His Services are very well known today and include settings in A, in B-flat, in C, in F, and in G. A Requiem Mass was composed for the Birmingham Festival of 1897. His anthems include 'The Lord is my Shepherd', 'Ye choirs of new Jerusalem', 'How beauteous are their feet who stand on Zion's hill' and 'Glorious and powerful God'. *Three Motets* (*Justorum Animae, Coelos ascendit hodie* and *Beati quorum via*) originally written as Graces for Trinity College, Cambridge are now used everywhere as anthems during Divine Service. Other items of church music include a Chant in A-flat and another in C, and the hymn tunes 'Orient', 'Engelberg', 'Alverstone' and 'Blackrock'. His evocative setting of the Irish traditional melodies to Mrs. Alexander's versification of 'St. Patrick's Breastplate' is found nowadays in many hymnals.

An oratorio *The Three Holy Children* was composed for the Birmingham Festival of 1885. There were nine operas, the first and last being *The Veiled Prophet of Khorassan* (produced in 1881) and *The Travelling Companion* (produced in 1926). A friend of Alfred, Lord Tennyson, who had commissioned incidental music for his play *Queen Mary* at the Lyceum, London in 1876.

Composed seven symphonies in all: his Irish Symphony was very popular abroad. His other instrumental works include eight string quartets, six Irish Rhapsodies, items for organ, chamber and piano music.

STANIFORTH, Thomas Worsley (1845-1909)

Born in Sheffield, Yorkshire on 7 June 1845; died in Sheffield on 25 March 1909. Organist of St. Peter's Church, London Docks, where the foundation stone was laid at a ceremony featuring the hymn 'Jerusalem, my happy home' to a tune by Staniforth. Organist of the churches of St. Paul, Brighton, Sussex and St. Paul, Regent's Park, London. Taught music at Highgate School, and was known as an organist and pianist. Composer of hymn tunes, including a setting of the hymn 'O Thou, our soul's Salvation,' which was sung at St. Paul's Cathedral on 27 February 1872 to celebrate the recovery from illness of the Prince of Wales.

STANISTREET, Dr. Henry Dawson (?-1883)

Died in Dublin on 1 August 1883. A chorister of York Minster. Graduated B.Mus. (1862), and D.Mus. (1878) at the University of Dublin. From 1862 he held an organistship in Shandon, Cork. From around 1871 until at least 1877 he was organist of Tuam Cathdral and was later organist of Trinity College, Dublin. Composer of anthems, settings of Psalms 16 'Preserve me, O God' and 69 'Save me, O God', and other items of church music.

STANLEY, Charles John (1713-1786)

John Stanley (some sources dispute the first name) was born in London on 17 January 1713; died in London on 19 May 1786. Following an accident at the age of two he was blind for the remainder of his life.

Studied music with **John Reading** and **Maurice Greene**, organist of St. Paul's Cathedral and graduated B.Mus. at the University of Oxford (1729).

His career centred in London: he lived in Hatton Garden and he was organist of the Churches of All Hallow, Bread Street (1723-1726 or 1727) and St. Andrew, Holborn (1726-1786) but he is best known as organist of the Temple Church (1739-1786), where it is said that up to 50 organists at a time would gather to hear the final

voluntary, including his friend **Handel**. The artist Gainsborough painted his portrait.

In 1779 he succeeded **William Boyce** as master of the Royal Band of Music. Had an excellent musical memory and after hearing an oratorio played through he could accompany it thereafter. An original member, from 1739, of the Royal Society of Musicians, and he was active as an organist into his old age.

Composed three oratorios including *Jephthah* (1757) and *Fall of Egypt* (1774), anthems including 'Hearken unto me, my people' and 'O Lord, my God', songs such as 'High Ho!', and organ works including voluntaries. His dramatic pastoral *Arcadia* was composed for the Wedding, on 26 October 1761, of George III.

STANLEY, Samuel (1767-1822)

Born in Birmingham in 1767, being baptised on 15 May; died in Birmingham on 29 October 1822.

At the age of 20, he was appointed precentor of the Carr's Lane Congregational Chapel, Birmingham, (1787-1820). In 1818 the Chapel moved to a larger site in Steelhouse Lane, known as the Ebenezer Chapel. The congregation had grown considerably, due at least in part to the high standard of music that Samuel Stanley had brought about.

A cellist of the Birmingham Theatre, the Birmingham Festival Choral Society (1802-1818) and the Vauxhall Gardens, London (from 1792). For a time he was landlord of the Crown Tavern, Great Charles Street, Birmingham. A Handel enthusiast, with an expert opinion as to performance of his works.

His hymn tunes include 'Calvary', 'Doversdale' and 'Warwick', which are found in the Revised Edition (1927) of *Church Hymnary*. A collector and editor of church music. His *Twenty-Four Tunes in Four Parts* (1819) included 'Warwick' as a setting of Psalm 23. In 1830 he issued three books of Psalm and hymn tunes, many of which were composed by him. His most famous tune is 'Simeon', which with four others is found in *Methodist Hymn Book* (1933).

STANTON, Dr. Walter Kendall (1891-1978)

Born in Dauntsey, Wiltshire on 29 September 1891; died in Sedgehill, Shaftesbury, Dorset on 30 June 1978.

At the age of 10 he became a chorister of Salisbury Cathedral under Charles South. Went on to study at Lancing College, Sussex and at Merton College, Oxford as organ scholar (1909-1913). Graduated B.A. (1915), B.Mus., M.A. (1915) and D.Mus. (1935) at the University of Oxford.

Taught at a number of public schools, including St. John's School, Leatherhead, Surrey (1914-1915), St. Edward's, Oxford (1915-1924) and Wellington College, Berkshire (1924-1937). Director of music at the University of Reading, Berkshire (1927-1937) and to the Midland Region of the B.B.C. (1937-1945).

Became, in 1947, the first professor of music at the University of Bristol and his first nomination as honorary Doctor of Music included the composer **Ralph Vaughan Williams**. Retired in 1957.

President of the Incorporated Society of Musicians (from 1953) and of the Union of Graduates in Music (1953-1957), an organisation which **John Stainer** and others had been instrumental in setting up to protect holders of British degrees in music from competition from those to whom foreign degrees of questionable merit had been awarded.

Composed a Cantate Domino and Deus Misereatur (1956), a Magnificat and Nunc Dimittis (1956), anthems, two motets for double choir *The spacious firmament* (1936) and *Sing we triumphant hymns* (1937). Contributed a total of 26 hymn tunes to *B.B.C. Hymn Book* (1951) of which he was editor-in-chief, and made a major contribution to the *Wellington College Hymn Book* of 1937. His tunes, amounting to nearly 50, include 'Hampton Lucy', 'Silchester', 'Linton' and 'Crudwell'.

STAPLES, Henry James (1891-1943)
Born in Poplar, London in 1891; died in Harrow, Middlesex on 2 December 1943. Published *The Choirmaster and Organist* in 1939. Composed, among others, the anthems 'Alleluia! now is Christ risen' (1933) for Easter-tide and 'Almighty and everlasting God' (1935), and songs. He lived in Nightingale Road, Poplar, after which he named the hymn tune 'Poplar', first published on a Sunday School Anniversary hymn sheet.

STARK, Humphrey John (1854-?)
Born on 22 May 1854. Graduated B.Mus. at the University of Oxford (1875). One of the founders of Trinity College of Music, London. Organist of Holy Trinity Church, Tulse Hill, London (from 1875). Presented various papers to the College of Organists and to other institutions. Composed an Evening Service with accompaniment for orchestra, other services, anthems including the festival anthem 'Praise the Lord, O my soul' (1875), a cantata *The rival seasons* (1885) and organ works.

STARMER, William Wooding (1866-1927)
Born in Wellingborough, Northamptonshire on 4 November 1866; died in Tunbridge Wells, Kent on 27 October 1927. Trained at the Royal Academy of Music. Organist to the Marquis of Northampton at Castle Ashby (from 1883) and of St. Mark's Church, Tunbridge Wells (from 1888). An expert on campanology, and he was professor of campanology at the University of Birmingham - believed to be the only such chair in the world. Contributed articles to Grove's *Dictionary of Music and Musicians*. Composed a Te Deum and Jubilate in D (1899), the anthem 'Come Holy Ghost, our souls inspire' (1904), a collection *Carols for Christmastide* (1892-1899), and hymn tunes.

STARNES, Percy James (1864-?)
Born in Lewes, Sussex in 1864; died in the U.S.A., where he is known still to have been alive in 1932. Composed the motet *Light of the world* (1902), and hymn tunes.

STATHAM, Francis Reginald (1844-1908)
Born in Everton, Liverpool on 6 February 1844; died in Richmond, Surrey on 4 March 1908. Emigrated to South Africa, where he was the minister of a Scottish Church. Wrote poems and novels, including *Mr. Magnus*. Composed a Magnificat and Nunc Dimittis in E-flat (1898), the anthem 'Rejoice in the Lord' (1892), hymn tunes and a cantata *Prosperity and Praise* (1892).

STATHAM, Dr. Heathcote Dicken (1889-1973)
Born in Holborn, London on 7 December 1889; died in Norwich, Norfolk on 29 October 1973. The son of H. Heathcote Statham, architect and author of *The Organ and its Position in Musical Art*. Attended St. Michael's College, Tenbury, Worcestershire (1900-1905) and Gresham's School, Holt, Norfolk (from 1905). Music scholar (1908) and deputy organist of Gonville and Caius College, Cambridge where he graduated Mus.B. (1911) and Mus.D. (1923).

Also studied for one year (1912) at the Royal College of Music with **Walter Parratt**.
Appointed C.B.E. in 1967.
Organist of the Cathedrals of Calcutta (from 1913) and Norwich (1928-1936). Between those appointments he was organist of St. Michael's College, Tenbury, Worcestershire (1920-1925) and St. Mary's Church, Southampton, Hampshire (1926-1928).
For 25 years (1936-1961) he was one of the conductors of the triennial Norwich Festival. Between 1943 and 1946 he conducted three seasons of concerts given by the London Symphony Orchestra. A local philharmonic society conductor.
His Preces and Responses are still popular today, and his other church music includes an Evening Service in E Minor, a Te Deum composed for the centenary of St. Michael's College, the anthems 'Praise the Lord' and 'Be glad and rejoice', and hymn tunes such as 'Arncliffe'. Also composed works for organ including Rhapsody on a Ground, and he was the editor of a set of 14 anthems by **John Blow**, issued in 1925.

STATHAM, Revd. Dr. William (1832-1898)
Born in Tarporley, Cheshire on 26 September 1832; died in Heswall, Cheshire on 7 January 1898. Educated at Marlborough College, Wiltshire and atUniversity College, Durham where he graduated B.A. (1856) and D.Mus. (1876). Ordained deacon in 1858. Having served as curate the Parish of Tunstall, Staffordshire, he was vicar and organist of Ellesmere Port, Cheshire (1866-1898). His church music is found in *Primitive Methodist Hymnal*, *Chants Ancient and Modern* and *Hymns Ancient and Modern*, which includes his tunes 'High Cliff', 'Latchford', 'Styall' and 'St. Margaret'. Also composed a Service in F (1869), an oratorio *The Beauty of Holiness* (1888), songs and organ arrangements.

STEANE, Bruce Henry Dennis (1866-?)
Born in Camberwell, London on 22 June 1866. A chorister of St. Augustine's Church, Forest Hill, London at the age of eight; from 12 he was assistant organist there. Organist of St. Mary's Church, Cuddington. Organist of the Kentish Churches of St. Bartholmew, Swanley; St. Mary, Kemsing (from 1903) and St. Peter, Seal, Sevenoaks. Organist of Whitechapel Parish Church, London and of St. Bartholomew's Hospital (from 1905). Organist and choirmaster of Combe Martin Parish Church, Devon (from 1918). Composed services, anthems, songs, part songs, a sacred cantata *The Ascension* (1895), organ works and items for piano.

STEED, Albert Orlando (1839-1881)
Born in 1839; died on 25 October 1881. Studied music with **William Sterndale Bennett**, Cambridge professor of music. A teacher of music at the Totteridge Park School, Hertfordshire (c1860-1862). Organist of Long Melford Parish Church, Suffolk (from 1865) and of Holy Trinity Church, Penge, Kent, where he was still in office at the time of his death. The author of *Music in Play* and *Music in Earnest* (1873). Composed and published as a collection *Seven Tunes to Popular Hymns and Two Kyries* (1878), songs including 'Before sunset'(1873) and duets. Composed the anthem 'Sing unto the Lord.

STEEL, Christopher Charles (1939-1991)
Born in London on 15 January 1939; died on 31 December 1991. Educated at Shrewsbury School and the Royal Academy of Music, and in Munich, Germany. Assistant director of music at Cheltenham College Junior School, Gloucestershire (1963-1965)

and at Bradfield College, Berkshire (1966-1969); director of music of Bradfield College (from 1968). Composer of a Mass In Five Movements (1968), the anthem 'O clap your hands together' (1971) and *The Lord's Prayer*. Also composed the cantata *Jerusalem*, and pieces for organ.

STEGGALL, Dr. Charles (1826-1905)

Born in London on 3 June 1826; died in Lambeth, Surrey on 7 June 1905. The father of **Reginald Steggall**.

In accordance with his father's wishes, Charles Steggall began his career in business rather than in music, but this was short-lived. Following a year's private organ tuition, he studied at the Royal Academy of Music (from 1847) with **William Sterndale Bennett**, who became a life long friend. Graduated Mus.B. (1851) and Mus.D. (also 1851) at the University of Cambridge: the treble soloist in the performance of his exercise for the doctorate was the young **John Stainer**, later organist of St. Paul's Cathedral.

A professor of harmony and organ at the R.A.M. (1851-1903), although on joining the R.A.M., organ was as yet unrecognised as a subject in its own right.. Is said to have trained more organists than any other teacher in the country and they include **Joseph Barnby**, **George Bennett**, Frederick Docker, E.H. Lemare and H.R. Rose. In 1882 he examined D.Mus. candidates at the University of Cambridge.

Organist in London of Christ Church, Maida Vale (from 1848); Christ Church, Lancaster Gate, where he was the first organist following the church's consecration (from 1855) and of Lincoln's Inn Chapel (from 1864). On his death his was succeeded by his son Reginald. Organist and choirmaster of Clapham Grammar School.

One of the founders of the College of Organists, giving the inaugural lecture on 18 October 1864. Honorary secretary of the Bach Society for the whole of its existence (1849-1870).

Charles Steggall had a life-long interest in hymns and hymnology and published his first collection of tunes while he was still a student. In 1852 he lectured at the Crosby Hall, Liverpool on 'Music as applied to Religion'.

Editor of *Church Psalmody* (1848) and succeeded **W.H. Monk** as musical editor of *Hymns Ancient and Modern*, where he worked on the Revision, starting in 1894. Steggall approved the proofs in 1904, which was one of his last acts of work.

Composed a Morning and Evening Service in F (1906), a Magnificat and Nunc Dimittis in C (1901), a Cantate Domino and Deus Misereatur in C for Voices and Orchestra (1880), settings of Psalm 105 'O give thanks' for Solo Voices, eight-part Chorus and Orchestra and Psalm 33 'Rejoice in the Lord'. His anthems include the harvest-tide work 'Praised be the Lord' (1869) and 'Remember now thy Creator', and he produced sets of Responses to the Commandments in F and in G.

His hymn tunes include 'Christchurch', 'Day of Praise', 'Morwellham', 'St. Ambrose' and 'Bonar'.

STEGGALL, Reginald (1867-1938)

Born in Bayswater, London on 17 April 1867; died in 1938. The son of **Charles Steggall**. Educated at Westminster Abbey and at the Royal Academy of Music (from 1884), winning a Balfe Scholarship in 1888. His teachers included **George Macfarren**, **Ebenezer Prout**, H.R. Eyers, Oscar Beringer and his father. Organist of St. Anne's Church, Soho, London (1886-1887) but gave up the position in order to assist his father at the Lincoln's Inn Chapel. In 1905, following the death of his father, he became organist there. Lived in the London suburb of Chiswick. A

professor of organ at the R.A.M. (from 1895). Composed a Mass for Voices, Organ and Orchestra, a Festival Evening Service for Voices and Orchestra in G (1895), anthems, two symphonies, and songs.

STEPHENS, Charles Edward (1821-1891)

Born in St. Marylebone, London on 18 March 1821; died in Paddington, London on 13 July 1891. A nephew of Catherine Stephens, Countess of Essex (1791-1882). Studied music at an early age with Cipriani Potter for composition, J.A. Hamilton for harmony and other subjects, and with Henry Blagrove. A piano recitalist. Organist of a number of London Churches: St. Mark's, Myddleton Square (from 1843); Holy Trinity, Paddington (from 1846); St. John's, Hampstead (from 1856); St. Mark's, Hamilton Terrace (1862-1863); St. Clement Danes, Strand (from 1864) and St. Saviour, Paddington (1872-1875). A member of the Royal Society of Musicians (from 1843), an original member of the Musical Association (from 1874), at which he presented papers, and of the Philharmonic Society, of which he was later director (from 1857). An examiner for musical degrees at the University of Cambridge (from 1885). Editor of *The Choir Chant Book* (1882), a publication containing 513 chants with biographies of their composers. Composed a Magnificat and Nunc Dimittis in F (1880), hymn tunes including 'Blagdon', 'Howley Place', 'In Storm' and 'Westbourne'. His Single Chant in E is found in *Cathedral Psalter Chants* (1875), His anthems include 'O praise the Lord, all ye nations' (?1860) and 'We have seen His star'. Composed orchestral works including two symphonies and piano works such as a Sonata in A-flat (1882).

STEPHENS, Dr. John (c1720-1780)

Born, possibly in Gloucester, around 1720; died in Salisbury, Wiltshire on 15 December 1780. Probably a chorister of Gloucester Cathedral. Held a doctorate in music, possibly from the University of Cambridge. Organist of St. James's Church, Bristol prior to his appointment as organist of Salisbury Cathedral, where he succeeded Edward Thompson. Conducted the Music Meeting in Gloucester (1766) and taught many of the gentry and the affluent in Gloucester and surrounding areas. **Highmore Skeats** the elder published *Cathedral Music* in 1805, containing the works of John Stephens. His anthems include 'Sing ye unto the Lord' and 'Like as the Hart'.

STEVENS, Revd. Arthur Henry (1857-?)

Born in Barnes, London in 1857. Organist and organ scholar of Worcester College, Oxford. Graduated B.A. (1881), M.A. (1881) and, at Worcester College, Oxford, B.Mus. (1883). Organist and choirmaster of Holy Trinity Church, Roehampton and St. John's Church, Hammersmith, London. Director of music, organist and precentor of Dover College, Kent (1882-1906). In 1887 he gave organ recitals in Canterbury Cathedral. Professor of singing at the Girls' Public Day School Trust (1888-1900); chairman of the Local Examiners of the Royal College of Music (1885-1906) and an examiner for the Kent County Scholarship at the R.C.M. (from 1892). Vicar of Chattisham, Ipswich (from 1906). Composed a Magnificat and Nunc Dimittis in G (1894), a Te Deum in chant form (1905), a prize hymn tune, anthems including 'Wherewithal shall a young man cleanse his way?' (1904), Christmas carols, school songs and a Scherzo for Organ. Composed as his degree exercise a cantata *The Song of Tobit* for Solo Voices, Chorus, Organ and Orchestra.

STEVENS, Richard John Samuel (1757-1837)
Born in London on 27 March 1757; died in Peckham, London on 23 September 1837. A chorister of St. Paul's Cathedral under **William Savage**. Organist of the Temple Church, London (1786-1810) and the Charter House. Gresham professor of music (from 1801) and, from 1831, a judge for the Gresham Prize, an award put up to encourage a high standard of composition in church music. The chairman was **William Crotch**, Oxford professor of music and the third judge was **William Horsley**, a founder of the Philharmonic Society. In 1833 the entry from **S.S. Wesley**, *The Wilderness*, was considered far too modern and unsuitable, much to Wesley's disgust. Compiled a collection of sacred music. His own compositions include a setting of the Collect for the first Sunday in Advent 'Almighty God, give us Grace' (1856), music for the stage, glees such as 'From Oberon in Fairyland' (1794) and 'Ye spotted snakes' (c1785), and songs. Won composition prizes from the Catch Club.

STEVENSON, Sir John Andrew (1761/2-1833)
Born in Dublin in 1761 or 1762; died in Headfort House, County Meath on 14 September 1833. His father, John Stevenson, was a violinist from Glasgow who had settled in Dublin. A chorister of St. Patrick's Cathedral, Dublin (1775-1780). Studied music with Samuel Murphy and Richard Woodward junior. Awarded the honorary D.Mus. at Trinity College, Dublin (1791).
The first Irish church musician to be knighted (1872) and the last until **R.P. Stewart**, Dublin professor of music was similarly honoured in 1872.
A vicar choral of the Dublin Cathedrals of St. Patrick (from 1783), where a memorial window was dedicated to him following his death, and Christ Church (from 1800). A bass singer.
Patronised by Mrs. Craddock, wife of the dean of St. Patrick's and became something of a fashionable figure in Dublin society. The first organist of the Chapel Royal, Dublin Castle (from 1814).
Thomas Moore was a poet who provided words for folk tunes collected by John Stevenson. The collaboration resulted in Moore's *Irish Melodies... Issued in 10 parts* plus a Supplement between the years 1807 and 1834. Later it was re-edited by **C.V. Stanford**.
Two volumes of John Stevenson's Morning and Evening Services and anthems were published in 1825. His anthems include 'O Lord, our Governor' (1899) and 'Lord, how are they increased that trouble me'. Also composed chants, and a set of Preces and Responses that was subsequently used by both Dublin Anglican Cathedrals on festive occasions. Also an oratorio *Thanksgiving*, canons, catches and songs. A revival of his works took place in English cathedrals in the early part of the 19th century.

STEVENSON, Peter Anthony Stanley (b.1928)
Born in Norwich, Norfolk on 28 August 1928. Educated at the City of Norwich School; Hatfield College, Durham - where he read music - and the Royal College of Music. Graduated B.A. (1951) and M.A. (1958) at the University of Durham. Organist of Berkhamstead Parish Church, Hertfordshire (1953-1956) and sub organist of Ripon Cathedral (1956-1958). Organist of Portsmouth Cathedral (1965-1969). Since then he has been a freelance lecturer, journalist and examiner for the Associated Board of the Royal Schools of Music (from 1969). A lecturer in the extra-mural department of the University of Southampton (from 1969). A special commissioner of the Royal School of Church Music (from 1965). Director of music of Wrekin College, Shropshire (1958-1965) and Portsmouth Grammar School (1965-1969). Extra-mural

lecturer for the University of Birmingham (1958-1965). Music master of Berkhamstead School (1953-1956). His works include a set of Ferial Versicles and Responses for Treble Voices.

STEVENSON, Dr. Robert (c1542-?)
Graduated B.Mus (1587) and D.Mus. (1596) at the University of Oxford. Organist of Chester Cathedral (1571-1597), and possibly before and after these dates. By Christmas 1571 he was master of the choristers. Composed the anthem 'When the Lord turned'.

STEWART, Arthur Charles Lestoc Hylton
See **HYLTON-STEWART**, Arthur Charles Lestoc (1884-1932)

STEWART, Dr. Haldane Campbell (1868-1942)
Born in London on 28 February 1868; died on 16 June 1942. A chorister of Magdalen College, Oxford (1879-1882) under **Walter Parratt**. Classics exhibitioner of Magdalen College (1887-1891) and graduated B.A. (1893), M.A. (1919), B.Mus. (1915) and D.Mus. (1919). Assistant master of Lancing School, Sussex (1891-1896) and of Wellington College, Berkshire (1896-1898). Director of music of Tonbridge School, Kent (1898-1919). Organist of Magdalen College (1919-1938) and choragus of the University. During World War II, Haldane Stewart acted as organist of Magdalen College in the absence on war service with the R.A.F. of **William Neil McKie**. Composed church music including a Magnificat and Nunc Dimittis (1939), a carol 'Penned are the sheep' (1926) and the anthem 'King of Glory'. His Latin motet *Veni, Sancte Spiritus* and his setting of the May morning hymn *Te Deum Patrem colimus* have both recently been published.

STEWART, Sir Robert Prescott (1825-1894)
Born in Dublin on 16 December 1825; died in Dublin on 25 March 1894.
The son of Charles F. Stewart, Librarian of King's Inns, Dublin.
A chorister of Christ Church Cathedral, Dublin, sometimes acting as organist in the absence of John Robinson.
At the age of eight or nine he could transpose at sight at the keyboard. Had a remarkable musical memory. Graduated with the Dublin B.Mus. (1846) and D.Mus. (1851).
Knighted in 1872.
In 1844, while still only in his 19th year, on the death of John Robinson, Stewart was appointed organist of Trinity College, Dublin and of Christ Church Cathedral. Remained in both positions until the year of his death.
At Christ Church he often strongly disagreed with the succentor's choice of music. At Trinity College he made the entrance examinations more stringent and he aimed 'to educate and make gentlemen of our professional musicians' and to raise their status from that of craftsmen to artists.
Unpaid organist of St. Patrick's Cathedral, Dublin (1852-1861), resigning in order to take up the offer of a half vicar choralship. The arrangement was that he would continue to play organ at services on Sunday evening, when his successor, William Murphy, would take his place in the choir.
Contributed essays to Cassell's *Biographical Dictionary* and articles to Grove's *Dictionary of Music and Musicians*.
Professor of music, at the age of 36, of the University of Dublin (from 1861). Raised the degree standards, insisting that candidates in music had a good general education. His was the first university in the British Isles to insist on a written paper as part of the examination for the bachelor's degree.

In 1865 he founded the Dublin Glee and Madrigal Union.

Succeeded **E.T. Chipp**, who had returned to England to become organist of Ely Cathedral, as organist of the Belfast Vocal Union, Belfast (1867). At the society's performances, Stewart played organ while a Dublin colleague, Joseph Robinson conducted. In 1872 he was invited to represent Ireland at the Boston Peace Festival, U.S.A. Declined, but sent instead an Ode composed especially for the occasion which combined Irish and American airs. In the same year he was appointed professor of theory of the Royal Irish Academy of Music.

Conductor of the Dublin Philharmonic Orchestra (from 1873). Travelled widely as a lecturer and a performer, aiming to escape at least once a year from what he considered the 'stagnant' musical atmosphere of Ireland. In 1876 he attended the first performance of the Ring cycle of operas at Bayreuth, Germany.

In 1878 he gave two recitals in Manchester Town Hall, the first of which was attended by some 800 people. As well as being an expert organist he was an authority on bagpipes.

Music editor of *Irish Church Hymnal* (1874), contributing 10 tunes of his own. Music adviser for the re-publication of the work in 1891. Edited a collection of chants which appeared in 1883 and contained 13 items by himself.

Composed a Service in E-flat for Double Choir (1878), a Service in C, a Service in G (1869), Chants, Responses to the Commandements in A, in E Minor and in G, anthems including 'Thou, O God, art praised in Zion' (1876), and 'O Lord, my God', motets, hymn tunes including 'Adrian,' 'Minster', 'Worship', 'St. Helen's' and 'Coeli Enarrant', cantatas and an Ode to Industry for the Cork Exhibition of 1852. In 1880 he admitted destroying most of what he had composed before then, confessing that he had 'spoiled as much music paper as most men of my age'.

STIDOLPH, Harold Edward (1845-?)

Born in Tonbridge, Kent in 1845. An articled pupil of **W.B. Gilbert**, organist of Tonbridge Parish Church where, at the age of eight, he was allowed to play at services. Attended Tonbridge Grammar School and played organ there. Organist and choirmaster of Speen Parish Church, Berkshire (from 1863); Chelmsford Parish Church in Essex (from 1864); Ealing Parish Church, London (from 1876) and Christ Church, Ealing (from 1880). Instituted a series of concerts in Ealing. Emigrated to South Africa in 1884. Settled firstly in Cape Town and then in Johannesburg, where he was organist of St. Augustine's Church, Doornfontein. Later moved to Wynberg, Cape Town. In 1887 he toured Cape Colony with Eduard Remenyi, the Hungarian violinist. An opera conductor and writer of verse. Composed church music including a Thanksgiving Hymn (1897), a national part song 'Around the throne of England'(1892), songs and a colonial national anthem.

STIMPSON, James (1820-1886)

Born in Lincoln on 29 February 1820; died in Birmingham on 4 October 1886. Brother of **Orlando Stimpson**. His father had been a lay vicar of Lincoln Cathedral. The family moved to Durham, where James became a chorister of the Cathedral (1822). Articled to Richard Ingham, organist of Carlisle Cathedral (from 1834). Organist of St. Andrew's Church, Newcastle-on-Tyne (from 1836) before he succeeded Ingham in 1841. The appointment was however short-lived. Moved to Birmingham, where he became organist of the Town Hall (from 1842) and of a number of Churches including St. Martin's (1852-1856) and St. Paul's. Founder, and the first conductor (1843-1855) of the Birmingham

Festival Choral Society and it was in this capacity that he trained the choir and played organ for the first performance of Mendelssohn's *Elijah* in 1846. Composed the anthem 'O Lord, rebuke me not'.

STIMPSON, Orlando John (1835-1916)

Born in Durham on 21 June 1835; died in Exeter, Devon on 16 November 1916. The brother of **James Stimpson**. A chorister of Durham Cathedral. Graduated B.Mus. (1871) at New College, Oxford and in the same year he was awarded the honorary B.Mus. at the University of Durham. Organist and choirmaster in Durham of Bethel Chapel (from 1855), St. Cuthbert's Church (from 1869) and St. Nicholas's Church (from 1872). Music master of Durham Diocesan Training College (from 1861). Organist and choirmaster of St. George's Church, Brandon Hill, Bristol (from 1875); St. James's Church, Bury St. Edmunds, Suffolk (from 1877) and Christ Church, Tunbridge Wells, Kent (1879-1882). Taught music in Tunbridge Wells and subsequently retired to Paignton, Devon. The author of *Singing Class Book for use in Elementary Schools* (1877). Composed Kyries and hymn tunes. His degree exercise was a setting of Psalm 1 'Blessed is the Man'.

STIRLING (Bridge), Elizabeth (1819-1895)

Born in Greenwich, London on 26 February 1819; died in London on 25 March 1895. Studied with W.B. Wilson, Edward Holmes, **George Macfarren** and **W.H. Holmes**. Studied organ and piano in Germany. Organist of All Saints' Church, Poplar, London (1839-1858) and of St. Andrew's Church, Undershaft (1858-1880).

In 1856 she submitted an exercise for Five Voices and Orchestra based upon Psalm 130 'Out of the deep' to the University of Oxford. It satisfied the examiners and had it been the work of a man, a B.Mus. would have been conferred. At the time however, the University had no powers to award the degree to a woman.

An expert organist, and one of the first to revive Bach's fugues, playing them in London churches and at the International Exhibition of 1862. She fulfilled the expectations of her expressed in *The Times* in 1837 when as a 17 year old she had given a recital at St. Sepulchre's Church in London: 'She must rise to a distinguished place in her profession.'

She composed a harvest hymn 'Now autumn strews on ev'ry plain' (1844) and part songs including 'All along the barley' (1851).

STOBBART, William James (1868-?)

Born in London in 1868. Graduated B.Mus. at the University of Durham (1898). He lived and taught in the town of Middlesbrough, Yorkshire where he was organist and choirmaster of the South Bank Wesleyan Church (1886-1894); the Grange Road Free Church (1894-1936) and the Park Presbyterian Church, Linthorpe (from 1936). A critic for *North East Gazette* and an honorary local examiner for the Royal College of Music. Composed church music including Vesper Hymn (1905), 'O God of mercy' (1909), prize hymn tunes, and pieces for organ and for piano. Submitted as his degree exercise a setting of Psalm 9 'I will give thanks unto Thee' for Solo Voices, Chorus and String Orchestra.

STOCK, Alfred Robert (1888-?)

Born in London in 1888. Studied music with Sydney Scott, and became a recitalist. Was on active service in World War I. Organist and choirmaster in London of the Bayswater United Methodist Church (1905-1909), the Congregational Churches of Chelsea, London (1909-1913) and Putney (1913-1914), and Essex Church,

Kensington (1914-1933). Composed anthems including 'The way of Zion' and 'Great and marvellous are Thy works,' and songs.

STOCK, Sarah Geraldina (1838-1898)

Born in Islington, London on 27 December 1838; died in Penmaenmawr, Caernarvonshire, Wales on 29 August 1898. Author of hymns and composer of hymn tunes.

STOCKS, Dr. George Gilbert (1877-1960)

Born in Huddersfield, Yorkshire in 1877; died in Surrey on 20 October 1960.

Trained privately in music and he graduated B.Mus. (1903) and D.Mus. (1908) at St. Edmund Hall, Oxford.

Organist of Almondbury Parish Church (1893-1900); St. John's Church, Cowley, Oxford (1900-1902) and St Edward's School, Oxford, where he also taught (1902-1912). Choirmaster of St. Margaret's Church, Oxford (1904-1906).

Chief music master of Repton School, Derbyshire (1912-1934). Then took up an appointment with the London College of Music as a travelling examiner, in connection with which he toured the U.K. In 1950 he retired and went to live in Croydon, Surrey at a home for retired professionals.

His *Hymns for use in Chapel* (1924) was designed as a supplement to *Hymns Ancient and Modern* for Repton School. It contained 22 of his own tunes for unison singing, five of his arrangements and a further 22 tunes by other composers. His hymn tune 'Village Sunset' was contained in the Revised Edition (1927) of *Church Hymnary*. 'Northleach' is found in *Hymns Ancient and Modern*. Composed a Holy Communion Service in F (1914) and a Magnificat and Nunc Dimittis in C (1903). His B.Mus. exercise was 'The Glories of Blood and State' while for his D.Mus. he submitted an Ode to the West Wind. Also composed part songs.

STOCKS, Dr. Harold Carpenter Lumb (1884-1956)

Born in Essendon, Hertfordshire on 21 October 1884; died in St. Asaph, Wales on 10 February 1956.

Educated at St. Asaph Grammar School and trained with Archibald Wilson and others. Graduated B.Mus. (1911) at the University of Oxford and D.Mus. (1921) at the University of Dublin.

Organist and choirmaster of Littleport Parish Church (1902-1906). Assistant organist of Ely Cathedral (1906-1909) to Archibald Wilson and he concurrently held the position of organist and choirmaster of St. Mary's Church, Ely. Played at the Reopening Service at Ely Cathedral (1908).

Organist and choirmaster of Yeovil Parish Church, Somerset (1909-1911) and of Ludlow Parish Church, Shropshire (1911-1917).

Served with the armed forces in World War I but was invalided home in 1916 after taking part in the campaigns of Salonika and Egypt.

Organist and choirmaster of St. Asaph Cathedral (1917-1956).

Author of a number of books, including *The Training of Boy Choristers*.

Composed settings of the Magnificat and Nunc Dimittis in D (1923) and in D Minor (1928), anthems including 'Grant, we beseech Thee' (1947) and 'Breathe on me, Breath of God' (1937), hymn tunes and songs. Submitted as his B.Mus. exercise a Symphonic Ode to Music.

STOCKS, William Henry (1860-1944)

Born in Chatteris, Cambridgeshire on 13 August 1860; died in Cambridge on 29 November 1944.

Trained in music with his father. At the age of 13 he was appointed music reader of the Royal Normal College for the Blind, Norwood, Surrey. Took pupils to Windsor Castle to perform before Queen Victoria.

Continued his studies with Oscar Beringer and Frits Hartvigson for piano and with **E.J. Hopkins** for organ and choir training. Also studied with **H.C. Banister** for harmony and composition and in Berlin with Hans von Bülow for piano.

In 1879, William Stocks was appointed private organist to Sir Robert Menzies. His other positions include that of assistant music master, of Dulwich College, London (from 1885) and organist of the College Chapel (from 1887); organist and choirmaster of the Clark Memorial Church, Largs, Ayrshire, Scotland (from 1912); Cardonald Parish Church, Renfrewshire (from 1920) and St. Mary's Episcopal Church, Newlands, Glasgow (from 1921).

The author of *A Short History of Organ, Organists and Services of the Chapel of Alleyn's College... at Dulwich* (1891).

Composer of hymn tunes and a setting of the Athanasian Creed (1899).

STOKES, Charles (1784-1839)

A chorister of St. Paul's Cathedral. An organist in Croydon, Surrey and elsewhere. Composer of the anthem 'I will lay me down'.

STOKES, Dr. Walter (1847-1916)

Born in Shipston-on-Stour, Worcestershire on 28 June 1847; died in Worcester on 25 November 1916.

Trained privately in music, his teachers being J. Bourne of Stourbridge and, for organ, **Roland Rogers**. His other instructors were W.T. Belcher, a Birmingham organist and, for composition, **C. Swinnerton Heap**. Graduated Mus.B. (1878) and Mus.D. (1882) at St. John's College, Cambridge.

Walter Stokes's parents were teachers. His father, as well as being a baritone singer was the choirmaster of the local parish church; his mother was organist there.

A pupil teacher before winning a scholarship to Saltley College, Birmingham.

He taught at schools in London and Birmingham, later settling in Worcester. Some of his estate was used to fund scholarships in theory and practice at the Royal Academy of Music.

Composed as his Mus.B exercise a setting of Psalm 84 'O how amiable are thy dwellings' for Solo Voices, Strings and Organ. His Mus.D. submission was the cantata *The Idol Bel* for Solo Voices, Double Chorus and Full Orchestra. Composer of hymn tunes, violin and piano sonatas, organ works, songs and part songs.

STOKOWSKI, Leopold (1882-1977)

Born in London on 18 April 1882, the year in which his parents (an Irish mother and a Polish father) settled in London; died in Nether Wallop, Hampshire on 13 September 1977.

A chorister of the Temple Church under **Walford Davies** who found him somewhat unruly. Attended the Royal College of Music where he studied theory with Walford Davies, composition with **C.V. Stanford** and organ with **W.S. Hoyte**. Graduated B.Mus. (1903) at Queen's College, Oxford.

Organist of the London Church of St. James, Piccadilly (from 1902). Emigrated to the U.S.A. in 1905 and became a U.S. citizen in 1915.

Organist and choirmaster of St. Bartholomew's Church, New York City (from 1905).

Conductor of the Cincinnati Symphony Orchestra (from 1906) and the Philadelphia Orchestra (from 1912). As music director (from 1931) he was given control over the selection of guest conductors and soloists. In a distinguished and high-profile career he gave the world premiere of *Amériques* by Varèse on 9 April 1926. Resigned in 1936 and was succeeded by Eugege Ormandy. Conducted the music for the Walt Disney film *Fantasia* (1939). After various appointments he became conductor of the American Symphony Orchestra, New York (1962-1975), during which period he conducted the orchestra in the first performance of the Fourth Symphony of Charles Ives.

Composed as his degree exercise the cantata *The Redeemer*. His church music includes a Benedicite in F (1948), and the Christmas carol 'When Christ was born' (1908).

STONARD (Stonnard), Dr. William (?-?1630)
In December 1608 he graduated B.Mus. at the University of Oxford, for which he composed a choral hymn in eight parts. Later graduated D.Mus. there. Organist of Christ Church Cathedral, Oxford from 1608 or before until the year of his death. A person of the same name - who may be the same person-was a lay clerk of Ely Cathedral from 1585. Of his compositions, 10 anthems are found in the collection by Clifford. His anthems include 'Hearken, all ye people' and 'Rejoice in the Lord'.

STONE, Francis Joseph (19th/20th century)
Graduated B.Mus. (1914) at the University of Durham. Choirmaster of the Church of the Sacred Heart, Hanley where he lived. A local choral society conductor and music master of Longton High School and Tunstall High School for Girls. Composed anthems including 'O sing unto the Lord' (1905) and songs. His degree exercise was 'Gloria in excelsis Deo'.

STONE, Robert (1516-1613)
As at 1553 he was a gentleman of the Chapel Royal. Composed a setting of The Lord's Prayer that has been perennially popular and is frequently used today.

STONEX, Henry (1823-1897)
Born in Norwich, Norfolk in 1823; died in Yarmouth, Norfolk on 10 January 1897. Studied under **J.A. Harcourt** and apprenticed to **Zechariah Buck**, organist of Norwich Cathedral. Organist of Yarmouth Parish Church (1850-1894). Gave the inaugural recital on the Church's new organ on 22 January 1883. A local music society conductor. In May 1893 he received a presentation for services to music in the town. He is particularly remembered for his Chant in F-sharp Minor.

STORER, Dr. John (1858-?)
Born in Hulland, near Derby on 18 May 1858
Soon after he was born, the family moved to Ashbourne. Became a chorister of Ashbourne Parish Church at the age of seven. The family moved once again, to Scarborough, Yorkshire, where he became a chorister of All Saints' Church (1869). An articled pupil of **John Naylor**, organist of All Saints' at the time, who was later appointed organist of York Minster. Graduated B.Mus. (1878) at the University of Oxford and D.Mus. at Trinity College, Toronto (1886).

Organist and choirmaster of St. Michael's Church, Whitby (1879-1881). Took a year out to study composition in London, returning to Yorkshire in 1882 as organist of Scarborough Parish Church (1882-1885). Conductor of a local philharmonic society.

Organist of Folkestone Parish Church, Kent (1885-1888). In the latter year he converted to Roman Catholicism and was appointed organist of the Church of the Redemptorist Fathers, Clapham, London. In 1891 he resigned in order to devote more time to composition.

Active in the London theatre, being director of music of The Globe, The Royalty, The Strand and The Olympic. Music critic and contributor to a number of newspapers.

His health failed in 1897 and his recuperation took 18 months. When able to return to work he became organist and choirmaster of St. Patrick's Church, Soho, London. Was then director of music of St. Gregory's College, Downside near Bath, Somerset. Organist of the Benedictine Chapel attached to the Monastery.

Organist and choirmaster of St. Marie's Roman Catholic Church, Sheffield (1904-1906) before being appointed organist of Waterford Cathedral, Ireland (1906-1916). Professor of Solesmes Plain Chant at St. John's Diocesan Ecclesiastical College, Waterford. Founded the Waterford Academy of Music.

Composed a number of Masses, including settings dedicated to St. Alphonsus (1888) and Our Lady of Ransom (1891) for Solo Voices, Chorus and Orchestra. A Grand Solemn Mass in F Minor was composed in 1895. Also composed a Magnificat in D (1889), anthems, a comic opera *The Punchbowl* (1887), songs, organ works and items for piano.

STRANG, Walter (1825-?)
Born in Edinburgh on 26 December 1825. Choirmaster of the Free St. George's Church, Edinburgh (1848-1885). For many years he was precentor to the General Assembly of the Free Church. Music master of the Free Church Normal School and other schools in Edinburgh. Composer of hymn tunes. Other works include school songs, some of which are found in his collection *School Music* (1853).

STRANGE, Charles Edward (b.1902)
Born in Oxford in 1902. Educated at New College, Oxford, and a chorister of Queen's College (1911-1916). Held a number of organ appointments in London. Assistant organist of Christ Church, Brondesbury (1917-1919) and of St. Mark's Church, North Audley Street (from 1924). Honorary organist (from 1923) and honorary choirmaster (1940-1945) of Bowes Park Congregational Church, and organist and choirmaster of St. George's Presbyterian Church of England, Palmers Green (from 1925). Organist and choirmaster of the Ministry of Transport Christian Fellowship (from 1946). Composer of hymn tunes.

STRATTON, John Henry (19th/20th century)
Graduated B.Mus. (1901) at the University of Durham. Principal of Sale Preparatory School, Cheshire; organist and choirmaster of Sale Parish Church (from 1901) and a local choral society conductor. Composed a Festival Evening Service (1903). His degree exercise was an Evening Song.

STRATTON, Stephen Samuel (1840-1906)
Born in London on 19 December 1840; died in Birmingham on 25 June 1906. A chorister of St. Mary's Church, Ealing, London. Studied piano under Elizabeth Chamberlaine, organ with Charles

Gardner and composition with **Charles Lucas**. Assistant organist of the London Church of St. Michael, Paddington (from 1862) and organist of St. Mary the Virgin, Crown Street, Soho (from 1863) and St. James's, Friern Barnet, Hertfordshire. Taught music at Totteridge Park School, and in 1866 he moved to Birmingham to take up a similar position. Organist of St. Barnabas Church, Birmingham (1866-1867); Edgbaston Parish Church (1867-1875); St. John's Church, Harborne (1876-1877) and the Church of the Saviour, Birmingham (1878-1882). In 1879 he founded a series of chamber concerts in Birmingham. Music critic for *Birmingham Post* and 'our own correspondent in Birmingham' for *Musical Times*. An original member of the College of Organists (1864-1894), and an associate of the Philharmonic Society (from 1882). Remembered today for his *British Musical Biography* (1897) which he compiled jointly with James D. Brown. His other works include notes on Mendelssohn for the 'Life' series published by Dent. Author of *Musical Curiosities*. Composed church music, songs and part songs. A collection of his hymn tunes and chants was published in 1874.

STREATFIELD, Sophia Charlotte (1829-1901)
Born in Speldhurst, Kent on 31 December 1829; died in Groombridge, Kent on 27 November 1901. Composer of hymn tunes.

STRINGER, Peter (1617-1669)
Baptised in Chester on 30 October 1617; died early in 1669. A chorister of Chester Cathedral in 1627. As an adult he was a conduct (singing man) and later, simultaneously organist, minor canon and precentor (1660-1673) of Chester Cathedral. Also deputy treasurer from 1666. Was succeeded as organist by his son, John Stringer. Composed anthems including 'I will magnify Thee' and 'Let God arise'.

STROGERS, Nicholas (17th century)
A church musician and composer of the 17th century, about whom little is known. Composed a Service in A, and the anthems 'O God, be merciful' and 'Praised be the God of love' (1664).

STRONG, Rt. Revd. Dr. Thomas Banks (1861-1944)
Born in West Brompton, London on 24 October 1861;. died in Kensington, London on 8 June 1944. Educated at Westminster School and Christ Church, Oxford where he graduated B.A. (1881) and M.A. (1886). Later graduated B.D. (1899) and D.D. (1902), and awarded honorary doctorates from the Universities of Durham and Leeds. Ordained deacon in 1885, priest in 1886. Appointed C.B.E. Bampton lecturer at the University of Oxford (from 1895) and dean of Christ Church (1901-1920). Vice Chancellor of Oxford University (1913-1917). As dean of Christ Church he took an interest in the young **William Walton**, a chorister (1911-1917) who had begun to compose around the age of 11. Bishop of Ripon (1920-1925) and of Oxford (1925-1938). One of the editors of *Oxford Hymn Book* (1908), to which he contributed his own tune 'Poplar'. His other hymn tunes include 'Hebdomadal'.

STROUD (Strode), Charles (1710-1726)
Born in 1710; died in London on 26 April 1726. A chorister of the Chapel Royal and a pupil of **John Blow**. Charles Stroud was a promising young musician who died prematurely at or around the age of 16. Had already become deputy organist of the Chapel

Royal, Whitehall. His anthems include 'Hear my prayer, O Lord' and 'I will lift up'.

STROUD, Edward (17th century)
Composed the anthem 'I will magnify Thee'.

STROVER, Martin Christopher Tinne (b.1932)
Born in 1932. Composer of hymn tunes. His other church music includes *Three Introits* (1969) for Boys' Voices and Organ.

STRUTT, Hon. Richard (1848-1927)
Born in Terling, near Chelmsford, Essex on 29 February 1848; died in Bath, Somerset on 14 October 1927. Son of the second Baron Rayleigh. Educated at Winchester College, Hampshire and at Magdalen College, Oxford where in 1876 he graduated M.A. Worked for an American bank in London before becoming a stockbroker. Warden and choirmaster of St. John's Church, Wilton Road, London for more than 30 years. A fellow of the Philharmonic, Horticultural and Zoological Societies and belonged to the Gregorian Association and the Church Music Society. Was on the Council of the Corporation of Church House. His hymn tunes include 'St. Catherine's Court,' which was composed for the Jubilee Celebration of the Girls' Friendly Society (1925).

STUBBES, Simon (16th/17th century)
The composer Stubbes has works in the collection The *Whole Booke of Psalmes* (1621) published by **Thomas Ravenscroft**. Composed the anthems 'Father of love' and 'Have mercy upon me'.

STURGEON, Nicholas (?-1454)
Died in London on 31 May 1454. From 1442 he was precentor of St. Paul's Cathedral. Owned the manuscripts found at Old Hall, near Ware, Hertfordshire, and may have been the copyist from the individual works. Seven are by him, of which two are incomplete. Composed a three-part Salve Mater Domini, which was probably composed for the journey of Henry V to France in 1416, in which Sturgeon was a member of the party.

STURGES, Edward (1808-1848)
Born in London on 25 February 1808; died in London on 15 February 1848. Attended the Choir School of St. Paul's Cathedral (1814 -1821). Organist of the Foundling Hospital (1833-1848). Editor of *Selections of Choruses by Handel* (1846) and *Organ Gems* (1845). Produced arrangements of anthems by **William Boyce** and of **Handel**'s *Creation*. Composed the anthem 'I know their sorrows'.

SUCH, Edwin Charles (1840-?)
Born in London on 11 August 1840. Attended the Merchant Taylors' School and London University College. Studied at the Cologne Conservatory, Germany (from 1861) under Ferdinand Hiller and Wilhelm Molique. Graduated Mus.B. (1877) at Trinity College, Cambridge and B.A. at the University of London. Lived in Bayswater, London. A professor of harmony at the Portman Academy, and a local choral society conductor. Composed anthems including 'Come, behold the Works of the Lord' (1878), a cantata *Narcissus and Echo* (1881), part songs, songs and piano items. His Mus.B. exercise was a setting of Psalm 46 'God is our Refuge' for Solo Voices, Chorus and Orchestra.

SUDLOW, William (1772-1848)
Born in 1772; died in Manchester in 1848. The son of a music dealer of Hanging Ditch, Manchester. A composer, organist, violinist and cellist. Organist and a singing man of Manchester Collegiate Church (1804-1848). The Church was elevated to cathedral status in 1847. Composed anthems including 'O God, my sins are manifold' (1862) and songs.

SULLIVAN, Sir Arthur Seymour (1842-1900)
Born in Lambeth, London on 13 May 1842; died in Westminster, London on 22 November 1900. At the age of 31 he dropped the use of his middle name, sensitive to the acronym formed by his initials. The son of Thomas Sullivan, a clarinettist of the Surrey Theatre, music teacher, copyist and Sergeant Bandmaster at the Royal Military College, Sandhurst, Surrey. Thomas Sullivan was later chief professor of clarinet at the Royal Military School of Music, Kneller Hall at Twickenham, Middlesex.
Arthur Sullivan attended Yorktown National School, Sandhurst. Learned to play piano and wind instruments. At the age of nine or ten he went as a boarder to a school in London run by William Plees.
A chorister of the Chapel Royal from under **Thomas Helmore**, master of the children (1854-1857).
Chapel Royal choristers were in demand as professional singers, and Sullivan sang at, among other events, the reopening of the Crystal Palace on 10 June 1855 by Queen Victoria and the Consecration of St. Michael's College, Tenbury, Worcestershire on 29 June 1856 when he sang the solo part in the anthem 'Praise the Lord' by **John Goss.**
Sullivan had already begun to compose and in May 1855 his anthem 'Sing unto the Lord and bless His name' was sung at the Chapel Royal under **George Smart**, one of the Chapel organists.
Like his friend **John Stainer**, Arthur Sullivan was a pupil of the organist **George Cooper**.
A Mendelssohn Scholarship had been established to provide a year's free tuition at the Royal Academy of Music, commencing in 1856. In July of that year, 17 candidates competed. Sullivan, who was then aged 14, tied with **Joseph Barnby** who was later a well-known London musician and principal of Guildhall School of Music. A deciding round was held, in which Sullivan was successful.
At the R.A.M. he studied piano under **William Sterndale Bennett**, harmony with John Goss, and violin with O'Leary, while continuing as a Chapel Royal chorister.
The scholarship was renewed, enabling Sullivan to study in Leipzig for two years. Studied piano with Louis Plaidy and Ignaz Moscheles, counterpoint with Moritz Hauptmann, organ under Ernst Richter, instrumentation and composition with Julius Rietz and violin with Raimund Dreyschock and Engelbert Röntgen.. Probably also studied conducting with Ferdinand David. In Leipzig he conducted his overture 'Lalla Rookh' on 25 May 1860.
Sullivan returned to London in 1861.
Awarded the honorary degrees of Mus.D. at the University of Cambridge (1876), and D.Mus. (1879) at the University of Oxford. Received the French decoration of Chevalier of the Legion of Honour (1878).
On his return to London he took pupils, but private teaching alone did not bring him sufficient income. Took up conducting and he became organist of St. Michael's Church, Chester Square from around 1861. Organist of St. Peter's Church, Onslow Gardens (1867-1872) and of the Opera House, Covent Garden.

He visited Ireland in 1864 which inspired him to compose an Irish Symphony, the first performance of which was given in London on 10 March 1866.
A professor of composition at the R.A.M. (from 1866). In 1876 he became principal and professor of composition of the newly-established National Training School of Music, continuing to teach at the R.A.M. By this time he was well known as a composer and it was feared that the additional administrative burden would encroach on the time available for composition.
From around 1866 he became a friend of George Grove. In 1867 he travelled with Grove to Germany to search out unpublished manuscripts of Schubert that were believed to be in existence. The expedition was a success: a bundle of part books of the work *Rosamunde* was found, having been put aside in September 1823 in Vienna. Copies were made and only weeks later the complete work was mounted at the Crystal Palace.
In January 1876, at the opening of the Royal Aquarium, Westminster, Sullivan was director of music. It had a concert hall and took on a salaried orchestra. Resigned in 1881.
Conductor of the Leeds Triennial Festival (1880-1898), although he had originally been third choice after Michael Costa and Charles Hallé. The first and last years were significant for different reasons.
In 1880, three telephonic transmitters, converging on one wire, were set up in Leeds Town Hall by the Yorkshire Telephone Company. During the performance of **Handel**'s *Samson* seven men in the company's office listened to the live performance on individual telephone receivers.
On 5 October 1898, the new cantata *Caractacus* by **Edward Elgar** was performed. In a note to Sullivan, the composer praised and thanked him for mounting the work when others were reticent. It was Elgar's first Leeds Festival performance and it was well-received.
Conductor of the London Philharmonic Society (1885-1887).
One of a number of distinguished musicians who signed a note calling for the inclusion of early works in cathedrals rather than modern ones that erred towards a light, secular style.
Arthur Sullivan contributed articles on **Frédéric Clay** and Louis Plaidy to the First Edition of George Grove's *Dictionary of Music and Musicians*.
Music editor of *The Hymnary* (1872) and *Church Hymns* (1874). Of the latter, to which he contributed 14 of his existing tunes plus 24 new ones, he observed, 'Had I known the wearisome labour of it, I would not have undertaken it for a thousand pounds'.
Something of a gambler, and liked to bet at the Orleans and Argus Clubs.
In all he composed some 56 hymn tunes, mainly during the period 1867-1874. 'St Gertrude' (1871), long associated with 'Onward, Christian soldiers' by **Sabine Baring-Gould** was named after the wife of Ernest Seymer, a lady of the congregation of St. Peter's, Onslow Gardens, where he was organist.
Composed a Te Deum, Jubilate and Kyrie in D (1866) and 16 anthems including 'We have heard with our ears' (c1860) and 'Sing, O Heavens' (1869). A Chant to Psalm 150 remains in manuscript. A Festival Te Deum was composed in 1872 following the recovery from illness of the Prince of Wales. Also composed carols.
Arthur Sullivan composed cantatas, including *Kenilworth* for the Birmingham Festival of 1864, and *The Prodigal Son* for the Three Choirs' Festival at Worcester in 1869. His first part song was published in 1855. Composed songs, part songs and other chamber works.

Best known for his compositions for the theatre, particularly operettas in collaboration with the librettist W.S. Gilbert. *Cox and Box* (1866) was with F.C. Burnand as librettist. *Ivanhoe* (1891), a full-length opera enjoyed a run of 160 nights.

Richard d'Oyly Carte founded a company in 1876 to produce works by Gilbert and Sullivan. The collaboration did not run entirely smoothly and there was a period from 1890 to 1893 when they refused to work with each other, following a disagreement ostensibly over a carpet in the Savoy Theatre, but actually because of artistic and personal tension. However, the partnership lasted for 25 years and produced a string of successful operettas. *Thespis* (1871) was the first Gilbert and Sullivan operetta. It was followed by *Trial By Jury* (1875), *The Sorcerer* (1877) *and H.M.S. Pinafore* (1878), which had 700 consecutive performances. *Pirates of Penzance* (1879), *Patience* (1881), *Iolanthe* (1882) and *Princess Ida* (1884) were followed by *The Mikado* (1885), which was the most popular of all his works in this genre. *Ruddygore* (1887), *The Yeomen of The Guard* (1888), *The Gondoliers* (1889), *Utopia (Limited)* (1893), and *The Grand Duke* (1896) were written by the same partnership.

SUMMERS, Dr. Joseph (1843-c1919)

Born in Somerset in 1843; died in Australia in 1916 or 1919.

A chorister of Wells Cathedral, where he was also responsible for copying out the anthems and services from manuscript.

Trained privately in music by **C.W. Lavington**, Cathedral organist of Wells and by **William Sterndale Bennett** and **H.J. Gauntlet**. Graduated B.Mus. at New College, Oxford (1887) and received the B.Mus. honorarily at the University of Melbourne. Accorded, in 1890, the Lambeth D.Mus.

Organist and choirmaster of St. Andrew's College, Bradfield, Berkshire (from 1861); Holy Trinity Church, Weston-super-Mare, Somerset (1864) and St. Peter's Church, Notting Hill, London (1865), at which point he emigrated to Australia.

He was government inspector of public schools in Victoria and became organist and choirmaster in Melbourne of St. Peter's Parish Church and of All Saints' Church, St. Kilda.

Composed anthems including 'O where shall Wisdom be found?' (1913). His hymn tunes are found in *Bristol Tune Book*, *Parish Tune Book* and *Worship Song*. They include 'Palmyra'. As his B.Mus. exercise he composed a setting of Psalm 31 'In Thee, O Lord, have I put my trust' for Solo Voices, Chorus, Double Quartet and Full Orchestra.

Also composed oratorios such as *Deborah*, cantatas including *The Bush Skeleton*, marches, songs and part songs.

SUMSION, Dr. Herbert Whitton (1899-1995)

Born in Gloucester on 19 January 1899; died in 1995.

A probationer (from 1908), and a full chorister (from 1910) of Gloucester Cathedral. An articled pupil (from 1914) and assistant (from 1915) of **A.H. Brewer**. Studied composition and piano at the Royal College of Music. Graduated B.Mus. (1920) at the University of Durham and received the Lambeth D.Mus. in 1947. Herbert Sumsion was appointed C.B.E. in 1961.

Director of music of Bishop's Stortford College, Hertfordshire (1924-1926) and organist and choirmaster of Christ Church, Lancaster Gate, London (1922-1926). At this time he was assistant instructor in music at Morley College, London. Lived in the Notting Hill district.

In July 1926 Herbert Sumsion took up an appointment in Philadelphia, U.S.A. as professor of harmony and counterpoint at the Curtis Institute of Music. At the same time, **R.O. Morris**, who had taught at the Royal College of Music since 1920, was appointed director of the Department of Composition at the Curtis Institute. Remained in the U.S.A. until 1928.

He then returned to the U.K. as organist of Coventry Cathedral in succession to Walter Hoyle. After Herbert Sumsion accepted the appointment but before his term of office commenced, Herbert Brewer, the organist of Gloucester Cathedral, died in office. Sumsion was released from his commitment to Coventry in order to take over at Gloucester, where he remained as organist until 1967.

He had to take on the burden of the Three Choirs' Festival of that year, which, by rotation, was held at Gloucester. A friend of **Edward Elgar**, Herbert Sumsion was the last surviving person to have worked with Elgar at the Three Choirs' Festival. His American wife, Alice, acquired fame by delivering a rebuke to an unrepentant George Bernard Shaw who had arrived late for a performance at the Three Choirs' Festival that he had been sent to review as music critic.

Director of music of Cheltenham Ladies' College, Gloucestershire (1935-1968). Retired to the Gloucestershire town of Stroud, where he continued to compose in retirement.

Composed a Festival Benedicite in D (1971), a Benedicite in B-flat (1955), Evening Services in G for All Voices, Men's and Boys' Voices. There were also Evening Services in A and in D. His anthems include 'They that go down to the sea in ships', 'Never weather beaten sail', 'We love the place, O God' and 'Fear not, O Land'. Also worthy of note are his *O Salutaris Hostia*, which was written for the Choir of Leeds Parish Church, and *Tantum ergo Sacramentum*. Composer of hymn tunes and an overture *In the Cotswolds*.

SURPLICE, Dr. Reginald Alwyn (1906-1977)

Born in Pangbourne, Berkshire on 20 August 1906; died in Winchester, Hampshire on 21 April 1977.

Educated at Reading Collegiate School and the University of Reading, where he studied music. Also studied music privately with **Malcolm Boyle, Harold Edwin Darke** and **Ernest Bullock**. Graduated B.Mus. (1938) at the University of Durham and, on his retirement, received the Lambeth D.Mus. (1971).

Organist of the Berkshire Parish Churches of Pangbourne (1922-1924) and Easthampstead (1924-1926). Organist of Holy Trinity Church, Windsor (1927-1945) and assistant organist of St. George's Chapel, Windsor Castle (1927-1932). Sub organist of St. George's Chapel from 1932 until 1945.

Organist of the Cathedrals of Bristol (1946-1949) and Winchester (1949-1971).

A professor of the Royal Academy of Music and a local philharmonic society conductor. Taught music at King Alfred's College, Winchester (from 1951).

Alwyn Surplice's works include anthems based on Psalm 15 'Lord, who shall dwell in Thy tabernacle?' (1953) and Psalm 121 'I will lift up mine eyes unto the hills' (1963). Composer of hymn tunes and the 'Stork Carol'.

SUTCLIFFE, Alfred Lister (1859-?)

Born in Leckhampstead, Buckinghamshire on 13 November 1859. Studied music with **L.G. Hayne**, who appointed him organist of Bradfied, Berkshire (from 1875) and of Mistley with Bradfield (from 1878) where Hayne was rector. Composed several hymn tunes.

SUTCLIFFE, Charles Thomas (1853-?)
Born in Manchester on 12 April 1853. A chorister of Manchester Cathedral, and attended Manchester Grammar School. Studied under the Cathedral organist, **Joseph John Harris,** for whom he played the early morning services and, for piano, Frederick Unger. Graduated B.Mus. (1893) at the University of Durham. Organist at the Bible Christian Church, Salford from the age of 11 (1864-1870); All Saints' Church, Manchester (from 1871) and St. John's Church, Longsight (1871-1876). Lived in Eccles, Lancashire, where he was organist and choirmaster of the Parish Church (1876-1883). Organist and choirmaster of St. Catherine's Church, Barton-on-Irwell, near Manchester (from 1884). Composed a Magnificat and Nunc Dimittis in F (1902), a Te Deum in C (1902), songs and piano works. His degree exercise was a setting of Psalm 104 'Praise the Lord,O my soul' for Solo Voices, Chorus, Piano and Strings.

SWANN, Donald Ibrahim (1923-1994)
Born in Llanelli, Glamorganshire, Wales on 30 September 1923; died in Clapham, London on 23 March 1994.
Of Russian parents: his father was a doctor and his mother, a nurse. The family moved to London when Donald was three years old. Educated at Westminster School and at Christ Church, Oxford (from 1941), where in 1948 he graduated in modern languages. Also graduated M.A.
Thereafter, he worked as a freelance singer, composer and pianist.
His name is associated with that of Michael Flanders, with whom he wrote and mounted the successful musical reviews *At the Drop of a Hat* (1956-1963) and *At the Drop of Another Hat* (1963-1967). He and Flanders knew and worked with each other at Christ Church. Composed a song cycle based on the works of. J.R.Tolkein *The Road goes ever On* (1968).
His books include *Space Between the Bars* (1968) and *Swann's Way Out* (1975).
Compiled two anthologies of carols, in which are some of his own compositions.
The hymn tune 'Flanders' is named after his former partner. Other hymn tunes include 'Jordan', composed for the Third Edition (1973) of *Church Hymnary*.
He has composed an opera *Perelandra* (1964) on the novel by C.S. Lewis, another Oxford friend. Other music to Lewis's words includes lyric settings and a *Requiem for the Living*.
Also composed a Festival Morning Service in F (1964) and others, and anthems including 'Praise the Lord, who reigns above' (1964).

SWANN, Stretton (19th/20th century)
Graduated B.Mus. (1897) at the University of Durham. Organist of a number of churches in and around London. They include St. John's, Horselydown (from 1880 and from 1895); Christ Church, Bermondsey (1880-1883); Holy Trinity, Gray's Inn Road (1883-1884); St. Mary's, Spital Square (1884-1887); St. Mark, Camberwell (1886-1887); St. Thomas's, Brentwood (from 1888); St. George the Martyr, Southwark (1889-1891); St. Olave, London Bridge (from 1891) and St. Anne, Bermondsey (1892-1895). Lived in Tooting, London. Composed a Holy Communion Service in E-flat (1899) and in D (1902), a Magnificat and Nunc Dimittis in D (1904), a harvest anthem 'How excellent is Thy Mercy, O Lord' (1911), hymn tunes and piano works. His degree exercise was a setting of Psalm 84 'Blessed are they that dwell'.

SWAYNE, Giles (b.1946)
Born in Hitchin, Hertfordshire on 30 June 1946. Educated at Ampleforth College, York (1955-1963), Trinity College, Cambridge (1964-1968) and Royal Academy of Music (1968-1971). Studied composition with Nicholas Maw, Alan Bush and Harrison Birtwistle. Attended Olivier Messiaen's composition classes at the Paris Conservatory (1976-1977). In 1990 went to live in Ghana, and now divides his time between Ghana and Britain. Has written chamber music, orchestral and vocal works and operas including 'Hamlet' (1998). His sacred music includes a Magnificat (1982), a Missa *Tiburtina* (1985), a Nunc Dimittis (1986), 'O magnum mysterium' (1986), and a Communion Service in D (1996).

SWEETING, Dr. Edward Thomas (1863-1930)
Born in Congleton, Cheshire on 16 September 1863; died in St. Albans, Hertfordshire on 8 July 1930.
Educated at the National Training School of Music (1876-1882) where he was Ward of Cripplegate Scholar and Novello Scholar. His tutors were **John Francis Barnett**, **Frederick Bridge** and **Ebenezer Prout**. Graduated B.Mus. (1889) and D.Mus. (1894) at New College, Oxford.
Organist and choirmaster of Rossall School, Fleetwood, Lancashire (1882-1897) where his pupils included the conductor Thomas Beecham.
Organist of St. Mary's Church, West Kensington at the age of 11 (1875-1882) and of St. John's College, Cambridge (1897-1901), where he succeeded **George Garrett**.
Master of the music of Winchester College, Hampshire (1901-1924), retiring in the latter year. When he joined the staff of the College, music was barely tolerated as a main curriculum subject. Sweeting developed it, increasing the music staff in the process. The composer **Henry Balfour Gardiner** taught at the college for a term during 1907, and dedicated his famous Evening Hymn of that year to Sweeting.
A temporary examiner for the Associated Board of the Royal Schools of Music.
Composed a Morning and Evening Service (1902), anthems, the hymn tune 'Wolvesey', songs and part songs. Composed as his B.Mus. exercise a setting of the hymn 'At even, ere the sun was set'. For his doctorate he submitted an ode The Passions.

SWIFT, George Henry (1856-?)
Born in Lambourn, Berkshire in 1856. Organist of Lambourn Parish Church, and a local choral society conductor. In 1884 he moved within the county to Hungerford. Composed an Evening Service in E (1886). His anthems include 'O sing unto the Lord' (1879) and 'Shew us Thy Mercy' (1881). Also composed a Sonata for Piano in C, and part songs.

SWIFT, James Frederick (1847-1931)
Born in Manchester on 28 December 1847; died in Wallasey, Cheshire on 9 January 1931. In 1851 his family moved to Liverpool, where he was educated. Studied at the Commercial School of Liverpool College. For a time, around the year 1881, James Swift was deputy organist at St. George's Hall, Liverpool to the famous organist, **W.T. Best.** An organ recitalist and a conductor for local music societies. Organist of the Cranmer Street Wesleyan Church, Liverpool from the age of 16 (1863-1876). Other church organistships followed at St. Andrew's, Renshaw Street (1876-1886) and St. Bride's, Percy Street (1886-1892). Composed anthems including 'All things praise Thee, Lord most high' (1925), and many hymn tunes. His 'Ernstein' appeared in the

Revised Edition (1927) of *Church Hymnary* with 'Holy Spirit, hear us'. 'Te laudant omnia' was composed around 1889 for a children's Service at St. Bede's Church, Liverpool. Under the pseudonym Godfrey Marks he composed more than two hundred songs including 'Sailing' and 'A brave heart'.

SWINSTEAD, Eric H. (1881-1950)
Born in 1881; died in Essex on 1 March 1950. Composer of hymn tunes.

SYDENHAM, Edwin Augustus (?-1891)
Died in Scarborough, Yorkshire on 18 February 1891. A chorister of Stratford-on-Avon Parish Church, Warwickshire. Studied at the Leipzig Conservatory. Organist of St. Martin's Church, Dorking, Surrey and St. Andrew's Farnham (from 1873). Organist of St. James's Church, Bury St. Edmunds (from 1879) and of All Saints' Church, Scarborough, Yorkshire (from 1882). Invented and patented a touch regulator for piano. A teacher in Scarborough. Composed an Evening Service in F (1885), anthems including the Easter-tide 'Christ is Risen' (1882) and 'O give thanks unto the Lord' (1905), a Battle Song (1884), part songs and chamber music.

SYKES, John Austen (1909-1962)
Born in India in 1909; died in Bath, Somerset on 20 June 1962. Attended Clifton College, the University of Oxford and the Royal College of Music. Graduated B.A. and B.Mus. Composer of hymn tunes.

SYMONDS, Daniel Philip (b.1929)
Born in Upwey, Dorset on 16 February 1929. Educated at St. Michael's College, Tenbury, Worcestershire under **Sydney Nicholson**, at Oundle School, Northamptonshire and, as organ scholar, at Hertford College, Oxford. A farmer in Gloucestershire. Composer of hymn tunes of which the most popular to date has been 'Mernle' which he composed in 1944 at the age of 15. It was composed for the hymn by Mrs. E. Miller 'I love to hear the Story'.

T, U

TAILOUR, Robert (?-1637)
A church musician and composer of the 16th and 17th centuries. He issued *Sacred Hymns... set to be sung in five partes...* (1615). His own compositions have been used as hymn tunes.

TALLIS, Thomas (c1505-1585)
Born around the year 1505; died in Greenwich, London on 23 November 1585.
Ioculator organorum of Dover Priory, Kent (1531-1532). From 1536 or 1537 Tallis was a conduct (singing man) of the Church of St. Mary-at-Hill, London. A member of the community of Waltham Abbey, and possibly, organist, but lost his position at the dissolution of the Abbey by Henry VIII (1540). From there he appears to have moved to Canterbury Cathedral as a lay clerk.
A gentleman of the Chapel Royal under Henry VIII from about 1542, retaining the position until the year of his decease. Tallis and **William Byrd** were organists together at the Chapel Royal from 1575 to 1585. Elizabeth awarded Tallis and Byrd a joint monopoly over the printing of music and music paper.
His anthems use Latin and English texts. His setting of Psalm 67 is familiar today as 'Tallis's Canon'. *Spem in alium* is a motet in 40 parts, possibly composed for the 40th birthday of Elizabeth I.

TAMBLYN, William (b 1941)
Born in Birmingham on 5 December 1941. Educated at University of Durham. Became principal lecturer at Colchester Institute School of Music (1974), chairman (1977), and professor (1995). Conductor of the Colchester Institute Choir. Has written music for film and television, choral and instrumental music. His sacred music includes a Jubilee Service, 'Afrika Gloria', 'Lumen Christi' and 'God of the living'.

TANNER, Laurence Edgar (1891-1941)
Born in Wandsworth, London in 1891; died in Portishead, Somerset on 17 June 1941. Composer of hymn tunes.

TANS'UR (Tanzer), William (c1706-1783)
Born in Dunchurch, Warwickshire probably in 1706, being baptised on 6 November of that year; died at St. Neots, Bedfordshire on 7 October 1783. Having established himself as a teacher of Psalmody in his youth, he taught classes at Barnes and

Ewell, Surrey, and while in Ewell he published the first edition of his *A Compleat Melody...* (1735). He went on to teach at a number of other places including Cambridge, Stamford, Boston and Leicester. He eventually settled in St. Neots as a bookseller. In 1760, he issued *The Psalm-Singer's Jewell* in conjunction with his son, and at other times brought out a number of works. Some hymn tunes bear his name, but many of these are adaptations rather than original compositions.

Tanymarian
See **JONES,** Edward.

TARGETT, James (1778-1803)
Born near Kidderminster, Worcestershire in October 1778; died in Chichester, Sussex on 15 May 1803. A chorister, and organist (1801-1803) of Chichester Cathedral. Composed anthems including 'Christ, being raised' and 'O Saviour of the world'.

TAVENER, John (b.1944)
Born in London on 28 January 1944.
Descended from **John Taverner**.
Attended Highgate School, London and studied under **Lennox Berkeley** at the Royal Academy of Music, and with the Australian composer David Lumsdaine.
A professor of music at Trinity College of Music (from 1969). Organist of St. John's Church, Kensington, London (from 1960).
Befriended by The Beatles, who recorded his works on their own Apple recording label.
In 1977, John Tavener joined the Russian Orthodox Church, and he has composed a number of works for its Liturgy since that time. His anthems include 'The Lamb' and 'The Tyger', first performed at St. George's Chapel, Windsor Castle. He has also composed an Akathist of Thanksgiving.

TAVERNER, John (c1495-1545)
Born in South Lincolnshire around the year 1495; died in Boston, Lincolnshire on 18 October 1545.
Organist of Boston Parish Church and, from November 1526, master of the choristers of Christ Church Cathedral, Oxford (then known as Cardinal College). Became embroiled in the Reformation. It is said that Wolsey, the founder of Cardinal

College, imprisoned him for heresy but later took pity on him and released him 'being but a musitian', but it is also claimed that this whole episode is a myth. At Oxford for some three to four years, after which he gave up music and settled in Boston.

One of the agents of Thomas Cromwell in the suppression of the monasteries and the killing of religious opponents.

He composed a considerable amount of church music, including Masses, motets and anthems including 'O Lamb of God' and 'O give thanks unto the Lord'.

TAWE-JONES, David (20th century)
Graduated B.Mus. at University College, Wales. Director of music of Carmarthen County Schools and of Preswylfa High School, Cardiff. Also involved in adult education. Organist and choirmaster of the Zion Church, Llanwrst and of the Water Street Church, Carmarthen. Composed a cantata *A Song of Praise*, anthems, hymn tunes, and more than 200 songs.

TAYLOR, Amram (19th century)
Published *The Sacred Harp...* (1842) and composed Psalm and hymn tunes.

TAYLOR, Dr. Cardinal (1871-?)
Born in Leicester in 1871. Trained privately in music and graduated D.Mus. at the University of Durham (1896). Organist of Holy Cross Church, Leicester (1887-1888). Organist and choirmaster of St. Mary's Church, Quorndon, Leicestershire (1889-1891); St. Peter's Church, Leicester (1891-1894); St. Mary's Church, Humberston, Leicestershire (1894-1899); St. Mary's Church, Whittlesey, Cambridgeshire (1899-1902); St. Paul's Church, Leicester (1902-1918) and St. Stephen's Presbyterian Church, Leicester (from 1918). He composed as his degree exercise a setting of Psalm 146 'Praise the Lord O my soul' for Solo Voices, Chorus and Strings. Also composed 'I thank Thee, gracious Lord' (1920), a hymn of thanksgiving.

TAYLOR, Revd. Cyril Vincent (1907-1991)
Born in Wigan, Lancashire on 11 December 1907; died in 1991.
Attended Magdalen College School, Oxford (1918-1926), where he was a chorister. Studied at Christ Church, Oxford (from 1926), where he graduated B.A. (1929) and M.A. (1939). Studied for the ministry of the Church of England at Westcott House, Cambridge (1930), following which he was ordained deacon (1931) and priest (1932). Curate within the Diocese of Leicester of the Churches of St. Mary, Hinkley (1931-1933) and St. Andrew, Kingswood (1933-1936).
Precentor of the Cathedrals of Bristol (1936-1939) and Salisbury.
From 1939 to 1953, Cyril Taylor was assistant to the head of religious broadcasting at the B.B.C.; warden and chaplain of the Royal School of Church Music, Addington, Croydon, Surrey (1953-1958) and priest in charge of Cerne Abbas, Dorset (from 1958). A fellow of St. Michael's College, Tenbury, Worcestershire (1953-1958).
One of the editors of *B.B.C. Hymn Book* (1951), to which he contributed some 20 tunes including 'Miniver' and 'Portland'. Among his best known hymn tunes are 'Abbot's Leigh' (1941) for the hymn 'Glorious things of Thee are spoken', and 'Belstead' (1941-1942). Served on the Committee for *Hymns Ancient and Modern*.

TAYLOR (Tayler), Daniel (17th century)
A singing man of Westminster Abbey at the time of the Funeral of James I in 1625. His anthem 'Sing we merrily' exists in manuscript at Durham Cathedral.

TAYLOR, Dr. Ebenezer William (1851-?)
Born in Stafford on 26 November 1851.
Studied music from the age of six. Trained at Hereford Cathedral, where he was articled to the Cathedral organist, George Townshend Smith. Studied with **C.W. Corfe** at the University of Oxford, where he graduated B.Mus. (Hertford College, 1876) and D.Mus. (New College, 1883).
Organist in Stafford of the Churches of St. Thomas (from 1872) and St. Mary (from 1880). A local examiner for the Royal College of Music, and the local representative of the Royal Academy of Music.
Composed a set of vocal score reading exercises, and of figured bass and melody exercises. His other educational works include *Pedal Scales and Arpeggios for Organ*, and *Introduction to Harmonising Melodies*.
His compositions include an Ave Maria, a setting of the Service of Holy Communion, hymn tunes - some of which were included in the *National Book of Hymn Tunes* - songs, and piano pieces. His degree exercises were the cantata *God our Refuge* (B.Mus.) and the oratorio *St. Stephen* (D.Mus.)

TAYLOR, John Prentice (1871-1936)
Born in Hamilton, Lanarkshire, Scotland on 28 September 1871; died in Cathcart, Glasgow on 13 February 1936. Composer of hymn tunes.

TAYLOR, John W.R. (20th century)
Composed the anthem 'O worship the Lord' (1965).

TAYLOR, Richard (1758-1813)
A composer and writer on musical subjects at Chelmsford, Essex. Composed anthems including 'Hear my crying' and 'I will give thanks'.

TAYLOR, Robert (1847-1915)
Born in 1847; died in Brighton, Sussex on 7 December 1915. While very young, Robert Taylor was organist of Badsey, Worcestershire and of Child's Wickham, Gloucestershire. Subsequently a chorister of Worcester Cathedral, where he was articled to the Cathedral organist, **William Done**, whom he also served as assistant. Moved to the Brighton area (1870). Director of the Brighton School of Music. Organist of St. Patrick's Church, Hove, and choirmaster of the Church of St. Michael and All Angels, Brighton. Established the Brighton Sacred Harmonic Society, and, with **Alfred King**, the Brighton School of Music. Composer of hymn tunes.

TAYLOR (Tayler), Captain Silas (1624-1678)
Composed anthems including 'I will give thanks' and 'The Lord is even at hand'.

TAYLOR, William (1832-1919)
Born in Kidderminster, Worcestershire on 8 December 1832; died in 1919. Studied with William Marshall. Graduated B.Mus. (1854) at Magdalen Hall, Oxford. Organist and choirmaster in Kidderminster, Worcestershire, of the Church of St. John the

Baptist (1849-1867) and of the Parish Church (1868-1903). Honorary borough organist of Kidderminster. Composed as his degree exercise a setting of Psalm 104 ' Praise the Lord' for Solo Voices, Chorus and Orchestra. His other works include settings of the Te Deum, Benedicite, Magnificat and Nunc Dimittis. His anthems include 'St. John the Baptist', and he also composed songs.

TEARNE, Theodore Stephen (19th/20th century)
Trained at Gloucester Cathedral and at St. George's Chapel, Windsor Castle. Graduated B.Mus. (1880) at New College, Oxford. Organist of the Churches of St. Mary, Chester (from 1876); St. Peter, Kirkley, Lowestoft, Suffolk (1881-1888); Edgbaston Church, Birmingham (1888-1900), Langley Green Church, Birmingham (1901-1904) and St. James, Handsworth, Birmingham (from 1904). Composed as his degree exercise a setting of Psalm 97: The Lord Is King for Solo Voices, Chorus and Strings. His other works include anthems, piano music and songs.

TERRY, Sir Richard Runciman (1865-1938)
Born in Ellington, Northumberland on 3 January 1865; died in Kensington, London on 18 April 1938.
The nephew of Lord Runciman.
A choral scholar of King's College, Cambridge. Graduated D.Mus. honorarily at the University of Durham (1911).
Knighted in 1922.
An external lecturer at the University of Oxford (from 1911). A lecturer at the University of Birmingham (from 1913). External examiner in music for the University of Ireland (1915-1918) and the University of Birmingham (1915-1918).
Organist and choirmaster of Elstow School, near Bedford (from 1890), and of St. John's Cathedral, Antigua, West Indies (1892-1896), an appointment he was forced to resign through ill-health. Organist and choirmaster of Downside Abbey and School (from 1896) and of Westminster Cathedral (1901-1924). At the time of his resignation, the cathedral choir was in decline in terms of numbers.
Editor of *Westminster Hymnal*, and chairman of the Committee for the preparation of the English Supplement to the *Vatican Antiphoner*. His other publications as editor include *Motets Ancient and Modern*, *Downside Motets*, *Downside Masses*, and *Musical News and Herald*.
An expert on the music of Palestrina.
Author of *Catholic Church Music*. He contributed articles to magazines and papers.
He composed five Masses. The carol 'Myn Liking' is the most famous of a set of 12. There are motets and hymn tunes, some of which are found in *Catholic Hymns* and *Catholic Church Hymnal* (U.S.A.). His hymn tunes include 'Highwood' which is found in *Methodist Hymn Book* (1933) and a number of other hymnals.

THACKERAY, Dr. Duncan (19th century)
Graduated B.Mus. at the University of Oxford (1870) and D.Mus. at Dublin (1871). Organist of the Churches of St. John, Perth, Scotland and Southgate Church, Middlesex. A tenor singer of Armagh Cathedral, Ireland. He composed a service, two sacred cantatas, and songs.

THACKWRAY, George Bayne (1846-1918)
Born in York in 1846; died in Scarborough, Yorkshire on 13 July 1918. Composer of hymn tunes.

THALBEN-BALL (Ball), Sir George Thomas (1896-1987)
Born in Sydney, New South Wales on 18 June 1896; died on 17 January 1987. Changed his name by deed poll to Thalben-Ball on 24 January 1924.
Knighted in 1982.
His parents, both musicians, were Cornish and the family returned to England when George was three years old.
After studying at Highfield School he won a Grove Scholarship to the Royal College of Music where he studied under **C.V. Stanford** and, **Hubert Parry** for composition, **Walter Parratt, Charles Wood** and **Frederick Bridge** for harmony and counterpoint, and **Walford Davies** for choir training. He had four piano teachers: Frits Hartvigson, Herbert Fryer, Franklin Taylor and Fanny Davies.
A chorister at the church of St. James, Muswell Hill, London, he was prepared for the R.C.M. Scholarship examination by the organist, G.D. Cunningham.
Awarded the Lambeth D.Mus. (1935) and appointed C.B.E. in 1957.
Succeeded G.D. Cunningham as City and University organist of Birmingham (1949).
Assistant organist of Whitefield's Tabernacle, Tottenham Court Road, London (1911-1914), and organist of the London Churches of Holy Trinity, Castelnau, Barnes (1914-1916) and St. James, Sussex Gardens, Paddington (1916-1919).
Acting organist of the Temple Church, London (1919-1923) before assuming full responsibility in the latter year. His famous recording of 'Hear my prayer', featuring the boy soprano Ernest Lough was made in 1927 and won a Gold Disc in 1963.
At the age of 18, in 1914, he gave organ recitals at the Alexandra Palace. His career as a recitalist flourished and he was well known for his performances at the Queen's Hall Promenade Concerts between the wars.
His organ pupils include **Sydney Watson** and James Dalton.
Religious music adviser to the B.B.C. from around 1940 until 1970. He retired in 1982.
Composed two books of introits, a Magnificat and Nunc Dimittis in G, a Te Deum and Jubilate in B-flat - written for the re-opening of the Temple Church in 1955 - hymn tunes including 'Llanherne' and the Polish carol 'Lullay, Lord Jesus'. Organ works include an Elegy in B-flat, and many volumes of introits for use in services of worship broadcast on B.B.C. Radio. He contributed to *For the Little Organ Book*, a posthumous tribute to **Hubert Parry** by the leading composers of the day, who each tendered a composition. His *Sursum Corda* was composed for the B.B.C. Chorus and Symphony Orchestra to commemorate the ending of World War II. One of the editors of *B.B.C. Hymn Book* (1951).

THATCHER, Sir Reginald Sparshatt (1888-1957)
Born in Midsomer Norton, Somerset on 11 March 1888; died in Cranleigh, Surrey on 6 May 1957.
He attended the Royal College of Music. Organ scholar of Worcester College, Oxford. Graduated M.A. and D.Mus (1923) at Worcester College, Oxford.
Awarded the Military Cross during World War I.
Knighted in 1952. Appointed Order of the British Empire.
Assistant music master of Clifton College, Gloucestershire. Director of music at the Royal Naval College, Osborne, Isle of Wight (from 1914). Organist and music master of Charterhouse (from 1919) and of Harrow School.
Warden (1943-1949) in succession to **Benjamin Dale** and, subsequently, principal of the Royal Academy of Music (1949-

1955) in succession to **Stanley Marchant**. He retired in 1955 through ill-health.

President of the Royal College of Organists (1954-1960) and an editor of *B.B.C. Hymn Book* (1951)

Composed hymn tunes. His anthem 'Come, ye faithful, raise the strain' is much sung. His degree exercise was a Choral Elegy.

THIMAN, Dr. Eric Harding (1900-1975)

Born in Ashford, Kent on 12 September 1900; died in Camden, London on 13 February 1975.

Educated at Caterham School, Surrey and at Guildhall School of Music.

For a time, Eric Thiman was a railwayman but he later pursued a career in music. Organist of Caterham Congregational Church (1917-1920); Elm Park Baptist Church, Beckenham (from 1920) and of the Park Chapel, Crouch End, London (from 1922). In 1958 he was organist and choirmaster of the City Temple, London.

Organist at the Annual Festival of the Free Church Choir Union (from 1930). These were at the Crystal Palace up to and including 1936, and thereafter at the Alexandra Palace. Conductor in 1938. The Annual Festivals were resumed after World War II, and Thiman held office as organist until his resignation in 1972.

A professor of harmony at the Royal Academy of Music (from 1930).

Eric Thiman was the author of textbooks on musical theory and was chairman of the Committee for the hymnal *Congregational Praise* (1951).

He composed anthems including 'Lo round the throne' and hymn tunes. There was said to be prejudice against him in cathedral circles but he has been given considerable credit for raising, almost single-handedly, the musical standards of the Free Church by his practical understanding of achievable targets and by the musical quality of his compositions.

THOMAS, Adelaide Louisa (?19th century)

Born in Clapham, London. Attended the National Training School of Music. Supplicated successfully for the Oxford B.Mus. (1892) with her Psalm setting 'The earth is the Lord's' for Solo Voices, Chorus, Strings and Piano but she was prevented by statute from being awarded the degree. A teacher of piano at Cheltenham Ladies' College, Gloucestershire (1886-1888) and she later became principal of the Scientific Training School for Music (from 1894). She lived in Brighton, Sussex. Gave piano recitals in London during 1883. Composed a Festival Magnificat and Nunc Dimittis.

THOMAS, Dr. Edwin Fugler (1896-?)

Edwin Thomas was born in Penzance, Cornwall in 1896. Studied music with **Mark Monk** and graduated D.Mus. at the University of Oxford. Organist and choirmaster of St. Paul's Church, Penzance (1916-1917; 1919-1933) and of Ludgran Church (from 1933). During World War I he was acting bandmaster of the 52nd Gordon Highlanders (1917-1919). He composed chants, Kyries, and songs.

THOMAS, Frank Lewis (1857-1918)

Born in London in 1857; died in Bromley, Kent on 22 May 1918. The younger son of the bass singer Lewis William Thomas.

Educated at the Royal Academy of Music under **William Cusins** for piano, Francis Ralph for violin and **H.C. Banister** for harmony. Continued his studies under A. H. Thouless for piano, J.S. Jekyll for organ and his father for singing. Organist of Christ Church, Lancaster Gate, London (from 1879). Organist and choirmaster of St. Mary's Church, Bromley, Kent (from 1880). An accompanist, taking part in the Covent Garden Promenade Concerts, and a music society conductor. He taught music in and around the town of Bromley. Composed a Benedicite, anthems, songs, piano works, and other items of chamber music.

THOMAS, Gertrude Evelyn (20th century)

Born in Bedwas, Wales. She studied music with, among others, **Joseph Parry**, W.E. Edwards and E.G. Richards. Organist and choirmaster of Bedwas Parish Church. Composed an Easter anthem 'I am He that liveth' and another for harvest: 'Father of mercies'. There were other anthems, Kyries, and chants.

THOMAS, John (Llanwrtyd: 1839-1922)

Born in Blaenannerch Cardiganshire, Wales on 11 December 1839; died in Llanwrtyd Wells, Breconshire, Wales on 22 February 1922. Known as John Thomas, Blaenannerch until 1921, in which year he married and moved to Llanwrtyd. An apprentice shopkeeper in Castellnewydd Emlyn but returned to work in his father's shop due to ill-health in the family. In 1871 he took over the running of the post office in Llanwrtyd Wells. A festival adjudicator and a close friend of David Lewis, the composer of hymn tunes and collector of Welsh melodies. John Thomas conducted festivals of congregational hymn singing throughout Wales and he was prominent in the *Cymanfa* Ganu movement (literally, a gathering for song - typically, for hymns but also oratorios) that had begun in 1858. Composer of hymn tunes including 'Blaencefn', anthems, glees, and part songs. From around the age of 30 he concentrated on writing poetry at the expense of further musical composition.

THOMAS, John Harries (1875-1950)

Born in Merthyr Tydfil, Glamorgan, Wales in 1875; died in Swansea, Glamorgan on 24 May 1950. A school teacher in Ammanford, Carmarthenshire, where he was organist and choirmaster of the local Baptist Church. Until the year of his death he was on the Music Committee for the *Welsh Baptist Hymnal* of 1955. Composer of hymn tunes.

THOMAS, John Lyddon (1910-1966)

Born in Haverhill, Suffolk in 1910; died in Chelsea, London on 11 June 1966.

As a boy he lived in Aberdare, Glamorgan, Wales, attending Aberdare County School. He later attended Tiffin's School, Kingston-on-Thames, Surrey. By profession he was an insurance underwriting clerk and he composed a number of hymn tunes including 'Harvest Song' (1956) for a Harvest Festival Service at Thames Ditton Congregational Church, Surrey where he was organist and choirmaster (1948-1966).

THOMAS, Dr. William Edwin (1867-?)

Born in Oxford in 1867.

From the age of seven he was a chorister of Christ Church Cathedral, Oxford, later becoming a pupil of the Cathedral organist, **C.W. Corfe**. As a Christ Church chorister he was selected by the founder of St. Michael's College, Tenbury, **F.A.G. Ouseley**, to sing at College Festivals. While still a chorister he played services at St. Nicholas's Chapel, Oxford. Graduated B.Mus. (1888) and D.Mus. (1893) at the University of Oxford, these being awarded partly on the strength of settings of Psalm 76 ('In Jewry is God known) and Psalm 71 (In Thee, O Lord, have I put my trust).

Deputy organist of St. Paul's Church, Oxford before becoming organist of Ellesborough Church, near Tring, Hertfordshire. After a few months at Ellesborough he was appointed organist and choirmaster of the Church of SS John and Mary, Oxford.

Organist and choirmaster of All Saints' Church, Banbury, Oxfordshire (from 1886) and of St. Clement's Church, Bournemouth, Dorset (from 1895). A local choral and philharmonic society conductor. Conducted examinations locally for the Royal College of Music.

Emigrated to New Zealand, where he was organist and choirmaster of All Saints' Church, Auckland (from 1900) and organist of Auckland Cathedral (from 1903). An examiner for the University of New Zealand.

His compositions include a Holy Communion Service in F, a Magnificat and Nunc Dimittis in D, a prize-winning madrigal 'And wilt thou weep', songs, part songs, and works for violin and for piano.

THOMPSON, Robert George (1862-1934)
Born in Stockton-on-Tees, County Durham on 5 November 1862; died in Middlesbrough, Yorkshire on 6 January 1934.

Attended the Wesleyan School, Middlesbrough and Westminster Training College. Graduated B.Mus. (1893) at the University of Durham.

A school teacher. He held organistships in Stockton-on-Tees at the Brunswick Wesleyan Church and Holy Trinity Church and in Middlesbrough at the Newport Road Baptist Church, the Grange Road United Methodist Church and the Park Methodist Church.

His degree exercise was the cantata *A Hymn of Faith* for Solo Voices, Chorus and Strings. His other works include anthems, hymn tunes including 'Blairgowrie' for *Methodist Hymn Book* (1933), an organ voluntary, school songs, a school operetta *The Rainbow Stair*, and piano items.

THOMSON, Revd. Andrew Mitchell (1778-1831)
Born in Sanquhar, Dumfriesshire, Scotland in June 1778 and was baptised on 11 July; died in Edinburgh on 9 February 1831.

Educated at the University of Edinburgh and in 1802 he was ordained into the Ministry of the Church of Scotland. He served congregations in Kelso (from 1802), Sprouston, Roxburgh (1805-1808) and Perth (East Church: 1808-1810), and the Edinburgh Churches of New Greyfriars (1810-1814) and St. George (1814-1831), the latter being newly-built.

Patron of the music teacher and viola player **Robert Archibald Smith** whom he persuaded to take up the position of precentor of St. George's. The two collaborated in the production of the collection *Sacred Harmony for the use of St. George's Church, Edinburgh...* (1820). Andrew Thomson did much to promote the use and improvement of Psalm singing within the Church of Scotland. He composed the Psalm tunes 'St George's', 'Edinburgh' and 'Redemption'.

THORLEY, Thomas (18th/19th century)
The singer and composer Thomas Thorley was active around the year 1800. He composed an Epitaph Hymn (1817) to mark the death of Princess Charlotte of Wales. Another notable work was *The Siege of Algiers* (1820) for Piano, simulating dramatically such events as the firing of rockets and bombs and the burning of ships.

THORN, Gilbert Charles (1890-1968)
Born in Cheltenham, Gloucestershire in 1890; died in Birmingham on 13 January 1968. Studied music under H. Marshall Sowry of Cheltenham. Organist of Salem Baptist Church, Cheltenham; Blenheim Baptist Church, Leeds; the Church of the Redeemer, Birmingham and Erdington Baptist Church, Birmingham. Composer of hymn tunes including 'Branksome' (1962) which appeared in *Baptist Hymn Book* of that year.

THORNE, Berthold George (19th/20th century)
Graduated B.Mus. (Durham: 1897) and B.Mus. (New College, Oxford: 1902). Organist and choirmaster of All Saints' Church, Wyke Regis, Weymouth, Dorset (1893-1895) and of Dunster Parish Church. Organist and assistant music master of Sherborne School, Dorset (1895-1902) and organist and music master of New College, Eastbourne, Sussex (1902-1904). Director of music of Trent College, Nottinghamshire (1904-1907), and organist and choirmaster of St. Mary's Church, Weymouth (from 1908). Composed Evening Services, anthems, and hymn tunes. His other works include songs, part songs, glees, organ works, and items for piano. His degree exercises were *A Song of Praise* (Durham) and *O quot undis lacrymarum* (Oxford).

THORNE, Dr. Edward Henry (1834-1916)
Born in Cranbourne, Dorset on 9 May 1834; died in Paddington, London on 26 December 1916.

The son of Edward Thorne, a musician.

A chorister at St. George's Chapel, Windsor Castle under **George Elvey**, to whom he was assistant organist from the age of 12. Awarded the Lambeth D.Mus. in 1913.

Organist of Henley-on-Thames Parish Church, Oxfordshire (1852-1862); St. Patrick's Church, Brighton, Sussex (from 1870) and the London Churches of St. Peter, Onslow Gardens, South Kensington (from 1873); St. Michael, Cornhill (from 1875) and St. Anne, Soho (from 1891), where he succeeded **Joseph Barnby**.

Organist of Chichester Cathedral (1862-1870).

A piano and organ recitalist and a teacher of piano and organ. His Bach organ recitals were well-known.

Composed a Magnificat and Nunc Dimittis for the annual Festival of the Sons of the Clergy in St. Paul's Cathedral, some 20 anthems including a setting of Psalm 57 'Be merciful unto me, O God', the hymn tunes 'Ira Justa' (1884), 'St. Bartholomew', 'St. Andrew' and 'We Give', Responses to the Commandments in E Minor and in G, and chamber and orchestral music.

THORNE, John (c1514-1573)
Born around the year 1514; died in York on 7 December 1573. Organist of York Minster (1541-1573). A poet and logician. Someone of the same name was clerk of the fabric (1567-1571) and a conduct (1539-1540) of the Church of St. Mary-at-Hill, London. He composed a Te Deum and other items of church music.

THORNTON, James (1824-1896)
Born in Bramley, Yorkshire in 1824; died in Horsforth, Yorkshire on 30 October 1896. Composer of hymn tunes.

THRELFALL, Thomas (1842-1907)
Born in Liverpool on 31 December 1842; died in Paddington, London on 3 February 1907. Graduated M.A. An amateur musician who was on the Management Committee of the Royal Academy of Music (from 1886). Later, he was chairman of the Committee for

20 years. Also chairman of the Associated Board of the Royal Schools of Music. Composer of the hymn tune 'Lancashire'.

THRUPP, Revd. Joseph Francis (1827-1867)
Born on 20 May 1827; died in Surbiton, Surrey on 24 September 1867. Educated at Winchester, Hampshire and at Trinity College, Cambridge. Vicar of Barrington, Cambridge. A Bible scholar. Published a collection of Psalm and hymn tunes *Ancient Jerusalem* (1853). He composed an Epiphany Hymn 'Brightest and best', and hymn tunes.

THUNDER, Henry G. (1832-1881)
Born near Dublin on 10 February 1832; died in New York City on 14 December 1881. Studied under Thalberg. On emigrating to New York he became organist of the Roman Catholic Churches of St. Augustine, St. Clement and St. Stephen. He composed items of church music, and songs.

THURLOW, Alan John (b.1947)
Born in Woodford Green, Essex on 18 May 1947.
Attended Bancroft's School, Woodford and the University of Sheffield as university organ scholar. Graduated B.A. (1968) in music. He then studied at Emmanuel College, Cambridge (1968-1971) where he undertook research into the Latin church music of **John Sheppard**.
In 1963, Alan Thurlow became organist of St. Barnabas Church, Woodford. From 1973 he was sub organist of Durham Cathedral and director of music of the choir school. Organist of St. Margaret's Church, Durham until 1976, and a part-time lecturer at the University of Durham.
Appointed organist of Chichester Cathedral in September 1980.
He has composed The *St. Barnabas* Mass, the anthems 'The Lord's Supper' and 'Delight thou in the Lord', and many arrangements of hymns and other items for use by brass bands in conjunction with organ.

THURNAM, Edward (1825-1880)
Born in Warwick on 24 September 1825; died in Reigate, Surrey on 25 November 1880. Organist of Reigate Parish Church, Surrey (1849-1880), and a local choral society conductor. He composed church music, songs, and items for piano.

TIDDEMAN, Maria C. (1837-1915)
Born in Croydon, Surrey in 1837 and baptised on 5 April of that year; died at Cowley, Oxfordshire on 8 January 1915. Her hymn tune 'Ibstone' was used in the 1875 edition of *Hymns Ancient and Modern* and was named after her father's parish of Fingest cum Ibstone. Composed a number of other hymn tunes, an anthem, songs and part songs.

TIDNAM, John Ellis (19th/20th century)
Graduated B.Mus. (1904) at the University of Oxford. Organist of Chard Parish Church (from 1893), Wimborne Minster (from 1897) and Stroud Parish Church (from 1902). Organist and music master of Dover College, Kent (from 1906). Composed church music and part songs. His degree exercise was a setting of L'Allegro by John Milton for Solo Voices, Chorus and Strings.

TILLEARD, James (1827-1876)
Born in Surrey in 1827; died in Lewisham, London on 17 January 1876. Editor of *Collection of Sacred Music for the Use of Schools* (1849), *Secular Music for Schools* (1851) and *The People's Chant Book* (1853). He composed Te Deums, a set of Responses to the Commandments in E, anthems including 'Star of morn and even' and 'Tho' nature's strength decay', hymn tunes, songs and part songs.

TILLMAN, June Boyce.
See **BOYCE-TILLMAN,** June.

TINNEY, Charles Ernest (1851-1925)
Born in Pimlico, London on 15 March 1851; died in East Grinstead, Sussex on 3 January 1925.
The son of Frederick George Tinney, a conductor.
A chorister of Westminster Abbey under **James Turle** and a pupil of **Charles Santley**. He studied at the Royal Academy of Music under Manuel Garcia.
A bass singer, he was a vicar choral of St. Paul's Cathedral (1877-1902) and, for two years, assistant master of the boys.
Principal English singing master at the New England Conservatory, Boston (1886-1890). Lived as a concert singer in Buenos Aires, Argentina for two years.
A professor of singing at the Royal Normal College for the Blind, and at Trinity College of Music, London. A professor of Guildhall School of Music (1883-1886) and a senior professor in singing at the R.A.M. (from 1913).
Choirmaster of All Saints' Church, Blackheath, London and associated with Loreto Abbey and Alexandra College. A glee club and madrigal club conductor.
He composed an Evening Service in D, anthems, and songs.

TIPPETT, Sir Michael Kemp (b.1905)
Born in London on 2 January 1905.
His father was of Cornish descent and his mother, who was associated with the suffragette movement, was from a Kentish family.
Spent much of his early childhood in Wetherden, Suffolk. His father then retired and bought a hotel in Cannes, where Michael learned to speak French fluently. His early education was from a governess and his mother.
Attended Fettes School, Edinburgh from the age of 13 but he was unhappy there. His parents withdrew him and sent him instead to Stamford School, Lincolnshire (1920). His parents were asked to remove him after Michael had refused to attend school prayers for a fortnight. He continued to have piano lessons from Frances Tinkler who had also taught the conductor Malcolm Sargent, but piano lessons were the only form of musical training he received prior to attending the Royal College of Music (1923-1928).
At the R.C.M. he studied composition initially under **Charles Wood** and, following Wood's death, with **C.H. Kitson**, with whom he was unable to build a rapport. He studied piano with Aubin Raymar, and conducting with Malcolm Sargent and Adrian Boult.
Michael Tippett was appointed C.B.E. (1959) and was knighted in 1966. He was made a Companion of Honour in 1979 and received the Order of Merit in 1983.
He founded a small choir in Oxted, Surrey (1928). A year later he was appointed as a part time teacher of French at Hazelwood School, Oxted, one of a number of appointments from which his income was sufficient to devote himself in his spare time to composition. In 1930 he put on a concert of his own works, as a result of which he decided that he still lacked the requisite training.

He therefore decided to resume his studies and returned to the R.C.M. (1930-1932) to work on composition with **R.O. Morris**.

In the early years of that decade he was in charge of the music at a work camp in North Yorkshire, an experience that consolidated his left-wing view of politics.

Michael Tippett led the South London Orchestra (1933-1940), a group of unemployed musicians based at Morley College. The College was almost totally destroyed by bombing in 1940. Tippett became director of music in the same year, a position he retained until 1952. From 1942, **Benjamin Britten** and Peter Pears became involved with Morley College. Tippett was the dedicatee of Britten's opera *Curlew River*. Tippett also ran the college choir, and his choristers included the future broadcasters, **Antony Hopkins** and John Amis. The teaching staff included Matyas Seiber and **Peter Racine Fricker**. A notable 'first' for the Choir and the College was the first English performance of Monteverdi's *Vespers* of 1610.

In 1940, Tippett joined the Peace Pledge Union. He registered as a conscientious objector and at about this time became a friend of the writer T.S. Eliot. At the inevitable tribunal in February 1942, **Ralph Vaughan Williams** spoke on his behalf but to no avail. Tippett was sentenced to six months' imprisonment in Wormwood Scrubs, commencing in June. Released on 21 August 1942, the day on which the first performance of his Second String Quartet was given, at Wigmore Hall, London. He organised some of his fellow-inmates into an orchestra and put on a concert which included **Handel**'s Largo and a Bach chorale.

Michael Tippett lived in Oxted (1928- 1951) and then at Wadhurst, Sussex (1951-1960). He subsequently lived in the Wiltshire towns of Corsham (1960-1970) and Calne (from 1970).

A broadcaster from 1951. Directed the Bath Festival, Somerset from 1969 to 1974.

Michael Tippett has composed a Magnificat and Nunc Dimittis (*St. John's College* Setting) and the anthem 'Plebs Angelica'. His other works include symphonies, eight operas, and oratorios including *A Child of our Time* (1944). Various of the five spirituals in this work are sung as separate anthems, including 'Go down, Moses' and 'Steal away'. His first major success was his Concerto for Double String Orchestra (1939), and he continues to compose in his 90s.

TIRBUTT, John Charles Brettel (1857-1908)

Born in Bromsgrove, Worcestershire on 30 March 1857; died in Reading, Berkshire, on 12 July 1908. Graduated B.Mus. (1891) at the University of Durham. Organist of All Saints' Church, Reading (from 1879) and lecturer in music at the University Extension College, Reading (from 1892). An amateur musical society conductor. He composed anthems, his degree exercise being a setting of Psalm 130 'Out of the deep have I called unto Thee' for Solo Voices, Chorus and Strings. His other works include cantatas, a ballad 'The phantom ship', songs, and part songs.

TOLHURST, George (1827-1877)

Born in1827; died in Barnstaple, Devon on 18 January 1877. Composed the anthem 'I will lay me down', an oratorio *Ruth* (1867), and songs.

TOMBLINGS, Philip Benjamin (b. 1902)

Born in London in 1902.

A chorister of Exeter Cathedral under D.J. Wood, and studied at the Royal College of Music, where his tutors included **Ernest Bullock**.

Director of music of St. Lawrence College, Ramsgate, Kent (1931-1946). Director of music of the Merchant Taylors' School, Northwood, Middlesex (1946-1966).

Organist and choirmaster in Exeter of Ide Parish Church (1919-1921) and St. Matthew's Church (1921-1923), and subsequently of St. Mary's Church, Berkeley Square, London (1923-1925).

Assistant master of Tonbridge School, Kent (1925-1929), and organist and music master of Bloxham School, Banbury, Oxfordshire (1929-1931).

A professor of harmony at the Royal Academy of Music (from 1966). An examiner to the Associated Board of the Royal Schools of Music (from 1948).

He has composed a Communion Service in D (the Missa *Sancti Matthaei*), a Benedicite in E-flat, a Te Deum in D, the anthems 'Come, my Way, my Truth, my Life' and 'Sing a song of joy' and his other works include songs and part songs. Also the carol 'Dost Thou in a manger lie?'.

TOMKINS, Giles (Gyles) (?-1668)

Buried in Salisbury, Wiltshire on 4 April 1668. Musician for virginals to Charles I from April 1630 until 1649. Resumed his post at the Restoration. Organist of King's College, Cambridge (1624-1626) and of Salisbury Cathedral (1630-1668). Composed the anthem 'In Thee, O Lord'.

TOMKINS, John (1586-1638)

Born in St. David's, Pembrokeshire, Wales in 1586. Graduated Mus.B. at the University of Cambridge. In 1625 he became a gentleman extraordinary of the Chapel Royal, with a view to securing the next organistship that fell vacant there, but it seems that this next step never took place. A vicar choral of St. Paul's Cathedral (from 1628), where he was a contemporary of **Adrian Batten**. Organist of King's College, Cambridge from 1606 until 1619 or 1621. He composed services for use at the Chapel Royal.

TOMKINS, Revd. Thomas (?-1627)

Born in Cornwall; died in Gloucester in 1627. A vicar-choral (1565), organist (c1570-c1586) and master of the children (from c1573) of St. David's Cathedral. Precentor of Gloucester Cathedral at some time during the early years of the 17th century. Also vicar of the Church of St. Mary de Lode, Gloucester. Composed the anthem 'O Lord I have loved' and his works feature in *The Triumphes of Oriana*.

TOMKINS, Thomas (c1572-1656)

Born in St. David's, Pembrokeshire, Wales around 1573; died in Martin Hussingtree, Worcestershire in 1656, being buried on 9 June.

Organist of the Chapel Royal (from 1621) and of Worcester Cathedral (1596-1656). It was intended that he should be composer-in-ordinary to Charles I following the death of **John Coprario**, but the position had already been promised to **Alphonso Ferrabosco**. The collection **Musica Deo Sacra**, published in 1668 after his death, contains five services and 95 anthems plus some madrigals. His anthems include 'Arise, O Lord God', 'My Shepherd is the Living Lord', 'O how amiable', 'Out of the deep' and 'Praise the Lord, ye servants'.

TOMLINSON, Richard (1822-1896)

Born in Sheffield, Yorkshire on 22 August 1822; died in Sheffield on 24 June 1896. Choirmaster of the Primitive Methodist Chapel,

Heeley, near Sheffield from around 1860. Composed hymn tunes and edited the collection *Original Tunes, Anthems, etc.* (1879).

TOMLYN, Alfred William (1860-?)
Born in Plaxtol, ·Kent on 19 August 1860. Studied at Trinity College of Music under **E.H. Turpin** and **C.W. Pearce**. Studied privately under **Philip Armes** at Durham. Graduated B.Mus. (1892) at the University of Durham. Organist of Girven Parish Church (1887-1892); Wallace Green Church, Berwick-on-Tweed (1892-1898); Braid Church, Edinburgh (from 1898), and St. Modoc's Church, Doune. A local choral society conductor. Composed as his degree exercise a Magnificat, Nunc Dimittis and Gloria for Chorus, Solo Voices and Quartet. His other works include an Evening Service, Holy Communion Services, anthems, a cantata *The Forerunner*, songs, part songs, and organ works.

TOMS, Sydney Weatherdon (1879-?)
Born in Acton, Middlesex on 10 November 1879. Educated at St. Paul's School, London; Temple Church; King's College London and the Royal College of Music, where he was organ exhibitioner (1901-1902), under **Walter Parratt, John Frederick Bridge** and **Henry Walford Davies**. Graduated B.Mus. (1908) at Queen's College, Oxford. Organist and choirmaster of the London Churches of St. Mary Magdalene, Chiswick (from 1894); St. Stephen, Shepherd's Bush (from 1900), Christ Church, Turnham Green (from 1901) and St. James, Piccadilly (from 1905). A local orchestral society conductor and organ recitalist, taking part in the Sunday Concert Series at the Royal Albert Hall. Composed a prize hymn tune for the London Church Choirs' Association (1907), and songs. His degree exercise was a setting of Psalm 3 'Lord, how are they increased that trouble me', for Solo Voices, Chorus and Strings.

TOPLIFF, Robert (1793-1868)
Born in 1793; died in London in 1868. Organist of Holy Trinity Church, Southwark, London. A blind organist and teacher of singing and piano. Editor of *Selection of the most Popular Melodies of the Tyne and Wear, harmonised...* (1820) and of *Six Sabbath Melodies* (1844). *Praise Offering* (1854) contained his own 'Enter not into judgement' and 'There were shepherds'. Composed church music, and songs including 'Consider the lilies'.

TORRANCE, Revd. Dr. George William (1835-1907)
Born in Rathmines, Dublin in 1835; died in Kilkenny, Ireland on 20 August 1907.
A chorister of Christ Church Cathedral, Dublin. In 1856 he travelled to Leipzig to study music, returning to Ireland in 1859 to study for the ministry of the Church of Ireland. Graduated B.A. (1864), and M.A. (1867); ordained deacon (1865) and priest (1866). Was awarded, honorarily, the Melbourne D.Mus. Graduated B.Mus. and Mus.D. at Trinity College, Dublin on the recommendation of **R.P. Stewart**.
Organist of three Dublin churches. A curate in Shrewsbury and Dublin. Incumbent of Holy Trinity Church, Blackrock, Dublin (until 1895). Emigrated to Australia and settled in Melbourne. Incumbent of St. John's Melbourne (from 1895), returning to Ireland two years later and becoming prebendary of Killamery and a canon of St. Canice's Cathedral, Kilkenny.
Composed a Te Deum and Jubilate, anthems, hymn tunes, oratorios including *Abraham* (1855), which he composed at the age of 19, songs and part songs.

TORRINGTON, Dr. Frederick Herbert (1837-1918)
Born in Dudley, Worcestershire on 20 October 1837; died on 20 November 1918.
An articled pupil of James Fitzgerald of Kidderminster. Graduated D.Mus. honorarily at the University of Toronto.
Organist and choirmaster of St. Anne's Church, Bewley (1853-1856).
In 1856 he emigrated to Canada, where he became organist and choirmaster of Great St. James Church, Montreal (1856-1868). Organist of the Metropolitan Church of St. James, Montreal, and the Metropolitan Church, Toronto where he remained for 40 years.
A violinist, and bandmaster of the 25th King's Own Borderers. With a small orchestra, he represented Canada at the Peace Jubilee in Boston (1872).
Organist and director of music at the King's Chapel, Boston, U.S.A. (1872-1876). A recitalist. Taught at the New England Conservatory of Music. In 1873 he became organist and choirmaster of the Metropolitan Church, Toronto, and conductor of the Toronto Philharmonic Society. Director of the first Toronto Festival (1886). Founder of the Toronto College of Music (1888) and its first director of music.
He composed services, hymn tunes, choruses, songs, and organ voluntaries.

TOURS, Berthold (1838-1897)
Born in Amsterdam on 17 December 1838; died in Fulham, London on 11 March 1897. His father was organist of St. Lawrence's Church, Amsterdam. Studied at the Conservatories of Brussels and Leipzig. Settled in London in 1861 as an orchestral violinist. Music editor of the publisher Novello, Ewer & Co. (from 1878). Author of *Primer of the Violin*. Organist of the Swiss Church, Holborn, London (from 1862). Composed anthems including 'God be merciful' and 'Rejoice in the Lord'. His hymn tunes include 'Haarlem', 'Holland' and 'Rotterdam.' He composed settings of the Responses to the Commandments in E-flat, in F and in G.

TOWERS, George Henry (b.1914)
Born in Leicester on 31 January 1914. Composer of hymn tunes.

TOZER, Dr. Augustus Edmonds (1857-1910)
Born in Sutton, Cheshire on 13 January 1857; died in Brighton, Sussex on 10 October 1910.
Trained at the Royal Academy of Music and at the National Training School of Music, where he was City of London scholar. Graduated B.Mus. (1893) at the University of Durham, and B.Mus. (1895) at New College, Oxford. Later awarded doctorates in music at both universities. He composed as his Durham B.Mus. exercise a Missa Brevis *Pro Pace* and for his Oxford B.Mus., four movements from a Mass in C Minor. His Oxford D.Mus. was gained with a Mass *of St. Francis of Assisi*.
A Knight of the Pontifical Order of St. Sylvester (1890) awarded by Pope Leo XIII, for services to the music of the Roman Catholic Church.
Associated with a number of churches in Sussex. Honorary organist of St. Mary's Church, Star of the Sea, Hastings (from 1884); choirmaster of Holy Trinity Church, Hastings (from 1876) and organist and choirmaster of the Church of St. Mary Magdalene, St. Leonards-on-Sea. Organist and choirmaster of St. Gregory's Priory Church, Cheltenham, Gloucestershire (from 1885). Returning to Sussex, he was organist and choirmaster of the Church of the

Sacred Heart, Brighton (1888-1893 and 1895-1901) and of the Church of Our Lady of Ransom, Eastbourne (1901-1905).
An honorary local representative of the Royal Academy of Music (from 1896).
Editor of *Catholic Hymns: Original and Translated with Accompanying Tunes*, *The Catholic Church Hymnal*, *Modern Church Music for Catholic Choirs*, *Antiphons of the Blessed Virgin Mary* and *Proper of the Mass to Simple Music*.
Composed six Masses, a set of Responses for High Mass, Latin Offertory Pieces, Benediction Services, Magnificats, Vespers, Compline Antiphons, anthems and hymn tunes. Also songs and works for organ and for piano.

TOZER, Dr. John Ferris (1858-1943)
Born in Exeter, Devon on 8 November 1858; died in Exeter on 15 December 1943. A chorister of Exeter Cathedral. Studied music with **Alfred Angel** and **D.J. Wood**. Graduated B.Mus. (1891) and D.Mus. (1896) at Queen's College, Oxford. A bank clerk by profession with the Devon and Cornwall Bank, Exeter. An active church musician until 1930. Organist of St. David's Church, Exeter (1875-1882) and of St. Michael's Church, Heavitree (1882-1930). A tenor singer. Composed many items of church music. These included a Morning and Evening Service in F, Kyries, a Benedicite, anthems and hymn tunes. His Lenten Cantata *The Way of the Cross* (1896) was well known and other sacred cantatas include *The last Advent* (1903). He also composed organ music. His degree exercises were a setting of Psalm 3 'Lord, how are they increased that trouble me' for Solo Voices, Chorus and Orchestra (B.Mus.), and *Balaam and Balaak* for the same forces (D.Mus.)

TOZER, Solomon (17th century)
Composed the anthem 'O Lord, let me know', the manuscript of which is in the collection of Durham Cathedral.

TRACEY, Ian (b.1955)
Born in Liverpool on 27 May 1955.
Attended Highfield School. Studied organ with **Noel Rawsthorne** before going up to Trinity College of Music, London (1973-1975). Studied with André Isoir and Jean Langlais under a scholarship. Trained in choral techniques by Ronald Woan in Liverpool. Qualified as a teacher at St. Katherine's College, Liverpool in 1976.
A professor of the Liverpool John Moores University.
Assistant organist (from 1976), organist (from 1980) and master of the choristers (from 1982) of Liverpool Cathedral.
Chorus master to the Royal Liverpool Philharmonic Society (from 1985) and city organist for Liverpool. An examiner in music (from 1988) for several boards.
His compositions include a Magnificat and Nunc Dimittis (Fauxbourdons) and Responses for Men's voices. Has composed several carols and many descants and arrangements, including a version of the popular football song 'You'll never walk alone' which caught the national imagination at the moving Memorial Service for the victims of the Hillsborough Stadium disaster.

TRANCHELL, Peter Andrew (1922-1993)
Born in Cuddalore, India on 14 July 1922; died on 14 September 1993.
Educated at Clifton College, Gloucestershire, where he was head boy, and at King's College, Cambridge, taking a first in music.

Served in the army during World War II and then resumed his studies at King's.
Taught at Eastbourne College, Sussex early in his career. A lecturer in music at Gonville and Caius College, Cambridge (1950-1989). A fellow and director of music (1960-1989), succeeding **Patrick Hadley** as precentor. His pupils included **Martin Neary**, subsequently organist of Westminster Abbey.
Contributed book reviews to the leading periodicals. A pianist and composer.
Between 1952 and 1961 he composed nine ballets for the Theatre Royal, Windsor. His ballets include *Falstaff* (1950). His other works include six musical comedies, and operas including *The Mayor of Casterbridge*. His church music consists of works and arrangements for the male voices of Gonville and Caius College. They include 17 Psalm settings, two Evening Services and the *St. Michael's* Mass.

TRAVERS, Henry (17th century)
Composer of the anthem 'Shall we receive?' which is in the collection of Ely Cathedral.

TRAVERS, John (1703-1758)
Born in Windsor, Berkshire in 1703; died in Westminster, London around 9 June 1758.
The son of Joseph Travers, a shoemaker.
A chorister of St. George's Chapel, Windsor Castle. Apprenticed to **Maurice Greene** (from 1719). Also studied under J.C. Pepusch, part of whose library he inherited.
Organist of St. Paul's Church, Covent Garden, London (from 1726), where his apprentices included the singer and composer **Thomas Barrow**. Organist of the King's Chapel and an original member of the Royal Society of Musicians. Organist of Fulham Parish Church (until 1737) and sub organist of St. Paul's Cathedral (from c1727).
Organist of the Chapel Royal (1737-1758). At the time there were two such posts and the other was held by Maurice Greene.
Composed anthems including 'Ascribe unto the Lord' and 'Ponder my words'. He also composed chants (examples are found in *Cathedral Psalter Chants* of c1875), and hymn tunes.

TREDINNICK, Noel (b.1949)
Director of music of the Church of All Souls, Langham Place, London. A composer of hymn tunes.

TREMBATH, Henry Gough (1844-1908)
Born in Penzance, Cornwall on 29 July 1844; died in Herne Bay, Kent on 31 July 1908. Educated at the Royal Academy of Music. Graduated B.Mus. at the University of Oxford (1869). He was appointed organist of the Church of St. John the Baptist, Woodlands, Isleworth, Middlesex (from 1874). A local choral society organist and conductor. Won a prize for his anthem 'Let not your heart be troubled'. He also composed hymn tunes.

TREPTE, Paul (b.1954)
Born in Morley, Yorkshire on 24 April 1954.
A chorister of Leeds Parish Church, studying under **Donald Hunt**. Attended Batley Grammar School and was organ scholar of New College, Oxford, where he graduated M.A. Accompanist to the Halifax Choral Society. Assistant organist of Worcester Cathedral (1976-1981) and organist of St. Mary's Church, Warwick (1981-1985).

Organist of St. Edmundsbury Cathedral (1985-1990) and of Ely Cathedral (from 1990).

His compositions include a Missa Parodia and the anthems 'People look East' and 'O perfect love'. His carol arrangements have also been published.

TRIMNELL, Thomas Tallis (1827-1897)
Born in Bristol, Gloucestershire on 13 October 1827; died in Wellington, New Zealand on 15 September 1897. The son of a lay clerk of Bristol Cathedral. At eight, Thomas Trimnell became a chorister of Bristol Cathedral. Apprenticed to the Cathedral organist, J.D. Corfe. Graduated B.Mus. (1875) at the University of Oxford. Organist of the Parish Churches of Clifton, Gloucestershire; Chesterfield, Derbyshire and Sheffield (1875-1886). A local choral society conductor. In 1886 he emigrated to New Zealand. Organist of St. Mary's Church, Parnell, Auckland and of St. Peter's Church, Wellington. He composed services; anthems including 'The earth is the Lord's' (1896), composed for the Wellington Exhibition and 'O clap your hands'; a set of Responses to the Commandments in C and hymn tunes.

TRIVETT, Vincent William (1882-?)
Born in Nottingham in 1882. Studied music with Arthur Page. Organist and choirmaster of St. Peter's Church, Nottingham (from 1906), and he was organist to the Duke of Portland Lodge of Freemasons. He composed items of church music.

TROMAN, Thomas (1839-1908)
Born in Old Hill, Cradley, Worcestershire on 21 March 1839; died in London on 29 October 1908.
Graduated B.Mus. (1875) at the University of Oxford.
Organist of a number of churches around Birmingham and the Black Country, including the Parish Churches of Cradley (from 1848), Rowley Regis (from 1855) and Halesowen (from 1862); Smethwick Old Church (from 1869); St. John's, Ladywood (from 1880); and Handsworth Parish Church (from 1882).
Organist of St. John's Church, Boulogne, France (from 1889) before returning to England and being appointed organist of the Church of St. George the Martyr, Deal, Kent (1892). A local choral society conductor and freemason.
Composed services and anthems. His degree exercise was a setting of Psalm 137 'By the waters of Babylon' for Solo Voices, Chorus and Orchestra. His other works include items for piano, and other chamber music.

TROTTER, George (1866-1917)
Born in Stockton-on-Tees, County Durham on 18 January 1866; died in Stockton-on-Tees on 25 July 1917. Composer of hymn tunes.

TROUTBECK, Revd. John (1832-1899)
Born in Blencowe, Cumberland on 12 November 1832; died in Westminster, London on 11 October 1899. In 1846, at the age of 14, he attended Rugby School, Warwickshire. Studied at University College, Oxford, where he graduated B.A. (1856) and M.A. (1858). Ordained deacon in 1855. Curate of St.Cuthbert's Church, Wells, Somerset (from 1855). He was vicar of Dacre, near Ullswater, Cumberland (from 1859). A minor canon (1864) and precentor (1865-1869) of Manchester Cathedral and subsequently a minor canon (from 1869) and precentor (from 1895) of Westminster Abbey. With **Reginald Dale** he compiled **Music Primer for**

Schools (1873). Published collections of music, including *The Manchester Psalter* (1868) and *Manchester Chant Book* (1871). He composed a Single Chant in C and a Double Chant in G, both of which are found in *Cathedral Psalter Chants* (1875).

TROWBRIDGE, Leslie (19th century)
Attended the Royal Academy of Music. Composed a Mass in D, and songs including 'My Rose'.

TROYTE (Acland), Arthur Henry Dyke (1811-1857)
Born in Killerton, near Exeter on 3 May 1811; died in Bridehead, Cheshire on 19 June 1857. The second son of Sir Thomas Dyke Acland of Killerton. Changed his name to Troyte in 1852. Educated at Eton and at Christ Church, Oxford, following which he read for the bar. Author of *Letters on Musical Notation* (1841). At the request of Bishop Hamilton of Salisbury, Troyte composed a number of chants: these were first published in *Salisbury Hymn Book* (1857), a publication to which he also contributed the hymn tune 'Salisbury'.

TUČAPSKÝ, Antonín (b.1928)
Born near Brno, Moravia in the former Republic of Czechoslovakia on 27 March 1928.
Educated at the Janacek Academy of Music and the University of Brno. Director of the Moravian Teachers' Choir for 10 years. After settling in London became a professor at Trinity College of Music.
He composed a Veni, Sancte Spiritus for the Cork International Festival of 1986 and his other works include a cycle of *Five Lenten Motets*, the oratorios *Misse Serena* and *Stabat Mater*, and the cantatas *The time of Christmas* and *The Sacrifice*, the latter in seven sections, a setting of verses by George Herbert describing in the first person the events leading up to the Crucifixion. *Missa de Angelis* is a collection of 10 Christmas carols.

TUCKER, Isaac? (1761-1825)
Precentor of the Baptist Church in Westbury Leigh, Wiltshire. Published the collections *Sacred Music... for three and four Voices* (1800) and *Sacred Music... Psalm and Hymn Tunes* (1810). His compositions include the hymn tunes 'Devizes', 'Old 100th' and 'Westbury Leigh'.

TUCKER, Revd. William (c1630-1678)
Born around 1630; died in London on 28 February 1678 and was buried in Westminster Abbey. A gentleman of the Chapel Royal. Precentor of Westminster Abbey (from 1660). A junior priest at the Coronation of James II. Composed anthems including 'Comfort ye, my people' and 'This is the day', and hymn tunes.

TUCKERMAN, Dr. Samuel Parkman (1819-1890)
Born in Boston, U.S.A. in 1819; died in 1890. A pupil of C. Zenner. Awarded the Lambeth D.Mus. Organist of St. Paul's Church, Boston (from 1841). In the 1850s, Samuel Tuckerman toured English cathedrals to learn the repertory and improve Amercian standards. Lived in Windsor (1850-1851) and, later, in Switzerland. Composed anthems including 'Lighten our darkness' and 'God so loved the world', and Responses to the Commandments in E-flat and in F.

TUDWAY, Dr. Thomas (c1650-1726)
Born around 1650; died in Cambridge on 23 November 1726.

A chorister of the Chapel Royal (from 1660) under **John Blow**. Graduated Mus.B. (1681) and Mus.D. (1705) at the University of Cambridge.

A tenor lay vicar at St. George's Chapel, Windsor Castle (from 1664). Organist (1670-1726) and instructor of the choristers (1679-1680) of King's College, Cambridge. Also at Cambridge he was organist of Pembroke College, and university professor of music (1704-1726). His professorship was suspended from 1706 to 1707 because of some disparaging remarks he had made about Queen Anne and her ministers.

He moved to London in 1726.

He formed a collection of cathedral music for Edward (Lord Harley), Earl of Oxford. This was entitled *A Collection of the most celebrated Service and Anthems...* and appeared in six volumes between 1715 and 1720.

Tudway's own compositions include services, anthems including 'Arise, shine', 'Man that is born', motets, and songs. He supplicated for his degrees in music with a setting of Psalm 2 'Quare fremunt gentes' and with the anthem 'Thou, O Lord hast heard'.

TURGES, Edmund (15th century)

Composed the anthem 'Enforce yourself as God's own knight'.

TURLE, James (1802-1882)

Born in Somerton, Somerset on 5 March 1802; died in Westminster, London on 28 June 1882.

A chorister of Wells Cathedral under Dodd Perkins and articled to John Jeremiah Goss, uncle of **John Goss** of St. Paul's Cathedral. An organ student of **G.E. Williams**.

Organist of the London Churches of Christ Church, Southwark (1819-1829) and St. James, Bermondsey (1829-1831). Organist of the Philanthropic Chapel (from 1819).

Assistant organist (1819-1831) to **Thomas Greatorex** at Westminster Abbey and succeeded him as organist (1831-1882). Held the organistship until his death but by 1875 it had become necessary to appoint a permanent deputy, **John Frederick Bridge**. James Turle was also music master of the School for the Indigent Blind (1829-1856).

Author, with Edward Taylor, of *The Art of Singing at Sight* (1846) and with Bridge he produced the *Westminster Abbey Chant Book*.

Composed a Service in D and another in E-flat. His anthems include 'Almighty and merciful God' and 'This is the day'. His other church music includes hymn tunes; chants; and Responses to the Commandments in C, in D, in E-flat and in F. A collection of his Psalm and hymn tunes was made after his death by his daughter. It was published in 1885.

TURNBULL, John (1804-1844)

Born in Paisley, Scotland on 12 January 1804; died in Glasgow on 1 November 1844. Precentor of New Church, Ayr (from 1827) and of St. George's Church, Glasgow (from 1833). Published *Easy and Progressive Exercises in Singing and in Reading Music*. He also published a collection of the music of **Robert Archibald Smith**. He composed Psalm tunes, anthems and songs including 'Jeannie Lee'.

TURNER, Austin T. (1823-?)

Born in Bristol, Gloucestershire in 1823. A chorister of Bristol Cathedral and a vicar choral of Lincoln Cathedral. In 1854 he emigrated to Australia, settling at Ballarat where he was the singing master of a local school, philharmonic society conductor and organist of Christ Church. Composed two Masses, a sacred cantata *Adoration*, and Two Marches for Orchestra (1868).

TURNER, John (19th century)

John Turner published *Manual of Instruction in Vocal Music...* (1833) and *Class Singing Book for Schools* (1844). He composed a Te Deum, and songs.

TURNER, John Bradbury (?-1898)

Born in Stockport, Cheshire; died in 1898.

Learned cello with S.W. Wilkinson. Played in a number of local orchestras. A pupil of the Royal Academy of Music (1852-1861), where he studied with **William Sterndale Bennett**, **George Macfarren** and **Charles Steggall**. Graduated Mus.B. (1865) at the University of Cambridge. Organist of St. Mary's Church, Primrose Hill, London and a founder of Trinity College of Music, where he became director of music. Composed anthems including 'But my trust is in Thy mercy' and 'Consider and hear me.' His other works include an overture, a Piano Trio in C Minor, and songs.

TURNER, Robert Henry (1859-1941)

Born in Scarborough, Yorkshire in 1859; died in Scarborough in 1941. His father was organist of Christ Church, Scarborough for 25 years. Robert Turner studied with **William Creser** and **George Garrett**. Graduated Mus.B. (1891) at Corpus Christi College, Cambridge (1886). A Cambridge M.A. Organist and choirmaster of St. Paul's Cathedral, Dundee (1881-1898) and of the Church of St. Thomas à Becket, Portsmouth, Hampshire (1898-1925). Organist of St. Peter's Church, Bishop Waltham for two years and of St. Simon's Church, Southsea, Hampshire (1930-1941). Composed an Evening Service (1883), an anthem 'Abide with me', hymns and part songs. His degree exercise was a setting of Psalm 95 'O come, let us sing unto the Lord'.

TURNER, Thomas Stanley (b.1913)

Born in Langley Mill, Nottinghamshire in 1913. He studied at University College, Nottingham, with **Gordon Slater** and Bernard Johnson. Organist and choirmaster of Ilkeston Parish Church, Derbyshire. Composed the anthems 'God be in my head' and 'The Lord is my Shepherd', and his other works include organ music.

TURNER, Dr. William (1651-c1739)

Born in Oxford in 1651; died in Westminster, London on 13 January 1739 or 1740.

The son of the cook of Pembroke College, Oxford.

A chorister of Christ Church Cathedral, Oxford under **Edward Lowe** and of the Chapel Royal under **Henry Cooke**, where he was one of the first of Cooke's boys. Graduated Mus.D. at the University of Cambridge (1696).

A gentleman and counter-tenor singer of the Chapel Royal (from 1669), serving a total of seven monarchs. Also a vicar choral of St. Paul's Cathedral and a lay vicar of Westminster Abbey.

Master of the choristers of Lincoln Cathedral (1667-1670).

Famous as one of the three composers of the so-called 'Club Anthem', the others being **John Blow** and **Pelham Humfrey**. Composed anthems including 'By the waters of Babylon' and 'Lord, Thou hast been our Refuge' and an Ode for St. Cecilia's Day (1685). He also composed hymn tunes, chants, and operas including *Presumptuous Lover* (1716).

TURPIN, Dr. Edmund Hart (1835-1907)

Born in Nottingham on 4 May 1835; died in Holborn, London on 26 October 1907.

The son of a local lace manufacturer, and brother of **James Turpin**.

Studied music with Charles Noble and a number of other local teachers before taking lessons in London with **John Hullah** and Ernst Pauer. Received the Lambeth D.Mus. in 1889.

Gave his first public organ recital at the Great Exhibition of 1851. Organist of St Barnabas's Roman Catholic Church, Nottingham (1850-1864). Organist of the London Churches of St. George, Bloomsbury (1869-1888) and St. Bride, Fleet Street (from 1888). A lecturer and concert pianist. An examiner for the College of Organists. Warden of Trinity College of Music (from 1892); an honorary member of the Tonic Sol-fa College (from 1885) and of the Royal Academy of Music (from 1890). Joint editor of *Musical News* (from 1891) and editor of *Musical Standard*.

Composed a Mass in A-flat and another in D for Solo Voices, Chorus, Brass, Drums and Organ; services, anthems, and hymn tunes including 'Clifton' and 'Mansfield'.

TURPIN, Dr. James (1840-1896)

Born in Nottingham on 15 December 1840; died on 29 July 1896. Brother of **Edmund Turpin**.

Graduated Mus.B. (1880) at the University of Cambridge.

Organist of Nottingham Roman Catholic Cathedral, and of Londonderry Cathedral, Northern Ireland. Then took up Parish Church appointments at St. Leonard's, Sussex, and Berkhamsted and Watford (St. Andrew's), Hertfordshire.

Pursued a full and active career, despite being paralysed for some years. Active as an organ recitalist, pianist and lecturer. A professor of harmony and counterpoint of Trinity College of Music, London. Influential in obtaining suitable buildings for the National Training School of Music and also for the College of Organists, of which he was secretary.

He composed a Service, songs and a piano sonata.

TURTON, Revd. Dr. Thomas (1780-1864)

Born in Hatfield, Yorkshire on 25 February 1780; died in Westminster, London on 7 January 1864. Educated at St. Catherine's Hall, Cambridge where he graduated B.A. (1805), M.A. (1808) and B.D. (1816). Cambridge professor of mathematics (from 1822) and of divinity (from 1827). Incumbent of Gimingham cum Trunch, Norfolk (1826-1827). Dean of Peterborough (1830-1842) and of Westminster (1842-1845), and Bishop of Ely (1854-1864). A controversial writer on matters of church politics, opposing the abolition of the religious test as part of the university admission procedure. He composed the hymn tune 'Ely St. Ethelreda', and a number of chants.

TWIGG, David (b.1956)

Born in Peterborough, Cambridgeshire on 18 July 1956. Educated at Deacon's School, Peterborough, at the University of Leeds where he was awarded a degree in music (1977), having studied composition with Alexander Goehr and Peter Paul Nash, and at the University of Birmingham where he continued his postgraduate studies with **John Joubert**. Organist and choirmaster of St. Mary's Parish Church, Selly Oak, Birmingham (1986-1989) and of Holy Trinity Parish Church, The Lickey. Also a freelance teacher and composer. A reviewer for *Choir and Organ*. Has written music for organ, for piano and for harp, incidental music to 'Peer Gynt' and

to the masque 'The flame of freedom'. His church compositions include settings of Psalms 23 and 24, and 'Welcome to a stranger'.

TYE, Revd. Dr. Christopher (c1500-c1572)

Born in Westminster, London around 1500; died in or around March 1572.

A chorister of the Chapel Royal. Graduated Mus.B. (1536) and Mus.D. (1545) at the University of Cambridge, and D.Mus. (1548), honorarily, at the University of Oxford.

A gentleman of the Chapel Royal for the entire reign of Edward VI (1547-1553). May have been one of the king's tutors. Organist of Ely Cathedral (1541-1562).

Ordained around 1560 and was subsequently appointed to three livings in the Diocese of Ely and county of Cambridgeshire: Little Wilbraham (1564), Newton (1567-1570) and Doddington-cum-March (1570-1572).

He set his own translations of the Acts of the Apostles to music (1553), and composed to both English and Latin texts. Wrote a Service in G Minor. His anthems include 'Praise the Lord ye children' and 'Once, only once'.

TYLER, James Sherman (1842-1917)

Born in Lambeth, Surrey on 20 October 1842; died in Sussex in 1917. Composer of hymn tunes.

TYSOE, Dr. Albert Charles (1884-1962)

Born in Northampton in 1884; died in Chichester, Sussex on 22 May 1962.

Studied with **Haydn Keeton**, graduating B.Mus. (1909) and D.Mus. (1915) at the University of Durham.

Organist and choirmaster of the Northampton Churches of St. Giles (1903-1914) and All Saints (1914-1920), and of Leeds Parish Church (1920-1937). Chorus master of the Leeds Festival. Conductor of the Halifax Choral Society (1922-1937), succeeding **C.H. Moody**.

Albert Tysoe was organist of St. Albans Cathedral (1937-1947).

He composed as his degree exercise a setting of texts from the Psalms for Solo Voices, Chorus and Strings. His works include a Morning Service in A and a hymn tune to 'Eternal Light, Eternal Light!'.

UGLOW, James (c1814-1894)

Born around 1814; died in Cheltenham, Gloucestershire on 6 May 1894. A chorister of Gloucester Cathedral from the age of six under **William Mutlow**. In 1824 he sang at a concert in Cheltenham given by Thomas Woodward, organist and choirmaster of Cheltenham Parish Church, to whom he was later articled. Studied under **William Crotch**, Neukomm, N. Mori and, for cello, William Lindley. James Uglow was an organist, violinist and cellist. Organist of the Cheltenham Churches of St. James, Trinity and St. John. In 1842 he travelled to Ireland, intending to settle there, but soon returned. Composer of hymn tunes.

V

VANN, Dr. William Stanley (b.1910)

Born in Leicester on 15 February 1910.

Attended Alderman Newton's Grammar School, Leicester, and Leicester College. Graduated B.Mus. at the University of London (1947). A fellow of Trinity College, London (from 1953). Awarded the Lambeth D.Mus. in 1971.

Chorus master of Leicester Philharmonic Society under **Henry Wood** (1931-1934) and subsequently under Sir Malcolm Sargent.

Assistant organist (1931-1933) to **George Gray** of Leicester Cathedral before becoming organist of Gainsborough Parish Church, Lincolnshire (and director of music at the High School and Queen Elizabeth's Grammar School) from 1933 to 1939 and Holy Trinity Church, Leamington Spa, Warwickshire (1939-1949) where he founded the Leamington Bach Choir and the Warwickshire Symphony Orchestra. During World War II he served in the Royal Artillery (1941-1946), rising to the rank of captain.

Organist of Chelmsford Cathedral (1949-1953) and a professor of harmony at Trinity College of Music, London. Organist of Peterborough Cathedral, a member of the Council of the Royal College of Organists and an examiner for T.C.M. (1953-1977), retiring in the latter year.

His published works include eight settings of the Mass or Holy Communion Service, 12 Evening Services and over a hundred motets, anthems, carols and organ pieces, including the 8-part motet *O sacrum convivium* (for the Choir of King's College, Cambridge) and such anthems as 'Behold, how good and joyful' and 'From Heaven's height'.

VAUGHAN WILLIAMS, Dr. Ralph (1872-1958)

Born in Down Ampney, Gloucestershire on 12 October 1872; died in St. Marylebone, London on 26 August 1958. His remains were interred in Westminster Abbey, close to those of Purcell and Stanford.

The son of a clergyman who died when Ralph was aged three. Related to Charles Darwin and the Wedgwood family.

Grew up at Leith Hill Place, Surrey, having moved from Down Ampney on the death of his father. Attended a preparatory school at Rottingdean, Brighton, Sussex; Charterhouse (1887-1890) and the Royal College of Music (1890-1892) before going up to Trinity College, Cambridge (1892-1895) to read history.

Graduated Mus.B. (1894), B.A. (1895) and Mus.D. (1901). Also awarded, honorarily, the Oxford D.Mus. (1919).

He learned to play the violin, piano and organ at preparatory school and at Charterhouse, he formed the ambition of becoming an orchestral viola player.

Having earlier declined a knighthood, Vaughan Williams was accorded the O.M. in 1935.

Organist of St. Barnabas's Church, South Lambeth Road, London (1896-1899).

At the R.C.M. his teachers included **Hubert Parry, C.V. Stanford** and **Charles Wood**. The latter formed the impression that Vaughan Williams did not have the makings of a composer. Vaughan Williams's difficulties were caused or accentuated by a lack of stimulation from the contemporary music scene and an awakening interest in folk origins. He also studied with Max Bruch in Berlin (1907), and with Maurice Ravel in Paris (1908).

During World War I, he served despite being 42 years old at the outset as a wagon orderly in the R.A.M.C., the forerunner of the Royal Artillery, and became an officer. He later served in Salonika and France. After the Armistice he had the responsibility of organising the amateur music-making of the British Expeditionary Force. He was demobilised in 1919 and appointed as a teacher of composition at the R.C.M. Prior to World War II, Vaughan Williams campaigned on behalf of the refugees from Germany and his music was banned by the Nazis in 1939.

Met **Gustav Holst** at the R.C.M. in 1895 and began a life-long friendship. Of similar views, each played through his compositions for critical comment by the other. Another close friend was Adrain Boult who later became one of the foremost interpreters of the music of Vaughan Williams.

Conductor of the Bach Choir (1920-1928).

Joined the Folk Song Society in 1904. Collected and published folk songs, particularly those of Norfolk, Essex and Sussex, the first such collection being *Bushes and Briars* (1903). President of the English Folk Dance and Song Society (from 1932).

He worked on many occasions with amateurs: for example, at the Leith Hill Festival, which he served as principal conductor from its inception in 1905 until 1953.

Lectured on national music at Bryn Mawr College, Pennsylvania, U.S.A. (1932). In 1954 he toured the U.S.A., lecturing at Cornell University and elsewhere.

Vaughan Williams made a major contribution to the music of the church as a hymnal editor. He was responsible for the *English Hymnal* (1906), *Songs of Praise* (1925) and *Oxford Book of Carols* (1928). He began to compose film music in 1940, when he worked on *The 49th Parallel*. His church music includes a motet for Choir, Organ, Brass and Percussion *O clap your hands, all ye people* (1921); the anthem 'O taste and see how gracious the Lord is'; a Te Deum in G (1928) for the enthronement of the Archbishop of Canterbury and a stirring arrangement of the Old Hundredth Psalm Tune 'All people that on earth do dwell' for the 1953 Coronation of Queen Elizabeth. His compositions include the famous *Fantasia on a theme by Thomas Tallis* (1910), and symphonies, three of which were composed late in life.

VERNON, John Richard (1833-1902)
Born in Louth, Lincolnshire in 1833; died in Williton, Somerset on 30 September 1902. Composed hymn tunes.

VERRINDER, Dr. Charles Garland (?-1904)
Born in Blakeney, Gloucestershire; died in Ealing, London on 27 June 1904.
A chorister of Salisbury Cathedral. Studied under **George Elvey**. Graduated B.Mus. at the University of Oxford (1862). The Lambeth D.Mus. was conferred upon him in 1873.
Organist of Holy Trinity Church, Windsor (from 1854) and of the London Churches of St. Giles-in-the-Fields (from 1856); Christ Church, Lancaster Gate (from 1866); St. Michael, Chester Square (from 1877) and St. Mary, West Kensington (from 1890). Organist of Ealing Congregational Church (1900-1904), the incumbent being W. Garrett-Horder. Organist of the Reformed Synagogue in London and the West London Synagogue (from 1859). A local choral society conductor.
Assisted Lady Elvey with the biography of her late husband.
Composed a Service in F, the anthems 'Seek ye the Lord' and 'The light hath shined upon us,' Kyries, the cantata *Israel*, Hebrew Services, organ works, songs and part songs.

VICARY, Walter (1770-1845)
Born in 1770; died in Oxford on 5 January 1845.
Studied with **James Nares** and graduated B.Mus. at the University of Oxford in 1805.
At the University of Oxford, Walter Vicary was organist of Magdalen College (1797-1845), a singing man of St. John's College (1816-1828) and lay chaplain of New College (1796-1844). Organist of St. Mary's Church, Oxford (from 1830). In 1805 he succeeded **William Crotch** as conductor of the Oxford Concerts.
He composed items of church music including 'The Heavens declare the glory of God' (which he may have submitted as his degree exercise), and songs.

VICKERS, Arthur Richard (1876-?)
Born in Wolstanton, in the Diocese of Lichfield, in 1876. Studied music with **George Oakey**, **Albert Peace**, and Theo Hemmings. Organist and choirmaster of St. Paul's Church, Burslem, Staffordshire. Composed settings of the Te Deum in F and in G, a Benedicite, hymns, organ works and songs. Also composed incidental music to the pantomime *Aladdin*.

VINCENT, Dr. Charles John (1852-1934)
Born in Houghton-le-Spring, Durham on 19 September 1852. died in Monte Carlo, Monaco on 23 February 1934.
Brother of **George Vincent**. His father was organist of St. Michael's Church, Houghton-le-Spring and his mother, a pianist.
Trained in music at Durham Cathedral (1864-1868) under **Philip Armes** and graduated B.Mus. (1878) and D.Mus. (1884) at the University of Oxford. Studied at the Leipzig Conservatory (1876-1878).
Organist and choirmaster of St. Mark's Church, Houghton-le-Spring.
Organist and choirmaster of Monkwearmouth Parish Church, Sunderland (1869-1875); Tavistock Parish Church (1877-1882) and Christ Church, Hampstead, London (1882-1892). Organist of Kelly College, Tavistock (from 1878).
A hymnal companion editor. An editor of the *Anglican Choir Series of Church Music*, and of *Organist and Choirmaster*, which he founded with **C.W. Pearce** and **E.J. Hopkins**. He edited the 1880 and 1893 versions of *The Chantbook Companion*.
A lecturer and examiner for Trinity College of Music, London, for which he visited South Africa in 1897, and Australia.
Founded the Vincent Music Company.
He composed as his B.Mus. exercise a setting of Psalm 68. His D.Mus. was achieved with his cantata *The Day of Rest*. His hymn tunes include 'Dunelm' and 'Whitstable'. He composed an oratorio *Ruth*. He composed services, anthems, cantatas including *Ishmail*, choruses, orchestral works, and items for organ.

VINCENT, Edwyn.
See **BONNER**, Carey

VINCENT, George Frederick (1855-1928)
Born in Houghton-le-Spring, Durham on 27 March 1855; died in Brentwood, Essex on 30 November 1928. Brother of **Charles Vincent**.
His father was organist of St. Michael's Church, Houghton-le-Spring and his mother, a pianist.. He attended Field House School, Sunderland and went on to study at the Leipzig Conservatory (1874-1876) under Carl Reinecke, R Papperitz, Oscar Paul, E. Wenzel and Ernst Richter.
Made his first public appearance as a violinist at the age of eight at the Athanaeum, Sunderland. His first London performance was in 1885 at the Inventions Exhibition, where he gave a number of organ recitals.
Organist of Sunderland Parish Church (1872-1874); Whitburn Parish Church, County Durham (1877-1882); St. Thomas's Church, Sunderland (1882-1900) and St. Michael's, Cornhill, London (from 1900). His Monday lunch-time recitals became a regular feature at St. Michael's.
An examiner in London for Guildhall School of Music and for Trinity College of Music.
Composed services, hymn tunes, operettas including *Peter's Pledge* (1878), cantatas, songs, piano works, and items for violin.

VINEN, Ernest Edward (1865-?)
Born in London on 12 October 1865. Studied at Guildhall School of Music, London. Organist and choirmaster of St. John's Church, Horsleydown (from 1881) when 16 years old; St. Augustine's Church, Bermondsey (from 1886) and of St. Augustine's, Honor Oak Park (from 1888). Composed an Evening Service in C, a Festival Te Deum for Solo Voices, Chorus and Orchestra; a cantata

The Legend of the Faithful Soul, chants, hymn tunes, songs, and orchestral works.

VINER, William Letton (1790-1867)
Born in Bath, Somerset on 14 May 1790; died in Westfield, Massachusetts, U.S.A. on 24 July 1867. The Wesley and Viner family were friends, and William Viner studied with Charles, the son of Revd. Charles Wesley. Organist of St. Michael's Church, Bath (from 1820) and of St. Mary's Church, Penzance, Cornwall (1838-1859). He then succeeded **S.S. Wesley** as organist of St. Mary's Chapel, Penzance (1859). In the same year he emigrated to the U.S.A. Editor of *A useful Selection from... Psalms*, and *The Chanter's Companion* (1857). His church music includes the hymn tunes 'Helston' (also known as 'Kingston'), and 'Dismissal'. He also composed organ works.

VINNING, William Skinner (19th century)
Born in Devon. A pupil of Charles Fowler of Torquay. Graduated Mus.B. at the University of Cambridge (1880). Organist of Torquay Parish Church and of St. Luke's Church, Torquay. Organist of St. Peter's Church, Bayswater, London (from 1884). Published papers on the subject of choir management. Composed services, a setting of Psalm 84 for Solo Voices, Chorus and Strings; the sacred cantatas *Song of the Passion* and *Song of the Nativity* and the operetta *Equality Jack* (1891).

VITTON, Arthur
See **CROWEST**, F.J.

VON HOLST, Gustav
See **HOLST**, Gustav Theodore.

VON MULLER, Hermann
See **BONNER**, Carey.

W

WADE, James Clift (1847-?).
Born in Coven, Staffordshire on 26 January 1847. Studied music with **Rowland Winn** and **Jacob Bradford**. Organist in his teens at Coven (1860-1865) and subsequently studied at Birmingham (1865-1866). Organist of Iver Parish Church, Buckinghamshire (1867-1869); private organist to W.S. Dugdale at Merevale, Warwickshire, and organist of St. Mary's Church, Maidenhead, Berkshire (from 1880). Conductor of the Maidenhead Orchestral Society. Composed church music, hymns, action songs for children and other vocal music.

WADE, John Francis (c1711-c1786)
Born around 1771; died in Douai, France in 1786 or 1787. A copyist of plainchant and other music at Douai for most of his life. Also a teacher of music. A composer of hymns tunes. 'Adeste Fideles ('O come, all ye faithful') has been traced as far back to a number of copies made by Wade, but it is no more than possible that he composed the tune.

WADE, Richard (19th/20th century)
Trained at the Royal College of Music. Graduated B.Mus. at the University of Durham. Lived in Willesden, London and was organist of Christ Church, Brondesbury (from 1903). Author of *The Harpsichord Illustrated and Improved...* His works include a Hymn for Peace (1915).

WADELY, Dr. Frederick William (1882-1970)
Born in Kidderminster, Worcestershire on 30 July 1882; died in Carlisle on 28 May 1970.
His father, W.E. Wadely, was a friend and contemporary of **Edward Elgar**.
Attended King Charles I School, Kidderminster. Organ Scholar at Selwyn College, Cambridge (1900). John Stewart of Rannoch scholar in sacred music (1901-1903). Graduated B.A. and Mus.B. (1903), M.A. (1907) and Mus.D. (1915) at Cambridge. Studied at the Royal College of Music with **C.V. Stanford**, **Walter Parratt**, **Charles Wood** and **C. Swinnerton Heap**.
Organist at the age of 13 of Wolverley Parish Church, Worcestershire (1895); Selwyn College, Cambridge (from 1900); St. Andrew's, Uxbridge, Midlesex (from 1903) and Malvern Priory, Worcestershire (1904-10).

Appointed organist of Carlisle Cathedral, out of 113 candidates, in February 1910, where he remained until 1960. Frederick Wadely, his predecessor Henry Ford and his successor **R. Andrew Seivewright** were in office for a collective total of some 150 years. A musical society conductor.
Appointed O.B.E. (1955).
Composer of anthems, including 'And thou, Bethlehem', 'At the Lamb's high feast we sing' and 'Christ is risen from the dead', carols and a Communion Service in G.

WAGHORNE, William Richard (?19th century)
Composer of the hymn tune 'Greystone', a Te Deum in A-flat and anthems including 'The Glory of the Lord', 'It is a good thing to give thanks', 'The Lord is my Shepherd' and 'O Lamb of God'.

WAINWRIGHT, Dr. John (c1723-1768)
Born in Stockport, Cheshire and baptised on 14 April 1723; buried in Stockport on 28 January 1768. The father of **Robert Wainwright** and **Richard Wainwright**. A chorister at Manchester Collegiate Church. Trained for a career in music. He settled in Manchester in 1746 and was a singing man in the Collegiate Church prior to 1750. Probably the organist of Stockport Parish Church in 1750. Organist of Manchester Collegiate Church (1767-1768). Composed anthems and hymns, and issued *Collection of Psalm tunes, anthems, hymns, and chants...* (1766), in which is found his 'Yorkshire' (originally known as 'Stockport'), long associated with 'Christians, awake!':

WAINWRIGHT, Richard (c1757-1825)
Baptised in Manchester on 8 July 1757; died in Liverpool on 20 August 1825. Son of **John Wainwright** and the brother of **Robert Wainwright**. Organist of Manchester Collegiate Church and probably St. Ann's, Manchester. Succeeded his brother, Robert, as organist of St. Peter's Church, Liverpool. Organist at St. James', Toxteth Park, Liverpool, for a time, but returned to St. Peter's.
Editor of *A Collection of Hymns with appropriate Symphonies* (1809). With Revd. J.J. Waite he edited *Hallelujah, a selection of tunes...* Composed the hymn tune 'Wainwright' also known as 'Newmarket', and other pieces of vocal music, including 'I heard a great voice as of a trumpet', an anthem for Easter Day.

WAINWRIGHT, Dr. Robert (1748-1782)

Born possibly in Manchester in 1748; died in Liverpool on 15 July 1782.

Son of **John Wainwright** and the brother of **Richard Wainwright**.

Graduated B.Mus. and D.Mus. at the University of Oxford in 1774. In 1768, he succeeded his father as organist of the Manchester Collegiate Church and was elected singing man and instructor of the choristers. In 1775, he became organist of St. Peter's Church, Liverpool. A candidate for the organistship of Halifax Parish Church in 1776, to which **F. W. Herschel** was appointed.

Composed a Te Deum as his degree exercise in 1774, an oratorio *The Fall of Egypt* and the Psalm or hymn tunes 'St. Gregory', 'Manchester', (also known as 'Charmouth'), 'Liverpool', and others.

WAIT, William M. (1854-?)

Born in Chester on 4 December 1854.

William Wait's parents were church singers in Chester and his uncle, William Wait, was a tenor lay clerk at Chester Cathedral for 33 years. As a chorister at Chester Cathedral, William Wait studied piano with John Munns, the sub organist. Later studied at Liverpool then took organ lessons with **John Frederick Bridge,** and **James Kendrick Pyne** at Manchester. Studied harmony and counterpoint with **R. H. Wilson**.

From 1870, he was appointed to various organistships in Manchester and London.

Compositions include the cantatas *St. Andrew* (1888), *The Good Samaritan* (1892) and *God with us*; an Evening Service in C and part songs.

WALCH, James (1837-1901)

Born in Egerton, near Bolton, Lancashire on 21 June 1837; died in 1901. Studied with **Henry Smart**. Organist of Duke's Alley Congregational Church, Bolton (1851); Walmsley Church (1857); Bridge Street Wesleyan Church (1858) and St. George's Parish Church, Bolton (1863). Became conductor of the Bolton Philharmonic Society in 1870. In 1877, he went to Barrow-in-Furness to work in a music business and was honorary organist of the Parish Church. A composer of hymn tunes and other church music. His best-known, 'Sawley', was composed in 1857 and printed for private circulation in 1860. Published *Sacred Melodies transcribed for the Pianoforte*.

WALE, William Henry (19th/20th century)

Conductor of the Orchestral Union in Leicester (1874-1879) and organist of St. Peter's Church, Leicester (1874-1882). In 1890, he emigrated to Australia. Became an examiner at Adelaide University and principal of the Sydney Conservatory. Composed 'God is our Hope and Strength' - a setting of Psalm 46 - and a Pater Noster in F.

WALENN, James Farquharson (1860-1884)

Born in London in January 1860; died in Hornsey, London on 10 February 1884. A chorister at All Saints', Margaret Street, London, and later a pupil of **W. S. Hoyte**. In December 1877, he won the Novello scholarship at the National Training School of Music. Two years later, he was appointed organist and choirmaster of St. Alban's, Holborn, London. Published *Melodies to certain Hymns in use at the Church of St. Alban,*. Composed church music

including a Sanctus, Benedictus, Agnus Dei and O Salutaris in E. Also two piano trios, and many songs.

WALFORD DAVIES, Sir Henry
see **DAVIES**, Sir Henry Walford.

WALKELEY, (Wakeley), Antony (1672-1718)

Born in 1672; died in Salisbury, Wiltshire on 16 January 1718. Probably from Wells, Somerset. Trained as a chorister of Wells Cathedral where he later became vicar choral. Appointed organist and instructor of the choristers (1700), succeeding **Daniel Roseingrave**. His compositions include 'Arise, shine!', 'O God, the heathen are come' and a Morning Service in E-flat, found in the collection by **Thomas Tudway**.

WALKER, Dr. Ernest (1870-1949)

Born in Bombay, India in 1870; died in Oxford on 21 February 1949.

Connected with music in various capacities at Balliol College, Oxford, for 34 years. At 17, when he arrived as a student, the University teaching staff included **John Farmer** (director of music) and **John Stainer** (professor). Director of music at Balliol (1901-1925). Choragus and examiner for degrees at the University. Graduated B.A. in classics (1891), B.Mus. (1893), M.A. (1894) and D.Mus. (1898).

Well-known as a pianist. Continued a series of Sunday evening chamber concerts which John Farmer began in 1885.

As an author, his works include *A History of Music in England*, published at the age of 37, *Free Thought and Church Music*, and a book on the subject of Beethoven.

His choral works include 'Lord, Thou hast been our Refuge' (which **Henry Walford Davies** considered the finest anthem of modern times), 'The earth is the Lord's', 'I will lift up mine eyes' and a Magnificat and Nunc Dimittis. Also wrote orchestral works and chamber music. His collection *The Lady Margaret Hall Hymn Tunes* features a number of his own, plus organ variations on them. The composer **Philip Heseltine** (Peter Warlock) found Ernest Walker a sympathetic teacher.

WALKER, Francis Geoffrey (b.1908)

Born in Leicester in 1908. Educated at St. Peter's School, Exmouth and Blundell's School, Tiverton, Devon. Studied with Frederick Green, Percy Wood and H. L. Read. Organist and choirmaster at Bank Street Methodist Church, Altrincham, Cheshire (1933-1934), Timperley Parish Church, Cheshire (1934-1936) and Withington Congregational Church, Manchester (from 1936). Composed anthems including 'Acquaint thyself with God', 'Christ whose Glory fills the skies' and 'Let all the world in every corner sing'; also wrote organ music and part songs.

WALKER, Reginald H. (1839-1876)

Born in 1839; died in Kingstown, Ireland in October 1876. Youngest son of J.H. Walker, music master of Rugby School, Warwickshire. His vocal compositions include the anthems 'Jerusalem is built as a city' and 'Open ye the gates'.

WALKER, Robert (b.1946)

Born in Northampton on 18 March 1946.

A chorister at St. Matthew's Church, Northampton; choral and organ scholar at Jesus College, Cambridge. Organist and schoolmaster in Lincolnshire and, (from 1975), a freelance composer. Vocal compositions include a setting of Psalm 150 (1974), a Requiem (1976), The *Norwich Service* (1977), a Magnificat and Nunc Dimittis in D (1985), a Missa Brevis (1985) and chants. His orchestral works include Variations on a Theme of Elgar (1982).

WALLIS, Ebenezer John (1831-1879)
Born in London on 9 May 1831; died in Sutton-at-Hone, Kent on 26 October 1879. Composed the hymn tune, 'Barossa', which was issued in *Anthems, Canticles and Hymns* (1869). Among his other works are the songs 'Glad Tidings' and 'Rend y'heart'.

WALMISLEY, Dr. Thomas Attwood (1814-1856)
Born in Westminster, London on 21 January 1814; died in Hastings, Sussex on 17 January 1856. Son of **Thomas Forbes Walmisley** and the godson and pupil of **Thomas Attwood**.
Graduated with the Cambridge degrees of Mus.B. (1833); B.A. (1838); M.A. (1841) and Mus.D. (1848).
After two years as organist of Croydon Parish Church, Surrey and an unsuccessful attempt (1832) to launch a career in London theatre music, he became organist of the Colleges of Trinity and St. John, Cambridge, succeeding Samuel Matthews. Concurrently organist of three Cambridge Colleges (Trinity, St. John's and King's) and the University Church, so that on Sundays he played at eight different services.
In 1836, at the age of 22, he became professor of music at the University of Cambridge. A friend of Mendelssohn, and a Bach enthusiast.
Wrote nine services including settings of the Evening Service in B-flat, in D and in D Minor; chants such as those published in *Cathedral Psalter Chants* (1875); anthems including 'Hear, O Thou Shepherd of Israel', 'From all that dwell below the skies' and the large-scale 'Remember, O Lord, what is come upon us' with its original quartet for tenors and basses and a moving treble solo before the final fugue. He also wrote odes on the installation as chancellors of Cambridge University of the Duke of Northumberland (1842) and Prince Albert (1849), a choral hymn and songs.

WALMISLEY, Thomas Forbes (1783-1866)
Born in London on 22 May 1783; died in London on 23 July 1866. Son of William Walmisley, clerk of the papers of the House of Lords and son of **Thomas Attwood Walmisley**. A chorister of Westminster Abbey and a pupil of **Thomas Attwood**. Organist of the Female Orphan Asylum (1810-1814) and of St. Martin-in-the-Fields, (1814-1854), succeeding **Robert Cooke**. Composed anthems including 'Hear me, O Lord' and 'When I was in trouble', a Morning and Evening Service, sacred songs, and glees.

WALMISLEY-LITTLE, Dr. Henry
See **LITTLE**, Dr. Henry Walmsley.

WALOND, William (c1750-c1836)
Born around 1750; died in Chichester, Sussex on 9 February 1836. Probably the son of the elder William Walond. Organist of Chichester Cathedral; composed some music for the church. Said to have died in extreme poverty.

WALTERS (Walter), John (17th/18th century)
Probably the John Waters who was one of the children of the Chapel Royal. Organist of Eton College about 1700; taught **John**

Weldon. His compositions include the anthems 'O God, Thou art my God' and 'O sing unto the Lord'.

WALTON, Emanuel, (19th century)
Said to be 'of Leeds'. He composed hymn tunes, anthems and an oratorio *Babylon*. Compiled *An original set of Psalm and Hymn Tunes arranged for four voices* (1810) and *Church Psalmody, selected and arranged for four voices* (1830), which went into a second edition five years later.

WALTON, Sir William Turner (1902-1983)
Born in Oldham, Lancashire in 1902; died in Ischia, Italy on 8 March 1983.
A chorister at Christ Church Cathedral, Oxford. Became an undergraduate at 16 but he did not graduate. Mostly self-taught, with advice (from Busoni and Ansermet). Encouraged at Christ Church by the dean **Thomas Strong**, the organist **H. G. Ley,** and the University professor of music, **H.P. Allen.** Graduated D.Mus. honorarily at the University of Oxford in 1942.
Knighted in 1951.
In 1922, he composed *Facade*, which was basically a parody of various forms and styles of music, as a setting of some of Edith Sitwell's poems. It was later enlarged and re-arranged.
William Walton's compositions include two symphonies and an opera *Troilus and Cressida*. The first performance of *Belshazzar's Feast* for Baritone Solo, Chorus and Orchestra took place at the 1931 Leeds Festival. The words are a paraphrase, by Osbert Sitwell, of the Book of *Daniel*. Also composed a Jubilate in B-flat for Christ Church Cathedral, Oxford; a Missa Brevis for Coventry Cathedral; a Magnificat and Nunc Dimittis for Chichester Cathedral; the anthems 'The Twelve' to words by W.H. Auden, 'Set me as a seal upon Thine heart' (1938) and 'Make we joy'; A Litany, also known as 'Drop, drop slow tears', and the carols 'All this night this song is best' and 'What cheer?'.

WANLESS (Wandlas, Wandlesse), Thomas (?-1712)
Died in York; buried on 2 February 1712. Graduated with the Cambridge degree of Mus.B. (1698). Became organist of York Minster in 1691. Composed the *York* Litany and anthems including 'Awake up my glory'. He is represented in *Cathedral Psalter Chants* (1875) by a Single Chant in F.

WARD, Cornelius (1814-?)
Born in Speen, Buckinghamshire on 29 June 1814. Organist and teacher at Speen and also composer and writer. Wrote an oratorio, *The Prodigal Son*, a cantata, *Nativity*, an ode, 'Seraphic Tidings'. Published *The Buckinghamshire Melodist...*(1844) and *The Wesleyan Minstrel...* (1854), collections of sacred music; five volumes of *The Chorister* and two volumes of *Choral Beauties*. He also composed anthems and songs.

WARD, Francis Marshall (1830-?)
Born in Lincoln on 26 December 1830.
A chorister at Lincoln Cathedral. Appointed organist of St. Peter in Eastgate, Lincoln in 1845. In 1851, he became principal bass at Hereford Cathedral and during the following 20 years he was an oratorio and concert singer.
In 1856, he became organist and choirmaster of Abergavenny Parish Church and, in 1857, of St. Mary's, Lincoln. In about 1867, he moved to Nottingham and became organist of Lenton Parish Church. He was organist and music master at the Blind Institution,

Nottingham for 10 years. In 1894, he became organist of Broad Street Wesley Chapel.

His compositions include services, anthems, songs and part songs, only a few of which are published. Composed 'Great and Marvellous', 'I have set the Lord always before me' and 'I will give thanks'.

WARD (Warde), John (1571-1638)

Born in Canterbury, Kent and baptised on 8 September 1571; died in 1638. 'A gentill man', according to **Adrian Batten**. In service to Sir Henry Fanshawe, to whom he dedicated *The First Set of English Madrigals...* (1613). Had madrigals in **Leighton's** Teares. Composed services and anthems, among which are 'I heard the voice of a great multitude' and 'O let me tread in the right path'.

WARD, John Charles (1835-?)

Born in Upper Clapton, London on 27 March 1835.

A chorister of the Temple Church, London (1842-1848). He studied piano with his father, violin with Howard Glover and concertina with George Case.

Organist of Bridewell Hospital Chapel (from 1852); St. John's Chapel, Hampstead, London (from 1853); Eaton Chapel, Eaton Square (from 1856); Christ Church, Hampstead (from 1863); Quebec Chapel (from 1868); Holy Trinity, Haverstock Hill (from 1884); Christ Church, Streatham Hill (from 1886) and St. Mary the Virgin, Primrose Hill (from 1890).

Member of the Leslie Choir (from its foundation in 1855); organist and assistant conductor (1856-1885).

His compositions include a motet *Thy word is a lantern* for Double Choir, 'Sanctus', also for Double Choir, a cantata *The Wood*, an anthem 'I am the Resurrection', services and works for organ.

WAREING, Dr. Herbert Walter (1857-?)

Born in Birmingham on 5 April 1857.

Educated at King Edward School, Birmingham and at Leipzig Conservatory, where he studied with Oskar Paul, Salomon Jadassohn, Ernst Richter and others. Also studied with **C. Swinnerton Heap**. Graduated with the Cambridge degrees of Mus.B. in 1882 and Mus.D. in 1886. A pianist.

Organist at St. John's, Wolverhampton (1876-1879), Edgbaston Parish Church (1881-1888) and King's Norton Parish Church (1891-1906). Director of music at Worcester Cathedral School (1890-1896).

Senior music master at Malvern College, Worcestershire (from 1909) and organist and choirmaster at Christ Church, Malvern (from 1911).

His String Quartet was performed in Leipzig Gewandhaus on 30 June 1876. His other compositions include anthems, a Service in G, an Evening Service in A, cantatas including *Wreck of the Hesperus*, for Solo Voices, Chorus and Orchestra (1895) and works for violin, cello and organ. He also wrote songs and part songs.

WARLOCK, Peter

see **HESELTINE**, Philip.

WARMAN, John Watson (1842-?)

Born in Canterbury, Kent on 12 August 1842.

Son of a private schoolmaster, descended from French Huguenot refugees. Took music lessons with **W.H. Longhurst** and **E. H. Thorne**. Articled to the trade of organ building from about 1858.

Became assistant organist of Ashford Church, Kent (from 1862), Hunton Bridge, near Watford, Hertfordshire (from 1865) and later in Faringdon, Berkshire and Hove, Sussex. In 1872, he went to Quebec and was organist of the Anglican Cathedral but returned after a year. In order to acquire practical knowledge, he worked for some months as an ordinary journeyman at Hill's organ factory, London then in 1877 he returned to Canterbury.

Author of a series of papers on counterpoint, published in *Musical Opinion*, and contributed to other periodicals. A local examiner for the Royal College of Music. Author of *The Organ, its Compass* (1884) and other works. A composer of hymn tunes and chants.

WARNER, Henry (Harry) Ernest (1859-?)

Born in Isleworth, Middlesex on 1 July 1859. Studied music with the organist of the Parish Church, to whom he became deputy at the age of 14. Later studied with Revd. Dr. Hayden. At 18 he was appointed organist and choirmaster of Brentford Parish Church, Middlesex, where he stayed for seven years before moving to the Royal Church, Kew, Surrey. An honorary local examiner for the Royal College of Music. Composed two cantatas for female voices *Merry May* (1891) and *The Golden Valley* (1893) and the anthems 'O God have mercy' and 'If ye love me'. He also wrote hymn tunes, part songs, music for string quartet, military band and piano.

WARRACK, Guy Douglas Hamilton (1900-1986)

Born in Edinburgh on 8 February 1900; died on 12 February 1986. Educated at Magdalen College, Oxford and at the Royal College of Music. Taught at the R.C.M. (from 1925) and was an orchestral society conductor. Composed a Te Deum in E-flat.

WARRELL, Arthur Sydney (1883-1939)

Born in Farmborough, near Bath, Somerset on 1883; died in Cotham, Bristol on 18 August 1939. Educated at Farmborough, at Merchant Venturer's Technical College, Bristol and at Bristol Cathedral where he was pupil assistant to Hubert Hunt. Organist and choirmaster at several Bristol churches: St. Matthias (1900-1901), St. Agnes (1901-1905), St. Alban (1905), St. Nicholas (from 1905) and Clifton Parish Church. Taught music at the department of education of the University of Bristol (from 1909) and founded the Bristol University Choir, Orchestra and Madrigal Singers. He promoted English works, and some composers dedicated pieces to him. Composed the anthems 'Bethlehem night', 'The day of the Lord', 'King of glory', 'The God of love' and songs including 'A sea song'.

WARRELL, Ernest Herbert (b.1915)

Born in London on 23 June 1915. Educated at Loughborough School, London (1927-1931); junior exhibitioner at Trinity College of Music, London (1927-1929). Appointed M.B.E. (1991). In 1938, became articled assistant to **E.T. Cook** at Southwark; later was sub-organist (1946-1954). Organist of St. Mary's, Primrose Hill (1954-1957) and St. John the Divine, Kennington (1961-1968). Organist of Southwark Cathedral (1968-1975). Lecturer in music and organist (from 1953), and lecturer in music in the theological department of King's College, London. Lecturer in plainsong at the Royal School of Church Music (1954-1959). Composed accompaniments to the Psalm Tones and was joint editor of *An English Kyriale*.

WARWICK, Thomas (17th century)

Assistant to **John Bull** at Hereford Cathedral. In 1625 became lute player to Charles I and succeeded **Orlando Gibbons** as organist of the Chapel Royal. He may have been organist of Westminster Abbey in 1642. Wrote the anthem 'O God of my salvation' and was the composer of a song in 40 parts, said to have been performed in 1635.

WASHINGTON-METCALFE, Thomas (1884-?)

Born in London in 1884. Educated at Cranleigh School, Surrey; Freiburg; Exeter Cathedral and Wakefield Cathedral where he was deputy organist. Organist and choirmaster of Saffron Walden Parish Church and School, Essex; the Royal Military College, Wantage, Berkshire and Barnstaple Parish Church, Devon. Private organist of Blenheim Palace. A choral society conductor. Composed a Te Deum in F, Evening Services in F and in E and an anthem 'They have taken away my Lord'.

WASSELL, Richard (1880-?)

Born in Tipton, Staffordshire in 1880. Studied with **C.W. Perkins**. Organist and choirmaster of Birmingham Parish Church. He was also an adjudicator at competitive festivals. His church compositions include the anthems 'Jesu, the very thought of Thee' and 'He that hath pity upon the poor'. He also wrote an overture for military band.

WATLEN, John (18th/19th century)

May have served in the Royal Navy. Worked for the music-sellers, Corri and Co., of Edinburgh, around 1788. First secretary of the Edinburgh Musical Fund, which was established in 1790. Started his own business as tuner, teacher and music-seller in Edinburgh but this business failed in 1798. He then went to London and started business in Leicester Place, Leicester Square. His works include an anthem 'Lord's Prayer', a Sonata for Harpsichord and Violin (1798) and Grand Sonata for Piano and Violin (1800).

WATSON, Ethel Leader

Ssee **EARLE**, Ethel Leader.

WATSON, Henry Piercy (1853-?)

Born in St. Marychurch, Devon in 1853. Educated with Tom Morley, **John Hullah** and J.B. Welch. Organist and choirmaster of the Church of the Good Shepherd, Leamington Spa, Warwickshire (1889-1909). A professor of singing at Comber House Ladies' School (1883-1906) and a visiting professor of singing and elocution in Oxford (1897-1914). His church compositions include three settings of the Benedictus and Agnus Dei, the Harvest anthem 'O praise the Lord', a Rogation Litany, and hymn tunes. He also wrote waltzes and songs.

WATSON, James (1816-1880)

Born in Glasgow on 10 June 1816; died in St. Pancras, London on 1 September 1880. Educated at Glasgow High School. In 1832, moved to London but returned to Scotland in 1838. Joined the Free Church Movement. Later joined the firm of Nisbet and Co., London publishers, as a partner (1845). Editor with Dr. H. Bonar of The Border Watch and was one of the editors of *Psalms and Hymns for Divine Worship* (1867). Composed the hymn tune 'Holyrood', which is usually included in Scottish collections.

WATSON, Dr. Sydney (1903-1991)

Born in Denton, Lancashire on 3 September 1903; died in 1991. Educated at Warwick School; the Royal College of Music (1921-1922) and Keble College, Oxford, where he was organ scholar (1922-1925). He graduated B.A. (1925), B.Mus. (1926), M.A. (1928) and D.Mus. (1932).

Assistant music master at Stowe School, Buckingham (1925-1928); music master at Radley College, Oxfordshire (1929-1933); organist of New College, Oxford 1933-1938; master of music at Winchester College, Hampshire, succeeding **George Dyson** (1938-1945); precentor and director of music at Eton College (1946-1955) and organist of Christ Church Cathedral, Oxford (1955-1970). Taught at the R.C.M. (from 1946) and lectured at the University of Oxford (from 1956). An orchestral society conductor. Appointed O.B.E. in 1970.

His church compositions include Evening Services in E-flat, in E and in F; Communion Services in F and in G and the anthem 'All my hope on God is founded'.

WATSON, William Michael (1840-1889)

Born in Newcastle-on-Tyne on 31 July 1840; died in East Dulwich, London on 3 October 1889. A composer and poet who studied painting at Leigh's School, London. In 1860 became a professional musician and in 1883 established the West End School of Music, London. His church compositions include the anthems 'Come near, ye nations' and 'Hear, O Lord'. Also wrote a cantata *Aladdin* (1885), songs including 'Quaker's daughter' and 'Winter story', part songs and piano music. Composed under the pseudonym Jules Favre.

WATTS, Dr. Harold Ernest (19th/20th century)

Lived for some time in Ladbroke Gardens, London. Trained at Worcester Cathedral. Graduated D.Mus. at the University of Oxford. Student-organist of St. John's College, Battersea (1899-1900). Deputy organist of the Church of St. Peter the Great, Worcester (1901-1903); organist and choirmaster of Wheathampstead Parish Church, St. Albans (from 1903) and St. Peter's, Paddington (from 1915). Composed the anthems 'From East to West', 'The God of Abraham praise' and 'Lord of the Harvest'.

WATTS, Joseph Virgo (1822-?)

Born in Wotton-under-Edge, Gloucestershire on 27 June 1822. Studied music with **John Hullah**, **Joseph Mainzer** and **G.W. Martin**. Organist at Chromhall, Lydney and Berkeley, all in Gloucestershire, then at Midsomer Norton, Somerset; Box Parish Church, Wiltshire; All Saints' Chapel, Bath and Kensington, London. Became choirmaster of the Abbey Church, Bath, retiring in 1885. Composed some church music and published *Original Hymn Tunes, Chants, Kyries and Chant Services* (1876).

WATTS, Thomas Isaac (1863-?)

Born in Broseley, Shropshire in 1863. Organ and choral scholar at Queens' College, Cambridge (1884-1887) and also studied at the Royal Academy of Music. Graduated Mus.B. (1886), B.A. (1887) and M.A. (1891) at the University of Cambridge. Became organist, choirmaster and assistant master at Trinity College, Glenalmond (1887-1895), then organist of Walsall Parish Church, Staffordshire (1895-1901) and of Epsom College Chapel, Surrey (from 1901). His compositions include an Ode *The Ages of Almond*, written for the 50th anniversary of the foundation of Trinity College (1892); a setting of Psalm 19 for Tenor Solo, Chorus and Strings; an Evening Service and hymn tunes.

WATTS-HUGHES, Megan (1842-1902)
Born in Dowlais, Glamorgan, Wales in 1842; died in 1902. Studied at the Royal Academy of Music with Manuel Garcia. Left the R.A.M. due to ill-health but sang and accompanied **Joseph Parry** on a musical tour of North Wales. Also sang duets with Jenny Lind. She and her husband later devoted their lives to humanitarian and religious work, founding an orphanage in London. Invented the musical device 'Voice Figures' and gave a demonstration of its use at a meeting of the Royal Society in London. Composed the hymn tune 'Wilton Square'.

WEALE (Wheal, Wheall) William (c1690-1727)
Born around 1690; buried in Bedford on 4 September 1727. Graduated Mus.B. at the University of Cambridge in 1719. Organist of St. Paul's, Church Bedford (1715-1727). Composed the Psalm tune 'Bedford', which was played on the bells of the Church at Bedford for over 100 years. A tune is also found in Timbrell's Divine Musick Scholars' Guide (c1723).

WEBB, Francis Gilbert (1853-1941)
Born in Isleworth, Middlesex in 1853; died in 1941.
Studied with **H.F. Frost**. An organist and composer but more widely known as a writer and theorist. He read papers before the Musical Association, was on the staff of *Musical Times* (from 1898), contributed to *Musical World* and other periodicals, was music critic of *The Lancelot* and *The Referee* and was a compiler of programme notes. He was on the staff of *The Standard* (from 1897) and was its principal music critic (1901-1905). He was on the staff of *The Morning Post* (1893-1901), *Daily Telegraph* (1905-1906), *The Observer* and *The Sunday Times*. He was for some years organist of St. Luke's, Brompton, London.
His compositions for the church include six settings of the Kyrie Eleison. He also wrote songs, part songs and pieces for violin and piano.

WEBB, George James (1803-1887)
Born in Rushmore Lodge, near Salisbury, Wiltshire on 24 June 1803; died in Orange, New Jersey, U.S.A. on 7 October 1887.
Studied with Alexander Lucas of Salisbury. Became an organist in Falmouth, Cornwall then in 1830 he emigrated to Boston, Massachusetts, U.S.A.
Became a Swedenborgian and helped to arrange the musical service for the Swedenborgian Church. Organist of Old South Church, Boston, which he co-founded with Dr. Lowell Mason, and was appointed professor at the Boston Academy of Music in 1833. He became president of the Handel and Haydn Society in 1840. In 1870 he went to Orange, New Jersey then worked in New York as a teacher (from 1876). He retired to Orange in 1885 where he died.
Author of *Vocal Techniques* and co-author with C.G. Allen of *Voice Culture*. Editor of *The Massachusetts Collection of Psalmody* (1840), *The American Glee Book* (1841), *The Psaltery* (1845) and *The National Psalmist* (1848). Composed a number of anthems and the hymn tunes 'Morning Light' and 'Tal-y-Llyn'.

WEBBE, Samuel (1740-1816)
Born in Minorca in 1740; died in London on 25 March or May 1816.
Father of **Samuel Webbe** the younger, with whom he collaborated.

Took lessons in music with Charles Barbandt, organist of the Bavarian Embassy in London. At the age of 11 he was apprenticed to a cabinet maker but later became a music copyist.
Chapel master of the Portuguese Chapel in London (from 1776) and organist of the Sardinian Embassy Chapel, London. Secretary of the Noblemen and Gentlemen's Catch Club (1794-1812).
The probable editor of the first two parts of *An Essay on the Church Plainchant* (1782).
Published *A Collection... as used in the Chapel of the King of Sardinia*, *A Collection of Masses...* (1792) and *A Collection of original Psalm tunes...* The latter work contained music by father and son. His anthems include 'Christ being raised' and 'The eyes of all wait'. Composed the hymn tune 'Benevento' and possibly 'Melcombe', although some attribute this to his son. He also wrote piano music, a concerto for harpsichord, and catches and glees including 'When winds breathe soft' and 'Glorious Apollo'.

WEBBE, Samuel (c1770-1843)
Born in London around 1770; died in Hammersmith, London on 25 November 1843.
Studied with his father **Samuel Webbe** and with Clementi. Lived in Liverpool (1798-1817) and was organist of the Unitarian Church, Paradise Street, Liverpool (from 1798) and St. Nicholas's Church and St. Patrick's Roman Catholic Church, Liverpool. In 1817 he returned to London and became music teacher at Logier's School of Music.
Like his father, he wrote glees and catches. He may have written the hymn tune 'Melcombe', although some sources suggest this was written by his father. He may also have written the anthem 'Ye servants of the all-bounteous Lord'.

WEBBER, Walter Gideon (1893-?)
Born in London in 1893. Studied at the Guildhall School of Music, London with **E.T. Cook** and **Harold Darke**. Published *Congregational Descant Book*. His anthems include 'I saw a new heaven' and 'Grant, we beseech Thee'.

WEBBER, William Southcombe Lloyd
See **LLOYD WEBBER**, William Southcombe

WEBSTER, Donald Frederick (b. 1926)
Born in Leeds in 1926. His early education was with **Melville Cook** at Leeds Parish Church, where he was later assistant (1962-1966) to **Donald Hunt**. He wrote the history of the choir of this church, 'Parish, past and present' (1988). His other books include 'Our Hymn Tunes' and 'The Hymn explosion and its aftermath'.
His career in music education has included posts at Morley High School, Leeds; Huddersfield University and Napier University, Edinburgh. In retirement from full-time teaching, he has served as music critic for the *Yorkshire Post*, *Musical Opinion* and *The Organ*.
His works for church include anthems, carol arrangements and canticle settings. His other music includes an Elegy for Strings.

WEBSTER, Harry (1878-1969)
Born in Halifax, Yorkshire in 1878; died in 1969.
At the age of 10 he worked part-time in a mill. Was later apprenticed to his father, a master joiner, and continued this work until 1947. Became organist of several Halifax churches: Trinity Wesleyan Chapel (from 1905), Mount Zion Methodist Church (from 1907), Mount Tabor Methodist Church (from 1911) and

Queen's Road Methodist Church (from 1918). Wrote several anthems and hymn tunes, including 'Nil nisi labore', which he wrote at the age of 76.

WEEKES, Dr. S. (1843-1932)
Born in 1843; died on 11 March 1932.
Studied at the Royal Academy of Music and was the last surviving pupil at the R.A.M. of Cipriani Potter. He graduated Mus.B. at the University of Cambridge (1873) and D. Mus. at Dublin (1896).
Organist of St. Peter's, Hammersmith, London (1861-1862) and moved to Plymouth, Devon in 1862. Organist of the Baptist Church, Plymouth (from 1876). Founded the Plymouth Choral Society (1863) and the Orchestral Society (1872) and was conductor of both. Became principal of the music school at Stoke, Devonport.
Author of *Questions on Acoustics* and a *Choral Primer*. His compositions include a cantata *Bless the Lord* for Solo Voices, Chorus and Orchestra, an oratorio *Nehemiah*, hymn tunes, songs and piano pieces.

WEELKES, Thomas (c1576-1623)
Born around 1576; died in London on 30 November 1623.
Graduated B.Mus. at New College, Oxford (1602).
May have been a chorister of Winchester Cathedral (1583-1584), as there is a record of a Thomas Wikes.
Organist of Winchester College (1598-1600 or later) and of Chichester Cathedral (1602-1623). By 1616, his swearing and drinking habits were apparently known. He seems to have remained as organist but he was deprived of his position as instructor of the choristers in January 1617.
Thomas Weelkes wrote ayres and madrigals. 'As Vesta was from Latmus Hill descending' is in the collection *The Triumphes of Oriana*. He also wrote services such as a Verse Service for Trebles and a Short Service (complete setting); anthems, including 'Gloria in excelsis Deo', 'Hosanna to the Son of David', 'Give ear O God' and 'O Lord grant the king'. Some of his anthems are in the collections of Clifford and Rimbault.

WEILAND, Douglas (b.1954)
Born in Malvern, Worcestershire in 1954. For many years a freelance violinist in London and abroad. In 1978 became a regular player in the Academy of St. Martin-in-the-Fields and (from 1985) was a founder member of the Australian Quartet, playing with them for five years. Studied composition throughout this time and since 1990 has worked solely as a composer.
Has written chamber works including a quintet 'In an Eden Hills garden' for String Quartet and Voice (1985); an Orchestral Suite (1995); church music including a Magnificat and Nunc Dimittis for Treble Voices (1995), an anthem 'The Lord's Prayer' (1982), two cantatas, and settings of Psalm 103 and Psalm 16.

WEIR, Dr. Judith (b.1954)
Born in 1954 of an Aberdeenshire family. While still at school in London, studied composition with **John Tavener** and played in the National Youth Orchestra. Studied at King's College, Cambridge (1973-1976) where her composition teacher was Robin Holloway. In 1975 she attended summer school at Tanglewood. Southern Arts Association's composer in residence (1976-1979). Taught in the music department at Glasgow University (1979-1982) and held a Creative Arts Fellowship at Trinity College, Cambridge (1983-1985). She was Guinness composer in residence at the Royal Scottish Academy of Music and Drama (1988-1991) and Fairbairn composer in association with the City of Birmingham Symphony Orchestra (1995-1997).
In 1995 she was appointed C.B.E., and received an honorary doctorate from the University of Aberdeen.
She has written operas including *A Night at the Chinese Opera*, orchestral works and music for theatre. She has written 'Ascending into Heaven' (1983), 'Illuminare, Jerusalem' (1985) and *Two Human Hymns* (1995), all for choir and organ.

WELDON, John (1676-1736)
Born in Chichester, Sussex on 19 January 1676; died in Westminster, London on 7 May 1736.
Pupil of **Henry Purcell** and, while a chorister at Eton, of **John Walters**.
Organist of New College, Oxford (1694-1701). Became a gentleman extraordinary of the Chapel Royal in 1701. On the death of **John Blow** he became one of the organists of the Chapel Royal (1708-1736). Also a composer there (from 1715). Organist of St. Bride's, Fleet Street, London (from 1702), and of St. Martin-in-the-Fields.
Won a prize of 100 guineas (£105) in a competition organised by *London Gazette* (1699) for a setting of Congreve's 'The Judgment of Paris'.
His compositions include the anthems 'O praise God in His Holiness', 'Hear my crying, O God' and 'O Saviour of the world'; chants, of which a Single Chant in G Minor is found in Cathedral Psalter Chants (1875); operas; songs and aires.

WELLS, Henry (Harry) Wharton (19th/20th century)
Organist of Long Ditton Parish Church, Surrey and of the London Churches of St. Clement, Fulham; St. Dionis, Fulham and St. Mary the Virgin, Putney (from 1889). Compositions include the Christmas carol, 'Hail! Hail! The heavenly light', eight settings of the Responses to the Commandments and a Chant for the Benedicite.

WELLS, Robin (b.1943)
Born in Bury St. Edmunds, Suffolk, in 1943. Educated at the Royal College of Music and the University of Reading. Studied with **Sydney Watson, H. Kenndy Andrews, Harold Darke** and, in Paris, with Marcel Dupré Director of Music at Charterhouse, Surrey (from 1987). An examiner for the Associated Board of the Royal Schools of Music. Conductor of the Petersfield Festival, Hampshire (from 1996). Composer of a number of carols, found in the *Novello Book of Carols*. Has also composed the anthem 'God is gone up', and a number of works in manuscript. Has edited a number of the organ works of **Herbert Howells** in three volumes.

WELSH, Thomas (c1780-1848)
Born in Wells, Somerset around 1780; died in Brighton, Sussex on 31 January 1848. Pupil of **J.B. Cramer** and Baumgarten. A chorister of Wells Cathedral. At the age of 12, he made his opera debut in London. Later became a bass singer, sang in oratorio and became a gentleman of the Chapel Royal. A singing teacher in London whose pupils included John Sinclair and Charles Horn. Author of *Vocal Instructor, or the art of singing exemplified...* (1825). His compositions include the anthem 'Awake up my glory' (1834) and 'Out of the deep', a Service in F, dramatic works, part songs, glees, duets and sonatas for piano.

WESLEY, Charles (1757-1834)

Born in Bristol on 11 December 1757; died in London on 23 May 1834.

Son of Charles Wesley the elder, brother and teacher of **Samuel Wesley**, uncle of **S.S. Wesley** and nephew of John Wesley. Studied with Rooke, **Thomas Kelway** and **William Boyce** and became a teacher in London. Organist of various London churches including St. George's, Hanover Square, and was organist in ordinary to George IV. Gave subscription concerts at his house in London. His Church compositions include the anthems 'Grant, we beseech Thee' and 'Lord remember David' and hymns. Also *A set of eight songs* (1784) and *A set of six Concertos for the Organ or Harpsichord'*.

WESLEY, Samuel (1766-1837)

Born in Bristol, Gloucestershire on 24 February 1766; died in London on 11 October 1837.

Son of Charles Wesley, younger brother of **Charles Wesley** (the younger), father of **S.S. Wesley** and nephew of John Wesley. A pupil of his brother, Charles, and, at the age of 6, of David Williams, organist of St. James' Church, Bath, Somerset.

A classical scholar. Temporarily joined the Roman Catholic church at the age of 18 and wrote much music for the Roman Catholic church. Deputy organist for a time of the Abbey Church, Bath and on coming to London as a teacher he became organist of Camden Chapel, now the Parish Church of Camden Town. In 1811 he conducted at the Birmingham Festival.

A friend of Mendelssohn. Said to have introduced the music of J.S. Bach to England.

At the age of 8, wrote the oratorio *Ruth*. Composed a Service in F; four Masses, anthems such as 'Exsultate Deo adjutori nostro', 'In exitu Israel de Aegypto' (from Psalm 114, partly founded on the 8th plainchant mode) and motets including *Sing aloud with gladness*, *When Israel came out of Egypt* and *My soul hath patiently*. He also wrote an opera (in manuscript), *The Misanthrope*, sonatas for piano, and organ voluntaries and fugues.

WESLEY, Dr. Samuel Sebastian (1810-1876)

Born in St. Marylebone, London on 14 August 1810; died in Gloucester on 19 April 1876.

Son of **Samuel Wesley**, with whom he appeared in concerts.

Attended Christ's Hospital from the age of six. Two years later, sang at the Chapel Royal under **William Hawes**, who described him as the best chorister who ever came under his care.

Graduated B.Mus. and D.Mus. at the University of Oxford (1839). His doctoral exercise *O Lord, Thou art my God* contains the anthem 'For this mortal must put on immortality'.

An organist from the age of 16 in various parish churches in and around London - St. James's, Hampstead Road (from 1826); St. Giles's, Camberwell (1829); St. John's, Waterloo Road (1829) and Hampton Parish Church, Surrey (from 1830).

A noted extempore organist, an enthusiastic teacher and a controversial figure. *A few words on Cathedral Music* (1849) made robust criticism of the style and standards of the day. Was once reprimanded for showing his contempt for the Dean and Chapter of Exeter Cathedral by playing 'Rule, Britannia' instead of the National Anthem at a special service. In reply, he denied responsibility, saying that he could not prevent the bellows from playing the former.

A professor of the Royal Academy of Music (from 1850).

Organist of Hereford Cathedral (1832-1835), Exeter Cathedral (1835-1842), Leeds Parish Church (1842-1849), Winchester Cathedral (1849-1865) and Gloucester Cathedral (1865-1876).

Edited and contributed tunes to Kemble's *Psalms and Hymns* (1864) and contributed to *European Psalmist* (1872). Composed Services in E (1845), in F, a Chant setting in F, and a Service in G. Composed hymn tunes including 'Aurelia', 'Harewood', 'Hereford', 'St. Sebastian', 'Radford' and 'Wimbledon'. Of his anthems the most enduring have proved to be 'Blessed be the God and Father of our Lord Jesus Christ', 'Thou wilt keep him in perfect peace' and 'Wash me thoroughly from my wickedness'. Of *The Wilderness*, with which Wesley confidently expected to win the Gresham Prize, **R.J.S. Stevens**, the glee writer and Prize Committee member, is quoted as saying, 'All very well, but not church music'. Also wrote glees, songs, organ pieces and part songs.

WEST, Edward Roberts (20th century)

Studied with **D.J. Wood** and at the Royal Academy of Music. Assistant organist of Exeter Cathedral and organist and choirmaster of St. Paul's Parish Church, Leamington Spa, Warwickshire. Private organist to the Dowager Countess of Warwick. A madrigal society conductor. Composed a Magnificat and Nunc Dimittis, and operettas. Published *The Psalm and Canticle Chant Book*.

WEST, John Ebenezer William (1863-1929)

Born in South Hackney, London on 7 December 1863; died in Westminster, London on 28 February 1929.

Parents were musicians and he received his early instruction from them. His father, William West, founded the North East London Academy of Music in 1863. He later studied organ with **John Frederick Bridge** and composition at the Royal Academy of Music with **Ebenezer Prout** (his uncle). He died while conducting a concert of the Railway Clearing House Male Voice Choir.

In 1884 he joined Novello and Co. as one of the musical editors and advisers. At Novello's he revived and adapted certain organ music from **Redford** to **Wesley**. He became organist and choirmaster of St. Mary's, Berkeley Square and between 1891 and 1902 he held similar positions at South Hackney Parish Church and St. Augustine's, Queen's Gate, London. As well as giving organ recitals he was known as a pianist.

His *Dictionary of Cathedral Organists* was published in 1899 and revised in 1921.

His compositions include the cantatas *The healing of the Canaanite's daughter* (1882) and *Seed time and harvest* (1892), a setting of Psalm 130 (1891), several services, the anthems 'The Lord is exalted' (St. Paul's Cathedral: 1883) and 'Lord, I call upon Thee' and a Festival Evening Service in E-flat, composed for the Festival of London Church Choir Association, St. Paul's in 1890. He also wrote works for organ including a Sonata in D Minor (1895) and a Fugue in E Minor, and songs and part songs.

WEST, Revd. Lewis Renatus (1753-1826)

Born in London on 3 May 1753; died in Tytherton, Wiltshire on 4 August 1826. Educated at the Moravian School, Leeds, where he was acquainted with **C.I. Latrobe**, one of the leading Moravian musicians. Became minister of the Moravian Church at Tytherton. His compositions include 'Have mercy, Lord' and 'Save me. O Lord'. Composed hymn tunes, including 'Tytherton' and other music for the church service.

WEST, William (1830-1906)

Born in Hackney, London on 17 September 1830; died in Stamford Hill, London on 24 January 1906. Father of **John Ebenezer West** and brother-in-law of **Ebenezer Prout**. Composer, teacher and lyric author (set by his son and other composers). In 1863 he founded the North East London Academy of Music. For 15 years was organist of the Congregational Church, Bethnal Green Road, resigning in 1885. Held for a time a similar appointment in Hackney. His compositions for the church include hymn tunes, chants and settings of the Sanctus. He also wrote songs and piano pieces.

WESTBROOK, Benjamin Vine (1859-1947)

Born in Greenwich, London in 1859; died in London on 8 April 1947. Educated with Hodges, B. Fisher and **H.C. Banister**. Organist of Holy Trinity, Greenwich (1880-86); Forest Hill Congregational Church (1886-89); Christ Church, East Greenwich (1889-1895) and St. George, Perry Hill, Catford (1895-1929). Organist of the private chapel of Ingleton House, Clapham, London (from 1929). His compositions include the anthems 'God is our refuge' and 'A Christmas prayer', and the wedding anthem 'Whither thou goest'. Also has works in *Congregational Hymn and Anthem Book* and *Bristol Tune Book*.

WESTBROOK, Dr. Francis Brotherton (1903-1975)

Born in Thornton Heath, Croydon on 16 June 1903; died on 19 September 1975.

Educated at Whitgift School, Didsbury Theological College and the University of Manchester. Graduated B.A. at the University of London and D.Mus. at Manchester.

Became principal of Williams' School of Church Music, Harpenden, Hertfordshire. Ministerial secretary of the Methodist Church Music Society (from 1945). A professor of harmony and counterpoint at the London College of Music (from 1968).

His compositions include the anthems 'Almighty Father, who dost give' and 'Christ for the world we sing' and the cantata for Passion-tide *Calvary*. His 'All glory to God in the sky' is found in *Hymns and Songs*. His arrangement in four part harmony of the Passion-tide Spiritual *Were you there when they crucified my Lord?* is found in many hymnals. Composed a Missa Brevis and a Christmas-tide cantata *The Birth of Christ*. His tune 'Benfield' is often found with 'Glory, love and praise and honour'

WESTBROOK, Dr. William Joseph (1831-1894)

Born in London on 1 January 1831; died in Sydenham, Surrey on 24 March 1894.

Graduated Mus.B. in 1876 and Mus.D. in 1878 at the University of Cambridge.

Organist of St. Bartholomew, Bethnal Green, London (from 1849) and of St. Bartholomew, Sydenham (f1851-1884). Became co-organist of Crystal Palace in 1860. In 1862 founded the *Musical Standard* with A.W. Hammond and John Crowdy. Conductor of the South Norwood Musical Society (1865-1878). Musical examiner to the College of Preceptors.

His works include the anthems 'God be merciful unto us' and 'With hearts renewed', an oratorio *Jesus* (1877), a cantata, *The Lord is my Shepherd* (1875) and services. He also wrote songs and part songs. His publications include *The Organist* (1876), *Young Organist*, *Practical Organist*, *Organ Journal*, *Ancient and Modern Fugues* (1865-1880) and *Practical Organ Tutor* (1872).

WESTERBY, Herbert (c1865-1949)

Born in Huddersfield, Yorkshire around 1865; died in Bath, Somerset in November 1949.

Educated with **E.H. Turpin**, James Higgs and Henry Parratt. Graduated B.Mus. at the University of London, his degree exercise being a Te Deum in five parts.

Organist at Gravesend, Kent; Stonehaven; St. George's Cathedral, Grahamstown, South Africa; Kimberley, South Africa; the Collegiate Church, Elgin, Scotland; Linthorpe Parish Church, Middlesbrough (1903); Kirkcaldy, Scotland and Erith, Kent. Organist and choirmaster of Christ Church, Ealing, London (from 1921).

A prolific writer on musical subjects. Author of *Liszt and his Piano Works* and *The History of Pianoforte Music*. Author of an article on *Christian Music* in *Hastings's Encyclopaedia of Religion and Ethics* and contributed articles to music magazines. Organising secretary of the Hymn Tune Association. A B.B.C. organ recitalist and a teacher and performer of piano, playing piano before royalty. Composed the anthem 'God be in my head'.

WESTLAKE, Frederick (1840-1898)

Born in Romsey, Hampshire on 25 February 1840; died in St. Marylebone, London on 12 February 1898.

Studied at the Royal Academy of Music (1855-1859). Became a sub-professor at the R.A.M. in 1860 and, three years later, professor of piano. A member of the Philharmonic Society and the Society of Musicians. His works include a Mass in E-flat and Mass *of the Holy Name* (Brompton Oratory: 1893). He contributed tunes to *Hymns Ancient and Modern*. Composed songs and part songs and completed the edition of Bach's 48 Preludes and Fugues commenced by **Sir William Sterndale Bennett**.

WESTMORLAND, John Fane, Earl of (1784-1859)

Born in London on 3 February 1784; died in Apthorpe House, Northamptonshire on 16 October 1859. As Lord Burghersh he succeeded to the title of Earl of Westmorland in 1841. Joined the army in 1803 and became general in 1854. Studied music in Lisbon with Marcos Portugal (1809-1812). A founder of the Royal Academy of Music and in 1861, a scholarship was founded in his memory. His compositions include a Cathedral Service (1841), Messa Solenne (1858) and a Requiem *to the Memory of Samuel Webbe*. He also wrote operas, symphonies, chamber music, madrigals and glees.

WESTON, Henry Walter (1864-1914)

Born in 1864; died in West Hill, Wandsworth, London on 15 June 1914. Graduated B.Mus. Organist and choirmaster of Holy Trinity, West Hill and became choirmaster of All Saints' Parish Church, Wandsworth (1902). Wrote two settings of the Vesper Hymn.

WESTROP, Henry John (1812-1879)

Born on 22 July 1812; died in London on 23 September 1879. Organist of St. Stephen's, Norwich, Norfolk; Little Stanmore (1831); Fitzroy Chapel (1833) and the Church of St. Edmund, King and Martyr (1834-1879). A violinist at the Italian Opera. Conductor of the Choral Harmonist's Society. A member of the Philharmonic Society and the Royal Society of Musicians, from whom he claimed relief in October 1875 when he suffered from paralysis. His daughter acted as his deputy at St. Edmund's until his death. He was also a teacher and pianist. His compositions include the anthem 'O taste and see'; *Winter*, a descriptive cantata for Bass Voice and Orchestra; operas and chamber music.

WESTROP, Thomas (1821-1881)
Born in 15 December 1821; died in London on 17 December 1881. Organist of St. Swithin, London Stone (1847-1881). A pianist and teacher of harmony. He edited *120 Selected Short Anthems* (1861). His compositions include the hymns 'Abide with me' and 'Have mercy on us, God most high', Psalms, sacred songs, a large number of comic and other songs, and piano pieces.

WESTRUP, Sir Jack Allan (1904-1975)
Born in London on 26 July 1904; died in Headley, Hampshire on 21 April 1975. Educated at Dulwich College, London and Balliol College, Oxford. Graduated B.Mus. (1926) and M.A. (1929). Assistant classics master at Dulwich College (1928-1934). A music critic for *The Daily Telegraph* (1934-1939). Editor of *Monthly Musical Record* (1933-1945). Gave classes and lectured in music in the Newcastle College of Durham University. Professor of music at Birmingham University (from 1944) and at Oxford (1946-1971). Knighted in 1960. Author of a work on **Henry Purcell**. Edited *New Oxford History of Music*. His compositions include the anthems 'Crossing the bar', 'God is our hope and strength' and 'God be merciful'.

WETTON, Dr. Henry Davan (1862-1928)
Born in Brighton, Sussex on 18 July 1862; died in London on 2 November 1928.
Educated at Islington Proprietary School, London. Trained at Westminster Abbey and studied with **Sir Frederick Bridge**. Graduated D.Mus. at the University of Durham in 1891.
A professor at the Royal College of Music and professor of organ at the Guildhall School of Music. Assistant organist of Westminster Abbey under Frederick Bridge (1881-1896) and sub-organist of Wells Cathedral (from 1890). He also held various other organistships: All Saints', Stoke Newington, London (1877); Christ Church, Woburn Square (1884); St. Gabriel's, Pimlico (1886-1889 and 1890-1893); Finchley Parish Church (1892) and the Alexandra Palace. Organist and director of music at the Foundling Hospital (from 1892) for 34 years.
Head of the Music Department of Battersea Polytechnic (from 1909) and of Northampton Institute, Clerkenwell. A member of the University of London Faculty of Music and Board of Studies in Music. Director of the Royal Philharmonic Society. Examiner for the Associated Board of the Royal Schools of Music.
His compositions include a setting of Psalm 9, for Solo Voices, Chorus, Strings and Piano; a Te Deum and Benedictus, an Evening Service for Men's Voices, anthems, carols, songs and piano pieces.

WHARMBY, Luther Tyndale (1865-1914)
Composer of the harvest-tide hymn, 'Come, ye thankful people, come'.

WHARTON-WELLS, Harry (1866-1942)
Born in Willesden, London in 1866; died in 1942. Educated at the Chapel Royal, St. James' Palace and at Trinity College of Music.
A 'recognised teacher in music and pedagogy at London University, Chelsea Polytechnic'. Organist and choirmaster at Long Ditton, Surrey and at Putney Parish Church (for 53 years). Wrote articles and books on music including *Handbook of Music and Musicians*. Wrote church music, songs and part songs.

WHATMOOR, Freeman (1856-1930)
Born in Bradford, Yorkshire in 1856; died in Leeds on 4 September 1930.
Studied at music initially in Leeds and with **William Spark** and **F.W. Hird**. Thereafter (from 1876) at the National Training School, Kensington, London where he won a scholarship. In 1887 he won a *Musical World* prize for his Organ Postlude. He graduated Mus.B. at the University of Cambridge in 1892.
Held organ appointments at Leeds; Southport, Lancashire; Gateshead Parish Church; St. Peter's Church, St. Albans, Hertfordshire; Birkenhead, Cheshire and Charlottenburg, South Africa. Sometime assistant to **Henry Farmer** at Harrow School. Later conductor and teacher in Watford, Hertfordshire. Also took part in chamber concerts and gave lectures.
Wrote the Christmas carol 'Hear ye not the angel legions?' and published school songs, part songs and pieces for piano and organ.

WHEELDON, Herbert Arthur (1869-1923)
Born in Derby on 6 June 1869; died in Hereford on 28 October 1923.
A pupil of (?E.H.) Turpin and articled pupil to **E.J. Crow** at Ripon Cathedral. Held posts in London; Eastbourne, Sussex; Ipswich, Suffolk and in Toronto and New York in his last years. Wrote a setting of the Magnificat and Nunc Dimittis in A and another in B-flat.

WHELAN, Revd. Ernest Hamilton (19th century)
Graduated B.Mus. (1887) and M.A. from the University of Dublin. Organist of Malahide Church, near Dublin (1868); Swords Parish Church (1869) and St. Andrew's, Dublin (1875-76). Conductor of the Dublin Diocesan Choral Festival in 1875. Curate of Powerscourt (1876-1883) and became rector of Kilbride, Bray in 1883. Composed a setting of Psalm 100 for Five Voices and Organ, the Vesper Hymn 'Glenart', hymn tunes that are found in *Irish Church Hymnal* and *Children's Hymnal*, and sacred songs.

WHETTAM, Graham Dudley (b.1927)
Born in Swindon, Wiltshire on 7 September 1927.
Did not have a formal musical education but was encouraged by, among others, Adrian Boult and Eric Fenby. Essentially self-taught as a composer.
In 1978 awarded the Gregynog Arts Fellowship (given jointly by the Welsh Arts Council and the University of Wales) which had not previously been awarded to a composer. One time chairman of the Composers Guild of Great Britain, and served as a vice-chairman of the British Copyright Council for almost 20 years.
His compositions include music for orchestra, chamber ensembles, brass band, piano and organ, and vocal and choral music. Composed film music including the orchestral score for *Genevieve*. His church music includes a Magnificat and Nunc Dimittis (1962), a Missa Brevis (1963), A Mass *for Canterbury* (1988) and the *Coventry* Service (Magnificat and Nunc Dimittis).

WHINFIELD, Revd. Walter Grenville (1865-1919)
Born in South Elkington on 6 November 1865; died in 1919. Studied at Magdalen College, Oxford. Graduated B.A. (1889) and B.Mus. (1890). Ordained deacon in 1890, priest in 1891. Held curacies in West Hackney, London (from 1890); Eastbourne, Sussex (from 1891) and Bromsgrove, Worcestershire (from 1898). Founder and first vicar of the new parish of Dodford, near Bromsgrove.

His hymn tune 'Wychbold' first appeared in *English Hymnal* (1906). 'Universal Praise' is an alternative to **Basil Harwood**'s 'Luckington' with 'Let all the world'. Also composed a Holy Harvest Song and a Chant setting of the Benedicite.

WHITBROKE, Revd. William (16th century)
Master of the Choristers of St. Paul's Cathedral in 1566. Composed a Magnificat and Nunc Dimittis and the anthem 'Let your light so shine'.

WHITE, Adolphus Charles (1830-?)
Born in Canterbury, Kent on 10 October 1830.
A chorister at Canterbury Cathedral. Studied organ, violin and other subjects with **W.H. Longhurst** and later studied in Ireland. Learned double-bass when he returned to Canterbury. Had lessons with James Howell in London, for whom he soon deputised. In 1853 he went to America. Returned to Britain and played at Her Majesty's Opera and elsewhere. When Howell died in 1879 Adolphus White succeeded him at the Handel Festival, Leeds Festival, Birmingham Festival (1876-1888) and Three Choirs' Festival. A professor of double-bass at the Royal Academy of Music and the Royal College of Music. Principal double-bass at the Royal Italian Opera until 1897. In 1890 he was appointed musician in ordinary to Queen Victoria. For 22 years was organist of St. Philip's Church, Waterloo Place, London. Composed church music, carols, songs, piano pieces and solos for double-bass. Author of a *Primer for Double-bass*.

WHITE, F. (16th century)
Composer of the anthem 'The Lord bless us'.

WHITE, Harold Robert (1872-?)
Born in Dublin in 1872. Educated at Christ Church Cathedral, Dublin with **R.P. Stewart**. A professor of singing and composition at the Leinster School of Music. Examiner for the Intermediate Board of Music Education. Wrote church music, chamber works, songs, part songs and an opera, sometimes using the pseudonym 'Dermot Macmurrough'.

WHITE, John Jesse (19th century)
Born in Bermondsey, London. A pupil of **James Stimpson** for organ and theory. Studied with Halévy in Paris. A contemporary namesake was active as a musician, and the biographical details have been difficult to distinguish. Spent many years in Chile and Peru as music director, composer and organist. Composed two large and four short Masses, operas, two symphonies and chamber music.

WHITE, Joseph (19th/20th century)
Organist of St. Sidwell's Church, Exeter, Devon. His compositions include an Epiphany cantata, *The Magi* (1888) and a setting of Robert Southey's 'Inchcape Rock' (1891).

WHITE, Lewis Meadows (1860-1950)
Composer of an anthem 'Brightest and best', three harvest-tide carols, a Communion Service in B-flat and an Easy Communion Service in C.

WHITE, Martin John (b.1941)
Born in Southall, Middlesex on 26 December 1941. Educated at the Mercers' School, Holborn, London (1953-1958) and at the

Royal Academy of Music (1961-1965). A B.Mus. graduate of Trinity College, Dublin (1982). Organist of Ruislip Parish Church, Middlesex and of Harrow Parish Church (1963-1968). Organist of St. Patrick's Church of Ireland Cathedral, Armagh, Northern Ireland. Composer of The *Celtic* Eucharist (1984), a setting of the I.C.E.T. text of the Mass, which was used at the Inaugural Service of the Church of Ireland's Alternative Prayer Book. It was followed some years later by A *Modal* Eucharist. Martin White has also arranged of carols, responsorial Psalms, and some orchestral pieces for youth orchestra use.

WHITE, Dr. Matthew (17th century)
Graduated B.Mus. and D.Mus. at the University of Oxford in 1629. Organist at Christ Church Cathedral, Oxford (1611-1613). A bass singer at Wells Cathedral and a gentleman of the Chapel Royal (until 1614) under James I. His compositions include the anthems 'Behold, new praise' and 'O praise God in his holiness' (also attributed to Robert White).

WHITE, Peter Gilbert (b.1937)
Born in Plymouth, Devon on 21 January 1937. Educated at Plymouth College and won an organ scholarship to the Royal Academy of Music. Studied at the Royal School of Church Music (1954-1956). Organ student at St. John's College, Cambridge (1956-1960). Read music and won the John Stewart of Rannoch Scholarship in Sacred Music. Graduated B.A. (1959), Mus.B. (1960) and M.A. (1964). Assistant organist of Chester Cathedral (1960-1962); headquarters choirmaster at the Royal School of Church Music (1962-1966); director of music at the Merchant Taylors' School, London (from 1966). Master of the music at Leicester Cathedral (from 1969). At the same time he was Head of Music at Alderman Newton's School, Leicester, subsequently moving to the City of Leicester School. His compositions include hymn tunes named after places in Leicestershire.

WHITE (Whyte), Robert (c1530-1574)
Born around 1530; died in Westminster, London in November 1574 and was buried on 11 November. Probably the son-in-law of **Christopher Tye**. Graduated B.A. and Mus.B. at the University of Cambridge (1560). Organist of Ely Cathedral, after Christopher Tye (1561-1566). Probably organist of Chester Cathedral (1567-1568) and then probably organist and master of the choristers at Westminster Abbey (1570-1574). His works include the anthems 'Praise the Lord' and 'Lord who shall dwell in thy tabernacle?'.

WHITE, Dr. Robert Thomas (19th/20th century)
Studied at Trinity College of Music, London. Graduated D.Mus. at the University of Oxford.
Organist and choirmaster at Marden Parish Church, Kent (1883-1889), St. James', Ratcliffe (1891-1893), Christ Church, Greenwich, London (from 1900); St. Mary Magdalene, St. Leonards-on-Sea, Sussex (from 1903) and Christ Church, Surbiton, Surrey (from 1904). Music master at Highbury House School, St. Leonards-on-Sea (1884-1889) and lecturer in music at the Diocesan Training College, New Cross, London (from 1906) and Goldsmiths' College (from 1921).
Composed a Magnificat and Nunc Dimittis in D, a Mass with English and Latin words, and an Office Hymn and Magnificat for Festivals of Our Lady.

WHITESIDE, John (1869-?)
Born in Calgate, near Lancaster in 1869. Studied at the Royal Normal College, Upper Norwood. Graduated B.Mus. at the University of Oxford. Organist at St. James, Tatham (1888-1892); Morecambe Parish Church, Lancashire (1892-1906) and St. George's, Kendal (from 1906). Edited a hymnal for the South African District Committee of the London Missionary Society. Composed an Evening Service in D.

WHITFELD, John.
See **CLARK-WHITFELD**, John.

WHITLOCK, Percy William (1903-46)
Born in Rochester, Kent on 1 June 1903; died in Bournemouth, Dorset on 1 May 1946.
Head boy of Rochester Cathedral and later assistant organist there. Won the Kent Scholarship to the Royal College of Music (1920-1924) where his tutors included **Ralph Vaughan Williams**.
Organist of St. Stephen's Church, Bournemouth, (from 1930), part-time organist of Bournemouth Pavilion (from 1933), and Borough organist (from 1935). Knew the technicalities of the organ and was good at extemporisation.
Wrote a set of five and a set of four organ pieces, the latter set including 'A Folk-Tune', much played. His anthems include 'Jesu, grant me this, I pray', 'Be still, my soul, for God is here', 'Here, O my Lord, I see Thee face to face' and 'Glorious in Heaven'. He also wrote a Solemn Te Deum, three Introits, a Communion Service and a Magnificat and Nunc Dimittis, plainsong with alternate verses in harmony. A frequent broadcaster whose compositions have enjoyed a considerable revival: a number of his organ works have recently been republished through the efforts of the Percy Whitlock Trust.

WHITTAKER, Dr. William Gillies (1876-1944)
Born in Newcastle-on-Tyne on 23 July 1876; died in Orkney Islands, Scotland on 5 May 1944.
Educated at Newcastle School of Art and Science, and Armstrong College, Newcastle (later, part of Durham University). Studied music with **C.F. Bowes** and **G..F. Huntley**. Graduated B.Mus. at the University of Durham. (1902), M.A. and D.Mus. at the University of Edinburgh.
Organist and choirmaster at St. George's Presbyterian Church, Newcastle (1894-1896) and St. Paul's Presbyterian Church, South Shields (1896-1909).
Music critic for *Newcastle Daily Leader* (from 1903). Music master for the Newcastle Education Committee in the Pupil Teachers' Centre (from 1904), singing master at Newcastle Central High School for Girls (from 1906) and music master at Rutherford College for Girls (from 1907). A choral and music society conductor.
Taught music at Armstrong College, Newcastle (1898-1938 and 1939-1941). Gardiner professor of music at the University of Glasgow and first principal of the Scottish National Academy of Music.
Had an intimate knowledge of Northern folk music and collected and edited volumes of North country folk songs. Composed a Festal Psalm 'O sing unto the Lord a new song', two song carols, 'Nunc gaudet Maria' and 'Lullay! Lullay!' and a Piano Quintet.

WHYTEBROKE, Thomas (c1495-1568)
Composer of a Magnificat and Nunc Dimittis and the anthem 'Let your light so shine'.

WHYTHORNE (Whithorne), Thomas (1528-1596)
Composer of some 12 two-part devotional songs and 15 anthems including 'I will yield thanks to Thee'.

WICKS, Dr. Edward Allan (b.1923)
Born in Harden, Yorkshire on 6 June 1923. The son of a clergyman. Allan Wicks was educated at St. John's School, Leatherhead, Surrey and Christ Church, Oxford (1941-1942 and 1945-1947) under an organ scholarship. Graduated B.A. (1947) and M.A. (1950).
Served in the army during World War II. Assistant organist of York Minster (1947-1954) under **Francis Jackson**; organist of Manchester Cathedral (1954-1961) and of Canterbury Cathedral (1961-1988). Awarded the Lambeth D.Mus. (1974), an Honorary D.Mus. (Kent) in 1985 and appointed C.B.E. in 1988.
Arranged a number of tunes for SSA or ATB. Composer of descants and chants, and a setting of the Alternative Service Book Rite A Eucharist based on plainsong. Being lively and short, it has been ideal for use in Canterbury Cathedral at extended services such as ordinations.

WICKSEY, James Thomas William (19th/20th century)
Composer of the anthem 'Delight thou in the Lord'.

WIDDOP, Accepted (c1749-1801)
Died at the age of 52 on 9 March 1801 and was buried at Ovenden, near Halifax, Yorkshire. Little is known about his background, although his Christian name suggests Puritan ancestry. A cloth worker by trade, who lived in Halifax. Composer of a number of anthems, and many Psalm tunes. His tune 'Ossett' is found in *Methodist Hymn Book* (1933).

WIGGINS, Christopher D. (b.1956)
Born in Leamington, Warwickshire on 1 February 1956.
Grandson of Lionel Wiggins, who was organist and choirmaster of All Saints' Parish Church, Leamington Spa (1922-1951).
Educated at Dursley Grammar School, Gloucestershire (1966-1969); King's School, Gloucester (1969-1973); Liverpool University (1974-1977 and 1978-1979); Bretton Hall College (1977-1978); Goldsmiths' College, London (1980-1982) and the University of Surrey (from 1991). Graduated B.A., B.Mus. and M.Mus.
Taught music at Putteridge High School, Luton (1979-1992) and Luton Sixth Form College (1990-1994).
Acting head of music at Icknield High School, Luton in 1995, later that year being appointed head of music at the International School of Berlin-Potsdam in Potsdam, Germany.
Member of several choirs including Dursley Parish Church Choir, Gloucestershire (1965-1975) and the City of London Choir (1982-1983).
Has written chamber works and concertos. Well known for his music for horn including a Concerto for Four Horns. His church music includes Exultate Deo (1993), a Magnificat and Nunc Dimittis (1981), a Missa Brevis (1986) and a Missa Paschalis (1990). He has also written motets and anthems. To date, six commissions have been received from Freiburg Cathedral, Germany.

WIGHT, Revd. Osborne (18th century)
A chaplain of New College, Oxford, around 1790. Composer of the anthem 'My God, my God'.

WIGTHORPE, William (16th/17th century)
Organist at New College, Oxford from 1598 until at least 1606. Graduated B.Mus. at the University of Oxford in 1605. Composer of the anthem 'My Shepherd is the living God'.

WILBY, Philip (b.1949)
Born in Pontefract, Yorkshire in 1949.
Educated at King's School, Pontefract and the University of Oxford. After orchestral and teaching appointments, he became a lecturer in music at Leeds University and later became senior lecturer in composition.
Many of his compositions are for the church, or inspired by religious subjects. Among his works are anthems, including 'God be in my head', and the carol-anthem 'The Word made Flesh', an Evening Service and a Service of Light. Larger-scale pieces include the cantata *The Temptations of Christ*. He also wrote substantial solo organ works such as 'Roses for the Queen of Heaven', and a Prelude, Fugue and Toccata.

WILBYE, John (1574-1638)
Born in Diss, Norfolk in 1574; died in Colchester, Essex in 1638. Lived in the house of Sir Thomas Kytson of Hengrave Hall, near Bury St. Edmunds. Remained there, and in the house of a young member of the family, until his death. In 1598 he was a teacher of music in Austin Friars, London. Published *Madrigals to three, four, five and six voices* (1598) and *The second set of madrigals...* (1609). His madrigal 'The Lady Oriana' is found in *The Triumphes of Oriana*. His church music includes the anthem 'If ye love Me'.

WILDBORE, Robert (17th century)
Succeeded **George Loosemore** as organist of Trinity College, Cambridge (1682-1688). Wrote music for the church, including the anthem 'Almighty and Everlasting God'.

WILDER, Philip van (16th century)
Composer of the anthem 'Blessed art Thou'.

WILKES, John Bernard (1823-?)
Born in Leominster, Herefordshire on 2 May 1823. Of a Moravian Family. Studied at the Royal Academy of Music (1842-1846).
Organist of Monkland, Herefordshire, where **H.W. Baker** was vicar. Organist of St. David's, Merthyr Tydfil, Wales (from 1854) and of Llandaff Cathedral (1861-1865). He appears still to have been alive in 1875. Composed the hymn tune 'Lyte', found in *Hymns Ancient and Modern* (1861).

WILKINS, George (1806-1897)
Organist of Ilfracombe Parish Church, Devon (from 1828); St. Nicholas's, Guildford (from 1837), Stoke Parish Church (from 1871) and Christ Church, Stoke (from 1878). His church compositions include the anthems 'Christ, our Passover' and 'The Lord is King'. Published *A collection of Psalms and Hymn tunes, Chants and Responses as used in St. Nicholas', Guildford, harmonised, arranged and composed by George Wilkins*.

WILKINSON, George (1808-1857)
Said to be 'of Huddersfield', Yorkshire. Composed the anthem 'The Lord is full of compassion'.

WILKINSON, Robert (1874-?)
Studied at the Royal College of Music. Graduated B.Mus. at the University of Oxford. Music master and organist of Christ's Hospital, Horsham (f1902-1929). Composer of the hymn tune 'His love', and 'O heavenly Jerusalem', a processional hymn for All Saints' Day.

WILLAN, Dr. James Healey (1880-1968)
Born in Balham, London on 12 October 1880; died in Toronto, Canada, in 1968.
Of Irish ancestry. Began to learn music around the age of 4. Accorded the Lambeth D.Mus. (1956).
At the age of eight, he went as a boarder to St. Saviour's Choir School, Eastbourne, Sussex and studied organ, piano and harmony with **W.H. Sangster**. In about 1899, he took organ lessons with **W.S. Hoyte** and piano lessons with Evlyn Howard-Jones.
Organist of St. Saviour's Church, St. Albans (1896/98-1900) and subsequently, choirmaster (from 1899). Organist of the St. Cecilia Society (1898-1900). Organist of Christ Church, Wanstead (1900-1903); organist and choirmaster of the Church of St. John the Baptist, Kensington, London (1903-1913).
Emigrated to Canada and held a number of appointments in the city of Toronto. Head of theory at the Conservatory (1913-1936). a lecturer and examiner (from 1914) and a professor of the (1937-1950) at the University. Organist of St. Paul's Anglican Church, Bloor Street (1913-1921) and of St. Mary Magdalene (1921-1968). Composed services including a Morning Service in D for Men's Voices, a Communion Service in D (1955), an Evening Service in E-flat and anthems such as 'Give ear, ye heavens' (1911). Composed many unaccompanied motets and responds in honour of the Blessed Virgin Mary, examples of which are *Fair of face* and *I beheld her, beautiful as a dove*. Also *The Apostrophe to the Heavenly Host*. Many Mass settings, mostly for unaccompanied singing. His Requiem has recently been published. Organ works include an Introduction, Passacaglia and Fugue, which has been described as a virtuoso *tour de force*; he also wrote chamber and orchestral music, songs and an opera *Deirdre*.

WILLCOCKS, Sir David Valentine (b.1919)
Born in Newquay, Cornwall on 30 December 1919. Father of **Jonathan Willcocks**.
A chorister at Westminster Abbey. Later won a music scholarship at Clifton College, Bristol and a Foundation Scholarship at King's College, Cambridge, where he also held the Dr. Mann Organ Studentship and a John Stewart of Rannoch Scholarship. He served in the army during World War II and was awarded the Military Cross in Normandy (1944). Graduated B.A. and Mus.B. (1946) and M.A. (1948). Also studied at the Royal College of Music and the Royal School of Church Music.
Organist of Salisbury Cathedral (1947-1950) and Worcester Cathedral (1950-1957). While at Worcester he was conductor of the City of Birmingham Choir. In Cambridge (1957-1974) as fellow and organist of King's College (1957-1973), university lecturer (1957-1974) and conductor of the Cambridge University Musical Society (1958-1973). Director of the R.C.M. (1974-1984) and Musical Director of the Bach Choir (from 1960).

David Willcocks was appointed C.B.E. in 1971 and knighted in 1977.
Composer of miscellaneous anthems and organ works; general editor of O.U.P. Church Music since 1961.

WILLCOCKS, Jonathan (b.1953)

Born in Worcester on 9 January 1953. Son of **David Willcocks**.
A chorister at King's College, Cambridge, a music scholar at Clifton College, Gloucestershire and a choral scholar at Trinity College, Cambridge. Graduated in music in 1974.
Director of music at Portsmouth Grammar School (1975-1978) and at Bedales School, Petersfield, Hampshire (1978-1989). Became director of the Junior Academy of the Royal Academy of Music. Conductor and musical director of Portsmouth Choral Union, Chichester Singers and Southern Pro Musica. Also works as freelance conductor and composer.
His larger works for the church include the *Worcester* Mass, *Great is the glory*, *Sing praises* and *Come rejoicing*. He has also written over 40 smaller sacred choral works including anthems.

WILLCOX, Scott (20th century)

Educated at Latymer Upper School, London and Trinity College of Music, studying composition with Richard Arnell. In 1987 he founded the St. Andrew's Music Festival in Shepperton, Middlesex. Directs the St. Andrew's Singers. Has written music for jazz Orchestra; a Brass Quintet; 'L'Avantreno' for harpsichord; and an opera *The Man from Heaven*, taking incidents from the life of Christ. He has also written settings of Psalm 29 (for two choirs), and Psalms 98, 126 and 150 (all for unaccompanied chorus), and a Short Mass for Chorus and Organ.

WILLIAMS, Aaron (1731-1776)

Born probably in London in 1731; died in London in 1776. Clerk to the Scotch Church in London Wall, a teacher of music, a music engraver and a publisher in West Smithfield. Compiled and published *The universal Psalmodist* (1763), *New universal Psalmodist* (1770) and *Psalmody in Miniature* (1778). His church compositions include the anthems 'Arise, shine O Zion' and 'Keep thy foot when thou goest'.

WILLIAMS, Adrian (b.1956)

Born in Watford, Hertfordshire on 30 April,1956.
Educated at Rickmansworth Grammar School, Hertfordshire and was a junior exhibitioner at the Royal Academy of Music. Won a double scholarship to the Royal College of Music where he studied with John Lill, John Russell, **Alan Ridout** and Bernard Stevens. Won several prizes for composition and for piano.
Composer in residence at Charterhouse, Surrey; taught at Ludlow School, Shropshire and directed the Presteigne Festival.
Has received commissions from the B.B.C., the Park Lane Group and the Three Choirs' Festival.
Has written orchestral and chamber music, and music for the church, including several Masses; carols such as 'There is no rose'; anthems among which are 'Send your Light and your Truth', 'The people that walked in darkness' and 'My heart is steadfast'; a Magnificat and Nunc Dimittis and a set of Preces and Responses.

WILLIAMS, Dr. Albert Edward (1864-?)

Born in Newport, Monmouthshire, Wales on 16 March 1864.
Educated in Newport and studied at with Carl Bathmann and **John Naylor**. Graduated B.Mus. (1891) and D.Mus. (1906). Bandmaster

of the Grenadier Guards (from 1897) He took a band to the St. Louis World's Fair, U.S.A. (1904) then toured the U.S.A. and Canada. A conductor for the Philharmonic Society. His compositions for the church include an oratorio, *Elisha* and a setting of Psalm 30 for Solo Voices, Chorus and Orchestra. Also wrote overtures and military marches.

WILLIAMS, Benjamin (1839-1918)

Born in Llandudno, Wales in 1839; died in 1918. Educated at the local British school and became a carpenter by trade. Later, a builder. He learnt the Tonic Sol-fa System and was a teacher of this method all his life. For 57 years he was precentor of the Welsh Presbyterian Church in Llandudno. Composed the hymn tune 'Deganwy'.

WILLIAMS, Charles Francis Abdy (1855-1923)

Born in Dawlish, Devon on 16 July 1855; died in Milford, Lymington, Hampshire on 27 February 1923.
Studied at the Leipzig Conservatory for 3 years (1882-1885). He was educated at Cambridge for a career in the church, studying music as an amateur. Graduated B.A. (1879), M.A. (1882) and Mus.B. (1891) at the University of Cambridge, and B.Mus. (1889) at the University of Oxford.
Organist of St. Mary's Church, Auckland, New Zealand (from 1879) and Dover College, Kent (from 1881). Organist and choirmaster of St. Mary's Boltons, London, (1885-1891) Organist and music master at Bradfield College, Berkshire (1895-1901).
Author of works on the history and theory of music. His compositions for the church include settings of Psalms 24 and 29 for Solo Voices, Chorus and Strings; a Communion Service in E-flat, Evening Services in F and in D and Chants for the Benedicite. He also wrote chamber music.

WILLIAMS, Dr. Charles Lee (1853-1935)

Born in Winchester, Hampshire on 1 May 1853; died in Gloucester on 29 August 1935.
The son of Revd. David Williams, rector of Barnes, Wiltshire.
A chorister of New College, Oxford (1862-1865) under **G.B. Arnold**, whom he followed to Winchester as a pupil. Deputy organist (to Dr. Arnold) of Winchester Cathedral (1865-1870) and at the age of 15 became organist of Ovington Parish Church, Winchester. Organist of Upton Church, Torquay, Devon (from 1870). Tutor and organist of St. Columba's College, Dublin (from 1872). In 1876 he graduated B.Mus. at the University of Oxford.
Awarded the Lambeth D.Mus. in 1929.
Organist of Llandaff Cathedral (1876-1882) and of Gloucester Cathedral (1882-1897), succeeding **C.H Lloyd**. Conductor of the Gloucester Festival until November 1896 and of the Worcester Festival of 1890. An examiner for the Associated Board of the Royal Schools of Music after his retirement from Gloucester. Retired totally in 1923.
For the church he wrote cantatas, a Te Deum (1895); services including an Evening Service in F; the anthems 'Thou wilt keep him', 'To Thee, O Lord' and others; and carols. He also wrote songs and part songs.

WILLIAMS, Evan 'Ifan' (1710-?)

A harpist. He assisted Edward Jones in his publications of his Welsh harp tunes. In 1770, he produced a collection of 24 tunes, printed at the end of the new edition of *Book of Common Prayer* in Welsh, of which eight were his compositions and the remainder were tunes already in existence. Editor of *Antient British Music* (1772), in association with Parry of Ruabon.

WILLIAMS, George Ebenezer (1783-1819)
Born in Clerkenwell Green, London on 30 August 1783; died in Westminster, London on 17 April 1819. A chorister at St. Paul's Cathedral under **Richard Bellamy**. A teacher at Hammersmith School in or before 1805. Deputy organist of the Temple Church (to **R.J.S. Stevens**) from 1805. Deputy organist to **Samuel Arnold** of Westminster Abbey. Later succeeded **Robert Cooke** as organist of Westminster Abbey (1814-1819). Author of *An Introduction to the Art of Playing on the Pianoforte* (1810; 2nd edition 1815), *Exercises for the Pianoforte* and *Examining Questions for School Classes* (1815). He composed church music including a number of chants. He also wrote secular vocal music.

WILLIAMS, John (1891-?)
Born in Rhos, Wrexham, Wales in 1891.
An extra-mural lecturer in the University College of North Wales, and lectured at summer schools. Adjudicated and conducted in musical festivals and was an accompanist for the Royal National Eisteddfod of Wales. He was organist and choirmaster of Bethlehem Congregational Church, Rhos; of Chester Street Congregational Church, Wrexham for over 17 years, and of the Tabernacle Chapel, Bangor. Composed hymn tunes, chants and piano works.

WILLIAMS, John (Dolgellau: 1740-1821)
Born in Llangelyn, Merionethshire, Wales in 1740; died in 1821. Learned trumpet and flute as a boy. Followed his father's trade of hat making until 1772 then became a solicitor's clerk. Proprietor of a number of schools. One of the best known musicians of his time. Composed hymn tunes including 'Brynhyfryd' (harmonised by **Samuel Wesley**)

WILLIAMS, Patrick (1905-1985)
Composed anthems including 'Lift up your heads, ye gates of brass', and songs.

WILLIAMS, Robert (Mynydd Ithel: 1781-1821)
Born in Anglesey, Wales in 1781; died in 1821. Blind from birth. A basket maker. Lived all his life on the island of Anglesey at Mynydd Ithel, Llanfechell. Composed the hymn tunes 'Bethel' and 'Llanfair'.

WILLIAMS, Thomas (Hafrenydd: 1807-1894)
Born in Llanidloes, Montgomeryshire, Wales on 7 December 1807; died in Llanidloes on 16 December 1894. Began to study music at the age of 10. Received a grant from the civil list in recognition of his services to music and literature. Published a number of collections of tunes, anthems (from 1845), and *Choruses of the Great Masters arranged to Welsh words*. Also published a *Musical Grammar and Dictionary*. Composed the hymn tune 'Nantmel' and Christmas hymns.

WILLIAMS, Thomas James (19th/20th century)
Born in Rhymney, Wales. A pupil of W. Lewis. Organist and choirmaster of St. Anne's Church, Ynshir, Rhondda; Old St. Mark's, Rhymney (aged 13); St. Matthew's, Rhymney; St. David's, Rhymney (from 1920) and St. Luke's, Porth, Rhondda (from 1927). Composer of anthems, descants and songs.

WILLIAMS, Thomas John (1869-1944)
Born in 1869; died in Llanelli, Wales in 1944. Studied music with David Evans of Cardiff. Organist of Zion Church, Llanelli (1903-1913) and Calfaria Church, Llanelli. Composed the hymn tune 'Ebenezer' (1896), taken from the anthem 'Golau yn y glyn' (Light in the valley). 'Ebenezer' was said by **Ralph Vaughan Williams** to be in the top hundred hymn tunes in the world.

WILLIAMS, Dr. Walter (19th/20th century)
Born in, Wrexham, Wales. Studied with **J. C. Bridge** and **Walter Carroll**. Graduated D.Mus. at the University of Oxford. Music master of Bury Grammar School and a professor of harmony at the Matthay School of Music. Organist and choirmaster of Bury Parish Church (from 1904) and of the Collegiate Church of St. Nicholas, Galway, Ireland and lectured in music at University College, Galway. An opera society conductor and a freemason.

WILLIAMS, William Aubrey (Gwilym Gwent: 1834-1891)
Born in Tredegar, Wales on 28 July 1834; died in Plymouth, Pennsylvania, U.S.A. on 3 July 1891. A working miner who was reputed to be the best glee writer in Wales. Chiefly responsible with **Thomas Jenkins** for the editing of the music in *Llwybraur Moliant* (Paths of praise) in 1872. A prolific writer whose compositions included several cantatas. *The Prodigal Son* won a prize at the National Eisteddfod, Aberystwyth (1865). Also composed anthems, choruses, hymn tunes, glees and part songs.

WILLIAMS, William Cecil (1885-?)
Born in Swansea, Wales in 1885. Educated at Newcastle-on-Tyne Cathedral with **George Huntley**, to whom he was a pupil assistant. Organist of St. Matthew's, Swansea. A teacher of piano, organ and violin. Played at the United Schools' Mission Festival, in Southwark Cathedral from the age of 15 and sang in the Choir of Westminster Abbey at the Coronation of George V (1911). Made arrangements of Welsh melodies for use in school. Composed a set of Versicles and Responses, sacred songs including 'Jesu, lover of my soul' and anthems including 'O Lord of heaven'.

WILLIAMSON, J. (1868-1947)
Composer of the hymn tune, 'St. Katrine', which first appeared in *The School Hymn Book of the Methodist Church* (1950).

WILLIAMSON, Sir Malcolm Benjamin Graham Christopher (b.1931)
Born in Sydney, Australia on 21 November 1931. Educated at the Sydney Conservatory with Eugene Goossens; Barker College, Hornsby, New South Wales; and (from 1953) in London with Elizabeth Lutyens and Erwin Stein. Composer-in-residence at Westminster Choir College, Princeton, New Jersey (1970-1971). In 1975, he became Master of the Queen's Music. A pianist, organist, composer and lecturer. Composer of music for the church including a Morning Service; a Mass *of St. Andrew*; a Mass *of Christ the King*, for Solo Voices, Chorus and Orchestra (1978); the anthems 'Dignus et agnus' and 'Let them give thanks', and a Jubilee Hymn for Chorus and Orchestra. Has also written operas and orchestral music. Published the collection *A Procession of Psalms*.

WILLING, Christopher Edwin Cumming (1830-1904)
Born in Devon on 28 February 1830; died in Southgate, Middlesex on 1 December 1904. Son of Christopher Willing, who was an alto singer and an assistant gentleman of the Chapel Royal. A chorister

of Westminster Abbey (1839-1845). Organist of Blackheath Park Church, London (from 1845); the Foundling Hospital (1848-1879); the Sacred Harmonic Society (from 1872). Assistant organist of Westminster Abbey. Organist of St. Paul's, Covent Garden, London (1857-1860) and All Saints', Margaret Street (1860-1868). In 1868 he edited *Book of Common Praise*. Composed the tune 'Alstone' to 'We are but little children weak' and a number of songs.

WILLS, Dr. Arthur William (b.1926)
Born in Coventry, Warwickshire on 19 September 1926.
Educated at St. John's School, Coventry and the College of St. Nicolas, Canterbury (which is now Royal School of Church Music and located in Dorking, Surrey).
Having played the organ frequently at St. Alban's Church, Leamington Spa from the age of 14, at 16 he was appointed organist. Took piano lessons with **Stanley Vann** and lessons in music theory with **Allen Blackall**. Graduated B.Mus. (1953) and D.Mus. (1957) at the University of Durham.
Appointed O.B.E. in 1990.
Assistant organist (1949-1958) of Ely Cathedral.
Director of Music at Ely Cathedral (1958-1990) and held a professorship at the Royal Academy of Music (1964-1992). Has toured extensively as a recitalist in Europe, the U.S.A., Australia and Hong Kong, and has broadcast, appeared on television and made recordings, both as a soloist and with the Ely Choir.
His secular music includes seven song cycles and an opera *1984* based on the George Orwell novel. He has composed extensively for organ, and his ensemble works include a Concerto with Strings and Timpani, a Concerto for Guitar and Organ, and a Symphonic Suite *The Fenlands* for Brass Band and Organ. His book *Organ* appeared in the *Menuhin Music Guide* Series in 1984, with a second edition in 1993.
Works for the church include Missa *Eliensis* (1960) and Evening Canticles on Plainsong Tones (1975); anthems include 'O praise God' (1964) and 'The Light invisible' (1976).

WILMOT, A. Raymond (1869-?)
Born in Withycombe Raleigh, Devon in 1869. Studied at Exeter with **D.J. Wood**, **Kellow Pye**, Herman Klein and Thomas Blackburn. Organist and choirmaster of St. John's Parish Church, Exmouth (from 1891). A professor of singing at the Metropolitan Academy of Music (1919-1925), and a choral and orchestral society conductor. Composed a Magnificat and Nunc Dimittis in B-flat and a number of cello and piano works.

WILSON, Revd. David Frederick Ruddell (1871-1957)
Born in Tyholland in 1871; died in 1957. Ordained in 1895. Succentor, and warden of the Cathedral Grammar School, of St. Patrick's Cathedral, Dublin (1899-1916). Later a residentiary canon and precentor of the Cathedral (from 1935). General editor of the *Irish Hymnal* and *Irish Chant Book*. Composed the hymn tune 'Tyholland'.

WILSON, Hugh (1766-1824)
Born in Fenwick, Ayrshire in 1766; died in Duntocher, Dumbartonshire, Scotland on 14 August 1824. An Ayrshire shoemaker. He occasionally acted as precentor in the Secession Church, Fenwick. One of the two founders of the first Sunday School in Fenwick. Around 1800 he moved to Pollokshaws, near Glasgow, and became accountant and draughtsman in+ the mills of

a Mr. William Dunn. Subsequently lived at Duntocher, working as manager of a mill. A teacher of music. Composed a number of Psalm tunes including 'Martyrdom' and 'Caroline'.

WILSON, Dr. John (1595-1674)
Born probably in Faversham, Kent on 5 April 1595; died in Westminster, London on 22 February 1674.
Graduated D.Mus. at the University of Oxford (1644).
Music master to the family of Sir William Walter of Sarsden, Oxfordshire (from 1646). Oxford professor of music (1656-1661). A singer, lute player and violist. A private musician to Charles I, and a gentleman of the Chapel Royal and chamber musician to Charles II (from 1662).
He may have been Shakespeare's Jack Wilson in *Much ado about Nothing*. He produced settings of several of the songs in Shakespeare's plays.
Published the collections *Psalterium Carolium* (1657) and *Divine Services and Anthems* (1663). Among his anthems are 'Blessed is He' and 'O Lord, Thou whose beauty'. He also wrote music for viols.

WILSON, John Whitridge (1905-1992)
Born in Bournville, Birmingham in 1905; died in July 1992. Studied at the Royal College of Music. Graduated M.A. and Mus.B. at the University of Cambridge. Assistant music master at Tonbridge School, Kent (1929-1932) and at Charterhouse, Surrey (from 1932). Published *Sixteen Hymns of today for use as simple Anthems*, carols including 'All poor men and humble' and two chorale preludes for organ. Composer of hymn tunes and descants, some of which are found in *Hymns and Psalms*. Choral versions also exist of some hymn tunes.

WILSON, Matthew (1812-1856)
Studied with **John Turnbull**. A Scottish amateur composer in Glasgow. Composed several hymn tunes including 'Drumclog', and contributed songs to collections.

WILSON, Robert Henry (1856-1932)
Born in Manchester in 1856; died on 19 January 1932. Studied with **Frederick Bridge** and graduated B.Mus. at the University of Oxford (from 1889). Chorus master of the Hallé Concert Society until his retirement in 1925, working with some of the foremost conductors including Hallé, **Cowen**, Richter, Balling, Beecham and Harty. Rehearsed the first Manchester performance of **Edward Elgar**'s The Dream of Gerontius. His compositions include the cantata *The Son of Man* and the harvest anthem 'Praised be the Lord daily'.

WILSON, Thomas (17th century)
Organist of Peterhouse, Cambridge and referred to in the Peterhouse books as 'organista Petrensis'. Composer of anthems including 'Behold how good and joyful' and 'Prevent us O Lord', a setting of Psalm 85, and a Litany in Latin.

WILSON, Dr. Thomas Brendan (b.1927)
Born in the U.S.A. in 1927.
Of British parents who returned to Britain and settled in the Glasgow area. Educated at St. Mary's College, Aberdeen and at Glasgow University. Served in the R.A.F. (1945-1948).

A lecturer (from 1957), reader (from 1971) and professor (from 1977) at the University of Glasgow, where he received an honorary D.Mus.

Has held executive and advisory positions in The Arts Council, The New Music Group of Scotland, The Society for the Promotion of New Music and The Composers Guild of Great Britain (Chairman 1986-1989). A founder member of the Scottish Society of Composers.

Appointed C.B.E. in 1990.

Has composed vocal music of various kinds, large-scale works, and compositions for a wide variety of chamber ensembles and solo instruments. Has received a number of commissions from, among others, the Promenade Concerts, Scottish Opera, and the Festivals of Edinburgh, Cheltenham and the City of London.

His works include a Te Deum (1971), 'Sequentiae Passionis' (1971), a Missa *pro mundo conturbato* (1970), *Songs of hope and expectation* (1977) and 'Amor Christi' (1989). His carol 'There is no rose' was first performed at King's College, Cambridge.

WILSON-DIXON, Dr. Andrew (b.1946)
Born in London in 1946.

Educated at Marlborough College, Wiltshire. Read music at the University of Cambridge (1963-1968), studying piano with Lamar Crowson and John Lill. Organ scholar of York Minster under **Francis Jackson**. Graduated D.Phil. at the University of York (1971).

A lecturer at the University of Leicester; principal lecturer (from 1984) and co-ordinator of early music at the Welsh College of Music and Drama.

Director of music of a number of Churches, including Holy Trinity, Leicester and Stanwell Road Baptist Church, Penarth, Wales.

Writes on the subject of Christian music for magazines and for the Royal School of Church Music. His *Story of Christian Music* was published in 1992.

Much of his church music is for congregational use. His works include some 30 congregational Psalm settings, anthems, motets, the *St. Albans* Gloria, the *East Anglian* Mass (1978) and a number of large-scale Christian music-dramas including *Revelation* (1979). There is also a String Quartet (1982).

WILTON, 2nd Earl of (Thomas Egerton) (1799-1882)
Born on 30 December 1799; died on 7 March 1882. Composer of the anthems 'O praise the Lord, all ye heathen' and 'When gathering clouds', a Hymn to Eros, a Kyrie in B-flat, chants and other vocal music.

WINCHESTER, Ernest Charles (1854-1916)
Born in Osborne, Isle of Wight on 22 May 1854; died in Bexley, Kent on 21 February 1916. Retired from the India Office and went to Bexley. Organist of Holy Trinity Church, Wimbledon, London, and organist and director of music at Christ Church, Southwark. His hymn 'Sing to the Lord' for Four Voices was the prize tune of the College of Organists in 1874. Composer of the anthems 'If ye love me', 'The Lord is my Shepherd' and 'I will give thanks' and a Te Deum and Benedictus. Also wrote a Grand Festival March for Organ, and other organ works.

WINGHAM, Thomas (1846-1893)
Born in London on 5 January 1846; died on 24 March 1893. Organist of St. Michael's Mission Church, Southwark at the age of 10 and of All Saints', Paddington (from 1864). Studied at the London Academy of Music (from 1863) and at the Royal Academy of Music (from 1867) with **William Sterndale Bennett** and Harold Thomas. In 1871 he became a professor of piano at the R.A.M. Also a professor at the Guildhall School of Music. Director of music at Brompton Oratory, London (1882-1893). His music for the church includes a Mass in D for Antwerp Cathedral (1876); a Te Deum for Voices, Orchestra and Organ; motets and Offertories. His *Vexilla Regis* is still sung at Brompton Oratory and elsewhere. He also wrote songs, orchestral music and chamber music.

WINN, Dr. Rowland Mellor (1856-?)
Born in Birmingham on 24 April 1856. An articled pupil of **AlfredGaul**. Graduated B.Mus. (1876) and D.Mus. (1883) at the University of Oxford. Organist and choirmaster of Harborne Parish Church, Birmingham (from 1874). A solo pianist and accompanist. His compositions include two Kyries; an oratorio *The Sea of Galilee*; part songs and piano pieces.

WINTER, John (b.1923)
Born in Bungay, Suffolk on 19 June 1923. Educated at Bungay Grammar School and at the Royal College of Music. Director of the Music School (from 1949), assistant organist, and organist (1971-1988) of Truro Cathedral. Composed a Magnificat and Nunc Dimittis in D.

WINTERBOTTOM, Joseph (1815-1859)
Organist of St. James's Church, East Compton, Lancashire. Composer of the anthem 'Thou wilt keep him.'

WINTLE, Revd. Ogle Richard (?-1860)
An M.A. graduate. A teacher at Uppingham School, Leicestershire, and headmaster of Bridgwater Grammar School, Somerset. His compositions include the anthems 'Come, my people' and 'O praise the Lord with me'. He also composed songs.

WISE, Charles Stanley (c1856-1939)
Died in Clarens, Switzerland in 1939.
Graduated Mus.B. at the University of Cambridge (1890). Organist of Petworth Parish Church, Sussex (from 1876); Godalming Parish Church, Surrey (from 1878); St. Michael's, Alnwick (from 1881); Christ Church, Clarens, Switzerland (from 1897) and All Saints', Vevey (from 1929). He also conducted the choral society in Wooler, Northumberland A correspondent of *The Times*. Attended the first Bayreuth performances of Wagner. Became acquainted with Stravinsky, who had connections with Clarens. He composed anthems including the Easter-tide 'Now upon the first day of the week' and services. He also wrote orchestral pieces, a String Quartet and songs.

WISE, Michael (c1648-1687)
Born in Salisbury, Wiltshire in 1648; died in Salisbury on 24 August 1687. Killed in a street disturbance.
A chorister of the Chapel Royal after the Restoration under **Henry Cooke**.
Organist and master of the choristers of Salisbury Cathedral (1668-1687).
A gentleman of the Chapel Royal (from 1676). At the Bishop's visitation in 1683 it was said that Michael Wise was notorious for intemperate drinking and other excesses, and he was suspended in 1685 at the time of the Coronation of James II.

Almoner and master of the choristers of St. Paul's Cathedral (1686-1687).

His church compositions include the anthems 'By the waters', 'Prepare ye the way of the Lord' and 'Blessed is he'; a Magnificat and Nunc Dimittis and a Magnificat in E-flat. It has been said of 'The ways of Zion do mourn' that the solos for Treble and Bass in semi-recitative style exquisitely depict the pathos of the famous text from Lamentations.

WISEMAN, Revd. Dr. Frederick Luke (1858-1944)
The son of a Methodist minister who was an accomplished amateur musician. Frederick Wiseman became a minister of the Methodist Church, and in 1933 was appointed president of the Methodist Conference. Minister of Wesley's Chapel, City Road, London. A member of the committee for *Methodist Hymn Book* (1904) and chairman of the Music Committee. He received the honorary degrees of D.D. at Mount Union University, Ohio and the Litt.D. at Leeds University. Composed the hymn tune 'Wonderful love'; the anthems 'Courage, brother, do not stumble' and 'Lift your glad voices'; a Rhapsody of the Resurrection and *Songs of the Twelve Hours*. The hymn tune 'Dallas' first appeared in *New People's Hymnary* (1922) and was in *Methodist Hymn Book* (1933) together with 'Fons amoris', first written for the *Methodist School Hymnal* (1910).

WISEMAN, Mary Jane
see **HORNABROOK**, Mary Jane.

WISHART, Peter Charles Arthur (1921-1984)
Born in Crowborough, Sussex on 25 June 1921; died on 14 August 1984. Educated at Bryanston School, Devon; Birmingham University and in Paris. He was visiting lecturer at Bath University of Technology, on the staff of the Birmingham School of Music (1948-1958), lecturer at Birmingham University (1950-1959), professor of composition at Guildhall School of Music (from 1961) and professor of music at Reading University. Composed a Benedicite and Te Deum, and, from a 14th century hymn text, 'Jesu, dulcis memoria'. Also songs and pieces for piano or organ. Composed carols including 'There is no rose' and, for unaccompanied voices, 'Alleluia! A new work is come on hand'.

WITCHELL, Peter (b.1945)
Born in Bromley, Kent on 22 November 1945.
Educated at Oundle School, Northamptonshire as Grocers' Company scholar; Lincoln College, Oxford, where he graduated M.A. in Mathematics and at the Royal Academy of Music where he won a number of prizes for piano and organ.
Assistant director of music at Sherborne School, Dorset (1971-1978); director of music (1978-1995) and subsequently head of academic music at Oakham School, Leicestershire.
Composer of instrumental, vocal and choral music for use in the theatre, and for orchestra and for chamber ensemble. His church music includes a Missa Brevis (1985) for Soprano, Baritone, Chorus and Orchestra; a Communion Service for Oakham School; carols and anthems including 'Fill Thou my life' (1995) and several organ pieces including Toccata Tropos, broadcast on BBC Radio 3.

WOAKES, W. H. (1780-?)
Organist of St. Peter's Church, Hereford. Published *A Catechism of Music* (1817). His compositions include anthems, dance music for piano, and songs.

WOLSTENHOLME (Wolstenhome), William (1865-1931)
Born in Blackburn, Lancashire on 24 February 1865; died in London on 23 July 1931.
Blind from birth. He became a friend of **Edward Elgar** who acted as amanuensis in copying his exercise for the University of Oxford B.Mus. (1887). His sister later acted as his amanuensis. Educated at Worcester College for the Blind. Organist of St. Paul's, Blackburn (from 1888); the King's Weigh House Congregational Church, London (from 1902); All Saints', Norfolk Square (from 1904) and All Saints', Finchley Road. In 1908 he made a recital tour in the U.S.A.
Composer of anthems including the Easter-tide 'Thou O God art praised in Zion', songs, part songs, an Intermezzo for Orchestra, a String Quartet and works for organ, violin, viola and cello.

WOOD, A. Rawlinson (1863-1948)
Born in Croydon, Surrey on 24 January 1863; died in Derby on 16 February 1948. Educated at Whitgift School, Croydon and at Trinity College of Music with **Benjamin Westbrook**. Graduated B.Mus. at the University of Durham (1895). Organist and choirmaster of St. John's, Caterham Valley (from 1879) and St. Luke's, Derby (from 1883). Director of music at Denstone College, Staffordshire (1902-1928). A choral and operatic society conductor. Contributed notes on public schools' music to *Musical Times* until his death. Composed the hymn 'Lead, kindly light'.

WOOD, Dr. Charles (1866-1926)
Born in Armagh, Ireland on 15 June 1866; died in Cambridge on 12 July 1926.
The third son of Charles Wood, lay vicar of Armagh Cathedral and brother of **W.G. Wood**.
Attended the Cathedral Choir School. Learned to play organ at an early age. Studied with **T.O. Marks**, organist of Armagh Cathedral (1880-1881). Won a Morley Scholarship to the Royal College of Music (1883-1887) where he studied composition with **C.V. Stanford**. Organ scholar of Selwyn College, Cambridge (1888) and studied also at Caius College (1889-1894), during which time he was also organist of the College. Graduated Mus.B. and B.A. (1890); Mus.D. and M.A. (1894). Became a fellow of Caius. He won several prizes including the Musical World Prize in 1887. Received an honorary L.L.D. at the University of Leeds (1904).
A lecturer in harmony and counterpoint (from 1897) and, succeeding Stanford, professor of music at the University of Cambridge (from 1924).
Co-editor with Revd. G.R. Woodward of *Songs of Syon* and of several carol books including *Cambridge Carol Book*. His interests, plainsong, Renaissance polyphony, and Psalm tunes of the 16th and 17th centuries, are said to have exercised an important influence on his compositional style.
Many of his works were composed at the turn of the century. There are some 20 sets of Evening Canticles and 30 anthems, and a Latin Mass. Composed a Magnificat and Nunc Dimittis in F (1915) for King's College, Cambridge and other Evening Services in C Minor, in D, two settings in E-flat and in G; a Service in G for Men's Voices; the anthems include 'O Thou, the Central Orb' and 'Great Lord of Lords'. His *St. Mark Passion*, composed in the course of nine days, was given its first performance on Good Friday, 1921 at King's College, Cambridge. He composed a song 'Ethiopia saluting the colours' but locked it away. Stanford took it from his desk and made it known.

The Charles Wood Summer School was founded in 1994 in Armagh, to highlight and promote Wood's Armagh connections.

WOOD, Dr. Daniel Joseph (1849-1919)
Born in Brompton, near Chatham, Kent on 25 August 1849; died in Exeter, Devon on 27 August 1919.
A chorister at Rochester Cathedral, and assistant organist and pupil of **John Hopkins** (1859-1864). Graduated B.Mus. at the University of Oxford (1874).
Awarded the Lambeth D.Mus. in 1896.
Organist of Holy Trinity, Brompton, Chatham (from 1864); Cranbrook Parish Church (from 1866); Lee Parish Church (from 1868); and Boston Parish Church, Lincolnshire (from 1869).
Organist of the Cathedrals of Chichester (1875-1876) and Exeter (1876-1919).
A teacher of harmony at Exeter University Extension College and a music, orchestral and oratorio society conductor. Joint editor of a new edition of *The Hymnal Companion*, to which he contributed tunes. A number of chants are found in *Chant Book Companion*. Composed organ and church music including an Evening Service in G, a Te Deum in G and the hymn 'Onward to Jerusalem'.

WOOD, David (18th century)
Organist of Ely Cathedral (1768-1774). May have been a gentleman of the Chapel Royal and a vicar choral of St. Paul's Cathedral. Composed the anthem 'Lord of all power and might'.

WOOD, Dr. Frederic Herbert (1880-1963)
Born in Berhampore, Orissa, India on 10 June 1880; died in May 1963. Graduated B.Mus. (1905) and D.Mus. (1913) at the University of Durham. A solo pianist and accompanist (from 1900). Organist and choirmaster of St. Paul's, Blackburn (1902-1905); St. John's, Blackburn (1905-1918) and Blackpool Parish Church (1918-1963). A lecturer in music at Liverpool University, a choral society conductor and a festival adjudicator. The author of works on psychic research and of *Ancient Egypt Speaks*. His compositions include 'The Ballad of Semmerwater' for Female Voices (1910), a cantata *Hymn to the Creator*, the anthem 'Around the throne of God in Heaven', carols, a violin concerto, songs and part songs.

WOOD, Sir Henry Joseph (1869-1944)
Born in London on 3 March 1869; died in London in 1944. Studied music with his father, who was an amateur cellist and solo tenor.
Deputy organist of St. Mary's, Aldermanbury at the age of 10 and organist of St. John's, Fulham at the age of 17. Studied at the Royal Academy of Music (from 1886) with **Ebenezer Prout, George Macfarren, Charles Steggall** and with Manuel Garcia and Duvivier.
He was knighted in 1911.
Became conductor of the Rousby Opera Company (1890), the Carla Rosa Opera Company (1891-1892) and the Georgina Burns Opera Company (1892). After a distinguished early conducting career he established a long-running series of promenade concerts at the Queen's Hall (from 1895), famous and firmly established today as 'The Proms' and centred at the Royal Albert Hall.
Composed a Mass in C, a Mass in E-flat, anthems and the hymn tune 'O God our strength' (1915).

WOOD, John (16th century)
Composer of the anthem 'O Lord, the World's Saviour'.

WOOD, Dr. Thomas (1892-1950)
Born in Chorley, Lancashire on 28 November 1892; died in Essex on 19 November 1950.
Educated at Barrow Grammar School, the Royal College of Music with **C.V. Stanford**, and at Exeter College, Oxford where he graduated M.A. and D.Mus. (1920). An assistant master (from 1918) and director of music (1919-1924) at Tonbridge School, Kent. Lecturer and precentor of Exeter College, Oxford (1924-1929). An examiner for the Associated Board of the Royal Schools of Music in Ceylon and Australia (1930-1932), and examiner for degrees in music at the University of Oxford (1933-1934) and in Canada (1937). He edited books of songs for boys, and the second volume of *Oxford Song Book*. Composed songs and the hymn tune 'St. Osyth'.

WOOD, William George (1859-1895)
Brother of **Charles Wood**. Studied at the Royal Academy of Music. Organist at St. Mary's, Hornsey Rise and at Highgate School, London. His works include the anthems 'O praise the Lord' and 'Praise the Lord, O Jerusalem'.

WOODD, Revd. Basil (1760-1831)
Born in Richmond, Surrey on 5 August 1760; died in London on 12 April 1831. Educated at Oxford. Acted as morning preacher at Bentinck Chapel, Lisson Grove, London (1785). Incumbent of Drayton, Beauchamp, Buckinghamshire (1808-1830). Published *A new metrical version of the Psalms of David* and composed a Psalm tune 'Paddington'.

WOODHAM, Twiford (?-1728)
A lay clerk at Ely Cathedral. Composer of the anthem 'I will praise Thy name'.

WOODS, Revd. Bertram Ernest (1900-?)
A Methodist minister who composed much sacred and secular music. He lived in the Shetland Islands for three years and composed many hymn tunes including 'Norwick', named after a hamlet in the Shetlands, which first appeared in *Methodist Hymn Book* (1933).

WOODS, Francis Cunningham (1862-1929)
Born in London on 29 August 1862; died in 1929.
Educated at the City of London School, in Neuwied-on-the-Rhine, and at the National Training School of Music (1877-1880) with **Arthur Sullivan, John Stainer, John Frederick Bridge, Ebenezer Prout, F.H. Cowen** and O'Leary. Went up to Brasenose College, Oxford (1883-1886). Graduated M.A. (1890) and B.Mus. (1891) at the University of Oxford.
Organist of Brasenose College, Oxford (1883-1886); organist and choirmaster at Exeter College, Oxford (1886-1895). Organist to the Duke of Marlborough (1891-1894) and teacher of organ and University of Oxford lecturer (1890-1895). In 1896 he became organist and music master at Highgate School, London. A choral society conductor.
Composed a Morning and Evening Service, anthems, cantatas including *King Harold* (1896), incidental music for *The Tempest*, a Suite in F for Small Orchestra, and songs.

WOODSON, Leonard (?-1641)
Organist of Eton College in 1615. His works include the anthems 'Arise, O Lord God' and 'Hear, O Lord'.

WOODWARD, Revd. Herbert Hall (1847-1909)
Born near Liverpool on 13 January 1847; died in London on 25 May 1909.
Studied at St. Peter's College, Radley. Took lessons in music with **E.G. Monk** and G. Wharton. A student of Corpus Christi, Oxford (from 1865), studying harmony for one year with **L. Hayne**. Graduated B.A., M.A., and B.Mus. at the University of Oxford (1866). He spent 15 months at Cuddesdon Theological College studying for the ministry of the Church of England under Canon King. Ordained in 1870. Curate at Wantage, Berkshire, for 11 years. In 1881 he became a minor canon at Worcester Cathedral, and Precentor from January 1890. Composed a Holy Communion Service in E-flat for Wantage Parish Church, Berkshire; a Unison Communion Service in A, a Te Deum in B-flat and the cantata *The radiant morn* (1881).

WOODWARD, Dr. Richard (1744-1777)
Born in Dublin in 1744; died in Dublin on 22 November 1777. His father, Richard, was master of the choristers of Christ Church Cathedral, Dublin. A chorister and apprentice of Christ Church. He became a vicar choral at St. Patrick's Cathedral in 1772. Organist of Christ Church Cathedral (1765-1777). In 1776 he succeeded his father as master of the choristers. Graduated B.Mus. (1768) at Trinity College, Dublin and D.Mus. (Dublin) in 1771. His works include the anthems 'Behold now praise' and 'Sing, O ye heavens', a Service in B-flat.

WOOLCOT, Charles (17th century)
Composer of the anthem 'O Lord, Thou hast cast us out'.

WOOLLEY, Edward Francis Reginald (1895-1954)
Born in Lincoln on 13 May 1895; died in Newark, Nottinghamshire on 12 January 1954.
Educated at Stamford School, Lincolnshire and Trinity College, Cambridge where he studied with **C.V. Stanford** and **Alan Gray**, and where he graduated M.A.. A pupil of Malcolm Sargent.
Assistant organist of Lincoln Cathedral under **George Bennett**. Organist and choirmaster of Newark Parish Church (1930-1954).
His works include the Modal, unaccompanied Short Communion Service (1926) and Evening Service; the carol 'When Christ took cloak of human form' and various other carols and hymn tunes. An unaccompanied Mass survives in manuscript, and other unpublished or privately-published works are still performed.

WORGAN, Dr. John (1724-1790)
Born in London in 1724 and baptised in November 1724; died in London on 24 August 1790.
A pupil 'of **Roseingrave**' and Geminiani. He was unsuccessful at the age of 11 in his application for the organistship of Christ Church, Spitalfields. He graduated Mus.B. (1748) and Mus.D. (1775) at the University of Cambridge.
Organist of St. Katherine, Cree End (1743-?1753); St. Andrew, Undershaft (1749-1790); St. Botolph's, Aldgate (1753-1790) and St. John's Chapel, Bedford Row (1760). Organist of the Vauxhall Gardens (1751-1774). Among his church compositions are the anthems 'It is good to give thanks' and 'Lord, Thou hast been our Refuge', hymns that are found in **William Riley**'s collection and, in Cathedral Psalter Chants (1875), a Double Chant in E-flat.

WORTON-STEWARD, Dr. Andrew (1948-1990)
Born in Kent on 20 February 1948; died on 30 March 1990.

Graduated B.A., and also D.Mus. at the Cincinnati Conservatory, U.S.A. (1976). His compositions include a Litany to the Holy Spirit, and 'Via crucis' (1983).

WRAY, Revd. Henry (?-1879)
Precentor of Winchester Cathedral and vicar of Holt, Denbighshire, Wales. Composed the anthem 'Come unto Me'.

WRENSHALL, William (1783-1854)
Organist of the Mayor's Chapel, Liverpool. Composed the anthem 'O Lord, who hast taught us'.

WRIGHT, Paul Leddington (b.1951)
Born in Taplow, Buckinghamshire on 28 August 1951.
Attended Desborough School, Maidenhead, Berkshire. Organ scholar of St. Catharine's College, Cambridge. Graduated B.A. (1973) and M.A. Director of music of the Methodist Association of Youth Clubs (1982-1984).
Organist of Coventry Cathedral (from 1984).
In 1996 he was appointed musical director of the Huddersfield Choral Society, Yorkshire.
His choral compositions include many commissioned anthems, among which are 'I will sing to the Lord'; also The *Coventry Litany*, these two items being written respectively for the 1994 and 1996 International Church Music Festivals. A Te Deum has been composed for Choir, Organ and Orchestra with its first performance in October 1996 at Broadway Baptist Church, Fort Worth, Texas.

WRIGHT, Thomas B. (1763-1829)
Born in Stockton-on-Tees, County Durham on 18 September 1763; died near Barnard Castle on 24 November 1829.
Son of Robert Wright, organist of Stockton Church (1766-1797) and grandson of Thomas Wright, also organist there (c1758-1760). Pupil and assistant organist (from 1774) and organist (1784-1785) of Sedgefield Church. Some time before 1784 he was pupil and assistant organist to **Thomas Ebdon** of Durham Cathedral. Succeeded his father at Stockton Church (from 1797). He invented a simple pocket metronome. His Concerto for Harpsichord (1795) was possibly the first piece of music to have metronome marks. Composer of anthems and Psalm tunes including 'Stockton', and also songs and an operetta.

WRIGLEY, John (1830-1902)
Born in Ashton-under-Lyne on 29 September 1830; died on 12 December 1902.
Studied music with his father, organist of Ashton Parish Church, and with, among other teachers, Richard H. Andrews. In 1849 he entered the Royal Academy of Music and studied composition with Cipriani Potter. Sometime organist of St. Saviour's Church, Chorlton-on-Medlock. In 1876 he became a local examiner for the R.A.M. and was examiner for the Royal College of Music at its foundation. President of the Victoria Glee Club. Vice president of the Manchester Vocal Union (from 1890). Composer of anthems including 'Make a joyful noise', 'Holy, Holy, Holy' for Solo Voices, Quartet and Chorus and 'He brought down my strength'. He also wrote songs, and works for piano and organ.

WYLDE, Dr. Henry (1822-1890)
Born in Bushey, Hertfordshire in 1822; died in London on 13 March 1890.

Son of Henry Wylde, a gentleman in ordinary to George IV. Graduated Mus.D. at the University of Cambridge (1851). Organist of SS Anne and Agnes, London (1844-1847). In 1852 he founded the New Philharmonic Society. He became Gresham Professor of Music in succession to Edward Taylor in 1863. In 1871 he established the London Academy of Music. He composed the cantatas *Praise and Prayer* and *Paradise Lost* (1850). He also composed chants, and a Piano Concerto in F Minor.

WYVILL, Zerubbabel (1763-1837)
Born in Maidenhead, Berkshire and was baptised on 4 September 1763; died in Hounslow, Middlesex on 14 May 1837. A teacher of music at Maidenhead, and organist of the Marquess of Huntingdon's Episcopal Chapel (where his son, Robert, was later organist) and at the Chapel of St. Mary Magdalene and St. Andrew. Composed anthems including 'O give thanks', and hymn tunes including 'Eaton'. He also wrote glees, a song 'The armed yeoman' (c1795) and a Berkshire March, composed for the Berkshire Militia (1793).

Y, Z

YARWOOD, Joseph (1829-?)
Born in Manchester on 6 May 1829. Composer of anthems, glees and piano music including polkas.

YATES, Charles James (1820-1889)
Organist of St. George's Church, Preston, Lancashire. He composed the anthems 'I will magnify Thee' and 'Unto Thee, O Lord'.

YOUNG, Revd. Edward (19th century)
Composer of a Te Deum, Jubilate, Magnificat and Nunc Dimittis and hymn tunes.

YOUNG, John Matthew Wilson (1822-1897)
Born in Durham on 17 December 1822; died in West Norwood, Surrey on 4 March 1897.
Was principal solo boy in Durham Cathedral choir, a pupil of **William Henshaw** and later his assistant.
For six years he was lecturer in music at York and Ripon Training College. Music master of St. Peter's College, York.
Organist and instructor of the boys at Lincoln Cathedral (1850-1895) and on his retirement he moved to London.
The Peterborough and Lincoln Oratorio Festival was established in 1888, the first Lincoln Festival taking place in June 1889 under the direction of Matthew Young.
Promoted the 'Speech Rhythm' Method of chanting the Psalms.
His church compositions include a sacred cantata *The return of Israel to Palestine*, produced at the Lincoln Festival on 15 June 1892; anthems including 'I will extol my God', 'Holy Eternal Spirit' and 'Sing with gladness'; a Service in A; a Festival Service in C; a Morning Service in D and several settings of the Te Deum.

ZOELLER, Carli (1840-1889)
Studied in Berlin and moved to England in 1873. Became bandmaster of the 2nd Life Guards and of the 7th Hussars in 1879. A viola d'amore player. His works include the anthems 'Bless the Lord, O my soul' and 'The Hosts of Heaven'.